# UNDERSTANDING PSYCHOLOGY

UNDERSTANDING

# PSYCHOLOGY

THIRD EDITION

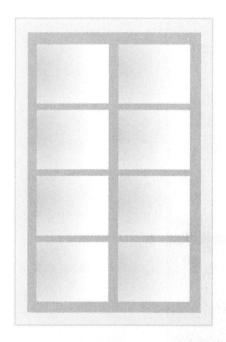

## CHARLES G. MORRIS

UNIVERSITY OF MICHIGAN

PRENTICE
HALL
Upper Saddle River, New Jersey 07458

*Library of Congress Cataloging-in-Publication Data*

Morris, Charles G.
Understanding psychology / Charles G. Morris —3rd ed.
p. cm.
Includes bibliographical references and indexes.
ISBN 0–13–432998–8
1. Psychology. I. Title.
BF121.M5987 1996
150—dc20 95-23618
CIP

*Editorial Team:* Peter Janzow, Marilyn Coco
*Development editor:* Robert Weiss
*Editorial/production supervision:* Shelly Kupperman
*Marketing Team:* Lauren Ward, Michael Alread, Aileen Ugural
*Buyer:* Tricia Kenny
*Art Director:* Leslie Osher
*Photo Editor:* Lori Morris-Nantz
*Photo Researchers:* Eloise Marion
*Interior and Cover Design:* Siren Design Inc.
*Medical Illustrator:* Alexander & Turner
*Eletronic Illustrations:* Siren Design Inc.

Printed in the United States of America
10 9 8 7 6 5 4 3 2 1

ISBN 0-13-432998-8 *(student version)*
ISBN 0-13-458654-9 *(professional version)*

Prentice-Hall International (UK) Limited, *London*
Prentice-Hall of Australia Pty. Limited, *Sydney*
Prentice Hall Canada, Inc. *Toronto*
Prentice-Hall Hispanoamericana, S.A., *Mexico*
Prentice-Hall of India Private Limited, *New Delhi*
Prentice-Hall of Japan, Inc. *Tokyo*
Simon & Schuster Asia Pte. Ltd., *Singapore*
Editoria Prentice-Hall do Brasil, Ltda., *Rio de Janeiro*

# OVERVIEW

Neurons Endocrine System Behavior Geneti ssenger l Neurons Endoc

# CONTENTS

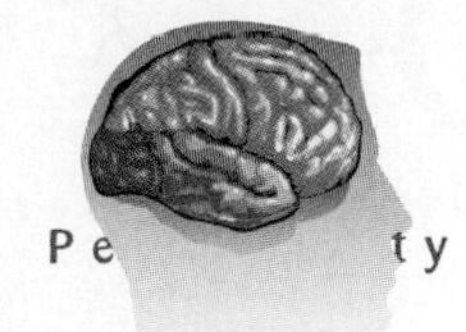

ychology Science Human Behavior Nervous System Con ing Pe ty C

## 5 LEARNING 161



## 6 MEMORY 201

## 11 STRESS AND HEALTH PSYCHOLOGY 417



## 12 ABNORMAL BEHAVIOR 447

# PREFACE

In the past 20 years more than a million and a half introductory psychology students have studied from and, I hope, enjoyed reading this textbook and its companion hardcover version. Over the years I've had the opportunity to listen to the suggestions of many of these student readers. I've also received feedback from instructors on their teaching experiences with this book. As a result of this ongoing dialogue this text has always enjoyed a reputation for reliable, well-written content that reflects the changing face of the general psychology course, its students and their instructors. The third edition is no exception; it represents the collective suggestions of students and instructors alike. Advances in research and in the practice of psychology have dictated additional content updates and organizational improvements.

I'm particularly excited about a few additions that reflect the impact and educational potential of the personal computer and network technologies that are changing the world around us every day. The proliferation of PCs and campus-wide—even worldwide—computer networks has afforded me the opportunity to develop some "high-tech" teaching methods, and I'm excited that this edition introduces a new **Online** debate feature based on my teaching experiences with these new media. Likewise, a comprehensive multimedia implementation of this text, **Multimedia Psych**, pioneers the use of new interactive teaching and learning techniques. Finally, the new edition introduces a related World Wide Web home page with a wide range of informational and interactive resources and capabilities.

While there is much that is new in the third edition, my original goals for this book remain unchanged: to present a scientific, accurate, and thorough overview of psychology in engaging language that the average student can easily comprehend; to be current without being trendy; and to write clearly about psychology and its applications without being condescending. In addition, three unifying themes run throughout the text: (1) Psychology is a science; (2) human behavior and thought are diverse, varied, and affected by culture; and (3) the study of psychology involves active thinking, questioning, and problem solving.

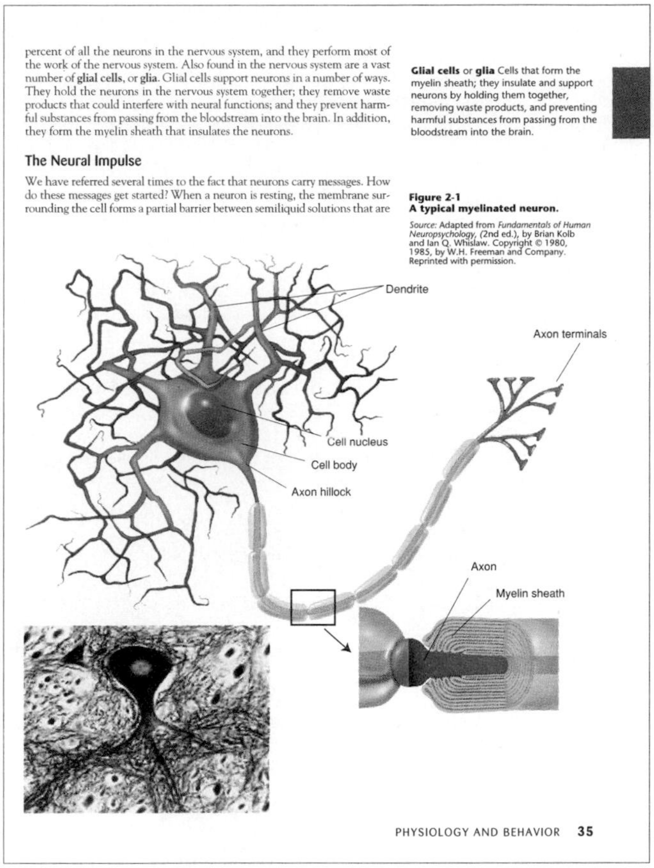

percent of all the neurons in the nervous system, and they perform most of the work of the nervous system. Also found in the nervous system are a vast number of **glial cells**, or **glia**. Glial cells support neurons in a number of ways. They hold the neurons in the nervous system together; they remove waste products that could interfere with neural functions; and they prevent harmful substances from passing from the bloodstream into the brain. In addition, they form the myelin sheath that insulates the neurons.

**Glial cells** or **glia** Cells that form the myelin sheath; they insulate and support neurons by holding them together, removing waste products, and preventing harmful substances from passing from the bloodstream into the brain.

### The Neural Impulse

We have referred several times to the fact that neurons carry messages. How do these messages get started? When a neuron is resting, the membrane surrounding the cell forms a partial barrier between semiliquid solutions that are

**Figure 2-1**
**A typical myelinated neuron.**

*Source:* Adapted from *Fundamentals of Human Neuropsychology*, (2nd ed.), by Brian Kolb and Ian Q. Whislaw. Copyright © 1980, 1985, by W.H. Freeman and Company. Reprinted with permission.

Dendrite
Axon terminals
Cell nucleus
Cell body
Axon hillock
Axon
Myelin sheath

PHYSIOLOGY AND BEHAVIOR 35

## The Science of Psychology

Every edition of this text has reflected my view of psychology as *the scientific study of behavior and mental processes*, and this new edition continues to reflect this belief. The third edition of *Understanding Psychology* presents key topics in a balanced, scientific manner, incorporating both classic studies and the most recent developments. Many of the changes I have introduced in this edition have made the book even more current and scientifically sound. For example, the chapter on abnormal psychology (Chapter 12) has been largely rewritten to accommodate both the new classification system introduced in *DSM-IV* and the current emphasis on the biopsychosocial (or integrated systems) approach. The chapter on physiology and neuroscience (Chapter 2) has an updated and expanded discussion of the workings of the brain and the nervous system. The memory chapter (Chapter 6) introduces an expanded discussion of recovered memories; and the chapter on stress (Chapter 11) now includes a more thorough discussion of the field of health psychology.

The third edition also brings with it a fresh, new, and interactive design. In keeping with the time-honored truism that "a picture is worth a thousand words," readers will discover an entirely reconceived, redrafted, and expanded anatomical art program in this edition, and completely new line art throughout the book.

This is only the beginning. Other content changes have been made in every chapter but are too numerous to detail in this space. (A complete list is available from the publisher.) Suffice to say that long-time users will likely find more new and updated material in the third edition than ever before. As was true for the previous editions, instructors looking for balanced, current scientific coverage of introductory psychology will find it in *Understanding Psychology*.

## Diversity

For today's students and instructors of introductory psychology, diversity is more than simply an issue for discussion and debate; it is a daily reality. Within a single classroom, students

**TABLE 12-2 Diagnostic Categories in DSM-IV**

**Disorders Usually First Diagnosed in Infancy, Childhood, or Adolescence**
Examples: mental retardation, learning disorders, autistic disorder, attention-deficit/hyperactivity disorder.

**Delirium, Dementia, and Amnestic and Other Cognitive Disorders**
Examples: delirium, dementia of the Alzheimer's type, amnestic disorder.

**Mental Disorders Due to a General Medical Condition**
Example: psychotic disorder due to epilepsy.

**Substance-Related Disorders**
Examples: alcohol dependence, cocaine dependence, nicotine dependence.

**Schizophrenia and Other Psychotic Disorders**
Examples: schizophrenia, schizoaffective disorder, delusional disorder.

**Mood Disorders**
Examples: major depressive disorder, dysthymic disorder, bipolar disorder.

**Anxiety Disorders**
Examples: panic disorder with agoraphobia, social phobia, obsessive-compulsive disorder, posttraumatic stress disorder, generalized anxiety disorder.

**Somatoform Disorders**
Examples: somatization disorder, conversion disorder, hypchondriasis.

**Factitious Disorders**
Example: factitious disorder with predominantly physical signs and symptoms.

**Dissociative Disorders**
Examples: dissociative amnesia, dissociative fugue, dissociative identity disorder, depersonalization disorder.

**Sexual and Gender-Identity Disorders**
Examples: male erectile disorder, female orgasmic disorder, vaginismus.

**Eating Disorders**
Examples: anorexia nervosa, bulimia nervosa.

**Sleep Disorders**
Examples: primary insomnia, narcolepsy, sleep terror disorder.

**Impulse-Control Disorders**
Examples: kleptomania, pyromania, pathological gambling.

**Adjustment Disorders**
Examples: adjustment disorder with depressed mood, adjustment disorder with conduct disturbance.

**Personality Disorders**
Examples: antisocial personality disorder, borderline personality disorder, narcissistic personality disorder, dependent personality disorder.

may vary in age from 16 to 60. Some come to their first psychology course having experienced poverty, racism, or sexism. Others have had to adjust to a new culture and language. The challenge confronting any textbook writer is to satisfy a heterogeneous audience without becoming "trendy" or unscientific. Over the last several years, the body of research examining issues of diversity has grown to significant levels, and as a result,

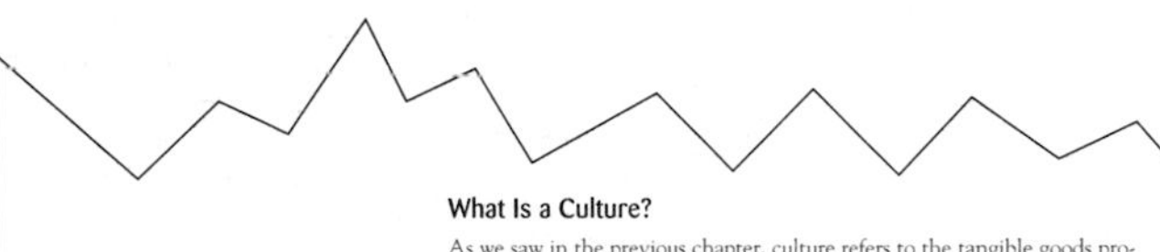

**What Is a Culture?**

As we saw in the previous chapter, culture refers to the tangible goods produced in a society, such as art, inventions, literature, and consumer goods. But it also refers to intangible processes such as shared beliefs, values, attitudes, traditions, and behaviors that are communicated from one generation to the next within a society (Barnouw, 1985). These cultural values, traditions, and beliefs in turn give rise to characteristic rules or norms that govern the behavior of people in that society, including what foods they eat, whom they may marry, and what they do on Saturday nights. These few examples should give you an idea of the extent to which cultural norms contribute to cultural diversity; we will see more examples in the pages that follow.

Diversity can exist within a culture as well as among cultures. This scene is from Nairobi, the capital of Kenya.

Moreover, there is room for diversity within a dominant culture in the form of *subcultures*, "cultural patterns that distinguish some segment of a society's population" (Macionis, 1993, p. 75). Texans, psychology professors, persons with AIDS, African-American women, homeless people, and teenagers all form subcultures within U.S. society. These subcultures have their own norms, values, and rituals, which may or may not be similar to those of the dominant culture. Moreover, many nations (such as the United States) are composed of various peoples with different backgrounds and traditions. Although we identify certain ideas, products, and behaviors as distinctly "American,"

I have expanded it as a key theme in this new edition. The most obvious addition to the book is the last chapter, titled "**Human Diversity.**" As its name suggests, it examines both gender and cultural diversity as they apply to such basic issues as cognitive skills, expression of emotions, and social behavior. The sections on cultural diversity address both diversity within the North American population and differences and similarities across cultures worldwide.

Rather than being confined to one chapter, however, *diversity is a recurring theme* throughout this text. Readers will find relevant research studies dealing with aspects of gender and cultural similarities and differences integrated in every chapter, wherever appropriate. Coverage begins with the first chapter, where I have expanded and updated the discussion of women in psychology. In later chapters I examine such topics as the relationships among stress, disease, and socioeconomic status (Chapter 11); the controversies surrounding intelligence tests (Chapter 7); cultural factors affecting clinical treatments (Chapter 13); and gender differences in sleep patterns and dream content (Chapter 4). As the composition of the student audience (and the psychology profession) has changed, *Understanding Psychology* has kept pace with these changes.

## Active Thinking: Promoting a Questioning Attitude

Education involves more than just memorizing information. A successful course in general psychology (and, for that matter, most other disciplines) helps students develop their ability to analyze, to ask questions, to evaluate the ideas of others, and ultimately to form their own ideas. Teaching active, critical thinking has long been a major objective of the courses I teach and of this text, and it remains a basic theme in the third edition.

**ONLINE: MODELS FOR ACTIVE THINKING** For the last 4 years I have introduced an online electronic bulletin board system (BBS) as an element in my courses here at Michigan. In addition to providing a convenient medium for routine course information, I've used the BBS to spur active thinking among my students. Students log on weekly to participate in online "discussions" of controversial topics. Of course, good instructors have used discussion/debate techniques in the classroom for years, but I've been quite happy with the results of our "high-tech experiment." The type of exchange that evolves online is quite similar to what you would encounter in a spirited classroom debate, but the digital medium affords an equal playing field to students who might be intimidated or otherwise reluctant to participate during in-class discussions. I'm also pleased with the writing practice this allows students. They appear to have taken to the new medium with great enthusiasm.

As a result of the strongly positive response I've had to these activities in my own classroom, this edition introduces in every chapter a new **Online** feature that highlights a controversy and provides a model of the active thought process for student readers: the *real* debates of other students. Each **Online** box introduces a discussion question, gives brief background information, and then presents excerpts from actual student communications about the issues. The questions, drawn directly from my teaching experience, will

**"Is the insanity defense ever valid?"**

In this chapter, we discuss the controversial insanity defense, which asserts that at the time of the crime the defendant was unable to understand the criminality of his or her act and to conform to the standards of the law. Among the issues the insanity defense raises are whether the mentally ill should be held responsible for their behaviors and whether people who successfully plead insanity and are later "cured" should then be punished by being sent to prison. In addition, because mental illness is a scientific term and insanity a legal one, an individual can be judged mentally ill yet be legally sane, as was the convicted serial killer Jeffrey Dahmer.

Insanity defenses are rare. When a defendant does enter such a plea, the court, as described in the chapter, tends to rely on expert testimony from psychologists and psychiatrists working for both sides. This practice has put psychology at the center of the insanity plea debate.

Do you think insanity should ever be considered a legal defense for criminal acts? Why or why not? After you have thought about these questions, take a few minutes to examine the opinions of some other students, which appear below.

•••••••

**KEISHA: I really don't think it should be called a defense for that implies an excuse. Just because you are considered insane does not mean you are not guilty.**

**PAT: The person is insane. Punishing him or her for being insane will not help. They must receive help, and if this is impossible, then they should be under supervision and cared for, but not punished.**

**TOM: I think if you know you are insane and potentially dangerous it's your societal responsibility to seek help beforehand, not after you've killed five people. If you were cognizant of your insanity, even if not of your act, you should be held to the same standards as everybody else.**

**MICHAEL: I think, by definition, an insane person does not know that he is insane, at least in most cases. It isn't really a loophole: it's not easy to prove that you were insane. . . . In most cases where it is not a genuine case of insanity, this comes out during a trial. . . . It is useless to set them free, as it is useless to throw them in jail, where they do not even understand why they are there, and will not comprehend the idea of punishment.**

**BOB: What is "temporary insanity"? How can you just say that when you killed someone, you were not yourself, but now you're okay? Does anyone who knows something about law know what temporary insanity is exactly? This is what I call a loophole because it seems like an excuse that anyone could use if they wanted to.**

**ANNMARIE: If it can be proven that the person was not thinking rationally and therefore could not control her actions, then punishing the person would be like punishing someone who had a heart attack while driving and hit someone when they lost control of the car.**

**MELISSA: There comes a point where the crimes are so hideous that they should be punished no matter what.**

**KARI: When a person is abused, even if their lives are not immediately in danger, the self-defense case becomes an issue, legally speaking. This is a very tough subject, but really has nothing to do with metal illness. Abuse of all sorts, mental and physical, may change a person's state of mind, but this is not necessarily a case of temporary insanity so much as a reasonable fear of the threat of violence.**

**BOB: I don't think temporary insanity is a good defense because these people also have shown that they have the capacity to do wrong, and when provoked again, they could repeat what they did.**

**AMAL: How can a person be responsible for his actions if he doesn't even know what it means to be responsible? The little boy who kills another child isn't old enough to understand; on TV people spring back to life, should the child assume that the neighbor child would not get up?**

**KEISHA: If you are taking a drug (maybe your doctor prescribed some outdated junk) and you kill someone, whose fault is it?**

•••••••

Did your views change after reading other students' views? If so, how? If not, why? How does your response to this discussion compare with your response to the discussion of alcoholism in Chapter 4? Are the two issues related? What can psychology teach us concerning the causes of human behavior?

appeal to today's students: Is the insanity defense valid (Chapter 12)? Are parents responsible for the way their children turn out (Chapter 8)? Is alcoholism a disease (Chapter 4)? Are permanent surgical or biological treatments ever justified for criminals (Chapter 13)?

For instructors and students who want to go one step further, the Instructor's Manual and student Study Guide contain additional discussion and writing activities related to the **Online** discussions. To allow interested instructors and students to participate actively in the **Online** process, Prentice Hall is establishing ongoing forums through America Online and the World Wide Web for students and instructors using this text. We hope to break down the walls of the classroom and encourage students across the country and around the world to engage in an ongoing exchange of ideas. (Point your web browser to this address: http:/ /www.prenhall.com/~morris.) The companion CD-ROM for this text, **Multimedia Psych** (discussed in detail later), features online program extensions that also allow students to engage in these activities. Further information can be requested directly from Prentice Hall either through local representatives or via the following Internet address: psych@prenhall.com.

## Other Active Thinking Elements

This edition contains some other critical thinking features based on cognitive research about effective learning from textbooks. At the start of every chapter readers will find **Think About It!** questions to get readers thinking about the material they will be reading. Students have told us that the questions serve as advance organizers while piquing their in-

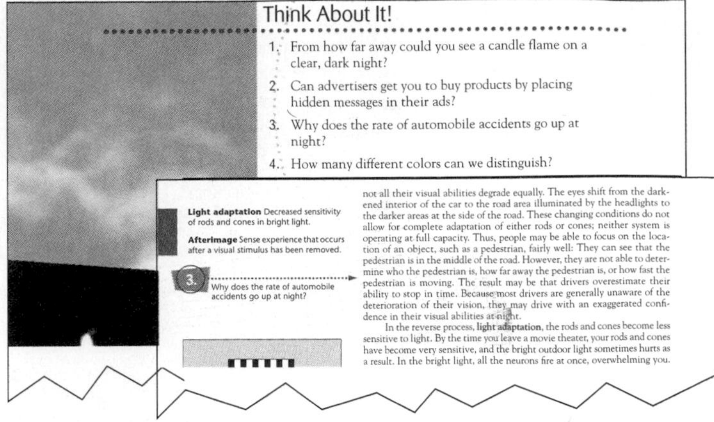
Think About It!

1. From how far away could you see a candle flame on a clear, dark night?
2. Can advertisers get you to buy products by placing hidden messages in their ads?
3. Why does the rate of automobile accidents go up at night?
4. How many different colors can we distinguish?

**Light adaptation** Decreased sensitivity of rods and cones in bright light.

**Afterimage** Sense experience that occurs after a visual stimulus has been removed.

3. Why does the rate of automobile accidents go up at night?

not all their visual abilities degrade equally. The eyes shift from the darkened interior of the car to the road area illuminated by the headlights to the darker areas at the side of the road. These changing conditions do not allow for complete adaptation of either rods or cones; neither system is operating at full capacity. Thus, people may be able to focus on the location of an object, such as a pedestrian, fairly well: They can see that the pedestrian is in the middle of the road. However, they are not able to determine who the pedestrian is, how far away the pedestrian is, or how fast the pedestrian is moving. The result may be that drivers overestimate their ability to stop in time. Because most drivers are generally unaware of the deterioration of their vision, they may drive with an exaggerated confidence in their visual abilities at night.

In the reverse process, **light adaptation**, the rods and cones become less sensitive to light. By the time you leave a movie theater, your rods and cones have become very sensitive, and the bright outdoor light sometimes hurts as a result. In the bright light, all the neurons fire at once, overwhelming you.

terest in the material that follows. Later in the chapter, each question is repeated in the margin opposite the text discussion where the related issue is addressed.

The critical perspective also pervades the narrative of the text. In many cases I examine a topic from different angles, showing my readers that there isn't always a "right" answer or approach to a psychological issue or problem. In addition, each chapter contains a new category of feature discussions, titled **Controversies**, that examine a specific issue or study from a variety of perspectives and then encourage students to develop their own ideas: How do we see forms and objects (Chapter 3)? Can illusions keep you healthy (Chapter 11)? Finally, each chapter now concludes with a number of **Critical Thinking and Applications** questions that require students to analyze, evaluate, and interpret some of the basic themes of the chapter.

## Student-friendly and Interactive

Throughout every edition of my text I have kept in mind that my final audience consists primarily of college undergraduates. Having taught undergraduates for more than 25 years, I realize that it is essential to make a textbook as accessible and helpful as possible. For this reason I have retained the clear, straightforward writing style to which students and reviewers have responded so positively over the years. Once again the text contains plenty of examples relevant to today's undergraduates. The tone is conversational without resorting to slang. Key terms are printed in **boldface** and defined in the margin where they first appear.

The chapters themselves contain many discussions that encourage activities, introduce strategies for personal change, or provide information for students seeking assistance with personal or family problems. Thus, we tell students what kinds of behaviors might indicate an alcohol-abuse problem (Chapter 4); how to improve their memories (Chapter 6); and how to deal with exam stresses (Chapter 11). The therapies chapter (Chapter 13) provides a long list of self-help organizations for all types of problems, along with addresses and phone numbers.

The teaching pedagogy integrated in every chapter has always made this book a student favorite. Cognitive psychology research has proved the value of structure and elaborative rehearsals in improving reading comprehension and retention. As a result, the chapter-opening **Overview** provides student readers with a road map for each chapter, then reinforce and help organize material for students when they appear again as the basic structure for end-of-chapter **Summaries.** **Summary Tables** of key concepts within chapters provide concise reviews of the most important concepts (for example, defense mechanisms, types of memory, theories of personality, and the structures and functions of the brain). The result is that students don't just process lists of unrelated facts, but instead have a cognitive map in which to contextualize, better understand, and more effectively relate and recall concepts.

## Supplements

It is increasingly true today that, as valuable as a good textbook is, it is still only one element of a comprehensive learn-

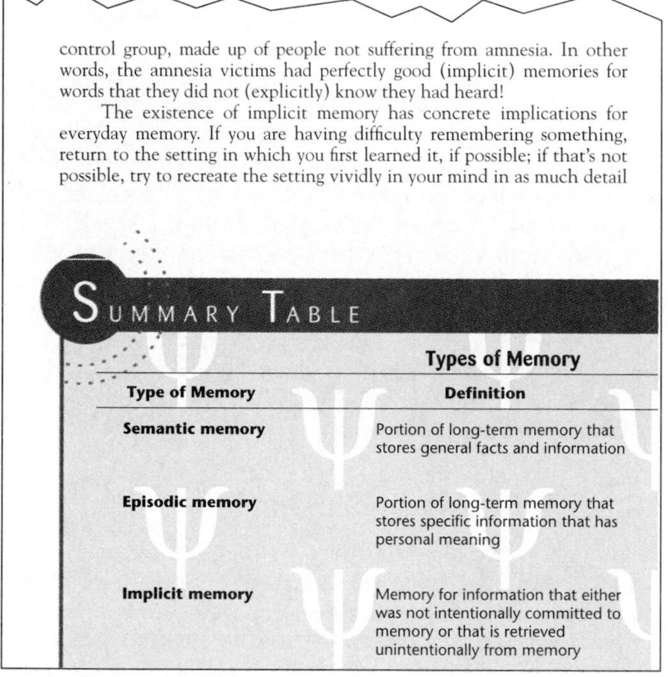

control group, made up of people not suffering from amnesia. In other words, the amnesia victims had perfectly good (implicit) memories for words that they did not (explicitly) know they had heard!

The existence of implicit memory has concrete implications for everyday memory. If you are having difficulty remembering something, return to the setting in which you first learned it, if possible; if that's not possible, try to recreate the setting vividly in your mind in as much detail

SUMMARY TABLE

Types of Memory

| Type of Memory | Definition |
|---|---|
| **Semantic memory** | Portion of long-term memory that stores general facts and information |
| **Episodic memory** | Portion of long-term memory that stores specific information that has personal meaning |
| **Implicit memory** | Memory for information that either was not intentionally committed to memory or that is retrieved unintentionally from memory |

ing package. Throughout the editions of my book, Prentice Hall and I have labored to produce not only a well-written text, but also a full range of supplemental learning tools. The supplements package that accompanies the third edition is the most comprehensive and impressive yet.

## For Instructors

***Test Item File*** (by Gary Piggrem and Charles G. Morris, ISBN 0-13-443425-0). The Test Item File for ***Understanding Psychology*** has always been among the strongest and most reliable available, thanks in large part to the careful, dedicated work of my colleague Gary Piggrem. (In fact, I'm happy to note that users of prior editions have called our Test Item File "bulletproof.") For the third edition, we have again incorporated the results of the extensive class-testing programs of prior editions. In addition to the detailed analysis and careful revision that resulted from this process, our own in-class experience using many questions from the Test Item File led us to modify the wording of a number of questions. Those revisions were also incorporated into the new test file. Finally, we engaged outside reviewers to comb through the entire Test Item File and identify incorrect or potentially ambiguous items that might otherwise have eluded detection. In each case, we made appropriate revisions to the items in question. New questions were added (most from items I have developed over the years for use in my own classes), and, as you would expect, the Test Item File reflects the many content changes in the third edition as well. The end result is a Test Item File that is stronger than ever before. We will continue our effort to improve and expand the Test Item File for future editions, and as always, I welcome your comments, suggestions, and teaching feedback. Send them directly to: Charles G. Morris, Department of Psychology, University of Michigan, Ann Arbor, MI 48109-1109.

In addition to this new Test Item File there is an updated supplemental test bank, **Core Test Item File III** (by Fred W. Whitford, ISBN 0-13-782640-0) consisting of over 3,000 additional class-tested items organized by major topics and accompanied by statistical item analysis available from Prentice Hall.

***Prentice Hall Custom Test for Windows, Macintosh, and DOS.*** The new testing software for this edition supports a full range of editing and graphics options, network test administration capabilities, and greater ease-of-use than ever before,.

***Toll-free Telephone Test Preparation Service*** is available to accompany this text. Interested instructors select up to 200 questions from the Test Item File, then call the Prentice Hall support staff (1-800-842-2958). Two distinct versions of the test are mailed within 48 hours, ready for duplication.

***Instructor's Resource Manual*** (by Traci Giuliano and Alan Swinkels, ISBN 0-13-443417-X). The paperbound, 3-hole punched Instructor's Resource Manual for this edition was extensively revised, rewritten, and expanded. In addition to lecture outlines and teaching suggestions for each chapter, the new manual contains all of the teaching annotations found in the previous edition's annotated instructor's edition. Authors Traci Giuliano and Alan Swinkels, who were also our chapter consultants for the new ***Human Diversity*** chapter, have added a wealth of information and resources related to diversity and teaching in a multicultural classroom. Instructors will find a wide array of new activities, exercises, and in-class demonstrations to enliven lectures and invigorate classroom discussions.

***Teaching Psychology, Second Edition*** (by Fred W. Whitford, ISBN 0-13-443193-6). This helpful manual covers many of the issues and questions related to teaching a general psychology course. The second edition includes a new chapter on Internetworking and Electronic Communications, along with additional information on the many teaching of psychology conferences and interest groups that have emerged in the last several years. Other new or expanded topics include sections on teaching to a diverse student population, an updated annotated bibliography, and expanded resource and reference lists throughout.

***Color Transparencies—Prentice Hall Series IV.*** An entirely new set of more than 180 full-color transparencies has been developed for this edition by David Steele. Drawn from illustrations within the third edition as well as from outside sources, Series IV was designed with lecture hall visibility and convenience in mind. (Some restrictions may apply. Contact your local Prentice Hall representative for details. )

***Digital Resource Library CD-ROM for Instructors*** (Release 1.0, ISBN 0-13-443201-0). The Digital Resource Library CD-ROM with Lecture Maker presentation software includes the entire set of digitized color transparencies, interactive Teaching Animations, and exciting new presentation software that allows instructors to assemble and sequence laser disc segments, digital graphics, and interactive animations in computer-driven lectures. (Some restrictions may apply. Contact your local Prentice Hall representative for details.)

***ABC News/Prentice Hall Video Libraries for Introductory Psychology.*** Several libraries ar eavailable, featuring more than 50 segments from award-winning ABC News programs, including *Nightline*, *20/20*, *Prime Time Live*, and *American Agenda*. (Some restrictions may apply. Contact your local Prentice Hall representative for details. )

***The Alliance Series: The Annenberg/CPB Collection*** is an extensive collection of professionally produced videos available with any Prentice Hall introductory psychology textbook. Selections include videos in the following Annenberg series: *The Brain, The Brain Teaching Modules, Discovering Psychology, The Mind, and The Mind Teaching Modules.*

Two Supplementary Laser Discs are available. ***LaserPsych for Introductory Psychology*** (ISBN 0-13-73538-1) and ***The Auxiliary Laser Disc for Psychology*** (ISBN 0-02-409612-1) provide an abundance of still graphics, demonstrations, animations, and video segments from classic experiments to enhance lecture presentations. (Some restrictions may apply. Contact your local Prentice Hall representative for details. )

**PSYCHActivities Software Simulations** features brief and entertaining activities and demonstrations through which students can participate in recreating psychological principles and concepts. Available in IBM and Macintosh versions. (IBM 3" ISBN 0-13-735622-6; Macintosh ISBN 0-13-73540-7)

***Psychology Simulations*** contains 15 interactive experiment programs for lab or in-class use. Each simulation helps teachers reinforce areas taught in class.

## For Students

***Multimedia PSYCH CD-ROM for Students*** (Windows ISBN 0-13-443250-9; Macintosh ISBN 0-13-443516-8) contains the complete text of the print version of the textbook, plus high-resolution, full-color graphics, interactive animations, an objective-driven, diagnostic/prescriptive student tutorial, digital video, and interactive World Wide Web and America Online components. **Multimedia Psych** features hypertext cross-references and other automated navigation tools, as well as a "talking" on-line glossary and detailed, hot-linked index.

***Study Guide,*** by Joyce Bishop, (ISBN 0-13-443508-7) includes study outlines, learning objectives, key concept reviews, and a range of multiple-choice, matching, and short-answer questions designed to promote mastery of the text. Author Joyce Bishop provides additional language-based activities for each chapter to facilitate learning for non-native speakers. The new edition features a variety of graphics drawn from diagrams in the text and provides writing exercises based on the student-to-student "Online" debate discussions in the text.

***How to Think Like a Psychologist: Critical Thinking in Psychology***, by Donald H. McBurney, University of Pittsburgh (ISBN 0-02-378392-3), is a unique supplementary text that uses a question-and-answer format to explore some of the most common questions students ask about psychology. A specially discounted combination package with this text is available.

***Forty Studies that Changed Psychology, Second Edition***, by Roger Hock, New England College (ISBN 0-13-3398896-X), is a widely adopted supplementary reader featuring 40 seminal research studies that have shaped the discipline. For each study, Hock provides an overview of the research, its methodology, its findings, and the impact these findings have had on current thinking in the discipline. A specially discounted combination package with this text is available.

The **New York Times *Supplement for General Psychology.*** When you adopt *Understanding Psychology, Third Edition*, Prentice Hall and *The New York Times* will provide you with a complimentary student newspaper in quantities for your class. This collection of articles is designed to supplement classroom lectures and improve student access to current real-world issues and research.

***The Guide to the Brain: A Graphical Workbook, Second Edition***, by Mark B. Kristal. This study aid helps students learn the names and location of the most important structures and functions of the brain and nervous system. The second edition offers more review exercises, expanded figures, and brief concept summaries. A full-color, digital version is available free for downloading, at Prentice Hall's psychology forum on America Online and at our World Wide Web site.

***Succeeding in Psych and in College,*** by Connie Schick, Eileen Astor-Stetson, and Brett L. Beck (ISBN 0-13-192394-

3). This practical supplement helps students to better prepare for the General Psychology course. It includes tips on: organizing for the semester, taking effective class notes, reading the assigned text productively, preparing for tests, and interacting effectively with professors.

***The Prentice Hall Critical Thinking Audio Study Cassette*** (ISBN 0-13-678335-X). This 60-minute cassette shows students how developing their critical thinking and study skills will improve reading, listening, note taking, test performance, job preparation, and job performance.

## Acknowledgments

As always, I am immensely grateful for the assistance I received from the many people who reviewed the previous edition and suggested improvements for this edition. I am deeply indebted to the small team of content specialists who provided detailed technical feedback, helped me to revise certain areas, and served as overall consultants for individual chapters. Their contributions were largely responsible for the thoroughness of this revision.

Matt Olson, Hamline University (Physiology, Sensation and Perception, and Learning)
John Benjafield, Brock University (Memory, Cognition, and Mental Abilities)
Neil Salkind, University of Kansas (Life Span Development)
Bob Emery, University of Virginia (Abnormal Behavior and Therapies)
Traci Giuliano, Southwestern University, and Alan Swinkels, St. Edward's University (Human Diversity)
Joyce Bishop, Golden West College (learning pedagogy throughout the text)
Joe Masucci, Nassau Community College (technical proofreading of the entire manuscript)

Let me also thank those individuals who completed user surveys and chapter reviews. Their comments and suggestions were an enormous help to me.

Philip Captain, Liberty University
Ed Cooperman, Kingsborough Community College
Susan S. Finlay, Suffolk Community College
Tony Fowler, Florence-Darlington Technical College
Bernadette Gadzella, East Texas State University
Jonathan Golding, University of Kentucky
George Grosser, American International College
Mary Grunke, Kansas City Kansas Community College
Greene P. Hankerson, Polk Community College
Charles Kaplan, University of North Carolina - Charlotte
Richard Lance, Haywood Community College
Al Maisto, University of North Carolina - Charlotte
James R. Marks, West Los Angeles College
Charles R. Martin-Stanley, Central State University
Marilyn Milligan, Santa Rosa Junior College
Ken Murdoff, Lane Community College
John Nield, Utah Valley State College
William Pelz, Herkimer County Community College
Paula M. Popovich, Ohio Univeristy
Camille M. Quinn, Tulsa Junior College
B. Tara Rao, Ferris State University
Richard Reardon, University of Oklahoma
Jeanne Riddell, Grossmont College
Carol Roberts, Springfield Technical Community College
Michael Rodman, Middlesex Community College
Eurston Rollins, Manatee Community College
Robert Russell, State University of New York - Delhi
Daniel Stern, York College
Stuart Taylor, Kent State University
Laura Uba, California State University, Northridge
Paul J. Wellman, Texas A & M University
Kay D. Young, North Iowa Area Community College

I would also like to express my gratitude to the team of people at Prentice Hall, all of whom made major contributions. Thanks especially to my "right hand" throughout the revision process, senior development editor Bob Weiss, whose intelligence and attention to detail are evident on every page of this edition. Editor in Chief Pete Janzow and his assistant, Marilyn Coco, guided the entire project with skill and insight. The production of the Ninth Edition was managed by Barbara Kittle and Bonnie Biller, and directly supervised by Shelly Kupperman, whose dedication, expertise, and quiet persistence assured an end product of very high quality, delivered on schedule! Thanks also to manufacturing buyer Tricia Kenny, and to Liz Kendall and Nicole Signoretti, who coordinated various aspects of the ancillary program for this edition. Leslie Osher and the team from Siren Design did a super job on the design of both the interior and the cover. The formatting of this edition, done in-house at Prentice Hall by Yvette Raven, enabled us to coordinate the complex aspects of producing the text and the companion CD-ROM at the same time. Lori Kane, Phyllis Bregman and Grace Walkus spearheaded this process and proved to be skillful troubleshooters whenever necessary. And photo researcher Eloise Marion and reference researcher Bryan Skib of the University of Michigan's Hatcher Library provided knowledgeable assistance in their assigned tasks. Finally, special thanks to Lauren Ward, Michael Alread, and Aileen Ugural for directing the marketing campaign for the book.

Charles G. Morris

## Think About It!

1. What are the major areas or subdivisions of psychology?
2. What is the scientific method, and how does it apply to psychology?
3. Is it ethical for people to use subjects in psychological experiments without telling them?
4. *True or false*: Sigmund Freud was the founder of psychology.
5. What is the difference between a psychologist and a psychiatrist?

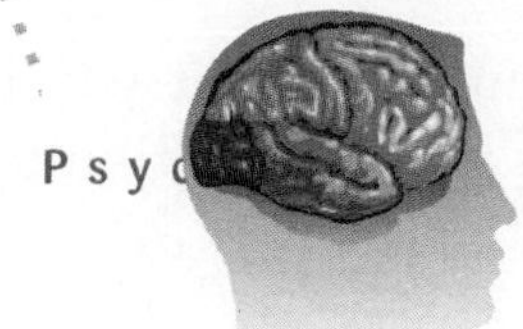

Psy... Case Study Behav... Ethics Survey P... trist Co...

# THE SCIENCE OF PSYCHOLOGY

# 1

## Overview

**Why are you taking a psychology course? What would you like to learn from it? What questions would you like to have answered?**

When students like you were asked what kinds of questions they hoped would be answered in their psychology course, they gave a broad range of responses:

- Why do some people have more motivation than others? Why does motivation sometimes disappear?
- How much of our behavior is inherited?
- How valid are IQ tests? Do they, and tests like the SAT and ACT, really predict how well we are likely to do in school?
- What is the most effective way to learn?
- What effects do different types of punishment have on children's behavior?
- What influence do parents have on their children's personalities?
- How does the brain function? How does it affect our behavior?
- Does ESP exist?
- Who determines what kind of behavior will be classified as "abnormal"?
- How successful is psychotherapy in curing psychological problems?
- Are human beings naturally aggressive?
- Do we shape our behavior, or does our behavior shape us?
- Does psychology have practical uses? How does psychology relate to other fields?

As you can see, psychology students wonder about a variety of issues relating to thought and behavior. Surely you are curious about some of the same things. Like most people, you have probably wondered about how heredity affects behavior, the uses of intelligence testing, the development of personality, and how psychologists treat "abnormal behavior." And like most students, you are no doubt interested in just what psychology is all about and whether it is a practical field of study.

## THE FIELD OF PSYCHOLOGY

What are the major areas or subdivisions of psychology?

Two major organizations deal with issues of interest to contemporary psychologists: the long-established American Psychological Association (APA), dating back to the last century, and the much younger American Psychological Society (APS), founded in 1988. The APA is made up of 48 divisions (see Table 1-1), each of which represents an area of particular interest to psychologists today. The APS takes a more targeted approach, promoting the academic and scientific bases of psychology. Among the broader specialty areas in this provocative field are the following:

**TABLE 1-1 American Psychological Association Divisions (1991)**

| DIVISION | |
|---|---|
| 1. General Psychology | 26. History of Psychology |
| 2. Teaching of Psychology | 27. Society for Community Research and Action |
| 3. Experimental Psychology | 28. Psychopharmacology and Substance Abuse |
| 5. Evaluation, Measurement, and Statistics | 29. Psychotherapy |
| 6. Physiological and Comparative Psychology | 30. Psychological Hypnosis |
| 7. Developmental Psychology | 31. State Psychological Association Affairs |
| 8. Society for Personality and Social Psychology | 32. Humanistic Psychology |
| 9. Society for the Psychological Study of Social Issues (SPSSI) | 33. Mental Retardation and Developmental Disabilities |
| 10. Psychology and the Arts | 34. Population and Environmental Psychology |
| 12. Clinical Psychology | 35. Psychology of Women |
| 13. Consulting Psychology | 36. Psychology of Religion |
| 14. The Society for Industrial and Organizational Psychology | 37. Child, Youth, and Family Services |
| 15. Educational Psychology | 38. Health Psychology |
| 16. School Psychology | 39. Psychoanalysis |
| 17. Counseling Psychology | 40. Clinical Neuropsychology |
| 18. Psychologists in Public Service | 41. American Psychology–Law Society |
| 19. Military Psychology | 42. Psychologists in Independent Practice |
| 20. Adult Devclopment and Aging | 43. Family Psychology |
| 21. Applied Experimental and Engineering Psychologists | 44. Society for the Psychological Study of Lesbian and Gay Issues |
| 22. Rehabilitation Psychology | 45. Society for the Psychological Study of Ethnic Minority Issues |
| 23. Society for Consumer Psychology | 46. Media Psychology |
| 24. Theoretical and Philosophical Psychology | 47. Exercise and Sport Psychology |
| 25. Experimental Analysis of Behavior | 48. Peace Psychology |
| | 49. Group Psychology and Group Psychotherapy |
| | 50. Psychology of Addictive Behaviors |

There are no divisions 4 or 11.

A psychologist talking with a patient (client). About half of all psychologists specialize in clinical or counseling psychology.

*Developmental psychology*, which explores the processes of mental and physical growth in humans from the prenatal period through childhood, adolescence, adulthood, and old age,

*Psysiological psychology*, which investigates the effects of organic processes and phenomena on behavior,

*Experimental psychology*, which delves into such basic psychological processes as learning, memory, sensation, perception, cognition, motivation, and emotion,

*Personality psychology*, which examines the differences among people in such traits as anxiety, sociability, self-esteem, the need for achievement, and aggressiveness,

*Clinical and counseling psychology*, which focuses on the diagnosis, causes, and treatment of psychological disorders (clinical psychology), or helps people cope with "normal" problems, such as choosing a career or dealing with marital difficulties (counseling psychology),

*Social psychology*, which probes the influence people have on one another,

*Industrial and organizational (I/O) psychology*, which addresses such issues as training personnel and improving working conditions and studies the effects of automation on humans.

**Psychology** The scientific study of behavior and mental processes.

**Scientific method** An approach to knowledge that relies on collecting data, generating a theory to explain the data, producing testable hypotheses based on the theory, and testing those hypotheses empirically.

**Theory** Systematic explanation of a phenomenon; it organizes known facts, allows us to predict new facts, and permits us to exercise a degree of control over the phenomenon.

**Hypotheses** Specific, testable predictions derived from a theory.

## THE GOALS OF PSYCHOLOGY

From time to time, most people have given thought to some or all of these issues, but does that mean that everyone is a psychologist? Not at all.

**Psychology** is the science of behavior and mental processes. The key word in this definition is *science*. Although psychologists share the average person's interest in behavior and the unseen mental processes that shape it, they rely on the **scientific method** when searching out answers to psychological questions. They collect data through careful, systematic observation; attempt to explain what they have observed by developing theories to explain their observations; make new predictions based on those theories; and then systematically test those predictions empirically to determine whether they are correct. Thus, like all scientists, psychologists use the scientific method to *describe*, *explain*, *predict*, and, eventually to achieve some measure of *control* over what they study. This method improves the critical thinking abilities of everyone who undertakes it (see the Highlights box titled "Critical Thinking: A Fringe Benefit of Studying Psychology").

An industrial/organizational psychologist might study this work team to see how the relations among its members affect motivation and performance on the job.

Let's see what this means by looking at how psychologists would approach the question of whether males and females differ when it comes to aggressiveness. Some people believe that males are naturally more aggressive than females. Others contend that this is merely a stereotype, or at least that it is not always true. First, psychologists would want to find out whether men and women actually differ in aggressive behavior. A number of research studies have addressed this question, and the evidence seems unequivocal: Males do behave more aggressively than females, particularly when we're talking about physical aggression (Eagly & Steffen, 1986; Frieze et al., 1978). Having established that there are sex differences in aggression, and having *described* those differences, psychologists would next seek to *explain* them. Physiological psychologists would tend to ascribe these differences to anatomy or body chemistry; developmental psychologists might look to early childhood experience and the way a child is taught to behave "like a boy" or "like a girl"; and social psychologists might explain the differences as a function of societal constraints against aggressive behavior in women.

2. What is the scientific method, and how does it apply to psychology?

Each of these explanations stands as a **theory** about the causes of sex differences in aggression; each attempts to distill from a large number of facts a few principles. And each theory allows us to make a number of new **hypotheses**, or predictions, about the phenomenon in question—in this case, aggressive behavior. For example, if gender differences in aggression arise because males have a greater amount of the male hormone testosterone than females do, as psychological psychologists might posit, then we would predict that reducing the level of testosterone would reduce aggressive behavior in men. If sex differences in aggression stem from early training, as developmental psychologists might assert, then we would predict

# HIGHLIGHTS

## Critical Thinking: A Fringe Benefit of Studying Psychology

Do you believe that

1. Gifted children are less well adjusted than other children?
2. Opposites attract?
3. Subliminal messages on self-help audiotapes have beneficial effects?

Since most of us believe in the virtue of common sense, you probably answered *yes* to each of these three popular commonsense assumptions. However, you may be amazed at how many of our commonsense assumptions prove false when subjected to critical thinking.

What exactly is critical thinking? It is the process of examining the information we have and then, based on this inquiry, making judgments and decisions. When we think critically, we define problems, examine evidence, analyze assumptions—our own as well as others'—consider alternatives, and ultimately find reasons to support or reject an argument.

To think critically, you must adopt a certain state of mind, one characterized by objectivity, caution, a willingness to challenge the opinions of others, and—perhaps most difficult of all—a willingness to subject your own deepest beliefs to searching scrutiny. If this process seems to you similar to the scientific method used by psychologists and other scientists,it is.

The ability to think critically is a learned behavior. Many people, including quite a few introductory psychology students, view psychology as nothing more than common sense thinly disguised by fancy jargon. As we have seen, however, psychology is based on data resulting from carefully designed research. As you read about some of that research in this text, your own critical thinking skills will be sharpened. In fact, according to recent research, training in psychology teaches people to think critically, perhaps because much of psychology is based on studies that subject commonsense beliefs to scientific scrutiny. In several studies of graduate students in psychology, medicine, law, and chemistry, it was the psychology students who improved their reasoning abilities the most during the first 2 years of graduate study and who emerged from graduate school especially well equipped to deal with statistical and methodological reasoning (Lehman, Lempert, & Nisbett, 1988; Nisbett et al., 1987).

Psychologists employ a number of strategies in questioning assumptions and examining data. Let's look at the following rules of psychological investigation and use them to judge whether the second statement above, "Opposites attract," is true.

1. *Define the problem or the question you're investigating.* (Do opposites attract each other?)
2. *Suggest a theory or a reasonable explanation for the problem.* (People who are dissimilar balance each other out in a relationship.)
3. *Collect and examine all the available evidence.* In doing so, be skeptical of people's self-reports, as they may be subjectively biased. If data conflict, try to find more evidence. (Research on attraction yields no support for the idea that opposites attract, whereas many studies confirm that people of similar looks, interests, age, family background, religion, values, and attitudes seek each other out.)
4. *Analyze assumptions.* (Since balancing different people's strengths and weaknesses is a good way to form a group, it is probably a good basis for personal relationships as well, and that is why people of opposite temperaments are naturally attracted to each other. Yet research evidence proves this commonsense assumption untrue. Why should similars attract? One important reason is that they often belong to the same social circles, and proximity is, research suggests, a big factor in attraction.)
5. *Avoid oversimplifying.* (Don't overlook the evidence that people of similar temperaments find living together rather difficult in some ways. For example, living with someone who is as tense as you are may be harder than living with someone of calm temperament—your opposite.)
6. *Draw conclusions carefully.* (It seems safe to conclude that, *in general*, opposites don't attract, but there are specific exceptions to this general rule.)
7. *Consider every alternative interpretation.* (People may cite cases they know of that conflict with your conclusion. Remember, however, that their arguments are based on subjective observations and a far narrower database than attraction researchers have used.)
8. *Recognize the relevance of research to events and situations.* (If you have been thinking of dating someone whose temperament seems quite different from yours, you may decide, on the basis of what you now know, not to rush into things but to go more slowly, testing your own observations against your knowledge of research findings.)

By the way, psychological research has proved that the other two statements are also false.

**Naturalistic observation** Research method involving the systematic study of animal or human behavior in natural settings rather than in the laboratory.

that there would be fewer sex differences in aggression in families where parents did not stress gender differences in behavior. Finally, if sex differences in aggression are traceable to societal constraints against aggression in women, a view social psychologists might support, then we would predict that removing or reducing those prohibitions would result in higher levels of aggressive behavior among women.

Each of these predictions or hypotheses may be tested through research, and the results should indicate whether one theory is better than another at accounting for known facts and predicting new facts. Assuming that one or more of the theories is supported by research evidence, it should be possible to *control* aggressive behavior to a greater degree than was possible before. For example, if people with a higher level of the hormone testosterone are indeed more aggressive than those with less of this hormone, it should be possible to make a highly aggressive person less aggressive by lowering the overall level of testosterone in that person's body.

## RESEARCH METHODS IN PSYCHOLOGY

In trying to understand people and their thoughts, feelings, and behaviors, psychologists use a variety of research methods, each of which has advantages and disadvantages compared to the others. In this section of the chapter, we will examine some of the techniques frequently used by psychologists as they pursue their research.

### Naturalistic Observation

Psychologists rely on **naturalistic observation** to study animal or human behavior in its natural context instead of under imposed conditions in the laboratory. Most of us use this method, too. When you watch dogs playing in the park or observe how your professors conduct their classes, you are using a form of naturalistic observation. One psychologist with this real-life orientation might observe behavior in a school or a factory; another might actually join a family to study the behavior of its members; still another might observe animals in their natural habitats instead of in cages. The primary advantage of naturalistic observation is that the behavior observed in everyday life will be more natural, spontaneous, and varied than that observed in a laboratory.

For example, W. H. Whyte (1956) wanted to know how people living in a suburban community chose their friends. He kept tabs on his subjects by reading the local newspaper. The social column told him when parties were being given and who was invited to each one. After collecting such data for some time, Whyte noticed that there were definite friendship patterns in the community. *Proximity*—people's nearness to one another—was the critical factor in determining which people became friends. Whyte concluded that all things being equal, people are more likely to make friends with those who live nearby. He might have been able to learn this by asking people, but he could not have discovered it in a laboratory.

The world-famous scientist Jane Goodall has spent most of her adult life observing chimpanzees in their natural environment in Africa.

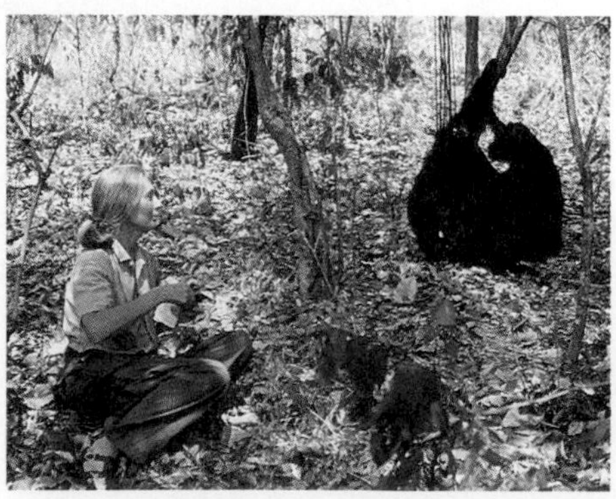

Whyte restricted his observations to one specific behavior: going to parties. It is not always possible, however, to make such restrictions. Because naturalistic observation does not constrain people's behavior, psychologists using this method have to take that behavior as it comes. Naturalistic observers cannot suddenly yell "Freeze!" when they want to study what is going on in more detail. Nor can psychologists tell people to stop what they are doing because it is not what they are interested in researching.

One of the central problems with naturalistic observation is *observer bias*. Any police officer will tell you how unreliable eyewitnesses can be. Even psychologists who are trained observers may subtly distort what they see to make it conform to what they were hoping to see. For this reason, the behavior of subjects in observational studies is often videotaped and the tapes scored by someone who does not know what the study is designed to find out. Another problem is that in their detailed notes of the observation psychologists may not record behavior they deem irrelevant. Therefore, it is sometimes preferable to rely on a team of trained observers who pool their notes. This strategy often generates a more complete picture than one observer could draw alone.

**Case study** Intensive description and analysis of a single individual or just a few individuals.

Researchers using naturalistic observation also run into the problem that the observed behavior depends on the particular time, place, and group of people involved. Unlike laboratory experiments that can be replicated over and over again, each natural situation is a one-time-only occurrence. Therefore, psychologists prefer not to make general statements based on information from naturalistic studies alone. They would rather test the information under controlled conditions in the laboratory before they apply it to situations other than the original one.

When people are unaware that they are being watched, they behave more naturally. A one-way mirror is therefore sometimes used for *naturalistic observation*.

Despite these disadvantages, naturalistic observation is a valuable tool for psychologists. After all, real-life behavior is what psychology is all about. Although the complexity of human interaction may be difficult to sort out, naturalistic observation is a boon to psychologists. It gives them new ideas, which can then be studied more systematically and in more detail in the laboratory than in the field. This method also helps researchers keep their perspective by reminding them of the larger world outside the lab.

## Case Studies

Another research method, which bears striking similarities to naturalistic observation, is the **case study** method. A researcher using this methods observes the real-life behavior of one person or just a few people at a time. For example, Gordon Allport described in some detail the relationship between a woman and her son as revealed in more than 300 letters written by the woman over a period of years (Allport, 1965). Case studies also helped Sigmund Freud forge his psychological theories and refine his therapeutic techniques. One of his patients was a 5-year-old boy whom he called "Little Hans" (Freud, 1909). Little Hans had a terrible fear of horses, which Freud later concluded stemmed from his fear of his father and sexual longing for his mother. This case not only confirmed Freud's suspicion that even very young children have sexual desires but also his belief that strong emotions that are pushed out of consciousness may surface in disguised form and cause psychological distress. Another famous psychologist, Jean Piaget, developed a comprehensive theory of cognitive development by carefully studying each of his three children as they grew and changed during childhood; his theory of cognitive development is described in the chapter called "Life Span Development."

Like naturalistic observation, case studies give researchers valuable insights but have some significant drawbacks. Observer bias is as much a problem here as it is with naturalistic observation. Moreover, since each person is unique, it is impossible to know whether we can confidently draw

**Surveys** Questionnaires or interviews administered to a selected group of people.

**Correlational method** Research technique based on the naturally occurring relationship between two or more variables.

general conclusions from a single case. Nevertheless, case studies figure prominently in psychological research. For example, in the next chapter, you will learn about the famous case of Phineas Gage, whose bizarre brain injury led researchers to believe that the front portion of the brain is important for the control of emotions and the ability to plan and carry out complex tasks. In 1959, Brenda Milner described another brain-damaged patient, called "H. M.," who could remember events that preceded the injury but had no long-term recall of events that happened after it. This observation prompted psychologists to posit that we have several kinds of memory that differ from one another in key ways, an idea that we will explore in greater detail in the chapter titled "Memory."

Surveys can generate a great deal of useful information, but only if the questions are unambiguous and the people surveyed are carefully selected and answer the questions honestly.

## Surveys

In some respects, **surveys** address some of the shortcomings of naturalistic observation and case studies. In survey research, a carefully selected group of people is asked a set of predetermined questions in face-to-face interviews or in the form of questionnaires. Perhaps the most familiar surveys are the polls taken before major elections: For weeks or months before the election, we are bombarded with estimates of the percentage of people likely to vote for each candidate. But surveys are used for other purposes as well. For example, a 1991 survey determined that 61 percent of the adults questioned by telephone believed that advertisers embedded subliminal messages in their ads, and 56 percent were convinced that such messages make people buy things they do not want (Lev, 1991). As we shall see in the chapter on sensation and perception, there is no scientific evidence supporting these beliefs. According to another 1991 survey, 38 percent of the American women polled said they had been "the object of sexual advances, propositions, or unwanted sexual discussions from men who supervised [them] or could affect [their] position at work" and that only 10 percent of that group had reported the incident at the time (Kolbert, 1991). This survey—and others like it—indicates that sexual harassment in the workplace is both widespread and underreported.

Surveys may generate a great deal of interesting and useful information at relatively low cost, but to have validity, the survey questions must be unambiguous and clear, and the people surveyed must be selected with great care. Moreover, the results can be seriously distorted if people are reluctant to talk about or admit to certain feelings, beliefs, or behaviors.

Naturalistic observations, case studies, and surveys can provide a rich set of raw data that *describes* behaviors, beliefs, opinions, and attitudes. But these research methods are not ideal for making *predictions*, and they are not at all well suited to *explaining*, or determining the causes of, behavior.

## Correlational Research

Suppose a psychologist, under contract to the air force, is seeking to predict which applicants for a pilot training program will make good pilots. The air force, which loses millions of dollars each year training potential pilots who subsequently fail to meet program standards, could save a great deal of money if it could accurately predict in advance which training candidates would make good pilots and which would not.

An excellent approach to this problem would be the **correlational method** of research: determining whether there is some characteristic or set of characteristics that is closely related to, or correlated with, eventual success as a pilot. For example, the psychologist might select several hundred present trainees, some of whom are shaping up to be superb pilots and others who are on the verge of being eliminated from the training program, and give them all a variety of aptitude and personality tests. Suppose he finds that the most successful trainees score higher than the unsuccessful trainees on mechanical aptitude tests and that they are also cautious people who do not like to take unnecessary risks. The psychologist has discovered that there is a **correlation**, or relationship, between these traits and success as a pilot trainee: Success as a trainee is related to high scores on a test of mechanical aptitude and a test designed to identify cautious people. High scores on these tests predict success as a pilot trainee. If these correlations are confirmed in a new group of trainees, then the psychologist could recommend with some confidence that the air force consider using these tests to select future trainees.

**Correlation** Relationship between two or more variables.

This psychologist has *described* a relationship between skill as a pilot and two other characteristics, and as a result he is able to use those relationships to *predict* with some accuracy which trainees will and will not become skilled pilots. Note that the psychologist may not be able to *explain* why these relationships exist, but for purposes of prediction, that is not necessary. Whatever the reason for the relationships, they can be used to select pilot trainees with a substantial degree of accuracy.

Note, too, that the psychologist has no basis for drawing conclusions about cause and effect from the data. Does the tendency to shy away fro'm risk-taking make a trainee a good pilot? Or is it the other way around: Learning to be a skillful pilot makes people cautious? Or is there some unknown factor that causes people to be both cautious and capable of acquiring the different skills needed in the cockpit? Correlational data do not permit the researcher to choose from among these various alternatives. Correlational research does not give experimenters the insight to draw conclusions about cause and effect, to explain the relationship between one set of variables and another.

Two homeless men: one in Tokyo, the other in New York City. Researchers might use a correlational study to understand the conditions under which passersby are more likely to stop and help such people. The same study undertaken in both countries might reveal significant cross-cultural differences, or it might show that Japanese and Americans respond similarly to the homeless.

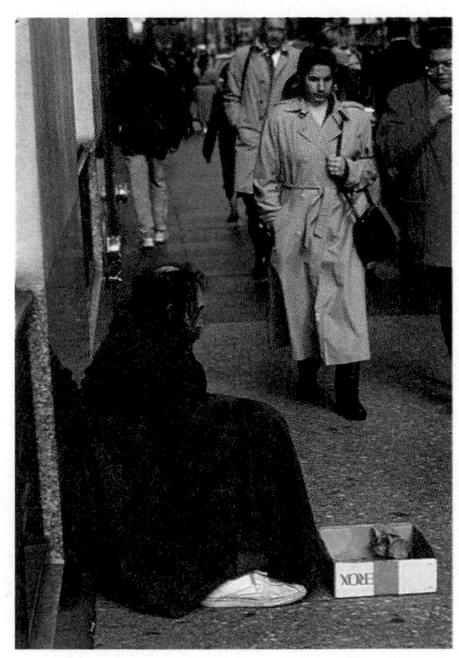

Correlational research often sheds light on psychological phenomena. In this book you will come across many examples of correlational research. People who are experiencing severe stress are more prone to develop physical illnesses than people who are not experiencing severe stress; people with schizophrenia are more likely to have schizophrenic children; the more similar people are to you, the more likely you are to like them; when someone needs help, the more bystanders there are who do nothing, the less likely it is that any one of them will come forward to offer to help.

Though these findings are interesting and allow us to make some predictions, most psychologists eventually want to move beyond simply making predictions. They want to delve into the *causes* of phenomena, to *explain* human thoughts, feelings, and behaviors. But none of the research methods we have examined so far give us much insight into the causes of behavior. The more powerful research methods we turn to next, however, are well suited to explaining, predicting, and controlling psychological phenomena.

## Experimental Research

A psychology instructor has noticed that on Monday mornings most students in her class do not remember material as well as they do later in the week. This psychologist has discovered a correlation between the day of the week and memory for course-related material. Based on this correlation, she could predict that next Monday and every Monday after that the students in her class will not absorb material as well as on other days. But she wants to go beyond simply predicting students' behavior; she wants to understand or explain *why* their memories are poorer on Mondays than on other days of the week.

Based on her own experiences and some informal interviews with students, she has come to suspect that students stay up late on weekends and

**Subjects** Individuals whose reactions or responses are observed in an experiment.

**Independent variable** In an experiment, the variable that is manipulated to test its effects on the other, dependent variables.

**Dependent variable** In an experiment, the variable that is measured to see how it is changed by manipulations in the independent variable.

**Experimental group** In a controlled experiment, the group subjected to a change in the independent variable.

**Control group** In a controlled experiment, the group not subjected to a change in the independent variable; used for comparison with the experimental group.

**Experimenter bias** Expectations by the experimenter that might influence the results of an experiment or their interpretation.

that this lack of sleep underlies their difficulty in remembering facts and ideas presented on Mondays. This theory makes sense, but the psychologist wants to prove her hypothesis: As a scientist, she needs to gather *evidence* that lack of sleep causes memory deficits. To compile that evidence, she turns to the experimental method.

Her first step is to pick **subjects**, people whom she can observe to find out whether her theory is right. She decides to use student volunteers. To keep her results from being influenced by sex differences or intelligence levels, she chooses a group made up of equal numbers of men and women who scored between 520 and 550 on the verbal section of their College Boards.

Next, she designs a memory task. She needs something that none of her subjects will know in advance. If she chooses a chapter in a history book, for example, she runs the risk that some of her subjects will be history buffs. Considering various possibilities, the psychologist decides to print a page of geometric shapes, each labeled with a nonsense word. Circles are "glucks," triangles, "rogs," and so on. She will give the students half an hour to learn the names, then take away the study sheets and ask them to assign those same labels to geometric shapes on a new page.

Now the psychologist is ready to devise *procedures*. Simply asking people if they have slept well is not a reliable measure: Some may say "no" so they will have an excuse for doing poorly on the test, others will say "yes" because they do not want a psychologist to think they are so unstable they cannot sleep. Then there are subjective differences: Two people who both say they slept well may not mean the same thing by that phrase. So the psychologist decides to intervene—that is, to control the situation more closely. Everyone in the experiment, she decides, will spend the night in the same dormitory. They will be kept awake until 4:00 A.M., and then they will be awakened at 7:00 A.M. sharp. She and her colleagues will patrol the halls to make sure that no one falls asleep ahead of schedule. By regulating the amount of time the subjects sleep, the psychologist is introducing and controlling an essential element of the experimental method: an **independent variable**. The psychologist believes that the students' ability to learn and remember her labels for geometric shapes will depend on their having had a good night's sleep. Performance on the memory task (the number of correct answers) thus becomes the **dependent variable**. According to the theory, changing the independent variable (the amount of sleep) should also change the dependent variable (performance on the memory task). This group of subjects, who get no more than 3 hours of sleep, should do quite poorly on the test.

At this point, the experimenter begins looking for loopholes in her experimental design. How can she be sure that poor test results mean that the subjects did less well than they would have done had they had more sleep? Their poor performance could be the result of knowing that they were participating in an experiment and therefore being closely observed. To be sure that her experiment measures *only* the effects of inadequate sleep, the experimenter divides the subjects into two groups. The two groups contain equal numbers of males and females of the same ages and with the same College Board scores. One of the groups, the **experimental group**, will be kept awake, as described, until 4:00 A.M. That is, they will be subjected to the experimenter's manipulation of the independent variable—amount of sleep. Members of the other group, the **control group**, will be allowed to go to sleep whenever they please. Because the only consistent difference between the two groups should be the amount of sleep they get, the experimenter can be much more confident that if the groups differ in their test performance, the difference is due to the length of time they slept the night before.

Finally, the psychologist questions her own objectivity. She is inclined to think that lack of sleep inhibits students' learning and memory, but she does not want to prejudice the results of her experiment; that is, she wants to avoid **experimenter bias**. So she decides to ask a neutral

## Summary Table

### Basic Methods of Research

| Research Method | Advantages | Limitations |
|---|---|---|
| **Correlational Research**<br>Employs statistical methods to examine the relationship between two or more variables. | May clarify relationships between variables that cannot be examined by other research methods. Allows prediction of behavior. | Does not permit researchers to draw conclusions regarding cause-and-effect relationships. |
| **Experimental Research**<br>One or more variables are systematically manipulated, and the effect of that manipulation on other variables is studied. | Strict control of variables offers researchers the opportunity to draw conclusions about cause-and-effect relationships. | The artificiality of the lab setting may influence subjects' behavior; unexpected and uncontrolled variables may confound results; many variables cannot be controlled and manipulated. |
| **Naturalistic Observation**<br>A human or an animal subject's behavior is observed in the environment in which it occurs naturally. | Provides a great deal of firsthand behavioral information that is more likely to be accurate than reports after the fact. The subject's behavior is more natural, spontaneous, and varied than behaviors taking place in the laboratory. A rich source of hypotheses as well. | The presence of an observer may alter the subjects' behavior; the observer's recording of the behavior may reflect a preexisting bias; and it is often unclear whether the observations can be generalized to other settings and other subjects. |
| **Surveys**<br>A large number of subjects are asked a standard set of questions. | Enables an emmense amount of data to be gathered quickly and inexpensively. | Sampling biases can skew results. Poorly constructed questions can result in answers that are ambiguous, so data are not clear. Accuracy depends on ability and willingness of subjects to answer questions accurately. |
| **Case Studies**<br>Behavior of one person or a few people is studied in depth. | Yields a great deal of detailed descriptive information. Useful for forming hypotheses. | The case(s) studied may not be a representative sample. Can be time-consuming and expensive. Observer bias is a potential problem. |

person, someone who does not know which subjects did or did not sleep all night, to score the tests.

The experimental method is a powerful tool, but it has its limitations. First, many intriguing psychological variables, such as love or grief, do not readily lend themselves to experimental manipulation. And even if it were possible to induce such emotion, serious ethical questions would arise if an experimenter were to cause subjects to experience profound grief, fear, or hatred as part of a psychological experiment. Second, because experiments are conducted in an artificial setting, they tend to constrain human behavior.

## Multimethod Research

Each of the research methods we have examined has its drawbacks. Thus, it should come as no surprise to you to learn that most psychologists use several methods to study a single problem. For example, a researcher interested in creativity might begin by giving a group of college students a creativity test that he invented to measure people's capacity to discover or

**Sample** Selection of cases from a larger population.

produce something new. He would compare the students' scores with their scores on intelligence tests and with their grades to see if there is a correlation between them. Then he would spend several weeks observing a college class and interviewing teachers, students, and parents to correlate classroom behavior and the adults' evaluations with the students' scores on the creativity test. He might decide to test some of his ideas with an experiment and to use a group of the students as his subjects. His findings might prompt him to revise the test, or they might give teachers and parents new insight into a particular student's creative abilities.

Interestingly, male and female researchers tend to have different preferences in their choice of research methods (Moses, 1991). Many women researchers dislike laboratory experiments that isolate psychological processes and study the processes outside of their natural context. Some issues of special interest to many female psychologists—rape, incest, sexual abuse, domestic violence—cannot be studied effectively in a laboratory; they are best understood in context. Thus, many female researchers are drawn more to naturalistic observation, case study, and correlational research methods than to laboratory experiments.

## ISSUES OF GENDER, RACE, AND CULTURE IN RESEARCH

In addition to becoming more sensitive to the context in which behavior is studied, psychologists have also taken steps to ensure that their findings reflect the diversity of the human population. They have also begun to consider what effects, if any, people's culture, race, ethnic background, and gender may have on their behavior. And, as we shall see, psychological researchers are working to uncover and overcome unintended biases in research related to the gender, race, and ethnicity of both researchers and their subjects.

### The Importance of Sampling

It is usually impossible, or at least impractical, to measure every single occurrence of a characteristic. No one could expect to measure the memory of every human being, or force all the mice or rats in the world to run mazes, or record the maternal behavior of all female monkeys. No matter what research method is used, whenever researchers conduct a study, they examine only a relatively small number of people or animals and hope that the results of that particular study can be used to predict behavior in similar groups that were not studied. In other words, regardless of the type of research method used, researchers almost always study a small **sample** of subjects and then use the results of that limited study to generalize about larger populations. The researchers cited earlier all assumed that the information they were gathering from a relatively small number of people would accurately reflect the feelings and behaviors of Americans as a whole. The psychologist who was trying to predict success in pilot training assumed that the trainees he was studying were representative of future groups of trainees. The psychology instructor who studied the effect of lack of sleep on memory assumed that her results would apply to other students in her classes (past and future), as well as to students in other classes and other colleges.

How realistic are these assumptions? How confident can you be that the results of research conducted on a relatively small sample of people accurately reflect the findings you would have come up with if much larger numbers of people were studied? One effective way to increase that is to randomly select the subjects in your study from the larger population. For example, the researcher studying pilot trainees might begin with an alphabetical list of all trainees and then select every third name or every fifth name on the list to be in his study. His subjects would constitute a **random sample** from the larger group of trainees because at the outset every trainee had an equal chance of being chosen for the study.

**Random sample** Sample in which each potential subject has an equal chance of being selected.

**Representative sample** Sample carefully chosen so that the characteristics of the subjects correspond closely to the characteristics of the larger population.

**Biased sample** Sample that does not truly represent a whole population.

Another way to make sure that your conclusions apply to the population is to pick subjects for the study that constitute a **representative sample** of that population. For example, researchers looking for a representative cross-section of Americans would have to make certain that the proportion of males and females in the study matched the national proportion, that the number of subjects from each state matched the national population distribution, and so on.

A **biased sample** does not truly represent the population in question. If we want to find out if a town's garbage is being collected efficiently, it would not be wise to stand outside the most fashionable department store in town at 3 o'clock on a workday afternoon and ask all the people who happened by how many times their garbage had been collected that week and at what times. The people who shop at that kind of department store in the middle of the afternoon on a weekday are unlikely to represent the town's population. We would have to figure out a way to make sure that all the town's neighborhoods were represented proportionally in our sample.

Generalizations based on biased samples can lead to erroneous conclusions. A classic instance is the presidential election of 1948, when newspaper headlines proclaimed the triumph of Thomas E. Dewey over Harry S. Truman. These headlines were based, not on election results, but on a telephone poll. As you can see from Truman's delighted expression in the photograph, this prediction was wrong. What happened? The sample was biased because many less wealthy voters did not have telephones at that time, and a large proportion of people without phones voted for Truman.

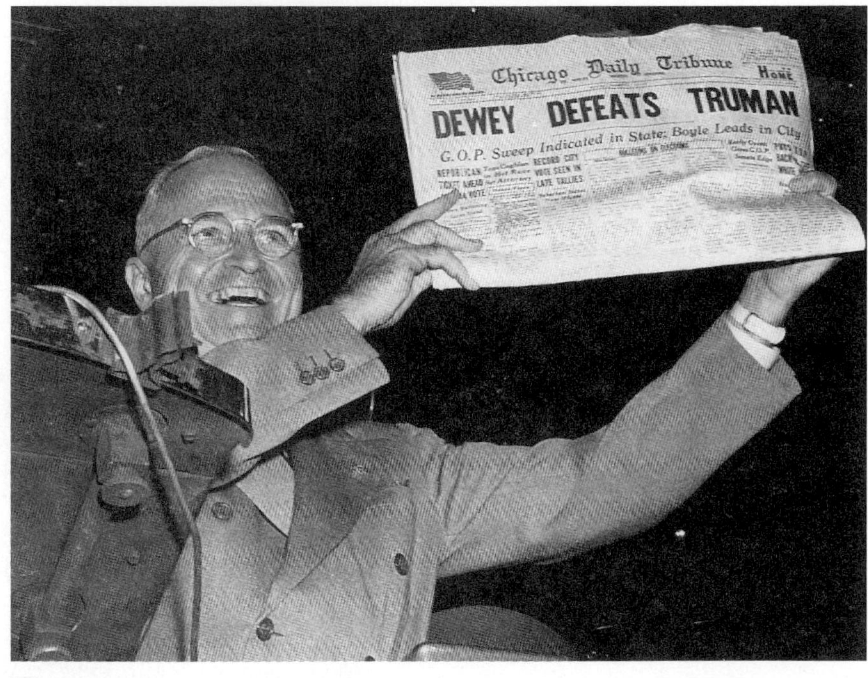


A classic case of biased sampling: This newspaper mistakenly announced a victory by Thomas Dewey over Harry S Truman in the 1948 presidential election.

Similarly, biased sampling in psychological research may produce results that do not reflect the behavior of the entire population. This issue has received a great deal of attention recently, particularly in relation to women and African Americans (e.g., Denmark, 1994; Gannon et al., 1992; S. Graham, 1992; Riger, 1992). Historically, most psychological researchers have been white American males, and most subjects used in psychological research have been white American male college students. The underlying assumption has been that the results of these studies would apply to women, to people of other racial groups, and to people of different cultures even though these groups were underrepresented—or frequently not represented at all—in the studies. Psychologists have now begun to question that assumption explicitly. Is the motivation to achieve really the same for men as it is for women? Do people from India, in fact, respond to stress the same way that Americans do? Since the 1970s, journals that publish psychological research have developed policies aimed at overcoming potential sampling bias, such as advocating that people of both sexes be used as subjects and taking care that researchers who study only male subjects do not generalize their findings to all human beings. Overall, we have seen better representation of women and better recognition of issues of gender in psychological research in recent years, although there are still some problems (Ader & Johnson, 1994; Gannon et al., 1992).

This new awareness has given rise to research on gender and cultural differences. However, the potential for bias exists here, too. For example, because so much research takes place on college and university campuses, the women in these studies often represent a biased sample of relatively well-to-do, white, college-educated women. Thus, the findings from these studies may not be applicable to other groups of women (Yoder & Kahn, 1993).

### Unintended Biases

Does the race, gender, or ethnicity of the experimenter influence the subjects or outcomes of research? New research is exploring the extent to which past studies by white, male experimenters may have been colored by subtle, unintended biases. For example, some early research concluded that women were more likely than men to conform to social pressure in the laboratory (e.g., Crutchfield, 1955). However, research now reveals no gender difference in this area when the experimenter is female (Eagly & Carli, 1981). Similarly, the findings of studies of African-American subjects may be affected by the race of the experimenter (Graham, 1992).

The examination of hidden biases such as these has prompted new studies designed specifically to assess racial, cultural, and sex differences when it comes to major psychological processes. For example, for many years, men were the sole subjects of studies of aggression, partly because research consistently shows that men are more aggressive than women. But the reasons for this sex difference had not been examined until recently. Sex differences in aggression are now being investigated in a number of research laboratories.

The systematic reappraisal of research studies and the methods used in conducting them has called into question the view of the scientist as an impartial or value-free observer (Riger, 1992). Though research methods and the scientific process strive for objectivity, subjective values—whether they derive from race, gender, or cultural background—influence human behavior, whether the human in question is the subject or the designer of psychological research.

Even decisions about which psychological processes to study may have been unintentionally biased in the past. Many issues of special concern to women (such as depression, domestic violence, sexual abuse, and pregnancy and childbirth) have received scant attention from researchers (DeAngelis, 1991a). For example, the rate of depression soars among girls during adolescence; there is no corresponding increase in depression among adolescent boys. But minimal research has been devoted to exploring this important sex-related finding.

Very little research has been done on differences in psychological processes from one society and culture to another, but this neglect is beginning to be remedied. A special effort has been made in this edition of the text to address concerns about and to report gender, race, and culture, and to report on research that bears on these issues. For example, we will consider findings on the physiological effects of racism (in "Stress and Health Psychology"), the cognitive advantages of bilingualism (in "Cognition and Mental Abilities"), and the effects of sexist language (also in "Cognition and Mental Abilities). Psychological research is broadening its scope to probe the full range and richness of human diversity, and this text mirrors that expansive and inclusive approach to questions of psychological concern.

## ISSUES OF ETHICS IN PSYCHOLOGY

### Ethics in Research on Humans

If the school you attend has a research facility, it is likely that you will have a chance to become a subject in an experiment in your psychology department. You will probably be offered a small sum of money or class credit to participate. But you may not learn the true purpose of the experiment until after it is over. Is this deception necessary to the success of psychology experiments? And what if the experiment causes you discomfort?

In response to ethical questions like these, more than 40 years ago the American Psychological Association (APA, 1953) drew up a code for treating experimental subjects. But in 1963 the issue of ethics came to the fore once again when Stanley Milgram published the results of several experiments he had conducted.

Milgram hired people to participate in what he said was a learning experiment. He told then they were to "teach" other people—called "learners,"—by giving them electric shocks when they came up with the wrong answers. The shocks could be administered in various intensities from mild to severe. The "teachers" administering the shocks were told by the experimenter to increase the intensity of the shock each time the learner made a mistake. As the shocks surged in intensity, the learners began to protest that the shocks were hurting them. They cried out in pain, and became more and more upset as the shocks continued. Some even appeared to pass out. The teachers, meanwhile, often became concerned and frightened, and asked if they could stop. In response, the experimenter politely but firmly pointed out that they were expected to continue, that this experiment was being conducted in the interests of science.

Unbeknown to the teachers—who were the real subjects of the experiment—Milgram was investigating obedience, not learning. He wanted to find out whether anyone in this situation would actually go all the way and jolt another person with the highest level of shock under the persistent prodding of an authority figure. Would they follow conscience, or would they obey the experimenter? Astonishingly, 65 percent of Milgram's subjects did administer the highest level of shock, even though some learners stopped answering toward the end and many teachers worried aloud that the shocks might be causing the learners serious damage.

To find out what he wanted to know, Milgram had to deceive his subjects. The stated purpose of the experiment—to test learning—was a lie. The shock machines were fake; the learners received no shocks at all. And the learners themselves were Milgram's accomplices who had been trained to act as though they were being hurt (Milgram, 1963).

Although the design of this experiment was not typical of the vast majority of psychological experiments, it sparked such a public uproar that the profession began to reassess its ethical guidelines. In the wake of this controversy, and amid new con-

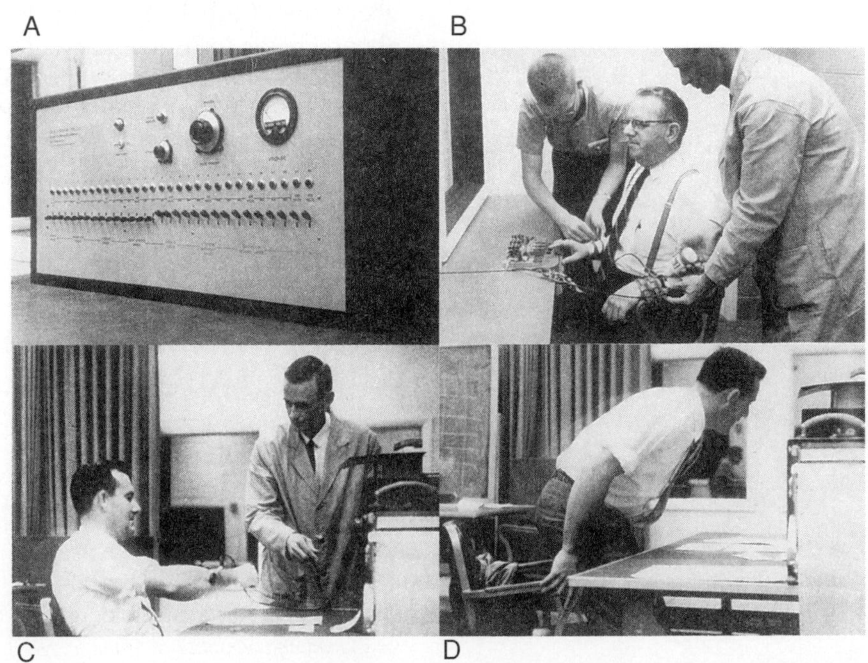


**Stanley Milgram's Obedience Experiment.** (A) The shock generator used in the experiment. (B) With electrodes attached to his wrists, the learner provides answers by pressing switches that light up on an answer box. (C) The subject administers a shock to the learner. (D) The subject breaks off the experiment. Milgram found out what he wanted to find out, but serious questions linger about the ethics of such experimentation.

cerns about the treatment of animals used in experiments, a new code of ethics on psychological experimentation was approved and subsequently revised (APA, 1982, 1985, 1992). Each year the code is reviewed to be sure that it is up-to-date, and periodically a more comprehensive review is undertaken to ensure that the code adequately protects subjects in research studies. In addition to outlining the ethical principles guiding research and teaching, the code spells out a set of ethical standards for psychologists who offer therapy and other professional services, such as psychological testing.

We will touch on some aspects of this code when we look at therapy (Chapter 13). The code covers all facets of psychologists' professional conduct, from teaching to sexual harassment, maintaining confidentiality, and obtaining informed consent in research, a topic that will be of interest to you if you are considering participating in a psychology experiment.

3. Is it ethical for people to use subjects in psychological experiments without telling them?

Among the key points in the APA code of ethics relating to informed consent are requirements that subjects be informed of the nature of research in clearly understandable language; that informed consent be documented; that risks, possible adverse effects, and limitations on confidentiality be spelled out in advance; that if participation is a condition of course credit, equitable alternative activities be offered; that subjects not be deceived about aspects of the research that would affect their willingness to participate, such as risks or unpleasant emotional experiences; and that deception about the goals of the research be used only when absolutely necessary to the integrity of the research.

In addition to these principles, which are specific to psychological research, the federal government has included in its Code of Federal Regulations an extensive set of regulations concerning the protection of human subjects in all kinds of research. Failure to abide by these federal regulations may result in the termination of federal funding for the researcher and penalties for the research institution.

Despite these sets of ethical and legal guidelines, controversy still rages about the ethics of psychological research on humans. Some people contend that research procedures should *never* be emotionally or physically distressing (Baumrind, 1985). Others assert that ethical guidelines that are too strict may undermine the scientific value of research or cripple future research (Gergen, 1973; D. Sears, 1994). Still others maintain that psychology, as a science, should base its ethical code on documented evidence about the effects of research procedures on subjects, not on conjecture about what is "probably" a good way to conduct research (Holmes, 1976b; Trice, 1986). Still another view is that the explanations necessary to produce informed consent may foster a better understanding of the goals and methods of research (Blanck et al., 1992).

The issues we have just addressed deal with research involving human beings. In recent years, there has also been considerable debate about the ethical treatment of animals used in research (e.g., Novak, 1991; K. Shapiro, 1991).

The use of animals in laboratory research has become highly controversial.

## Ethics in Research on Nonhuman Animals

Studies of the behavior of animals have shed light on human behavior. Crowding mice into small cages, for example, has yielded valuable insights into the effects of overcrowding on humans. Animals are also used in experiments where it would be clearly unethical to use human subjects, such as studies involving brain lesions (requiring cutting into the brain) or electric stimulation of parts of the brain. Yet animal-rights advocates and others have questioned whether it is ethical to use animals in psychological research considering that, unlike humans, they cannot give their consent to serve as subjects.

Concerns have been voiced about the suffering that experimentation causes animals. A number of animal-rights groups, including Psychologists for the Ethical Treatment of Animals (PsyETA), are urging legislators to curb harmful experimentation on animals on the ground that it is inhumane (K. Shapiro, 1991).

Their opponents contend that the goals of scientific research—to reduce or eliminate human suffering, for example—justify some animal suffering, even though they agree that animals should be made to suffer as little as possible (Gallistel, 1981; Novak, 1991). They argue that procedures now in place, including the use of anesthesia in many experiments, already minimize animal suffering.

The APA has addressed this issue in its ethical guidelines noting that psychologists using animals in research must ensure "appropriate consideration of [animal's] comfort, health and humane treatment" (APA, 1992). Under these guidelines, animals may not be subjected to "pain, stress, or privation" when an alternative procedure is available.

But animal-protection activists believe these guidelines fall short. They charge that psychological researchers unnecessarily repeat many experiments on animals, that there is little evidence that this work ultimately benefits humans, and that researchers rarely seek out alternative means of gathering data.

Ironically, the National Institutes of Health (NIH), which opposes animal protectionists' views and funds about 40 percent of biomedical research in the United States, has instituted new, more stringent policies governing animal research. A project will not receive NIH funding unless it has been sactioned by an animal-research committee. This committee must include someone not affiliated with the institution conducting the research, as well as the research institution's attending veterinarian and a scientist experienced in laboratory animal medicine.

These debates on research ethics have forced psychologists to confront many difficult questions and reconsider their treatment of both human and nonhuman subjects. Although unanimous acceptance of a formal code of ethics is a long way off, most experimenters find the current APA ethical code a step in the right direction.

## THE GROWTH OF PSYCHOLOGY AS A SCIENCE

It has been said that psychology has a long past but a short history. For centuries, dating back to the time of Plato and Aristotle, people have wondered about human behavior and mental processes. But not until the late 1800s did they begin to apply the scientific method to questions that had been puzzling philosophers for centuries. Only then did psychology come into being as a formal discipline separate from philosophy. We now take a look at how psychology evolved over the past hundred years.

### Wilhelm Wundt and Edward Bradford Titchener: Structuralism

In 1879, Wilhelm Wundt, a physiologist and philosopher at the University of Leipzig in Germany, founded the first formal psychological laboratory. He was striving to develop techniques to uncover the natural laws of the human mind. To isolate the basic units of thought, Wundt examined the process by which we create meaningful patterns out of sensory stimuli. When we look at a banana, for example, we immediately think, "Here is a fruit, something to peel and eat." But these are associations based on past experience. All we *see* is a long, yellow object.

Wilhelm Wundt

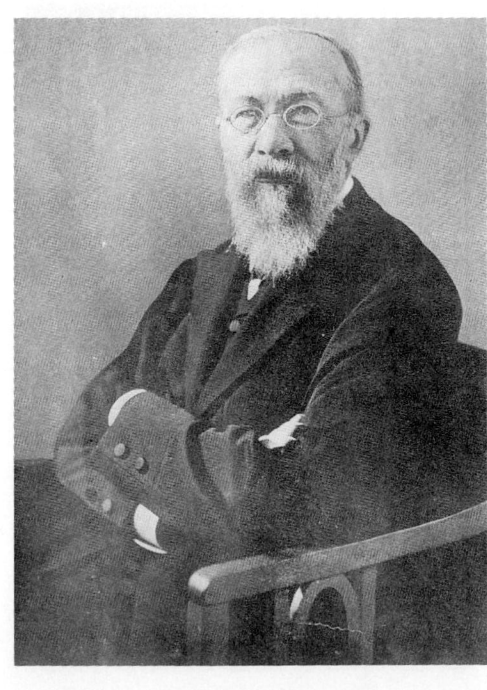

**Structuralism** School of psychology that stresses the basic units of experience and the combinations in which they occur.

**Functionalist theory** Theory of mental life and behavior that is concerned with how an organism uses its perceptual abilities to function in its environment.

Wundt's students went forth from Leipzig and spread the word about the new science of psychology around the world. Among Wundt's protégés was Edward Bradford Titchener, who was British by birth but became the leader of American psychology soon after he was appointed professor of psychology at Cornell University, a post that he held until his death in 1927.

Psychology, Titchener wrote, is the science of consciousness—physics with the observer kept in. In physics, an hour or a mile is an exact measure. To the *observer*, however, an hour may seem to pass in seconds, while a mile may seem endless. Titchener viewed psychology as the study of such experiences. When we recognize a banana, according to Titchener's, we combine a physical sensation (what we see) with feelings (liking or disliking bananas) and images (memories of other bananas). Even the most complex thoughts and feelings, he argued, can be reduced to these simple elements. Psychology's role is to identify these elements and show how they fit together. Because it stresses the basic units of experience and the combinations in which they occur, this school of psychology is called **structuralism**.

William James

## William James: Functionalism

William James, the first American-born psychologist, found fault with Wundt's and Titchener's basic approach. He concluded that Wundt's "atoms of experience"—pure sensations without associations—simply do not exist. Our minds are constantly weaving associations, revising experience, starting, stopping, jumping back and forth in time. Consciousness, James argued, is a continuous flow in which perceptions and associations, sensations and emotions, cannot be separated. When we look at a banana, we see a banana, not a long, yellow object. If we could not recognize a banana, we would have to figure out what it was each time we saw one. Thus, James asserted, mental associations allow us to benefit from previous experience.

With this insight, James arrived at a **functionalist theory** of mental life and behavior. Functionalist theory goes beyond mere learning, sensation, and perception to explore how an organism uses its learning or perceptual abilities to function in its environment. James also argued for the value of subjective (untrained) introspection and insisted that psychology should focus on real-life experiences.

Sigmund Freud

## Sigmund Freud: Psychodynamic Psychology

Sigmund Freud, a Viennese neurologist whose first love was research, was forced to develop a private medical practice to meet the financial needs of his growing family. Freud noticed that many of his patients' ailments appeared to have psychological rather than physiological origins. In 1900, he published *The Interpretation of Dreams*, in which he described how dreams provide clues to the unconscious desires and conflicts that he believed lay at the root of many of his patients' neurological symptoms. Freud had forged his clinical discoveries into a comprehensive theory of mental life that differed radically from the views of American psychologists. This theory—that unconscious processes guide much human thought and action—has had a profound impact on psychology and the other social sciences, as well as on the arts, starting in the late 1920s.

Freud also became well known for his approach to psychotherapy (discussed in Chapter 13) in which the patient lies on a couch and freely says whatever comes to mind. His technique (called psychoanalysis) seeks to uncover the unconscious desires and motivations that affect people's behavior. As we shall see in Chapter 10, Freud's posited that personality develops in a series of critical stages during the first few years of life. If we successfully resolve the conflicts that we encounter at each of these stages, we can avoid psychological problems in later life. But if we become "fixated" at any one of these stages, we may carry related feelings of anxiety or exaggerated fears with us into adulthood. This view that behavior stems from unconscious dynamics—such as conflicts—within the individual is known as *psychodynamic psychology*.

**Behaviorism** School of psychology that studies only observable and measurable behavior.

In addition to emphasizing the impact of childhood experiences on adult neuroses, Freud maintained that many unconscious desires and conflicts have their roots in sexual repression. A 5-year-old boy, Freud argued, sexually desires his mother and wishes to destroy his father, whom he sees as his rival for her affection. Yet at the same time, he loves his father. These two feelings give rise to a conflict. Of all Freud's theories, the influence of the sexual drive on the formation of personality has sparked the greatest controversy. As we will see in the chapter on personality, many of Freud's colleagues and successors rejected this viewpoint. Alfred Adler, for instance, felt that the child's struggle to overcome a sense of inferiority was central to forming personality. Carl Jung focused on the individual's drive for self-realization in the context of the history and religious impulses of the human species. Karen Horney asserted that the need for basic security (e.g., to feel loved and nurtured by one's parents) supersedes the sexual drive as a guiding force in the development of personality. Despite these differences, psychodynamic theory has had a huge impact on academic psychology, particularly on the study of personality and abnormal behavior, and is highly influential today.

4. *True* or *false:* Sigmund Freud was the founder of psychology.

## John B. Watson: Behaviorism

Challenging both the structuralist and functionalist schools then thriving in the United States, John B. Watson argued that the whole idea of consciousness, or mental life, was mere superstition, a relic left over from the Middle Ages. You cannot define consciousness any more than you can define a soul, Watson contended. You cannot locate it or measure it, and therefore it cannot be the object of scientific study. For Watson, psychology was the study of observable, measurable behavior—and nothing more.

Watson's view of psychology, known as **behaviorism**, was based largely on well-known experiments conducted by the Russian physiologist Ivan Pavlov. Pavlov had noticed that the dogs in his laboratory began to drool as soon as they heard their feeder coming—even before they could see their dinner. He decided to try to teach the dogs to drool at the sound of a ringing bell even when no food was in the room. He succeeded by first pairing the bell with the presence of food and then eventually ringing the bell without introducing any food. Pavlov explained his results as follows: All behavior is a response to some stimulus or agent in the environment. In ordinary life, food makes dogs salivate. All Pavlov did was to train his animals to respond to the sound of a bell as they had previously responded to the presence of food. He called this training *conditioning*.

John B. Watson

One obvious question concerning Pavlov's experiments is whether the same type of conditioning can be applied to humans. In a famous experiment with an 11-month-old child, Watson showed that human behavior can also be conditioned. Little Albert was a secure, happy baby who had no reason to fear soft, furry white rats. But each time Albert reached out to pet the rat that Watson offered him, Watson made a loud noise that frightened Albert. It wasn't long before Albert was afraid of white rats (Watson & Rayner, 1920). Thus, conditioning changed the child's behavior radically.

Watson took Pavlov's findings a step further, showing that fears in humans could both be induced and eliminated by conditioning. Mary

**Gestalt psychology** School of psychology that studies how people perceive and experience objects as whole patterns.

**Reinforcement** Anything that follows a response and makes that response more likely to recur.

**Existential psychology** School of psychology that focuses on the meaninglessness and alienation of modern life, and how these factors lead to apathy and psychological problems.

Cover Jones (1924), one of his graduate students, successfully reconditioned a boy who showed a fear of rabbits (not caused by laboratory conditioning) to overcome this fear. Her technique, which involved presenting the rabbit at a great distance and then gradually bringing it closer while the child was eating, is similar to the desensitization techniques used today with people who have phobias.

In the 1920s, when Watson's behaviorist theory was first published, American psychologists had all but exhausted the structuralist approach. So Watson's orthodox scientific approach (if you cannot see it and measure it, forget about it) found a warm audience.

## Gestalt Psychology

Meanwhile, a group of psychologists in Germany was attacking structuralism from another direction. Max Wertheimer, Wolfgang Köhler, and Kurt Koffka were all interested in perception, but particularly in certain tricks that the mind plays on itself. Why, they asked, when we are shown a series of still pictures flashed at a constant rate (for example, movies or "moving" neon signs), do the pictures seem to move? The eye *sees* only a series of still pictures. What makes us *perceive* motion?

Phenomena like these propelled a new school of thought, **Gestalt psychology**. Roughly translated from the German, *Gestalt* means "whole" or "form." When applied to perception, it refers to our tendency to see patterns, to distinguish an object from its background, to complete a picture from a few cues. Like James, the Gestalt psychologists thought that the attempt to break down perception and thought into their elements was misguided. When we look at a tree, we see just that, a tree, not a series of isolated leaves and branches.

Mary Cover Jones

## B. F. Skinner: Behaviorism Revisited

B. F. Skinner, like Watson, fervently believed that psychology should study only observable and measurable behavior (Skinner, 1938, 1987, 1989, 1990). He, too, was primarily interested in changing behavior through conditioning—and in discovering natural laws of behavior in the process. But his approach differed in subtle ways from that of his predecessor.

Skinner added a new element to the behaviorist repertoire: **reinforcement**. He rewarded his subjects for behaving the way he wanted them to behave. For example, an animal (rats and pigeons were Skinner's favorite subjects) was put into a special cage and allowed to explore it. Eventually, the animal reached up and pressed a lever or pecked at a disk on the wall, whereupon a food pellet dropped into the box. Gradually, the animal learned that pressing the bar or pecking at the disk always brought food. Why did the animal learn this? Because it was reinforced, or rewarded, for doing so. Skinner thus made the animal an active agent in its own conditioning.

## Existential and Humanistic Psychology

**Existential psychology**, as the name suggests, draws on the existential philosophy made popular in the 1940s by, among others, the French philosopher, playwright, and novelist Jean-Paul Sartre. Existential psychologists are concerned with meaninglessness and alienation in modern life, for they believe that these feelings lead to apathy, fear, and other psychological problems. Psychoanalyst Rollo May, for example, held that modern Americans are lost souls—a people without myths and heroes. R. D. Laing, another existentialist, believed that we must reevaluate our attitude toward psychotic behavior: Such behavior, far from being abnormal, constitutes a reasonable,

# HIGHLIGHTS

## Missing: Women in Psychology?

As you read the brief history of modern psychology in this chapter, it is difficult not to conclude that the founders of the new discipline were all men. But did psychology really have only fathers and no mothers? If there were women pioneers, why are their names and accomplishments absent from historical accounts?

In fact, psychology has profited from the contributions of women from its beginnings. Women presented papers and joined the national professional association as soon as it was formed in 1892 (Furumoto & Scarborough, 1986). Often, however, they faced gender-based obstacles: Some colleges and universities did not grant degrees to women, professional journals were reluctant to publish their work, and teaching positions were often closed to them (O'Connell & Russo, 1990; Russo & Denmark, 1987; Stevens & Gardner, 1982).

Despite these barriers, a number of early women psychologists made important contributions, and were acknowledged by at least some of the men in the growing discipline of psychology. In 1906, James McKeen Cattell published *American Men of Science*, which, despite its title, included a number of women, among them 22 female psychologists. Cattell rated three of these women as among the 1,000 most distinguished scientists in the country: Mary Whiton Calkins (1863-1930), Christine Ladd-Franklin (1847–1930), and Margaret Floy Washburn (1871–1939).

Despite their eminence, the careers of these three exceptional women illustrate the ways discrimination against women served to keep them and their work in the background. Ladd-Franklin and Calkins were admitted to all-male graduate schools only after men interceded on their behalf. Washburn transferred from Columbia to Cornell, where the opportunities for women were greater (Furumoto & Scarborough, 1986). Only Calkins and Washburn went on to have academic careers. Though both taught at distinguished schools (Calkins at Wellesley and Washburn at Wells and Vassar), neither gained a place on the faculty of a major research institution. All three grappled with the competing demands of family and career. Denied a doctorate from Harvard because of her sex—although the university's most eminent psychologist, William James, described her as his brightest student—Mary Whiton Calkins developed an influential system of self psychology (Furumoto, 1980). She also developed the paired associate technique, a significant research tool in the study of memory, and in 1891 she inaugurated the psychology laboratory at Wellesley College.

Unlike Calkins, Christine Ladd-Franklin received a Ph.D., but only in 1926—more than 40 years after she had completed the degree requirements—when Johns Hopkins finally lifted its restrictions against granting doctoral degrees to women. Although she developed an influential theory of color vision, Ladd-Franklin never received a permanent academic position, largely because of the prevailing prejudice against women combining a professional career with marriage and motherhood (Furumoto & Scarborough, 1986).

In contrast to Calkin and Ladd-Franklin, Margaret Floy Washburn received her Ph.D. in psychology from Cornell soon after completing her degree requirements. She subsequently taught at Wells and Vassar for 34 years. Washburn went on to write several important books, including *Movement and Mental Imagery* (1916), which anticipated current research on the role of imagery in directing thought and activity.

Today women receive over half of the Ph.D.'s granted in psychology (APA, 1991a) and perform key research in all of psychology's subfields. You will find their work referred to throughout this text. Terry Amabile has studied creativity, in particular the positive effect exposure to creative role models can have on people (in the chapter on "Cognition and Mental Abilities"). Karen DeValois studies color vision; her work and that of her husband is discussed in the chapter on "Sensation and Perception." Elizabeth Loftus studies memory; her work has uncovered how unreliable eyewitness accounts of a crime can be (in the chapter "Memory"). Carol Nagy Jacklin has studied the role that parents' expectations can play in girls' (and boys') perceptions of the value of mathematics (in the chapter "Human Diversity"). Judith Rodin's research examines eating behavior, in particular bulimia and obesity (in the chapter "Life Span Development"). Eleanor Maccoby, Alice Eagly, and Jacqueline Eccles are prominent among the growing number of women and men who are studying sex differences in a variety of areas, such as emotionality, influenceability, math and verbal ability, and helping behavior. Throughout this text we will be looking at this work to see what part biology and society play in differences in the behavior of women and men.

Although women are increasing in number and influence in psychology, women's experiences as psychologists are often considerably different from those of men. Women graduate students tend to receive less financial support from their institutions than men do (Cohen & Gutek, 1991). After graduation, men are more likely to secure full-time employment in psychology and to be employed by the government and business, while women more often work in schools (APA 1991a; Stapp & Fulcher, 1984 cited in A.G. Cohen, & B. A. Gutek, 1991). The most recent available statistics indicate that the median annual salary for male psychologists is $58,900, while that for female psychologists is $50,300 (National Science Foundation, 1991). Encouragingly, salary differences are smaller among more recent graduates (A.G. Cohen & B. A.Gutek, 1991).

**Humanistic psychology** School of psychology that emphasizes nonverbal experience and altered states of consciousness as a means of realizing one's full human potential.

**Cognitive psychology** School of psychology devoted to the study of mental processes in the broadest sense.

**Evolutionary psychology** An approach to, and subfield of, psychology that is concerned with the origins of behaviors and mental process, their adaptive value, and the purposes they continue to serve.

normal response to an abnormal world. Existential psychology guides people toward an inner sense of identity, which allows them to take responsibility for their actions and, in the process, to achieve freedom.

**Humanistic psychology** is closely related to existential psychology. Both schools insist that people must learn how to realize their human potential. But where existential psychology emphasizes restoring an inner sense of identity and willpower, humanistic psychology focuses on the possibilities of nonverbal experience, the unity of mind, altered states of consciousness, and "letting go."

Existential and humanistic viewpoints have never predominated in American psychology, but they remain influential to this day, particularly when it comes to understanding personality and the treatment of abnormal behavior.

## Cognitive Psychology

Over the past 2 decades, several new perspectives have emerged and begun to reshape the field of psychology. **Cognitive psychology** is the study of our mental processes in the broadest sense: thinking, feeling, learning, remembering, making decisions and judgments, and so on. Thus, cognitive psychologists are especially interested in the ways in which people perceive, interpret, store, and retrieve information.

In contrast to the behaviorists, cognitive psychologists believe that mental processes can and should be studied scientifically. Although we cannot observe cognitive processes directly, we can observe behavior and make inferences about the kinds of cognitive processes that underlie that behavior. For example, we can read a lengthy story to people and then observe the kinds of things that they remember from that story, the ways in which their recollections change over time, and the sorts of errors in recall they are prone to make. On the basis of systematic research of this kind, it is possible to gain insight into the cognitive processes underlying human memory.

Although cognitive psychology is relatively young, it has already had an enormous impact on almost every area of psychology (Sperry, 1988). Even the definition of psychology has changed as a result. Twenty years ago, most introductory psychology texts defined psychology simply as the scientific study of behavior. Now revised editions of many of those same texts point out that "behavior" encompasses thoughts, feelings, experiences, and so on. Other texts, including this one, define psychology as the scientific study of behavior *and* mental processes. You will see the influence of cognitive psychology throughout this book.

Another very recent perspective is **evolutionary psychology**. As its name suggests, evolutionary psychology looks to the origins of certain behaviors and mental processes, exploring what adaptive value they have and what purposes they serve (DeKay & Buss, 1992). Evolutionary psychologists focus on such diverse behaviors and mental processes as helping others, mating and mate selection, and jealousy. By studying such phenomena over time and among different species, cultures, and sexes, evolutionary psychologists have expanded our understanding of cultural and gender differences, as well as the effects of socialization, and have established the links between human and animal behavior (DeKay & Buss, 1992; Scarr, 1993). Take jealousy, for example. According to evolutionary psychology, because men are never certain of their paternity, they are more likely to become jealous over issues involving the sexual fidelity of their partners. Women, as childbearers, are confident of their maternity, so they are more jealous of the potential loss of a partner's commitment and investment in raising offspring (Daly & Wilson, 1988; Symonds, 1979; cited in DeKay & Buss, 1992).

**"Is the concept of free will compatible with science?"**

In this chapter, we have defined psychology as the science of behavior and mental processes. A major philosophical issue that psychologists must address is the causes of human behavior. Because psychology is a science, researchers focus on observable or measurable factors that affect the ways in which people behave. But psychologists disagree about the extent to which these external, observable factors *determine* human behavior. Recall our discussion of behaviorism. Behaviorists argue that human actions are caused entirely by external factors in the environment (or at most the interaction of environmental and genetic forces). The argument that human behavior is the product of external forces beyond our control is known as *determinism*.

But think of all the things you do, all the decisions you make, in a typical day. Are these thoughts and actions all "caused" by environmental and genetic factors beyond your control? Throughout history, many people have argued that human beings exercise free will, that we mediate among all the forces that act on us and ultimately choose to act in particular ways. According to this argument, environmental and genetic forces may help shape our behavior, but they don't totally determine it.

What are your feelings on this issue? Do you believe in free will, or do you think we merely respond to internal and external cues that are beyond our control? Can there ever be a "science of human behavior" if human behavior is the result of free will? After you have thought about these questions, take a few minutes to examine the opinions of some other students, which appear below.

• • • • • • •

**LEE: Without cause, everything is random, and I think psychologists need to assume cause (and lack of free will) in order to study why people behave the way they do.**

**PAT: Just because science, guided by men with human brains, has determined that all things have a cause, including our behavior and thought, does not necessarily mean that this humanly conceived principle is valid in the universal scheme of things.**

**JOEL: Saying that humans lack free will is kind of reckless. It allows us to avoid taking personal responsibility for our actions.**

**BILL: I think that most psychologists would assume that people have some degree of free will but also that all realize that biological processes play a significant role in decision making. The debate over which one has more effect on us is simply unsolvable and a time-consuming debate for psychologists.**

**LEE: You cannot have *some* free will. You either have it or you don't.**

**KEISHA: I'm not saying that we can train our minds to control a reflex [an example given of behavior beyond a person's control or will], but I am saying that many of the things we consider reflexes are in fact very controllable.**

**ETHAN: The idea that psychologists must assume humans have no free will seems absurd to me since they are not reaching a conclusion about all humans. In fact, it seems they must assume we *do* have free will for their experiments to be valid. An assumption of no free will would force the effect of the independent variable to be all or nothing.**

**CAROL: The relationship between two things does not mean a subject had no free will, but rather that there was some influence. If one assumes there is no such thing as free will, psychology becomes much less interesting. In that instance one would only be looking for a formula. Free will is what makes the human mind so intriguing.**

**KATE: Our upbringing and biochemical structure and previous experiences predispose us to making certain decisions, but do not necessarily predict the behavior.**

**MICHAEL: Psychologists must believe that the mind is a sort of machine, which follows a predictable pattern, or their work makes no sense.**

**ANNMARIE: I think that high predictability signifies an absence of free will, because in many cases people freely choose to do the same thing that other people would freely choose to do . . . it is not the presence of free will that is essential to many psychological experiences, but the extent to which the decision that we make of our own free will can be influenced.**

• • • • • • •

Now that you've been exposed to other students' views, you might want to reconsider your position on this issue. Has your opinion changed? If so, how? If not, why not? Which arguments did you find most convincing? How should psychologists treat the issue of free will?

## THE MULTIPLE PERSPECTIVES OF PSYCHOLOGY TODAY

For many years, psychologists clashed over the merits of the various approaches to psychology. Contemporary psychologists are less likely to advocate one theoretical perspective to the exclusion of all others (Friman et al., 1993). Though most psychologists continue to work within a particular theoretical framework—focusing, say, on the biological mechanisms for memory—they generally take into account other factors—such as the role cultural context or motivation plays in memory—as well. Rather than viewing these disparate approaches as conflicting, the tendency today is to see them as complementary, with each approach contributing in its own way to our understanding of human behavior. When we think about the wide variety of behaviors and mental processes that psychology seeks to explain, it is not surprising that no single approach can account for them all.

Consider the study of aggression. Psychologists no longer circumscribe their thinking by noting that aggressive behavior is simply learned from one's parents as a consequence of reward and punishment (the behavioral view), or that it constitutes an expression of unconscious hostility toward a parent (Freud's perspective). Instead, many, if not most, contemporary psychologists trace aggression to a number of influences, including not only learning and the effects of past experiences, but also the culture in which people grow up (including the television shows they watch and the religious beliefs they hold) and the immediate circumstances surrounding the aggressive behavior (such as abusive treatment by parents, the level of violence in the neighborhoods, or the frustrations of unemployment and poverty). These sociocultural influences on behavior dovetail with people's perceptions and interpretations ("That guy is making fun of me" or "She's asking for it")—both cornerstones of cognitive psychology—as well as with the physiological origins of aggression, grounded in genetics and biochemistry.

By now you may be thinking that psychology is a vast field teeming with different approaches and covering an enormous range of human behavior, thought, and emotion. If so, you are right. Sometimes these theoretical perspectives mesh beautifully, with each one enhancing the others in an arena of dynamic interaction; at other times adherents of one approach challenge their peers, arguing for the primacy of one viewpoint over all the others.

This chapter has outlined some of the main research areas in psychology, given a capsule history of the field, and suggested some of the major approaches that have emerged to explain human behavior. It has also described the research methods used most often by psychologists in their efforts to discover more about human behavior and mental life. Before we conclude the chapter, we must examine one more important topic: what you can do with a background or an advanced degree in psychology.

## CAREERS IN PSYCHOLOGY

What kinds of jobs do psychology graduates look for and find with their newly minted degrees? People holding bachelor's degrees in psychology may seek to assist psychologists working in mental-health centers, vocational rehabilitation, and correctional centers. They may also take positions as research assistants, teach psychology in high school, or land jobs as trainees in government or business.

Community college graduates with associates degrees in psychology are well qualified for paraprofessional positions in state hospitals, mental-health centers, and other human-service settings. Job responsibilities may include screening and evaluating new patients, record keeping, and assisting in consultation sessions.

Many other careers outside psychology draw on a person's knowledge of psychology without requiring postgraduate study. A sample: (1) Personnel administrators deal with employee relations. (2) Vocational rehabilitation counselors help people with disabilities find employment. (3) Directors of volunteer services recruit and train volunteers. (4) Probation officers work with parolees. (5) Day-care-center supervisors oversee the care of preschool children of working parents.

### Work in Academic, Applied, and Clinical Settings

For those who pursue advanced degrees in psychology, career opportunities span a wide range. Many of these people join the faculties of colleges and universities. Others put their knowledge to work in applied settings such as business and industry. Nearly half of those people with advanced degrees in psychology, generally a master's degree or doctorate, are clinicians who treat people experiencing mental or emotional difficulties. Recently, the American Psychological Association (APA) developed standards that require professionals working in institutions, such as clinics and hospitals, and in private practice to be supervised by a doctoral-level psychologist. Such regulations limit the opportunities for those with master's degrees to move into higher positions.

### Psychologists, Psychiatrists, Psychoanalysts

When we look at careers in psychology, it is important to distinguish among psychiatrists, psychologists, and psychoanalysts. A *psychiatrist* is a medical doctor who, in addition to 4 years of medical training, has completed 3 years of residency training in psychiatry, most of which is spent in supervised clinical practice. Psychiatrists specialize in the diagnosis and treatment of abnormal behavior. Besides giving *psychotherapy*—the treatment of personality and behavior disorders with psychological techniques—they take medical responsibility for their patients, including prescribing drugs, if necessary. A *psychoanalyst* is a psychiatrist or psychologist who has received additional specialized training in psychoanalytic theory and practice. Most, but not all, *psychologists* hold Ph.D.'s in psychology—the result of 4 to 6 years of study in a graduate program in psychology.

What is the difference between a psychologist and a psychiatrist?

Finally, social workers may also offer treatment for psychological problems. Typically they have a master's degree (M.S.W.) or doctorate (D.S.W.). Social workers often work under another mental-health professional, though in some states they may be licensed to practice independently.

A free booklet titled *Careers in Psychology* is available from the Order Department, American Psychological Association, P.O. Box 2710, Hyattsville, MD 20784-0710, or by calling 1-800-374-2721.

## LOOKING FORWARD

The field of psychology is as vast and varied as human experience itself. This chapter traced some of the major routes through that sprawling terrain and described its subfields. The chapters that follow will explore the work being done in some of those subfields. Along the way, you will become familiar with points of connection among these psychological communities.

In its relatively brief history, psychology has undergone a number of significant shifts in approach and emphasis. These differences in perspective persist to some extent. Rather than believe that one all-encompassing view will be able to explain all behavior, however, many psychologists today are more inclined to think that behavior, thought, and emotion are best explained as the products of several kinds of processes, from longstanding evolutionary adaptation to environmental or situational influences like culture, gender, and socioeconomic status. Throughout the chapters of this book, in each of the neighborhoods of psychology that we visit, we will become familiar with the rich, subtle, and diverse workings of the human mind—the territory that makes up the world of psychology.

# SUMMARY

## THE FIELD OF PSYCHOLOGY

This chapter introduces the field of psychology by describing issues of interest and concern to contemporary psychologists and the research methods they use to explore those issues, as well as the goals of psychology and its origins and growth as a science.

The American Psychological Association consists of 48 divisions, each representing an area of special interest to psychologists. The discipline's major subfields include developmental psychology, physiological psychology, experimental psychology, personality psychology, clinical and counseling psychology, social psychology, and industrial and organizational psychology.

## THE GOALS OF PSYCHOLOGY

Psychologists rely on the **scientific method** to unravel the causes of human behavior and to describe, explain, predict, and, eventually, achieve some measure of control over human thought and action. **Psychology** is the science of behavior and mental processes, with the emphasis on *science*. Like all scientists, psychologists develop **theories** to systematically explain a phenomenon, and then derive testable predictions, or **hypotheses**, from those theories.

## RESEARCH METHODS IN PSYCHOLOGY

Psychologists use a variety of methods to study behavior and mental processes. Each method has its own advantages and disadvantages.

### Naturalistic Observation

The **naturalistic-observation** method calls for observing the behavior of human or animal subjects in a natural setting, with minimal interference from the researcher. This method generates a good deal of first-hand information because behavior in the natural setting is likely to be more spontaneous and varied than behavior observed in a laboratory. Naturalistic observation also serves as a rich source of hypotheses. However, observers may allow preexisting biases to influence their recording of events.

### Case Studies

A researcher using the **case study** method undertakes an in-depth study the behavior of one person or a few people. While this method yields much detailed, descriptive information that is useful for forming hypotheses, it, too, may suffer from observer bias. In addition, the case or cases studies may not be representative of the larger population.

### Surveys

In a **survey,** a large number of subjects are asked a standard set of questions. This method yields a substantial amount of data quickly and inexpensively. However, unless care is taken, sample bias may skew results, and poorly constructed questions may produce ambiguous answers, making any conclusions drawn from the data suspect.

### Correlational Research

**Correlational research** investigates the relationship, or **correlation**, between two or more variables. This method may clarify relationships between preexisting variables that cannot be ascertained by other research methods. Thus, it allows for prediction of behavior. But it does not explain cause-and-effect relationships.

### Experimental Research

In **experimental research**, one variable—the **independent variable** is systematically manipulated and the effect of that manipulation on another variable—the **dependent variable**—in an **experimental group**. For comparison purposes, a **control group**, which is not subjected to change in the independent variable, is also used. To reduce **experimenter bias**, results are recorded by someone who does not know which subjects are from which group. This method enables the researcher to draw conclusions about cause-and-effect relationships. However, subjects' behavior may be constrained by the artificial setting of the laboratory. Also, many variables do not lend themselves to experimental manipulation.

### Multimethod Research

Since each research method has benefits as well as limitations, many psychologists use multiple methods to study a single problem.

## ISSUES OF GENDER, RACE, AND CULTURE IN RESEARCH

Regardless of the research method chosen, researchers almost always study a small **sample** of subjects and then generalize their results to larger populations. To ensure that their results will have broader application, researchers compile **random samples**, in which subjects are chosen randomly, and **representative samples**, in which subjects are chosen to reflect the general characteristics of the population as a whole.

A **biased sample** is one that fails to truly represent the population in question; the results of a study that use such a sample may be erroneous. Many researchers are now examining effects that sexually, racially, and culturally biased sampling may have on psychological research, as well as how the gender, race, and ethnic background of the researcher may affect both the subjects and the outcomes of research.

### Ethics in Research on Humans

More than 40 years ago, the American Psychological Association drew up a code of ethics for psychological experimentation, with emphasis on obtaining the informed consent of subjects. Each year the code is updated, and periodically a more comprehensive reevaluation is undertaken. Although many psychologists believe that such an ethical code is both necessary and appropriate, controversy still smolders over the ethics of research.

### Ethics in Research on Nonhuman Animals

Animal research has given us valuable insights into such psychological phenomena as the effects of overcrowding. Animal research is undertaken when it would be clearly unethical to use human subjects, such as in studies involving brain lesions. It is this aspect of animal research that sparks controversy. Though there are APA and federal guidelines governing the treatment of laboratory animals, many animal-rights advocates feel that nonhuman animals deserve the same treatment and safeguards as humans.

## THE GROWTH OF PSYCHOLOGY AS A SCIENCE

Philosophers since the time of Aristotle and Plato have grappled with questions about mental processes, but it was not until the late 1800s that the scientific method came to be used to probe these questions. Only then did psychology emerge as a formal discipline separate from philosophy.

### Wilhelm Wundt and Edward Bradford Titchener: Structuralism

In 1879, Wilhelm Wundt established the first formal laboratory for psychological research, at the University of Leipzig in Germany. He and one of his students, Edward Bradford Titchener, founded the school of **structuralism**, which stressed that psychology's role was to identify the basic elements of experience and the combinations in which they occur.

### William James: Functionalism

William James, the first American-born psychologist, developed a **functionalist theory** of psychology that was a significant departure from Wundt's structuralism. James believed that sensations cannot be separated from the mental associations that allow us to benefit from previous experience, and therefore all mental activity and behavior are functional.

### Sigmund Freud: Psychodynamic Psychology

The theories of Sigmund Freud added a new dimension to the understanding of human psychology. Freud's psychodynamic psychology posits that much human behavior is governed by hidden motives, internal conflicts, and unconscious desires. His theories and therapeutic approach (psychoanalysis) did not win wide acceptance right away. In fact, Freud's emphasis on the role of the sexual drive in personality formation remains widely disputed to this day.

### John B. Watson: Behaviorism

John B. Watson rejected both the structuralist and the functionalist schools, on the ground that we cannot define consciousness any more than we can define the soul. Psychology, he maintained, should concern itself only with observable, measurable behavior. Watson based much of his work on Pavlov's conditioning experiments and sought to explain all behavior in stimulus-response terms—thus founding the school of psychology known as **behaviorism**.

### Gestalt Theory

According to **Gestalt psychology**, perception depends on the human tendency to see patterns, to distinguish an object from its background, to complete pictures from a few clues. In this emphasis on wholeness, the Gestalt school differed significantly from structuralism.

### B.F. Skinner: Behaviorism Revisited

B. F. Skinner's beliefs were similar to Watson's, but by adding **reinforcement** to the learning process, he made the subject an active agent in the conditioning process.

### Existential and Humanistic Psychology

**Existential psychology** attributes psychological problems to feelings of meaninglessness and alienation in modern life, and it calls for people to take responsibility for their actions in order to achieve freedom. **Humanistic psychology** has concerns and goals similar to those of existential psychology, but it emphasizes nonverbal experience and altered states of consciousness as a means of realizing one's full potential.

### Cognitive Psychology

**Cognitive psychology** is the study of mental processes in the broadest sense, focusing on how people perceive, interpret, store, and retrieve information. Unlike the behaviorists, cognitive psychologists believe that mental processes can and should be studied scientifically. Although cognitive psychology is relatively young, its influence on the study and definition of psychology is far-reaching. Today psychology examines human behavior as well as mental processes.

A very recent perspective known as **evolutional psychology** explores the origins of behaviors and mental processes with an eye toward discovering the effects on human behavior of socialization and cultural and gender differences, as well as establishing links between human and animal behavior.

## THE MULTIPLE PERSPECTIVES OF PSYCHOLOGY TODAY

While the early psychologists tended to embrace one theoretical view and shun all others, contemporary psychologists bring to their research a keen appreciation for the discipline's various perspectives. In fact, many psychologists today use more than one research method or theoretical outlook to study psychological phenomena.

## CAREERS IN PSYCHOLOGY

Jobs abound for people who graduate with degrees in psychology. People holding associate's degrees are qualified for paraprofessional positions; those with bachelor's degrees may assist psychologists working in various settings, teach psychology in high school, or find jobs as trainees in government or business. Those who earn an advanced degree in psychology have several career options, including teaching at a college or university, working in business or industry, and doing clinical or counseling work in a mental-health setting.

Psychologists, most of whom hold Ph.D.'s in psychology, differ in training and practice from psychiatrists—medical doctors who may complement psychotherapy with drug therapy. Psychoanalysts are psychologists or psychiatrists with specialized training in psychoanalytic theory and practice. In some states, social workers, too, may offer treatment for psychological problems.

# REVIEW QUESTIONS

## MULTIPLE CHOICE

1. Psychologists rely on the ______ method to obtain answers to questions concerning human behavior and mental processes.
2. The four goals common to all psychologists are to ______, ______, ______, and ______ behavior.
3. A method of research known as ______ allows psychologists to see how behavior operates in real-life situations.
4. The ______ variable in an experiment is manipulated to see how it affects a second variable; the ______ variable is the one observed for any possible effects.
5. The experimental method is associated with all of the following except:

   a. hypotheses
   b. variables
   c. experimenter bias
   d. subjects

6. The ______ method of research is used to identify naturally occurring relationships among variables without having to manipulate any variable.
7. ______ is a major shortcoming of the case study method.
8. Naturalistic observation, case studies, and surveys are not well suited to ______ and ______ behavior.
9. To ensure that the results of a particular study apply to a larger population, researchers use ______ or ____ samples.
10. Which of the following is a *true* statement about ethics in research?

    a. Controversy over ethical standards has almost disappeared.
    b. The APA code of ethics in use today is unchanged since 1953.
    c. Ethical questions apply only to laboratory experiments.
    d. Failure to follow federal regulations can result in penalties.

11. It was not until the late ______ that psychology came into its own as a separate discipline, with the use of the scientific method.

12. Match the following terms with their appropriate descriptions:

____ Structuralism
____ Functionalism
____ Behaviorism
____ Psychoanalysis
____ Existential psychology
____ Humanistic psychology
____ Gestalt psychology
____ Cognitive psychology

a. Concerned with how an organism uses its perceptual abilities to function in its environment.

b. Stresses the whole character of perception.

c. Concerned with alienation and meaninglessness in modern life and resulting psychological problems.

d. Studies only observable and measurable behavior.

e. Stresses the basic elements of experience and the combinations in which they occur.

f. Emphasizes nonverbal experience and altered states of consciousness in realizing one's potential.

g. Studies mental processes in the broadest sense.

h. Maintains that hidden motives and unconscious desires govern much of our behavior.

13. B. F. Skinner added the new element of ______ to conditioning.

14. Freud established ____ as a form of patient treatment.

15. As a result of the influence of the cognitive school, psychology is now defined as the study of _____ and ______.

## CRITICAL THINKING AND APPLICATIONS

16. What does the phrase "critical thinking in psychology" mean? How can you benefit from developing your critical thinking skills?

17. One day in your psychology class you notice that some students take more notes than others, and you become curious about whether note taking ultimately affects grades. How would you use the scientific method to determine if there is a relationship between not taking and grades? What types of research methods would you consider? What would each of these methods tell you about this issue? What are the drawbacks of each method?

18. A renowned psychologist developed a theory of moral development that claimed that throughout the course of their lives people pass through a series of moral stages, beginning with basic definitions of right and wrong and ultimately progressing to a higher level based on such abstract concepts as justice, liberty, and equality. Critics later pointed out that this theory was based almost entirely on work with male subjects. Assuming that this criticism was valid, how would it affect your appraisal of the theory?

19. How do you feel about animal research and experimentation in psychology? When, if ever, is animal research justified? Do you approve of the current regulations concerning animal research? Why or why not?

*(Answers to the Review Questions can be found in the back of the text.)*

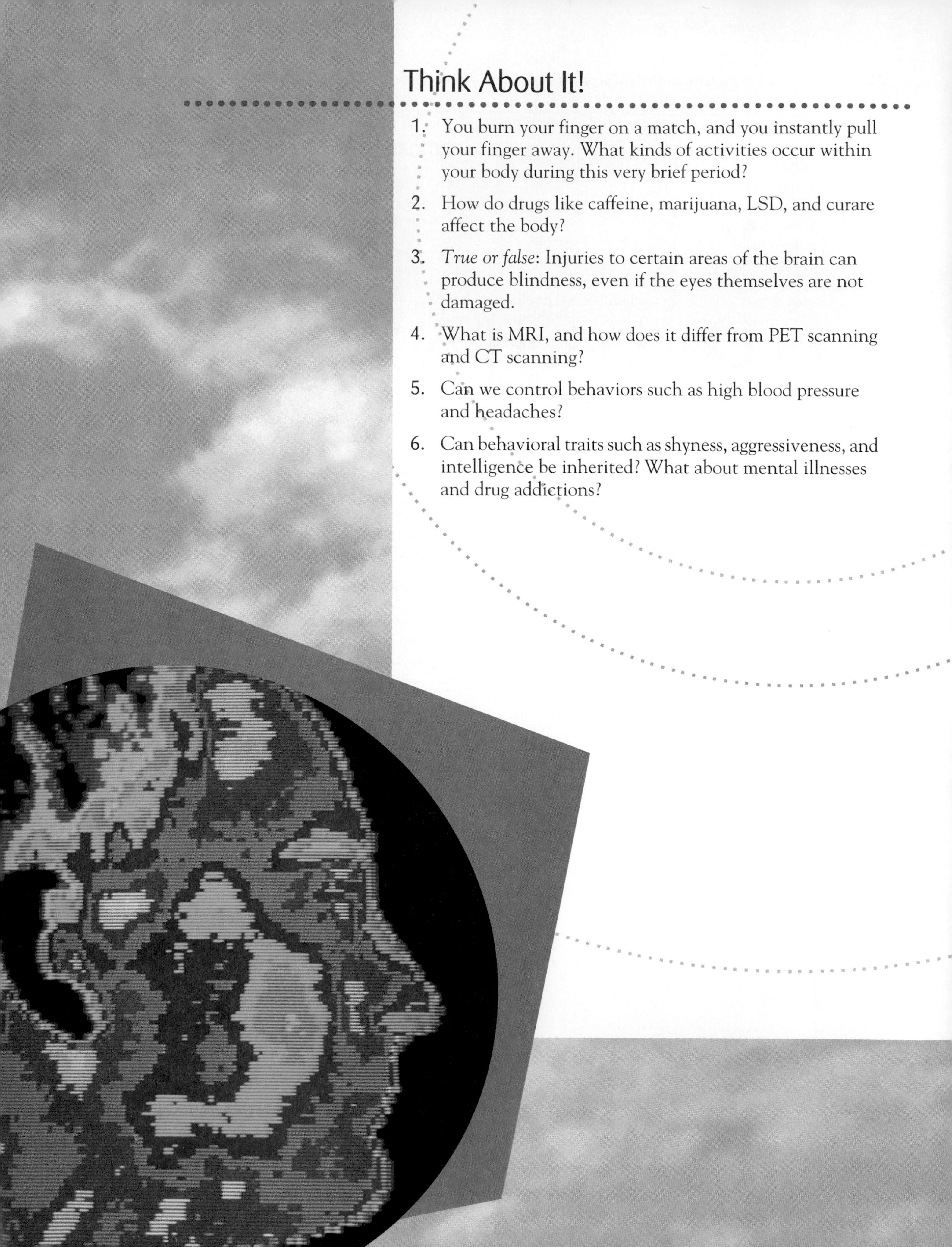

## Think About It!

1. You burn your finger on a match, and you instantly pull your finger away. What kinds of activities occur within your body during this very brief period?
2. How do drugs like caffeine, marijuana, LSD, and curare affect the body?
3. *True or false*: Injuries to certain areas of the brain can produce blindness, even if the eyes themselves are not damaged.
4. What is MRI, and how does it differ from PET scanning and CT scanning?
5. Can we control behaviors such as high blood pressure and headaches?
6. Can behavioral traits such as shyness, aggressiveness, and intelligence be inherited? What about mental illnesses and drug addictions?

# PHYSIOLOGY AND BEHAVIOR

# 2

## Overview

**John P. has suffered a stroke that damaged the back part of his brain. Although he seems to be a friendly, talkative, and healthy man, he works with an occupational therapist four times each week to learn skills that will help compensate for the damage done by the stroke. When his therapist arrives, he greets her happily: "Hey, Doc, you are working too hard—I thought I told you to take the day off!"**

Later, in the hospital lunchroom, the therapist pushes a saltshaker toward him and asks him what it is. "It's a. . . you know. . .what you call. . .I just can't think of the word right now." John takes the saltshaker and shakes salt onto the table. "You know. . .like this! I just can't seem to remember the name." After several minutes, the exercise is repeated with a paper napkin, and the results are remarkably similar. "Isn't that funny?" John nervously wipes at his fingers and mouth with the napkin. "I keep forgetting words today!" Later, as John and his therapist leave the lunchroom, a hospital orderly passes by. John waves and calls, "Hey, Doc, you are working too hard—I thought I told you to take the day off!"

Gayle G. expected that she would be tired after the birth of her baby, but her friends and family told her that when she held her newborn baby, she would feel wonderful. Things turned out much differently than she thought they would. Unlike many new mothers, Gayle felt no sense of joy when she was with her baby. Instead, she felt indifferent, and she continued to experience extreme fatigue even 3 and 4 days after her daughter was born.

When Gayle and the baby came home from the hospital, conditions worsened. Gayle was annoyed when the baby cried, and she felt terribly guilty for "not having the experiences that new mothers are supposed to have." Gayle began to feel a deep sense of depression and loss. She became convinced that the baby was an evil force. She also became convinced that her husband and mother were plotting against her. When her family realized that Gayle might actually harm the baby, they informed her doctor of her condition, and she was hospitalized.

Howard M. was admitted to a hospital emergency room in a very agitated condition. He was crying, fearful, and confused. The medical staff gave him a powerful sedative that helped him sleep. Later Howard recalled taking a small pill he believed to be LSD, a powerful drug that can induce disorientation and hallucinations. Nearly an hour after he took the pill, he joined friends at the college dormitory cafeteria, and that was when the drug seemed to take effect.

"I sat down and looked at my food and it was crawling off the plate! It looked horrible—the most disgusting colors you've ever seen. It was, like, I knew it wasn't real, so I closed my eyes to make it go away. But every time I closed my eyes, I could still *see* everybody at the table—they were laughing, throwing food, making this big riot. I was laughing so hard—it was a huge food fight right out of some movie. And then I would open my eyes, and nobody was throwing food and there was no mess or anything. Pretty soon, I couldn't tell which was really happening. I was sitting there laughing and it seemed like everyone was watching me. . .I guess I got pretty scared."

These three stories are about real people and real events, and they all have something in common. In each case, we see that profound changes in psychological functions can result from changes in physiological or biological systems. In John's case, brain injury has left him unable to recognize objects and people's faces. Gayle experienced an abnormal reaction to the changes in her body during labor and delivery. The result was a dramatic change in her mood and energy level, along with a frightening misperception of the conditions and people around her. Howard swallowed a pill that he estimated to be about one-half the size of an aspirin tablet. This tiny amount of chemical produced remarkable alterations in his perceptions, emotions, and behavior.

**Nervous system** The brain, the spinal cord, and the network of nerve cells that transmit messages throughout the body.

**Endocrine system** Internal network of glands that release hormones directly into the bloodstream to regulate body functions.

Psychology is the study of behavior, but often we cannot understand behavior unless we know a little about what goes on inside the human body. Most of the time—when the body is functioning normally—we tend to forget about the complex activities that are constantly going on, but they continue nonetheless. The cells keep functioning and reproducing themselves; the organs and glands keep regulating such diverse activities as digestion and growth. We tend to become concerned with these complex activities only when we are sick or injured. When they are healthy, the brain and nervous system act, along with other biological systems, to receive, interpret, and send messages so effortlessly and accurately that we do not even stop to wonder how they work. Only when something goes wrong, as it did for John, Gayle, and Howard, are we are likely to think about how interactions among different biological systems affect our everyday psychological life.

How does the body coordinate the different systems that play important roles in the ways that we see, hear, think, feel, and remember? In general, the body possesses two major systems for coordinating and integrating behavior. One is the **nervous system**, which relays messages in the form of nerve impulses throughout the body. The second is the **endocrine system**, which consists of a number of glands that secrete chemical messages into the bloodstream. These chemicals perform a variety of functions, including preparation of nerves and muscles to act, control of metabolism, and regulation and development of secondary sexual traits. The more we learn about the nervous system and the endocrine system, the more we understand how they work together to integrate the body's extraordinarily complex activities.

To understand how intricate these activities are, imagine that you burn your finger on a match. What happens next? "It's simple," you might say. "I automatically snatch my hand away from the heat." But, in fact, your body's response to a burn is not simple at all. It involves a highly complex set of activities. First, special sensory cells pick up the message that your finger is burned. They pass this information along to the spinal cord, which triggers a quick withdrawal of your hand. Meanwhile, the message is being sent to other parts of your nervous system. Your body goes on "emergency alert": You breathe faster, your heart pounds, your entire body mobilizes itself against the wound. At the same time, the endocrine system gets involved: Chemicals are released into the bloodstream and carried throughout the body to supplement and reinforce the effects of nervous system activity. Meanwhile, your brain continues to interpret the messages being sent to it: You experience pain, perhaps you turn your hand over to examine the burn, you might walk over to the sink and run cold water over your hand. In other words, even a simple event such as burning your finger results in an extremely complex, coordinated sequence of activities involving the body's nervous system working hand in hand with its endocrine system.

**1.** You burn your finger on a match, and you instantly pull your finger away. What kinds of activities occur within your body during this very brief period?

In our effort to understand how biology affects psychological processes, we will first look at the nervous system. We will then take a look at the endocrine system. Finally, we will consider the extent to which genes influence our behavior.

## NEURONS, THE MESSENGERS

**Neurons** Individual cells that are the smallest unit of the nervous system.

**Dendrites** Short fibers that branch out from the cell body and pick up incoming messages.

**Axon** Single long fiber extending from the cell body; it carries outgoing messages.

**Nerve** Group of axons bundled together

**Myelin sheath** White fatty covering found on some axons.

**Sensory** or **afferent neurons** Neurons that carry messages from sense organs to the spinal cord or brain.

**Motor** or **efferent neurons** Neurons that carry messages from the spinal cord or brain to the muscles and glands.

**Interneurons** or **association neurons** Neurons that carry messages from one neuron to another and do most of the work of the nervous system.

The nervous system is composed of a number of parts that work together to form a remarkable communication network. These parts are numerous and complex, and in some cases their functions are still a mystery. Before we consider the larger parts of the nervous system, we will examine the system's smallest unit, the individual nerve cell or **neuron**, which underlies the activity of the entire nervous system.

There may be as many as 100 billion nerve cells or neurons in the brain of an average human being. In addition, there are billions more neurons in other parts of the nervous system. Like most other cells, each neuron has a *cell body*, which contains a nucleus where metabolism takes place. Unlike other cells, however, neurons have tiny fibers extending from the cell body that enable the neuron to receive messages from surrounding cells and pass them on to other cells. Figure 2-1 contains an actual photograph of a neuron as well as a stylized drawing that illustrates the various parts of a typical neuron.

Many small fibers called **dendrites** branch out from the cell body. The dendrites pick up messages coming in from surrounding areas and carry them to the cell body. Also extending from the cell body of the neuron is a single long fiber called an **axon**. The axon is very thin and is usually much longer than the dendrites. For example, in adults, the axons that run from the brain to the base of the spinal cord or from the spinal cord to the tip of the thumb may be as long as 3 feet. Most axons, however, are only 1 or 2 inches long. A group of axons bundled together like parallel wires in an electric cable is called a **nerve**. The axon carries outgoing messages from the cell and either relays them to neighboring neurons or directs a muscle or gland to take action. Although there is just one axon per neuron, near its end the axon splits into many terminal branches. Because there may be hundreds or thousands of dendrites on a single neuron, and because the axon itself may branch out in numerous directions, one neuron can be in touch with hundreds or thousands of others at both its input end (dendrites) and its output end (axon).

Look at the neuron in Figure 2-1. Its axon is surrounded by a white fatty covering called a **myelin sheath**. Not all axons are covered by myelin sheaths, but myelinated axons are found throughout the body. The myelin sheath appears pinched at intervals, which makes the axon resemble a string of microscopic sausages. Because of this white covering, tissues made up of lots of myelinated axons are often referred to as "white matter," whereas tissues with lots of unmyelinated axons look gray and thus are called "gray matter." As we will soon see, the sheaths help neurons act with greater efficiency as well as provide insulation for the neuron.

A photomicrograph showing the cell bodies, dendrites, and axons of several neurons.

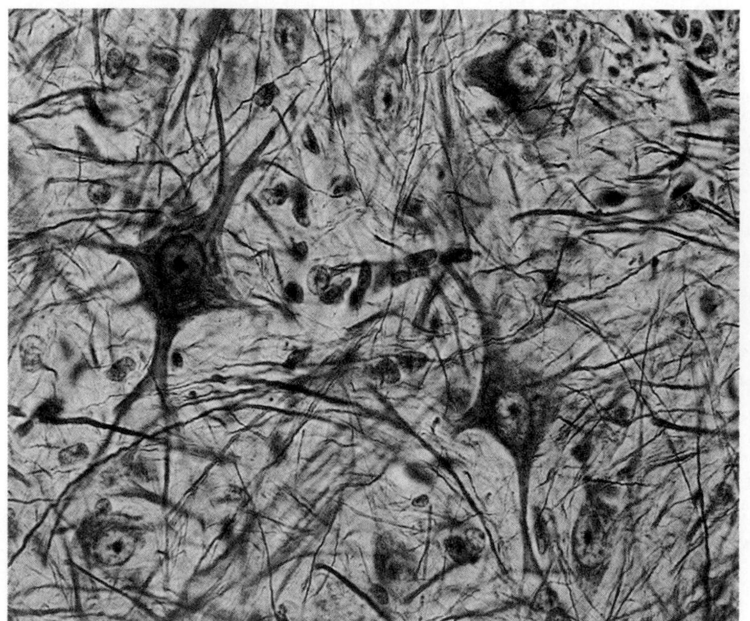

Although all neurons relay messages, the kind of information they collect and the places to which they carry it help us distinguish among different types of neurons. Neurons that collect messages from sense organs and carry those messages *to* the spinal cord or the brain are called **sensory** (or **afferent**) **neurons**. Neurons that carry messages *from* the spinal cord or the brain to the muscles and glands are called **motor** (or **efferent**) **neurons**. And neurons that carry messages from one neuron to another are called **interneurons** (or **association neurons**). Interneurons account for more than 99 percent of all the neurons in the nervous system, and they perform most of the work of the nervous system. Also found in the nervous system are a vast number of **glial cells**, or **glia**. Glial cells support neurons in a number of ways. They hold the neurons in the nervous system together; they remove waste products that could interfere with neural functions; and they prevent harmful substances from passing from the bloodstream into the brain. In addition, they form the myelin sheath that insulates the neurons.

**Glial cells** or **glia** Cells that form the myelin sheath; they insulate and support neurons by holding them together, removing waste products, and preventing harmful substances from passing from the bloodstream into the brain.

## The Neural Impulse

We have referred several times to the fact that neurons carry messages. How do these messages get started? When a neuron is resting, the membrane surrounding the cell forms a partial barrier between semiliquid solutions that are

**Figure 2-1**
**A typical myelinated neuron.**

*Source:* Adapted from *Fundamentals of Human Neuropsychology,* (2nd ed.), by Brian Kolb and Ian Q. Whislaw. Copyright © 1980, 1985, by W.H. Freeman and Company. Reprinted with permission.

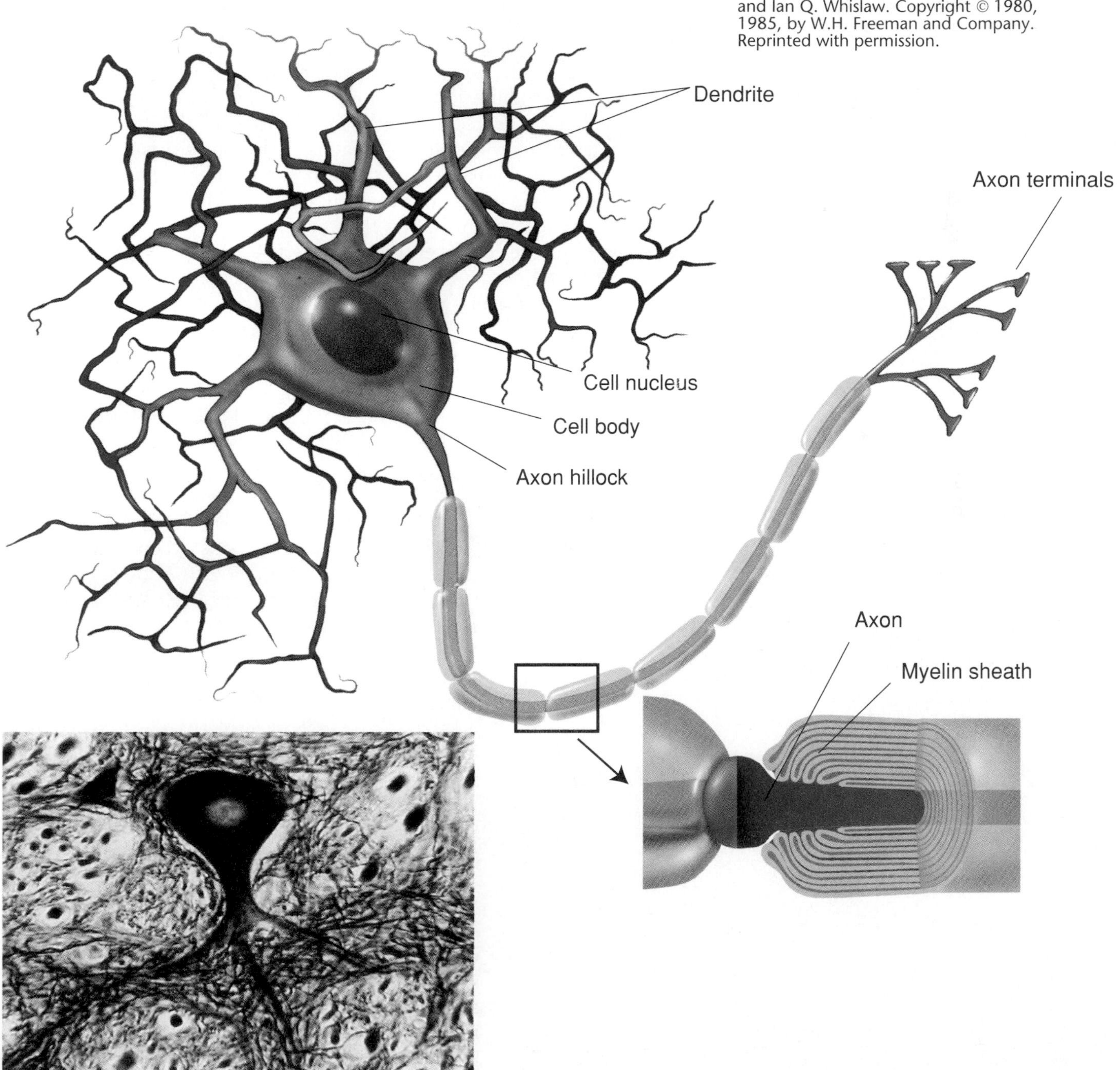

**Ions** Electrically charged particles found both inside and outside of the neuron.

**Resting potential** Electrical charge across a neuron membrane when sodium ions concentrate on the outside and potassium ions concentrate on the inside.

**Polarization** The condition of a neuron when the inside is negatively charged relative to the outside; for example, when the neuron is at rest.

inside and outside the neuron. Both solutions contain electrically charged particles, or **ions**. These include positively charged sodium and potassium ions. There are also large, negatively charged organic ions, found only inside the cell. When the cell is resting, or at its **resting potential**, these ions exist in an unbalanced state that causes a small electrical tension between the inside and outside of the cell. There is a greater concentration of sodium ions on the outer surface of the cell than on the inner surface, and there is a greater concentration of potassium ions on the inner surface than on the outer surface. This imbalance, along with the negatively charged organic ions inside the cell, creates an electrical charge inside the neuron that is negative relative to the outside. Thus, the resting neuron is said to be in a state of **polarization**. Figure 2-2A shows a resting neuron in a state of polarization.

In its resting state, a polarized neuron is like a spring that has been compressed or a guitar string that has been pulled but not released. All that is needed to generate a neuron's signal is the release of the tension stored in the polarized state.

When a small area on the cell membrane is adequately stimulated by an incoming message, pores (or channels) in the membrane at the stimulated area allow sodium ions to move across the cell membrane. When enough sodium ions have entered the neuron to make the inside positively charged relative to the outside—that is, it becomes *depolarized*—those pores close, and no more sodium ions can enter at that time. Meanwhile, as sodium ions are moving into the cell, potassium ions begin to flow out of the cell, and they continue to do so even after the sodium ions have stopped entering the cell. Eventually, enough positively charged potassium ions leave the cell so that the inside again becomes slightly negative compared to the outside; thus, the cell returns to its resting potential.

The breakdown of the cell membrane does not occur at just one point. In fact, as soon as the cell membrane allows sodium to enter the cell

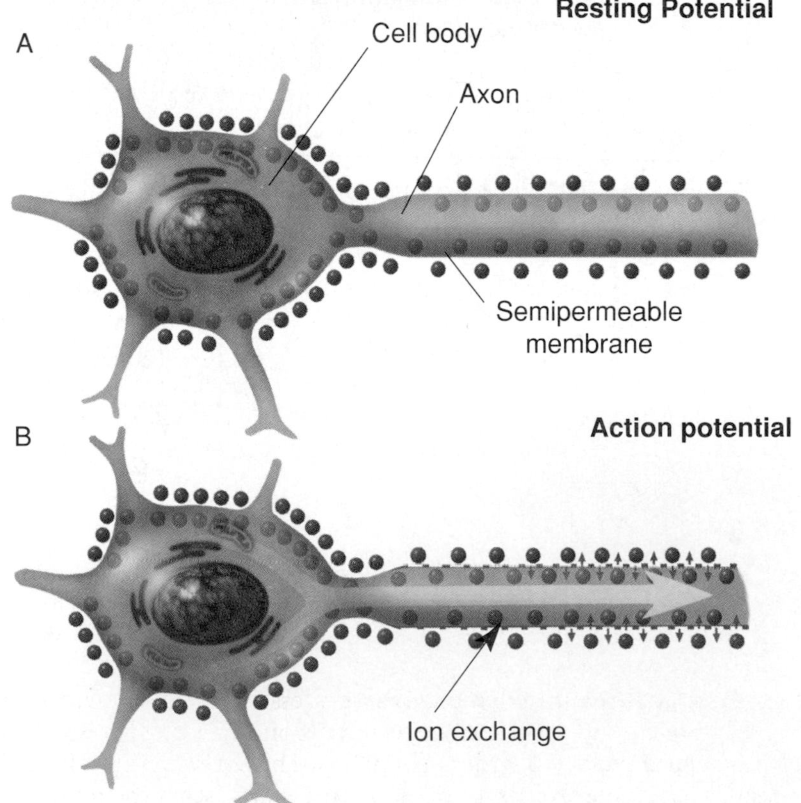


**Figure 2-2**
**The neural impulse—communication within the neuron.** When a point on the semipermeable *neural membrane* is adequately stimulated by an incoming message, the membrane opens at that point, and positively charged sodium ions flow in. This process is repeated along the length of the membrane, creating the neural impulse that travels down the axon, causing the neuron to fire.

*Source:* Adapted from *Psychology* (2nd ed.), by John G. Seamon and Douglas Kenrick. Copyright© 1994, p. 45. Reprinted by permission of Prentice Hall, Inc.

at one point, the next point on the membrane also opens. More sodium ions flow into the neuron at the second spot and depolarize this part of the neuron, and so on. The process is repeated along the length of the neuron, creating a **neural impulse**, or **action potential**, that travels down the axon, much like a fuse burning from one end to the other (see Figure 2-2B). When this happens, we say that the neuron has fired.

As a general rule, single impulses received from neighboring neurons do not make a neuron fire. Incoming impulse messages cause temporary small shifts in the electrical charge in areas of the neuron that receive the impulse. These **graded potentials** are transmitted along the cell membrane and may simply fade away, leaving the neuron in its normal polarized state. However, if the graded potentials caused by impulses from many neighboring neurons—or even from one other neuron firing repeatedly—combine to exceed a certain minimum **threshold of excitation**, the neuron will fire. Just as a light switch requires a minimum amount of pressure to be activated, an incoming message must be above the minimum threshold to make a neuron fire.

Immediately after firing, during the **absolute refractory period**, the neuron will not fire again no matter how strong the incoming messages may be. In the **relative refractory period**, when potassium ions are leaving the cell, the neuron will fire, but only if the incoming message is considerably stronger than is normally necessary to make it fire. Finally, the neuron is returned to its resting state, ready to fire again, as shown in Figure 2-3.

Although individual action potentials occur very quickly, there is a wide range in the speed with which individual neurons conduct impulses. In some of the largest myelinated axons, the fastest impulses may travel at speeds of nearly 400 feet per second. Axons with myelin sheaths can conduct impulses very rapidly because the impulses leapfrog along the string of pinched intervals, or *nodes*, that lie along the sheaths. Neurons without myelin sheaths tend to conduct impulses more slowly, in a steady flow like a fuse. Impulses in the slowest of these unmyelinated neurons poke along at little more than 3 feet per second.

At any instant, a neuron may be in any number of states determined by the overall pattern of graded potentials. For example, it may be engaged in an action potential, it may be moving toward an action potential, or it may even be moving below a resting potential. Although we are just beginning to study the messages in graded potential activities of neurons, we can, to some extent, interpret the messages transmitted in action potentials.

We know, for example, that strong incoming signals do not cause stronger neural impulses. Neurons either fire or they do not, and every firing of a particular neuron produces an impulse of the same strength. This is called the **all-or-none law**. However, the neuron is likely to fire more often when stimulated by a strong signal. The result is rapid neural firing that communicates the message "There's a very strong stimulus out here."

## The Synapse

We have been discussing the operation of a single neuron. But the billions of neurons in the nervous system work together to coordinate the body's activities. How do they interact? How does a message get from one neuron to another?

Imagine a single neuron that receives its messages from just one other neuron and transmits messages to just one neuron. The dendrites or cell body of the neuron pick up a signal. Then, as we have seen, if the signal is strong enough, the neuron fires, and an impulse starts down the axon and

**Neural impulse** or **action potential** The firing of a nerve cell.

**Graded potential** A shift in the electrical charge in a tiny area of a neuron.

**Threshold of excitation** The level an impulse must exceed to cause a neuron to fire.

**Absolute refractory period** A period after firing when a neuron will not fire again no matter how strong the incoming messages may be.

**Relative refractory period** A period after firing when a neuron is returning to its normal polarized state and will fire again only if the incoming message is much stronger than usual.

**All-or-none law** Principle that the action potential in a neuron does not vary in strength; the neuron either fires at full strength or it does not fire at all.

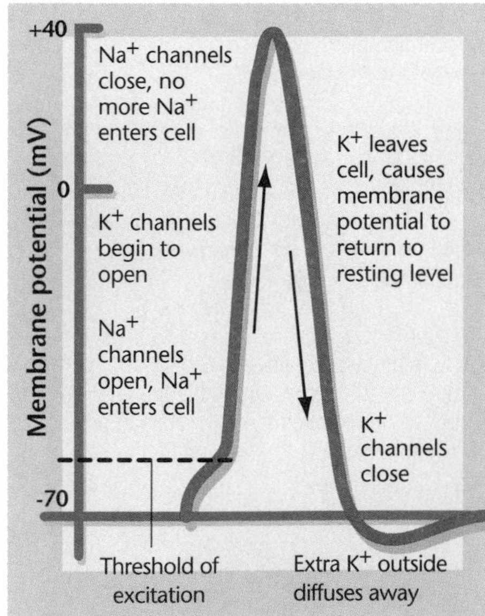


**Figure 2-3**
**Electrical changes during the action potential.** The incoming message must be above a certain threshold to cause a neuron to fire. After it fires, the cell body begins to pump potassium *ions* out of the neuron until the neuron is returned to its resting state. This process happens very quickly, and within a few thousandths of a second the neuron is ready to fire again.

*Source:* Adapted from *Physiology of Behavior*, 5/E by Neil R.Carlson. Copyright©1994 by Allyn & Bacon. Reprinted by permission.

**Axon terminal** or **synaptic knob** Knob at the end of an axon terminal branch.

**Synaptic space** or **synaptic cleft** Tiny gap between the axon terminal of one neuron and the dendrites or cell body of the next neuron.

**Synapse** Area composed of the axon terminal of one neuron, the synaptic space, and the dendrite or cell body of the next neuron.

**Synaptic vesicles** Tiny sacs in a synaptic knob that release chemicals into the synapse.

**Neurotransmitters** Chemicals released by the synaptic vesicles that travel across the synaptic space and affect adjacent neurons.

**Receptor site** A location on a receptor neuron into which a specific neurotransmitter fits like a key into a lock.

out to the end of the terminal branches. At the end of each branch is a tiny knob called an **axon terminal** or **synaptic knob**. In most cases, there is a tiny gap between this knob and the next neuron. This tiny gap is called a **synaptic space** or **synaptic cleft**. The entire area composed of the axon terminal of one neuron, the synaptic space, and the dendrite or cell body of the next neuron is called the **synapse** (see Figure 2-4).

If the neural impulse is to travel on to the next neuron, it must somehow cross the synaptic space. It is tempting to imagine that the neural impulse simply leaps across the gap like an electric spark, but in reality the transfer is made by chemicals. What happens is this: Most axon terminals contain a number of tiny oval sacs called **synaptic vesicles** (see Figure 2-4). When the neural impulse reaches the end of the axon, it causes these vesicles to release varying amounts of chemicals called **neurotransmitters**. The neurotransmitters diffuse randomly into the synaptic space, where they can affect the next neuron.

There are many different neurotransmitters, and their functions are still being investigated. For each such substance there are matching **receptor** (or hookup) **sites** on the other side of the synaptic space. Each neurotransmitter fits into its corresponding receptor sites just as a key fits into a lock. Some neurotransmitters "excite" the next neuron, making it more likely to fire. For example, *acetylcholine (ACh)* acts as an excitatory transmitter where neurons meet skeletal muscles. It also appears to play a critical role in such psychological processes as arousal, attention, memory, and motivation (Panksepp, 1986). Alzheimer's disease, which involves loss of memory and severe language problems, is thought to be due to a reduction in ACh and the loss in certain portions of the brain of cells that respond to ACh.

Other transmitter substances "inhibit" the next neuron, making it less likely to fire. *Dopamine* is one prevalent inhibitory transmitter that seems to

A photograph taken with a scanning electron microscope, showing the synaptic knobs at the ends of axons. Inside the knobs are the vesicles that contain neurotransmitters.

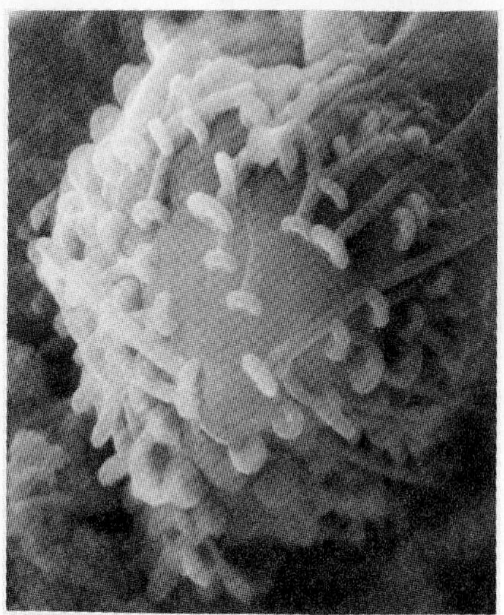

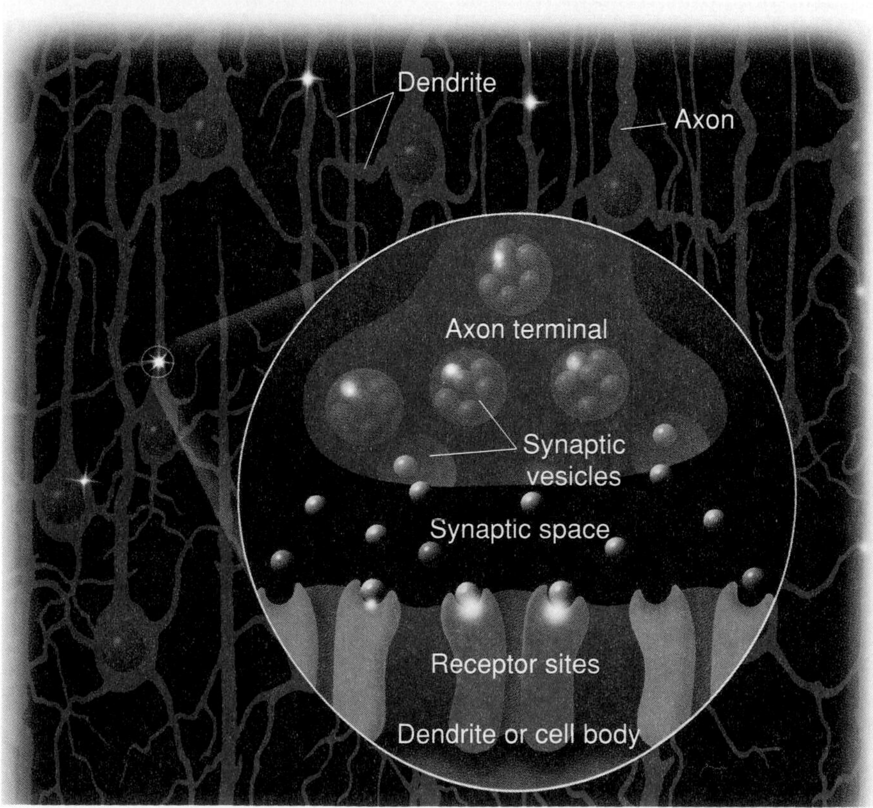


**Figure 2-4**
**Synaptic transmission—communication between neurons.**
When a neural impulse reaches the end of an axon, tiny oval sacs, called *synaptic vesicles*, at the end of most axons release varying amounts of chemical substances called *neurotransmitters*. These substances travel across the synaptic space and affect the next neuron.

play an important role in schizophrenia and the motor disorder known as Parkinson's disease. *Serotonin* is another inhibitory neurotransmitter that affects emotions, arousal, and sleep. *Norepinephrine* similarly plays a role in wakefulness and arousal, as well as in learning, memory, and emotional mood. (See the Summary Table for a more detailed list of major neurotransmitters and their effects.)

Some transmitter substances have widespread effects on the nervous system. They seem to regulate or adjust the sensitivity of large numbers of synapses, in effect "turning up" or "turning down" the activity level of whole portions of the nervous system. This process is especially clear in the case of substances that are involved in the body's relief of pain. Both *endorphins* and *enkephalins* appear to reduce pain by inhibiting, or "turning down," the neurons that transmit pain messages in the brain. Endorphins are chains of amino acids that act like neurotransmitters. One endorphin was found to be 48 times more potent than morphine when injected into the brain and 3 times more potent when injected into the bloodstream (S.H. Snyder, 1977). Enkephalins also occur naturally in the brain, but they seem to have smaller and shorter-term pain-relieving effects (R. Bolles & Fanselow, 1982).

Once a chemical transmitter has been released into the synaptic space and has performed its job, what happens to it? If it remains loose or if it continues to occupy receptor sites, it will continue to affect other neurons indefinitely, long after the initial message or signal is over. There are two ways that the action of most neurotransmitters is terminated. First, some neurotransmitters are broken down by other chemicals. In some cases, the by-products are recycled to

Endorphins, which are released into the body during exercise, are neurotransmitters that act as natural painkillers.

## Summary Table

### Major Neurotransmitters and Their Effects

| | | |
|---|---|---|
| **Acetylcholine (ACh)** | Generally excitatory | Affects arousal, attention, memory, motivation, movement. Too much: spasms, tremors. Too little: paralysis, torpor. |
| **Dopamine** | Inhibitory | Inhibits wide range of behavior and emotions, including pleasure. Implicated in schizophrenia and Parkinson's disease. |
| **Serotonin** | Inhibitory | Inhibits virtually all activities. Important for sleep onset, mood, eating behavior. |
| **Norepinephrine** | Generally excitatory | Affects arousal, wakefulness, learning, memory, mood. |
| **Endorphins and enkephalins** | Inhibitory | Inhibits transmission of pain messages. |

make new neurotransmitters; in other cases, they are treated as wastes and are removed from the body. Second, many neurotransmitters are simply reabsorbed into axon terminals to be used again. In either case, the synapse is cleared up and returned to its normal state.

## Synapses and Drugs

How do drugs like caffeine, marijuana, LSD, and curare affect the body?

Most drugs and toxins that affect psychological functions alter the way in which synapses work. Some substances impede the release of transmitter chemicals from neurons into the synaptic space. For example, the toxin produced by the microorganism that causes botulism prevents the release of ACh. The result is paralysis and sometimes rapid death. Drugs such as reserpine cause transmitter chemicals to leak out of the synaptic vesicles and be rapidly broken down. The result is a shortage of transmitters and decreased activity at the synapse. Reserpine is often prescribed to reduce blood pressure because it decreases the activity of neurons that excite the circulatory system.

In contrast to toxins or drugs that reduce the amount of neurotransmitters, some drugs speed up the release of transmitter chemicals into the synaptic space. For example, the poison of the black widow spider causes ACh to be poured into the synapses of the nervous system. As a result, neurons fire repeatedly, causing spasms and tremors. Amphetamines have a similar effect on neurons containing norepinephrine, and the results can be jitteriness, high arousal, an exaggerated sense of self-confidence, and insomnia. Caffeine increases release of excitatory, arousing neurotransmitters by blocking the action of adenosine, a transmitter substance that inhibits the release of these substances. In fact, two or three cups of coffee provide enough caffeine to block half the adenosine receptors for several hours, producing a high state of arousal in the nervous system. In some cases, the arousal is so high that we say the person is suffering from "coffee nerves."

The substances just mentioned produce their effects by increasing or decreasing the amount of neurotransmitters in the synapse. Other drugs work directly on the receptor sites at the other side of the synaptic gap. Lysergic acid diethylamide (LSD), for example, attaches to receptor sites on neurons that release serotonin and inhibits the activity of those neurons. It may also affect levels of dopamine, although scientists do not know exactly how. You may be wondering how suppressing of the activity of serotonin-releasing neurons could produce the spectacular sensations of an LSD "trip." Some psychologists (N. Carlson, 1994) have speculated that, under normal waking conditions, some of these neurons suppress dreaming. When LSD inhibits or interferes with those neurons, they are no longer able to suppress dreaming, even though the user is actually awake. Other investigators warn, however, that the process might be more complex (J.R. Cooper, Bloom, & Roth, 1991; Shepherd, 1994).

Some drugs act by blocking receptors so that neurotransmitters can neither excite nor inhibit their targets. For example, atropine, a poison derived from belladonna and other plants, blocks receptor sites for ACh in the brain, often disrupting memory functions. Curare, the poison with which some native peoples of South America traditionally have tipped their arrows, blocks the ACh receptors that control skeletal muscle function and rapidly produces paralysis.

Still other drugs interfere with the removal of neurotransmitters after they have done their job. Recall that once transmitter chemicals have bonded to receptor sites and have stimulated or inhibited the neuron, they are normally either removed from the body or returned to the axon terminals from which they came. A number of stimulant drugs interfere with this process. Cocaine, for example, prevents dopamine from being reab-

## HIGHLIGHTS

### New Connections for Old Neurons

During adulthood, the body does not create new neurons. In fact, with each passing day the number of neurons actually decreases. How, then, do we create new neural circuits that allow us to learn and remember?

Research suggests one possible answer: By growing new synapses—or by strengthening already-existing ones—the brain can store information about new experiences. For example, British scientist Timothy Bliss and his colleagues have reported an interesting phenomenon that they have called *long-term potentiation (LTP)* (Bliss & Dolphin, 1982). In a typical experiment, Bliss used a single electrical pulse to stimulate nerves in the hippocampus—a structure in the brain that is involved in the formation of new memories—and then measured the resulting current in the nerves. Although the initial current was extremely weak, when Bliss subsequently stimulated the same pathway with a series of high-frequency pulses, it responded vigorously. Weeks later it still retained this ability. Old brain tissue had learned a new trick.

Since Bliss's work, researchers have hypothesized that LTP may represent a crude kind of memory. Both William T. Greenough and Gary Lynch at the University of California at Irvine have found that LTP not only strengthens existing synapses, it also creates new ones (Lynch et al., 1988). Because of these discoveries, one of the recent focuses of neuroscientific research is to discover how the brain accomplishes such feats.

Investigators feel confident the answer will be expressed biochemically. Although signals travel through a neuron in the form of electrical pulses, messages between neurons are biochemical—after they reach a synapse, they become neurotransmitters and cross the synaptic gap, binding to the next neuron's receptors. If there is a sufficient amount of excitatory neurotransmitter substance present, this neuron fires.

Researchers now think that LTP (and therefore possibly learning) may occur when neurotransmitters activate a special kind of receptor called the NMDA receptor. After such a receptor has been turned on, a number of chemical reactions take place that appear to increase the receiving cell's sensitivity.

sorbed. As a result, excess amounts of dopamine accumulate in the nervous system, producing heightened arousal of the entire nervous system.

Sometimes our investigations of drug effects lead to surprising discoveries about the brain and its neurotransmitters. For example, in attempting to explain the effects of *opiates*—painkilling drugs like morphine and heroin that are derived from the opium plant—Candace Pert and Solomon Snyder discovered that the central nervous system contained receptor sites for these substances (Pert & Snyder, 1973). They reasoned that such receptor sites would not exist unless the body somehow was able to produce its own natural painkillers. Not long after, researchers discovered that our brains actually do produce such substances—the enkephalins and endorphins discussed above. It turns out that morphine and other narcotics are able to lock into the receptors for endorphins and have the same painkilling effects. Similarly, people researching the effects of marijuana found brain receptors for a chemical called tetrahydrocannabinal (THC), the active ingredient in marijuana (Devane et al., 1988; Herkenham et al., 1990; Matsuda et al., 1990). They, too, reasoned that there should be a natural substance in the body that would fit into these receptor sites. Sure enough, researchers later discovered a natural transmitter substance produced by the brain, called *anandamide*, that binds to those same receptors (Devane et al., 1992). Although its natural functions are not yet known, anandamide should have at least some of the effects of marijuana, since it locks into the same receptors as THC.

Another fascinating discovery is that imbalances in some neurotransmitters may contribute to certain kinds of mental illness. Schizophrenia, for

**Central nervous system** Division of the nervous system that consists of the brain and spinal cord.

**Peripheral nervous system** Division of the nervous system that connects the central nervous system to the rest of the body.

example, seems to be associated with an overactivity of dopamine. Some drugs that have been developed to treat schizophrenia seem to reduce the symptoms of this disorder by blocking dopamine receptors. Similarly, some theories link depression to reduced serotonin activity. Antidepressant drugs such as Prozac may reduce the symptoms of depression by blocking reabsorption of serotonin, thus increasing the overall level of serotonin in the synapses of the nervous system. We will explore these interesting discoveries more fully in the chapters on abnormal behavior and therapies.

## THE CENTRAL NERVOUS SYSTEM

If the brain alone has as many as 100 billion neurons, and if each neuron can be "in touch" with thousands of other neurons, then our bodies must contain trillions of synapses through which each neuron is indirectly linked to every other neuron in the nervous system. Although it is impossible to comprehend such an immense system of interconnected neurons, there really is some structure, some organization, to it all. As we noted earlier in this chapter, the **central nervous system** consists of the brain and spinal cord. The **peripheral nervous system** connects the brain and spinal cord to everything else in the body: sense organs, muscles, glands, and so on (see Figure 2-5).

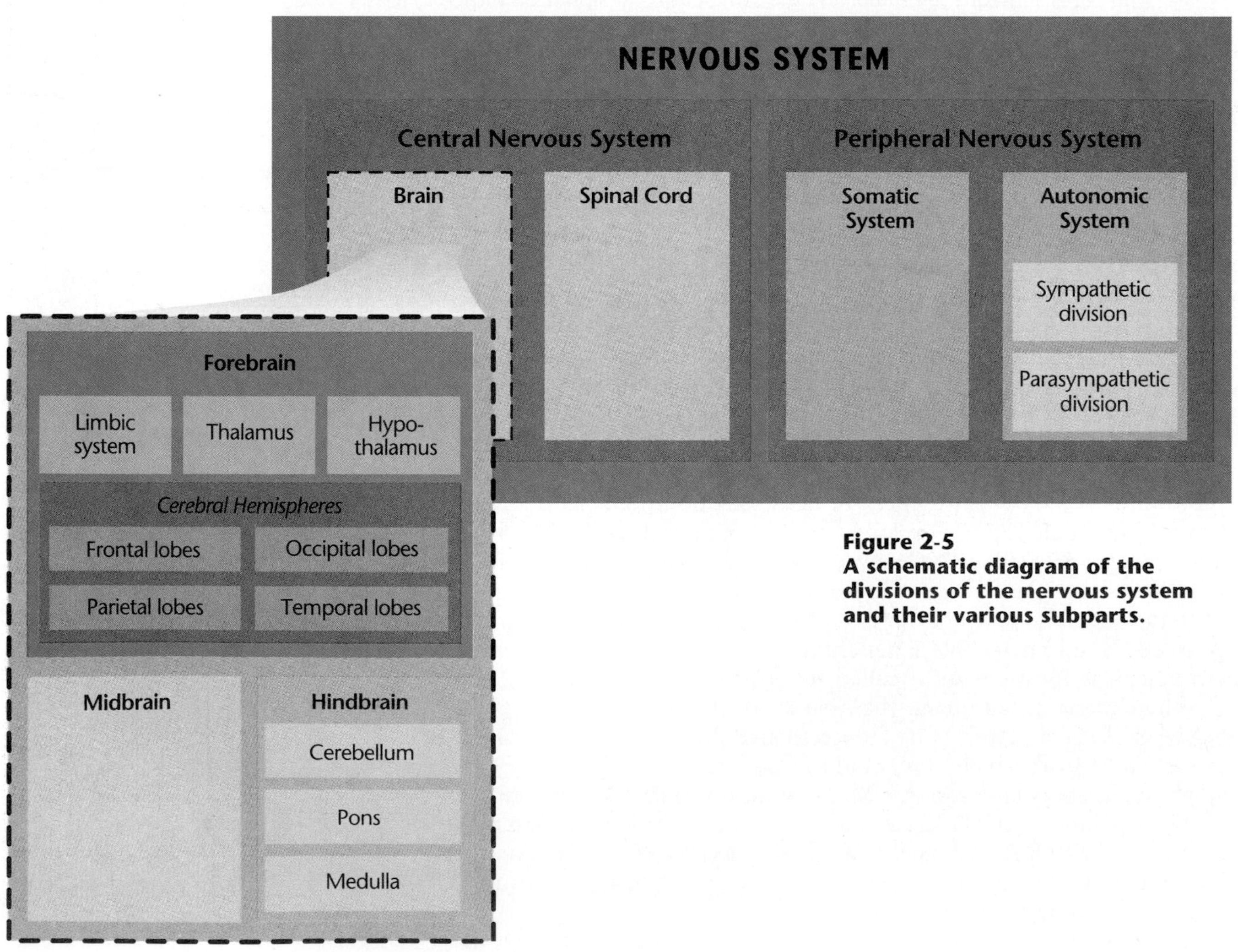


**Figure 2-5**
**A schematic diagram of the divisions of the nervous system and their various subparts.**

## The Brain

The brain is the most fascinating part of the nervous system. Containing more than 90 percent of the body's neurons, the brain is the seat of awareness and reason, the place where learning, memory, and emotions are centered. It is the part of us that decides what to do and whether that decision was right or wrong. And it imagines how things might have turned out if we had acted differently.

As soon as the brain begins to take shape in the human embryo, we can detect three distinct parts: the hindbrain, midbrain, and forebrain. These three parts are still present in the fully developed adult brain, although they are not so easily distinguished from one another (see Figure 2-6). We will use these three basic divisions to describe the parts of the brain, what they do, and how they interact to influence our behavior.

Because the **hindbrain** is found in even the most primitive vertebrates, it is believed to have been the earliest part of the brain to evolve. The part of the hindbrain nearest to the spinal cord is the **medulla**, a narrow structure about 1.5 inches long. The medulla controls such things as breathing, heart rate, and blood pressure. The medulla is also the point at which many of the nerves from the body cross over on their way to the higher brain centers; axons from neurons on the left part of the body cross to the right side of the brain and vice versa.

**Hindbrain** Brain area containing the medulla, pons, and cerebellum.

**Medulla** Part of the hindbrain that controls such functions as breathing, heart rate, and blood pressure.

**Figure 2-6**
**A cross section of the brain,** showing the areas that make up the hindbrain midbrain, and forebrain.

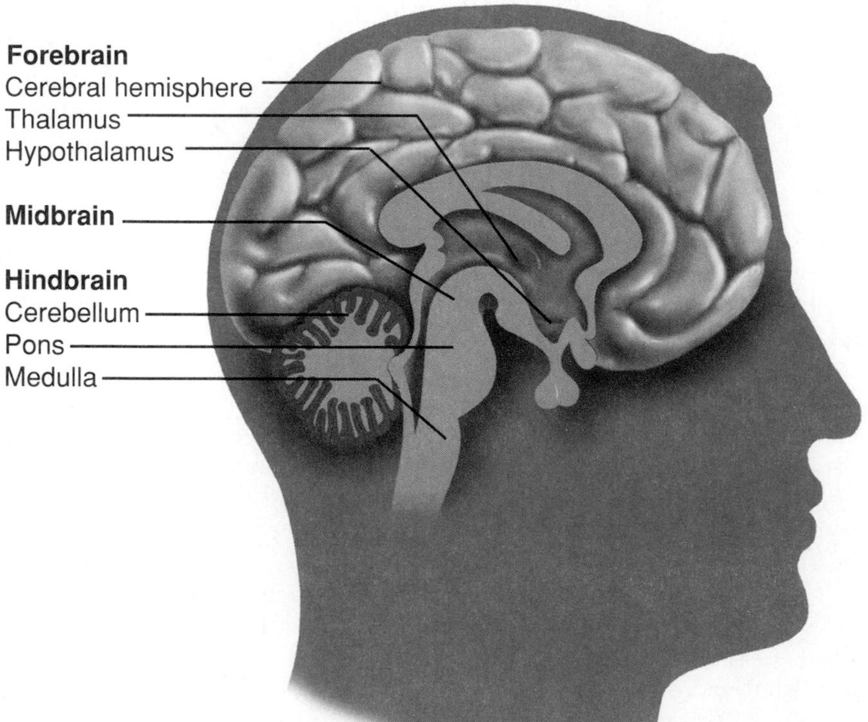

**Pons** Part of the hindbrain that connects the cerebral cortex at the top of the brain to the cerebellum.

**Cerebellum** Two hemispheres in the hindbrain that control certain reflexes and coordinate the body's movements.

**Brain stem** The top of the spinal column; it widens out to form the hindbrain and midbrain.

**Midbrain** Region between the hindbrain and the forebrain; it is important for hearing and sight, and it is one of several places in the brain where pain is registered.

**Forebrain** Top part of the brain, including the thalamus, hypothalamus, and cerebral cortex.

**Thalamus** Forebrain region that relays and translates incoming messages from the sense receptors, except those for smell.

**Hypothalamus** Forebrain region that governs motivation and emotional responses.

**Cerebral cortex** The outer surface of the two cerebral hemispheres that regulate most complex behavior.

Above the medulla lies the **pons**, which connects the top of the brain to the section of the hindbrain called the **cerebellum**. Chemicals produced in the pons help maintain our sleep-wake cycle (discussed in Chapter 4). The cerebellum is composed of two hemispheres and performs a wide range of functions. It handles certain reflexes, especially those that have to do with balance, and it coordinates the body's actions to ensure that movements go together in efficient sequences. Damage to the cerebellum causes severe problems in movement, such as jerky motions, loss of balance, and lack of coordination.

Above the pons and cerebellum, the **brain stem** widens to form the **midbrain**. As its name implies, the midbrain is in the middle of the brain, between the hindbrain at the base and the forebrain at the top. The midbrain is especially important for hearing and sight. It is also one of several places in the brain where pain is registered.

Supported by the brain stem, budding out above it and drooping over somewhat to fit into the skull, is the **forebrain**. In the center of the forebrain, and more or less directly over the brain stem, are the two egg-shaped structures that make up the **thalamus**. The thalamus relays and translates incoming messages from sense receptors (except those for smell) throughout the body. Many of these messages that travel from one part of the brain to another also pass through the thalamus. Some of the neurons in the thalamus seem to be important for regulating the activity of brain centers in the cortex. Others control the activities of those parts of the nervous system outside the brain and spinal cord.

Below the thalamus is a smaller structure called the **hypothalamus**. This part of the forebrain exerts an enormous influence on many kinds of motivation. Portions of the hypothalamus govern eating, drinking, sexual behavior, sleeping, and temperature control. The hypothalamus is also directly involved in emotional behavior such as rage, terror, and pleasure. Also, the hypothalamus appears to play a central role in times of stress, coordinating and integrating the activity of the nervous system.

Above the brain stem, thalamus, and hypothalamus are the two cerebral hemispheres, the outer surface of which is called the **cerebral cortex**. These are what most people think of first when they talk about "the brain," though, as we've seen, the "brain" actually consists of the forebrain, midbrain, and hindbrain taken together. As you can see in Figure 2-7 and Figure 2-8, the two cerebral hemispheres take up most of the room inside the skull. They balloon out over the brain stem, fold down over it, and actually hide most of it from view. The cerebral hemispheres are the most recently evolved part of the nervous system, and they are more highly developed in humans than in any other animal. They account for about 80 percent of the weight of the human brain, and they contain about 70 percent of the neurons in the central nervous system. If they were spread out, they would cover 2 to 3 square feet and would be about as thick as an uppercase letter on a typed page. To fit inside the skull, the cerebral hemispheres have developed an intricate pattern of folds—hills and valleys called *convolutions*. In each person, these convolutions form a pattern that is as unique as a fingerprint.

Despite each cerebral hemisphere's unique appearance, a number of large landmarks on the cortex allow us to identify common functional areas. As seen in Figure 2-7, the cerebral cortex is divided approximately into front and rear halves by a vertical "valley" or "crack." Cortical areas in front of this dividing line (motor areas) are devoted to the planning, sequencing, and execution of body movement. The cortical areas to the rear of this boundary (sensory areas) are involved in processing and combining inputs from our senses. The cerebral hemispheres can each be

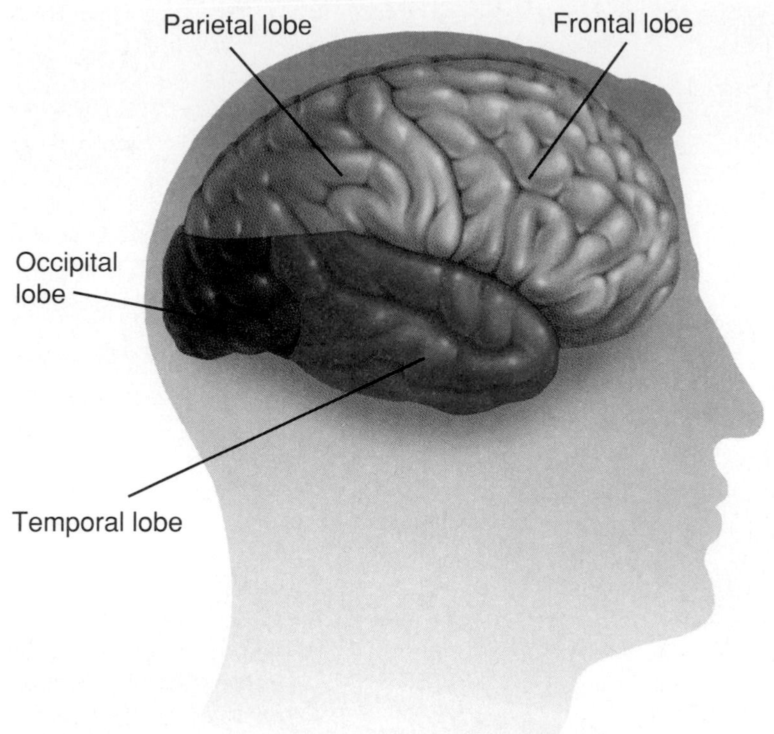


**Figure 2-7**
**The four lobes of the cerebral cortex.** Deep fissures in the cortex separate these areas or lobes.

**Association areas** Areas of the cerebral cortex where incoming messages from the separate senses are combined into meaningful impressions and outgoing messages from the motor areas are integrated.

**Occipital lobe** Part of the cerebral hemisphere that receives and interprets visual information.

**Temporal lobe** Part of the cerebral hemisphere that helps regulate hearing, smell, balance and equilibrium, and certain emotions and motivations.

divided into four large parts, or "lobes," which are separated from one another by the deep*fissures* or cracks on the cortex (see Figure 2-7). Three of these lobes are in the rear portion of each hemisphere, the portion that primarily processes sensory information. The remaining lobe in each hemisphere lies in the front half, which is involved primarily with integration of our movement. Also, there are large areas on the cortex of all four lobes called **association areas**. Experts generally believe that information from diverse parts of the cortex is integrated in the association areas and that these areas are the sites of mental processes such as learning, thinking, remembering, and comprehending and using language.

The **occipital lobe**, located at the very back of the cerebral hemispheres, receives and processes visual information. It is in the occipital lobe that we actually experience shapes, color, and motion in the environment. Damage to the occipital lobe can produce blindness, even though the eyes and their neural connections to the brain are perfectly healthy. The **temporal lobe**, located in front of the occipital lobe, roughly behind the temples, plays an important role in complex visual tasks such as recognizing faces. It is the primary "smell center" in the brain. It also receives and processes information from the ears, contributes to balance and equilibrium, and regulates emotions and motivations such as anxiety, pleasure, and anger. In addition, the ability to understand and comprehend language is thought to be concentrated primarily in the rear portion of the temporal lobes, though recent research indicates that some language comprehension may also occur in the parietal lobe and the frontal lobe (Ojemann et al., 1989). See the Controversies box for a discussion of language centers in the brain.

3.

*True or false*: Injuries to certain areas of the brain can produce blindness, even if the eyes themselves are not damaged.

**Parietal lobe** Part of the cerebral cortex that responds primarily to sensations of touch and bodily position.

**Sensory projection areas** Areas of the parietal lobe where messages from the sense receptors are registered.

**Frontal lobe** Part of the cerebral cortex that is responsible for voluntary movement; it is also important for attention, goal-directed behavior, and appropriate emotional experiences.

**Motor projection areas** Areas of the cerebral cortex where response messages from the brain to the muscles and glands begin.

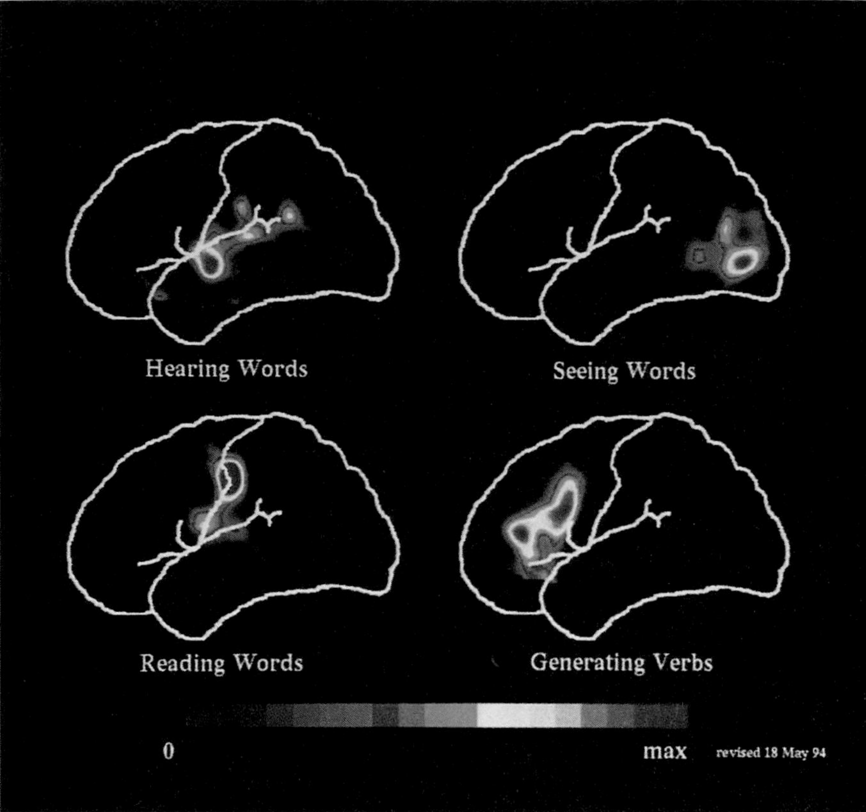


PET scans of the human brain as it processes language. The scans actually spotlight the areas of the brain most active in hearing, seeing, thinking, and speaking.

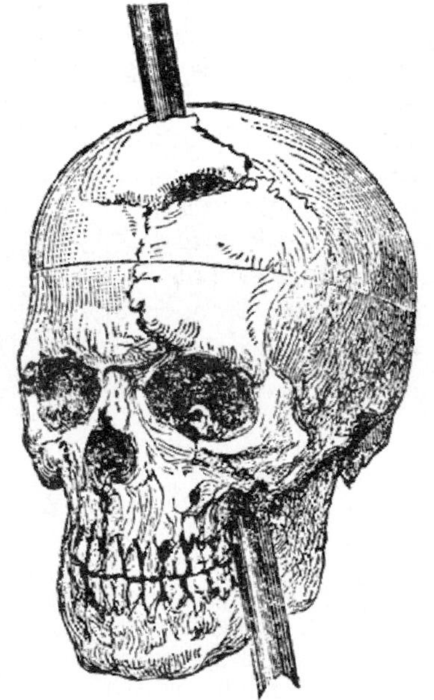

The skull of Phineas Gage, showing where the tamping iron passed through it.

The **parietal lobe** sits on top of the temporal and occipital lobes and occupies the top back half of each hemisphere. This lobe receives sensory information from all over the body—from sense receptors in the skin, muscles, and joints. Messages from these sense receptors are registered in areas called **sensory projection areas**. The parietal lobe also seems to play a role in spatial abilities, such as the ability to follow a map or to tell someone how to get somewhere (A. Cohen & Raffal, 1991).

The **frontal lobe**, located just behind the forehead, accounts for about half the volume of the human brain. Response messages from the brain start their return trip in the **motor projection areas** of the frontal lobe, and from there they go to the various muscles and glands in the body. Scientists are still uncertain of all the functions performed by this portion of the brain. In part, this is because much of our knowledge about brain function comes from research on animals, whose frontal lobes are relatively undeveloped, or from studying the rare cases of people with some kind of frontal lobe damage. One such famous case became public in 1848. It involved a bizarre accident that happened to a man named Phineas Gage.

Gage, who was the foreman of a railroad construction gang, made a careless mistake while using some blasting powder and a tamping iron. As a result, the tamping iron tore through his cheek and severely damaged his frontal lobe. Gage remained conscious, walked part of the way to a doctor, and, to the amazement of those who saw the accident, suffered few major aftereffects. There was no physical impairment, and his memory and skills seemed to be as good as ever. He did, however, undergo major personality changes. Once a steady worker, he lost interest in work and drifted from job to job. Other personality changes were so great that, in the view of his friends, Gage was no longer the same man.

# HIGHLIGHTS

## Growing Brain Cells

Each year thousands of people suffer injuries to the spinal cord and to the brain itself. Traditionally, such injuries have been considered permanent and beyond medical help. The time may be near, however, when it will be possible to treat these injuries successfully

Unlike cells in other body organs, neurons do not divide and repair themselves. At birth or shortly thereafter, we have as many neurons as we will ever have. Many of the neurons that are present at birth die, and those that die are not replaced. Thus, it is critical to keep the surviving neurons in good repair.

In view of these facts, scientists have been puzzled for many years by the observation that injuries in the peripheral nervous system do sometimes heal themselves. Since neurons in the central nervous system are basically just like neurons in the peripheral nervous system, how is it that one group of neurons repair themselves while the other cannot? The answer seems to be that the peripheral nervous system has a type of glial cell called a *Schwann cell* that responds to injury by producing a chemical called *nerve growth factor* or *NGF*. This chemical stimulates and guides the growth of damaged axons so that they grow toward and establish new synapses with their former targets. Thus, neurons in the peripheral nervous system are able, to some extent, to repair themselves. In contrast, glial cells in the central nervous system actually inhibit axon growth and thus are unable to repair themselves (Schwab & Catoni, 1988). Researchers are presently exploring the possibility of treating injured cells in the central nervous system with a substance that blocks the growth-inhibiting substance and stimulating them with a substance like NGF in hopes that the neurons might then be able to recover from their injuries (Schnell & Schwab, 1990).

Other avenues to repairing damage to the central nervous system include implanting fetal brain tissues into damaged areas in adult brains. For reasons that are still unknown, fetal nerve tissues are not rejected by the brain into which they are implanted. They seem to ignore growth-inhibiting substances and readily establish new connections in recipient brains, thus replacing existing tissue that is damaged or missing. Fetal tissue implants offer hope for arresting or slowing the course of Parkinson's disease and may even prove to be of use in treating Alzheimer's disease. The use of fetal tissues for these purposes raises many ethical issues, however, and therefore remains highly controversial.

Still other researchers are attempting to grow brain cells in the laboratory (Snyder, 1990), with the hopes of using these "test-tube" cells for drug testing and possibly for transplantation. In addition, two Canadian researchers have discovered that a group of immature cells, capable of dividing and growing, is kept in reserve in the brains of adult mice (B.A. Weiss & Reynolds, 1992). This finding is a surprise because it has long been assumed that such cells did not exist in the mammalian brain after birth. If such cells exist in the human brain, then they might be used to repair damage to the spinal cord or brain, thus resolving both the controversy and medical difficulties inherent in transplanting cells from "donor" brains.

Since Gage's time, careful research has refined these early impressions of the functions of the frontal lobe. This part of the brain seems to permit and anticipate goal-directed behavior. Patients with damage to the frontal lobe have trouble completing tasks that involve following complex directions or performing tasks in which the directions change during the course of the job. Low levels of activity in portions of the frontal lobe are associated with hyperactivity and attention deficits in some people (Zametkin et al., 1990), and abnormalities in frontal lobes are often observed in patients with schizophrenia (Raine et al., 1992).

The frontal lobe also appears necessary for a person to lead a normal emotional life. People whose frontal lobe has been severed often seem apathetic and capable of only shallow emotions, although this apathy may be interrupted by periods of boastfulness and silliness. Moreover, some people with injuries to the frontal lobe experience explosive anger afterward: They react with inappropriate, purposeless, and instantaneous anger to the slightest provocation and often feel embarrassed about their behavior afterward (Damasio, Tranel, & Damasio, 1990b). And some research suggests that the

**Corpus callosum** Band of nerve fibers that connects the two cerebral hemispheres and coordinates their activities.



**Figure 2-8**
**The two cerebral hemispheres.** The left hemisphere controls movements of the right hand, and the right hemisphere controls the left hand. The left hemisphere is usually dominant in verbal tasks, while the right hemisphere is typically superior at nonverbal, visual, and spatial tasks.

frontal lobe is linked to emotional temperament (being cheerful and optimistic or melancholy and alarmist) (Tomarken, Davidson, & Henriques, 1990). The frontal lobe also receives and coordinates messages from the other three lobes of the cortex. And it seems to play a role in the ability to keep track of previous and future movements of the body. Much more research needs to be done before psychologists can understand how this part of the cortex contributes to such a wide and subtle range of mental activities.

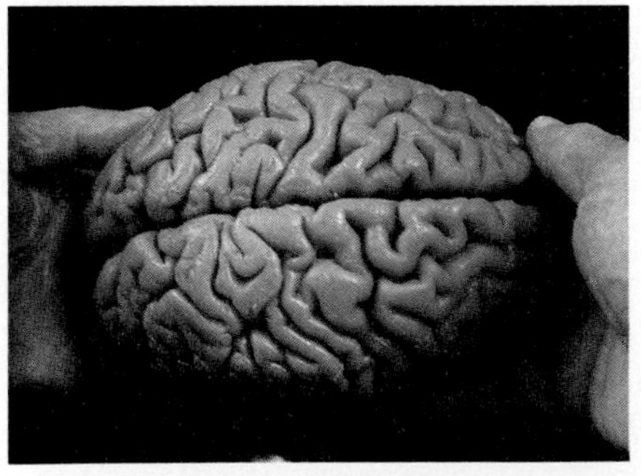

The human brain, viewed from the top.

## Hemispheric Specialization

As we saw earlier, most of what we normally consider "the brain" consists of two separate cerebral hemispheres. In a sense, humans have a "right half-brain" and a "left half-brain." The two hemispheres are connected at several locations, but the primary connection between the left and right cortex is a thick, ribbonlike band of nerve fibers under the cortex called the **corpus callosum**, which is illustrated in Figure 2-13 on page 56.

Under normal conditions, the left and right cerebral hemispheres are in close communication through the corpus callosum, and they work together as a coordinated unit (Semrud-Clikeman & Hynd, 1990; Hellige, 1993). Nonetheless, some evidence suggests that the cerebral hemispheres are not really equivalent (see Figure 2-8). For example, damage to the left hemisphere often results in severe language problems, whereas similar damage to the right hemisphere seldom has that effect. More dramatic evidence comes from research carried out on people with epilepsy in the early 1960s by Sperry and his colleagues at the California Institute of Technology. In some cases of severe epilepsy, surgeons cut the corpus callosum in an effort to stop the spread of epileptic seizures from the cortex of one hemisphere to the other. But this operation also cuts the only direct communication link between the two hemispheres and thus makes it possible to watch each hemisphere work on its own (Sperry, 1964, 1968, 1970). The results proved startling.

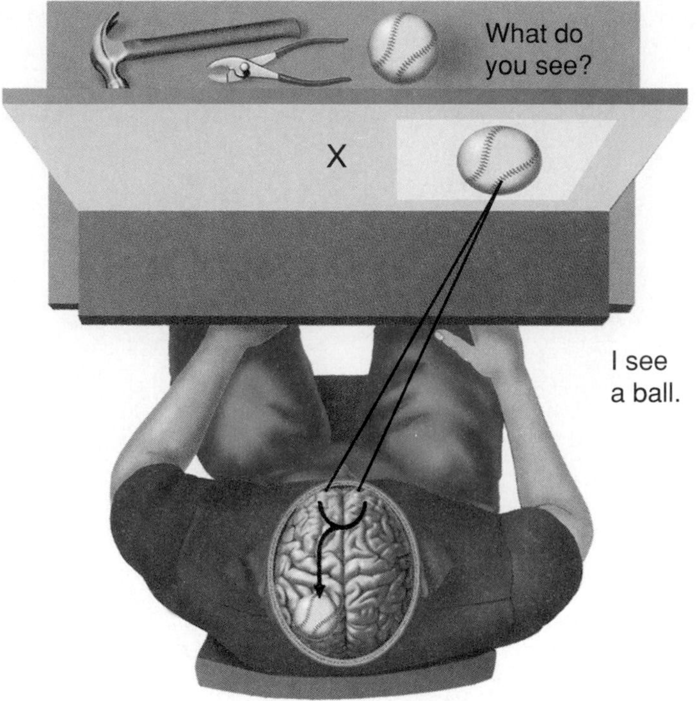


**Figure 2-9**
When split-brain patients stare at the "X" in the center of the screen, visual information projected on the *right* side of the screen goes to the patient's *left* hemisphere, which controls language. When asked what he or she sees, the patient can reply correctly.

*Source:* Adapted from Carol Ward ©*Discover* Magazine, 1987.

When such "split-brain patients" are asked to stare at a spot on a projection screen while pictures of various objects are projected to the *right* of that spot, they are able to identify the objects verbally, and they are able to pick them out of a group of hidden objects, using their right hands to feel each object in turn (see Figure 2-9). However, when pictures of objects are shown on the *left* side of the projection screen, subjects can pick out the objects by feeling them with their left hands, yet they are unable to say what the objects are! In fact, most often when objects are projected on the left side of the screen, split-brain patients report verbally that they see "nothing" on the screen, even though they can accurately identify the objects when given a chance to touch and feel them with their left hands (see Figure 2-10).

The explanation for these startling results is to be found in the way each hemisphere of the brain operates. The left cerebral hemisphere receives information only from the right side of the body and the right half of the visual field. Thus, it can match an object shown in the right visual field with information received by touch from the right hand. However, the left hemisphere is unaware of (and thus unable to identify) objects shown in the left visual field or touched by the left hand. Conversely, the right hemisphere of the brain receives information only from the left side of the visual field and the left side of the body. Thus, the right hemisphere can match an object shown in the left visual field with information received by touch from the left hand. But it is unaware of any objects shown in the right visual field or touched with the right hand.

This description of the two hemispheres explains all of Sperry's findings except one: When an object is shown in the left visual field, why can't split-brain patients identify the object verbally? The answer seems to be that, for the great majority of people, language ability is concentrated primarily in the left cortex of the brain (Hellige, 1990, 1993). In most split-brain patients, the right hemisphere of the brain cannot verbally identify the object that it is "seeing" in the left visual field, even though the object

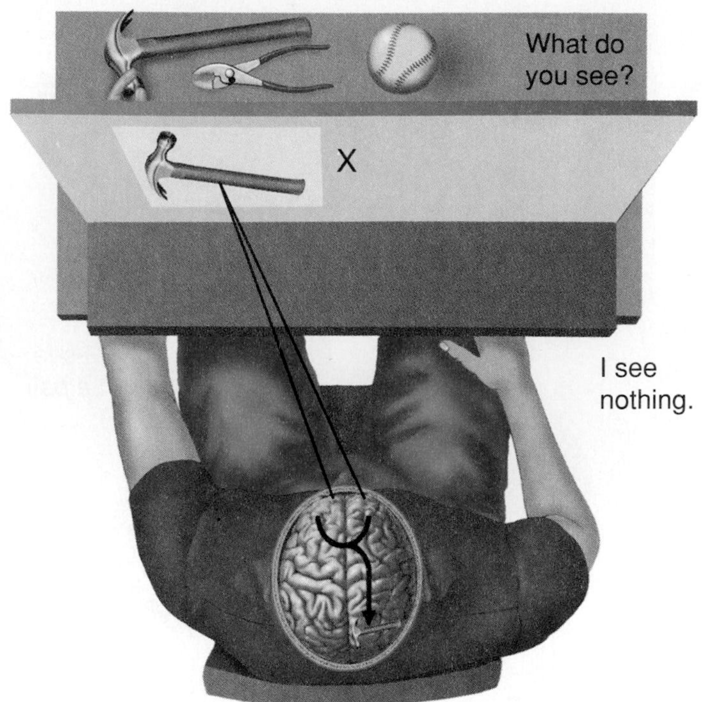


**Figure 2-10**
When split-brain patients stare at the "X" in the center of the screen, visual information projected on the *left* side of the screen goes to the patient's *right* hemisphere, which does not control language. When asked what he or she sees, the patient cannot name the object but can pick it out by touch with the *left* hand.

PET scans of a person at rest (top) and using language (bottom). The "hot" colors (red and yellow) indicate greater brain activity. This photo indicates that language activity is located primarily, but not exclusively, in the left hamisphere of the brain.

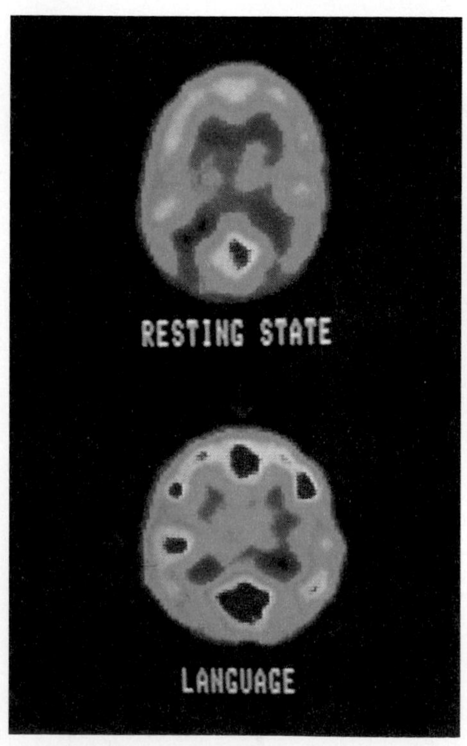


can be picked out by touch using the left hand. When the person is asked, "What do you see?" the left hemisphere (which monitors the right visual field) correctly reports, "Nothing."

In other words, the two hemispheres not only receive from and send information to different sides of the body, but they also seem to excel at somewhat different functions. In most people, the left hemisphere is dominant in verbal tasks, such as identifying spoken and printed words and speaking (Figure 2-8) (Hellige, 1990, 1993; Semrud-Clikeman & Hynd, 1990; Springer & Deutsch, 1989). It has been suggested that the left hemisphere may also operate more analytically, logically, rationally, and sequentially than the right hemisphere, though clearly demonstrating such differences is difficult, if not impossible (Beaton, 1985; Hellige, 1990, 1993). In contrast, research indicates that the right hemisphere excels at visual and spatial tasks, nonverbal imagery (such as visual images, music, and environmental noises), face recognition, and the perception and expression of emotion (Hellige, 1990, 1993; Kalat, 1988; Semrud-Clikeman & Hynd, 1990.)

One intriguing line of contemporary research suggests that the left and right frontal lobes may play quite different roles in emotional reactivity and temperament. Using a wide variety of research techniques, Richard Davidson and his colleagues at the University of Wisconsin have discovered that people whose left frontal lobe is more active than the right tend to be more cheerful, sociable, ebullient, and self-confident; they also respond more positively to events around them, take delight in other people and novel situations, and are less upset by unpleasant events. In contrast, people with more right frontal lobe activity are more easily stressed, frightened, and upset and threatened by unpleasant events around them; they (not surprisingly) tend to shrink from encounters with other people and novel situations. They also tend to be more suspicious and depressed than people with predominantly left frontal lobe activity (Henriques & Davidson, 1990; Tomarken, et al.

## Summary Table

### Parts of the Brain and Their Function

| | | |
|---|---|---|
| **Hindbrain** | Medulla<br>Pons<br>Cerebellum | Breathing, heart rate, blood pressure<br>Sensory nerves crossover<br>Regulation of sleep–wake cycle<br>Reflexes (e.g., balance)<br>Coordinates movement |
| **Midbrain** | | Hearing, vision relay point<br>Pain registered |
| **Forebrain** | Thalamus<br>Hypothalamus<br>Cerebral cortex<br>Occipital lobe<br>Temporal lobe<br>Parietal lobe<br>Frontal lobe | Major message relay center<br>Regulates higher brain centers and peripheral nervous system<br>Motivation<br>Emotion<br>Stress reactions<br>Temperature control<br>Receives and processes visual information<br>Complex vision<br>Hearing<br>Balance and equilibrium<br>Emotions and motivations<br>Some language comprehension<br>Sensory projection and association areas<br>Visual/spatial abilities<br>Goal-directed behavior, concentration<br>Emotional control<br>Motor projection and association areas<br>Temperament |

1990). Rather dramatic supporting evidence comes from studies of patients suffering from seizure disorders. Patients whose right hemisphere is anaesthetized frequently laugh and express positive emotions. Conversely, anaesthetizing the left hemisphere often produces crying (Lee et al., 1993).

It is important to note that not everyone shows the same pattern of differences between the left and right hemispheres; in particular, there is some evidence that the differences between the hemispheres may be greater in men than in women (Hellige, 1993; Seamon & Kenrick, 1992; Semrud-Clikeman & Hynd, 1990). Moreover, even though the differences between the two hemispheres are intriguing, we must remember that under normal conditions, the right and left halves of the brain are in close communication through the corpus callosum and thus work together in a coordinated, integrated way. Nevertheless, in recent years, a good deal of popular literature has seized on the highly publicized split-brain research and drawn all kinds of unwarranted conclusions about human behavior. In particular, some authors have inaugurated what is sometimes called a "right-brain movement" to promote the uses and virtues of supposedly right-brain skills like intuition and creativity. In response, Michael Gazzaniga, one of the pioneers in split-brain research, simply points out: "You don't have to invoke one cent's worth of experimental psychological data or neuroscience to make the observation that there are some people in this world who are terribly intuitive and creative, and some who aren't" (McKean, 1985, p. 34).

# CONTROVERSIES

## Do Men and Women Speak Different Languages?

The notion that human language is controlled primarily by the left cerebral cortex was first set forth in the 1860s by a French physician named Paul Broca. Broca's ideas were modified a decade later by a scientist named Karl Wernicke. Thus, it should come as no surprise that the two major language areas in the brain have traditionally been called *Broca's area* and *Wernicke's area* (see Figure 2-11).

Wernicke's area lies toward the back of the temporal lobe. This area seems to be especially important for processing and understanding what others are saying. In contrast, Broca's area, found in the frontal lobe, is considered to be essential to our ability to talk. To oversimplify a bit, Wernicke's area seems to be important for listening, and Broca's area seems to be important for talking. One line of evidence in support of these distinctions comes from patients who have suffered left-hemisphere strokes and resulting brain damage. Such strokes often produce language problems, called *aphasias*, that can be quite predictable. If the brain damage primarily affects Broca's area, the aphasia tends to be "expressive." That is, the patients' language difficulties lie predominantly in sequencing and producing language (talking). If the damage mostly affectsWernicke's area, the aphasia tends to be "receptive," and patients may have profound difficulties understanding language (listening).

Broca's area

Wernicke's area

**Figure 2-11**
**Broca's area and Wernicke's area.**

*Source:* Adapted from *Physiology and Behavior* (5th ed.), by Neil R. Carlson. Copyright © 1994 by Allyn & Bacon. Reprinted by permission.

Recent research suggests, however, that this model of the brain may apply only to males. For example, Doreen Kimura of the University of Western Ontario has shown that women who have brain damage near Wernicke's area rarely, if ever, experience language difficulties (Kimura, 1985; E. Hampson & Kimura, 1992). Kimura suggests that, in women, an area in the frontal lobe quite close to Broca's area actually combines the functions of both Broca's area and Wernicke's area. Other brain-mapping studies have provided support for this view (Mateer et al., 1982; Vignolo et al., 1986).

These data, along with reports that men's and women's brains differ in other ways as well (see Breedlove, 1994), raise a number of questions. Do all males have separate Broca and Wernicke areas for language, and do all females have the more economical, single frontal language area described by Kimura? If so, can we distinguish male and female ways of understanding and producing language? More generally, do different types of brain structures make the sexes think differently? Do experience and culture help bring about distinct "male" and "female" ways of thinking and speaking? Or, are different patterns of thought and speech based on individual, rather than gender, differences? Scientists know that male and female brains differ in certain ways. Whether these physical differences necessarily lead to behavioral differences is a question that requires a lot more research.

## New Tools for Studying the Nervous System

Much of the information that we have discussed thus far was generated by our increasingly sophisticated technology for studying the structure and functions of the brain. Most of these brain-studying techniques were developed only in recent decades or, in some cases, in recent years. For centuries, our understanding of the brain depended entirely on observing patients who suffered from brain injury or on examining the brains of cadavers. Then, in 1929, Hans Berger developed the *electroencephalograph (EEG)*, which provided insight for the first time into the living, fully functioning brain. Since that time, there has been a virtual explosion of techniques for studying the nervous system. These techniques include microelectrode, macroelectrode, structural imaging, and functional imaging techniques.

**MICROELECTRODE TECHNIQUES** *Microelectrode recording techniques* are used to study the functions of single neurons. A microelectrode is a tiny glass or quartz pipette (smaller in diameter than a human hair) that is filled with a conducting liquid. When technicians place the tip of this electrode on the surface of a neuron or even inside a neuron, they can study changes in the electrical conditions of that particular neuron. Microelectrode techniques have been used to discover the dynamics of action potentials, the effects of drugs or toxins on neurons, and even processes that occur in the neural membrane.

In an EEG, electrodes attached to the scalp are used to create a picture of neural activity in the brain.

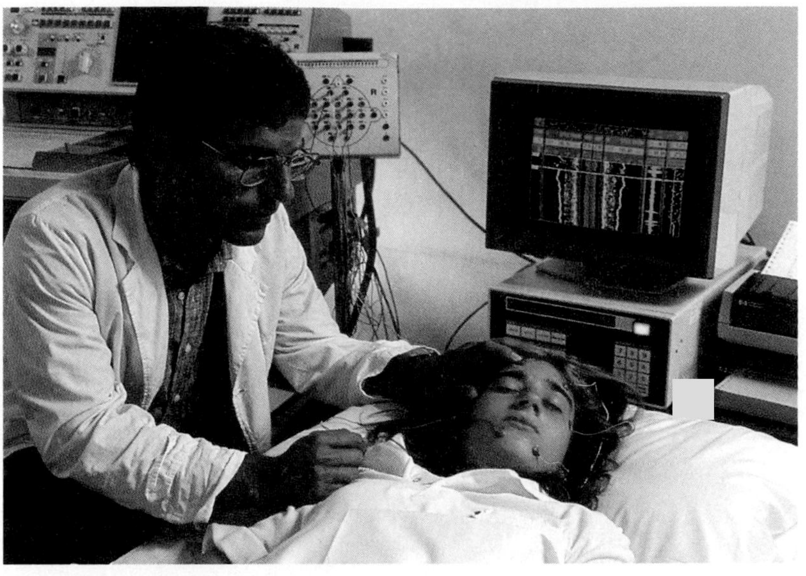

**MACROELECTRODE TECHNIQUES** Berger's EEG is an example of a *macroelectrode* technique used in studying the brain. Macroelectrode techniques involve the use of large recording devices that are placed directly on the surface of the scalp, where they can detect the collective activity of millions of neurons in the underlying cortex. These so-called brain waves provide an index of both the size and the rhythm of neural activity in the cerebral cortex. The shape and pattern of these waves vary depending on what you happen to be doing at the time. *Alpha waves* are commonly found when you are relaxing with your eyes closed. Alphas change to higher-frequency *beta waves* when you are awake and still but with your eyes open. At the other extreme are the low-frequency *delta waves*, which occur during deepest sleep. As we will see in the chapter titled "States of Consciousness," the changes that occur in brain waves during sleep have proved to be a valuable tool for researchers interested in learning more about sleep and dreaming.

An EEG presents a continuous picture of the brain over an extended period. Sometimes, however, technicians want to see what the brain is doing when it is responding to a specific stimulus. To accomplish this, they take a series of EEG traces during the stimulus event. These traces are then analyzed by computer to produce an *event-related potential (ERP)* or *evoked potential (EP)*, a pattern representing a specific cortical response to the stimulus. Researchers have discovered that certain components of the ERP (see Figure 2-12) appear in the interval between some type of warning signal and a response, such as pressing a button. This seems to suggest that brain waves can reflect subtle psychological processes, such as a state of expectancy (Rosenzweig & Leiman, 1982). Because of this, the waves can be "read" as indicators of a person's psychophysiological state; however, they do not provide information about a person's actual thoughts (Donchin, 1987).

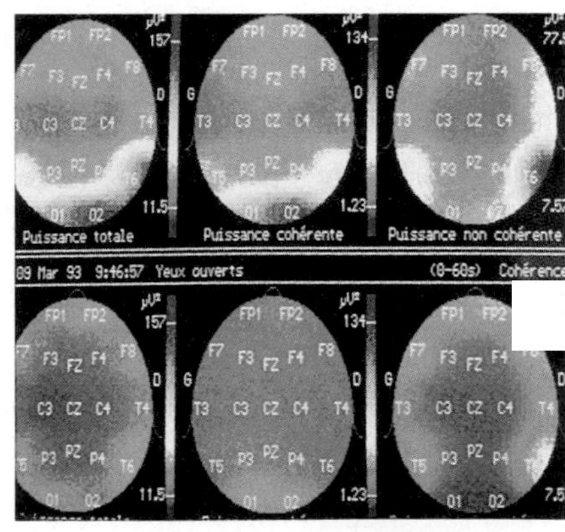


An EEG recording of one person's alpha brain waves. Red and violet colors indicate greater alpha-wave activity.

**STRUCTURAL IMAGING** *Computerized axial tomography (CT) scanning* allows scientists to create three-dimensional images of a human brain without actually performing surgery. To create a CT scan, an X-ray photography unit rotates around the patient, moving from the top of the head to the bottom; a computer then combines the resulting images. Even more successful at producing pictures of the inner regions of the brain—its ridges, folds, and fissures—is an imaging technique called *magnetic reso-*

What is MRI, and how does it differ from PET scanning and CT scanning?

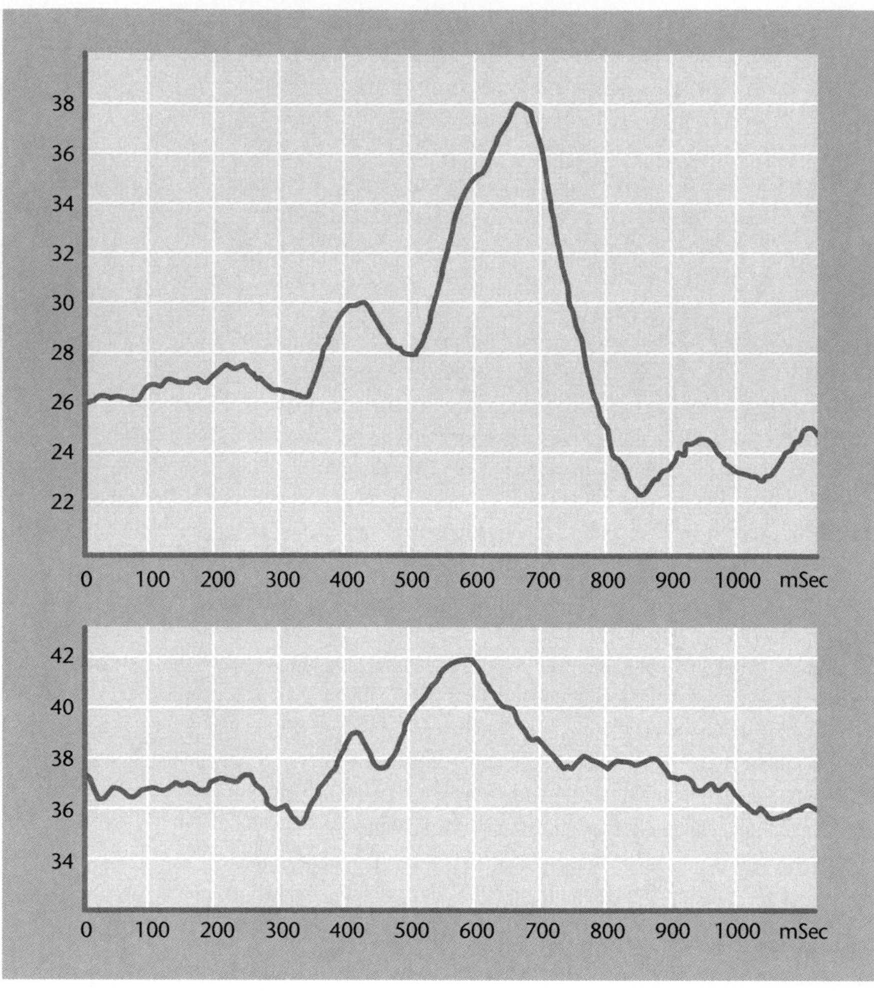


**Figure 2-12**
The ERP trace of a male nondrinker (top) and a male with an alcohol-abuse problem (bottom).

*Source:* Courtesy of S. M. Matsui and M. H. Olson.

*nance imaging (MRI)*. In the MRI technique, the patient's head is placed in a magnetic field, and the brain is exposed to radio waves. When the radio waves stop, hydrogen atoms in the brain release energy. The energy released by different structures in the brain generates an image that appears on a computer screen.

CT scan of a normal human brain.

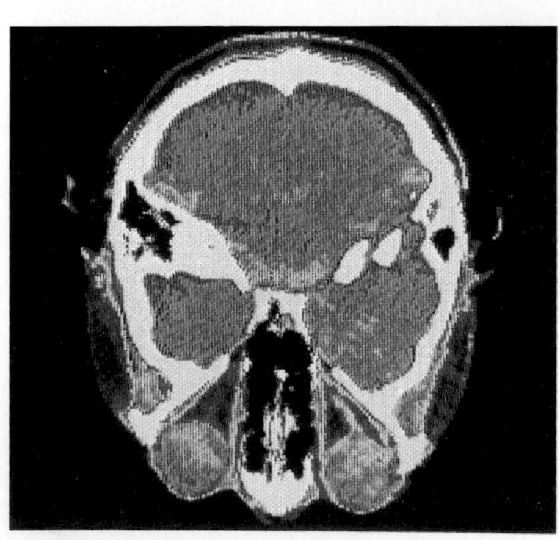

**FUNCTIONAL IMAGING** Both CT scanning and MRI permit unparalleled mapping of the brain's structures in living human beings. Neither technique, however, can provide a picture of the brain's activity. Several techniques allow researchers to observe the overall activity of the cortex as it actually reacts to sensory stimuli such as pain, tones, and words. In one technique, called *EEG imaging*, measurements of the actual functioning of the brain are made "on a millisecond-by-millisecond basis" (Fischman, 1985, p. 18). In this technique, more than 2 dozen electrodes are placed at important locations on the scalp. These electrodes record brain activities, which are then converted by a computer into colored images on a television screen. These images show the distributions of alpha, beta, and other activity. For example, the technique has been extremely useful for detecting abnormal cortical activity such as that observed during an epileptic seizure.

Two related techniques, called *magnetoencephalography (MEG)* and *magnetic source imaging (MSI)*, take the procedure a step further. In standard EEG, electrical signals are distorted as they pass through the skull, and it is difficult to determine exactly where they come from. However, those same electrical signals create magnetic fields that are unaffected by bone. Both MEG and MSI actually measure the strength of the magnetic field and are able to identify its source with considerable accuracy. Using these procedures, biopsychologists hope to be able to determine exactly which parts of the brain actually do most of the work in such psychological processes as memory, language processing, and reading. In turn, that research may shed new light on such disorders as amnesia and dyslexia (a reading disorder). Researchers also hope to be able to locate the areas of the brain affected by various drugs, such as those used to treat severe psychological disorders like schizophrenia. This knowledge would be particularly valuable in understanding the side effects these drugs sometimes produce.

**Reticular formation (RF)** Network of neurons in the hindbrain, midbrain, and part of the forebrain whose primary function is to alert and arouse the higher parts of the brain.

Another family of techniques—*positron emission tomography (PET) scanning*, *radioactive PET*, and *single photon emission computed tomography (SPECT)*—uses radioactive energy to map brain activity. In all these techniques, a person first receives an injection of a radioactive substance. Brain structures that are especially active immediately after the injection absorb most of the substance. When the substance starts to decay, it releases subatomic particles. By studying where most of the particles come from, physicians can determine exactly which portions of the brain were most active. Some of the findings produced by these techniques have been surprising. For example, it turns out that in general the brains of people with higher IQ scores are actually *less* active than those of people with lower IQ scores, perhaps because they process information more efficiently (Haier, 1988). Progress has also been made in locating the damaged brain region in which reduced levels of the neurotransmitter dopamine contribute to Parkinson's disease. Hopefully, these techniques will also increase our knowledge of the effects of psychoactive drugs such as tranquilizers.

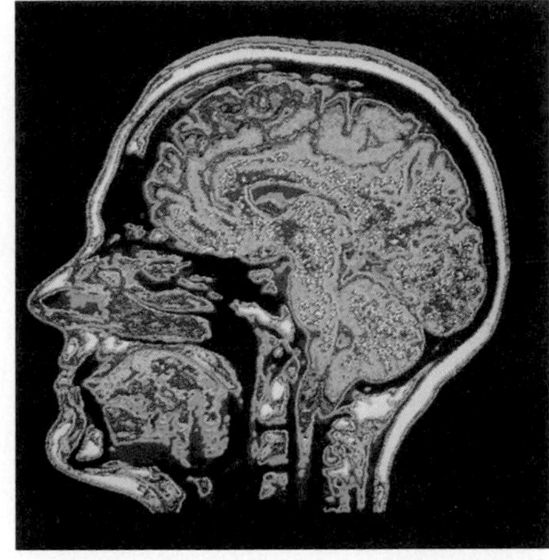

MRI image of the human head.

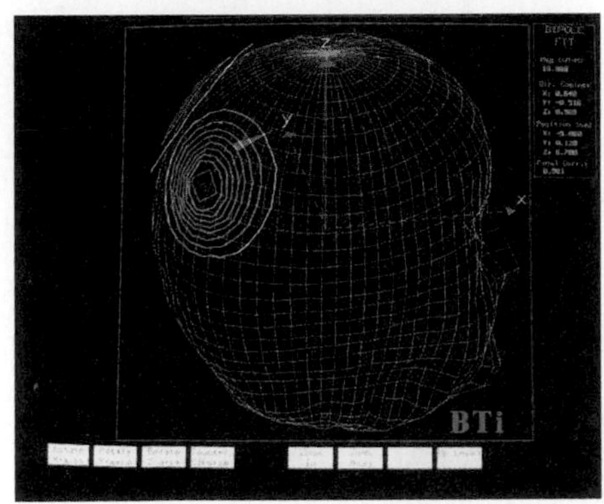


A computer printout of an MEG.

Even more recent techniques measure the movement of blood molecules and water molecules as neurons work. Because these methods enable us to collect images rapidly, and because they do not use radioactive chemicals, they seem to be especially promising as new research tools.

By combining these various techniques, neuroscientists can simultaneously observe anatomical structures (from CT and MRI), sites of energy use (PET, SPECT, MEG), blood and water movement, and areas of electrical activity in the brain (EEG and ERP). When all these data are put together, scientists may finally be able to study with unprecedented detail the impact of drugs on the brain, the formation of memories, and the sites of many other mental activities.

## The Reticular Formation

We separated the brain into hindbrain, midbrain, and forebrain to simplify our discussion. But the brain itself often ignores such distinctions and sets up systems that jump across these boundaries, drawing together its different parts to perform certain functions. One such system is the **reticular formation (RF)**.

The RF is made up of a netlike bundle of neurons running through the hindbrain, midbrain, and part of the forebrain. Its main job seems to be to send "Alert!" signals to the higher parts of the brain in response to incoming messages. The RF can be shut down. An anesthetic, for example, works largely by shutting down this system. Permanent damage to the RF can cause a coma.

**Limbic system** Ring of structures around the brain stem; it plays a role in learning and emotional behavior.

**Spinal cord** Complex cable of neurons that runs down the spine, connecting the brain to most of the rest of the body.

## The Limbic System

Another example of the interconnected nature of parts of the central nervous system is the **limbic system**, a ring of structures around the brain stem (see Figure 2-13). Two of the structures—the *amygdala* and the *hippocampus*—play an essential role in the formation of new memories. People with severe damage in these regions cannot form new memories, though they can still remember names, faces, and events that they learned before they were injured. Animals with damage in these areas seem to be unable to recognize where they have just been; as a result, they will explore the same small part of their environment over and over again, as if it were constantly new to them.

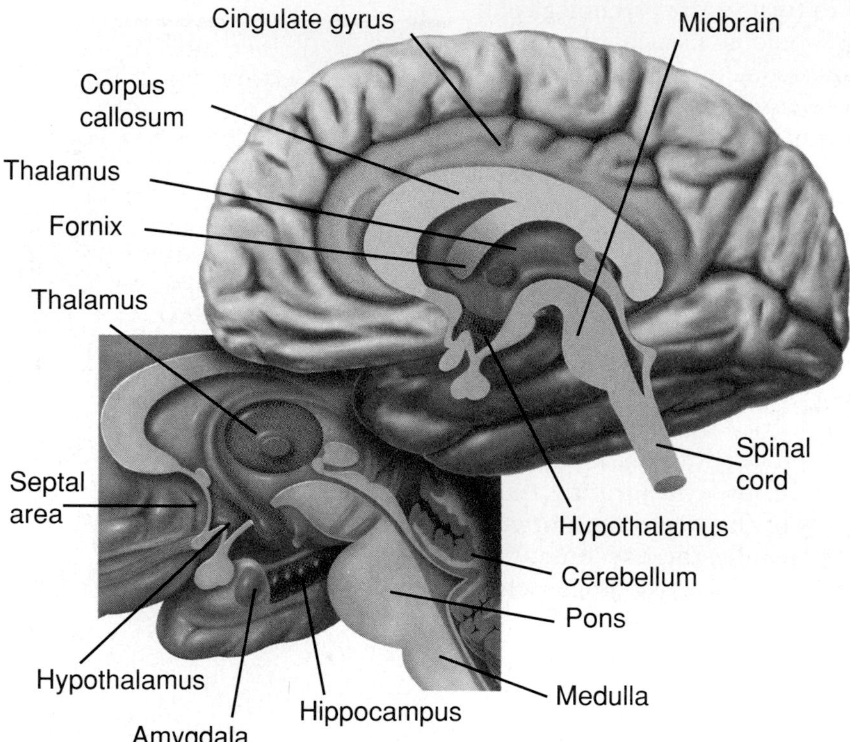


**Figure 2-13**
**The limbic system,** a ring of structures around the brain stem that work together to play an essential role in the formation of new memories as well as influencing motivation and emotion.

The limbic system is also important to emotion and motivation (topics that we will discuss more fully in the chapter "Motivation and Emotion"). The amyg–dala and the hippocampus are critical to emotions that are related to self-preservation (MacLean, 1970). When portions of these structures are damaged or removed, hostile animals, for example, become tame, unaggressive, and docile; in contrast, when portions of these two structures are electrically stimulated, animals show signs of fear and panic, while stimulation to other portions of these structures triggers attack behavior. Two other limbic structures, the *cingulate gyrus* and the *septum*, seem to be especially important to the experience of pleasure and to inhibiting aggression. Destruction of areas in these two structures can lead to high levels of aggressive activity. Electrical stimulation of portions of the septum especially seems to result in intense pleasure: Animals that are given the opportunity to electrically stimulate themselves in these areas will do so endlessly, even to the point of ignoring all food and water. Evidence suggests that humans also experience pleasure when some areas of the septum are electrically stimulated, though apparently it is not as intense an experience as it is for nonhumans. The limbic system is also closely connected to the *hypothalamus*, which, as we saw earlier in this chapter, plays a central role in a wide variety of motivational and emotional activities such as hunger, thirst, sexual motivation, fear, and anger.

## The Spinal Cord

The complex cable of neurons that connects the brain to most of the rest of the body is known as the **spinal cord**. We talk of the brain and the spinal cord as two distinct structures, but there is no clear boundary between them since, at its upper end, the spinal cord enlarges and merges into the hindbrain and midbrain. Moreover, although the spinal cord tends to receive less attention than the brain, without it we would be severely limited. People who have accidentally severed their spinal cords by breaking their necks provide tragic evidence of the importance of the spinal cord to normal functioning. When the cord is severed, parts of the body are literally disconnected from the brain. Accident victims lose all sensations from

## HIGHLIGHTS

### Brain Structure Associated with Schizophrenia

For the first time, researchers have found an apparent link between the physical structure of the brain and schizophrenia. This disabling and at present incurable mental disorder, which afflicts about 2.8 million Americans, is characterized by distortions in thought and perceptions of reality, as well as by delusions and hallucinations.

Although abnormalities had previously been detected in the brains of people with schizophrenia, many of these features were also observed in at least some normal people as well. But some recent research, using 15 sets of identical twins in which only one twin in each set suffered from schizophrenia, discovered subtle differences in brain anatomy between normal and disturbed twins (Suddath et al., 1990). Using magnetic resonance imaging, the researchers found evidence suggesting that people with schizophrenia have a smaller brain volume than do people who do not suffer from this disorder. The difference was so notable that in 12 sets of twins the investigators correctly identified which twin had schizophrenia simply by looking at brain size. In a control group, consisting of 7 sets of normal twins, no such differences were observed.

The biggest difference was that the twins with schizophrenia had larger ventricles, or cavities, within the brain and broader spaces between the folds found at the surface of the cortex. The result of each of these differences: less brain tissue. These twins also had a smaller left temporal lobe and part of the hippocampus was also smaller. The temporal lobes and hippocampus are essential to memory, emotion, decision making, and attention—all psychological processes that are severely disrupted in schizophrenia.

The investigators believe these differences were not caused by either the disease itself or its treatment. For example, the changes seemed unrelated to length of illness or amount of medication received. Instead, the study's findings suggest that brain damage causes at least some of the symptoms of schizophrenia. But how did the brain damage arise in the first place? Possible causes may be a viral infection, prenatal oxygen deprivation, birth difficulties, or trauma, any of which could lead to early brain tissue loss. Another possibility is a slow virus, which after remaining dormant during much of an individual's life attacks the brain. Whatever the eventual explanation, the new findings have made many scientists more optimistic about eventually uncovering the biological bases of schizophrenia.

the parts of the body that can no longer send information to higher brain areas. Similarly, they can no longer control the movements of those body parts, and many times the result is total paralysis. Some spinal accident patients also experience problems with bowel and bladder control, and they may exhibit lowered blood pressure, which makes it difficult to maintain comfortable body temperature.

The spinal cord is made up of bundles of long nerve fibers and has two basic functions: to permit some reflex movements and to carry messages to and from the brain. Let's return to the example at the beginning of this chapter. When you burn your finger on a match, a message signaling pain comes into your spinal cord and causes the almost instantaneous reaction of pulling your hand away. A similar reaction occurs when the doctor taps your knee with a rubber mallet (see Figure 2-14). The pain message also travels up the spinal cord to your brain, but even before it gets there, your hand is being pulled out of the flame. Most of these spinal reflexes are protective: They enable the body to avoid serious damage and maintain muscle tone and position.

## THE PERIPHERAL NERVOUS SYSTEM

Recall from Figure 2-5 that the nervous system is made up of two major parts: the central nervous system (the brain and spinal cord) and the peripheral nervous system. In our discussion so far, we have seen some of the roles that the peripheral nervous system plays in transmitting messages to

**Somatic nervous system** The part of the peripheral nervous system that carries messages from the senses to the central nervous system and between the central nervous system and the skeletal muscles.

**Autonomic nervous system** The part of the peripheral nervous system that carries messages between the central nervous system and the internal organs.

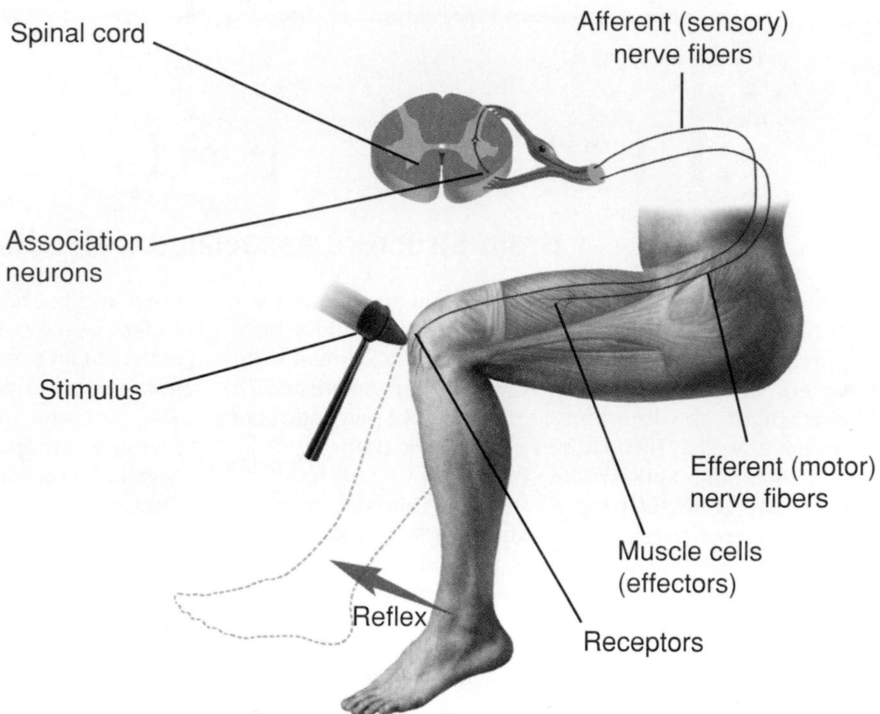


**Figure 2-14**
Simple reflexes are controlled by the *spinal cord*. The message travels from the sense receptors near the skin through the afferent nerve fibers to the spinal cord. In the spinal cord, the messages are relayed through association neurons to the efferent nerve fibers, which carry them to the muscle cells that cause the reflex movement.

and from the central nervous system. In this section, we will examine in greater detail the two branches of the peripheral nervous system. These are called the somatic and the autonomic nervous systems.

## The Somatic Nervous System

The **somatic nervous system** is composed of all the afferent, or sensory, neurons that carry information to the central nervous system and all the efferent, or motor, neurons that carry messages from the central nervous system to the skeletal muscles of the body. All the things that we can sense—sights, sounds, smells, temperature, pressure, and so on—have their origins in the somatic part of the peripheral nervous system. In later chapters, we will see how the somatic nervous system affects our experience of the world both inside and outside our bodies.

## The Autonomic Nervous System

The **autonomic nervous system** is composed of all the neurons that carry messages between the central nervous system and all the internal organs of the body (the glands and the smooth muscles such as the heart and digestive system). The autonomic nervous system obviously is necessary to such body functions as breathing and assuring a proper flow of blood. But it is also important in the experience of various emotions—a fact that makes it of special interest to psychologists.

To understand the autonomic nervous system, we must make one more distinction. The autonomic nervous system consists of two branches: the *sympathetic* and *parasympathetic divisions* (see Figure 2-15). Both branches are directly involved in controlling and integrating the actions of the glands and the smooth muscles within the body.

The nerve fibers of the **sympathetic division** are busiest when you are frightened or angry. They carry messages that tell the body to prepare for an emergency and to get ready to act quickly or strenuously. In response to messages from the sympathetic division, your heart pounds, you breathe faster, your pupils enlarge, and your digestion stops. As we will see shortly, the sympathetic nervous system also tells the endocrine system to start pumping chemicals into the bloodstream to further strengthen these reactions. Sympathetic nerve fibers connect to every internal organ in the body—a fact that explains why the body's reaction to sudden stress is so widespread. However, the sympathetic division can also act selectively on a single organ.

**Sympathetic division** Branch of the autonomic nervous system; it prepares the body for quick action in an emergency.

**Parasympathetic division** Branch of the autonomic nervous system; it calms and relaxes the body.

Parasympathetic nerve fibers connect to the same organs as the sympathetic nerve fibers, but they cause just the opposite effects. The **parasympathetic division** says, in effect, "Okay, the heat's off, back to normal." The heart then goes back to beating at its normal rate, the stomach muscles relax, digestion starts again, breathing slows down, and the pupils of the eyes get smaller. Thus, the parasympathetic division compensates for the sympathetic division and lets the body rest after stress.

Often these two systems work in tandem: After the sympathetic division has aroused the body, the parasympathetic division follows with messages to relax. In many people, however, one division or the other may dominate. In ulcer patients, for example, the parasympathetic division tends to dominate: They salivate heavily, their hearts beat rather slowly, their digestive systems are often overactive. People whose sympathetic division dominates show the opposite symptoms: Their mouths are dry, their palms moist, and their hearts beat quickly even when they are resting. Moreover, recent findings suggest that the sympathetic and parasympathetic divisions do not always act in opposition to each other: Sometimes they can act independently of each other, and at other times they can even act simultaneously (Berntson, Cacioppo, & Quigley, 1993).

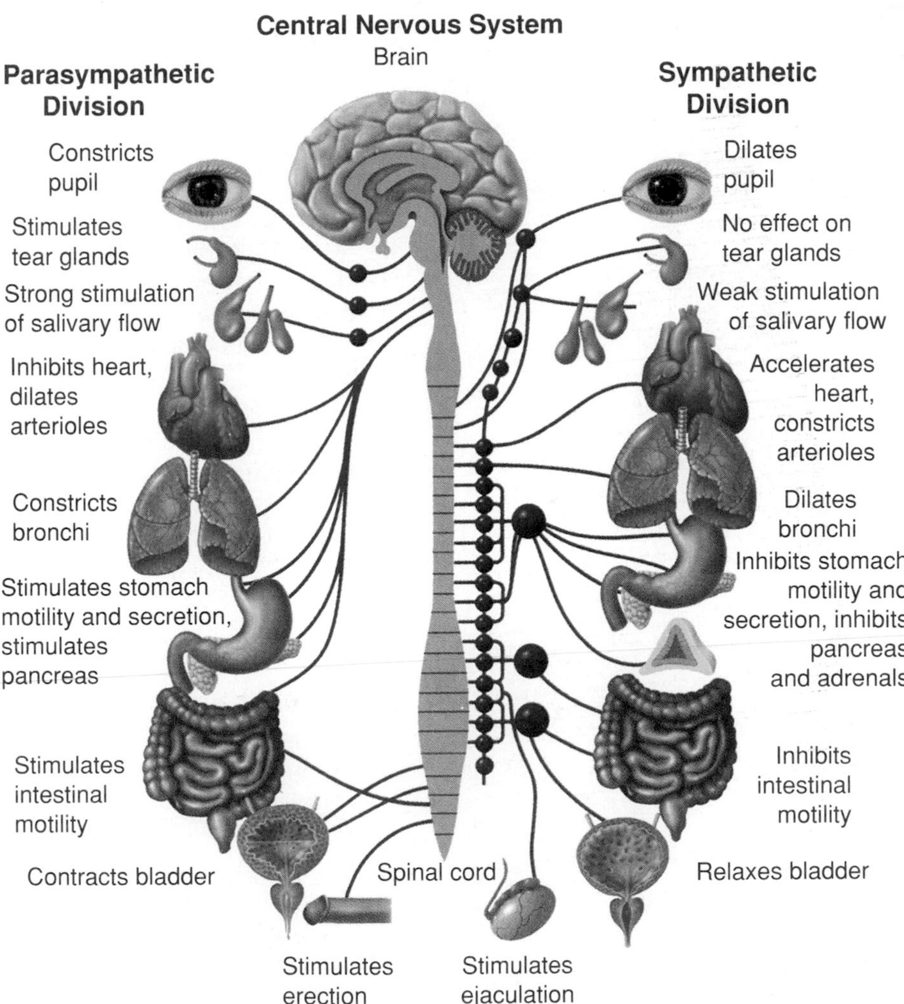


**Figure 2-15**
**The sympathetic and parasympathetic divisions of the autonomic nervous system.** The sympathetic division generally acts to arouse the body, and the parasympathetic follows with messages to relax.

*Source:* Adapted from *General Biology*, revised edition by Willis Johnson, Richard A. Laubengayer, and Louis E. Delanney, Copyright ©1961 by Holt, Rinehart, and Winston, Inc. and renewed 1989 by Willis H. Johnson and Louis E. Delanney. Reproduced by permission.

The autonomic nervous system was traditionally regarded as the "automatic" part of the body's response mechanism. You could not, it was believed, tell your own autonomic nervous system when to speed up or slow down your heart's beating or when to stop or start your digestive processes. These things were thought to run as automatically as a thermostat controlling the temperature of a room. Evidence suggests, however, that we have more control over the autonomic nervous system than we think. Many studies seem to show that people (and animals) can indeed manipulate this so-called automatic part of the nervous system. For example, it is possible to learn to control such things as high blood pressure, migraine headaches, and

Can we control behaviors such as high blood pressure and headaches?

**Hormones** Chemical substances released by the endocrine glands; they help regulate bodily activities.

**Endocrine glands** Glands of the endocrine system that release hormones into the bloodstream.

**Thyroid gland** Endocrine gland located below the voice box; it produces the hormone thyroxin.

**Thyroxin** Hormone that regulates the body's rate of metabolism.

**Parathyroids** Four tiny glands embedded in the thyroid; they secrete parathormone.

**Parathormone** Hormone that controls the levels of calcium and phosphate in the blood and tissue fluids.

even ulcers. Some people have even learned to control their own heart rate and brain waves. These are all cases in which the autonomic nervous system is brought under deliberate control. We will look more closely at these possibilities when we discuss biofeedback in Chapter 5.

## THE ENDOCRINE SYSTEM

The nervous system is not the only mechanism that regulates the functioning of our bodies. Let's return one more time to our earlier example. When you burn your finger on a match, you quickly withdraw your finger from the heat. But your response to the burn does not end with the nervous system. Chemical substances called **hormones** are also released into your bloodstream by internal organs called **endocrine glands**. These hormones are carried throughout your body, where they have widespread effects on a variety of organs. Hormones are of particular interest to psychologists for two reasons. First, at certain stages of our development, hormones *organize* the nervous system and body tissues. Consider, for example, the dramatic hormone-induced changes that occur at puberty and at menopause. Second, hormones *activate* behaviors. They affect such things as alertness or sleepiness, excitability, sexual behavior, the ability to concentrate, aggressiveness, reactions to stress, and even the desire for companionship. Hormones can also have dramatic effects on mood, emotional reactivity, the ability to learn, and even the ability to resist disease. Radical changes in some hormones may even be involved in, and contribute to, serious psychological disorders like depression.

The locations of the endocrine glands are shown in Figure 2-16. Our discussion will focus on those glands whose functions are best understood and those whose effects are most closely related to the way we behave.

### The Thyroid Gland

The **thyroid gland** is located just below the larynx, or voice box. It produces one primary hormone, **thyroxin**, which regulates the body's rate of metabolism; that is, it determines how fast or how slowly the foods we eat are transformed into the energy that we need to function normally. Differences in metabolic rate determine how alert and energetic people are and how fat or thin they tend to be.

An overactive thyroid can produce a great variety of symptoms: overexcitability, insomnia, reduced attention span, fatigue, agitation, acting out of character, and making snap decisions, as well as reduced concentration and difficulty focusing on a task. Little wonder, then, that there was considerable concern in the spring of 1991 when it was discovered that President George Bush was suffering from an overactive thyroid. Too little thyroxin leads to the other extreme: You will want to sleep and sleep and will still feel constantly tired. Without enough thyroxin, your body is unable to maintain normal temperature, muscle tone is reduced, and metabolism is sluggish.

### The Parathyroid Glands

Embedded in the thyroid gland are the **parathyroids**—four tiny, pea-shaped organs. They secrete **parathormone**, which controls and balances the levels of calcium and phosphate in the blood and tissue fluids. The level of calcium in the blood has a direct effect on the excitability of the nervous system. A person with too little parathormone will be hypersensitive and may suffer from twitches or muscle spasms. Too much parathormone, on the other hand, can lead to lethargy and poor physical coordination.

## The Pineal Gland

The **pineal gland** is a pea-sized gland that apparently regulates activity levels over the course of a day. Increased levels of light in the morning stimulate the pineal gland, which in turn reduces the amount of the hormone *melatonin* it releases into the bloodstream. As a result, body temperature rises, and the organism becomes more active—it "wakes up" and prepares for a new day. At the end of the day, as light levels decrease, the pineal gland releases more melatonin, which lowers body temperature and reduces the organism's overall level of activity in preparation for sleep. These effects (which we will study in greater detail in Chapter 4) are most evident in lower animals such as birds and rats; in fact, in birds sunlight can shine right through the skull onto the pineal gland (Levinthal, 1990). It is possible that the pineal gland has similar effects on humans, though research evidence is not yet available on this point. There is some speculation that people who suffer from *seasonal affective disorder*—that is, who become depressed during the dark winter months—may be suffering from too much melatonin released by the pineal gland in response to the reduced light in that season, though research on this hypothesis is only in its early stages.

**Pineal gland** A gland located roughly in the center of the brain that appears to regulate activity levels over the course of a day.

**Pancreas** Organ lying between the stomach and small intestine; it secretes insulin and glucagon.

**Insulin** and **glucagon** Hormones that work in opposite ways to regulate the level of sugar in the blood.

**Pituitary gland** Gland located on the underside of the brain; it produces the largest number of the body's hormones.

**Posterior pituitary** Part of the pituitary that affects thirst, sexual behavior, and perhaps paternal and maternal behavior.

## The Pancreas

The **pancreas** lies in a curve between the stomach and the small intestine. The pancreas controls the level of sugar in the blood by secreting two regulating hormones: **insulin** and **glucagon**. These two hormones work against each other to keep the blood-sugar level properly balanced.

When the pancreas secretes too little insulin so that there is too much sugar in the blood, the kidneys attempt to get rid of the excess sugar by excreting a great deal more water than usual. The tissues become dehydrated, and poisonous wastes accumulate in the blood. These symptoms are characteristic of *diabetes mellitus*. People with diabetes must take insulin and maintain a special diet to keep their blood-sugar level normal. Oversecretion of insulin leads to the chronic fatigue of *hypoglycemia*, a condition in which there is too little sugar in the blood.

**Figure 2-16**
**The glands of the endocrine system.**

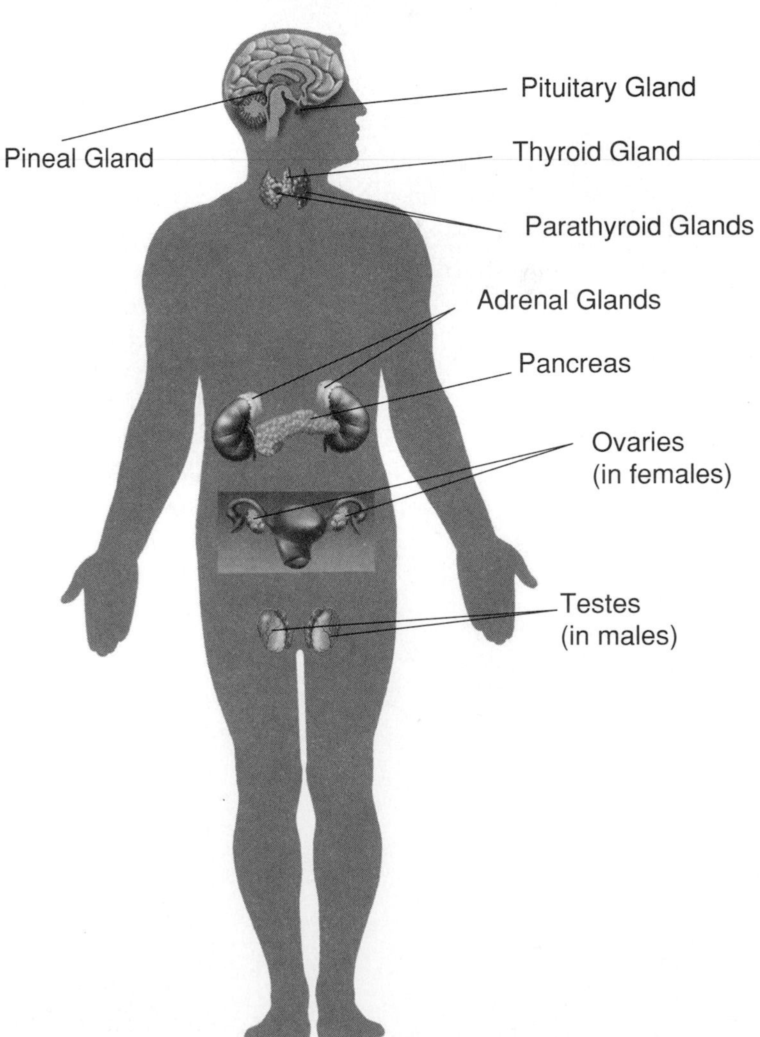


## The Pituitary Gland

The endocrine gland that produces the largest number of different hormones, and thus has the widest range of effects on the body's functions, is the **pituitary gland**. This gland is located on the underside of the brain and is connected to the hypothalamus. The pituitary gland has two parts that function quite separately.

The **posterior pituitary**, so called because it is located toward the back of the pituitary gland, is controlled by the nervous system. It secretes two hormones. One, *vasopressin*, causes blood pressure to rise and regulates the amount of water in the body's cells. Too little vasopressin results in extreme thirst. The other, *oxytocin*, has long been known to cause the uterus to contract during childbirth and the mammary glands to start producing milk. But scientists have been puzzled by the fact that males also have significant levels of oxytocin in their bodies, suggesting that

**Anterior pituitary** Part of the pituitary known as the "master gland" because it produces numerous hormones that trigger the action of other glands; it regulates body growth and also affects motives and emotions.

**Gonads** The reproductive glands—testes in males and ovaries in females.

Production of too much growth hormone by the pituitary results in giantism; too little hormone results in dwarfism.

this hormone plays other roles beyond childbirth and nursing. Research now indicates that oxytocin has a powerful effect on sexual behavior, grooming, maternal and paternal behavior, and social companionship: Animals with higher levels of oxytocin or increased numbers of receptors for oxytocin in the brain are more sexually active, they engage in much more grooming, they pay greater attention to their young, and they seem to crave companionship from other animals (Caldwell et al., 1989; Drago et al., 1986; T.R. Insel & Harbaugh, 1989; Jirikowski et al., 1989; Witt & Insel, 1991). Whether oxytocin plays a similar role in humans is still being researched, but we do know that during sexual intercourse oxytocin levels in men are from three to five times greater than normal and that people who have lost interest in sex can regain that interest when the level of oxytocin in the body is increased.

The **anterior pituitary**, located toward the front of the pituitary gland, is controlled by chemical messages from the bloodstream and is often called the "master gland." It produces numerous hormones that trigger the action of other endocrine glands. Among the functions of the anterior pituitary is the production of the body's growth hormone, through which it controls the amount and timing of body growth. Dwarfism and giantism are the result of too little and too much growth hormone, respectively.

The functioning of the anterior pituitary provides a good example of the interaction between the endocrine system and the nervous system. The operation of the anterior pituitary is partly controlled by hormones that are released by the hypothalamus—part of the nervous system (Schally, Kastin, & Arimura, 1977). Hormones released from the anterior pituitary cause the reproductive glands to produce still other hormones, which, in turn, affect the hypothalamus, producing changes in behavior or feeling. Thus, the hypothalamus affects the anterior pituitary, which indirectly affects the hypothalamus. This circular route is typical of the kind of two-way interaction that often takes place between the body's nervous system and endocrine system.

## The Gonads

The **gonads**—the *testes* in males and the *ovaries* in females and, to a lesser extent, the adrenal glands—secrete hormones that have traditionally been classified as masculine and feminine. These are the *androgens* and *estrogens*, respectively. Although both sexes produce both types of hormone, androgens predominate in males, whereas estrogens predominate in females. These hormones play a number of important organizing roles in human development. For example, in humans, if the hormone *testosterone* is present during the third and fourth month after conception, the fetus will develop as a male; otherwise it will develop as a female (Kalat, 1988). Testosterone and other androgens are also linked to sexual interest and behavior in adults of both sexes.

Testosterone also seems to play a role in aggression and violence, although the evidence concerning human behavior is complex, and the ways in which this hormone interacts with other important factors such as education, social and economic status, and environment are not yet clear (Dabbs & Morris, 1990). We do know, however, that violence is greatest among males between 15 and 25 years of age, the years when testosterone levels are at their highest. Both male and female prisoners with high levels of testosterone are likely to have committed crimes at an earlier age and to have committed more violent crimes (Dabbs & Morris, 1990; Dabbs et al., 1988). Even in a noncriminal population, men with higher levels of testosterone "more often reported having trouble with parents, teachers, and classmates. . . ."(Dabbs & Morris, 1990, p. 209).

Although estrogen is related to testosterone, it does not seem to affect aggressive behavior in women, and its roles in sexual behavior are unclear. Most female mammals, including humans, are more sexually receptive during the ovulatory phase of their estrous (nonhuman) or menstrual (human) cycles, when estrogen is highest (D.B. Adams et al., 1978). However, in cases where the ovaries have been surgically removed, which dramatically lowers levels of estrogen, human female sexual activity and interest do not diminish significantly. Thus, researchers have concluded that estrogen does not affect sexual behavior directly (Dennerstein & Burrows, 1982; Martin et al., 1980).

Perhaps more intriguing, estrogen seems to have cognitive effects. It has been associated with increased performance on certain tests of manual dexterity, verbal skills, and perceptual speed. Thus, women do better at these sorts of cognitive tasks during the ovulatory phase of their menstrual cycles. In addition, postmenopausal women show improvement at these tasks when they undergo estrogen replacement therapy (E. Hampson & Kimura, 1992; Kimura & Hampson, 1994). Beyond the cognitive effects of estrogen, it is commonly observed that the rate of strokes and heart attacks in premenopausal women is lower than that in men, but that after menopause, when estrogen levels decline, strokes and heart attacks increase in women. These findings suggest that estrogen may have some "protective" function in women that is not shared by males.

**Adrenal glands** Two endocrine glands located just above the kidneys.

**Adrenal cortex** Outer covering of the two adrenal glands that releases hormones important for dealing with stress.

**Adrenal medulla** Inner core of the adrenal glands that also releases hormones to deal with stress.

**Beta endorphin** One of the endorphins, a natural painkiller released by the body.

**ACTH** Hormone released by the anterior pituitary; it stimulates hormone production of the adrenal cortex.

**Epinephrine** Adrenal hormone that is released mainly in response to fear and causes the heart to beat faster.

## The Adrenal Glands

The two **adrenal glands** are located just above the kidneys. Each adrenal gland has two parts: an outer covering, called the **adrenal cortex**, and an inner core, called the **adrenal medulla**. Both the adrenal cortex and the adrenal medulla are important in the body's reaction to stress. Imagine that you are walking down the street when you see a professor to whom you owe an overdue paper. As you approach the professor, you realize that there is no graceful escape. You begin to experience stress. The hypothalamus secretes a hormone that causes the anterior pituitary gland to release two more hormones. One is **beta endorphin**, one of the body's natural painkillers. The other is **ACTH**, a messenger hormone that goes to the adrenal cortex. Alerted by ACTH from the pituitary, the adrenal cortex in turn secretes hormones that increase the level of blood sugar, help to break down proteins, and help the body respond to injury. Meanwhile, the adrenal medulla is stimulated by the autonomic nervous system so that it also pours several hormones into the bloodstream: **Epinephrine** activates the sympathetic nervous system, making the heart beat faster, digestion stop, the pupils of the eyes enlarge, more sugar flow into the bloodstream, and preparing the blood to clot fast if necessary. Another hormone, norepinephrine (which we previously discussed as a neurotransmitter), not only raises the blood pressure by causing the blood vessels to become constricted but is also carried by the bloodstream to the anterior pituitary, where it triggers the release of still more ACTH, thus prolonging the response to stress. The result is that your body is well prepared to deal with the stress. It may even mobilize you to finish and submit that overdue paper.

The complicated details of all these hormonal processes are much less important for our purposes than an understanding that the endocrine system plays a major role in helping to coordinate and integrate complex psychological reactions. In fact, as we have said before, the nervous system and the endocrine system work hand in hand. We will see other examples of this in the chapter "Motivation and Emotion," where we talk about motivation.

In our overview of the nervous system and endocrine system, we have seen a very close connection between biology and psychology. There are still other connections: For example, the genes that we inherit from our parents can affect important psychological processes, as we will now discover.

**Behavior genetics** Study of the relationship between heredity and behavior.

**Genetics** Study of how traits are passed from one generation to the next.

**Traits** Characteristics on which organisms differ.

**Heredity** The transmission of traits from one generation to the next.

# BEHAVIOR GENETICS

Charles Darwin was one of the first to recognize the impact of heredity on such psychological characteristics as intelligence, personality, and mental illness. For example, in a discussion of gestures, he described the following case:

> A gentleman of considerable position was found by his wife to have the curious trick, when he lay fast asleep on his back in bed, of raising his right arm slowly in front of his face, up to his forehead, and then dropping it with a jerk so that the wrist fell heavily on the bridge of his nose. The trick did not occur every night, but occasionally. ( Darwin, 1872, p. 34)

To protect the gentleman's nose it was necessary to remove the buttons from the cuff of his nightgown. Years after the man's death, his son married a woman who observed precisely the same behavior in him. And their daughter exhibited the same behavior as well.

Darwin heard about this case from his half-cousin, Francis Galton, who was the first person to try to demonstrate systematically how behavior characteristics can be transmitted genetically. Galton was especially interested in the transmission of mental traits. In an effort to show that high mental ability is inherited, he identified about 1,000 men of eminence in Great Britain—judges, political leaders, scholars, scientists, artists, and so on—and found that they belonged to only 300 families. Because only 1 in 4,000 people in the British population was "eminent," Galton concluded that eminence must be an inherited trait.

Galton's findings were challenged by others, who claimed that environmental factors such as educational and social advantages could have accounted for the concentration of eminence in just a few hundred families. In the early twentieth century, Galton's assumptions about the inherited nature of behavioral traits came under more fundamental attack from the behaviorists. The founder of behaviorism, John Watson, argued that

> We have no real evidence of the inheritance of traits. I would feel perfectly confident in the ultimately favorable outcome of careful upbringing of a *healthy, well-formed* baby born of a long line of crooks, murderers and thieves, and prostitutes. Who has any evidence to the contrary? (Watson, 1930, p. 103)

The question of how much influence heredity has on various behaviors is at the heart of modern **behavior genetics**, and, as we will see, psychologists still disagree on the answer to the question, though recent research indicates that environment is at least as important as heredity in causing behavioral differences among people (Plomin, 1989, 1990; Plomin & Rende, 1991). To begin to appreciate the "nature-nurture controversy," we need to become familiar with some of the basic mechanisms of inheritance.

## Genetics

**Genetics** is the study of how plants, animals, and people pass **traits** from one generation to the next. A trait is a characteristic that differs from one organism to the next: curly hair, aggressiveness, brown eyes, intelligence, schizophrenia, or even an allergy to poison ivy. The transmission of traits from one generation to the next is known as **heredity**.

Gregor Mendel, an Austrian monk, gave modern genetics its beginning in 1867 when he reported the results of his research on many years of systematically breeding peas. Mendel believed that every trait was controlled by elements that were transmitted from one generation to the next. He called these elements **genes**.

Much more is known today about genes and how they work. We know, for example, that within a cell nucleus genes are lined up on tiny threadlike bodies called **chromosomes**, which are visible under a microscope. The chromosomes are arranged in pairs, and each species has a constant number of pairs. Mice have 20 pairs, monkeys have 27, peas have 7. Human beings have 23 pairs of chromosomes in every normal cell.

The main ingredient of chromosomes and genes is **deoxyribonucleic acid (DNA)**, a complex molecule that looks like two chains twisted around each other. The order of this twisting DNA forms a code that carries all our genetic information. The individual genes, which are the smallest message units of the DNA, carry instructions for a particular process or trait. We now understand that the nucleus of every cell contains DNA with enough genetic coding to direct the development of that single cell into a fully grown adult with billions of cells!

Chromosomes, as we said, are arranged in pairs, and each pair carries a complete set of genes. Because each pair provides the coding for the same kinds of traits, a gene for a given trait may therefore exist in two alternate forms. We can think of a gene for eye color, for example, as having one form, *B*, which will result in brown eyes, and another form, *b*, which will result in blue eyes. If a girl receives *b* genes from both parents, her eyes will be blue. But if she inherits a *b* gene from one parent and a *B* gene from the other, her eyes will be brown (see Figure 2-17).

The *B* form is thus said to be the **dominant gene**, whereas the *b* form is **recessive**. Although the girl with one *B* gene and one *b* gene has brown eyes, the recessive *b* gene is still present in her and can be passed on to her offspring, thus producing a blue-eyed child, if it is paired with a recessive *b* gene from the other parent.

We have been talking about characteristics such as eye color that are controlled by single genes. In fact, however, most of our important traits, such as intelligence, height, and weight, cannot be traced back to a single gene. Rather, a number of genes make a small or moderate contribution to the trait in question in a process known as **polygenic inheritance**. Just as each of the instruments in a symphony orchestra contributes separate notes to the sound that reaches the audience, each of the genes in a polygenic system contributes separately to the total effect (McClearn et al., 1991).

It is important to note that the effects of heredity need not be immediately or fully apparent. In some cases, expression of a trait is delayed until later in life. For example, many men inherit "male-pattern baldness" that does not become apparent until middle age. Moreover, quite often genes predispose a person to develop a particular trait, but environmental factors play a major role in altering or suppressing expression of the trait. Having the proper genes provides a person with the potential for a trait, but that trait may not appear unless the environment cooperates. A person with an inherited tendency to gain weight may or may not be obese depending on diet, exercise program, and overall health. With these general principles in mind, let's look at how psychologists study the relation between genetics and behavior and see what they have learned so far.

## Genetics and Behavior

To this point, we have primarily examined the role of genetics in determining differences among people in various physical characteristics, such as eye color, height, and weight. But there is increasing evidence that heredity also plays an important role in differences between people over a wide range of behavior, including hypertension, epilepsy, hyperactivity,

**Genes** Elements that control the transmission of traits; they are found on the chromosomes.

**Chromosomes** Pairs of threadlike bodies within the cell nucleus that contain the genes.

**Deoxyribonucleic acid (DNA)** Complex molecule that is the main ingredient of chromosomes and genes and forms the code for all genetic information.

**Dominant gene** Member of a gene pair that controls the appearance of a certain trait.

**Recessive gene** Member of a gene pair that can control the appearance of a certain trait only if it is paired with another recessive gene.

**Polygenic inheritance** Process in which several genes interact to produce a certain trait; responsible for our most important traits.

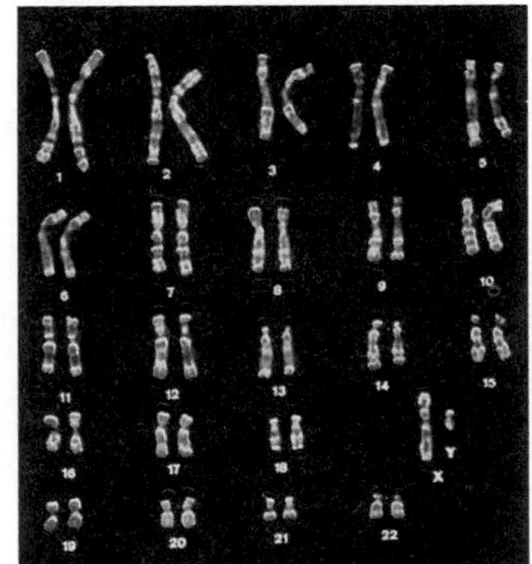

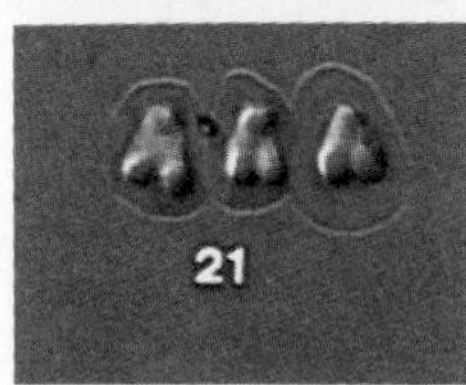


The 23 pairs of human chromosomes found in every normal cell. Twenty-two of the 23 pairs of chromosomes look exactly alike. The members of the 23rd pair, the sex chromosomes, may or may not look alike. Females have equivalent X chromosomes, while males have only one X and one Y chromosome, named for their distinctive appearance. The presence of an additional number-21 chromosome will result in Down syndrome, as in the inset below.

**Strain studies** Studies of the heritability of behavioral traits using animals that have been inbred to produce strains that are genetically very similar to one another.

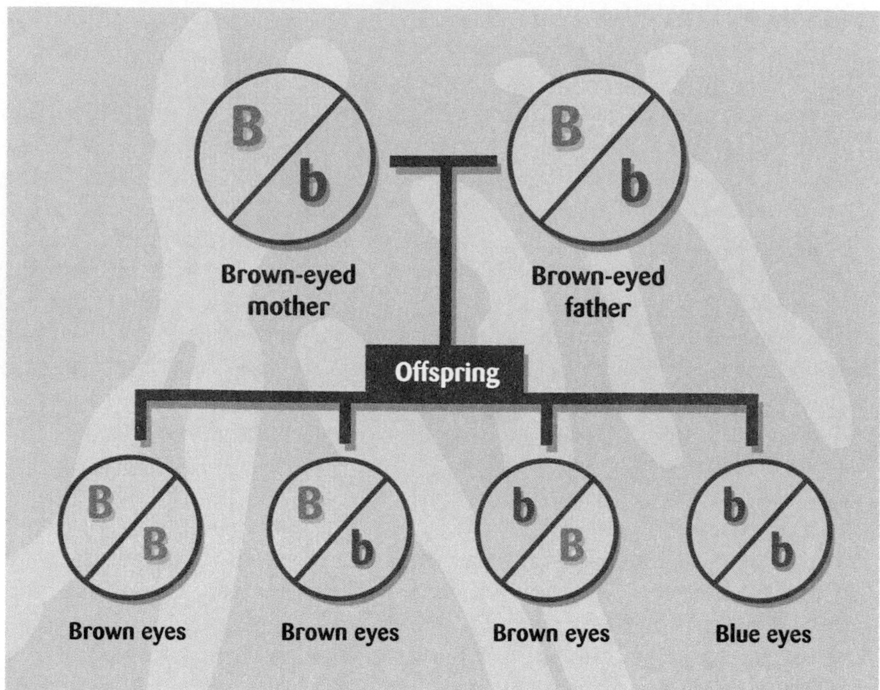


**Figure 2-17**
**Transmission of eye color by dominant (*B*) and recessive (*b*) genes.** This figure represents the four possible mixtures of eye-color genes in these parents' offspring. Because three out of the four combinations result in brown-eyed children, the chance that any child will have brown eyes is 75 percent.

A photomicropraph of DNA molecules, showing the twisted strands. They have been magnified 6233 times.

6. Can behavioral traits such as shyness, aggressiveness, and intelligence be inherited? What about mental illnesses and drug addictions?

some forms of mental retardation, emotionality and responsiveness to stress, nervousness, shyness, aggressiveness, intelligence, some forms of mental illness, and perhaps alcohol dependence and other drug addictions (D. Johnson, 1990; Loehlin, Willerman, & Horn, 1988; Plomin, DeFries, & McClearn, 1990; Plomin & Rende, 1991; Wimer & Wimer, 1985). Of course, genes do not directly cause behavior. Rather, they affect both the development and operation of the nervous system and the endocrine system, which, in turn, influence the likelihood that a certain behavior will occur under the proper circumstances.

In the remainder of this chapter, we will look at some of the methods used by behavior geneticists as well as some of their more interesting discoveries. We will start with methods appropriate for animal studies and then examine the techniques used to study behavior genetics in humans.

**Animal Behavior Genetics** Psychologists have devised several methods to approach the problem of determining the *heritability* of behavioral traits, that is, the extent to which particular traits can be passed on from one generation to the next (Henderson, 1982; Parke & Asher, 1983; Plomin, et al., 1990). **Strain studies** are often used with animals to determine the heritability of traits. Close relatives such as siblings are intensively inbred over many generations to create strains of animals that are genetically very similar to one another and different from other strains. Mice are often used because they breed quickly and yet have relatively complex behavior patterns. When animals from different strains are raised together in the same environment, differences between them largely reflect genetic differences in the strains. Using this method, it has been shown that differences between mice with respect to such things as sense of smell, susceptibility to seizures, and performance on a number of learning tasks are all affected by heredity.

**Selection studies** can also be used with animals to estimate heritability. If a trait is closely regulated by genes, then when animals having the trait are bred with one another, more of their offspring should have the trait than one would normally find in the general population. By measuring changes in the proportion of successive generations that have the trait, scientists can estimate the heritability of that trait.

Artificial selection has been used for thousands of years to create breeds of dogs and many other animals that have desirable traits. Terriers, for example, were originally bred to crawl into burrows and chase out small animals living there. In France, dogs have been bred for specialized aspects of farm work, and in the United Kingdom, dogs have been bred for centuries to point to hidden prey or to retrieve downed birds. The fact that dog breeds differ greatly in many respects, including the development of social relationships, excitability, and trainability, suggests that these psychological characteristics are at least to some extent genetically controlled (Plomin, DeFries, & McClearn, 1990).

**Selection studies** Studies that estimate the heritability of a trait by breeding animals with other animals that have the same trait.

**Family studies** Studies of heritability in humans based on the assumption that if genes influence a certain trait, close relatives should be more similar on that trait than distant relatives.

**Twin studies** Studies of identical and fraternal twins to determine the relative influence of heredity and environment on human behavior.

**Identical twins** Twins developed from a single fertilized ovum and therefore identical in genetic makeup at the time of conception.

**HUMAN BEHAVIOR GENETICS** Of course, for the purpose of studying the genetic basis of human behavior, both strain and selection studies are out of the question. However, many new molecular genetics techniques can be used with humans. For example, it is now possible to study, and even change, the genetic code directly. In fact, the so-called Human Genome Project has set out to map all 23 pairs of human chromosomes (the entire human genome) and to determine which areas of which specific genes control which characteristics (D. Johnson, 1990; Plomin & Rende, 1991). By using these genetic markers, researchers expect that eventually we will be able to determine the role of heredity in even the most complex behaviors (Plomin et al., 1990).

Although the results of those studies lie in the future, a good deal has already been learned indirectly about human behavior genetics by analyzing the behavioral similarities of members of the same family. **Family studies** are based on the assumption that if genes influence a trait, close relatives should be more similar on that trait than distant relatives because close relatives share more genes. So far, family studies have uncovered strong evidence that heredity plays a role in some forms of mental illness. Siblings of people with schizophrenia, for example, are about eight times more likely to develop schizophrenia than someone chosen randomly from the general population. And children of schizophrenic parents are about ten times more likely to develop schizophrenia than are other children. Moreover, a recent controversial study in the Netherlands (Brunner et al., 1993) found what appears to be a genetic link in one family between aggressive and violent tendencies on the one hand and mutations in a gene responsible for one of the enzymes that deactivate dopamine, norepinephrine, and serotonin on the other. Although findings such as these may lead to greater understanding of some types of behavior, there is no claim that a genetic flaw lies at the base of every case of schizophrenia or of all human violence. Moreover, such findings do not completely rule out the role of environment. Growing up in a household in which both parents have schizophrenia might cause a child to develop the disorder even if that child does not have a genetic potential for schizophrenia (Plomin et al., 1990). Similarly, we cannot rule out the behavioral effects of growing up in a family in which violence is common.

People clearly can inherit physical traits from their parents. Whether—and to what extent—they also inherit behavioral traits remains uncertain.

In an effort to separate more clearly the influence of heredity from that of environment on human behavior, psychologists often use **twin studies**. Twins can be either identical or fraternal. **Identical twins** develop from a single fertilized ovum, and at the moment of conception they are therefore identical in genetic makeup. Any differences between them

**Fraternal twins** Twins developed from two separate fertilized ova and therefore different in genetic makeup.

should be due to environmental differences. **Fraternal twins**, however, develop from two separate fertilized egg cells and are no more similar genetically than are other brothers and sisters. The differences between fraternal twins are thus due to both heredity and environment. Assuming the various pairs of twins studied have similar environments, if identical twins are no more alike on some characteristics than fraternal twins are, then heredity cannot be very important for that trait.

Twin studies have provided evidence for the heritability of a number of behaviors. Let's return to the example of schizophrenia. Among the general population, the baseline occurrence of schizophrenia is expected to be only 1 to 2 percent (L.N. Robins et al., 1984). In cases where one identical twin develops schizophrenia, however, the other twin will develop the disorder about 50 percent of the time. For fraternal twins, the chances are about 15 percent that the second twin will develop the disorder (Gottesman & Shields, 1982). The much higher rate exhibited by twins, particularly identical twins, suggests that heredity plays an important role in schizophrenia.

Mental abilities also seem to be affected by heredity. Evidence from numerous studies shows that genetics plays an extremely important role in general intelligence (Loehlin & Nichols, 1976; R.S. Wilson, 1983). In Chapter 8, we will examine this relationship much more closely. Genetic differences also play a major role in specific cognitive abilities, such as verbal and spatial skills, and memory. Evidence has also been found in twin studies for genetic influences on temperament and personality, such mannerisms as the strength of a handshake, smoking and drinking habits, and even tastes in food (Farber, 1981).

Identical twins develop from a single ovum and consequently have the same genetic material. Fraternal twins develop from two different fertilized ova and so are as different in genetic makeup as any two children of the same parents.

Similarities between twins, even identical twins, are not automatically due to genetics, however. Twins generally are reared in the same environment; thus, similarities in their behaviors can reflect the fact that they are often treated alike. It would be easier to separate the effects of heredity from those of the environment if we could study identical twins who were separated at birth or in very early childhood and then raised in different homes. A University of Minnesota research team led by Professor Thomas Bouchard has done just that for more than 10 years (T.J. Bouchard, 1984; T.J. Bouchard et al., 1990). The Minnesota team has confirmed that genetics plays a major role in such things as mental retardation, schizophrenia, depression, and intelligence. It has also found evidence that genetics plays a key role in such things as complex personality traits, interests, and talents, and even the structure of brain waves. The studies of twins reared apart became a source of heated debate, however, when researchers suggested that their data also showed that such things as ability to tell a good story, preference in dogs and cigarette brands, use of specific aftershaves, selection of hobbies, preference for automobile brands, attraction to tattoos, and even preferred names for children had some genetic basis.

Critics of twin studies are numerous (see, for example, Ford, 1993; Wyatt, 1993), and their criticisms are important to consider. For example, even identical twins reared apart are likely to share similar environments because adoption agencies usually try to place siblings in similar homes. If these twins turn out to be similar in some respects, how do we know whether the similarity is due to genetics or to the similarities of the homes in which they were reared? Moreover, people with a certain characteristic (such as intelligence or attractiveness) are likely to be treated in similar ways by other people. How can we tell with confidence whether their similarities are due to genetics or to the ways that others

**Should society prohibit individuals with certain heritable conditions from having children?**

We have seen that heredity influences a number of traits and behaviors, including some mental disorders such as schizophrenia. As we shall see in Chapter 13, many of these disorders are severe and cannot be cured. Some people have argued that individuals who exhibit a severe physical or psychological disorder that might be passed on genetically to their children should be prohibited from having children. Critics of this position view such restrictions as an invasion of personal rights.

To complicate matters, people often possess recessive genes for various conditions, meaning they do not exhibit the conditions themselves, but can pass these conditions on to subsequent generations. To prevent this from happening, should all couples undergo genetic screening before they have children? If the tests disclose that otherwise healthy people have a recessive gene for a serious disorder, should society prohibit them from reproducing?

After you have thought about these issues, take a few minutes to examine the opinions of some other students.

•••••••

**MARIA: Why should I control someone else's reproductive rights? Is it really any of my business? If someone had a physical history of high blood pressure, would we say "No, you can't reproduce, it's not healthy"? I think controlling people's babies based on "disorder" is analogous to the Nazis trying to produce a "perfect" race. Who are we to say what is "normal" or "better" anyway?**

**JOEL: Screening would allow couples to decide whether they could handle a "special" child and all the responsibilities that such a child entailed, rather than flinging the child and its social burdens upon the rest of society without a family to support him or her. Prohibiting reproduction would neither be enforceable nor ethical. As animals, human beings have a natural drive to reproduce, and, I think, feel a great proportion of life's enjoyment when a child is created.**

**ANDY: I don't know that laws banning reproduction are ridiculous—China in a way does it (and has to) and the rest of the world is rapidly coming to that point. There are too many people for the earth to support. . . and someday something will have to be done. . . . I agree humans are a part of nature, but in nature, these disabled people would be dead, along with a lot of the nondisabled people who are alive today. . . . Is it right to prevent death if nature ordains it?. . . People who argue for survival of everyone don't argue for nature.**

**JOHN: The state makes decisions all the time that deal with what we can or cannot do, such as a drinking age, driver's license, where we can smoke. . . . You have to grant the fact that the state is already a large part of our lives, so, as Plato says, we are not trying to make the individual happy but the state happy.**

**ERIN: The fact is that we are trying to sustain a society, not moral idealism. If we have the technology to screen out people who are dangerous to the security of society, why not make use of it?. . . But why bring a person into this world who is going to suffer her whole life and burden all of those around her? I'm talking of the extreme cases here—severe mental retardation or the screening of genes such as those causing schizophrenia. Yes, we're messing with nature, but we have the opportunity to reduce suffering here.**

**STEVE: A study was done on the views of adolescents who contracted a genetic disease that invariably kills the afflicted in middle age. When asked whether they would rather have been informed that they had the disorder or not, the majority said that they were glad they had been informed and that they were content living until middle age as opposed to not living at all. An outsider might look at these people as being a tragedy and perhaps would say that they should never have been brought into this world, but to those afflicted, it is the only life they know, and who is to say their life is not worth living if they are content?**

**ERIN: [in response to another student's proposal to prohibit the mentally handicapped from reproducing] Lots of people are bad parents without being mentally handicapped—so how do you draw lines between them? Something else to think about—we don't prohibit mothers who have AIDS or are addicted to crack from reproducing—isn't that a similar situation in a way?**

•••••••

What are the critical issues in this debate? How do you feel about these issues? Who is qualified to make decisions concerning the right to have children? What can the study of psychology contribute to this debate?

**Adoption studies** Research carried out on children adopted at birth by parents not related to them to determine the relative influence of heredity and environment on human behavior.

**Amniocentesis** Technique that involves collecting cells cast off by the fetus into the fluid of the womb and testing them for genetic abnormalities.

have reacted to them during the course of their lives? Do studies of twins raised separately really remove environmental variables and focus exclusively on heredity? Or do they instead demonstrate the extent to which similar environments and life experiences interact with similar genetic codes to produce similar traits and behaviors?

Recently, researchers have become interested in **adoption studies**. Adoption studies focus on children who were adopted at birth and brought up by parents not genetically related to them. Adoption studies provide additional evidence for the heritability of intelligence and some forms of mental illness (J. Horn, 1983; Scarr & Weinberg, 1983). For example, one study located 47 people who had mothers with schizophrenia but who had been adopted at birth and reared by normal parents. Of these 47, 5 subsequently suffered from schizophrenia. In another group of people who had been adopted at birth but whose parents did not have schizophrenia, there was not a single case of schizophrenia (Heston, 1966). Studies of biological and adoptive families have also suggested that chronic alcoholism and suicide—two phenomena that would at first appear to be tightly tied to environmental influences—have a strong genetic basis. This might help explain why most people who drink do not develop chronic alcoholism, and why only a few people turn to suicide when they despair (Kety, 1979).

## Social Implications

Science is not simply a process that takes place in a laboratory; it can have widespread effects on society at large. To the extent that we can trace such human traits as intelligence, temperament, and mental illness to their origins in chromosomes and genes, we increase the extent to which we can control human lives. And because this control permits choices that were previously not available, we face new ethical dilemmas.

Advances in genetics, for example, have improved our ability to predict birth defects in babies not yet conceived. Genetic counselors using family histories can spell out the likelihood that the children of a given marriage will inherit genetic problems. Before deciding to have a child, therefore, a high-risk couple must weigh some very serious ethical questions.

Once conception has occurred, a technique called **amniocentesis** permits detection of many genetic problems before the baby is born. Amniocentesis involves collecting some of the cells that the fetus has cast off into the fluid surrounding it in the womb and testing them for chromosomal or genetic abnormalities. In about 2 percent of the cases, genetic problems are found. Does the child nonetheless have a right to life? Do the parents have a right to abort the fetus? Should society protect all life, no matter how imperfect it is in the eyes of some? If not, which defects are so unacceptable that abortion is justified? Most of these questions have a long history, but recent progress in behavior genetics and in medicine has given them a special urgency.

The study of behavior genetics makes many people uneasy. Some fear that it may lead to the conclusion that who we are is written in some kind of permanent ink before we are born. Some people also fear that research in behavior genetics could be used to undercut movements toward social equality. It is important to note that far from finding human behavior to be genetically predetermined, the recent work of behavioral geneticists actually shows just how important the *environment* is in determining which genetic predispositions come to be expressed and which do not. The emerging picture is that *both* heredity and environment play an important role in shaping most significant behaviors and traits.

## LOOKING FORWARD

At the very center of our psychological experience is the human brain. Yet only in the last 100 years or so have we really engaged in scientific exploration of the brain as the organ of our thoughts, memories, language, emotions, and even our deepest fears and our dysfunctions. As we have seen, studies of the brain raise new questions, even as they answer existing ones. Just 20 years ago, we knew of a handful of neurotransmitters and only suspected that there might be more. Today we know of more than 50 substances that serve as transmitters or modulators of neuron signals, and this number is increasing. We are finding that many neurons secrete and receive information from more than one transmitter substance. What events are communicated in these double, triple, or even quadruple chemical messages? We have pieced together evidence from brain-injured patients, brain-scanning studies, and research with nonhuman subjects to form a picture of how the various parts of the brain work as interrelated systems, and we are beginning to view the brain and endocrine system as a network that can communicate with and affect virtually every cell in the body. We are only beginning to understand how this vast network is involved in illness, healing, and pain control. We have found ways to overcome the central nervous system's own blockades against healing processes after injury, and we look forward to a time when spinal and brain injuries are no more serious than a broken arm or an inflamed appendix. We must now concern ourselves with what will happen when we attempt to repair a system that naturally defends against repair.

At the heart of our exploration of the brain lie two fundamental issues that will continue to be the focal points of debate in psychology—as well as in other disciplines—for years to come. One of these is the *nature-nurture* question. How much of what we are is determined by our genes and innate biological makeup, and how much comes from continuous, skillful adaptation to social and environmental forces? The other issue, much more at the core of Western philosophical and psychological traditions, is the *mind-body problem*. Is the brain really the mind? If it is, how can 3 pounds of cell tissue and its fluids be conscious, self-reflective, embarrassed, loving, and creative?

## SUMMARY

This chapter presents the basic biological processes that are at the root of our thoughts, feelings, and actions. The body possesses two systems for coordinating and integrating behavior: the **nervous system** and the **endocrine system**.

### NEURONS, THE MESSENGERS

The billions of **neurons**, or nerve cells, that underlie all the activity of the nervous system form a communication network that coordinates all the systems of the body and enables them to function. Neurons usually receive messages from other neurons through short fibers, called **dendrites**, that pick up messages and carry them to the neuron's cell body.

#### The Neural Impulse

When the neuron is at rest, there is a slightly higher concentration of negative **ions** inside the membrane surrounding the cell body than outside, so there is a negative electrical charge inside relative to the outside. When an incoming message is strong enough, this electrical charge is changed, an **action potential** is generated, and the neuron is depolarized. An electrical impulse is sent down the **axon** of a neuron and stimulates the release of chemical messengers called **neurotransmitters**.

#### The Synapse

Neurotransmitter molecules cross the tiny **synaptic space** between the axon of the sending neuron and the dendrite of the receiving neuron, where they latch on to a receptor site, much the way a key fits into a lock, thus passing on their **excitatory** or **inhibitory** messages.

#### Synapses and Drugs

Certain drugs produce psychological effects by increasing or decreasing the amount of neurotransmitters at the synapse, preventing the neurotransmitters' destruction (cocaine) or reabsorption (caffeine). Drugs that block the dopamine receptors and reduce the symptoms of schizophrenia have also been developed.

## THE CENTRAL NERVOUS SYSTEM

The billions of neurons in the brain are connected to neurons throughout the body by trillions of synapses. This nervous system is organized into two parts: the **central nervous system**, which consists of the brain and the spinal cord, and the **peripheral nervous system**, which connects the central nervous system to the rest of the body.

### The Brain

The brain contains more than 90 percent of the body's neurons. Physically, the brain has three distinct areas: the hindbrain, midbrain, and forebrain. The functions of these areas often overlap.

The **hindbrain** is found in even the most primitive vertebrates. It is made up of the cerebellum, pons, and medulla. The **medulla** is a narrow structure nearest the spinal cord; it is the point at which many of the nerves from the left part of the body cross to the right side of the brain and vice versa. The medulla controls such functions as breathing, heart rate, and blood pressure. The **pons** is just above the medulla and connects the top of the brain to the cerebellum. Chemicals produced in the pons help maintain our sleep-wake cycle. The **cerebellum** is divided into two hemispheres and handles certain reflexes, especially those that have to do with balance. It also coordinates the body's actions.

The **midbrain** lies between the hindbrain and forebrain and is important for hearing and sight.

The **forebrain** is supported by the brain stem and buds out above it, drooping somewhat to fit the skull. It consists of the thalamus, hypothalamus, and cerebral cortex. The **thalamus** relays and translates incoming messages from the sense receptors—except those for smell. The **hypothalamus** governs motivation and emotion and appears to play a role in coordinating the responses of the nervous system in times of stress.

The cerebral hemispheres, located above the thalamus and hypothalamus, take up most of the room inside the skull. The outer covering of the cerebral hemispheres is known as the **cerebral cortex**. The cerebral hemispheres are what most people think of when they think of the brain. They are the most recently evolved portion of the brain, and they regulate the most complex behavior. Each cerebral hemisphere is divided into four lobes, delineated by deep fissures on the surface of the brain. The **occipital lobe** of the cortex, located at the back of the head, receives and processes visual information. The **temporal lobe**, located roughly behind the temples, is important to the sense of smell; it also plays a role in helping us perform complex visual tasks, such as recognizing faces. The **parietal lobe** sits on top of the temporal lobe and occipital lobes. It receives sensory information from all over the body and seems to play a role in spatial abilities. The ability to comprehend language is concentrated in two areas in the parietal and temporal lobes. The **frontal lobe** is the part of the cerebral cortex responsible for voluntary movement and attention as well as goal-directed behavior. It may be linked to emotional temperament.

These four lobes are both physically and functionally distinct. Each lobe contains areas for specific motor or sensory function as well as **association areas**. The association areas—areas that are free to process all kinds of information—make up most of the cerebral cortex and enable the brain to produce behaviors requiring the coordination of many brain areas.

### Hemispheric Specialization

The two hemispheres of the cerebral cortex are linked by the **corpus callosum**, through which they communicate and coordinate. Nevertheless, they appear to have some separate functions. The right hemisphere of the cortex appears to excel at nonverbal and spatial tasks, whereas the left hemisphere is usually more dominant in verbal tasks such as speaking and writing. The right hemisphere controls the left side of the body, and the left hemisphere controls the right side.

### New Tools for Studying the Nervous System

In recent decades science has developed an increasingly sophisticated technology for investigating the brain and nervous system. Among the most important tools are microelectrode techniques; macroelectrode techniques (EEG, ERP); structural imaging (CT scanning, MRI); functional imaging (EEG imaging, MEG, MSI), and tools that such as PET scanning that use radioactive energy to map brain activity. Scientists often combine these techniques to study brain activity in unprecedented detail.

### The Reticular Formation

The **reticular formation** is a network of neurons running through the hindbrain, midbrain, and forebrain that serves to arouse the higher parts of the brain.

### The Limbic System

The **limbic system** contains structures that are important for forming memories and experiencing pleasure, as well as for various motivational and emotional activities.

### The Spinal Cord

The **spinal cord** is a complex cable of nerves that connects the brain to most of the rest of the body. It is made up of bundles of long nerve fibers and has two basic functions: to permit some reflex movements and to carry messages to and from the brain.

## THE PERIPHERAL NERVOUS SYSTEM

The second major division of the nervous system, the peripheral nervous system, carries messages to and from the central nervous system. It is made up of two parts: the somatic and the autonomic nervous systems.

## THE SOMATIC NERVOUS SYSTEM

The **somatic nervous system** is composed of the sensory (afferent) neurons that carry messages to the central nervous system and the motor (efferent) neurons that carry messages from the central nervous system to the skeletal muscles of the body.

## THE AUTONOMIC NERVOUS SYSTEM

The **autonomic nervous system** is itself broken into two parts: the **sympathetic** and **parasympathetic** divisions. The first acts primarily to arouse the body; the second, to relax and restore the body to normal levels of arousal.

## THE ENDOCRINE SYSTEM

The endocrine system is the other communication system in the body. It is made up of **endocrine glands** that produce **hormones**, chemical substances released into the bloodstream to affect such processes as metabolism, growth, and sexual development. Hormones are also involved in regulating emotional life.

### The Thyroid Gland

The **thyroid gland** secretes **thyroxin**, a hormone that can reduce concentration and lead to irritability when the thyroid is overactive and cause drowsiness and a sluggish metabolism when the thyroid is underactive.

### The Parathyroid Glands

Within the thyroid are four tiny pea-shaped organs, the **parathyroids**, which control and balance the levels of calcium and phosphate in the blood and tissue fluids. This, in turn, affects the excitability of the nervous system.

### The Pineal Gland

The **pineal gland** is a pea-sized gland that apparently responds to exposure to light and regulates activity levels over the course of the day.

### The Pancreas

The **pancreas** lies in a curve between the stomach and the small intestine and controls the level of sugar in the blood.

### The Pituitary Glands

The **pituitary gland** produces the largest number of different hormones and therefore has the widest range of effects on the body's functions. The **posterior pituitary** is controlled by the nervous system. It produces two hormones: vasopressin, which causes blood pressure to rise and regulates the amount of water in the body's cells; and oxytocin, which causes the uterus to contract during childbirth and lactation to begin. The **anterior pituitary** is often called the "master gland." It responds to chemical messages from the bloodstream to produce numerous hormones that trigger the action of other endocrine glands.

### The Gonads

These reproductive glands—the testes in males and ovaries in females, and, to a lesser extent, the adrenal glands—secrete androgens and estrogens.

### The Adrenal Glands

The two **adrenal glands** are located one above each kidney. Each has two parts: an outer covering, the **adrenal cortex**, and an inner core, the **adrenal medulla**. Both are important to the body's responses to stress.

### Genetics and Behavior

**Behavior genetics** is the study of the relationship between heredity and behavior. There is a good deal of disagreement among psychologists regarding the degree to which behavior is inherited.

### Genetics

**Genetics** is the study of how plants, animals, and people pass on **traits** from one generation to the next through **genes**. Each gene is lined up on tiny threadlike bodies called **chromosomes**, which are, in turn, made up predominantly of **deoxyribonucleic acid (DNA)**.

### Genetics and Behavior

Psychologists use a variety of methods to study the relationships between genes and various behaviors. They use **strain studies** to determine the heritability of certain traits in animals, and **family studies**, particularly those containing twins, to examine genetic influences on human behavior.

### Social Implications

The study of behavior genetics makes many people uneasy. Some fear that research in behavior genetics will undercut movements to social equality; others fear that it will lead people to conclude that who we are is written in some kind of permanent ink before we are born.

# REVIEW QUESTIONS

## MULTIPLE CHOICE

1. Match the following terms with the correct definition:

| | |
|---|---|
| ___ neuron | a. group of axons bundled together |
| ___ nerve | b. receives incoming messages from surrounding neurons |
| ___ axon | c. carries outgoing messages away from the nerve cell |
| ___ dendrite | d. single nerve cell |

2. When a neuron is in a polarized state, there are mostly ______ ions on the outside of the cell membrane and mostly ______ ions on the inside.

3. During the ______ period, the neuron will fire only if the incoming message is considerably stronger than usual:
a. absolute refractory b. relative refractory

4. A very strong incoming signal will cause a neuron to fire more strongly than before and in turn cause neighboring neurons to fire more strongly. T / F

5. When a neural impulse reaches the end of the axon, it is transferred to the next neuron chemically through the release of ______.

6. Match the following drugs with the ways they affect neurotransmission.

| | |
|---|---|
| ___ Amphetamines | a. occupy or block receptor sites |
| ___ Curare, LSD, and Atropine | b. increase release of neurotransmitter |
| ___ Antidepressants | c. interfere with the reabsorption of neurotransmitter |

7. The ______ nervous system connects the central nervous system to all parts of the body beyond the brain and spinal cord.

8. Which brain structure is a vital center for such important biological functions as temperature control, eating, drinking, and sexual behavior?
a. cerebral cortex c. cerebellum
b. pons d. hypothalamus

9. Which brain structure is a "relay station" for sensory systems?
a. thalamus c. corpus callosum
b. hypothalamus d. pons

10. In the cerebral cortex the ____ lobe receives sensory information from all over the body, and the _____ lobe send messages to various muscles and glands in the body.

11. Which of the following is not part of the brain's structure?
a. hypothalamus c. limbic system
b. corpus callosum d. parathyroid

12. Although the left and right hemispheres of the brain are specialized, they are normally in close communication through the:
a. midbrain c. corpus callosum
b. temporal lobe d. cerebellum

13. In the great majority of humans, the _______ side of the cortex is specialized for language.

14. Current evidence suggests that the _____ frontal lobe is associated with positive emotions and the ____ frontal lobe is associated with negative emotions.

15. Communication in the endocrine system is dependent on _________, chemicals secreted directly into the bloodstream.

16. Depression, schizophrenia, intelligence, and general emotional reactivity may all be influenced by genes. T / F

## CRITICAL THINKING AND APPLICATIONS

17. In the previous chapter we examined various schools of psychology, including behaviorism, psychoanalytic psychology, and cognitive psychology? Which school or schools did you find most convincing before you read this chapter? Now that you have been exposed to the physiological and hereditary bases of behavior, have you changed your opinion? If so, how and why?

18. What are some of the most current methods for studying the brain and nervous system? What can they teach us? When do you think they should be used?

19. In this chapter we discussed possible biological and hereditary bases for schizophrenia. Do you think scientists will eventually find biological causes for some—or most—mental illnesses? If so, is the use of drugs to treat these disorders appropriate? Why or why not?

20. What do behavioral scientists mean when they state that certain behaviors have a genetic component? How do you feel about explaining human behavior in terms of inherited characteristics?

*(Answers to the Review Questions can be found in the back of the text.)*

## Think About It!

1. How far away can you see a candle flame on a clear, dark night?
2. Can advertisers persuade you to buy products by placing hidden messages in their ads?
3. Why does the rate of automobile accidents go up at night?
4. How many different colors can we distinguish?
5. Which sense is more sensitive, taste or smell?
6. What kinds of visual cues do we use to judge distance and depth?

# Sensation and Perception

# 3

## Overview

**Sensation** Experience of sensory stimulation.

**Perception** Process of creating meaningful patterns from raw sensory information.

**Suppose you wanted to figure out how far off a thunderstorm was. How would you get the necessary information? If you lived on a prairie, you could use your visual sense to pick up relevant information, though at night you would have to rely more on your sense of hearing. Some people claim that they can "smell" a storm coming or that they experience a tingling sensation on their skin as a storm is rolling in. But sensation alone is not enough to give us a good grasp of the external world. Sounds, colors, tastes, and smells are just random sensory impressions until we interpret them in some meaningful way. Our *perceptual processes* are the tools we use to understand and make sense of the countless sensations that we are continually experiencing; without these perceptual processes, even the most mundane tasks would become impossible. Take driving a car, for example. As you negotiate traffic, you focus on visual cues about your surroundings. From a complicated array of colors, shapes, and patterns, you must be able to distinguish a road sign that tells you how to get to your destination from one that tells you to stop. You depend on visual cues to judge the distances of other cars, bicycles, and pedestrians. If you see a motorist trying to enter the flow of traffic from a driveway just ahead of you, you must be able to determine whether that car and yours are on a collision course. And as you drive, if you hear a siren, you must determine quickly where it is coming from and how close it is so that you can yield the right of way if necessary. In all these cases, you have to make sense out of raw sensory information and act accordingly.**

In this chapter, we will discover how we interpret the raw data picked up by our senses from the outside world. First, we will discuss **sensation**—that is, the basic experience of stimulation of the body's senses: sight, hearing, smell, taste, balance, touch, and pain. We will examine each of the body's senses and learn how each one converts physical energy—light or sound waves, for example—into nerve impulses. Then, by exploring how our perceptual processes organize and interpret elementary sensations, we will see how we arrive at our **perception** of meaningful events. In the process, we will discuss how we perceive patterns, distance, and movement, and how we are able to identify an object despite changing or even contradictory information. And finally, we will examine how our personal characteristics influence the way we perceive the world..

## THE NATURE OF SENSORY PROCESSES

### The Character of Sensation

Described in general terms, the sequence of events that produces a sensation seems quite simple. Initially, some form of energy, either from an external source or from inside the body, stimulates a receptor cell in one of the sense organs, such as the eye or the ear. A receptor cell is designed to respond to one particular form of energy—light waves, in the case of vision, or vibration, in the case of hearing. The energy must be sufficiently intense for the receptor cell to react to it. But given sufficient energy, the receptor responds to the energy by sending to the brain a coded electrochemical signal, which varies according to the characteristics of the stimulus. For instance, a very bright light might be coded by the rapid firing of a set of nerve cells, whereas a dim light would set off a much slower firing sequence. As the neural signal passes along the sensory nerves to the central nervous system, it is coded still further, so that by the time it reaches the brain, the message is precise and detailed. Thus, the coded signal that the brain receives from a flashing red light differs significantly from the message signaling a soft yellow haze. And both of these signals are coded in a much different way from a loud, piercing noise.

**Absolute threshold** The least amount of energy that can be detected as a stimulation 50 percent of the time.

Our sensory experiences, then, are the result of patterns of neural signals. In a way, every sensory experience is an illusion created in the brain. The brain sits within the skull, isolated from the external events; yet, bombarded by the "clicking" of coded neural signals coming in over millions of nerve fibers, this nerve center creates images. The clicks on the optic nerve are no more "visual" than the clicks on an auditory nerve. But clicks on the optic nerve reliably produce an experience we call vision, just as clicks moving along an auditory nerve produce the experience we call hearing, or *audition*. Even if the clicks on the optic nerve are caused by something other than light, the result is still a visual experience. Gentle pressure on an eye, for instance, results in signals from the optic nerve that the brain interprets as visual patterns. In the same way, both a symphonic recording and a stream of water trickling into the ear stimulate the auditory nerve, and both cause us to hear something. In 1842, Johannes Müller, an influential German physiologist, discovered this one-to-one relationship between stimulation of a specific nerve and the resulting type of sensory experience, a concept now known as *the doctrine of specific nerve energies*.

The interaction of sensation and perception. Our mental, perceptual processes help us interpret the physical sensations—the sounds, the smells, the particular quality of light—that accompany the coming of a storm. You may even have a sense in your "mind's eye" of what the air in this photograph would smell like.

## Sensory Thresholds

Earlier we noted that the energy reaching a receptor must be sufficiently intense for it to have a noticeable effect. The minimum intensity of physical energy required to produce any sensation at all in a person is called the **absolute threshold**. Any stimulation below the absolute threshold will not be experienced.

How much sensory stimulation is needed to produce a sensation? How loud does a sound have to be, for example, for a person to hear it? How bright does a "blip" on a radar screen have to be for the operator to see it? To answer these kinds of questions, psychologists present a stimulus at different intensities and ask people whether they sense anything. You might expect that there would come a point where people would suddenly say, "Now I see the flash" or "Now I hear a sound." But actually there is a range of intensities over which a person sometimes, but not always, can sense a stimulus. For a variety of reasons, psychologists have agreed to set the absolute threshold at the point where a person can detect the stimulus 50 percent of the time that it is presented (see Figure 3-1).

Although there are differences among people, and even differences from moment to moment for the same person, the absolute threshold for each of our senses is remarkably low. According to McBurney and Collings (1984), the approximate absolute thresholds are as follows:

- *Taste*: 1 gram (.0356 ounce) of table salt in 500 liters (529 quarts) of water.
- *Smell*: One drop of perfume diffused throughout a three-room apartment.

**Adaptation** Adjustment of the senses to the level of stimulation they are receiving.

**Difference threshold** or **just noticeable difference (jnd)** The smallest change in stimulation that can be detected 50 percent of the time.

From how far away can you see a candle flame on a clear, dark night?

- *Touch*: The wing of a bee falling on your cheek from a height of 1 centimeter (.39 inch).
- *Hearing*: The tick of a watch from 6 meters (20 feet) in very quiet conditions.
- *Vision*: A candle flame seen from 50 kilometers (30 miles) on a clear, dark night.

Of course these figures apply only under ideal circumstances—in extremely quiet or dark or "taste-free" or "smell-free" conditions. Under more normal conditions, absolute thresholds vary depending on the level and nature of ongoing sensory stimulation. For example, your threshold for the taste of salt would be considerably higher after you had eaten salted peanuts or potato chips; it would take much more than just 1 gram of salt in 500 liters of water for you to notice the salty taste. In the same way, your vision threshold would be much higher in the middle of a bright, sunny day than at midnight on a moonless night; you certainly wouldn't see a candle flame 30 miles away during the daytime! In both these cases, the absolute threshold would rise because of sensory **adaptation**. Our senses automatically adjust to the overall, average level of stimulation in a particular setting. When confronted by a great deal of stimulation, they become much less sensitive than when the overall level of stimulation is low. By the same token, when the level of stimulation drops, our sensory apparatus becomes much more sensitive than under conditions of level of high stimulation. This process of adaptation allows all our senses to be keenly attuned to environmental conditions, picking up a multitude of cues without getting overloaded. When we enter a hushed room, we are able to hear the faint tick of a wristwatch. But when we go out onto a busy city street at rush hour, the noise of street traffic would be deafening or even painful unless our ears adapted and became less sensitive to noise. Similarly, through visual adaptation, we can move from a dark room into the bright sunshine without experiencing great pain or damaging our visual system. Later in this chapter we will examine various kinds of adaptation in more detail.

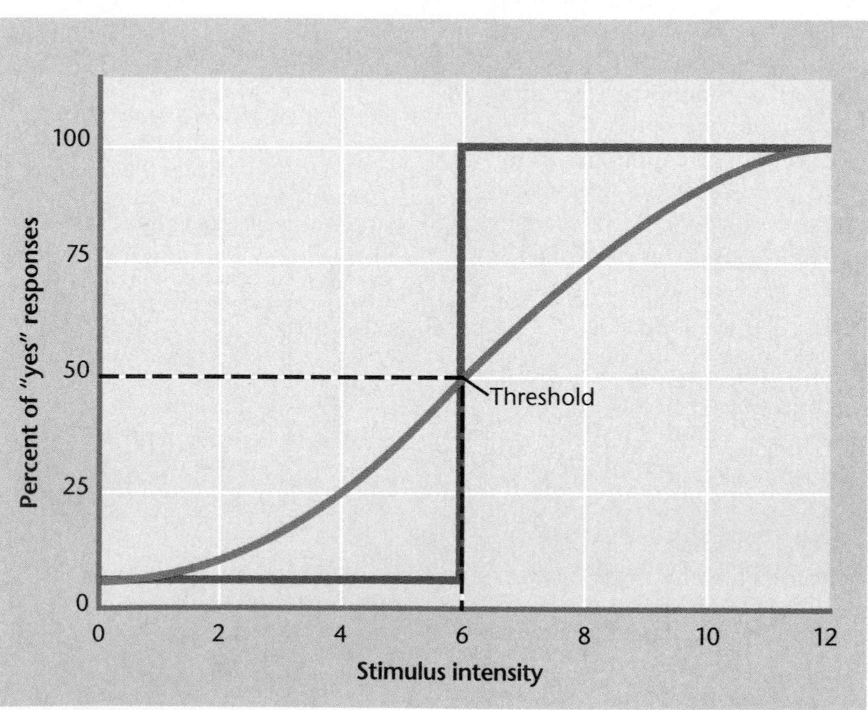


**Figure 3-1**
**Determining a sensory threshold.** The red line represents an ideal case—at all intensities below the threshold, the subject reports no sensation or no change in intensity; at all intensities above the threshold, the subject does report a sensation or a change in intensity. In actual practice, the ideal of the red line is never realized. The blue line shows the actual responses of a typical subject. The threshold is taken as the point where the subject reports a sensation or a change in intensity 50 percent of the time.

Imagine now that you can hear a particular sound. How much stronger must the sound become before you notice that it has grown louder? The smallest change in stimulation that you can detect 50 percent of the time is called the **difference threshold**, or the **just noticeable difference, (jnd)**. Like the absolute threshold, the difference threshold varies from person to person and from moment to moment for the same person. And like absolute thresholds, difference thresholds tell us something about the flexibility of sensory systems. For example, adding 2 pounds to a 10-pound load will certainly be noticed, so we might assume that the difference threshold must be considerably *less than* 2 pounds. Yet adding 2 pounds to a 100-pound load probably would not make much of a difference, so we might conclude that the difference threshold must be considerably *more than* 2 pounds. But how can the difference threshold (jnd) be both less than and greater than 2 pounds? It turns out that the difference threshold varies according to the strength or intensity of the original stimulus. The greater the stimulus, the greater the change necessary to produce a jnd. In the 1830s, Ernst Weber concluded that the difference threshold is a constant *fraction or proportion* of the specific stimulus. The theory that the jnd is a constant fraction of the original stimulus is known as **Weber's law**. It is important to note that the values of these fractions vary significantly for the different senses. Hearing, for example, is very sensitive: We can detect a change in sound of 0.3 percent (1/3 of 1 percent). By contrast, producing a jnd in taste requires a 20 percent (1/5) change. To return to our earlier example of weight, a change in weight of 2 percent (1/50) is necessary to produce a jnd. Thus, adding 1 pound to a 50-pound load would produce a noticeable difference 50 percent of the time; adding 1 pound to a 100-pound load would not.

**Weber's law** The principle that the jnd for any given sense is a constant fraction or proportion of the stimulation being judged.

**SUBLIMINAL PERCEPTION** The idea of a threshold implies that certain events in the real world occur below our level of conscious experience. But does stimulation below the sensory threshold influence behavior in some way? According to a 1991 survey, nearly two-thirds of Americans believe that advertisers put hidden messages and images in their advertisements to increase sales of their products (Lev, 1991). Such messages are called *subliminal* because they occur below the threshold of awareness. Are subliminal messages actually used in advertisements and in motivational products such as self-help tapes? If so, do they have the power to change people's behavior?

In a classic example of subliminal advertising, a movie theater in Fort Lee, New Jersey, allegedly flashed messages such as "Drink Coca-Cola" and "Eat Popcorn" between frames of the 1950s movie *Picnic*. Although the messages flashed too quickly for moviegoers to pick up them consciously, legend has it that soft drink and popcorn sales increased dramatically at that theater. In fact, there was no change in sales, but the story has circulated for decades nonetheless.

More recently, the sale of audiotapes with subliminal self-help messages has become a big business, constituting anywhere from a quarter to a third of spoken-word audiocassette sales. Rather than manipulating behavior in some sinister way, however, the tapes are designed to improve it. These tapes claim to incorporate *affirmations*, messages that are not perceptible to the ear but that nonetheless affect behavior. A weight-loss tape might carry the subliminal message "Eat less," while a tape geared toward improving self-esteem might subliminally convey the message "I am capable."

Can people be influenced by information of which they are not consciously aware? The answer is a qualified yes: Under carefully controlled conditions, individuals have responded briefly to sights and sounds outside their conscious awareness. For example, in a recent study, one group of people was shown a list of words related to competition, while a second group was exposed to a list of neutral words. In both cases, the words were flashed so rapidly that the subjects could not identify them. Later, when the subjects were playing a game, researchers found that the subjects who had been shown to the subliminal list of words with competitive overtones became especially competitive (Neuberg, 1988). In another study, one group of subjects was subliminally exposed to words conveying honesty (a positive trait), while other subjects were subliminally exposed to words conveying meanness (a negative trait). Subsequently, all the subjects read a description of a woman whose behavior could be looked at as either honest or mean. When asked to assess various personality characteristics of the woman, the subjects who had been subliminally exposed to "honest" words

Can advertisers persuade you to buy products by placing hidden messages in their ads?

rated her as more honest, and those who had been subliminally exposed to "mean" words judged her as being more mean (Erdley & D'Agostino, 1988). Thus, people's behaviors and judgments seem to be affected by subliminal exposure to lists of words.

Another line of evidence for subliminal perception comes from research in which a message intended to elicit feelings of security and safety (such as "Mommy and I Are One") is projected on a screen too quickly for subjects to report seeing anything other than a flash of light. In a review of more than 50 studies of this sort, Hardaway (1991) concluded that subliminal presentations of this phrase (and others similar to it) tended to reduce feelings of anxiety, hostility, and threat and to promote recall of more positive memories.

Finally, a group of students at the University of Michigan was shown a series of geometric figures so rapidly—one every 0.001 second—that the subjects reported seeing only a pulse of light (Kunst-Wilson & Zajonc, 1980). Later, however, these students expressed a preference for the figures they had been exposed to subliminally compared to ones they were seeing for the first time.

These studies, and others like them, indicate that in a controlled laboratory setting people can process and respond to information of which they are not consciously aware. It does not follow, however, that advertisers using such techniques will influence consumer behavior or that subliminal phrases embedded in self-help tapes will succeed in changing behavior. So far, there is no independent scientific evidence that subliminal messages in advertising or self-help tapes have any appreciable effect (Beatty & Hawkins, 1989; Greenwald et al., 1991; T.E. Moore, 1982; T.G. Russell, Rowe, & Smouse, 1991; Vokey & Read, 1985). For example, in one representative study, half the subjects saw an advertisement that had no sexual images, while the other half viewed the identical advertisement with a subliminal sexual image incorporated. The addition of the sexual imagery made no difference in people's preference ratings of the product (Gable et al., 1987).

In another series of studies, volunteers used self-improvement tapes with subliminal messages for several weeks; about half said they felt better about themselves and had improved as a result of listening to the tapes. However, objective tests detected no measurable change. Moreover, the perceived improvement seemed to have more to do with the label on the tape than its subliminal content: About half the people who received a tape labeled "Improve Memory" said their memory had improved, even though many of them had actually received a tape intended to boost self-esteem; and about one-third of the people who listened to tapes labeled "Increase Self-Esteem" said their self-esteem had gone up, though many of them had actually been listening to tapes designed to improve memory (Greenwald et al., 1991).

In response to research like this, the National Academy of Science issued a report in 1991 that concluded that there is no evidence that self-help tapes are useful for their stated purposes (Druckman & Bjork, 1991). Moreover, officers of the Institute of Canadian Advertisers and the American Association of Advertising Agencies (AAAA) have consistently denied that subliminal messages figure in any advertising campaign, adding that such messages are not effective. The president of the AAAA recently concluded, "There is no such thing [as subliminal advertising]. In 36 years in advertising, I've never heard the issue seriously discussed" (Lev, 1991).

So far, we have been talking about the general characteristics of sensation, but each of the body's sensory systems works a little differently. Each of these sensory systems contains receptor cells that specialize in converting a particular kind of energy into neural signals. The threshold at which this conversion occurs varies from system to system. So do the mechanisms by which sensory data are processed and coded and sent to the brain for still more processing. We now return to the unique features of each of the sensory systems.

## VISION

Different animal species depend more on some senses than on others. Dogs rely heavily on the sense of smell, bats on hearing, some fish on taste. But for humans, vision ranks as the most important sense; and therefore, it has received the most attention from psychologists. To understand vision, we need to look first at the parts of the visual system, beginning with the structure of the eye.

### The Visual System

The structure of the human eye, including the cellular path to the brain, is shown in Figure 3-2. Light enters the eye through the **cornea**, the transparent protective coating over the front part of the eye. It then passes through the **pupil**, the opening in the center of the **iris**, the colored part of the eye. In very bright light, the muscles in the iris contract to make the pupil smaller and thus protect the eye from damage. This contraction also helps us see better in bright light. In dim light, the muscles relax to open the pupil wider and let in as much light as possible.

Inside the pupil, light moves through the **lens**, which focuses it onto the **retina**, the light-sensitive inner lining of the back of the eyeball. The lens changes shape to focus on objects that are closer or farther away. Normally the lens is focused on a middle distance, at a point neither very near nor very far away. To focus on an object that is very close to the eyes, tiny muscles around the lens contract and make the lens rounder. To focus on something far away, the muscles work to flatten the lens.

On the retina and directly behind the lens lies a depressed spot called the **fovea** (see Figure 3-3). The fovea occupies the center of the visual field, and images that pass through the lens are in sharpest focus here. Thus, the words that you are now reading are hitting the fovea, while the rest of what you see—a desk, walls, or whatever—is striking other areas of the retina.

**Cornea** The transparent protective coating over the front part of the eye.

**Pupil** Small opening in the iris through which light enters the eye.

**Iris** Colored part of the eye.

**Lens** Transparent part of the eye inside the pupil that focuses light onto the retina.

**Retina** Lining of the eye containing receptor cells that are sensitive to light.

**Fovea** Area of the retina that is the center of the visual field.

**Receptor cell** Specialized cell that responds to a particular type of energy.

**Rods** Receptor cells in the retina responsible for night vision and perception of brightness.

**Cones** Receptor cells in the retina responsible for color vision.

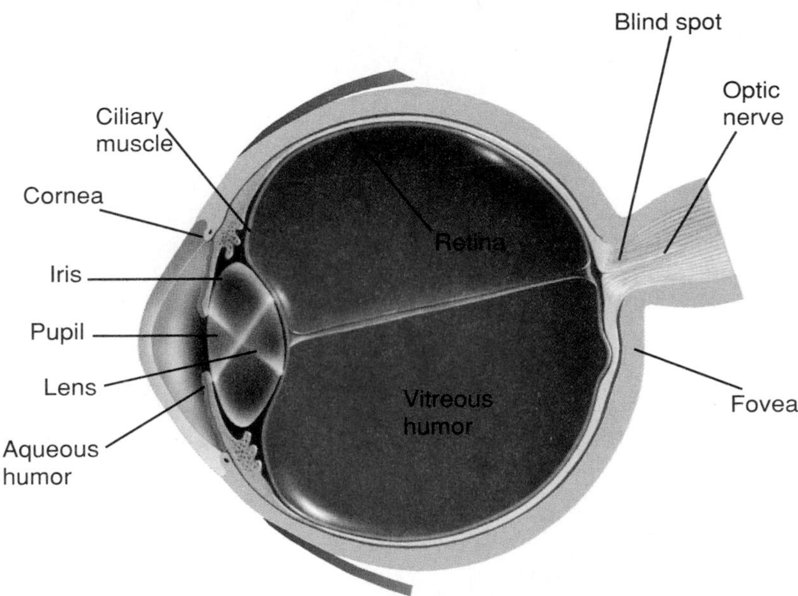


**Figure 3-2**
**A cross section of the human eye.** Light enters the eye through the cornea, passes through the pupil, and is focused by the lens onto the retina.

*Source:* Adapted from Hubel, 1963.

**THE RECEPTOR CELLS** The retina of each eye contains the **receptor cells** responsible for vision. These cells are sensitive to only a fraction of the spectrum of electromagnetic energy, which includes light along with other energies (see Figure 3-4). We generally refer to energies in the electromagnetic spectrum by their wavelengths. The shortest wavelengths that we can see are experienced as violet-blue colors; the longest appear as reds.

There are two kinds of receptor cells in the retina—**rods** and **cones**—named for their characteristic shapes (see Figure 3-5). About 120 million rods and 8 million cones are focused in the retina of each eye. Rods respond only to varying degrees of light and dark, not to colors. They are chiefly responsible for night vision. Cones, on the other hand, allow us to see light and dark as well as colors. Operating chiefly in day-

**Bipolar cells** Neurons that have only one axon and one dendrite; in the eye, these neurons connect the receptors on the retina to the ganglion cells.

light, cones are less sensitive to light than rods are (MacLeod, 1978). In this regard, cones, like color film, work best in relatively bright light. The more sensitive rods, like black-and-white film, respond to much lower levels of illumination.

Rods and cones differ in other ways as well. Cones are found mainly, but not exclusively, in the fovea, which contains no rods. And the greatest density of cones is in the very center of the fovea, which, as you recall, is where images are projected onto the retina in sharpest focus. Rods predominate just outside the fovea. As we move outward from the fovea toward the edges of the retina, both rods and cones get sparser. At the extreme edges of the retina, there are almost no cones and only a few rods.

Rods and cones also differ in the ways that they connect to the nerve cells leading to the brain. Both rods and cones connect to specialized neurons called **bipolar cells**, which have only one axon and one dendrite (see Figure 3-6). In the fovea, cones generally connect with only one bipolar cell—a sort of "private line" arrangement. Rods are usually on a "party line"—several may share a single bipolar cell.

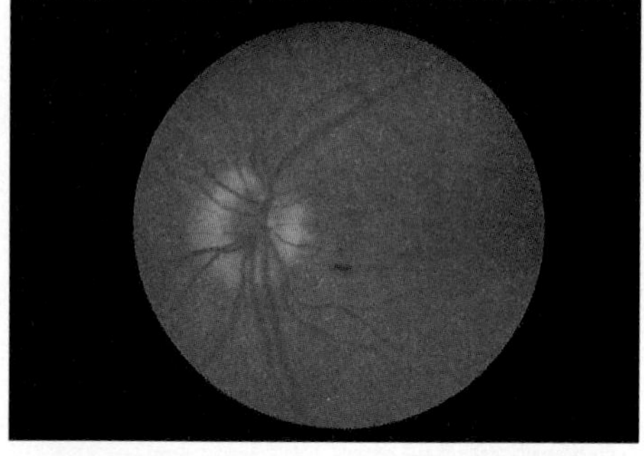

**Figure 3-3**
**The retina.** A view of the retina through an ophthalmoscope, an instrument used to inspect blood vessels in the eye. The central dark area is the *fovea*. The yellow circle marks the *blind spot*, where the optic nerve leaves the eye.

Knowing these facts about rods and cones can help you understand some of the more common experiences in seeing. For example, you may have noticed that at night you can see a dimly lit object better if you look slightly to one side of it rather than directly at it. This has to do with the location of the rods and cones. When you look directly at an object, its image falls on the fovea, which consists only of relatively light-insensitive cones. However, when you look slightly to one side of the object, its image falls next to the fovea and onto the highly light-sensitive rods. Moreover, a weak stimulus will prompt only a weak response in the cones, and this probably will not be sufficient to fire their bipolar cells. But because many rods converge on a single bipolar cell, that neuron is much more likely to fire and thereby initiate a sensory message to the brain in dim light.

At other times, vision gets better when more cones are stimulated. Have you ever tried to examine something and been unable to make out the details? You probably found that by increasing the amount of light on

**Figure 3-4**
**The electromagnetic spectrum.** The eye is sensitive to only a very small segment of the spectrum, known as visible light.

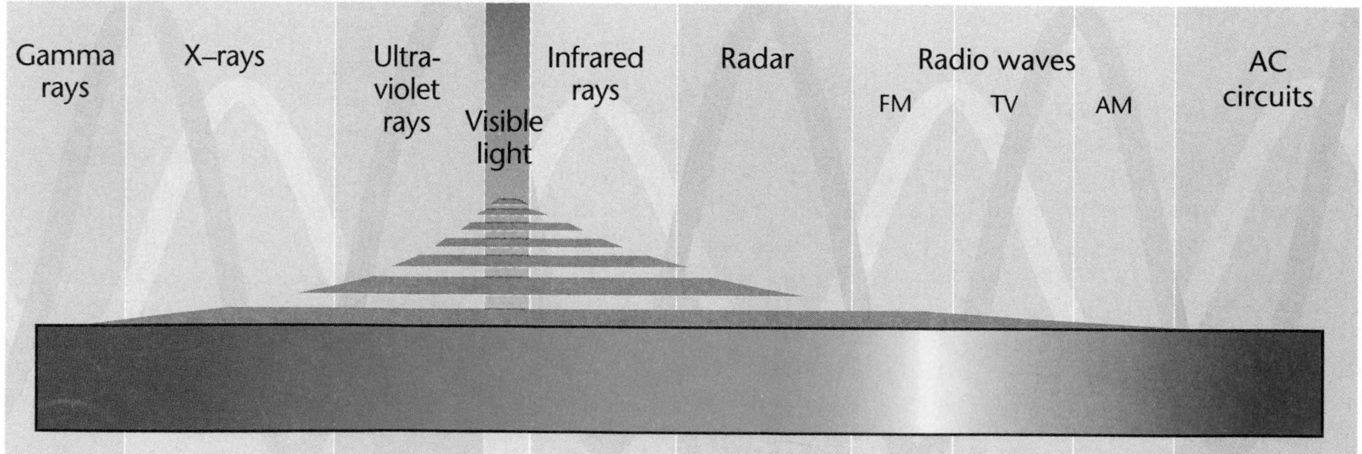

the object—perhaps by moving it into direct sunlight or under a lamp—you could see it better. That's because the better the illumination, the greater the number of cones stimulated; the greater the number of cones stimulated, the more likely they are to stimulate the bipolar cells, starting a message to the brain. Our ability to see improves as light intensity increases. So for "close" activities like reading, sewing, and writing, the more light, thebetter.

**Visual acuity** The ability to distinguish fine details visually.

For related reasons, vision is sharpest—even in normal light—whenever you look directly at an object and its image falls on the fovea. In the fovea, the one-to-one connection between cones and bipolar cells allows for maximum **visual acuity**—the ability to visually distinguish fine details. You can easily see how acuity works by conducting the following experiment: Hold the book about 18 inches from your eyes and look at the "X" in the center of the line below. Notice how your vision drops off for words and letters toward the left or right end of the line.

This is a test to show how visualXacuity varies across the retina.

Your fovea picks up the "X" and about four letters to either side. This is the area of greatest visual acuity. The letters at the left and right ends of the line fall well outside the fovea, where there are many more rods than cones. Rods, as you remember, tend to "pool" their signals on the way to the bipolar cells; and while this increases sensitivity, it cuts down on the fine details in the signal that goes to the brain. Outside the fovea, acuity drops by as much as 50 percent!

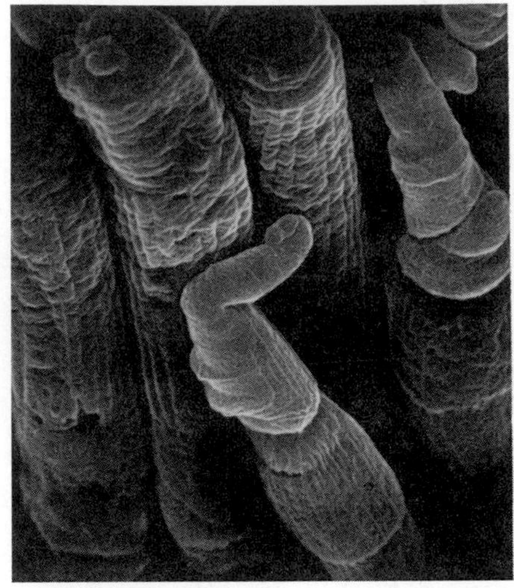

**Figure 3-5**
**Rods and cones.** As you can see from this photomicrograph, the rods and cones are aptly named.

**ADAPTATION** Earlier in the chapter we discussed *adaptation*, the process by which our senses adjust to different levels of stimulation. In the case of vision, adaptation occurs as the sensitivity of rods and cones changes according to how much light is available. When you go from bright sunlight into a dimly lit theater, your cones are initially fairly insensitive to light: You can see little or nothing as you look for a seat. But during the first 5 or 10 minutes in the dark, the cones become more and more sensitive to the dim light. After about 10 minutes, you will be able to see things directly in front of you about as well as you are going to: The cones do not get any more sensitive after this point. But the rods, which have also been adapting, continue to become more sensitive to the light for another 20 minutes or so. They reach maximum sensitivity about 30 minutes after you

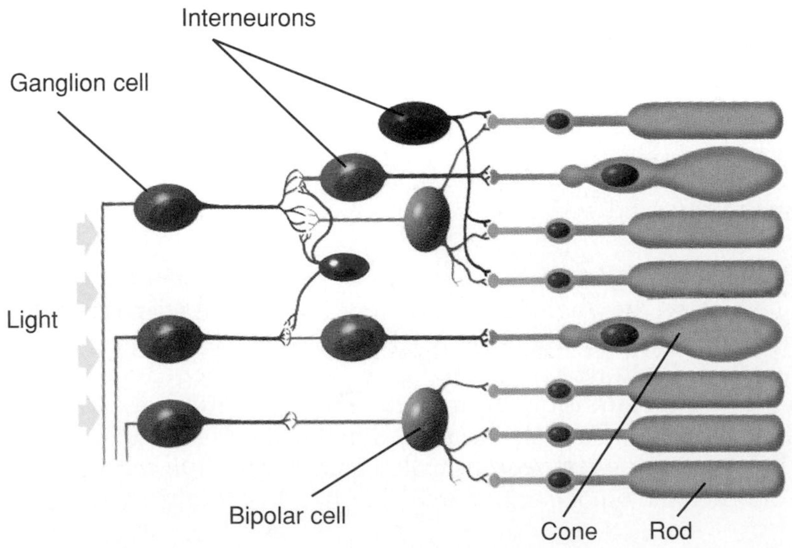


**Figure 3-6**
**A close-up of the layers of the retina.** Light must pass between the *ganglion cells* (both the large M-cells and the smaller P-cells) and the *bipolar cells* in order to reach the *rods* and *cones*. The sensory messages then travel back out again from the receptor cells, through the bipolar cells, to the ganglion cells. The axons of the ganglion cells gather together to form the *optic nerve*, which carries the messages from both eyes to the brain (see Figure 3-2).

**Dark adaptation** Increased sensitivity of rods and cones in darkness.

**Light adaptation** Decreased sensitivity of rods and cones in bright light.

**Afterimage** Sense experience that occurs after a visual stimulus has been removed.

enter a darkened room. The process by which rods and cones become more sensitive to light in response to lowered levels of illumination is called **dark adaptation**. But even with dark adaptation, there is not enough energy in very dim light to stimulate the cones to respond to colors. When your eyes are adapted to the dark, then, you see only a black-and-white-and-gray world of different brightnesses.

Problems with dark adaptation account in part for the much greater incidence of highway accidents at night (Leibowitz & Owens, 1977). When people drive at night, not all their visual abilities degrade equally. The eyes shift from the darkened interior of the car to the road area illuminated by the headlights to the darker areas at the side of the road. Unlike the situation in a darkened movie theater, these changing night-driving conditions do not allow for complete adaptation of either rods or cones; so neither system is operating at full capacity. Thus, people may be able to focus on the location of an object, such as a pedestrian, fairly well: They can see that the pedestrian is in the middle of the road. However, they are not able to determine who the pedestrian is, how far away the pedestrian is, or how fast the pedestrian is moving. As a result, drivers may overestimate their ability to stop in time. Because most drivers are generally unaware of the deterioration of their vision at night, they may drive with an exaggerated confidence in their visual abilities.

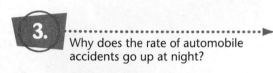

3\. Why does the rate of automobile accidents go up at night?

In the reverse process, **light adaptation**, the rods and cones become less sensitive to light. By the time you leave a movie theater, your rods and cones have grown very sensitive, and the bright outdoor light sometimes hurts as a result. In the bright light, all the neurons fire at once, overwhelming you. You squint and shield your eyes, and each iris contracts, all of which reduces the amount of light entering your pupils and striking each retina. As light adaptation proceeds, the rods and cones become less sensitive to stimulation by light, and within about a minute, both rods and cones are fully adapted to the light. At this point, you no longer need to squint and shield your eyes.

You can observe the effects of dark and light adaptation by staring continuously at the dot in the center of the upper square in Figure 3-7 for about 20 seconds. Then shift your gaze to the dot in the lower square. A gray-and-white pattern should appear in the lower square (when looking at the lower square, if you blink your eyes or shade the book from bright light, the illusion will be even stronger). When you look at the lower square, the striped areas that were black in the upper square will now seem to be light, and the areas that were white in the upper square will now appear gray. The **afterimage** appeared because the part of the retina that was exposed to the dark stripes of the upper square became more sensitive (it dark-adapted), and the area exposed to the white part of the upper square became less sensitive (it light-adapted). When you shifted your eyes to the lower square, the less sensitive parts of the retina produced the sensation of gray rather than white. This afterimage fades within a minute as the retina adapts again, this time to the solid white square.

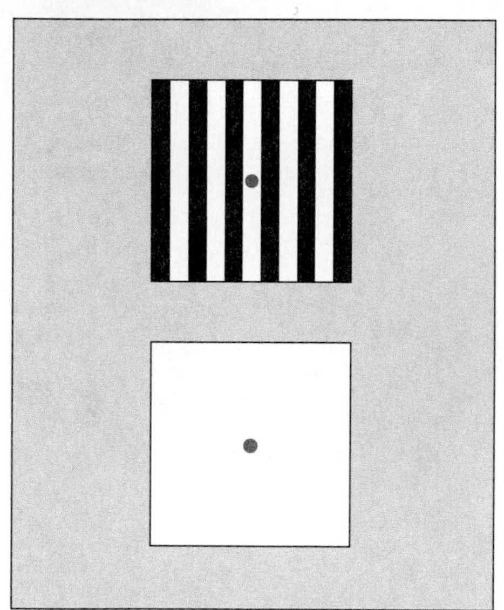

**Figure 3-7**
**An afterimage.** First stare continuously at the center of the upper square for about 20 seconds. Then shift your gaze to the dot in the lower square. Within a moment, a gray-and-white *afterimage* should appear inside the lower square.

**From Eye to Brain** Up to now, we have been focusing on the eye itself and the origins of visual processing in the retina. But messages from the eye must eventually reach the brain for a visual experience to occur. As you can imagine from Figure 3-6, the series of connections between eye and brain is quite intricate. To begin with, rods and cones are connected to bipolar cells in many different numbers and combinations. In addition, sets of neurons called *interneurons* link receptor cells to one another and bipolar cells to one another. Eventually these bipolar cells hook up with the **ganglion cells**, leading out of the eye. The axons of the ganglion cells join to form the **optic nerve**, which carries messages from each eye to the brain.

The place on the retina where the axons of all the ganglion cells join to leave the eye is called the **blind spot**—it contains no receptors. Even when light from a small object is focused directly on it, the object will not be seen (see Figure 3-8). After they leave the eyes, the fibers that make up the optic nerves separate, and some of them cross to the other side of the head at the **optic chiasm** (see Figure 3-9). The nerve fibers from the right side of each eye travel to the right hemisphere of the brain; those from the left side of each eye travel to the left hemisphere. Thus, as shown in Figure 3-9, visual information about any object in the *left visual field*, the area to the left of the viewer, will go to the right hemisphere (the pathway traced by the blue line in Figure 3-9). Similarly, information about any object in the *right visual field*, the area to the right of the viewer, will go to the left hemisphere (the pathway traced by the red line). You may refer back to Figures 2-10 and 2-11 to recall how researchers took advantage of the split-processing of the two visual fields to study split-brain patients.

The optic nerves carry their messages to various parts of the brain. Some messages reach the segment of the brain that controls the reflex movements that adjust the size of the pupil. Others find their way to the part of the brain that directs the eye muscles to change the shape of the lens. But the main destinations for the messages from the retina are the visual projection areas of the cerebral cortex, where the complex coded messages from the retina are registered and interpreted.

Scientists have come up with several kinds of evidence showing that the sensory messages entering the brain are routed along multiple pathways for simultaneous processing in a number of different areas. As an example of how sensory messages work their way through the brain, consider stroke victims who suffer from a disorder called *prosopagonsia*. These people lose their ability to recognize faces but otherwise can still see as well as any normal person. All but the most severely brain-damaged are able to tell whether faces in photographs are happy, sad, surprised, disgusted, fearful, or angry; they could also estimate age as accurately as anyone else could (Damasio, Tranel, & Damasio, 1990a; Tranel, Damasio, & Damasio, 1988). This suggests that sensory information goes to at least two areas in the brain: one that allows us to recognize faces, and one that enables us to assess whether faces appear happy or sad, male or female, old or young, and so on.

Another way researchers have determined that sensory messages follow several pathways is through studies of patients with severe damage to the *visual cortex*, the parts of the cortex responsible for vision. These "cortically blind" patients may have healthy retinas and optic nerves, but they report partial or total blindness. A few of these patients demonstrate an odd phenomenon called *blindsight*: They behave as if they can see

**Ganglion cells** Neurons that connect the bipolar cells in the eyes to the brain.

**Optic nerve** The bundle of axons of ganglion cells that carries neural messages from each eye to the brain.

**Blind spot** Place on the retina where the axons of all the ganglion cells leave the eye and where there are no receptors.

**Optic chiasm** Point near the base of the brain where some fibers in the optic nerve from each eye cross to the other side of the brain.

**Figure 3-8**
**Finding one's blind spot.** To locate your *blind spot*, hold the book about a foot away from your eyes. Then close your right eye, stare at the "X," and slowly move the book toward you and away from you until the red dot disappears.

X

forms, colors, and motion—even though they claim that they cannot see at all (Poppel et al., 1973; Weiskrantz, 1978, 1986). Some researchers have speculated that these patients' ability to see stems from lower brain areas rather than the visual cortex, leading scientists to conclude that parts of the brain other than the cortex receive and help process visual messages (Gazzaniga et al., 1994; Zeki, 1992, 1993).

Finally, studies of monkeys show that information from the retina about movement and depth goes to one area of the visual cortex, whereas detailed information about color and shape goes to nearby, but different, areas of the visual cortex (Hubel & Livingstone, 1987; Livingstone & Hubel, 1988a; Zeki, 1992, 1993). As a result, researchers contend that parts of the visual cortex specialize in color vision, other parts are used in detecting motion, and still others see specific forms in motion. If the color area is damaged, patients develop a special type of colorblindness called *achromatopsia*, in which they can neither see color nor remember color experience they had before the injury. In all other ways, however, they can see as well as anybody else—further evidence that many different areas in the brain process visual information.

Our knowledge about the way visual information is coded and relayed to the brain has some valuable practical applications. For example, in a condition known as *glaucoma*, fluid pressure inside the eye builds up and can cause permanent damage to the optic nerve and consequent loss of vision. Recent research indicates that people in the early stages of glaucoma tend to lose their dim-light vision before any permanent damage is done to the optic nerve or to daylight vision. Thus, researchers are hopeful that loss of dim-light vision can be used as an early warning sign of glaucoma, prompting physicians to initiate treatment long before there is any permanent damage to daylight vision (Dadona, Hendrickson, & Quigley, 1991).



**Figure 3-9**
**The neural connections of the visual system.** Messages about the blue-colored area in the left visual field of each eye travel to the right occipital lobe; information about the red area in the right visual field of each eye goes to the left occipital lobe. The crossover point is the *optic chiasm.*

*Source:* Adapted from "The Split Brain of Man," by Michael S. Gazzaniga. Copyright© 1967 by Scientific American, Inc.

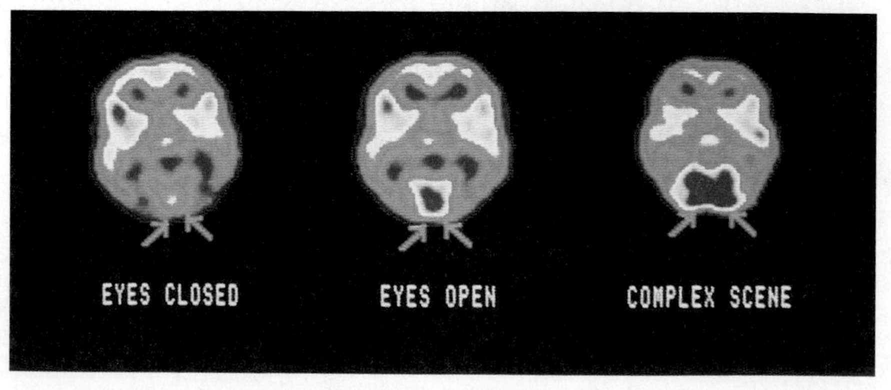


Nerve fibers from each eye cross to opposite sides of the brain, enabling the optic nerves to carry visual information to different parts of the brain. As these PET scans show, the more complex the scene, the more the visual areas of the brain are engaged in visual processing. (High levels of brain activity are shown as yellow and red; low levels of activity are shown as green and blue.)

## Color Vision

Like most mammals, humans can see a range of colors. In the following pages, we will first explore characteristics of color vision and then consider how the eyes convert light energy into sensations of color.

**Hue** The aspect of color that corresponds to names such as red, green, and blue.

**Saturation** The vividness or richness of a hue.

**Brightness** The nearness of a color to white as opposed to black.

**PROPERTIES OF COLOR** Look at the color solid in Figure 3-10. What do you see? Most people say they see a number of different colors: some oranges, some yellows, some reds, and so forth. Psychologists call these different colors **hues**, and to a great extent, what hues you see depends on the wavelength of the light reaching your eyes (see Figure 3-4).

Now look at the triangle of green colors in Figure 3-10. Although each color patch on the triangle is the same hue, the blue color is deepest or richest toward the left side of the triangle. Psychologists refer to the vividness or richness of a hue as its **saturation**.

Finally, notice that the colors near the top of the color patches are almost white, while those close to the bottom are almost black. This is the dimension of **brightness**, which depends largely on the strength of the light entering your eyes. If you squint your eyes and look at the color solid, you will reduce the apparent brightness of all the colors in the solid, and many of them will appear to become black.

Hue, saturation, and brightness are three separate aspects of our experience of color. Although people can distinguish only about 150 hues (Coren, Porac, & Ward, 1984), gradations of saturation and brightness within those 150 hues allow us to see more than 300,000 different colors (Hochberg, 1978; Kaufman, 1979). Some of this variety is captured in Figure 3-10.

**THEORIES OF COLOR VISION** Think for a moment about what you already know about color vision. You know that roughly 8 million cones in the retina are responsible for color vision. And you also know that we can distinguish approximately 300,000 different kinds of colors. But in the fovea there are only about 150,000 cones. So there are not enough cones in the fovea to have even one cone for every color! Somehow a relatively few cones must be able to combine their messages in a way that provides both the full range of color and the clear, sharp images we perceive when we look directly at objects. How does this occur?

**4.** How many different colors can we distinguish?

One hint at an answer to this question comes from the fact that for centuries scientists have known that it is possible to produce all 150 basic hues by mixing together only a few lights of different colors (see Figure 3-11).

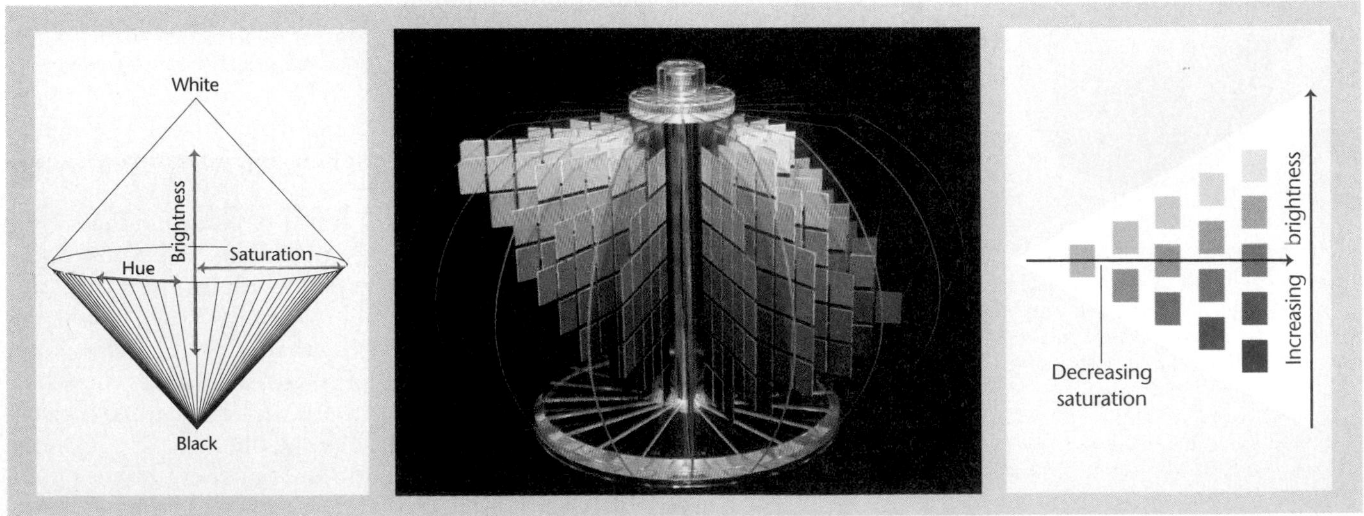


**Figure 3-10**
**The color solid.** The dimension of *hue* is represented around the circumference. *Saturation* ranges along the radius from the inside to the outside of the solid. *Brightness* varies along the vertical axis. The drawing (bottom right) illustrates this schematically.

**Additive color mixing** The process of mixing lights of different wavelengths to create new hues.

**Subtractive color mixing** The process of mixing pigments, each of which absorbs some wavelengths of light and reflects others.

**Trichromatic theory** Theory of color vision that holds that all color perception derives from three different color receptors in the retina (usually red, green, and blue receptors).

**Colorblindness** Partial or total inability to perceive hues.

**Opponent-process theory** Theory of color vision that holds that three sets of color receptors (yellow-blue, red-green, black-white) respond to determine the color you experience.

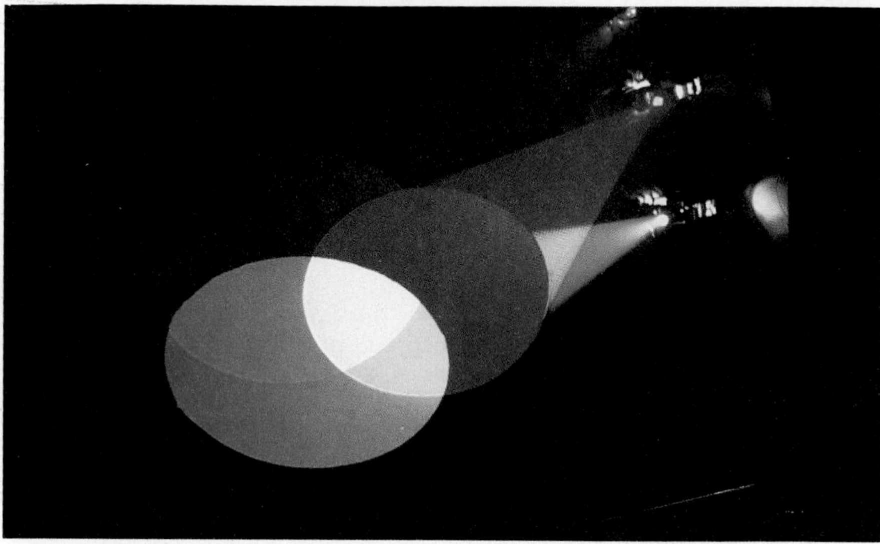

**Figure 3-11**
**Additive color mixing.** Mixing light waves is an *additive process*. When red and green lights are combined, the resulting hue is yellow. Adding blue light to the other two results in white light.

**Figure 3-12**
**Subtractive color mixing.** The process of mixing paint pigments rather than lights is a *subtractive process,* because the pigments absorb some wavelengths and reflect others. A mixture of the three primary pigments (red, yellow, and blue) absorbs all wavelengths, producing black.

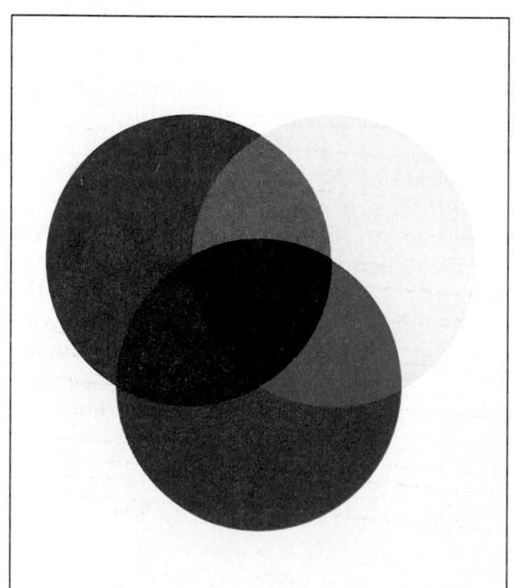

Specifically, red, green, and blue lights, the *primary colors* for light mixtures, can be combined to create any hue. For example, red and green lights combine to give yellow; red and blue lights combine to give purple. Combining red, green, and blue lights in equal intensities gives white. Television picture tubes use this principle to provide a full range of colors: If you look closely at the screen, you will see that the picture is actually made up of tiny red, green, and blue dots that blend together to give all possible hues. The process of mixing lights of different wavelengths is called **additive color mixing**, since each light adds additional wavelengths to the mixture.

The rules for mixing paints (or pigments) differ from those for lights (see Figure 3-12). For example, mixing red and green paints will give you gray, not yellow. That is because the red paint absorbs light from the blue end of the spectrum (see Figure 3-4), whereas the blue paint absorbs light from the red end of the spectrum. Together they absorb all the light, leaving only a dull gray surface. This is called **subtractive color mixing**, since each paint subtracts or absorbs light from various portions of the spectrum. For paint pigments, the primary colors are red, yellow, and blue.

In the 1800s, the German physiologist Hermann von Helmholtz drew on his knowledge of additive color mixing to propose that the eye contains some cones that are sensitive to reds, others that pick up greens, and still others that respond most strongly to blue-violet. According to this view, color experiences in the brain come from mixing the signals from the three receptors. Helmholtz's explanation of color vision is known as the **trichromatic theory**.

Trichromatic theory accounts for some kinds of **colorblindness**—the partial or total inability to perceive hues (see Figure 3-13). Yet because it falls short of explaining all color vision experiences, including afterimages (see Figure 3-14), another German scientist, Ewald Hering, proposed an alternative theory in 1878. Hering's **opponent-process theory** postulated that our visual response system comprised three pairs of color receptors: a yellow-blue pair and a red-green pair that determine the hue a person sees, and a black-white pair that assesses the brightness of colors. Contemporary scientific research has established that both trichromatic and opponent-process theories of color vision are valid, although at two different stages in the visual pro-

**Sound waves** Changes in pressure caused when molecules of air or fluid collide with one another and then move apart again.

**Figure 3-13**
**Experiencing colorblindness.** People who are colorblind have a partial or total inability to perceive *hue.* To show what this means in everyday life, we have printed a photo of a hot-air balloon both in normal color (left) and as someone with red-green colorblindness would see it (right).

cess. As trichromatic theory asserts, there are three kinds of cones for color (some are most sensitive to violet-blue light, others are most responsive to green light, and still others are most sensitive to yellow light—not red light, as Helmholtz contended). Opponent-process theory comes into effect higher up the visual pathway, where some neurons respond only to brightness, not to color. Taken together, trichromatic and opponent mechanisms in the visual system can explain almost all color phenomena.

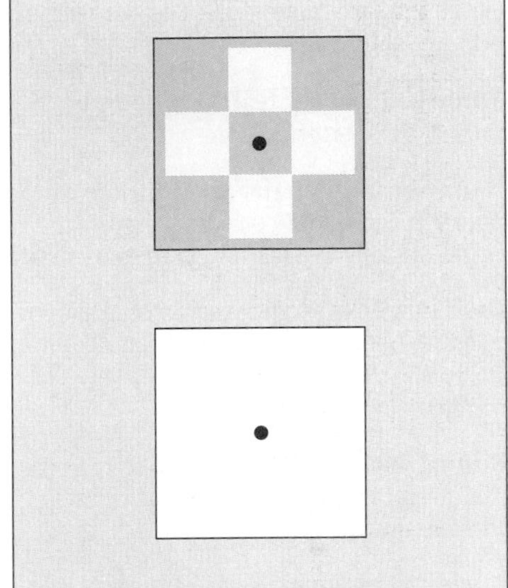

**Figure 3-14**
**Complementary afterimages.** An afterimage always appears in complementary colors. After staring at the center of the top square for about 30 seconds and then shifting your gaze to the center dot of the bottom square, you will see *complementary afterimages.* The small yellow squares will appear as blue, and the blue squares will appear as yellow.

## HEARING

An ancient question asks, "If a tree falls in the forest and no one is there, does the tree make a sound?" A psychologist would answer, "There are sound waves, but there is no sound or noise." Sounds and noise are psychological experiences created by the brain in response to stimulation. In this section, we will examine hearing, an important sense that is sometimes shortchanged because of the extensive focus on vision. First, we will see what kinds of stimuli cause us to hear sounds, and then we will explore how those stimuli are converted into neural signals.

### Sound

The physical stimuli that prompt the sense of hearing are **sound waves** — changes in pressure caused when molecules of air or fluid collide with one another and then move apart again, transmitting energy at every collision. The simplest sound wave—what we hear as a pure tone—can be pictured as a sine wave (see Figure 3-15). The tuning fork vibrates, causing the mol-

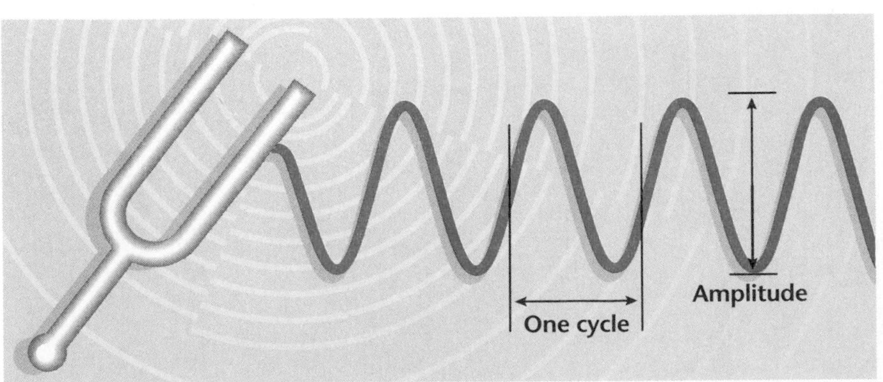


**Figure 3-15**
**Sound waves.** As it vibrates, the tuning fork alternately compresses and expands the molecules of air, creating a *sound wave.*

**Frequency** The number of cycles per second in a wave; in sound, the primary determinant of pitch.

**Hertz (Hz)** Cycles per second; unit of measurement for the frequency of waves.

**Pitch** Auditory experience corresponding primarily to frequency of sound vibrations, resulting in a higher or lower tone.

**Decibel** Unit of measurement for the loudness of sounds.

**Amplitude** The magnitude of a wave; in sound, the primary determinant of loudness.

**Overtones** Tones that result from sound waves that are multiples of the basic tone; primary determinant of timbre.

**Timbre** Quality or texture of sound; caused by overtones.

**Hammer, anvil, stirrup** The three small bones in the middle ear that relay vibrations of the eardrum to the inner ear.

**Oval window** Membrane across the opening between the middle ear and inner ear that conducts vibrations to the cochlea.

**Round window** Membrane between the middle ear and inner ear that equalizes pressure in the inner ear.

**Cochlea** Part of the inner ear containing fluid that vibrates, which in turn causes the basilar membrane to vibrate.

**Basilar membrane** Vibrating membrane in the cochlea of the inner ear; it contains sense receptors for sound.

ecules of air first to compress and then to expand. The **frequency** of the waves is measured in cycles per second, expressed in a unit called **hertz (Hz)**. Frequency primarily determines the **pitch** of the sound—how high or how low it is. The human ear responds to frequencies from about 20 Hz to 20,000 Hz. A double bass can reach down to about 50 Hz, a piano as high as 5,000 Hz.

The perceived *loudness* of a sound, measured in **decibels** corresponds closely to the **amplitude** of the wave. Prolonged exposure to sounds above 85 decibels—an air raid siren, a jackhammer, live rock music—can cause permanent damage to the ears. Sound waves also resonate with **overtones,** waves that are different multiples of the frequency of the basic tone. A violin string, for example, not only vibrates as a whole, it also vibrates in halves, thirds, quarters, and so on, all at the same time. This complex pattern of overtones determines the **timbre**, or "texture" of the sound.

## The Ear

Hearing begins when sound waves strike the eardrum (see Figure 3-16) and cause it to vibrate. The quivering of the eardrum causes three tiny bones in the middle ear—called the **hammer**, the **anvil**, and the **stirrup**—to hit each other in sequence and to carry the vibrations to the inner ear. The last of these three bones, the stirrup, is attached to a membrane called the **oval window**. Just below the oval window is another membrane, called the **round window**, which equalizes the pressure in the inner ear when the stirrup strikes the oval window.

The air waves are magnified during their trip through the middle ear. Thus, when the oval window starts to vibrate at the touch of the stirrup, it has a powerful effect on the inner ear. There the vibrations are transmitted to the fluid inside a snail-shaped structure called the **cochlea**. The cochlea is divided lengthwise by the **basilar membrane** (see Figure 3-16). The basilar membrane is stiffer near the oval and round windows and gets gradually more flexible toward its other end. When the fluid in the cochlea begins to move, the basilar membrane is pushed up and down, rippling in response to the movement of the cochlear fluid.

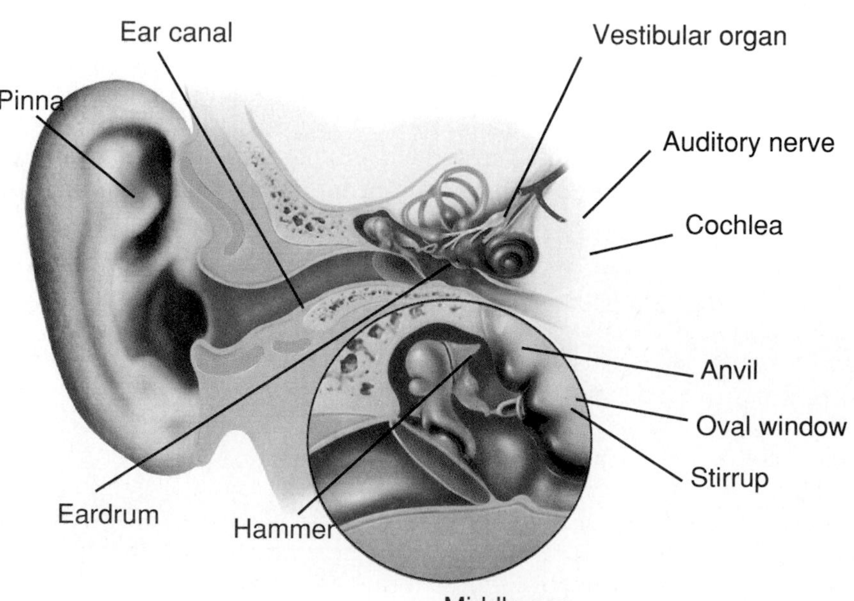


**Figure 3-16**
**The structure of the human ear.** This drawing shows details of the middle ear.

*Source:* Adapted from Carol Donner.

Lying on top of the basilar membrane, and moving in sync with it, is the **organ of Corti**. It is here that the messages from the sound waves finally reach the receptor cells for the sense of hearing: thousands of tiny hair cells that are embedded in the organ of Corti (Spoendlin & Schrott, 1989). As you can see in Figure 3-17, each hair cell is topped by a bundle of fibers. These fibers are pushed and pulled by the vibrations of the basilar membrane. If the fibers bend by so much as 100 trillionths of a meter, the receptor cell sends a signal to be transmitted through the **auditory nerve** to the brain. The brain pools the information from thousands of these cells to create sounds. Scientists now know that each hair cell not only sends messages *to* the brain but also receives messages *from* the brain. The brain apparently can send the hair cells signals that reduce their sensitivity to sound in general or to sound waves of particular frequencies. The brain can, in effect, "shut down" the ears somewhat, but for what purpose remains one of the mysteries of research on hearing (Hudspeth, 1983; Kim, 1985).

**Organ of Corti** Structure on the surface of the basilar membrane that contains the receptor cells for hearing.

**Auditory nerve** The bundle of neurons that carries signals from each ear to the brain.

**NEURAL CONNECTIONS** The sense of hearing is truly bilateral. Each ear sends messages to both cerebral hemispheres. The switching station where the nerve fibers from the ears cross over is in the medulla, part of the hindbrain (see Figure 2-6). From the medulla, other nerve fibers carry the messages from the ears to the higher parts of the brain. Some messages go to the brain centers that coordinate the movements of the eyes, head, and ears. Others travel through the reticular formation (which we examined in the previous chapter), which probably tacks on a few special "wake-up" or "ho-hum" postscripts to the sound messages. The primary destinations, of course, are the auditory areas in the temporal lobes of the two cerebral hemispheres.

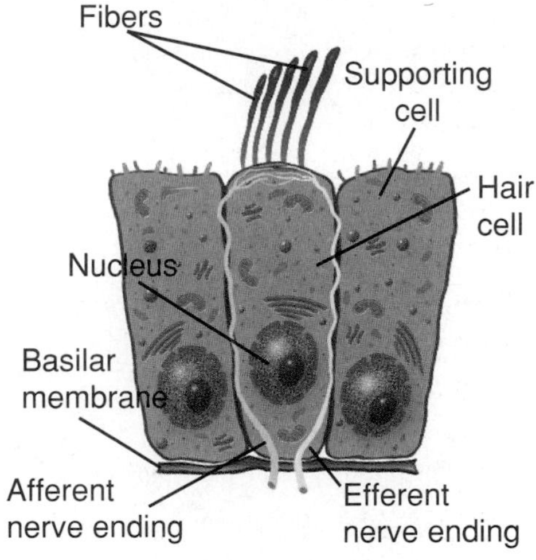


**Figure 3-17**
**A detailed drawing of a hair cell, the receptor for hearing.** At the top of each hair cell is a bundle of fibers. If the fibers bend so much as 100 trillionths of a meter, the receptor cells transmit a sensory message to the brain.

*Source:* Adapted from "The Hair Cells of the Inner Ear," by A.J. Hudspeth, ©1983 by Scientific American, Inc. All rights reserved.

## Theories of Hearing

The thousands of tiny hair cells in the organ of Corti send messages about the infinite variations in the frequency, amplitude, and overtones of sound waves. But how are the different sound-wave patterns coded into neural messages? One aspect of sound, loudness, seems to depend on how many neurons are activated—the more cells that fire, the louder the sound seems to be. The coding of messages about pitch is more complicated. There are two basic views of pitch discrimination: place theory and frequency theory. *Place theory* states that the brain determines pitch by noting the place on the basilar membrane at which the message is strongest. This theory proposes that for any given sound wave, there is a point on the basilar membrane at which vibrations are most intense. Thus, high-frequency sounds cause the greatest vibration at the stiff base of the basilar membrane; low-frequency sounds do the same at the opposite end (Zwislocki, 1981). The brain detects the location of most intense nerve-cell activity and uses this to determine the pitch of a sound.

The *frequency theory* of pitch discrimination holds that the frequency of vibrations of the basilar membrane as a *whole*, not just *parts* of it, is translated into an equivalent frequency of nerve impulses. Thus, if a hair bundle is pulled or pushed rapidly, its hair cell sends a high-frequency message to the brain. Neurons cannot fire as rapidly as the frequency of the highest-pitched sound that can be heard, however, and this problem has led theorists to modify the frequency theory to include a *volley principle*. According to this view, auditory neurons can fire in sequence: One neuron fires, then a second one, then a third. By then, the first neuron has had time to recover and can fire again. In this way, the three neurons together can send a more rapid series of impulses to the brain than any single neuron could send by itself.

Because neither place theory nor frequency theory alone fully explains pitch discrimination, some combination of the two is needed. Frequency theory, for example, accounts for the ear's responses to frequencies up to about 4,000 Hz. Above that, however, place theory provides a better explanation of what is happening.

**Hearing Disorders** Because the mechanisms that allow us to hear are so subtle and complicated, the number of possible problems that can compromise our hearing is large. Deafness is one of the most common concerns. Some instances of deafness result from defects in the outer or middle ear—for instance, the eardrum may be damaged, or the small bones of the middle ear may not work properly. Other cases of deafness occur because the basilar membrane in the cochlea or the auditory nerve itself has been damaged. Disease, infections, and even long-term exposure to loud noise can harm the ear and cause partial or complete deafness. In fact, of the estimated 28 million Americans with some loss of hearing, approximately 10 million are the victims of protracted loud noise on the job or at home, with the chief culprits leaf blowers, chain saws, snowmobiles, and personal stereo systems (Leary, 1990).

Far from not hearing enough sound, some people hear too much of the wrong kind of sound and suffer greatly because of it. Almost everybody has at some time heard a steady, high-pitched hum that persists even in the quietest room. This sound seems to come from inside the head. In about 1 percent of the population, this tone, called a *tinnitus*, becomes unbearably loud—like the screeching of subway brakes—and does not go away (Dunkle, 1982). In a few cases, tinnitus is caused by blood flowing through vessels near the inner ear. Generally, though, tinnitus originates somewhere in the brain.

Unfortunately, medical research has not yet found a cure for tinnitus, although many people who suffer from this problem gain some relief from *masking*. In this process, a device mounted in the ear much like a hearing aid produces a sound that mutes the annoying hum. Oddly enough, in about a third of the cases, just about any weak sound has the desired effect (McFadden & Wightman, 1983). The tinnitus often remains masked for seconds or even minutes after the masking tone has been withdrawn. Researchers are at a loss to explain how masking devices work, but it is clear that they do not simply drown out the tinnitus. Another line of attack has been drugs, but none tested so far have not proved to be very effective.

## THE OTHER SENSES

Psychologists and other scientists have focused most of their attention on the senses of vision and hearing because humans rely primarily on these two senses to gather information about their environment. However, we also use other senses, such as smell, taste, balance, motion, pressure, temperature, and pain. Let's look briefly at each of these senses, starting with the chemical senses, smell and taste.

### Smell

Which sense is more sensitive, taste or smell?

The sense of smell in humans is extremely sensitive. According to one estimate, it is about 10,000 times as sensitive as that of taste (Moncrieff, 1951). Only a few molecules of a substance reaching the smell receptors are necessary to cause humans to perceive an odor. Certain substances, such as decayed cabbage, lemons, and rotten eggs, can be detected in minute amounts. As another example, mercaptan, a foul-smelling substance added to natural gas, can be smelled in concentrations as small as 1 part per 50 billion parts of air.

Despite this great sensitivity, the sense of smell undergoes adaptation much like the other senses. The perfume that was so pleasant to its wearer early in the evening seems to have "worn off" after a few hours. Others continue to notice it, however. Similarly, the enticing aroma that led you to a restaurant seems to have disappeared by the time your meal begins. However, it continues to draw other patrons to the restaurant. Fortunately, the ability to smell some substances—like the mercaptan added to natural gas—adapts more slowly than our ability to smell other substances.

**Olfactory epithelium** Nasal membranes containing receptor cells sensitive to odors.

**Olfactory bulb** The smell center in the brain.

Most mammals, including humans, have two different sensory systems devoted to the sense of smell. The first allows us to detect and discriminate among common odors. This branch of our olfactory (smell) system helps us to tell the difference between the citrus scents of lemon and orange and the sour smell of spoiled milk. The second branch of the smell sense is used in communicating sexual, aggressive, or territorial scent signals. As we will see, even though humans have this system, it is much more important to nonhuman animals.

Certain animal species rely more on their sense of smell than humans do. This dog has been trained to use its keen sense of smell to detect bombs hidden in luggage.

**DETECTING COMMON ODORS** Our sense of smell is activated by a complex protein produced in a nasal gland. As we breathe, a fine mist of this protein, called *odorant binding protein (OBP)*, is sprayed through a duct in the tip of the nose. The protein binds with airborne molecules that then activate the receptors for this sense, located high in each nasal cavity in a patch of tissue called the **olfactory epithelium** (see Figure 3-18). The olfactory epithelium is only about one-half the size of a postage stamp, but it is packed with millions of receptor cells. Interestingly, these nerve cells die and are replaced by new ones every few weeks (Graziadei, Levine, & Graziadei, 1979)—the only neurons known to be replaced in the human body.

The axons from these millions of receptors go directly to the **olfactory bulb**, where some recoding takes place. From the olfactory bulb, messages are routed to the temporal lobes of the brain, resulting in our awareness of the smells. But messages are also routed to lower brain centers such as the amygdala and the hippocampus, which, as we saw in the previous chapter, figure prominently in emotion and memory.

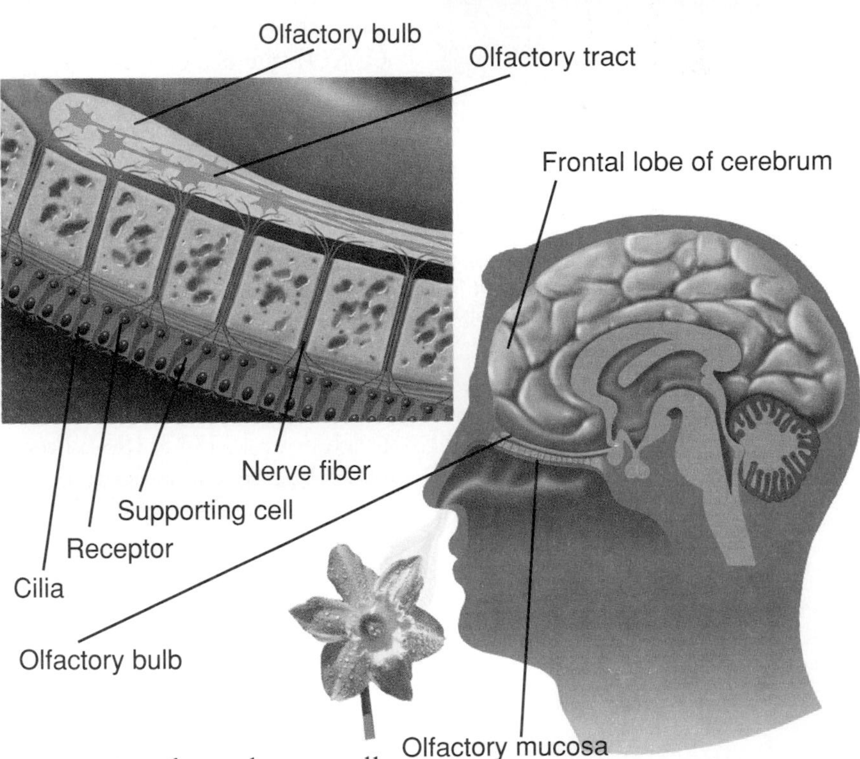


**Figure 3-18**
**The human olfactory system.** The sense of smell is dependent on odor molecules in the air reaching the olfactory receptors located inside the top of the nose. Inhaling and exhaling odor molecules from food does much to give food its flavorful "taste."

*Source:* From *Human Anatomy and Physiology* by Anthony J. Gaudin and Kenneth C. Jones. Copyright © 1989 by Holt, Rinehart, and Winston, Inc. Reprinted by permission.

Researchers have uncovered some interesting facts about smell. First, although people can discriminate a large number of odors, they find it much more difficult to identify the sources of many familiar odors. For example, more than 90 percent of people can correctly identify the smell of coffee, but only 80 percent can identify leather, only about 70 percent can identify bubble gum or mustard, and 60 percent can identify bologna. Less than 50 percent of people can correctly identify turpentine, vinegar, honey, and vanilla extract (Cain, 1982; Engen, 1982).

Odor sensitivity also appears to be related to gender. Numerous studies confirm that women generally have a better sense of smell than men do. For example, William Doty and his research team (1984) found that women were better at determining the sex of people on the basis of breath

**Pheromone** Chemical that communicates information to other organisms through smell.

**Vomeronasal organ (VNO)** Location of receptors for pheromones in the roof of the nasal cavity.

odor. A subsequent study found that women were also better at identifying a set of 40 common smells (Doty et al., 1985). Women were also better at identifying the wider range of smells used in the Cain (1982) study.

Age also makes a difference in ability to detect and identify odors (Doty, 1989). Generally, the ability to smell is sharpest during the early adult years (ages 20 to 40) (Doty et al., 1984). Of the people tested by Doty and his colleagues, one-quarter of those over the age of 65 and one-half of those over the age of 80 had completely lost their ability to smell. The complete loss of smell, known as *anosmia*, can be devastating. In almost all cases, it causes people to lose interest in food; in some cases, it can even reduce the desire for sexual activity. And it can also be dangerous: People who are unable to smell are unable to detect such things as escaped natural gas, spilled gasoline, spoiled food, and smoke.

**PHEROMONE COMMUNICATION** One of the more exotic aspects of the sense of smell is the fact that some animals use smells for communication. Certain chemicals called **pheromones** can have quite specific and powerful effects on behavior. For example, ants use pheromones to mark trails, and queen bees have a distinctive smell that sets them apart from all other bees. Many animals, including domestic dogs and wolves, also use pheromones to mark their territory. Moreover, pheromones signal sexual receptivity in female mice, rats, cattle, and pigs. Research indicates that pheromones are sensed by receptors in the **vomeronasal organ (VNO)** that is located in the roof of the nasal cavity. The VNO sends messages to a second olfactory bulb that is specialized for pheromonal communications (Bartoshuk & Beauchamp, 1994; Wysocki & Meredith, 1987).

An example of pheromones in the animal world: Queen bees have a distinctive smell that sets them apart from other bees. It is unclear what role, if any, pheromones play in the control of human behavior.

It is intriguing to note that humans, like other mammals, have a VNO (Takami et al., 1993), but so far no one has conclusively established what role (if any) pheromones play in human interaction. For example, there is no evidence that pheromones affect human sexual response (Quadagno, 1987). However, we do know that women who live together tend over time to synchronize their menstrual cycles (McClintock, 1971), and there is considerable experimental evidence from studies involving both humans and nonhumans supports the contention that *menstrual synchronicity* occurs as a result of some kind of pheromone communication (McClintock, 1978, 1984; Preti et al., 1986; M.J. Russell et al., 1980).

We also know that humans are capable of some other remarkable feats involving the sense of smell, although we do not yet know which of the two olfactory systems is responsible. For example, mothers can identify their babies by smell after only a few hours of contact (R.H. Porter, Cernich, & McLaughlin, 1983). In turn, newborn infants can discriminate between their mothers' body odors and the odors of other mothers (Schaal, 1986), and they will even turn their heads toward the scent of a perfume that has been worn by their mothers while ignoring a different perfume (Schleidt & Genzel, 1990). Scent recognition may even bind families throughout life: Adults can recognize clothing worn by their relatives, even after they have been separated for several years (R.H. Porter et al., 1986).

## Taste

To understand taste, we must first distinguish it from *flavor*. The flavor of food arises from a complex combination of taste and smell. If you hold your nose when you eat, most of the food's flavor will disappear, even though you will still experience sensations of *bitterness*, *saltiness*, *sourness*, or *sweetness*. In other words, you will get the taste, but not the flavor. The importance of flavor is clear from a study conducted by Mozel et al. (1969). When subjects were allowed to taste and smell substances dropped on their tongues, more than half were able to identify correctly coffee, cherry, garlic, root beer, and chocolate. But when they were prevented from smelling the substances, only 1 to 3 percent of the subjects could identify those same substances. The effect was much less pronounced for strong-tasting substances such as vinegar, whiskey, and lemon; more than 35 percent of subjects could still correctly identify those substances without using smell.

The receptor cells for the sense of taste are housed in the **taste buds**, most of which are found on the tip, sides, and back of the tongue. An adult has about 10,000 taste buds. The number of taste buds decreases with age, a fact that partly explains why older people often lose interest in food—they simply cannot taste it as well as they used to.

The taste buds are embedded in the tongue's **papillae**, bumps that you can see if you look at your tongue in the mirror. Each taste bud contains a cluster of taste receptors or taste cells (see Figure 3-19), which die and are replaced about every 7 days. The chemical substances in the foods we eat dissolve in saliva and fall into the crevices between the papillae of the tongue, where they come into contact with the taste receptors. The chemical interaction between food substances and the taste cells causes adjacent neurons to fire, sending a nerve impulse to the parietal lobe of the brain and to the limbic system. This happens very fast: People can accurately identify a taste within one-tenth of a second after something salty or sweet has touched the tongue (Cain, 1981). The same nerves that carry messages about taste also conduct information about chewing, swallowing, and the temperature and texture of food.

We experience only four primary taste qualities: sweet, sour, salty, and bitter. All other tastes derive from combinations of these four. The tip of the tongue is most sensitive to sweetness and saltiness, the back to bitterness, and the sides to sourness. But each area can distinguish all four qualities to some degree. The middle of the tongue does not respond to taste at all.

Taste, like the other senses, also displays adaptation. You might have noticed that when you first start eating salted peanuts, the saltiness is quite strong, but after a while it becomes less noticeable. Furthermore, exposure to one quality of taste can modify other taste sensations in a process called *cross-adaptation* (Bartoshuk, 1974). For example, many people find that after eating fresh artichokes, other foods, as well as plain water, tend to have a sweet taste. Conversely, after brushing your teeth in the morning, you may notice that your orange juice has lost its sweetness. That's partly because toothpaste contains an ingredient that reduces our sensitivity to sweetness and heightens our sensitivity to the sourness of the juice's citric acid.

**Taste buds** Structures on the tongue that contain the receptor cells for taste.

**Papillae** Small bumps on the tongue that contain taste buds.

**Kinesthetic senses** Senses of muscle movement, posture, and strain on muscles and joints.

**Vestibular senses** Senses of equilibrium and body position in space.

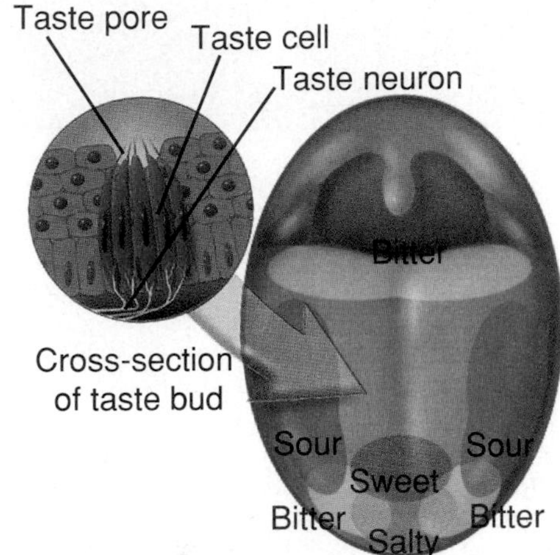


**Figure 3-19**
**The structure of a taste bud.** The sensory receptors for taste are found primarily on the tongue. Taste cells can detect only sweet, sour, salty, and bitter qualities. All other tastes result from different combinations of these qualities.

## Kinesthetic and Vestibular Senses

The **kinesthetic senses** provide information about the speed and direction of our movement in space. More specifically, they relay information concerning muscle movement, changes in posture, and strain on muscles and joints. Specialized nerve endings attached to muscles and to tendons (which connect muscle to bones) provide constant feedback from the stretching and contraction of individual muscles. The information from these receptors travels via the spinal cord to the brain, where it is ultimately represented on the cortex of the parietal lobes, the same area of the cortex where the sense of touch is represented.

The **vestibular senses** provide information about our orientation or position in space. We use this information to determine which way is up and which way is down. Birds and fish also rely on these senses to determine in which direction they are heading when they cannot see well. Like hearing, the vestibular senses originate in the inner ear, and the sense organs are hair cells that send their signals out over the auditory nerve. There are actually two kinds of vestibular sensation. The first concerns the speed and direction of body rotation. The second gives us information about *gravitation and movement* forward and backward, up and down. The nerve impulses from the several vestibular organs travel to the brain along the auditory nerve, but their ultimate destinations in the brain are still something of a mystery. Certain messages from the vestibular system go to the cerebellum, which controls many of the reflexes involved in coordinated movement. Others reach the areas that regulate to the internal body organs, and some find their way to the parietal lobe of the cerebral cortex for analysis and response.

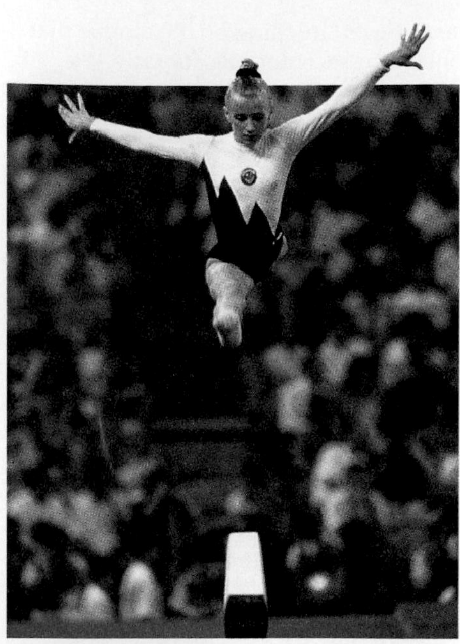

This Olympic gymnast is utilizing information provided by both her kinesthetic and her vestibular senses. Her kinesthetic senses are relaying messages pertaining to muscle strain and movements; her vestibular senses are supplying feedback about her body position in space.

## Sensations of Motion

Motion sickness arises in the vestibular organs. Certain kinds of motion (riding in ships, cars, airplanes, even on camels and elephants) trigger strong reactions in some people. According to one theory, motion sickness stems from discrepancies between visual information and vestibular sensations. To experience this conflict between visual and vestibular information, try reading a book while your body is being jolted up and down in a bus.

Occasionally the vestibular sense can be completely overwhelmed by visual information. This is what happens when we watch an automobile chase scene that was filmed from inside a moving car. We feel a sensation of movement because our eyes are telling our brain that we are moving, even though the organs in our inner ear insist that we are sitting still. In fact, the sense of motion can be so strong that some people experience motion sickness while sitting absolutely still as they watch a movie filmed from an airplane or a boat! This visual trick has an advantage: People who have had one or even both vestibular organs removed can function normally as long as they have visual cues on which to rely.

## The Skin Senses

Our skin is actually our largest sense organ. A person 6 feet tall has about 21 square feet of skin. Aside from protecting us from the environment, holding in body fluids, and regulating our internal temperature, the skin is a sense organ with numerous nerve receptors distributed in varying concentrations throughout its surface. The nerve fibers from all these receptors travel to the brain by two routes. Some information goes through the medulla and the thalamus and from there to the sensory cortex in the parietal lobe of the brain—which is presumably where our experiences of touch and pressure and so on arise. Other information goes through the thalamus and then on to the reticular formation, which, as we saw in the previous chapter, is responsible for arousing the nervous system or quieting it down.

The various skin receptors give rise to what are called the *cutaneous sensations* of pressure, temperature, and pain. But the relationship between the receptors and our sensory experiences is a subtle one. Researchers believe that our brains draw on complex information about the *patterns* of activity on many different receptors to detect and discriminate among skin sensations. For example, there are cold fibers that speed their firing rate as the skin cools down and slow down their firing when the skin heats up. Conversely, there are warm fibers that accelerate their firing rate when the skin gets warm and slow down when the skin cools. The brain may use the combined information from these two sets of fibers as the basis for determining skin temperature. If both sets are activated at once, the brain may read their combined pattern of firings as "hot." Thus, you might sometimes think that you are touching something hot when you are really touching something warm and something cool at the same time. This phenomenon is known as *paradoxical heat* (see Figure 3-20).

The skin senses are remarkably sensitive. For example, skin displacement of as little as .00004 inch can result in a sensation of pressure. Moreover, various parts of the body differ greatly in their sensitivity to pressure: Your face and fingertips are extremely sensitive, while your legs, feet, and back are much less so (Weinstein, 1968). It is no wonder, then, that when we examine things with our hands, we tend to do so with our fingertips. It is this remarkable sensitivity in our fingertips that makes possible Braille touch reading, which requires identifying patterns of tiny raised dots distributed over a very small area.

Like other senses, the skin senses undergo various kinds of sensory adaptation. When we first sit in a hot bath, it may be too hot to tolerate, but in a few minutes, we adapt to the heat, just as our eyes adapt to darkness. Similarly, when we put on an article of clothing that is a bit tight, we may feel uncomfortable at first but not even notice it later. How soon this adaptation occurs, or whether it occurs at all, appears to depend on how large an area of the skin is being stimulated and the intensity of the pressure (Geldard, 1972): The larger the area and the more intense the pressure, the longer it takes for us to adapt.

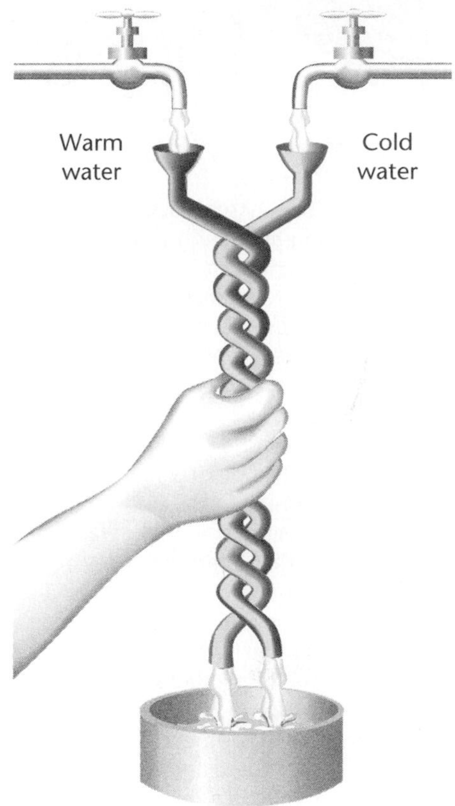


**Figure 3-20**
**Paradoxical heat.** Touching a warm pipe and a cold pipe at the same time causes two sets of skin receptors to signal at once to the brain. The brain reads their combined pattern of firings as "hot," a phenomenon known as *paradoxical heat.*

## Pain

The sensation of pain is an extraordinarily complex sensory event. For example, it seems reasonable to assume that body damage causes pain, yet in many cases actual physical injury is not accompanied by pain. And conversely, people may experience a clear sense of pain even though they have not suffered any physical harm.

We might also assume that pain occurs when some kind of pain receptor is stimulated. But there is no simple relationship between pain receptors and the experience of pain. In fact, scientists have had great difficulty even finding pain receptors. The most likely candidate for a pain receptor is the simple *free nerve ending*, but this receptor also contributes to our sense of touch or pressure. Perhaps chemicals released from damaged tissues somehow convert free nerve endings from touch and pressure sensors into pain sensors.

Because pain also differs from the other senses in the ways in which people react to it, some psychologists question whether pain should even be considered a basic sensation like pressure and temperature (Melzack, 1992). For example, certain people appear to be completely insensitive to pain (Manfredi et al., 1981). In one famous case, a young Canadian girl felt nothing when she inadvertently bit off part of her tongue and suffered third-degree burns as a result of kneeling on a hot radiator (Baxter & Olszewski, 1960; McMurray, 1950). Moreover, people perceive and react to pain in strikingly different ways. If you burn your hand, you might calmly run cold water over the burn; someone else might scream out loud. Our beliefs about pain can also affect our experience of it. For example, one study (DiMatteo & Friedman, 1982) found that hospital patients who believed that a particular medical procedure was not painful actually reported experiencing less pain. Finally, emotional or motivational conditions have an impact on our perception of pain. Beecher (1972) noted that only 25 percent of soldiers wounded during battle requested pain medication, whereas more than 80 percent of surgical patients asked for painkillers for comparable "wounds." Athletes injured on the field of play often feel no pain until the excitement of competition has passed.

A person reading in Braille uses his or her fingertips because they are highly sensitive.

# HIGHLIGHTS

## The Importance of Touch

Of all our senses, touch may be the most comforting. By touching and being touched by others, we bridge, at least momentarily, our isolation and our loneliness by giving and receiving tenderness and care. This explains to some extent why in most societies hellos and goodbyes are accompanied by gestures involving touch—shaking hands, brushing lips against cheeks, or hugging—and why lovers express their affection by kissing, holding hands, and caressing.

Indeed, research such as psychologist Harry Harlow's work with monkeys has affirmed the vital importance of touch in human development. In a series of classic experiments, Harlow (1958; Harlow & Zimmerman, 1959) showed that infant primates deprived of maternal contact suffered psychologically and physically (this research is explored in greater detail in the chapter titled "Motivation and Emotion"). More recent research that examines the neurochemical effects of skin-to-skin contact suggests that the experience of being touched may play a crucial role in human development: It may directly affect the growth of an infant's mind and body. In one study (Field, 1986), premature infants who were massaged three times a day for 15 minutes at a time gained weight much more quickly than did a control group that was left untouched. The massaged babies were subsequently more responsive to faces and rattles and were generally more active than the other babies. Because of their comparatively rapid growth, the massaged infants were discharged from the hospital an average of 6 days earlier than the nonmassaged infants were. And 8 months later, the massaged infants maintained their weight advantage while performing better on tests of motor and mental ability. Significantly, the massaged infants did not eat more than the others: Their accelerated weight gain appears to be due solely to the effect of physical touch on their metabolism.

This new research has significant implications for hospital care of premature infants. Traditionally, these babies have been placed in incubators, fed intravenously, and touched only minimally, because when approached or handled, premature babies often become agitated, which can put a life-threatening strain on their lungs. But Field found that gentle massage of the babies immediately restored their calm.

Why does touch produce such beneficial effects? Studies of rats, whose basic neural and tactile (touch) systems are similar to those of humans, indicate that a specific pattern of touch by the mother rat—especially licking—inhibits the baby's manufacture of beta endorphin, a chemical that reduces levels of growth hormone (Schanberg & Field, 1987). In response to maternal licking, the infant rats' levels of beta endorphin decreased, and levels of growth hormone increased. If the rat pups were separated from their mothers, levels of beta endorphins increased, growth hormones decreased, and the baby rats' growth was inhibited. When the pups were reunited with their mothers and maternal licking resumed, beta endorphin levels decreased once again, and growth speeded up.

In related studies, S. Levine, Johnson, and Gonzales (1985) found that when infant rats and monkeys are separated from their mothers, they show a stress response that disappears when maternal contact is resumed. According to Levine, skin-to-skin contact may reduce the level of stress hormones, soothing all infants, not just premature babies. It may be that both the mental and physical development of all infants could be enhanced if they were touched more (Wachs & Smitherman, 1985).

Each of us, of course, differs in the degree of physical contact we welcome. The uniqueness of our nervous systems may account for some of this difference, but our past experiences with touch undoubtedly play a role as well. In one study, the nerve cells in the area of the cortex that controls touch sensations were better developed in rats that had experienced more physical contact than in rats that had less contact (Rosenzweig, Bennett, & Diamond, 1972). Researchers suspect that those who have had little physical contact may become hypersensitive to touch, so much so that they find the experience of touching physically uncomfortable.

Culture and belief systems play a dramatic role in how we respond to bodily injury. Kosambi (1967) and Melzack (1973) describe a religious ceremony, practiced in parts of India, in which a young man swings from a ceremonial platform, supported by hooks embedded in his back, seemingly without pain. It should not be surprising, then, that in cases of serious injury the perception of pain is not related to the amount of tissue damage sustained (Schiffman, 1982). And because of the great variability in the ways that people experience pain, scientists encounter difficulty in measuring typical pain thresholds and studying how individuals adapt to pain (Irwin & Whitehead, 1991).

**Gate control theory** Theory that a "neurological gate" in the spinal cord controls the transmission of pain messages to the brain.

How do psychologists explain our varying sensitivities to pain? One commonly accepted view is the **gate control theory** of pain (Melzack, 1980). According to this theory, a "neurological gate" in the spinal cord controls the transmission of pain impulses to the brain. If the gate is open, we experience more pain than we do if it is closed. Whether the gate is closed or open depends on a complex competition between two different types of sensory nerve fibers. On the one hand, there are large fibers that tend to "close the gate" when they are stimulated, thus preventing pain impulses from reaching the brain. But there are also small fibers that "open the gate" when they are stimulated, letting the pain messages get through to the brain. Moreover, certain areas of the brain stem can also close the gate from above, so to speak, by sending down signals to fibers in the spinal cord to close the gate. Finally, by focusing our attention away from pain, we may also experience greatly diminished feelings of pain. All these mechanisms may be at work when, in the same circumstances, one person experiences excruciating pain while another feels no pain at all. We cannot pinpoint why some individuals experience pain differently than others. From the perspective of gate control theory, these differences might be due to the numbers of small fibers or large fibers that a person has, or varying levels of control exerted on the gate mechanism from higher brain areas. It may also turn out that some people have faulty gates.

Despite its complexities, the gate control process is already being used to develop new techniques for the control of pain. For example, some dentists are experimenting with devices that electrically stimulate large nerve fibers and block the action of small fibers, thus closing the gate on pain. Patients can adjust the amount of stimulation based on their own needs.

Studies of pain relief suggest that there are two other pain-controlling systems that may be independent of or in some way related to the spinal pain gate. In the first case, if you give pain sufferers a chemically neutral pill, or *placebo*, but tell them that it is an effective pain reducer, they will often experience less pain after taking it. No doubt many home remedies and secret cures rely on the *placebo effect*. In addition, traditional Chinese and Korean medicine have demonstrated that *acupuncture* treatments, involving the insertion of thin needles into parts of the body, can reduce or eliminate pain. Research indicates that both placebos and acupuncture work through the release of endorphins, the pain-blocking neurotransmitters that we examined in the previous chapter. There are a number of drugs that block the effects of endorphins and if these blockers are given before administering placebos or acupuncture, these pain reducers are far less effective. As a result, scientists assert that endorphins somehow contribute to the pain relief provided by placebos and acupuncture (Coren et al., 1994; He, 1987).

However, some other pain-reduction techniques have nothing to do with endorphins. For example, pain can be reduced through hypnosis or related concentration exercises (as in the Lamaze birth technique). These concentration techniques are just as effective when endorphin blockers are administered, which suggests that there is a second pain-control system that works independently of the brain's chemical painkillers (Akil & Watson, 1980; D.J. Mayer & Watkins, 1984). Pain researchers suspect that these concentration techniques act to close the spinal pain gate, but nobody knows how.

As noted in the introduction to this chapter, our senses provide us with raw data about the external world. However, unless we interpret this raw in-

**Figure** Entity perceived to stand apart from the background.

**Ground** Background against which a figure appears.

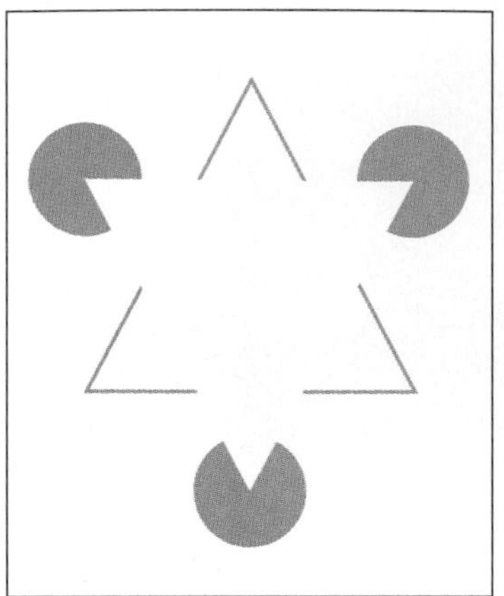

**Figure 3-21**
When sensory information is incomplete, we tend to create a complete perception by supplying the missing details. In this figure, we fill in the lines that let us perceive a white triangle in the center of the pattern.

**Figure 3-22**
Knowing beforehand that the black blotches in this figure represent a person riding a horse changes our perception of it.

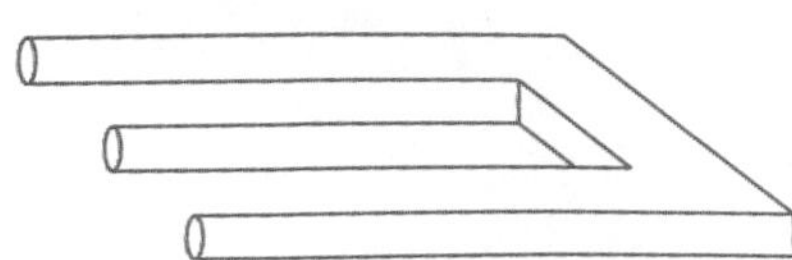

**Figure 3-23**
**An optical illusion.** In the case of the trident, we go beyond what is sensed (blue lines on flat white paper) to perceive a three-dimensional object that isn't really there.

## PERCEPTION

formation, it remains what William James (1890) called "a booming, buzzing confusion." The eye records patterns of light and dark, but it does not "see" a bird flittering from branch to branch. The eardrum vibrates in a particular fashion, but it does not "hear" a symphony. Deciphering *meaningful* patterns in the jumble of sensory information is what we mean by *perception*.

Ultimately, the brain interprets the complex flow of information from the various senses. Using sensory information as raw material, the brain creates perceptual experiences that go beyond what is sensed directly. For example, looking at Figure 3-21, we tend to perceive a white triangle in the center of the pattern, although the sensory input consists only of three circles from which "pie slices" have been cut and three 60-degree angles. Or take Figure 3-22. At first glance, most people see only an assortment of black blotches. If you are told that the blotches represent a person riding a horse, suddenly your perceptual experience changes. What was meaningless sensory information now takes shape as a horse and rider.

Sometimes, as in certain optical illusions, you perceive things that could not possibly exist. The trident shown in Figure 3-23 exemplifies such an "impossible" figure; on closer inspection, you discover that the object that you "recognized" is not really there. In all these cases, the brain actively creates and organizes perceptual experiences out of raw sensory data—sometimes even from data we are not aware of receiving. We will now explore how perceptual processes organize sensory experience.

### Perceptual Organization

Early in this century, a group of German psychologists, calling themselves *Gestalt psychologists*, set out to discover the principles through which we interpret sensory information. The German word *gestalt* has no exact English equivalent, but essentially it means "whole," "form," or "pattern." The Gestalt psychologists believed that the brain creates a coherent perceptual experience that is more than simply the sum of the available sensory information and that it does so in predictable ways.

In one important facet of the perceptual process, we distinguish **figures** from the **ground** against which they appear. A colorfully upholstered chair stands out from the bare walls of a room. A marble statue is perceived as a whole figure separate from the red brick wall behind it. The illusory trident in Figure 3-23 stands out from the white page. In all these cases, we perceive some objects as "figures" and other sensory information as "background."

The figure-ground distinction pertains to all our senses, not just vision. We can distinguish a violin solo against the ground of a symphony orchestra, a single voice amid cocktail party chatter, and the smell of roses in a florist's shop. In all these instances, we perceive a figure apart from the ground around it.

Sometimes, however, there are not enough cues in a pattern to permit us to easily distinguish a figure from its ground. The horse and rider in Figure 3-22 illustrate this problem, as does Figure 3-24, which shows a spotted dog investigating shadowy surroundings. It is hard to distinguish the dog because it has few visible contours of its own, and as a result, it seems to have no more form than the background. This is the principle behind camouflage—to make a figure blend into its background (see Figure 3-25).

Sometimes a figure with clear contours can be perceived in two very different ways because it is unclear which part of the stimulus is the figure and which the ground. Examples of such reversible figures are shown in Figures 3-26 and 3-27 on page 104. At first glance, you perceive figures against a specific background, but as you stare at the illustrations, you will discover that the figures eventually dissolve into the ground, making for two very different perceptions of the same illustration.

Figure 3-28 on page 105 demonstrates some other important principles of perceptual organization. In every case, our perceptual experience makes a leap beyond the raw sensory information available to us. In other words, we use sensory information to create a perception that is more than just the sum of the parts. While sometimes this can cause problems, this perceptual tendency to "fill in the blanks" usually broadens our understanding of the world. As creatures searching for meaning, we tend to fill in the missing information, to group various objects together, to see whole objects and hear meaningful sounds rather than just random bits and pieces of raw sensory data. The box titled "The Human Factor in Engineering and Design" spotlights how our appreciation of perceptual processes is changing the practice of engineering.

**Figure 3-24**
There are not enough cues in this pattern to allow us to easily distinguish the *figure* of the Dalmatian dog from the *ground* behind it.

*Source:* Gregory, 1970.

**CORTICAL CODING AND PERCEPTION** Important research undertaken decades after the original work of the Gestalt psychologists has begun to shed light on how neurons in the brain organize perceptual experiences. One pivotal study was conducted by David H. Hubel and Torsten N. Wiesel (1959, 1979), who received the Nobel Prize for their work. Hubel and Wiesel inserted an electrode into the visual areas of the brain of an anesthetized cat. They were then able to record the activity of individual neurons when certain stimuli—such as a vertical or horizontal line—were projected onto a screen in front of the cat's eye. They found that certain cells, called *simple cells*, would respond to a line presented only at a certain angle or orientation. For example, some cells fired only when the line was tilted 45 degrees from the vertical. When the line was displayed vertically, for example, simple cells specialized for that orientation started to respond. Cells that respond to orientation are just one type among a variety of cells called *feature detectors*, which are highly specialized to respond to particular elements in the visual field. For example, some feature detectors are sensitive to movement: Frogs have "bug detector" cells that are especially well suited for picking out small, dark, moving objects.

In addition to simple feature detectors, *complex cells* appear to coordinate information drawn from a number of simple cells—for example, some complex cells respond only to a 45-degree line moving from left to right. Furthermore, *hypercomplex* cells are believed to coordinate information at a still higher level of complexity, such as two different lines forming an angle.

As yet, researchers have not confirmed the existence of cells specialized to respond to such aspects of Gestalt organization as closure and proximity. But some psychologists believe that just as the frog has its "bug detector" cells, humans and other higher animals must have neural structures sensitive to the complex patterns that these species must perceive in order to survive. Through evolution, we may be prewired to perceive many of the complex shapes and movements that appear in our natural environment. For example, as we will see in Chapter 9, newborns, given the choice, will spend sig-

**Figure 3-25**
It is difficult for predators to see the figure of the walking stick against the background of its natural environment.

**Perceptual constancy** Tendency to perceive objects as stable and unchanging despite changes in sensory stimulation.

**Figure 3-26**
The *reversible* figure and ground in this Escher woodcut cause us to see first black devils and then white angels in each of the rings.

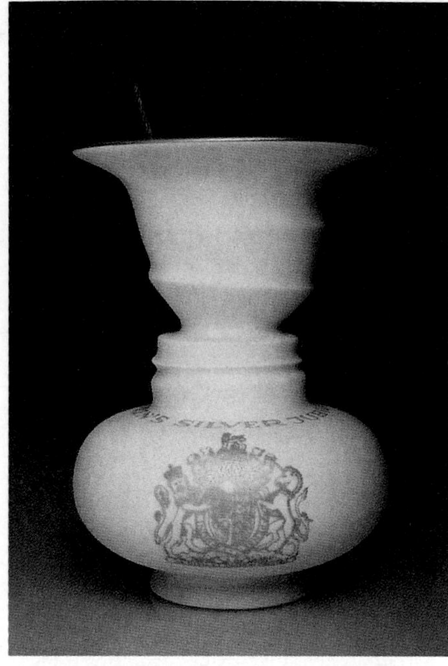

**Figure 3-27**
**Figure-ground relationship . . . How do you perceive this figure?**
Do you see a vase or the silhouettes of a man and a woman? Both interpretations are possible, but not at the same time. Reversible figures such as this work because it is unclear which part of the stimulus is the *figure* and which is the neutral *ground* against which the figure is perceived.

nificantly more time gazing at sketches of human faces than at other types of patterns or figures. Yet, because we could not possibly be born with an innate grasp of all the different objects that we encounter in the world around us, learning and experience clearly play an important part in the way we organize perception. Perceptual constancies, to which we turn next, serve as one illustration of the role of experience in perception.

## Perceptual Constancies

Surprisingly, we often continue to have the same perceptual experience even as the sensory data change. **Perceptual constancy** refers to the tendency to perceive objects as relatively stable and unchanging despite changing sensory information. Without this ability, we would find the world very confusing. Once we have formed a stable perception of an object, we can recognize it from almost any position, at almost any distance, under almost any illumination. A white house looks like a white house by day or by night and from any angle. We see it as the same house. The sensory information may change as illumination and perspective change, but the object is perceived as constant.

We also tend to perceive objects at their true size regardless of the size of the image that they cast on the retina. As Figure 3-29 on page 106 shows, the farther away an object is from the lens of the eye, the smaller the retinal image it casts. For example, a 6-foot-tall man standing 20 feet away casts a retinal image that is only 50 percent of the size of the retinal image he casts at a distance of 10 feet. Yet he is not perceived as having shrunk to 3 feet.

Memory and experience play important roles in perceptual constancy. For example, look at Figure 3-30, a slightly altered photograph of former British prime minister Margaret Thatcher. Before reading further, turn the book upside down, and look at the picture again. An essentially normal face has taken on a gruesome aspect. Your experience in recognizing people and interpreting their facial expressions has accustomed you to focus on certain perceptual cues (particularly eyes and mouths). When you look at the upside-down picture, the eyes and mouth are normal, so you perceive the entire face as normal. In other words, you use your experience in perceiving normal human faces to perceive this (very unusual) face, and as a result, you do not perceive it as grossly distorted until you look at it rightside up.

**Size constancy** Perception of an object as the same size regardless of the distance from which it is viewed.

**Size constancy**, too, depends partly on experience—information about the relative sizes of objects is stored in memory—and partly on distance cues. When there are no distance cues, size constancy has to rely solely on what we have learned from our previous experience with an object. Naturally, more errors occur when there are no distance cues, but fewer than we might expect in view of the radical changes in the size of the retinal image. We might guess that a woman some distance away is 5 feet 4 inches tall when she is really 5 feet 8 inches, but hardly anyone would

**Figure 3-28**
**Gestalt principles of perceptual organization.**

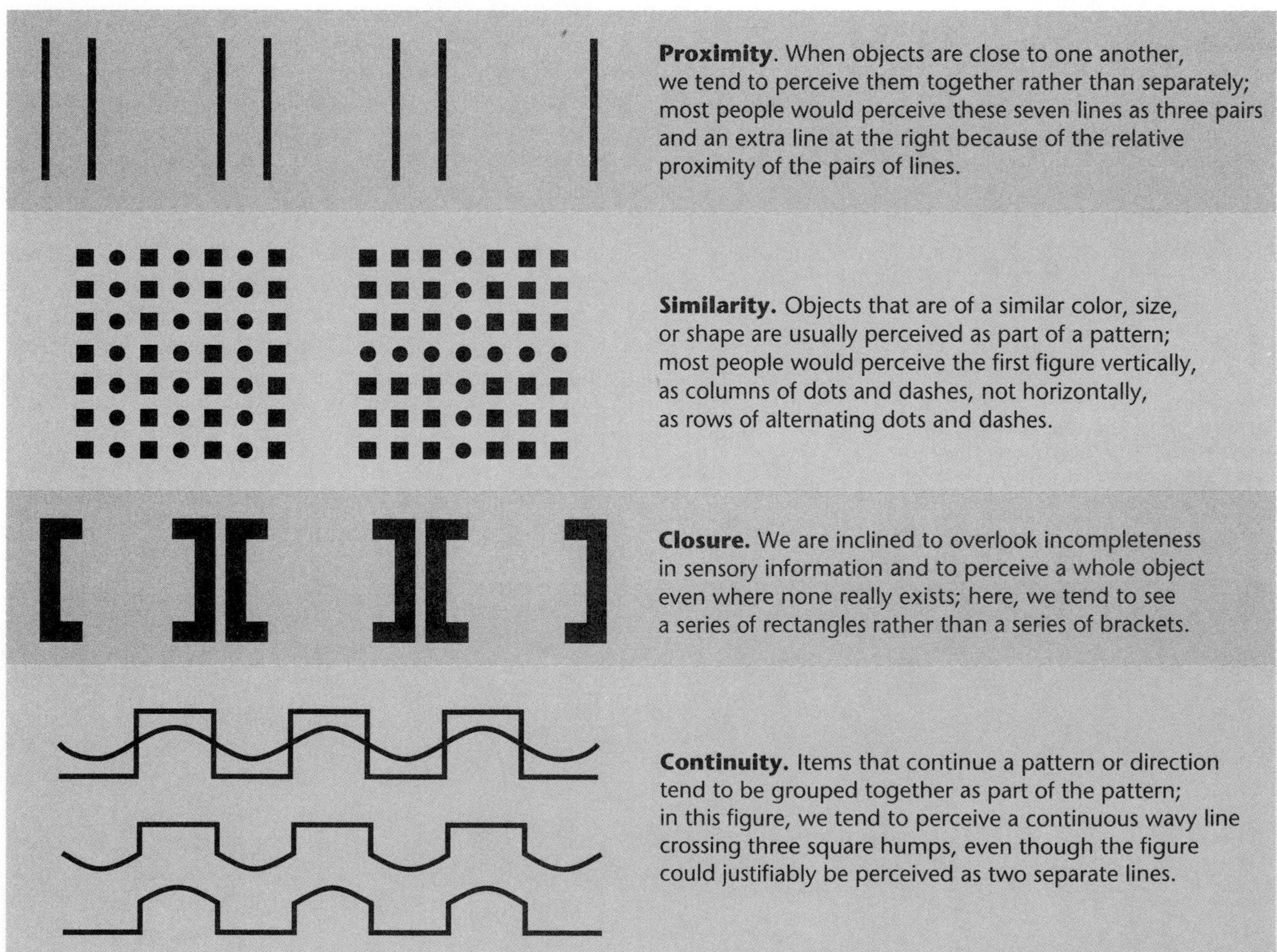

**Proximity**. When objects are close to one another, we tend to perceive them together rather than separately; most people would perceive these seven lines as three pairs and an extra line at the right because of the relative proximity of the pairs of lines.

**Similarity.** Objects that are of a similar color, size, or shape are usually perceived as part of a pattern; most people would perceive the first figure vertically, as columns of dots and dashes, not horizontally, as rows of alternating dots and dashes.

**Closure.** We are inclined to overlook incompleteness in sensory information and to perceive a whole object even where none really exists; here, we tend to see a series of rectangles rather than a series of brackets.

**Continuity.** Items that continue a pattern or direction tend to be grouped together as part of the pattern; in this figure, we tend to perceive a continuous wavy line crossing three square humps, even though the figure could justifiably be perceived as two separate lines.

**Shape constancy** Tendency to see an object as the same shape no matter what angle it is viewed from.

**Brightness constancy** Perception of brightness as the same, even though the amount of light reaching the retina changes.

**Color constancy** Inclination to perceive familiar objects as retaining their color despite changes in sensory information.

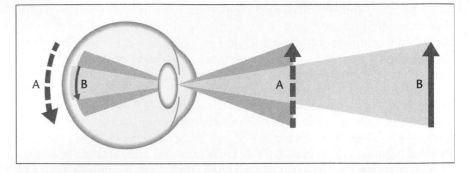

**Figure 3-29**
**Retinal image.** The relationship between distance and the size of the retinal image. Object A and object B are the same size, but A, being much closer to the eye, casts a much larger image on the retina.

perceive her as being 3 feet tall, no matter how far away she is. We know from experience that adults are seldom that short.

Familiar objects also tend to be seen as having a constant shape, even though the retinal images that they cast change as they are viewed from different angles. A dinner plate is perceived as a circle even when it is tilted and the retinal image is oval. A rectangular door will project a rectangular image on the retina only when it is viewed directly from the front. From any other angle, it casts a trapezoidal image on the retina, but it is not perceived as having suddenly become a trapezoidal door. These are all examples of **shape constancy** (see Figure 3-31).

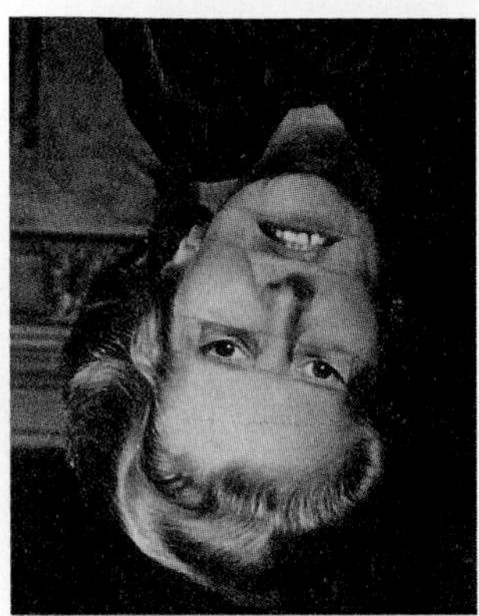

**Figure 3-30**
Look at the picture and then turn the book upside down so that the picture is rightside up. Experience leads you to use certain perceptual cues to recognize facial expressions, and the upside-down picture looks normal. Those same cues cause the rightside-up picture to look grossly distorted.

Two other important perceptual constancies are **brightness constancy** and **color constancy**. The former principle means that even though the amount of light available to our eyes varies greatly over the course of a day, the perceived brightness of familiar objects hardly varies at all. We perceive a sheet of white paper as brighter than a piece of coal whether we see these objects in candlelight or under bright sunlight. This may seem obvious, but bear in mind that coal in sunlight reflects more light than white paper in candlelight, yet we always perceive white paper as being brighter. Brightness constancy occurs because a white object—or a black or gray one—will reflect the same percentage of the light falling on it whether that light is from a candle, a fluorescent lamp, or the sun. Rather than basing our judgment of brightness on the *absolute* amount of light that the object reflects, we assess how the *relative* reflection compares to the surrounding objects.

Similarly, we tend to perceive familiar objects as keeping their colors, regardless of information that reaches the eye. If you own a red automobile, you will see it as red whether it is on a brightly lit street or in a dark garage, where the small amount of light may send your eye a message that the color is closer to brown or black than red. But color constancy does not always hold true. When objects are unfamiliar or there are no customary color cues to guide us, color constancy may be distorted—as when we buy a pair of pants in a brightly lit store, only to discover that in ordinary daylight they are not the shade we thought they were.

**Figure 3-31**
**Examples of shape constancy.** Even though the image of the door on the retina changes greatly as the door opens, we still perceive the door as being rectangular.

*Source:* Boring, Langfeld, & Weld, 1976.

In exploring these various principles, we have noted that perceptual experiences often go far beyond the available sensory information. In fact, our perceptual experiences rarely if

# CONTROVERSIES

## How Do We See Objects and Shapes?

Stop reading for just a moment, and look at your opened psychology text. Almost without thinking, you see a book. Your perception of the book is extraordinarily reliable. The book remains a book if you view it from different angles, if the lighting in the room changes, if you grasp it and move it closer, if it's open or closed. You can close your eyes and come up with a fairly accurate mental image of the book; you can imagine viewing the book from several angles, in different lighting, and in motion. Not even the most sophisticated computer can do these things, yet we do them effortlessly. What have psychologists learned about the processes that enable us to create complex and meaningful perceptual experiences from sensory information?

First, psychologists assume that perception begins with some real-world object with real-world properties "out there." Psychologists call that object, along with its important perceptual properties, the *distal stimulus*. We never experience the distal stimulus directly, however. Energy from it (or in the case of our chemical senses, molecules from it) must activate our sensory system. Psychologists call the information that reaches sensory receptors the *proximal stimulus*. Strangely enough, even though the distal stimulus and the proximal stimulus are never the same thing, our perception of the distal stimulus is usually very accurate. So, as we view the book on the desk, how does the pattern on the retina (the proximal stimulus) become an integrated perception of the book (the distal stimulus)—one that captures all the important aspects of "bookness"?

The discovery of detector cells by Hubel and Wiesel, noted previously, puts us a step closer to answering that question. But recall that detector cells provide only fundamental information about lines, positions, angles, motion, and so on. Somehow we take the very basic information provided by detector cells and use it to create coherent perceptual experiences. Scientists have advanced a number of theories to explain how this process works.

According to some theorists, at least a two-stage process occurs in which the image on the retina is literally decomposed and then reassembled in the brain. Anne Treisman, for example, believes that an automatic "preattentive" stage of processing first breaks a proximal stimulus into independent, fundamental properties such as color, curves, positions, and motion. Then "focused attention" is required to reassemble the image by combining the independent parts (Treisman, 1986; Treisman et al., 1990). In a similar way, Irving Biederman asserts that three-dimensional objects can be broken down into 36 basic geometric shapes (cylinders, blocks, pyramidal shapes, and so on) that can be combined to represent thousands of real-world objects. Biederman contends that if we can visually recognize the basic shapes of an object, then we can completely and correctly recognize the object (Biederman, 1987; Hummel & Biederman, 1992).

In contrast to the "take it apart and then put it back together" schemes of Treisman and Biederman, other theorists assert that perception occurs via *parallel distributed processing networks* or *neural networks* (Rummelhart & McClelland, 1986). Rather than looking at the raw data taken from the retinal image, these theories posit that thousands or even millions of neurons in the brain act in coordinated weblike patterns in which some parts of the web represent the color, other parts the curves, and yet others the positions, shapes, or other fundamental information in a stimulus. Whereas Treisman and Biederman argue that the various parts of a stimulus are analyzed separately and then reassembled, the neural networks approach maintains that the parts are processed simultaneously, or in parallel. Thus, because these parts are never separated, they need not come back together. All the important features of a stimulus are simultaneously represented in the network, and the entire web of neural activity *is* the perceptual image.

Theories like those proposed by Treisman and Biederman envision only one large perceptual system that is used to perceive everything from faces to landmarks. Other theories, however, hold that multiple, specialized subsystems come into play in object perception. For example, Stephen Kosslyn of Harvard University suggests that the brain has one system for "what" and one system for "where." That is, one specialized system recognizes the kind or category of thing that we see, while the other provides information about its spatial position and spatial relationships. He further maintains that the two systems operate differently in each of the cerebral hemispheres (Kosslyn, 1980, 1987).

An entirely different approach to understanding form vision is called *computational neuroscience*. The late David Marr (1982), one of the more influential researchers in this area, advanced the theory that visual perception emerges from the brain's complex mathematical analysis of patterns of light and dark areas, edges, ends of segments, and positions. Through sophisticated calculations, this analysis eventually produces a finished visual image. Marr's perspective has been influential in shaping more recent theories of how we create meaningful perceptual experiences (see Kosslyn, 1994; Kosslyn & Koenig, 1992).

No one knows which of these approaches—or some as-yet-undiscovered theoretical explanation—will shed the most light on our understanding of perception. Whatever the final explanation, we must acknowledge that the brain accomplishes a remarkable feat when it creates a clear and cohesive world of objects and shapes from the information it receives from the eyes.

ever correspond exactly to the information that we receive through our senses. We have already seen how neural structures organize sensory information. Now we turn to the ways certain "personal" variables also influence and organize sensation.

## Observer Characteristics

While we clearly draw on past experience and learning when it comes to perception, several other factors can also affect our perceptual experiences, including our own motivations, values, expectations, cognitive style, and preconceptions grounded in our culture. In this section, we will probe how these sorts of variables influence the perceptual organization of sensory information.

**MOTIVATION** Oftentimes, our desires and needs strongly shape our perceptions. People in need are more likely to perceive something that they think will satisfy that need. For example, several interesting experiments have tested the influence of hunger on perception. Sanford (1937) found that if people were deprived of food for some time and were then shown vague or ambiguous pictures, they were apt to perceive the pictures as being related to food. Similarly, McClelland and Atkinson (1948) showed blurred pictures to people who had not eaten for varying lengths of time. Some had eaten 1 hour before; others had gone as long as 16 hours without food. Those who had not eaten for 16 hours perceived the blurred images as pictures of food more often than those who had eaten just 1 hour before.

**VALUES** In an experiment that revealed how strongly perceptions can be affected by a person's values, nursery-school children were shown a poker chip. Each child was asked to compare the size of the chip to the size of an adjustable circle of light until the child said the chip and the circle of light were the same size. The children were then brought to a machine with a crank that, when turned, produced a poker chip that could be exchanged for candy. Thus, the children were taught to value the poker chips more highly than they had before. After the children had been rewarded with the candy for the poker chips, they were again asked to compare the size of the chips to a circle of light. This time, the chips seemed larger to the children (Lambert, Solomon, & Watson, 1949).

**EXPECTATIONS** Preconceptions about what we are supposed to perceive can also influence perception. For example, in a well-known children's game, a piece of cardboard with a red stop sign is flashed in front of you. What did the sign say? Nearly everyone will say that the sign read "STOP." In fact, however, the sign is misprinted "STOPP." Because we are accustomed to seeing stop signs reading "STOP," we tend to perceive the familiar symbol rather than the misprint. Lachman (1984) demonstrated this phenomenon by asking subjects to copy a group of stimuli similar to this one:

PARIS<br>IN THE<br>THE SPRING

When the expressions were flashed briefly on a screen, the vast majority of subjects tended to omit the "extra" words and to report seeing more familiar (and more normal) expressions, such as PARIS IN THE SPRING. This phenomenon of *perceptual familiarization* or *perceptual generalization* reflects a strong tendency to see what we expect to see even if our expectation conflicts with external reality.

**COGNITIVE STYLE** As we mature, we develop a *cognitive style*—our own way of dealing with the environment—and this also affects how we see the world. Some psychologists distinguish between two general approaches that people use in perceiving the world (Witkin et al., 1962). People taking the *field-dependent* approach tend to perceive the environment as a whole and do not clearly delineate in their minds the shape, color, size, or other qualities of individual items. If field-dependent people are asked to draw a human figure, they generally draw it so that it blends into the background. By contrast, people who are *field independent* are more likely to perceive the elements of the environment as separate and distinct from one another and to draw each element as standing out from the background.

Cognitive styles can also be viewed from the perspective of "levelers" and "sharpeners"—those who level out the distinctions among objects and those who magnify them. To investigate the differences between these two cognitive styles, G.S. Klein (1951) showed people sets of squares of varying sizes and asked them to estimate the size of each one. One group, the "levelers," failed to perceive any differences in the size of the squares. The "sharpeners," however, picked up the differences in the size of the squares and made their size estimates accordingly.

**Monocular cues** Visual cues requiring the use of one eye.

**Binocular cues** Visual cues requiring the use of both eyes.

**Superposition** Monocular distance cue in which one object, by partly blocking a second object, is perceived as being closer.

**EXPERIENCE AND CULTURE** Cultural background also influences people's perceptions. As we will see in the chapter on cognition, the language people speak affects the ways in which they perceive their surroundings. Cultural differences in people's experiences can also influence how people use perceptual cues. Historically, for example, the Mbuti pygmies of Zaire seldom left the Ituri Rain Forest and rarely encountered objects that were more than a few feet away. On one occasion, anthropologist Colin Turnbull (1961) took a pygmy guide named Kenge on a trip onto the plains. When Kenge looked across the plain and saw a herd of buffalo, he asked what kind of insects they were. He refused to believe that the tiny black spots he saw were buffalo. As he and Turnbull drove toward the herd, Kenge believed that magic was making the animals grow larger. Because he had no experience of distant objects, he could not perceive the buffalo as having constant size.

Let us now look at a basic perceptual phenomenon—distance and depth—to see how we use both stimulus information and past experience to create perceptual experiences.

## Perception of Distance and Depth

We are constantly judging the distance between ourselves and other objects. When we walk through a classroom, our perception of distance helps us avoid bumping into desks or tripping over the wastebasket. If we reach out to pick up a pencil, we automatically judge how far to extend our arms. And as a matter of course, we also assess the depth of objects—how much total space they occupy. We use many cues to determine the distance and the depth of objects. Some of these cues depend on visual messages that one eye alone can transmit; these are called **monocular cues**. Others, known as **binocular cues,** require the use of both eyes. Having two eyes allows us to make more accurate judgments about distance and depth, particularly when objects are relatively close. But monocular cues alone are often sufficient to allow us to judge distance and depth quite accurately, as we will see in the next section.

What are some of the visual cues we use to judge distance and depth?

**MONOCULAR CUES** **Superposition**, when one object partly blocks a second object, is an important relative distance cue. The first object is perceived as being closer, the second as more distant (see Figure 3-32).

As all students of art know, there are several ways in which perspective can help in estimating distance and depth. Two parallel lines that extend

**Linear perspective** Monocular cue to distance and depth based on the fact that two parallel lines seem to come together at the horizon.

**Aerial perspective** Monocular cue to distance and depth based on the fact that more distant objects are likely to appear hazy and blurred.

**Elevation** Monocular cue to distance and depth based on the fact that the higher on the horizontal plane an object is, the farther away it appears.

**Texture gradient** Monocular cue to distance and depth based on the fact that objects seen at greater distances appear to be smoother and less textured.

**Stereoscopic vision** Combination of two retinal images to give a three-dimensional perceptual experience.

**Retinal disparity** Binocular distance cue based on the difference between the images cast on the two retinas when both eyes are focused on the same object.

into the distance seem to come together at some point on the horizon. This cue to distance and depth is known as **linear perspective**. In **aerial perspective**, distant objects have a hazy appearance and a somewhat blurred outline. On a clear day, mountains often seem to be much closer than on a hazy day, when their outlines become blurred. The **elevation** of an object also serves as a perspective cue to depth. An object that is on a higher horizontal plane seems to be farther away than one on a lower plane (see Figure 3-33).

Still another useful monocular cue to distance and depth is **texture gradient**. An object that is close seems to have a rough or detailed texture. As distance increases, the texture becomes finer, until finally the original texture cannot be distinguished clearly, if at all. A man standing on a pebbly beach, for example, can distinguish among the gray stones and gravel in front of his feet. As he looks down the beach, however, the stones appear to become smaller and finer until eventually he cannot make out individual stones at all.

**Binocular Cues** All the visual cues examined so far depend on the action of only one eye. Many animals, such as horses, deer, and fish, rely entirely on monocular cues. Although they have two eyes, the two visual fields do not overlap because their eyes are located on the sides of the head rather than in front. Humans, apes, and many predatory animals—such as lions, tigers, and wolves—have a distinct physical advantage over these animals. Because both eyes are set in the front of the head, the visual fields overlap. The **stereoscopic vision** derived from combining the two retinal images makes the perception of depth and distance more accurate.

Because our eyes are set approximately 2-1/2 inches apart, each one has a slightly different view of things. The difference between the two images that the eyes receive is known as **retinal disparity**. The left eye receives more information about the left side of an object, and the right eye receives more information about the right side. You can easily prove that each of your eyes receives a different image. Close one eye and line up a finger with some vertical line, like the edge of a door. Then open that eye and close the other one. Your finger will appear to have moved a great distance. When you look at the finger with both eyes, however, the two different images become one.

One binocular cue to distance comes from the muscles that control the

**Figure 3-32**
**Superposition.** Because the king of clubs appears to have been superimposed on the blank card, we perceive it as being closer to us than the king of spades. When the cards are spaced out, however, we can see that the king of spades is actually no farther away than the king of clubs. It appears to be farther away because the other two cards seem to be superimposed on it.

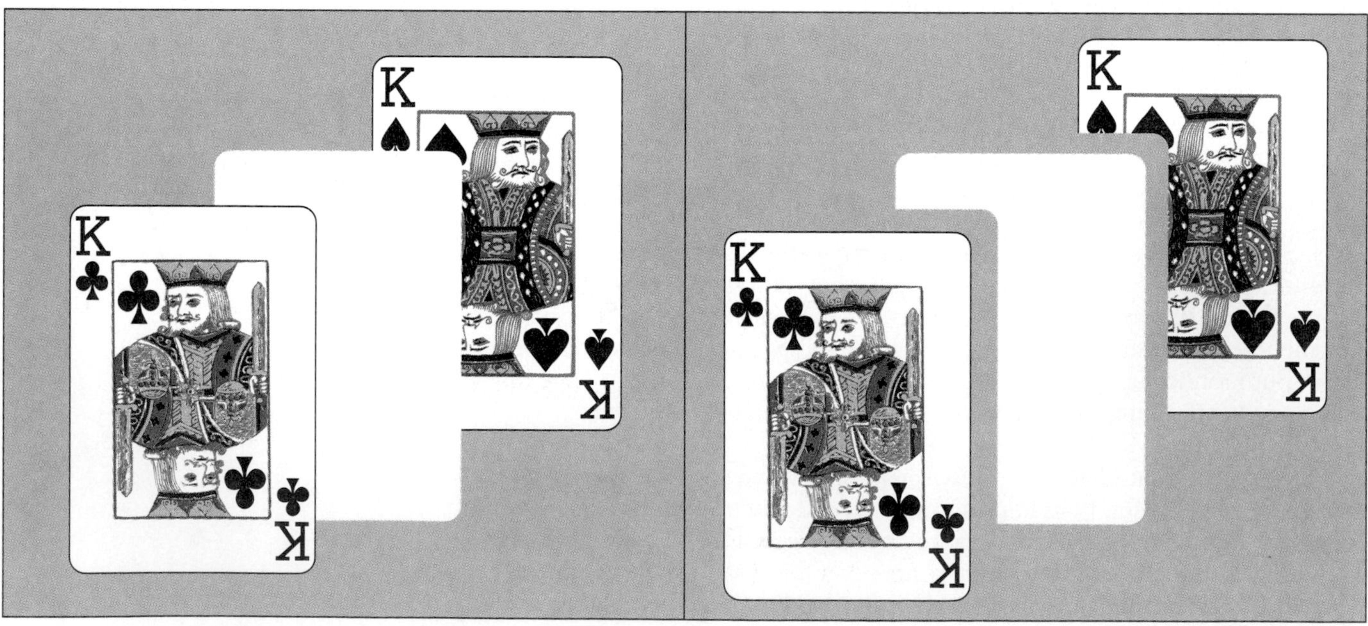

**Figure 3-33**
**Elevation as a visual cue.** Because of the higher elevation and the suggestion of depth provided by the road, the tree on the right is perceived as being more distant and about the same size as the tree at lower left. Actually, it is appreciably smaller, as you can verify if you measure the heights of the two trees.

**Convergence** A visual depth cue that comes from muscles controlling eye movement as the eyes turn inward to view a nearby stimulus.

**Monaural cue** Cue to sound location that requires just one ear.

**Binaural cue** Cue to sound location that involves both ears working together.

**convergence** of the eyes. When we look at objects that are fairly close to us, our eyes tend to converge—to turn slightly inward toward each other. The sensations from the muscles that control the movement of the eyes thus provide another cue to distance. If the object is very close, such as at the end of the nose, the eyes cannot converge, and two separate images are perceived. If the object is more than a few yards (meters) away, the sight lines of the eyes are more or less parallel, and there is no convergence.

**LOCATION OF SOUNDS** Just as we use monocular and binocular cues to establish visual depth and distance, we draw on **monaural** (single-ear) and **binaural** (two-ear) **cues** to locate the source of sounds (see Figure 3-34). In one monaural cue, load sounds are perceived as closer than faint sounds, with changes in loudness translating into changes in distance. Binaural cues work on the principle that because sounds off to one side of the head reach one ear slightly ahead of the other, the brain processes the time difference between sound waves reaching the two ears and uses that difference to make accurate judgments of location.

Most of us rely so heavily on visual cues that we seldom pay much attention to the rich set of auditory information available in the world around us. Blind people, who often compensate for their lack of vision by sharpening their ability to perceive sounds, can figure out where obstacles lie in their paths by listening to the echoes from a cane, their own footsteps, and their own voices. In one notable case, a blind boy had grown so adept at avoiding obstacles by sound that he could safely ride a bicycle in public places. Many blind people can judge the size and distance of one object in relation to another using nothing more than sound cues. They can also discriminate between contrasting surfaces, such as glass and fabric, by listening to the difference in the echo produced when sound strikes them.

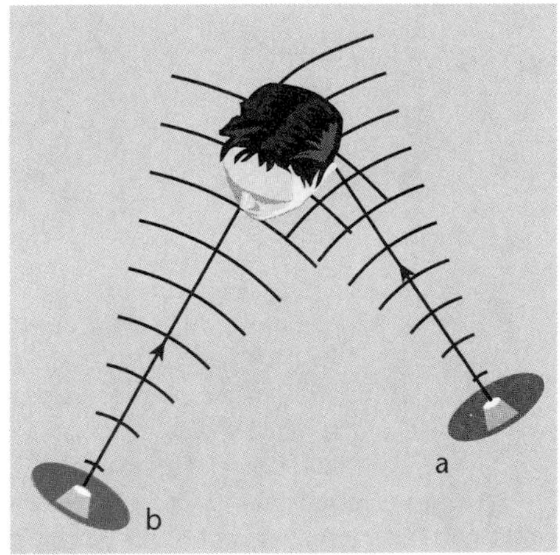


**Figure 3-34**
**Cues used in sound localization.**
Sound waves coming from source (b) will reach both ears simultaneously. A sound wave from source (a) reaches the left ear first, where it is also louder. The head casts a "shadow" over the other ear, thus reducing the intensity of the delayed sound in that ear.

*Source:* Langfeld & Weld, 1976.

## Perceptual Illusions

Visual illusions graphically demonstrate the ways in which we use a variety of sensory cues to *create* perceptual experiences that may (or may not) correspond to what is out there in the real world. By understanding how we are fooled into

**Physical illusion** Illusion due to distortion of information reaching receptor cells.

**Perceptual illusion** Illusion due to misleading cues in stimuli that cause us to create perceptions that are inaccurate or impossible.

"seeing" something that isn't there, psychologists can figure out how perceptual processes work in the everyday world and under normal circumstances.

Psychologists generally distinguish between *physical* and *perceptual* illusions. One example of a **physical illusion** is the bent appearance of a stick when it is placed in water—an illusion easily understood because the water acts like a prism, bending the light waves before they reach our eyes.

On the other hand, some illusions depend primarily on our own perceptual processes, of which we are not ordinarily aware, and these illusions can be quite startling. **Perceptual illusions** occur because the stimulus contains misleading cues that give rise to inaccurate or impossible perceptions.

In Figure 3-35, for example, a false and misleading depth cue makes us perceive the strange triangle as a three-dimensional figure that clearly cannot exist. Another graphic that fools us by presenting false depth cues is Figure 3-36E, in which the top line is perceived as shorter than the bottom. Our experience tells us that objects appear smaller when they are far away. In Figure 3-36F, both monsters cast the same-size image on the retina in our eyes. But the depth cues in the tunnel suggest that we are looking at a three-dimensional scene and that therefore the top monster is much far-

## ONTROVERSIES

### Extrasensory Perception

Some people claim to have an extra power of perception, one beyond those of the normal senses. This unusual power, known as *extrasensory perception*, or *ESP*, has been defined as "a response to an unknown event not presented to any known sense" (McConnell, 1969). ESP refers to a variety of phenomena, including *clairvoyance*—awareness of an unknown object or event; *telepathy*—knowledge of someone else's thoughts or feelings; and *precognition*—foreknowledge of future events. The operation of ESP and other psychic phenomena is the focus of a field of study called *parapsychology*.

Much of the research into ESP has been criticized for poor experimental design, failure to control for dishonesty, selective reporting of results, or inability to obtain replicable results (Cornell, 1984; Hansel, 1969). But a recent research paper has added new fuel to the controversy because it cannot be challenged on those grounds (Bem & Honorton, 1994). Daryl Bem, a research psychologist and an ESP skeptic, visited the New Jersey laboratory of the late Charles Honorton, a researcher and advocate of the reality of psychic phenomena, to examine his claims of improved controls and procedures. Bem was so impressed with Honorton's approach to ESP research that he agreed to conduct some joint experiments with him.

Bem and Honorton used an *autoganzfeld* procedure to test for telepathy. In this procedure, a "sender," isolated in a soundproof room, concentrates on a picture or video segment randomly selected (by a computer) from a set of 80 photos or 80 videotape segments. A "receiver" is placed alone in another soundproof room. The receiver engages in deep relaxation while wearing a half Ping-Pong ball over each eye and headphones playing a hissing sound (to provide uniform visual and auditory stimulation). The receiver then tries to experience any message or image coming from the sender. The experiment concludes with a test in which a computer displays four photos or videotape segments to the receiver, who rates them for similarity to impressions or images received during the sending phase of the experiment. Although receivers did not identify all the actual photos and videos that the senders were looking at, they performed significantly better than would be expected by chance alone.

Although Bem and Honorton's studies are intriguing, Ray Hyman, a leading skeptic of psychic research, has criticized them on the grounds that items were not appropriately randomized during the test phase of the experiment and that the authors failed to control for the tendency of receivers to pick certain images—for example, the first or last one—regardless of a match between the test item and a mental image (Hyman, 1994).

According to surveys, psychologists and other scientists do not discount ESP entirely. In fact, one survey (Wagner & Monnet, 1979) indicated that 34 percent of psychologists accepted ESP as either an established fact or a likely possibility. Even many of those who remain skeptical do not dismiss ESP out of hand but rather point out that experimentation has not yet given scientific credence to these phenomena.

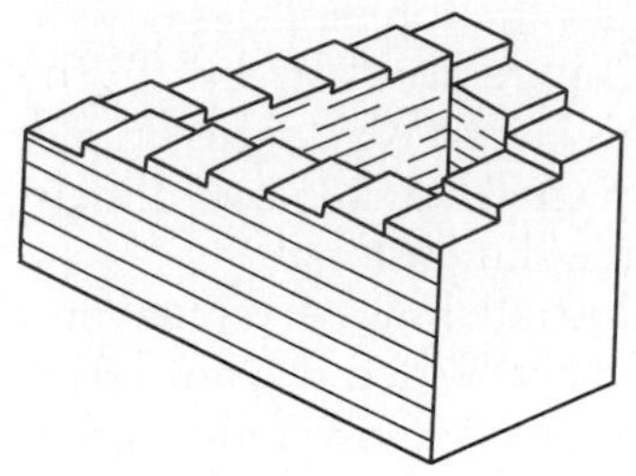
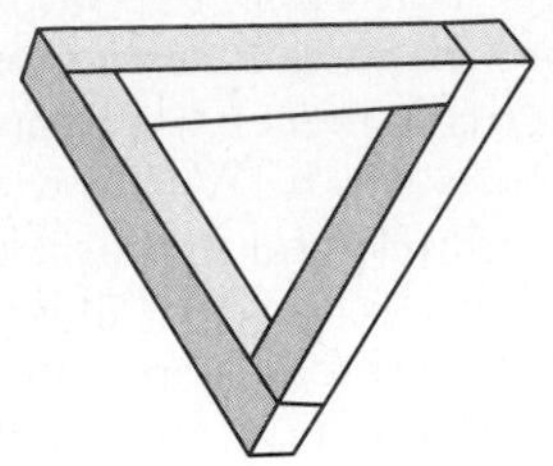

**Figure 3-35**
**Visual illusions using misleading depth cues.** In these visual illusions, there are misleading *depth cues*. For example, the strange triangle is constructed so that a fake depth cue signals a three-dimensional object that cannot exist.

*Source:* Adapted from Gregory, 1978.

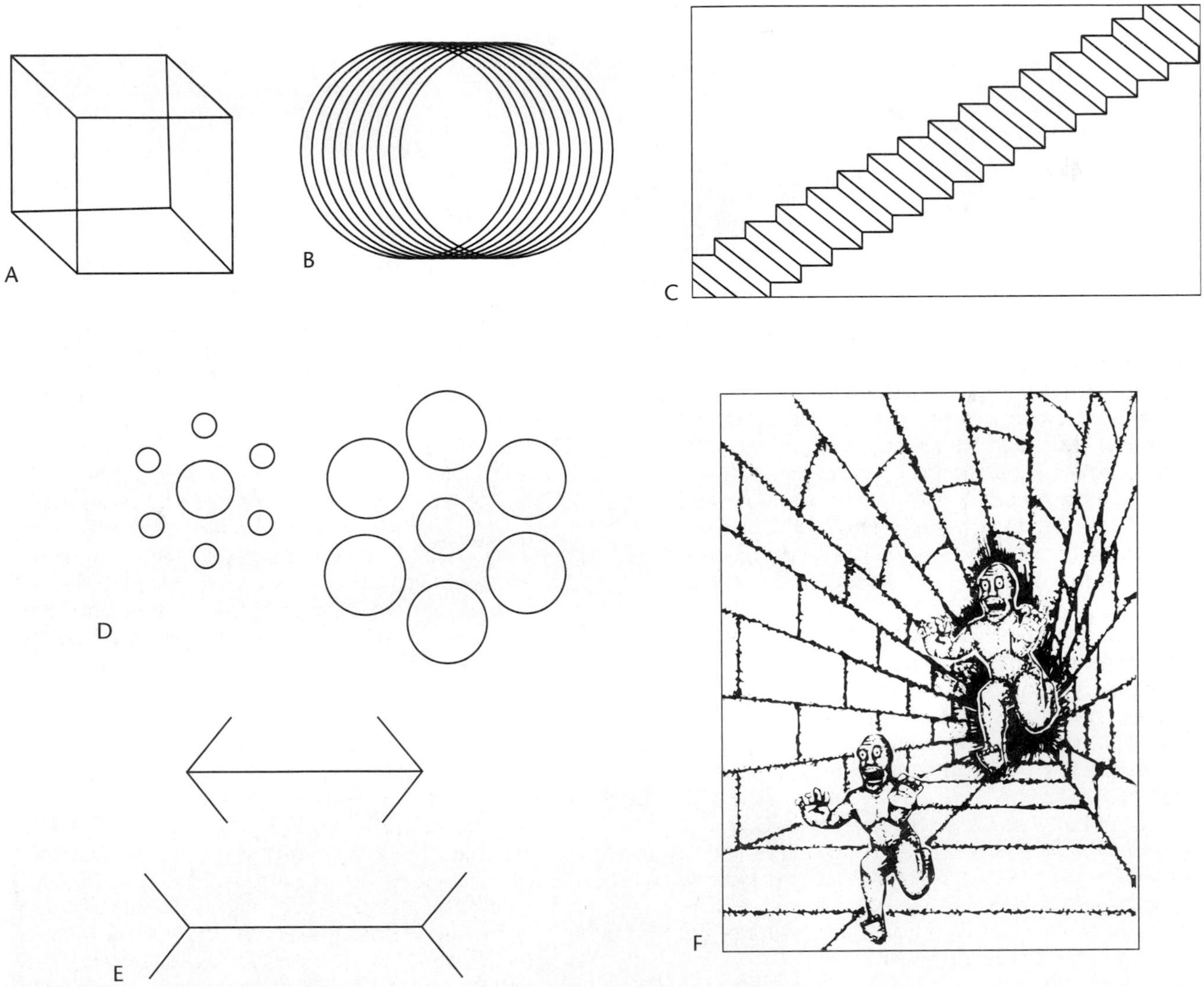

A B C

D

F

E

**Figure 3-36**
**Reversible figures and misleading depth cues.** A, B, and C are examples of *reversible figures*. D, E, and F show how through the effects of misleading *depth cues* we misjudge the size of objects. The middle circles in D are exactly the same size, as are the lines in E and the monsters in F.

ther away. In the real world, this would mean that the top monster is actually much larger than the bottom monster. Therefore, we "correct" for the distance and actually perceive the top monster as larger. We do this despite other cues to the contrary: We know that the image is actually two-dimensional, but we still respond to it as if it were three-dimensional.

There are also "real-world" illusions that illustrate how perceptual processes work, such as the illusion of *induced movement*. When you are sitting in a stationary train and the train next to you begins to move forward, you seem to be moving backward. Because you have no reference point by which to tell if you are standing still, you are confused as to which train is actually moving. However, if you look down at the ground, you can establish an unambiguous frame of reference and make the situation clear to yourself.

Artists rely on many of these perceptual phenomena both to represent reality accurately and to distort it deliberately. In paintings and sketches drawn on a two-dimensional surface, it is almost always necessary to distort objects for them to be perceived correctly by viewers. For example, in representational art, railroad tracks, sidewalks, and tunnels are always drawn closer together in the distance. In Figure 3-37, you can

**Figure 3-37**
The artist has manipulated distance cues to create the *perceptual illusion* of water traveling uphill.

**"Can we ever know an objective reality, or can we know only what we perceive through our senses?"**

The discussion of perception in Chapter 3 stresses our dependence on sensory input and our interpretation of sensory messages. Recall the definitions of noise and sound on p. 99. To what extent do we perceive what is "really" there, and to what extent do we "create" our own worlds through perception? How do we "know" anything? What are the implications of the section on illusions?

What are your thoughts about this issue? Do you believe that we really perceive all or some of an external objective reality, or do you think that we simply create our own subjective worlds? Can we alter behavior by altering our perceptions? What factors that psychologists could change influence people's perceptions? After you have thought about these questions, take a few minutes to examine the opinions of some of your fellow students.

• • • • • • •

**LEE: I think that IF there is an outside world, then it is absolute, but that our perception of it is entirely dependent on how our brain processes information.**

**PAT: If you and I observe the same table, but you view it with spots on it and I claim that there are no spots, who is perceiving the right reality? Perhaps you can use a portion of your brain that allows you to see things I cannot; perhaps your brain is tricking you into seeing spots. We can never know the absolute reality of the table, because we are all dependent on those tools of perception and the brain which we have not even come close to understanding. But, if and when we are able to fully explain the brain, we will still be limited by the fact that our brain is just one vehicle for understanding and perceiving the world. Our reality may not coincide with the absolute condition or reality of the world.**

**KELLY: But how do you know that you are not just living in a dream? If your body is just a figment of your imagination, why can you not say that your self-consciousness is just a figment of your imagination as well? But then, what is your imagination?**

**CARVER: Absolute reality is (or is not) an oxymoron. You can't say anything about it, and to refer to it as anything at all is just plain presumptuous. And if your idea of absolute reality was not derived (in terms of final causes) from your subjective reality of sensory experience, then where do you think it came from?**

**ANN: What I am concluding is that all reality is relative to how educated we are and what we choose to believe and how much we trust or rely on our senses.**

**CARVER: Reality changes along with us. We are in fact a part of this reality and change it as we observe it. Moreover, we perceive ourselves as part of reality.**

**MARIA: I think our perception totally creates our reality. No one can know what "reality" really is. Reality for me is not reality for you. I notice my dad only notices when a woman cuts him off on the road, but when a man does it, he only complains. I'm sure that if we actually took count, more men than women have cut him off, but he still thinks women are worse drivers than men. If we actually do take count, he may change his mind, but I think he's too stubborn to do so. In this case, I'm not sure how else I would change his perceptions and actually get a change in behavior or attitude.**

**LESLIE: I think it is possible for psychologists to change people's perceptions. I think with conditioning, subjects could perceive something differently—they may perceive something which they once thought positive to be negative because the psychologist has ingrained it in their minds.**

**SCOTT: I heard that if you turn a baby upside down for a while (say a couple of weeks), he/she starts seeing the world right side up from that upside-down position. When the baby is turned right side up, everything seems upside down. Well, I just wanted to say that perception in some ways can be altered, but I don't know about changing behaviors by changing perception.**

• • • • • • •

Now that you've been exposed to other students' views, have your opinions changed at all? Which questions and ideas did you find most compelling? In what ways can psychology contribute to our understanding of perception and reality?

readily see how an artist can use distance cues not only to give realistic depth to a picture but also to create perceptual experiences that don't correspond to anything in the real world. Three-dimensional movies also work on the principle that the brain can be deceived into seeing three dimensions if slightly different images are presented to the left and right eyes (working on the principle of retinal disparity). Thus, our understanding of perceptual illusion enables us to manipulate images for deliberate effect—and to delight in the results.

Other species are also fooled by monocular depth cues. For example, Virginia Gunderson and her colleagues showed two identical toys to infant rhesus monkeys who were wearing an eye patch over one eye. The toys were placed against a background pattern of squares and trapezoids that produces depth cues like those in the "tunnel" of Figure 3-36. One of the toys was placed lower than the other against the photograph to exaggerate the effect—just like the "smaller" monster in the tunnel illusion. Even though the toys were the same distance from the monkeys, the infant monkeys tended to reach for the lower toy, suggesting that they perceived it to be closer (Gunderson et al., 1993).

## LOOKING FORWARD

Students often take a psychology course because they are interested in psychological disorders and mental dysfunctions. The study of sensation and perception, however, is the study of order rather than disorder and function rather than dysfunction. In this chapter, we have seen that no simple relationship exists between an external event and our experience of it. Even when we examine a single sensory system, we see that it is designed to respond to different aspects of a stimulus—to break the stimulus down into its most primitive parts. In turn, systems in the brain are designed to synthesize the basic components of an experience and somehow compose a whole and unified experience. As we pursue better explanations of sensory and perceptual events, we make discoveries with practical applications for improving our lives. Researchers have been experimenting for a number of years with mechanisms to restore sight to people with damaged eyes or optic nerves; other scientists are working on ways to restore—not just aid—hearing. Chronic pain interrupts the normal lives of thousands of people each year, and some researchers have applied our understanding of pain mechanisms to provide relief to those people. Even the remarkably sharp picture on a giant color television screen owes its clarity to research into sensory function.

However, most of the research in the fields of sensation and perception is aimed at figuring out how the fundamental processes of our senses work and how we use sensory information to understand the world around us. Underlying most of this research is a curiosity about human experience. Though we usually take our sensory and perceptual experiences for granted, as soon as we begin systematically to investigate the seemingly simple processes of vision or smell, for example, we see that they are magically complex. More than anything else, it is the need to unravel the complexity—to solve the puzzles—that drives research in sensation and perception.

## SUMMARY

This chapter examines sensation and perception, the phenomena that enable us to gather and understand information from numerous sources. **Sensation** refers to the raw sensory data from the senses of sight, hearing, smell, taste, balance, touch, and pain. **Perception** is the process of creating meaningful patterns from that raw sensory data.

### THE NATURE OF SENSORY PROCESSES

#### The Character of Sensation

In all sensory processes, some form of energy stimulates a receptor cell in one of the sense organs. The receptor cell converts that energy into a neural signal, which is further coded as it travels along sensory nerves. By the time it reaches the brain, the message is quite precise.

### Sensory Thresholds

The energy reaching a receptor must be sufficiently intense to produce a noticeable effect. The least amount of energy needed to generate any sensation at all in a person 50 percent of the time is called the **absolute threshold**. The **difference threshold** or the **just noticeable difference (jnd)** is the smallest change in stimulation that is detectable 50 percent of the time. Generally, the stronger the stimulation, the bigger the change must be to be sensed. In most cases, our senses adjust to the level of stimulation they are experiencing, a process known as **adaptation**.

Subliminal messages are messages that fall below the threshold of conscious perception and are therefore assumed to be perceived subconsciously. Some studies have indicated that in a controlled laboratory setting people can be influenced briefly by sensory messages that are outside their conscious awareness. No scientific studies support the claims, however, that advertisers can use subliminal messages to influence consumer choices or that subliminal phrases in self-help tapes can significantly change a person's behavior.

## VISION

Unlike most animals, humans rely most heavily on their sense of vision to relate to the world.

### The Visual System

In the process leading to vision, light enters the eye through the **cornea**, then passes through the **pupil** and the **lens**, which focuses it onto the **retina**. The lens changes its shape to allow light to be focused sharply on the retina. Directly behind the lens and on the retina is a depressed spot called the **fovea**, which lies at the center of the visual field.

The retina of each eye contains the two kinds of **receptor cells** responsible for vision: **rods** and **cones**. Rods, chiefly responsible for night vision, respond to varying degrees of light and dark but not to color. Cones respond to light and dark as well as to color, and operate mainly in daytime. Only cones are present in the fovea.

Rods and cones connect to the nerve cells, called **bipolar cells**, leading to the brain. In the fovea, a single cone generally connects with one bipolar cell. Rods, on the other hand, share bipolar cells. The one-to-one connection between cones and bipolar cells in the fovea allows for maximum **visual acuity**, the ability to distinguish fine details. Vision is thus sharpest whenever the image of an object falls directly on the fovea; outside the fovea, acuity drops dramatically.

The sensitivity of rods and cones changes according to the amount of light available. **Light adaptation** helps our eyes adjust to bright light; **dark adaptation** allows us to see, at least partially, in conditions of darkness.

Neural messages originating in the retina must eventually reach the brain for a visual sensation to occur. The bipolar cells connect to **ganglion cells**, whose axons converge to form the **optic nerve** that carries messages to the brain.

There are more than 100 million rods and cones in each retina, but only about 1 million ganglion cells to receive and transmit information from them. Two kinds of ganglion cells divide between themselves the type of information that is sent to the brain. Approximately 100,000 magnocellular cells (M-cells) code general information about an object's distance and movement. The remaining (nearly 1 million) parvocellular cells (P-cells) encode detailed information about color, shape, and form.

### Color Vision

The human vision system allows us to see an extensive range of colors. **Hue, saturation**, and **brightness** are three separate aspects of our experience of color. Hue refers to colors (red, green, blue, etc.); saturation indicates the vividness or richness of the hues, and brightness is the intensity of the hues. Humans can distinguish only about 150 hues, but through gradations of saturation and brightness, we can perceive about 300,000 colors.

Theories of color vision attempt to explain how the cones, which number only about 150,000 in the fovea, are able to distinguish some 300,000 different colors. One clue lies in color mixing: **Additive color mixing** is the process of mixing only a few *lights* of different wavelengths to create many new colors; **subtractive color mixing** refers to mixing a few *pigments* to come up with a whole palette of new colors.

Based on the principles of additive color mixing, the **trichromatic theory** of color vision holds that the eye contains three different kinds of color receptors that are most responsive to either red, green, or blue light. By combining signals from these three basic receptors, the brain can detect any color and even subtle differences among nearly identical colors. By contrast, the **opponent-process theory** maintains that receptors are specialized to respond to either member of the three basic color pairs: red-green, yellow-blue, and black-white (dark and light).

Drawing on elements of the two theories, current knowledge holds that while there are three kinds of receptors for colors in the retina (for violet-blue, green, and yellow light), the messages they transmit are coded by other neurons in the visual system into opponent-process form.

## HEARING

Sounds and noises we hear are psychological experiences created by the brain in response to stimulation.

## SOUND

The physical stimuli for the sense of hearing are **sound waves**, which produce vibration in the eardrum. **Frequency** is the number of cycles per second in a wave, expressed in a unit called **hertz**. Frequency is the primary determinant of **pitch**—how high or low the tone seems to be. **Amplitude** is the magnitude of a wave; it largely determines the loudness of a sound. Loudness is measured in **decibels**.

### The Ear

Hearing begins when sound waves strike the eardrum and cause it to vibrate. This vibration, in turn, makes three bones in the middle ear—the **hammer**, the **anvil**, and the **stirrup**—to vibrate in sequence. These vibrations are magnified in their passage through the middle ear deep into the inner ear. There the vibrations cause the fluid inside the **cochlea** to vibrate, pushing the **basilar membrane** and **organ of Corti** up and down.

Inside the organ of Corti are tiny hair cells that act as sensory receptors for hearing. Stimulation of these receptors produces auditory signals that are transmitted to the brain through the **auditory nerve**. The brain pools the information from thousands of these cells to create the perception of sounds.

## THE OTHER SENSES

### Smell

The sense of smell is activated by substances carried by airborne molecules into the nasal cavities, where the substances activate highly specialized receptors for smell, located in the **olfactory epithelium**. From here messages are carried directly to the **olfactory bulb** in the brain, where they are sent to the brain's temporal lobe, resulting in our awareness of smells.

### Taste

The receptor cells for the sense of taste are housed in the **taste buds** on the tongue, which, in turn, are found in the **papillae**, the small bumps on the surface of the tongue. Each taste bud contains a cluster of taste receptors, or hair cells, that cause their adjacent neurons to fire when they become activated by the chemical substances in food, sending a nerve impulse to the brain.

We experience only four primary taste qualities: sweet, sour, salty, and bitter. All other tastes derive from combinations of these four. Flavor is a complex blend of taste and smell.

### Kinesthetic and Vestibular Senses

The **kinesthetic senses** relay specific information about muscle movement, changes in posture, and strain on muscles and joints. They rely on feedback from two sets of specialized nerve endings: **stretch receptors**, which are attached to muscle fibers, and **Golgi tendon organs**, attached to the tendons.

The **vestibular senses** control equilibrium and create an awareness of body position. The receptors for these senses are located in the vestibular organs in the inner ear. The sensation of body rotation arises in the three **semicircular canals** of the inner ear. The sensation of gravitation and movement forward and backward, as well as up and down, is generated by the two **vestibular sacs** that lie between the semicircular canals and the cochlea. Both are filled with fluid.

### Sensations of Motion

The vestibular organs are also responsible for motion sickness, which triggers strong reactions in some people. Motion sickness may be caused by the discrepancies between visual information and vestibular sensation.

### The Skin Senses

The skin is the largest sense organ, with numerous nerve receptors distributed in varying concentrations throughout its surface. The nerve fibers from these receptors travel to the brain.

Skin receptors give rise to what are known as the *cutaneous sensations* of pressure, temperature, and pain. Research has not established a simple connection between the various types of receptors and the separate sensations. Because the brain uses complex information about the patterns of activity on many different receptors to detect and discriminate among skin sensations, a direct connection between receptors and sensations has so far eluded researchers.

### Pain

People have varying degrees of sensitivity to pain. The most commonly accepted explanation of pain is the **gate control theory**, which holds that a "neurological gate" in the spinal cord controls the transmission of pain impulses to the brain.

## PERCEPTION

There are several ways in which the brain interprets the complex flow of information from the various senses and creates perceptual experiences that go far beyond what is sensed directly.

### Perceptual Organization

One important way our perceptual processes work is through distinguishing **figures** from the **ground** against which they appear. The figure-ground distinction pertains to all our senses, not just vision. For instance, a violin solo stands out against the "ground" of a symphony orchestra. When we use sensory information to create perceptions, we fill in the missing information, group various objects together, see whole objects, and hear meaningful sounds.

### Perceptual Constancies

**Perceptual constancy** is our tendency to perceive objects as unchanging in the face of changes in sensory stimulation. Once we have formed a stable perception of an object, we can recognize it from almost any angle. Thus, **size, shape, brightness**, and **color constancies** help us relate to the world better. Memory and experience play an important part in perceptual constancy, compensating for confusing stimuli.

### Observer Characteristics

In addition to past experience and learning, several personal factors influence our perception. For example, our familiarity with a symbol or object affects our expectation of how the object should look, even if we observe subtle changes in its appearance. Our perceptions are also influenced by our individual method of dealing with the environment and by our cultural background, values, and cognitive style.

### Perception of Distance and Depth

We can perceive distance and depth through **monocular cues**, from one eye, or **binocular cues**, which depend on the interaction of both eyes.

**Superposition** is a monocular distance cue in which one object, by partly blocking a second, appears closer. **Linear perspective** is another monocular cue to distance and depth based on the fact that two parallel lines seem to come together at the horizon. Other monocular cues include **aerial perspective, elevation,** and **texture gradient**.

With binocular cues, the **stereoscopic vision** obtained from combining the two retinal images makes perceptions of depth and distance clearer. **Convergence** is another binocular cue. Humans, apes, and some predatory animals with the ability to use binocular cues have a distinct advantage over animals whose vision is limited to monocular cues.

Sounds, too, add to our sense of space. **Sound localization** is our ability to determine where a sound originates. **Monaural cues**, such as loudness and distance, require only one ear. On the other hand, **binaural cues**, such as discrepancies in the arrival time of sound waves and their volume, which help us to locate the source of a sound, depend on the collaboration of both ears.

### Visual Illusions

Visual illusions occur when we use a variety of sensory cues to create perceptual experiences that do not actually exist.

More easily understood are **physical illusions**, an example of which is the bent appearance of a stick when placed in water. **Perceptual illusions** depend primarily on our own perceptual processes and occur because the stimulus contains misleading cues.

# REVIEW QUESTIONS

## MULTIPLE CHOICE

1. The ______ threshold is the smallest change in stimulation that can be detected 50 percent of the time.
   a. absolute　　b. difference

2. Match the following terms with their definitions:

| | |
|---|---|
| ______ cornea | a. colored part of the eye |
| ______ pupil | b. center of the visual field |
| ______ iris | c. receptor cell responsible for color vision |
| ______ lens | d. protective layer over front part of the eye |
| ______ fovea | e. contains the receptor cells that respond to light |
| ______ retina | f. focuses light onto the retina |
| ______ rod | g. receptor cell responsible for night vision |
| ______ cone | h. opening in the iris through which light enters |

3. The process whereby the rods and cones adjust to become more sensitive to lowered levels of illumination is known as ________________.
   a. dark adaptation　　b. light adaptation

4. The place on the retina where the axons of all the ganglion cells come together to leave the eye is called the ______ .
   a. fovea　　c. optic chiasm
   b. blind spot　　d. visual cortex

5. ______ , ______ , and ______ are three separate aspects of our experience of color.

6. The process of mixing pigments is known as ______ color mixing.
   a. additive　　b. subtractive

7. Trichromats can mix ______ , ______ , and ______ lights to create virtually any hue.

8. The theory of color that best explains color afterimages is ____________________ .
   a. the volley theory
   b. trichromatic theory
   c. opponent-process theory
   d. subtractive color theory

9. As a sound wave moves from the outer ear to the inner ear, number the following in the order that it would reach them:
   ______ oval window
   ______ anvil
   ______ cochlea
   ______ auditory nerve
   ______ round window

10. Match the following theories with their definitions:

| | |
|---|---|
| ____frequency theory | a. groups of cells fire in sequence, not each individually |
| ____volley principle | b. rate at which hair cells in the cochlea fire determines pitch |
| ____place theory | c. different parts of basilar membrane respond to different frequencies |

11. The receptor cells for taste lie in the ______ ______ on the tongue and give rise to the four basic taste sensations: ______ , ______ , ______ , and ______ .

12. The sense of pain can be affected by ______ , ______ , ______ , and ______ .

13. Placebos and acupuncture may affect pain by ______ .
    a. closing the pain gate
    b. releasing endorphins
    c. blocking pain receptors in the skin

14. The process by which we create meaningful experiences out of the jumble of sensory information is called ______ .

15. In the case of reversible figures, we have difficulty distinguishing the ______ from the ______ behind it.

16. Match the following principles of perception with their definitions:

| | |
|---|---|
| ____ similarity | a. tendency to perceive a whole object even where none exists |
| ____ continuity | b. objects in motion together appear to stand out from their surroundings of the visual field |
| ____ common fate | c. elements that continue a pattern are likely to be seen as part of the pattern |
| ____ proximity | d. objects that are like one another tend to be grouped together |
| ____ closure | e. elements found close together tend to be perceived as a unit |

17. Next to each depth cue, put B if it is a binocular cue and M if it is a monocular cue.
    ______ retinal disparity
    ______ texture gradient
    ______ shadowing
    ______ convergence
    ______ motion parallax
    ______ stereoscopic vision
    ______ linear perspective
    ______ superposition

18. The perception of loud sounds as being closer than faint sounds is a common ______ cue to sound localization.
    a. monaural   b. binaural

19. Autokinetic illusion, stroboscopic motion, and the phi phenomenon are three examples of ______ movement.

## CRITICAL THINKING AND APPLICATIONS

20. When we look directly at an object, the image is focused on each eye's fovea. Why is this advantageous?

21. When we are reading or studying, we often seem to be very aware of movements off to our sides. Why is it so easy to sense these events?

22. What is the difference between the vestibular sense and the kinesthetic sense? What kinds of activities require both?

23. Adults seem to enjoy the flavors of many things that children find disgusting. What kinds of things might contribute to changes in taste preference throughout the life span?

24. "Flavor" is thought of as the combination of the taste sense with the sense of smell. How could you demonstrate the difference between flavor and taste? Between flavor and smell?

25. What sorts of emotional or motivational factors affect our sense of pain? Do these same factors have similar effects on other senses?

26. Examine a few passages of your favorite song. Explain how the Gestalt principles of organization (proximity, similarity, closure, etc.) operate in the perception of music.

*(Answers to the Review Questions can be found in the back of the text.)*

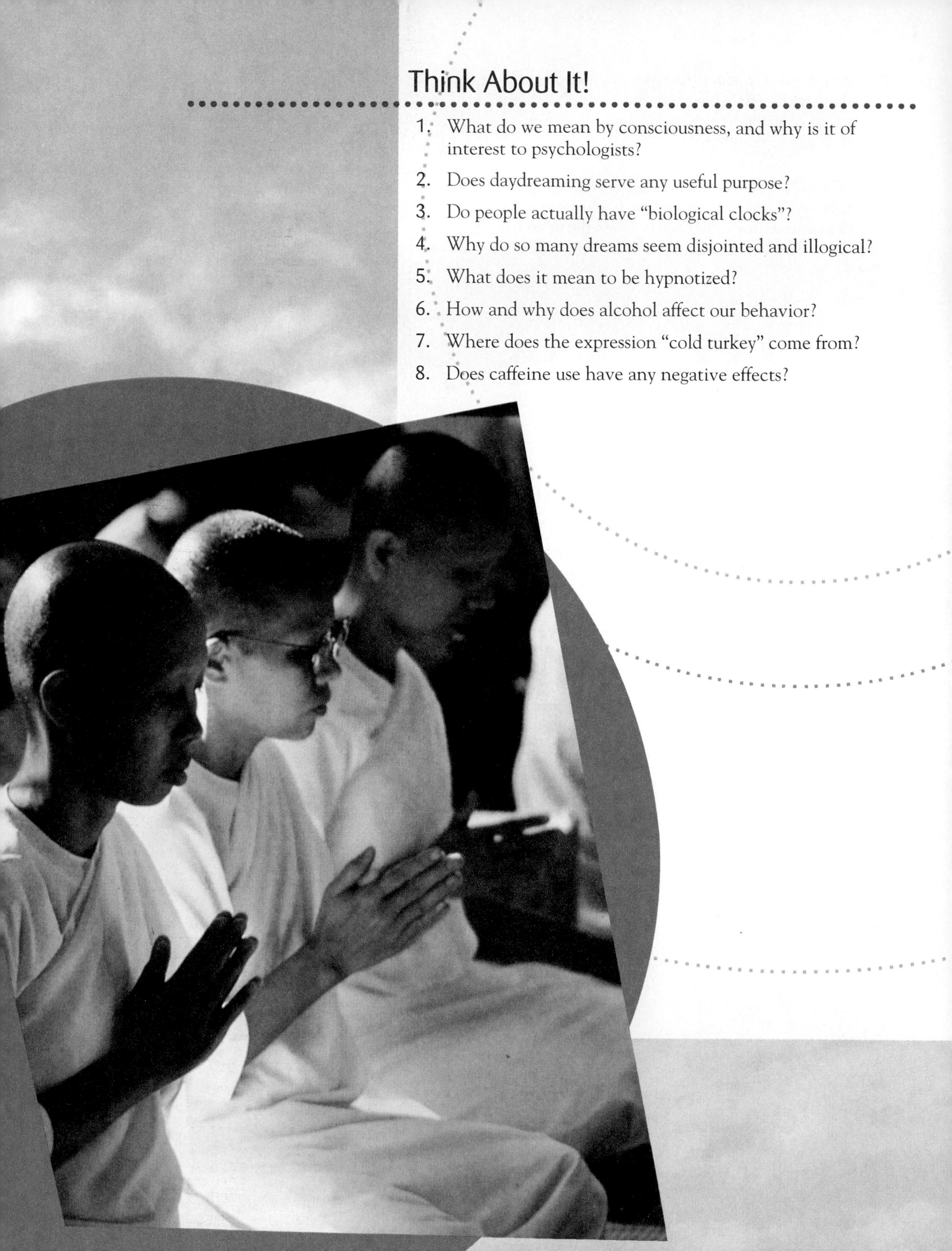

## Think About It!

1. What do we mean by consciousness, and why is it of interest to psychologists?
2. Does daydreaming serve any useful purpose?
3. Do people actually have "biological clocks"?
4. Why do so many dreams seem disjointed and illogical?
5. What does it mean to be hypnotized?
6. How and why does alcohol affect our behavior?
7. Where does the expression "cold turkey" come from?
8. Does caffeine use have any negative effects?

# STATES OF CONSCIOUSNESS

4

## Overview

**Consciousness** Our awareness of various cognitive processes, such as sleeping, dreaming, concentrating, and making decisions.

**Waking consciousness** Mental state that includes the thoughts, feelings, and perceptions that occur when we are awake and reasonably alert.

**Altered state of consciousness (ASC)** Mental state that differs noticeably from normal waking consciousness.

**Consider the following scenario. You wake up and start your day by deciding what to eat for breakfast and what to wear. After breakfast, you sit down to memorize some facts for an upcoming history exam, but you soon find yourself daydreaming about last night's date or next summer's vacation. You realize your mind is wandering, and you make a deliberate effort to refocus your attention on your history test. During lunch, you drink a cup of coffee or tea to stay alert. After lunch, you spend some time reflecting on bigger questions, such as what subject to major in or what direction you want your life to take. You meditate to ease your anxiety over the upcoming test. Later you decide to go out for dinner, and you have a glass of wine or beer with your meal. Finally, at the end of the day, you fall asleep and, shortly thereafter, experience the first of several dreams you will have before morning.**

This depiction of an ordinary day in the life of a student illustrates the great variety of cognitive processes that occur in human beings: Making decisions, remembering, daydreaming, concentrating, reflecting, sleeping, and dreaming are but a few of the mental processes we commonly experience. Our awareness of these various mental processes is called **consciousness**.

From an evolutionary perspective, consciousness has had important survival value. Slow and weak compared to many other animals, humans have compensated for these physical disadvantages by developing mental skills that enable them to think, reason, remember, plan, and predict.

What do we mean by consciousness, and why is it of interest to psychologists?

Throughout human history, philosophers, theologians, artists, and, most recently, scientists have all tried to grasp the elusive nature of consciousness. From William James's early characterization of consciousness as a kaleidoscopic flow or "stream" mingling internal and external information, to behaviorists John B. Watson and B.F. Skinner's outright rejection of consciousness as a subject of scientific inquiry, contemporary scientific psychology has settled on a middle ground of sorts. Pioneering techniques like electroencephalography (EEG), PET and CT scans, magnetic resonance imaging (MRI), and magnetoencephalography (MEG) cast new light on brain activity during various states of consciousness, allowing us to study these states with a measure of precision. By linking data from these techniques with subjective reports of conscious processes, scientists have made tremendous strides in understanding human consciousness.'

All these technological and cultural developments stimulated the study of consciousness (Hilgard, 1980). Generally speaking, contemporary psychologists divide consciousness into two broad areas. **Waking consciousness**—or conscious awareness—includes all the thoughts, feelings, and perceptions that occur when we are awake and reasonably alert. Such waking consciousness encompasses sensation and perception, learning, memory, thinking, problem solving, decision making, intelligence, and creativity—all processes so pivotal in contemporary psychology that whole chapters are devoted to them in this book.

But there are times when we experience **altered states of consciousness (ASC)**; then our mental state differs markedly from our normal waking consciousness. Some altered states (such as daydreaming, sleep, and dreaming) occur routinely, even spontaneously. Other ASCs (such as hypnosis, meditation, and intoxication) are brought on by deliberate attempts to alter normal consciousness. In this chapter we will begin by examining natural variations in consciousness. Then we will turn our attention to strategies people use to deliberately alter normal states of consciousness.

## NATURAL VARIATIONS IN CONSCIOUSNESS

Even when we are fully awake and alert, we are usually conscious of only a small portion of what is going on around us. At any given moment, we are exposed to a great variety of sounds, sights, and smells from the outside world. At the same time, we experience all sorts of internal sensations (such as heat and cold, touch, pressure, pain, equilibrium) as well as an array of thoughts, memories, emotions, and needs. Normally, however, we are not aware of all these competing stimuli; after all, to survive and make sense of our environment, we are forced to select only the most important information to attend to and then filter out everything else. At times we pay such close attention to what we are doing that we are wholly absorbed in it and oblivious to what is going on around us (see the Highlights box titled "Going with the Flow"). How this process of attention works is examined at some length in the chapter on memory. Here it is enough to note that the hallmark of normal waking consciousness is the highly selective nature of attention.

We are subject to numerous cognitive processes, undergo all sorts of experiences, and perform numerous tasks without being consciously aware of them. For example, we are rarely attuned to such vital bodily processes as

### Going with the Flow

Most of us have experienced moments of total absorption when we are so focused on what we are doing that our sense of time passes unnoticed and we are filled with happiness. New research suggests that such wholehearted absorption—whether in reading a book, skiing, building something, or playing the piano—leads to an altered state of consciousness in which our minds function at peak effectiveness and we experience a feeling of effortless engagement.

Mike Csikszentmihalyi, a psychologist at the University of Chicago, refers to these moments of absorption as "flow states," periods when everything falls into place perfectly and you feel most alive and fully intent on what you're doing. In one study, Csikszentmihalyi and his colleagues at Chicago and at the Milan Medical School found that people enter the flow state when the demands on them are a little higher than usual, so they are not bored, but not so great that they become anxious (Massimini, Csikszentmihalyi, & Della Fave, 1988). Certain techniques promote the flow state. One method is to make a task more challenging. For example, an assembly-line worker whose job is tightening screws escaped the boredom inherent in the daily repetition by experimenting with ways to cut a few seconds from the time it took to complete the task. Another method is to pay strict attention to a task; initially, this is a struggle, but then the person relaxes into an effortless flow state.

Flow researchers distinguish between strained and effortless attention. Findings by scientists at the National Institute of Mental Health indicate that these two kinds of attention correspond to opposing patterns of brain function (J. A. Hamilton, Haier, & Buchsbaum, 1984). Strained concentration is accompanied by increased cortical arousal, while the effortless concentration typical of flow is associated with decreased arousal.

The deep concentration of the flow state bears a striking similarity to the altered state of hypnosis. Research shows that people who are drawn to fantasizing or who easily become absorbed in a painting are more readily hypnotized than other people (Pekala & Kumar, 1984). Once hypnotized, such individuals frequently report feelings mirroring those in altered states—joy, a sense of deep meaningfulness coupled with rich imagery, a distorted sense of time, and profound attentiveness (Pekala & Kumar, 1986).

**Daydreaming** Alteration in consciousness that occurs seemingly without effort, typically when we want to momentarily escape the demands of the real world.

blood pressure and respiration. And most of us can walk down the street or ride a bicycle without consciously thinking about every movement we are making. In fact, we carry out certain tasks better when we are not consciously aware of performing them. You probably have no trouble signing your name; you may do it several times in a day "without giving it a thought." But if you think carefully about each movement you are making with your pen or pencil, you will find that signing your name so that it looks normal becomes exceedingly difficult. Similarly, if you are driving your car along the familiar route that you always take to work or school, the process may be so automatic that you remain largely unaware of your surroundings en route.

Many psychologists believe that certain key mental processes, such as recognizing a word or a friend's face, also go on outside of normal waking consciousness. As we saw in the first chapter, Sigmund Freud thought that many of the most important influences on our behavior—such as erotic feelings for our parents—are screened from our consciousness even though they underlie much of our behavior. According to Freud, the conscious part of our minds is only the tip of the iceberg. The real driving forces behind human actions are sexual and aggressive instincts that remain largely hidden—though they may come to the fore in such altered states of consciousness as hypnosis and dreaming. We will explore the notion of nonconscious mental processes as we consider various ASCs in this chapter, and when we delve into behavior disorders in the chapter on abnormal behavior.

## Daydreaming and Fantasy

While it takes a deliberate effort to enter an ASC via hypnosis, drugs, or meditation, **daydreaming** is an ASC that occurs seemingly without effort. For example, in your psychology class, you may suddenly find yourself preoccupied with thoughts of lunch or a recent conversation with a friend.

Typically, we daydream when we would rather be somewhere else or be doing something else—it is a momentary escape from the demands of the real world. You may reminisce pleasantly about last year's vacation while doing an unpleasant chore or mentally flee the daily college grind to fantasize about your future as a business tycoon. Your daydreams give you the opportunity to write, star in, and stage-manage a private drama for which you are the only audience.

**2.** Does daydreaming serve any useful purpose?

Are daydreams random paths your mind travels? Not at all. Psychologists have discovered that people's daydreams fall into several distinct categories and that different people prefer particular kinds of daydreams (Singer, 1975). People who score high on measures of anxiety often have fleeting, loosely connected daydreams related to worrying, which give them little pleasure. By contrast, people who are achievement oriented tend to replay in their daydreams recurring themes of achievement, guilt, fear of failure, and hostility, reflecting the self-doubt and competitive envy that accompanies great ambition. Still other people derive considerable enjoyment from their daydreams and use them to solve problems, think ahead, or distract themselves. These "happy daydreamers" stage for themselves pleasant fantasies uncomplicated by guilt or worry. Finally, people with unusual curiosity about their environment who also value objective thinking and experience daydreams filled with scenes from the objective world and marked by controlled lines of thought.

About 4 percent of us are considered *fantasy-prone*, meaning we spend more than half our time not merely daydreaming but lost in elaborate reveries. Studies of fantasy-prone people reveal that they are generally highly creative (Lynn & Rhue, 1988). One fantasy-prone woman actually found herself shivering uncontrollably while watching the movie *Dr. Zhivago*, much of which takes place during a Siberian winter.

Does daydreaming, which is nearly universal, serve any useful function? Some psychologists argue that daydreams have little or no positive or practical value. They regard daydreaming as nothing more than a retreat from the real world, especially when that world is not meeting our needs. One study, for example, found that television viewing stimulates spontaneous daydreaming, but decreases the purposeful use of creative imagination (Valkenburg & van der Voort, 1994).

Other psychologists stress the positive value of daydreaming and fantasy (Klinger, 1990). According to Freudian theorists, daydreams allow us to express and deal with desires—generally relating to sex or hostility—that would otherwise make us feel guilty or anxious (Giambra, 1974). And Pulaski (1974) speculates that daydreaming builds cognitive and creative skills; for example, it is difficult to imagine an artist or a writer becoming a success without an active fantasy life. Pulaski also notes that daydreaming helps people endure difficult situations; prisoners of war have used it to survive torture and deprivation. In her view, then, daydreaming and fantasy provide welcome relief from everyday—often unpleasant—reality and reduce internal tension and external aggression.

Singer goes one step further, proposing that daydreams are more than just a substitute for reality or a means of relieving tension; they are also an important way of dealing with information (see the chapter on memory). Every day we process a vast, potentially overwhelming array of information received through the senses. When the chance arises—either during a dull moment in the day or in dreams at night—we reshape some of this information into new and more useful forms. Daydreams and dreams, then, provide a forum for us to handle "unfinished business." Although daydreaming temporarily distracts us from the real world, Singer believes that in the long run this hiatus allows us to take a step back and reassess things so we are better able to cope when real-world crises bear down.

## Sleep and Dreaming

We spend about one-third of our lives in the altered state of consciousness known as sleep. Throughout history, cultures had paid varying degrees of respect to sleep and the dreams that inhabit it. In some societies people believed that universal truths are revealed in dreams; members of other societies view sleep as a nonproductive, though essential, activity. Only recently have sleep researchers started to analyze the fascinating complexity of sleep, its functions, and its psychological and biological value.

**CIRCADIAN CYCLES: THE BIOLOGICAL CLOCK** Like many other biological functions, sleep and waking follow a daily, or *circadian*, cycle (from the Latin expression *circa diem*, meaning "about a day") (Moore-Ede, Czeisler, & Richardson, 1983). The time we spend asleep and awake depends on a 24-hour cycle influenced by the sun. Sleep-wake cycles change as the days grow longer or shorter with the seasons. Metabolism, stomach acidity, alertness, body temperature, blood pressure, and the level of most hormones also vary predictably over the course of a day. Together, these rhythms are often referred to as our *biological clock*. Not all body cycles follow the same pattern. For example, the level of the hormone epinephrine (which causes the body to go on alert) reaches a peak in the late morning hours and then steadily declines until around midnight, when it suddenly drops to a very low level and remains there until morning. By contrast, levels of melatonin (which figures in the onset of sleep) surge at night and drop off during the day.

3. Do people actually have "biological clocks"?

Normally, the rhythms and chemistry of all these different cycles interact smoothly, so that a shift in one brings about a corresponding shift in others (Moore-Ede, Czeisler et al., 1983). In fact, we rarely notice these circadian rhythms until they are disturbed. Jet lag is a familiar example: You might take a nine-hour transatlantic flight departing from New York at 7 P.M. New York time and arriving in London at 9 A.M. London time—just in time to start the day, even though, according to your biological clock it's really 4 A.M. and long past your bedtime. Shift work serves as another example: Workers who are transferred from the day shift to the midnight shift often experience weight loss and suffer from irritability, health problems, insomnia, and extreme drowsiness around the clock for a very long time (Richardson, Miner, & Czeisler, 1989–1990). These disruptions of the biological clock pose a threat to safety in the case of pilots or workers operating dangerous equipment. Even the change from standard time to daylight saving time and back again creates temporary problems of adjustment for most people.

Researchers recently found a way to adjust our biological clocks. It seems that light inhibits the production of melatonin (Lewy, 1992), which, as we mentioned earlier, goes up as the sun goes down. A small dose of melatonin taken in the morning (the time when the hormone is usually tapering off) sets back or slows down the biological clock. Taken in the evening, melatonin speeds up the biological clock, making the person fall asleep earlier than usual (Lewy, 1992). Someday a melatonin pill, perhaps used in conjunction with exposure to sunlight or darkness, may help people adjust their circadian rhythms at will.

**SLEEP** Nobody who has tried to stay awake longer than 20 hours or so can doubt the necessity of sleep. There are people who claim they never sleep, but, when they are observed under laboratory conditions, some actually sleep soundly without being aware of it, while others engage in short periods of "microsleep," dozing for a second or two at a time. Merely resting doesn't satisfy us. When an organism is sleep-deprived, it craves sleep just as strongly as it would food or water after a period of deprivation.

So we certainly need to sleep, yet nobody knows exactly why. Many scientists believe that sleep restores effective functioning of the body and brain. This view implies that during waking life the body is depleted of certain chemicals that are replenished during sleep, but little evidence supports this idea. While protein synthesis in the brain speeds up during sleep, no one has determined that protein depletion causes sleep. A chemical called the *s-factor*, which has been isolated from the brains of animals and from human urine, induces deep sleep when injected into the brain (Maugh, 1981). But again, scientists can point to no evidence that a buildup of the s-factor brings on sleep or even that sleep reduces the level of s-factor in the body. Some psychologists, working from an evolutionary perspective, see sleep as an adaptive mechanism that evolved to encourage organisms to remain inactive and conserve energy during times of the day when their food supplies were low or their predators were especially numerous. So far scientists have been unable to piece together a satisfactory explanation of the role of sleep from these provocative hypotheses.

Sleep researchers monitor volunteers' brain waves, muscle tension, and other physiological functions.

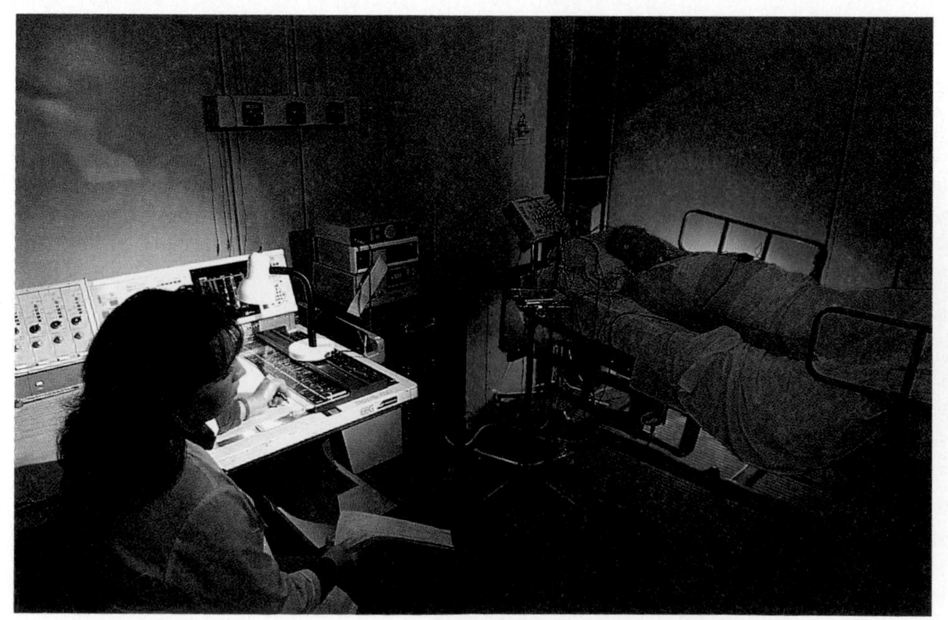

Although still uncertain about the function of sleep, scientists have learned a great deal about the rhythms of sleep and the dreams that occur as we sleep. Researchers do not usually enter people's homes to study how they sleep. Instead, they recruit volunteers who are willing to spend one or more nights in what is called a "sleep lab." With electrodes painlessly attached to their skulls, the volunteers sleep comfortably as their brain waves, eye movements, muscle tension, and other physiological functions are monitored. Data from such studies show that although there are significant individual differences in sleep behavior, almost everyone goes through several stages of sleep (Anch et al., 1988) and that each stage is marked by characteristic patterns of brain waves, muscular activity, blood pressure, and body temperature. Figure 4-1 illustrates the electrical activity related to the brain, heart, and facial muscles at each stage.

"Going to sleep" means losing awareness and failing to respond to a stimulus that would produce a response in the waking state. As measured by an EEG, brain waves during this "twilight" state are characterized by irregular, low-voltage *alpha waves*. This brain-wave pattern mirrors the sense of relaxed wakefulness that we experience while lying on a beach or in a hammock or when resting after a big meal. In this twilight state with the eyes closed, people often report seeing flashing lights and colors, geometric patterns, and visions of landscapes. Sometimes they also experience a floating or falling sensation, followed by a quick jolt back to consciousness.

After this initial twilight phase, the sleeper enters Stage 1 of sleep. Stage 1 brain waves are "tight" and of very low amplitude, resembling those recorded when a person is alert or excited. But in contrast to normal waking consciousness, Stage 1 of the sleep cycle is marked by a slowing of the pulse, muscle relaxation, and side-to-side rolling movements of the eyes—the last being the most reliable indication of this first stage of the sleep process (Dement, 1974). Stage 1 usually lasts only a few moments. The sleeper is easily aroused at this stage and, once awake, may be unaware of having slept at all.

Stages 2 and 3 are characterized by progressively deeper sleep. Brain waves increase in amplitude and become slower. At these stages, the sleeper is hard to awaken and does not respond to stimuli such as noises or lights. Heart rate, blood pressure, and temperature continue to drop.

In Stage 4 sleep, the brain emits very slow *delta waves*. Heart rate, breathing rate, blood pressure, and body temperature are as low as they will

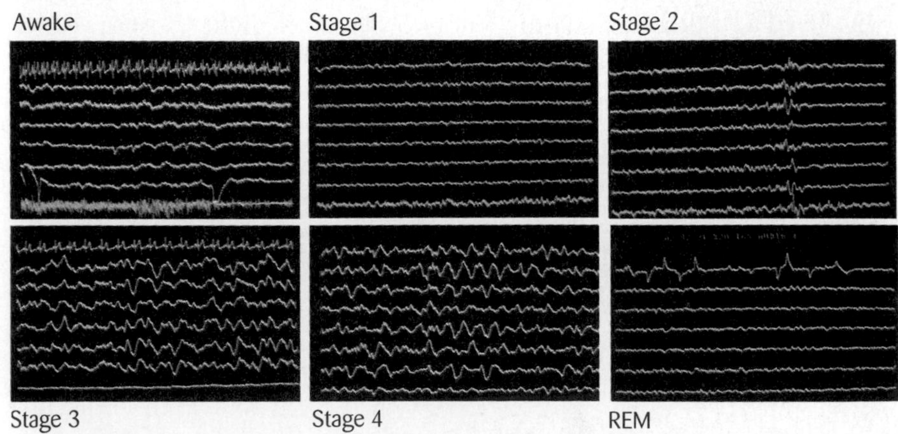


**Figure 4-1**
**Waves of sleep.** This series of printouts illustrates electrical activity in the brain, heart, and facial muscles during the various stages of sleep. Levels of activity are lowest during Stage 4 (delta) sleep.

**REM (paradoxical) sleep** Sleep stage characterized by rapid eye movement; it is during this stage that most vivid dreaming occurs.

**Non-REM (NREM) sleep** Non–rapid-eye-movement stages of sleep that alternate with REM stages during the sleep cycle.

get during the night. In young adults, delta sleep occurs in 15- to 20-minute segments—interspersed with lighter sleep—mostly during the first half of the night. Delta sleep time lessens with age but continues to be the first sleep to be made up after sleep has been lost.

About an hour after falling asleep, the sleeper begins to ascend from Stage 4 sleep to Stage 3, Stage 2, and back to Stage 1—a process that takes about 40 minutes. The brain waves return to the low-amplitude, sawtoothed shape characteristic of Stage 1 sleep and waking alertness. Heart rate and blood pressure also increase, yet the muscles of the body are more relaxed than at any other point in the sleep cycle, and the person is very difficult to awaken. The eyes move rapidly under closed eyelids. This **rapid eye movement (REM)** sleep stage is distinguished from all other stages of sleep (called **non-REM** or **NREM**) that precede and follow it.

REM sleep is also called **paradoxical sleep**, because while measures of brain activity, heart rate, blood pressure, and other physiological functions closely resemble those recorded during waking consciousness, the person in this stage appears to be deeply asleep and is incapable of moving since the body's voluntary muscles are essentially paralyzed. This is also the stage when most vivid dreaming occurs. When researchers made lesions on the brain stems of cats to prevent this paralysis from occurring, the results were spectacular. After they entered the REM stage, although otherwise sound asleep, the cats raised their heads, tried to stand up, and in some cases even searched for and attacked prey (Morrison, 1983). Obviously, the normal inhibition of this kind of movement through muscle paralysis makes REM sleep safer for all of us.

The first Stage 1-REM period lasts about 10 minutes, and is followed by Stages 2, 3, and 4 of NREM sleep. This sequence of sleep stages repeats itself all night long, averaging 90 minutes from Stage 1-REM to Stage 4 and back again. Normally, a night's sleep consists of four to five sleep cycles of this sort. But the pattern of sleep changes as the night progresses. At first Stages 3 and 4 dominate; but as time passes, the Stage 1-REM periods gradually become longer and Stages 3 and 4 become shorter, eventually disappearing altogether. Over the course of a night, then, about 45 to 50 percent of the sleeper's time is spent in Stage 2, while REM sleep takes up another 25 percent of the total.

Sleep requirements and patterns vary considerably from person to person, though. Some adults need hardly any sleep. Researchers have documented the case of a Stanford University professor who slept for only 3 to 4 hours a night over the course of 50 years and that of a woman who lived a healthy life on only 1 hour of sleep per night (Rosenzweig & Leiman, 1982). Sleep patterns also change with age (see Figure 4-2).

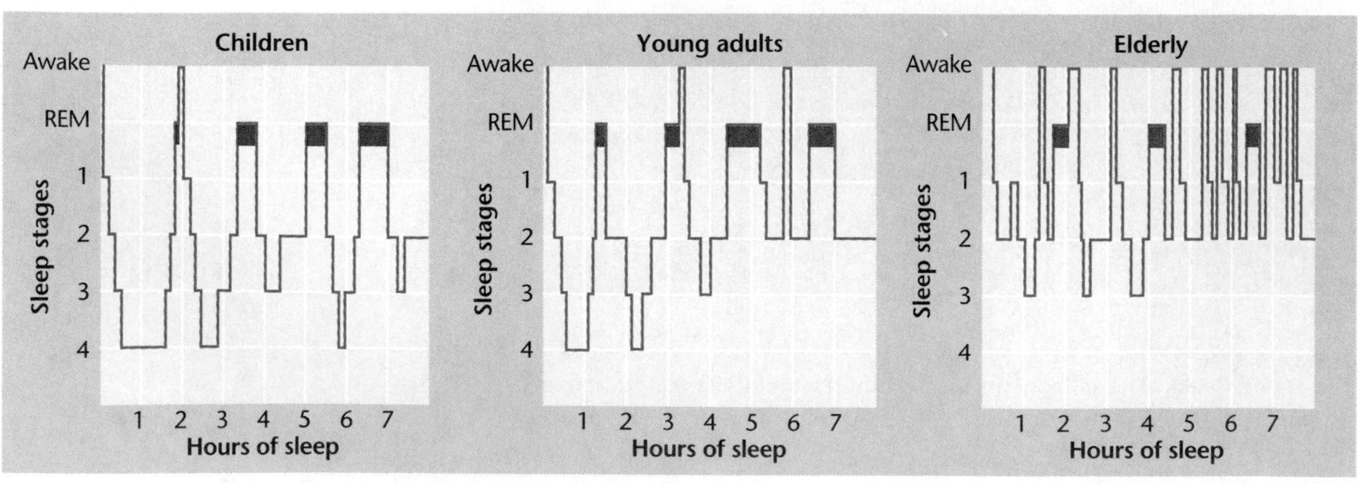


**Figure 4-2**
**A night's sleep across the life span.** Sleep patterns change from childhood to young adulthood to old age. The red areas represent REM sleep, the stage of sleep that varies most dramatically across age groups.

*Source:* Adapted by permission of *The New England Journal of Medicine, 290*, 487, 1974.

Infants sleep much longer than adults—13 to 16 hours during the first year—and much more of their sleep is REM sleep (see Figure 4-3). Unlike adults, infants enter the REM stage immediately after falling asleep and change sleep stages often. The elderly, on the other hand, tend to sleep less than younger adults, wake up more often during the night, and spend much less time in the deep sleep of Stages 3 and 4. Finally, men generally sleep less well than women do: During early adulthood, they awaken more often and sleep less restfully; after age 60, their sleep patterns are more disturbed and they engage in less Stage 3 and 4 sleep than women do (Paulson, 1990).

**Dreams** Vivid visual and auditory experiences that occur primarily during REM periods of sleep.

**DREAMS** On average, people dream for about 2 hours every night, though most dreams are quickly forgotten. **Dreams** are vivid visual and auditory experiences that our minds conjure up primarily during REM periods; subjects awakened during REM sleep report graphic dreams about 80 to 85 percent of the time (R. J. Berger, 1969). Less striking experiences that resemble the thinking done during normal wakeful consciousness tend to occur during NREM sleep.

At times REM dreams can be so vivid that it is hard to distinguish them from reality. In some cultures, in fact, dreams are considered to be

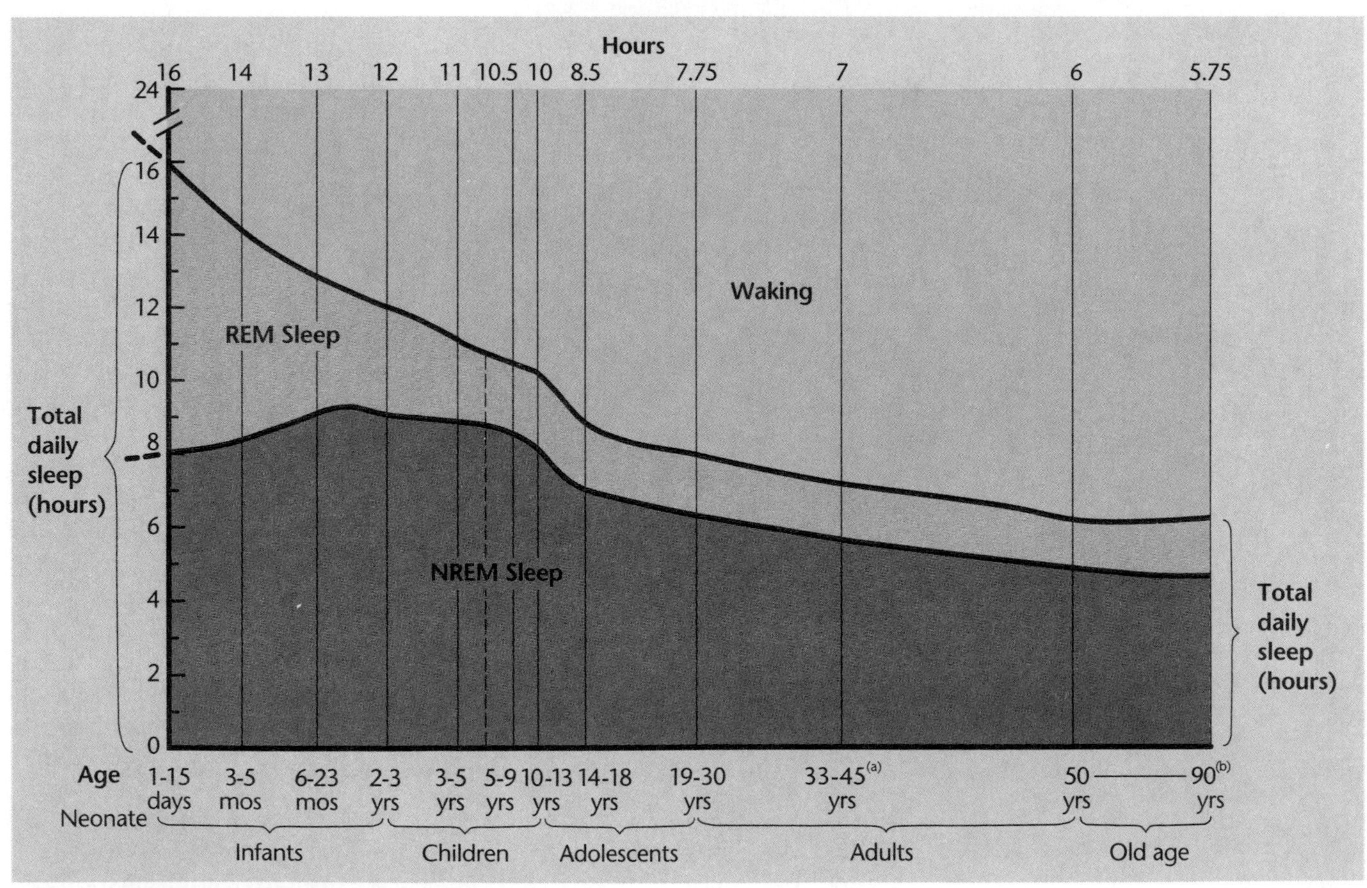


**Figure 4-3**
**Changes in REM and NREM sleep.** As people age, they need considerably less REM sleep. REM sleep accounts for about 8 hours, or 40 percent of total sleep, at birth, and falls to just one hour, or about 20 percent of total sleep, in old age.

*Source:* Adapted from H. P. Roffwarg, "Ontogenetic Development of the Human Sleep-Dream Cycle." *Science, 152,* p. 60. Copyright ©1966 by the American Association for the Advancement of Science. Reprinted with permission.

real experiences of a world that is inaccessible to us in our waking lives. Similarly, most young children have great difficulty distinguishing between dreams and waking experiences. REM dreams seem so real to the dreamer because the state of brain arousal during REM sleep mirrors that of normal waking consciousness. But during REM sleep, the brain is relatively insensitive to outside sensory input. Thus, during REM sleep, the brain is alert and excited, but its only input is internal images from memory (Koulack & Goodenough, 1976).

Psychologists have long been fascinated by dream activity and the contents of dreams. Sigmund Freud (1900), whose theories are explored more comprehensively in the chapter on personality, called dreams the "royal road to the unconscious." Believing that dreams represent wishes that have not been fulfilled in reality, he asserted that people's dreams shed light on the motives guiding their behavior—motives of which they may not be consciously aware. Freud distinguished the *manifest*, or *surface*, *content* of dreams from their *latent content*—the hidden, unconscious thoughts or desires that he thought were expressed indirectly through dreams. In dreams, according to Freud, people permit themselves to express primitive desires that are relatively free of moral controls. For example, someone who is not consciously aware of hostile feelings toward a loved one (say, a sister), may have dreams about murdering her. However, even in a dream, such hostile feelings may be censored and transformed into a highly symbolic form. For example, the desire to terminate one's sister (the dream's latent content) may be recast into the dream image of seeing her off at a train "terminal" (the dream's manifest content). According to Freud, this process of censorship and symbolic transformation accounts for the highly illogical nature of many dreams. Deciphering the disguised meanings of dreams is one of the principal tasks of psychoanalysts in their work with clients.

**4.** Why do so many dreams seem so disjointed and illogical?

Though there is some evidence that dreams are generated by random outbursts of nerve cell activity, some experts argue that dreams often just *seem* illogical and disjointed because we don't remember them very well.

*Source:* Marc Chagall "Over Vitebsk." 1915–20 (after painting of 1914). Oil on canvas, 26 3/8 x 36 1/2. The Museum of Modern Art, New York. Acquired through the Lillie P. Bliss Bequest.

Others have offered a neurophysiological interpretation for the disjointed nature of so many dreams. J. Allan Hobson and Robert McCarley (1977) hold that dreams are generated by random outbursts of nerve-cell activity. In responding to these internal stimuli—many of which involve brain cells used in vision and hearing—the brain attempts to synthesize or make sense of them by drawing on memory to create the images and scenes we experience as dreams. The brain of a dreaming person is sufficiently aroused to sketch a narrative of events, but it can do this only in a primitive, concrete fashion.

Other researchers have suggested that the bizarre content of dreams reflects the brain's effort to free itself of irrelevant, repetitious thoughts or associations during sleep so that it will be more open to new information during waking consciousness (Crick & Mitchison, 1983). In this view, dreams are filled with spurious information that is being purged from memory as the brain goes about its "housecleaning."

A more recent neurophysiological hypothesis comes to the opposite conclusion: that in our dreams we reprocess information gathered during the day, as a way of strengthening the memory of information that is crucial to the survival of the organism (Winson, 1990). How does this work? Oswald (1973, 1974) believes that at the neurophysiological level REM sleep may be related to brain "restoration" and growth, and researchers have indeed confirmed that protein synthesis proceeds at a faster rate during REM sleep than during NREM sleep. Protein synthesis may be the neurophysiological process that enables us to combine new and old information into imaginatively restructured patterns. Rossi (1973) argues that this biochemical activity "serves as the organic basis for new developments in the personality." Other research has demonstrated not only that both human and nonhuman subjects spend more time in REM sleep after learning difficult material but also that interfering with REM sleep in the days immediately after subjects initially learn something severely disrupts their memory for the newly learned material (C. T. Smith, 1985; C. T. Smith & Lapp, 1986; C. T. Smith & Kelly, 1988). Thus, if you study hard during the week and then stay up all night on Friday and Saturday, you are likely to forget up to one-third of the material you would have remembered had you had a more restful weekend.

Whatever the ultimate explanation for dream content, we do know that it is related to several factors. For example, when you are closest to waking, your dreams are apt to center on recent events. Since the last dream that you have before waking is the one you are most likely to remember, it follows that most of the dreams you remember deal with recent events. In the middle of the night, however, dreams generally focus on childhood or past events.

The content of men's and women's dreams also differs to some extent. Women not only tend to recall more dreams than men do; they also more frequently report dreams with characters, emotions, and friendly interaction as well as dreams that take place indoors and deal with home and family. By contrast, men more often remember dreams about aggression and overt hostility as well as successful striving for achievement (Brenneis, 1970; D. B. Cohen, 1973; Winget, Kramer, & Whitman, 1972). Before the onset of menstruation, women often dream about waiting; before childbirth, they generally dream more about babies or their mothers than about their husbands. On the other hand, both sexes dream equally about being pursued or victimized.

Dream content also varies by age (Foulkes, 1982). Very young children (ages 2 to 5) tend to have brief dreams, many of which involve animals, but the images are usually unrelated to one another and there is seldom any emotion or narrative or story line. In children between the ages of 5 and 9, dreams become considerably longer; a few narrative, storylike dreams appear around ages 5 to 7, but it is not until the child is 7 to 9 years old that most dreams take this narrative, sequential form. Feelings and emotions also make their appearance in dreams in the years between 7 and 9, and children more often appear as a character in their own dreams at that age. In those aged 9 to 15, dreams become more adultlike: Narratives follow well-developed story lines, other people play important roles, and there are many verbal exchanges in addition to motor activity. At the other end of the age scale, people over 65 report significantly more dreams dealing with death (Anch et al., 1988).

Some children also experience *sleep terrors*, a form of nocturnal fright that makes them suddenly sit up in bed, often screaming out in fear. Sleep terrors are altogether different from *nightmares*. Children generally cannot be awakened from night terrors and will push away anyone trying to comfort them. Unlike nightmares, sleep terrors cannot be recalled the next morning upon waking. They also occur more often if the child is very tired. Though sleep terrors are usually seen in children between 4 and 12 years old, they may continue into adulthood (Hartmann, 1984). Adults who have night terrors are more likely to suffer from a personality disorder (Kales et al., 1980) or to abuse drugs or alcohol. Brain injuries associated with epilepsy may also contribute to night terrors in adults.

Neither nightmares nor night terrors alone are evidence of psychological problems. Anxious people have no more nightmares than other people do. And like night terrors, nightmares become less frequent with age (J. M. Wood & Bootzin, 1990). People whose nightmares stem from a traumatic experience, however, may be plagued by these terrifying nighttime episodes for years.

Most dreams last about as long as the events would in real life; they do not flash on your mental screen just before waking, as was once believed. Generally, dreams consist of a sequential story or a series of stories. Stimuli, both external and internal, may modify an ongoing dream, but they do not initiate dreams.

Are all the dreams dreamt in a single night related to one another? Unfortunately, experimenters encounter a methodological problem when they try to answer this question: Each time the subject is awakened to be asked about a dream, the natural course of the dream is interrupted and is usually lost forever. If one particular problem or event weighs heavily on the dreamer's mind, however, it will often show up in dreams throughout the night (Dement, 1974).

If you set up a tape recorder to play back information while you sleep, will you painlessly absorb this material? Unfortunately, research has never confirmed that people can learn complex material while sleeping. Even experiments designed to teach sleepers simple pairs of words have failed. Very rudimentary forms of learning may be possible, however. The first time a stimulus such as a loud noise is presented to a sleeper, it produces signs of arousal. Repetition of the stimulus causes less and less arousal, suggesting that the sleeper has learned that the stimulus is not a cause for alarm.

Attempts to influence dream content through presleep suggestions have also had mixed results. Success seems to depend on such subtleties as the phrasing of the suggestion, the tone in which it is given, the relationship between the suggester and the subject, and the setting (P. C. Walker & Johnson, 1974). If these variables could be refined and controlled, the presleep suggestion technique could be an important tool for both sleep researchers and psychotherapists.

**Need for Dreams** As we have already noted, scientists are uncertain about why we need to sleep. They are even more uncertain about why we dream. Freud suggested that dreams serve as a psychic safety valve. That is, they allow us to give harmless expression to otherwise disturbing thoughts—sometimes so disturbing that they need to be transformed into highly symbolic forms even in dreams. If this theory is correct, depriving people of the opportunity to dream should have significant effects on their waking lives. Dement (1965) studied the effects of dream deprivation by awakening subjects just as they entered REM sleep. He found that those who were deprived of REM sleep became anxious, testy, and hungry, had difficulty concentrating, and even hallucinated in their waking hours. But since Dement's study, we have learned that some dreams occur in NREM sleep, so we know that eliminating REM sleep is not equivalent to eliminating all dreams. Thus, REM deprivation studies do not provide the full answer to the question of why we dream (Anch et al., 1988).

This does not mean that preventing people from entering REM sleep has no effect on them. As we saw earlier, there is evidence that REM sleep is important for learning and memory. Interestingly, when people deprived of REM sleep are finally allowed to sleep undisturbed, the amount of REM sleep nearly doubles—a phenomenon called *REM rebound.* However, people with schizophrenia show little or no REM rebound, and people who show signs of dreaming during the day show less REM rebound than the norm (D. B. Cohen, 1976). These findings suggest that we can make up for the loss of REM sleep either in NREM sleep or in dreamlike fantasies during waking life (Dement et al., 1970). In passing, it is worth noting that REM rebound may be one reason it is difficult for some people to break the habit of using sleeping pills or a "nightcap" to fall asleep. Alcohol and most sleep medications are central nervous system depressants that reduce the amount of REM sleep and dreaming in users. The sharp increase in bizarre dreams—the rebound effect that occurs when these drugs are discontinued—is so disturbing to many people that they are driven back to the drugs in an attempt to avoid dreaming. The hallucinations that sometimes accompany alcohol withdrawal, may, in fact be a kind of REM rebound during waking life (Greenberg & Pearlman, 1967).

Dreams usually reflect the personality, interests, concerns, and emotional experiences of the dreamer. Some people seem able to use them to solve intricate work problems. For instance, the chemist Friedrich August von Kekule figured out the structure of the benzene molecule after he dreamt about a snake that grabbed its own tail: He awoke with the inspiration that the molecule must be configured in the shape of a ring, an insight that proved to be true. Dreams may also help us process emotional information. In dreams, emotionally significant events may be assimilated with previous experiences (Farthing, 1992). For example, children's first experience of a carnival or amusement park is usually a blend of terror and excitement. Later in life, whenever they undergo experiences that are exciting but also somewhat frightening, carnival rides or images may dominate their dreams. That we cannot yet definitively state why we need dreams may only reflect how variable are both dreams themselves and their uses.

**SLEEP DEPRIVATION** Inadequate sleep is a "national epidemic" in the United States (Webb & Agnew, 1975; Angier, 1990). It is estimated that between one-third and one-half of all adults regularly fail to get enough sleep, and the problem is getting worse: Americans were sleeping an average of 8 to 12 hours a night in the 1950s, but by 1990, they were down to only 7 hours a night. Moreover, although there were only 25 accredited sleep-disorder clinics in the United States in 1980, 10 years later there were 140, with still more on the way (Angier, 1990; Dotto, 1990).

Losing an hour or two of sleep every night, week after week, month after month, makes it more difficult for people to pay attention (especially to monotonous tasks) and to remember things. Reaction time slows down, behavior becomes unpredictable, accidents and errors in judgment increase, and productivity and the ability to make decisions decline (Angier, 1990; Webb & Levy, 1984; Borbély, 1984; C. Evans, 1983; Babkoff et al., 1991).

These research findings have important implications. For example, experts estimate that sleep loss is a contributing factor in 200,000–400,000 car accidents each year and in 15–20 percent of deaths from car accidents, making it the most common contributing factor after alcohol (Brody, 1994; Richardson et al., 1989–1990; Wald, 1995). Sleep deprivation may also routinely affect the performance of those in high-risk positions, such as pilots, hospital staff, and nuclear-power-plant operators, who often have to make critical decisions on short notice. A dramatic example of the effects of sleep deprivation on the ability to cope is the 1979 accident at the nuclear power plant at Three Mile Island in

**Insomnia** Sleep disorder characterized by difficulty in falling asleep or remaining asleep throughout the night.

Pennsylvania. The three control-room operators on duty the morning of the accident were working a "slow-shift rotation": They were on during the daytime for one week, then evenings for a week, and then late nights for a third week. According to biologists, such a work schedule may result in the worst possible human performance because it severely disrupts the body's biological clock and sleep cycle.

During the first 100 minutes of the accident, the operators made an unusual number of errors. Fourteen seconds after the trouble began, one of them failed to notice two warning lights. A few seconds later, none of the operators realized that a valve that should have closed was open. The presidential commission that investigated the Three Mile Island incident concluded that human error had transformed a minor mishap into a major nuclear accident.

Based on the new awareness of the relationship between sleep deprivation and accidents, policy makers have changed the working patterns of high-risk personnel. For example, regulations restricting the hours of hospital residents have already been put in place in some parts of the country.

Anyone who has spent a sleepless night tossing and turning has first-hand knowledge that getting a good night's sleep is not always possible. But people do not always know when they are not getting enough sleep. In one recent study by the National Transportation Safety Board, most truck drivers involved in accidents that clearly resulted from their falling asleep at the wheel claimed they felt rested at the time (Wald, 1995). In a laboratory study, one group of normal, healthy college students who were getting 7 to 8 hours of sleep a night showed no apparent signs of sleep deprivation. Yet 20 percent of them fell asleep immediately when they were put into a dark room, a symptom of chronic sleep loss. Another group for a period of time went to bed 60 to 90 minutes earlier than their normal bedtime. These students reported that they felt much more vigorous and alert and, indeed, they performed significantly better on tests of psychological and mental acuity (Carskadon & Dement, 1982).

**SLEEP DISORDERS** Up to this point, we have emphasized average sleep patterns. But the scientific study of typical sleep patterns has given us new insight into sleep disorders such as **insomnia**, which afflicts as many as 35 million Americans. Most episodes of insomnia grow out of stressful events and are temporary. But for some sufferers, insomnia constitutes a persistent life disruption. Taking sleeping pills is often counterproductive, because sleeping pills lose their effectiveness over time Moreover, Halcion, one of the most widely prescribed remedies for insomnia, frequently causes severe side effects, including anxiety, memory loss, hallucinations, and violent behavior.

For some people, insomnia is rooted in longstanding psychological problems, such as depression (A. Kales et al., 1976), so its cure requires treating the underlying disorder. Other people with insomnia have a different physiological makeup from normal sleepers in that their biological system is always overaroused. A biological predisposition to insomnia may combine with associated distress over the sleeplessness to create a cycle in which biological and emotional factors reinforce one another. People may worry so much about not sleeping that their bedtime rituals, such as brushing teeth and getting dressed for bed, "become harbingers of frustration, rather than stimuli for relaxation" (Hauri, 1982). Furthermore, bad sleep habits—such as varying bedtimes—and distracting sleep settings may aggravate or even cause insomnia.

Often a simple alteration in routine (such as changing the temperature of the bedroom or avoiding certain foods before bedtime) markedly improves the quality of sleep for insomnia sufferers. Among the keys: maintaining regular bedtime hours and not sleeping late on weekends, abstaining from drugs (including alcohol and caffeine and the routine use of sleeping pills), avoiding anxious thoughts while in bed, and not fighting insomnia when it occurs. The old saying "If I can't sleep, I mop the kitchen floor" makes sense to sleep researchers, who counsel their clients to get out of bed and engage in an activity for an hour or so until they feel sleepy again. Another strategy for people who suffer from insomnia is to set aside regular times during the day—well before bedtime—to mull over their worries. This technique may be supplemented by relaxation training in using such methods as biofeedback, hypnosis, or meditation. Finally, tryptophan, a substance that promotes sleep, may be taken as a sleep aid in the form of warm milk, confirming another folk remedy for sleeplessness.

Another sleep disorder, **apnea**, affects 2 to 4 percent of the population. This condition is associated with breathing difficulties at night: in severe cases, the victim actually stops breathing after falling asleep. When the level of carbon dioxide in the blood rises to a certain point, apnea sufferers are spurred to a state of arousal just short of waking consciousness. Because this may happen hundreds of times a night, apnea patients typically feel exhausted and fall asleep repeatedly the next day. They may also complain of depression, sexual dysfunction, difficulty concentrating, and headaches. Apnea is particularly prevalent among the elderly, who are also the major consumers of sleeping medications.

People suffering from insomnia and apnea may envy those who have no trouble sleeping. But too much sleep has serious repercussions as well. **Narcolepsy** is a hereditary disorder whose victims nod off without warning in the middle of a conversation or other alert activity. People with narcolepsy often experience a sudden loss of muscle tone upon expression of any sort of emotion. A joke, anger, sexual stimulation—all bring on a feeling of weakness. Another symptom of the disorder is immediate entry into REM sleep, which produces frightening hallucinations that are, in fact, dreams the person is experiencing while still partly awake. Narcolepsy is believed to arise from a defect in the central nervous system.

**Apnea** Sleep disorder characterized by breathing difficulty during the night and feelings of exhaustion during the day.

**Narcolepsy** Hereditary sleep disorder characterized by sudden nodding off during the day and sudden loss of muscle tone following moments of emotional excitement.

**Meditation** Any of various methods of concentration, reflection, or focusing of thoughts undertaken to suppress the activity of the sympathetic nervous system

## ARTIFICIAL ALTERATIONS IN CONSCIOUSNESS

### Meditation

For centuries, people have used various forms of **meditation** to experience an alteration in consciousness (Benson, 1975). Each form of meditation focuses the meditator's attention in a slightly different way. Zen meditation concentrates on respiration, for example, while Sufism relies on frenzied dancing and prayer (G. E. Schwartz, 1974). In transcendental meditation (TM), practitioners intone a mantra, which is a sound specially selected for a student by the teacher of TM, to keep all other images and problems at bay and allow the meditator to relax more deeply (Deikman, 1973; Schwartz, 1974).

In all its diverse forms, meditation suppresses the activity of the sympathetic nervous system, the part of the nervous system that prepares the body for strenuous activity during an emergency. Meditation also lowers the rate of metabolism (see Figure 4-4) and reduces heart and respiratory rates. Alpha brain waves (which accompany relaxed wakefulness) increase noticeably during meditation, and there is a decrease in blood lactate, a chemical linked to stress.

Meditation may relieve anxiety and promote peace of mind and a sense of well-being in practitioners.

Meditation has been used to treat certain medical problems, including drug abuse. Some studies have found that a high percentage of people who used drugs stopped using them after taking up meditation. For example, Benson and Wallace (1972) found that among people who practiced TM, mari-

**Hypnosis** Trancelike state in which the subject responds readily to suggestions.

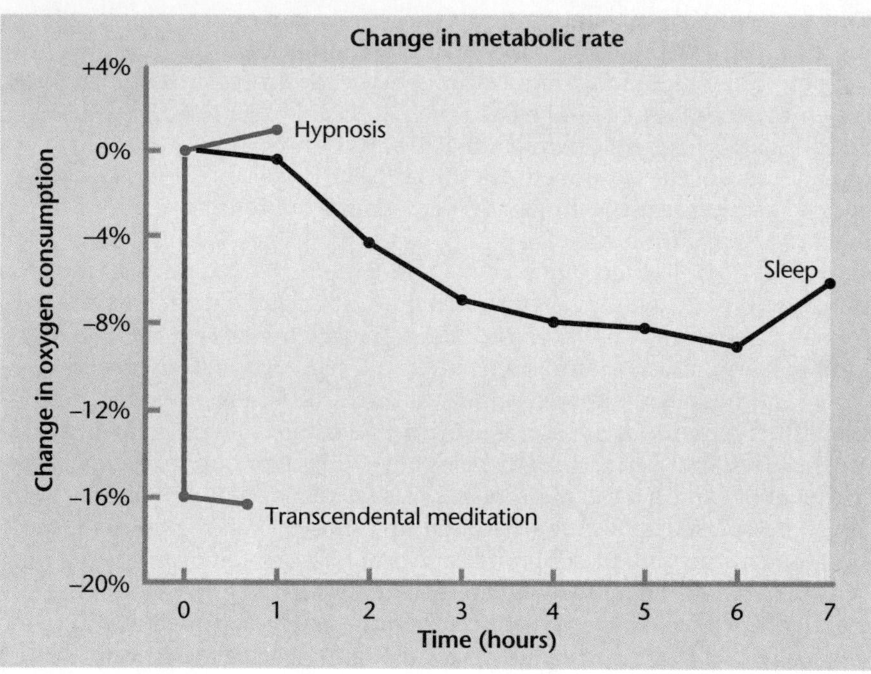


**Figure 4-4**
**A graph depicting the lowered rate of metabolism during meditation** as measured by reduced absorption of oxygen in the bloodstream.

*Source:* From *The Physiology of Meditation*, by Robert Keith Wallace and Herbert Benson. Copyright ©1972 by Scientific American, Inc. All rights reserved.

juana use fell from 78 percent to 22 percent after 21 months; of those taking LSD, 97 percent had ceased using the drug after an average of 22 months of meditation. However, the subjects of this study were already committed to TM when they were surveyed; among other populations, the effects are not always so dramatic (Benson et al., 1979). Meditation has also been shown to reduce high blood pressure (Benson, Alexander, & Feldman, 1975; R. A. Stone & DeLeo, 1976).

Besides physiological benefits, people who practice some form of meditation may gain certain emotional and even spiritual advantages: They often report increased sensory awareness, euphoria, strong emotions, and a sense of timelessness and expanded awareness (Deikman, 1973). Peace of mind, a sense of well-being, and total relaxation have also been reported by meditators (S. R. Dean, 1970).

Some investigators question whether meditation significantly alters normal states of consciousness, because the same physical changes can be brought about simply by deep relaxation (D. S. Holmes, 1984). Advocates of meditation reply that this fact does not rule out the possibility that meditation produces some uniquely beneficial psychological effects. And in fact a meta-analysis comparing TM with other forms of meditation and physical relaxation techniques such as biofeedback (see Chapter 5) did demonstrate that TM is superior when it comes to reducing anxiety (Eppley, Abrams, & Shear, 1989).

## Hypnosis

**Hypnosis**, while sharing some attributes with other ASCs, has a distinct history dating back to mid-eighteenth-century Europe, where Anton Mesmer, a Viennese physician, fascinated audiences by putting patients into trances in order to cure their illnesses. Hence, the term *mesmerism* was first used to describe the phenomenon, though *hypnosis* has since become the preferred term (Hypnos was the Greek god of sleep). Mesmer's abilities were initially discredited by a French commission chaired by Benjamin

Franklin; but in the nineteenth century, some respectable physicians revived interest in hypnosis when they discovered it could be used to treat certain forms of mental illness. Even today, however, considerable disagreement persists about how to define hypnosis and even about whether it constitutes a valid ASC.

One of the reasons for the controversy is that, from a behavioral standpoint, there is no simple definition of what it means, to be hypnotized. Different individuals believed to have undergone hypnosis describe their experiences in very different ways. The following quotations (Farthing, 1992, p. 349) from hypnotized subjects illustrate some of these experiential disparities:

> "Hypnosis is just one thing going on, like a thread . . . focusing on a single thread of one's existence . . . "
>
> "I felt as if I were 'inside' myself; none of my body was touching anything . . . "
>
> "I was very much aware of the split in my consciousness. One part of me was analytic and listening to you (the hypnotist). The other part was feeling the things that the analytic part decided I should have."

**HYPNOTIC SUGGESTIONS** Given these variations in experience among hypnotized individuals, it is difficult to arrive at a single definition for the state of hypnosis. It appears that consciousness *is* altered by hypnosis, though the exact means by which this occurs and the ways in which it is felt vary from one individual to another. Some people who are told they cannot move their arms or that their pain has vanished do, in fact, experience paralysis or anesthesia; if told they are hearing a certain piece of music or are unable to hear anything, they may hallucinate or become deaf temporarily. Other hypnotized people remember events from their early childhood and say they feel as though they are experiencing those events all over again, as when a hypnotist tells a 40-year-old subject that she is 6 years old. Finally, in some people it is possible to induce amnesia, which lingers even after they are no longer hypnotized, through instructions such as "You will remember nothing that happened under hypnosis until I tell you." In still other cases, instructions received while under hypnosis can temporarily diminish the person's desire to smoke or overeat.

What does it mean to be hypnotized?

Note that some of these results are easier to achieve than others. It is usually relatively easy to convince suggestible people that they cannot open their eyes or that their arms are too heavy to lift. It is more difficult to produce anesthesia in people so that they become insensitive to pain, such as that produced by a pinprick (Spiegel, Bierre, & Rootenberg, 1989). And it is still more difficult to coax people to recall lost memories or to generate hallucinations (Hilgard, 1965). Hypnotic suggestion, it seems, is most effective when it comes to simpler behaviors or mental processes.

**INDUCING HYPNOSIS** To induce hypnosis, the hypnotist usually begins by focusing a willing subject's attention on the hypnotist's voice. The subject may also be asked to concentrate on a specific object or to visualize a particular scene, such as a relaxing day at the beach. Guided imagery may be used to bring the scene into sharp focus; for example, a subject imagining stretching out at the beach might be told to think about becoming progressively more relaxed while lying on the sand. As the subject enters the hypnotic trance, its effects may be heightened and tested by some preliminary suggestions. For instance, the subject may be told that at the count of 10, it will be impossible to open his or her eyes. Sometimes these suggestions are put in "paradoxical" form. Subjects are told, for example, that the harder they try to open their eyes, the more tightly shut their eyes will remain. More suggestions of relaxation follow until eventually the subject appears to be in a state of complete relaxation.

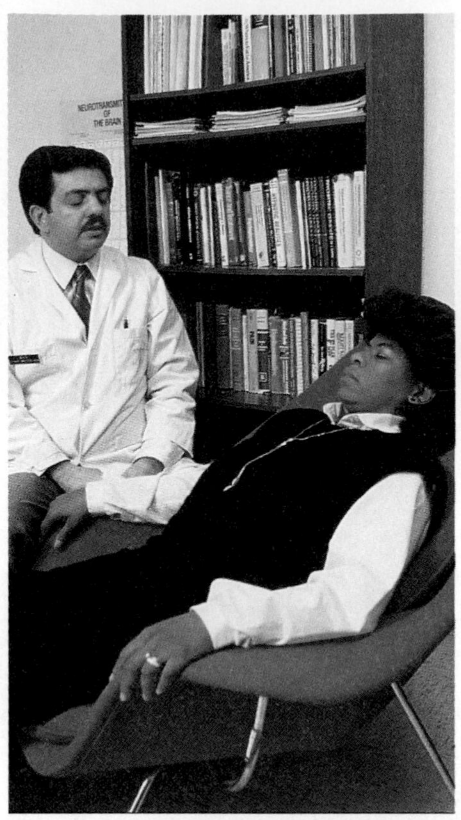

Although hypnosis is often used in clinical situations, psychologists disagree about whether it actually constitutes an altered state of consciousness.

**Hypnotic Susceptibility** People vary greatly in their susceptibility to hypnosis. If you're easily carried away by a book or a movie you're probably extremely susceptible to hypnosis. How deeply a subject enters a hypnotic trance is measured more precisely by means of Hilgard's Stanford Susceptibility Scale. About 10 percent of the people tested show almost no response to hypnosis. At the other extreme, about 25 percent undergo deep hypnosis, including such effects as anesthesia. But only about 5 to 10 percent experience the most dramatic effects, such as hallucinations (Hilgard, 1965). Hypnotic susceptibility appears to be partly learned and partly inherited. Growing up with parents who have fertile imaginations and who encourage imaginative play in their children seems to contribute to hypnotic susceptibility (Kihlström, 1985). But so does growing up with severely punishing parents, perhaps because such a childhood makes people highly obedient to instructions from authority, including the hypnotist's suggestions. As for genetic predispositions to hypnotic susceptibility, some evidence indicates that identical twins are more similar to each other in hypnotic suggestibility than are fraternal twins (Morgan, 1973). Susceptibility also varies according to age. On the whole, children are more susceptible to hypnotic induction than adults are (Banyai & Hilgard, 1976). Finally, scientists have established that hypnotic behavior is greatly affected by contextual cues, including the setting in which the hypnosis is carried out and the exact words used by the hypnotist (Kihlström & McConkey, 1990; Spanos, 1986; Spanos & Chaves, 1989).

**Clinical Applications of Hypnosis** Since hypnotic susceptibility varies significantly from one person to another, it stands to reason that hypnosis in clinical and therapeutic settings will not be universally effective. Nevertheless, hypnosis is being used in a variety of medical and counseling situations; in fact, hypnosis has been found more effective as an anesthetic than morphine for certain types of pain. Dentists have been using it as an anesthetic for years. More recently hypnosis has been used to alleviate pain in children with leukemia who have to undergo repeated bone-marrow biopsies: Those who are able to imagine themselves living temporarily in a world outside their bodies can learn to tolerate this extremely painful procedure quite well (Hilgard, Hilgard, & Kaufmann, 1983).

Can hypnosis make someone change or eliminate bad habits? The jury is still out on this question. Critics point out that if people really want to change a behavior, they are likely to do so without hypnosis. Hypnosis may shore up their will, but so might joining a support group such as Weight Watchers. In other words, posthypnotic suggestions may be no more effective than other kinds of supportive help.

**Hypnosis: An Altered State?** For some time, controversy has swirled around the question of whether the hypnotic trance *is* actually an altered state of consciousness (Kihlström & McConkey, 1990). Those who challenge the notion that hypnosis is an ASC assert that hypnosis is simply a special setting in which otherwise normal cognitive processes, such as imagination, take place (Farthing, 1992). Bolstering their argument, critics also point out that hypnosis has no clearly measurable effects on blood pressure, heart rate, brain waves, or other vital signs that would allow us to distinguish a hypnotic trance from a normal resting state (Hilgard, 1974). And while subjects of hypnosis do experience greater suggestibility, critics note that nonhypnotized individuals, under orders from a person in authority, take direction in much the same way as hypnotized subjects do.

Does the *experience* of hypnosis then, qualify it as altered state of consciousness? One study (Zamansky & Bartis, 1985) demonstrated that people who are hypnotized perceive their experience while performing feats differently than people not under hypnosis: Hypnotized subjects see themselves as if looking from the outside in, as though they were not themselves. But this same sort of division of consciousness occurs in everyday life, according to some experts. As an example, you might be consciously planning dinner while driving home from work (Hilgard, 1986). Following this logic, a hypnotized subject is simply putting certain aspects of consciousness (such as awareness of pain) on hold while focusing attention elsewhere, and, if so, then hypnosis may merely be an extreme form of an otherwise normal kind of divided consciousness.

No consensus has been reached among psychologists about whether the "hypnotic trance" constitutes a separate, definable state of consciousness or whether suggestibility alone explains "hypnotic" behaviors.

**Psychoactive drugs** Chemical substances that change moods and perceptions.

## DRUG-ALTERED CONSCIOUSNESS

So far, our discussion has focused on ASCs produced without using drugs. Meditation, hypnosis, daydreams, sleep, and dreaming can all occur without chemical intervention. In this final section of the chapter, we will look at ASCs that are induced by **psychoactive drugs**, chemical substances that change moods and perceptions.

Since ancient times, people have used drugs to alter their consciousness for social, religious, and personal reasons. Wine is mentioned often in the Bible and plays a sacramental role in several major religions. Marijuana is alluded to in the herbal recipe book of a Chinese emperor in 2737 B.C.; and the Jivaro Indians of Ecuador, who consider the world of the senses an illusion, habitually use drugs to contact the "real world" of supernatural forces. In our own culture, the use of some substances to alter mood or behavior is, under certain circumstances, regarded as normal behavior. This includes moderate intake of alcohol and of the caffeine in coffee, tea, or cola. Smoking tobacco, which is not illegal, is nonetheless becoming anathema as people increasingly recognize the dangers of secondhand smoke. In some circles, illegal substances such as marijuana, cocaine, and amphetamines are used on a regular basis as well.

Even animals in the wild seek out and use drugs (R. Siegel, 1989). Goats and horses eat the hallucinogenic mescal beans that grow wild in the Texas desert, and horses also enjoy the aptly named locoweed that is found throughout the southwestern United States. And during the late fall, robins and cedar waxwings regularly fly into the windows of my house in a state of high confusion, apparently brought on by eating too many fermented crabapples.

The problems associated with the abuse of drugs have also been recognized since ancient times. The Greeks advocated moderation in all things, including the drinking of wine, and the Bible preaches against the sin of alcohol abuse. A recent national survey showed that more than 60 percent of adult Americans believe that all drug use is immoral and should be illegal ("61% of Americans," 1990). These concerns about drug abuse are not without foundation. For example, substance abuse among employees costs U.S. businesses more than $100 billion a year through absenteeism from work, lost productivity, and medical expenditures (Freudenheim, 1988). More than 15,000 Americans die every year, and more than a million more are injured, in alcohol-related car accidents. Smoking is at least partly responsible for the deaths of more than a quarter of a million people each year—which is more than one out of every six deaths in the United States.

**Substance abuse** A pattern of drug use that diminishes the ability to fulfill responsibilities at home or at work or school, that results in repeated use of a drug in dangerous situations, or that leads to legal difficulties related to drug use.

**Substance dependence** A pattern of compulsive drug taking that results in tolerance, withdrawal symptoms or other specific symptoms for at least a year.

**Tolerance** Phenomenon whereby higher doses of a drug are required to produce its original effects or to prevent withdrawal symptoms.

**Withdrawal symptoms** Unpleasant physical or psychological effects that follow the discontinuance of a dependence-producing substance.

## Substance Use, Abuse, and Dependence

If we define drugs as broadly as we did earlier—that is, to include caffeine and alcohol—clearly most people throughout the world use some type of drug on an occasional or regular basis. People who take drugs in moderation or for health-related purposes do not usually suffer ill effects or become excessively dependent on these substances. Unfortunately, however, for many others, substance use escalates into substance abuse. The term **substance abuse** refers to a pattern of drug use that diminishes one's ability to fulfill one's responsibilities at home or at work or school, that results in repeated use of a drug in dangerous situations, or that leads to legal difficulties related to drug use (Oltmanns & Emery, 1995, p. 338). For example, people who regularly go on drinking binges severe enough to cause ill health in themselves and problems within their families or on their jobs are abusing alcohol.

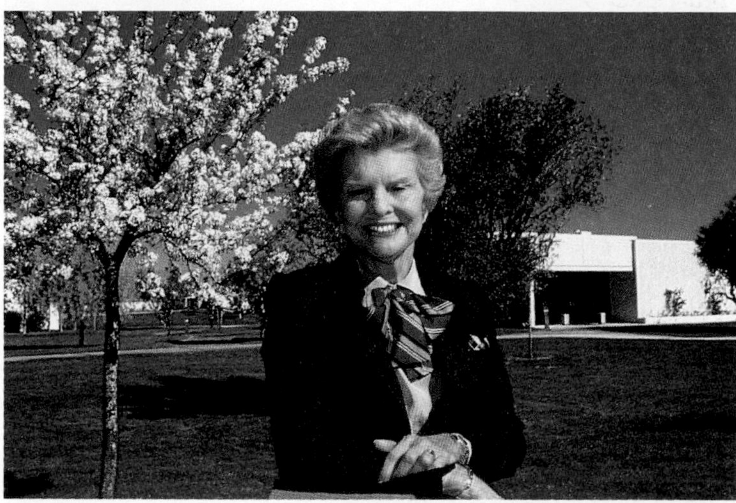

Former First Lady Betty Ford founded a clinic that treats people with substance-abuse and dependence problems. Although some cases are treated successfully, the causes of substance abuse are complex and difficult to pinpoint.

The ongoing abuse of many drugs, including alcohol, may lead to compulsive use of the substance, or **substance dependence** (also known as "addiction"). Although not everyone who abuses a substance develops dependence, dependence usually follows a period of abuse. Dependence often includes **tolerance**, the phenomenon whereby higher doses of the drug are required to produce its original effects or to prevent **withdrawal symptoms**, the unpleasant physical or psychological effects following discontinuance of the substance.

The most recent clinical definition of dependence (APA, 1994) describes a broad pattern of drug-related behaviors characterized by at least three of the following seven symptoms over a 12-month period:

1. Developing tolerance: needing increasing amounts of the substance to gain the desired effect *or* experiencing a diminished effect when using the same amount of the substance. For example, the person might have to drink an entire six-pack to get the same effect formerly experienced after drinking just one or two beers.
2. Experiencing withdrawal symptoms—physical and psychological problems that appear if the person tries to stop using the substance. Withdrawal symptoms range from anxiety and nausea to convulsions and hallucinations.
3. Using the substance for a longer period or in greater quantities than intended.
4. Having a persistent desire or making repeated efforts to cut back on use of the substance.
5. Devoting a great deal of time to obtaining or using the substance.
6. Giving up or reducing social, occupational, or recreational activities as a result of drug use.

7. Continuing to use the substance even in the face of ongoing or recurring physical or psychological problems likely to be caused or made worse by use of the substance.

The causes of substance abuse and dependence are complex and generally are rooted in some combination of biological, psychological, and social factors that varies for each individual and for each substance. Also keep in mind that the development of substance dependence does not follow an established timetable. One person might drink socially for years before abusing alcohol, whereas someone else might become addicted to crack (a crystalline form of cocaine) in a matter of weeks. But before we proceed to examine specific drugs and their effects, we need to look at how psychologists study drug-related behaviors.

**How Drug Abuse Is Studied** In the past our knowledge of the effects of drug use and abuse came largely from anecdotal reports of drug experiences. Today the effects of particular drugs are usually studied under carefully controlled scientific conditions. In most cases, experimenters compare people's behavior prior to the administration of the drug to their behavior afterward, taking special precautions to ensure that any observed changes in behavior are due to the drug alone. Sometimes, simply *expecting* that a drug will yield a particular effect is enough to produce that effect. If, unbeknownst to subjects the active ingredient is removed from marijuana or the caffeine is removed from coffee, the substance will usually have the same effects that the actual drug would. That is, the subjects act just as though they had actually used marijuana or caffeine! Similarly, if experimenters expect that alcohol will slow down behavior, they are more likely to look for and observe that phenomenon in subjects who consume alcohol.

To eliminate such sources of research error, most drug researchers use a **double-blind procedure**, in which some subjects receive the active drug, while others take a neutral, inactive substance called a **placebo**. Neither the researcher nor the subjects know which people took the active drug and which got the placebo. After data are collected, the researcher compares the behavior of subjects who actually received the drug with the behavior of those who unknowingly took the placebo. Then, if the groups differ in their behavior, the cause is likely to be the active ingredient in the drug.

In examining the effects of particular drugs, it is useful to group them into the categories of *depressants*, *stimulants*, and *hallucinogens*. Even though these are not rigid categories, this division helps organize our knowledge about drugs.

**Double-blind procedure** Experimental design, useful in studies of the effects of drugs, in which neither the subject nor the researcher knows at the time of administration which subjects are receiving an active drug and which are receiving an inactive substitute.

**Placebo** Chemically inactive substance used for comparison with active drugs in experiments on the effects of drugs.

**Depressants** Chemicals that slow down behavior or cognitive processes.

**Alcohol** Depressant that is the intoxicating ingredient in whiskey, beer, wine, and other fermented or distilled liquors.

## Depressants

**Depressants** are chemicals that retard behavior and thinking by either speeding up or slowing down nerve impulses. Generally speaking, alcohol, barbiturates, and the opiates have depressant effects.

**Alcohol** Our society recognizes many appropriate occasions for the consumption of alcohol: to celebrate milestone events, to break down social isolation and inhibitions, and to promote group harmony. Perhaps because of its social acceptability and legality, **alcohol** is widely used in our society: About 500 million gallons of alcoholic beverages are consumed annually in the United States. Much of this drinking is done by American youth, despite age restrictions on the purchase and consumption of alcohol: In 1989, 60 percent of high school seniors and more than 75 percent of college students reported drinking alcohol at least once in the previous month (Berke, 1990; Carmody, 1990). More recent studies reveal

Statistics indicate that alcohol consumption is a major contributing factor in automobile accidents.

that alcohol consumption among students is on the rise, though not so dramatically as the use of other drugs (Janofsky, 1994).

Alcohol *is* a drug, and the social costs of abusing it are high. Alcohol is implicated in more than two-thirds of all fatal automobile accidents, two-thirds of all murders, two-thirds of all spouse beatings, and more than half of all cases of violent child abuse. Alcohol abuse costs society more than $100 billion a year through lost productivity, crime, accidents, and medical treatment (Steele & Josephs, 1990). A study conducted by the National Institute on Alcohol Abuse and Alcoholism (NIAAA) found that more than 40 percent of all "heavy drinkers" die before the age of 65 (compared to less than 20 percent of nondrinkers), and that even light to moderate drinking is associated with shorter life spans ("Study Links," 1990). In addition, there is the untold cost for the nearly 30 million children of alcohol abusers. Eric Ryerson, whose experience growing up in an alcoholic household was in many ways typical, wrote: "I lived with a daily dread—about how bad the drinking would be that day, about how much shouting, crying or fighting there might be and about when, or if, it was ever going to end. I never knew what to expect next. I lived with constant fear and worry. I felt ashamed and confused. But more than anything else, I felt alone" (cited in Brody, 1987).

Even though alcohol is a depressant, it is often experienced as a stimulant. People *expect* drinking to help them become less inhibited in social situations, and that expectation may affect their behavior.

Its dangers not withstanding, alcohol continues to be a popular drug because of its short-term effects. As a depressant, it calms down the nervous system very much like a general anesthetic (McKim, 1986). Thus, some people consume alcohol to relax, to enhance their mood, to put them at ease in social situations, and to relieve the stress and anxiety of everyday living (Steele & Josephs, 1990). Paradoxically, although it is a depressant, alcohol is often experienced subjectively as a stimulant because it inhibits centers in the brain that govern critical judgment and impulsive behavior. To the drinker, the long-term negative consequences of alcoholism pale beside the short-term positive consequences, such as the sense that alcohol makes them feel more courageous, less inhibited, and more spontaneous (Steele & Josephs, 1990).

A study by Muriel Vogel-Sprott (1967) demonstrated how strong these short-term effects of alcohol are. Vogel-Sprott conducted an experiment in which the subjects received both painful shocks and money for engaging in certain behaviors. Some subjects were given alcohol before the experiment began; others received only a placebo. The subjects who received a placebo sharply reduced the behaviors that caused them to receive shocks—the money just wasn't worth the pain. But the subjects under the influence of alcohol showed no such inhibition—they weathered the shocks to get the money. Apparently, the negative consequences of their behavior (the shocks) were no longer important to them. Steele and his colleagues use the term *alcohol myopia* to refer to the alcohol-induced shortsightedness that makes drinkers oblivious to many behavioral cues in the environment and less able to make sense of those cues they do perceive (Steele & Josephs, 1990).

Several dozen research studies have clearly demonstrated that alcohol use is correlated with an increase in aggression, hostility, violence, and abusive behavior (Bushman, 1993; Bushman & Cooper, 1990). In all these studies, alcohol dulled the effects of environmental cues to proper behavior and made the users less aware of and less concerned about the negative consequences of their actions.

**6.** How and why does alcohol affect our behavior?

Physiologically, alcohol first affects the frontal lobes of the brain, which figure prominently in inhibitions, reasoning, and judgment. As consumption continues, alcohol affects the cerebellum, the center of motor control and balance. Eventually, alcohol consumption affects the spinal cord and medulla, which regulate such involuntary functions as breathing, body temperature, and heart rate. A blood-alcohol level of 0.50 percent or more may cause this part of the nervous system to shut down, leading to death from alcohol poisoning (see Table 4-1).

Alcohol compromises perception, motor processes, and memory. It diminishes visual acuity, depth perception, and the perception of the differences between bright lights and colors; interestingly, it seems to improve the ability to perceive dim lights. Some aspects of hearing, such as the perception of loudness, are not affected by alcohol consumption, but the ability to discriminate between different rhythms and pitches is impaired by just a single dose of the drug. Smell and taste perception are uniformly diminished, and the perception of time also becomes distorted. Most peo-

**TABLE 4-1 The Behavioral Effects of Blood Alcohol Levels**

| LEVELS OF ALCOHOL IN THE BLOOD | BEHAVIORAL EFFECTS |
|---|---|
| 0.05% | Feels good; less alert |
| 0.10% | Slower to react; less cautious |
| 0.15% | Reaction time much slower |
| 0.20% | Sensory-motor abilities suppressed |
| 0.25% | Staggering (motor abilities severely impaired); perception is limited as well |
| 0.30% | Semistupor |
| 0.35% | Level for anesthesia; death is possible |
| 0.40% | Death is likely (usually as a result of respiratory failure) |

*Source:* Data from *Drugs, Society, and Human Behavior* (3rd ed.) by Oakey Ray, 1983, St. Louis: The C.V. Mosby Co.

ple report that time seems to pass more quickly when they are "under the influence" (National Commission on Marijuana and Drug Abuse [NCMDA], 1973b)146.

Alcohol interferes with memory storage: People find it difficult to recall what happened after having only two or three drinks (E. S. Parker, Birnbaum, & Noble, 1976). Prolonged drinking impairs retrieval of memories—that is, heavy drinkers have difficulty recalling memories they once could retrieve easily. In heavy drinkers, alcohol may also produce *blackouts*, which make them unable to remember any of the events that occurred when they were drinking.

We still don't know exactly how alcohol affects the brain and memory, but a recent study in Denmark has suggested that alcohol does not kill brain cells but rather "disconnects" the fibers that link the cells to one another. Why is this significant? Recall from the Highlights box in Chapter 2 that the brain cannot replace nerve cells after they have died, but it can strengthen existing synapses or create new ones. Thus, if alcohol does not actually kill brain cells, it may be possible for the brain to heal—to some extent—the physiological damage often caused by alcohol abuse. For this to occur, of course, the person must stop drinking (Pakkenberg, 1993).

Although many of these effects can be traced to the ways in which alcohol operates on the central nervous system, they also reflect people's expectations about how alcohol will affect them (Critchlow, 1986; Goldman et al., 1991; Leigh, 1989; Leigh & Stacy, 1991). For example, experimental evidence indicates that men become more aggressive, more sexually aroused, and less anxious in social situations when they *believe* they are drinking alcohol, even if they are not actually doing so (Marlatt & Rohsenow, 1980).

Does alcohol have stronger effects on women than on men? Yes, partly because the same quantity of alcohol will have a greater impact on a lighter person than on a heavier person. Since women generally weigh less than men, the same dose of alcohol has a stronger effect on the average woman than on the average man. But research has shown that even when the effect of weight is canceled out, a given dose of alcohol has a more pronounced effect on women than on men. Why? It turns out that the amount of alcohol reaching the bloodstream is regulated by an enzyme in the stomach. The more of this enzyme the body contains, the smaller the quantity of alcohol that passes through the stomach into the bloodstream, where it spreads throughout the body. Most women have less of this stomach enzyme than men do, so more alcohol reaches their bloodstream. (In similar fashion, drinking alcohol on an empty stomach has more pronounced effects because less of this enzyme is present in an empty stomach [Frezza et al., 1990].) Putting these facts together, we can conclude that one drink is likely to have the same biological and psychological effects on the average woman as two drinks on the average man.

Despite its social and legal acceptance, alcohol is a highly addictive drug with potentially devastating long-term effects. Approximately 13 percent of U.S. adults (about 20 million people) either abuse alcohol or are dependent on it, making alcohol abuse and dependence the most serious substance-abuse problem in the United States. (See the Highlights box titled "What Are the Signs of Alcoholism?") One study found the rate of alcohol dependence among men between the ages of 18 and 44 to be 27 percent. Long-term abuse of alcohol can cause memory loss, decreased sexual drive or impotence, menstrual problems, liver and kidney damage, damage to the stomach and intestine, cancers of the mouth and esophagus, anxiety, insomnia, and brain damage. Long-term heavy use may also bring on a form of mental illness known as Korsakoff's syndrome, which is characterized by hallucinations, confusion, and severe memory problems

# IGHLIGHTS

## What Are the Signs of Alcoholism?

The following test is excerpted from a more comprehensive self-test published by the National Council on Alcoholism and designed to point up many of the common symptoms of alcoholism. This test will help you determine if you or someone you know needs to find out more about alcoholism, but this it is *not* intended to be used to establish the diagnosis of alcoholism.

1. Do you ever drink heavily when you are disappointed, under pressure, or have had a quarrel with someone?
2. Can you handle more alcohol now than when you first started to drink?
3. Have you ever been unable to remember part of the previous evening, even though your friends say you didn't pass out?
4. When drinking with other people, do you try to have a few extra drinks the others won't know about?
5. Has a family member or close friend ever expressed concern or complained about your drinking?
6. Have you been having more memory "blackouts" recently?
7. Do you often want to continue drinking after your friends say they've had enough?
8. Do you usually have a reason for the occasions when you drink heavily?
9. When you're sober, do you sometimes regret things you did or said while drinking?
10. Have you tried switching brands or drinks or following different plans to control your drinking?
11. Have you sometimes failed to keep promises you made to yourself about controlling or cutting down on your drinking?

If your answer to any of these questions is "yes" you may be at risk for alcoholism. More than one affirmative answer may signal an alcohol-related problem and the need to consult with an alcoholism counselor. To find out more, contact the National Council on Alcoholism and Drug Dependence in your area.

For further information about drug addiction or for help in dealing with an addiction, call the following numbers:

| | |
|---|---|
| National Council on Alcoholism | (800) 622-2255 |
| Psychiatric Institutes of America | (800) COCAINE |
| American Cancer Society (nicotine) | (800) 227-2345 |
| McDonald Center for Alcoholism and Drug Addiction | (800) 382-4357 |

Additional resources are listed in the box on getting help in the chapter on therapy.

(Bowden, 1990; see the discussion in the chapter on memory). Ultimately, chronic abuse of alcohol may lead to death: Approximately 100,000 Americans die each year as a result of using alcohol with other drugs or from alcohol-related breathing difficulties, heart failure, pneumonia, automobile accidents, and suicide (Van Natta et al., 1985).

Are some people especially prone to alcohol abuse? Researchers have no clear answers (Newlin & Thomson, 1990). Alcoholism does run in families: Children whose parents do not use alcohol tend to abstain or to drink only moderately; to a lesser extent, children whose parents abuse alcohol also tend to drink heavily (Cotton, 1979; Harburg, DiFranceisco et al., 1990; Harburg, Gleiberman et al., 1990; Webster et al., 1989). Moreover, there is some direct evidence of a genetic basis for alcohol abuse. For example, identical twins are far more likely to have similar drinking patterns than are fraternal twins. Moreover, people whose biological parents have alcohol-abuse problems are likely to abuse alcohol even if they are adopted and raised by people who do not abuse alcohol (McGue, 1993; Shields, 1977).

Psychologists have reached no consensus on the exact role heredity plays in the tendency to alcoholism. Some point to hereditary differences in

**"Is alcoholism a disease?"**

We have considered the enormous physiological and social costs of alcohol use and abuse. Yet why some people develop drinking problems and others do not remains a mystery. In trying to unravel this mystery, experts must address the question of whether alcoholism is a disease. People who consider alcoholism a disease point out that the disorder appears to have a genetic component. Critics of this approach respond that although many people may be predisposed toward alcoholism, not all of them develop the disorder. Moreover, many chronic alcohol abusers show no evidence of a hereditary predisposition to alcoholism. Thus, the critics conclude, something other than genetics must be at work.

What are your feelings about these issues? Do you think alcoholism is a disease? If so, to what extent should people who abuse alcohol be held responsible for their behavior? And if you think alcoholism is a disease, would you say a heavy smoker also has a disease? How about a person dependent on caffeine? After you have thought about these questions, take a few minutes to examine the opinions of some other students, which appear below:

• • • • • • •

**LISA: Alcoholism is a disease. It is often uncontrollable by the afflicted, and is a sickness that, I believe, stems from inheritance and your own genetic makeup.**

**BOB: Alcoholism can be thought of as a disease, but not a biological one. This disease is both a biological and social disease. We can consider society's pressures to drink as the virus or bacteria that transmits the disease. Once this pressure breaks through, it takes over the body biologically. I can see how a person's body chemistry may cause them to have an "affinity" for alcohol, but if the idea never penetrates the mind, the person won't become an alcoholic.**

**PAT: I agree that there are strongly contributing social and cultural influences here, but might there be some people who are just born with alcoholism as a genetically inherited trait? Social influences are not significant, because once they take that first drink, the disease is activated.**

**MARIA: I think that if we can have mental "illness," then alcoholism is a disease, whether social or genetic.**

**KELLY: Alcoholism is certainly a disease. It is a "condition in which there is an incorrect function resulting from the effect of heredity (infection), (diet), or environment." (*Random House Dictionary*). Alcoholics do have an "incorrect function"—they have no willpower but are helplessly in need and addicted to alcohol.**

**ANDRE: I think that smoking and caffeine addiction are diseases. It's just that society has decided that these diseases are not harmful to society in the way alcoholism is.**

**MICHAEL: The reason we don't call nicotinism a disease is that chain smoking is a lot more socially acceptable than constant drunkenness. Though smoking kills more people, we don't see the effects as much.**

**ERIN: One good thing about calling it a disease is that it takes the blame off the individuals who are alcoholic. They can feel that they are good people who have a disease rather than awful people who are completely responsible for their condition. This is much more conducive to recovery.**

**TOM: I feel a lot more pity for the children of alcoholics than I do for the alcoholics themselves. And for this reason, I think it's wrong to label something like that a disease. Or at least promote the idea of helplessness and destiny along with it.**

**BILL: It's funny that a lot of people think that the term "disease" takes guilt off the person who is an alcoholic. I saw it the other way around. "Disease" has negative connotations and is something which makes a person abnormal and being physically or psychologically hurt. Alcoholism is something that people at some point probably had control over or at least can do something about now. So I saw it as laying more blame by saying that they let themselves become "infected" by a disease that they could have prevented, so at least now they better do all they can to destroy the disease.**

**MICHAEL: We shouldn't use the genetic predisposition to alcoholism as evidence for it being a disease, because those who call it a disease extend it to those who have no family history as well.**

**KATE: I really think alcoholism should still be considered an addiction rather than a disease. It causes disease, such as mental problems and cirrhosis, but I think in itself it is just a problem of addiction.**

• • • • • • •

Now that you've read through other students' views, you might want to reconsider the distinctions, if any, between addiction and disease. What are the implications for both personal responsibility and treatment if you define alcoholism as a disease? As an addiction?

levels of the stomach enzyme mentioned earlier, deducing that people born with higher levels of the enzyme have to drink more alcohol to achieve the same psychological effects as those with lower levels of the enzyme. People may also differ genetically in their tolerance for alcohol in the blood and in the ways they react to alcohol. There was a flurry of excitement in the spring of 1990 when it was reported that a single gene that puts people at risk for alcoholism had been identified (K. Blum et al., 1990), but subsequent research failed to confirm the finding. Instead, it appears that the genetic basis of alcoholism is considerably more complex (Bolos et al., 1990).

**Barbiturates** Potentially deadly depressants, first used for their sedative and anticonvulsant effects, now used only to treat such conditions as epilepsy and arthritis.

Other researchers cite nonbiological factors as the keys in determining who is likely to abuse alcohol. Some researchers have identified an "alcoholic personality," one that is emotionally immature and needy, low in self-esteem, and unable to tolerate frustration well (Coleman et al., 1984). But this personality profile cannot be the whole answer because many people who have these characteristics do not abuse alcohol. Another line of research holds that specific psychological disorders underlie the propensity for addiction to alcohol and other drugs. According to this view, people who are so cut off from their own feelings that they are unable to form relationships with others are likely to be attracted to alcohol because it helps them experience and express affection, aggression, and closeness. By contrast, people who are depressed or hyperactive are more likely to be drawn to stimulants such as amphetamines, and people who have difficulty controlling their anger and hostility favor the opiates (Khantzian, 1990).

Culture, too, may steer people toward or away from alcoholism. Parents and spouses may introduce people to a pattern of heavy drinking. Alcohol is also more acceptable in some ethnic cultures than in others. As an example, Orthodox Jews, who frown on the use of alcohol, and Muslims, who prohibit it, have low rates of alcoholism.

**BARBITURATES** **Barbiturates**—commonly known as "downers"—include such medications as Amytal, Nembutal, and Seconal. Discovered about a century ago, this class of depressants was first prescribed for its sedative and anticonvulsant qualities. But when researchers realized that barbiturates had potentially deadly effects—particularly in combination with alcohol—their use declined in the 1950s. At the same time, pharmaceutical companies introduced a new group of sedatives—the "minor tranquilizers," which include the widely prescribed drug Valium. Nonetheless, barbiturates are sometimes used today to treat such diverse conditions as insomnia, anxiety, epilepsy, arthritis, and bedwetting (Reinisch & Sanders, 1982).

The effects of barbiturates bear striking similarities to those of alcohol: Taken on an empty stomach, 150 mg will cause lightheadedness, silliness, and poor motor coordination (McKim, 1986). Larger doses—400 mg to 700 mg—may bring on such effects as slurred speech, loss of inhibition, and increases in aggressive behavior (Aston, 1972). As with alcohol, the effect of the drug varies from one setting to another: A dose that prompts aggressive behavior at a party may cause only drowsiness when taken in the privacy of one's home. Though they are often prescribed to help people sleep, barbiturates actually disrupt the body's natural sleep patterns and cause dependence when used for long periods. Frequently prescribed for elderly people, who tend to take them chronically along with their other medications, barbiturates may produce significant side effects such as confusion and anxiety (Celis, 1994).

Strangely enough, barbiturates sometimes enhance memory. While barbiturates may cause amnesia (as can alcohol does in the form of blackouts), in smaller doses these drugs are the "truth serums" of contemporary spy thrillers.

**Opiates** Drugs, such as opium and heroin, derived from the opium poppy, that dull the senses and induce feelings of euphoria, well-being, and relaxation. Synthetic drugs resembling opium derivatives are also classified as opiates.

**Stimulants** Drugs, including amphetamines and cocaine, that stimulate the sympathetic nervous system and produce feelings of optimism and boundless energy.

7. Where does the expression "cold turkey" come from?

**THE OPIATES** Historians believe that opium use dates back more than 6,000 years. The **opiates**—a group of substances derived from the opium poppy or synthetic substances resembling it—came into widespread use in the United States in the nineteenth century. *Laudanum*—opium dissolved in alcohol—was sold over the counter, and morphine, a chemical derivative of opium, was readily obtained by prescription. Ironically, heroin—a further refinement of opium developed in 1898—was originally marketed as a cure for morphine addiction. Even though the nonmedicinal distribution of opiates was banned early in this century, because of their highly addictive character, opiate dependence remained a social problem and appears to be on the rise today (Kantrowitz et al., 1993).

Generally, the opiates produce subjective feelings of euphoria, well-being, and relaxation. However, controlled studies reveal that these pleasant effects are short-lived and are quickly replaced by undesirable changes in mood and behavior. A study by R. E. Meyer and Mirin (1979), for example, demonstrated that addicts who are given relatively free access to heroin do experience euphoria and reduced tension for the first few days of use. However, tolerance soon sets in so that users need more of the drug to experience the positive effects and reduce the unpleasant sensations associated with withdrawal. The subjects of Meyer and Mirin's study also reported that after several days of use, the pleasant feelings associated with heroin lasted for only a short time and that more frequent injections became necessary to sustain the "high." The researchers also observed more aggressive behavior and social isolation in these subjects, along with less general physical activity.

Extremely unpleasant withdrawal symptoms follow discontinuance of heroin. The first symptom of withdrawal is restlessness, accompanied by fits of yawning, chills, and hot flashes. The skin often breaks out into goose bumps resembling the texture of a plucked turkey (hence the term "cold turkey"). This is generally followed by periods of prolonged sleep lasting up to 12 hours. When awake, the addict experiences severe cramps, vomiting, and diarrhea, along with convulsive shaking and kicking. All this is accompanied by profuse sweating. In about a week's time, the withdrawal symptoms diminish and then disappear.

Heroin addicts must take larger and larger doses to obtain the same positive mood-altering effects as they did when they first used the drug. Lesser doses simply provide some limited relief from the terrible pains of withdrawal. In advanced stages of addiction, heroin becomes less a means to alter consciousness than a painkiller to stave off withdrawal symptoms. Because heroin is illegal and expensive, addicts must spend a great deal of time—often engaged in criminal activities—obtaining the wherewithal to buy it. These factors underlie policy makers' concerns about heroin as a social problem.

## Stimulants

The drugs classified as **stimulants**—caffeine, nicotine, amphetamines, and cocaine—have legitimate uses, but since they produce feelings of optimism and boundless energy, the potential for abuse is high.

**CAFFEINE AND NICOTINE** Coffee and cigarettes contain powerful mind-altering drugs. Aside from their harmful physical effects, they share many characteristics of the "more serious" drugs we have been examining. Caffeine, which occurs naturally in coffee, tea, and cocoa, belongs to a class of drugs known as *xanthine stimulants*. Nicotine, which occurs naturally only in tobacco, also has stimulant effects, although, paradoxically, at higher doses it acts as a depressant.

Although caffeine is popularly believed to maintain wakefulness and alertness, many of its stimulant effects are illusory. In one study, subjects were asked to perform a series of motor and perceptual tasks after taking 151a dose of caffeine. All thought they were doing better when they were on caffeine, but their actual performance was no better than it had been without caffeine. The primary ingredient in over-the-counter stimulants, caffeine reduces the total number of sleep minutes and increases the time it takes to fall asleep. Interestingly, it is the only stimulant that does not appear to alter sleep stages or cause REM rebound, making it much safer than amphetamines.

**8.** Can caffeine use have any negative effects?

Caffeine is generally considered a benign drug, although large doses—more than 600 mg a day (see Figure 4-5), the equivalent of five or six cups of strong coffee—may cause *caffeinism*, or "coffee nerves." Symptoms include anxiety, headaches, heart palpitations, insomnia, and diarrhea. Since caffeine works in part by suppressing the transmission of naturally occurring chemicals that have calming effects, it also interferes with the action of prescribed medications such as tranquilizers and sedatives. Moreover, caffeine appears to aggravate the symptoms of many psychiatric disorders. Without the knowledge of either patients or staff, DeFreitas and Schwartz (1979) switched patients on a psychiatric ward to decaffeinated coffee. Following the switch, they observed a decrease in symptoms like anxiety and an increase in socially appropriate behavior. These effects were reversed when regular coffee was served once again.

Many coffee drinkers are dependent on caffeine and experience headaches, lethargy, and depression if they stop consuming it. Though it is not clear what percentage of coffee drinkers qualify as dependent on the substance, it is known that those who are dependent experience tolerance, physical and psychological distress, and an inability to give up caffeine, whether in caffeinated soda, coffee, or tea (Blakeslee, 1994). Since drinking or eating anything is usually forbidden for several hours before an operation, caffeine withdrawal may explain why some patients experience postoperative headaches (E. Rosenthal, 1992).

Nicotine is far more dangerous than caffeine. Besides immediate effects of increased heart rate and constricted blood cells, which cause smokers to lose skin color and to have cold hands, it accelerates the process

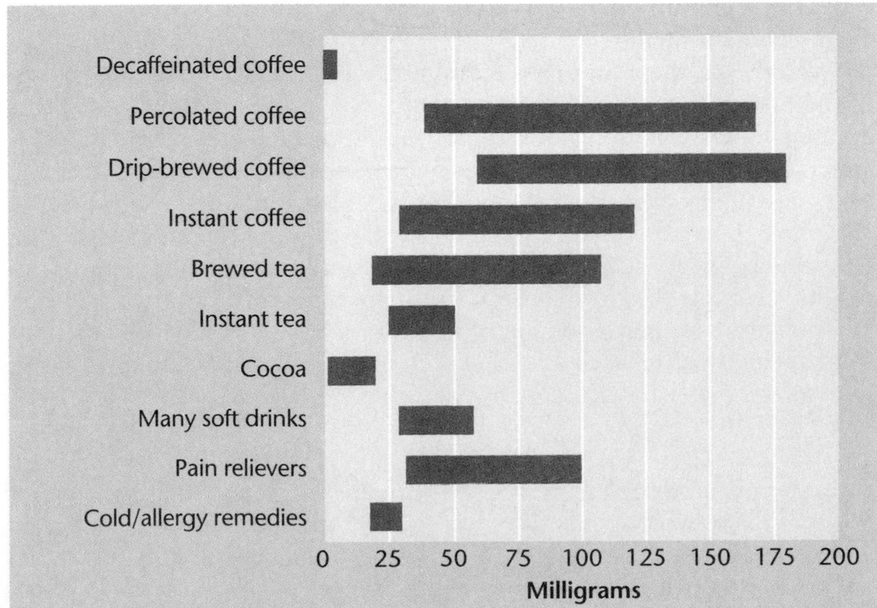


**Figure 4-5**
**The amount of caffeine in some common preparations.** Americans consume about 200 mg of caffeine a day, the equivalent of about three cups of coffee.

*Source:* Copyright ©1991 by The New York Times Company. Reprinted by permission.

**Amphetamines** Stimulant drugs that initially produce "rushes" of euphoria often followed by sudden "crashes" and, sometimes, severe depression.

**Cocaine** Drug derived from the coca plant that, while producing a sense of euphoria by stimulating the sympathetic nervous system, also leads to anxiety, depression, and addictive cravings.

of wrinkling and aging (Daniell, 1971). Its long-term physical effects include placing users at increased risk for lung cancer and other cancers as well as for cardiovascular disease. Nicotine increases levels of endorphins, norepinephrine, and acetylcholine in the nervous system (see Chapter 2); it also raises levels of dopamine in the areas of the brain affecting mood (Brandon, 1994). When ingested through smoking, nicotine tends to arrive at the brain all at once following each puff. This rush, which is similar to the "high" experienced by heroin users, makes the brain crave more nicotine.

Users tend to become highly dependent on nicotine. In one study, smokers were required to pull a plunger a number of times in order to take a puff of a cigarette. When the number of pulls required to get a puff was gradually increased, most subjects simply inhaled more during each puff. One subject, however, pulled the plunger 14,000 times over 45 minutes to get just two puffs of tobacco (T. Adler, 1993a).

This research points up how strong the craving for nicotine is and how difficult it is to quit. The withdrawal symptoms for nicotine users include nervousness, insomnia and drowsiness, headaches, irritability, and an intense craving for nicotine (Brandon, 1994). Research on treatment outcomes indicates that as few as 15 percent of smokers manage to quit permanently. Certain conditions and behaviors increase a user's likelihood of quitting. Nicotine patches and nicotine gum, which deliver smaller doses of the drug, may lessen the physical addiction while also helping to break the habit of lighting up. Those who have quit previously and started smoking again also have a higher success rate. According to one study, 18 percent of smokers who had quit for a time later quit completely, compared to only 10 percent of those who had never quit for even a week. However, the majority of smokers do *not* succeed in giving up smoking for good. Nicotine is highly addictive and there are no miracle cures for smokers who want to quit.

**AMPHETAMINES** While reports of amphetaminelike substances date back more than 5,000 years, researchers did not discover the medicinal value of amphetamines until the early part of the 20th century. At the chemical level, **amphetamines** resemble epinephrine, a neurotransmitter that stimulates the sympathetic nervous system (see the chapter on physiology and behavior). Because of this chemical similarity, amphetamines are used to treat asthma: They open respiratory passages and ease breathing. Amphetamines have also been prescribed for narcolepsy because of their stimulant qualities.

However, these drugs have a tremendous potential for abuse because of their effects on consciousness and behavior. As one of their side effects, amphetamines bring on a feeling of euphoria; higher doses amplify this effect. But after the drug's effects wear off, users may experience a "crash" and subsequent severe depression (Gunne & Anggard, 1972). To head off this unpleasant experience, users tend to take more amphetamines, leading to a condition called *amphetamine psychosis*, similar to paranoid schizophrenia and characterized by delusions, hallucinations, and paranoia. Habitual amphetamine use may also prompt aggressive, violent behavior, caused not so much by the drug itself as by the profound personality changes—particularly paranoia—that accompany excessive use (Leccese, 1991).

**COCAINE** **Cocaine** is also a stimulant and, like the amphetamines, can cause euphoric moods. Cocaine is extracted from the leaves of the coca plant, which is native to the Andes Mountains in South America. The original method for ingesting this drug, which is still practiced today in South America, involves chewing the leaves of the coca bush. Today, cocaine use has become more widespread, particularly in its crystalline

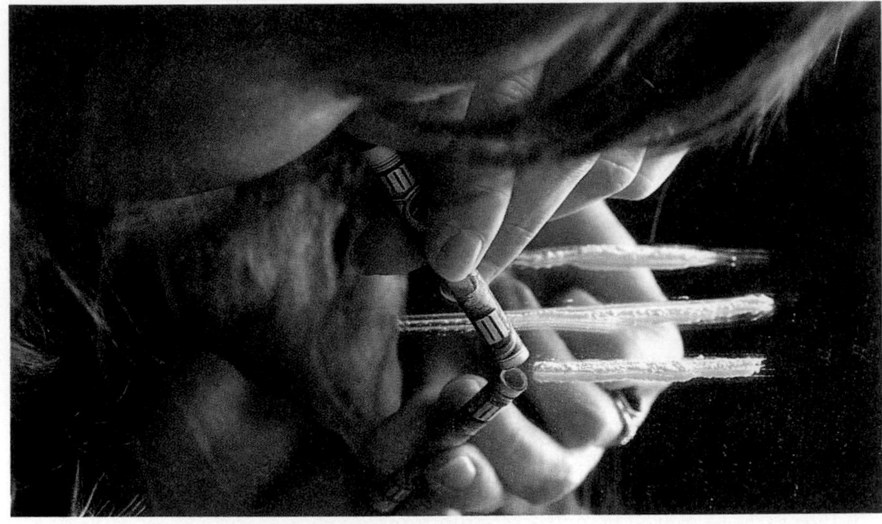

A cocaine user about to inhale the white powdery substance.

form known as "crack," which can be smoked easily in a pipe or cigarette. What makes crack such a serious problem is that many users report becoming dependent on the drug almost immediately, and because of the way the drug acts on the brain, the craving for it is difficult to break.

The effects of cocaine mirror those of the amphetamines, although they are shorter in duration. The effects of crack, however, are even faster and more intense than those produced by amphetamines. Along with the feelings of euphoria, energy, and perceived clarity of thought, physiological effects include stimulation of the sympathetic nervous system, an increase in heart rate and blood pressure, and constriction of the blood vessels. Large doses also raise the body temperature and dilate the pupils. After relatively large doses wear off, some users experience a "crash" characterized by anxiety, depression, and a strong craving for more cocaine. R. K. Siegel (1982) surveyed habitual users and discovered that one-third to one-half also experienced such mood and behavioral symptoms as paranoia, visual hallucinations, cravings for the drug, and attention and concentration problems. When smoked as crack, molecules of cocaine reach the brain in less than 10 seconds, producing a high that lasts from 5 to 20 minutes and is followed by a swift and equally intense depression. Crack and cocaine stimulate a pleasure center in the base of the brain—an area that, as we will see in the chapter on motivation and emotion, is responsible for our emotions. As the levels of cocaine in the brain drop, users begin to feel depressed and anxious. With crack, this pleasureless state begins to set in within 30 minutes. Because cocaine interferes with the chemistry of this pleasure center in the brain, and subsequently with the brain's ability to reestablish emotional balance, the craving for the drug is doubly painful and difficult to overcome. The compulsion to take more and more of this expensive drug may impoverish even wealthy users.

Cocaine use creates problems not only for users but also for their unborn children. Women addicted to crack and cocaine often give birth to premature, low-birthweight babies. These "crack babies" were once believed to be born addicted because of their small size and agitated, trembling behaviors. However, research has found that though cocaine and crack use often prevents women from carrying their babies to term, children born to mothers dependent on crack are actually less likely to be born addicted than are children of women who use alcohol, nicotine, or marijuana. It turns out that the agitation and shaking that were originally viewed as evidence of drug dependence are typical of premature babies in general (Coles, 1992).

In many parts of the country, the use of crack, a crystalline form of cocaine, has become epidemic. Because they stimulate pleasure centers in the brain, crack and cocaine produce a feeling of euphoria that is quickly followed by a pleasureless "crash" that fosters even greater craving for, and dependency on, the drug.

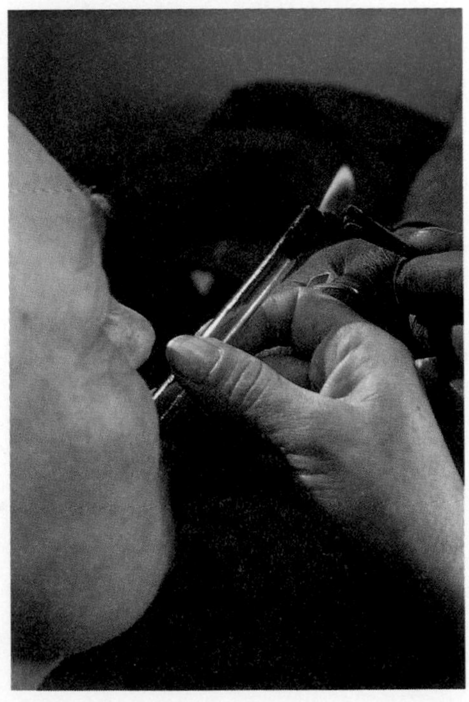

## Hallucinogens and Marijuana

**Hallucinogens** Any of a number of drugs, such as LSD and mescaline, that distort visual and auditory perception.

**Lysergic acid diethylamide (LSD)** Hallucinogenic or "psychedelic" drug that produces hallucinations and delusions similar to those occurring in a psychotic state.

The hallucinogens include lysergic acid diethylamide (LSD, also known as "acid"), mescaline, peyote, psilocybin, and phencyclidine (PCP, or "angel dust"). Marijuana is sometimes included in this group, although its effects are normally less powerful. Even in very small doses, these drugs often produce striking visual effects that resemble hallucinations, giving rise to the term *hallucinogen*. Although many other drugs will, in large enough doses, also bring on hallucinatory or delusional experiences, mimicking those that occur in severe mental illnesses, hallucinogens do so in far less than toxic quantities.

These Native-American women in Mexico are grinding dry peyote that will be mixed with water and drunk during an upcoming festival. Many Native-American peoples have traditionally included peyote in their religious ceremonies.

**HALLUCINOGENS** Many of the **hallucinogens** occur in natural forms such as mushrooms and other fungi. In natural form, they share with other consciousness-altering drugs an ancient history. Mescaline, for example, occurs in the peyote cactus, and historians believe that it has been used for at least 8,000 years by Native Americans.

By contrast, the story of **lysergic acid diethylamide (LSD)**, the drug that triggered the current interest in the hallucinogens, begins in this century. In 1943, an American pharmacologist synthesized LSD, and after ingesting it, he reported experiencing "an uninterrupted stream of fantastic pictures and extraordinary shapes with an intense, kaleidoscopic play of colors." His report led others to experiment with LSD as a means of altering normal consciousness. In the 1960s, the development of LSD as a street drug was prompted in large part by Timothy Leary, a Harvard psychologist who, after trying the chemically related drug psilocybin, began spreading what became the gospel of the 1960s hippie movement—"Turn On, Tune In, Drop Out". After a steady decline in use since the 1970s, LSD and marijuana have recently become popular once again with high school and college students (Janofsky, 1994).

Studying the consciousness-altering effects of the hallucinogens is particularly difficult for several reasons. As with other drugs, setting, mood, and expectations have a profound effect on people's reactions to these drugs. But unlike cocaine and the opiates, which produce "rushes," the hallucinogens give rise to more subtle effects, and their onset is often delayed for an hour or more after the drug is ingested. After taking LSD, subjects sometimes find researchers' questions hilarious or irrelevant; at other times, they either refuse to answer questions or are unable to do so (NCMDA, 1973a). Finally, there is the problem of trying to measure subtle changes in perceptual experiences.

LSD changes users' auditory perceptions in a variety of ways. Some people report hearing imaginary conversations, fully orchestrated original symphonies, or foreign languages previously unknown to them. Auditory acuity may be increased, making the person keenly aware of low sounds like breathing, heartbeat, and the light rustle of leaves in the wind.

Unlike depressants and stimulants, LSD and the other hallucinogens appear to produce no withdrawal effects in the user. On the other hand, tolerance builds up quite rapidly: If LSD is taken repeatedly, after a few days no amount of the drug will produce its usual effects until administration is halted for about a week (McKim, 1986). This rapid development of tolerance is a built-in deterrent to continuous use—a fact that helps explain why LSD is generally taken episodically rather than habitually. After a time, users seem to get tired of the experience and decrease or discontinue taking the drug, at least for a period of time.

One strong negative effect of some hallucinogens is "bad trips," or unpleasant experiences that may be set off by a change in dosage or an alteration in setting or mood. During a bad trip, the user may not realize that the experiences are being caused by the drug, and panic may set in. More serious are the stories of users who kill themselves because the drug makes them think they can fly out a window or who commit murders while under the influence of the drug. *Flashbacks*, or recurrences of hallucinations that occur weeks after ingesting LSD, are also relatively common.

In rare cases, people have developed enduring mental illnesses from repeated use of hallucinogens—apparently because the drug triggers a powerful emotional response that, in turn, sets off a preexisting tendency toward disturbed behavior. Other consequences include memory loss, paranoia, panic attacks, nightmares, and aggression (Seligmann et al., 1992).

**Marijuana** A mild hallucinogen that produces a "high" often characterized by feelings of euphoria, a sense of well-being, and swings in mood from gaiety to relaxation; may also cause feelings of anxiety and paranoia.

**MARIJUANA** **Marijuana**, a drug produced from the *cannabis* plant, was cultivated as long as 5,000 years ago in China and there are reports of its use in the Bible. The ancient Greeks also were aware of its existence, and it has been used in India for centuries because of its intoxicating effects. Only in this century did it become popular in the United States. During the 1920s, the spreading use of marijuana generated alarm, as reflected in the propaganda film *Reefer Madness*, which proclaimed that the drug could seduce innocent youth into violence and madness. By the end of the 1930s, the drug had all but disappeared from American culture. Marijuana was revived in the 1960s, and flourished in the youth culture of that time. Since then, an estimated 50 million Americans have tried the drug at least once. Currently, marijuana is the fourth most popular drug among students, after alcohol, caffeine, and nicotine. In 1989, 17 percent of high school seniors and 16 percent of college students reported using marijuana within the previous 30 days (Berke, 1990; Carmody, 1990). More recently, the percentage of high school seniors who reported using marijuana during the previous year rose from 22 percent in 1992 to 26 percent in 1993 (Treaster, 1994).

Although the active ingredient in marijuana, *tetrahydrocannabinol* (*THC*), shares some chemical properties with hallucinogens like LSD, it is far less potent and affects consciousness much less profoundly. The marijuana "high" is often marked by euphoric feelings and a sense of well-being accompanied by swings from gaiety to relaxation. But some people experience feelings of anxiety and paranoia. Whether the user is suffused with happiness or filled with anxiety and paranoia depends in large part on the overall setting and the mood of others in that setting.

Marijuana has a number of demonstrated physiological effects. It dilates the blood vessels in the eyes, making the eyes appear bloodshot. Since it is generally smoked, users frequently experience a dry mouth and coughing, as well as increased thirst and hunger and mild muscular weakness, often in the form of drooping eyelids (Donatelle & Davis, 1993). Among the drug's psychological effects is a distortion of time, which has been confirmed under experimental conditions. In addition, marijuana may produce alterations in attention and memory, including an inability to concentrate on many types of tasks—a fact that contributes to concern about people's ability to drive a car after using marijuana (DeLong & Levy, 1974). One-third of car-accident victims admitted to the trauma unit of one hospital had noticeable levels of THC in their blood (Donatelle & Davis, 1993). The drug also interferes with short-term memory: Users often cannot retain information for later use (Hollister, 1986), which bring on anxiety and even panic (Leccese, 1991).

The chief negative physiological effects of marijuana are potential respiratory and cardiovascular damage (Wu et al., 1988)—effects found in smokers of any substance. However, some studies have observed "apathy, loss of effectiveness, and diminished capacity to carry out complex, long-term plans, endure frustration, concentrate for long periods, follow routines, or successfully master new material" in marijuana users (McGothlin

& West, 1968). It is difficult to determine from such reports whether these changes are produced by marijuana in normal people or whether people who are predisposed toward apathy are more likely to select and use marijuana for a long period of time.

## Summary Table

### Drugs: Characteristics and Effects

| | Typical Effects | Effects of Overdose | Tolerance/Dependence |
|---|---|---|---|
| ***Depressants*** | | | |
| **Alcohol** | Biphasic: tension-reduction "high," followed by depressed physical and psychological functioning. | Disorientation, loss of consciousness, death at extremely high blood-alcohol levels. | Tolerance: physical and psychological dependence, withdrawal symptoms. |
| **Barbiturates**<br>**Tranquilizers** | Depressed reflexes and impaired motor functioning, tension reduction. | Shallow respiration, clammy skin, dilated pupils, weak and rapid pulse, coma, possible death. | Tolerance: high psychological and physical dependence on barbiturates, low to moderate physical dependence on such tranquilizers as Valium, although high psychological dependence; withdrawal symptoms. |
| ***Stimulants*** | | | |
| **Amphetamines**<br>**Cocaine**<br>**Caffeine**<br>**Nicotine** | Increased alertness, excitation, euphoria, increased pulse rate and blood pressure, sleeplessness. | For amphetamines and cocaine: agitation and, with chronic high doses, hallucinations (e.g., "cocaine bugs"), paranoid delusions, convulsions, death. | For amphetamines and cocaine: tolerance, psychological but probably not physical dependence. |
| | | For caffeine and nicotine: restlessness, insomnia, rambling thoughts, heart arrhythmia, possible circulatory failure. For nicotine: increased blood pressure. | For caffeine and nicotine: tolerance; physical and psychological dependence; withdrawal symptoms. |
| ***Opioids*** | | | |
| **Opium**<br>**Morphine**<br>**Heroin** | Euphoria, drowsiness, "rush" of pleasure, little impairment of psychological functions. | Slow, shallow breathing, clammy skin, nausea, vomiting, pinpoint pupils, convulsions, coma, possible death. | High tolerance; physical and psychological dependence; severe withdrawal symptoms. |
| ***Hallucinogens*** | | | |
| **LSD**<br>**PCP (dissociative anesthetic)** | Illusions, hallucinations, distortions in time perception, loss of contact with reality. | Psychotic reactions, particularly with PCP; possible death with PCP. | No physical dependence for LSD; degree unknown for PCP; psychological dependence for PCP; degree unknown for LSD. |
| **Marijuana** | Euphoria, relaxed inhibitions, increased appetite, possible disorientation. | Fatigue, disoriented behavior, possible psychosis. | Psychological dependence. |

# LOOKING FORWARD

Long relegated to the murky depths of psychological inquiry, consciousness has once again surfaced as a topic of great interest among research psychologists. Psychologists today are intensely curious about how we think, solve problems, and make decisions. They are also intrigued by altered states of consciousness, including sleep, meditation, and hypnosis. Although some of these processes might seem to elude scientific analysis, they can often be observed and measured scientifically by studying people's physiological reactions. For example, modern technology enables medical researchers to monitor brain, nerve, and muscular activity during sleep or altered states of consciousness; information gathered in this way, in turn, holds promise of both medical and psychological benefits. As an example, hypnosis has been used clinically to relieve pain among those with painful chronic conditions and to control bleeding among dental patients with hemophilia. Thus, we should avoid splitting psychology into two warring camps of consciousness "versus" physiology; the two are closely interrelated.

The study of altered states of consciousness figures prominently in this area of inquiry because it dovetails with a number of key social and scientific issues of contemporary concern. Take substance abuse, which has become a major problem in U.S. society. By studying both the personalities of people who abuse dangerous substances as well as the action of drugs within the body, psychologists hope to shed light on the underlying causes of substance abuse and develop better preventive and treatment procedures. Psychologists have also alerted us to the dangers associated with sleep deprivation, including its deleterious effects on driving ability and job performance. The study of consciousness, then, has become a critical area of psychological research—one that offers benefits to people throughout society.

# SUMMARY

**Consciousness** is our awareness of the various cognitive processes that operate in our daily lives: making decisions, remembering, daydreaming, concentrating, reflecting, sleeping, and dreaming, among others. Psychologists divide consciousness into two broad areas: **waking consciousness**, which includes the thoughts, feelings, and perceptions that arise when we are awake and reasonably alert; and **altered states of consciousness (ASC)**, during which our mental state differs noticeably from normal waking consciousness.

## NATURAL VARIATIONS IN CONSCIOUSNESS

To make sense of our complex environment, we choose what to absorb from the myriad happenings around us and filter out the rest. This applies to both external stimuli such as sounds, sights, and smells, and internal sensations such as heat, cold, pressure, and pain. Even our thoughts, memories, emotions, and needs are subjected to this selective process. We also perform familiar tasks, such as signing our names, without deliberate attention. Many psychologists believe that important mental processes go on outside of normal waking consciousness, perhaps as a form of automatic processing.

### Daydreaming and Fantasy

**Daydreaming** occurs without effort, often when we prefer to escape the demands of the real world briefly. Some psychologists see no positive or practical value in daydreaming. Others contend that daydreams and fantasies allow us to express and deal with hidden desires without guilt or anxiety. Still others believe that daydreams build cognitive and creative skills that help us survive difficult situations—that they are a useful substitute for reality or a beneficial way of relieving tension. Finally there are those who view daydreaming as a mechanism for processing the vast array of information we take in during the day, enabling us to retrieve thoughts put aside for later review and to transform them into new and more useful forms.

### Sleep and Dreaming

Research into sleep patterns shows that normal sleep consists of several stages.

Following the initial "twilight" state, which is characterized by irregular, low-voltage alpha waves and a state of relaxed wakefulness, the sleeper enters Stage 1 of sleep. This stage, which is marked by a slowing of the pulse, muscle relaxation, and side-to-side rolling movements of the eyes, lasts only a few moments. The sleeper is easily awakened from Stage 1 sleep.

Stages 2 and 3 are characterized by progressively deeper sleep. In these stages, the sleeper is hard to awaken and does not respond to noise or light. Heart rate, blood pressure, and temperature continue to drop.

During Stage 4 sleep, heart and breathing rates, blood pressure, and body temperature are as low as they will get during the night. About an hour after first falling asleep, the sleeper begins to ascend through the stages back to Stage 1—a process that takes about 40 minutes. At this stage in the sleep cycle, heart rate and blood pressure increase, the muscles become more relaxed than at any other time in the cycle, and the eyes move rapidly under closed eyelids. It is this rapid eye movement (REM) that gives this stage of sleep its name.

**REM sleep** is also called **paradoxical sleep** because while brain activity and other physiological symptoms resemble those recorded during waking consciousness, the sleeper appears to be deeply asleep and is incapable of moving because of paralysis of the body's voluntary muscles. **Non-REM**, or **NREM sleep**, refers to the non–rapid-eye-movement stages of sleep that alternate with REM stages during the sleep cycle.

**Dreams** are vivid images or experiences that occur primarily during REM periods of sleep. According to Freud, dreams have two kinds of contents: manifest (the surface content of the dream itself) and latent (the disguised, unconscious meaning of the dream). Less vivid experiences that resemble conscious thinking tend to occur during NREM sleep. One theory to explain why REM dreams are so vivid cites the level of brain arousal during REM sleep: The brain's activity closely resembles that of normal waking consciousness, but because of its relative insensitivity to outside sensory input, it draws on nothing but internal images from memory.

Several theories have been developed to explain the nature and content of dreams. One recent hypothesis suggests that dreams arise out of the mind's reprocessing of information absorbed during the day—information that is important to the survival of the organism. Thus, dreaming strengthens our memories of important information. At the neurophysiological level, REM sleep may be related to brain "restoration" and growth.

Many people are afflicted by sleep disorders. **Insomnia** is characterized by difficulty in falling asleep or remaining asleep throughout the night. **Apnea** is marked by breathing difficulties during the night and feelings of exhaustion during the day. **Narcolepsy** is a hereditary sleep disorder characterized by sudden nodding off during the day and sudden loss of muscle tone following moments of emotional excitement.

## ARTIFICIAL ALTERATIONS IN CONSCIOUSNESS

### Meditation

**Meditation** refers to any of several methods of concentration, reflection, or focusing of thoughts intended to suppress the activity of the sympathetic nervous system. Meditation not only lowers the rate of metabolism but also reduces heart and respiratory rates. Brain activity during meditation resembles that experienced during relaxed wakefulness, and the accompanying decrease in blood lactate reduces stress.

### Hypnosis

**Hypnosis** is a trancelike state in which the person responds readily to suggestions. People's susceptibility to hypnosis depends on how suggestible they are. Hypnosis has several practical applications; for instance, it eases the pain of certain medical conditions and can help people stop smoking and break other habits.

## DRUG-ALTERED CONSCIOUSNESS

Some ASCs are induced with the help of **psychoactive drugs**.

### Substance Use, Abuse, and Dependence

It is important to distinguish between substance use and substance abuse: *Substance use* may be essential for medical reasons and it may also be culturally approved and valued. By contrast, **substance abuse** is a pattern of drug use that diminishes the person's ability to fulfill responsibilities at home or at work or school, that results in repeated use of a drug in dangerous situations, or that leads to legal difficulties related to drug use.

Continued abuse over a period of time can lead to **substance dependence**, a pattern of compulsive drug taking that is much more serious than substance abuse. It is often marked by **tolerance**, the need to take higher doses of a drug to produce its original effects or to prevent withdrawal symptoms. **Withdrawal symptoms** are the unpleasant physical or psychological effects that follow discontinuance of the substance.

To study the effects of drugs scientifically, most researchers use a **double-blind procedure** to eliminate biases that might arise out of the experimenter's or subject's prior knowledge or expectations about a drug. Neither the subjects nor the researcher knows at the time of administration which subjects are receiving the active drug and which are receiving a **placebo**—a neutral, chemically inactive substance used for comparison with active drugs in experiments on the effects of drugs.

Consciousness-altering drugs are grouped into three broad categories: depressants, stimulants, and hallucinogens.

## DEPRESSANTS

**Depressants** are chemicals that slow down behavior or cognitive processes. **Alcohol**, a depressant, is the intoxicating ingredient in whiskey, beer, wine, and other fermented or distilled liquors. It is responsible for tens of thousands of deaths each year and contributes to a great deal of crime and domestic violence.

**Barbiturates**, popularly known as "downers," are potentially deadly depressants. They were first used for their sedative and anticonvulsant effects, but today their use is limited to the treatment of such conditions as epilepsy and arthritis.

The **opiates** are highly addictive drugs such as opium, morphine, and heroin that dull the senses and induce feelings of euphoria, well-being, and relaxation.

## STIMULANTS

**Stimulants** are drugs such as caffeine, nicotine, amphetamines, and cocaine that stimulate the sympathetic nervous system and produce feelings of optimism and boundless energy, making the potential for their abuse significant.

Caffeine occurs naturally in coffee, tea, and cocoa;

nicotine occurs naturally only in tobacco. Caffeine is considered to be a benign drug, but in large doses it can cause anxiety, insomnia, and other unpleasant conditions. Although nicotine is a stimulant, it acts like a depressant when taken in large doses.

**Amphetamines** are stimulants that initially produce "rushes" of euphoria often followed by sudden "crashes" and, sometimes, depression. **Cocaine** brings on a sense of euphoria by stimulating the sympathetic nervous system, but it can also cause anxiety, depression, and addictive cravings. Its crystalline form—crack—is highly addictive.

### HALLUCINOGENS AND MARIJUANA

**Hallucinogens** are any of a number of drugs, such as LSD, phencyclidine (PCP, or "angel dust"), and mescaline, that distort visual and auditory perception.

Many of the hallucinogens occur naturally in mushrooms or other fungi. In these forms, they share an ancient history with other consciousness-altering drugs of natural origins. By contrast, **lysergic acid diethylamide (LSD)** is an artificial hallucinogen that produces hallucinations and delusions similar to those that occur in a psychotic state.

**Marijuana** is a mild hallucinogen that is capable of producing feelings of euphoria, a sense of well-being, and swings in mood from gaiety to relaxation to paranoia. Currently, marijuana is the fourth most popular drug among students, following alcohol, caffeine, and nicotine. Though similar to hallucinogens in certain characteristics, marijuana is far less potent and its effects on consciousness are far less profound.

# REVIEW QUESTIONS

### MULTIPLE CHOICE

1. We experience ______ consciousness when our mental state differs noticeably from the state we experience when we are awake and alert.
2. The hallmark of normal waking consciousness is highly selective ______ .
3. According to Freud, the real driving forces behind human actions are ______ instincts that are hidden but brought into consciousness through such states as dreaming and hypnosis.
4. True or false: Psychologists have a clear understanding of the biological and psychological necessity for sleep.
5. REM sleep is usually called ______ sleep, because during it such physical functions as heart rate closely resemble those of waking consciousness, even though the sleeper's voluntary muscles appear to be paralyzed.
6. The increase in dreaming that occurs after the cessation of dream deprivation is known as ______ ______ .
7. Match the sleep disorder with the symptoms:

    ____insomnia
    ____apnea
    ____narcolepsy

    a. excessive, unpredictable sleeping sessions
    b. breathing difficulties and day-after exhaustion
    c. acute or chronic inability to sleep

8. In all its diverse forms, meditation reduces the activity of the ______ system.
9. Many psychologists believe that the effects of hypnosis can be accounted for by the variable of ______ .
10. Although alcohol is a ______ , it is sometimes experienced subjectively as a ______ .
11. ______ are commonly known as "downers."
12. The crystalline form of cocaine is known as:

    a. LSD
    b. angel dust
    c. crack
    d. opium

13. Match the following categories of drugs with their descriptions:

    ___alcohol
    ___amphetamines
    ___barbiturates
    ___opiates
    ___cocaine
    ___hallucinogens

    a. produces feelings of optimism and boundless energy
    b. addictive drugs that dull the senses
    c. effects vary with quantity consumed and manner and setting in which it is taken
    d. responsible for the most serious drug problem in the United States today
    e. profoundly affects visual and auditory perception
    f. depressants that compromise memory and perception of time

### CRITICAL THINKING AND APPLICATIONS

14. Should psychologists study consciousness? Is it a valid subject for scientific research? Why or why not?
15. A close friend informs you that she has been having a number of unusual dreams in recent weeks. What would you advise her to do? Do you believe that dreams offer insights into our innermost thoughts and feelings? Should psychologists study dreams or discuss the content of dreams with their clients?
16. What, in your opinion, are the major causes of substance abuse and dependence? How should society deal with these problems?

*(Answers to the Review Questions can be found in the back of the text.)*

## Think About It!

1. How can a household pet learn to identify the sound of a can opener?
2. What do we mean by reinforcement of behaviors? Is reinforcement the same as punishment?
3. How do we learn superstitions? Do animals other than humans exhibit superstitious behaviors?
4. What do we mean when we say that money is a secondary reinforcer?
5. *True or false*: Punishing a child for aggressive behavior by slapping or spanking can teach the child to act more violently.
6. *True or false*: Humans are the only species that can cognitively process information.

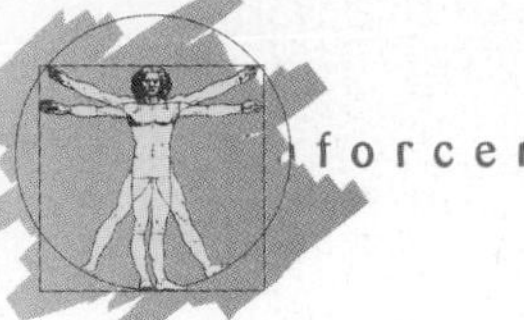

# LEARNING

# 5

## Overview

**Learning** The process by which experience or practice results in a relatively permanent change in behavior or potential behavior.

**Conditioning** The acquisition of specific patterns of behavior in the presence of well-defined stimuli.

**Classical** or **Pavlovian conditioning** Type of learning in which a response naturally elicited by one stimulus comes to be elicited by a different, neutral stimulus.

**Operant** or **instrumental conditioning** Type of learning in which behaviors are emitted (in the presence of specific stimuli) to earn rewards or avoid punishments.

**As unlikely as it may seem, the following situations have something in common:**

- On completion of a training course at the National Zoo, the star students demonstrate their newly acquired behaviors: Junior, a young orangutan, cleans up his cage for the chance to blow a whistle; a pair of 18-inch-long lizards jump 2 feet in the air to snatch insects from the tip of a forceps; a chinchilla weighs itself by hopping into a basket on top of a scale; and Peela the tiger retrieves a floating keg from the moat in his exhibition area.
- In the chronic schizophrenia ward of a mental hospital, patients who once had to be fed, cleaned, and clothed by caretakers now do their own laundry, eat meals together in a dining room, and wash and comb their own hair. The ward operates as a token economy: For performing tasks, patients earn tokens that will buy things like candy, soap, magazines, and trinkets.
- Joey goes away to summer camp for the first time, a city kid, he hasn't done much boating, hiking, or camping. But by the end of 8 weeks at Camp Winnepesaka, Joey can row a canoe and sail a Sunfish sailboat, pitch camp, and blaze a trail; he can even distinguish poison ivy from poison sumac and pick out constellations in the nighttime sky.

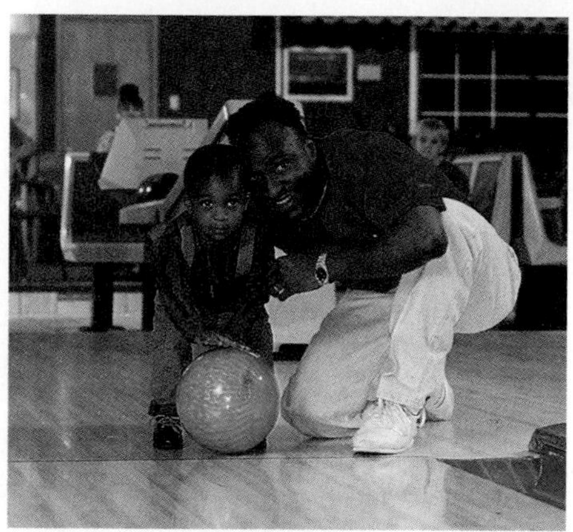

Learning is the process by which experience or practice results in a relatively permanent change in behavior or potential behavior.

Although these situations took place outside the confines of a school classroom, all are instances of **learning.** Most people equate learning with studying. But psychologists define learning more broadly, as the process by which experience or practice results in a relatively permanent change in behavior or potential behavior. This definition certainly encompasses classroom learning and studying, but it covers many other types of learning as well: learning to turn off lights when we leave a room, learning which way to put the key into the front door lock, learning how to avoid falling down on skis, learning how to dance.

In this chapter, we will explore several different kinds of learning. We will begin with a basic form of learning known as conditioning. **Conditioning** is a general term—used for animals as well as for human beings—that refers to the acquisition of fairly specific patterns of behaviors in the presence of well-defined stimuli. In one type of conditioning, called **classical conditioning**, or **Pavlovian conditioning**, *reflexive* behaviors—involuntary responses that would automatically follow one type of stimulus—are *elicited* by other, formerly neutral stimuli. For example, you might become tense or anxious when you hear the kind of music that always precedes a frightening or startling scene in a scary film, because you have come to identify this music with such scenes. In a second type of conditioning, known as **operant conditioning** or **instrumental conditioning**, selected, voluntary behaviors come to be *emitted* in the presence of specific stimuli in order to gain a reward or to avoid a punishment. Teaching a dog to sit or heel on command is an example of operant conditioning. In both cases, past experience in the presence of well-defined stimuli (the music or the command to sit) causes corresponding changes in behavior. Although the examples we have used to introduce conditioning may seem simplistic or unimportant, Hergenhahn and Olson (1993) state:

> No organism would survive long if it did not *learn* which environmental objects could be used to satisfy its basic needs. Nor could an organism survive long if it could not learn which environmental objects were safe and which were dangerous. . . . In general, it is through

classical conditioning that we learn which environmental objects are conducive to survival and which are not; and it is through instrumental or operant conditioning that we learn how to acquire or avoid desirable and undesirable objects. (p. 10)

Thus, classical and operant conditioning are essential to our ability to survive in and adapt to a changing world.

After delving into classical and operant conditioning, we will probe more complex forms of learning that are not tied to the immediate environment. Grouped under the heading of *cognitive learning* because they depend on thinking and reasoning processes, these include *insight* and *observational learning*, or *vicarious learning*. When, after pondering a math problem or similar puzzle, you suddenly see the solution in its complete form, you are experiencing insight. When you take to the dance floor and imitate the steps of professional dancers you saw last night on television, you are demonstrating observational learning. Like conditioning, cognitive learning is one of our survival strategies. Through cognitive processes, we learn which events are safe and which are dangerous without having to experience those events directly. Cognitive learning also gives us access to the wisdom of people who lived hundreds of years ago, and it will give people living hundreds of years from now some insight into our experiences and way of life.

Our discussion begins with the first of these learning processes: classical conditioning. This simple kind of learning serves as a convenient starting point for examining what learning is and how it can be observed.

## CLASSICAL CONDITIONING

### Pavlov's Conditioning Experiments

Classical conditioning was discovered almost by accident by Ivan Pavlov (1849–1936), a Russian physiologist who was studying digestive processes. Because animals salivate when food is placed in their mouths, Pavlov inserted tubes into the salivary glands of dogs to measure how much saliva they produced when they were given food. He noticed, however, that the dogs salivated before the food was in their mouths: The mere sight of food made them drool. In fact, they even drooled at the sound of the experimenter's footsteps. This aroused Pavlov's curiosity. What was making the dogs salivate even before they had the food in their mouths? How had they learned to salivate in response to the sound of the experimenter's approach?

To answer these questions, Pavlov set out to teach the dogs to salivate when food was not present. He devised an experiment in which he sounded a bell just before the food was brought into the room. A ringing bell does not usually make a dog's mouth water, but after hearing the bell many times just before getting fed, Pavlov's dogs began to salivate as soon as the bell rang. It was as if they had learned that the bell signaled the appearance of food, and their mouths watered on cue even if no food followed. The dogs had been conditioned to salivate in response to a new stimulus, the bell, that would not normally have prompted that response (Pavlov, 1927). In Figure 5-1, we see an improved procedure devised by Pavlov, in which the bell has been replaced by a tactile (touch) stimulus, applied to the dog's leg, just before food is presented.

### Elements of Classical Conditioning

Generally speaking, classical conditioning involves pairing a response that is usually evoked by one stimulus with a different, previously neutral stimulus. Pavlov's experiment illustrates the four basic elements of classical condition-

**Unconditioned stimulus (US)** Stimulus that invariably causes an organism to respond in a specific way.

**Unconditioned response (UR)** Response that takes place in an organism whenever an unconditioned stimulus occurs.

**Conditioned stimulus (CS)** Originally neutral stimulus that is paired with an unconditioned stimulus and eventually produces the desired response in an organism when presented alone.

**Conditioned response (CR)** After conditioning, the response an organism produces when only a conditioned stimulus is presented.

**1.** How can a household pet learn to identify the sound of a can opener?

ing. The first is an **unconditioned stimulus (US)**, like food, which invariably causes a certain reaction—salivation, in this case. That reaction—the **unconditioned response (UR)**—is the second element and always results from the unconditioned stimulus: Whenever the dog is given food (US), its mouth waters (UR). The third element is the neutral stimulus—the ringing bell—which is called the **conditioned stimulus (CS)**. At first, the conditioned stimulus is said to be "neutral" with respect to the desired response (salivation) because dogs do not salivate at the sound of a bell unless they have been conditioned to react in this way by repeatedly presenting the CS and US together. Frequent pairing of the CS and US produces the fourth element in the classical conditioning process: the **conditioned response (CR)**. The conditioned response is the behavior that the animal has learned in response to the conditioned stimulus. Usually, the unconditioned response and the conditioned response are slightly different versions of the same response—salivation, in our example (see Figure 5-2).

Without planning to do so, you may have conditioned your own pet the same way very that Pavlov trained his dogs. Your cat may begin to purr when it hears the sound of a can being opened in the kitchen. The taste and smell of food are unconditioned stimuli (USs) that cause, among other responses, purring (the unconditioned response or UR). Based on experience, your cat associates the sound of the can opener (the conditioned stimulus, or CS) with the food; over time, the CS by itself causes your cat to purr even before food is presented (the conditioned response, or CR).

**Figure 5-1**
**Pavlov's apparatus for classically conditioning a dog to salivate.** The experimenter sits behind a one-way mirror and controls the presentation of the conditioned stimulus (touch applied to the leg) and the unconditioned stimulus (food). A tube runs from the dog's salivary glands to a vial, where the drops of saliva are collected as a way of measuring the strength of the dog's response.

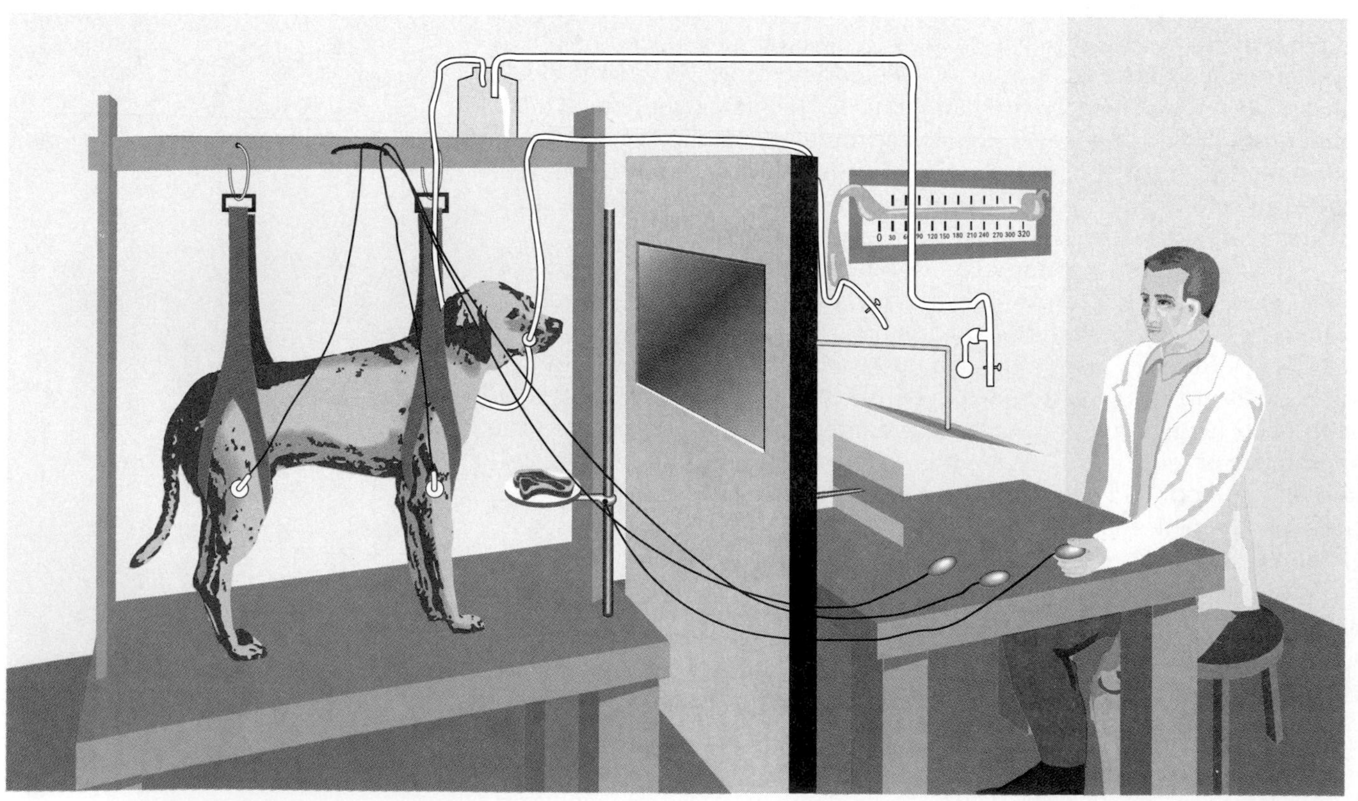

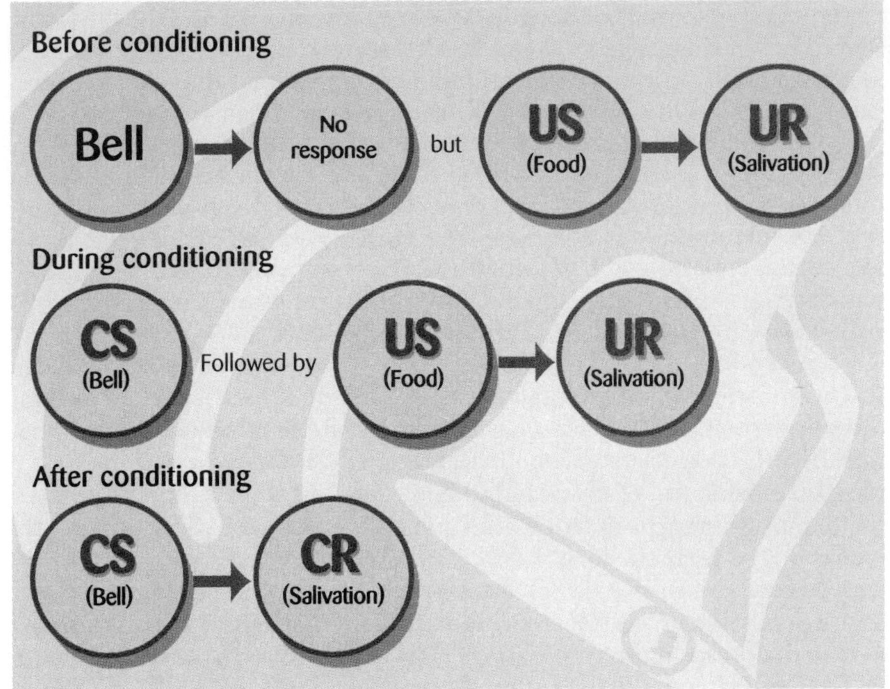


**Figure 5-2**
**A paradigm of the classical conditioning process.**

Dog owners who have used physical punishment with their pet may notice that the dog cringes or trembles when they speak in a loud and angry voice. In the past, physical pain (US)—which causes a number of responses, including cowering and trembling (URs)—may have been paired with shouting (a CS). Now, merely the sound of a loud voice can evoke a fear response (the CR).

## Classical Conditioning in Humans

You might wonder what Pavlov's dogs and reflexive responses have to do with human learning. Quite simply, human beings also learn behaviors through classical conditioning. Consider, for example, the positive thoughts and feelings that we associate with the smell of fresh-baked bread or cake.

As another example of classical conditioning in humans, let's think for a moment about *phobias*—irrational fears of particular things, activities, or situations, such as cats, spiders, or snakes, or high places (acrophobia), closed places (claustrophobia), or busy public places (agoraphobia). Many of us approach a visit to the dentist or the prospect of making a speech with fear, but for some people, these situations can provoke a major panic attack, which leaves sufferers unable to catch their breath, perspiring profusely or shaking from uncontrollable chills. Some victims of phobias even have convulsions and pass out when seized by an irrational fear.

Sigmund Freud, the father of psychoanalysis, explained phobias in terms of unresolved inner conflicts in which the phobic object (the thing that is feared) represents some other problem or situation that troubles the patient. As we will see, however, phobias may also be acquired through observational learning (Cook et al., 1985). Another view, advanced by Wolpe and Rachman (1960), considers phobias an instance of classical conditioning: An object comes to be feared after being linked with a frightening stimulus.

To see how phobias might develop through classical conditioning, consider a classic experiment conducted by John Watson and Rosalie Rayner (Watson & Rayner, 1920). In this famous study, an 11-month-old-boy, called "Little Albert," was taught to fear a harmless laboratory rat. The

**Desensitization therapy** Conditioning technique designed to gradually reduce anxiety about a particular object or situation.

experimenters started by showing Albert a white rat. At first the child displayed no apparent fear of the rodent. The infant crawled toward the rat and tried to play with it. But every time he approached the rat, the experimenters made a loud noise by striking a steel bar. Because nearly all children are afraid of loud noises, Albert's natural reaction was fear. After just a few of these experiences, Albert would cry whenever he saw the rat and quickly withdraw from it in fear. This is a simple case of classical conditioning. An unconditioned stimulus—the loud noise—caused the unconditioned response of fear. Next, the loud noise was associated several times with the rat (conditioned stimulus). Soon the rat alone caused Albert to behave as if he were afraid (conditioned response).

Several years later, psychologist Mary Cover Jones demonstrated a method by which children's fears can be unlearned by means of classical conditioning (Jones, 1924). Her subject was a 3-year-old boy named Peter who, like Albert, had a fear of white rats. Jones paired the sight of a rat with a pleasant experience—eating candy. While Peter sat alone in a room, a caged white rat was brought in and placed far enough away so that the youngster would not be frightened. At this point, Peter was given plenty of candy to eat. On each successive day of the experiment, the cage was moved closer and was followed by the presentation of candy, until eventually Peter showed no fear of the rat. In this case, eating candy (US) elicited a pleasant response (UR). By pairing the candy with the sight of the rat (CS), Jones was able to teach Peter to respond with pleasure (CR) when the rat appeared.

Many years later, psychiatrist Joseph Wolpe adapted Jones's method to the treatment of certain kinds of anxiety (Wolpe, 1973, 1982). Wolpe reasoned that because irrational fears and anxieties are learned or conditioned, it should also be possible to unlearn them through conditioning. He noted that it is not possible to be both fearful and relaxed at the same time; therefore, if people could be taught to relax in fearful or anxious situations, their anxiety should disappear. His **desensitization therapy** begins by teaching the person a system of deep-muscle relaxation techniques. Then the therapist helps the person construct a list of situations that prompt various degrees of fear or anxiety. These situations are then rated on a scale from zero (the person would feel absolutely calm and relaxed) to 100 (the person would be terrified). For example, people who are afraid of heights might rate "standing on top of the Empire State Building" near the top of the scale, while "standing on the first rung of a ladder" might be rated near the bottom. Then they enter a state of deep relaxation during which they imagine the least distressing situation on the list. When they succeed in remaining relaxed while imagining that situation, they progress to the next one, and so on until they experience no anxiety even when imagining the most frightening situation on the list. We will examine desensitization therapy in greater detail in the chapter on therapies, but for the moment, let's just realize that it is one way in which classical conditioning can be used to change human behavior.

In another example of classical conditioning in humans, researchers have devised a novel way to treat a group of diseases, called *autoimmune disorders*, which cause the immune system to attack healthy organs or tissues. While powerful drugs can be used to suppress the immune system and thus reduce the impact of the autoimmune disorder, these drugs may have serious side effects: They may produce nausea and headaches and may actually damage organs such as the pancreas and liver, so they must be administered sparingly. The challenge, then, was to find a treatment that could suppress the immune system without damaging vital organs. Fortunately, researchers working on the treatment of autoimmune disorders like lupus discovered that through classical conditioning techniques they could use formerly neutral stimuli either to elevate or to suppress the activity of the immune system (Markovic et al., 1993). Here's how it works: The researchers use immune-suppressing drugs as USs and pair them with a specific CS, such as a distinctive smell or taste. After only a few pairings of the drug (US) with the smell or taste (CS), the CS alone suppresses the immune system (the CR) without any dangerous side effects!

**Conditioned food** or **taste aversion** Conditioned avoidance of poisonous food even if there is a lengthy interval between eating the food and becoming ill and even if there is only one pairing of conditioned and unconditioned stimuli.

## Classical Conditioning Is Selective

Think back to the examples of phobias learned through classical conditioning. If any object can come to be feared after being linked with a frightening or anxiety-arousing stimulus, why don't people have phobias about almost everything? As M.E.P. Seligman notes, "Only rarely, if ever, do we have pajama phobias, grass phobias, electric-outlet phobias, hammer phobias, even though these things are likely to be associated with trauma in our world" (1972, p. 455). Why should this be?

To Seligman, the answer lies in *preparedness* and *contrapreparedness*. Some stimuli serve readily as CSs for certain kinds of responses (preparedness), and other stimuli do not (contrapreparedness). All the common objects of phobias—heights, snakes, cats, the dark, and so on—are "related to the survival of the human species through the long course of evolution" (Seligman, 1972, p. 455). Thus, humans may be prepared to develop fear responses and phobias about these things while we are very unlikely to acquire phobias about flowers.

Recent studies of preparedness both confirm and moderate Seligman's views. For example, some stimuli unrelated to human survival through evolution but which we have learned to associate with danger, can serve as CSs for fear responses. Pictures of handguns and butcher knives, for example, are as effective as pictures of snakes and spiders in conditioning fear in some people (Lovibond et al., 1993). Other studies have shown that people who do not suffer from phobias can rather quickly unlearn fear responses to spiders and snakes if those stimuli appear repeatedly without painful or threatening USs (Honeybourne et al., 1993). These studies suggest that preparedness may be the result of learning rather than evolution. However, Seligman's basic claim still stands: Our evolutionary history and our personal learning histories interact to increase the likelihood of certain kinds of conditioning while making other kinds of conditioning less likely to occur.

Preparedness also underlies **conditioned food aversion** or **taste aversion.** Classical conditioning generally requires many presentations of the CS and US with a short interval between the appearance of the two. Conditioned food aversion is a notable exception to these rules. Animals rarely require more than one occasion of being poisoned to learn not to eat a particular food. This phenomenon was discovered by accident by John Garcia in the midst of experiments on the effects of exposure to radiation (Garcia et al., 1956). Garcia was exposing rats in a special chamber to high doses of radiation that made them sick. He noticed that the rats were drinking less and less water when in the radiation chamber, although they drank normally in their "home" cages. Garcia realized that the water bottles in the radiation chamber were plastic, perhaps giving the water a different taste from the water contained in glass bottles in the home cages. He theorized that the taste of the water from the plastic bottles had served as a conditioned stimulus (CS) that the rats associated with radiation (US); as a result of this conditioning, the plastic-tasting water by itself made the rats feel ill (CR).

Conditioned taste aversion has been demonstrated in a wide variety of animals by Garcia and a number of other researchers; as a result, a great deal has been learned about this phenomenon (Braveman & Bronstein, 1985). We now know, for example, not only that conditioned food aversion can take place after only one bad experience but also that the interval between eating the food (the CS) and falling ill (the US) can be quite long—up to 12 hours among rats. In one experiment, after rats experienced a single pairing of salty water (CS) with illness (US) induced by drugs, they avoided salty water for more than a month (Garcia, Hankins, & Rusiniak, 1974). And oddly enough, an animal that has been poisoned learns to avoid only the food it ate, not any of the other stimuli that were present while it was eating, such as the room in which it ate the food or the container in which the food was kept (Dickinson & Mackintosh, 1978). In fact, if the animal eats both familiar and novel foods before it becomes ill, it subsequently avoids only the novel foods!

Why do taste-illness combinations produce such rapid and long-lasting learning? Garcia traces the answer to evolution: Rapid learning of taste-illness combinations increases some animals' chances of survival. Rats, for example, are scavengers: They will nibble at almost anything, so they are quite likely to come into contact with potentially toxic foods. It makes sense that over thousands of generations rats would have evolved a nervous system that is especially good at remembering taste-illness combinations (Garcia & Koelling, 1966). By contrast, birds depend on vision to find and identify their food; it follows that birds should have evolved a nervous system that is especially good at remembering sight-illness combinations—and, in fact, this turns out to be the case. In one study, both rats and quail were fed water that was flavored with salt, colored blue, and contained a chemical that would make both animals ill. Later they were offered a choice between water just colored blue and water just flavored with salt. The rats chose the blue water and avoided the salty water; the quails did the reverse. The rats seemed to have associated the salty *flavor* cue with their illness, whereas the birds associated the blue *visual* cue with their illness (Wilcoxon, Dragoin, & Kral, 1971). In other words, each species seems to have been prepared or preprogrammed for certain types of learning that are critical to its own survival.

Of course, the learning of food aversions is not limited to nonhumans. People have been found to develop food aversions based on a variety of cues, including taste, appearance, and smell. For example, if you become ill after trying a new dressing on your salad, you will probably develop a strong aversion to that dressing, no matter how much you enjoyed it. One study found that over half the college students surveyed had at least one conditioned taste aversion (Logue, Ophir, & Strauss, 1981). The conditioned aversion response is so ingrained that even when we know food was not the cause of an illness to which we succumbed, we are still tend to form an aversion to the food we ate before we got sick. One psychologist described a dinner party at which he and several other guests all picked up an intestinal virus that left many of them with an aversion to tarragon chicken (the main dish) or any food with tarragon spicing (Mazur, 1994). Even though they knew that the tarragon chicken was not the source of their illness, they were unable to overcome the powerful conditioned response. Similarly, patients undergoing treatment for cancer frequently develop taste aversions. Because the drugs used in chemotherapy often produce nausea, patients commonly develop strong taste aversions for foods eaten both before and after injections of these chemicals, even though they know that the foods did not bring on their nausea (Jacobsen et al., 1994).

## OPERANT CONDITIONING

Classical conditioning is concerned with behavior that invariably follows a particular event: the salivation that automatically occurs when food is placed in the mouth, the blink of the eye that always results when a puff of air strikes the eye. In classical conditioning, we usually learn to transfer this reaction to another stimulus that would not normally produce it: salivating at the sound of a bell, blinking to a tone. In a sense, classical conditioning is passive. The behavior is initially *elicited* by the unconditioned stimulus.

**Operant behavior** Behavior designed to operate on the environment in a way that will gain something desired or avoid something unpleasant.

Most overt behavior, however, initially seems to be *emitted* rather than elicited; that is, most behavior is usually voluntary rather than triggered by outside events. You wave your hand in a particular way to signal a taxi or bus to stop for you. Children pick up their toys either to avoid punishment or to gain some particular reward from their parents. We put money into machines and pull on levers or push buttons to obtain soft drinks, food, entertainment, or a chance to win money. These and similar actions can be classified as **operant behavior**. They are learned behaviors that are designed to *operate* on the environment in a way that will gain something desired or avoid something unpleasant; they are not automatic reflexes caused by biologically important stimuli. This kind of learning is called *operant* or *instrumental conditioning*. We now turn to the basic principles of operant conditioning.

## Thorndike's Conditioning Experiments

Around the turn of the century, while Pavlov was busy with his dogs, Edward Lee Thorndike, an American psychologist and educator, was using a "puzzle box," or simple wooden cage, to determine how cats learn (Thorndike, 1898). As illustrated in Figure 5-3, Thorndike placed a hungry cat in the close quarters of the puzzle box, with food just outside the cage where the cat could see and smell it. To get to the food, the cat had to figure out how to open the latch on the cage door, a process Thorndike timed. In the beginning, it took the cats quite a while to discover how to open the door. But each time a cat was put back into the puzzle box, it took less time to open the door, until the cat eventually could escape from the box in almost no time.

**Figure 5-3**
**A cat in a Thorndike "puzzle box."** The cat can escape and be rewarded with food by tripping the bolt on the door. As the graph shows, Thorndike's cats learned to make the necessary response more rapidly after an increasing number of trials.

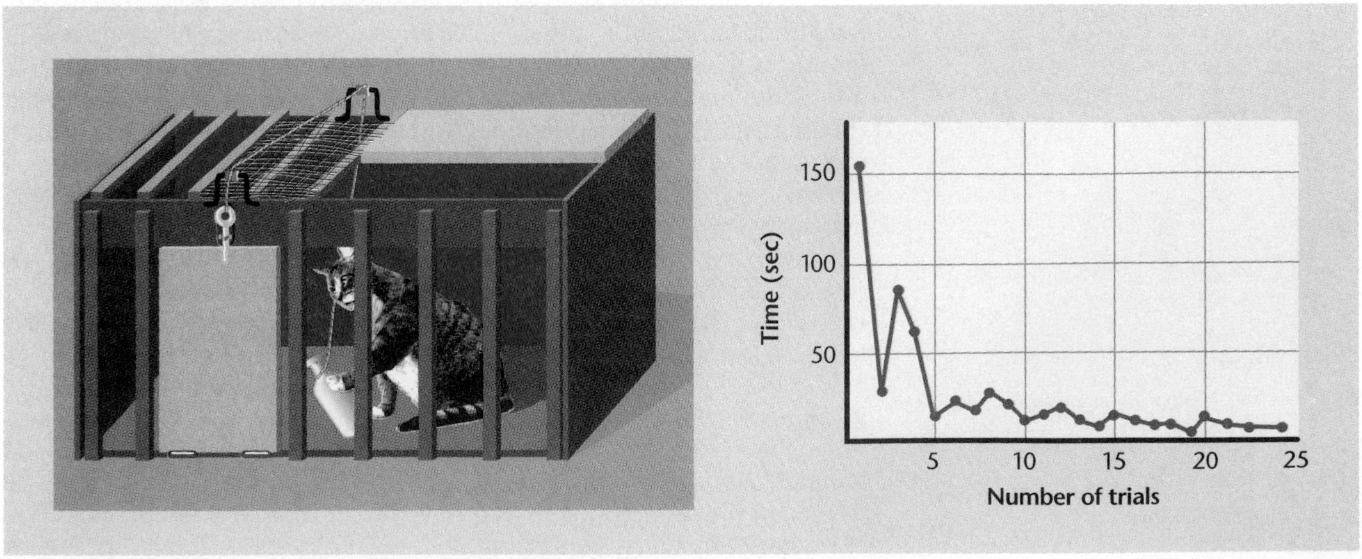

## Elements of Operant Conditioning

**Reinforcer** A stimulus that follows a behavior and increases the likelihood that the behavior will be repeated.

**Punisher** A stimulus that follows a behavior and decreases the likelihood that the behavior will be repeated.

**Law of effect** Thorndike's theory that behavior consistently rewarded will be "stamped in" as learned behavior, and behavior that brings about discomfort witll be *stamped out.*

**Positive reinforcer** Any event whose presence increases the likelihood that ongoing behavior will recur.

**Negative reinforcer** Any event whose reduction or termination increases the likelihood that ongoing behavior will recur.

What do we mean by reinforcement of behaviors? Is reinforcement the same as punishment?

Thorndike's experiments illustrate two factors that are essential in operant or instrumental conditioning. The first is the operant response. When we analyze operant learning—whether it be using conditioning principles to acquire good work habits or avoiding the street where we once received a speeding ticket—we realize it occurs when we choose a particular response, called the *operant response*, from a wide variety of behaviors and then focus on observing and changing that response.

The second essential element in operant conditioning is the *consequence* that follows the behavior. Thorndike's cats gained either freedom or a piece of fish for escaping from their constraining puzzle boxes; your dog may receive a food treat for sitting on command; and a child may receive praise or a chance to play a computer game for helping to clear the table. Consequences such as these that increase the likelihood that the behavior will be repeated are called **reinforcers**. By contrast, consequences that decrease the chances that a behavior will be repeated are called **punishers**. Imagine how Thorndike's cats might have performed had they been greeted by a large, snarling dog when they escaped from their puzzle boxes, or what might happen if a dog that sits on command is scolded for doing so or if a child who has helped to clear the table is sent to sit in a "time-out" corner. Thorndike's understanding of the importance of reinforcement is reflected in his **law of effect**: "Responses which are accompanied or closely followed by satisfaction to the animal will, other things being equal, be . . . more likely to recur; those which are accompanied or closely followed by discomfort to the animal will, other things being equal,. . . be less likely to occur" (Thorndike, 1911, p. 244). In a given stimulus situation, a response that consistently brings about a satisfying effect (reinforcement) will be stamped in, and responses that bring about discomfort (punishment) will be stamped out. Contemporary psychologists often refer to the *principle of reinforcement* rather than the law of effect, but the two terms refer to the same phenomenon.

## Types of Reinforcement

**POSITIVE AND NEGATIVE REINFORCEMENT** Psychologists distinguish among several kinds of reinforcers. **Positive reinforcers,** such as food or pleasant music, *add* something rewarding to a situation. By contrast, **negative reinforcers** *subtract* something *un*pleasant from the situation; the reinforcement, that is, consists of *removing* the stimulus. You might find it helpful to use the plus symbol (+) to refer to a positive (+) reinforcer that adds (+) something rewarding to the environment and the minus sign (–) to refer to a negative (–) reinforcer that subtracts (–) something negative or unpleasant from the environment. Animals will learn to press bars and open doors not only to obtain food and water (positive reinforcement) but also to avoid electric shocks or loud noises (negative reinforcement).

Both positive and negative reinforcement result in the learning of new behaviors or the strengthening of existing behaviors. Remember, in everyday conversation when we say that we have "reinforced" something, we mean we have strengthened it. "Reinforced concrete" is strengthened by the addition of steel rods or steel mesh; generals "send reinforcements" to strengthen a military force; people "reinforce" their arguments by marshaling facts that strengthen them. Similarly, in operant conditioning, all reinforcements—whether positive or negative—strengthen behavior. A boy might practice the piano to receive praise (positive reinforcement) or to escape doing tedious homework for a while (negative reinforcement). If a girl is scolded for eating spaghetti with her fingers and the scolding stops when she picks up a fork and uses it, she is more likely to use a fork in the future. This is an example of a negative reinforcer, because reducing or terminating unpleasant events (such as a scolding) increases the likelihood that the behavior going on at the time (eating with a fork) will recur. And if at the same time you add positive reinforcement ("Good girl! That's the way grown-ups eat their spaghetti!"), the new behavior is even more likely to happen again in the future.

**Punishment** Any event whose presence decreases the likelihood that ongoing behavior will recur.

## Punishment

Up to this point, we have concentrated on the effects of reinforcers on behavior. A reinforcer can be anything that increases the likelihood that a response will be repeated when it is presented after the response. Praise, food, money, a smile—all are positive reinforcers for most of us. When they follow some behavior, we are more likely to behave that way in the future.

But behavior can also be controlled by **punishment**. For most of us, receiving a fine for speeding or littering reduces the likelihood that we will speed or litter in the future. Being rudely turned down when we ask someone for a favor makes it less likely that we will ask that person for a favor again. In both these cases, the unpleasant aftereffect reduces the likelihood that we will repeat that behavior. Be sure you understand the difference between punishment and negative reinforcement: Reinforcement of whatever kind *strengthens* (reinforces) behavior; negative reinforcement strengthens behavior by removing something unpleasant from the environment. By contrast, punishment adds something unpleasant to the environment, and as a result it tends to *weaken* behavior. Turning off a loud, unpleasant sound is likely to be reinforcing (you are more likely to turn off future unpleasant sounds as a result of the reinforcement you received); accidentally turning on a loud, unpleasant sound is likely to be punishing (as a result, you are less likely to make the same mistake again in the future).

Although the examples listed above suggest that punishment works, we can all think of situations where punishment clearly does not work. Children often continue to misbehave even after they have been punished repeatedly for that misbehavior. Some drivers persist in driving recklessly despite repeated fines. The family dog may sleep on the couch at night despite being punished for this behavior every morning. And criminals continue to commit crimes when facing both threatened and real punishment. So an important question comes to mind: Under what conditions does punishment work?

For punishment to be effective, it must be imposed properly. First, punishment should be *swift*. Children who misbehave should be punished right away so they know that what they have done is wrong. If punishment comes too long after the offensive action, it may not be clear to children why they are being punished. Punishment should also be *sufficient* without being cruel. If a parent merely warned a child not to bully other children, the effect might be less pronounced than if the warning were accompanied by the threat of being "grounded" for a day. Moreover, the common practice of making the punishment for each successive misdeed more severe than the last is not as effective as maintaining a constant level of punishment. Effective punishment, then, is also consistent, or *certain*. Parents should try to punish children each and every time they misbehave. Otherwise the misbehavior may persist.

Punishment imposed properly can change behavior quickly, which is critical in certain cases. A child who likes to play in the street or who enjoys poking things into electric outlets must be stopped quickly, and in these instances, punishment may be the best course of action. Similarly, some severely disturbed children repeatedly injure themselves by bang-

Merely paying attention to someone's behavior can be reinforcing, particularly if the person is "starved for attention." Withdrawal of the reinforcing attention results in the elimination of the behavior.

*Source:* Drawing by Opie; ©1961, 1989. The New Yorker Magazine, Inc.

**Avoidance training** Learning a desirable behavior to prevent the occurrence of something unpleasant such as punishment.

ing their heads against the wall or by hitting themselves in the face with their fists. Punishment may stop this self-destructive behavior so that other forms of therapy can proceed. But even in situations like these, punishment has significant drawbacks (Skinner, 1953). First, punishment only suppresses behavior: It doesn't prompt someone to unlearn the offensive behavior, and it doesn't teach a more desirable behavior. If the punisher or the threat of punishment is removed, the negative behavior is likely to recur. Drivers who are speeding on a highway generally slow down when they see a radar-equipped police car on the side of the road—the police car introduces the threat of punishment. But as soon as the threat is past, they tend to speed up again. Thus, punishment rarely works when long-term changes in behavior are sought. Second, punishment often stirs up unpleasant emotions that can impede learning of the behavior we want to teach in place of the punished behavior. For example, when children are learning to read and a teacher or parent scolds them every time they mispronounce a word, they may become frightened and confused. As they become more frightened and confused, they mispronounce more words and get scolded more often. In time, they may become so overwhelmed with fear that they do not want to read at all. Third, punishment may convey the notion that inflicting pain on others is justified, thereby inadvertently teaching undesirable aggressive behavior. In laboratory studies, monkeys that are punished tend to attack other monkeys, pigeons other pigeons, and so on (B. Schwartz, 1989). In addition, punishment often makes people angry, and angry people frequently become more aggressive and hostile.

If punishment must be used to suppress undesirable behavior, it should be terminated when more desirable behavior occurs (to negatively reinforce that behavior). Positive reinforcement (praise, rewards) should also be used to strengthen the desired behavior. This approach is more productive than punishment alone, because it teaches an alternative behavior to replace the actions that prompted the punishment. Positive reinforcement also makes the learning environment less threatening overall.

As a method for controlling behavior, punishment is one of the least pleasant options because it is often ineffective, and it can have negative side effects. Most of us would prefer to avoid using punishment at all, relying instead on the *threat* of punishment when behavior is getting out of control. If the threat of punishment induces a change to more desirable behavior, punishment need not be imposed at all. Psychologists call this **avoidance training**.

Avoidance training with animals usually includes some sort of warning device, like a light or a buzzer. For example, an animal might be placed in a box with a wire floor that can deliver a mild shock. The experimenter first sounds a buzzer and then a few seconds later turns on the shock. If the animal presses a bar after hearing the buzzer, no shock will be delivered. Pressing the bar after the shock has already started will have no effect. The animal must learn to press the bar after hearing the buzzer, but before the shock starts, to prevent the shock from occurring. At first this usually happens accidentally. But once the animal learns that pressing the bar prevents the shock, it will run to the bar whenever it hears the buzzer, thus avoiding the shock altogether.

We, too, derive lessons from avoidance training, as when we learn to carry an umbrella when it looks like rain or not to touch a hot iron. But sometimes avoidance learning outlives its usefulness. Children taught not to go into deep water may avoid deep water even after they have learned how to swim. In other cases, avoidance behavior may persist long after the fear has been removed. So while fear is essential for learning the avoidance response, it is not always necessary for sustaining the learned response.

Remember that we do not know if a particular entity is reinforcing or punishing until we see whether it increases or decreases the occurrence of a response. We might assume that candy, for example, is a reinforcer for children, but some children don't like candy. In addition, an event or object might not be consistently rewarding or punishing over time. So even if candy is initially reinforcing for some children, if they eat large amounts of it, it can become neutral or even punishing. We must therefore be very careful in labeling items or events as reinforcers or punishers.

The so-called dancing "chicken" illustrates the importance of preparedness in operant conditioning: Learning is less likely for those behaviors that would not typically occur in the training situation.

## Operant Conditioning Is Selective

In our discussion of preparedness in classical conditioning, we saw that some stimuli serve readily as CSs for certain kinds of responses while other stimuli do not. Classical conditioning is more likely to occur when a natural fit exists between the stimulus and the response—for example, a fear response to snakes or an aversive response to an unpleasant odor. Similarly, in operant conditioning, some behaviors are easier to train than others. In general, the behaviors that are easiest to condition are those that animals typically would perform in the training situation. For example, Shettleworth (1975) used food pellets to teach food-deprived hamsters to spend more time doing a variety of things: washing their faces, digging, scent marking, scratching, rearing up on their hind legs, and scraping a wall with their paws. The hamsters quickly learned to spend much more time rearing up on their hind legs, scraping walls, and digging, but there was only a slight increase in the amount of time they spent washing their faces, scratching, and scent marking. The first three behaviors are responses that hamsters typically make when they are hungry, whereas the last three behaviors usually occur less often when a hamster is hungry. Thus, learning was most successful for those responses that are most likely to occur naturally in the training situation. Other examples of preparedness in operant conditioning come from Breland and Breland (1972), a husband-and-wife team who trained animals to perform in shows. They tried to condition a bantam chicken to stand still on a platform for 12 to 15 seconds as part of a complex stunt, but the chicken insisted on scratching. The Brelands finally gave up and billed their bantam as a "dancing chicken." A raccoon was trained to insert a coin into a container for food but then reverted to its natural "washing" response. The animal was content to rub the coins together and handle them, and it refused to give them up to the food dispenser.

These cases illustrate the remarkable differences among species concerning which behaviors they can learn and the circumstances under which learning will occur. These species differences put significant constraints on both classical and operant conditioning.

Skinner found that the bird would repeat whatever action it had been doing just before food was dropped into the box—a form of *superstitious behavior.*

## Superstitious Behavior

Whenever something we do is followed closely by a reinforcer, we will tend to repeat the action—even if the reinforcement is not produced directly by what we have done. In an experiment by the American psychologist B.F. Skinner (1948), a pigeon was placed in a cage that contained only a food hopper. There was nothing the bird could do directly to get food, but at random intervals Skinner dropped a few grains of food into the hopper. He found that the pigeon began to repeat whatever it had been doing just before it was given food: standing on one foot, hopping around, or strutting around with its neck stretched out. None of these actions had anything to do with getting the food—it was pure coincidence that the food appeared when the bird was standing on one foot, for example, but that action would usually be repeated. Skinner labeled the bird's behavior *superstitious*.

How do we learn superstitions? Do animals other than humans exhibit superstitious behaviors?

**Response acquisition** "Building phase" of conditioning during which the likelihood or strength of the desired response increases.

Some human superstitions are learned in the same way. If we happen to be wearing a particular piece of jewelry or carrying a rabbit's foot when something good happens to use, we may come to believe that these incidental factors caused the positive incident, or reinforcement. We may even develop elaborate cognitive explanations for accidental or randomly occurring reinforcements. This is known as magical thinking.

## COMPARING CLASSICAL AND OPERANT CONDITIONING

Despite the clear differences between classical and operant conditioning, the two forms of learning have many important processes in common. Let's look first at how responses are acquired in classical and operant conditioning.

### Response Acquisition in Classical Conditioning

With the exception of conditioned food aversions based on one fearful experience—learning experiences—which are relatively rare—classical conditioning requires repeated pairing of the CS and US. Each pairing builds on the learner's previous experience. Psychologists refer to this "building phase" of learning as **response acquisition;** each pairing of the US and CS is called a *trial*. Learning does not increase indefinitely or by an equal amount on each successive trial. At first the likelihood or strength of the conditioned response increases significantly each time the conditioned stimulus and the unconditioned stimulus are paired. But learning eventually reaches a point of diminishing returns: The amount of each increase gradually becomes smaller until finally no further learning occurs, and the likelihood or strength of the CR remains constant despite further pairings of the US and CS. For example, imagine that we first direct a mild puff of air into the subject's eye (the US); the resulting reflexive eye blink is the UR. Then we sound an annoying "buzz" (the CS) just before the puff of air hits the eye. After only 10 trials, we test for conditioning by presenting the "buzz" (CS) alone. In all likelihood, some of the participants in our experiment will blink when they hear the buzzing sound, others may only partially blink, and still others may not blink at all. But after 50 pairings, most or all of the people in the experiment will respond to the buzz with a full and forceful eye blink. At that point, if we continue to pair the US (air puff) and CS (buzz), we will probably see little or no evidence of additional learning. Thus, in general classical conditioning is a cumulative process that eventually reaches a point of diminishing returns.

Barry Schwartz (1989) has pointed out that the cumulative nature of most classical conditioning works to our benefit. There are always lots of different environmental stimuli present when we experience pain, for example, yet most of those stimuli are irrelevant to the pain. If conditioning occurred on the basis of single events, then these irrelevant stimuli would all generate some type of CR, and we would soon become overwhelmed by the amount of learning—most of it inappropriate or unnecessary—that would take place. Because a number of pairings are usually required to produce a CR, however, in most cases only the relevant cues consistently produce this reaction. We have seen that, up to a point, the more often the US and CS are paired, the stronger the learning. It turns out that the *spacing* of trials—that is, the time between one pairing and the next—is at least as important as their number. If the trials follow one another rapidly, or if they are very far apart, the subject may need many trials to achieve the expected response strength. If the trials are spaced evenly—neither too far apart nor too close together—learning will occur after fewer trials. It is also important to ensure that the CS and US rarely, if ever, occur alone. Pairing the CS and US on only some of the learning trials and presenting them separately on other trials is called **intermittent pairing**, a procedure that reduces both the rate of learning and the final level of learning achieved.

**Intermittent pairing** Pairing the conditioned stimulus and the unconditioned stimulus on only a portion of the learning trials.

**Skinner box** Box often used in operant conditioning of animals. That limits the available responses and thus increases the likelihood that the desired response will occur.

## Response Acquisition in Operant Conditioning

Response acquisition in operant conditioning is somewhat more difficult than in classical conditioning. In classical conditioning, the US invariably elicits the UR, which is the behavior we want to link to the CS. But in operant conditioning, the behavior we want to teach is usually voluntary and is not inevitably triggered by outside events. As a result, ensuring that the behavior occurs at all often poses a significant challenge. Sometimes you simply have to wait for the subject to hit on the correct response. Thorndike's cats, for example, were capable of opening the latch on the cage; Thorndike simply waited for them to trip the latch and then reinforced that behavior. Similarly, most babies on their own will eventually make a sound like "mama" in the course of their babbling. If parents just wait long enough, the sound will occur spontaneously, and then they can reinforce the baby with smiles and hugs in order to increase the likelihood that the baby will say "mama" again in the future.

Waiting for the correct response to occur spontaneously can be a slow and tedious process, however. If you were an animal tamer for a circus, imagine how long you would have to wait for a tiger to decide to jump through a flaming hoop so that you could reinforce that behavior! There are several ways to speed up the process and make it more likely that the desired response will occur so that it can then be reinforced. One possibility is to increase motivation: A hungry laboratory rat is more active and thus more likely to give the response you're looking for than is a well-fed rat. Similarly, an alert and motivated child is more likely to perform some desired behavior than is a passive, unmotivated child.

Another way to speed up the process of operant learning is to reduce or eliminate the opportunities for making irrelevant responses, thereby boosting the chances that the correct response will occur. This can be done by limiting the subject's range of action and then allowing the subject to respond freely within those boundaries. Thorndike's puzzle boxes for cats served this purpose: Because the boxes were essentially bare except for the latch mechanisms, the cats had little to do other than to work on the latches. More recently, researchers interested in operant conditioning have made extensive use of the **Skinner box**, a device named after B. F. Skinner, who pioneered the study of operant conditioning. As you can see from Figure 5-4, a Skinner box for rats is small, with solid walls, and it is bare except for a bar with a cup underneath it. In this simple environment, it doesn't take long for an active, hungry rat to happen to step on the bar, thereby releasing food pellets into the cup, which reinforces the rat's bar-pressing behavior. A Skinner box for pigeons is also bare except for a round disk on one wall and a cup underneath the disk. When a pigeon, exercising its natural food-finding behavior, eventually pecks at the disk, food is released into a cup, and the pecking behavior is reinforced.

**Figure 5-4**
**A rat in a Skinner box.** By pressing the bar, the rat releases food pellets into the box, which reinforces its bar-pressing behavior.

**Shaping** Reinforcing successive approximations to a desired behavior.

**Extinction** Decrease in the strength or frequency of a learned response due to failure to continue pairing the US and CS (classical conditioning) or to withholding of reinforcement (operant conditioning).

Yet another way to speed up response acquisition during operant conditioning is to reinforce successive approximations to the desired response. This approach is called **shaping**. In a Skinner box, for example, we might first reward a rat for turning toward the response bar. Once the rat has learned this behavior, we might withhold reinforcement until the rat moves toward the bar. Later, we might reward it only for sniffing the bar or touching it with its nose or paw, and so on. In this way, by reinforcing successive approximations to the desired behavior, we gradually shape the bar-pressing response without waiting passively for the response to occur on its own. Shaping was used to teach a 6-year-old boy named Dickey to wear eyeglasses. Dickey had just had cataracts removed from his eyes, and his physicians feared that without the glasses his vision would deteriorate permanently. At the mere mention of eyeglasses, however, Dickey threw terrible temper tantrums. Researchers at the University of Washington tried a shaping procedure to ease him into the idea of wearing glasses. Dickey was deprived of his breakfast so that food could be used as a reward for behavior in the right direction. Then a pair of empty eyeglass frames was left in Dickey's room, and he received a bit of food each time he picked them up. Later in the procedure, he had to put the glasses on to receive a reward, and finally he had to keep the glasses on to gain reinforcement. Within 18 days, Dickey had learned through these gradual steps to wear his glasses for 12 hours a day (Wolf, Mees, & Risley, 1964).

The first problem in operant conditioning is to make the desired response occur so that it can be reinforced and learned. The animal trainer uses *shaping*, reinforcing smaller bits of behavior, to teach animals complicated behaviors.

Animal training exemplifies the process of shaping in a dramatic way. For instance, to teach a circus tiger to jump through a flaming hoop, the tiger might first be reinforced for simply jumping up on a certain pedestal. After that behavior has been learned, the tiger might be reinforced only for leaping from that pedestal to another. Next, the tiger might be required to jump through a hoop between the pedestals to gain its reward. Finally, the hoop might be set on fire and the tiger required to leap through the burning hoop to be rewarded.

In operant conditioning, once the desired response occurs, we increase the likelihood that it will recur by providing reinforcement. As with classical conditioning, this process of response acquisition is cumulative, and it eventually reaches a point of diminishing returns. If you look back to Figure 5-3, you will see that the first few reinforcements produced quite large improvements in performance, as indicated by the rapid drop in time required to escape from Thorndike's puzzle box. But each successive reinforcement produced less of an effect. Thus, just as in classical conditioning, the greatest learning in operant conditioning occurs in the first few trials; later trials are more limited in their effects. Eventually a point is reached where continued reinforcement brings no evidence of further learning. For example, in Figure 5-3, after 25 trials or so, the cats were escaping from the box no more quickly than they had been after 15 trials.

Shaping can also be used for some types of human learning. A diver's movements are developed and perfected through a series of successive approximations.

## Extinction and Spontaneous Recovery in Classical Conditioning

Once a behavior is conditioned, does the learning persist forever, even if the US or the reinforcement is stopped? Let's go back to Pavlov's dogs, which had learned to salivate upon hearing a bell. What do you think happened over time when the dogs heard the bell (CS) but no food (US) appeared? The conditioned response to the bell—the amount of salivation—gradually decreased until eventually it stopped altogether: The dogs no longer salivated when they heard the bell. This process is known as **extinction**. If the conditioned stimulus (the bell) appears alone so often that the learner no longer associates it with the unconditioned stimulus (the food) and stops making the conditioned response (salivation), extinction has taken place. If the

# CONTROVERSIES

## Shaping Better Health Through Biofeedback

For 20 of her 29 years, a woman had suffered from tension headaches. The dull aching would begin in the morning and last all day. Members of the clinic where she sought help traced her problem to excessive contraction of the frontalis muscle, the main muscle in the forehead. They then set about teaching her to relax this muscle by providing her with *biofeedback*. Electrodes attached to her forehead measured the degree of contraction in the frontalis muscle. The machine registered the contraction with an audible tone—the less the contraction, the lower the pitch of the tone. If the patient relaxed the muscle even slightly, the tone dropped noticeably. The patient worked to relax the muscle more and more, using the dropping pitch of the tone as her guide. Over the course of several dozen 30-minute training sessions spread over 9 weeks, the woman became increasingly adept at controlling frontalis contraction. At a follow-up session 3 months after therapy had begun, the woman reported virtually no further tension headaches (Budzynski, Stoyva, & Adler, 1970).

Biofeedback training has been used for a wide variety of disorders. NASA combined a program of biofeedback with cognitive therapy (such as mental messages) to reduce the motion sickness astronauts experience at zero gravity (Cowlings, 1989). And more recently, researchers have drawn on biofeedback techniques to treat a painful bowel condition in infants (Cox et al., 1994) and migraine headaches in adults (Lisspers et al., 1992).

Biofeedback training is an operant conditioning procedure in which instruments are used to inform learners about some biological response over which they wish to gain control. A device collects information about a biological response—for example, muscle contractions, blood pressure, or heart rate—of which people normally have little or no awareness. Information about the response is provided to the subject in the form of a light, a tone, or some other signal that can be varied according to the measured level of the response. The feedback information—the tone or light—serves as a secondary reinforcer, and the response is learned bit by bit, as in shaping techniques of learning.

The effectiveness of biofeedback depends on some of the same factors that determine success in other forms of operant conditioning. Feedback should be rapid, consistent, and precise. When feedback is *rapid*, reinforcement is most effective. Each time the tone drops, for example, it immediately reinforces the muscle-relaxation response. *Consistent* feedback is also crucial. Suppose that early in the headache sufferer's training, the tone dropped several times, but her frontalis muscle had actually contracted rather than relaxed. Learning how to relax the muscle would have been much harder for her, if not entirely impossible. Finally, especially at the start of training, feedback must be *precise*, indicating even the slightest changes in response. This permits the shaping of the desired behavior by successive approximations.

Biofeedback has become a well-established treatment for a number of medical problems, including tension headaches and migraine headaches as well as asthma and peptic ulcers. In addition to serving as a medical therapy, biofeedback has been used by athletes, musicians, and other performers to control the anxiety that can interfere with their performance. For marathon runners, biofeedback helps overcome the tight shoulders and shallow breathing that can prevent them from finishing races. While most reports of the effectiveness of biofeedback in sports are based on personal accounts, rather than controlled studies, this anecdotal evidence strongly suggests that biofeedback offers real benefits (Peper, 1990).

Biofeedback treatment has some drawbacks however. Patients must invest considerable time and effort in practicing the technique, which demands patience and discipline. Nevertheless, biofeedback places control of treatment in the patient's own hands, a major advantage over other methods of treatment, and it has achieved impressive results in alleviating certain medical problems (Olton & Noonberg, 1980).

Biofeedback has been hailed as a panacea by some and rejected as quackery by others in a debate that still rages (A.H. Roberts, 1985). Critics challenge the scientific rigor of studies that have evaluated biofeedback and the professional caliber of the technicians who operate the various biofeedback instruments. In addition, some conditions, such as high blood pressure, do not respond well to biofeedback training. Further research may reveal other conditions for which this type of treatment is not appropriate. Advocates of the procedure have responded by arguing that when biofeedback is viewed properly—as a way to learn self-regulation of biological processes rather than as a therapy—and when it's evaluated on those terms, it can stand up to the most rigorous scientific scrutiny (Norris, 1986).

sound of a can being opened or a cupboard door opening (CS) is no longer associated with the sight or smell of food (US), your cat may no longer purr (CR) when it hears the CS. If scary music in films (CS) is not associated with frightening events on screen (US), you will eventually stop becoming tense

**Spontaneous recovery** The reappearance of an extinguished response after the passage of time, without further training.

and anxious (CR) when you hear that kind of music. These are all examples of extinction of classically conditioned responses.

Once such a response has been extinguished, is the learning gone forever? Pavlov trained his dogs to salivate when they heard a bell, then extinguished the learning. A few days later, the same dogs were again taken to the laboratory. As soon as they heard the bell, their mouths began to water. The response that had been learned and then extinguished reappeared on its own, with no retraining. This phenomenon is known as **spontaneous recovery**. The dogs' response was only about half as strong as it had been before extinction, but the fact that the response occurred at all indicated that the original learning was not completely lost during extinction (see Figure 5-5). Similarly, if your cat is away for a while and then returns home, it may run to the kitchen and start purring the first few times it hears cans or cupboard doors being opened. And if you stop going to the movies for some time, you may find, the next time you go, that scary music once again makes you tense or anxious. In both cases, responses that were once extinguished have returned spontaneously after the passage of time. Note, however, that responses reappearing during spontaneous recovery do not return at full strength and that generally they extinguish very quickly.

How is it possible for extinguished behavior to disappear, only to reappear again at some later time? According to Mark Bouton (1993, 1994), extinction does not erase conditioned responses. Rather, extinction occurs because *new* learning during extinction interferes with the previously learned response. That is, stimuli that were paired with conditioned responses come to elicit responses different from, and sometimes incompatible with, those original conditioned responses. A buzzer paired with electric shock initially means "Pain is coming!" and comes to elicit a number of responses—changes in heart rate and blood pressure, for example—that accompany painful stimulation. During extinction, the association between the buzzer and pain disappears, and the buzzer therefore elicits another set of responses, which may be entirely different from the originally learned responses. In fact, these new responses may even antagonize or oppose those original responses. For example, if one response during training was an

**Figure 5-5**
**Response acquisition and extinction in classical conditioning.** From point *A* to point *B*, the conditioned stimulus and the unconditioned stimulus were paired, and learning increased steadily. From *B* to *C*, however, the conditioned stimulus was presented alone. By point *C*, the response had been extinguished. After a rest period from *C* to *D*, spontaneous recovery occurred—the learned response reappeared at about half the strength that it had at point *B*. When the conditioned stimulus was again presented alone, the response extinguished rapidly (point *E*).

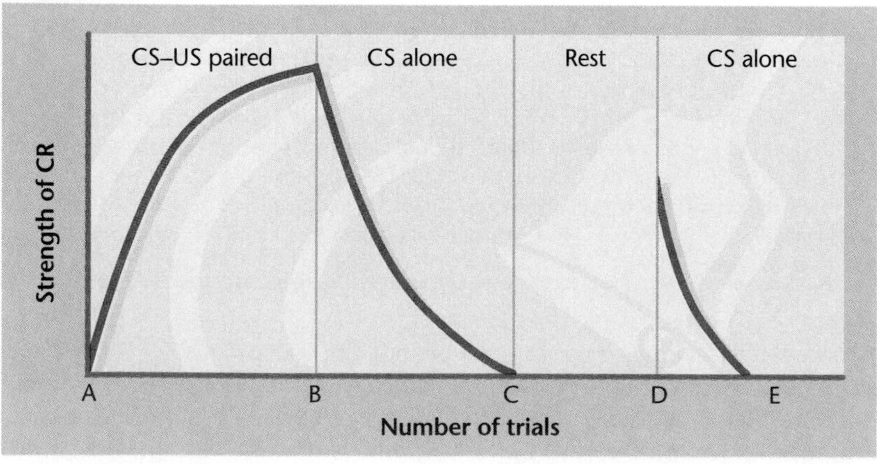

increased heart rate but the new response during extinction is a decreased heart rate, the two clearly cannot happen at the same time. The result is *interference*, and spontaneous recovery consists of overcoming this interference. According to Bouton, we overcome this interference in one of two ways. The first is called the *renewal effect*. Imagine that you are conditioned in one setting (for example, a dim and dark laboratory), and then your conditioned response is extinguished in a very different setting (for example, a bright and cheerful room). Even with total extinction in the new setting, if you return to the original laboratory room, your conditioned response will immediately return. This occurs because the new, interfering responses learned during extinction are associated with stimuli in the new setting and not with stimuli in the original lab room. The originally learned stimulus-response connections, then, are still intact.

Or imagine that your conditioned response has been totally extinguished (the CR never occurs when the CS is presented). Now, if you are presented with the US that was used during your initial conditioning, the CR suddenly reappears! It is as if the US acts as a sort of "reminder" of your earlier conditioning and refreshes or renews the connections between stimuli and responses learned prior to extinction. The US, that is, overcomes the interfering effects of responses learned during extinction. As you might expect, "reminder" stimuli work particularly well if they are presented in the original conditioning setting.

## Extinction and Spontaneous Recovery in Operant Conditioning

Extinction and spontaneous recovery also occur in operant conditioning. In operant conditioning, extinction happens as a result of withholding reinforcement. Yet withholding reinforcement does not usually produce an immediate decrease in the frequency of the response; in fact, when reinforcement is first discontinued, there is often a brief *increase* in responding before the strength or frequency of the response declines. The behavior itself also changes at the start of extinction: It becomes more variable and often more forceful. For instance, if you put coins in a vending machine and it fails to deliver the goods, you may pull the lever more violently or slam your fist against the glass panel. If the vending machine still fails to produce the item for which you paid, your attempts to get it to work will decrease, and you will finally stop trying altogether.

Just as in classical conditioning, however, extinction does not erase a response forever. Spontaneous recovery may occur if a period of time passes after initial extinction. And once again, both extinction and spontaneous recovery may be understood in terms of interference from new behaviors. If a rat is no longer reinforced for pressing a lever, it will start to engage in other behaviors—turning away from the lever, biting at the corners of the operant chamber, attempting to escape, and so on—and these new behaviors will interfere with the operant response of lever pressing causing extinction. Spontaneous recovery is a brief victory of original training over these interfering responses.

Numerous factors affect how easy or how hard it is to extinguish behaviors learned through operant conditioning. The stronger the original learning, the longer it takes for the response to extinguish. If you spend many hours training a puppy to sit on command, you will not need to reinforce this behavior very often once the dog grows up. Also, the greater the variety of settings in which learning takes place, the harder it is to extinguish it. Rats trained to run in a single straight alley for food will stop running sooner than rats trained in several different alleys that vary in width, brightness, floor texture, and other features. Complex behavior is also much more difficult to

**Stimulus generalization** Transfer of a learned response to different but similar stimuli.

**Stimulus discrimination** Learning to respond to only one stimulus and to inhibit the response to all other stimuli.

extinguish than simple behavior: Because complex behavior consists of many actions, every action contributing to the total behavior must be extinguished. Also, as we will see later, the pattern of reinforcement used during operant conditioning has a major effect on the extinction process. Responses that are reinforced only occasionally during acquisition are usually more resistant to extinction than responses that are reinforced every time they occur. Finally, behaviors learned on the basis of punishment rather than reinforcement are especially hard to extinguish. If you have been repeatedly attacked by a particularly nasty dog when jogging down one street, you may change your route and jog down a different street. Now that you always follow the new route, you have no way of knowing whether the dog's owner has moved away and made it safe for you to run your original course. In fact, your learning may never extinguish (you may never return to running the original route).

One way to speed up the extinction of any kind of learning is to put the learner in a situation that is different from the one in which the response was learned. The response is likely to be weaker in the new situation, and therefore it will disappear more quickly. When the learner is returned to the original learning setting after extinction has occurred elsewhere, however, the response may show spontaneous recovery, just as in classical conditioning; but it is likely to be weaker than it was initially, and it should be relatively easy to extinguish once and for all.

## Generalization and Discrimination in Classical Conditioning

Recall the case of Little Albert and his conditioned fear of white rats. When the experimenters later showed Albert a white rabbit, Albert cried and tried to crawl away, even though he had not been taught to fear rabbits. Similarly, Pavlov noticed that after his dogs had been conditioned to salivate when they heard a bell, their mouths would often water when they heard a buzzer or the ticking of a metronome, even though they had not been taught to salivate to buzzers or ticking sounds. Oftentimes in classical conditioning we see that a response learned to one CS also occurs in the presence of other, similar objects or situations. Reacting to a stimulus that is similar to the one to which you have learned to respond is called **stimulus generalization**. In Pavlov's case, the conditioned response generalized from the ringing of a bell to other unusual noises in the testing room. Albert's learned fear of white, furry rats generalized not only to white, furry rabbits but also to all kinds of white, furry objects—he came to fear cotton balls, a fur coat, and even a white-bearded Santa Claus mask.

Wolpe's desensitization therapy, mentioned earlier, also exemplifies stimulus generalization. In the example we used previously, people who most feared great heights (such as standing on top of a tall building), had generalized the fear response to a wide variety of more or less similar situations: flying in an airplane, standing on a ladder, perhaps even watching a circus high-wire performer. Even photos shot from the tops of tall buildings may trigger fear in vulnerable people sitting safely at home while looking at them.

Stimulus generalization is not inevitable. In a process called **stimulus discrimination**, we can train animals and people not to generalize but rather to give a learned response only to a single specific object or event. If we present several similar objects, only one of which is followed by the unconditioned stimulus, the subject will learn over time to respond only to that stimulus and to inhibit the response in the presence of all other stimuli. If Albert had been presented with a rat and a rabbit and cotton balls and other white, furry objects, but the loud noise (US) had occurred only when the rat appeared, he would have learned to discriminate the white rat from the other objects, and the fear response would not have generalized as it did.

Learning to discriminate is essential in everyday life. As we noted earlier, most children fear loud noises. Because thunder cannot harm a child, however, it would be helpful if children learned not to be afraid every time they heard it. Similarly, not all mushrooms are good to eat, and not all strangers are unfriendly. Thus, discrimination is crucial to learning.

**Response generalization** Giving a response that is somewhat different from the response originally learned to that stimulus.

### Generalization and Discrimination in Operant Conditioning

Stimulus generalization may also occur in operant conditioning. For example, a baby who is hugged and kissed for saying "Mama" when he sees his mother may begin to call everyone "Mama"—males and females alike. Although the person whom the baby sees—the stimulus—changes, he responds with the same word. In the same way, the skills you learn when playing tennis may be generalized to badminton, Ping-Pong, and squash.

In addition, in operant conditioning, we often encounter situations in which the same stimulus triggers responses that are different from, but similar to, the one that was taught. This process is called **response generalization**. For example, the baby who calls everyone "Mama" may also call his mother "Gaga" or "Baba"—the learning has generalized to other sounds that are similar to the correct response, "Mama." Note that in classical conditioning, response generalization does not occur. If a dog is taught to salivate when it sees an orange light, it will salivate less when it sees a reddish or orange-yellow light, but the response is still salivation rather than some other response.

Discrimination is an important element of learning—as any wild mushroom fancier will tell you.

Discrimination in operant conditioning is accomplished by reinforcing only the specific, desired response, and then only in the presence of specific stimuli. In this way, pigeons have been trained to peck at a red disk but not at a green one. First, the pigeon is taught to peck at a disk. Then it is presented with two disks, one red and one green. The bird gets food when it pecks at the red one but not when it pecks at the green one. Eventually, it learns to discriminate between the two and will peck only at the red disk. And if it is reinforced only for pecking, and not for other behaviors, it will learn that pecking is the only correct response in this situation. Similarly, babies can learn to say "Mama" only for their own mothers if they are reinforced for using "Mama" correctly and not reinforced when they use the term for other people. In the same way, if they are reinforced only when they say "Mama" and not when they say "Gaga" or "Baba," they will learn that those responses are not appropriate.

## NEW LEARNING BASED ON ORIGINAL LEARNING

Learning would be severely limited if learned responses were elicited (or emitted, in operant conditioning) only in the presence of the specific stimuli that are present during training. We have already seen how stimulus generalization expands the environment in which learning can be demonstrated. In this section, we explore other ways that original learning serves as the basis for new learning. We will see that in classical conditioning a conditioned response to one US can be transferred to a different US. Similarly, in operant conditioning, objects that have no intrinsic value can nevertheless become reinforcers because of their association with other, more basic reinforcers.

### Higher-order Conditioning in Classical Conditioning

Let's begin with classical conditioning. Once subjects have learned a conditioned response in the presence of a conditioned stimulus, they can build on that learning to acquire new kinds of learning. For example, after Pavlov's dogs had learned to salivate when they heard a bell, Pavlov was able to use the bell (without food) to teach the dogs to salivate at the sight of a black square. Instead of showing them the square and following it with food, he showed them the square and followed it with the bell until the dogs learned

**Higher-order conditioning** Conditioning based on previous learning; the conditioned stimulus serves as an unconditioned stimulus for further training.

**Primary reinforcer** Reinforcer that is rewarding in itself, such as food, water, and sex.

**Secondary reinforcer** Reinforcer whose value is learned through association with other primary or secondary reinforcers.

to salivate when they saw the square. In effect, the bell served as a substitute unconditioned stimulus and the black square became a new conditioned stimulus. This procedure is known as **higher-order conditioning**, not because it is more complex or because it incorporates any new principles, but simply because it is conditioning based on previous conditioning.

Higher-order conditioning is difficult to achieve because it races against extinction. The original US, the foundation of the original conditioning, is no longer presented along with the CS and, as we saw earlier, that is precisely the way to extinguish a classically conditioned response. During higher-order conditioning, Pavlov's dogs were exposed to the square and the bell, but no food was presented. In fact, the square became a signal that the bell would *not* be followed by food, so the dogs soon stopped salivating to the square/bell pairing. For higher-order conditioning to succeed, then the US has to be reintroduced occasionally: Food must be given to the dogs once in a while at the sound of the bell, so that they will continue to salivate when they hear the bell.

## Secondary Reinforcers in Operant Conditioning

As you have probably already noticed, there are a number of areas in which classical conditioning and operant conditioning act in concert. Specifically, we can use classical conditioning principles to explain why operant learning, particularly human operant learning, is not restricted to food reinforcers and painful punishers.

Some reinforcers, such as food, water, and sex, are intrinsically rewarding in and of themselves. These are called **primary reinforcers**. No prior learning is required to make them reinforcing. Other reinforcers have no intrinsic value, but they acquire value or rewarding properties through association with primary reinforcers. These are called **secondary reinforcers** not because they are less important, but because prior learning or conditioning is required before they will function as reinforcers. A rat learns to get food by pressing a bar; then a buzzer is sounded every time food drops into the dish. Even if the rat stops getting the food, it will continue to press the bar for a while just to hear the buzzer. Although the buzzer by itself has no intrinsic value to the rat, it has become a secondary reinforcer through association with food, a primary reinforcer.

**4.** What do we mean when we say that money is a secondary reinforcer?

Money is also a secondary reinforcer. Although money is just paper or metal, through its association with food, clothing, and other primary reinforcers, it becomes a powerful reinforcer. Children come to value money only after they learn that it will buy such things as candy (a primary reinforcer). Chimpanzees will learn to work for poker chips, which they insert into a vending machine to obtain a primary reinforcer, raisins. The poker chips, then, serve as secondary reinforcers for the chimps. Tokens have been used successfully as reinforcers for patients suffering from chronic schizophrenia. As we will see in Chapter 13, these *token economies* have proved especially effective in encouraging institutionalized mental patients to improve their personal hygiene and to engage in more social interactions (Schaefer & Martin, 1966).

# CONTINGENCIES ARE IMPORTANT

## Contingencies in Classical Conditioning

Pavlov's theory emphasized that the CS and US must occur closely together in time for classical conditioning to take place. More recent research, however, has shown that a brief time lapse between CS and US is not sufficient; rather, the CS must also precede and provide predictive information about the US. Robert Rescorla (1966, 1967, 1988) refers to this relationship between CS and US as a **contingency**. It works like this: If animals are exposed to a tone (CS) just before they receive a mild electrical shock (US), they will develop a clear startle or fear response when they hear the tone alone. This is a straightforward example of classical conditioning. It is also a clear example of a contingency between CS and US: When the tone (CS) always precedes the shock (US), the tone predicts that the shock is coming. But if the animals hear the tone *after* the shock or at the same time as the shock, they will show little, if any, conditioned fear because the meaning of the tone is ambiguous. In fact, if the CS (tone) always follows the US (shock), *backward conditioning* may occur, according to Rescorla. The animals learn that the tone means the shock is over and will not occur again for some time. Thus, the tone comes to produce a conditioned relaxation response rather than a fear response!

The idea that a CS must provide information about the US in order for conditioning to occur was confirmed when Leon Kamin (1969) discovered that the rat experiencing a noise (CS) followed by a brief shock (US) would indeed quickly learn to react with feat to the onset of the noise. Then, he added a second CS—a light—along with the noise. Contrary to what you might expect, the rats showed no conditioned fear when only the light was presented; it was as if they did not realize that the light was also a signal that a shock was forthcoming. Kamin concluded that the original learning (noise means shock) had a **blocking** effect on new learning (light also means shock). Since the light provided no new information about the likelihood of shock, no new learning took place.

**Contingency** A reliable "if-then" relationship between two events such as a CS and US.

**Blocking** A process whereby prior conditioning prevents conditioning to a second stimulus even when the two stimuli are presented simultaneously.

**Schedule of reinforcement** In operant conditioning, the rule for determining when and how often reinforcers will be delivered.

**Fixed-interval schedule** Reinforcement schedule in which the correct response is reinforced after a fixed length of time since the last reinforcement.

## Contingencies in Operant Conditioning

Contingencies also figure prominently in operant conditioning. Seldom, either in life or in the laboratory, are we rewarded every time we do something. And this is just as well. Experiments demonstrate that *partial* or *intermittent reinforcement* results in behavior that will persist longer than behavior learned by *continuous reinforcement*. When they receive only occasional reinforcement, subjects learn not to expect reinforcement with every response, so they continue responding in the absence of reinforcement in hopes that they will eventually gain the desired reward. Vending machines and slot machines illustrate the effects of continuous and partial reinforcement on extinction. Each time you put the correct change into a vending machine, you get something such as food in return (reinforcement); if a vending machine is broken and you receive nothing for your coins, you are unlikely to drop additional coins into it! By contrast, casino slot machines pay off only occasionally; therefore, you might continue putting coins into a slot machine for a long time even though you are not receiving anything in return.

Whenever partial reinforcement is given, the rule for determining when and how often reinforcers will be delivered is called the **schedule of reinforcement**. Schedules are either fixed or variable, and may be based on either the number of correct responses or the elapsed time between correct responses. The most common reinforcement schedules are fixed-interval and variable-interval schedules, which are based on time, and fixed-ratio and variable-ratio schedules, which are based on the number of correct responses.

On a **fixed-interval schedule**, subjects are reinforced for the first correct response only after a certain time has passed following the previous correct response; that is, they have to wait for a set period before they can be reinforced again. With fixed-interval schedules, performance tends to fall off immediately after each reinforcement and then to pick up again as the time for the next reinforcement draws near. For example, when exams are given

**Variable-interval schedule** Reinforcement schedule in which the correct response is reinforced after varying lengths of time following the last reinforcement.

**Fixed-ratio schedule** Reinforcement schedule in which the correct response is reinforced after a fixed number of correct responses.

**Variable-ratio schedule** Reinforcement schedule in which a varying number of correct responses must occur before reinforcement is presented.

at fixed intervals—like midterms and finals—students tend to increase the intensity of their studying just before an exam and then decrease it sharply right after the exam until shortly before the next one (see Figure 5-6).

A **variable-interval schedule** reinforces correct responses after varying lengths of time following the last reinforcement. One reinforcement might be given after 6 minutes, the next after 4 minutes, the next after 5 minutes, the next after 3 minutes. Subjects learn to give a slow, steady pattern of responses, being careful not to be so slow as to miss all the rewards. Thus, if several exams are given during a semester at unpredictable intervals, students have to keep studying at a steady rate all the time, because on any given day there might be an exam.

On a **fixed-ratio schedule**, a certain number of correct responses must occur before reinforcement is again available. This results in a high response rate because making many responses in a short time yields more rewards. Being paid on a piecework basis is an example of a fixed-ratio schedule. Farm workers might get $3 for every ten baskets of cherries they pick. The more they pick, the more money they make. Under a fixed-ratio schedule, a brief pause after reinforcement is followed by a rapid and steady response rate until the next reinforcement.

On a **variable-ratio schedule**, the number of correct responses necessary to gain reinforcement is not constant. The casino slot machine is a good example of a variable-ratio schedule: It may pay off, but you have no idea when. And because there is always a chance of hitting the jackpot, the temptation to keep playing is great. Subjects on a variable-ratio schedule tend not to pause after reinforcement and have a high rate of response over a long period of time. Because they never know when reinforcement may come, they keep on trying. Similarly, salespeople working on commission know that every attempt will not produce a sale, but it is certain that the more customers they approach, the more sales they will make.

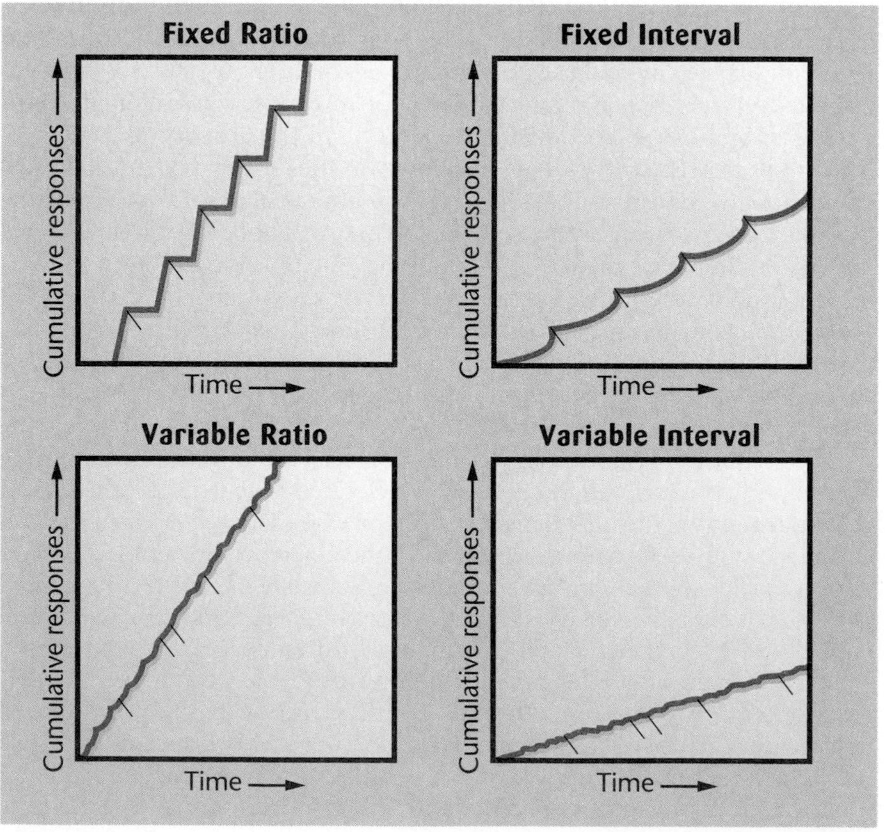


**Figure 5-6**
**Response patterns to schedules of reinforcement.** The *fixed-ratio* schedule is characterized by a high rate of response and a pause after each reinforcement. On a *fixed-interval* schedule, as the time for reinforcement approaches, the number of responses increases, and the slope becomes steeper. A *variable-ratio* schedule produces a high rate of response with little or no pause after each reinforcement. On a *variable-interval* schedule, the response rate is moderate and relatively constant. Notice that each tick mark on the graph represents one reinforcement.

## A REVIEW OF CLASSICAL CONDITIONING AND OPERANT CONDITIONING

In the preceding discussion, we noted a number of similarities and some differences between classical and operant conditioning. Both focus on building of associations between stimuli and responses. Both are subject to extinction and spontaneous recovery as well as to generalization and discrimination. In these respects, operant conditioning and classical conditioning bear some striking resemblances as learning processes. In other ways, however, the two seem to differ significantly. The main difference is that in classical conditioning, the learner is passive and the desired behavior is usually involuntary, while in operant conditioning, the learner is active and the desired behavior is usually voluntary.

However, some psychologists play down these differences, suggesting that classical and operant conditioning are simply two different ways of bringing about the same kind of learning. For example, classical conditioning can be used to shape voluntary movements (P.L. Brown & Jenkins, 1968). Moreover, operant conditioning of involuntary processes has occurred in automatic conditioning studies in which both humans and animals have been taught to control certain biological functions, such as blood pressure, heart rate, and skin temperature. Finally, in operant conditioning, once the operant response becomes linked to a stimulus, the response looks and acts very much like an unconditioned response. If you have been reinforced repeatedly for stepping on the brake when a traffic light turns red, the red light comes to elicit braking behavior just as an unconditioned stimulus elicits an unconditioned response in classical conditioning.

The slot machine is a classic example of a variable-ratio schedule: Because subjects never know when reinforcement may come, they maintain a high rate of response over a long period of time.

These facts, together with the evidence that there are few differences between classical and operant conditioning in such things as extinction and generalization, suggest that classical and operant conditioning may simply be two different procedures for achieving the same end (Hearst, 1975). If this is so, psychologists have been overstressing the differences and paying too little attention to the similarities between the two. Learning occurs in both cases, and the nature of learning itself remains open to new theories. In the next section, we discuss several of these new theories.

Classical and operant conditioning concern the learning of observable, external, objectively measurable responses. But it would appear that, at least in the case of humans, there's often more to learning than meets the eye, as we shall see in the next section.

## COGNITIVE LEARNING

Classical and operant conditioning both emphasize direct experience and stimulus control. Classical conditioning requires that a learner be exposed to a CS and a US; without a US, classical conditioning cannot occur. Similarly, operant conditioning requires that a response be followed by a consequence; if there is no reinforcer or punisher, then operant conditioning cannot occur. Some psychologists insist that because the elements of these types of learning can be observed and measured, they are the only legitimate kinds of learning to study scientifically. However, other psychologists point up the importance of mental activities such as attention, expectation, thinking, and remembering as part of the process of learning. We learn to find our way around a building or neighborhood, we learn what to expect from a given situation, we learn abstract concepts, and we can even learn about situations that we have never experienced firsthand. These kinds of **cognitive learning** are impossible to observe and measure directly, but they can be *inferred* from behavior; thus, the argument goes, they, too, are legitimate subjects for scientific inquiry. As we will see, much of the recent research in the area of learning has focused on identifying what cognitive learning is and how it works—what goes on *inside* us when we learn.

**Cognitive learning** Learning that depends on mental processes that are not directly observable.

**Latent learning** Learning that is not immediately reflected in a behavior change.

**Cognitive map** A learned mental image of a spatial environment that may be called on to solve problems when stimuli in the environment change.

## Latent Learning and Cognitive Maps

Research into cognitive learning actually began shortly after the earliest work in both classical and operant conditioning. Edward Chace Tolman, one of the pioneers in the study of cognitive learning, acknowledged in his presidential address to the American Psychological Association (1938) that the psychology of learning "has been and still is primarily a matter of agreeing or disagreeing with Thorndike, or trying in minor ways to improve upon him." For his part, Tolman disagreed with Thorndike on two key points. First, Tolman felt that Thorndike's law of effect neglected the inner drives or motives that made learners pursue the "satisfying state," and he felt that the concept of response needed to include a range of behaviors—a *performance*, in Tolman's word—that would allow learners to reach their goal. Second, Tolman felt that learning occurs even before the subject reaches the goal and occurs whether or not the learner is reinforced. Tolman called this concept **latent learning**.

*Source:* Drawing by Chas. Adams, ©1981. The New Yorker Magazine, Inc.

Tolman demonstrated latent learning in a famous experiment conducted with C.H. Honzik in 1930. Two groups of hungry rats were placed in a maze and required to find their way from a start box to an end box. The first group found food pellets (a reward) in the end box; the second group found nothing there. According to the principles of operant conditioning, the first group would learn the maze better than the second group—which was, indeed, what happened. But when Tolman took some of the rats from the second, unreinforced group and started to give them food at the goal box, almost immediately they started running the maze as well as the rats in the first group (see Figure 5-7). He explained these dramatic findings by noting that the unrewarded rats had actually learned a great deal about the maze, but their learning was *latent*—stored internally in some way but not yet reflected in their behavior. When they were given a good reason to run the maze quickly, they put their latent learning to use.

Since Tolman's time, there has been a great deal of work on just what the nature of this latent learning might be. From their studies of how animals or humans find their way around a maze, a building, or a neighborhood with many available routes, psychologists have proposed that latent learning is stored in the form of a mental image, or **cognitive map**, of the whole area. When the proper time comes, the learner can call up the stored image or map and put it to use.

In response to Tolman's theory of latent learning, Thorndike proposed an experiment to test whether a rat could learn to run a maze and store a cognitive image of the maze without experiencing the maze firsthand. His experimental design envisioned researchers carrying each rat through the maze in a small wiremesh container and then rewarding the rat at the end of each trail as if it had run the maze itself. He predicted that the rat would show little or no evidence of learning compared to rats that had learned the same maze on their own through trial and error. Neither he nor Tolman ever conducted the experiment.

Two decades later, however, researchers at the University of Kansas picked up on Thorndike's idea (McNamara, Long, & Wike, 1956). But instead of taking the passive rats through the "correct" path in a simple

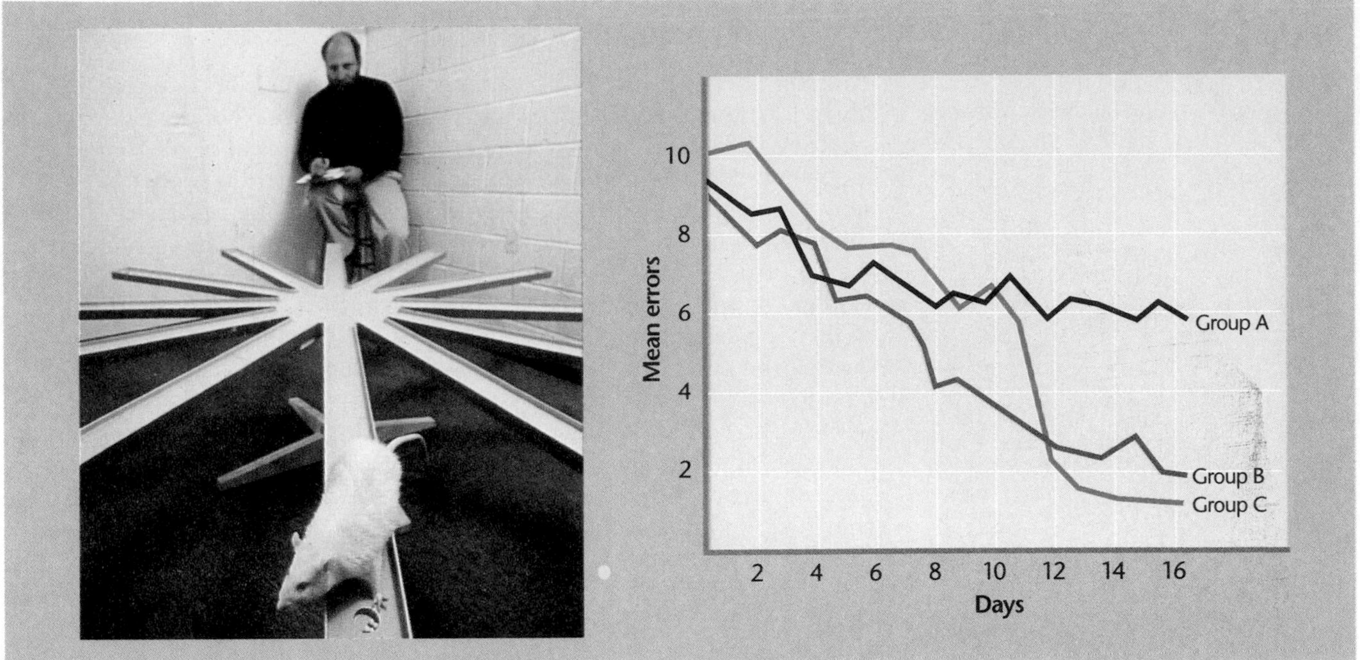


**Figure 5-7**
**Maze used to study latent learning in rats.** The results of the classic Tolman-Honzik study are revealed in the graph. Group A never received a food reward; Group B was rewarded each day. Group C was not rewarded until the eleventh day, but note the significant change in the rats' behavior on Day 12. These results suggest that Group C had been learning all along, although this learning was not reflected in their performance until they were rewarded with food for demonstrating the desired behaviors.

*Source:* From Tolman and Honzik, 1930.

maze, they carried each passenger rat over the same path that a free-running partner rat had taken on the same trail. Contrary to Thorndike's prediction, the passenger rats learned the maze just as well as their active counterparts.

In a second version of the experiment, the experimenters covered windows and masked the lights in the room so that the passenger rats would have only the directional cues to orient them to the maze. Under these conditions, the passenger rats seemed not to have learned to run the maze at all, performing only as well as they might by chance.

The first experiment seems to confirm Tolman's view of latent learning of cognitive maps. The second experiment suggests that rats use information from their surroundings as an important part of their cognitive maps. More recent research reconfirms this picture of cognitive spatial learning in animals. It appears that animals have a great deal more flexibility when it comes to solving problems and making choices than can be explained by simple conditioning (Domjan, 1987). In a series of experiments with rats in a radial maze, the rats consistently recalled which arms they had previously traveled down and which they hadn't, even when scent cues were removed and all arms contained a bait reward. Researchers concluded that these rats had developed a cognitive map or spatial memory of their experiences in the maze (Olton & Samuelson, 1976). The pivotal point for our purposes is that, even in rats, learning involves more than a change in observable behavior. It also appears to involve changes in unobservable mental processes that may (or may not) be reflected at some future time in the subject's behavior.

## Insight and Learning Sets

**Insight** Learning that occurs rapidly as a result of understanding all the elements of a problem.

Another phenomenon that highlights the importance of cognitive processing in learning is **insight**, the sudden "coming together" of the elements of a situation so that the most efficient path is instantly clear or the solution to a problem suddenly strikes the learner. In this case, learning does not progress slowly and gradually on a smooth curve as a result of practice but suddenly shoots up from unsuccessful trial and error to instant success.

During World War I, the German Gestalt psychologist Wolfgang Köhler conducted a series of experiments on the nature of insightful learning. He placed a chimpanzee in a cage with a banana on the ground just outside the cage, but not within reach. When the animal realized that it couldn't reach the banana by stretching out its arms, it initially reacted with frustration. After a while, the chimp started looking at what was in the cage, including a stick left there by the experimenters. Sometimes quite suddenly, the chimp would grab the stick, poke it through the bars of the cage, and drag the banana within reach. The same kind of sudden insight occurred when the banana was hung from the roof of the cage, just out of the chimp's grasp. This time, inside the cage were some boxes, which the chimp quickly learned to move to the spot under the banana and stack up high enough so it could climb up to snatch the food.

One of Köhler's insightful chimps has arranged a stack of boxes in order to reach some bananas hanging from the roof of the cage.

Are the complex cognitive processes that produce insight limited to higher animals such as apes and humans? In 1984, four Harvard University psychologists (R. Epstein et al., 1984) presented the banana-and-box problem to a small group of pigeons to see if they, too, were capable of insight learning. Because moving boxes around is not as natural a behavior for pigeons as it is for chimps, the researchers first conditioned the pigeons, through standard shaping procedures, to push a box toward a particular target—a green spot on the wall of the training cage. On separate occasions, the pigeons were also taught to climb onto a box that was stuck to the floor and to peck at a small picture of a banana to receive a food reward. The question then was: Could the pigeons put the two new behaviors together to solve the problem of the banana and the box? When the pigeons were presented with an out-of-reach hanging picture of a banana and with a box, Epstein and his co-workers reported that each pigeon initially showed confusion and, just like Köhler's chimps, looked for a while from the hanging picture to the box. Then, fairly suddenly, each pigeon began to push the box toward the picture, stopping now and then to sight the picture and to check the direction in which to push the box. When they had the box underneath the picture of the banana, each of the pigeons then climbed on top and pecked at the picture to receive its reward.

Epstein and his co-workers felt that the main reason pigeons couldn't solve the problem without preliminary training is that pigeons (unlike chimps) don't already know how boxes can be pushed around and used in various ways, nor do they normally value bananas. When pigeons are given the right tools and are taught how to use them, however, they show that they can solve quite complex cognitive problems. In other words, in this view, Köhler's chimps quickly learned how to reach the banana because they already knew how to use sticks and boxes to get at objects and because they valued bananas.

Previous learning can also be used to speed up new learning, a process demonstrated clearly in a series of studies by Harry Harlow with rhesus monkeys (Harlow, 1949). Harlow presented each monkey with two boxes—say, a round green box on the left side of a tray and a square red box on the right side. A morsel of food was put under one of the boxes. The monkey was permitted to lift just one box; if it chose the correct box, it got the food. On the next trial, the food was put under the same box (which had been moved to a new position), and the monkey again got to choose just one box. Each monkey had six trials to figure out which box covered the food no matter where that box was located. Then the monkeys were given a new set of choices—say, between a blue triangular box and an orange pentagonal one—and another six trials, and so on with other shapes and colors of boxes.

How long did it take for the monkeys to figure out that in any set of six trials, food was always under the same box? Initially, the monkeys chose boxes randomly, by trial and error; sometimes they would find food, but just as often they would not. However, after a while their behavior changed: In just one or two trials, they would find the correct box, which they chose consistently thereafter until the experimenter supplied new boxes. They seemed to have learned the underlying principle—that the food would always be under the same box—and they used that learning to solve almost instantly each new set of choices presented by the experimenter.

Harlow concluded that the monkeys had "learned how to learn" or that they had established **learning sets**: Within the limited range of choices, they had discovered how to tell which box would give them what they wanted. By extension, Köhler's chimps could be said to have established learning sets for various ways of obtaining food that was just out of reach. When presented with the familiar problem of reaching the banana, the chimps simply called up the appropriate learning sets and solved the problem. By contrast, Epstein's pigeons first had to be taught the appropriate learning sets, and then they, too, were able to solve the problem. In both cases, the animals seemed to have learned more than just specific behaviors—they apparently learned how to learn. Whether this means that animals can think is an issue that is still being studied and debated (see further discussion of this point in Chapter 7).

**Learning set** Ability to become increasingly more effective in solving problems as more problems are solved.

**Social learning theory** View of learning that emphasizes the ability to learn by observing a model or receiving instructions, without firsthand experience by the learner.

**Observational** or **vicarious learning** Learning by observing other people's behavior.

## LEARNING BY OBSERVING

In the past 2 decades, another group of psychologists, known as *social learning theorists*, has challenged the idea that most or all human learning stems from classical or operant conditioning. **Social learning theory** focuses on the extent to which we learn not just from firsthand experience—the kind of learning explained by classical and operant conditioning—but also from watching what happens to other people or by hearing about something. In fact, we can learn new behaviors without ever actually carrying them out or being reinforced for them. The first time you drive a car, you tend to drive carefully because you have been told to do so, you have been warned about driving carelessly, you have watched people drive carefully, and you've seen what happens when people drive carelessly. In other words, you have learned a great deal about driving before you ever sat behind the wheel of a car.

This kind of **observational** or **vicarious learning** is quite common. By watching models, we can learn such things as how to start a lawn mower and how to saw wood. We also learn how to show love or respect or concern, as well as how to show hostility and aggression. When the Federal Communications Commission (FCC) banned cigarette commercials on TV, the commissioners were acting on the belief that modeling a behavior—lighting up a cigarette—prompted people to imitate it. They removed the model to discourage the behavior.

In *observational* or *vicarious learning,* we learn by watching a model perform a particular action and then trying to imitate that action correctly.

**Vicarious reinforcement** and **vicarious punishment** Reinforcement or punishment experienced by models that affects the willingness of others to perform the behaviors they learned by observing the models.

Of course, we do not imitate everything that other people do. Social learning theory accounts for this in several ways (Bandura, 1977, 1986). First, you must not only see but also *pay attention* to what the model does; this is more likely if the model commands attention (as does a famous or attractive person or an expert). Second, you must *remember* what the model did. Third, you have to *convert* what you learned into action: You may learn a great deal from watching a model but have no particular reason to convert what you have learned into behavior. This distinction between *learning* and *performance* is crucial to social learning theorists: They stress that learning can occur without any change in outward behavior. Finally, the extent to which we display behaviors that have been learned through observation can be affected by **vicarious reinforcement** and **vicarious punishment**. That is, our willingness to perform acts that we learn by observation depends in part on what happens to the people we are watching. So when children watching TV or movies see people using drugs or engaging in unsafe sex, there is cause for concern whether or not the actors are punished for their behavior.

The foremost proponent of social learning theory is Albert Bandura, who refers to his learning theory as a *social cognitive theory* (Bandura, 1986). In a classic experiment, Bandura (1965) demonstrated that people can learn a behavior without being reinforced for doing so and that learning a behavior and performing it are not the same thing. Bandura randomly divided a group of 66 nursery-school children (33 boys and 33 girls) into three groups of 22 subjects each. Each child individually watched a film in which an adult model walked up to an adult-size plastic doll and ordered it to move out of the way. When the doll failed to obey, the model became aggressive, pushing the doll on its side, punching it in the nose, hitting it with a rubber mallet, kicking it around the room, and throwing rubber balls at it.

The film ended differently for children in each of the three groups, however. Children in the *model-rewarded condition* saw the model showered with candies, soft drinks, and praise by a second adult—an example of vicarious reinforcement. Those in the *model-punished condition* witnessed the second adult shaking a finger at the model, scolding, and spanking him—an example of vicarious punishment. Youngsters in the *no-consequences condition* saw a version of the film that ended with the scene of aggression—no second adult appeared, so there were no consequences for the model.

Immediately after seeing the film, the children were individually escorted into another room where they found a doll, rubber balls, a mallet, and many other toys. As the child played alone for 10 minutes, observers recorded the youngster's behavior from behind a one-way mirror. Every time a child spontaneously repeated any of the aggressive acts seen in the film, that child was coded as *performing* the behavior. After 10 minutes, an experimenter entered the room and offered the child treats in return for imitating or repeating things the model had done or said to the doll. Bandura used the number of successfully imitated behaviors as a measure of how much the child had *learned* by watching the model.

Analysis of the data revealed that (1) children who had observed the model being rewarded were especially likely to *perform* the models' behavior spontaneously; but (2) children in all three groups had *learned* to imitate the model's behavior equally well, and quite accurately at that (see Figure 5-8).

Notice that the children in this study learned aggressive behavior without being reinforced for it. Although reinforcement of a model is not necessary for vicarious learning to occur, seeing a model reinforced or punished nonetheless provides us with useful information that may then affect our willingness to show or perform what we have learned. Vicarious reinforcement and punishment tell us what the correct or incorrect behavior is and

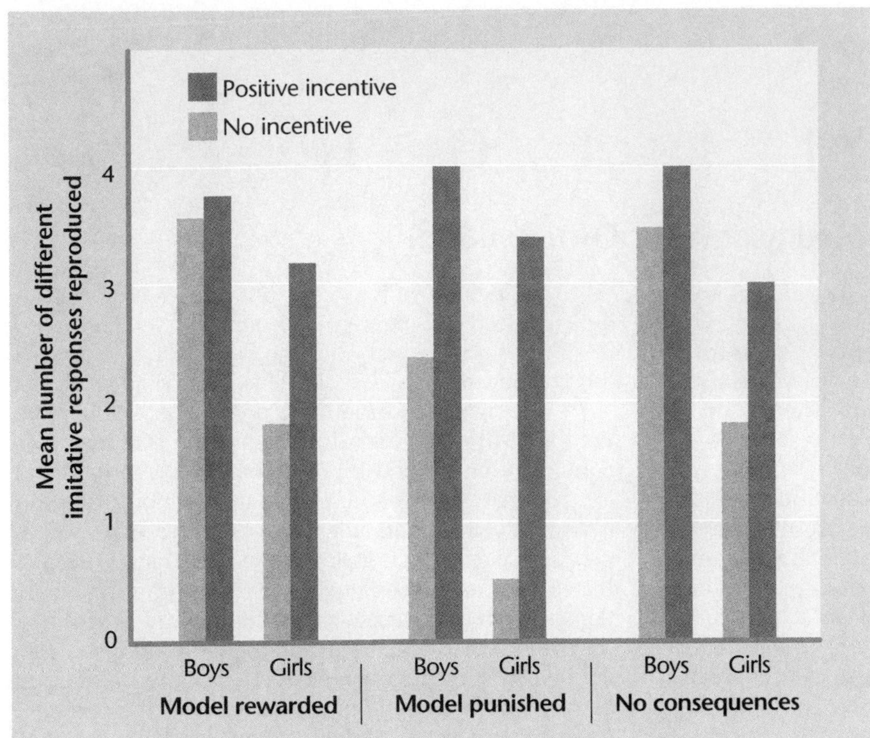


**Figure 5-8**
As the graph shows, even though all of the children in Bandura's study of imitative aggression learned the models' behavior, they *performed* differently depending on whether the model was rewarded or punished.

*Source:* Bandura, 1965, p. 592. Copyright© 1965 by the American Psychological Association. Reprinted by permission.

what is likely to happen to us if we imitate the model. Moreover, Bandura stresses that human beings are capable of setting performance standards for themselves and then rewarding (or punishing) themselves for achieving or failing to achieve those standards as a way to regulate their own behavior. (See the Highlights box titled "Modifying Your Own Behavior.")

Because of its emphasis on expectations, insight, information, self-satisfaction, and self-criticism, social learning theory promises not only to broaden our understanding of how people learn skills and gain abilities but also to help us grasp how attitudes, values, and ideas pass from person to person. According to this view of learning, human beings use the powers of sight as well as insight, hindsight, and foresight to interpret our own experiences and those of others (Bandura, 1962). By drawing attention to the importance of modeling, social learning theory also points out how *not* to teach something unintentionally. For example, suppose you want to teach a child not to hit other children. You might think that slapping the child as punishment would change the behavior, while reinforcing more desirable behavior. But social learning theory maintains that slapping the child only demonstrates that hitting is an effective means of getting one's way. You and the child would both be better off if your actions reflected a less aggressive way of dealing with other people (Bandura, 1973, 1977).

*True or false*: Punishing a child by slapping or spanking can teach the child to act more violently.

## COGNITIVE LEARNING IN NONHUMANS

Contemporary approaches to conditioning emphasize that conditioned stimuli, reinforcers, and punishers provide *information* about the environment. According to this view, classical and operant conditioning are not purely mechanical processes that can proceed without at least some cognitive activity. Thus, the fact that all animals can be conditioned implies

## HIGHLIGHTS

### Modifying Your Own Behavior

Can people modify their own behavior? The answer is yes. The first thing to do is to decide what behavior you want to acquire—the "target" behavior. What if you want to stop behaving in a particular way? Much better results are achieved when you focus on a new behavior to be acquired rather than on a behavior to be eliminated. For example, instead of setting a target of being less shy, you might define the target behavior as becoming more outgoing or more sociable. Other possible target behaviors are behaving more assertively, studying more, and getting along better with your roommates. In each case, you have spotlighted the behavior that you want to acquire rather than the behavior that you want to reduce or eliminate.

The next step is to define the target behavior precisely: What exactly do you mean by "assertive" or "sociable"? Start by imagining situations in which the target behavior could be performed. Then describe in writing these situations and the way in which you now respond to them. For example, in the case of shyness, you might write: "When I am sitting in the lecture hall, waiting for class to begin, I don't talk to the people around me." Next, write down how you would rather act in that situation: "Ask the people sitting next to me how they like the class or the professor, or ask if they have seen any particularly good films lately."

Then you need to monitor your present behavior by keeping a daily log of activities related to the target behavior to establish your present rate of behavior. At the same time, try to figure out if your present, undesirable behavior is being reinforced in some way. For example, if you find yourself unable to study, record what you do instead and try to determine how that undesirable behavior is being reinforced.

The next step—the basic principle of self-modification—is to provide yourself with a positive reinforcer that is contingent on specific improvements in the target behavior. You may be able to use the same reinforcer that now maintains your undesirable behavior, or you may want to pick a new reinforcer. D.L. Watson and Tharp (1985) cite the example of a student who wanted to improve his relationship with his parents. He first counted the times he said something pleasant to them and then rewarded himself for improvement by making his favorite pastime, playing pool, contingent on predetermined increases in the number of pleasant remarks he made. You can also use tokens: Give yourself one token for every 30 minutes of studying and cash in those tokens for reinforcement. For an hour of TV, you might charge yourself three tokens, while the privilege of going to a movie might cost six.

Remember that behavior need not be learned all in one piece. You can use shaping, or successive approximations, to change your behavior bit by bit over a span of time.

If you would like to attempt a program of self-improvement, a book by David Watson and Roland Tharp titled *Self-Directed Behavior* (1985) offers step-by-step instructions and exercises.

6. *True or false*: Punishing a child by slapping or spanking can teach the child to act more violently.

that all animals are capable of at least minimal cognitive processing of information. We have also seen that animals can perform whole patterns of operant behaviors, even when the pattern as a whole has never been reinforced. And animals are capable of latent learning, learning cognitive maps, and insight, all of which involve cognitive processes. Do nonhuman animals also exhibit other evidence of cognitive learning? The answer seems to be a qualified yes. For example, rats that watch other rats try a novel or unfamiliar food show an increased tendency to eat the new food (Galef, 1993). In a different experiment, one group of rats watched another group experience extinction; as a result, the observer rats themselves extinguished faster than if they had not watched the model rats (Heyes et al., 1993). Apparently, the observer rats learned something about the absence of reward simply by seeing what happened to the other rats. These surprising results, along with reports that animals as diverse as chickens and octopi learn by watching, further support the notion that nonhuman animals do indeed learn in ways that fit well with the cognitive theory of learning.

**"Can we make people into anything we want them to be?"**

Within the field of psychology there has been an ongoing debate about the relative effects of nature (heredity) and nurture (learning) in shaping human behavior. Consider, for example, the skills involved in learning to play the violin. Is nature or nurture more important in the acquisition of these skills? Why do so many people have difficulty learning to play a musical instrument, while still others find it impossible?

What are your feelings on this issue? If human behavior can be conditioned, then can we make people into anything we want them to be? Or can behavior be conditioned only up to a point? If so, to what point? How does the concept of conditioning affect the notion of free will? After you have considered these questions, take a few minutes to examine the opinions of some other students.

• • • • • • •

**KARI: Some behaviors are genetically linked, and others are not as easily influenced as others.**

**SUNI: I had the experience of teaching piano for a few months, and there were some kids who had great interest in music and the supportive environment of the family, and yet they just could not advance.**

**ANDRE: There are definitely gifted people in the world who are good at one thing. But I do think you can make a person anything he wants to be to an extent.**

**MELISSA: I think that there are genetic predispositions—for example: intrinsic personality characteristics or an aptitude for a specific vocation such as art or music.**

**JOSÉ: There aren't really any genetic predispositions towards medicine or engineering or computer science. These are man-made fields. There are, however, natural abilities in math, language, music, art, athletics, etc. You take an unshaped child, you could probably make it into anything you want. I bet Michael Jordan could have been a decent concert violinist—maybe not the greatest, and probably he wouldn't be as good in it as he is in basketball—but the ability is there, and if from birth you trained him in violin instead of letting him play basketball, he would be a good violinist but bad at basketball.**

**LISA: I think that genetically we have certain talents and attributes that cannot be completely altered by environment. I'm not entirely creative, but my sister, who grew up in exactly the same environment as me, is extremely artistic and creative.**

**CARVER: We are exactly what we make of ourselves through our experience. We exist and then take on more. Only things like watches, skyscrapers, and stock markets are set in their function from the moment of their conception. People are continuously becoming, always being determined.**

**LEE: What about right-/left-brained people who seem to have a natural talent for language skills or spatial (perhaps artistic) skills? These seem to be connected to how the body is put together and may have something to do with "inborn talents."**

**KATE: There are still going to be some people that will not be capable of, say, becoming a ballerina. Anyway, there's a girl on my hall that wants to be a ballerina, and I suppose she is very good, but hasn't anyone told her that she is too short?**

**ETHAN: The best people in a profession have probably been conditioned already. That's why they're the best at what they do. For instance, a superb ball player probably had all kinds of positive and negative reinforcers as a child, both from friends and parents that led him/her to focus their energies on ball. This is why I think that a person could be conditioned to be as good as the best players, but not better, as they would both have received pretty much the same conditioning. One just would have gotten it by chance, and one on purpose.**

**PAT: I happen to find much greater happiness in theater than in science. Because of my enthusiasm, I excel at one and don't put the effort forth in order to excel at the other. My family is analytical and scientific, not artistic and theatrical, so if anything, I've been more conditioned to be a "science" person. Therefore, I believe my love of the arts is an inherent part of my genetically influenced personality.**

• • • • • • •

Now that you've been exposed to other students' views, you might want to reconsider your position on this issue. Do you think people have inborn talents? Or can a person can be anything he or she wants to be? Consider the skills and behaviors that you've developed over the course of your lifetime. Are thy primarily the result of learning on your part, or do they reflect inborn aptitudes?

## LOOKING FORWARD

We come into the world with a marvelous capacity to change in response to experience and to store those changes so we can function more effectively in our environments. Without the ability to learn, our survival would rest on a few rudimentary instinctive behaviors that would not sustain life. Thus, our very existence depends on learning. Psychologists began the systematic study of learning by examining the phenomena of classical and operant conditioning. It was once believed that these two kinds of learning were simple, miniature models of the wide variety of learning that we exhibit throughout life, and that we could develop a complete understanding of all learning by generalizing from the rules that underlie both classical and operant conditioning. Instead, we have found that these models of learning are in no way *simple*, and that even in their surprising complexity, they do not account for the vast array of learning experiences that we have. In recent years, as we have delved further into conditioning, we have also developed a growing understanding that much learning stems from the internal world of cognition rather than on the external world of stimuli and reinforcement. Yet, even after nearly a century of study, psychologists are only starting to learn about learning.

## SUMMARY

This chapter concentrates on **learning**, the process by which experience or practice produces a relatively permanent change in behavior or potential behavior.

### CLASSICAL CONDITIONING

#### Pavlov's Conditioning Experiments

Russian psychologist Ivan Pavlov hit upon **classical conditioning** almost by accident when studying digestive processes. He trained a dog to salivate at the sound of a bell by presenting the sound just before food was brought into the room. Eventually the dog began to salivate at the sound of the bell alone.

#### Elements of Classical Conditioning

Classical conditioning involves pairing a response naturally caused by one stimulus with another, previously neutral stimulus. There are four basic elements to this transfer: The **unconditioned stimulus (US)**, often food, invariably causes an organism to respond in a specific way. The **unconditioned response (UR)** is the reaction (such as salivation) that always results from the unconditioned stimulus. The **conditioned stimulus (CS)** is a stimulus (such as a bell) that is originally neutral—the CS alone, that is, does not bring about the desired response—but that over the course of conditioning comes to produce the desired response when presented alone. Finally, the **conditioned response (CR)** is the behavior that the organism learns to exhibit in the presence of a conditioned stimulus.

#### Classical Conditioning in Humans

Humans also learn to associate certain sights or sounds with other stimuli. John Watson conditioned a little boy, Albert, to fear white rats by making a loud, frightening noise every time the boy was shown a rat. Using much the same principle, Mary Cover Jones developed a method for unlearning fears: She paired the sight of a caged rat, at gradually decreasing distances with a child's pleasant experience of eating candy. This method evolved into **desensitization therapy**, a conditioning technique designed to gradually reduce anxiety about a particular object or situation. Recently, scientists have discovered that the immune system may respond to classical conditioning techniques, thus allowing doctors to use fewer drugs in treating certain disorders.

#### Classical Conditioning Is Selective

Classical conditioning is not a simple, mechanistic process that stamps in the stimulus-response connection whenever any unconditioned stimulus and conditioned stimulus are paired. Martin Seligman uses the terms *preparedness* and *contrapreparedness* to account for the observation that some kinds of conditioning are accomplished very easily, while other kinds may never occur. Research demonstrating that we develop phobias about snakes and spiders, for example, but almost never about flowers or cooking utensils illustrates the principles of preparedness and contrapreparedness, respectively. The ease with which we develop **conditioned food aversions** also exemplifies learning preparedness. Conditioned food aversions are exceptions to the general rules about classical conditioning. Animals can learn to avoid poisonous food even if there is a lengthy interval between eating the food and becoming ill. Moreover, in many cases, only one pairing of conditioned and unconditioned stimuli is necessary for learning to take place.

## OPERANT CONDITIONING

While classical conditioning focuses on a behavior that invariably follows a particular event, **operant conditioning** concerns the learning of behavior that operates on the environment so that the person or animal will gain something desired or avoid something unpleasant. This behavior is initially *emitted* rather than elicited—you wave your hand to flag down a taxi, dogs beg at the dinner table to get food.

### Thorndike's Conditioning Experiments

Psychologist Edward Lee Thorndike was the first researcher to study operant behavior systematically. He proposed the **law of effect**, which states that behavior that is consistently rewarded will become *stamped in* as learned behavior and behavior that is consistently punished will be *stamped out*.

### Elements of Operant Conditioning

Thorndike's work still serves as an important foundation in the investigation of effects of both **reinforcers** and **punishers**. In operant conditioning, reinforcement (such as food) is used to increase the probability that a particular response will occur in the future. To decrease the probability that a particular response will recur, punishers (such as scolding) are used.

### Types of Reinforcement

There are several kinds of reinforcers; all of them *strengthen* behavior just as steel rods reinforce or strengthen concrete.

The presence of **positive reinforcers** (like food) adds to or increases the likelihood that a behavior will recur. **Negative reinforcers** (such as electric shocks) also increase the likelihood that a behavior will recur, but they do so by reducing or eliminating something unpleasant from the environment.

### Punishment

While all reinforcers (both positive and negative) increase the likelihood that a behavior will occur again, **punishment** is any event whose presence decreases the likelihood that ongoing behavior will recur. Reinforcement always *strengthens* behavior; punishment *weakens* it. **Avoidance training** involves learning a desirable behavior that prevents an unpleasant condition, such as punishment, from occurring.

### Operant Conditioning Is Selective

Studies have revealed that in operant conditioning the behaviors that are easiest to condition are those that animals typically would perform in the training situation. These behaviors vary from species to species; and put significant constraints on both classical and operant conditioning.

### Superstitious Behavior

When something we do is followed closely by a reinforcer, we tend to repeat that behavior, even if it was not actually responsible for producing the reinforcement. Such behaviors are called *superstitious*. Nonhumans as well as humans exhibit superstitious behaviors.

## COMPARING CLASSICAL AND OPERANT CONDITIONING

A number of phenomena characterize both classical conditioning and operant conditioning, and there are several terms and concepts common to both kinds of learning.

### Response Acquisition

In classical conditioning, responses occur naturally and automatically in the presence of the unconditioned stimulus. During the phase of the experiment called **response acquisition**, these naturally occurring responses are attached to the conditioned stimulus by pairing that stimulus with the unconditioned stimulus. In operant conditioning, response acquisition refers to the phase of the learning process in which desired responses are followed by reinforcers. To speed up this process and make the occurrence of a desired response more likely, motivation may be increased by letting the animal become hungry, or the number of potential responses may be reduced by restricting the environment.

For behaviors outside the laboratory, which cannot be controlled so conveniently, the process of **shaping** is often useful: Reinforcement is given for successive approximations to the desired behavior. There are differences, however, among species in what behaviors can be learned and the circumstances under which learning will take hold.

### Extinction and Spontaneous Recovery

If the unconditioned stimulus and conditioned stimulus cease to be paired, **extinction** occurs, meaning the strength and/or frequency of the learned response diminishes. When Pavlov's dogs received no food after repeatedly hearing the bell, they ceased to salivate at the sound of the bell. However, after a while, this extinguished response may reappear without retraining, in a process called **spontaneous recovery**. Extinction is complete when the subject no longer produces the conditioned response.

Extinction occurs in operant conditioning when reinforcement is withheld. However, the ease with which a behavior is extinguished varies according to several factors: the strength of the original learning, the variety of settings in which learning takes place, and the schedule of reinforcement used during conditioning. Especially hard to extinguish is behavior learned through punishment rather than reinforcement.

### Generalization and Discrimination

In classical conditioning, situations or stimuli may resemble each other enough that the learners will react to one the way they have learned to react to the other through a process called **stimulus generalization**. On the other hand, the process of **stimulus discrimination** enables learners to perceive differences among stimuli so that not all loud sounds, for example, provoke fear.

Just as in classical conditioning, responses learned through operant conditioning can generalize from one stimulus to other, similar stimuli. **Response generalization** occurs when the same stimulus leads to different but similar responses. Discrimination in operant conditioning is taught by reinforcing a response only in the presence of certain stimuli.

## NEW LEARNING BASED ON ORIGINAL LEARNING

In both classical and operant conditioning, original learning serves as a building block for new learning.

### Higher-order Conditioning in Classical Conditioning

**Higher-order conditioning** in classical conditioning uses an earlier conditioned stimulus as an unconditioned stimulus for further training. For example, Pavlov used the bell to condition his dogs to salivate at the sight of a black square. This sort of conditioning is difficult to achieve because of extinction: Unless the first unconditioned stimulus is presented occasionally, the initial conditioned response will be extinguished.

### Secondary Reinforcers in Operant Conditioning

In operant conditioning, neutral stimuli can become reinforcers by being paired or associated with other reinforcers. A **primary reinforcer** is one that, like food and water, is rewarding in and of itself. A **secondary reinforcer** is one whose value is learned through its association with primary reinforcers or with other secondary reinforcers. Money is an example of a secondary reinforcer—in and of itself, it is not rewarding; it is valuable only for what it can buy.

## CONTINGENCIES ART IMPORTANT

The "if-then" relationship between conditioned stimuli and unconditioned stimuli in classical conditioning or between responses and reinforcers (or punishers) in operant conditioning is called a **contingency**.

### Contingencies in Classical Conditioning

Robert Rescorla has demonstrated that classical conditioning requires more than merely presenting an unconditioned stimulus and a conditioned stimulus together in time. His work shows that in order for conditioning to occur, a conditioned stimulus must provide information about the unconditioned stimulus—that is, there must be a CS-US contingency.

### Contingencies in Operant Conditioning

In operant conditioning, response contingencies are sometimes referred to as **schedules of reinforcement**. We rarely receive reinforcement every time we do something. Interestingly, it turns out that *partial reinforcement*, in which rewards are given for some correct responses but not for every one, results in behavior that persists longer than that learned by continuous reinforcement. The schedule of reinforcement specifies when a reinforcer will be delivered. Reinforcers may be delivered on the basis of time since last reinforcement (the *interval* between reinforcements). Or reinforcement may depend on the number of correct responses since the last reinforcement (the *ratio* of reinforcement per correct response).

A **fixed-interval schedule** provides reinforcement of the first correct response after a fixed, unchanging period of time. A **variable-interval schedule** reinforces the learner for the first correct response that occurs after various periods of time, so the subject never knows exactly when a reward is going to come. In a **fixed-ratio schedule**, behavior is rewarded each time a fixed number of correct responses is given; in a **variable-ratio schedule**, reinforcement is provided after a varying number of correct responses.

## A REVIEW OF CLASSICAL CONDITIONING AND OPERANT CONDITIONING

Despite their differences, classical and operant conditioning share many similarities: Both involve associations between stimuli and responses; both are subject to extinction and spontaneous recovery as well as generalization and discrimination. In fact, many psychologists now question whether classical and operant conditioning are not simply two ways of bringing about the same kind of learning.

## COGNITIVE LEARNING

Both human and nonhuman animals also demonstrate **cognitive learning**, learning that is not tied to immediate experience by stimuli and reinforcers. Albert Bandura contends that **observational learning**—learning by watching others—accounts for many aspects of human learning. His highly influential theory of learning holds that although reinforcement is unrelated to learning itself, reinforcement may influence whether or not learned behavior is actually displayed. In general, cognitive theories of learning assert that learning is an ongoing process that proceeds independently of reinforcement.

### Latent Learning and Cognitive Maps

Early experiments by Edward Chace Tolman and other psychologists demonstrated that learning takes place even before the subject reaches the goal and occurs whether or not the learner is reinforced. Tolman proposed the concept of **latent learning**, which maintains that subjects store up knowledge even if this knowledge is not reflected in their behavior because it is not elicited by reinforcers. Later research suggested that latent learning is stored as a mental image, or **cognitive map**. When the proper time comes, the learner calls up this map and puts it to use.

### Insight and Learning Sets

One phenomenon that highlights the importance of cognitive processing in learning is **insight**, in which learning happens quickly and seems to occur in a "flash." Through insight learning, human and some nonhuman animals suddenly discover whole patterns of behavior or solutions to problems. **Learning sets** refer to the increasing effectiveness at problem solving that comes about as more problems are solved.

## LEARNING BY OBSERVING

**Social learning theory** argues that we learn not just from firsthand experience, but also from watching others or by hearing about something. Such **observational** or **vicarious learning** stresses the importance of models in our lives. To imitate a model's behavior, we must (1) pay attention to what the model does; (2) remember what the model did; and (3) convert what we learned from the model into action. **Social cognitive theory** emphasizes that learning a behavior from observing others does not necessarily lead to performing that behavior. We are more likely to imitate behaviors we have seen rewarded.

## COGNITIVE LEARNING IN NONHUMANS

Research has demonstrated that nonhuman animals can be classically conditioned, that they can be taught to perform whole patterns of operant behaviors, and that they are capable of latent learning. All this evidence lends support to the argument that nonhuman animals use cognitive processing in learning.

# REVIEW QUESTIONS

## MULTIPLE CHOICE

1. The simplest type of learning is called ______ . It refers to the establishment of fairly predictable behavior in the presence of well-defined stimuli.

2. For the most effective learning in classical conditioning, should the conditioned stimulus (CS) be presented before or after the unconditioned stimulus (US)?

3. To extinguish classical conditioning, you must break the association between which pair?
   a. CS and US
   b. US and UR
   c. US and CR

4. Recent work indicates that a CS must provide ______ about the US.

5. After extinction and a period of rest, a CS may again elicit a CR; this phenomenon is known as ______ ______ .

6. The process by which a learned response to a specific stimulus comes to be associated with different but similar stimuli is known as ______ .

7. A type of learning that essentially involves reinforcing the desired response is known as ______ .

8. In the technique called ______ , a new response is acquired by successively reinforcing partial responses.

9. Which kind of conditioning technique is administered when an aversive stimulus is turned off?
   a. positive reinforcement
   b. negative reinforcement
   c. positive punishment
   d. negative punishment

10. Classify the following as (1) primary or (2) secondary reinforcers:
_____ food _____ diploma
_____ money _____ sex

11. You offer your two roommates a box of their favorite cookies each time they leave the room clean. What type of conditioning technique are you using?
a. positive reinforcement
b. negative reinforcement
c. stimulus generalization
d. punishment

12. You like to listen to loud music when you are at your parents' home. If you turn off the music only when your parents offer you money to go to the movies, what type of conditioning technique are you experiencing?
a. positive reinforcement
b. negative reinforcement
c. stimulus generalization
d. punishment

13. Identify the following schedules of reinforcement as (FI) fixed interval, (VI) variable interval, (FR) fixed ratio, or (VR) variable ratio:
_____ The subject is reinforced on the first correct response after 2 minutes have passed since the last reinforcement.
_____ The subject is reinforced on every sixth correct response.
_____ The subject is reinforced after four correct responses, then after six more correct responses, then after five more correct responses.
_____ The subject is reinforced on the first correct response after 3 minutes have passed since the last reinforcement, then the first correct response after 6 minutes since reinforcement, then the first correct response after 5 minutes since reinforcement.

14. Unreinforced, or latent, learning may be stored internally. Particularly when this learning concerns spatial relationships, it is stored as_____ _____ .

15. An ape examines a problem and the tools available for solving it. Suddenly, the animal leaps up and quickly executes a successful solution. This is an example of
a. insight
b. operant conditioning
c. trial-and-error learning

16. Which of the following factors have been identified by contingency theorists as necessary for learning?
a. a CS that provides new information about the likelihood of the US occurring
b. strong reinforcement
c. blocking

17. According to social learning theorists, what is the source of reinforcement?
a. internal standards of behavior
b. external rewards
c. both a and b

18. _____ is likely to happen whether we see someone else punished or rewarded for behavior.

19. _____ occurs when we see someone else punished for a behavior.

20. What kinds of evidence indicate that all learning is cognitive?

## CRITICAL THINKING AND APPLICATIONS

21. If you imagine biting into a large dill pickle or a slice of lemon, you might notice that your mouth puckers and that you secrete saliva. Use classical conditioning principles to explain this phenomenon.

22. Many people dread going to the dentist. How would classical conditioning explain this?

23. Explain how a sound—a siren, for example—could be a conditioned stimulus for fear on the one hand and for relief on the other.

24. Think about your daily schedule. What kinds of things do you do every day that can be called "operant behaviors"?

25. Imagine that you want to keep your dog from barking and annoying the neighbors. What kind of reinforcement would you use to do this? How would you use the principles of extinction to do this?

26. Describe a cognitive map that you use in your daily activities. Were you reinforced for learning it? For navigating it correctly?

27. What kinds of skills might be taught best through observational learning rather than through operant learning? Why would observational learning be better in the examples you cite?

*(Answers to the Review Questions can be found in the back of the text.)*

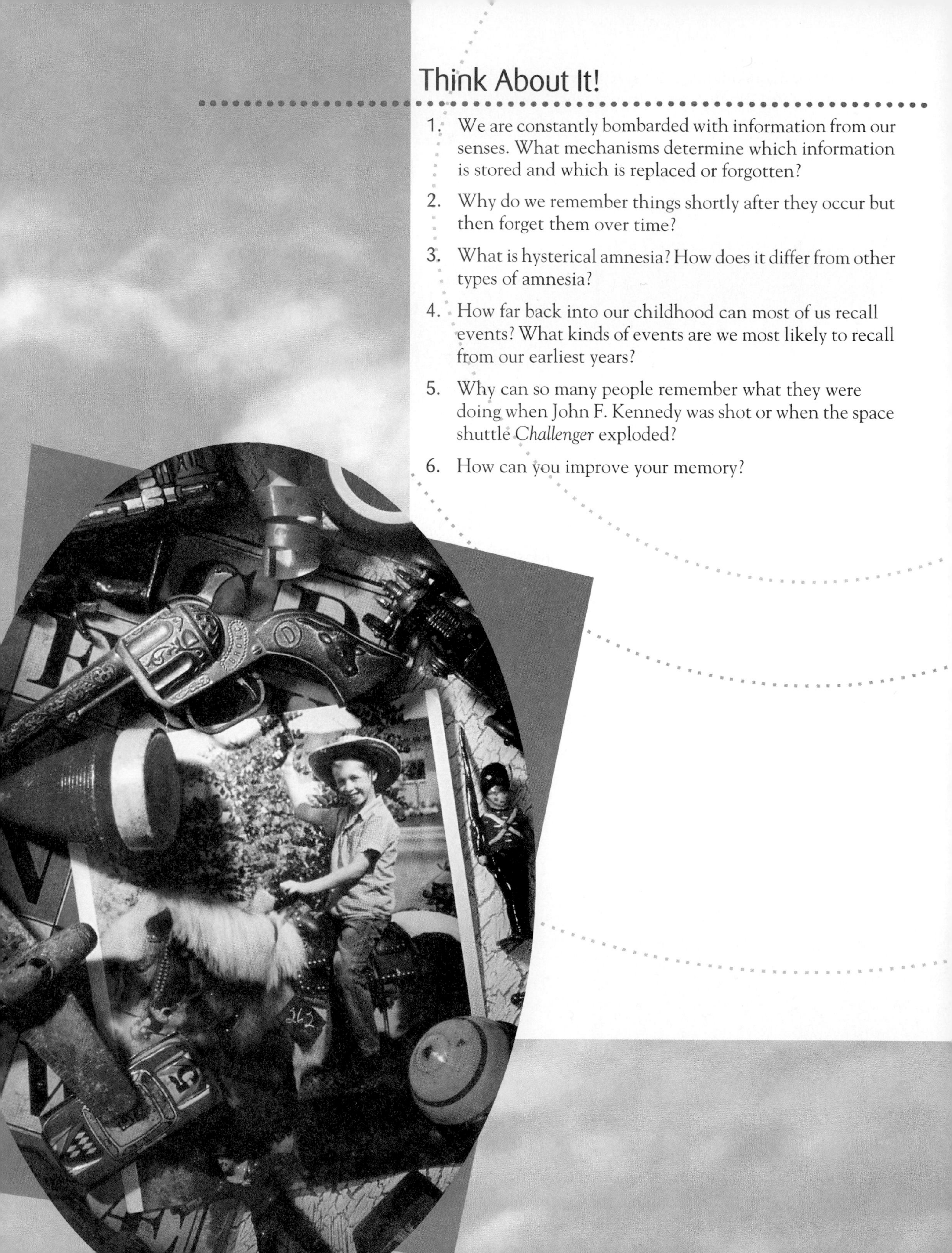

## Think About It!

1. We are constantly bombarded with information from our senses. What mechanisms determine which information is stored and which is replaced or forgotten?
2. Why do we remember things shortly after they occur but then forget them over time?
3. What is hysterical amnesia? How does it differ from other types of amnesia?
4. How far back into our childhood can most of us recall events? What kinds of events are we most likely to recall from our earliest years?
5. Why can so many people remember what they were doing when John F. Kennedy was shot or when the space shuttle *Challenger* exploded?
6. How can you improve your memory?

Mem ention Mnemonics ata Interference ia Chunking R

# MEMORY

# 6

## Overview

**We tend to take memory for granted. Only when confronted with people whose memories are exceptional do we begin to realize how much we rely on this multifacted mental faculty.**

- The world-renowned conductor Arturo Toscanini memorized every single note written for every instrument in some 250 symphonies and all the music and lyrics for more than 100 operas. Once, when he could not locate a score of Joachim Raff's Quartet No. 5, he sat down and reproduced it purely from memory—even though he had not seen or played the score for decades. When a copy of the quartet was finally found, people were astonished to discover that with the exception of a single note, Toscanini had reproduced it perfectly (Neisser, 1982).

- A waiter named John Conrad routinely handled parties of 6 to 8 in a busy Colorado restaurant, remembering every order from soup to salad dressing. He once waited on a party of 19, serving 19 complete dinners to his customers without a single error (Singular, 1982).

- Before being stricken with a viral illness, a 29-year-old woman known as MZ told researchers she could remember "the exact day of the week of future or past events of almost anything that touched my life . . . all personal telephone numbers . . . colors of interiors and what people wore . . . pieces of music . . . . recalling a picture, as a painting in a museum, was like standing in the museum looking at it again" (Klatzky, 1980).

These accounts of people with extraordinary memories raise numerous questions about the nature of memory itself. Why are some people so much better at remembering things than others? Are they simply born with good memories, or do they hone the skill of precise recall? Could any of us learn to remember as much as these people do? And why is it that remembering may sometimes be so simple (think how effortlessly baseball fans remember the batting averages of their favorite players) and other times so difficult (as when we grope for answers on an exam)? Why do we find it so hard to remember something that happened only a few months back, yet we can recall in vivid detail some other event that happened 10, 20, even 30 years ago? Just how does memory work, and what makes it fail? We will explore all these and other questions about memory in this chapter.

Scientific research on memory began in the middle of the nineteenth century when psychology was still considered a branch of philosophy. Hermann Ebbinghaus, a German psychologist, designed the first memory experiments with well-defined independent and dependent variables and controls for other factors. Although he studied only his own memory processes, many of his findings have since been confirmed by other experimenters (Slamecka, 1985).

Ebbinghaus composed lists of "nonsense syllables" (meaningless combinations of a consonant, a vowel, and then another consonant, such as PIB and WOL). He memorized lists of 13 nonsense syllables each until he could recite each list perfectly. After varying amounts of time, he then tried to relearn the syllables on each list. As you might expect, Ebbinghaus noted that the longer he waited after first learning a list, the more he forgot (that is, the longer it took him to relearn that list). However, he also found that this memory loss did not progress at a steady rate: He lost the most information in the first few hours; after that, his memory tended to level out, as shown in the learning curve in Figure 6-1.

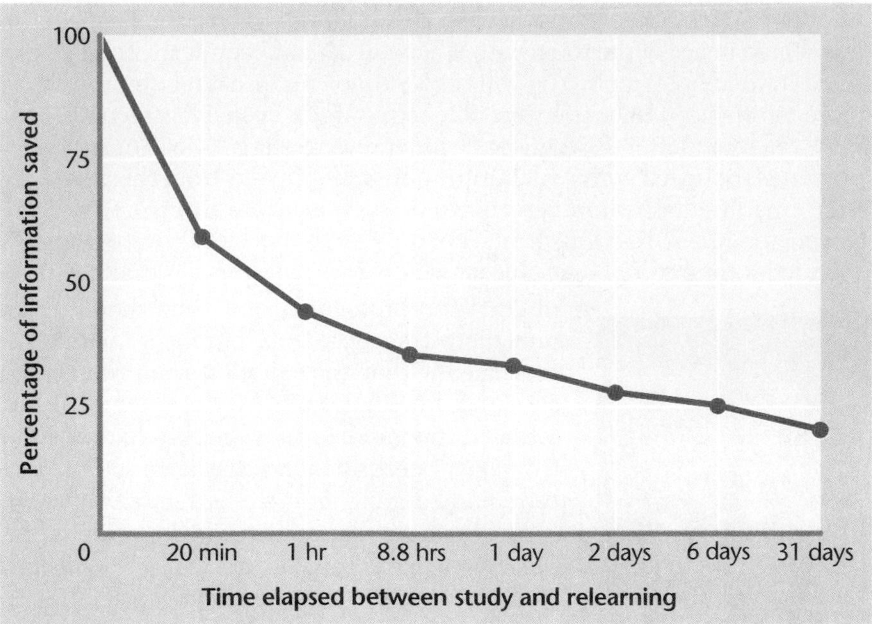


**Figure 6-1**
**The learning curve from Ebbinghaus's experiment.** Ebbinghaus found that the amount of previously learned material that could be retrieved decreased systematically over time, but not at a steady rate.

**Sensory registers** Entry points for raw information from the senses.

While Ebbinghaus's contributions dominated memory research for many years, more recently psychologists have adopted an information-processing approach to studying memory (Massaro & Cowan, 1993), which views memory as a series of stages. Vast amounts of information continually bombard our senses, and we cannot process all of it. So the first stage of information processing involves selecting some of this information to think about and, if appropriate, to remember.

## THE SENSORY REGISTERS

If you look slowly around the room, you will see that each glance—which may last for only a fraction of a second—takes in an enormous amount of visual information, including colors, shapes, textures, relative brightness, and shadows. At the same time, you pick up sounds, smells, and other kinds of sensory data. All this raw information flows from your senses into what are known as the **sensory registers**. These registers are like waiting rooms in which information enters and stays for only a short time. Whether we remember any of this information depends on which operations we perform on it, as you will see throughout this chapter. Although there are registers for each of our senses, the visual and auditory registers have been studied most extensively, and therefore we begin with them.

We are constantly bombarded with information from our senses. What mechanisms determine which information is stored and which is replaced or forgotten?

### Visual and Auditory Registers

Although the sensory registers have virtually unlimited capacity (Cowan, 1988), information disappears from them quite rapidly. To understand how much visual information we take in, and how quickly it is lost, bring an instant camera into a darkened room and take a photograph using a flash. During the split second that the room is lit up by the flash, your visual register will absorb a surprising amount of information about the room and its contents. Try to hold on to that visual image, or *icon*, as long as you can. You will find that it fades rapidly, in a few seconds it is gone. Then compare your remembered image of the room with what you actually saw at the time, as captured in the photograph. You will notice that your visual register took in far more information than you were able to retain for even a few seconds.

A clever set of experiments by George Sperling (1960) clearly demonstrates the speed with which information disappears from the visual register. Sperling flashed groups of letters, such as those in Figure 6-2, on a screen for just a fraction of a second. When the letters were gone, he sounded a tone to tell his subjects which row of letters to recall: A high-pitched tone indicated that they should try to remember the top row of letters, a low-pitched tone meant that they should recall the bottom row, and a medium-pitched tone signaled them to recall the middle row. Using this *partial-report technique*, Sperling found that if he sounded the tone immediately after the letters were flashed, his subjects could usually recall 3 or 4 of the letters in any of the three rows; that is, they seemed to have at least 9 of the original 12 letters in their visual registers. But if he waited for even 1 second before sounding the tone, his subjects were able to recall only 1 or 2 letters from any single row—in just 1 second, then, all but 4 or 5 of the original set of 12 letters had vanished from their visual registers.

Visual information may actually disappear from the visual register even more rapidly than Sperling thought (Cowan, 1988). In everyday life, new visual information keeps coming into

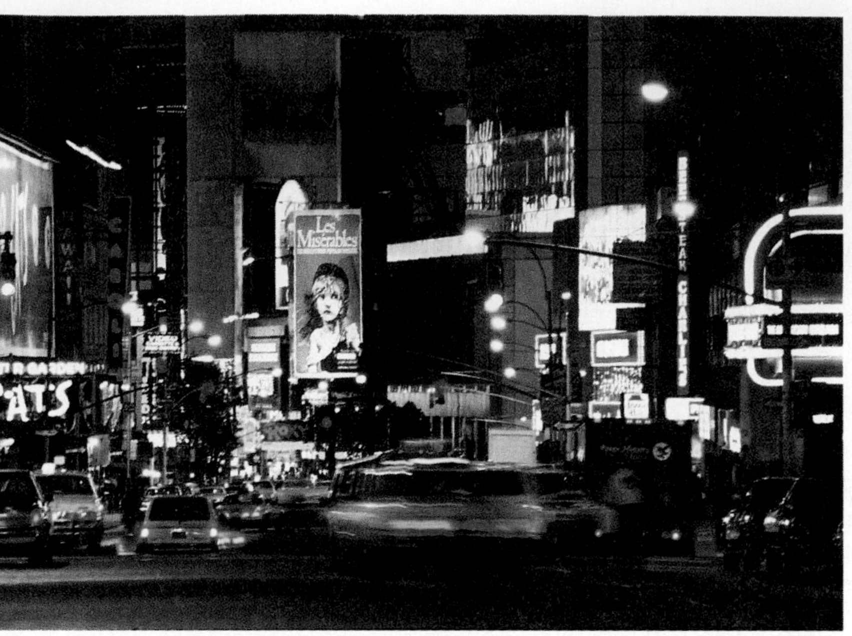


While our *sensory registers* constantly take in an enormous amount of visual and other sensory information, we rely on the element of *attention*—the process of sensing selectively and giving meaning to incoming sensory information—to help us function and make sense of our experiences.

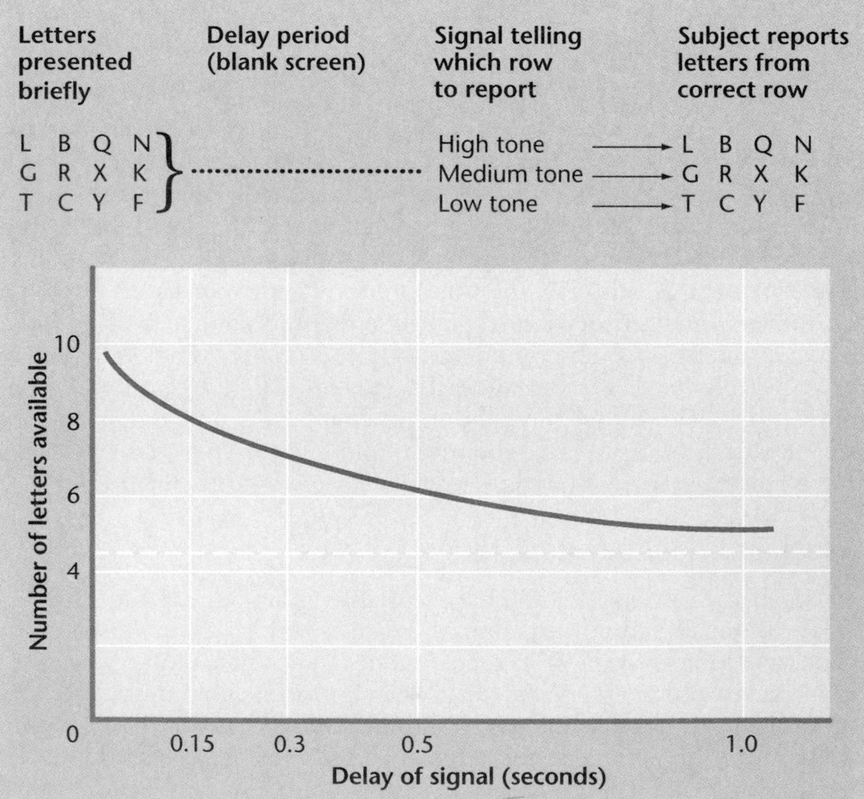


**Figure 6-2**
**Sperling's partial-report technique** is illustrated at the top; the results are given in the graph. The longer the signal was delayed, the more the number of recalled letters decreased.

the register, and this new information replaces the old information almost immediately, a process often called *masking*. This is just as well, because otherwise the visual information would simply pile up in the sensory register and get hopelessly scrambled. Under normal viewing conditions, visual information is erased from the sensory register in about a quarter of a second and is replaced by new information long before it would have a chance to fade out by itself.

Auditory information fades more slowly than visual information. The auditory equivalent of the icon, the *echo*, tends to last for several seconds, which, given the nature of speech, is certainly fortunate for us. Otherwise, "*You* did it!" would be indistinguishable from "You *did* it!" because we would be unable to remember the emphasis on the first words by the time the last words were registered.

**Attention** Selection of some incoming information for further processing.

## Initial Processing

If information disappears from the sensory registers so rapidly, how do we remember anything for more than a second or two? One way we select some of the incoming information for further processing is called **attention** (see Figure 6-3). Attention is the process of selective looking, listening, smelling, tasting, and feeling. In the process of attending, we also give *meaning* to the information that is coming in. Look at the page in front of you. You will see a series of black lines on a white page. Until you recognize these lines as letters and words, they are just meaningless marks. For you to make sense of this jumble of data, the information in the sensory registers must be processed for meaning.

How do we select what we are going to pay attention to at any given moment, and how do we give that information meaning? Donald Broadbent (1958) suggested that a filtering process at the entrance to the nervous system allows only those stimuli that meet certain requirements to pass through. Those stimuli that get through the filter are compared with what we already know, so that we can recognize them and figure out what they mean. If you and a friend are sitting in a restaurant talking, you filter out all other conversations taking place around you, a practice known as

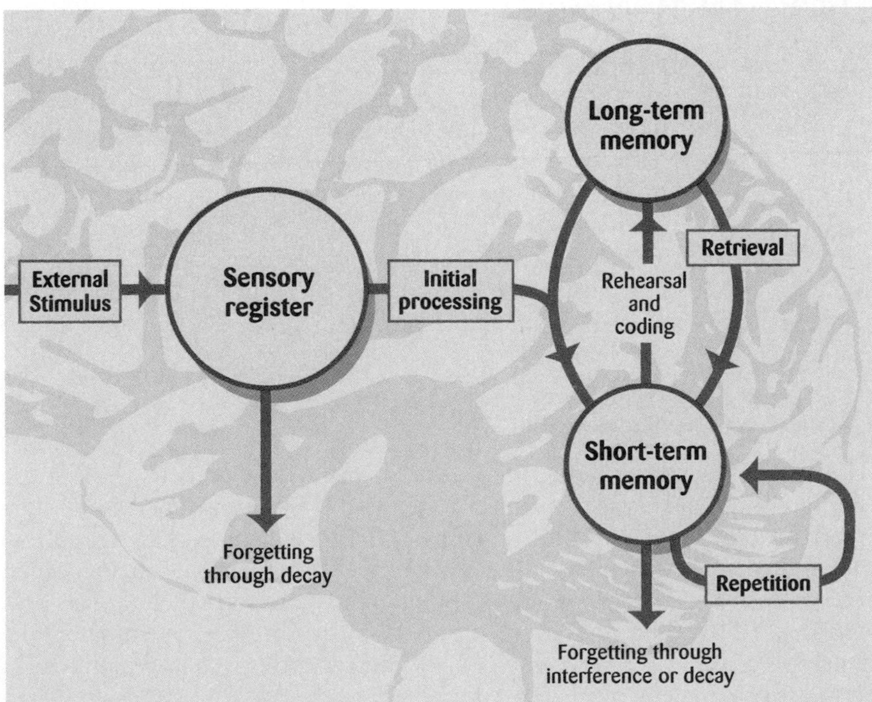


**Figure 6-3**
**The sequence of information processing in explicit memory.**
Raw information flows from the senses into the *sensory registers*, where it is processed in terms of existing knowledge and information. Information that is determined to be meaningful is passed on for further processing in *short-term memory*; the rest is discarded. Once in short-term memory, information is either forgotten or transferred into *long-term memory*, where it can be stored and retrieved when necessary.

**Short-term memory (STM)** Working memory; briefly stores and processes selected information from the sensory registers.

the *cocktail-party phenomenon* (Cherry, 1966). Although you might be able to describe certain characteristics of those other conversations, such as whether the people speaking were men or women and whether the words were spoken loudly or softly, according to Broadbent you normally would not be able to recount what was being discussed, even at neighboring tables. Because you filtered out those other conversations, processing of that information did not reach the point at which you could understand the meaning of what you heard.

While Broadbent's filtering theory helps explain some aspects of attention, sometimes unattended stimuli capture our attention nonetheless. To return to the restaurant example, if someone around you were to mention your name, in all likelihood your attention would shift to that conversation. Anne Treisman (1960, 1964) modified the filter theory to account for phenomena like this. She contended that the filter is not a simple on/off switch but rather a variable control, like the volume control on a radio, that can "turn down" unwanted signals without rejecting them entirely. According to this view, although we may be paying attention to only some incoming information, we monitor the other signals at a low volume. In this way, we can shift our attention if we pick up something particularly meaningful. This automatic processing works even when we are asleep: Parents often wake up immediately when they hear the baby crying, but sleep through other, louder noises. Similarly, most of us would jump out of a sound sleep if we heard the words "The house is on fire," but we would probably snooze through less important phrases like "The car is for sale."

To summarize, we consciously attend to very little of the information in our sensory registers; instead, we select some information and process those signals further as we work to recognize and understand them. However, unattended information receives at least some initial processing, so that we can shift our attention to focus on any element of our surroundings that strikes us as potentially meaningful.

But what happens to the information that we do attend to? It enters our short-term memory.

## SHORT-TERM MEMORY

**Short-term memory (STM)** holds the information we are thinking about or are aware of at any given moment (Stern, 1985). It was originally called *primary memory* by William James (1890; Waugh & Norman, 1960). When you listen to a conversation or a piece of music, when you watch a ballet or a tennis tournament, when you become aware of a leg cramp or a headache—in all these cases, you are using STM both to hold on to and to think about new information coming in from the sensory registers. STM therefore has two primary tasks: to store new information briefly and to work on that (and other) information. Thus, STM is sometimes called *working memory* (Baddeley, 1986).

### Capacity of STM

The arcade fanatic absorbed in a video game is oblivious to the outside world. Chess masters at tournaments demand complete silence while they ponder their next move. You shut yourself in a quiet room to study for final exams. All these examples illustrate that STM can handle only so much information at any given moment. Some forty years ago psychologists posited that STM could hold at most 5 to 10 bits of information at the same time (Miller, 1956; Sperling, 1960). More recently, researchers have asserted that it may be more accurate to say that STM can hold as much information as can be repeated or rehearsed in 1.5 to 2 seconds (Baddeley, 1986; Schweickert & Boruff, 1986).

To get a better idea of the limits of STM, read the first row of letters in the following list just once. Then close your eyes and try to remember the letters in the correct sequence before going on to the next row:

**Chunking** Grouping of information into meaningful units for easier handling by short-term memory.

1. C X W
2. M N K T Y
3. R P J H B Z S
4. G B M P V Q F J D
5. E G Q W J P B R H K A

Like most people, you probably found rows 1 and 2 fairly easy, row 3 a bit harder, row 4 extremely difficult, and row 5 impossible to remember after just one reading. This gives you an idea of the relatively limited capacity of STM.

Now try reading through the following set of 12 letters just once and see if you can repeat them: TJYFAVMCFKIB. How many letters were you able to recall? In all likelihood, not all 12. But what if you had been asked to remember the following 12 letters instead: TV FBI JFK YMCA. Could you do it? Almost certainly the answer is yes. These are the same 12 letters as before but here they are grouped into four separate "words." This way of grouping and organizing information so that it fits into meaningful units is called **chunking**. The 12 letters have been chunked into four meaningful elements that can readily be handled by STM—they are well below the 5-10-item limit of STM, and they can be repeated in less than 2 seconds. Here's another example of chunking. Try to remember this list of numbers:

1 0 6 6 1 9 4 5 1 8 1 2

Remembering 12 separate digits is usually very difficult, but try chunking the list into three groups of four:

1066 1945 1812

For those who take an interest in military history, these three chunks will be much easier to remember than 12 unrelated digits.

By chunking words into sentences or sentence fragments, we can process an even greater amount of information in STM (Tulving & Patkau, 1962; Aaronson & Scarborough, 1976, 1977). For example, suppose you want to remember the following list of words: *tree, song, hat, sparrow, box, lilac, cat*. One strategy would be to cluster as many of them as possible into phrases or sentences: "The sparrow in the tree sings a song"; "a lilac hat in the box"; "the cat in the hat." But isn't there a limit to this strategy? Would five sentences be as easy to remember for a short time as five single words? Simon (1974) found that as the size of any individual chunk increases, the number of chunks that can be held in STM declines. Thus, STM can easily handle five unrelated letters or words simultaneously, but five unrelated sentences are much harder to remember.

Data such as these lend support to the view that the limit of STM might better be conceived as a 2-second limit rather than a 5-to-10-item limit: In both cases, there are only five items of information to be remembered, but it takes longer to repeat five sentences than it does to repeat five words. If there is a 5-to-10-item limit on STM, the sentences should be just as easy to remember as the individual words. But if there is a 2-second limit on information in STM, the sentences should be more difficult to remember than the individual words—and this is what research confirms.

A dramatic example of the power of chunking was reported by Chase and Ericsson (1981). The subject in this case, known as SF, was a young man who had spent more than 250 hours in the laboratory over 2 years, purposefully using chunking to increase his short-term memory for strings of digits. At the time of the report, SF could accurately recall strings of more than 80 digits. He accomplished this feat by associating groups of digits with his already vast knowledge of common and record times for running races of particular lengths. The digit string 3492 might be broken out, for instance, as a chunk associated with a near-record time for the mile, 3 minutes, 49.2 seconds. SF, by the way, was no better than average at remembering strings that he could not relate to running, such as strings of letters.

Keep in mind that STM usually has more than one task to perform at once. During the brief time you spent memorizing the rows of letters on page 207, you probably gave them your full attention. But normally, you have to attend to new incoming information while you work on whatever is already present in short-term memory. Competition between these two tasks for the limited work space in STM means that neither task will be done as well as it could be. In one experiment, subjects were given 6 random numbers to remember and repeat while performing a simple reasoning task. As a result, they performed their reasoning task more slowly than subjects who had simply been asked to repeat the numbers 1 through 6 throughout the task (Baddeley & Hitch, 1974). Similarly, if you had been asked to count backward from 100 while trying to learn the rows of letters in our earlier example, you would have been much less successful in remembering them. Try it and see.

## Coding in STM

Just how do we *code* information for storage in STEM? This question has sparked controversy for years. Research confirms that strings of letters or numbers are stored *phonologically* in STM, that is, in a manner based on speech (Baddeley, 1986). In other words, we code verbal information according to how it sounds even if we see the word, letter, or number on a page rather than hear it spoken. Numerous experiments have shown that when people try to retrieve material from STM, they generally mix up items that sound alike and that are spoken alike, even if they are visually dissimilar (Sperling, 1960). Moreover, words that sound alike and are pronounced alike are often confused in STM. For example, a list of words such as *mad, man, mat, cap* is much tougher for most people to recall accurately than is a list like *pit, day, cow, bar* (Baddeley, 1986).

But not all material in short-term memory is stored phonologically. At least some material is stored in visual form, while other information is retained based on its meaning (Cowan, 1988; Matlin, 1989). For example, we don't have to convert visual data like maps, diagrams, and paintings into sound before we can code them into STM and think about them. And, of course, deaf people rely primarily on shapes rather than sounds to retain information in STM (Conrad, 1972; Frumkin & Ainsfield, 1977). In fact, it appears that the capacity for visual coding in STM actually exceeds that for phonological coding (Reed, 1992). A good illustration of the superiority of visual coding in STM is an experiment done by Nielsen and Smith (1973). They asked subjects to pay close attention either to a verbal description of a face or to an actual picture of a face for 4 seconds. The subjects were then asked to match features of a test face with the features they had just seen or heard described. Because it took much longer to recognize the face from the verbal description ("large ears," "small eyes," etc.), researchers concluded that visual images tend to be more efficiently coded and decoded than verbal ones.

**Decay theory** A theory that argues that the passage of time causes forgetting.

**Interference theory** A theory that argues that interference from other information causes forgetting.

## Retention and Retrieval in STM

Why do we forget material stored in short-term memory? According to the **decay theory**, the mere passing of time causes the strength of memory to decrease, thereby making the material harder to remember. Most of the evidence supporting the decay theory comes from experiments known as *distracter studies*. For example, Peterson and Peterson (1959) gave subjects a sequence of letters to learn, like PSQ. Then subjects were given a 3-digit number, such as 167. They were then asked to count backwards from 167 by threes: 167, 164, 161, and so on, for up to 18 seconds. At the end of that period, they were asked to recall the three letters. The results of this test astonished the experimenters. The subjects showed a rapid decline in their ability to remember the letters (see Figure 6-4). Counting backwards was assumed *not* to interfere with remembering, so the researchers could only account for the forgotten letters by noting that they had simply faded from short-term memory in a matter of seconds. Decay, then, seems to be at least partly responsible for forgetting in short-term memory.

2. Why do we remember things shortly after they occur but then forget them over time?

In subsequent studies, Shiffrin and Cook (1978) found that interference may also lead to forgetting in STM. In contrast to decay theory, **interference theory** holds that information gets mixed up with, or pushed aside by, other information and thus becomes harder to remember. Some of this forgetting may be due simply to the limited capacity of STM, as new information pushes out old. This process is most pronounced, however, when

**Figure 6-4**
**The results of Peterson and Peterson's (1959) distracter study.**
The experiment measured the length of time that short-term memory lasts without rehearsal. Subjects showed a rapid decline in their ability to remember a sequence of letters.

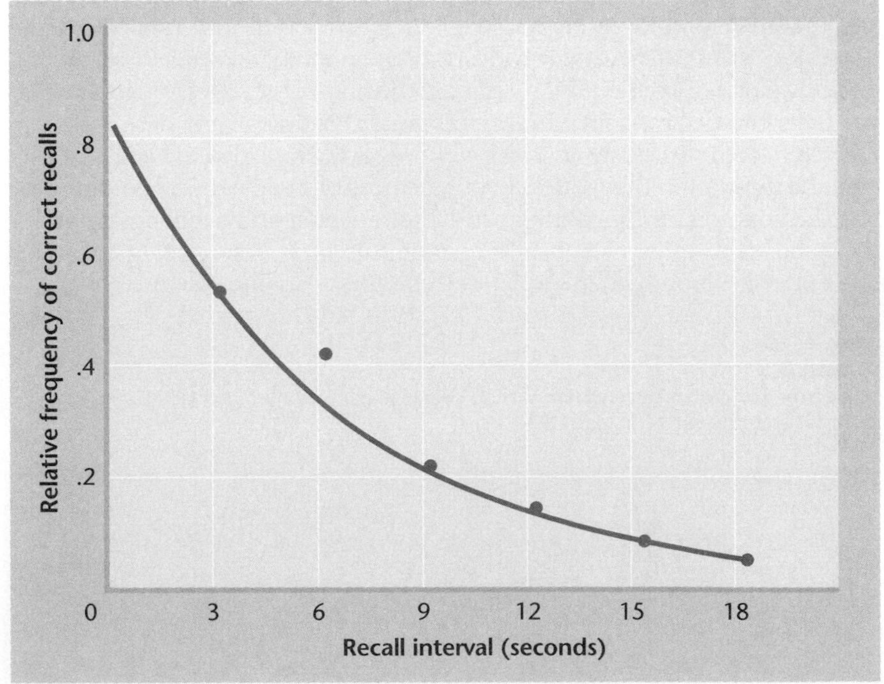

**Rote rehearsal** Retaining information in STM simply by repeating it over and over.

the new information resembles the old in some way. If you are counting items, keeping a running total in your head, or repeating a phone number over and over to remember it, you may not lose your train of thought if some friends start talking to you about the beautiful poem they have just read. But if, someone begins counting another set of items or calls your attention to some other group of numbers, you will quickly become confused about which set of digits was yours.

Now, without looking back, try to recall the five rows of letters you learned on page 207. In all likelihood, you will not be able to remember them. That's because material in short-term memory disappears in 15 to 20 seconds unless it is rehearsed or practiced (Bourne et al., 1986).

It is probably just as well that we lose much of what is initially stored in STM. Not only does this process provide space in STM for new information, but it keeps us from being overwhelmed with a jumble of irrelevant, trivial, or unrelated data. In this sense, loss of information from STM is usually not a "problem." However, sometimes we want to hold on to some information for a bit longer than 15 or 20 seconds, and at other times we want to remember a new piece of information permanently. How do we guard against forgetting in these cases?

## Rote Rehearsal

If you want to hold on to information for just a minute or two, the most effective way to do this is through **rote rehearsal**, also called *maintenance rehearsal* (Greene, 1987), meaning you talk to yourself, repeating information over and over, silently or out loud. Although this is hardly the most efficient way to remember something permanently, it can be quite effective for a short time. In fact, if you repeat something to yourself long enough, but cannot recall it later, you may still recognize the information when you hear or use it again. If you look up a telephone number and then 20 minutes later you are asked, "What was that telephone number?" you are not likely to recall it. But if someone asks instead, "Were you dialing 555-1356?" you might recognize the number if you had repeated it often enough (Glenberg, Smith, & Green, 1977).

Rote rehearsal—simply repeating material over and over—is a very common memory strategy. Millions of students have learned the alphabet and multiplication tables by doggedly repeating letters and numbers. Mere repetition without any intent to learn does enhance subsequent recall, but not very much (Greene, 1987). Think of the number of times in your life that you have handled (and presumably recognized) pennies. Stop here and try to draw from memory the front side of a U.S. penny. Now look at Figure 6-5 and pick the illustration that matches your memory of a real penny. For most people, this task is surprisingly difficult: Despite seeing and exchanging tens of thousands of pennies, most people cannot accurately draw one, or even pick one out from among other, similar objects (Nickerson & Adams, 1979).

Rote rehearsal—simply repeating material over and over—is a very common memory strategy. Repetition without any intent to learn, however, does not enhance memory.

**Figure 6-5**
**A penny for your thoughts.** Which of these accurately illustrates a real U.S. penny? The answer is on page 211.

### Elaborative Rehearsal

If simple rote repetition is not sufficient, what do we have to do to ensure that information in STM will be remembered for a long time? Most researchers believe that we need to practice **elaborative rehearsal** (Postman, 1975), a method of relating new information to something that we already know. Suppose that you had to remember that the French word *poire* means *pear*. You are already familiar with *pear*, both as a word and as a fruit. *Poire*, however, means nothing to you. To remember what it means, you have to connect it to *pear*, either by telling yourself that "*pear* and *poire* both begin with p, or by associating *poire* with the familiar taste and image of a *pear*."

You can see that elaborative rehearsal calls for a deeper and more meaningful processing of new data than does simple rote repetition (Craik & Lockhart, 1972). Unless material gets rehearsed in this way, it will probably be forgotten quickly. For example, consider what happens when elaborative rehearsal is either interrupted or prevented. Frequently, people in accidents who suffer concussions cannot recall events just before the injury even though they can remember what happened some time earlier. This condition is known as **retrograde amnesia**. The events right before the accident were at the short-term memory level and had not been rehearsed enough to be remembered for more than a short time. Thus, they were forgotten.

Another example of rehearsal failure is probably more familiar to you. Have you ever been in a group where people were taking turns speaking up—perhaps on the first day of class when all present are asked to introduce themselves briefly, or at the beginning of a panel discussion when the speakers are asked to do the same in front of a large audience? Did you notice that you forgot virtually everything that was said by the person who spoke just before you did? According to recent research, your failure to remember was due to the fact that you did not elaboratively rehearse what that person was saying (Bond, Pitre, & Van Leeuwen, 1991). As the time for your own introduction approached, your attention shifted increasingly to what you yourself were going to say, and as a result you spent little or no time elaboratively rehearsing what the person before you was saying. That person's comments simply "went in one ear and out the other" while you were preoccupied with thinking about your own remarks.

Elaborative rehearsal is crucial to future recall. But before we delve further into understanding the nature of this process, we need to know more about long-term memory. By the way, the accurate illustration of a penny in Figure 6-5 is the third from the left.

## LONG-TERM MEMORY

Everything that we "know" is stored in **long-term memory (LTM)**: the words to a popular song; the results of the last election; the meaning of "justice"; the fact that George Washington was the first president of the United States; the meaning of abbreviations such as TV, FBI, JFK, and YMCA; what you ate for dinner last night; the date you were born; and what you are supposed to be doing tomorrow at 4 P.M. Endel Tulving (1972, 1985) of the University of Toronto contended that LTM should be divided into separate *memory systems*. One system, called **semantic memory**, is much like a dictionary or encyclopedia, filled with general facts and information, such as the first five examples in this paragraph. When you see the words *George Washington*, you call up all sorts of additional information from LTM: 1776, the first president, Father of Our

**Elaborative rehearsal** The linking of new information in short-term memory to familiar material stored in long-term memory.

**Retrograde amnesia** The inability to recall events immediately preceding an accident or injury, but without loss of earlier memory.

**Long-term memory (LTM)** Portion of memory that is more or less permanent corresponding to everything we "know."

**Semantic memory** Portion of long-term memory that stores general facts and information.

**Episodic memory** Portion of long-term memory that stores more specific information that has personal meaning.

Country, Mt. Vernon, crossing the Delaware, a holiday in February. This kind of information is stored in semantic memory. Still other information in LTM is more personal and specific. This personal memory system known as **episodic memory** (Tulving, 1972, 1985), encompasses specific events that have personal meaning for us, like the last three examples that began this paragraph. If we compare semantic memory to an encyclopedia or dictionary, episodic memory can be viewed more like a diary, although it may also include events in which you did not participate but that are still important to you. Episodic memory lets you "go back in time" to a childhood birthday party, to the day you were in a car accident, to the story of how your parents met, to the great time you had with your best friend last President's Day.

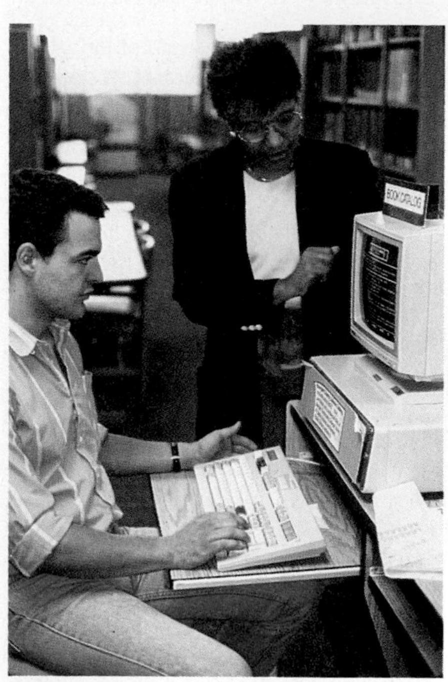


Information in LTM is highly organized and cross-referenced, like a cataloguing system in a library. The more carefully we organize information, the better the chance that we can retrieve it later.

## Coding in LTM

Can you picture the shape of Florida? Do you know what a trumpet sounds like? Can you imagine the smell of a rose or the taste of coffee? When you answer the telephone, can you sometimes identify the caller immediately, just from the sound of the voice? Your ability to do most or all these things means that at least some long-term memories are coded in terms of nonverbal images: shapes, sounds, smells, tastes, and so on (Cowan, 1988).

Yet most of the information in LTM seems to be coded in terms of meaning. If material is especially familiar (the national anthem, say, or the opening of the Gettysburg Address), you may have stored it verbatim in LTM, and oftentimes you can retrieve it word for word when you need it. Generally speaking, however, we do not use verbatim storage in LTM. If someone tells you a long, rambling story, complete with flashbacks, you may listen to every word, but you certainly will not try to remember the story verbatim. Instead, you will extract the main points of the story and try to remember those. Even simple sentences are usually coded in terms of their meaning. Thus, when people are asked to remember that "Tom called John," they often find it impossible to remember later whether they were told "Tom called John" or "John was called by Tom." They usually remember the meaning of the message but not the exact words (Bourne et al., 1986).

Information in STM gets transferred to LTM if it is rehearsed. Through elaborative rehearsal, you extract the meaning of the information and then link the new information to as much of the material already in LTM as possible. The more links or associations you can make, the more likely you are to remember the new information later, just as it is easier to find a book in the library if it is catalogued under many headings rather than just one or two. This is one reason we tend to remember semantic material better than episodic material: Episodic material is quickly dated; we code fewer cross-references for it. For instance, you may remember that you ate a hamburger last night, but normally there is no good reason to relate that piece of information to anything else in LTM, so it is not something you are likely to remember for very long. But if you had been a vegetarian for years and found the very thought of eating beef repulsive, then eating that hamburger was a very meaningful event, and it is probably linked to all kinds of other facts in your LTM. As a result, you are unlikely to forget it for quite some time.

We have been talking as if there were only one kind of elaborative rehearsal, but in fact there are many different ways of rehearsing material. Think for a moment about how you might study for an examination in this course. If you expected a multiple-choice test, the way you would study is likely to be quite different than if you expected a fill-in-the-blank or short-answer test. And if the professor promised to ask you essay questions, you would undoubtedly shift your approach to the task of studying. Research confirms that the way we encode material for storage in LTM affects the ease with which we can retrieve it later on (Flexser & Tulving, 1978; Leonard & Whitten, 1983). We will examine this principle in greater detail later in the chapter when we look at how to improve memory.

**Explicit memory** Memory for information that was intentionally committed to memory or intentionally retrieved from memory.

**Implicit memory** Memory for information that either was unintentionally committed to memory or was unintentionally retrieved from memory.

## Implicit Memory

Most of the memories we've considered so far are things that you intended to remember, at least at one time. Psychologists call such memories **explicit memory**. But you also acquire a great deal of information that you never intended to remember. For example, have you ever misplaced something like a pair of eyeglasses and then retraced your steps in an effort to find it? "Let's see, I came in the door, put down my keys, then I went to the kitchen, where I put down the packages. . . ." And then you go to the kitchen and find your glasses, although you may not actually recall having left them there. Or perhaps you have had the experience of recalling exactly where on a page a particular piece of information appeared, even though you did not try to remember the item or its placement. If you stop to think about it, the fact that you have such memories is really quite remarkable. You made no deliberate effort to remember either of these things, yet in each case memories were apparently formed outside your awareness and without any conscious elaborative processing on your part (Cowan, 1988; Adler, 1990). Similarly, memories are sometimes called up spontaneously (Roediger, 1990). The smell of a particular perfume or the taste of a distinctive cake may bring back a flood of memories. In these cases, too, you first stored and then retrieved information without any conscious intention to do so. Moreover, the recall of stored information does not include any conscious awareness of the occasion when it was acquired. Psychologists call such unintentional memories **implicit memory** (Jacoby & Witherspoon, 1982; Graf & Schacter, 1985; Tulving & Schacter, 1990; Squire, Knowlton, & Musen, 1993).

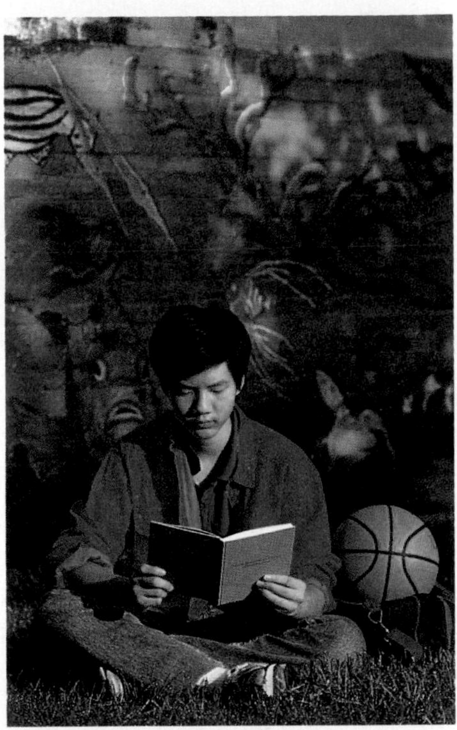

Understanding the concept of implicit memory can help us remember things we are trying to learn. For example, if this student imagines himself back in this setting while taking a test, he might recall more of the material he is now studying.

The importance of implicit memory might become clearer if you think about the following experiment. Schab (1990) presented a group of subjects with a list of 40 adjectives; he asked them to write down the opposite of each word and informed them that the next day he would ask them to recall the words they had written. The smell of chocolate permeated the air surrounding one group of students while they were writing their list of words. The next day, adding a chocolate smell to the air significantly increased the number of words these students recalled from the previous day. In other words, the smell of chocolate somehow became linked to the words they wrote, and the smell then became an effective cue or "hint" that helped them find and recall the correct words. Although this may seem odd, it happens all the time: Whenever we try (explicitly) to commit something to memory, we are also unintentionally (implicitly) picking up facts about the context in which the learning is taking place, and those facts, lodged in implicit memory, may serve as useful retrieval cues when we later try to retrieve the corresponding information from explicit memory.

Let's consider one way that implicit memory works in the world of medicine. It turns out that anesthesia blocks explicit memory but does not completely block implicit memory of events or verbal exchanges that occur during an operation. Patients who are put under general anesthesia have no conscious recall of events during surgery, but they do sometimes show indirect signs of remembering and responding to comments made while they were under anesthesia. In one study of this phenomenon, patients heard lists of word pairs while under general anesthesia (Kihlstrom et al., 1990). They had no explicit recall of the words on the lists, but later on when they were read one word from each pair and asked to say the first

## Summary Table

**Types of Memory**

| Type of Memory | Definition | Example |
|---|---|---|
| **Semantic memory** | Portion of long-term memory that stores general facts and information | Recalling the capital of Ohio |
| **Episodic memory** | Portion of long-term memory that stores specific information that has personal meaning | Recalling where you went on your first date |
| **Implicit memory** | Memory for information that either was not intentionally committed to memory or that is retrieved unintentionally from memory | Suddenly thinking of a friend's name without knowing why |

word that came to mind, they tended to report the other word in the pair more often than would be expected by chance.

Interestingly, people suffering from some forms of amnesia (which is a failure of explicit memory) have nothing wrong with their implicit memory (Graf, Squire, & Mandler, 1984; Graf, Shimamura, & Squire, 1985). Warrington and Weiskrantz (1970), for example, gave several people with amnesia a list of words to remember; when they asked these people to recall the words or pick them out of longer lists, they performed poorly, as one might expect. But when the experimenters showed the amnesia sufferers fragments of the words or just the first three letters of the words and asked them simply to guess what the word might be or to say the first thing that popped into their heads, they "remembered" just as many of the words on the list as did the control group, made up of people not suffering from amnesia. The researchers' conclusion: The amnesia victims had perfectly good (implicit) memories for words that they did not (explicitly) know they had heard!

Understanding the workings of implicit memory has concrete implications for everyday memory. Say you are having difficulty remembering something. If possible, return to the setting in which you first learned it; otherwise try to recreate the setting vividly in your mind in as much detail as possible, including the thoughts and feelings you were having at the time. Your implicit memory of the setting should help trigger your memory of the fact you are trying to recall.

### Storage and Retrieval in LTM

We saw earlier that information in short-term memory disappears in less than 20 seconds unless it is rehearsed. But at least some information placed in long-term memory does not disappear over time. In fact, under the proper circumstances, we can often dredge up an astonishing amount of information from LTM. In one study, for example, adults who had graduated from high school more than 40 years earlier were still able to recognize the names of 75 percent of their classmates (Bahrick, Bahrick, & Wittlinger, 1974). Not everything stored in LTM can be remembered when we need it, however. A classic example of this is the *tip-of-the-tongue phenomenon*, or *TOT* (Brown & McNeil, 1966). Everyone has had the experience of knowing a word but not quite being able to recall it. We say that such a word is "right on the tip of my tongue." If you want to experience TOT yourself, try naming the Seven Dwarfs (Meyer & Hilterbrand, 1984).

**Retroactive interference** Process by which new information interferes with old information already in memory.

**Proactive interference** Process by which old material already in memory interferes with new information.

The TOT phenomenon has several intriguing characteristics (R. Brown & McNeil, 1966; R. Brown, 1991). While everyone experiences TOTs, these experiences become more frequent during stressful situations and as people get older. Moreover, other words—with a sound or meaning similar to the word you are seeking—occur to you while you are in the TOT state. These words interfere with and sabotage your attempt to recall the desired word. The harder you try, the worse the TOT state gets. The best way to recall a blocked word, then, is to stop trying to recall it! The word you were searching for may just pop into your head minutes, or even hours, after you stopped consciously searching for it (Norman & Bobrow, 1976).

The TOT phenomenon demonstrates the power of *interference* to disrupt memory. The TOT phenomenon occurs most often with words that are seldom used. Researchers believe that it is the infrequent use of these words that weakens the link between their meaning and their pronunciation (Burke, McKay, Worthley & Wade, 1991). When you try to remember one of these words, lots of other words that sound like them or mean roughly the same thing come to the surface of your mind and interfere with your ability to retrieve the word you want. When you stop trying to recall the word, the interference decreases, and the word you were seeking "pops" to the surface.

The effects of interference are not limited to TOTs. In fact, interference is responsible for many cases in which people are unable to retrieve information from long-term memory. Interference can come from two directions. First, new material may interfere with material already in long-term memory, this is known as **retroactive interference**. If you learn a new way of doing something, you may find it difficult to recall how you had done it for years. Second, interference may also proceed the other way, with old information blocking a similar new memory: We call this **proactive interference**. These two processes are illustrated in Figure 6-6.

Because interference strains our ability to retrieve information from long-term memory, it would be useful to know how to reduce or overcome interference. As the TOT phenomenon suggests, *similarity* is the primary determinant of interference: Items are likely to interfere with one another to the extent that they are similar to one another. In this light, consider the following experiment, conducted by Bower & Mann (1992). Subjects learned two lists of 21 letters each. The first list was SOJFNUGPAHWMSELICBQTA, and the second was YADILOHSREKNABYHTLAEW. Then the subjects were asked to recall the first list. Retroactive interference occurs because the second list consists of a sequence of letters just like the first list and thus interferes with it. But when some of the subjects were told that the second list spells WEALTHY BANKERS HOLIDAY backwards, interference dropped significantly. With the new information, the second list could be distinguished from the first list, so there was less interference between the two lists. You can see that to learn something successfully you should try to avoid interference—or at least keep it to a minimum—by making the new material as distinctive as possible. The more dissimilar something is from other things you have already learned, the less likely it will be to mingle and interface with other material in memory.

**RECONSTRUCTIVE MEMORY** In the early 1930s, Sir Frederic Bartlett pioneered the study of how long-term memory changes over time, and we will look more closely at this research in the final chapter of this book. Bartlett posited that people "reconstruct memories" as time passes.

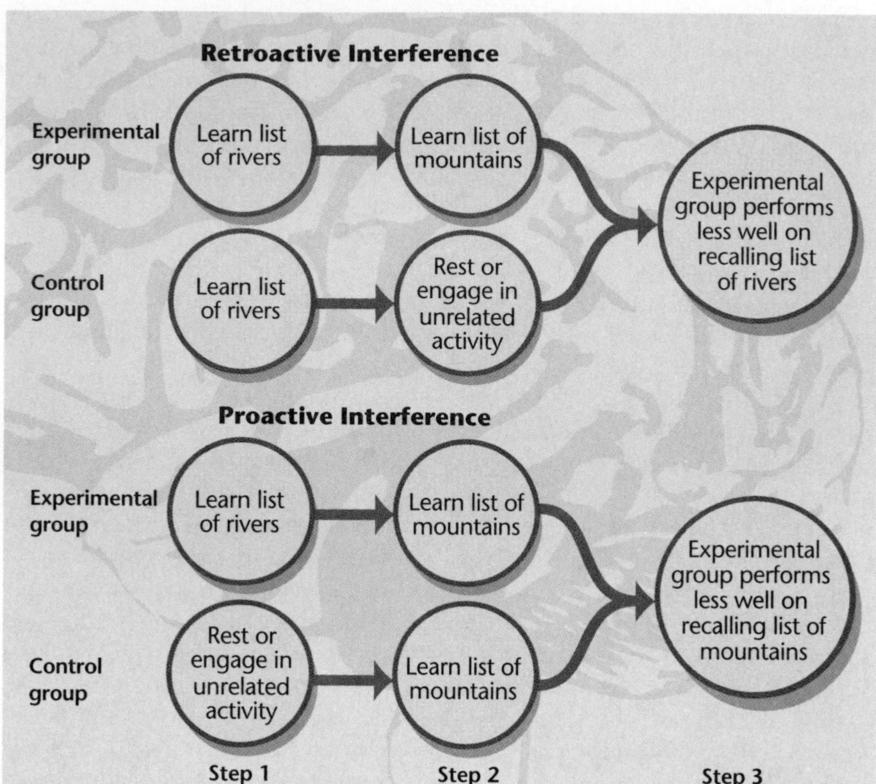


**Figure 6-6**
**Diagram of experiments measuring retroactive and proactive interference.** In the case of *retroactive interference*, the experimental group usually does not perform as well on tests of recall as those in the control group, who experience no retroactive interference from the list of words in step 2. In the case of *proactive interference*, people in the experimental group suffer the effects of proactive interference from the list in step 1 and, when asked to recall the list from step 2, perform less well than those in the control group.

Culture influences our reconstructive memory. People who are not Chinese rarely have an accurate memory of a Chinese New Year celebration. Because of their lack of familiarity with the traditions and ceremony that give meaning to this holiday, they will distort or drop certain details of the event in their memories.

This phenomenon of reconstructive memory has been well documented in the accounts of witnesses to, or victims of, crimes and accidents (see the Controversies box titled "Eyewitness Testimony and Recovered Memories" on page 218). People also unknowingly rewrite their memories of past events to fit their current image or their desired image of themselves. This is not always a bad thing. A study of children whose home life had been so troubled that they had been placed for a time in a child guidance clinic found that changing or "rewriting" their memories of early childhood made a difficult, disadvantaged life less of a liability. For example, when these children were interviewed 30 years later, those who incorrectly recalled their childhood as fairly normal were also the ones who had been able to develop a basically stable, conventional life of their own (Robins et al., 1985).

Like the children from troubled homes in the Robins study just mentioned, any of us may reconstruct memories for social or personal self-defense. Each time you tell someone the story of an incident, you may unconsciously make subtle changes in the details of the story—you like to think of yourself as more reasonable than that; maybe the other guy wasn't quite that big—and these changes are encoded as part of your memory. When an experience doesn't fit our view of the world or ourselves, we tend, unconsciously, to adjust it or to blot it out of memory altogether. This is the phenomenon Freud described as *repression*.

What is hysterical amnesia? How does it differ from other types of amnesia?

At its most extreme, repression can cause *hysterical amnesia*, a type of memory loss that has no known neurological origin. The plots of many movies and television shows center around people with hysterical amnesia: A man wakes up in a strange city, unable to remember his name or where he came from or how he got there, but he is perfectly capable of reciting the alphabet or frying an egg. Yet the memory of any personal information is gone. In hysterical amnesia, there is no apparent organic reason for the failure of memory. Usually, a terribly frightening or traumatic incident in a person's life has prompted the mind to totally repress all personal memories rather than remember that one incident.

**Schema** (plural: **schemata**) Set of beliefs or expectations about something that is based on past experience.

USING SCHEMATA Recognizing that past reactions and experiences may affect memory, Bartlett developed the *schema theory*, a theory of the way in which people use past reactions and past experiences to organize and interpret their perceptions of an episode in the present. Modern schema theory has refined Bartlett's ideas somewhat, but the concept of schema still stands at the center of how psychologists view memory. A **schema** (plural: **schemata**) is like a script that past experience has begun writing for you, with details to be filled in by your present experience. It is an unconscious mental representation of an event, object, situation, person, process, or relationship that is stored in memory and that leads you to expect your experience to be organized in certain ways. For example, you may have a schema for going to the mall, for eating in a restaurant, for driving a car, or for attending a class lecture. A class lecture schema might include a large room, seating arranged in rows, a space in the front of the room where the professor or lecturer will stand, a podium or lectern, a chalkboard, a screen, and other characteristics common to your experience of attending lectures. You enter, sit down, open your notebook, and expect the professor or lecturer to come in and address the class from the front of the room.

Schemata such as these serve memory in several ways (Brewer & Nakamura, 1984). They provide a framework into which incoming information is fitted. For example, if you enter a restaurant and see that there are no servers, that people are placing their orders at a long counter and then seating themselves, you might reasonably conclude that this is a "fast-food restaurant." Later in the day when a friend asks you where you had lunch, you might recall that it was "at a fast-food place." Schemata may also influence the amount of attention you pay to a given event. If you attend a lecture on environmental pollution, you will probably pay more attention than if you overhear a conversation on the same topic in the cafeteria. Schemata may color what you recall as well. In this way, schemata may prompt you to form stereotypes; that is, to ascribe certain characteristics to all members of a particular group. The process of stereotyping will be examined in the social psychology chapter. Finally, schemata may help you fill in missing information or draw inferences. If Bob was in a really bad mood one day and you found out later that he had a flat tire while rushing to an important appointment dressed in his best clothes, your schema or mental representation of what it is like to fix a tire in such a situation would help you understand why Bob was not his usual cheerful self that day.

In the preceding examples, schemata influenced the content of long-term memory. Schemata can also affect the ways in which information is retrieved from memory. For example, in one study, college undergraduates read a story about two boys playing hooky from school. The story related what the boys did at one of their homes, and many details about the home were given in the course of the story. Later, some students were asked to recall as many details about the home as possible from the point of view of someone looking to buy a new home, while other students were asked to recall as many details as possible from the point of view of a burglar. Those who recalled the details from a home buyer's viewpoint tended to remember such things as the leaky roof; those who recalled the details from a burglar's viewpoint tended to remember the possessions in the home, such as jewelry and crystal. When

# ONTROVERSIES

## Eyewitness Testimony and Recovered Memories

Jurors in court cases tend to believe eyewitnesses. Faced with conflicting or ambiguous testimony, they are tempted to put their faith in people who actually "saw" an event with their own eyes. However, this faith in eyewitnesses may be misplaced (McCloskey & Egeth, 1983). Although eyewitness accounts are essential to courtroom testimony, studies clearly show that people who say, "I know what I saw," often mean, "I know what I *think* I saw." And these people may be wrong.

Consider this scenario. Two women enter a bus station and leave their belongings unattended on a bench while they check the bus schedule. A man enters, reaches into their baggage, stuffs something under his coat, and leaves. One of the women returns to her baggage and, after checking its contents, exclaims, "My tape recorder was stolen!" Eyewitnesses sitting nearby confirm her story when contacted by insurance investigators; many of the eyewitnesses provide a description of the missing tape recorder, including its color, size, and shape. In fact, there never was a tape recorder! The "thief" and the women "travelers" were assisting psychologist Elizabeth Loftus in a study of the fallibility of eyewitness testimony (Loftus, 1983).

Increasingly, courts are recognizing the flaws in eyewitness testimony. For example, judges instruct juries to be skeptical about eyewitness testimony and to evaluate it critically. But how serious are judges' reservations about this form of courtroom testimony? Take the case of Father Bernard Pagano, a Roman Catholic priest who found himself accused of a series of armed robberies in Wilmington, Delaware. After one witness told police that Father Pagano looked a lot like the man in a sketch being circulated by the local media, no less than seven eyewitnesses positively identified the priest as the perpetrator. In the middle of the trial, however, another man—whose resemblance to Father Pagano was not even close—confessed to the crime (see the accompanying photographs). How did the judicial system nearly carry out such a travesty of justice? First of all, the media had made a point of noting that the perpetrator was unusually "gentlemanly": polite, articulate, well dressed, and so on. Furthermore, in presenting pictures of suspects to eyewitnesses, the police had apparently let slip that the culprit could be a priest. When Father Pagano was the only suspect in clerical garb, witnesses' memories apparently adjusted to accommodate the notion that a priest might, in fact, be guilty of the crime spree. Needless to say, Father Pagano was more fortunate than many falsely accused people. Commenting on over 1,000 cases in which innocent people were convicted of crimes, Wells (1993) concludes that errors made by eyewitnesses were the single most persuasive element leading to false conviction.

Father Bernard Pagano (right) was identified as an armed robber by seven eyewitnesses and was nearly convicted for crimes actually committed by the man on the left.

For more than 20 years, Elizabeth Loftus (1993a; Loftus & Hoffman, 1989) has been the most influential researcher into eyewitness memory. In a classic study, Loftus and Palmer (1974) showed subjects a film depicting a traffic accident. Some subjects were asked, "About how fast were the cars going when they hit each other?" Other subjects were asked the same question, but with the words *smashed into, collided with, bumped into,* and *contacted* in place of *hit*. The researchers discovered that people's reports of the cars' speed depended on which word was inserted in the question. When they were asked about cars that "smashed into each other," they reported that the cars were going faster than if they were asked simply about cars that "contacted" each other. In another experiment, subjects were also shown a film of a collision, and then asked either, "How fast were the cars going when they hit each other?" or "How fast were the cars going when they smashed into each other?" One week later, subjects were asked some additional questions about the accident they had seen on film the week before. One of the questions was "Did you see any broken glass?" More of the subjects who had been asked originally if the cars had *smashed into* each other reported that they had seen broken glass than did the subjects who had been asked simply if the cars had *hit* each other. These findings illustrate how police, lawyers, and other investigators may, often unconsciously, sway witnesses and influence subsequent eyewitness accounts. Based on studies like these, Loftus and Palmer concluded that eyewitness memory is unreliable because witnesses cannot disentangle their memory of the original event from information and suggestions they receive after the event.

When people reconstruct memories, is their memory of the original event destroyed and then replaced with a new memory—some composite of the original event and new information received after the event? According to Johnson and Raye (1981) and Lindsay and Johnson (1989),

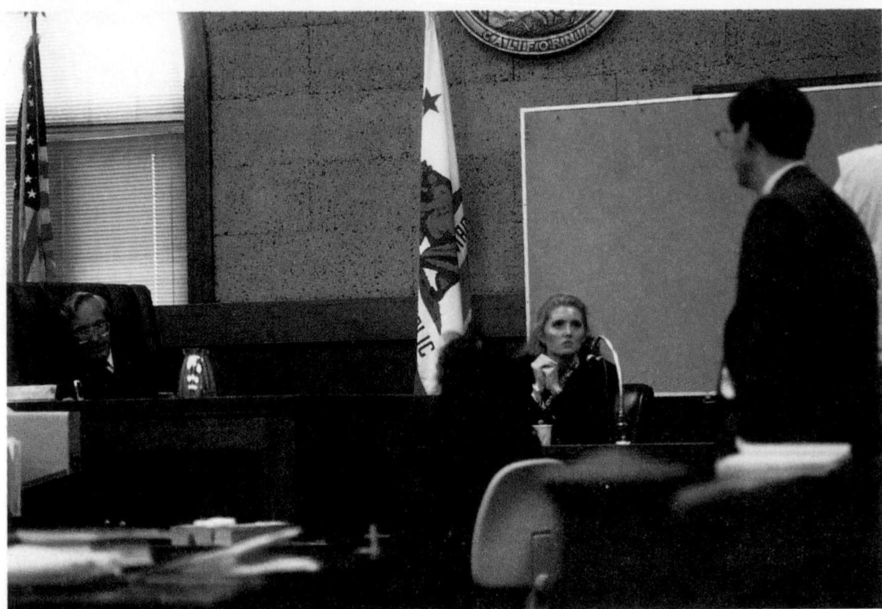

The issue of recovered memories has legal as well as psychological implications. In 1990, a woman named Eileen Franklin testified that she had recovered memories of her father killing her friend 20 years earlier. Her father was eventually convicted of murder.

the original memory is not destroyed; instead, people are sometimes unable to tell the difference between what actually happened and what they merely heard about or imagined. If you imagine an event in a particularly vivid way, you may later have difficulty remembering whether the event really happened or you simply imagined it. Similarly, if, after witnessing an event, you hear information about that event, you might later confuse your memory of that subsequent information with your memory of the original event. Lindsay (1993) contends that if people paid more attention to the source of their memories, eyewitness accounts and memories in general would be less biased by information and suggestions picked up after an event.

Eyewitness research may cast light on the veracity of recovered memories of traumatic events, such as childhood sexual abuse. Nobody denies the severity of the problem of sexual abuse of children or the intensity of the suffering of incest survivors. And because of repression, memories of such events sometimes do not surface until many years later. The phenomenon of repressed memories has legal as well as psychological repercussions, because individuals who recover memories may accuse other people of abuse or other criminal behavior that allegedly occurred far in the past. Some observer, including Loftus, 1993b), question the accuracy of memories recovered so many years after the original event. Although Loftus does not doubt that many such memories accurately reflect actual incidents, she also notes that, in at least some instances other sources (such as the media and even psychotherapists) may shape people's recollections of early childhood experiences. For example, in some cases, well-meaning psychotherapists may unwittingly create false memories by leading patients to imagine vividly incidents that never happened.

Other researchers (e.g., Byrd, 1994; Olio, 1994) criticize Loftus for appearing not to take the stories of incest survivors seriously enough. They argue that false accusations are rare and that it is destructive to make incest survivors doubt the reality of their memories. This volatile issue, will only be resolved as we learn more about the nature of long-term memory and the extent to which it changes over time.

the students were then asked to do the same thing all over again, but this time from the other perspective, they suddenly remembered details that they had previously "forgotten," even though in both cases they were asked to recall as many details from the original story as they could (Anderson & Pichert, 1978). This experiment demonstrates how schemata streamline the process of retrieving information from memory: People tend to recall only what they need to know in a particular situation and filter out memories that are not pertinent.

**The Effects of Cues on Retrieval from LTM** Two other factors also affect retrieval from long-term memory. The more extensively the information was linked to other material when it was first entered into LTM, and the more cues we have to work with at the time of retrieval, the more likely it is that our search will end in success. Recall our earlier example of the vegetarian who eats a hamburger. For someone who has chosen to follow a vegetarian diet, this act becomes very meaningful, and it is probably linked to all kinds of other facts in

**"At some point do we create or embellish memories?"**

In Chapter 3, we discussed whether reality can ever be objective or whether it is always subjective. For many psychologists, the subjectivity of memory is also an issue. For example, in this chapter, we discussed the phenomenon of reconstructive memory—memories that were significantly revised over time or even generated by the individual—and the reasons why people rewrite their memories of certain events.

What are your thoughts about this issue? Can you recall and describe examples in your own life of reconstructive memories? Do you know of any people who "remember" things that never actually happened? Why do you think these memories developed as they did? Can psychology explain this phenomenon? After you have thought about these questions, take a few minutes to examine the options of some other students in the following exchange.

• • • • • • •

**KARI: Sometimes I'm sure my whole life is reconstructive memory. I think such memories evolve due to the necessity to create a cause for an inexplicable response. . . . Maybe a child who feels frightened walking to school will fabricate in memory a cemetery to give him a reason for having been frightened in the past. Phobias may often be rationalized by reconstructed memories.**

**AMY: The book mentions someone who recreated her childhood to be that of a normal, well-adapted family. She did this to forget about the abuse she really endured. So reconstructive memory can be useful.**

**MELISSA: The other day I was telling a story about an event that had happened a few years ago. I had told this story quite a few times and it had become almost a recitation. Then somebody asked me a question about a detail of the story and I found that I couldn't answer. It took me a few moments to actually remember the *event* and not just the *story*. It was kind of unnerving because I realized that I had been "living" the story for the past few years.**

**BOB: I think some reconstructive memories are formed out of photographs. I sometimes think that I remember things from when I was really young, but then I see a picture of the event and I wonder if I really did remember that event or if the event was created by my brain in response to the picture. Maybe the guy from the cemetery story had seen a picture of the cemetery and somehow he correlated that photo to his walk to school every day.**

**MARIA: I think not only the immediate emotions and impressions affect memory, but also what happens afterwards. For example, you have a fight with a best friend, then later make up. Now you don't quite remember why the nasty things she/he said were so mean, you were at fault too. You lost your anger in your memory.**

**BOB: I always thought that my grandparents' old house was a mansion. But when I saw a picture of it recently, it was a really dinky house. I guess point of view has a big part in memory. The book talks about how the brain makes maps of places. I guess a small person's map would look different from a big person's map because of the point of view. Maybe some reconstructive memories are formed by the overlap of some of these maps causing something that is in one map to be transferred to another map.**

**CARVER: Fabrications are to make us feel that we are consistent and that we are how we would like ourselves to be. I've seen this in myself with car accidents, filling in details of stories and constantly revising what I thought I experienced.**

**MARIA: I remember reading where Freud asked all these little girls these questions and found out they'd all been molested by their fathers. Later he discovered that most of them had made it all up but really believed it.**

**BOB: Last summer we were on the Pennsylvania Turnpike at night and in the rain. Our van slipped out of control, and we swerved and almost hit an oncoming semi. This incident must have taken 4 seconds at max, but why do I think that it took much longer? I think that since my brain was not ready to take in the sensations of swerving, I was not able to record it well in my memory. Since this was a life-threatening situation, maybe my brain went back to the bits of information it had and filled in the gaps with what it thinks had happened.**

**ANN: There are times I could swear that someone told me something, when it was not real and only happened in a dream. It's really freaky at times. I would say this could be how a lot of memories are reconstructed, or at least my own are!**

• • • • • • •

Have your views changed at all as a result of reading the thoughts of other students? What are some of the problems associated with the study of reconstructive memories? How might psychologists deal with these problems?

LTM (such as the value of animals as a form of life, the importance of consuming protein from plants to ensure an environmentally sustainable society, and our responsibility to other species on the planet. Or take another example. If you are asked, "Who was the twenty-second president of the United States?" you might have difficulty recalling his name, since the only useful retrieval cue is "twenty-second." If you were told, "His name is the same as that of a large city in Ohio," the additional cue might help you recall his name. But if you were asked, "Was it John Sherman, Thomas Bayard, or Grover Cleveland?" you would probably recognize the correct answer as Grover Cleveland immediately. His name is a powerful retrieval cue.

## Autobiographical Memory

Long-term memory enables us to recall events that occurred throughout our lifetime. Yet are we more likely to recall events from particular periods of our life. *Autobiographical memory* refers to our recollection of events that happened in our life and when those events took place. Crovitz and Schiffman (1974) conducted a classic study of autobiographical memory in which they asked young adults to report the earliest personal memory that came to mind when they saw each of 20 words, and then to estimate how long ago each event had occurred. The words were all common nouns, such as *hall* and *oven*, for which people can easily create images. Crovitz and Schiffman found that, in general, most personal memories concerned relatively recent events: The longer ago an event occurred, the less likely people were to report it.

You might like to try Crovitz and Schiffman's technique yourself. You and a friend should each make up a list of 20 nouns, like *table*, *robin*, and *Brussels sprouts*, that can be easily pictured, and then generate one personal memory for each of the other person's words. Try to date each memory as accurately as possible. Did you have more memories for recent events than for events early in your life? Did you have any memories for events in the first 3 or 4 years of your life? Research shows that, in general, our earliest personal memories tend to be date back to between 3 and 4 years of age (Kihlstrom & Harackiewicz, 1982)

Recent research also indicates that certain kinds of events are more likely to be remembered than others from those first few years of life. For example, Usher and Neisser (1993) found that college students could often recall the birth of a sibling or being hospitalized as early as age 2, while the death of a family member or making a family move could be recalled as early as age 3. Generally speaking, the earliest memories are those for events that significantly change one's life story (for instance, a sibling's birth) or are particularly frightening (such as hospitalization). However, it is extremely rare for people to recall events that occurred before they were 2 years old. This phenomenon is sometimes called *infantile amnesia*.

**4.** How far back into our childhood can most of us recall events? What types of events are we most likely to recall from our earliest years?

Corvitz and Schiffman concluded that personal memories primarily center on relatively recent events. Research reviewed by Holland and Rabbitt (1990), however, shows that people over 50 years of age exhibit a tendency toward *reminiscence*; that is, they are more likely than younger people to recall events from relatively early in life. Yet this doesn't mean that the memories they consider most important necessarily come from those years. When Mackavey, Malley, and Stewart (1991) analyzed the autobiographies of 49 well-known psychologists, written when the psychologists were between 54 and 86 years of age, they discovered that 80 percent of the psychologists'—*autobiographically consequential experi-*

**TABLE 6-1 Memory as an Information-Processing System**

| SYSTEM | MEANS BY WHICH INFORMATION IS ENCODED | STORAGE ORGANIZATION | STORAGE DURATION | MEANS BY WHICH INFORMATION IS RETRIEVED | FACTORS IN FORGETTING |
|---|---|---|---|---|---|
| **SENSORY REGISTERS** | Visual and auditory registers | None | From less than 1 second to only a few seconds | Reconsideratio nof registered information | Decay or masking |
| **SHORT-TERM MEMORY** | Visual and phonological representation | None | Usually 15 to 20 seconds | Rote or maintenance rehearsal | Interference or decay |
| **LONG-TERM MEMORY** | Comprehensio nof meaning, elaborative rehearsal | Logical frameworks, such as hierarchies or categories | Perhaps for an entire lifetime | Retrieval cues linked to organized information | Retrieval failure or interference |

*ences*—or formative decisions—occurred between the ages of 18 and 35; very few occurred during early childhood or after age 50. The researchers concluded that because the most pivotal life choices (such as those concerning marriage and career) are typically made in late adolescence and young adulthood and the outcomes of these choices shape the rest of our lives, makes sense for us to focus on this period when we look back to summarize and evaluate our lives.

We have seen that long-term memory offers a vast storage space for information that we can retrieve in a variety of ways. Its capacity is immense, and material stored in LTM never seems to decay, although it may be transformed. By comparison, short-term memory has a sharply limited capacity; information may disappear from STM as a result of decay or interference or simply because the storage space is full. To keep information in STM, we must refresh it constantly through rote rehearsal. If we want to retain information for a long period of time, we must transfer it to long-term memory through the process of elaborative rehearsal. The sensory registers can take in an enormous volume of less permanent information but they have no ability to process memories. Together, these three stages of memory—the sensory registers, STM, and LTM—comprise the information-processing view of memory (see Table 6-1). Let us now take a brief look at some special topics in memory, including ways in which memory may be improved.

## SPECIAL TOPICS IN MEMORY

### Flashbulb Memories

"I was standing by the stove getting dinner; my husband came in and told me." "I was fixing the fence, can go within a rod of the place where I stood. Mr. W. came along and told me. It was 9 or 10 o'clock in the morning." "It was in the forenoon; we were at work on the road by K's mills: A man driving past told us." These were three responses to the question, "Do you recall where you were when you heard that Abraham Lincoln was shot?" Other accounts were even more detailed. In fact, of 179 people interviewed, 127 recalled precisely the time and place at which they first heard of the assassination. That is a very high percentage, considering that the question was asked by a researcher 33 years after the event (Colegrove, 1982).

**Flashbulb memory** A vivid memory of a certain event and the incidents surrounding it even after a long time has passed.

A **flashbulb memory** is the experience of remembering vividly a certain event and the incidents surrounding it even after a long time has passed. Events that are shocking or otherwise highly significant are often remembered in this way. The death of a close relative, a time when we were seriously hurt, a graduation or wedding day, may all elicit flashbulb memories. So can dramatic events in which we were not personally involved, such as the assassination of President John F. Kennedy in November 1963 or the explosion of the space shuttle *Challenger* in January 1986.

5. Why can so many people remember what they were doing when John Kennedy was shot or when the *Challenger* exploded?

Researchers have developed several theories about how people form such memories. According to the *now print* theory, a mechanism starts up in the brain when something especially significant, shocking, or noteworthy is at hand. The entire event is captured and then "printed," much like a photograph. The "print" is then stored, like a photograph in an album, for long periods, perhaps for a lifetime. It is periodically reinforced, because such an important event is bound to be remembered and discussed many times throughout the years.

This theory raises other questions, however. Why are all sorts of insignificant features remembered along with the main event—"standing by the stove," "fixing the fence"? The answer given by the *now print* theory is that the entire event is registered, not just the primary subject. Again, this is like a photograph. You may decide to photograph your mother sitting on the couch on her silver wedding anniversary. Your mother is the main subject, yet that same picture may capture the arrangement of the living room furniture, the antics of the family dog who climbed into the picture, a small crack in the plaster of the back wall that looms much larger in memory than it really was. You did not intend to include those things in your picture, but because they were there in the background, they, too, were registered on film (Brown & Kulik, 1977).

Even years from now, many people will have a *flashbulb memory* of where they were and what they were doing at 11:30 A.M. EST on January 28, 1986—if they are reminded that this is the moment when the space shuttle *Challenger* exploded.

The *now print* theory implies, among other things, that flashbulb memories are accurate, that they are created at the time of an event, and that they are remembered better because of their highly emotional content. All these implications have come under criticism. First of all, flashbulb memories are certainly not always accurate. Although this is a difficult contention to test, let's consider just one case. Psychologist Ulric Neisser vividly recalled what he was doing on the day in 1941 that the Japanese bombed Pearl Harbor. He clearly remembered that he was listening to a baseball game on the radio, which was interrupted by the shocking announcement. But baseball is not played in December, when the attack took place, so this sharp flashbulb memory was simply incorrect (Neisser, 1982).

Moreover, even if an event is registered accurately, it may undergo periodic revision, just like other long-term memories. We are bound to discuss and rethink a major event many times, and we probably also hear a great deal of additional information about that event in the weeks and months after it occurs. As a result, the flashbulb memory may undergo reconstruction and become less accurate over the years until it sometimes bears little or no resemblance to what actually occurred.

Beyond flashbulb memories, what can we do to improve our overall memory? We address this topic in the next section.

## Improving Your Memory

At a cocktail party, you're embarrassed when a familiar-looking person comes over and hugs you but you can't remember her name. You're describing a movie you've just seen, but you can't recall its title. After returning

## HIGHLIGHTS

### Aging Memory Better than Expected

Most of us believe that when we grow old our memory will inevitably deteriorate, but current studies paint a different picture of memory among the elderly. Recent research suggests that just one kind of memory declines with age: episodic memory.

One study that compared episodic, semantic, and implicit memory found that only episodic memory tends to fade with age (Graf, 1990). While people with physical diseases may show significant loss of memory at an early age, for physically healthy people, episodic memory remains stable through the mid-60s, and then worsens noticeably during the 70s. Episodic memory, as you recall, is memory for specific events that have personal meaning for us, such as where we put our glasses, what we had for dinner last night, who visited us last week, and where we are supposed to be at 3:00 this afternoon. Implicit memory (things we unintentionally recall) tends to decline minimally, and semantic memory (general knowledge and facts) actually improves with age (Katzman & Terry, 1983). In fact, even the falloff in episodic memory may not be inevitable, except in older people with an illness such as Alzheimer's disease. In physically healthy people, any decline in episodic memory may be caused primarily by social events, such as retirement, that typically occur when people are in their 60s. Some researchers speculate that retired people don't exercise their episodic memories as much as they did when they worked, and that this lack of practice leads to a decline in the quality of episodic memory.

Can elderly people take steps to compensate for memory declines that they do experience? Many older people use the kinds of memory-enhancing techniques we will be discussing in this section of the chapter to head off memory problems. For example, they may write notes to remind themselves about particular things they want to remember, or talk or think about an event afterward to reinforce their memory of the day. One memory researcher, psychologist Daniel Schacter, asserts that many elderly people have problems committing information to long-term memory if events rush by too quickly or happen in a confusing way (Schacter et al., 1991). When events threaten to overwhelm you, psychologists advise trying to focus on what's happening and to minimize distractions. People of all ages who can focus their attention in this way generally find that their memory is better than they thought!

from the grocery store, you realize that you've forgotten to pick up garlic and rosemary for tonight's stew.

What kinds of things can you do to improve your memory?

Has your memory always been bad, or is it deteriorating? Many people worry that their memory is not what it used to be. But studies of memory show that most people, even those who are older, have better memories than they realize (see the Highlights box titled "Aging Memory Better than Expected"). Here are some factors psychologists say interfere with memory, and some remedies for them.

1. *You lack motivation.* If you forget to put the car in the garage, perhaps you'd simply rather not go outside. Without a strong desire to learn or remember something, you probably won't. But if you find a way to keep yourself alert and stimulated, you will have an easier time learning and remembering things.

2. *You need practice.* To stay sharp, memory skills, like all skills, must be practiced and used. Memory experts recommend exercises such as crossword puzzles, acrostics, anagrams, Scrabble, Monopoly, Trivial Pursuit, and bridge. Or you might learn Japanese, join a chess club, or make a point of discussing current events regularly with friends.

3. *You lack confidence in your ability.* Self-doubt often leads to anxiety, which, in turn, interferes with the ability to retrieve information

from memory. Relaxation exercises, experts agree, may substantially boost your ability to retrieve information from memory. Also, if you're convinced that you won't remember something, you probably won't. For example, people who are sure they won't remember the parts of the nervous system for a psychology test will undoubtedly have more difficulty mastering this material than people who adopt a more positive attitude toward the task.

**Mnemonics** Techniques that make material easier to remember.

**Mnemonist** Someone with highly developed memory skills.

4. *You're distracted.* While some people can study for an exam and listen to the radio simultaneously, most people find that outside distractions interfere with both learning and remembering. If you are being distracted, look for a quiet, even secluded, setting before attempting to commit something to memory.

5. *You're not focused.* Paying close attention to details, focusing on your surroundings, emotions, and other elements associated with an event, will help you remember it clearly.

6. *You're not making enough connections between new material and other information already stored in your long-term memory.* One key to improving memory lies in organizing and coding material more effectively when it first enters LTM. Discuss things you want to remember with other people. Think about or write down ways in which the new information is related to things you already know. The more links you forge between new information and old information already in LTM, the more likely you are to remember the new material.

   In some situations, special techniques called **mnemonics** may help you to tie new material to information already in LTM. Some of the simplest mnemonic techniques are the rhymes and jingles that we often use to remember dates and other facts. "Thirty days hath September, April, June, and November . . . " enables us to recall how many days are in a month. We are also familiar with other simple mnemonic devices in which we make up words or sentences out of the material to be recalled. The colors of the visible spectrum—red, orange, yellow, green, blue, indigo, and violet—are easily remembered by using their first letters to form the name ROY G. BIV. Some people dazzle others with seemingly impossible feats of memory. Known as **mnemonists**, these individuals are not born with a special gift for remembering things; rather, they have carefully honed their memory techniques following certain principles. Because it takes time and effort to develop an exceptional memory, mnemonists generally have strong motivation for sharpening their memory skills. Consider for a moment the importance of a superior memory for actors and chess masters, for example.

7. *You're not using mental imagery effectively.* Imagery works wonders as an aid to recalling information from memory. Whenever possible, form mental pictures of the items, people, words, or activities you want to remember. For example, to remember that someone's last name is Glass, you might imagine her holding a glass or looking through a glass. If you were asked to recall the word pair "man-horse," your best bet would be to imagine a horse and a man interacting in some unusual way (you might, for example, visualize the horse trying to throw the man). If you have a sequence of stops to make, picture yourself leaving each place and heading for the next. Greek and Roman orators used a similar mnemonic technique to memorize long speeches. They would visit a large house or temple and walk through

the rooms in a specific order, noting where particular objects were placed in each room. When the orator had memorized the plan of the building and its contents, they would go through the rooms in their mind, placing images of material to be remembered at different spots in the rooms. To retrieve the material in the proper sequence during the speech, the orator would imagine themselves going through the rooms in order and, by association, would recall each point of their speech as they came to each object in each room.

**Eidetic imagery** The ability to reproduce unusually sharp and detailed images of something one has seen.

People with exceptional—or *photographic*—memories make use of **eidetic imagery**, creating unusually sharp and detailed visual images of a picture, a scene, even a page of text they have seen, which they can reproduce in minute detail. Eidetic imagery is much more common in children, but some adults also have this extraordinary talent.

People who develop exceptional memories usually have a strong need or desire to do so. Successful actors, for example, are called on to memorize parts in sometimes long and complicated scripts. What kinds of cues and mnemonic devices do you think they use to help them remember their lines?

8. *You're not using retrieval cues effectively*. As we saw earlier, the more retrieval cues you have, the more likely it is that you will remember something. One way to establish automatic retrieval cues is to create routines and structure. For example, when you come in the door, put your house and car keys in the same place every time. Then when you ask yourself, "Where did I put my keys?" the fact that you have a special place for the keys serves as a retrieval cue. Similarly, if you want to remember to do something before you go to bed, leave something unusual on your bed (perhaps a shoe or a sock); when it's time to go to bed, you'll see the unusual object and that should help you remember what you wanted to do.
9. *You're relying to heavily on memory alone*. Human memory is less than perfect, so it's wise not to rely entirely on memory when there are alternatives. Write down the things you need to remember, and then post a note or list of those things somewhere obvious, such as on your bulletin board or refrigerator door. Put all the dates you want to remember on a calendar, and then put the calendar in a conspicuous place. If you witness an accident, immediately write down everything you saw and heard in as much detail as you can; then use your written account to refresh your memory periodically.

Most memory-improvement books are filled with suggestions and techniques such as these, and they do work if you are willing to devote the time and energy to learning how to use them. For example, a study by Bower (1973) showed that mnemonic techniques were far more effective than simple rehearsal for remembering long lists of items. College students were asked to study five successive "shopping lists" of 20 unrelated words each. They were given 5 seconds to memorize each word and additional time to study each list as a whole. At the end of the session, they were asked to recall all 100 items. Subjects using mnemonic techniques remembered an average of 72 items, but the control group—generally relying on simple rehearsal—remembered only 28. The subjects trained in mnemonic techniques were also much more successful at recalling the position of each item in the list on which it appeared.

**IMPROVING YOUR MEMORY FOR TEXTBOOK MATERIAL** You can use all the principles spelled out in this chapter to help you remember material from textbooks like this one. We have seen that the key to storing new material in long-term memory is making associations between that material and information that is already in LTM. If you simply passively reread the chapter over and over, you are not likely to store, retain, or retrieve information effectively. Highlighting or underlining passages makes for a slight improvement, if only because you are at least thinking about which material is most important.

A more effective technique, however, is to prepare an outline of the chapter before reading it so that you have associations and links ready to be made when you actually read the material. Some textbooks (including this one) provide you with a ready-made outline at the beginning of the chapter, but you are better off putting one together for yourself, because that forces you to start thinking about the content of the chapter and how one section relates to another. How would you compose a chapter outline? You might scan the various headings in the chapter, or read the first few sentences of each paragraph, or look at the end-of- chapter summary for ideas to insert in your outline. Then, as you read, enter brief comments under the various headings of your outline as a way of summarizing each portion of the chapter. Not only will your personal summary help you remember material but it will also prove useful when you are reviewing the material for a test.

Another simple technique is to engage actively in a form of elaborative rehearsal of the material as you read the chapter. As an example, you might write in the margin of the text as you go along, recording your reactions, questions, ideas about how the new material may relate to other material, thoughts about how you might apply what you are learning in your own life, and so on. Try to relate the new material to all sorts of things you already know and to express this relationship in your own words. You can also work with a friend, taking turns challenging each other with questions that draw on material from different sections or paragraphs. However you go about it, integrating and elaborating on the textual material forces you to process it and to form new associations among the pieces of information that you are storing. This approach to learning offers two distinct benefits: It ties the new material to information already in memory and it generates a multitude of retrieval cues to help you put your finger on the material when you need it.

A more ambitious, but even more effective, system for studying is known by the letters of its five stages: *SQRRR* (or *SQ3R*, for short). SQRRR involves the following steps:

> *(1) Survey*. Before you even start to read, look quickly at the chapter outline, the headings of the various sections in the chapter, and the chapter summary. This gives you an overview of what you will be reading, and helps you organize and integrate the material as you go along.
>
> *(2) Question*. Before you start to read, translate each heading in the chapter into questions about the text to follow, as a way to compare the new material with what you already know. This process gets you actively involved in thinking about the topic and helps bring the main points into sharp relief. Before reading this chapter, for example, you might have recast the heading "Short-Term Memory" on page 206 into questions such as "Why is it called 'short-term'?" "Is there another type of memory that lasts longer?" "What good is memory if it's only short-term?" "Why do memories fade?" It is usually helpful to write these questions down.
>
> *(3) Read*. Now read the first section in the chapter, looking for answers to the questions you have posed. If you discover major points not directly related to your questions, either revise or refine your old questions to encompass the new material or make up new questions more specifically targeted to the new material.

*(4) Recite.* Once you finish reading the section, close the book, and recite from memory the answers to your questions and any other major points that you can remember. You may want to jot down your answers in outline form or even recite them aloud to someone else. Then open the book and check to make sure that you have covered all the key points raised in the section. Repeat steps 2, 3, and 4 for each section of the chapter.

*(5) Review.* After reading through the chapter, review your notes, and then recite your questions and answers from memory. Relate the material to other ideas, to experiences in your own life, or to things with which you are familiar. Try to think of particularly good examples or illustrations of the points brought out in the chapter. Get involved.

The SQ3R method forces you to react—to enter into a dialogue with the text. This interaction makes the material more interesting and meaningful and improves your chances of recalling it. Although this method may strike you as too time-consuming, you will probably spend less time studying overall if you use it because studying for exams later on should go much more quickly.

## BIOLOGICAL BASES OF MEMORY

What physiological processes take place inside of us when we are remembering something? Where is memory stored and retrieved? We turn to these questions now.

For nearly 200 years, psychologists have attempted to determine if memory is localized in a certain part of the brain. In Chapter 2, "Physiology and Behavior," we learned that some psychological functions, such as vision and speech, are indeed localized in this way. Early in the nineteenth century, many scientists believed this was also true of memory.

In fact, some memories may be localized in certain portions of the brain. For example, some of the learning that takes place in classical conditioning (see Chapter 5) is apparently stored in the cerebellum (McCormick et al., 1982). However, research also reveals that in many cases memories are not stored in any single part of the brain. In an attempt to trace memory to a specific location in the brain, Lashley (1950) performed a pivotal experiment in which he removed various parts of rats' brains. Although their memories were found to be weakened by losing any part of the brain, the memories were still present. The amount of memory remaining seemed to depend primarily on the amount of brain tissue that Lashley removed, not on the particular portion of the brain that was excised. Lashley concluded that a single memory may be stored in numerous parts of the brain, so that removal of any one part may diminish but not erase the whole memory.

Why would most memories be stored in various parts of the brain? First of all, several different senses usually contribute to any one memory: A single experience, that is, might be stored in the brain's visual centers, auditory areas, and centers for smell and touch—all at the same time. Secondly, the processing centers that retrieve stored material are widely distributed, so damaging the brain may interfere with only some retrieval mechanisms.

Yet even if most memories are stored throughout the brain and retrieval processes are widely scattered, recent evidence points to specific centers in the brain, which are essential for the formation of memories in the first place. In humans, the part of the brain called the *hippocampus* is instrumental in transferring factual information from short-term to long-term memory (see Figure 2-14 on page 58). People with hippocampal damage can remember events that have just occurred (STM), but they often have to write everything down to remember it for any length of time (LTM). For example, electroconvulsive shock therapy (see the chapter on therapies) disrupts the hippocampus, and patients who undergo this therapy for severe depression have difficulty remembering things that happened to them 2 or 3 hours before the treatment (an example of retrograde amnesia). Researchers account for this phenomenon by noting that information that was still being processed by the hippocampus when it was disrupted vanishes from memory entirely.

Scientists now believe that the hippocampus helps the brain forge memories by stimulating it to form new synapses, to make new connections, that is, among the neurons in the brain. Neurons in the adult brain do not reproduce. However, they do form new synapses, which is one reason we are able to learn new ideas, to improve our throwing arm, and to form new memories long after our brains have fully developed. How are these new connections engraved in the brain's circuitry? Researchers have found that when a portion of the hippocampus is stimulated by an electric current, a small response can be measured farther down a neural pathway. If the same area of the hippocampus is stimulated again, these neural circuits react much more vigorously, as if sensitized by the earlier stimulation. So researchers conclude that stimulation through the hippocampus causes new synapses to form and strengthens the synapses that already exist. This process is called *long-term potentiation*, or *LTP*, underlies learning and, consequently, the formation of memories.

Once these new neural connections have been formed and long-term potentiation has taken place, the hippocampus is no longer figures in that particular memory—the memory and all its connections to other information have become an integral part of the brain's structure and will persist even if the hippocampus is totally destroyed (Zola-Morgan & Squire, 1990; Squire & Zola-Morgan, 1991).

## LOOKING FORWARD

Memory is the central process by which we acquire and use information. We acquire information selectively, but once it is lodged in LTM, we are usually able to access it quite effectively. Yet sometimes we pick up memories unintentionally, and at times we are blocked from recalling desired information (as in the case of TOT). Moreover, our recall is not always accurate (think back, for example, to the controversies box on eyewitness testimony), and we occasionally engage in imaginative reconstruction of the past (as did the people in the Robins study who grew up in troubled homes). Current research on memory focuses on two areas: broadening our understanding of the biological bases of memory and learning how we form and reconstruct autobiographical memories.

## SUMMARY

This chapter opened with an explanation of the information-processing model of memory. This model describes how information is encoded, organized, and stored in memory, and how it is retrieved from memory. We also considered memory systems, such as episodic, semantic and implicit memory, as well as the process of reconstructive memory.

### THE SENSORY REGISTERS

**Sensory registers** are the entry points for raw information from the senses. After information enters the sensory registers, either it is processed further or it disappears. While the visual and auditory registers have received the most attention, there are registers for each of our senses.

### Visual and Auditory Registers

Although the sensory registers have virtually unlimited capacity, information disappears from them quite rapidly. As new visual information enters the registers, old information (the *icon*, or visual image) is "masked" almost immediately. Otherwise, the registers would overload as visual information piled up and became scrambled. Auditory information (the *echo*) fades more slowly than visual information does; the echo may last for several seconds.

### Initial Processing

From the mass of incoming information, we select some elements and hold them for further processing; we may choose to remember them permanently. In this process, called **attention**, we also give meaning to the information.

## SHORT-TERM MEMORY

**Short-term memory (STM)** is also called *primary memory* and *working memory* because it not only briefly stores information but also processes that information further. STM contains everything that we are consciously aware of at any instant.

### Capacity of STM

STM has its limits. Researchers have found that STM can hold only as much information as can be repeated or rehearsed in 1.5 to 2 seconds, which is usually 5 to 10 separate bits of information.

In STM, information can be grouped into larger meaningful units for easier handling, a process called **chunking**. Chunking helps us process more information than would otherwise be possible.

### Coding in STM

Information can be coded for temporary storage in STM *phonologically*, (according to the way it sounds), in visual form, or in terms of its meaning. Researchers conclude that STM has a greater capacity for material coded visually than for information coded phonologically.

### Retention and Retrieval in STM

Material in STM disappears in 15 to 20 seconds unless it is rehearsed or practiced. According to **decay theory**, material is lost from STM simply because of the passage of time. **Interference theory**, on the other hand, contends that interference from other information leads to forgetting from STM: Earlier information gets mixed up with, or pushed aside by, new information. Memory loss from STM is permanent. This prevents us from becoming overwhelmed with a mass of irrelevant, trivial, or unrelated data.

### Rote Rehearsal

Through **rote rehearsal**, or **maintenance rehearsal**, we retain information in STM by repeating it over and over again. However, rote memorization does not promote long-term memory, which requires a different type of rehearsal.

### Elaborative Rehearsal

**Elaborative rehearsal**, or the linking of new information in STM to familiar material stored in long-term memory, enables us to retain information for a longer period of time in STM. Through elaborative rehearsal, we process new data in a deeper and more meaningful way than through simple rote repetition.

An accident or severe interference can make unrehearsed information disappear. **Retrograde amnesia** (the inability to recall events immediately preceding an accident or injury) is caused by an interruption in elaborative rehearsal.

## LONG-TERM MEMORY

**Long-term memory (LTM)** is more or less permanent and corresponds to everything we "know." **Semantic memory** is the portion of LTM that stores general facts and information in dictionary or encyclopedia form. Another facet of LTM, **episodic memory**, stores more specific information from our personal lives and other information rich with personal meaning. The information in LTM is highly organized, enabling us to retrieve information almost instantaneously.

### Implicit Memory

**Implicit memory** refers to "unintentional" memories of information that either was not intentionally committed to LTM or is retrieved unintentionally from LTM. By contrast, **explicit memory** allows us to recall information that is intentionally committed to LTM and retrieved from LTM. Implicit memory means the memories we acquire without trying to remember anything; this form of memory tends to occur to us unbidden.

### Storage and Retrieval in LTM

Most, if not all, of the information in LTM remains there more or less permanently, though there is some evidence that information lasts longer in LTM if more effort is put into encoding it in the first place.

To the extent that information is apparently lost from LTM, researchers do not cite decay as the cause; rather, interference from competing information seems a more likely explanation. Such interference accounts for the *tip-of-the-tongue phenomenon.* Interference may come from two directions: In **retroactive interference,** new information interferes with old information already in LTM; **proactive interference** refers to the process by which old information already in LTM interferes with new information.

Interference may hinder the retrieval of information from LTM in two ways. Retrieval failure occurs when information still lodged in LTM can't be retrieved because of interference from other information. Storage failure occurs when interfering information simply wipes out other information in LTM. Retroactive interference stems from storage failure or loss, in which new information pushes out the old. Proactive interference can be traced to problems in retrieval—both the old and the new information may be present in LTM, but "seniority" dictates which information will be recalled, so the newer information is difficult or impossible to retrieve.

Recognizing that past reactions and experiences affect memory, researchers developed the *schema theory*. A **schema** (plural: **schemata**) is a set of beliefs or expectations about something based on past experience. As an unconscious, stored mental presentation of a situation, the schema serves as a basis or standard for comparison with a new experience or expectation of an experience. Using schemata, we not only comprehend and interpret present circumstances but also streamline our retrieval processes.

### Autobiographical Memory

*Autobiographical memory* refers to your recollection of events that happened in your life and when those events took place. Research indicates that people generally cannot remember events that occurred prior to age 2 and that our earliest memories frequently concern events that significantly changed our lives or that were particularly frightening.

## SPECIAL TOPICS IN MEMORY

### Flashbulb Memories

Years after a dramatic or significant event occurs, people often have vivid memories of that event as well as the incidents surrounding it. These memories are known as **flashbulb memories**. According to the *now print* theory, these memories are created at the time of the event and remain essentially accurate and unchanged through the years because of their highly emotional content. Recent research has challenged all these assumptions.

### Improving Your Memory

The key to improving memory lies in organizing and coding information more effectively when we first place it in LTM. Techniques called **mnemonics**, make it easier to organize and code such information. Mnemonic devices provide ready-made ways to impose order on new information. Familiar mnemonic methods include rhymes and jingles like those used for remembering dates and similar facts; other mnemonics rely on sophisticated imagery in which special meanings are attached to the material.

Techniques designed to bolster recall of textbook material encourage more active engagement with or elaborative rehearsal of the material than a simple rereading (even of a summary such as this) does. Highlighting the key points helps, but preparing an outline of the chapter before reading it works better. Other tips: write down questions and reactions to new material in the margin of the text as you read, and spell out, in your own words, how the new material relates to what you already know.

Finally, the highly effective *SQ3R* method (survey, question, read, recite, review) forces you into a sort of dialogue with the text.

## BIOLOGICAL BASES OF MEMORY

While some memories may be localized in certain portions of the brain (for example, some of the learning that takes place in classical conditioning is stored in the cerebellum), in many cases a single memory is stored in numerous parts of the brain. Thus, damage to or removal of any one part of the brain may diminish but not erase the whole memory.

According to recent studies, however, specific centers in the brain are essential for the formation of memories. In humans, the brain's hippocampus transfers factual information from STM to LTM. People who suffer damage to the hippocampus can remember events stored in STM, but their ability to remember things for any length of time is seriously impaired.

Most recent studies of memory show that the

hippocampus plays a role only during the memory-formation stage; once a memory has been well formed, it persists even if the hippocampus is destroyed.

# REVIEW QUESTIONS

## MULTIPLE CHOICE

1. Raw information from the senses reaches the ______ before it disappears or is further processed.

2. The selection process that allows us to retain information after it has arrived from the senses is termed ______ .

3. We are able to focus on some information while ignoring other information. This is called the ______ ______ phenomenon.

4. ______ ______ memory is what we are thinking about at any given moment. Its function is to briefly store new information and to work on that and other information.

5. According to ______ theory, the mere passing of time in itself will cause the strength of memory to decrease. By contrast, ______ theory holds that information gets mixed up with, or pushed aside by, other information and thus becomes harder to remember.

6. ______ rehearsal, or simply repeating information over and over, is an effective way of retaining information for just a minute or two.

7. To ensure that information in short-term memory will be remembered for a long time, the best strategy to use is ______ rehearsal, which involves relating new information to something that we already know.

8. Long-term memory includes ______ memory, which is filled with general facts and information, and ______ memory, made up of events that have personal meaning for us.

9. Most psychologists agree that the tip-of-the-tongue phenomenon is due to ______ .

10. When the operator gives you the telephone number you requested, you have trouble remembering it because the sequence of numbers is close to that of your friend. This is an example of ______ interference.

11. The psychological term for the detailed visual images that serve as the basis for photographic memory is ______ imagery.

12. Arrange the following steps of the SQ3R method in the proper sequence: question, read, review, survey, recite.

13. True or false: Some memories are stored in specific regions of the brain, while others are stored throughout many regions.

14. The inability to recall events prior to a certain age is called ______ .

## CRITICAL THINKING AND APPLICATIONS

15. Suppose a friend gave you a vivid account of a traffic accident she had witnessed. How would you verify that her account was accurate? Which interviewing techniques would you avoid in questioning her? What kinds of questions might you pose if you wanted to try to change her memory of the accident?

16. What are flashbulb memories? Have you ever experienced one? If so, what characteristics

did it have? How could you tell if it was accurate or not?

17. Compare and contrast episodic, semantic, and implicit memory. Give examples from your own experience of each type of memory. For which kinds of situations is each type of memory most useful?

*(Answers to the Review Questions can be found in the back of text).*

# Think About It!

1. Is trial and error an effective way of solving problems?
2. *True or false*: People often make decisions based on whatever information is most readily available, even if that information is not accurate.
3. How do psychologists define intelligence? Do psychologists and laypeople define intelligence in the same way?
4. What does IQ mean? How is it measured? Is IQ the same as intelligence?
5. What are some of the most common criticisms of IQ tests?
6. Are highly creative people more intelligent than less creative people?

# COGNITION AND MENTAL ABILITIES

7

## Overview

**Cognition** The processes whereby we acquire and use knowledge.

**Phonemes** The basic sounds that make up any language.

**Morphemes** The smallest meaningful units of speech, such as simple words, prefixes, and suffixes.

**Perhaps you know the following riddle. "A man married 20 different women in the same small town. All these women are still alive, and he never divorced a single one of them. How did this happen?" The solution to the riddle is that the man was a member of the clergy. When you hear the answer for the first time, you are liable to groan because the solution is so obvious once you know it, even though it is difficult to see at first. In the first part of this chapter, we will consider the processes that enable us to solve little problems, such as riddles, as well as bigger, more complicated problems. These processes are all part of cognition.**

Psychologists use the term **cognition** to refer to all the processes by which we acquire and use information. In previous chapters, we have already considered some important cognitive processes, such as perception and memory. Later in this book we will explore the crucial roles cognition plays in coping and adjustment, abnormal behavior, and interpersonal relations. For now, we will focus on a family of cognitive processes that are all related to thinking: language, imagery, conceptualization, evaluation or interpretation, problem solving, and decision making. Here are some examples of cognitive processes at work: "I think this town is like the one I grew up in" indicates conceptualization. The question, "What does she think of all this?" seeks an evaluation. "Aha! I think I have the answer!" reflects problem solving and insight. "I think I'll buy the red one" shows decision making.

In probing cognition and mental abilities in this chapter, we will first examine the building blocks of thought—how we think and what we think about—and then look at how these building blocks figure in problem solving and decision making. Turning to intelligence and other mental abilities, we will focus on what constitutes intelligence, the underpinnings of and the controversy over intelligence testing, and, finally, the connection between intelligence and creativity.

What images and thoughts come to mind when you think of your mother?

## BUILDING BLOCKS OF THOUGHT

Language, images, and concepts are the three most important building blocks of thought. When you say that you are thinking about your mother, you may have in mind complex linguistic statements such as "I think she would like to hear from me sometime soon" or "I wish I could be more like her." You may also have an image of her—probably her face, but perhaps also the sound of her voice or the scent of her favorite perfume. Or you may think of your mother by using various concepts or categories such as *woman, successful, strong, caring, dynamic, gentle*. In the first part of this chapter, we will consider how language and images underlie thinking. Then we will explore concepts and their relationship to thought.

### Language

Ordinary language is based on universal sound units, such as the sounds of *t*, *th*, and *k*. These are called **phonemes**. There are about 45 phonemes in English, and as many as 85 in some other languages (Bourne et al., 1986). Standing alone, phonemes are meaningless: The sound *b*, for example, has no inherent meaning. But phonemes may be grouped together to form words, prefixes (*un-*, *pre-*), and suffixes (*-ed*, *-ing*), known as **morphemes**—the smallest meaningful units in a language. Morphemes play a key role in human cognition. By themselves, they can represent important ideas such as "red" or "calm" or "hot." The suffix *-ed* captures the idea of "in the past" (as in *mowed* or *liked* or *cared*). The prefix *pre-* reflects the idea of "before" or "prior to" (as in *preview* or *predetermined*).

Morphemes may also be combined to create complex words that represent quite complex ideas, such as *pre-exist-ing*, *un-wal-ed*, *psycho-logy*. In turn, words may be combined to form phrases and sentences, which can represent even more complex thoughts.

Sentences have both a **surface structure**—the particular words and phrases—and a **deep structure**—the underlying meaning. The same deep structure can be conveyed by various different surface structures, as in the following example:

The ocean is unusually calm tonight.

Tonight the ocean is particularly calm.

Compared to most nights, tonight the ocean is calm.

When you wish to communicate an idea, you start with a thought, then choose words and phrases to express the idea, and finally produce the speech sounds that make up those words and phrases. This is sometimes called *top-down processing*, and you can see from the left arrow in Figure 7-1 that the movement is indeed from top to bottom. When you want to understand a sentence, your task is reversed. You must start with speech sounds and work your way up to the meaning of those sounds. This is sometimes called *bottom-up processing*, as shown by the right arrow in Figure 7-1.

Rules govern how we combine phonemes and morphemes, just as rules specify how we structure sentences so their meaning is clear. While such rules underlie both spoken and sign languages, we will focus primarily on spoken language. These rules comprise what linguists call a **grammar** (Chomsky, 1957). The work of the linguist Noam Chomsky (1957) has significantly broadened our understanding of the way grammar functions. The rules of grammar enable speakers and listeners to move easily from surface to deep structure performing what Chomsky calls *transformations*. To accomplish this, we draw on two major components of a grammar—semantics and syntax. **Semantics** describes how we assign meaning to the morphemes we use. Some semantic rules specify how a word may refer to an object—for

**Surface structure** The particular words and phrases used to make up a sentence.

**Deep structure** The underlying meaning of a sentence.

**Grammar** The language rules that determine how sounds and words can be combined and used to communicate meaning within a language.

**Semantics** The criteria for assigning meaning to the morphemes in a language.

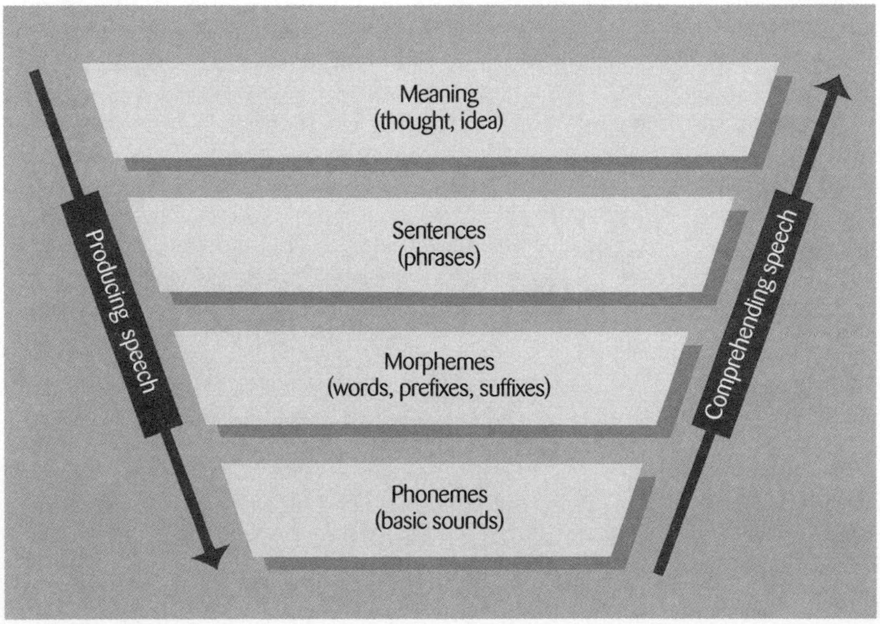

Meaning
(thought, idea)
Sentences
(phrases)
Morphemes
(words, prefixes, suffixes)
Phonemes
(basic sounds)
Producing speech
Comprehending speech

**Figure 7-1**
**The direction of movement in speech production and comprehension.**
When we produce a sentence, we move from thoughts and ideas to basic sounds; to understand a sentence, we move from basic sounds back to the underlying thoughts and ideas.

**Syntax** The rules for arranging words into grammatically correct sentences.

example, that a large, striped cat is a *tiger*. Other semantic rules govern how different combinations of morphemes affect meaning: Adding the suffix *-ed* to a verb like *play*, for example, puts the action in the past; adding the prefix *un-* to *necessary* reverses its meaning. **Syntax** is the system of rules that dictates how we combine words to form grammatically correct sentences. After all, a random jumble of individually meaningful words wouldn't communicate very much! In the English language, for example, adjectives come before nouns. The reverse is true in some European languages.

In Chapter 9, we will probe more deeply into language and how people learn to use it to think and to communicate. For the moment, it is sufficient for us to recognize that words, phrases, and sentences form major building blocks of thought. Knowing more than one language may actually contribute to a person's ability to think in general (see the Highlights box titled "The Cognitive Advantages of Bilingual Education"). Language is

# IGHLIGHTS

## The Cognitive Advantages of Bilingual Education

Nearly 5 million students in the United States come from homes where a language other than English is spoken (*The New York Times*, 1985). Which language to use when teaching such children has been the subject of heated debate in recent years. Lining up on one side are educators who believe that for non–native-speaking children to be assimilated into U.S. culture, they should be placed in classes where only English is taught. Some educators supporting this position have also argued that bilingual education confuses children. On the other side of this thorny debate are educators who advocate that non–native speakers be taught in both English and their native language so they don't lose touch with their culture.

Nationwide, schools have been eliminating bilingual-education programs. As a result, children from non–English-speaking homes have become fluent in English while losing familiarity with their native language.

However, some research evidence bolsters the argument for bilingual education. For example, a study of Latino children in New Haven showed a positive correlation between bilingualism and superior cognitive abilities (Hakuta, 1987). The more children used both Spanish and English, the researcher observed, the greater their intellectual grasp of reading and nonverbal logic. In addition, bilingual children showed a more sophisticated understanding of language than other children did, and they scored higher on tests of mental flexibility than children who spoke only English. Mental flexibility refers to skill in considering objectively more than one solution to a problem (Hakuta, 1987).

The greater cognitive abilities of bilingual children, in Hakuta's view, indicate that a wide range of intellectual experience enriches the mind. These studies also show that rather than confusing children, material learned in Spanish seemed to enhance their intellectual development in English. Hakuta concludes that bilingualism apparently has no negative cognitive effects, leading him to call for U.S. schools to instruct non–English-speaking children in their native language for at least 3 years, while only gradually introducing instruction in English. Some school systems have already begun to heed this call. For example, the Detroit public schools have instituted an experimental program in which children whose native language is Arabic are taught half the day in Arabic and the other half in English.

In reviewing a number of bilingual education programs, Genesee (1994) arrived at the same conclusion as Hakuta. In Canada, where bilingual education in English and French has been the norm for many years, these programs have been extensively evaluated. Regardless of whether English or French is the student's native language, training in a second language does not interfere with normal learning of the first language. Moreover, educators confirm that bilingual courses of study enhance overall academic achievement and bolster cognitive processes.

Bilingualism need not always involve two spoken languages; in fact, some important findings have been generated by research into the effects of learning sign language in childhood (Mayberry & Eichen, 1991). Deaf children have great difficulty in learning *spoken* language, but they learn *sign* language relatively easily. In fact, the earlier children acquire sign language, the more effectively they will communicate later in life. One interesting contrast was observed between (1) children who learned a spoken language before they became deaf and subsequently learned sign language in adolescence, and (2) children who were born deaf but who also acquired sign language in adolescence. Even though both groups learned sign language at the same age, the first group learned it more easily. This shows the positive effect that learning one language in childhood can have on learning a second language later on.

not the only building block of thought, however, as we will see in the next section of the chapter.

**Image** A mental representation of a sensory experience.

**Concept** A mental category for classifying objects, people, or experiences.

## Images

Stop reading and think for a moment about Abraham Lincoln. Then think about being outside in a summer thunderstorm. Your thoughts of Lincoln may have ranged from "wrote the Gettysburg Address," to "president during the Civil War," and "assassinated by John Wilkes Booth." But in addition to these words and phrases you probably also came up with some mental images of Lincoln: his bearded face, perhaps, or his lanky body, or a log cabin. When you thought about the thunderstorm, you probably formed mental images of wind, rain, and lightning. An **image** is a mental representation of a sensory experience; it can be used to think about things. We can visualize the Statue of Liberty or astronauts hopping around on the surface of the moon; we can smell Thanksgiving dinner; we can hear Martin Luther King, Jr., saying "I have a dream!" In short, we can think by using sensory images.

Images allow us to think about things in nonverbal ways. Albert Einstein relied heavily on his powers of visualization to understand phenomena that he would later describe by complex mathematical formulas. Although few of us can approach Einstein's visionary genius, we all use imagery and solve problems. The power of images comes through most clearly when concrete forms give shape to complex and abstract ideas. For example, in Figure 7-2 a pie chart illustrates the composition of households in the United States, based on data from the 1990 census. Each type of household is represented by a wedge, the size of which varies according to its percentage of the total number of households. You can mentally compare the size of each wedge and imagine how the pie would change if the percentage of a particular form of household grew or shrank in comparison to the others. Thus, images figure prominently in thinking and cognition. Now let's examine concepts, another important building block of thought.

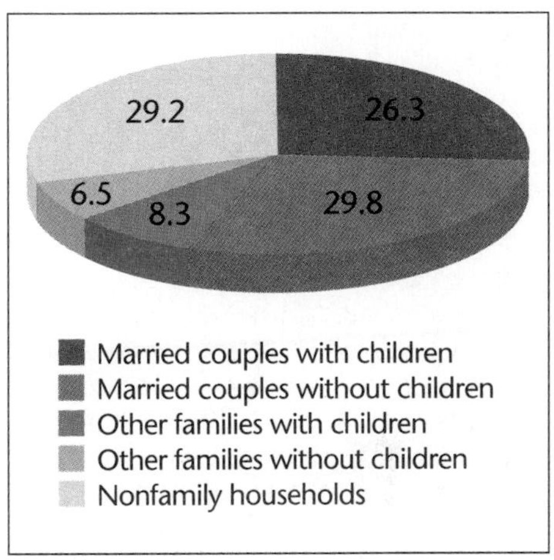


**Figure 7-2**
**The composition of U.S. households in 1990.** How might the sizes of the wedges have differed 25 years ago? What are the advantages of presenting numerical data in this visual form?

## Concepts

**Concepts** are mental categories for classifying specific people, things, or events (Komatsu, 1992). *Dogs*, *books*, and *cars* are all concepts that let us categorize objects in the world around us. *Fast*, *strong*, and *interesting* are also concepts that we use in categorizing objects. When you think about an object—say, a Ferrari—you usually think of the concepts that apply to it, such as, *fast*, *sleek*, *expensive car*. Thus, concepts help us think more efficiently about things. Without the ability to form concepts, we would need a different name for every individual object.

Concepts also give meaning to new experiences. We do not stop and form a new concept for every new experience we have. We draw on concepts we have already formed and place the new object or event into the appropriate categories. In the process, we may modify some of our concepts to better match the world around us. Consider, for example, the concept of *professor*. You probably had some concept of *professor* before you ever attended any college classes. In all likelihood, your concept changed somewhat after you actually met some professors and took your first college courses. You might realize now that professors are not all absentminded, that some professors are not even 30 years old—in fact, that the majority of professors are not very different from most other people. Your concept will become more subtle and intricate as you add new information about professors based on your experiences in college. Conceptualizing *professor* (or anything else) is a way of grouping or categorizing experiences so that every new experience need not be a surprise. We know, to some extent, what to think about it.

**Prototype** According to Rosch, a mental model containing the most typical features of a concept.

**PROTOTYPES** It is tempting to think of concepts as simple and clear-cut. But, as Eleanor Rosch (1973, 1978) discovered, most of the concepts that people use in thinking are neither simple nor unambiguous. Rather, they are "fuzzy": They overlap one another and are often poorly defined. For example, most of us can tell a mouse from a rat, but we would be hard-pressed to come up with an accurate list of the significant differences between mice and rats.

If we cannot explain the difference between a mouse and a rat, how can we use these concepts in our thinking? One possibility that Rosch proposed is that we construct a mental model, or **prototype**, of a representative mouse and a representative rat, which we then use in our thinking. Our concept of bird, for example, does not consist of a list of key attributes like "feathered," "winged," "two feet," and "lives in trees." Instead, most of us have a model bird, or prototype, in mind—such as a robin or a sparrow—that captures for us the essence of *bird.* When we encounter new objects, we compare them to this prototype to determine if they are, in fact, birds. And when we think about birds, we usually think about our prototypical bird.

Most people would agree that a robin somehow expresses "birdness" more than a penguin does—it more nearly fits our prototypical image of a bird. But prototypes are seldom perfect models. Robins, thus, do not embody every single feature that can be possessed by birds. For example, they do not have the talons of an eagle. Because natural categories are fuzzy, prototypes are only the best and most suitable models of a concept, not perfect or exclusive representations of it. As Lindsay and Norman (1977) point out, "The typical dog barks, has four legs, and eats meat. We expect all actual dogs to be the same. Despite this, we would not be too surprised to come across a dog that did not bark, had only three legs, or refused to eat meat" (p. 386). We would still be able to recognize such an animal as a dog.

How, then, do we know which objects belong to a concept? For instance, how do we know that a lion is not a bird but that a penguin is a bird? The answer is that we decide what is most probable or most sensible, given the facts at hand. This is what Rosch calls relying on the *degree of category membership*. For example, a lion and a bird both have two eyes. But the lion does not have wings, it does not have feathers, and it has four feet and a mouth full of teeth—all of which indicate that it is quite unlike our prototype of a bird. Thus, we are able to eliminate lions from the general category of birds. On the other hand, penguins share many features that belong to our prototype of a bird. As a result, we recognize these Arctic creatures as members of the bird family even though they don't fly.

So far, we have seen that words, images, and concepts form the building blocks of thought. But human cognition goes beyond just passively thinking about things; it also involves actively using words, images, and concepts to solve problems and make decisions. In the next two sections of the chapter, we will examine how this works.

## PROBLEM SOLVING

Consider the following problems:

**PROBLEM 1** You have three measuring spoons (see Figure 7-3). One is filled with 8 teaspoons of salt; the other two are empty but have a capacity of 2 teaspoons each. Divide the salt among the spoons so that only 4 teaspoons of salt remain in the largest spoon.

**Figure 7-3**

**PROBLEM 2** You have a 5-minute hourglass and a 9-minute hourglass (see Figure 7-4). How would you use them to time a 14-minute barbecue? (Adapted from Sternberg, 1986)

Most people find these problems very easy to solve. (The answers to these problems appear at the end of the chapter.) But now consider more elaborate versions of the same two problems:

**Problem representation** The first step in solving a problem; it involves interpreting or defining the problem.

**PROBLEM 3** You have three measuring spoons (see Figure 7-5). One (spoon A) is filled with 8 teaspoons of salt. The second and third spoons are both empty; the second spoon (spoon B) can hold 5 teaspoons, and the third (spoon C) can hold 3 teaspoons. Divide the salt among the spoons so that spoon A and spoon B each have exactly 4 teaspoons of salt and spoon C is empty.

**PROBLEM 4** You have a 5-minute hourglass and a 9-minute hourglass. How would you use them to time a 13-minute barbecue? (Adapted from Sternberg, 1986)

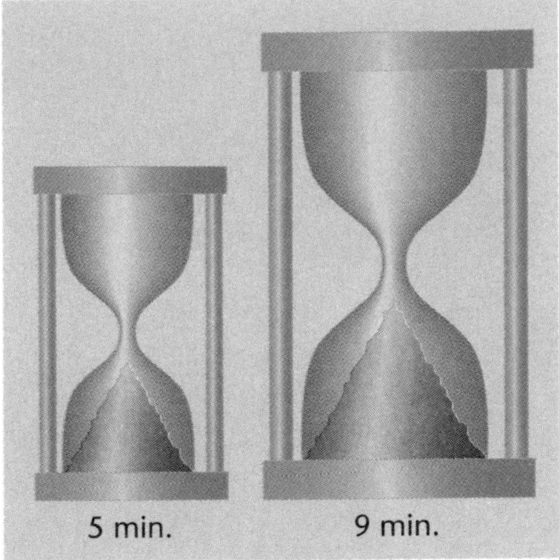


**Figure 7-4**

Most people find the last two problems much more difficult to solve than the first two. Why? In part, this is because the solutions to Problems 3 and 4, simply take longer to work out than the solutions to the first two problems. But there is more to it than that. The first two problems are considered trivial because the solution is obvious; the strategy for solving them is simple and easily identified, and with each step you know you are moving closer to a solution. The last two problems, however, require some interpretation, the strategy for solving them is not at all clear-cut, and it is much harder to figure out whether any given step has actually propelled you closer to a solution. (Solutions to these last two problems can also be found at the end of the chapter.)

Let's examine each of these aspects of the problem-solving process. After we look at the principles of solving a problem and the steps and strategies underlying this process, we will turn to common obstacles that people encounter when they tackle a problem. To conclude, this section will present several techniques for sharpening your skills at problem solving.

**Figure 7-5**

## The Interpretation of Problems

The first step in solving a problem is called **problem representation**, which means interpreting or defining the problem. It is tempting to leap ahead and try to solve a problem just as it is presented, but this impulse often yields poor solutions. For example, if your business is losing money, you might focus on ways to cut costs. But by defining the solution narrowly as an issue of cost cutting, you have ruled out the possibility that the best way to stop losing money might be to increase income rather than to cut costs. A better representation of this problem would be to discover ways to cut costs or increase income or do both.

Now consider these problems:

**PROBLEM 5** You have four pieces of chain, each of which is made up of 3 links (see Figure 7-6). It costs 2 cents to open a link and 3 cents to close a link. All links are closed at the beginning of the problem. How would you join all 12 links together into a single, continuous circle without paying more than 15 cents?

**PROBLEM 6** Arrange six kitchen matches into four equilateral triangles (see Figure 7-7). Each side of every triangle must be only one

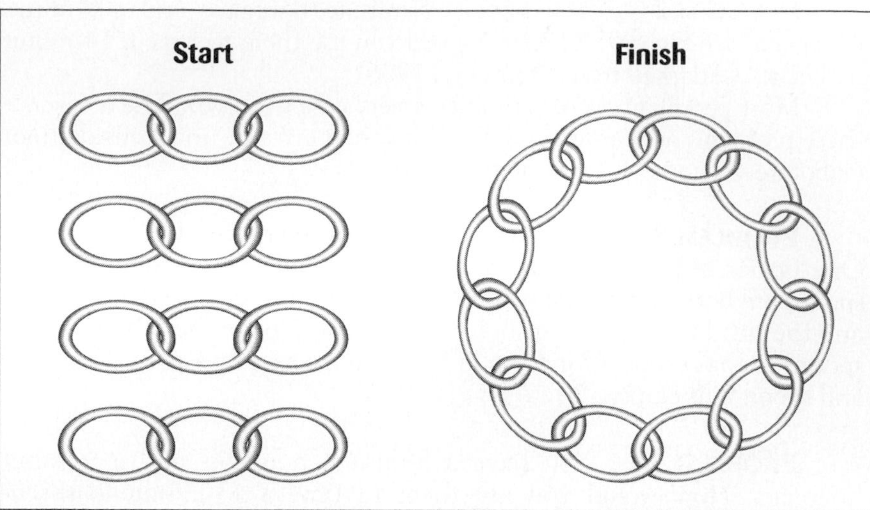


**Figure 7-6**

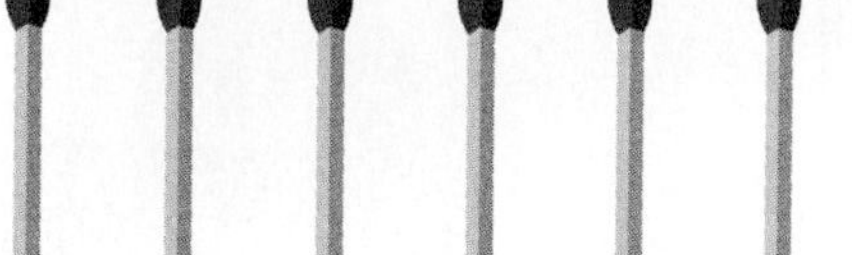

**Figure 7-7**
**The six-match problem.** Arrange the six matches so that they form four equilateral triangles. The solution is given in Figure 7-12.

match length. Before going on, stop and try to work out solutions to Problems 5 and 6.

These two problems are difficult because most of us are looking at them in ways that make them impossible to solve. For example, in Problem 5, most people assume that the best way to proceed is to open and close the end links on the various pieces of chain. As long as this "conceptual block" stands in their way, they are unable to solve the problem. If the problem is represented differently, however, the solution becomes almost instantly clear. Similarly, for the kitchen match problem, most people assume that they can work only in two dimensions—that is, that the triangles must lie flat on a surface—or that one match cannot serve as the side of two triangles. When the problem is presented differently, the solution becomes much easier to figure out. (The solutions to both these problems appear at the end of the chapter). In each case, a narrow definition of the problem sets up conceptual blocks that make solving the problem impossible.

Before you proceed, see if you can solve the following problem:

**Problem 7** A monk wishes to reach a retreat at the top of a mountain. He starts climbing the mountain at sunrise and arrives at the top of the mountain at sunset of the same day. During the course of his ascent, he travels at variable speeds and stops often to rest and eat the food he has brought with him. He spends the night engaged in meditation. The next day he starts his descent at sunrise, following the same narrow path that he used to climb the mountain. As before, he travels at various speeds and stops often to rest and to eat. Because he takes great care not to trip and fall on the way down, the trip down takes as long as the trip up, and he does not arrive at the bottom until sunset. Prove that there is one place on the path that the monk passes at exactly the same time of day on the trip up and on the trip down.

Have you worked out an answer to Problem 7? This problem is extremely difficult to solve if it is represented verbally or mathematically. It is considerably easier to solve if it is represented visually, as you can see from the explanation that appears at the end of the chapter.

Oftentimes, people with a knack for solving problems actually excel at interpreting and representing them in effective ways. Star chess players, for example, can readily categorize a new game situation by comparing it to various standard situations stored in their long-term memories. This strategy helps them interpret the pattern of chess pieces they're facing now with greater speed and precision than the novice chess player. Likewise, a seasoned football coach may quickly recognize that a certain situation on the gridiron calls for a particular kind of defense. He has interpreted the game in terms of familiar categories. To a great extent, gaining expertise in any field, from football to physics, consists of increasing your ability to represent and categorize problems so you can solve them more quickly and effectively (Mayer, 1983).

**Trial and error** A problem-solving strategy based on the successive elimination of incorrect solutions until the correct one is found.

**Information retrieval** A problem-solving strategy that requires only the recovery of information from long-term memory.

**Algorithm** A step-by-step method of problem solving that guarantees a correct solution.

**Heuristics** Rules of thumb that help in simplifying and solving problems, although they do not guarantee a correct solution.

## Producing and Evaluating Solutions

Once you have properly interpreted a problem, the next step is to select a solution strategy that best suits the problem. When casting about for the right strategy, you must choose from a rich assortment of possibilities. In the following pages, we will examine a number of these strategies.

**TRIAL AND ERROR** One way to solve problems is through simple **trial and error**. This strategy works best when we have only a limited set of choices. For example, if you had only three or four keys to choose from, trial and error would be the best way to find out which one unlocked your uncle's garage door. In most cases, however, trial and error usually wastes time because it may take hours or even days for the solution to appear. Moreover, many problems can never be solved through this scattershot approach. How many guesses would it take, for example, to come up with the name of the seventh caliph of the Islamic Abbasid dynasty? Or, how soon could you guess the square root of the product of two sides of a given triangle? You could probably go on guessing for the rest of your life and never come up with the correct answers.

1\. Is trial and error an effective way of solving problems?

To solve most problems, you have to go beyond trial and error. Let's look at some of the other problem-solving strategies at our disposal.

**INFORMATION RETRIEVAL** In some cases, the solution to a problem may be as simple as retrieving information from long-term memory. **Information retrieval** is often critical when a solution must be found quickly. For example, a pilot is expected to memorize the slowest speed at which she can fly a particular airplane before it stalls and heads for the ground. When she needs this information, she has no time to sit back and calculate the correct answer. She simply refers to her long-term memory for an immediate answer.

**ALGORITHMS** Solving more complex problems requires more complex strategies. In some cases, an **algorithm** will yield the right answer. Algorithms are problem-solving methods that guarantee a solution if they are appropriate for the problem and are properly carried out. For example, to calculate the product of 323 and 546, we multiply them according to the rules of multiplication (the algorithm). If we do it accurately, we are sure to get the right answer. To convert temperatures from Fahrenheit to Celsius, we use the formula $C = 5/9(F-32)$. This formula, like all mathematical formulas, is an algorithm.

**HEURISTICS** Many of the problems that we encounter in everyday life, however, cannot be solved by algorithms. In these cases, we often turn to **heuristics**—rules of thumb that help us simplify problems. Heuristics do not guarantee a solution, but they may bring it within reach. Some heuristic methods work better in some situations than in others. Particular heuristics have special purposes only, such as those applied to chess or word

**Hill climbing** A heuristic problem-solving strategy in which each step moves you progressively closer to the final goal.

**Subgoals** Intermediate, more manageable goals used as one heuristic strategy to make it easier to reach the final goal.

puzzles. But other, more general heuristics may be applied to a wide range of human problems. One key element of problem solving is deciding which heuristic best suits a given problem (Bourne et al., 1986).

As an example, consider the very simple heuristic method known as **hill climbing**. In this process, we continually move closer to our final goal without digressing or going backward. At each step, we evaluate how far "up the hill" we have come, how far we still have to go, and precisely what the next step should be to bring us closer to the goal. One useful strategy in answering questions on a multiple-choice test, for example, would be to eliminate the alternatives that are obviously incorrect. Even if this method does not leave you with the one correct answer, you are certainly closer to a solution. In trying to balance a budget, too, each reduction in expenses brings you closer to the goal and leaves you with a smaller overall deficit.

Yet the hill-climbing heuristic is far from optimal in many cases, including Problem 3 on page 241. In solving this problem, there comes a point where you must digress, or actually move backward, to make ultimate progress toward your goal.

Let's consider some other examples for which the hill-climbing strategy is inappropriate. You have probably played checkers at one time or another. At a decisive moment you may have had to "give up" a piece to maneuver toward a more strategic position on the board. Although losing that one piece seemed to push you further from victory, the move in fact nudged you closer to your goal. In baseball, a pitcher can prevent a good hitter from driving in runs at a critical point in the game by giving him or her an "intentional walk." This tactic puts an extra player on base and seems to work against the goal of keeping runners off base. But a shrewd pitcher knows that by conceding a walk to a strong batter, he will instead be pitching to a weaker hitter, next in the lineup, who is less likely to drive in runs.

If you were facing a stellar hitter like Ken Griffey, Jr., you might opt to walk him intentionally. Even though that strategy does not move you directly toward your goal of keeping runners off base, it might ultimately prevent a run from scoring.

Another problem-solving heuristic involves creating **subgoals**. By setting subgoals, we can often break a problem into smaller, more manageable parts, each of which is easier to solve than the problem as a whole. Consider the problem of the Hobbits and the Orcs:

**PROBLEM 8** Three Hobbits and three Orcs are on the bank of a river. They all want to reach the other side of the river, but their boat will carry only two creatures at a time. Moreover, if at any time the Orcs outnumber the Hobbits on the boat or on the river bank, the Orcs will attack the Hobbits. How can all the creatures get across the river without endangering the Hobbits?

We can solve this problem by dividing it into a series of subparts, each with its own goal. Consider what has to be done to get just one or two creatures across the river at a time—setting aside, temporarily, the overriding goal of transporting everyone to the opposite side. We could first send two of the Orcs across and have one of them return. That gets one Orc across the river. Now we can think about the next trip. It's clear that we can't then send a single Hobbit across with an Orc because the Hobbit would be outnumbered as soon as they landed on the opposite shore. So that means we have to send either two Hobbits or two Orcs. By working on the problem in this fashion—concentrating on subgoals—we can eventually get everyone across safely.

Once you have mastered Problem 8, you might want to try your hand at Problem 9, which is considerably more difficult (the answers to both problems can be found at the end of the chapter):

**PROBLEM 9** This problem is identical to Problem 8, except that there are five Hobbits and five Orcs, and the boat can carry three creatures at a time across the river.

Subgoals help us solve a variety of everyday problems. For example, a student whose goal is to write a term paper might set subgoals by breaking the project into a series of separate tasks: choosing a topic, doing research and taking notes, preparing an outline, writing the first draft, editing, rewriting, and so on. Even the subgoals can sometimes be broken down into separate tasks. For example, writing the first draft of the paper might be broken down into subgoals such as writing the introduction, describing the position to be taken, supporting the position with evidence, drawing conclusions, composing a summary, and compiling a bibliography. In this case, the subgoals need not be reached in any particular order: It might be easier to start spelling out the evidence in support of a position, then back up and write a detailed description of the position to be taken, and only then write the introduction and summary. This strategy works extremely well if you find yourself struggling to begin writing your opening. Skip the introduction and write some other section of the paper first, and then come back to the opening paragraphs later when you have a better idea of what you want to say and how best to say it. In any situation, subgoals simplify problem solving because they free us from the burden of having to "get to the other side of the river" all at once. This tactic allows us to set our sights on closer, more manageable goals. Of course, the overall purpose of setting subgoals is still to reach the ultimate goal—the solution to the problem.

**Working backward** A heuristic strategy in which the problem solver works backward from the desired goal to the given conditions.

**Set** The tendency to perceive and to approach problems in certain ways.

Another heuristic approach is called **working backward** (Bourne et al., 1986). Using this strategy, we search for a solution by starting at the goal and working backward toward the "givens." This method has distinct advantages when the goal offers more information than the givens and when the operations can work both forward and backward. If, for example, we wanted to spend exactly $100 on clothing, it would be difficult to reach that goal simply by buying some items and hoping that they totaled exactly $100. A better strategy would be to purchase one item, subtract its cost from $100 to determine how much money we have left, then purchase another item, subtract its cost, and so on, until we have spent $100.

Up to this point, we have been concentrating on how to use various strategies to solve problems. Yet in real life, problem solving often bogs down: We're either unable to arrive at any solution or we're stuck with an ineffective or unworkable solution. In the next section, we will examine various obstacles to problem solving.

## Obstacles to Solving Problems

Success in solving problems is affected by many factors other than those we have already touched on. One of these factors is a person's level of motivation, or emotional arousal. As will be noted in the chapter called "Motivation and Emotion," we usually reach the "peak" or optimal state of performance in problem solving at intermediate levels of excitement or arousal. Moreover, we need to keep our emotions in check to solve complex problems: The more intricate the problem-solving task, the lower the level of emotion that can be tolerated without interfering with performance. Generally speaking, we must generate a surge of excitement—but not too much—to motivate ourselves to solve a problem.

Another factor that can either help or hinder problem solving is **set**, which refers to our tendency to perceive and to approach problems in specific ways. Our set determines which information we will be able to retrieve from memory in a given situation. Set, therefore, can be helpful if we have learned certain operations and ways of perceiving in the past that we can apply in the present situation. For example, people tend to do better when they solve problems for the second or third time because they have learned more effective strategies for addressing the problem and because they have

**Functional fixedness** The tendency to perceive only a limited number of uses for an object; it interferes with the process of problem solving.

come to understand the problem better (Reed, Ernst, & Banerji, 1974). Much of our education has to do with learning sets and ways to solve problems (i.e., heuristics and algorithms), even though it may seem that we are only learning specific information. We are taught to integrate new information into forms that we already know or to use methods that have proved effective in the past. In fact, the strategies that we use in problem solving are themselves a set. We have learned that approaching a problem in a certain logical order is the best way to solve it.

But sets do not always help solve problems. If a problem calls for applying your previous experience in a new and different way, a strong set could pose a serious obstacle. Oftentimes, people who are most successful in solving problems have many different sets at their disposal and can figure out quickly when to change sets or when to give up a set entirely. Great ideas and inventions emerge from such a delicate balance. For example, the renowned astronomer Copernicus was familiar with all the sets of his time, but he saw beyond the confines of his contemporaries' views and realized that they might not be relevant to his work. Only by rejecting these sets could he discover that the earth revolves around the sun, rather than the other way around, as his contemporaries believed.

The point that sets are useful as long as they do not obscure novel approaches to solving problems.

One characteristic of sets that can seriously hinder problem solving is **functional fixedness**. Consider Figure 7-8. Do you see a way to mount the candle on the wall? The more you use an object in one way, the harder it is to see new uses for it. When you get used to seeing or using something in only one way, you have assigned a fixed function to it. To some extent, of course, learning is a process of assigning correct functions to objects. We teach a child that the "right" function of a spoon is stirring, not pounding.

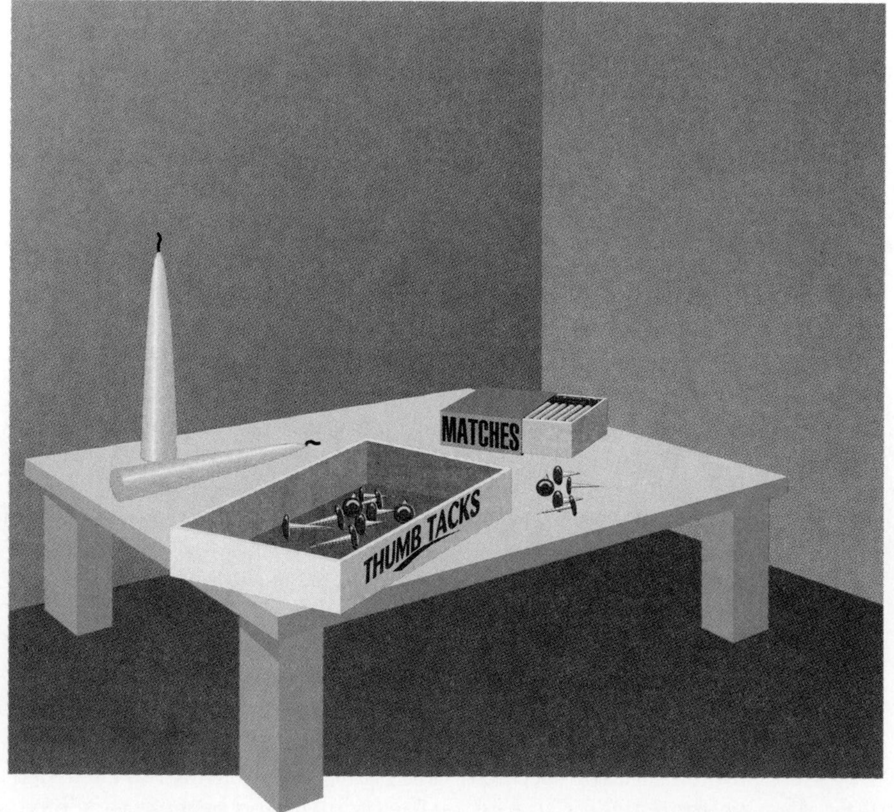


**Figure 7-8**
In order to test the effects of *functional fixedness,* subjects might be given the items shown on the table and asked to mount a candle on the wall. A solution is given in Figure 7-16.

But to solve problems we must keep an open mind to see that an object can indeed be used for an entirely different function if need be. (The solution to this problem appears at the end of the chapter.)

We have been talking about functional fixedness in terms of objects, but the idea can also be applied to problems with people. For example, the problems of the elderly have commanded much attention recently. Older people who are placed in institutions often feel useless and depressed. Unwanted children who live in institutions rarely receive the attention and care they need to thrive. Instead of seeing the elderly as people who are no longer productive and need to be looked after, someone came up with the clever idea of asking them to serve as foster grandparents for the children in institutions. This idea grew out of suspending the fixed function of both groups and viewing them, instead, in a new light. The "grandparents" gave the children love and attention, and the children gave the older people the feeling that they were needed and useful. By moving past functional fixedness, two human problems were addressed with one wise, novel, and compassionate strategy.

Despite the many pitfalls we may encounter when trying to solve problems, we can sharpen our problem-solving skills in a number of ways. Let's take a look at some of the techniques that can help us become better and more efficient problem solvers.

**Tactic of elimination** A problem-solving strategy in which possible solutions are evaluated according to appropriate criteria and discarded as they fail to contribute to a solution.

**Visualizing** A problem-solving strategy in which principles or concepts are drawn, diagrammed, or charted so that they can be better understood.

## Becoming Better at Problem Solving

Recall that the first step in successfully solving a problem is to interpret or represent the problem correctly. You can then experiment with a number of solution strategies, shifting your perspective on the problem from one angle to another. Let's look more closely at how some of these strategies work.

**TACTIC OF ELIMINATION** If in solving a given problem you are more sure of what you do not want than of what you do want, the **tactic of elimination** can be very helpful. The best approach is first to create a list of all the possible solutions you can think of. Then discard all the solutions that take you where you definitely do not want to go. That leaves a smaller number of potential solutions for you to examine much more closely. This strategy will only work if your list of possible solutions contains at least one good solution to the problem. Otherwise you'll end up eliminating all the possible solutions on your list, and you'll have to start all over again from scratch! Also, you have to be careful not to scrap a solution that *seems* on the surface to lead to an undesirable outcome but, on closer examination, might turn out to be an excellent solution to the problem.

**VISUALIZING** Other useful tactics include **visualizing**, diagramming, and charting various courses of action (J. L. Adams, 1980). For example, in the Hobbit and Orc problem, it might help to draw a picture of the river and show the Hobbits and Orcs at each stage of the problem as they are ferried back and forth. By drawing a diagram of a problem, or even constructing a simple model of it, you may find it easier to grasp the principle of the problem and to avoid irrelevant or distracting details. Some chess masters, for example, can visualize chess games in their heads; as a result, they are able to play as many as 50 simultaneous games blindfolded!

**CREATIVE PROBLEM SOLVING** Many problems, of course, do not lend themselves to straightforward solutions but rely more on flexible and original thinking. For example, how many unusual uses can you think of for an ordinary object like a brick? It's easy to imagine a few good uses for a brick but quite another task to come up with 50 or 60 distinct uses.

**Divergent thinking** Thinking that meets the criteria of originality, inventiveness, and flexibility.

**Convergent thinking** Thinking that is directed toward one correct solution to a problem.

**Brainstorming** A problem-solving strategy in which an individual or a group produces numerous ideas and evaluates them only after all ideas have been collected.

**Compensatory model** A rational decision-making model in which choices are systematically evaluated based on various criteria.

Psychologists sometimes refer to this type of thinking as **divergent thinking**, as opposed to **convergent thinking** (Guilford, 1967). A problem requiring convergent thinking has only one or a very few solutions—like a math problem. Convergent thinking is required when a problem has a known solution. By contrast, problems that have no single correct solution and that require a flexible, inventive approach call for divergent thinking.

Because creative problem solving requires thinking up new and original ideas, the process is not always aided by planning or the deliberate use of problem-solving strategies. Solutions to many problems rely on insight, a seemingly arbitrary flash "out of the blue" that reveals the solution to a problem. Therefore, if you simply cannot arrive at a solution to a problem after careful preparation and step-by-step efforts at problem solving, it might be wise to stop thinking about the problem for a while and return to it later, approaching it from a new angle (Murray & Denny, 1969). Sometimes you get so enmeshed in the details of a problem that you lose sight of an obvious solution. Taking a rest from the problem may allow a fresh approach to surface.

It is also important to develop a questioning attitude toward problems. Ask yourself, "What is the real problem here? Can the problem be interpreted in other ways?" By *redefining* the problem, you may find that you have opened up new avenues to creative solutions. And try to maintain an uncritical attitude toward potential solutions: Don't reject a prospective solution because at first glance it doesn't seem to fit that problem. On closer examination, the solution may turn out to be highly effective, or it may bring to mind similar solutions that would work. This is the rationale behind the technique called **brainstorming**: When solving a problem, produce lots of ideas without evaluating them prematurely. Only after lots of ideas have been collected should you review and evaluate them (Haefele, 1962).

Finally, people may become more creative when they interact with creative peers and teachers who serve as role models (Amabile, 1983). Although some creative people work well in isolation, many others find it stimulating to collaborate with other creative people.

## DECISION MAKING

Decision making refers to a special kind of problem solving in which we already know all the possible solutions (choices). Therefore, the task is not to come up with new solutions, but rather to identify the best available solution or choice based on a predetermined set of criteria. This might sound like a fairly simple process, but sometimes we have to juggle a large and complex set of criteria as well as a multitude of possible choices. As the number of criteria and choices grows, so does the difficulty of making a good decision. For example, suppose you are looking for an apartment. There are hundreds of apartments to choose from. And while the monthly rent is important, so are the neighbors, location, level of noise, and cleanliness. If you find a noisy apartment with undesirable neighbors but a bargain-basement rent, should you take it? Is it a better choice than an apartment in a more desirable location with less noise but a higher rent? How do you weigh all these factors to make the best possible choice among all the available apartments?

The logical way to proceed in making any decision is to rate each of the available choices based on all the criteria and to rank each choice overall according to how well it matches your criteria. For each choice the attractive features may offset or compensate for the unattractive features; thus, this approach to decision making is called a **compensatory model**. For example, if you are buying a house, one element you might be looking for is a brick exterior. You might, however, end up buying a wood frame house if it is located in a good school district, has a pleasing floor plan, and is reasonably priced. In this case, the attractive features offset or compensate for the lack of brick construction.

**Noncompensatory model** A decision-making model in which weaknesses in one or more criteria are not offset by strengths in other criteria.

Table 7-1 illustrates one of the most useful compensatory models. The various criteria are listed, and each one is assigned a weight according to its importance. Here the decision involves the purchase of a new car, and only three criteria are considered: price (which is not weighted heavily), and gas mileage and service record (which are weighted much more heavily). Each car is then rated from 1 (poor) to 5 (excellent) on each of the criteria. You can see that Car 1 has an excellent price (5) but relatively poor gas mileage (2) and service record (1); Car 2 has a less desirable price but a fairly good mileage and service record. Each rating is then multiplied by the weight for that criterion (e.g., for Car 1, the price rating of 5 is multiplied by the weight of 4), and the result is put in parentheses next to the rating. Then the numbers in parentheses are added to give a total for each car. Clearly Car 2 is the better choice: It has a less desirable price, but that factor is offset by its superior mileage and service record—two criteria that are more important than price to this particular buyer.

Designing a table like this one allows you to evaluate a large number of choices based on many criteria. This model may be extremely helpful in making choices such as which college to attend, which job offer to accept, which career to pursue, and where to take a vacation. If you have properly weighted the various criteria and correctly rated each alternative in terms of each criterion, then you can be sure that the alternative with the highest total score is, in fact, the most rational choice, given the information available to you.

Most people, however, do not follow such a precise system when it comes to making decisions. Rather, they use various **noncompensatory models** in which shortcomings on one criterion are not offset by strengths on other criteria. Especially popular is the *elimination-by-aspects* tactic (S.K. Reed, 1988). In the case of buying a car, you might toss out specific choices if they do not meet one or two of your requirements, regardless of how well they stack up on other criteria. So you might eliminate Car 2, regardless of all its advantages, simply because it costs more. Noncompensatory models tend to be shortsighted. Because they do not help you weigh the values of particular features, nor do they invite you to compare all the alternatives, such decision-making models can lead to decisions that are merely adequate but not optimal.

Sometimes it is useful to combine compensatory and noncompensatory strategies to arrive at a decision. When faced with many alternatives and many criteria, a noncompensatory approach could eliminate any choices that were especially weak on one or more key criteria, even though they might be strong on other criteria. Once you narrowed the field to a few alter-

**TABLE 7-1 Compensatory Decision Table for Purchase of a New Car**

| | Price (weight = 4) | Gas Mileage (weight = 8) | Service Record (weight = 10) | Weighted Total |
|---|---|---|---|---|
| **Car 1** | 5(20) | 2(16) | 1(10) | (46) |
| **Car 2** | 1(4) | 4(32) | 4(40) | (76) |
| **Ratings:** | 5=Excellent<br>1=Poor | | | |

**Representativeness** A heuristic by which a new situation is judged on the basis of its resemblance to a stereotypical model.

**Availability** A heuristic by which a judgment or decision is based on information that is most easily retrieved from memory.

natives, all of which ranked at least average on the various criteria, then you might adopt some form of compensatory decision model to identify the best choice from among the remaining alternatives. For example, in purchasing a car, you might scratch all the choices that clearly were too expensive or all those with especially poor service records (noncompensatory strategy). You could then evaluate and choose from among the remaining choices based on a number of specific criteria (compensatory strategy).

Choosing an appropriate decision-making model often depends on how much is at stake. A compensatory model is usually favored when the stakes are high: buying a home or choosing a college. When the stakes are low, the noncompensatory model helps us make quick decisions about such casual matters as which shoes to wear or who we think will win an Academy Award.

Even in crucial matters, however, making rational decisions is not always easy. Sometimes, for example, information about an alternative option is unavailable or vague. When choosing between two cars, for instance, you may not have access to the repair record of either car, perhaps because both are new models. In this case, you have to make some estimates based on information about past repair records for cars of that make, which then help you predict how much downtime these new models might need for repairs. In the absence of any reliable information at all, you may have to venture a guess about some of the facts that you need to make a sound decision, and research indicates that guesses in these situations are often incorrect (Gilovich, 1991).

The heuristic of **representativeness** is widely used in making judgments and reaching decisions. We draw on the principle of representativeness whenever we make a decision based on information that matches our model of the typical member of a category. Representativeness can help simplify the decision-making process. For example, if every time you went shopping you consistently purchased the least expensive items, and if all these items turned out to be of poor quality, you might eventually decide not to buy any item that falls into the category "very cheap."

One shortcoming of representativeness is the tendency to stereotype; that is, to attribute certain characteristics to all members of a specific group. For example, when it comes to hiring, many people discriminate against all elderly people without considering a particular individual's ability to do the job. Their stereotype of the elderly casts these people as incapable of certain tasks, and they therefore judge all older people as representative of the general model. (Stereotypes are examined in greater detail in Chapter 14.)

**2.** *True or false*: People often make decisions based on whatever information is most readily available, even if that information is not accurate.

Another common heuristic used in decision making is **availability**. In the absence of full and accurate information, we often make decisions based on whatever information we can most easily retrieve from memory, even though this information may not be accurate. In one experiment, subjects were asked whether the letter *r* appears more frequently as the first or third letter in English words. Most people said first, but the correct answer is third. Their estimates were incorrect because they relied on the most readily available information in their memories, and it is easier to recall words that begin with *r* than words that have *r* as their third letter.

Everyday examples of the availability heuristic can be spotted all the time (Gilovich, 1991). For example, consider the so-called subway effect: It seems to be a law of nature that if you are waiting at a subway station, one train after another will come along headed the opposite way. Similarly, if you are trying to hail a taxi, it always seems as if most of those traveling the way you want to go are occupied or off-duty. The problem here is that once a subway train or a taxi does come your way, you leave the scene, so you never see the overall situation: several subway trains going in your direction before one comes the other way or a long string of empty taxis heading the way you're going. As a result, you tend to assume that those situations seldom or never occur! Consider another example: If you are driving at the speed limit on a busy highway, it is natural for you to conclude that you are virtually the only person driving at that speed and that almost everyone on the road is driving either faster or slower than you are. Why? Because even if there are hundreds of cars going the same speed as you are, you will see very few of them: You'll never pass them, and they'll never pass you. Thus, most of the cars that you notice are those that are going faster or slower than you are and that either pass you or are passed by you. The natural conclusion, based on the limited evidence available to you, is that nearly everyone is going faster or slower than you are.

**Confirmation bias** The tendency to look for evidence in support of a belief and to ignore evidence that would disprove a belief.

Another faulty heuristic that is closely related to availability is **confirmation bias**—the tendency to seek evidence in support of our beliefs and to ignore evidence that contradicts them.

Confirmation bias is one of the processes that perpetuates stereotypes in the face of contradictory evidence. Suppose that you believe all elderly people are frail and mentally incompetent. Every time you see an elderly person in need of care or assistance, you take it as evidence in support of your belief. But what about all the elderly people who are active, healthy, and leading very productive lives? You'll probably discount them as exceptions to the rule. As long as you discount contradictory evidence, your stereotype of the elderly is likely to remain intact.

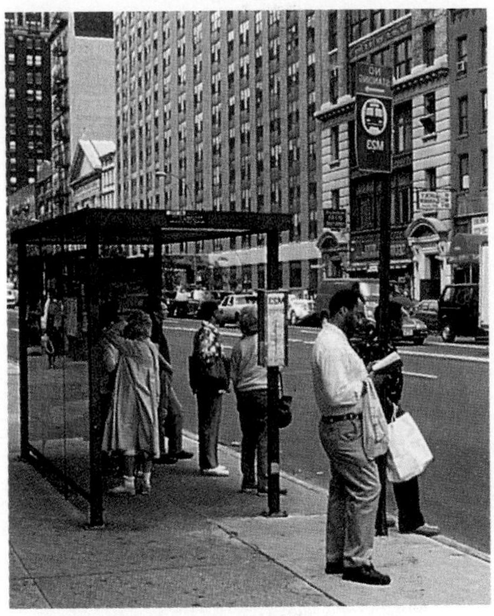

When we are waiting for a bus, taxi, or subway train, they all *seem* to be going in the opposite direction. This distortion exemplifies the availability heuristic.

Even though faulty heuristics guide much of our decision making, for the most part people still manage to make reasonably satisfactory decisions in the real world (Kleinmuntz, 1991). After all, we can usually revise decisions if it appears that an initial choice was not optimal. Moreover, real-world decisions often don't have to be ideal or optimal, as long as the results are acceptable.

In certain situations, however, *close* is not good enough. For example, Spettle and Liebert (1986) studied the potential for error in decision making among operators at nuclear power plants. They found that in addition to the kinds of heuristic errors that we have been exploring, the stress of an emergency situation causes decision making to deteriorate further. Great stress may even erode performance to the point of panic. According to Spettle and Liebert, training that simulates actual emergency conditions may prepare people to make efficient and effective split-second decisions not only in those situations but also in novel situations where quick and accurate decisions are crucial. Preparatory training is also central to the Outward Bound program. a wilderness-training program originally developed because British sailors, whose boats were torpedoed, panicked and died when calm decision making would have ensured their survival. Outward Bound places people in a variety of stressful wilderness situations in the belief that they will learn effective survival and decision-making strategies that can be applied to a wide variety of everyday situations. A recent review of the research literature confirms that trained experts performing familiar tasks are less likely to be swayed by judgmental biases than is the average person faced with an unfamiliar task (J. F. Smith & Kida, 1991).

So far in this chapter, we have examined language, images, and concepts, and the ways in which these three building blocks of thought can be used in problem solving and decision making. In the next section, we will delve into the relationship between language and thought. Then we will turn to what psychologists know about intelligence and other mental abilities and ways to measure these abilities.

**Linguistic relativity hypothesis** Whorf's contention that patterns of thinking are determined by the specific language one speaks.

## LANGUAGE AND THOUGHT

We have seen that language is closely tied to the expression and understanding of thoughts. Many words in our language—such as *friend, family, airplane, love*—correspond to concepts, which serve as the building blocks of thought. By stringing words together into sentences, we link concepts to other concepts to form complex thoughts and ideas. Because our language determines not only the words we use but also the ways in which we combine those words into sentences, does language also determine how we think and the range of material we can think about?

Some theorists believe that language does indeed affect the way we think and the things we think about. Recall from the chapter on memory that language affects long-term memory. To illustrate how this works, R. W. Brown and Lenneberg (1954) asked subjects to look at color patches and assign each one a name. Colors that were quickly and easily named (like blue) were more readily coded and retrieved from memory than were those that took longer to name and were given less common labels (like sky blue or pale blue). The researchers concluded that the easier and quicker it is for us to name and encode an experience, the stronger our memory of that experience will be. As P. H. Lindsay and Norman (1977) point out, "memory for single perceptual experiences is directly related to the ease with which language can communicate that experience" (p. 483).

If language affects our ability to store and retrieve information, it should also affect our ability to think about things. Benjamin Whorf (1956) was the strongest spokesperson for this position. According to Whorf's **linguistic relativity hypothesis**, the language that we speak determines the pattern of our thinking and our view of the world. For Whorf, if a language lacks a particular expression, the thought to which the expression corresponds will probably not occur to the people who speak that language. Whorf noted, for example, that the Hopi, a Native-American people of the southwestern United States, have only two nouns for everything that flies. One noun refers to birds; the other is used for everything else, whether airplanes, kites, or dragonflies. Thus, according to Whorf, the Hopi would interpret all flying things in terms of either of these two nouns—something in the air would be either a bird or a nonbird.

Yet some critics of the linguistic relativity hypothesis point out that a society's need to think about things differently changes a language rather than the language dictating how people think. For example, if the Hopi had been subjected to air raids, undoubtedly they would have created a word to distinguish a butterfly from a bomber! In fact, Berlin and Kay (1969) discovered that the more complex a society is, the more terms its language contains. That is, as societies become more sophisticated, their people simply add words to accommodate their expanded concepts. Closer to home, most English-speaking people know only one word for snow. But skiers, realizing that different textures of snow affect a downhill run, have coined specific words for snow of various consistencies—*powder, corn,* and *ice*. So, to some

To support his *linguistic relativity hypothesis,* Whorf cited the Hopi, whose language has only two words to describe everything that flies.

extent at least, experience shapes language: People create new words as the need arises. And while language efficiently organizes human thought, language certainly does not necessarily reflect all the experiences of the people who speak it. For example, although nonskiers may call all kinds of snow simply "snow," they can nonetheless envision and think about the differences among icy snow, powdery snow, and slush. The Dani of New Guinea have no words for colors—everything is either dark/cool or light/warm. Nonetheless, they remember basic colors like red, green, and yellow better than other colors. Furthermore, when taught the names of these basic colors, they learn them faster than they learn the names of other colors. Moreover, the Dani judge the similarity of colors as well as English-speaking people do (E. R. Heider, 1972; E. R. Heider & Oliver, 1972; Rosch, 1973). Thus, people from other cultures whose languages bear no resemblance to ours can think about some things, such as color, much as we do, even if their language includes no words for those things.

In summary, it is clear that language and thought are intertwined. People create words to reflect important aspects of their experiences, and once words make their appearance, they may indeed influence how people think and what they think about. Experience shapes language, and language, in turn, affects subsequent experience. But people can also think about things for which they have no words, so thoughts are not limited to the words in one's language.

## TESTS OF INTELLIGENCE AND MENTAL ABILITIES

Earlier in this chapter, we looked at the ways in which people solve problems and make decisions. But people clearly differ in the extent to which they think intelligently and creatively. We now turn to what psychologists know about intelligence and mental abilities. But before we begin, take a few minutes to answer the following questions:

1. Describe the difference between *laziness* and *idleness.*
2. Which direction would you have to face so your right hand would be toward the north?
3. What does *obliterate* mean?
4. In what way are an *hour* and a *week* alike?
5. Select the item that completes the following series of four figures:

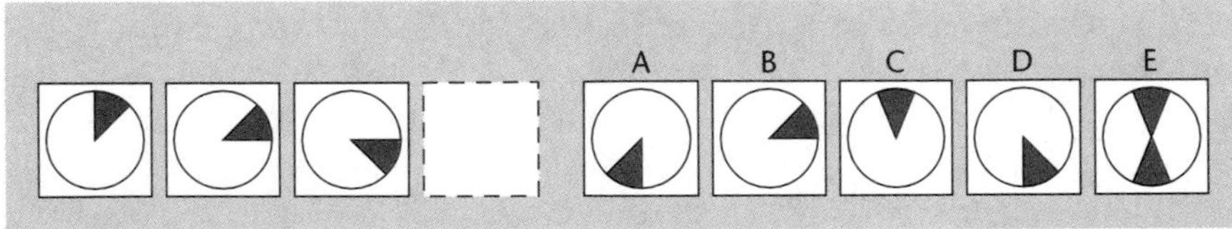


6. If three pencils cost 25 cents, how many pencils can be bought for 75 cents?
7. Choose the word that is most nearly *opposite* in meaning to the word in capital letters:
   SCHISM: (a) majority (b) union (c) uniformity (d) conference (e) construction

**Intelligence tests** Tests designed to measure a person's general mental abilities.

**Intelligence** A general term referring to the ability or abilities that figure in learning and adaptive behavior.

8. Choose the set of words that, when inserted in the sentence, best fits in with the meaning of the sentence as a whole: From the first, the islanders, despite an outward ______ , did what they could to ______ the ruthless occupying power.

   (a) harmony . . . assist (b) enmity . . . embarrass

   (c) rebellion . . . foil (d) resistance . . . destroy

   (e) acquiescence . . . thwart

9. Select the lettered pair that best expresses a relationship similar to that expressed in the original pair:

   CRUTCH: LOCOMOTION: (a) paddle: canoe

   (b) hero: worship (c) horse: carriage (d) spectacles: vision

   (e) statement: contention

10. The first three figures are alike in some way. Find the figure at the right that goes with the first three.

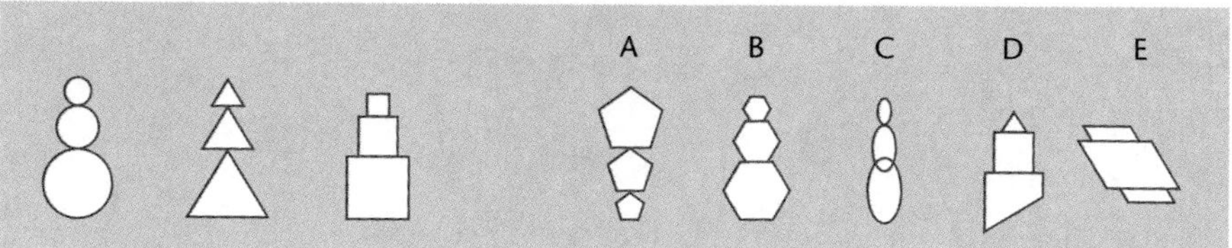


11. Decide how the first two figures are related to each other. Then find the one figure at the right that goes with the third figure in the same way that the second figure goes with the first.

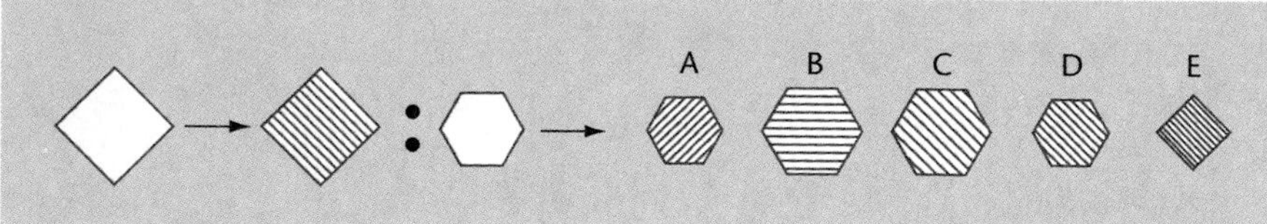


These questions were drawn from various **intelligence tests** designed to measure general mental abilities (the answers appear at the end of the chapter). What do these tests actually tell us? Do they sample all of the kinds of ability that we consider **intelligence**? Because we cannot see the complex mental processes that underlie intelligence, we have to approach the subject indirectly—by watching how people respond when situations call for the use of intelligence. But what exactly is intelligence? Is it related to creativity? Do intelligence tests such as the *Scholastic Aptitude Test (SAT)* measure all aspects of intelligence needed for success in school? Do these standardized tests predict how well you will succeed on the job or in your personal life? We will address these and related questions in this section of the chapter.

## INTELLIGENCE

Intelligence is notoriously difficult to define. What does "intelligence" mean to you? Before reading further, write down on a sheet of paper some behaviors that you believe reflect intelligence. How do these behaviors differ from those that reveal a lack of intelligence?

Most people agree that intelligence refers to a collection or family of *mental abilities*, but there is some disagreement about which abilities should be considered elements of overall intelligence. For example, Robert Sternberg and his associates (Sternberg, 1982; Sternberg et al., 1981) discovered that laypeople with no expertise in psychology generally think of intelligence as a combination of practical problem-solving skills, verbal ability, and social competence (see Table 7-2 on page 257). Practical problem-solving ability includes using logic, connecting ideas, and viewing a problem in its entirety. Verbal ability encompasses using and understanding both written and spoken language in well-developed ways. Social competence means interacting well with others—being open-minded about people different from us and showing interest in a variety of topics. Psychologists who are experts in the area of intelligence generally agree with laypeople that overall intelligence includes verbal intelligence and problem-solving ability, but they part company when it comes to social competence as an indicator of intelligence. Instead of social competence, psychologists focus on practical intelligence as a key factor. A later study revealed that the majority of experts list creativity and the ability to adapt to the environment as additional components of intelligence (Snyderman & Rothman, 1987).

3. How do psychologists define intelligence? Do psychologists and laypersons define intelligence in the same way?

Before we go on, you might find it interesting to compare your own description of intelligent behaviors with those of Sternberg's laypeople and experts. Was your description closer to that of the laypeople or the experts? Which characteristics of intelligence do you think are most important? Why do you think so?

In the next section, we will look more closely how psychologists think about intelligence and how those formal theories of intelligence affect the content of intelligence tests.

## FORMAL THEORIES OF INTELLIGENCE

For more than a century, psychologists have pondered and argued about what constitutes general intelligence—or even if this notion has any validity at all. One of the most basic questions facing anyone who tries to understand intelligence is this: Is intelligence a general aptitude or ability or, rather, is it composed of many separate and distinct aptitudes or abilities? Charles Spearman, a British psychologist who lived early in the 20th century, maintained that intelligence is quite general—a kind of wellspring of mental energy that flows into every action. Spearman noted that people who are bright in one area are often bright in other areas as well. The intelligent person understands things quickly, makes sound decisions, carries on interesting conversations, and tends to behave intelligently in a variety of situations. Although each of us is quicker in some areas than in others, Spearman saw these differences simply as ways in which the same underlying general intelligence comes through in different activities. To return to our earlier image, according to Spearman, general intelligence is the fountain from which specific abilities flow like streams of water in many directions.

In the 1930s, American psychologist L. L. Thurstone took issue with Spearman's thesis. Thurstone argued that intelligence comprises seven distinct kinds of mental abilities (Thurstone, 1938):

- S—Spatial ability*
- P—Perceptual speed
- N—Numerical ability
- V—Verbal meaning
- M—Memory
- W—Word fluency
- R—Reasoning

*Spatial ability is the ability to perceive distance, recognize shapes, and so on.

**Triarchic theory of intelligence** Sternberg's theory that intelligence involves mental skills (componential aspect), insight and creative adaptability (experiential aspect), and environmental responsiveness (contextual aspect).

**Componential intelligence** According to Sternberg, the ability to acquire new knowledge, to solve problems effectively.

**Experiential intelligence** Sternberg's designation of the ability to adapt creatively in new situations, to use insight.

**Contextual intelligence** Sternberg's term for the ability to select contexts in which you can excel, to shape the environment to fit your strengths.

Unlike Spearman, Thurstone believed that these abilities are relatively independent of one another. Thus, a person with exceptional spatial ability might perform poorly when it comes to word fluency. But taken together, Thurstone felt, these primary mental abilities are what we mean when we speak of general intelligence.

In contrast to Thurstone, psychologist R. B. Cattell asserted that there are just two clusters of mental abilities (Cattell, 1971). The first cluster comprises what Cattell called *crystallized intelligence*, or abilities like reasoning and verbal and numerical skills. Because these are the kinds of skills stressed in school, Cattell noted that the scores on tests of crystallized intelligence are greatly affected by experience and formal education. The second cluster of abilities makes up what Cattell calls *fluid intelligence*, or skills such as spatial and visual imagery, the ability to notice visual details, and rote memory. Scores on tests of fluid intelligence are much less affected by experience and education.

More recently, Robert Sternberg (1985, 1986) has advanced a **triarchic theory of intelligence**, which holds that human intelligence encompasses a much broader variety of skills than imagined by previous theorists and that skills necessary for effective performance in the real world are just as important as the more limited skills assessed by traditional intelligence tests. We can see Sternberg's theory in action by considering three graduate students he worked with, whom he calls Alice, Barbara, and Celia. Alice fit the standard definition of intelligence perfectly. She scored extremely well on tests of intelligence and achieved nearly a 4.0 average as an undergraduate. Her analytical abilities were superb. Alice excelled in her first year of graduate work, but by the second year of graduate school, she was having trouble developing her own research ideas and had dropped from the top of the class to the lower half. By contrast, Barbara's undergraduate record was far from exemplary, and her admission test scores were quite low by Yale's standards. Nevertheless, she had received excellent recommendations from those who had worked with her as an undergraduate: They pointed out that she was highly creative, came up with imaginative new ideas, and did fine research. Barbara proved to be the model associate Sternberg had hoped for. In fact, he credits his collaboration with her for producing some of his most important work. The third graduate student, Celia, fell somewhere between the other two: She had good recommendations and fairly high admission test scores. Celia conducted good (but not great) research work, yet she turned out to have the easiest time landing a good job after graduate school.

These three students seemed to have different kinds of intelligence, prompting them to excel in different ways. Alice, Barbara, and Celia each represent one of the three aspects of Sternberg's triarchic theory. Alice exemplifies **componential intelligence**—the mental processes emphasized by most theories of intelligence, such as the ability to learn how to do things or acquire new knowledge and carry out tasks effectively. Barbara showed particular strength in what Sternberg calls **experiential intelligence**—the ability to adjust to new tasks, to use new concepts, to respond effectively in new situations, to gain insight, and to adapt creatively. Celia had the easiest time finding a job because she excelled in **contextual intelligence**. According to Sternberg, people high in contextual intelligence are very good at capitalizing on their strengths and compensating for their weaknesses. They make the most of their talents by seeking situations that match their skills, by shaping those situations so that they can best showcase and maximize their skills, and by knowing when to seek out new situations that better suit their talents.

For Sternberg, then, intelligence is tightly tied to a broad range of skills that allow us to function effectively in the real world. In this sense, Sternberg's theory of intelligence mirrors the informal view that most laypeople have of intelligence (see Table 7-2).

**Theory of multiple intelligences** Howard Gardner's theory that there is not one intelligence, but rather many intelligences, each of which is relatively independent of the others.

An influential alternative to Sternberg's theory of intelligence is the **theory of multiple intelligences** advocated by Howard Gardner and his associates (H. Gardner, 1983a, 1993). Gardner's theory resembles Thurstone's theory of intelligence in that Gardner believes that intelligence comprises many separate abilities or *multiple intelligences*, each of which is relatively independent of the others. It is difficult to determine precisely how many separate intelligences there are, but Gardner (1993) lists seven: *logical-mathematical intelligence*, *linguistic intelligence*, *spatial intelligence*, *musical intelligence*, *bodily-kinesthetic intelligence*, *interpersonal intelligence*, and *intrapersonal intelligence*. The first two of these intelligences should be familiar to you because they are included in the other theories of intelligence we have examined so far. Spatial intelligence refers to the ability to imagine the relative location of objects in space; it is particularly strong in people with artistic ability. Exceptional musical intelligence is demonstrated by people with a rare gift for music, such as musical prodigies. Bodily-kinesthetic abilities distinguish outstanding sports performers and dancers. People who are extraordinarily talented at understanding and communicating with others, such as exceptional teachers and parents, exemplify interpersonal intelligence. Intrapersonal intelligence reflects the ancient adage "Know thyself." People who understand themselves and who use this knowledge effectively to attain their goals are likely to be high in intrapersonal intelligence.

Here are some of Gardner's examples of well-known people who have possessed one of these intelligences to an extreme degree. You can probably think of many other examples.

**TABLE 7-2 Some Characteristics of Intelligence as Seen by Laypersons and Experts**

| | |
|---|---|
| **LAYPERSONS** | I. **Practical problem-solving ability**: reasons logically, makes connections among ideas, can see all sides of a problem, keeps an open mind, responds thoughtfully to the ideas of others, good at sizing up situations, interprets information accurately, makes good decisions, goes to original source for basic information, good source of ideas, perceives implied assumptions, deals with problems in a resourceful way. |
| | II. **Verbal ability**: speaks articulately, converses well, is knowledgeable about a particular field, studies hard, reads widely, writes without difficulty, has a good vocabulary, tries new things. |
| | III. **Social competence**: accepts others as they are, admits mistakes, shows interest in the world at large, arrives on time for appointments, has social conscience, thinks before speaking and acting, shows curiosity, avoids snap judgments, makes fair judgments, assesses the relevance of information to the problem at hand, is sensitive to others, is frank and honest with self and others, shows interest in the immediate environment. |
| **EXPERTS** | IV. **Practical intelligence**: sizes up situations well, determines how best to achieve goals, shows awareness of world around him or her, shows interest in the world at large, uses self-knowledge of own motives to select the tasks that will best accomplish own goals. |
| | V. **Verbal intelligence**: has a good vocabulary, reads with high comprehension, is intellectually curious, sees all sides of a problem, learns rapidly, shows alertness, thinks deeply, shows creativity, converses easily on a wide range of subjects, reads widely, sees connections among ideas. |
| | VI. **Problem-solving ability**: makes good decisions, displays common sense, shows objectivity, is good at solving problems, plans ahead, has good intuition, gets to the heart of problems, appreciates truth, considers the results of actions, approaches problems thoughtfully. |

*Source*: Sternberg, 1982; Wagner & Sternberg, 1986.

**Binet-Simon Scale** The first test of intelligence, developed for testing children.

The title character in the movie *Forrest Gump* clearly had limited cognitive abilities. According to Gardner's system, however, he would have scored high when it comes to bodily-kinesthetic intelligence. What does this suggest about the concept of intelligence?

- Logical-mathematical intelligence: Albert Einstein; Nobel Prize–winning microbiologist Barbara McClintock
- Linguistic intelligence: poet T. S. Eliot, whose ability to manipulate language won him a Nobel Prize in Literature
- Spatial intelligence: Nadia, an autistic child (see Chapter 13) whose drawings reminded some observers of those of Leonardo da Vinci
- Musical intelligence: violinist Yehudi Menuhin, who was internationally renowned by the age of 10
- Bodily-kinesthetic intelligence: Babe Ruth; Wayne Gretzky
- Interpersonal intelligence: Anne Sullivan, Helen Keller's teacher
- Intrapersonal intelligence: Novelist Virginia Woolf, who could describe her inner life so vividly that it came alive for other people.

Let's stop briefly to compare and contrast the formal theories of intelligence we have considered in this section. We began with Spearman, who had the simplest view of intelligence. He believed that people differed in the extent to which they possessed the "mental energy" he called general intelligence. Subsequent theorists, such as Thurstone and Cattell, attempted to specify the structure of mental abilities in more detail than Spearman did. The two most influential contemporary theorists are Sternberg and Gardner. Their theories are similar in that both emphasize practical abilities that help us navigate the real world. Despite this similarity, however, the two theories differ in some basic ways. Sternberg has shown great ingenuity in the invention of mental tests to measure different aspects of intelligence. Gardner, by contrast, has relied more on a case-history approach that explores the development of a specific intelligence in a particular person. It is entirely possible that future work will lead to a synthesis of these two approaches (Gardner, 1993, p. 40).

One reason that formal theories of intelligence are so important is that they shape the content of intelligence tests and tests of mental abilities and these tests, in turn, are often used to help evaluate the abilities of millions of people, including students. Therefore, it is essential to consider not only how these tests are developed and administered but also whether they accurately measure intelligence at all and how the results should be used. In the next section, we will look closely at some of the most widely used intelligence tests.

## INTELLIGENCE TESTS

### The Stanford-Binet Intelligence Scale

The first "intelligence test" was designed for the French public school system by Alfred Binet, director of the psychological laboratory at the Sorbonne, and his colleague, Theodore Simon. Binet and Simon developed a number of questions and tested them on schoolchildren in Paris to find out which children were retarded or had trouble learning.

The first **Binet-Simon Scale** was issued in 1905. It consisted of 30 tests arranged in order of increasing difficulty. With each child, the examiner started at the top of the list and worked down until the child could no longer answer questions. By 1908, enough children had been tested to predict how the average child performed at each age level. From these scores

Binet developed the concept of mental age. A child who scores as well as an average 4-year-old has a mental age of 4; a child who scores as well as an average 12-year-old has a mental age of 12.

In the next 10 years, numerous Binet adaptations were developed, the best known of which was prepared at Stanford University by L. M. Terman and issued in 1916. Terman introduced the now-famous term **intelligence quotient**, or **IQ**, to establish a numerical value of intelligence, setting the score of 100 for a person of average intelligence. Figure 7-9 shows an approximate distribution of IQ scores in the population.

The **Stanford-Binet Intelligence Scale** has been revised four times since 1916, for several reasons. First, any test must be updated as the meanings and usages of words change. Second, Terman and his colleagues found that some questions were easier for people from one part of the country than for those from another, that some were harder for boys than for girls (and vice versa), and that some failed to discriminate among age levels because nearly everyone tested could answer them. Such questions were replaced. In 1972, the norms for scoring the test were restandardized and included the scores of nonwhites for the first time. The test items themselves were not changed (Sattler, 1982). The latest version of the Stanford-Binet was released in 1985. Questions that were determined to be biased against ethnic groups or against males or females were replaced with neutral questions, and new questions were added that allow testers to identify mentally retarded and mentally gifted people as well as those with specific learning disabilities (Sattler, 1988). The 15 different subtests of the Stanford-Binet are designed to measure four kinds of mental abilities that are almost universally considered to be characteristics of intelligence: verbal reasoning, abstract/visual reasoning, quantitative reasoning, and short-term memory. Questions 1 and 2 at the opening of this section were drawn from an earlier version of the Stanford-Binet.

The Stanford-Binet test is not simply passed out to a roomful of students. Instead, each test is administered individually by trained examiners. The test resembles an interview. It takes about 30 minutes for young children and up to an hour and a half for older ones. The standard procedure is to begin by testing just below the expected mental age of the subject. If the person fails that test, he or she is then given the test at the next lowest level, and so on, until he or she can pass the test. This level is then established as the person's basal age. Once the basal age is known,

**Intelligence quotient (IQ)** A numerical value given to intelligence that is determined from the scores on an intelligence test; based on a score of 100 for average intelligence.

**Stanford-Binet Intelligence Scale** Terman's adaptation of the Binet-Simon Scale.

What does IQ mean? How is it measured? Is IQ the same as intelligence?

Alfred Binet, along with his associate, Theodore Simon, developed the first intelligence test* in France.

**Figure 7-9**
**The approximate distribution of IQ scores in the population.**

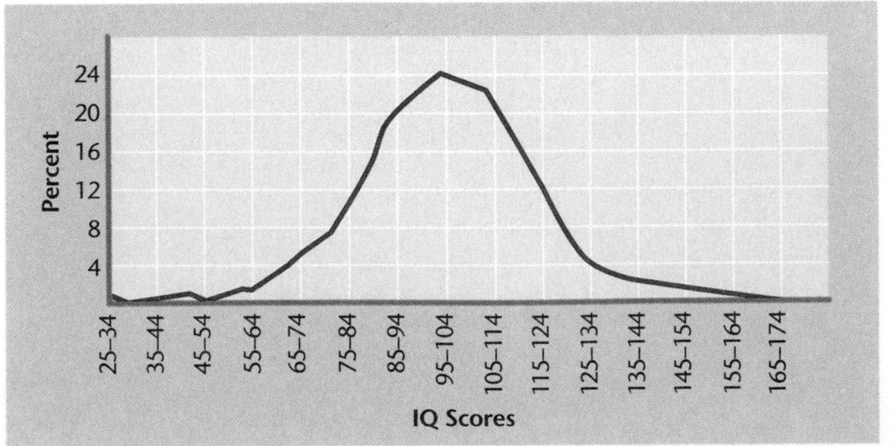

**Wechsler Adult Intelligence Scale–Revised (WAIS–R)** Individual intelligence test developed especially for adults; measures both verbal and performance abilities.

the examiner continues testing at higher and higher levels until the person fails all the tests. Then the tests stop. After scoring the tests, the examiner determines the subject's mental age by adding to the basal age credits for each test passed above that age level. Notice that the ages in Table 7-3 go up only to 26 years. Although the Stanford-Binet has been used with older people, it is best suited for children, adolescents, and very young adults.

## The Wechsler Intelligence Scales

The individual test most often given to adults is the **Wechsler Adult Intelligence Scale–Revised (WAIS–R)**. The original WAIS was developed by David Wechsler, a psychologist at Bellevue Hospital in New York City.

The WAIS-R is divided into two parts. One part stresses verbal skills, the other performance skills. The verbal scale includes tests of information ("Who wrote *Paradise Lost?*"), tests of simple arithmetic ("Sam had three pieces of candy, and Joe gave him four more. How many pieces of candy did Sam have then?"), and tests of comprehension ("What should you do if you see someone forget a book on a bus?"). All these tests require a verbal or a written response. The performance scale also measures routine tasks. People are asked to "find the missing part"—buttonholes in a coat, for example; to copy patterns; and to arrange three to five pictures so that they tell a story. Questions 3 and 4 at the start of this section are similar to questions on the WAIS–R.

Although the content of the WAIS–R is somewhat more sophisticated than that of the Stanford-Binet, Wechsler's chief innovation was in scoring. First, the subject is given separate verbal and performance scores as well as an overall IQ score. Second, on some items the test taker can earn one or two extra points, depending on the complexity of the answer given.

**TABLE 7-3 Areas, Subsets, and Age Spans for Stanford-Binet: Fourth Edition**

| DESIGNATED AREA | SUBTEST | AGE SPAN |
|---|---|---|
| Verbal reasoning | Vocabulary | 2 – 23 |
| | Comprehension | 2 – 23 |
| | Absurdities | 2 – 14 |
| | Verbal relations | 12 – 23 |
| Abstract/visual reasoning | Pattern analysis | 2 – 23 |
| | Copying | 2 – 13 |
| | Matrices | 7 – 23 |
| | Paper folding and cutting | 12 – 23 |
| Quantitative reasoning | Quantitative | 2 – 23 |
| | Number series | 7 – 23 |
| | Education building | 12 – 26 |
| Short-term memory | Bead memory | 2 – 23 |
| | Memory for sentences | 2 – 23 |
| | Memory for digits | 7– 23 |
| | Memory for objects | 7– 23 |

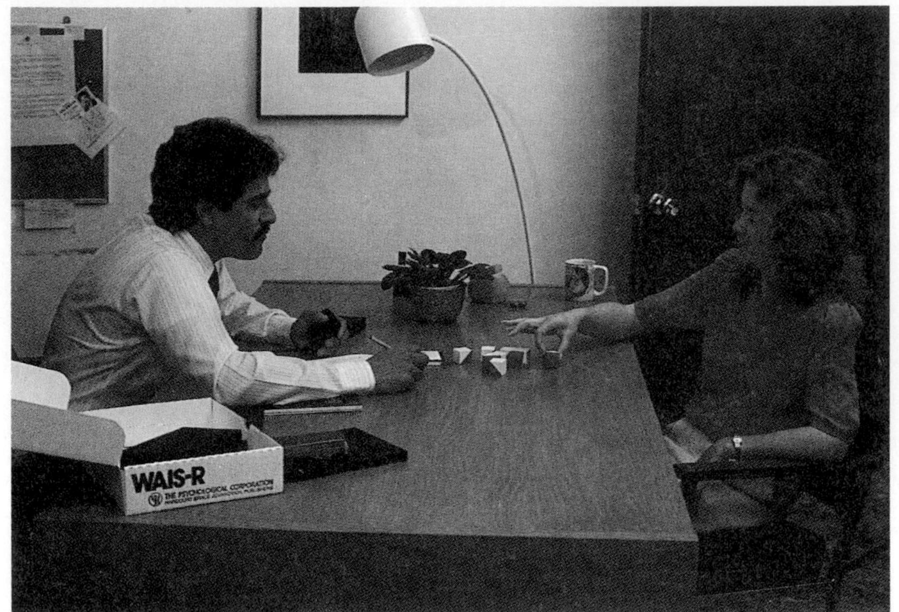

The *Wechsler Intelligence Scales* are designed for both adults (WAIS–R) and children (WISC–III).

**Wechsler Intelligence Scale for Children–Third Edition (WISC–III)** Individual intelligence test developed especially for school-aged children; measures verbal and performance abilities and also yields an overall IQ score.

**Group tests** Written intelligence tests administered by one examiner to many people at one time.

This unique scoring system gives credit for the reflective qualities that we expect to find in intelligent adults. Third, on some questions, both speed and accuracy affect the score.

Wechsler has also developed a similar intelligence test for use with school-aged children. Like the WAIS–R, the 1991 version of the **Wechsler Intelligence Scale for Children–Third Edition (WISC–III)** yields separate verbal and performance scores as well as an overall IQ score.

## Group Tests

The Stanford-Binet, the WAIS–R, and the WISC–III are individual tests. The examiner takes the person to an isolated room, spreads the materials on a table, and spends from 30 to 90 minutes administering the test. The examiner may then spend another hour or so scoring the test according to detailed instructions in the manual. Clearly, this is a time-consuming, costly operation. Moreover, the examiner's behavior in the one-on-one test-taking situation may greatly influence the score.

For these reasons, test makers have devised **group tests**. These are written tests of mental abilities that a single examiner may administer to a large group of people at the same time. Instead of sitting across the table from a person who asks you questions, you receive a test booklet that contains questions for you to answer within a certain amount of time. Questions 5 through 11 at the beginning of this section are from group tests.

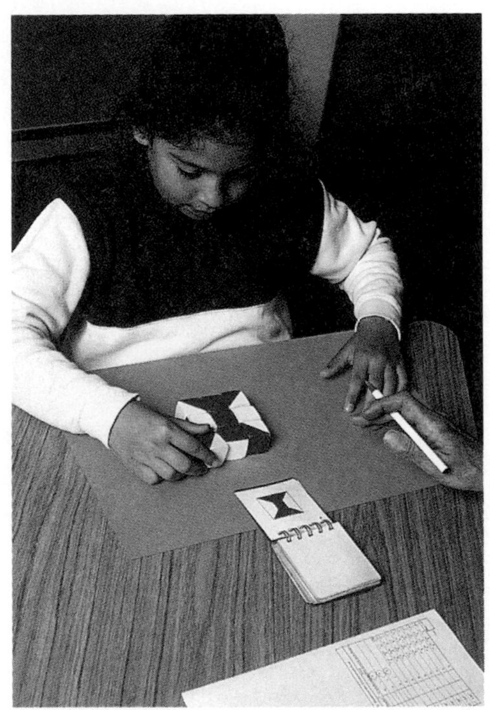

When most people talk about "intelligence" tests, they are usually referring to group tests, because this is generally the means by which they themselves were tested in school. Schools are among the biggest users of group tests. From fourth grade through high school, tests such as the *School and College Ability Tests (SCAT)* and the *California Test of Mental Maturity (CTMM)* are used to measure students' specific abilities. The *Scholastic Aptitude Tests (SAT)*—questions 7 through 9 at the beginning of this section—and the *American College Testing Program (ACTP)* are designed to assess a student's ability to handle college-level work. The *Graduate Record Examination (GRE)* serves the same function on the graduate level. Group tests are also widely administered in industry, the civil service, and the military.

**Performance tests** Intelligence tests that minimize the use of language.

**Culture-fair tests** Intelligence tests designed to eliminate cultural bias by minimizing assessment of skills and values that vary from one culture to another.

Group tests have some distinct advantages over individualized tests. They eliminate bias on the part of the examiner; answer sheets can be scored quickly and objectively; and because greater numbers of people can be tested in this way, more useful norms can be established. But there are also some clear disadvantages to group tests. The examiner is less likely to notice if a person is tired, ill, or confused by the directions. People who are not used to being tested tend to do worse on group tests than on individual tests. Finally, emotionally disturbed children seem to do better on individual tests than on group tests (Anastasi, 1982).

## Performance and Culture-fair Tests

The intelligence tests we have highlighted thus far share one common element: To perform well, people must be able to read, speak, or understand English. In many situations, however, people might experience language problems that are not necessarily related to intelligence. For example, infants and preschool children are too young to understand directions or answer questions. Deaf children take longer to learn words than do children who can hear. Immigrants who have been lawyers or teachers in their own countries may need time to learn English How, then, do we test these people? Psychologists have designed two general types of tests for such situations: performance tests and culture-fair tests.

**Performance tests** consist of problems that minimize or eliminate the use of words. One of the earliest performance tests, the *Seguin Form Board*, was devised in 1866 to test mentally retarded people. The form board is essentially a puzzle. The examiner removes specifically designed cutouts, stacks them in a predetermined order, and asks the person to replace them as quickly as possible. A more recent performance test, the *Porteus Maze*, consists of a series of increasingly difficult printed mazes. Examiners ask the people taking the test to each trace their way through the maze without lifting the pencil from the paper. Such tests require the test taker to pay close attention to a task for an extended period and continuously plan ahead so as to make the correct choices that solve the maze.

One of the most effective tests administered to very young children is the *Bayley Scales of Infant Development*. The Bayley Scales are used to evaluate the developmental abilities of children from 2 months to 2 1/2 years of age. One scale tests perception, memory, and the beginning of verbal communication; another measures sitting, standing, walking, and manual dexterity. The Bayley Scales can detect early signs of sensory and neurological defects, emotional problems, and troubles in a child's home environment (J. R. Graham & Lilly, 1984).

**Culture-fair tests** are designed to measure the intelligence of people who are outside the culture in which the test was devised. Like performance tests, culture-fair tests minimize or eliminate the use of language. Culture-fair tests also downplay skills and values—such as the need for speed—that vary from culture to culture.

Cattell's *Culture-Fair Intelligence Test* combines some questions that demand verbal comprehension and specific cultural knowledge with other questions that are culture-fair. By comparing scores on the two kinds of questions, cultural factors can be isolated from general intelligence. An example of a culture-fair item from the Cattell test is question 5 at the start of this section.

Another culture-fair test, the *Progressive Matrices*, consists of 60 designs, each with a missing part. The person is given six to eight possible choices to replace the part. The test calls for an understanding of various logical relationships, requires discrimination, and can be administered to one person or to a group.

## WHAT MAKES A GOOD TEST?

All the tests that we have looked at so far claim to measure a broad range of mental abilities, or "intelligence." But how can we tell if they do measure what they claim to be measuring? And how can we decide whether one test is better than another? Psychologists address these questions by referring to a test's reliability and validity.

**Reliability** Ability of a test to produce consistent and stable scores.

**Split-half reliability** A method of determining test reliability by dividing the test into two parts and checking how well the scores match on both parts.

### Reliability

By **reliability** psychologists mean the dependability and consistency of the scores yielded by a given test.

But how do we know if a test is reliable? The simplest way to find out is to give the test to a group and then, after a short time, give the same people the same test again. If they score the same each time, the test is reliable. For example, look at Table 7-4, which shows the IQ scores of eight people who took the same test one year apart. This is a very reliable test. Although the scores did change slightly, none changed by more than 6 points.

This way of determining reliability poses is a serious problem, however: Because the exact same test was used on both occasions, people might simply have remembered the answers from the first time they took the test and repeated them the second time around. To avoid this shortcoming, psychologists prefer to give alternate forms of a test. In this method, two equivalent tests are designed to measure the same ability. If a person receives the same score on both tests, the tests are deemed reliable. One way to create alternate forms is to split a single test into two parts—for example, to assign odd-numbered items to one part and even-numbered items to the other. If scores on the two halves match, the test is said to have **split-half reliability**. Most intelligence tests do, in fact, have alternate equivalent forms, just as each college admission test has many versions.

How reliable are intelligence tests? In general, people's IQ scores on most intelligence tests are about as stable as the scores in Table 7-4. Performance tests and culture-fair tests are somewhat less reliable. However, scores on even the best tests vary somewhat from one day to another. Therefore, many testing services now report a person's score along with a range of scores that allows for variations due to chance. One person might

**TABLE 7-4 IQ Scores on the Same Test Given 1 Year Apart**

| PERSON | FIRST TESTING | SECOND TESTING |
|---|---|---|
| A | 130 | 127 |
| B | 123 | 127 |
| C | 121 | 119 |
| D | 116 | 122 |
| E | 109 | 108 |
| F | 107 | 112 |
| G | 95 | 93 |
| H | 89 | 94 |

**Validity** Ability of a test to measure what it has been designed to measure.

**Content validity** Refers to a test's having an adequate sample of the skills or knowledge it is supposed to measure.

be told that her score was 105 with a range of 95–115. This implies that the true score almost certainly lies somewhere between 95 and 115 but is most likely within a few points of 105. But even with the best intelligence tests, differences of a few points in IQ scores have little meaning and should not be the basis for major decisions, such as putting a child in an accelerated or remedial program.

We have seen that many intelligence tests are reliable. But do these tests really measure "intelligence"? We know that the scores on intelligence tests are fairly consistent from day to day, but how do we know that the consistency is due to "intelligence" and not to something else? When psychologists ask these questions, they are concerned with test validity.

## Validity

**Validity** refers to a test's ability to measure what it has been designed to measure. How can we determine if a given test actually measures what it claims to measure?

**Content Validity** One measure of validity is known as **content validity**—whether the test contains an adequate sample of the skills or knowledge that it is supposed to measure.

Do IQ tests adequately measure the kinds of mental abilities that they set out to assess? The answer is somewhat mixed. Alfred Binet specifically designed his test to measure qualities like judgment, comprehension, and reasoning, so the test focused more heavily on verbal skills than on perceptual or sensory abilities. As we saw earlier, Binet's original test has been revised and updated several times. At the earliest age levels, the test now measures eye-hand coordination, discrimination, and the ability to follow directions.

Most people would agree that the content of the Stanford-Binet is at least part of what we commonly consider "intelligence," so we would conclude that the Stanford-Binet has at least some content validity. But because of its heavy emphasis on verbal skills, the test may not adequately assess all aspects of intelligence equally well.

The WAIS–R and WISC–III cover many of the primary abilities that Thurstone included under "intelligence" and that Cattell grouped under the headings of "fluid" and "crystallized" intelligence. Thus, the WAIS–R and WISC–III also appear to have some content validity as intelligence tests.

Most group intelligence tests, such as those from which questions 5 through 11 at the beginning of this section were taken, also seem to measure at least some of the mental abilities that make up intelligence.

In general, then, the content of most intelligence tests spans many of the abilities that most people consider to be components of intelligence. These abilities include concentration, planning, memory, understanding language, and writing (J. B. Carroll & Horn, 1981). Yet intelligence tests do not measure every type of mental ability. Some tests focus on skills that other tests leave out, and each intelligence test emphasizes the abilities that it measures in a slightly different way.

**Criterion-Related Validity** Is test content the only way to determine if an intelligence test is valid? Fortunately, it is not. For example, if both the Stanford-Binet and the WISC–III measure intelligence in children, high scorers on one should be high scorers on the other. Think of two rulers, one that measures in inches and one that measures in centimeters. The measurements obtained by one ruler should correspond with those obtained by the other because both rulers are measuring the same thing—length. Similarly, two different measures of intelligence should be correlated with each other, because they should both be measuring the same thing. In fact, various intelligence tests do relate well with one another despite the differences in their content: People who score high on one test tend to score high on the others.

**Criterion-related validity** Validity of a test as measured by comparing the test score with independent measures of what the test is designed to assess.

However, just because intelligence tests tend to correlate with one another does not mean they are related: Conceivably the tests could be measuring the same things but these things do not constitute intelligence. To demonstrate that the tests are valid, we need an independent measure of intelligence against which to compare intelligence test scores. The most common independent measure is academic achievement. Ever since Binet invented the intelligence test, these tests have been used to predict school achievement. The underlying idea is that individual differences in school grades must reflect individual differences in intelligence, at least to some extent. Therefore, students with good grades should get high scores on the Stanford-Binet and other intelligence tests, and students with poor grades should do worse on such tests. Academic achievement is a "direct and independent measure of that which the test is designed to predict" (Anastasi, 1982, p. 137). Using such a procedure to determine the validity of a test is called **criterion-related validity**.

Do IQ tests predict academic achievement? Even the strongest critics agree that IQ tests do indeed correlate well with performance in school (Aiken, 1988).

We have seen that intelligence tests are quite reliable: Scores on these tests are consistent from day to day. These tests also seem to measure many of the areas that psychologists define as components of intelligence. And intelligence test scores seem to agree with one another and with other indicators of intelligence, such as school grades. Nonetheless, in recent decades, intelligence tests have come under severe criticism.

## Criticisms of IQ Tests

**5.** What are some of the most common criticisms of IQ tests?

**Test Content and Scores** One major criticism of IQ tests focuses on their content. Many critics argue that intelligence tests assess ability in only a very narrow range of skills: passive verbal understanding; the ability to follow instructions; common sense; and, at best, scholastic aptitude (Ginsberg, 1972; Sattler, 1975). For example, one critic observes, "Intelligence tests measure how quickly people can solve relatively unimportant problems making as few errors as possible, rather than measuring how people grapple with relatively important problems, making as many productive errors as necessary with no time factor" (J. M. Blum, 1979, p. 83).

These critics charge that if there is one thing that all intelligence tests measure, it is the ability to take tests. This would explain why people who do well on one IQ test also tend to do well on others. And it would also explain why intelligence test scores correlate so closely with school performance: Academic grades depend heavily on test scores as well. Notice that this criticism of intelligence tests challenges the assumption that academic achievement stems from intelligence. Advocates of this argument contend that neither academic achievement nor intelligence tests measure abilities that come into play during real-life situations that require intellectual activity. Thus it should not be surprising that there is a tendency to "abandon the term IQ and replace it with a more accurate descriptor, such as school ability or academic aptitude" (Reschly, 1981, p. 1097). However, recent reviews of the evidence have reasserted the claim that both school grades and intelligence tests are good predictors of occupational success (Barret & Depinet, 1991). Thus, this particular criticism of intelligence tests may have to be reconsidered.

Still other critics argue that the content and administration of IQ tests discriminate against minorities. After all, high scores on most IQ tests require considerable mastery of standard English, which biases the tests in favor of middle- and upper-class white people (J. M. Blum, 1979). Moreover, white middle-class examiners may not be familiar with the speech patterns of lower-income black children, or children from homes where English is not the primary language, a complication that may compromise test performance as well (Sattler, 1975). In addition, certain questions may have very different meanings for children of different social classes. The Stanford-Binet, for instance, asks, "What should you do if another boy hits you without meaning to do it?" The "correct" answer is, "Walk away." But for a child who lives in an environment where survival depends on acting tough, the "correct" answer might be, "Hit him back." This answer, however, receives zero credit on the Stanford-Binet.

Some people argue that intelligence tests measure only the ability to take tests. Other critics assert that both the content and the methods of administering intelligence tests discriminate against minorities.

Even presumably culture-fair tests may accentuate the very cultural differences that they were designed to minimize (Linn, 1982). For example, when given a picture of a head with the mouth missing, one group of Asian-American children responded by saying that the body was missing, thus receiving no credit. To them, the absence of a body under the head was more remarkable than the absence of the mouth (Ortar, 1963).

Although some investigators believe that the most widely used and thoroughly studied tests are not biased against minorities (Bersoff, 1981; Cole, 1981; Herrnstein & Murray, 1994; Reschly, 1981), this conclusion is not universally accepted. Janet Helms (1992) argues that a proper study of cultural equivalence in testing has yet to be made. By *cultural equivalence*, Helms means that items on a test have the same meaning in different cultures and subcultures. She calls for sampling equivalence (e.g., Were samples of each racial and ethnic group used to develop and validate the test items?); equivalence of testing condition (e.g., Was the examiner of the same race as the subject?); and contextual equivalence (e.g., Are the abilities being tested evaluated in the same way in different cultures?). Looking closely at these sources of potential bias may shed light on why individuals from disparate cultures give different answers to test items than people brought up in the cultural mainstream (Helms, 1992, p. 1092).

If IQ tests were used only for obscure research purposes, perhaps the criticisms we have just mentioned would carry less weight. But because IQ tests have been used for so many significant purposes, it is critical that we understand both their strengths and their weaknesses. Let's examine the ways in which IQ test scores are used and the effects they may have on people's lives.

**USE OF IQ SCORES** Alfred Binet developed the first IQ test to help the French public school system identify students who needed to be placed in special classes. In fact, Binet believed that courses of "mental orthopedics" would help those with low IQ scores. But the practice of using IQ tests to assign a person to a "track" or "slot" in school, may backfire. To the extent that children obtain low scores on IQ tests because of test bias, language barriers, their own lack of interest in test taking, the administrative decision to label these children as "slow" or "retarded" and place them in special classes apart from "normal" students may have a disastrous effect—one that may grow worse, not better, over time. Of course, such tracking may also have the opposite effect on those identified early on as having high IQ scores. Such children may come to believe that they will be high achievers, and, like a self-fulfilling prophecy, this expectation may figure prominently in their subsequent success (Dahlstrom, 1993). Thus, IQ test scores may not simply predict subsequent achievement or the lack of it; they may also be partly responsible for it.

Although IQ tests are useful for predicting academic performance and for reflecting past learning, they do not measure other elements underlying academic achievement—motivation, emotion, and attitudes, for example. Yet in many situations, these characteristics may have more to do with an individual's success and productivity than IQ does. Let's look briefly at the relationship between IQ scores and success.

**IQ AND SUCCESS** Despite their limitations, IQ tests do a good job of predicting future school performance. What does this fact mean, and how important is it?

IQ scores should correlate well with academic performance because both call for intellectual activity and both stress verbal ability. Moreover, both academic achievement and high IQ scores require similar kinds of motivation, attention, and continuity of effort. And as we noted earlier, because academic success depends largely on test-taking ability, the correlation is not surprising. But critics contend that there may be another, less savory, reason for the high correlation between school performance and IQ test scores. If teachers expect particular students to do well in school on the basis of their IQ scores, the teachers may encourage those students. By the same token, if teachers expect students with low IQ scores not to perform well, they may neglect those students.

Whatever the reason, IQ scores do predict success in school with some accuracy. Moreover, people with high IQ scores generally enter high-status occupations: Physicians and lawyers tend to have high IQs, whereas truck drivers and janitors usually do not. However, this pattern may be explained in various ways. For one thing, because people with higher IQs tend to do better in school, they stay in school longer and earn advanced degrees, which, in turn, opens the way to high-status jobs. Moreover, children from wealthy families are more likely to have the money needed for graduate school and other advanced occupational training. They also benefit from family connections. Most important, they grow up in environments that encourage academic success and reward good performance on tests (J. M. Blum, 1979).

Research confirms that people with high IQ scores are more successful in school and tend to get higher-status jobs, but are they also more likely to succeed in their careers? In a classic paper, David C. McClelland (1973), argued that IQ scores and grades in college have very little to do with later occupational success. His review of the research evidence indicated that when education and social class were held constant, on a wide range of jobs people with high IQs did not perform better than people with lower IQs. A more recent survey of the relevant research data contradicts McClelland's conclusions, however. Barrett and Depinet (1991) found considerable evidence that grades and results on tests of intellectual ability do predict occupational success. They concluded that "test results were not an artifact of social status, nor were they unfair to minorities" (p. 1021). Similarly, Ree and Earles (1992) point to evidence that measures of general intelligence serve as excellent predictors of job performance.

In response to these studies, McClelland (1993) has reiterated his earlier views, charging that these recent investigations fail to control for the influence of such variables as family advantage and achievement motivation. According to Robert J. Sternberg, some of whose work we considered earlier, and his colleague, Richard K. Wagner (1993), new tests should be developed specifically to measure skills relevant to job performance.

In this section, we have reviewed several criticisms that have been leveled at IQ tests and their use. But not all critics of IQ tests want to see them eliminated. Many simply want to improve IQ tests so they better reflect what they're trying to measure. For example, J. R. Mercer developed the *System of Multicultural Pluralistic Assessment (SOMPA)*, designed for

**"What is the proper use—if any—for standardized tests?"**

We have seen that psychologists disagree on what constitutes intelligence. Nevertheless, for almost a century psychologists have developed a number of tests designed to measure intelligence or mental aptitudes. Supporters of standardized tests like the Stanford-Binet and the Wechsler scales argue that the ultimate purpose of these tests is not to measure intelligence, but rather to predict performance in school or college. Questions persist, however, as to what these tests actually measure and how well they measure it.

What are your feelings on this issue? What do you think intelligence or aptitude tests really measure? Should these tests include racially, sexually, or culturally biased questions if those questions raise the predictive validity of these tests? After you have thought about these issues, take a few minutes to ponder the opinions of some other students.

• • • • • • • •

**AMY: I think we have to decide what is more important, the validity of the test or complete fairness on all the questions. If we want validity, we may have to sacrifice the desire for fairness. Colleges could be told then that some groups may perform slightly better than others and scores could then be adjusted.**

**BILL: I think it's OK to make a test valid—as long as it is recognized that that's what it is. Maybe the purpose of the ACT, etc., is to predict performance in college. But the consensus is that it is supposed to measure intelligence. Though related to an extent, these are just not the same things.**

**LEE: I'm not sure I understand just how biased questions *could* increase predictability. . . . A biased question may increase the predictability of the test for the in-group, but it will decrease the predictability for the out-group, which doesn't understand the question. This will give too high a score for members of the in-group and too low scores for members of the out-group. This actually keeps the predictability at status quo, as there is an increase and corresponding decrease. The only result I see is that the in-group will *appear* to be even more intelligent than the out-group did before the inclusion of the biased questions.**

**MALCOLM: The test is supposed to predict performance in college. By saying that a biased test would increase predictability, we also say that colleges themselves are biased. In other words, a white American male would do better in college because of the way the curriculum is set. Thus, with a biased test you could more accurately predict their performance in college. This is not the same as saying they are more intelligent.**

**ERIN: The tests are probably MORE valid for being biased, which only indicates that the colleges themselves are the problem. However, allowing them to continue being biased only worsens the situation and enables the vicious cycle to continue.**

**LISA: I suppose that if SATs are now valid and reliable, do we really need to alter them all that much? We can't really bias certain questions so that someone can get them right just so they'll get a better score if this doesn't really correlate with their grades in college. Is this really all that fair to them or to the college recruiters?**

**CARVER: Biased items should not be included. Aptitude tests should reflect aptitude, not how well someone's grades might turn out 5 years later. There may be a correlation between the two, but so what!**

**AMY: If the purpose of the SAT is to predict college performance, then that should be its stated purpose, instead of saying it's to [measure] aptitude. So then if a biased question helps for this prediction, then don't get rid of it.**

• • • • • • • •

Now that you've read through other students' views, you might want to reconsider your position on this issue. What do standardized tests predict? Can these tests be used in positive ways? If not, why not? If so, should questions that might be racially, sexually, or culturally biased still be included on these tests?

children between the ages of 5 and 11. SOMPA involves collecting a wide range of data on a child, including information about health and socioeconomic status, that provides the context within which IQ test scores are interpreted. SOMPA takes into account both the dominant school culture and the child's family background, and then adjusts the child's IQ score (based on the Wechsler Scales) accordingly (B. Rice, 1979). And Sternberg is developing new intelligence test items that will tap a much broader set of skills that may underlie intelligence.

It is important to remember that an IQ score is not the same as intelligence. IQ tests measure people's ability level at a certain point in time and in relation to the norms for their age group. IQ scores do not tell us why someone performs poorly or well. Moreover, as we have seen, most psychologists today look on "intelligence" not as a singular entity but; rather, as a combination of abilities and aptitudes required for adaptation to, and effective behavior in, the real world (Anastasi, 1982; Frederickson, 1986; Sternberg, 1985a, 1986). And these abilities vary to some extent from culture to culture, with skills considered most important in one culture tending to predominate in that culture, while abilities that are deemphasized tend to fade out (B. M. Levinson, 1959). Finally, an IQ score is a highly simplistic way of representing an extremely complex set of abilities. Maloney and Ward (1976) point out that we do not describe a person's personality with a 2- or 3-digit number. Why, then, they ask, should we try to sum up something as complex as intelligence by labeling someone "90" or "110"? As Sternberg (1992) points out, we have come to rely too much on single tests yielding a single score. What is required are more differentiated measures of different types or aspects of intelligence, especially in the area of practical intelligence.

## DETERMINANTS OF INTELLIGENCE

### Heredity

Is intelligence inherited? As we saw in Chapter 2, scientists use studies of identical twins to measure the effects of heredity in humans. Twin studies of intelligence begin by comparing the IQ scores of identical twins who have been raised together. As you can see in Figure 7-10, the correlation

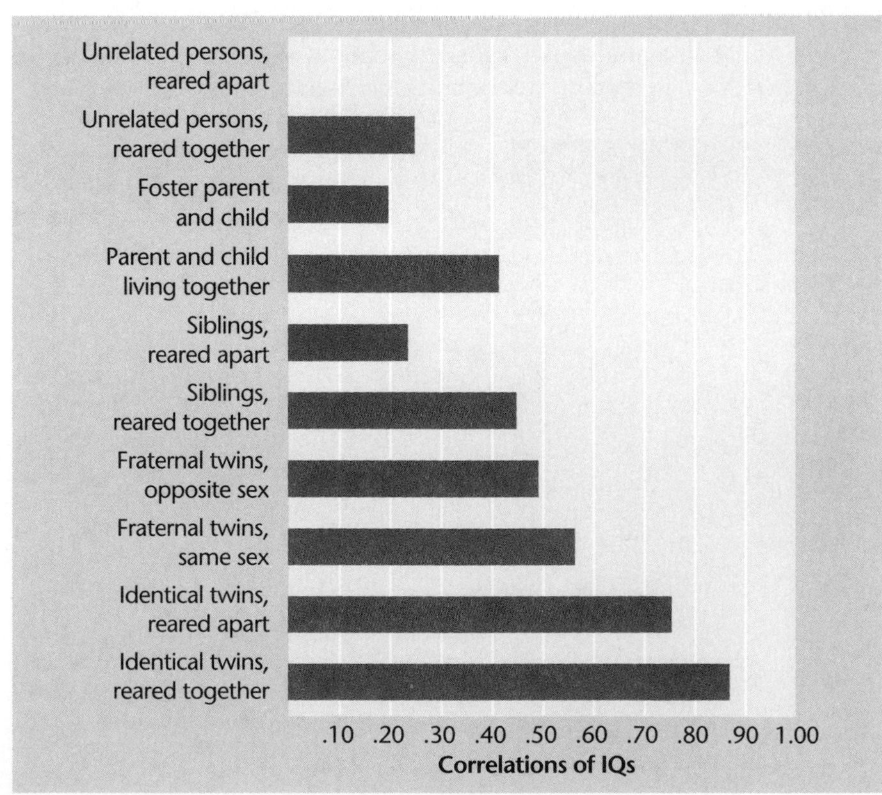


**Figure 7-10**
**Correlations of IQ scores and familial relationships.**

*Source:* Adapted from "Genetics and Intelligence: A review," by Erlenmeyer-Kimling and L.F. Jarvik 1963, *Science, 142*, pp. 1477–1479. Copyright © 1963 by the American Association for the Advancement of Science.

between their IQ scores is very high. But these twins grew up in the same environments: They shared parents, home, schoolteachers, vacations, and probably friends and clothes, too. These common experiences could explain their similarity on IQ scores. To check this possibility, researchers look for identical twins who were separated early in life—generally before they were 6 months old—and raised in different families. As you can see from Figure 7-10, even when identical twins are reared in different families, they tend to have very similar IQ scores; in fact, the similarity is much greater than that between siblings who grew up in the same home.

At this point, the case for heredity seems to be ironclad: Identical twins have very similar IQ scores even when they have not been raised together. For several reasons, however, twin studies do not constitute "final proof." First, finding identical twins who were separated at birth or soon after is very difficult; therefore, very few such pairs have been studied. Drawing conclusions about the influence of heredity based on such a small sample of subjects is hazardous at best (Loehlin, 1989). Second, adoption agencies tend to match natural and adoptive parents. If twins are born to educated middle-class parents, the adopted twin would most likely be placed with educated middle-class adoptive parents. Finally, even if twins grow up in radically different environments, they lived for 9 months inside the same mother: Their prenatal experiences were virtually identical, and it is difficult to determine the extent to which those shared experiences might contribute to their similarities. Therefore, even among identical twins, at least some of their similarity may actually be due to similarity of environment. It is here that the case for environmental influence begins.

## Environment

Proponents of the environmental influence on intelligence do not deny that, to some degree, intelligence is inherited, but they feel this is only the beginning. Each of us inherits a certain body build from our parents, but our actual weight depends largely on what we eat and how much we exercise. Similarly, even though we inherit certain mental capacities, how we develop our intellectual abilities depends on what we see around us as infants, how our parents respond to our first attempts to talk, the schools we attend, the books we read, the television programs we watch—even what we eat.

If children do not consume an adequate diet early in their development, both their mental and their physiological growth will be stunted.

Environment has an impact on children even before birth: A number of studies show that prenatal nutrition affects IQ scores (Hack et al., 1991). In one study of pregnant women who were economically deprived, half were given a dietary supplement, and half were given placebos. When given intelligence tests between the ages of 3 and 4, the children of the mothers who had taken the supplement scored significantly higher than the other children (Harrell, Woodyard, & Gates, 1955).

Extreme malnutrition during infancy can lower IQ scores. For example, severely undernourished children in South Africa had IQs that averaged 20 points lower than the IQs of their peers with adequate diets (Stock & Smythe, 1963). This leads to the conclusion that children do not get an adequate diet early in their development, both their mental and their physiological growth will be stunted. Subsequent research in Great Britain (Benton & Roberts, 1988) and in California (Schoenthaler, Amos, Eysenck, Peritz, & Yudkin, 1991) has suggested that the addition of vitamin supplements to the diet can increase IQ test scores, possibly even among children who are not experiencing malnutrition.

Quite by chance, psychologist H.M. Skeels found evidence in the 1930s that IQ scores among children also depend on environmental stimulation. While investigating orphanages for the state of Iowa, Skeels noticed that the wards where the children lived were very overcrowded and that the few adults charged with caring for the children had almost no time to play with them, talk to them, or read them stores. Many of these children were classified as "subnormal" in intelligence. Skeels followed the cases of two girls who, after 18 months in the orphanage, were transferred to a ward for severely retarded adult women. Originally, the girls' IQs were in the range of retardation, but after a year on the adult ward, as if by magic, their IQs had risen to normal. He repeated the experiment by placing 13 slow children as house guests in adult wards (Skeels, 1942). Again, within a scant 18 months, the mean IQ of these children had soared from 64 to 92 (within the normal range). What accounts for these remarkable results? Skeels concluded that once these deprived children finally had someone to play with them, to read to them, to cheer them when they took their first steps, and to encourage them to talk, they approached their full potential. Meanwhile, the mean IQ of a group of children who had been left in orphanages dropped from 86 to 61.

A more recent study that reinforces Skeels's findings was conducted in France by Capron and Duyme (1989). Half the children in this study had been born to parents of high socioeconomic status (SES), and half had been born to parents of low SES. Half the children born to high-SES parents were adopted and raised by parents of similar status, and half were adopted and raised by low-SES parents. Similarly, half the children born to low-SES parents were adopted and raised by high-SES parents, and half

Advocates of the environmental influence on intelligence claim that intellectual development depends on environmental stimulation and encouragement. This is true for everyone, although the specific form of stimulation varies from culture to culture.

were adopted and raised by other low-SES parents. The results showed that the socioeconomic status of the adoptive parents had an effect on their adopted children's IQs. Regardless of the socioeconomic status of the child's biological parents, those children adopted by high-SES parents had higher IQs than did those children adopted by low-SES parents. Why? High-SES families tend to provide children with better nutrition and heightened stimulation; thus, these results mirror the outcome of earlier studies showing the importance of an adequate diet and intellectually stimulating surroundings.

**INTERVENTION PROGRAMS** Advocates of the influence of environment draw support from the success of *intervention programs* that set out deliberately to bolster people's mental abilities and thereby to improve their scores on ability tests. For example, in 1961 the so-called Milwaukee Project was launched. Its purpose was to see if intervening in a child's family life could offset the negative effects on IQ scores of cultural and socioeconomic deprivation. Rick Heber (Garber & Heber, 1982; Heber et al., 1972) and his associates at the University of Wisconsin Infant Center worked with 40 poor pregnant women in the Milwaukee area. On average, the women initially scored less than 75 on the Wechsler intelligence scales. The women were then split into two groups. One group was given job training and sent to school. As they found jobs, they were also instructed in child care, home economics, and personal relationships. The other group received no special tips on handling children and no job training. After all 40 women had their babies, the research team turned to the children. Starting when they were 3 months old and continuing for the next 6 years, the children of the mothers who were chosen for special training spent the better part of each day in an infant education center, where they received nourishing meals and participated in a daily program that featured a wide range of educational toys. They were cared for by paraprofessionals who behaved like nonworking mothers in affluent families. The other group of children, whose mothers were not receiving any special training, were not given access to the education center.

Periodically, all the children were given IQ tests. Children in the experimental group, whose mothers were given special training and who themselves had access to the education center, ended up with an average IQ score of 126—51 points higher than their mothers' average scores. By contrast, children in the control group, whose mothers received no special training and who did not have access to the education center, ended up with an average IQ score of 94—not as high as the experimental group, but still much higher than their mothers' average scores, perhaps, in part, because they had become accustomed to taking tests, an experience their mothers had never had.

Another study evaluated the impact of the Perry Preschool Program in Ypsilanti, Michigan. Included in this study were 123 preschoolers from low-income families, 58 of whom attended the program while 65 did not. The children who participated in the program scored higher on tests of academic skill, were more likely to finish high school and plan to go to college, and had a higher employment rate than those who did not take part in the program (Schweinhart & Weikart, 1980).

Head Start, the largest intervention program, began in 1965 and today provides "comprehensive services for 721,000 children lasting at least a half a day for 128 days a year" (Kassebaum, 1994). Head Start, which focuses on preschoolers between the ages of 3 and 5 who live in low-income families, is designed to provide these children with some important educational and social skills before they get to school, plus offer information about nutrition and health to both the children and their families. Parents get involved in all aspects of Head Start, from daily activities to administration of the program itself, and some studies indicate that this parental involvement has been crucial to the program's success (Ryan, 1974).

Numerous researchers have evaluated the long-term effects of Head Start. After reviewing much of the early research, Brown and Grotberg (1981) concluded that the program had boosted the children's cognitive abilities. Today, however, some experts voice reservations about the program's success, noting that these improvements may not be lasting. For example, some evidence suggests that improvements in IQ as a result of Head Start tend to be modest or short-term. Nevertheless, there seems to be no question that children leaving Head Start are in a better position to profit from schooling than they would be otherwise (Zigler & Styfco, 1994). In one important study, Schweinhart, Barnes, and Weikart (1993) followed Head Start graduates until age 27. Among the long-term benefits they ascribed to Head Start was higher academic achievement: They found that the Head Start graduates tended to stay in school longer and were more likely to graduate from college. Thus, even if the IQ gains brought on by Head Start fade in times, the program still offers substantial long-term, practical benefits, according to researchers.

Based on assessments of various intervention programs, intellectual ability can be enhanced through extensive training, particularly if the training starts in the preschool years. Moreover, some researchers contend that older children, adolescents, and adults might also benefit from such training (Anastasi, 1989; Hobbs & Robinson, 1982). Considering that the development of mental abilities proceeds over a lifetime rather than stopping at some point during childhood, it seems plausible that problem-solving skills and abstract thinking abilities, too, can be improved throughout adolescence and into adulthood.

## The IQ Debate: A Continuing Controversy

We have seen evidence that both heredity and environment have important effects on mental abilities. But which is more important than the other?

When IQ test scores were collected from soldiers in World War I, psychologists discovered large differences in scores among various ethnic groups (C. Brigham, 1923; Yerkes, 1921/1948). For example, men who traced their ancestry to northern European countries such as England and Germany scored higher than men whose families originated in southern European countries, including Greece and Italy. Some psychologists believed strongly that these differences arose because some ethnic groups had lived in the United States longer than others and thus were more familiar with the cultural norms reflected in the tests. Other psychologists argued vehemently that differences among ethnic groups could only be explained by genetics.

In the years following World War I, the intensity of the argument over the connection between race and ethnicity, on the one hand, and intelligence, on the other, subsided. Decades later, however, public and scholarly debate erupted once again after the publication of an article in 1969 by psychologist Arthur Jensen. In his article, Jensen asserted that heredity accounts for roughly 80 percent of the variation in IQ test scores among various racial groups.

Over the next two decades the conflict over nature versus nurture when it comes to intelligence died down, but it did not go away. Then, in 1994, the dispute burst out into the open once again with the publication of a controversial book titled *The Bell Curve: Intelligence and Class Structure in American Life* by Richard Herrnstein and Charles Murray. Herrnstein and Murray argued that intelligence is largely inherited, that different people inherit different levels of intellectual ability, and that levels of intelligence vary among ethnic and racial groups. They further maintained that U.S. society has become increasingly stratified based on intelligence and dominated by an elite group with superior cognitive abilities.

**Mental retardation** Condition of significantly subaverage intelligence combined with deficiencies in adaptive behavior.

It is difficult to sort out the conflicting data and claims involved in this debate, but one point of common ground emerges clearly: Almost all the participants agree that both heredity and environment affect IQ scores. Consider the following analogy, adapted from Turkheimer (1991). Suppose you grow one group of plants in enriched soil, and another group of plants in poor soil. The enriched group will grow to be larger and stronger than the nonenriched group; the difference between the two groups in this case is due entirely to differences in their environments. However, within each group of plants, differences among individual plants primarily have to do with genetics, because all plants in the same group share essentially the same environment. Nevertheless, the size and strength of any single plant will reflect both heredity and environment. Similarly, group differences in IQ scores may be traced to environmental factors, differences among people within racial groups may be due primarily to genetics, and the IQ scores of particular people almost certainly reflect the effects of both heredity and environment.

Of course, this example assumes that the plants have been distributed randomly between the two groups; thus, general differences between the groups are due entirely to the environment. It is possible, however, to select plants with different genetic characteristics for each group; for example, tall plants in one group and short plants in another. In this case, differences between the two groups would be the products of both environment and heredity. As you can see from these examples, sorting out environmental influences on IQ scores from genetic influences is a thorny business, and scientists likely will continue to debate this issue for years to come (see, for example, Humphreys, 1992, pp. 272-73).

One final note on this issue. Both Humphreys (1992) and Jensen (1992) note that IQ scores have *gone up* in the population as a whole. They cite evidence gathered by Flynn (1984,1987) showing that between 1932 and 1978 IQ scores rose about 3 points per decade. Several explanations have been advanced for this finding. Perhaps people are simply getting better at taking tests. By the same token, environmental factors, such as improved nutrition and health care, may account for the improvement. Some theorists also contend s that our culture is now richer and more stimulating than it ever was before.

## EXTREMES OF INTELLIGENCE

In general, the average IQ score on intelligence tests is 100. Nearly 70 percent of all people have IQs between 85 and 115, and all but 5 percent of the population have IQs that fall between 70 and 130. In this section, we will focus on people who score at the two extremes of intelligence—people who are mentally retarded and those who are gifted.

### Mental Retardation

**Mental retardation** encompasses a vast array of mental deficits with a wide variety of causes, treatments, and outcomes. The American Psychological Association (1994, p. 39) defines mental retardation as "significantly subaverage general intellectual functioning . . . that is accompanied by significant limitations in adaptive functioning"; in addition, the condition must appear before the individual is 18 years old. It is important to note that a low IQ score, by itself, does not mean a person is mentally retarded; rather, that individual must also lack the kinds of daily living skills that everyone needs to function independently (Wielkiewicz & Calvert, 1989). Individuals placed in the classification of "mild retardation" have IQs in the range of the low 50s to 70s and may be able to function adequately in society, gaining academic skills comparable to those of a sixth-grader. Those with IQs from the mid-30s to the low 50s fall into the category of "moderate retardation,"; they can learn on a second-grade level and perform skilled work in a sheltered workshop with supervision. People whose IQs range from the low 20s to the mid-30s are placed in the category of "severe retardation," and while they cannot learn vocational skills, they can carry out simple tasks with supervision. In the classification of "profound retardation" fall those with IQs below 25. These individuals require constant care and supervision.*

What causes mental retardation, and what can be done to prevent or overcome it? In most cases, the causes are simply not known (Hallahan, Kauffman, & Lloyd, 1985). This is especially true in cases of mild retardation, which account for nearly 90 percent of all retardation. In instances where causes can be identified, most often the retardation is traced to nonbiological causes—environmental, social, nutritional, and other risk factors have been shown to produce mental retardation of varying degrees of severity (Scott & Carran, 1987).

About 25 percent of the cases, however, stem from genetic or biological disorders; these tend to be the more severe forms of retardation. For example, a genetically based disease known as *phenylketonuria*, or *PKU*, brings on retardation. When a person suffers from PKU, the liver fails to produce a certain enzyme necessary for early brain development. PKU occurs in about one person out of 25,000 (Minton & Schneider, 1980). Another cause of severe mental retardation is chromosomal abnormality; this underlies *Down syndrome*, a form of mental retardation affecting 1 in 600 newborns. These people are born with defects on part of chromosome 21 (see the photo on p. 65 in Chapter 2). Down syndrome, named for the nineteenth-century British physician Langdon Down, who first described the symptoms, is characterized by severe mental retardation together with a characteristic pattern of physical deformities, including skinfolds on the hands, feet, and eyelids. Research evidence indicates that in the great majority of cases of Down syndrome, the egg from which the baby developed either was defective at the time of the mother's birth or developed defects during ovulation. In about 5 percent of the cases, the defect seems to originate with the father's sperm (Antonarakis, 1991).

As you might guess, little can be done to reverse the biological damage that underlies many cases of severe mental retardation once it has developed. But steps can be taken to reduce the effects of retardation, whether mild or severe, through education and training. Today the majority of students with their physical disabilities are educated in their local school systems (Schroeder, Schroeder, & Landesman, 1987), a process called *mainstreaming*, which allows these students to interact with nondisabled peers. In a similar way, efforts have been made to move mentally retarded people out of large, impersonal institutions and to place them in smaller community homes that offer them a greater opportunity for normal life experiences and personal growth (Landesman & Butterfield, 1987). And more and more of these people are being trained to hold jobs in the community as well.

A highly complex phenomenon, mental retardation eludes simplistic categories. Just as intelligence tests fail to measure certain abilities, such as artistic talent, people classified as retarded sometimes exhibit exceptional skills in areas outside of general intelligence. The most dramatic and intriguing examples of this center around *savant performance*, in which certain individuals who are mentally retarded or who suffer from mental handicaps or brain injuries demonstrate remarkable abilities in specialized areas, such as numerical computation, memory, art, or music (O'Connor &

---

*·Categories of mental retardation are based on APA, DSM-IV, 1994.

**Giftedness** Refers to superior IQ combined with demonstrated or potential ability in such areas as academic aptitude, creativity, or leadership.

Hermelin, 1987). Savant performances range from making mental calculations using large numbers almost instantly to determine the day of the week for any date over many centuries, and playing back a long musical composition after hearing it played only once. Whatever its origins, savant performance constitutes an intriguing mixture of retardation and giftedness, the topic to which we now turn.

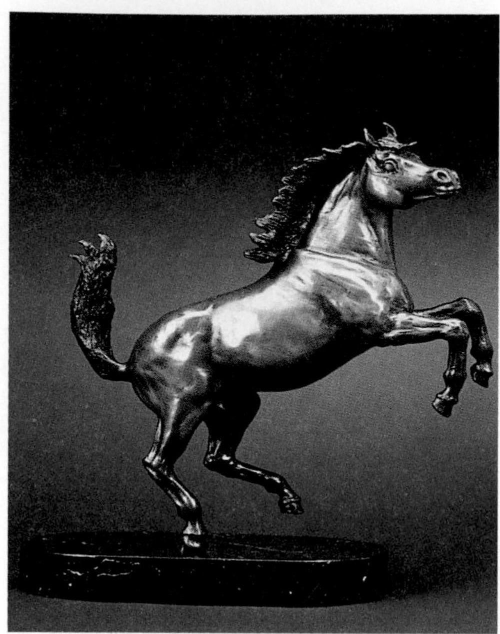

An example of savant performance. Alonzo Clemons, the sculptor who created this work, suffered brain injury in a childhood fall. The brain injury resulted in a lowered IQ and limited language development. Nevertheless, he is an accomplished artist whose work has appeared in exhibits throughout the country.

## Giftedness

At the other extreme of the intelligence scale are "the gifted"—those with exceptional mental abilities as measured by scores on standard intelligence tests. As with mental retardation, the causes of **giftedness** are largely unknown.

Lewis Terman and his colleagues launched the first and now-classic study of giftedness in the early 1920s. Terman's (1925) was the first major research study in which giftedness was defined in terms of academic talent and measured by an IQ score in the top 2 percentile. More recently, some experts have sought to broaden the definition of giftedness to encompass more than simply a high IQ. Renzulli (1978), for instance, proposes thinking of giftedness as the interaction of above-average general ability, exceptional creativity, and high levels of commitment. Sternberg and Davidson (1985) define giftedness as especially effective use of what we earlier called componential aspects of intelligence: planning, allocating resources, acquiring new knowledge, and carrying out tasks effectively. In 1971, Congress drafted a significantly broadened definition of giftedness. Gifted children were identified as those with demonstrated achievement or potential ability in any of the following areas, singly or in combination: (1) general intellectual ability, (2) specific academic aptitude, (3) creative or productive thinking, (4) leadership ability, and (5) fine arts.

But how do children demonstrate giftedness? Most school districts use a combination of intelligence tests, teacher recommendations, achievement tests, diagnostic tests, interviews, and evaluation of academic and creative work before labeling a child as gifted. While this series of assessments does identify students with a broad range of intellectual and creative gifts, it tends to slight those whose talent lies in specific areas such as mathematics or music.

Despite questions about the accuracy of assessment, momentum began to build in the 1970s for a national movement to establish targeted educational programs for gifted children, a movement that gained strength in the 1980s (Horowitz & O'Brien, 1985, 1986; Sternberg & Davidson, 1986). Yet because there has been little systematic study of programs for gifted children (Reis, 1989), many critics have challenged the fundamental assumptions underlying these programs. Take the assumption that gifted people, as a group, are demonstrably superior to other people in all areas of intelligence and creativity. Critics note that people gifted in one area are not necessarily gifted in others. Gardner (1983) found that gifted children performed no better than other bright children on tests of moral and social reasoning.

In addition, some critics charge that the methods currently used to identify gifted children may overlook gifted students in minority populations (Baldwin, 1985). To address this concern, experts have devised alternative measures for minority students, including an abbreviated Standford-Binet for youngsters with disadvantaged backgrounds (Bruch, 1971) and the Mercer and Lewis (1987) *System of Multicultural Pluralistic Assessment*, both of which adjust intelligence test scores to take into account a child's sociocultural group. It is still too soon to assess the effectiveness of these alternatives.

One further reservation about programs for gifted children: Just how do students themselves feel about being labeled as exceptional? Some children would rather not be thought of as "brains," while others may resent the pressure to perform. Finally, a controversy is growing over creativity and its relationship to giftedness. Guilford (1967), among others, has pointed out that the ability to do creative problem solving is not adequately measured by achievement and aptitude tests. And Getzels and Jackson (1962) have found that some children who score only moderately high on intelligence tests, but exceptionally high on creative measures, are capable of outstanding achievement. We will look more closely at the relationship between creativity and intelligence in the next section.

**Creativity** The ability to produce novel and unique socially valued ideas or objects.

## CREATIVITY

**Creativity** is the ability to produce novel and unique socially valued ideas or objects ranging from philosophy to paintings, from music to mousetraps (Mumford & Gustafson, 1988).

Some researchers view creative ability simply as one aspect of intelligence. For example, the study by Sternberg and his associates (1981) referred to earlier in the chapter, found that experts on intelligence generally considered creativity as part of verbal intelligence (see Table 7-1). Sternberg also saw creativity and insight as important elements in the experiential component of human intelligence.

Recent definitions of giftedness have broadened the concept beyond scores on intelligence tests. These young people at the Moscow School of Music, for example, have demonstrated exceptional musical abilities since childhood.

What, exactly, is the relationship between intelligence and creativity? Are people who score high on IQ tests likely to be more creative than those who score low? Early studies typically found little or no relationship between creativity and intelligence (e.g. Getzels & Jackson, 1962; Wing, 1969). Critics point out, however, that these early studies were flawed because their subjects were all bright students. For example, the average IQ score of the students tested by Getzels and Jackson was 132. Perhaps creativity and intelligence are linked until IQ reaches a certain level, or threshold, after which there is little or no relationship between them. Called the *threshold theory* of creativity and intelligence, this theory has garnered substantial support. However, studies supporting the threshold theory relied heavily on tests of creativity. Thus, any conclusions drawn from them must assume that scores on creativity tests reflect real-life creativity, an assumption that many people question. But other studies of people who have demonstrated outstanding creativity in their lives also lend credence to the threshold theory of creativity and intelligence. These studies (e.g., Barron, 1963; Cattell, 1971; Helson, 1971; Bachtold & Werner, 1973) show that creative people tend to be highly intelligent—that is, highly creative artists, writers, scientists, and mathematicians tend, as a group, to score high on intelligence tests. But for individuals in this special group, there is little relationship between IQ scores and levels of creative achievement, just as the threshold theory would predict.

Are highly creative people more intelligent than less creative people?

In general, creative people are *problem finders* as well as problem solvers (Mackworth, 1965; Getzels, 1975). In school and on the job, other people often give us problems to solve. The more creative people are, the less they like to work on problems given to them by other people, and the more they like to puzzle out problems they have set for themselves. Thus, creative scientists such as Charles Darwin may work for years on a problem, such as evolution, that was not assigned to them, but that they freely chose to delve into. Creative people also show a willingness to take risks. These two traits of creative people—problem finding and risk taking—fit together neatly; after all, working for years on a problem of your own choosing involves real risks because there is no guarantee that you will succeed.

## ANSWERS TO PROBLEMS IN THE CHAPTER

**PROBLEM 1** Fill each of the smaller spoons with salt from the larger spoon. That will require 4 teaspoons of salt, leaving exactly 4 teaspoons of salt in the larger spoon.

**PROBLEM 2** Turn the 5-minute hourglass over; when it runs out, turn over the 9-minute hourglass. When it truns out, 14 minutes have passed.

**PROBLEM 3** As shown in Figure 7-11, fill spoon C with salt from spoon A (now A has 5 teaspoons of salt and C has 3). Pour the salt from spoon C into spoon B (now A has 5 teaspoons of salt and B has 3). Again fill spoon C with salt from spoon A (leaving A with only 2 teaspoons of salt, while B and C each have 3). Fill spoon B with salt from spoon C (this leaves 1 teaspoon of salt in spoon C while B has 5 teaspoons and A has only 2). Pour all the salt from spoon B into spoon A (now A has 7 teaspoons of salt and C has 1). Pour all the salt from spoon C into spoon B, and then fill spoon C from spoon A (this leaves 4 teaspoons of salt in A, 1 teaspoon in B, and 3 teaspoons in C). Finally, pour all the salt from spoon C into spoon B (this leaves 4 teaspoons of salt in spoons A and B, which is the solution).

**PROBLEM 4** Start both hourglasses. When the 5-minute hourglass runs out, turn it over to start it again. When the 9-minute hourglass runs out, turn over the 5-minute hourglass. Since there is 1 minute left in the 5-minute hourglass when you turn it over, it will run for only 4 minutes. Those 4 minutes, together with the original 9 minutes, add up to the required 13 minutes for the barbecue.

**PROBLEM 5** Take one of the short pieces of chain shown in Figure 7-12 and open all three links (this costs 6 cents). Use those three links to connect the remaining three pieces o f chain (closing the three links costs 9 cents).

**PROBLEM 6** Join the matches to form a pyramid as seen in Figure 7-13.

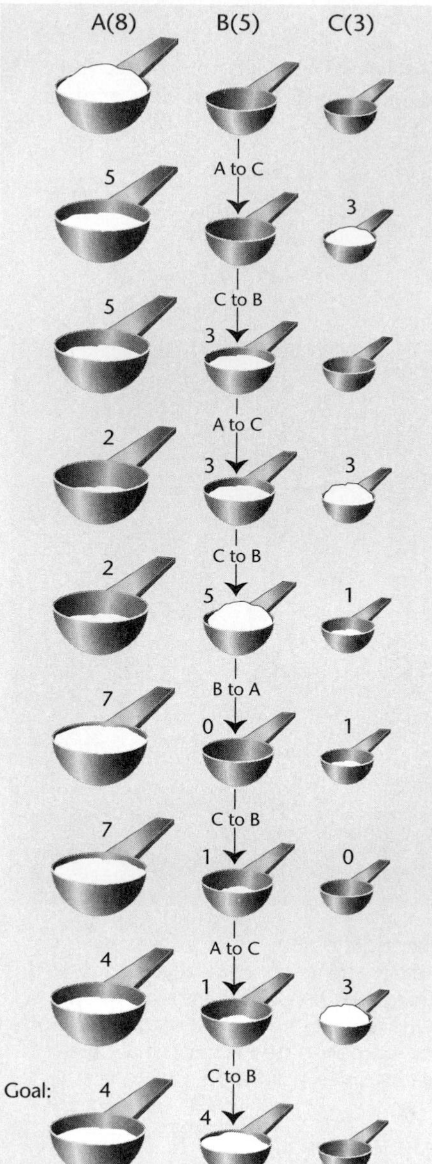


**Figure 7-11**

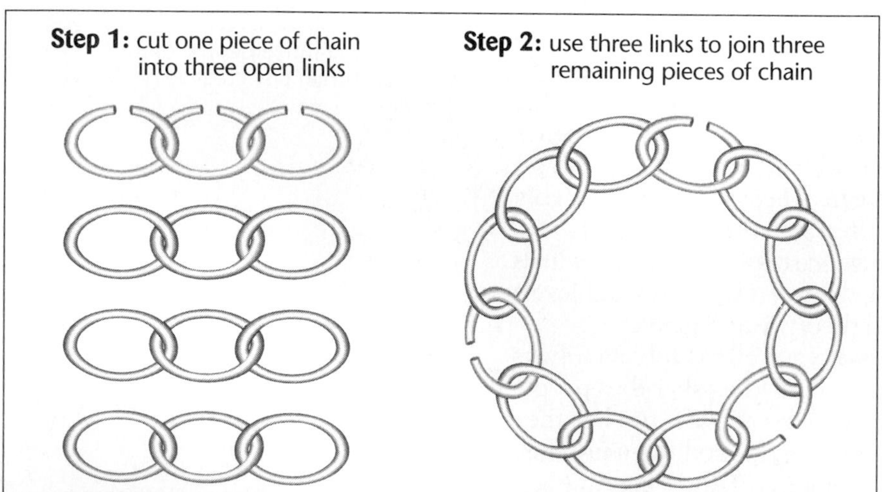


**Figure 7-12**

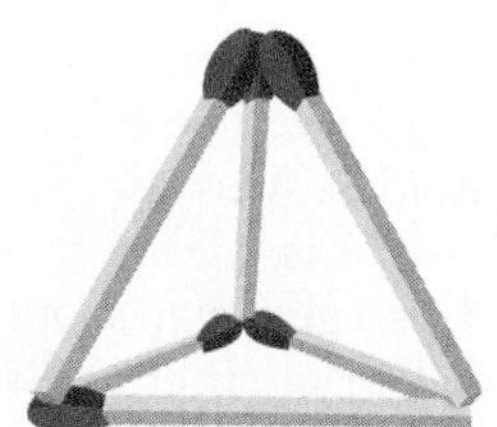

**Figure 7-13**

**PROBLEM 7** One way to solve this problem is to draw a diagram of the ascent and the descent as in Figure 7-14. From this drawing, you can see that indeed there is a point that the monk passes at exactly the same time on both days. Another way to approach this problem is to imagine that there are two monks on the mountain; one starts ascending at 7 A.M. while the other starts descending at 7 A.M. on the same day. Clearly, sometime during the day the monks must meet somewhere along the route.

**PROBLEM 8** There are four possible solutions to this problem, of which one is shown in Figure 7-15 (the other three solutions differ only slightly from this one).

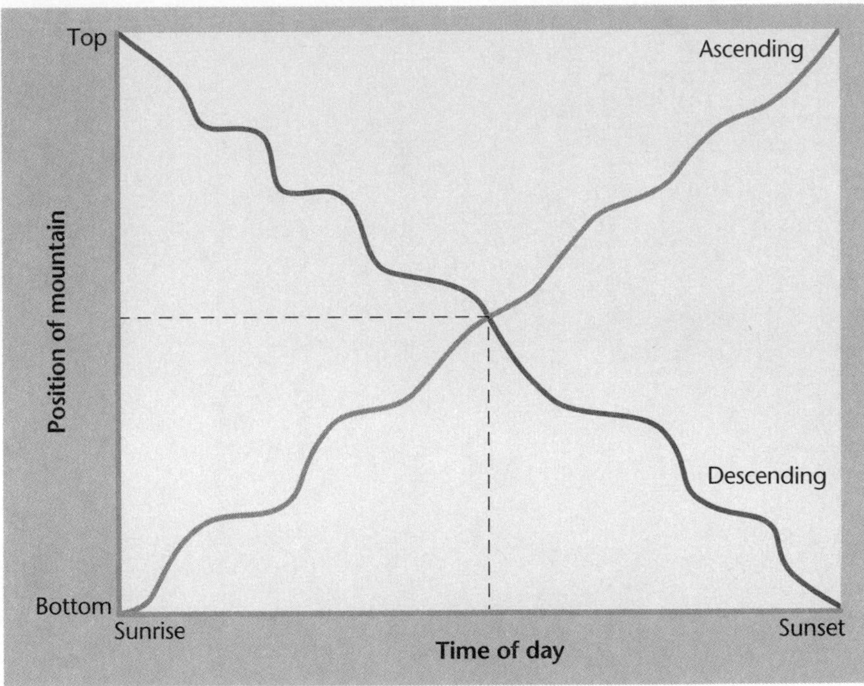


**Figure 7-14**

**PROBLEM 9** There are 15 possible solutions to this problem, of which this is one: One Hobbit and one Orc cross the river in the boat; the Orc remains on the opposite side while the Hobbit rows back. Next, three Orcs cross the river; two of those Orcs remain on the other side (making a total of three Orcs on the opposite bank) while one Orc rows back. Now three Hobbits and one Orc row the boat back. Again three Hobbits row across the river, at which point al five Hobbits are on the opposite bank with only two Orcs. One of the Orcs then rows back and forth across the river twice to transport the remaining Orcs to the opposite side.

**SOLUTION TO FIGURE 7-8.** In solving the problem given in Figure 7-8, many people have trouble realizing that the box of tacks can also be used as a candleholder, as shown in Figure 7-16.

## ANSWERS TO INTELLIGENCE-TEST QUESTIONS

1. *Idleness* refers to the state of being inactive, not busy, unoccupied; *laziness* means an unwillingness or reluctance to work. Laziness is one possible cause of idleness, but not the only cause.
2. If you face west, your right hand will be toward the north.
3. *Obliterate* means to erase or destroy something completely.
4. Both an hour and a week are measures of time.
5. Alternative D is correct. Each sector starts where the previous sector left off and extends 45 degrees clockwise around the circle.
6. 75 cents will buy nine pencils.
7. Union (b) is most nearly opposite in meaning to chism. *Union* means a uniting or joining of several parts into a whole; *schism* means a splitting apart or dividing of something that was previously united.

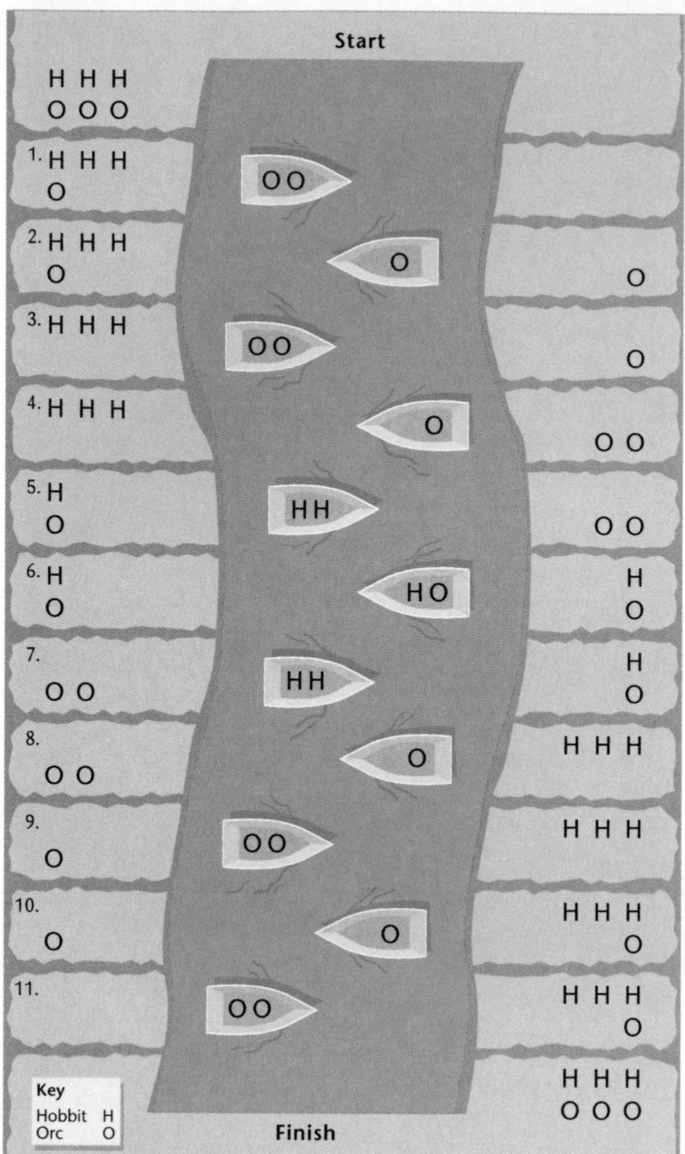


Figure 7-15

Figure 7-16

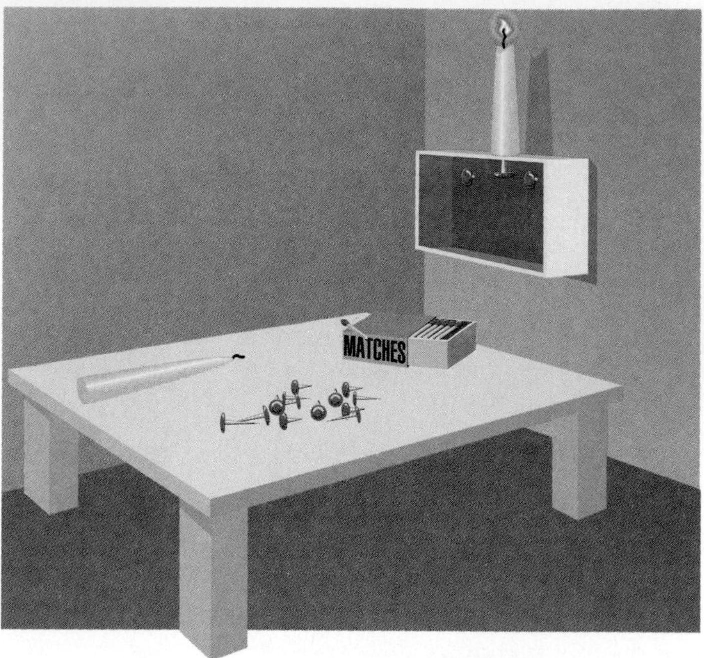


8. Alternative (e) makes the most sense. The phrase "despite an outward" implies that the words in the blanks should form a contrast of some sort. *Acquiescence* (agreeing, consenting without protest) certainly contrasts with thwarting (opposing, hindering, obstructing).

9. Alternative (d) is correct. A crutch is used to help someone who has difficulty with locomotion; spectacles are used to help someone who has difficulty with vision.

10. Alternative B is correct. In each case, the figure is made up of three shapes that are identical except for size; the largest shape goes on the bottom and the smallest on top, with no overlap between the shapes.

11. Alternative D is correct. The second figure is the same shape and size but with diagonal crosshatching from upper left to lower right.

## LOOKING FORWARD

As we think, we draw on language, images, and concepts. Language makes use of a very powerful system of rules to enable us to express a virtually limitless range of ideas. We can manipulate images and extract new information from them by examining them from different perspectives. Much current research focuses on helping people use their intrinsic imaging skills more effectively. Our conceptual framework is extremely malleable, enabling us to categorize events in ways that best suit a specific occasion.

Problem solving lies at the core of thinking. As long as we are open to conceiving of problems in novel ways, we can devise new and ingenious strategies to tackle and solve even the most difficult problems. Our decision-making capabilities, however, are prone to a wide range of errors, which we must make a special effort to avoid. Cognitive psychologists focus on identifying the strengths and weaknesses of our problem-solving and decision-making abilities.

The language we use can subtly influence the ways we think about things; as a result, different cultures approach problems and perceive reality in very different ways. Studying the interplay between language and thought may help people from far-flung cultures better understand one another.

Intelligence is a complex and controversial concept. Some theorists regard it as a singular entity—"general intelligence"—while sometimes conceding that it may have multiple facets. Other theorists believe that there is no such thing as general intelligence, only multiple intelligences. Recent research increasingly has focused on various kinds of practical intelligence—skills and abilities that are closely related to performance outside the walls of the classroom. This line of inquiry is also receiving a great deal of attention because psychologists want to establish their usefulness and expertise in "real-world" settings.

Over the years, psychologists have developed sophisticated tests to measure various aspects of intelligence. In the process, the IQ-test industry has exerted a tremendous impact on society, generating ongoing controversy over the proper role of intelligence testing. Although heredity and environment both affect mental abilities, the ways in which they interact and the degree to which each one contributes to intelligence are still being intensely explored and debated.

## SUMMARY

This chapter first examines **cognition**, or the process of thinking, and its role in problem solving and decision making. Thinking involves language, imagery, reflection, conceptualization, evaluation, and insight, among other processes. Thus, in addition to the retrieval and processing of information from memory, cognition requires the manipulation of information in various ways.

### BUILDING BLOCKS OF THOUGHT

The mental constructs we use to think and the kinds of things we think about form the basis of the building blocks of thought. Of these building blocks, language, images, and concepts are the three most important. That is, when we think about an object or a person, we think in terms of verbal statements, an image, or a concept consisting of certain attributes of the object or person.

#### Language

Language is based on **phonemes**, the basic sounds that make up a language. Phonemes themselves are meaningless unless they are grouped together to form **morphemes**, the smallest meaningful units of speech, such as simple words, prefixes, and suffixes. When we wish to communicate an idea, we start with a thought, then choose words and phrases that will express the idea, and produce the speech sounds of those words and phrases. To understand speech, the task is reversed.

The rules that determine the meaning and form of words and sentences are called **grammar**. Semantics and syntax are the two major components of grammar. **Semantics** refers to the criteria for meaning in a language—how we assign meaning to the morphemes we use. **Syntax** is the system of rules governing the structure of word forms and sentences.

#### Images

An **image** is a mental representation or recollection of a sensory experience. Imagery is an effective aid in thinking about and solving problems. Images also give us the power of visualization.

#### Concepts

A **concept** is a mental category for classifying objects, people, and experiences based on their common elements. Concepts help us think more efficiently about things; without the ability to form concepts, we would need a different, previously unused name for every individual object.

Concepts also help clarify new experiences since we draw on previously formed concepts to place new objects or events into appropriate categories. In the process, the concepts themselves may undergo some modification as they incorporate new information.

In general, concepts lack clear-cut boundaries and frequently overlap with one another. Therefore, we often use **prototypes**, mental models of the most typical examples of a concept. We mentally compare a new object to this prototype to determine if the object is indeed what we think it is based on features the object and our prototype have in common.

## PROBLEM SOLVING

In addition to thinking about things, human cognition involves the active use of language, images, and concepts—the building blocks of thought—for solving problems and making decisions.

### The Interpretation of Problems

**Problem representation**, defining or interpreting the problem, is the first step in problem solving. We must decide whether to view the problem verbally, mathematically, or visually; and we must decide what class or category a given problem belongs to, since properly categorizing a problem sheds light on how to solve it.

### Producing and Evaluating Solutions

After interpreting a problem, we select an optimum strategy for solving that problem.

**Trial and error** is a problem-solving strategy based on the successive elimination of incorrect solutions until the correct one is found. But trial and error is time-consuming, and its scattershot approach is unsuitable in many problem situations.

**Information retrieval** is a problem-solving technique that requires only the recovery of information from long-term memory. This strategy works best when a factual solution must be found quickly.

An **algorithm** is a step-by-step method of problem solving that guarantees a correct solution if the method is the right one for the problem and if it is carried out properly. Solving a mathematical problem by means of a formula exemplifies the use of an algorithm.

For many everyday problems that cannot be solved by algorithms, heuristics are useful. **Heuristics** are rules of thumb that simplify problems and lead to solutions, even though they do not guarantee a correct solution. **Hill climbing** is a heuristic in which each step moves the problem solver closer to the final goal. Another heuristic strategy involves creating **subgoals**—intermediate goals that may make it easier to reach the final goal.

**Working backward**, another heuristic, traces steps from the desired goal back to the given conditions. This method works well when the goal offers more information than the givens and the operation can work both forward and backward.

### Obstacles to Solving Problems

Effective problem solving depends on many factors, including the proper level of motivation or emotional arousal. Too little emotion does not motivate us to solve the problem; too much may interfere with the problem-solving process.

Another factor that can help or hinder problem solving is **set**, the tendency to perceive and to approach problems in certain ways. Sets enable us to draw on past experience to solve a problem now, but a strong set may also block out new and different ways to solving specific problems when those novel tacks would be most appropriate.

One set that can seriously hamper problem solving is **functional fixedness**— the tendency to perceive only a limited number of uses for an object.

### Becoming Better at Problem Solving

Several strategies help us analyze and solve problems by shifting our perspective on the problem from one angle to another.

Using the **tactic of elimination**, we evaluate possible solutions according to appropriate criteria and discard those that fail to contribute to a solution. This approach is particularly valuable if we have a better grasp of what we do not want than of what we do want. In **visualizing**, various courses of action are drawn, diagrammed, or charted so we can better understand and analyze them.

In solving most problems, we need to be creative. Problems that have no single correct solution call for **divergent thinking**, thinking that is original, inventive, and flexible. By contrast, the highly focused process of **convergent thinking** works better for problems that have just one correct solution.

When people, either individually or in groups, float all sorts of ideas without rejecting any of them outright, they're **brainstorming**. Through this technique, numerous ideas are gathered and problem solvers only begin to evaluate the prospective solutions after all possible ideas have been proposed.

## DECISION MAKING

Unlike other kinds of problem solving, decision making starts off with a knowledge of all the possible solutions or choices. The task is to select the best alternative based on a predetermined set of criteria.

In the **compensatory model**, which is a rational approach to decision making, choices are systematically evaluated based on various criteria. In this model, we assess how the attractive features of each choice might compensate for the unattractive ones, and then decide which of the options best matches our ideal choice. An alternative approach that is not so precise is the **noncompensatory model**, which does not systematically compare each option against the others. When we use the elimination-by-aspects tactic, for example, we toss out choices that do not meet one or two of our requirements, even though they may be excellent choices on other grounds. Noncompensatory models can lead to shortsighted decisions because the values of all features are not weighed nor are all the alternatives systematically compared.

Oftentimes, we lack complete or accurate information about one or more alternatives. In such a case, we must rely on guesses that may or may not be correct. We may then end up judging a new situation in terms of its resemblance to a more familiar, stereotypical model—this is called the **representativeness** heuristic. Another common decision-making heuristic is **availability**, in which a judgment or decision is based on information that is most easily retrieved from memory, whether or not that information is accurate. Finally, we often rely on intuition or "gut instincts"—a mix of objective information and subjective emotions.

In the real world, the use of faulty heuristics does not always spell disaster. First of all, such decisions are rarely final; secondly, we often do not need to make an absolutely perfect decision as long as the results are satisfactory.

### Language and Thought

Language is crucial to the expression and understanding of thought. There are several theories concerning the relationship between language and thinking. According to Benjamin Whorf, patterns of thinking are determined by the language wespeak. His theory, called the **linguistic relativity hypothesis**, states that if a language lacks a particular expression, the thought to which the expression corresponds rarely, if ever, occurs to the people who speak that language. Some critics of this theory maintain that an idea may, indeed, spring to mind before someone learns the corresponding word or phrase. Others point out that the need to think about particular things changes a language rather than the language dictating what we think about. However, most researchers agree that once new phrases for an object come into everyday use, we are then able to think about the object in those terms.

## INTELLIGENCE

**Intelligence** and mental abilities are cognitive abilities that promote learning and adaptive behavior. The only way to study the complex processes that make up mental abilities is indirectly, through a person's actions in situations requiring their use. **Intelligence tests** are designed to measure a person's general mental abilities.

Recent research indicates that experts do not yet agree on a single definition of "intelligence." Moreover, the meaning of intelligence apparently differs somewhat among experts and nonexperts. In the early 1980s, Sternberg and his associates discovered that both experts and nonexperts described an intelligent person as someone with practical problem-solving ability and verbal ability. But laypeople included social competence in their concepts of intelligence, while experts put more emphasis on practical intelligence.

## FORMAL THEORIES OF INTELLIGENCE

Intelligence theorists fall into two categories: In one group are those who argue for a "general intelligence" that characterizes a person's actions and thinking in all areas. Their critics believe that intelligence is composed of many separate types of aptitudes and abilities, and that a person who excels in one area will not necessarily excel in all areas.

In an attempt to simplify theories of intelligence, R. B. Cattell in the early 1970s divided mental abilities into two clusters. The first is crystallized intelligence, or abilities such as reasoning and the verbal and numerical skills that are stressed in school. The second is fluid intelligence, or skills such as spatial and visual imagery, the ability to notice visual details, and rote memory.

In the mid-1980s, psychologist Robert Sternberg proposed a **triarchic theory of intelligence** that encompasses a much broader range of skills and abilities. According to this theory, intelligence consists of three aspects: **componential intelligence**, the traditional mental processes or skills emphasized by earlier theories of intelligence, such as the ability to acquire new knowledge and perform tasks efficiently; **experiential intelligence**, which incorporates insight and creative adaptability as well as efficient and quick processing of information without conscious thought; and **contextual intelligence**, characterized by responsiveness to the environment. Intelligent people, according to Sternberg, are adept at making the most of their strengths and compensating for their weaknesses.

Howard Gardner has advanced the hypothesis that what we refer to as intelligence actually consists of many separate abilities, or **multiple intelligences**, each of which is relatively independent of the others.

Formal theories of intelligence serve as the foundation for the design and administration of intelligence tests. And because experts do not view intelligence in exactly the same way as nonexperts do, most tests of intelligence do not cover areas that many nonexperts perceived as part of intelligence.

## INTELLIGENCE TESTS

### The Stanford-Binet Intelligence Scale

The **Binet-Simon Scale**, the first test of intelligence, was developed in France by Alfred Binet and Theodore Simon for testing children. First issued in 1905, it consisted of 30 tests arranged in order of increasing difficulty. From the average scores of children, Binet developed the concept of mental age.

The best-known Binet adaptation is by Stanford University's L. M. Terman in 1916 and is called the **Stanford-Binet Intelligence Scale**. Terman introduced the term **intelligent quotient (IQ)**, which is a numerical value given to scores on an intelligence test (a score of 100 corresponds to average intelligence).

The Stanford-Binet scale has been revised four times since it was first issued, most recently in 1985. The 15 different subtests of the Stanford-Binet are designed to measure skills in the four areas of verbal reasoning, abstract/visual reasoning, quantitative reasoning, and short-term memory.

### The Wechsler Intelligence Scales

The **Wechsler Adult Intelligence Scale–Revised (WAIS–R)**, was developed by David Wechsler especially for adults. The test measures both verbal and performance abilities. Wechsler also created the **Wechsler Intelligence Scale for Children–Third Edition (WISC–III)**, which is meant to be used with school-aged children. It measures verbal and performance abilities separately, though it also yields an overall IQ score.

### Group Tests

Unlike the Stanford-Binet and the Wechsler tests, which are administered and scored on an individual basis, **group tests** are administered by one examiner to many people at one time. Group tests are most commonly used by schools. The California Test of Mental Maturity (CTMM) and the Scholastic Aptitude Test (SAT) are examples of group tests.

Group tests aim to overcome the problems of time and expense associated with individual tests and to eliminate bias on the part of the examiner. However, the examiner is less likely to notice if a test taker is tired, ill, or confused by the directions. In general, emotionally disturbed children and people who have less experience taking tests do better on individual tests than on group tests.

### Performance Tests and Culture-Fair Tests

Some intelligence tests may discriminate against certain cultural or ethnic groups. **Performance tests** are intelligence tests that do not involve language, so they can be useful for testing people who do not have a strong command of English. The Seguin Form Board, Porteus Maze, and Bayley Scales of Infant Development are examples of performance tests.

**Culture-fair tests** are designed to eliminate cultural bias by minimizing skills and values that vary from one culture to another. The Progressive Matrices exemplify culture-fair tests.

## WHAT MAKES A GOOD TEST?

Psychologists use reliability and validity as measures of a test's quality, and for purposes of comparing different tests.

### Reliability

**Reliability** is the ability of a test to produce consistent and stable scores. The simplest way to determine a test's reliability is to give the test to a group and then, after a short time, give it again to the same group. If the group scores the same each time, the test is reliable. The problem with this way of determining reliability is that the group may have remembered the answers from the first testing. One way to eliminate this problem is to divide the test into two parts and check the consistency of people's scores on both parts. If the scores generally agree, the test is said to have **split-half reliability**.

### Validity

**Validity** is the ability of a test to measure what it has been designed to measure. **Content validity** exists if a test contains an adequate sample of the skills or knowledge it is supposed to measure. In general, most intelligence tests measure many of the abilities considered to be components of intelligence: concentration, planning, memory, language comprehension, and writing. However, a single test may not cover all the areas that make up intelligence, and tests differ in their emphasis on the abilities they do assess.

**Criterion-related validity** refers to the relationship between test scores and independent measures of whatever the test is designed to measure. In the case of intelligence, the most common independent measure is academic achievement. Despite their differences in surface content, most intelligence tests are good predictors of academic success. Based on this criterion, these tests do seem to have adequate criterion-related validity.

### Criticisms of IQ Tests

Much of the criticism of intelligence tests has focused on their content. Critics point out that most intelligence tests are concerned with only a narrow set of skills and may, in fact, measure only the ability to take tests. Critics also maintain that the content and administration of IQ tests are shaped by the values of white middle-class society and that, as a result, they may discriminate against minorities. IQ tests come under criticism because the results are often used to label some students as slow learners. Finally, IQ tests do not shed light on an individual's motivation, emotion, attitudes, and other similar factors that may have a strong bearing on a person's success in school and in life.

Other critics hold that intelligence is far too complex to be precisely measured by tests. IQ tests are also criticized for neglecting to account for social influences on one person's performance. However, high scores on IQ tests may seldom predict occupational success, so it is likely that these tests will continue to be used.

## DETERMINANTS OF INTELLIGENCE

### Heredity

Historically, research on the determinants of intelligence has focused on identical twins, some of whom have been reared together, and others of whom have been reared apart in separate households. The correlation between the IQs of identical twins is usually very high, suggesting that their identical genetic inheritance is a more powerful determinant of intelligence than their experiences. But critics of this research point out that (1) it is difficult to find identical twins who have been separated at birth, so that there are only a few such studies; (2) identical twins tend to be placed in households similar in socioeconomic backgrounds to those of their biological parents; and (3) even twins who are separated at birth have had nearly identical prenatal experiences.

### Environment

Research strengthens the case for environment as a factor in the development of superior intellectual ability. Thus, even though certain mental abilities are inherited, without the necessary stimulation a child's intelligence will not develop fully. This is important because lower-income families don't have access to the kinds of resources that better-off families do. Significantly, when they are placed in more stimulating environments, economically deprived children show an improvement in their level of intelligence. For example, children born to lower-income parents but raised in middle-class homes reveal significant gains in IQ. Similarly, children who participate in intervention programs such as Head Start frequently exhibit improvements in cognitive abilities; however, questions have been raised about whether such programs offer any substantial long-term benefits.

### The IQ Debate: A Continuing Controversy

Psychology has been unable to clearly account for group differences in IQ. This debate burst into the public consciousness in 1969 with the publication of an article by psychologist Arthur Jensen claiming that differences in IQ scores along with racial lines are largely the result of heredity. Jensen's article raised a storm of controversy, which came raging back to the fore in 1994 with the publication of a book on this topic by Richard Herrnstein and Charles Murray. Significantly, most participants in this debate agree that both heredity and environment affect IQ scores.

## EXTREMES OF INTELLIGENCE

The IQs of nearly 70 percent of the general population fall between 85 and 115, and all but 5 percent of the population have IQs between 70 and 130. People who are mentally retarded and the gifted score at the two extremes of intelligence.

### Mental Retardation

**Mental retardation** is a condition of significantly subaverage intelligence combined with deficiencies in adaptive behavior. The condition includes very different kinds of deficiencies with a wide variety of causes, treatments, and outcomes. There are varying degrees of mental retardation: A person may fall anywhere along the spectrum from moderately to profoundly retarded. In addition to having a low IQ, to be considered mentally retarded a person must also lack skills essential for independent daily living.

In most cases, the causes of mental retardation are not known. Where causes can be identified, the majority of cases stem from variety of environmental, social, nutritional, and other risk factors. About 25 percent of mental retardation cases can be traced to biological causes, including Down syndrome.

### Giftedness

**Giftedness** refers to superior IQ combined with demonstrated or potential ability in academic aptitude, creativity, leadership, and fine arts. The recent movement to identify and assist gifted children in schools has come under criticism, as have the assumptions underlying notions of giftedness. Critics say, among other things, that gifted people may not be a distinct group superior to the general population in all areas, but rather people who excel only in some areas, and that it is erroneous to assume that career success comes automatically to the gifted.

## CREATIVITY

**Creativity**—the ability to produce novel and unique socially valued ideas or objects—is regarded by some psychologists as one aspect of intelligence. But there is some disagreement about the link between creativity and intelligence. The threshold theory of the relationship between intelligence and creativity states that although creativity requires a certain amount of intelligence, once intelligence rises above the threshold level, creativity and intelligence correlate only moderately, if at all.

# REVIEW QUESTIONS

## MULTIPLE CHOICE

1. The term that psychologists use to refer to all the processes whereby we gather and use information is ______ .

2. ______ , ______ , and ______ are the three most important building blocks of thought.

3. Categories for classifying specific people, things, or events are

   a. concepts  c. phonemes
   b. images  d. morphemes

4. True or false: Images help us think about things because images are more concrete than words.

5. True or false: People decide which objects belong to a concept by comparing the facts to a model or prototype.

6. Match each problem-solving strategy with its definition:
   ______ algorithm
   ______ heuristics
   ______ hill climbing
   ______ working backward
   a. rules of thumb that help in simplifying and solving problems, although they do not guarantee a correct solution
   b. strategy in which each step moves you progressively closer to a solution
   c. step-by-step method that guarantees a solution
   d. strategy in which you move from the goal to the starting point

7. All of the following are potential obstacles to problem solving except
   a. sets
   b. excitement
   c. functional fixedness
   d. hill climbing

8. Bill is trying to decide between taking a ski vacation in Vermont and a beach vacation in the Caribbean. To make the choice, he sets up some criteria for a good vacation and then rates the two alternatives on each criterion to see how they stack up against each other. Bill is using a ______ model of decision making.

9. Our tendency to perceive and to approach problems in certain ways is called a ______ .

10. The tendency to perceive only a limited number of uses for an object, a tendency that interferes with the process of problem solving, is known as ______ ______ .

11. Decision-making models that do not try to systematically weigh comparisons among alternatives are ______ models.

12. People are most likely to use a compensatory model when
    a. the stakes are low
    b. the stakes are high
    c. others are observing them
    d. the problem is simple

13. In language, universal sounds, called ______ , are combined to form the smallest meaningful units, which are called ______ . These meaningful units may then be combined to create words, which, in turn, are used to build phrases and whole ______ .

14. We use ______ to link concepts with other concepts and thus form more complex thoughts.

15. According to Whorf's ______ hypothesis, the language we speak determines the pattern of our thinking and our view of the world.

16. According to Chomsky, language users employ rules or ______ to allow them to go from the surface to the deep structure of language.

17. The tendency to look for confirming rather than contradictory evidence for our beliefs is called ______ .

18. Match each of the following with his concept of intelligence:
    ____ Cattell
    ____ Spearman
    ____ Sternberg
    ____ Thurstone
    ____ Gardner
    a. proposed a triarchic theory of intelligence
    b. identified seven somewhat independent mental abilities
    c. argued that intelligence is general
    d. specified two clusters of mental abilities
    e. advanced a theory of multiple intelligences

19. According to Sternberg, the three complex aspects of intelligence are the ______ aspect, which enable us

to acquire new knowledge; the ______ aspect, which includes the ability to understand new concepts; and the ______ aspect, which encompasses the ability to adapt to or reshape the environment.

20. In 1916, the Stanford psychologist L. M. Terman introduced the term ______ and established the score of ______ for a person of average intelligence. His test was based on the first intelligence test, the ______ ______, designed by Alfred Binet.

21. True or false: The IQ test that L. M. Terman constructed is called the Stanford-Binet Intelligence Scale.

22. The individual IQ test most often given to adults is the ______ ______ ______ ______.

23. Written tests of intelligence designed to be administered by a single examiner to many people at one time are called ______ ______. Which of the following is not such a test?

    a. GRE c. Wechsler Adult Intelligence Scale
    b. SAT d. SCAT

24. ______ tests eliminate or minimize the use of words. They are designed for people who cannot speak English and for preschoolers and handicapped people. Like these tests, ______ ______ tests minimize the use of language, but they also include questions that downplay the use of skills and values that vary across cultures.

25. If you take a test several times and score about the same each time you take it, your results suggest that the test is ______.

26. ______ is a test's ability to measure what it has been designed to measure.

27. IQ scores predict success in ______ pretty well.

28. The ability to produce novel and unique ideas or objects, ranging from philosophy to painting, from music to mousetraps, is called

    a. creativity c. fluid intelligence
    b. IQ d. wit

29. Two important features of creative people are:
    a. They take risks and like to work on problems they invent themselves.
    b. They are perceived as less intelligent and more irresponsible than other people.
    c. They excel at art, but are poor at science.

## CRITICAL THINKING AND APPLICATIONS

30. You must decide whether to rent an inexpensive, noisy apartment with neighbors who are a nuisance, or a quieter, more expensive apartment with nice neighbors. How would you go about making your decision using a compensatory model?

31. Think for a moment about the last time you were confronted with a difficult problem. What kinds of thinking or reasoning did you use to deal with that problem? Now that you have read this chapter, how would you respond differently if you were faced with a similar problem?

*(Answers to the Review Questions can be found in the back of the text.)*

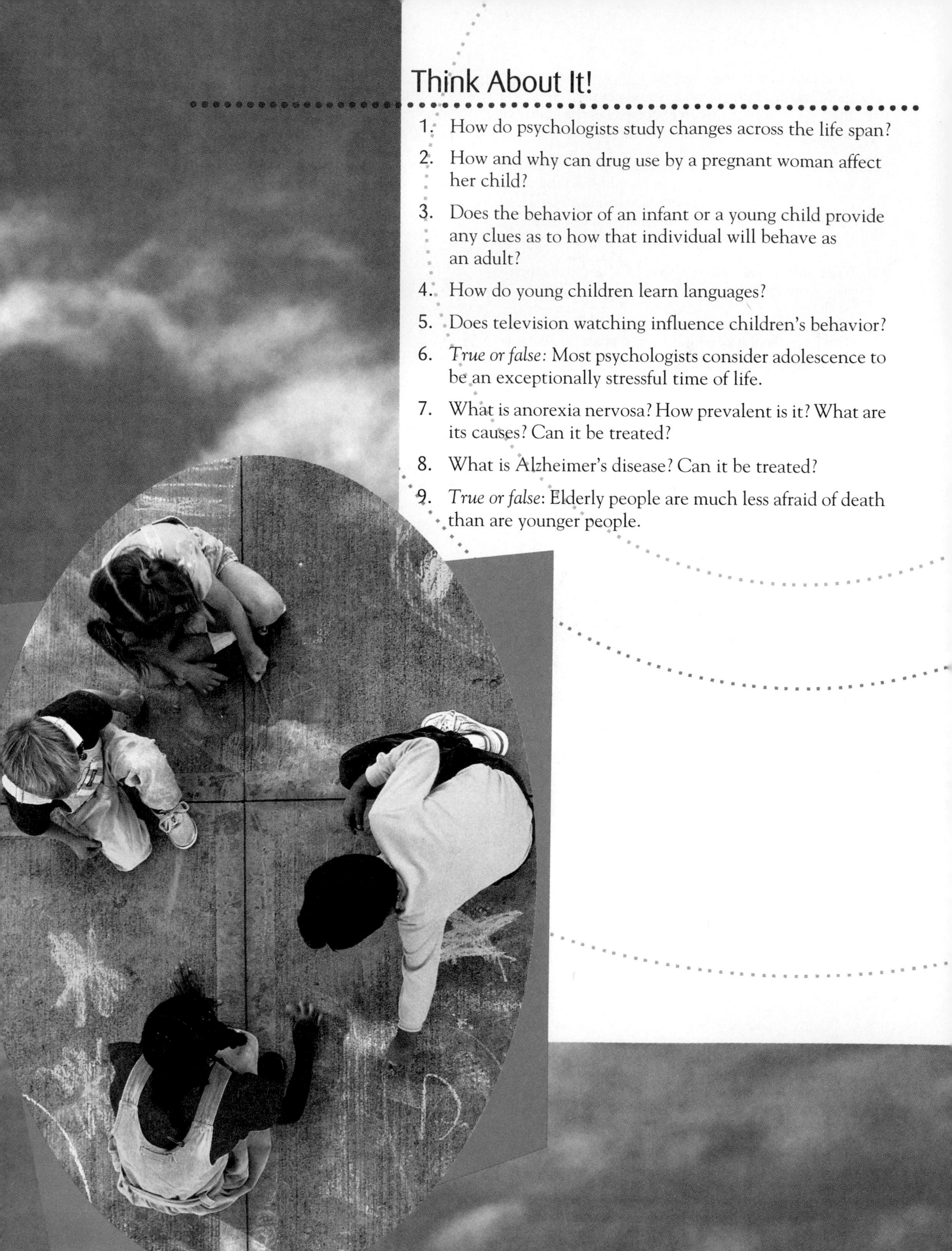

## Think About It!

1. How do psychologists study changes across the life span?
2. How and why can drug use by a pregnant woman affect her child?
3. Does the behavior of an infant or a young child provide any clues as to how that individual will behave as an adult?
4. How do young children learn languages?
5. Does television watching influence children's behavior?
6. *True or false:* Most psychologists consider adolescence to be an exceptionally stressful time of life.
7. What is anorexia nervosa? How prevalent is it? What are its causes? Can it be treated?
8. What is Alzheimer's disease? Can it be treated?
9. *True or false*: Elderly people are much less afraid of death than are younger people.

Long al Study Age Coho enta Neonate Ad nce Gender Identity

# LIFE SPAN DEVELOPMENT

8

## Overview

**Developmental psychology** Study of the changes that occur in people from birth through old age.

**Cross-sectional study** Method of studying developmental changes by examining groups of subjects who are of different ages.

**Cohort** Group of people born during the same period in historical time.

**Longitudinal study** Method of studying developmental changes by examining the same group of subjects two or more times, as they grow older.

How do psychologists study changes across the life span?

**For thousands of years, people have been fascinated by the changes that take place in an individual over the course of a lifetime. In Greek mythology, the Sphinx posed a riddle to Oedipus: "What goes on four feet in the morning, two feet in the afternoon, and three feet in the evening?" Oedipus had the answer: "Man, who crawls on all fours in infancy, walks on two legs in adulthood, and leans on a cane in old age."**

The study of how people change, from birth through old age, is called **developmental psychology**. Because virtually everything about a person alters during the life span, the field of developmental psychology includes all the other topics that psychologists study, such as cognition, language, intelligence, and social behavior. But a developmental psychologist who studies cognition, for example, is interested not just in cognition itself but also in how it changes during childhood or adulthood.

Researchers studying development use the same methods employed in other kinds of psychology: the naturalistic-observational method, the correlational method, and the experimental method (see Chapter 1). However, because developmental psychologists are interested in processes that change over time, they utilize these methods in three special types of studies: *cross-sectional*, *longitudinal*, and *biographical*.

In a **cross-sectional study**, researchers examine developmental change by observing or testing people of different ages at the same point in time. For example, they might study the development of logical thought by testing a group of 6-year-olds, a group of 9-year-olds, and a group of 12-year-olds, and then look for differences among the age groups. Or, if they are interested in cognitive changes during adulthood, they might study 40-year-olds, 60-year-olds, and 80-year-olds. The problem with cross-sectional studies is that they do not distinguish age differences from *cohort differences*. A **cohort** is a group of people born during the same period of historical time—all Americans born in 1940, for example, form a cohort. Cohort differences are differences between individuals who were born and grew up at different times. If we found that 40-year-olds were able to solve harder math problems than 80-year-olds, we wouldn't know whether this result was due to the difference in their ages or to the fact that the 80-year-olds grew up in an era when educational opportunities were more limited and there were no calculators or computers.

**Longitudinal studies** examine developmental changes by testing the same people two or more times, as they grow older. Thus, researchers who are interested in the development of logical thought might begin their study testing a group of 6-year-olds, wait 3 years and test the same children again at age 9, then wait another 3 years to test them again at age 12. The problem with longitudinal studies is that they do not distinguish age differences from differences that arise from improved assessment or measurement tools. For example, the researchers retesting the cohort referred to above at age 9 might have access to a more sensitive measure of logical thought than they did when they tested that cohort at age 6. Thus, if they found significant improvement in logical thought over this 3-year period, they wouldn't know to what extent it reflected the advance in age and to what extent it reflected the more sensitive measuring tool.

Obviously, carrying out a longitudinal study takes considerable time even if the researchers are interested only in development during childhood. If they are studying changes that take place over the course of adulthood, a longitudinal study could require 50 years or more. To avoid the huge expense of such a long study, researchers have devised a third way of studying adulthood: the **biographical** or **retrospective study**. Whereas a longitudinal study might start with some 20-year-olds and follow them as they grew older, a biographical approach might start with some 70-year-olds and pursue their lives *backward*. That is, the researchers would try to reconstruct their subjects' past by interviewing them and by consulting various other sources, much as a biographer does when writing someone's life. Biographical data are less trustworthy than either longitudinal or cross-sectional data, however, because people's recollections of the past are not always accurate.

**Biographical** or **retrospective study** Method of studying developmental changes by reconstructing subjects' past through interviews and investigating the effects of past events on current behaviors.

Each of these three kinds of studies has both advantages and disadvantages, which are summarized in Table 8-1. But each is highly useful in its way, and together they have provided us with a wealth of information about human development. You will come across examples of all three methods in this chapter.

Besides using different methods to study human development, psychologists approach their research from various points of view. Some emphasize the importance of heredity; others stress experience or environmental influences; still others concentrate on the interaction between heredity and the environment. Some see developmental change as abrupt and discontinuous; others view it as a gradual, steady process. In this chapter, we will consider these differing viewpoints as we discuss various aspects of human development across the life span. And because development begins not at birth but at conception, we will start at the point when a woman's egg combines with a man's sperm to form a fertilized egg.

**TABLE 8-1 Advantages and Disadvantages of Different Types of Developmental Research Methods**

| METHOD | ADVANTAGES | DISADVANTAGES |
|---|---|---|
| CROSS-SECTIONAL | • Inexpensive<br>• Takes relatively little time to complete<br>• Avoids high attrition rate (dropout of subjects from study) | • Different age groups are not necessarily very much alike<br>• Subjects of the same chronological age might not be of the same maturational age<br>• *Cohort* differences and *age* differences are confounded |
| LONGITUDINAL | • Generates detailed information about individuals<br>• Allows for the study of developmental change in great detail | • Expensive<br>• Potential for high attrition rate—subjects drop out over such a long period of time |
| BIOGRAPHICAL OR RETROSPECTIVE | • Generates rich detail about one individual's life<br>• Allows for in-depth study of one individual | • Individual's recall often cannot be trusted<br>• Can be very time-consuming and expensive |

**Prenatal development** Development from conception to birth.

**Embryo** Developing human between 2 weeks and 3 months after conception.

**Fetus** Developing human between 3 months after conception and birth

**Placenta** Organ by which an embryo or fetus is attached to its mother's uterus and that nourishes it during prenatal development.

**Critical period** Time when certain internal and external influences have a major effect on development; at other periods, the same influences will have little or no effect.

**Neonate** Newborn baby.

How and why can drug use by a pregnant woman affect her child?

This human fetus can be affected by anything its mother eats, drinks, or inhales.

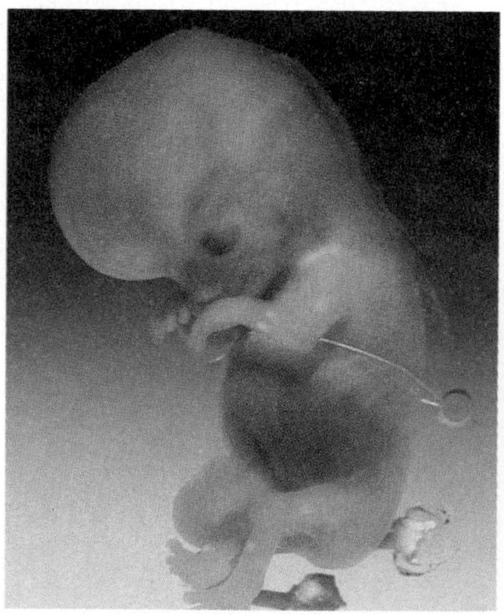

## PRENATAL DEVELOPMENT

During the earliest period of **prenatal development**—the stage of development from conception to birth—the fertilized egg divides, embarking on the process that will transform it, in just 9 months, from a one-celled organism into a complex human being. The dividing cells form a hollow ball, which implants itself in the wall of the uterus. Two weeks after conception, the cells begin to specialize: Some will form the baby's internal organs, others will form muscles and bones, and still other cells will form the skin and the nervous system. No longer an undifferentiated mass of cells, the developing organism is now called an **embryo**.

The embryo stage ends 3 months after conception, when the stage of the **fetus** begins. At this point, although it is only 1 inch long, the fetus roughly resembles a human being, with arms and legs, a large head, and a heart that has begun to beat. Although it can already move various parts of its body, another month is likely to pass before the mother will become aware of its movements.

The embryo and the fetus are nourished by an organ called the **placenta**. Within the placenta, the mother's blood vessels transmit substances to the embryo and carry waste products away from it. Although the mother's blood never actually mingles with that of her unborn child, almost anything she eats, drinks, or inhales is capable of being transmitted through the placenta. If she develops an infection such as syphilis, rubella ("German measles"), or AIDS, the microorganisms that cause these diseases can cross the placenta and infect the fetus, often with disastrous effects. If she smokes cigarettes, drinks alcohol, or uses other drugs during pregnancy, her baby may be born too early or, in extreme cases, it may die (Harris & Liebert, 1991).

Alcohol is the drug most often abused by pregnant women. In the last few decades, scientists have recognized the devastating effects alcohol can have on the developing child (Steinhausen, Willms, & Spohr, 1993). Pregnant women who consume alcohol—particularly in large doses—risk giving birth to a child with *fetal alcohol syndrome (FAS)*, a condition characterized by facial deformities, heart defects, stunted growth, and cognitive impairments. The effects of other drugs on the developing fetus are less clear. For example, although several studies have shown that smoking crack cocaine by pregnant women increases the risk for birth defects and sudden infant death syndrome (SIDS) in their babies (E.R. Brown & Zuckerman, 1991), other studies (Chasnoff, Griffith, Frier, & Murray, 1992) have not found these results.

In any event, there seems to be a **critical period** during which the introduction of many potentially harmful substances is most likely to have a major effect on the fetus. At other times, the same substance may have no effect at all. For example, if a woman contracts rubella during the first 3 months of pregnancy, the effects can range from the spontaneous aborting of the fetus to congenital deafness in the child. However, if the woman contracts rubella during the final 3 months of her pregnancy, severe damage to the fetus is unlikely.

Pregnancy is most likely to have a favorable outcome when the mother takes good care of herself during those crucial 9 months. That means getting good nutrition, good medical care, and adequate rest and exercise, and avoiding alcohol, tobacco, and all other unnecessary drugs.

## THE NEWBORN BABY

Research has disproved the old idea that **neonates**, or newborn babies, do nothing but eat, sleep, and cry, while remaining oblivious to the world around them. It is true that they sleep much of the time—up to 16 or 20 hours a day, though this varies considerably from one baby to the next. It is also true that they are totally dependent on the care of the adults around them.

But babies are not as incompetent as they look. For one thing, they come equipped with a number of useful reflexes. Many of these reflexes, such as those that control breathing, are essential to life outside the uterus. Other reflexes enable the baby to nurse. The **rooting reflex** causes the baby to turn its head toward the touch of a nipple on its cheek and grope around with its mouth. The **sucking reflex** causes the baby to suck on anything that enters its mouth, and the **swallowing reflex** enables it to swallow milk and other liquids without choking. These feeding movements are performed awkwardly at first, but within a few days of birth, babies have acquired the knack of sucking and swallowing efficiently and rhythmically.

Other reflexes have purposes that are less obvious. The **grasping reflex** causes newborns to cling vigorously to an adult's finger or to any object placed in their hands. The **stepping reflex** causes very young babies to take what looks like walking steps if they are held upright with their feet just touching a flat surface. These reflexes normally disappear after 2 or 3 months, reemerging later as voluntary grasping (at around 5 months of age) and real walking (at the end of the first year).

Very young babies are also capable of a surprisingly complex kind of behavior: imitating the facial expressions of adults. If an adult opens his mouth or sticks out his tongue, newborn babies often respond by opening their mouths or sticking out their tongues too(McCall, 1979; A.N. Meltzoff & Moore, 1985). When this ability to imitate was first noted in newborn babies, psychologists could hardly believe it. How could babies carry out such complex responses at an age when they can have no idea of how their own face looks, much less how to contract various muscles to make specific facial expressions! It now appears that this early imitation response is only a primitive reflex, like the grasping and stepping reflexes. It disappears after a few weeks, and then reemerges in more complex form many months later (Bjorklund, 1989; Wyrwicka, 1988).

Almost all newborns respond to the human face, the human voice, and the human touch. After all, babies are totally dependent on the people who take care of them, so it is essential that their social relationships get off to a good start. From the very beginning, they have a means of communication that serves to get their needs across to the people they live with: They can cry. Also, shortly after birth, they can follow an adult with their eyes. And very soon—in only about 6 weeks—they have an even better method of communication, one that serves as a thank-you to the people who are working so hard to keep them happy: They can smile.

**Rooting Reflex** Reflex that causes a newborn baby to turn its head toward something touching its cheek and to grope around with its mouth.

**Sucking reflex** Reflex that causes the newborn baby to suck on objects placed in its mouth.

**Swallowing reflex** Reflex that enables the newborn baby to swallow liquids without choking.

**Grasping reflex** Reflex that causes newborn babies to close their fists around anything that is put in their hands.

**Stepping reflex** Reflex that causes newborn babies to make little stepping motions if they are held upright with their feet just touching a surface.

**Temperament** Term used by psychologists to describe the physical/emotional characteristics of the newborn child and young infant; also referred to as *personality.*

## Temperament

It is tempting to talk about babies as if they are all the same, but babies display individual differences in **temperament** (Goldsmith & Harman, 1994; Piontelli, 1989). Some cry much more than others do; some are much more active than their peers. Some babies love to be cuddled, whereas others seem to dislike being held and will wriggle out of their parents' arms.

In a classic study of infant temperament, Alexander Thomas and Stella Chess (1977) identified three different types of babies: "easy," "difficult," and "slow-to-warm-up." They described "easy" babies as good-natured and adaptable. These babies are likely to turn into good-natured, adaptable children who enjoy new experiences and get along well in school. "Difficult" babies, on the other hand, were described as moody and intense, reacting to new people and new situations both negatively and strongly. These babies adapt poorly to change and stress. Thomas and Chess described "slow-to-warm-up"

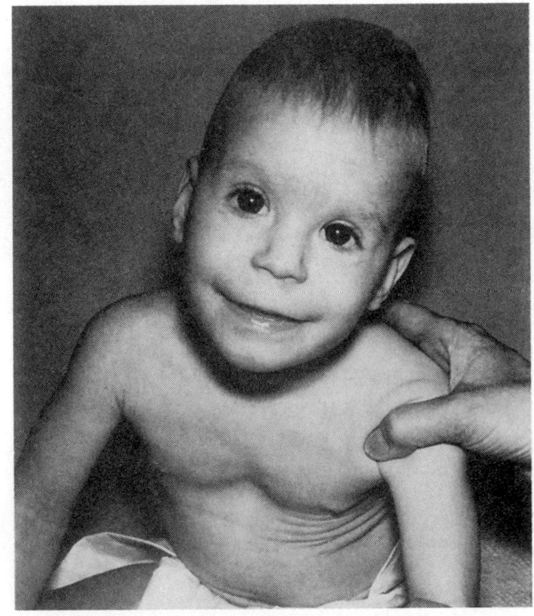

Children born with *fetal alcohol syndrome* often exhibit facial deformities, heart defects, stunted growth, and cognitive impairments.

babies as relatively inactive and slow to react. When they do react, their reactions are mild. Recently, Jerome Kagan and his associates (Kagan et al., 1988; Kagan & Snidman, 1991) identified another temperament type: the "shy child." According to Kagan, shy children are timid and inhibited, fearful of anything new or strange. Their nervous systems react to stimuli in a characteristically hypersensitive way.

These basic temperament types may turn out to be universal, although the surface characteristics of each type may differ significantly from one culture to another. For example, mothers of Italian children described "difficult" children as demanding and inflexible rather than "moody and intense" (Attili, Vermigli, & Travagila, 1991). Whether similar differences exist in other cultures remains to be seen.

Thomas and Chess believe that temperament is largely innate. If temperament is determined primarily by heredity, it should remain fairly stable over time. In fact, one study (Pedlow, Sanson, Prior, & Oberklaid, 1993) that looked at temperament from infancy through 8 years of age as reported by mothers found that characteristics such as degree of irritability, flexibility, and persistence were quite stable. Moreover, other research has shown that the fussy or difficult infant is likely to turn into a "problem child" who has difficulties in school and displays aggressive behavior (Guérin, 1994; G.R. Patterson & Bank, 1989; Persson-Blennow & McNeil, 1988). And a longitudinal study of shy children and some of their less inhibited peers showed that most of the shy infants continued to be relatively shy and inhibited at age 8, just as most of the uninhibited infants remained relatively outgoing and bold at that age (Kagan & Snidman, 1991).

**3.** Does the behavior of an infant or a young child provide any clues as to how that individual will behave as an adult?

What kind of person a child becomes, however, also depends on home environment and parental behavior. For example, most parents can rear an "easy" baby, but rearing a "difficult" baby is much more demanding. Because difficult babies are so hard to care for, their parents are likely to find themselves tired, frustrated, and often angry. Moreover, cultural practices may also affect temperament (Shwalb, Shwalb, & Shoji, 1994). For example, children in traditional Japanese homes are taught early to revere their grandparents and to be reserved in matters of emotion.

Since environment, experience, and culture all play a role in determining temperament, an individual's temperament can change over time. For example, not all difficult infants become problem children, and not all children who are easy as infants sail through childhood without difficulty. In one study, about 25 percent of the shy children had become considerably braver, and a similar proportion of the uninhibited children had become hesitant and quiet (Kagan, Snidman, & Arcus, 1992). The researchers attributed these changes to environmental influences. For instance, some parents of shy children tried very hard to get their children to be more outgoing. As for the uninhibited children who became inhibited, some may have been pressured to behave in a quieter, more reserved fashion, and others may have been affected by problems in the home. These results, and similar results from other studies, illustrate that even if all children are born with a particular temperament, they need not have that temperament for life. Each child's personality interacts with the environment in a particular way, and how the child turns out is the result of that interaction.

## The Perceptual Abilities of Infants

We now know that newborn babies can see, hear, and understand far more than previous generations gave them credit for. Their senses work fairly well at birth and rapidly improve to near-adult levels. Neonates begin to absorb and process information from the outside world as soon as they enter it—or, in some cases, even before they enter it.

**VISION** Unlike puppies and kittens, babies are born with their eyes open and functioning. However, the world looks a bit fuzzy to them at first, and they focus their eyes on distant objects or very close ones (such as their own hand approaching their face). Newborns see most clearly when faces or objects are 8 to 10 inches away from them. Their visual acuity (the clarity of their vision) improves rapidly, and so does their ability to focus. By 6 or 8 months of age, babies can see almost as well as the average college student, though their visual system takes another 3 or 4 years to develop fully (Maurer & Maurer, 1988).

For a long time, psychologists assumed that newborns were colorblind because they show so little interest in color. But newer techniques have demonstrated that babies can see some colors even in the first week of life, and that color vision, like other aspects of the visual system, develops very rapidly. At birth, babies can distinguish yellow, orange, red, and green from gray. By the time they are 4 months old, they can see all the colors an adult can see (Maurer & Maurer, 1988).

Researchers have found that very young babies already have definite preferences in regard to visual stimuli. They would rather look at a new picture or pattern than one they have seen many times before. If given a choice between two pictures or patterns, both of which are new to them, they generally prefer the one with the clearest contrasts. Thus, most newborn babies prefer to look at a black-and-white pattern than at a colored one. The pattern cannot be too complex, however: A large black-and-white checkerboard pattern is preferred to one with smaller squares because the smaller squares tend to blur in the baby's vision. As babies get older and their vision improves, they prefer more and more complex patterns, perhaps reflecting their need for an increasingly complex environment (Acredolo & Hake, 1982; Fantz, Fagan, & Miranda, 1975).

Babies also prefer patterns with curved lines to patterns with straight lines. Perhaps this is another indication of their interest in the human face (which is composed of curves). At any rate, by the time they are 2 or 3 months old, babies can recognize a line drawing of a human face (Dannemiller & Stephens, 1988). Newborns also prefer to look at their own mother rather than at a stranger (Walton, Bower, & Bower, 1992).

Several psychologists have tried to explain how very young babies manage to recognize their mother's face so quickly. Walton and Bower (1993) suggest that infants form a *prototypical scheme*, or collection of mental images that represent "Mom." Since infants are likely to see their mother more often than anyone else following birth, they acquire sets of different images of the mother (from various angles and so on) so that she becomes the most familiar and most preferred person in their environment.

**DEPTH PERCEPTION** Depth perception is the ability to see the world in three dimensions—with some objects nearer, others farther away. Although researchers have been unable to find evidence of depth perception in babies younger than 4 months (Aslin & Smith, 1988), the ability to see the world in three dimensions is well developed by the time the baby learns to crawl at between 6 and 12 months of age. This was demonstrated in a classic experiment using a device called a *visual cliff* (Walk & Gibson, 1961). Researchers divided a table into three parts. The center was a solid runway, raised above the rest of the table by about an inch. On one side of this runway was a solid surface decorated in a checkerboard pattern and covered with a sheet of clear glass. The other side was also covered with a thick sheet of clear glass, but on this side—the visual cliff—the checkerboard surface was not directly under the glass, but 40 inches below it. An infant of crawling age was placed on the center runway, and its mother stood on one side or the other, encouraging the infant to crawl toward her across the glass.

When placed on the *visual cliff*, babies of crawling age will not cross the deep side, even to get to their mothers. This is evidence that babies of crawling age (about 6 to 14 months) can perceive depth.

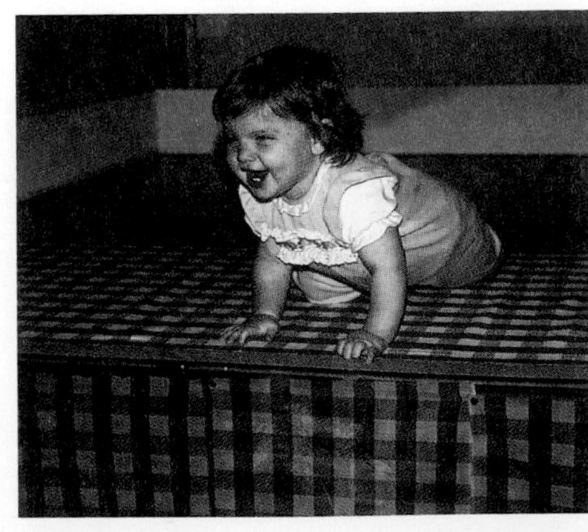

All of the 6- to 14-month-old infants tested by Walk and Gibson refused to crawl across the visual cliff when their mothers stood on the deep side of the table. Some cried; others peered down at the surface below the glass or patted the glass with their hands. But when their mothers stood on the shallow side of the table, the babies were willing to crawl across the glass. Obviously, then, 6-month-olds can perceive depth. But what about younger babies? Because infants younger than 6 months cannot crawl, they were placed on the shallow and then the deep side of the apparatus, and their pulse rates were measured in both positions. When the infants were moved from the shallow to the deep side of the table, their heart rates slowed down, a reaction typical of both infants and adults who stop to orient themselves in new situations (Campos, Langer, & Krowitz, 1970). Thus, although they did not know precisely how to react, babies younger than 6 months did seem to realize that something was different about the deep side of the table.

**Other Senses** Even before babies are born, their ears are in working order. Babies can hear sounds in the uterus and will startle at a sudden, loud noise in the mother's environment. More surprising is the evidence that fetuses are capable of learning about the sounds they hear. Researchers asked women in the last 6 weeks of pregnancy to read aloud, twice a day, from the children's book *The Cat in the Hat*. After the babies were born, the researchers tested them to see whether they recognized the story in that book. By sucking on a pacifier at a certain rate, the babies could signal their desire to hear a recording of someone reading from a children's book. The babies modified their rate of sucking to hear a recording of *The Cat in the Hat*, but not to hear a recording of another children's book (DeCasper & Spence, 1986). Thus, the babies seemed both to recognize and to prefer the familiar book that was read to them before they were born.

Newborns not only can hear but can also tell from which direction a sound is coming; they will turn their heads toward a sound source (Muir, 1985). By 4 months, they can even locate the source of a sound in the dark (where there are no visual cues) (Hillier, Hewitt, & Morrongiello, 1992). Moreover, babies are more likely to turn their heads toward their mother's voice than toward their father's, perhaps because they are better at localizing high-pitched sounds than low-pitched ones, or perhaps because they recognize their mother's voice from having heard it before they were born (DeCasper & Fifer, 1980).

Infants are particularly tuned in to the sounds of human speech. One-month-olds can distinguish among similar sounds such as "pa-pa-pa" and "ba-ba-ba" (Eimas & Tartter, 1979). In some ways, infants are even better at distinguishing sounds than older children and adults are. As children grow older, they lose their ability to hear the difference between two speech sounds that are not distinguished in their native language. For example, Japanese infants have no trouble hearing the difference between "ra" and "la," sounds that are not distinguished in the Japanese language. By the time they are 1-year-old, however, Japanese infants can no longer tell these two sounds apart (Werker, 1989).

With regard to taste and smell, newborns have clear-cut likes and dislikes. They like sweet flavors, a preference that persists through childhood. A baby only a few hours old will show pleasure at the taste of sweetened water but will screw up its face in disgust at the taste of lemon juice (J.E. Steiner, 1979). Babies also seem to prefer many of the smells that adults find pleasant, although some things that smell good to most adults (shrimp, for example) provoke expressions of disgust in babies.

As infants grow older, their perceptions of the world become keener and more meaningful. Two factors are important in this development. The first is the physical maturation of the sense organs and the nervous system.

The second is gaining experience in the world: Babies learn about the people and objects in their environment and experience a variety of sights, sounds, textures, smells, and tastes. As a result, their perceptions are increasingly enriched by a growing fund of memories and understanding.

**Maturation** Automatic biological unfolding of development in an organism as a function of the passage of time.

**Developmental norms** Ages by which an average child achieves various developmental milestones.

## INFANCY AND CHILDHOOD

During the first dozen or so years of life, a helpless baby becomes a competent member of society. Many important kinds of development occur during these early years. Scientists use the term **maturation** to refer to the biological process that results in an orderly sequence of changes, such as the progression from crawling to toddling to walking. Maturation accounts for many of the changes in physical and motor development that we will consider in this section—changes in which environmental influences (such as the opportunity to practice) play little or no role. As you will see later in the section, however, numerous other developmental changes are the products of the interaction between maturation and experience. We will begin our examination of infancy and childhood by looking at physical growth.

### Physical Development

In the first year of life, the average baby grows 10 inches in height and gains 15 pounds in weight. By 4 months of age, its birth weight has doubled, and by its first birthday, its birth weight has tripled. During the second year, physical growth slows considerably. Rapid increases in height and weight will not occur again until early adolescence.

Recent research tells us that an infant's growth does not occur in the smooth, continuous fashion depicted by growth charts hanging on the pediatrician's wall. Rather, growth takes place in fits and starts (Lampl, Veidhuis, & Johnson, 1992). In this research, infants were measured daily, weekly, and monthly up to 21 months of age. Most children showed no growth 90 percent of the time, but when they did grow, their growth was rapid—sometimes startlingly so. Incredible though it may sound, some children gained as much as 1 inch in height overnight!

Changes in the baby's size are accompanied by marked changes in body proportions (see Figure 8-1). During the first 2 years after birth, babies and toddlers have heads that are large relative to their bodies. This rapid growth of the head reflects the rapid development of the central nervous system: An infant's brain reaches three-quarters of its adult size by about the age of 2, at which point head growth slows down and the body does most of the growing. Head growth is virtually complete by age 10, but the body continues to grow for several more years.

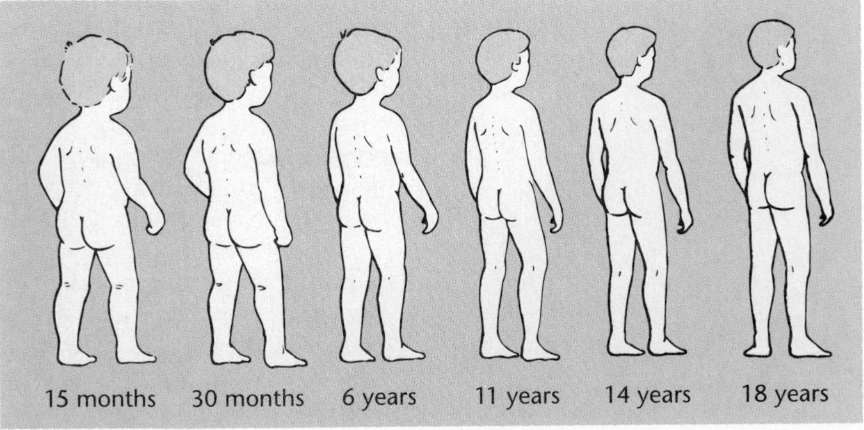


**Figure 8-1**
**Body proportions at various ages.** Young children are top heavy: They have large heads and small bodies. As they get older, the body and legs become longer, and the head is proportionately smaller.

*Source:* Adapted from Bayley, 1956. Reprinted with the permission of the Society for Research in Child Development, Inc.

### Motor Development

Motor development refers to the acquisition of abilities such as grasping, walking, skipping, and balancing. Since motor development follows a fairly predictable timetable during infancy, physicians and psychologists have been able to establish **developmental norms**, indicating the ages by which an *average* child achieves various developmental milestones. By about 9 months, for example, the average infant can stand up

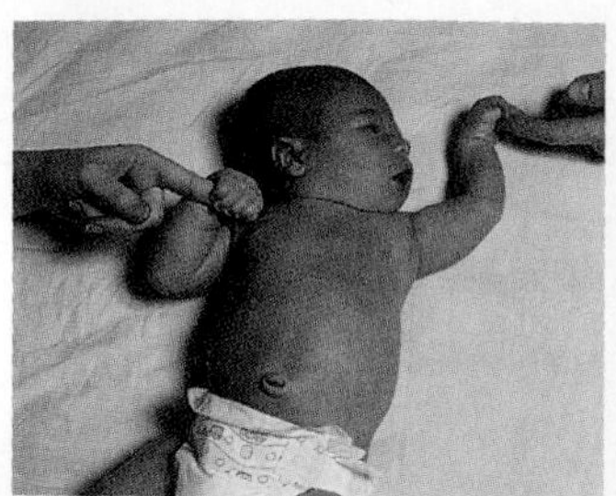

The normal sequence of *motor development.* At about 2 months, babies can lift their head and shoulders. They can sit up by themselves at about 6 1/2 months, and can stand up (holding onto something) at about 9 months. Crawling begins, on average, at 10 months, and walking at 1 year.

while holding onto something. Crawling occurs, on average, at 10 months, and walking at about 1 year. However, some normal infants develop much faster than average, while others develop more slowly. A baby who is 3 or 4 months behind schedule may be perfectly normal, and one who is 3 or 4 months ahead is not necessarily destined to become a star athlete.

Much early motor development consists of substituting voluntary actions for reflexes. As we noted earlier, the grasping reflex and stepping reflex of the newborn infant give way to voluntary grasping and walking in the older infant. Moreover, motor development proceeds in a *proximodistal* fashion—that is, from nearest the center of the body (proximal) to farthest from the center of the body (distal). For example, the infant initially has much greater control over gross arm movements than over movements of the fingers. Babies start batting at nearby objects as early as 1 month, but they cannot reach accurately until they are about 4 months old. It takes them another month or two before they are consistently successful in grasping objects they reach for (von Hofsten & Fazel-Zandy, 1984). At first, they grasp with the whole hand, but by the end of the first year, they can pick up a tiny object with the thumb and forefinger.

Most evidence suggests that practice or training has relatively little effect on early motor development. In a classic study of a pair of identical twin girls, researchers gave one twin practice in climbing stairs. At the age of 1 year, the trained twin could climb stairs noticeably faster than her untrained sister. But in only 2 weeks, the untrained twin had caught up (Gesell & Thompson, 1929). Another study looked at the development of walking in Hopi Indian children whose parents had reared them in the traditional way by keeping them strapped to a stiff cradle board for most of their first year of life. These babies had been prevented from crawling or standing up until they were freed from the cradle board, yet they learned to walk at about the same age as other Hopi infants whose parents had not adhered to the cradle-board custom (Dennis & Dennis, 1940).

As children's coordination improves, they learn to run, skip, climb, and balance themselves. At 3 and 4, they begin to use their hands for increasingly complex tasks, first learning how to put on mittens and shoes, then grappling with buttons, zippers, and shoelaces. Gradually, through a combination of practice and the physical maturation of the body and the brain, they acquire increasingly complex motor skills, such as bike riding, roller blading, and swimming.

**Sensory-motor stage** In Piaget's theory, the stage of cognitive development between birth and 2 years of age, in which the individual develops object permanence and acquires the ability to form mental representations.

**Object permanence** The concept that things continue to exist even when they are out of sight.

## Cognitive Development

Under this heading, we look at changes in the way children think about the world. The most influential view of children's cognitive development is that of the Swiss psychologist Jean Piaget. We will examine his theory in some detail.

Jean Piaget (1896–1980) was trained as a biologist, and the biological perspective was an important influence on his cognitive theory. He became interested in cognitive development while watching his own three children at play. Later, he observed and studied other children, playing games with them, asking them questions, and devising tests to learn how they were thinking. Gradually, Piaget discerned a series of stages that he thought all children pass through.

Piaget believed cognitive development is a way of adapting to the environment. Unlike animals, children do not have many built-in responses. This gives them more flexibility in adapting to their environment. As they get older, their approach to environmental problems changes.

**SENSORY-MOTOR STAGE (BIRTH TO 2 YEARS)** According to Piaget, babies spend the first 2 years of life in the **sensory-motor stage** of development. They start out by simply applying the skills they are born with—primarily sucking and grasping—to a broad range of activities. Small babies delight in taking things into their mouths—their mother's breast, their own thumb, or anything else within reach. Gradually, they divide the world into what they can suck on and what they cannot. Similarly, young babies will grasp a rattle reflexively. When they eventually realize that the noise comes from the rattle, they begin to shake everything they can get hold of in an effort to reproduce the sound. Eventually, they distinguish between things that make noise and things that do not. In this way, infants begin to organize their experiences, fitting them into rudimentary categories such as "suckable" and "not suckable," "noise making" and "not noise-making."

Jean Piaget

Another important outcome of the sensory-motor stage is the development of **object permanence**, which is the awareness that objects in the real world continue to exist even when they are out of sight. For a newborn child, objects that disappear simply cease to exist—"out of sight, out of mind." But as children gain experience with the world, they develop a sense of object permanence. Piaget believed that this change takes place in six steps:

1. *Birth to 1 month*: No signs of object permanence.
2. *1 to 4 months*: Although babies show no interest or surprise if an object vanishes, they do seem to expect that if they look away from something, it will still be there when they look back a few seconds later.

**Mental representation** Mental image or symbol (such as a word) used to think about or remember an object, a person, or an event.

**Preoperational stage** In Piaget's theory, the stage of cognitive development between 2 and 7 years of age, in which the individual becomes able to use mental representations and language to describe, remember, and reason about the world, though only in an egocentric fashion.

**Egocentric** Unable to see things from another's point of view.

3. *4 to 8 months*: At this point, if an infant drops a toy, he or she may look for it on the floor. The child is beginning to understand that even if something is no longer visible, it may still exist.
4. *8 to 12 months*: The first signs of object permanence appear. If you cover up an object with a cloth, the infant will lift the cloth to search for it. However, if you do this a few times and then let the child see you hide the object in a new place, the infant may nonetheless still search for it in the old location under the cloth. Thus, the permanence of the object, or the child's mental representation of it, is not yet established.
5. *12 to 18 months*: Now infants search for a hidden toy wherever they see you hide it, but at this point they understand only the motions of real objects they can see and touch. An infant of this age cannot think that a make-believe ball might also roll out of sight under the sofa and then imagine it coming out on the other side.
6. *18 to 24 months*: Finally, the child becomes capable of forming a **mental representation** of an object and can follow its movement in his or her imagination. Object permanence is now complete.

By the end of the sensory-motor stage, the child has also developed a sense of self-recognition—that is, is able to recognize the child in the mirror as "myself." In one famous study, researchers asked mothers to put a dab of red paint on their child's nose while pretending to wipe the child's face. Then each child was placed in front of a mirror. Babies under 1 year of age stared in fascination at the red-nosed baby in the mirror; some of them even reached out to touch the reflection of their red nose. But babies between 21 and 24 months of age reached up and touched their *own* reddened noses, showing that they knew the red-nosed baby in the mirror was "me" (Brooks-Gunn & Lewis, 1984).

**Preoperational Stage (2 to 7 Years)** When children leave the sensory-motor stage and enter the **preoperational stage** of cognitive development, their thought is still tightly bound to their physical and perceptual experiences. But their increasing ability to use mental representations lays the groundwork for the development of language—using words as symbols to represent events in the world and to describe, remember, and reason about experiences. In a later portion of this chapter, we will look closely at exactly how language develops.

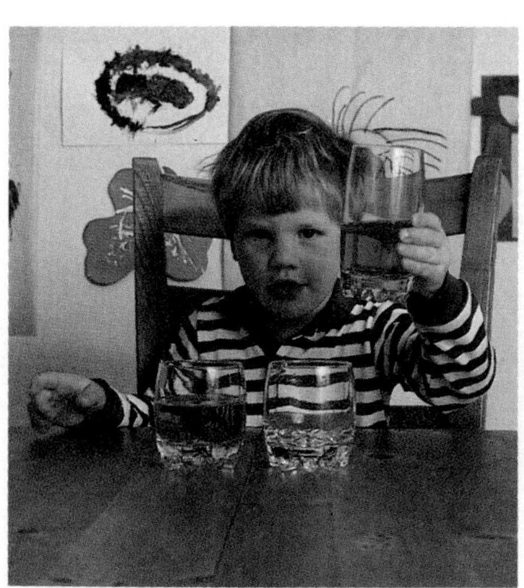

**Figure 8-2**
In this famous experiment by Piaget, the child has to judge which holds more juice: the tall, thin one or the short, wide one. Children in the preoperational stage (like this little boy) say that the tall, thin glass holds more, because they focus their attention on only one thing: the height of the juice in the glass.

According to Piaget, preoperational thinking differs not only from sensory-motor thought but also from the thinking of older children and adults. For example, small children are **egocentric**. They have great difficulty seeing things from another person's point of view or putting themselves in someone else's place. They also find it hard to distinguish between things as they appear to be and things as they really are (Flavell, 1986). They are easily misled by appearances and tend to concentrate on the most outstanding aspect of a display or event, ignoring everything else. In a famous experiment, Piaget showed preoperational children two identical glasses, filled to the same level with juice (Figure 8-2). The children were asked which glass held more juice, and they replied (correctly) that both had the same amount. Then Piaget poured the juice from one glass into a tall, narrow container. Again the children were asked which glass held more juice. This time the children looked at the two containers, saw that the level of the juice in the tall, narrow container was much higher than in the short, wide one, and replied that the narrow container had more! An older child would have realized that no juice had been added to the narrow container or taken away from the wider container. But the preoperational child focuses on only one thing at a time: the way the two containers look *now.* According to Piaget, children at this stage cannot consider the past (Piaget simply poured all the juice from one container into another) or the future (if he poured it back again, the levels of juice would be identical). Nor can they consider a container's height and width at the same time. Thus, they can't understand how an increase in one dimension (height) might be offset by a decrease in another dimension (width).

**Concrete-operational stage** In Piaget's theory, the stage of cognitive development between 7 and 11 years of age, in which the individual can attend to more than one thing at a time and can understand someone else's point of view, though thinking is limited to concrete matters.

**Formal-operational stage** In Piaget's theory, the stage of cognitive development between 11 and 15 years of age, in which the individual becomes capable of abstract thought.

**CONCRETE OPERATIONS (7 TO 11 YEARS)** During the **concrete-operational stage**, children become more flexible in their thinking. They learn to consider more than one dimension of a problem at a time and to look at a situation from someone else's point of view. Yet they are still very much stuck in the "here and now," often being unable to solve problems without concrete reference points.

An experiment Piaget conducted with his associate, Bärbel Inhelder, illustrates the difference between the cognitive abilities of a preoperational child and those of a concrete-operational child. A child was seated at a table on which there was a display consisting of three papier-mâché mountains that differed in size and color. Placed in another chair, on the other side of the table, was a doll. The child was asked to judge what the three mountains would look like from the *doll's* point of view by choosing from among pictures of the mountains the one that showed the perspective from the other side of the table. Children in the preoperational stage selected the picture that showed their *own* perspective of the three mountains. This is a good example of egocentric thought; the children could only envision the mountains from their own point of view. Children in the concrete-operational stage, on the other hand, chose the correct picture, the one that showed what the mountains would look like from the doll's side of the table (Piaget & Inhelder, 1956).

**FORMAL OPERATIONS (11 TO 15 YEARS)** Although children in the concrete-operational stage are able to use logic to solve problems, they can think only in terms of concrete things they can handle or imagine handling. In contrast, adolescents at the **formal-operational stage** of cognitive development can think in abstract terms. They can formulate hypotheses, test them mentally, and accept or reject them according to the outcome of these mental experiments. Therefore, they are capable of going beyond the here-and-now to understand things in terms of cause and effect, to consider possibilities as well as realities, and to develop and use general rules, principles, and theories.

To illustrate formal-operational thinking, Piaget and Inhelder gave children of various ages a number of different objects and asked them to separate the objects into two piles: things that would float and things that would sink. The objects included blocks made of different materials, sheets of paper, nails, pebbles, and a lid. After the children finished sorting, the researchers had them test their predictions by putting the objects into a pail of water and then asked them to explain why some things floated while others sank (Inhelder & Piaget, 1958). The younger children, who were still in the concrete-operational stage, were neither good at predicting which objects would float and which would sink nor able to explain why. The older children, who had reached the formal-operational stage, were better at predicting. And when asked for an explanation, they would make comparisons, gradually concluding that neither weight nor size alone determined if an object would float, but rather the relation between those two dimensions.

**CRITICISMS OF PIAGET'S THEORY** Piaget's work has produced a great deal of controversy. Developmental psychologists question his assumption that there are distinct stages in cognitive development and that a child must pass through one stage before entering the next. Some researchers (Brainerd, 1978; L. Siegel, 1993) argue that development does not always progress in an orderly, sequential way and that a child can reach a later developmental stage, and perform the tasks associated with it, without having gone through Piaget's earlier stages. Other researchers (Paris & Weissberg, 1986) maintain that cognitive development is a gradual process, resulting from the slow acquisition of experience and practice rather than the abrupt emergence of distinctly higher levels of ability.

Piaget's theory has also been criticized for assuming that young infants understand very little about the world. In one study (LAS, no date), for example, babies demonstrated that they could understand cause-and-effect relationships much earlier than Piaget's theory predicted.

Other critics have questioned whether preoperational children are confined to egocentric thought and are really incapable of adopting another person's point of view. Although this may be true in complex situations, in simple situations even 4-year-olds seem able to take account of the perspectives of other people. In one study, for example, 4-year-olds were asked to choose birthday presents for their mothers. Egocentric thinking would have led these children to pick gifts they themselves would like to receive, but that is not what they did. They chose presents that were appropriate for their mothers (Marvin, 1975).

Finally, although Piaget's theory gives us a schematic road map of cognitive development, the interests and experiences of a particular child—including exposure to television—may influence the development of cognitive abilities in ways not accounted for in the theory.

## Moral Development

One of the important changes that occurs during childhood and adolescence is the development of moral reasoning. Lawrence Kohlberg (1979, 1981) studied this kind of development by telling his subjects stories that illustrate complex moral issues. The "Heinz dilemma" is the best-known of these stories:

> In Europe, a woman was near death from cancer. One drug might save her, a form of radium that a druggist in the same town had recently discovered. The druggist was charging $2,000, ten times what the drug cost him to make. The sick woman's husband, Heinz, went to everyone he knew to borrow the money, but he could only get together about half of what it cost. He told the druggist that his wife was dying and asked him to sell it cheaper or let him pay later. But the druggist said, "No." The husband got desperate and broke into the man's store to steal the drug for his wife. (Kohlberg, 1969, p. 379)

The children and adolescents who heard this story were asked, "Should the husband have done that? Why?"

On the basis of his subjects' replies to these questions (particularly the second one, "Why?"), Kohlberg theorized that moral reasoning develops in stages, much like Piaget's account of cognitive development. Preadolescent children are at what Kohlberg called the *preconventional level* of moral reasoning: They tend to interpret behavior in terms of its concrete consequences. Very young children at this level base their judgments of "right" and "wrong" behavior on whether it is rewarded or punished. Somewhat older children at this level define "right" behavior as that which satisfies needs, particularly their own.

With the arrival of adolescence and the shift to formal-operational thought, the stage is set for the individual's progression to the second level of moral reasoning, the *conventional level*. At this level, the adolescent at first defines right behavior as that which pleases or helps others and is approved by them. Around midadolescence, there is a further shift toward considering various abstract social virtues, such as "doing one's duty," being a "good citizen," respecting authority, and maintaining the social order. Both forms of conventional moral reasoning require an ability to think about such abstract values as "duty" and "social order," to consider the intentions that lie behind behavior, and to put oneself in the "other person's shoes."

The third level of moral reasoning, the *postconventional level*, requires a still more abstract form of thought. This level is marked by an emphasis on principles such as justice, liberty, and equality. Personal and strongly felt moral standards become the guideposts for deciding what is right and wrong. Whether these decisions correspond to the rules and laws of a particular society at a particular time is irrelevant. For the first time, individuals may become aware of discrepancies between what they judge to be moral and what the society has determined to be legal.

Kohlberg's views have been criticized on several accounts. First, research indicates that many people in our society, adults as well as adolescents, never progress beyond the conventional level of moral reasoning (Conger & Petersen, 1991). And some societies appear to exhibit *no* postconventional moral reasoning.

Second, Kohlberg's theory does not take account of cultural differences in moral values. For example, Kohlberg puts considerations of "justice" at the highest level of moral reasoning. In Nepal, however, researchers discovered that a group of adolescent Buddhist monks placed the highest moral value on alleviating suffering and showing compassion, concepts that have no place in Kohlberg's scheme of moral development (Huebner, Garrod, & Snarey, 1990).

Third, Kohlberg's theory has been criticized as sexist. A highly influential book by Carol Gilligan (1982) points out that Kohlberg based his theory almost entirely on work with male subjects. Subsequently, Kohlberg found that boys usually scored higher than girls on his test of moral development. According to Gilligan (1992), this was because boys base their moral judgments on the abstract concept of justice, while girls base theirs on different, equally valid criteria: caring about other people and the importance of maintaining personal relationships. These different approaches lead male and female adolescents to make different decisions regarding moral issues. For example, a teenage boy might decide to report a classmate who breaks a school rule, while a teenage girl might instead offer help and advice to the rule breaker (Gilligan & Attanucci, 1988).

Other researchers (Cohn, 1991; Eisenberg, 1989) have confirmed Gilligan's findings that adolescent girls are more caring and concerned about the feelings of others than boys of the same age are. However, they attribute this difference to the fact that boys mature more slowly than girls, psychologically as well as physically. They have found that while girls start understanding and caring about the feelings of others at an earlier age, boys eventually catch up. As adults, males and females are equally able to use either caring or justice as the criterion in making moral decisions (Cohn, 1991).

Finally, it should be pointed out that there is no necessary connection between someone's moral reasoning and that person's *behavior*. However, an individual who can reason on a postconventional moral level is somewhat more likely to behave in a fashion that most people in our society consider moral (M.H. Bornstein & Lamb, 1988).

## Language Development

**Babbling** A baby's language that consists of repetition of consonant-vowel combinations.

**Holophrases** One-word sentences, commonly used by children under 2 years of age.

The development of language follows a predictable pattern. At about 2 months of age, an infant begins to coo (a nondescript word for nondescript sounds). In another month or two, the infant enters the **babbling** stage and starts to repeat sounds such as *da* or even meaningless sounds that developmental psychologists refer to as "grunts"; these sounds are the building blocks for later language development (Dill, 1994). A few months later, the infant may string together the same sound, as in *dadadada*. Finally, the infant will form combinations of different sounds, as in *dabamaga* (Ferguson & Macken, 1983).

How do young children learn languages?

Recent research by psychologists Laura Pettito and Paula Marentette (1991) has shown that even babies who are deaf and who have deaf parents engage in a form of babbling. In such families, the parents communicated with each other and with their infants through a manual sign language. Pettito and Marentette found that these deaf infants, like hearing infants, began to babble before they were 10 months old—but they babbled with their hands! Like hearing infants who utter sounds like "dadadada" over and over, the deaf babies made repetitive movements with their hands. One baby, for example, repeatedly performed a hand motion that resembled the sign-language word "okay."

Gradually, an infant's babbling takes on certain features of adult language. At about age 4 to 6 months, the infant's speech begins to show signs of *intonation*, the rising and lowering of pitch that allows adults to distinguish, for example, between questions ("You're tired?") and statements ("You're tired."). Also around this time babies learn the basic sounds of their native language, well before they utter their first words. In other words, very young children develop an understanding of the role that sounds play in words long before they comprehend the words themselves (Kuhl, Williams, & Lacerda, 1992). By around their first birthday, babies begin to use intonation to indicate commands and questions (Greenfield & Smith, 1976). At about the same age, children show signs of understanding what is said to them, and they begin not only to imitate what others say but also to use sounds to get attention. Vocalization also becomes more and more communicative and socially directed. Parents facilitate this process by speaking to their babies in what is called *motherese*. This "mother talk" is slowly spoken, and uses simple sentences, a higher-pitched voice, repetition, and exaggerated intonations—all of which engage babies' attention and help them to distinguish the sounds of their language (J. Hampson & Nelson, 1993). Songs often sung to children, such as "This Little Piggy," contain such characteristic repetition and lots of intonation.

The culmination of all this preparation is the utterance of the first word, usually *dada*, at about 12 months. During the next 6 to 8 months, children build a vocabulary of one-word sentences called **holophrases**: "Up!"; "Out!"; "More!" At first, these words are used to describe the child's own behavior, but later they are employed to describe the actions of others (Huttenlocher, Smiley, & Charney, 1983). Children may also use compound words such as *awgone* [all gone]. To these holophrases they add words used to address people—*Bye-bye* is a favorite—and a few exclamations, such as *Ouch*!

In the second year of life, children begin to distinguish between themselves and others. Possessive words become a big part of the vocabulary: [The shoes are] "Daddy's." But the overwhelming passion of children from 12 to 24 months old is naming. With little or no prompting, they will name virtually everything they see in their environment, though not always correctly! Children at this age are fascinated by objects. If they don't know the name of an object, they will simply invent one or use another word that is almost right. Feedback from parents ("No, that's not a dog, it's a cow") enhances vocabulary and helps children understand what names can and cannot be assigned to classes of things ("dog" is not used for big four-legged animals that live on farms and moo rather than bark). L.J. Stone and Church (1984) described a child who called all red cars *engines*—apparently because he was accustomed to red fire engines—long before he used the word *red* or had grasped the more abstract concept of colors or the differences between cars and fire engines.

**Language acquisition device** An internal mechanism for processing speech that is "wired into" all humans.

During the third year of life, children begin to form two- and three-word sentences such as "See daddy," "Baby cry," "My ball," and "Dog go woof-woof." Recordings of mother-child conversations show that children from 24 to 36 months old noticeably omit auxiliary verbs and verb endings ([Can] "I have that?"; "I [am] eat[ing] it up") as well as prepositions and articles ("It [is] time [for] Sarah [to] take [a] nap") (Bloom, 1970). Apparently, children this age seize on the most important parts of speech, those that contain the most meaning.

After 3 years of age, children begin to fill in their sentences ("Billy school" becomes "Billy goes to school"), and language production increases dramatically. Children start to use the past tense as well as the present. They ask more questions and learn to employ "Why?" effectively (and sometimes monotonously). By the age of 5 or 6, most children have a vocabulary of over 2,500 words and can construct sentences of 6 to 8 words. This increase in the number of words a child uses when communicating is only one aspect of language development. Complexity of speech is a much more sensitive indicator of a child's level of language development. For example, the number of words that a child uses *per sentence* is an excellent index of language development (R. Brown, 1973). If you compare the sentence complexity of a 1-year-old with that of an almost-4-year-old, you will note a dramatic difference.

**THEORIES OF LANGUAGE DEVELOPMENT** We have seen that children enjoy making sounds and learning words, and that they readily pick up the complex rules for putting words together into sentences. But what prompts them to learn to talk in the first place, and how do they learn to speak so well so quickly?

There are two very different theories about how language develops. B. F. Skinner (1957) believed that parents and other people listen to the infant's cooing and babbling and *reinforce*, or reward, the infant for making those sounds that most resemble adult speech. If the infant says something that sounds like *mama*, Mommy reinforces the behavior with a smile or a hug. As children get older, the things they say must sound more and more like adult speech in order to be reinforced. Children who call the wrong person "Mama" are less likely to be smiled at; they are reinforced only when they use the word appropriately. In the same way, Skinner believed that children learn by trial and error where words belong in a sentence, how to use prefixes and suffixes, and so on.

Most psychologists and linguists now believe, however, that reinforcement alone cannot explain the speed, accuracy, and originality with which children learn to use language. Noam Chomsky (1965) has been the most influential critic of the notion that children must be *taught* language. Instead, he argues that children are born with a **language acquisition device**, an internal mechanism for processing speech that is "wired into" all humans, and that infant speech is therefore universal (Kuhl, Kuhl, & Williams, 1992). This language acquisition device enables children to understand the basic rules of grammar, to make sense of what they hear, and to form their own sentences. It is like an internal "map" of language: All the child has to do is to fill in the blanks with information supplied by the environment. An American child fills in the blanks with English words, a Mexican child with Spanish words, and so on.

But the environment must do more for children than provide words to fill in the blanks in their internal map. Without the social stimulus of people to talk to, children are slow to pick up the words and rules of their language. Babies reared in institutions, without smiling adults around to reward their efforts, babble like other children but take much longer to begin talking than children reared in families (R. Brown, 1958). The greater attention paid to first-born children may explain why these children tend to be more advanced in their language development than those born later. Mothers speak differently to first-borns, asking more questions and making more requests: "Where is the duck?" "Say thank-you" (C.P. Jones & Adamson, 1987).

Some aspects of children's speech are highly resistant to adult influence. Early errors in pronunciation are especially hard to correct. Children who say "mouse" instead of "mouth" can hear the difference between the two words, they just haven't learned how to pronounce the difficult *th* sound. One researcher recorded a story about a toddler who used the word "fis" when talking to an adult. The adult, puzzled, said "fis?" The child became annoyed. "Fis!" exclaimed the child in frustration. Finally the adult guessed "fish?" and the child, satisfied at last, said "Yes, fis" (Moskowitz, 1978).

During the first years of life, children also have a grammar of their own that guides their use of language. A 3-year-old might announce, "I saw some sheeps" or "I digged a hole." The words *sheeps* and *digged* were not learned by imitating adults. Instead, they are an indication that the child has figured out how our language usually forms the plural of a noun and the past tense of a verb. Quite an achievement for a small person who has no idea of what a "noun" or a "verb" is!

**BILINGUALISM AND THE DEVELOPMENT OF A SECOND LANGUAGE** It's fascinating to listen to a bilingual child switch from one language to another as need dictates. For example, the child may speak English at school, but switch to Spanish, Polish, or Vietnamese at home. Or the child of deaf parents may sign with them but speak English with other people. There are almost 10 million school-aged children in the United States for whom English is not the primary language; in some states, 25 percent of all school-children have a primary language other than English. As a result, bilingual education has become a pressing concern.

Monitoring how children learn a second language is important for several reasons. First, it improves our understanding of how language develops, because linguists can watch the parallel development of two different languages and compare the development of each. Second, it allows educators to design curricula to maximize the school success of children whose primary language is not English. Finally, bilingualism is an important social issue. Should parents try to provide equal exposure to both languages in their home, perhaps sacrificing some of the family's cultural identity in the process? Or should the family use only its native language at home, perhaps making it more difficult for their child to "fit in" at school and in peer groups?

The answers to those questions are not yet clear. Neither is it clear how bilingual children might best be educated. Should all their classes be taught in English, or should at least some of their classes be taught in their primary language? One recent report on bilingual education in New York City showed that students who take most of their classes in English learn English better than those who are taught different subjects in their primary language. Another interesting finding is that students from groups that place a high value on learning English—such as Russian, Korean, and Chinese immigrants—pass through bilingual classes much faster than students from groups that place a lower value on English literacy (Dillon, 1994).

**Imprinting** Form of primitive bonding seen in some species of animals; the newborn animal has a tendency to follow the first moving thing (usually its mother) it sees after it is born or hatched.

**Critical Periods in Language Development** Earlier in the chapter we discussed the notion of *critical periods*, the hypothesis that certain experiences have a more profound effect on development at certain periods of time than at others. It has been suggested that there is a critical period during which a child must be exposed to language in order for language acquisition to proceed normally. If exposure does not occur during this period, the child's acquisition of language will likely be imperfect and incomplete.

The acquisition of sign language in children who are severely hearing impaired provides a natural context in which to test the critical period hypothesis. Sign language is acquired in much the same way as any other language. It starts with babbling, progresses to more complex sentences, and culminates in completely effective communication. Deaf children whose parents are also deaf have sign language as their primary language from birth. In contrast, deaf children whose parents are not themselves deaf receive less exposure to sign language because their hearing parents do not normally use sign language to communicate between themselves. Many children in this second group do not learn to sign until they reach school age or are placed in some type of residential program, long after the critical period for learning language has passed. Research shows there is a strong relationship between the age at which people first learn American Sign Language and their skill at using it. Those who were exposed to sign language during early childhood are usually more proficient than those who were not exposed to sign language until adolescence or adulthood (Emmorey, 1994). These results are not due to differences in the length of time the two groups have used sign language. Among people who have used sign language for the same length of time, those who acquired the language during early childhood usually have a greater mastery of the language than those who learned it later in life. These and similar data clearly support the critical period hypothesis: To learn any language, the child's exposure to it should begin as early in life as possible.

## Social Development

One of the central aspects of human development is the process whereby a child learns to relate to other people. Early in life, children's most important relationships are with their parents and other caregivers. By the time children are 3 years old, their important relationships have usually expanded to include siblings, playmates, and other children and adults outside the family circle. Children's social world is further enlarged when they start school. As we will see, social development involves both ongoing relationships and new or changing ones.

**Parent-Child Relationships in Infancy: The Development of Attachment** In nature, young animals of many species follow their mothers around. They do this because of **imprinting**. Shortly after they are born or hatched, these young animals form a strong bond to the first moving object they see. In nature, this object is normally the mother, the first source of nurturance and protection. But in laboratory experiments, certain species of animals, such as geese, have been hatched in incubators and have imprinted on decoys, mechanical toys, and even on human beings (H.S. Hoffman & DePaulo, 1977; Lorenz, 1935). Such goslings faithfully follow their human "mother," showing no interest whatever in adult females of their own species (Figure 8-3).

**Attachment** Emotional bond that develops in the first year of life that makes human babies cling to their caregivers for safety and comfort.

**Autonomy** Sense of independence; a desire not to be controlled by others.

Bonding does not occur in the same way with human newborns, nor does it occur as quickly. A newborn child separated from its mother will not imprint on any moving object that happens to pass by! But human infants do gradually form an **attachment**, or emotional bond, to the people who take care of them (regardless of the caretakers' gender). The process may begin with the baby's very effective and well-developed ability to "lock on" to an adult's eyes. Some *ethologists* (experts in the biological and social basis of animal behavior) believe that the human baby's disproportionally large eyes help to ensure that a bond is formed between caretakers and infants and that, in turn, this bond ensures that the baby will be well cared for.

An infant will gradually develop an attachment to his primary caregiver during his first year of life. By 6 months of age or even earlier, he will react with smiles and coos at the caregiver's appearance and with whimpers or cries when the caregiver goes away. At around 7 months, attachment behavior becomes more intense. The infant will reach out to be picked up and will crawl into his mother or father's lap and cling, especially when he is tired, frightened, or in pain. He will begin to be wary of strangers, sometimes reacting with loud wails at even the friendliest approach by an unfamiliar person. He also begins to react negatively if separated from a parent or another caregiver for even a few minutes, especially in an unfamiliar place.

**Figure 8-3**
**Imprinting.** Goslings follow biologist Konrad Lorenz, on whom they have imprinted. He was the first moving thing they set eyes on after they hatched.

Parents are often puzzled by this new behavior in their previously nonchalant infants, but it is perfectly normal. In fact, anxiety over separation from the mother indicates that the infant has developed a sense of "person permanence" along with the sense of object permanence. For the 5-month-old, it's still "out of sight, out of mind" when Mother leaves the room. But the 9-month-old knows that Mother continues to exist, even when he can't see her, and he announces at the top of his lungs that he wants her to come back!

Ideally, infants eventually learn that Mother always comes back and that there are other things of interest in the world. They crawl away, cautiously at first, then more boldly, to investigate objects and people around them. This exploration is an indication of children's developing **autonomy**, or sense of independence and trust in their own abilities and powers.

Autonomy and attachment may seem to be opposites, but in a way they are actually different sides of the same coin. The child who has formed a secure attachment to a caregiver can explore the environment without fear. Such a child knows that the caregiver will be there when really needed, and so the caregiver serves as a "secure base" from which to venture forth (M.D.S. Ainsworth, 1977).

Unfortunately, not all children form secure attachments. Perhaps the primary caregiver is unresponsive to the child's needs or is absent much of the time. Whatever the reason, children who are insecurely attached to their mothers are less likely to explore an unfamiliar environment, even when their mother is present. Moreover, if left in a strange place, most young children will cry and refuse to be comforted, but the insecurely attached child is more likely to continue crying even after the mother returns, either pushing her away angrily or ignoring her altogether. In contrast, a securely attached 12-month-old is more likely to rush over to the mother for a hug or a smile when she returns and then happily begin to play (M.D. Ainsworth et al., 1978).

The importance of secure attachment early in life is evident for many years afterward. Studies of children from 1 through 6 years of age have shown that those who formed a secure attachment to their mothers by the age of 12 months were later more at ease with other children, more interested in exploring new toys, and more enthusiastic and persistent when presented with new tasks (Harris & Liebert, 1991). Thus, secure attachments, far from being a sign of excessive dependency, actually strengthen the child's developing autonomy.

**Socialization** Process by which children learn the behaviors and attitudes appropriate to their family and their culture.

At about 2 years of age, children begin to assert themselves by becoming very negative. They refuse everything: getting dressed ("No!"), going to sleep ("No!"), using the potty ("No!"). The usual outcome of these first efforts at independence is that the parents begin to discipline the child. Children are told they have to eat and go to bed at a particular time, they must not pull the cat's tail or kick their sister, and they must respect other people's rights. The conflict between the parents' need for peace and order and the child's desire for autonomy often creates difficulties. But it is an essential first step in **socialization**, the process by which children learn the behaviors and attitudes appropriate to their family and their culture.

**PARENT-CHILD RELATIONSHIPS IN CHILDHOOD** As children grow older, their social world expands. They play with siblings and friends, they go off to nursery school or a day-care center, and they eventually enter elementary school. But parents continue to play a central role in social development, teaching their child both by direct instruction (which becomes more and more verbal as the child gets older) and by serving as models of behavior. Of the two, modeling is almost always more effective because children tend to pay greater attention to what a parent *does* than to what he or she *says*.

Parents also control children's behavior through rewards (such as praise and affection) and punishments (such as reprimands and spankings). However, as we saw in the chapter on learning, punishment, even when used correctly, is likely to have a number of undesirable side effects. It tends to disrupt learning, and it often triggers anger and aggression. Moreover, a parent who physically strikes a child is modeling aggressive behavior. The child is likely to learn an unintended lesson: "The way to get people to do what you want is to hurt them."

How parents discipline their children and the demands they make of them have lasting effects on children's behavior. Diana Baumrind (1972), who has done extensive research on parenting styles, found that *authoritarian* parents, who control their children's behavior rigidly and insist on unquestioning obedience, are likely to produce children who are withdrawn and distrustful. But *permissive* parenting can also have negative effects: When parents exert too little control, their children tend to be overly dependent and lacking in self-control. The most successful parenting style is what Baumrind calls *authoritative*. Authoritative parents provide firm structure and guidance without being overly controlling. They listen to their children's opinions and give explanations for their decisions, but it is clear that they are the ones who make and enforce the rules. Parents who use this approach are most likely to have children who are self-reliant and socially responsible.

It is important to note that the parent-child relationship is not determined solely by the parent: Children also affect the relationship. Parents do not act the same way toward every child in the family, because each child is a different individual. A thoughtful, responsible child is more likely to encourage authoritative parenting, whereas an impulsive child who is difficult to reason with is more likely to elicit authoritarian parenting. It is easier and more rewarding to listen to and reason with a thoughtful child. Conversely, it is easier to deal with an impulsive child by issuing commands and insisting they be followed without question.

**Solitary play** A child engaged in some activity alone; the earliest form of play.

**Parallel play** Two children playing side by side at the same activities, paying little or no attention to each other; the earliest kind of social interaction between toddlers.

**Cooperative play** Two or more children engaged in play that requires interaction.

**Gender identity** A little girl's knowledge that she is a girl, and a little boy's knowledge that he is a boy.

## Relationships with Other Children

At a very early age, infants begin to show an interest in other children. However, the social skills required to play with another child develop only gradually. Children first play alone, participating in **solitary play**. Between 1 1/2 and 2, children begin to engage in **parallel play**—that is, they play side by side, doing the same things, but not interacting much with each other. Around the age of 2, imitation becomes a game: One child throws a toy into the air, the other does the same, and then they both giggle. At around 2 1/2, children begin to use language to communicate with their playmates, and their play becomes increasingly imaginative. By age 3 or 3 1/2, they are engaging in **cooperative play**, including games that involve group imagination such as "playing house" (Eckerman, Davis, & Didow, 1989).

Peer influences grow much stronger when children start school. Now they are under a great deal of pressure to be liked, or at least accepted, by their peers. Inability to get along well with one's classmates has long-lasting consequences. Psychologists studying unpopularity and its effects have found that children whose classmates dislike them are more likely to drop out of school, to engage in criminal behavior, and to become mentally ill later in life. This is particularly true of children who are disliked because they are aggressive (J.G. Parker & Asher, 1987). However, not all children who lack friends are actually disliked by their peers: It is important to distinguish between *rejected* children, whose classmates actively dislike them, and *neglected* children, whose classmates simply never notice them. Rejected children run the greatest risks; they tend to be unpopular in every group they enter. On the other hand, children who are neglected by their classmates may be popular in other contexts (in the neighborhood, for example) and may have a close friend in another class or another school (Harris & Liebert, 1991).

As children get older, they develop a deeper understanding of the meaning of friendship. For those under the age of 7, a "friend" is someone who lives nearby, who has nice toys, and who plays with them. At this stage, "friend" means "someone I play with." Around age 7, children define friends as "people who do things for me"; thus, friends are important because they meet the child's needs. Later, at about age 9, children come to understand that friendship is a two-way street and that, while friends do things for us, we are also expected to do things for them. During these early years, friendships often come and go at dizzying speed; they endure only as long as needs are being satisfied. It is not until late childhood or early adolescence that friendship is viewed as a stable and continuing social relationship that requires mutual support, trust, and confidence (Selman, 1981).

Along with the social experience it provides, school is a major influence on a child's sense of competence and achievement. The school years are when children begin to compare themselves to others and to develop a greater awareness of their own personal characteristics: "I'm good in sports" or "I'm the most popular girl in the class." In this way, they become aware of their own strengths and weaknesses (Ruble, Parsons, & Ross, 1976). Children who are successful in school are likely to develop a positive outlook on life, whereas those who encounter constant frustration in the school environment may lower their expectations of personal success in life or even give up (M.E.P. Seligman, 1975). Success or failure during the school years can exert a lifelong influence on self-image.

**SEX-ROLE DEVELOPMENT** By about the third birthday, both boys and girls have developed a **gender identity**; that is, a little girl knows that she is a girl, and a little boy knows that he is a boy. At this point, however, children have little understanding of what it means to be a girl or a boy. A 3-year-old boy, for example, might think that he can grow up to be a mommy, or that if you put a dress on him and a bow in his hair, he will turn into a girl. By the age of 4 or 5, most children know that gender depends on what kind of genitals a person has. They have acquired **gender constancy**, the realization that gender cannot be changed. In fact, modern children are so sophisticated about these matters that many 4-year-olds now know that it all depends on the genitals and not on what a person is wearing or how a person styles her or his hair (S.L. Bem, 1989).

**Gender constancy** The realization by a child that gender cannot be changed.

**Sex-role awareness** Knowledge of what behavior is appropriate for each gender.

**Sex-typed behavior** Socially prescribed ways of behaving that differ for boys and girls.

**Sex-role awareness**, the knowledge of what behavior is appropriate for each gender, involves much more than gender identity or constancy. Children learn, as they get older, what kinds of behaviors are expected of males and of females in their society. As they learn this, they develop sex stereotypes: Girls are clean and polite, whereas boys are rough and noisy; women are kind, caring, and emotional, whereas men are competitive, domineering, and aggressive. Moreover, they develop sex-typed behavior themselves: Girls play with dolls, while boys play with trucks; girls put on pretty clothes and fuss with their hair, while boys run around and wrestle with one another.

Behavioral differences between girls and boys appear early in development. By the age of 3, girls are playing mostly with other girls and boys mostly with other boys. Furthermore, they are playing in different ways. The boys are more active and aggressive, and tend to play in larger groups. The girls talk more, shove less, and tend to interact in pairs. Of course, there are some active, aggressive girls and some quiet, polite boys, but they are not in the majority.

We have been describing **sex-typed behavior**, the source of which is a matter of considerable controversy. Some researchers attribute sex differences in behavior to the fact that adults treat girls and boys differently and *expect* different kinds of behavior from them. In one study, for example, adults saw a videotape of a 9-month-old infant dressed in unisex clothing reacting to a jack-in-the-box. Those who had been told that the baby was a boy tended to interpret the baby's reaction as anger, while viewers who thought the baby was a girl tended to attribute the same reaction to fear (Condry & Condry, 1976). More recent studies, however, have challenged the assumption that parents encourage different behaviors in sons and daughters. This issue is examined in greater detail in the Controversies box.

Whatever the role of parental expectations, there are several other factors that influence sex-role development. For example, popular culture, including advertisements, books, children's toys, and television, reflects sex-typed behavior. Even our use of language helps perpetuate traditional attitudes toward gender differences. As we saw in the chapter titled "Language and Cognition," for example, the use of the generic "he" when referring to doctors and business executives encourages the belief that these are "male" professions.

Because so many factors affect sex-role development, it is exceedingly difficult to determine exactly how much of the difference between girls and boys is the result of environmental influences and how much is biologically determined. There is some evidence that whatever differences are present at birth are likely to be magnified and increased by later experiences. One recent study that explored sex differences from infancy through 8 years of age (Prior, Smart, Sanson, & Obeklaid, 1993) found that though there were minimal differences between boys and girls in infancy, major differences developed as the children got older. For example, girls had begun to excel in language and motor skills by age 3, while boys of the same age were more likely to have developed problems with social and adaptive behav-

## ONTROVERSIES

### Do Boys and Girls Behave Differently Because Their Parents Treat Them Differently?

Hugh Lytton and David Romney (1991) recently reviewed 172 studies of differential treatment of boys and girls in order to find out whether there were any systematic differences in the way parents act toward sons and daughters. Here is what they concluded:

First, in most areas of parent-child interaction, there were *no overall differences* between the ways girls and boys were treated. For example, in encouragement of achievement and independence, discouragement of aggressiveness, amount of strictness and affection, amount of verbal interaction, and total amount of interaction with their children, parents behaved very much the same toward sons and daughters.

Second, for North American parents, the only significant difference between the ways girls and boys were treated was in regard to the encouragement of sex-typed behavior. Parents—especially fathers—tended to expect girls to do "girl things" and boys to do "boy things," both in their play activities and in their household chores. Hofferth and colleagues cautioned, however, that "such encouragement may build on the child's already existing preferences" (Hofferth et al., 1990, p. 287). In other words, it is possible that parents buy a daughter a doll and a son a toy truck because they have observed that their children prefer those toys.

Notice that there was no evidence that parents encouraged achievement or aggression in boys or dependency in girls. Aggression was discouraged in both sexes; achievement and "politeness" were encouraged. These results do very little to explain the considerable differences we see in male and female children.

Eleanor Maccoby, a specialist in sex differences, has an interesting hypothesis: The everyday differences in behavior we see between boys and girls on the playground are more the result of peer influences than pressure from parents or other adults. She has noticed that girls and boys are not very different in behavior if they are tested or observed one at a time. Their behavior is most different, most sex-typed, when they are playing in all-male or all-female groups.

E.E. Maccoby (1990) points out that girls and boys have different styles of interaction. In all-boy groups, the children tend to form a hierarchy in which issues of dominance are important; they are concerned about not "losing face" in front of their friends. Girls' groups are less competitive, and because girls are not so concerned about "losing face," they are more willing to reveal themselves to their friends. Thus, the two groups develop different "cultures," and those who become members of such groups are under pressure to conform to the group's cultural norms.

Since the different styles of interaction appear very early in development (even before the age of 3), Maccoby believes that they are at least partly biological in origin. But she thinks the biological differences are small at first, and later become exaggerated because of the different kinds of socialization experienced by boys and girls when they play with members of their own sex.

iors. Teachers also rated boys as having more problems in school. From this study and others like it, it seems increasingly clear that the psychological differences between boys and girls (and men and women, for that matter) are, to a very great extent, the result of their experiences.

## Television and Children

5. Does television watching influence children's behavior?

American children spend more time watching television than they do engaging in any other activity besides sleeping (Huston, Watkins, & Kunkel, 1989). Children who watch 2 hours of TV per day (well below our national average) will see about 8,000 murders and 100,000 other acts of violence by the time they leave elementary school (American Psychological Association, 1992). On average, children between 2 and 5 years of age watch about 4 hours of TV each day (Lande, 1993).

It is hardly surprising, then, that psychologists, educators, and parents are concerned about television's influence on children's development. Their concern has focused on two issues: (1) Does watching television make children more aggressive, and if so, does the violence so commonplace on TV account, at least in part, for the rapid rise in violent crime among adolescents in recent years? (Lande, 1993) (2) Does watching television make children less intelligent?

The answer to the first part of question 1 is clear: If children's television fare consists of programs such as *Sesame Street* and *Mr. Rogers*, watching TV does *not* make them more aggressive. The answer to the second part of the question is less certain, but there is convincing evidence that children who frequently watch *violent* TV shows behave more aggressively than other children (Eron, 1982; Singer & Singer, 1983). Indeed, the evidence suggests that viewing fictional violence on television can lead to copycat behavior in the real world. For example, one study linked 13 movies and 13 television programs to 58 acts of violence of exactly the same kind as shown on the screen (W. Wilson & Hunter, 1983).

Perhaps the best evidence for a causal link between TV watching and violent behavior comes from a study that compared rates of violence in three similar towns, one of which did not have television until 1973 (Will, 1993). Two years after television was introduced into that remote community, the rate of physical aggression soared by 45 percent for both boys and girls, while it did not change in the two other towns that already had television.

## HIGHLIGHTS

### Youth Violence: Origins and Interventions

Here are some of the findings published in *Violence and Youth*, a recent report of the American Psychological Association (APA, 1993).

- More than 25,000 Americans are murdered each year.
- The probability that a young African-American female will be murdered is four times higher than that of a non-African-American female.
- In a study of first- and second-graders in Washington, D.C., 45 percent of the children said they had witnessed muggings, 31 percent said they had witnessed a shooting, and 39 percent said they had seen a dead body.

Violence has always been a problem of young people in this country, both as perpetrators and as victims, but never at the levels being recorded today. And, as is true of so many other troubling social problems, no single factor seems to be responsible; rather, violence is the product of a combination of factors that interact in a complex fashion.

One of the strongest predictors of violent behavior in a young person is a history of previous violence (APA, 1993). How violent or antisocial the child is when young seems to predict how violent the child will be when older. A family history of violent and/or criminal behavior by parents also predicts early aggressive behavior in children. We have discussed at several points in this textbook the powerful role modeling plays in children's socialization. When a parent or other role model is violent, children learn violence and antisocial behaviors.

In addition, children who are highly impulsive and fearless are more likely to act aggressively and violently later in life. Children who are difficult to comfort as infants and who have temper tantrums in early childhood also show a higher propensity to violence as they grow older.

Finally, harsh and continuous physical punishment encourages aggressive behavior. Not only does the parent model the use of aggressive behavior to settle disputes. Such aggressive parental behavior also teaches the child that aggression is a way of life, and the continuous nature of the punishment teaches that there is no other effective way to resolve disputes.

Still, even children who are most at risk for violent behavior can be helped to change. Intervention and community programs—including visits to the homes of children at risk for violence, school-based programs, and programs that work with the family—have all been shown to reduce violent behavior. We have the knowledge to help troubled children gain the attention and emotional support they crave without resorting to violence.

The most convincing theoretical argument that violent behavior is linked to television watching is based on social learning theory, which we discussed in Chapter 5. Social learning theory leads us to expect that children who see fictional characters on TV being rewarded for their violent behaviors will not only learn those behaviors but will also perform them when given the opportunity. Children need not directly participate in a behavior or be personally rewarded for it in order to learn it. They can learn the behavior simply by watching someone else do it, and if the model is rewarded, they are more likely to perform that behavior themselves in the future in similar situations. The Highlights box further explores the origins of youth violence and interventions that have worked to stem it.

The second question of concern about the effects of television viewing on children involves their intellectual lives—their IQs, cognitive development, and academic achievement. Scores on a number of standardized tests taken by American children and adolescents have been declining for years. Many educators blame these declines on the fact that children no longer read books; instead, they watch television (DeWitt, 1991). But a study of TV viewing by preschoolers found no correlation between their IQ scores and how much TV they watched (Plomin, Corley et al., 1990). Also, despite the general increase in television viewing over the past few decades, IQ scores haven't declined. Rather, they have increased—all over the world (Flynn, 1987).

Moreover, there is evidence that children can learn worthwhile things from watching television. For example, infants only 14 months old learned how to take apart a toy after they saw the action demonstrated on a television screen (A.N. Meltzoff, 1988). In another study, 12- to 18-month-old babies learned new words by hearing them used on a TV show. The researchers concluded that television can serve as a kind of "talking picture book" for infants (Lemish & Rice, 1986). In another study, children who watched *Mr. Rogers* exhibited increased prosocial behavior (Tower et al., 1979). In addition, the content of some children's shows has been shown to promote good health and nutrition (Calvert & Cocking, 1992).

There are other concerns about television's possible negative effects on children's development. Some critics think that children are especially

Studies confirm that watching television can make children act more aggressively, but only if the content of the shows is violent. There is no evidence linking television watching to lower IQ scores.

vulnerable to TV messages, particularly commercials (Huston et al., 1989). Children under the age of 8 have a very difficult time understanding when the TV show stops and the commercial begins. But even older children are easily misled by the kinds of subtle deception used by advertisers (Kunkel, 1988). In addition, children who watch a lot of TV are more likely to become obese (Dietz, 1987), not only because they get less exercise than they should, but also because they tend to munch on the kind of high-calorie, high-fat foods featured in TV commercials while they are watching.

To summarize, television is a significant influence on children's development. It presents both "good" and "bad" models for them to copy, and it provides vast amounts of information. Many experts feel the medium has not begun to reach its potential as a teaching tool. On the downside, children who watch a lot of television spend less time doing other productive and useful things, may learn undesirable behaviors, and may be unduly influenced by advertisements.

**Growth spurt** A rapid increase in height and weight that occurs during adolescence.

**Puberty** Onset of sexual maturation, with accompanying physical development.

## ADOLESCENCE

Adolescence is that awkward period of life when a person is neither a child nor an adult. At the beginning of adolescence, young people are still quite dependent on their parents. By the end, friends and romantic partners have come to play a central role in their lives. Along the way, they have made many important decisions, some of which may be irrevocable.

Of the many differences between a 12-year-old and a 20-year-old, the physical ones are the most conspicuous. What changes take place in the body during adolescence, and what are the effects of these changes on the young people who experience them?

### Physical Changes

Adolescence is ushered in by a series of dramatic physical milestones. The most obvious is the **growth spurt**, a rapid increase in height and weight that begins, on average, at about age 10 1/2 in girls and 12 1/2 in boys, and reaches its peak at age 12 in girls and 14 in boys (see Figure 8-4). The typical adolescent attains his or her adult height about 6 years after the start of the growth spurt (Tanner, 1978).

The growth spurt begins with a lengthening of the hands, feet, arms, and legs, which produces the awkward, gangly look of young adolescents. This stage is followed by the growth of the torso, which brings the body back into proportion. In boys, the final stage of growth results in a broadening of the chest and shoulders and the development of heavier muscles. For girls, changes in body shape occur as the hips widen and fat is deposited on the breasts, hips, buttocks, and thighs. All these changes result from an increase in hormones which, as we saw in Chapter 2, are chemicals released by the endocrine system (Dyk, 1993).

In both sexes, changes also occur in the face. The chin and nose become more prominent, and the lips get fuller. Increases in the size of oil glands in the skin can contribute to acne; sweat glands produce a more odorous secretion. The heart, lungs, and digestive system all expand.

**SEXUAL DEVELOPMENT** As you can see from Figure 8-4, the visible signs of **puberty**—the onset of sexual maturation—occur in a somewhat different sequence for boys and girls. In boys, the initial sign of approaching sexual maturity is the growth of the testes, which starts, on average, at around 11 1/2, about a year before the beginning of the growth spurt. This is followed by the growth of the penis. Development of pubic

**Menarche** First menstrual period.

hair comes a little later, and facial hair later still. Deepening of the voice is one of the last noticeable changes of male maturation.

In females, the beginning of the growth spurt at an average age of 10 1/2 is typically the first sign of approaching puberty. Shortly thereafter, the breasts begin to develop; some pubic hair appears at around the same time. **Menarche**, the first menstrual period, occurs between 12 1/2 and 13 for the average American girl (Powers, Hauser, & Kilner, 1989). The timing of menarche is affected by health and nutrition, with fatter girls maturing earlier than thinner ones.

The onset of menstruation does not necessarily mean that a girl is biologically capable of becoming a mother, for it is uncommon (though not unheard of) for a girl to become pregnant during her first few menstrual cycles. Female fertility increases gradually during the first year after menarche. The same is true of male fertility. Boys achieve their first ejaculation at an average age of 13 1/2, often during sleep. But first ejaculations contain relatively few sperm (Tanner, 1978). Nevertheless, adolescents are capable of producing babies long before they are mature enough to take care of them.

**Figure 8-4**
**The growth spurt and sexual development in girls and boys during puberty.** The period of rapid growth is indicated by the blue line. The bars show the average age at which each kind of development begins and ends.

*Source:* Adapted from "Growing Up," by J.M. Tanner, 1973. Copyright ©1973 by Scientific American, Inc. All rights reserved.

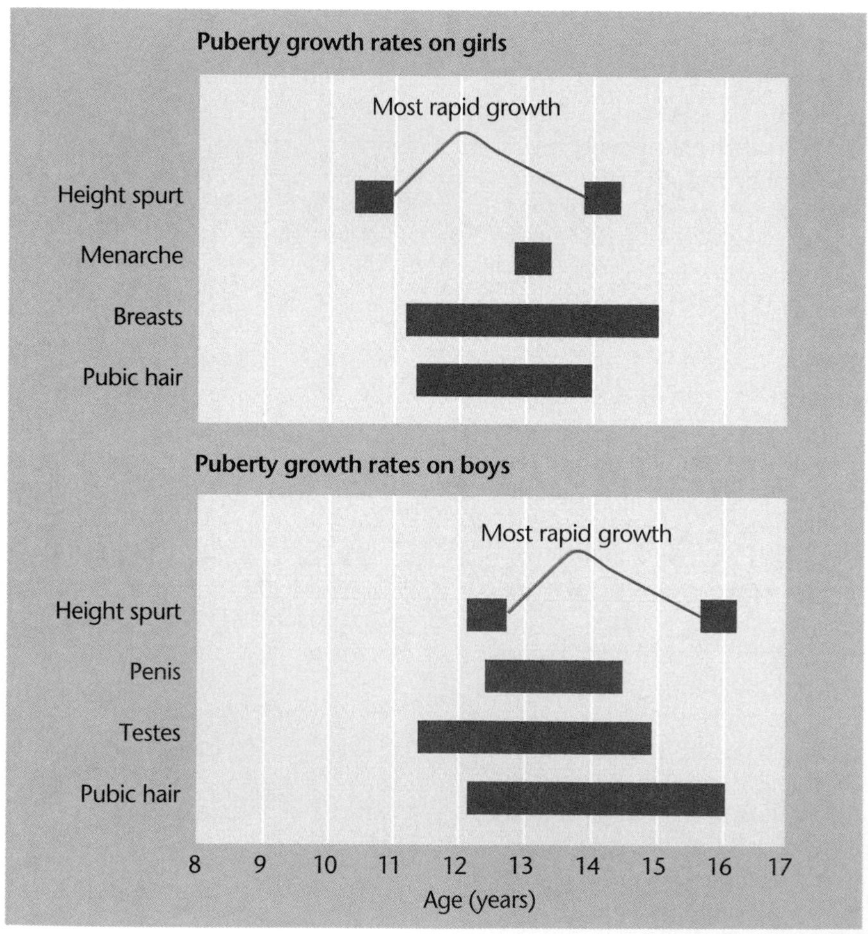


**REACTIONS TO PHYSICAL CHANGES** Teenagers are acutely aware of the changes taking place in their bodies. Many become anxious about whether they are the "right" shape or size and obsessively compare themselves with the models and actors they see on television and in magazines. Since few adolescents can match these ideals, it is not surprising that when young adolescents are asked what they most dislike about themselves, physical appearance is mentioned more often than anything else (Conger & Petersen, 1991). Approximately one-third of boys and one-half of girls in early adolescence are unhappy about some aspect of their physical appearance. Among adolescent girls especially, satisfaction with one's appearance is tied to satisfaction with oneself. Adolescents who are least satisfied with their physical appearance have the lowest self-esteem (G.R. Adams & Gullota, 1983).

Sexual maturation has other psychological consequences for adolescents. Among boys, the increasing frequency of erections and ejaculations is often a source of pride, though it may also be a source of embarrassment. For an adolescent girl, the onset of menstruation is a sign that she is becoming a woman. But menarche has its negative side. A negative reaction is more likely to occur if menarche is accompanied by physical discomfort, if it arrives unusually early or late, or if the girl has received little or no preparation for it (Greif & Ulman, 1982).

**EARLY AND LATE DEVELOPERS** Individuals differ greatly in the age at which the growth spurt begins and in how rapidly they progress through the sequence of pubertal changes. Thus, some 12-year-old girls and 14-year-old boys still look like children, while others their age already look like young women and men. Among boys, early maturing has definite psychological advantages. Boys who mature earlier do better in sports and in social activities and receive greater respect from their peers (Conger & Petersen, 1991). However, at least one study (Peskin, 1967) found that late-maturing boys develop a stronger sense of identity during early adulthood. For girls, early maturation appears to be a mixed blessing. A girl who matures early may be admired by other girls but is likely to be subjected to embarrassing treatment as a sex object by boys (Clausen, 1975).

**ADOLESCENT SEXUAL ACTIVITY** The achievement of the capacity to reproduce is probably the single most important developmental event of adolescence. But sexuality is a confusing issue for adolescents in our society. Fifty years ago, young people were expected to postpone expressing their sexual needs until they were responsible, married adults. Since then, drastic changes in social customs have led to new patterns of sexual behavior. Although there are no comprehensive data on adolescent sexual activity, you can see from Figure 8-5 that the majority of adolescents of both sexes (66 percent of males and 50 percent of females) have had intercourse by the time they reach 17 (Alan Guttmacher Institute, 1990).

Moreover, some recent data suggest that there are significant differences between the ways boys and girls view their early sexual behavior (T. Lewin, 1994a). In a random sample of 504 teenagers in grades 9 through 12, 46 percent of the girls responded that they felt good about their sexual experiences, whereas 65 percent of the boys responded similarly. Also, 65 percent of the girls expressed the feeling that they should have waited until they were older before having sex compared to only 48 percent of the boys.

**TEENAGE PREGNANCY** One consequence of the trend toward earlier intercourse is a tremendous increase in unwanted pregnancies. In

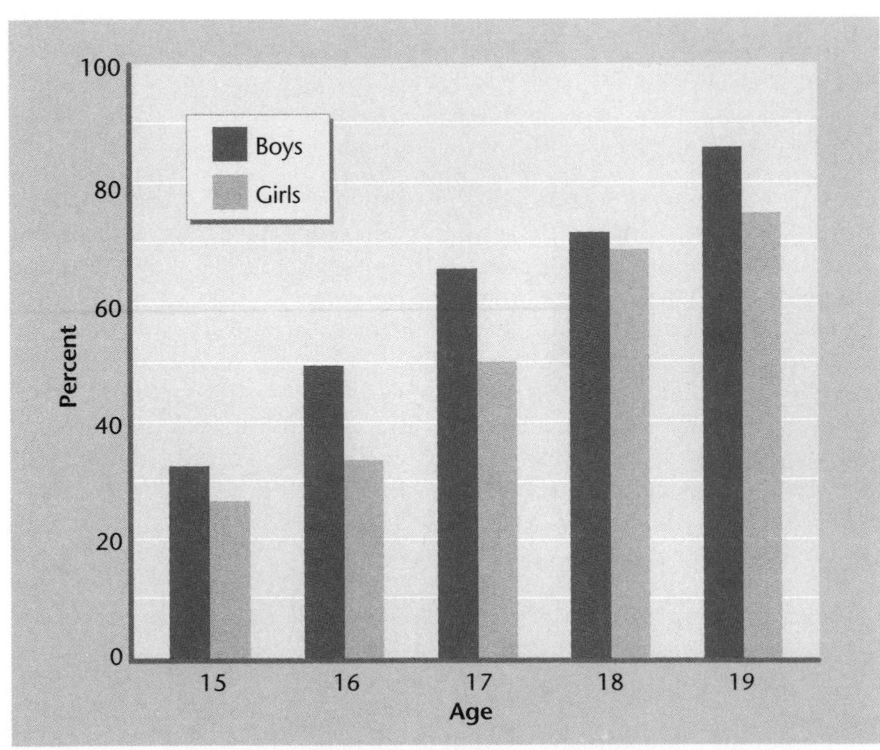


**Figure 8-5**
**Percentage of adolescents age 15–19, who have had intercourse.**

*Source:* Adapted from Alan Guttmacher Institute, 1990.

the United States, there are more than 1 million births a year among teenage girls. In fact, every year, 127 out of every 1,000 adolescent girls becomes pregnant (Alan Guttmacher Institute, 1990). Moreover, 4 out of 5 of these young women are unmarried.

One reason for our high levels of unwanted pregnancies is ignorance of the most basic facts concerning reproduction among our young people. In countries such as England, Sweden, and the Netherlands, which have extensive programs of sex education, teenage pregnancy rates are much lower (Hechtman, 1989), even though the rates of intercourse are about the same as those for American teenagers. However, even U.S. adolescents who know all the facts are at risk for unwanted pregnancy if they become sexually active at an early age, partly because of the false belief many of them harbor that "nothing bad can happen to me." Teenagers tend to feel invulnerable in general, and this sense of invulnerability blinds them to the possibility of becoming a teenage parent (Quadre, Prouadrel, Fischoff, & Davis, 1993). Yet another possible explanation for this rising teenage pregnancy rate is the fact that more and more adolescents have an older sister who is a teenage mother. One study (East & Felice, 1992) found that the younger sisters of childbearing teenagers are at increased risk for adolescent pregnancy themselves. The study identified three possible explanations for this finding: (1) sibling ties promote modeling and imitation; (2) the possibility that the sisters' parents themselves were teenage parents; and (3) the exposure of both sisters to the same risk factors, such as low income and living in a single-parent home. It's important to keep in mind that such conditions don't *cause* adolescent pregnancy; rather, they may place a young woman at heightened risk for becoming pregnant.

For an unmarried teenage mother, the consequences can be devastating. Particularly if she has no parental support or is living in poverty; motherhood is likely to have serious negative effects on her entire future. She is less likely to graduate from high school, less likely to improve her economic status, and less likely to get married and stay married than a girl who postpones childbearing. In addition, infants born to adolescent mothers are more likely to be of low birth weight, which is associated with learning disabilities and later problems in school, childhood illnesses, and neurological problems (Furstenberg, Brooks-Gunn, & Chase-Lansdale, 1989).

## Cognitive Changes

Although adolescents sometimes behave thoughtlessly and with apparent disregard for their own future, some important cognitive advances occur during this period. As we noted earlier in the chapter, Piaget (1969) described this development as a change from concrete-operational thought to formal-operational thought—that is, the individual advances from concrete thinking to abstract thinking about the world. Adolescents can understand and manipulate abstract concepts, speculate about alternative possibilities, and reason in hypothetical terms. If you listen in on an informal "rap" session, you may hear adolescents talking about such problematical issues as abortion, sexual behavior, and AIDS. These kinds of issues force young people to think in abstract terms and exercise their mental schema, adding to, subtracting from, and otherwise changing their world views. However, as we saw in the section criticizing Piaget's theory, not all adolescents reach the stage of formal operations, and even among those who do, many fail to apply formal-operational thinking to the everyday problems they face (H. Gardner, 1982). Younger adolescents especially are unlikely to be objective about matters concerning themselves and have not yet achieved a deep understanding of the difficulties involved in moral judgment.

In those who do achieve formal-operational thought, this advance has its hazards, among them overconfidence in new mental abilities and a tendency to place too much importance on one's own thoughts. Some adolescents also fail to realize that everyone does not share their mental processes and that other people may hold different views (Harris & Liebert, 1991). Piaget called these tendencies the "egocentrism of formal operations" (Piaget, 1967).

**Imaginary audience** Elkind's term for adolescents' delusion that they are constantly being observed by others.

**Personal fable** Elkind's term for adolescents' delusion that they are unique, very important, and invulnerable.

David Elkind (1968, 1969) uses Piaget's notion of adolescent egocentrism to account for two characteristic fallacies of thought he noticed in this age group. He calls the first the **imaginary audience**. This refers to the tendency of teenagers to feel they are constantly being observed by others, that people are always judging them on their appearance and behavior. Elkind believes this feeling of always being "onstage" is the source of much self-consciousness and showing off in adolescence. The strong role the imaginary audience plays in adolescent's lives explains why so many of them spend a good deal of time primping in front of the mirror.

The other fallacy of adolescent thinking identified by Elkind is the **personal fable**—an unrealistic sense of self-importance that makes adolescents think they are unique and so important that nothing bad can ever happen to them. This feeling of invulnerability explains much of the reckless risk taking among people in this age group. It leads some adolescents to make mistakes that will affect the entire course of their lives (Arnett, 1991). The personal fable is one reason why so many adolescents who have accurate birth control information ignore it on the grounds that pregnancy "can't happen to me."

## Personality and Social Development

Adolescence is a time of transition on almost every level of personality and every dimension of social growth and development. Adolescents are eager to establish their independence from their parents, but at the same time they fear the responsibilities of adulthood. They have many important tasks ahead of them and many important decisions to make. Particularly in a technologically advanced society like ours, this period of development is bound to involve some stress. But not all psychologists see adolescence as an exceptionally stressful time of life.

**THE "STORM AND STRESS" VIEW OF ADOLESCENCE** In the early part of this century, adolescence was seen by many psychologists as a stage of life characterized by instability and strong emotions. For example, G. Stanley Hall (1904), one of the first developmental psychologists, called adolescence a period of "storm and stress," portraying it as fraught with suffering, passion, and rebellion against adult authority. Opponents of this view, including the famous anthropologist Margaret Mead (1928), saw adolescence as a time of casual relationships and easy transition from childhood to adulthood.

*True or false:* Most psychologists consider adolescence to be an exceptionally stressful time of life.

Although the controversy between these two opposing viewpoints still rages, recent research suggests that the "storm and stress" description is inaccurate for most adolescents. True, adolescence is accompanied by some stress related to school, family, and peers, and this stress can be difficult to manage at times. For example, one survey of more than 4,000 eleventh-graders in the United States, Taiwan, and Japan showed that American and Taiwanese students considered school a source of stress, while Japanese students were less likely to feel so. U.S. teenagers also mentioned sports and part-time jobs as sources of stress (Crystal et al., 1994). Still, the great majority of adolescents do not describe their lives as rent by turmoil and chaos (J. Eccles et al., 1993). Most adolescents, particularly those whose development has pro-

**Identity formation** Erikson's term for the development of a stable sense of self necessary to make the transition from dependence on others to dependence on oneself.

**Identity crisis** Period of intense self-examination and decision making; part of the process of identity formation.

**Peer group** A network of same-aged friends and acquaintances who give one another emotional and social support.

ceeded smoothly up to this point in the life cycle, manage to keep stress in check and experience little disruption in their everyday lives (Bronfenbrenner, 1986; Offer & Offer, 1975). Nonetheless, some individuals find adolescence very difficult. Research data show that between 15 and 30 percent of adolescents drop out of high school, that teenagers have the highest arrest record of any age group, and that many adolescents regularly abuse drugs (Office of Educational Research and Improvement, 1988). Those whose prior development has been stressful are likely to experience a stressful adolescence. Moreover, some adolescents suffer from serious emotional or behavioral problems, and others live in environments so harsh or chaotic that they must struggle for their very survival.

**FORMING AN IDENTITY** To make the transition from dependence on parents to dependence on oneself, the adolescent must develop a stable sense of self. This process is called **identity formation** (Erikson, 1968). Adolescents discover that some of the behaviors and beliefs they grew up with—acquired from their family, friends, or ethnic group—no longer seem to fit them. The overwhelming question becomes "Who am I?"

James Marcia (1980) believes that to find a satisfactory answer to this question, young people must go through an intense period of self-exploration and decision making called an **identity crisis**. He identified four possible statuses for adolescents attempting to achieve a stable sense of identity.

Those in *identity achievement status* have passed through the identity crisis and succeeded in making personal choices about what they believe and what goals they should pursue. They are comfortable with their decisions and confident that their values and actions meet with the approval of others.

Adolescents in *foreclosure status* have prematurely settled on an identity provided for them by others. They have made the decision to become what those others want them to be without ever going through an identity crisis.

Adolescents in what Marcia calls *moratorium status* are in the midst of an identity crisis, and while it is ongoing, they put off making important decisions. In the meantime, they explore various alternatives and choices.

Finally, some adolescents avoid the issue altogether by remaining in *identity diffusion status*. They are dissatisfied with their present condition, but unable to develop a new identity that feels right to them. These young people who can't seem to "find themselves" may resort to escapist activities such as drug or alcohol abuse in a futile attempt to quell their anxieties (G.R. Adams & Gullota, 1983).

**GAY AND LESBIAN ADOLESCENTS** By some estimates (Desiher, 1993), as many as 10 percent of adolescents identify themselves as gay and lesbian, compared to 7 percent of all males and females (Hunt, 1974). For these adolescents, the problems associated with establishing an identity are magnified. Not only must they cope with the usual dramatic changes in physical, social, and cognitive development, but they must also wrestle with the dilemma of whether to hide or express their attraction to the same sex. Such difficulties can have a profound impact on their behavior. For example, a disproportionate number of adolescents who commit suicide are gay or lesbian (30 percent), and suicide attempts are two to three times higher for gay and lesbian youths than for other adolescents (Herdt & Boxer, 1993). Furthermore, gay and lesbian adolescents are at high risk for being victimized by their peers (Gentry & Eron, 1993).

**RELATIONSHIPS WITH PEERS** For most adolescents, the **peer group** of agemates provides a network of social and emotional support, while at the same time making it possible for them to become autonomous and to experiment with different roles and values. By choosing to associate with a particular group of friends, adolescents define themselves and create their own social style (P.R. Newman, 1982). Young teenagers feel an almost desperate need for their friends to approve of their choices, views, and behavior. The result is often a rigid conformity to peer and friendship group values that peaks around the ninth grade (Perry, 1990).

**Clique** Group of adolescents with similar interests and strong mutual attachment.

The nature of friendship changes significantly during the adolescent years. Friendship groups in early adolescence tend to be small unisex groups, called **cliques**, of three to nine members. While cliques provide adolescents with the intimacy they crave, they also exert significant control over their lives (McLellan, Haynie, & Strauss, 1993). One study found that the same-sex preference shown by most early adolescents stems from a liking for same-sex peers rather than a dislike of other-sex peers (Bukowski, Gauze, Hoza, & Newcomb, 1993). Thus, for the adolescent girl, it's not "I don't like boys," but rather "I like girls."

*Peer groups* help adolescents develop identities apart from family influences; cliques are small friendship groups that provide closeness but can exert significant control over adolescents' lives.

In midadolescence, unisex cliques generally break down and are replaced by mixed-sex groups. And these are usually replaced, in turn, by groups consisting of couples. At first, adolescents tend to have short-term heterosexual relationships within the group that fulfill short-term needs without exacting the commitment of "going steady" (Sorensen, 1973). Such relationships do not demand love and can dissolve overnight. But between the ages of 16 and 19, most adolescents settle into more stable dating patterns. No longer group oriented, and more confident of their sexual maturity, they begin to gain competence at longer-term relationships. Some even decide to get married while still in their teens. But these early marriages have a very high failure rate compared with marriages between people in their 20s or 30s (Cavanaugh, 1990).

**RELATIONSHIPS WITH PARENTS** Because most adolescents have not yet achieved a stable sense of identity or developed an independent lifestyle, they are badly in need of stability and structure in their lives. And because they are often unable to think through the long-term consequences of their actions, they require guidance and discipline. Thus, in order to cope effectively with the challenges they are likely to encounter, adolescents need involved, caring parents.

Being the parent of an adolescent is far from easy. Young children believe their parents know everything and are powerful and good, but adolescents are all too aware of their parents' faults and weaknesses. In their struggle for independence, they question everything and test every rule. It takes many years for adolescents to see their mothers and fathers as real people with their own needs and strengths as well as weaknesses (Smollar & Youniss, 1989). In fact, many people find themselves thinking in young adulthood that their parents have gotten a lot smarter in the last 7 or 8 years!

The low point of parent-child relationships generally occurs in early adolescence, when the physical changes of puberty are occurring. Then the

**"Are parents responsible for the way their children turn out?"**

Who or what is responsible for the person each of us becomes? In this chapter, we described the roles of peers, media, and teachers, as well as parents, in how children turn out. None of these interactions, we emphasized, is one-way: The child is always an active participant. We can see this especially in parent-child interchanges. Because every child is unique, parents behave differently toward each of their children. For example, authoritative parents may rely mainly on reasoning with a quiet, introspective son but insist that a rebellious daughter obey their commands. But even if these parents managed to treat their two children identically, the children would not respond identically.

Recently, a 25-year-old man sued his parents for $350,000 in damages, alleging that they reared him so poorly he would need therapy for the rest of his life. Do you think parents should be considered basically responsible for how their children turn out? Why or why not? If so, what would you accept as evidence of "parental malpractice"? After you have thought about these questions, take a few minutes to examine the opinions of some of your fellow students.

•••••••

**LEE: Parental malpractice would consist of things like child abuse and severe and intentional mistreatment. "Parent" isn't a professional occupation. [The plaintiff] ought to be bright enough to realize that his parents were nothing more than inexperienced amateurs (even if he had previous brothers or sisters). He has or had no reason to expect expert parenting from people who were not trained or educated to be expert parents.**

**AMY: If he [the plaintiff] went to college, lived on his own, had friends, then I don't see how he could blame the misfortunes of his life entirely on his parents. If parents refused to send their child to school or wouldn't let him have any friends, that would probably be abuse.**

**BOB: I think that blaming only our parents for all of our problems is like blaming the president for the bad economy. There are many factors involved in a person's development.**

**LISA: You could be the most loving, attentive parent in the world and your child may still turn out to be a mass murderer.**

**GREG: In this society where the individual is so highly stressed and there is a strong-sense of self-empowerment, I don't think that [the plaintiff] has much of a chance and his legal action against his parents would be taken as a mere cop-out.**

**PAT: My view is that parents have the potential to completely shape their children. They are not necessarily to blame for their children's problems or, on the other end of the spectrum, stability, but if they choose to be, they can be. In other words, parents can control their child's behavior, even when the child is exposed to outside forces. By developing a strong support system in the home, by communicating with their children clearly, parents can be the dominant influence in a child's life. If they don't do this, the child is at the mercy of uncertain outside influences and the parents are indirectly responsible for any shortcomings the child might develop because of the untamed outside world.**

**LESLIE: I agree with Pat about the amount of influence that parents can and do have on their children. I don't think that children can just realize it and walk away if there's a problem. They are dependent on their parents financially and also in a way which is different than anyone else they knew. . . . Anyway, if I were the judge, I'd definitely need proof of out-of-the-ordinary treatment, which can be considered either physical or psychological abuse.**

**MARIA: What about hereditary factors?. . . then again, I suppose someone could then sue their parents for giving them those genes in the first place.**

**LISA: There are many other factors that influence a child's development other than the parents, like peers, teachers, other authority figures, culture, and their own personality.**

**AMY: It seems like [the plaintiff] can't take responsibility for his own actions. If his life isn't going the way he wants, then it can't be anything he did, so it must be his parents' fault.**

•••••••

Have you changed your own views after reading these students' views? If so, how? Are parents primarily responsible for their children's problems? Why or why not? At what point in life does personal responsibility for one's problems start? What role, if any, can psychology play in addressing social/legal issues of this sort?

warmth of the parent-child relationship ebbs and conflict rises. Some researchers note that warm and caring relationships with adults outside the home, such as those at school or at a supervised community center, are valuable to adolescents during this period (J. Eccles et al., 1993). However, conflicts with parents tend to be over minor things and are usually not intense. Only in a small minority of families does the relationship between parents and children show a marked deterioration in adolescence (Paikoff & Brooks-Gunn, 1991).

## Problems of Adolescence

Adolescence is a time of experimentation, whether it be with sex, alcohol and drugs, hair color, or various kinds of rule breaking. Delinquent acts such as shoplifting and writing graffiti are relatively common during this period, but minor problems can become major ones. For reasons we still do not understand, psychiatric disorders such as schizophrenia and depression often first appear during adolescence. Moreover, many problems of adolescence such as depression, substance abuse, and eating disorders tend to occur together. In this section, we will examine three representative problems of adolescence: loss of self-esteem (particularly among females), depression and suicide, and eating disorders.

Minor acts of delinquency are relatively common during adolescence.

**SELF-ESTEEM** A 1988 study released by the American Association of University Women (AAUW) reported the disturbing finding that girls experience a sharp drop in self-esteem during adolescence. To a large extent, girls felt this way because they were ignored by teachers, believed they were not being given an equal chance at intellectual challenges, and found it hard to compete in the classroom with their more assertive male classmates. Boys' self-esteem drops too during adolescence, but not nearly as much. The result is that by midadolescence, the average boy has a much better opinion of himself than the average girl. For example, 46 percent of high school boys say they feel "happy the way I am" versus only 29 percent of high school girls (Daley, 1991).

More recent evidence has contributed to our understanding of these gender differences in self-esteem (J. Block & Robbins, 1993). In one study, the same group of young people completed a self-esteem test at 14, 18, and 23 years of age. The findings were only partially consistent with those of the AAUW study. From ages 14 to 23, one-fifth of the boys displayed a substantial loss of self-esteem, while one-third reported a gain. Overall, then, this study, unlike the AAUW report, found an increase in average self-esteem among boys. In contrast, fully half the girls cited a decline in self-esteem, and only one-fifth reported an increase: This represents a significant decrease in female self-esteem between early adolescence and adulthood, which is consistent with the AAUW findings.

Other studies have raised questions about the AAUW findings. For example, the AAUW study surveyed only 3,000 children. In contrast, a longitudinal study of 25,000 adolescents by the U.S. Department of Education found that more girls than boys feel the teacher is interested in them; moreover by the tenth grade, 72 percent of girls compared with 68 percent of boys said that teachers listen to what they have to say (Sommers, 1994). Given the contradictory nature of these different findings, we obviously need more research on the question of self-esteem among adolescents before we can form any firm conclusion.

**DEPRESSION AND SUICIDE** The rate of suicide among adolescents has increased more than 600 percent since 1950. Suicide is now the third leading cause of death among adolescents, after accidents and homicides (Blumenthal, 1990). According to one survey, 27 percent of high school students had thought seriously about suicide. A smaller proportion (16 percent) had made a specific plan for killing themselves, and a still smaller percentage (8 percent) had actually attempted suicide. One quarter of the attempts were serious enough to require medical attention. Although successful suicide is more common in males than in females, more females attempt suicide (Centers for Disease Control, 1991a).

The considerable research done on adolescents who tried to commit suicide make it clear that suicidal behavior (including thinking about suicide as well as actually attempting it) is not an isolated phenomenon. Rather, it is often linked to other psychological problems, such as depression, substance abuse, and disruptive behaviors (see Table 8-2) (Andrews & Lewinson, 1992). For example, one study of more than 1,700 adolescents revealed that a set of related factors put an adolescent at risk for attempting suicide. Among these are being female, thinking about suicide, mental disorders (such as depression), poor education of the father, and the absence of the father from the home. Again, it's important to remember that these factors are *not* causal and the presence of one or more of them does not mean that a child will attempt suicide. The presence of these factors does, however, make a suicide attempt *more likely.*

The complex intertwining of factors that predispose an adolescent to think about or attempt suicide make it difficult to know which troubled adolescents are at high risk. For example, we know that depression in and of itself rarely leads to suicidal behavior: Data indicate that 3 percent of adolescents at any one time suffer severe depression, but the suicide rate among adolescents is only .01 percent (Connelly, Johnston, Brown, Mackay, & Blackstock, 1993). It seems the combination of depression and other factors, such as those cited in the paragraph above, makes suicide more likely, but exactly which factors are most important and what kind of intervention might reduce adolescent suicides are still unclear.

**7.** What is anorexia nervosa? How prevalent is it? What are its causes? Can it be treated?

**EATING DISORDERS** "When people told me I looked like someone from Auschwitz [the Nazi concentration camp], I thought that was the highest compliment anyone could give me." This is from the confession of a young woman who as a teenager suffered from a serious eating disorder

**TABLE 8-2 Mental Disorders Among People Who Attempt Suicide**

| | MALES | | FEMALES | |
|---|---|---|---|---|
| **DISORDER** | **% of Attempters** | **% of Nonattempters** | **% of Attempters** | **% of Nonattempters** |
| Major depression | 65 | 10 | 56 | 21 |
| Alcohol abuse | 20 | 4 | 14 | 4 |
| Drug abuse | 29 | 6 | 14 | 5 |
| Disruptive behaviors | 32 | 9 | 12 | 4 |
| Adjustment disorder | 6 | 5 | 10 | 4 |
| Anxiety disorder | 10 | 6 | 19 | 4 |

*Source:* Adapted from "Suicidal attempts among older adolescents: Prevalence and co-occurence with psychiatric disorders" by J.A. Andrews and P.M. Lewinsohn, 1992, *Journal of the American Academy of Child and Adolescent Psychiatry, 31,* pp. 655-662.

known as **anorexia nervosa**. She was 18 years old, 5 feet 3 inches tall, and weighed 68 pounds. This young woman was lucky. She managed to overcome the disorder and has since maintained normal body weight. Others are less fortunate. In 1983, the singer Karen Carpenter died of cardiac arrest following a long battle with anorexia. More recently, the world-class gymnast Christy Henrich succumbed to the disease, weighing just 61 pounds at her death (Pace, 1994).

**Anorexia nervosa** A serious eating disorder that is associated with an intense fear of weight gain and a distorted body image.

**Bulimia** An eating disorder characterized by binges of eating followed by self-induced vomiting.

People with anorexia nervosa perceive themselves as overweight and strive to lose weight, usually by severely limiting their intake of food. Even after they become very thin, they constantly worry about weight gain. The American Psychiatric Association's *Diagnostic and Statistical Manual of Mental Disorders (DSM–IV)* lists four symptoms of anorexia nervosa (APA, 1994):

1. Intense fear of becoming obese, which does not diminish as weight loss progresses.
2. Disturbance of body image (for example, claiming to "feel fat" even when emaciated).
3. Refusal to maintain body weight at or above a minimal normal weight for age and height.
4. In females, the absence of at least three consecutive menstrual cycles.

Approximately 1 percent of all adolescents suffer from anorexia nervosa; about 90 percent of these are white upper- or middle-class females (Brumberg, 1988; E.H. Gilbert & DeBlassie, 1984; Romeo, 1984). Before the development of more successful treatment methods in recent years, perhaps as many as 6 percent of people with anorexia died from the disorder (Agras & Kraemer, 1983). Generally, people suffering from anorexia enjoy an otherwise normal childhood and adolescence. They are usually successful students and cooperative, well-behaved children. They have an intense interest in food but view eating with disgust. They also have a very distorted view of their own body.

Anorexia is frequently compounded by another eating disorder known as **bulimia**. The *DSM–IV* lists the following diagnostic criteria for bulimia (APA, 1994):

1. Recurrent episodes of binge eating (rapid consumption of a large amount of food in a discrete period of time, usually less than 2 hours).
2. Recurrent inappropriate behaviors to try to prevent weight gain, such as self-induced vomiting.
3. The binge eating and compensatory behaviors must occur at least twice a week for 3 months.
4. The person's self-image is excessively influenced by body shape and weight.
5. These behaviors do not occur only during episodes of anorexia.

This photo of gymnast Christy Henrich was taken about a year before her death in June 1994. Henrich suffered from the eating disorder known as *anorexia nervosa*.

It is estimated that 4 to 8 percent of all adolescent females and up to 2 percent of adolescent males suffer from bulimia (Gwirtsman, 1984; Heatherton & Baumeister, 1991; C. Johnson et al., 1984).

The binge-eating behavior usually begins at about age 18, when adolescents are facing the challenge of new life situations. Not surprisingly, residence on a college campus is associated with a higher incidence of bulimia (S. Squire, 1983). This is partly due to the fact that the socioeconomic group at high risk for bulimia—again, primarily upper-middle- and upper-class women—is highly represented on college campuses. College campuses also foster social as well as academic competition; there is some evidence that bulimia is more prevalent on campuses where dating is emphasized than on those where it is not (Rodin, Striegel-Moore, & Silberstein, 1985).

Although anorexia and bulimia are apparently much more prevalent among females than males, newer evidence suggests that many more men are affected by these disorders than was once suspected (A.E. Anderson, 1990; Gwirtsman, 1984). For example, in a 1992 survey of people who had graduated from Harvard University in 1982, reported cases of eating disorders had dropped by half for women, over the decade but had doubled for men (J. Seligman, Rogers, & Annin, 1994). The higher numbers for men did not indicate that eating disorders have become more prevalent among males since 1982, but rather that they were more likely to be diagnosed or reported in the 1990s than in the 1980s. One reason for the underreporting of eating disorders in males is that men are generally more reluctant than women to seek help for their problems. Moreover, physicians are less likely to diagnose eating disorders in their male patients because men often characterize their weight loss as an attempt to improve their athletic performance, to meet occupational weight requirements, or to make themselves more attractive to women (A.E. Anderson, 1990). In addition, men don't exhibit some of the obvious symptoms that women do, particularly amenorrhea (the absence of menstrual cycles). Moreover, many men with eating disorders start out overweight, so their weight loss brings them closer to their ideal weight and does not, on the surface, represent a significant medical problem. In contrast, many women with eating disorders start out below their ideal weight and become seriously underweight as a result of their disorder.

Since attempts to understand the causes of eating disorders have focused almost entirely on females, we know very little about what might predispose an adolescent male to develop such a disorder. Among adolescent women, several factors appear to contribute to the likelihood of eating disorders (Brooks-Gunn, 1993). The media promote the idea that a woman must be thin to be attractive. Rarely do fashion magazine covers feature a well-proportioned woman of normal weight for her height. Interestingly, an analysis of height-to-weight ratios of *Playboy* centerfolds and Miss America pageant contestants shows that the trend toward taller and thinner models of feminine beauty parallels the rise of eating disorders in the population at large (Agras, 1987). Perhaps because of the media emphasis on weight, American women are prone to overestimate their body size (H. Bruch, 1980; Fallon & Rozin, 1985). Thompson and his colleagues (1986) found that over 95 percent of their female subjects believed they were about one-fourth larger than they actually were in the waist, thighs, and hips.

Psychological factors also contribute to the risk of eating disorders. The general portrait of the adolescent with an eating disorder (again, based mostly on women) is of an individual with an obsessive-compulsive disorder (see the chapter on abnormal psychology) who feels personally ineffective and depends on others (Phelps & Bajorek, 1991). Feelings of vulnerability and helplessness apparently dispose people to adopt inappropriate ways of controlling the world around them.

Eating disorders are notoriously hard to treat, and there is considerable disagreement on the most effective approach to therapy (Garfinkel & Garner, 1982). Obviously, the first step in cases of anorexia is to get the victim to gain weight, because the disorder can be life-threatening. Cognitive-behavior modification therapy (see the chapter on therapies) has been successful in increasing food intake and somewhat successful in treating physical stress (Telch et al., 1990) in cases of anorexia. Some forms of cognitive-behavior therapy have also helped people with bulimia, especially when coupled with techniques to prevent vomiting. Treatments that ask the subject to eat in the presence of an observer help make people with bulimia more aware of their behavior (C.P. Herman, Polivy, & Silver, 1979). Other attempts to make subjects more aware include requiring them to count candy wrappers after binge eating (Polivy et al., 1983). Some psychologists admit, however, that the prognosis for eating disorders is not optimistic in a culture bombarded with the message that "thin is in," reinforced by numerous self-help diet plans.

## ADULTHOOD

Compared to adolescent development, development during adulthood is much less predictable, much more a function of the individual's decisions, circumstances, and even luck. In adulthood, unlike in childhood and adolescence, developmental milestones do not occur at a particular age, although there are certain experiences and changes that take place sooner or later in nearly everyone's life and certain needs that nearly every adult tries to fulfill.

### Love, Partnerships, and Parenting

Nearly all adults form a long-term, loving partnership with another adult at some point in their lives. This may happen after graduation from college, during middle age, or even in later adulthood. According to Erikson, a person is not ready to form such an intimate bond until he or she has developed a firm sense of identity. Erikson (1963) defined the word *intimacy* as a person's "capacity to commit himself" to a partnership. Thus, according to Erikson, young people are not capable of truly loving another person until they have answered the "Who am I?" question.

Carol Gilligan (1982) doesn't agree that a sense of identity is a prerequisite for forming a loving relationship. Moreover, she argues that the path to love is different for males and females. Gilligan believes that young men tend to find intimacy and commitment frightening. Before they can take such risks, they must first develop a sense of identity as separate individuals. Young women, on the other hand, fear most the isolation that accompanies the absence of intimate relationships. Because they are more concerned about forming connections to other people and less worried about defining themselves as separate individuals, they need not follow Erikson's rule of "identity before intimacy."

Gilligan implies that it is all right for a young woman to seek love before she has a clear sense of her own identity. There is some evidence that argues against this view, however. Marriages between teenagers, for instance, are more likely to end in divorce than marriages between those in their 20s and 30s (Cavanaugh, 1990). Plausibly, early marriages fail so often because very young people do not know enough about themselves to make a sensible decision about what kind of person they ought to marry. On the other hand, teenage couples are also more likely than older couples to face financial troubles, parental disapproval, clashing goals and aspirations, and these problems rather than identity problems may be responsible for the relatively high divorce figures.

**FORMING PARTNERSHIPS** More than 90 percent of Americans eventually get married (Doherty & Jacobson, 1982), but those who marry are waiting longer to do so. In 1970, only 15 percent of men and women aged 25 to 29 had never married; by 1988, the percentage had increased to

36 percent (U.S. Bureau of the Census, 1990). Moreover, increasing numbers of adults are involved in long-term, intimate partnerships without marriage, and still others choose to live alone but to maintain meaningful relationships with other people. While heterosexual marriage is still the statistical norm, other types of partnerships and relationships are increasingly meeting the needs of different types of adults. Unfortunately, because relatively little research has been done on these nonmarital partnerships and relationships, much of our knowledge of intimate and loving relationships is based solely on studies of married couples.

The decision about whom to marry is not a random one. Research indicates that most people marry someone of similar race, religion, education, and background (Gagnon, Laumanm, Michael, & Kolata, 1994). That is because people with similar characteristics and backgrounds are more likely to meet, and once they meet, they are more likely to discover shared interests and compatibility (Murstein, 1986). Not surprisingly, choice of a partner for cohabitation (living together) seems to proceed in much the same way. Often there is a spoken or unspoken assumption among couples that "if things work out, then we'll marry." Interestingly, couples who live together before marriage are generally less satisfied with their marriages and more likely to divorce later than couples who married without first living together (DeMaris & Rao, 1992).

Most people marry someone of similar race, religion, education, and background.

Marriage is one of several important determinants of overall life satisfaction, but research suggests that forming and maintaining any kind of close relationships is important to living a long and happy life. In one 6-year study of men aged 24 to 60, those who had good social support networks outlived those who lacked such support (W.S. Kaplan & Novorr, 1994). People who didn't join social organizations were twice as likely to die during the same period as those who did join such groups. And those men who were dissatisfied with the quality of their interpersonal relationships were twice as likely to die as those who were satisfied with their relationships.

**PARENTHOOD** In an intimate partnership such as marriage, the birth of children signals a major turning point. As children grow, most parents experience a sense of achievement and pride. And for most parents, loving and being loved by one's children is an unparalleled source of fulfillment. However, the birth of the first child requires many adjustments by the parents. Friendship and romance give way to a more serious relationship in which duty often takes precedence over pleasure. Young children demand a lot of time and energy, which may leave parents with little time or energy for each other. Inexperienced parents in particular may feel inadequate and worry about the fact that they sometimes have mixed emotions about their baby.

Parenthood may also heighten conflicts between the parents' pursuit of careers and their responsibilities at home. This is especially likely to be a problem for a woman who has had an active career outside the home. She may suddenly be thrown into conflict, feeling frustrated if she abandons her career, and anxious or guilty if she continues to work. This

## HIGHLIGHTS

### Adult Sexual Behavior

Here's the news that everyone's been waiting for. Until recently, the only comprehensive studies done on the sexual behavior of adults were the Kinsey Report, completed back in 1948, and the work of Masters and Johnson in the 1960s. Although both studies were carried out on a generally nonrandom and therefore unrepresentative sample of all adults, their results have been used for years to form conclusions about adult sexual behavior. They have also been used to formulate public policies concerning AIDS and other sexually transmitted diseases.

Now we have a report (Gagnon, et al., 1994) based on 3,432 *randomly selected* men and women, aged 18 to 59, who were interviewed at length about their sexual behaviors. Some of the results obtained from this more representative study are surprising. For example, contrary to the popular view that extramarital affairs and casual sex are the norm in contemporary America, 85 percent of the married women and 74 percent of the married men reported being faithful to their spouses. Moreover, married people reported having sex more often than their single counterparts, with 41 percent of all married couples saying they had sex at least once a week. Unmarried couples who lived together had sex most often; 56 percent of such respondents reported having sex twice a week or more.

Some other important findings from this study:

- More than half of the men interviewed said they thought about sex at least once a day, compared with only 19 percent of the women.
- More than 80 percent of the sample said they had had only one sexual partner over the last year.
- Among marriage partners, 93 percent are of the same race, 82 percent are of the same educational level, and 72 percent share the same religion.

conflict between outside employment and home responsibilities is added to the usual worries about being an adequate spouse and parent (Warr & Perry, 1982). Thus, it is no wonder that women feel the need for their partner's cooperation more strongly during this period of life than men do (Belsky, Lang, & Rovine, 1985). And while today's fathers spend more time with their children than *their* fathers did, mothers still bear the greater responsibility for both child rearing and housework. For all these reasons, a woman's marital satisfaction is likely to decline sharply after her first child is born (Ruble et al., 1988).

Parenthood is a source of fulfillment and pride, but it requires major adjustments by both partners.

Once children leave the home, however, many parents experience renewed marital satisfaction. Research shows that rather than lamenting over their "empty nests," most women breathe a sigh of relief (Rovner, 1990) when the last child leaves home. For the first time in years, the husband and wife can be alone together and enjoy one another's company. In a study of older couples, more than 50 percent said that their marriage had improved with time, and most of those polled felt that the later years of their marriage were the best of all (Stinnett, Carter, & Montgomery, 1972).

**Ending a Relationship** Intimate relationships frequently break up. Although this is true for all types of couples—married and unmarried, heterosexual and homosexual—most of the research on ending relationships has focused on divorced couples. The bad news is that almost half of today's marriages will eventually end in divorce. The good news is that the divorce rate has apparently stabilized after rising for several decades (Darnton, 1992).

Rarely is the decision to separate a mutual one. Most often, one partner takes the initiative in ending the relationship after a long period of slowly increasing unhappiness. Making the decision does not necessarily bring relief. More often, in the short term, it brings turmoil, animosity, and apprehension. However, in the longer term, most divorced adults report that the divorce was a positive step that eventually resulted in greater personal contentment and healthier psychological functioning, although a substantial minority seem to suffer permanent negative effects (Kelly, 1982).

Divorce can have serious and far-reaching implications for children as well. Although thousands of studies have been conducted on the effects of divorce on children, so many factors are involved (such as the age and sex of the child, the family's socioeconomic status, and the degree of parental conflict before, during, and after the divorce) that it's difficult to draw any general conclusions. Perhaps the most that can be said is that in many cases divorce has profound effects on children's school performance, self-esteem, gender-role development, and attitudes toward marriage (Barber & Eccles, 1992). One study found that people whose parents divorced are *not* any more likely to divorce than other couples, but they are more likely to be anxious about their marriages (Vaughn, 1993). Other studies have found that children adapt more successfully to divorce when they have good support systems, when the divorcing parents maintain a good relationship, and when sufficient financial resources are made available to the children (P.A. Miller, Kliewer, & Burkeman, 1993; Salkind, 1983).

## The World of Work

Three or four generations ago, choosing a career was not an issue for most young adults. Men followed in their fathers' footsteps or took whatever apprenticeships were available in their communities. Women were occupied in child care, housework, and helping with the family farm or business, or they pursued such "female" careers as secretarial work, nursing, and teaching. Today career choices are far more numerous for both men and women. In 1990, for example, women were 25 percent of full-time employed physicians, 27 percent of lawyers, and 30 percent of college professors. All told, women accounted for about 39 percent of the labor force (L.A. Gilbert, 1994). However, on average, women get paid 30 percent less than men for doing the same job. Moreover, many women experience discrimination or sexual harassment at work. And women typically have fewer opportunities to change jobs or receive a promotion, two ways by which men tend to get out of an unsatisfactory job (Aranya, Kushnir, & Valency, 1986).

**The Effects of Work** Studies of job satisfaction indicate that the vast majority of workers are moderately or highly satisfied with their jobs and would continue to work even if they didn't have to, because work gives meaning to their lives. Jobs also provide economic independence and self-esteem. In addition, people in all occupational groups say they value the relationships they form with their colleagues at work. For these and other reasons, men and women who are employed are healthier than those who are not employed.

Losing a job is a terrible blow to a person's self-esteem, even if the job loss occurs as a result of company "downsizing" rather than because of inadequate performance. Although unemployment places the most stress on couples with young children, people over 45 are more likely to require psychiatric care as a result of long-term unemployment (Cavanaugh, 1990).

**Dual-career Families** Over the last 50 years, the number of married women who work outside the home has increased dramatically: 71 percent of married women with school-aged children and 60 percent of women with children under 6 now have jobs outside the home (L.A. Gilbert, 1994; Harris & Liebert, 1991). However, the two-paycheck family is not always a matter of choice. Rather, with increasingly unstable economic conditions and the rising costs of essentials such as health care and education, it is not unusual for both adults in a family to have to work simply to make ends meet.

Balancing the demands of career and family is a problem in many families, especially for women. Even when the wife has a full-time job outside the home, she is likely to end up doing far more than half of the housework and child care. She is also likely to be aware of this imbalance in responsibilities and to resent it (Benin & Agostinelli, 1988). The "double shift"—one at paid work outside the home and another at unpaid labor in the home—is the common experience of millions of women throughout the world (A. Mednick, 1993). True equality—the hopeful goal of the dual-career movement—has yet to be achieved (L.A. Gilbert, 1994).

Despite the stress associated with the "double shift," most women report increases in self-esteem when they are employed (Baruch & Barnett, 1986). In one recent study women in the fields of medicine, law, accounting, and engineering reported that the demands of running a home did not keep them from progressing professionally or from deriving satisfaction from their busy lives (J. Brody, 1992). The majority said they would continue to work even if they didn't need the money. Mothers who are employed are as healthy as those who are not, and they are less likely to suffer from depression.

**CHILDREN IN DUAL-CAREER FAMILIES** Most dual-career families must entrust their young children to the care of someone else for a sizable percentage of the children's waking hours. About 5 million American children under the age of 5 are now being cared for in day-care centers, preschools, or a relative's home (see Figure 8-6) (Hofferth, 1991). Is it a good idea to leave infants and very young children with substitute caregivers?

Some research shows clear benefits for the children of mothers who work, even if the children are still very young (Greenstein, 1993). For example, the children of employed mothers tend to be more independent and self-confident and to have less stereotyped views of males and females (Harris & Liebert, 1991). Nonetheless, some researchers are concerned that being entrusted to caregivers outside the immediate family may interfere with the development of secure attachments and put children at greater risk for emotional maladjustment (Barglow, Vaughn, & Molitor, 1987; Belsky & Rovine, 1988). Others disagree, maintaining that the risks have been exaggerated and that there may even be benefits for the children, such as the development of increased social skills (Clarke-Stewart, 1989; D.A. Phillips et al., 1987). According to Alison Clarke-Stewart, research has consistently shown that "infants of working mothers do form attachments to their mothers and prefer their mothers to their substitute caregivers" (1989, p. 266). She does concede that some studies have suggested that infants of mothers with full-time jobs outside the home are less securely attached to their mothers than are infants whose mothers either did not work outside the home or worked part-time. These conclusions are open to debate, however. In addition, Clarke-Stewart points out that on other measures of emotional adjustment, the children of working mothers do as well as other children and show no signs of being insecure.

Which is better for a child—being cared for at home or being cared for in a day-care center? The answer is that regardless of the setting, quality counts: Any secure, affectionate, stimulating environment is likely to

**Figure 8-6**
**Percentage of children in different child-care arrangements in the United States.**

*Source*: Adapted from Hofferth et al., 1990.

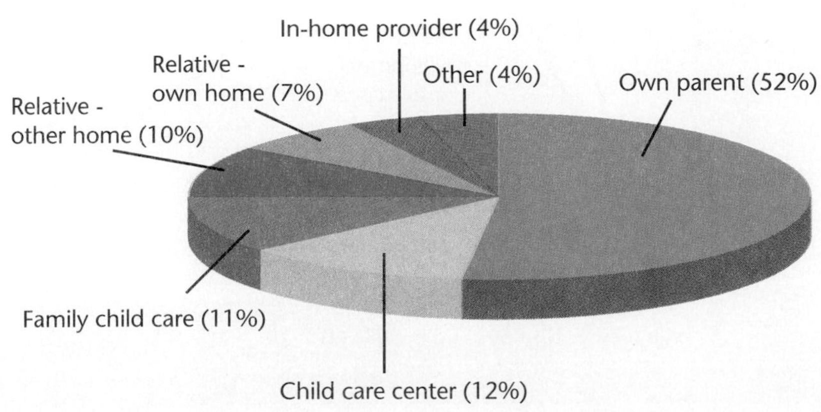

produce children who are healthy, outgoing, and ready to learn; any environment fraught with doubts and emotional and physical threats is likely to stunt development.

## Cognitive Changes

Earlier in the chapter, we noted that the last stage of Piaget's cognitive development model is formal operations. Piaget (1967) hinted that there might be further changes in styles of thinking during adulthood, but only recently have investigators begun to explore the ways in which an adult's thinking differs from that of an adolescent.

The development of the ability to think abstractly allows adolescents to test alternatives and to arrive at what they see as the "correct" solution to a problem. In adulthood, people gradually come to realize that there isn't a single correct solution to every problem—there may, in fact, be no correct solution, or there may be several. Adolescents rely on authorities to tell them what is "true," but adults realize that "truth" often varies according to the situation and one's point of view. Adults are also more practical: They know that a solution to a problem must be realistic as well as reasonable (Cavanaugh, 1990). No doubt these changes in adult thinking derive from greater experience of the world. Dealing with the kinds of complex problems that arise in adult life requires moving away from the literal, formal, and somewhat rigid thinking of adolescence and young adulthood (Labouvie-Vief, 1986).

Just as physical exercise is necessary for optimal physical development, so is mental exercise necessary for optimal cognitive development. Nancy Denney (1984) proposed a model of change in cognitive abilities over the life span that focuses on the importance of exercise, broadly defined as repeatedly practicing certain cognitive tasks such as memorizing words. Figure 8-7 illustrates her model. The upper curve represents optimal performance, or what people can achieve with regular exercise of their cognitive skills, while the lower curve represents performance without benefit of exercise. Notice that both curves begin to descend at about 20 to 30 years of age, reflecting the general decline in performance on cognitive tasks after young adulthood, but there is a significant gap between the curves throughout life. This gap represents the benefits of regular cognitive exercise. In one study (Schaie, 1994), for example, adults who received training in spatial orientation skills improved their performance by 40 percent. Thus, although some decline in cognitive skills is inevitable, as people age, the decline can be minimized with sufficient exercise.

**Figure 8-7**
**Denney's model of change in cognitive and physical abilities over time.**

*Source*: Adapted from "Model of cognitive development across the life span" by N. Denney, 1984. *Developmental Review, 4*, pp. 171–191.

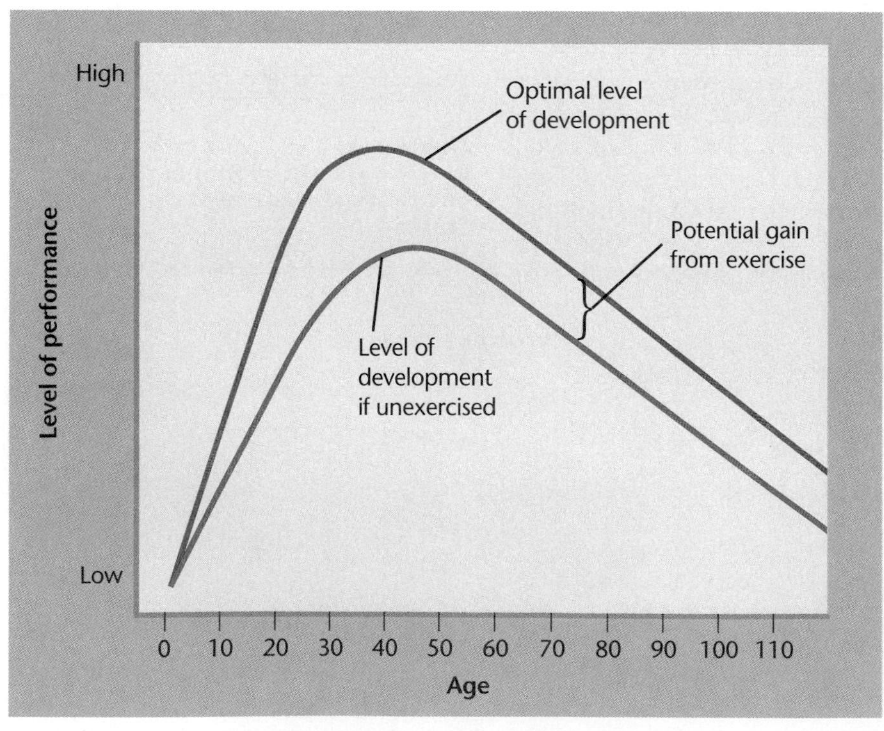


## Personality Changes

We have seen that major life events in adulthood require considerable adaptation. Do these events also lead to significant changes in personality? Relatively few studies have systematically examined the effects of specific life events on adult personality development, but the existing data suggest that both men and women become less self-centered and develop better coping skills with age (Neugarten, 1977). One longitudinal study found that people are more sympathetic, giving, productive, and dependable at 45 than they were at 20 (J. Block, 1971). Another found that people in their middle years feel an increasing commitment to and responsibility for others, develop new ways of adapting, and are more comfortable in interpersonal relationships (Vaillant, 1977).

Orderly changes in adaptive strategies and moral growth also occur throughout adult life (D.J. Levinson, 1978, 1986, 1987). Daniel Levinson described male adult personality development as a stepwise progression through three eras, each of which is initiated by a major transition: *early adulthood* (17 to 45), *middle adulthood* (40 to 65), and *late adulthood* (60 and older). (The overlap in ages signifies that not all adults go through these eras at exactly the same time.) Levinson's view of the tasks that males must master within each era appear in Table 8-3.

Sometimes middle-aged people who have achieved most or all of their goals discover that they are no longer satisfied in their personal lives or careers. Instead, they feel bored, fatigued, and trapped. This period

**TABLE 8-3 Levinson's Model of the Developmental Sequences of Adult Life**

| STAGE | TASK |
|---|---|
| Entering the adult world (22–28) | Resolution of the conflict between exploring available options and establishing a stable life structure—"I will keep my options open." |
| Age 30 . . . transition (28–33) | Tentative commitments and life goals reexamined and questioned—"Did I make the right choices?" |
| Settling down and becoming one's own man (33–40) | Achieving stability, security, and comfort—actively carving out niche in society—"I want to make my place in this world." |
| Midlife transition (40–45) | Assessment of accomplishments and evolvement of another life structure—"What is it I really want?" |
| Midlife (45–50) | Accepting one's fate—"What I have achieved is OK." |
| Age 50 . . . transition and midlife culmination (50–60) | Finding security and self-acceptance—"What I have become is OK." |
| Late adult transition (60+) | Achieving a satisfactory life outlook—"My life has been OK and will continue to be OK." |

*Source*: Adapted from *The Season's of a Man's Life* by Daniel L. Levinson, 1978. Copyright © 1978 by Daniel J. Levinson. Reprinted by permission of Sterling Lord Literistic, Inc., and Alfred A. Knopf. Inc.

**Midlife crisis** A time when adults discover they no longer feel fulfilled in their jobs or personal lives and attempt to make a decisive shift in career or lifestyle.

**Midlife transition** According to Levinson, a process whereby adults assess the past and formulate new goals for the future.

**Menopause** Time in a woman's life when menstruation ceases.

when success in one area of life leaves the individual feeling unfulfilled and ready for a decisive shift in career or lifestyle has been called the **midlife crisis**. Researchers have found, however, that the midlife crisis is not typical: Most people do not make dramatic changes in middle adulthood. In fact, many use this time to make renewed commitments to marriage, work, and family (B. M. Newman, 1982). Levinson preferred the term **midlife transition** for this period when adult males assess their accomplishments, determine whether they have been satisfying, formulate new goals, and evolve a revised structure for their future lives.

## The "Change of Life"

During middle age, there is a decline in the function of the reproductive organs. In women, the amount of estrogen (the principal female hormone) produced by the ovaries drops sharply at around age 45 (the exact age varies considerably from woman to woman). Breasts, genital tissues, and the uterus begin to shrink, and menstrual periods become irregular and then cease altogether at around age 50. The cessation of menstruation is called **menopause**.

The hormonal changes that accompany menopause often cause a characteristic pattern of physical symptoms, of which the most noticeable is "hot flashes." In some women, menopause also leads to a serious thinning of the bones, making them more vulnerable to fractures. Both of these symptoms can be prevented by estrogen replacement therapy (a pill or a skin patch that must be prescribed by a physician). Although this therapy may slightly increase a woman's risk for breast and uterine cancer (K.K. Steinberg et al., 1991), it appears to significantly *decrease* her risk for heart disease (Barrett-Connor & Bush, 1991). Some women are apprehensive about the "change of life," but others revel in their newfound freedom from fear of pregnancy.

Experts disagree about whether there is such a thing as a "male menopause." Men never experience as severe a drop in testosterone (the principal male hormone) as women do in estrogen. Instead, studies have found a more gradual decline—perhaps 30 to 40 percent—in testosterone in men between 48 and 70 (Angier, 1992). Some gerontologists (people who study the process of aging) see the "male menopause" as equivalent to the "midlife crisis" we discussed earlier. In any case, there is much disagreement about whether men should be treated, as menopausal women commonly are, with hormones. Some are concerned that hormone therapy could increase men's risk of prostate cancer and heart disease.

# LATE ADULTHOOD

Older adults constitute the fastest-growing and one of the most politically powerful segments of the U.S. population. In 1991, 17 percent of Americans were 60 or older; it is estimated that this proportion will climb to 25 percent by the year 2020 (U.S. Bureau of the Census, 1991). At present, 3.3 million Americans are over the age of 65; by the year 2080, there could be as many as 72 million Americans *over the age of* 85 (Kolata, 1992). This dramatic rise in the numbers of older adults stems from increases in life expectancy due primarily to better health care and nutrition (see Figure 8-8) (Downs, 1994).

Since older adults will become a more and more visible part of U.S. society over the next century or so, it is important to understand development in later adulthood. Unfortunately, our views of older adults are often heavily colored by myths. For example, many people believe that most older adults are lonely, poor, and troubled by ill health. Even doctors and other health professionals sometimes assume that it is *natural* for elderly patients to feel ill; as a result, physical, cognitive, or psychological symptoms that would indicate treatable disease in younger people are taken as the inevitable signs of decay and frequently go untreated. The false belief that "senility" is inevitable in old age is another damaging myth. A third is the belief that most older adults are helpless and dependent on their families for care and financial support. As you will see in the following pages, these inaccurate beliefs, cause unnecessary problems for older adults.

Late adulthood generally brings an accentuation of early- and middle-adulthood characteristics rather than an alteration of them. Nonetheless, the later years of life require the individual to change, develop, and adapt. All the research done on people in this stage of development points in one direction: Late adulthood is a successful time of life for people who learn to manage it and use it to the fullest.

## Physical Changes

Beginning in middle adulthood and continuing through late adulthood, physical appearance and the functioning of every organ change. But in contrast to the physical changes of adolescence, the changes of middle and late adulthood are only loosely controlled by a person's biological clock. The physical well-being of older adults is affected by many factors, some of which they can influence and some of which are beyond their control. The hair thins and turns white or gray. The skin wrinkles. Bones become fragile and more easily broken. Muscles lose power, and joints stiffen or wear out. Circulation slows, blood pressure rises, and because the lungs hold less oxygen, the older adult has less energy. The body shape and posture change, and the reproductive organs atrophy. Difficulties in falling asleep and staying asleep become more common, and reaction times are slower. Vision, hearing, and the sense of smell all become less acute (Cavanaugh, 1990; LaRue & Jarvik, 1982). Most people are at first unaware of these changes, because they occur gradually and there is plenty of time to develop strategies for coping with them. But the decline eventually becomes undeniable.

**Figure 8-8**
**Life expectancy for males and females, 1900–1990.**

*Source:* Adapted from H. Downs, 1994. Copyright © 1994 by *Parade*. Reprinted by permission.

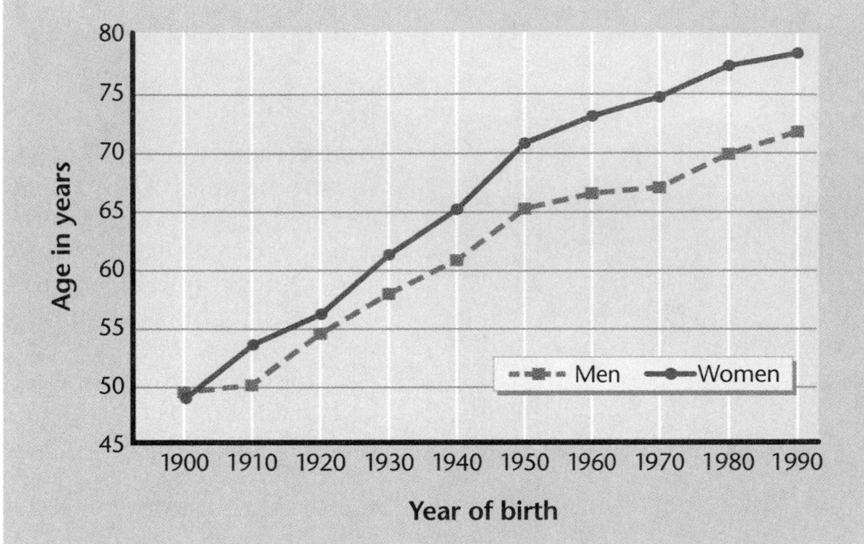


The inevitable physical changes of late adulthood need not be incapacitating. The important thing is how the individual *responds* to these changes. Research shows that people who have a continuing sense of usefulness, who maintain old ties, investigate new ideas, and take up new activities, and who feel in control of their lives have the lowest rates of disease and the highest survival rates (Butler & Lewis, 1982; Caspi & Elder, 1986). So there's a good deal of truth in the saying "You're only as old as you feel." In fact, psychologists are starting to use *functional* or *psychological age*, rather than *chronological age*, to predict an older adult's responses to life's demands.

Late adulthood can be a successful and productive time of life. Pianist Eubie Blake, for example, continued to perform well into his 90s.

## Social Development

Opposed to the stereotype of the elderly as weak and dependent is the fact that most men and women over 65 live independently and maintain a satisfactory lifestyle. In a survey of people 65 years and older done in 1975, more than half the respondents reported being just as happy as they were when younger. Three-quarters said they were involved in activities that were as interesting to them as any they had engaged in in their younger years (Birren, 1983). Political interest certainly does not decline with age: Almost 90 percent of older adults are registered to vote, and two-thirds vote regularly—the greatest percentage turnout of any age group. The American Association of Retired People (AARP) has more than 8 million active members and uses its political force to ensure that entitlement programs for older adults, like Social Security, are maintained (Butler & Lewis, 1982).

Still, gradual social changes do take place in late adulthood. Cumming and Henry (1961) have described these changes as a process of "disengagement" that occurs in three stages. The first stage is *shrinkage of life space*: Individuals interact with fewer people and perform fewer social roles. The second stage is *increased individuality*: Behavior is less influenced by social rules and expectations than it was earlier in life. The third and final stage involves *acceptance of the changes in the first two stages*: Individuals step back and assess their lives, realize there is a limit to their capacity for social involvement, and learn to live comfortably with those restrictions.

## Retirement

Another major change that most people experience in later adulthood is leaving the world of paid employment. People's reactions to retirement differ greatly, partly because society has no clear idea of what retirees are supposed to do. Should they sit in a rocking chair and watch life go by, or should they play golf, become foster grandparents, and study Greek? The advantage to this lack of clear social expectations is that older adults have the flexibility to structure their retirement as they please.

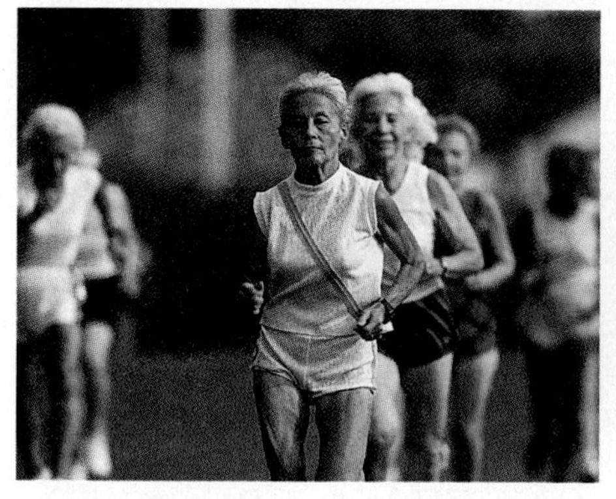

Although physical changes are inevitable during late adulthood, how people respond to these changes can have a major effect on their quality of life.

Of course, the nature and quality of retired life depend in part on financial status. If retirement means a major decline in a person's standard of living, that person will be less eager to retire and will lead a more limited life after retirement. Another factor in people's attitudes toward retirement is their feelings about work. People who are fulfilled by their jobs are usually less interested in retiring than people whose jobs are unrewarding (Atchley, 1976).

## Sexual Behavior

A common misconception about the aged is that they have outlived their sexuality. This myth reflects our stereotypes about the elderly. To the extent that we see them as physically unattractive and frail, we find it difficult to believe that they are sexually active. It is true that older people respond more slowly and are less sexually active than younger people, but the majority of older adults can enjoy sex and have orgasms. Earlier surveys found that 70 percent of married 70-year-old men were sexually active (Clanan, 1966; Pfeiffer, 1977), and one recent survey revealed that 37 percent of married people over 60 have sex at least once a week, 20 percent have sex outdoors, and 17 percent swim in the nude (Woodward & Springen, 1992).

Nonetheless several factors work against sexual satisfaction in old age. First, some older adults accept the myth that they should no longer be interested in sex, and as a result deny their sexual urges. Second, because women tend to outlive men, many older women do not have an available partner. Poor health is another factor that can curb sexual activity. Further, while menopause does not halt a woman's sexual interests, the physical effects of declining hormones can produce bodily changes that require some adjustment in technique or timing. For some women, intercourse becomes actually painful because of the thinning and drying out of vaginal tissues. Estrogen replacement therapy and the use of jellied lubricants may help this problem (J.E. Brody, 1990). Finally, there are cohort differences to consider. Today's older adults grew up in the early part of this century, when attitudes toward sexuality were quite different from what they are now. Thus, their sexual attitudes and behaviors are likely to reflect generational differences as well as age.

**Alzheimer's disease** A disorder common in late adulthood that is characterized by progressive losses in memory and cognition and changes in personality and that is believed to be caused by a deterioration of the brain's structure and function.

## Cognitive Changes

Researchers have found that healthy people who remain intellectually involved maintain a high level of mental functioning in old age (Schaie, 1984). The aging mind works a little more slowly (Salthouse, 1991), and as we saw in the chapter on memory, certain types of memories are a little more difficult to store and retrieve. But these changes are not serious enough to interfere with the ability to enjoy an active, independent life. Furthermore, training and practice can greatly reduce the decline in cognitive performance in later adulthood (Willis, 1985; Willis & Schaie, 1986).

A group of men now in their 70s have been studied since they were identified in 1921 as "gifted children." The researcher who interviewed these men in late adulthood concluded that, at least for bright people who have remained mentally active, the 70s bring no noticeable declines in intellect or vocabulary. He added: "The 70s are not as 'old' when one is in them as they appeared to be when one was young" (Shneidman, 1989, p. 692).

The psychologist K. Warner Schaie has spent his entire career studying the course of adult intellectual development (Schaie, 1994). He has collected longitudinal data on 5,000 adults, looking for patterns of changes and the factors that might be responsible for these changes. Among his most interesting findings is that while there is a general decline in intellectual abilities over a long period of time (more than 50 years), different abilities decline at a different rates. For example, the sharpest decline is in the area of mathematics: At age 74, men tested about one-third lower than they had when they were in their 50s. The smallest decline was seen in spatial ability (for example, reading a map): At age 80, men tested only about one-eighth lower than they had at age 50.

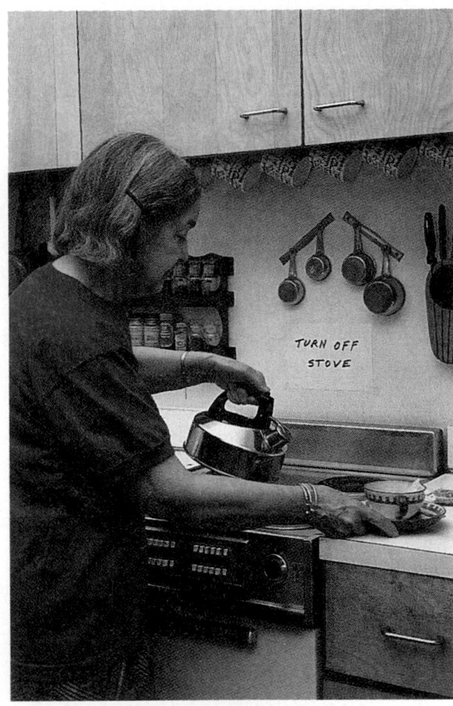


Because people with Alzheimer's disease suffer memory loss, they sometimes use signs to remind themselves to perform everyday activities.

Unfortunately, there are many people in late adulthood who are *not* functioning so well. They forget the names of their children or are unable to find their way home from the store. Some even fail to recognize their husband or wife. The word *senile* was used in the past to describe the condition of such people, but this term is inaccurate. In fact, these people are not suffering from the normal consequences of aging; rather, they are victims of Alzheimer's disease.

**ALZHEIMER'S DISEASE** The disorder known as **Alzheimer's disease** is named for the German neurologist Alois Alzheimer. Alzheimer's most famous case involved a woman who died in her 50s after suffering a progressive loss of the ability to communicate and to reason. When Alzheimer performed an autopsy on her brain, he observed certain abnormalities. Some of the neurons had clumped together in tangles, while others were shrunken or dead. For many years, Alzheimer's disease was considered to be rare, and it was diagnosed only in people under 60 who developed the symptoms of memory loss and confusion. But now Alzheimer's is recognized as a common disorder and as the cause of what used to be called "senility" when it appears in older people. According to current estimates, 5 to 7 percent of adults over 65 (some 4 million people) and at least 20 percent of adults 85 or older suffer from Alzheimer's disease (Anthony & Aboraya, 1992).

What is Alzheimer's disease? Can it be treated?

Alzheimer's usually begins with minor memory losses, such as difficulty in recalling words and names or in remembering where one put something. As it progresses—and this may take anywhere from 2 to 20 years—personality changes are also likely. First, the person's family may notice a kind of emotional withdrawal or flatness. In the later stages, Alzheimer's patients may develop delusions, such as thinking their relatives are stealing from them. They become confused, and may not know where they are or what time of day it is. Eventually, these people lose the ability to speak, to care for themselves, and to recognize family members. If they do not die of other causes, Alzheimer's will eventually prove fatal, as their bodies "forget" how to swallow and how to breathe.

There is at present no known cure for the disorder, but researchers are making progress in searching for its causes and have compiled a set of risk factors as a first step toward understanding the epidemiology of the disease (Kokmen, 1991). Known risks are a family history of *dementia*, defined as a general decline in physical and cognitive abilities; Down syndrome or Parkinson's disease; maternal age at time of birth, with children born to mothers over 40 having an increased likelihood of getting Alzheimer's; and head trauma, especially an incident that resulted in unconsciousness.

It is important to bear in mind that Alzheimer's disease is not the only cause of mental impairment in older people. Conditions such as depression, deafness, alcoholism, stroke, anemia, kidney failure, reactions to certain prescription drugs, and even a vitamin deficiency can produce symptoms that resemble those of Alzheimer's disease—though these other conditions are often treatable (Gruetzner, 1988).

## Facing the End of Life

**9.** *True or false*: Elderly people are much less afraid of death than are younger people.

Fear of death is seldom a central concern for people in later adulthood. In fact, such fear seems to be a greater problem in young adulthood or in middle age, when the first awareness of mortality coincides with a greater interest in living (Kimmel, 1974). For example, one study of attitudes toward death found that 19 percent of young adults were afraid of dying, compared with less than 2 percent of people over age 65 (D. Rogers, 1980). Older people spend more time taking stock of past accomplishments than worrying about death (Butler, 1963). This does not mean that the elderly are constantly brooding about the past. Rather, review of one's life goes on alongside concerns about the present.

The elderly do have some major fears associated with *dying*. They fear the pain, indignity, and depersonalization they might experience during a terminal illness, as well as the possibility of dying alone. They also worry about burdening their relatives with the expenses of their hospitalization or nursing care. As for their relatives, they have their own fears about dying, and these fears, combined with the psychological pain they feel watching a loved one die, sometimes makes them depersonalize the loved one just at the time when that person most needs comfort and compassion (Kübler-Ross, 1975).

**STAGES OF DYING** Psychiatrist Elisabeth Kübler-Ross (1969) interviewed more than 200 dying people of all ages to try to understand the psychological aspects of dying. From these interviews, she described a sequence of five stages through which she believed people pass as they react to their own impending death.

> *Denial*: The individual denies the diagnosis, refuses to believe that death is approaching, insists that an error has been made, and seeks other, more acceptable opinions or alternatives.
>
> *Anger*: The individual now accepts the reality of the situation, but expresses envy and resentment toward those who will live to fulfill their plans and dreams. The question becomes "Why me?" Anger may be

directed at the doctor or randomly in all directions. The patience and understanding of other people are particularly important at this stage.

*Bargaining*: The individual desperately tries to buy time, negotiating with doctors, family members, clergy, and God in a healthy attempt to cope with the realization of death.

*Depression*: As bargaining fails and time is running out, the individual may succumb to depression, lamenting failures and mistakes that can no longer be corrected.

*Acceptance*: Tired and weak, the individual at last enters a state of "quiet expectation," submitting to fate.

According to Kübler-Ross, Americans have a greater problem coping with death than people in some other cultures because we fear and deny it. She observes that while some cultures are *death affirming*, American culture is *death denying*: "We are reluctant to reveal our age; we spend fortunes to hide our wrinkles; we prefer to send our old people to nursing homes" (1975, p. 28). We also shelter children from knowledge of death and dying. By trying to protect them from these unpleasant realities, however, we may actually make them more fearful of death.

Some observers have found fault with Kübler-Ross's model of dying. Most of the criticisms have focused on her methodology. She studied only a relatively small sample of people, and provided little information about how they were selected and how often they were interviewed. Also, all her patients were suffering from cancer, leading some critics to wonder whether Kübler-Ross's model applies as well to people dying from other causes. Finally, some critics question the universality of her model, noting that different cultures have very different ways of thinking about death. Death itself is universal, but reactions to dying may differ greatly from one culture to another.

Despite these legitimate questions, there is nearly universal agreement that Kübler-Ross deserves credit for pioneering the study of the transitions people undergo during the dying process. She was the first to investigate an area long considered taboo, and her research has made dying a more "understandable" experience, and perhaps one that is easier to deal with.

**WIDOWHOOD** The death of one's spouse may be the most severe challenge people face during adulthood. Especially if it was unexpected, people respond to such a loss with initial disbelief, followed by numbness. Only later is the full impact of the loss felt, and that can be severe. The incidence of depression rises significantly following the death of a spouse (F.H. Norris & Murrell, 1990). Moreover, a long-term study of several thousand widowers 55 years of age and older revealed that nearly 5 percent of them died in the 6-month period following their wife's death, a figure that is well above the expected death rate for men that age. Thereafter, the mortality rate of these men fell gradually to a more normal level (Butler & Lewis, 1982).

Perhaps because they are not as used to taking care of themselves, men seem to suffer more than women from the loss of a mate. But because women have a longer life expectancy, there are many more widows than widowers. Thus, men have a better chance of remarrying. More than half the women over 65 are widowed, and half of them will live another 15 years without remarrying. Thus, for somewhat different reasons, the burden of widowhood falls heavily on both men and women (Feinson, 1986).

## LOOKING FORWARD

Throughout this book you will be introduced to many new ideas about human behavior. The study of human growth and development, however, becomes particularly personal, because almost all the concepts described in this chapter can at one time or another apply to each of us. In this chapter, we charted the human life span, from infancy through old age. Within each of these stages, such topics as language development, physical growth, and emotional change are always present, undergoing change, and have formed the focus on subdisciplines within the study of human growth and development.

Perhaps what is most fascinating about these changes is that people are always developing, as psychologists strive to identify the underlying processes that are responsible for these changes. In fact, developmental psychologists have spent almost 100 years trying to map these changes and to refine techniques to help us to understand why they occur. The next 100 years, guided by new developments in such areas as neurosciences, biology, and medicine, are sure to have an impact on the ways in which developmental psychologists look at how human beings change throughout the life span.

## SUMMARY

This chapter deals with **developmental psychology**, the study of the changes that occur in people from birth through old age. To examine changes that take place over time, developmental psychologists use three different methods. In **cross-sectional studies**, researchers test groups of subjects of different ages. In **longitudinal studies**, researchers test the same subjects—usually a **cohort**, or group of people born during the same historical period—as they grow older. For studying adulthood, researchers sometimes use **biographical** or **retrospective studies**, in which subjects' lives are examined *backward* through interviews. Each of these methods has certain advantages and disadvantages. Psychologists also have different views of development. Some believe that changes occur in a series of steplike stages; others see development as a smooth, steady progression. Some believe that heredity is of primary importance; others assign the major role to experience and environment.

### PRENATAL DEVELOPMENT

Development begins at conception. The period from conception to birth is called **prenatal development**. Two weeks after conception, the fertilized egg has become an **embryo**; 3 months after conception, the developing organism is called a **fetus**. The fetus is nourished by an organ called the **placenta**. Disease-producing organisms and substances the mother eats, drinks, or inhales can pass through the placenta and, at **critical periods**, do major harm to the fetus. Pregnancy is most likely to have a favorable outcome if the mother gets good nutrition, proper medical care, and adequate rest and exercise, and if she also refrains from smoking, drinking alcohol, and using illegal drugs.

### THE NEWBORN BABY

**Neonates** (newborn babies) come equipped with a number of reflexes, such as those that help them breathe and nurse. The **rooting reflex** causes a newborn, when touched on the cheek, to turn its head in that direction and grope around with its mouth. The **sucking reflex** causes the newborn to suck on anything that is placed in its mouth, and the **swallowing reflex** enables it to swallow liquids without choking. The **grasping reflex** causes a newborn to close its fist around anything that is put in its hand. The **stepping reflex** causes the newborn to make little stepping motions if held upright with its feet just touching a surface.

#### Temperament

Babies are born with personalities that are often referred to by developmental psychologists as **temperament**. The pioneering work of Thomas and Chess identified three basic types of temperament in newborns—easy, difficult, and slow-to-warm—and a great deal of research has examined the differences among them.

#### The Perceptual Abilities of Infants

Infants can see as soon as they are born. Vision is fuzzy at first, but visual acuity improves rapidly. Some color vision is present at birth; by 4 months, babies can see all the colors an adult can see. Newborns prefer patterns with clear contrasts, so they like looking at black-and-white patterns better than at colored ones. They also prefer a new picture to one they've seen many times before. By 2 or 3 months, a baby will look at a drawing of a human face in preference to a random pattern that has the same contrast and complexity. A classic experiment using a device called the *visual cliff* showed that infants of crawling age can perceive depth.

Fetuses can hear sounds in the uterus, and newborns can tell from what direction a sound is coming. Infants are so tuned in to the sounds of human speech that they can distinguish between some speech sounds that are indistinguishable to an adult. Infants also have clear-cut preferences in taste and smell.

## INFANCY AND CHILDHOOD

**Maturation**—the automatic biological unfolding of development as a function of time—accounts for most physical and motor development in babies and children. Cognitive, moral, language, and social development depend on the interaction between maturation and environmental influences.

### Physical Development

Growth of the body is most rapid during the first year, when it can occur in startling spurts. It then slows down and remains slow until early adolescence. During the prenatal period and the first 2 years of life, the head grows rapidly, making the young child's head large in proportion to his or her body. Head growth slows down after the age of 2, and the body does most of the growing from then on. Physical development proceeds a little faster in girls than in boys.

### Motor Development

Motor development refers to the acquisition of abilities such as grasping and walking. **Developmental norms** indicate the ages at which the average child achieves certain developmental milestones; however, development that is slower or faster than the norm tells us little or nothing about the child's future characteristics. During early motor development, the reflexes of the newborn give way to voluntary action.

### Cognitive Development

Cognitive development refers to changes in the way children think about the world. The Swiss psychologist Jean Piaget saw cognitive development as a way of adapting to the environment, and theorized that it proceeds in a series of distinct stages.

During the **sensory-motor stage** (birth to age 2), infants develop **object permanence**, the concept that things continue to exist even when they are out of sight. At birth, there is no sign of object permanence, but the concept is fully developed by 18 to 24 months, when the child acquires the ability to form **mental representations**—mental images or symbols (such as words) used in thinking and remembering. The development of self-recognition also occurs during the sensory-motor stage.

In the **preoperational stage** (ages 2 through 7), children are able to use mental representations and language assumes an important role in describing, remembering, and reasoning about the world. But preoperational thought is **egocentric**: Children of this age are unable to see things from another person's point of view. They are also easily misled by appearances and tend to focus on the most striking aspect of an object or event.

Children in the **concrete-operational stage** (7 to 11) can pay attention to more than one thing at a time and are able to understand someone else's point of view. However, their thinking is limited to concrete matters that they can handle or imagine handling.

When they enter the **formal-operational stage** (between 11 and 15), adolescents can think in abstract terms and test their ideas internally, using logic. Thus, they can grasp theoretical cause-and-effect relationships and consider possibilities as well as realities.

Piaget's theory has been criticized on two grounds: The content of the stages has been disputed, and his assumption that all children proceed through the stages in the same order has been questioned. Some researchers believe that cognitive development proceeds gradually through experience and practice rather than in a series of distinct stages.

### Moral Development

Like Piaget, Lawrence Kohlberg developed a stage theory, although his involves moral development. Kohlberg's stages—preconventional, conventional, and postconventional—hinge on the different ways the developing child views morality. The preconventional child sees doing right and wrong as a function of physical consequences; the conventional child sees it as a function of what others think; and the postconventional individual sees right behavior as based on a system of values and justice.

### Language Development

Language begins with cooing and progresses to **babbling**, the repetition of speech-like sounds. The first word is usually uttered at about 12 months; at the same age, infants show signs of understanding what is said to them. In the next 6 to 8 months, children build a vocabulary of one-word sentences, called **holophrases**. Between 2 and 3, children begin to put words together into simple sentences, though they leave out unimportant parts of speech such as auxiliary verbs. Between 3 and 4, children fill out their sentences and are able to use past and present tenses. By 5 or 6, most children have a vocabulary of over 2,500 words and can create sentences of 6 to 8 words.

There are two different theories of language development. Skinner proposed that parents listen to their infant's babbling and reinforce (reward) the infant for making sounds that most resemble adult speech. Chomsky, on the other hand, maintained that children are born with a **language acquisition device**, an innate mechanism that enbles them to understand the rules of grammar, make sense of the speech they hear, and form intelligible sentences themselves. Most researchers agree with Chomsky's view.

The critical period hypothesis postulates that

there is a critical time for the acquisition of language. If language is not acquired during that time, it will be very difficult for the child to master it later.

### Social Development

A baby duck or goose follows its mother because of a phenomenon called **imprinting**, a primitive form of bonding. Bonding in humans is a more complex process called **attachment**. This emotional bond that develops in human infants during the first year of life makes them cling to their caregiver for safety and comfort. The first attachment is likely to be to the infant's primary caregiver, usually the mother. It develops during the first year of life, usually along with a wariness of strangers.

Infants who are securely attached to their mothers are better able to develop **autonomy**, a sense of independence and a desire not to be controlled by others. Children who are insecurely attached to others are less likely to explore an unfamiliar environment.

At about 2 years of age, the child's desire for autonomy clashes with the parents' need for peace and order. These conflicts are a necessary first step in **socialization**, the process by which children learn the behaviors and attitudes appropriate to their family and culture. Parenting style affects children's behavior and self-image. The most successful parenting style is authoritative, in which parents provide firm guidance but are willing to listen to the child's opinions. However, parents do not act the same way toward every child in the family because children are different from each other and elicit different parental responses.

The earliest kind of play is **solitary play**—children engaging in some activity all by themselves. Children's interest in other children shows up very early in life, but the skills necessary for playing together develop only gradually. The earliest kind of social interaction is **parallel play**, in which two toddlers play side by side at the same activity but largely ignore each other. At around 2 or 2 1/2, children begin to use language to communicate with each other. By 3 or 3 1/2, they are engaging in **cooperative play** involving group imagination. As children get older, they develop a deeper understanding of the meaning of friendship.

By age 2, a child has developed a **gender identity**, a girl's knowledge that she is a girl and boy's knowledge that he is a boy. But children that age have little idea of what it means to be a girl or a boy; some toddlers think that a change in clothing or hairstyle will transform them into a child of the opposite sex. By 4 or 5, most children develop **gender constancy**, the realization that gender depends on what kind of genitals one has and cannot be changed.

**Sex-role awareness**—the knowledge of what behavior is appropriate for each gender—develops as children interact with their society. From an early age, children show **sex-typed behavior**—behavior that is typical of females (for example, playing with dolls) or of males (for example, playing with trucks). It is not clear whether this sex-typed behavior is innate or due to the fact that adults behave differently toward girls and boys.

#### TELEVISION AND CHILDREN

American children spend more time watching television than engaging in other activity except sleeping. A child who watches 2 hours of TV per day will see about 8,000 murders and 100,000 other acts of violence before leaving elementary school. If television viewing consists of watching nonviolent programs, it does not make children more aggressive. But if TV viewing involves constant exposure to scenes of violence, the evidence suggests that children become more aggressive in their behavior.

The most convincing theoretical argument linking violent behavior with TV watching is based on modeling and social learning theory. Viewing behaviors on television that are violent and characters who are reinforced for such violence leads children to imitate that behavior.

## ADOLESCENCE

During this awkward period of life, the individual is neither a child nor an adult. Among the many differences between a 12-year-old and an adult, the physical ones are probably the most conspicuous.

### Physical Changes

The **growth spurt** is a rapid increase in height and weight that begins, on the average, at about age 10 1/2 in girls and 12 1/2 in boys, and reaches its peak at age 12 in girls and 14 in boys. Growth is essentially complete about 6 years after the start of the growth spurt. During this period, changes occur in body shape and proportions as well in size.

Signs of **puberty**—the onset of sexual maturation—begin at around 11 1/2 in boys, about a year before the start of the growth spurt. In girls, the growth spurt typically precedes the other signs of approaching puberty. **Menarche**, the first menstrual period, occurs between 12 1/2 and 13 for the average American girl. Age at menarche is influenced by health and nutrition.

Teen pregnancy is a serious problem in the United States, with more than 1 million births per year to teenagers, 80 percent of whom are unmarried.

### Cognitive Changes

The cognitive abilities of adolescents undergo an important transition from the concrete-operational to the formal-operational stage. Adolescents can understand and manipulate abstract concepts, reason using general rules, and speculate about alternatives. These new mental abilities often make them overconfident and overimpressed with their own importance. Elkind described two patterns of thought characteristic of this age: the

**imaginary audience**, which makes teenagers feel they are constantly being watched and judged; and the **personal fable**, which gives young people the sense that they are unique and invulnerable and encourages them to take needless risks.

### Personality and Social Development

The classical view of adolescence as a period of "storm and stress" fraught with conflict, anxiety, and tension is not borne out in most teenagers' lives. A child whose development has gone smoothly up to adolescence is likely to do well during adolescence.

**Identity formation** is the process by which a person develops a stable sense of self. According to Marcia, identity formation takes place during an intense period of self-exploration called an **identity crisis**. People who are in identity achievement status have passed through the identity crisis and formed a clear and satisfactory sense of who they are. Those who have taken on an identity provided for them by others, without going through an identity crisis, are in foreclosure status. People in moratorium status are in the midst of an ongoing identity crisis; they put off important decisions in order to have time and room to explore various alternatives. Those in identity diffusion status are avoiding the identity issue entirely. Uncertain or dissatisfied with their present place in society, they may resort to escapist activities such as drug or alcohol abuse to calm their anxieties.

Most adolescents rely on a **peer group**, a network of agemates, for social and emotional support. They often rigidly conform to the values of their friends. From small unisex **cliques** in early adolescence, friendship groups change to mixed-sex groups in which short-lived romantic interests are common. Later stable dating patterns emerge.

Parent-child relationships are difficult during adolescence. Teenagers become aware of their parents' faults and question every parental rule. Conflicts are most common during early adolescence, though only in a minority of families does the parent-child relationship show a severe deterioration. The transition to adulthood is most clearly marked by leaving home. When a young person goes to college, takes a job, or gets married, the child-parent relationship generally improves.

### Problems of Adolescence

Psychiatric disorders often show up for the first time in adolescence. A sizable number of adolescents think about committing suicide; a much smaller proportion attempt it. Depression and eating disorders such as **anorexia nervosa** and **bulimia** affect a large percentage of adolescents.

## ADULTHOOD

Unlike childhood and adolescence, adulthood is not marked by clear, predictable milestones. Still, there are certain experiences and changes that nearly everyone goes through and certain needs that nearly everyone tries to fulfill.

### Love, Partnerships, and Parenting

Almost every adult forms a long-term loving partnership with at least one other adult at some point during his or her life. More than 90 percent of all Americans eventually get married, although they are waiting longer to do so. Most people select a marriage or cohabitation partner of similar race, religion, education, and background. According to Erikson, people are not ready for love until they have achieved a firm sense of identity. Evidence in favor of Erikson's view is the fact that marriages between people who are still in their teens are less successful than those between older people.

For a long time, our understanding of sexual behavior in adulthood was based on the surveys of such people as Kinsey and Masters and Johnson, whose respondents were not very representative of the general population. A newer report, based on a more representative study population, challenges some earlier conclusions. For example, most people stay within one relationship for sex, and sex is a vibrant and enjoyable aspect of the lives of the majority of older Americans.

### The World of Work

The dual-career family is now typical. A married woman who works outside the home is likely to be burdened with child care and housework as well as a job; moreover, her job is likely to be less prestigious than her husband's. Nevertheless, most women derive satisfaction from their jobs. The emergence of the dual-career family has raised many questions concerning the availability of child care and the effects on children of spending much of their early years with adults other than their parents.

### Cognitive Changes

An adult's thinking is more flexible and practical than an adolescent's. Whereas adolescents search for the one "correct" solution to a problem, adults realize that there may be several "right" solutions or none at all. Adults place less faith than adolescents in authorities.

One model of cognitive change maintains that cognitive exercises can minimize the inevitable decline in cognitive functioning as people age.

### Personality Changes

Late adulthood is more likely to involve an accentuation of existing personality characteristics than the development of new ones. But people have to be able to adapt and to change during this period of life. In the process, some people experience a **midlife crisis**, as success in one area of life leaves them feeling unfulfilled and ready for a decisive shift in career or lifestyle. More commonly, people go through a **midlife transition**, a period of taking stock of one's life and formulating new goals.

### The Change of Life
Middle adulthood brings a decline in the functioning of the reproductive organs. Women go through **menopause**, the cessation of menstruation accompanied by a sharp drop in estrogen. Men experience a slower decline in testosterone.

### Late Adulthood
Older adults are the fastest-growing segment of the U.S. population. Development in late adulthood consists more of an accentuation of early- and middle-adulthood characteristics than an alteration of them.

### Physical Changes
The physical changes of late adulthood affect outward appearance and the functioning of every organ. Although aging is inevitable, heredity and lifestyle play a role in the timing of this process.

### Social Development
Most older adults have an independent and satisfactory lifestyle and engage in social activities that interest them. But they gradually go through a process of disengagement and life assessment and accept necessary limitations on their social involvement.

### Retirement
People's reactions to leaving the world of paid employment differ, depending on their financial status and their feelings about work. Those who found their greatest fulfillment in work and those for whom retirement means a sharp drop in income are generally less eager to retire than others.

### Sexual Behavior
Sexual responses are slower in older adults, but most recent information indicates that people continue to enjoy sex in their 60s and 70s.

### Cognitive Changes
The aging mind works a little more slowly, and certain kinds of memory are more difficult to store and retrieve, but these changes are generally not serious enough to interfere with normal activities. Older adults who engage in intellectually stimulating activities remain mentally alert.

Old people who used to be called "senile" are now recognized as having a specific disorder called **Alzheimer's disease**, which causes progressive losses in memory and cognition and changes in personality. This disorder is quite common in people 85 or older. However, it is important to distinguish Alzheimer's disease from other causes of mental impairment that may be treatable.

### Facing the End of Life
Elderly people fear death less than younger people. What they do fear are the pain, indignity, depersonalization, and loneliness associated with a terminal illness. They also worry about being a financial burden to their families.

Kübler-Ross described a sequence of five stages that people go through when they are dying: denial, anger, bargaining, depression, and acceptance. Other researchers do not believe that everyone passes through these five stages, but no one denies that Kübler-Ross has made a very important contribution in increasing our awareness of death as a natural event.

# REVIEW QUESTIONS

## MULTIPLE CHOICE

1. In a ______ study the researcher studies a group of subjects two or more times as they grow older.
2. Neonates are only capable of simple reflexes and are relatively unresponsive to the outside world. T/F
3. Newborn babies will sometimes imitate the facial expressions of adults. T/F
4. Very young infants prefer a black-and-white pattern to a colored one. T/F
5. Put Piaget's stages of cognitive development in the right order and describe how thinking changes at each stage.
   Formal operational stage
   Preoperational stage
   Sensory-motor stage
   Concrete operational stage
6. What makes a duckling follow its mother? Why is this an important activity for ducklings?
7. What makes a human baby 12 months old cling to her mother when he or she is frightened or hurt?

8. The process by which children learn the behaviors and attitudes appropriate to their family and their culture is called ______ .

9. The growth spurt begins at an average age of ______ in girls and ______ in boys.

10. An important milestone for a girl is ______ , her first menstrual period.

11. In the conventional level of moral reasoning, adolescents judge "right" and "wrong" in terms of whether they are rewarded or punished for their actions. T/F

12. Eating disorders are characteristic only of adolescent females. T/F

13. The most important milestone in the transition to adulthood is ______ .

## CRITICAL THINKING AND APPLICATIONS

14. Serena, a pregnant woman, says that the fetus inside her is safe and oblivious to what is happening, either to itself or to Serena. She says that the baby will "wake up" when he or she is born. Briefly respond to these statements.

15. What are some of the things that you might look for in a friend's behavior if you suspect that he or she is suffering from an eating disorder such as anorexia or bulimia? How do you account for the prevalence of these disorders in U.S. society?

16. With the expansion of dual-income families, what kinds of the child-care arrangements have been developed in U.S. society? Do you think they help or hurt children?

17. Rick and Ann's adult children blush at the suggestion that their 65-year-old parents still have sex together. What evidence could you present to convince them that it's likely Rick and Ann are not only sexually active but very much enjoy making love to each other?

*(Answers to the Review Questions can be found in the back of the text.)*

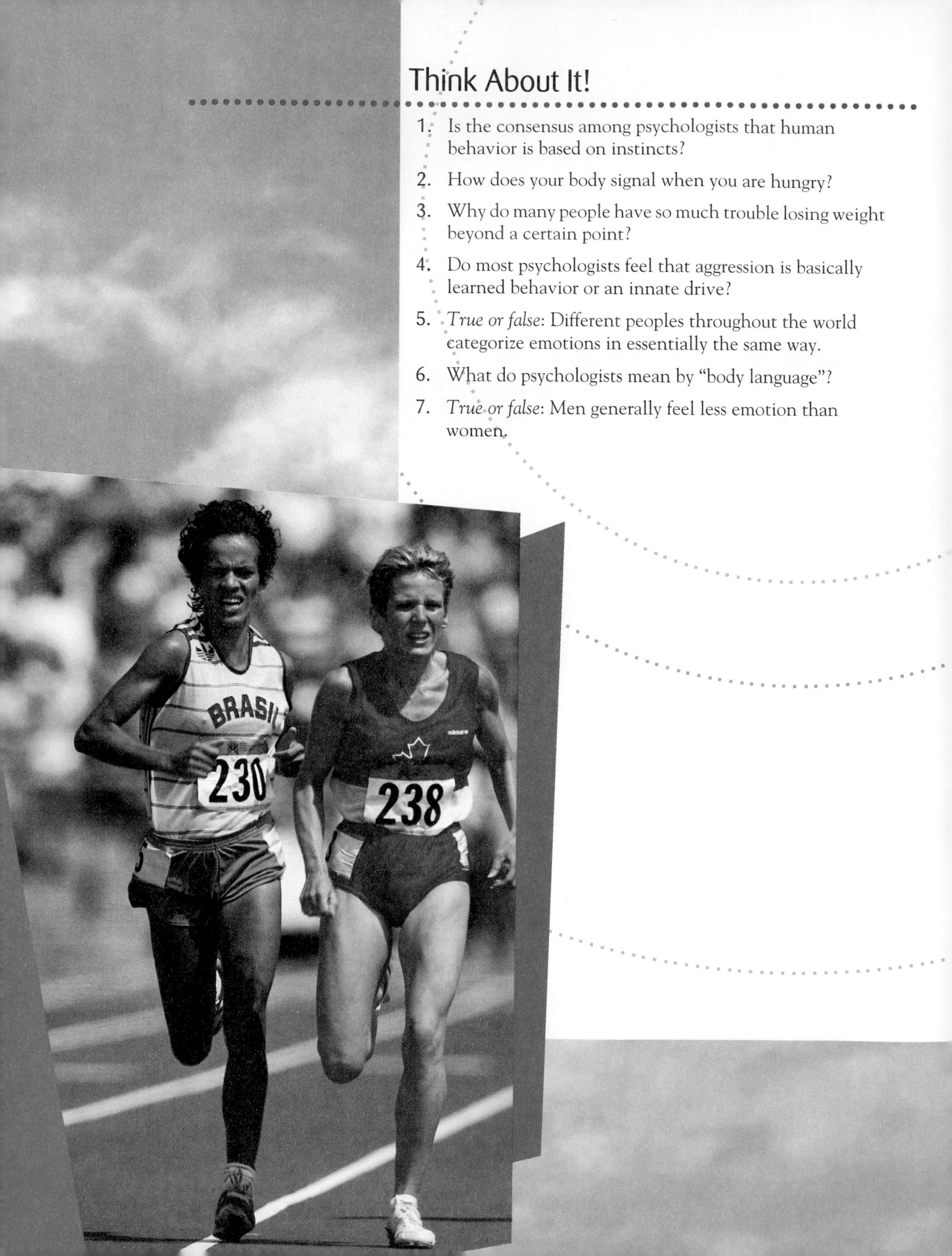


## Think About It!

1. Is the consensus among psychologists that human behavior is based on instincts?
2. How does your body signal when you are hungry?
3. Why do many people have so much trouble losing weight beyond a certain point?
4. Do most psychologists feel that aggression is basically learned behavior or an innate drive?
5. *True or false*: Different peoples throughout the world categorize emotions in essentially the same way.
6. What do psychologists mean by "body language"?
7. *True or false*: Men generally feel less emotion than women.

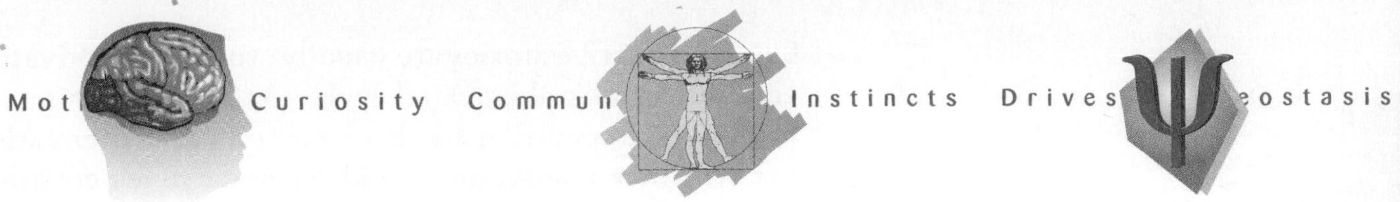


# MOTIVATION AND EMOTION

# 9

## Overview

**Motive** Specific need, desire, or want, such as hunger, thirst, or achievement, that prompts goal-oriented behavior.

**Emotion** Feeling, such as fear, joy, or surprise, that underlies behavior.

**Classic detective stories are usually studies of motivation and emotion at a sophisticated level. At the beginning, all we know is that a murder has been committed: After eating dinner with her family, sweet old Amanda Jones collapses and dies of strychnine poisoning. "Now, why would anyone do a thing like that?" everybody wonders. The police ask the same question, in different terms: "Who had a *motive* for killing Miss Jones?" In a good mystery, the answer is: "Practically everybody."**

The younger sister—now 75 years old—still bristles when she thinks of that tragic day 50 years ago when Amanda stole her sweetheart. The next-door neighbor, a frequent dinner guest, has been heard to say that if Miss Jones's poodle tramples his peonies one more time, he intends to . . . The nephew, who stands to inherit a fortune from the deceased, is deeply in debt. The parlor maid has a guilty secret that Miss Jones knows. All four people were in the house on the night that Amanda Jones was poisoned. All four had easy access to strychnine, which was used to kill rats in the basement. All four had strong emotional reactions to Amanda Jones—envy, anger, shame, guilt. All of them had a motive for killing her.

Motivation and emotion also play a role in some of the less dramatic events in the story. Motivated by hunger, the family sits down together to eat a meal. The poodle, motivated by curiosity or the call of nature, is attracted on repeated occasions to the neighbor's peonies. The next-door neighbor visits because he is lonely and longs for company. The parlor maid's guilt stems from activities engaged in to satisfy sexual urges. The tragedy of Amanda Jones's death brings the four suspects closer together out of a need for affiliation, but the fear generated by the murder prompts the self-preservation drive to kick in, making each of the suspects suspicious of the others.

In this story, motivation and emotion are so closely intertwined that it is difficult to draw distinctions between them. A **motive** is an inner directing force—a specific need or want—that arouses the organism and directs its behavior toward a goal. All motives are triggered by some kind of stimulus: a bodily need, such as hunger or thirst; a cue in the environment, such as the peonies in the garden; or a feeling, such as loneliness, guilt, or anger. When one or more stimuli create a motive, the result is goal-directed behavior (see Figure 9-1). **Emotion** refers to the experience of such feelings as fear, joy, surprise, or anger. Like motives, emotions also activate and affect behavior, but it is more difficult to predict the *kind* of behavior that a particular emotion will prompt. If a man is hungry, we can be reasonably sure that he will seek food. If, however, this same man experiences a feeling of joy or surprise, we cannot know with certainty how he will act.

The important thing to remember about both motives and emotions is that they push us to take some kind of *action*—from an act as drastic as murder or a habit as mundane as drumming our fingers on a table when we

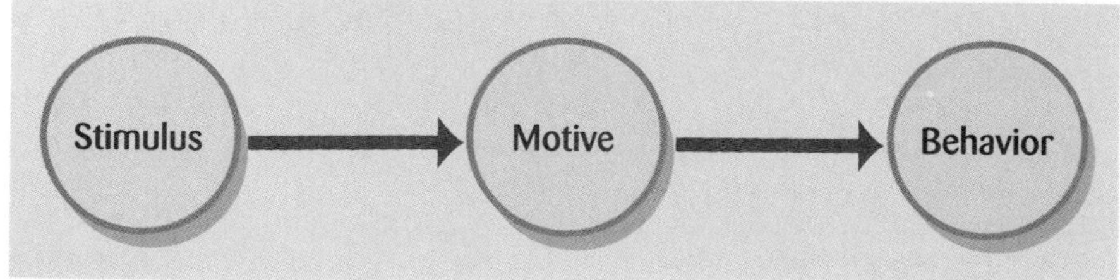


**Figure 9-1**
**How motivation works.** A *motive* is triggered by some kind of *stimulus*—a bodily need or a cue in the environment. A motive, in turn, activates and directs *behavior.*

are nervous. Motivation occurs whether we are aware of it or not. We do not think about feeling hungry to make a beeline for the refrigerator or focus on our need for achievement to study for an exam. We do not have to consciously recognize that we are afraid to step back from a growling dog or know that we are angry before raising our voice at someone. Moreover, the same motivation or emotion may produce different behaviors in different people. Ambition might motivate one person to go to law school and another to join a crime ring. Feeling sad might lead one person to cry alone and another to talk to a friend. On the other hand, the same behavior might arise from different motives or emotions: You may buy liver because you like it, because it is inexpensive, or because you know that your body needs the iron it contains. You may go to a movie because you are happy, bored, or lonely. The workings of motives and emotions are very complex.

In this chapter, we will first look at specific motives that play an important role in human behavior. Then we will turn our attention to emotions and the various ways they are expressed.

**Instinct** Inborn, inflexible, goal-directed behavior that is characteristic of an entire species.

**Drive** State of tension or arousal brought on by biological needs.

**Drive-reduction theory** Theory that motivated behavior is aimed at reducing a state of bodily tension or arousal and returning the organism to homeostasis.

**Homeostasis** State of balance and stability in which the organism functions effectively.

## PERSPECTIVES ON MOTIVATION

Early in the twentieth century, psychologists were inclined to attribute behavior to **instincts**—specific, inborn behavior patterns characteristic of an entire species. Animal instincts include salmon swimming upstream to spawn and spiders spinning webs. In 1890, William James proposed such diverse human instincts as hunting, rivalry, fear, curiosity, shyness, love, shame, and resentment. But by the 1920s, instinct theory began to fall out of favor as an explanation of human behavior for two reasons: (1) Most significant human behavior is not inborn but learned through experience; and (2) human behavior is rarely rigid, inflexible, unchanging, and characteristic of the species. In addition, ascribing every conceivable human behavior to a corresponding instinct really explains nothing (calling a person's propensity to be alone an "antisocial instinct," for example, merely describes the behavior without pinpointing its origins) So after World War I, psychologists started looking for more credible explanations of human behavior.

1. Is the consensus among psychologists that human behavior is based on instincts?

One alternative view of motivation holds that bodily needs (such as the need for food or the need for water) create a state of tension or arousal called a **drive** (such as hunger or thirst). According to **drive-reduction theory**, motivated behavior is an attempt to reduce this unpleasant state of tension in the body and to return the body to a state of **homeostasis**, or balance. When we are hungry, we look for food to reduce the hunger drive. When we are tired, we go to sleep. When we are thirsty, we find something to drink. In each of these cases, behavior is directed toward reducing a state of bodily tension or arousal.

Drive reduction doesn't explain all motivated behavior, however. When we are bored, for instance, we may actually seek out activities that *heighten* tension and arousal. Some people go to horror movies, take up skydiving, and pursue all kinds of new challenges just to raise their level of arousal. These thrill seekers enjoy a higher-than-normal level of stimulation; they feel especially alive when they are taking part in some dangerous activity. As we can see from these examples, human beings strive to maintain an optimal state of arousal: If arousal is too high, we will make efforts to reduce it; if arousal is too low, we will take steps to increase it.

Salmon swimming upstream to spawn exemplify instinctive behavior. Psychologists argue that human behavior cannot be explained solely in terms of instincts.

To complicate matters further, some behavior isn't triggered by internal states at all. For example, the smell from a bakery may prompt us to eat, even if we have just finished a satisfying meal; a sample copy of a new magazine, a demonstration of a new product, or a store window display may lead us to buy something we would not have otherwise bought. In other words,

**Incentive** External stimulus that prompts goal-directed behavior.

**Primary drive** Physiologically based unlearned motive, such as hunger.

Thrill seekers apparently need a different level of stimulation than other people. Thrill-seeking behaviors defy the theory of drive reduction.

objects in the environment—called **incentives**—can also motivate behavior (R.C. Bolles, 1972; Rescorla & Solomon, 1967). Moreover, some psychologists believe that much of our behavior is motivated by unconscious drives. A middle-aged man may buy a new sports car claiming that the car is fun to drive and well designed. But the purchase may also reflect his concerns about growing older, insecurity about his or her attractiveness, or an aggressive desire to be behind the wheel of the fastest car on the road.

The next section of this chapter begins with a look at hunger. Two motives we are generally conscious of and that are primarily guided by internal biological states. From there we will turn to sexual behavior, which is responsive to both internal states and external incentives. We then examine several behaviors, such as curiosity and manipulation, that depend heavily on external environmental cues. Finally, we describe several learned motives that figure prominently in human social relationships.

## PRIMARY DRIVES

As we have seen, all motives are aroused by some kind of stimulus—a bodily need, such as hunger or thirst, or a cue in the environment, such as a picture of a juicy hamburger and a frosty milkshake. Once a motive is aroused, we pursue a goal-directed behavior—perhaps a trip to the nearest fast-food restaurant. Thus, one or more stimuli create a motive, which in turn activates and directs behavior. But motivation is far from a simple, predictable process the same stimuli may arouse different motives in different people, just as the same motives may prompt strikingly different behaviors from one person to the next.

In some cases, a biological need triggers a corresponding state of psychological arousal or tension (a drive), which, in turn, activates and directs behavior. Unlearned drives of this sort are common to every animal, including humans, these are called **primary drives**. Primary drives—principally hunger, thirst, and sex—are strongly influenced by stimuli within the body that are part of the biological programming for survival of the organism—or, in the case of sex, with the survival of the species.

### Hunger

When you are hungry, you eat. If you don't, your need for food will increase the longer you are deprived of it. But your appetite, your feeling of hunger, will not necessarily increase. Suppose you decide to skip lunch to study at the library. Your *need* for food will not go away; in fact, it will increase throughout the day. But your *hunger* will come and go. You will probably be hungry around lunchtime; then your hunger will likely abate while you are at the library. But by dinnertime, no concern will seem as pressing as eating. The *psychological* state of hunger, then, is not the same as the *biological* need for food, although the psychological state is often set in motion by biological processes.

Two centers in the brain are pivotal in our experience and response to hunger. One, the *hunger center*, stimulates eating; while the other, the *satiety center* ("satiety" means being full to satisfaction), reduces the feeling of hunger. Both centers are located in the hypothalamus.

Since the 1950s, scientists have been exploring how these two centers function. We now know that when the neurons in one of these centers are stimulated, the neurons in the other center fire less often. Thus, if your hunger center "tells" you that you are hungry, you will pick up few signals from the satiety center to contradict this message (see Figure 9-2). Scientists have also discovered that the sensation of hunger derives from more than just these two centers alone do not regulate hunger. Neurons that pass through the hunger and satiety centers on their way to other parts of the brain also have some influence. So does another part of the brain near the hypothalamus, called the *amygdala*, though its exact role has not been defined.

**Glucose** Simple sugar that is the main source of body energy.

How do these areas of the brain "know" when to signal hunger? Scientists believe that the brain monitors the level in the blood of a simple sugar called **glucose**. When the glucose level falls, neurons in the hunger center are stimulated and those in the satiety center are inhibited. Researchers see the same effect when the level of fats in the blood increases as the body draws down reserve energy supplies.

How does your body signal when you are hungry?

The brain also monitors the amount and kind of food that you have eaten, with some help from the stomach. Receptors in the stomach sense not only how much food the stomach is holding but also how many calories that food contains. (A stomach full of salad is far less satisfying to most people than a stomach full of turkey with all the trimmings.) Signals from these receptors are sent to the brain, where they stimulate the satiety center, and if your stomach is full from a big meal, you feel less hungry. In addition, some researchers have noted that when food enters the small intestine, a hormone is released into the bloodstream and carried to the brain, where it, too, stimulates the satiety center (Albus, 1989; G.P. Smith & Gibbs, 1976; Takaki et al., 1990). Researchers have developed a drug that mimics the action of this hormone and reduces hunger; other researchers have come up with drugs that increase hunger by blocking this hormone (Wolkowitz et al., 1990). If these drugs prove safe for humans, they might provide an effective mechanism for controlling hunger in people who eat too much or too little, as well as people with serious eating disorders.

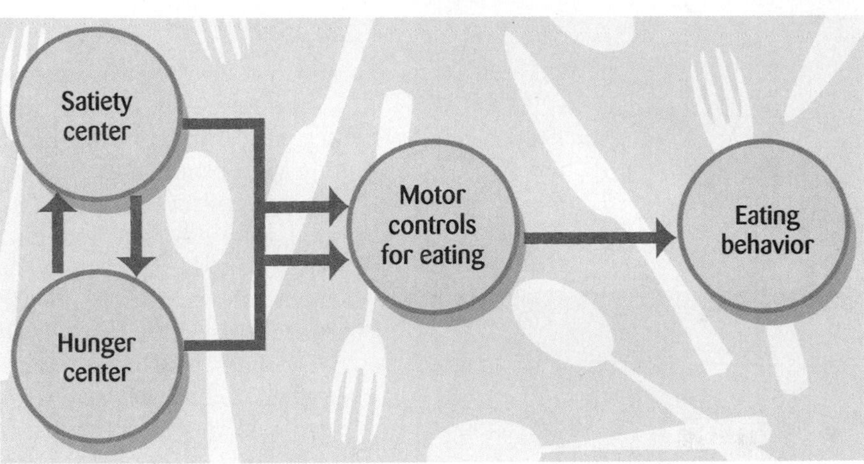


**Figure 9-2**
**A diagram of the dual mechanisms in the brain that control hunger and eating.** The *hunger center* signals when you are hungry and stimulates eating. The *satiety center* reduces the feeling of hunger and the desire to eat.

These hunger mechanisms regulate our day-to-day intake of food. But there appears to be yet another hunger regulator, one that operates on a long-term basis to regulate the body's weight. Have you ever noticed that very few animals besides humans and some domesticated animals become grossly overweight? The body seems to have a way of monitoring its own fat stores and regulating the intake of food to provide just enough energy to maintain normal activities without storing excessive fat deposits.

As we saw earlier, hunger does not always stem from a biological need for food. External cues, like the smell of a cake baking in the oven, may trigger the desire to eat at almost any hour of the day. Sometimes just looking at the clock and realizing that it is dinnertime may make us feel hungry. One intriguing line of research suggests that such external cues set off internal biological processes that mimic real internal needs. For example, Rodin (1985) found that the mere sight, smell, or thought of food causes an increase in insulin production, which, in turn, lowers glucose levels in the body's cells, mirroring the body's response to a physical need for food. So the aroma from a nearby restaurant may serve as more than an incentive to eat; it may actually arouse the primary drive of hunger.

The precise role played by the brain in hunger is not known, but after lesions were made in the hypothalamus of this rat, it ate so much that it increased its body weight to over three times its normal level.

The hunger drive may be affected by emotions as well. Suppose you are very hungry, but in the midst of preparing dinner, you have a serious argument with your boyfriend or girlfriend. If you become extremely upset by the argument, you may not want to eat for hours. Or imagine that you

**Set point** A homeostatic mechanism in the body that regulates metabolism, fat storage, and food intake so as to maintain a preprogrammed weight.

are sitting down to dinner when you receive a phone call notifying you that one of your favorite relatives has just died. You probably would not have much appetite after hearing that news. On the other hand, there are people who become hungry whenever they are anxious or nervous.

Social influences also affect our motivation to eat. Say you are at an important business lunch where you are intent on impressing a prospective client. You may not feel very hungry, even though this lunch is taking place an hour past your usual lunchtime. Conversely, social situations may prompt you to eat when you are not hungry. Imagine that on a day when you have slept late and eaten a large breakfast, you are invited to your grandparents' house. When you arrive, you discover, much to your dismay, that a wonderful home-cooked meal is being served in a few minutes. Although you are not at all hungry, you may decide to eat merely out of courtesy toward your grandparents.

Like hunger, thirst is stimulated by both internal and external cues. Internally, thirst is controlled by two regulators that interact and complement each other. One monitors the level of fluids inside the cells of the body, prompting activation of the thirst drive when the cells become dehydrated. The other thirst regulator monitors the amount fluid outside the cells. When the level of extracellular fluid drops, less blood flows to the kidneys, which, in turn, release a substance into the bloodstream that triggers the thirst drive (Epstein, Fitzsimmons, & Simmons, 1969)

Just as we become hungry in response to external cues, we sometimes get thirsty when we see a TV commercial featuring people savoring tall, cool drinks in a lush, tropical setting. Seasonal customs and weather conditions also affect our thirst-quenching habits: Ice-cold lemonade is a summer staple, while hot chocolate warms cold winter nights.

In satisfying, hunger or thirst we rely on social, psychological, environmental, and cultural influences as well as on physiological needs. For example, the Japanese tea ceremony is concerned more with restoring inner harmony than with slaking thirst. Do you think this office worker is drinking coffee because she is thirsty?

**CULTURAL DIFFERENCES** How you respond when you are hungry will vary according to your experiences with food, which are mostly governed by learning and social conditioning. The majority of Americans eat three meals a day at regular intervals. A typical American family eats breakfast at 7 A.M., lunch around noon, and dinner about 6 P.M. But in Europe, people often have dinner much later in the evening. Italians, for example, rarely eat dinner before 9 P.M.

What we choose to eat is also influenced by our culture, while most Americans will not eat horse meat, it is very popular in several European countries. Some preindustrial peoples traditionally ate insect larvae, the thought of which would disgust most Americans. Yet many Americans consume pork, which violates both Islamic and Jewish dietary laws (Scupin, 1995). So while hunger is basically a biological drive, it is not merely an internal state that we satisfy when our body tells us to. Both the motivation to eat and overeating behavior are guided by psychological, cultural, and environmental considerations in addition to biological factors.

**WEIGHT LOSS** Based on what we know about the hunger drive and the relationship between eating and body weight, how should someone go about losing excess weight?

3. Why do many people have so much trouble losing weight beyond a certain point?

According to one theory, a homeostatic mechanism in the body known as the **set point** regulates metabolism, fat storage, and food intake (Bennett & Gurin, 1982). Set-point theory argues that the body is preprogrammed for certain weight. If you regularly weigh about 150 pounds and gain 10 pounds on vacation, it will be relatively easy for you to lose the additional pounds because you will be returning to a weight that is consistent with your body's set point. Set-point theory helps explain plateauing and backsliding among dieters, as well as why a thin person can consume the same number of calories as an overweight person and stay thin. It may also offer insights into how genes influence weight (see the Highlights box titled "Obesity: More than Consuming Calories").

Set-point theory and the finding that there may be a genetic basis for body weight should not discourage those who are considerably overweight from trying to lose weight because obesity may lead to serious health risks (Bray, 1986) as well as depression. Research has shown that even small weight losses in people who are obese can bring about significant improvements in blood pressure and blood sugar levels (Brownell & Rodin, 1994).

# HIGHLIGHTS

## Obesity: More than Consuming Calories

Fitness is an American obsession: People now worry about cellulite the way they used to worry about crabgrass. Thin is in, as the media constantly remind us.

Nevertheless, many Americans are overweight, and some are heavy enough to be considered obese. Why do people become fat? Certainly, one cause of obesity is high caloric intake relative to the body's needs: The person who leads a sedentary life and who also consumes large quantities of high-calorie foods is an excellent candidate for obesity! But this explanation merely skims the surface of the obesity problem: Two people may consume the same number of calories and maintain the same level of activity, but one will gain weight and the other will not (Rodin, 1981b). Why is this?

Recent research indicates that heredity has a great deal to do with who is likely to become overweight and who is not. In one study (Stunkard et al., 1990), researchers found that identical twins had nearly identical weight (corrected for height) whether they were reared together or apart, while fraternal twins differed greatly in body weight no matter whether they grew up together or separately. In other words, sharing the same childhood environment counts for very little compared to genetics; essentially, thin people were born to be thin, and overweight people were born to be overweight.

Several factors underlie the connection between heredity and body weight. Apparently, some people are born with an oversupply of fat cells, which increases their ability to store excess calories and promotes weight gains. Others are born with a metabolism that burns excess calories by turning them into muscle tissue rather than fat (C. Bouchard et al., 1990). Since it takes nearly ten times as much energy to convert food into muscle as it does to convert it into fat, more of the excess calories are burned off right at the start. Moreover, since muscle is more dense than fat, a pound of muscle takes up less space than a pound of fat; thus, a person who gains 10 pounds of muscle will appear trimmer than someone who puts on 10 pounds of fat. Finally, animal studies point to a genetic link between the satiety hormone were referred to in the text and overeating. McLaughlin, Peikin, and Boile (1984) discovered that obesity may be caused by a hormone-related inability to sense fullness. Although they found that the hormone that signals satiety, cholecystokinin (CCK), is present in adequate amounts in obese rats, these rats did not have enough receptors to which the hormone could bind. Thus, the obese rats never experienced satiety, and they continued eating long after ordinary rats would have been satisfied.

Eating experiences during childhood also affect body weight over one's lifetime. People who are overfed as children may acquire extra fat cells that stay with them throughout life. In addition, poor eating habits learned during childhood often persist into adulthood. However, research reveals that environmental factors outside the family, such as having friends who favor video games over sports and high-fat snack foods over fruit, weigh more heavily than family influences when it comes to someone's overall tendency toward obesity (Grilo, Pogue-Geile, 1991).

Individual differences in sensitivity to internal and external cues may play a secondary role in determining body weight. Schachter (1971a, 1971b) suggested that overweight people are less sensitive than people of normal weight to internal signals of hunger, such as hunger pangs and low blood sugar, and more responsive to *environmental* cues. For them, the sight of a big bowl of ice cream on a table is triply enticing: It gives them the incentive to eat, the means to eat, and the prospect of great enjoyment from eating. We are all receptive to such stimuli, but Schachter contends that obese people are more vulnerable to such external cues. The evidence suggests that in some cases Schachter's hypothesis may be correct, though not all overweight people are overresponsive to external cues, and some normal-weight people are not very responsive to internal signals of hunger and satiety (Rodin, 1981a, 1985).

**Testosterone** Hormone that is the primary determinant of the sex drive in both men and women.

**Pheromones** Substance secreted by some animals; when scented they enhance the sexual readiness of the opposite sex.

To be successful, a program of weight control has to be long-term and work with, rather than against, the normal tendency of the body to maintain weight at all costs. That means finding a way to increase the body's metabolism. The most effective metabolism raiser is a regular program of exercise—20 to 30 minutes of moderate activity several times a week in which only 200 to 300 calories are burned off during each session (Craighead, 1990; Pi-Sunyer, 1987). Coupled with such an exercise program, dietary changes do reduce weight. A moderate reduction in calories is beneficial, but even more important is reducing the consumption of fats (particularly saturated fats) and substances (such as table sugars and syrups) that trigger an increase in the body's level of insulin. Recall that high levels of fat and insulin in the blood stimulate the hunger center, and that dietary fats are more easily stored by the body as fat than as muscle.

Finally, it is essential to set realistic goals for weight loss and to focus at least as much on *maintaining* the lower weight that you reach as on losing more weight. If you need to lose weight, try to shed just 1 pound a week for 2 or 3 months, and then concentrate on maintaining that new, lower weight for the rest of the year before moving on to further weight loss. And most important, reward yourself—in ways unrelated to food— for small improvements. Use some of the behavior-modification techniques brought out in the chapter on learning: Reward yourself not only for each pound of weight loss, but also for each day or week that you maintain that weight loss.

## Sex

Sex is the primary drive that motivates reproductive behavior. Like the other primary drives, it can be turned on and off by biological conditions in the body and by environmental cues. But it differs from them in one important way: Hunger and thirst are vital to the survival of the individual, but sex is vital only to the survival of the species.

The way in which we become sexually aroused and respond is controlled internally, both by the nervous system and by the level of certain hormones in the bloodstream. However, unlike lower animals whose sexual activity is largely controlled by hormones and is tied to the female's reproductive cycle, humans are capable of sexual arousal at any time. Erotic fantasies, the sight of one's lover, the smell of perfume or after-shave lotion—all of these can stimulate sexual excitement. As with the other drives, experience shapes human responses to the sexual drive. Ideas about what is moral, appropriate, and pleasurable also help guide our sexual behavior.

**Biological Factors in Sexual Response** Chemical messengers secreted into the bloodstream by the endocrine glands strongly influence the human sex drive. For both men and women, the hormone **testosterone** has the greatest biological impact on the sex drive (Masters, Johnson, & Kolodny, 1982). However, testosterone level alone does not determine sexual desire. Despite low testosterone levels, some people maintain an active interest in sex. As we shall see, psychology has at least as much sway in human sexuality as biology.

Scientists suspect that, as in other animals, the sex drive in humans may be affected by subtle smells. In Chapter 2, Physiology and Behavior, we saw that many animals secrete substances called **pheromones** that, when smelled by the opposite sex, promote sexual readiness. Some indirect evidence suggest that humans, too, secrete pheromones, in the sweat glands of the armpits and in the genitals (LeMagnen, 1952; Michael, Bonsall, & Warner, 1974). Research with rhesus monkeys has shown that females secrete fatty acids called *copulins* that have an aphrodisiac effect on males. It now appears that human females also secrete copulins (N.M.

Morris & Udry, 1978). However, researchers have not reached any consensus about what role, if any, these secretions play in human sexual arousal.

The nervous system also figures in the human sex drive. In the male, signals are sent to an "erection center" at the base of the spinal cord, which, in turn, transmits neural messages to the muscles that control erection. A similar reflex center, higher in the spine, stimulates ejaculation; this process, however, is subject to some voluntary control. Little is known about how comparable mechanism work in women (Hyde, 1982). The brain exerts a powerful influence on the sex drive, too. In particular, the limbic system, located deep within the brain, main influence sexual excitement. When experimenters implanted electrodes into the limbic system of male monkeys, they located three areas that, when stimulated, caused erections (Hyde, 1982). Two human subjects, who had electrodes placed in their limbic systems for therapeutic reasons, reported sexual pleasure when the electrodes were electrically stimulated (R.C. Heath, 1972).

**PSYCHOLOGICAL AND CULTURAL INFLUENCES ON SEXUAL MOTIVATION** While hormones and the nervous system do figure in the sex drive, human sexual motivation, especially in the early stages of excitement and arousal, is much more dependent on experience and learning than on biology.

What kind of stimuli activate the sex drive in humans? It need not be anything as immediate as a sexual partner. People respond sexually to fantasies, pictures, and words, as well as to things they can see, touch, or hear. According to a recent survey by the National Opinion Research Center (NORC), more than half of the men surveyed said they thought about sex every day or several times a day, while only 19 percent of women reported thinking about sex so often (Lewin, 1994).

Some psychologists believe that evolution has had a hand in men's greater interest in sex and their tendency to have more partners than women. Because sperm are plentiful and eggs are scarce, it makes evolutionary sense for the male to inseminate many females (thereby perpetuating his genetic heritage as widely as possible), and for the female to very selective about the genes that will be paired with hers (as she seeks out a partner who will stand by her and their offspring). Others embrace the psychoanalytic view proposed by Nancy Chodorow, which is covered in more detail in the next chapter. Briefly, they see gender differences in sexuality as stemming from the disparate developmental tasks facing boys and girls as they separate from their (generally) female caregiver: This childhood experience puts males on a track toward independence and signals females to strive for relationships and connectedness. Still others maintain that these differences reflect learning and social influences, such as the "double standard" whereby women are more likely to be punished and ostracized for sexual activities. This double standard gives women less freedom than men to engage in a variety of sexual behaviors.

Just as society dictates standards for sexual conduct, culture guides our views of sexual attractiveness. Culture and experience may influence the extent to which we find particular articles of clothing or body shapes sexually arousing. As creatures grounded in individual societies and cultures, our primary biological drives, including sex, are strongly guided by environmental cues. By the same token, sexual dysfunctions—including diminished or nonexistent sexual drive—may be traced to both biological and psychological factors. We will examine sexual dysfunctions in depth in the chapter on abnormal behavior. In our discussion so far, we have moved from motives that are heavily dependent on biological needs (hunger and thirst) to a motive that (in humans, at least) is considerably more sensitive to external cues (sex). In the next section, we will continue this progression by examining some motives that are even more responsive to environmental cues.

**Stimulus motive** Unlearned motive, such as curiosity or activity, that prompts us to explore or change the world around us.

## STIMULUS MOTIVES

Like the primary drives, **stimulus motives** are largely unlearned, but in all species, these motives are more dependent than primary drives on external stimuli—things in the world around us. Whereas primary drives are associated with the survival of the organism or the species, stimulus motives are associated with obtaining information about the environment. Motives such as *activity*, *curiosity*, *exploration*, *manipulation*, and *contact* push us to investigate, and often to change, our environment.

### Exploration and Curiosity

Where does that road go? What is in that dark little shop? How does a television set work? How will a real-life mystery be solved? What is the answer to the question about Hobbits and Orcs on page 244? Answering these questions has no obvious benefit: You do not expect the road to take you anywhere you need to go or the shop to contain anything you really want. You are not about to start a TV repair service or use an unknown tool. You just want to know. *Exploration* and *curiosity* are motives sparked by the new and unknown and directed toward no more specific goal than "finding out." The family dog will run around a new house, sniffing and checking things out, before it settles down to eat its dinner. Even rats, when given a choice, will opt to explore an unknown maze rather than run through a familiar one (see Figure 9-3).

*Curiosity* is a stimulus motive that pushes us to investigate unfamiliar stimuli. As we learn more about our environment, our curiosity becomes more ambitious.

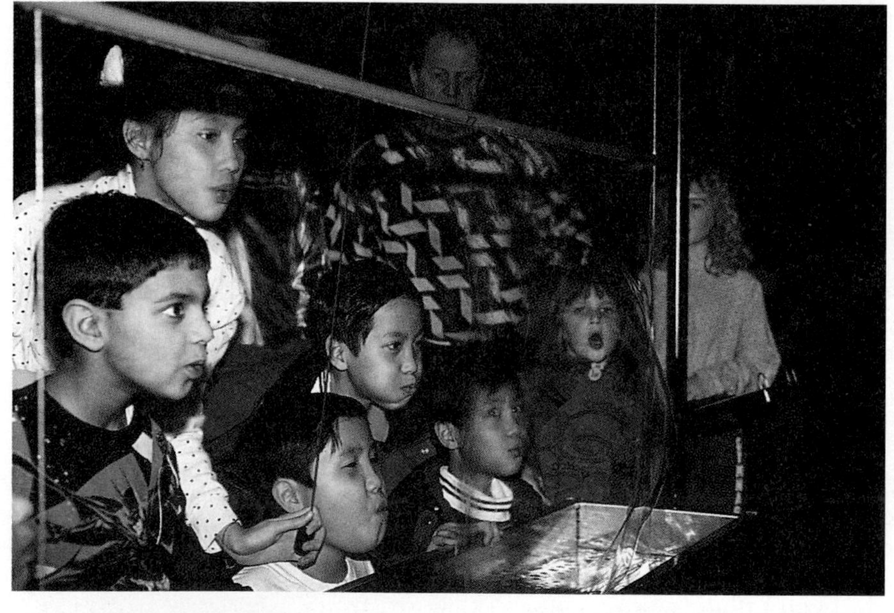

Psychologists disagree about the nature and causes of curiosity (Loewenstein, 1994). William James viewed it as an emotion; Freud considered it as a socially acceptable expression of the sex drive. Others have seen it as a response to the unexpected and as evidence of a human need to make sense of or find meaning in life. We might assume that curiosity is a key component of intelligence, but studies attempting to establish a positive correlation between the two have been inconclusive. However, curiosity has been linked to creativity (Loewenstein, 1994). While curiosity occurs naturally, it also springs from specific situations. For example, people who have been subjected to boredom by sensory deprivation will ask to listen to something as boring as old stock reports simply to gain some stimulation (Hebb, 1958). Thus, our level of curiosity is not stable, but it fluctuates situation to situation.

Curiosity can also varies according to our familiarity with events and circumstances. At times, we have all perceived the unknown as more distressing than stimulating or found something—an argument, a symphony, a chess game—too complex for us. A young child accustomed only to her parents may withdraw from a new face and scream with terror if that face has a beard. Unusual clothing or a radical piece of art or music may be rejected, scorned, even attacked. But greater familiarity and understanding may change the face, clothing, or symphony from something unacceptable to

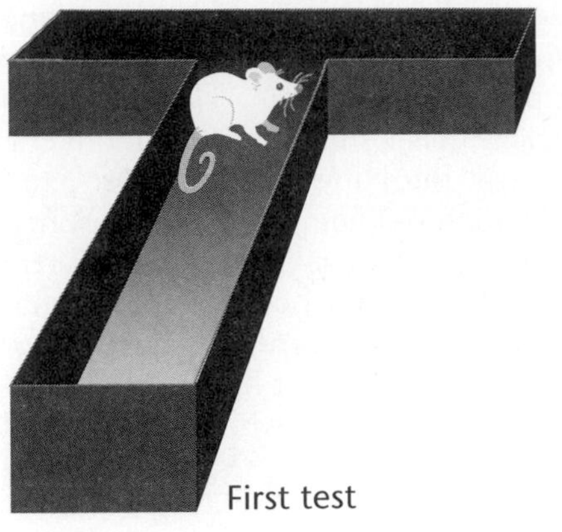


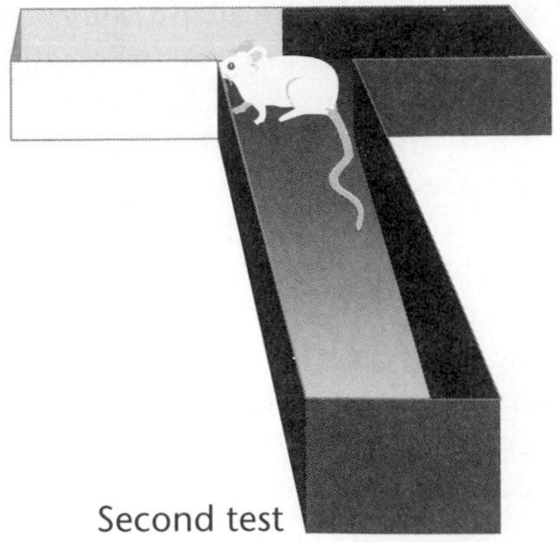


**Figure 9-3**
**Curiosity at work.** On a first trial, a rat will explore either one of the black arms of the maze at random. On a second trial, however, given a choice between a black arm and a white one, a rat will consistently choose the unfamiliar one.

something interesting and praiseworthy. Someone who at age 2 responds happily to "Three Blind Mice" may be intrigued by the complex rhythms of a popular song at age 12 and embraces the subtleties of a Mozart string quartet at age 22. As we continually explore and learns from our environment, and learn from it, we raise our threshold for the new and complex, and our explorations and our curiosity become much more ambitious. In this respect, curiosity dovetails with cognition. When something eludes our understanding, it may stimulate our curiosity. But as our curiosity is satisfied and the unfamiliar becomes familiar, we tend to become bored. This, in turn, prompts us to explore our surroundings further (Loewenstein, 1994).

## Manipulation

Why do you suppose that museums have *Do Not Touch* signs everywhere? It is because the staff knows from experience that the urge to touch is irresistible. Unlike curiosity and exploration, *manipulation* focuses on a specific object that must be touched, handled, played with, and felt before we are satisfied. Manipulation is a motive limited to primates, which have agile fingers and toes.

Psychologists trace the desire to manipulate to two things: the need to know about something at the tactile level and the need to be soothed. Greek "worry beads"—a set of beads on a short string that are moved back and forth during a conversation—exemplify manipulation as a calming action. Under stress, people "fiddle" with a cigarette, a napkin, a fountain pen. Children are always manipulating objects around them to learn how they work and how they fit into the overall scheme of things. Eyeglasses, earrings, flowers, dogs' tails—everything must be touched and played with. The brighter the object, the more vivid its colors, the more irregular its shape, the more appealing it is as an object for manipulation.

## Contact

People also want to touch other people. The need for *contact* is more universal than the need for manipulation. Furthermore, it is not limited to touching with the fingers—it may involve the whole body. Manipulation is an active process, but contact may be passive.

In a famous series of experiments, Harry Harlow demonstrated how important our need for contact is (Harlow, 1958; Harlow & Zimmerman, 1959). Newborn baby monkeys were separated from their mothers and given two "surrogate mothers." Both "mothers" were the same shape, but one was made of wire mesh and had no soft surfaces. The other was cud-

An infant monkey with Harlow's "surrogate" mothers—one made of wire mesh, the other covered with terry cloth. The monkey clings to the terry-cloth "mother," even though the wire-mesh "mother" provides both food and warmth, while the soft terry-cloth "mother" provides only warmth. These experiments suggest that the need for closeness and affection goes deeper than a need for mere warmth and food.

**Social motive** Learned motive associated with relationships among people, such as the needs for affiliation, achievement, and power.

**Aggression** Behavior aimed at doing harm to others; also the motive to behave aggressively.

dly—layered with foam rubber and covered with terry cloth. A nursing bottle was put in the wire-mesh "mother," and both "mothers" were warmed by means of an electric light placed inside them. Thus the wire-mesh "mother" fulfilled two physiological needs for the infant monkeys: the need for food and the need for warmth. But baby monkeys most often gravitated to the terry-cloth "mother," which did *not* provide food: When they were frightened, they would run and cling to it as they would to a real mother. Since both mothers were warm, the researchers concluded that the need for affection, cuddling, and closeness goes deeper than a need for mere warmth. More recently, the importance of contact has been demonstrated with premature infants. Low-birthweight babies who were held and massaged gained weight faster and were calmer than those who were touched only minimally (Field, 1986).

## LEARNED MOTIVES

We are not born with all our motives intact. In fact, as we have already seen, some motives that appear to be innate—such as hunger, thirst, and sex—are actually partly learned. As we develop, our behavior is governed by new motives that are almost entirely learned, yet these new motives, such as aggression, may exert just as much influence over our behavior as unlearned drives and motives do. In probing the field of learned motives, we will first look at aggression. Then we will consider some of the most crucial **social motives**, which center on our relationships with other people.

### Aggression

**Aggression** in human beings encompasses all behavior that is *intended* to inflict physical or psychological harm on others. Intent is a key element of aggression (R. Beck, 1983). If you accidentally hit a pedestrian with your car, you have inflicted harm, but without intent to do so. If, however, you spot the person who mugged you last week and try to hit him with your car as he crosses the street, you are doing something intentionally harmful. This is an act of aggression.

Judging from the statistics (which often reflect underreporting of certain types of crimes), aggression is disturbingly common in this country. According to the FBI, there were approximately 1,800,000 violent crimes in the United States in 1990: 24,000 murders, 100,000 rapes, 640,000 robberies, and 1,000,000 aggravated assaults (*The New York Times*, April 29, 1991). Family life also has a violent underside: One-quarter of families experience some form of violence. Some 3 to 4 million women are battered by their partners each year, with more than 25 percent of these battered women seeking medical attention for their injuries; over 2 million cases of child abuse are reported each year, and more than 1,000 children die annually as a result of abuse (*Newsweek*, December 12, 1988, and July 16, 1990).

A scene from a shelter for battered women: In the United States, women are frequent targets of aggression: Between 3 and 4 million women are battered by their partners each year.

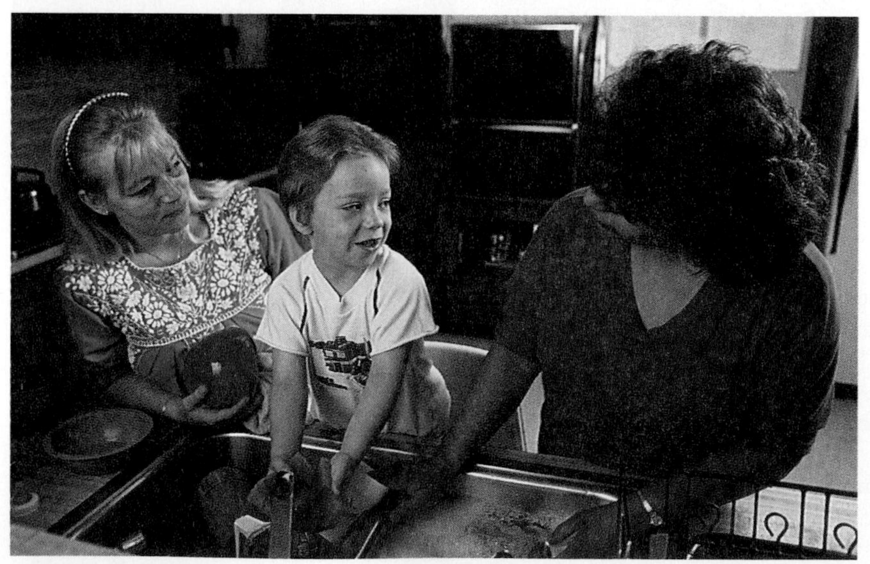

Why is aggression so widespread? According to one view, it is a vestige of our evolutionary past that is triggered by pain or frustration (Lorenz, 1968). There is some evidence that pain and frustration may prompt aggressive behavior. In one experiment, a pair of rats received painful electric shocks through a grid in the floor of their cage; frustrated in their efforts to escape, they started to fight each other. As the frequency and intensity of the shocks increased, so did the fighting (Ulrich & Azrin, 1962). Frustration plays a role in human aggression as well. In one experiment, Kulik and Brown (1979) divided subjects into two groups who were both told they could earn money by soliciting charitable donations over the telephone. One group was informed that previous callers had been quite successful in eliciting pledges; the other group was told that its predecessors had met with only scant success. Each group was given a list of prospective donors, all of whom were the experimenters' accomplices who had instructions to refuse to pledge any money. The subjects who had been led to believe that success would come easy tended to express considerable anger, arguing with uncooperative respondents and even slamming down the phone.

Most psychologists believe that aggression is largely a learned behavior. Professional athletes in contact sports often serve as models of aggressive behavior.

While studies like this one reveal a link between frustration and aggression, frustration does not always produce aggression. In fact, individuals have very different responses to frustration: Some seek help and support, others withdraw from the source of frustration, and some choose to escape into drugs or alcohol. In other words, frustration seems to generate aggression only in people who have learned to be aggressive as a means of coping with unpleasant situations (Bandura, 1973). Moreover, aggression may be a learned response to a number of different stimuli. According to L. Berkowitz (1983), research indicates that almost any unpleasant event may prompt an aggressive outburst. Foul odors, high room temperature, frightening information, and exposure to cigarette smoke have all been found to increase hostility in human subjects. Thus, frustration is only one of many types of unpleasant experiences that may provoke aggression.

Freud considered aggression an innate drive, similar to the hunger and thirst drives, that builds up until it is released. In his view, one important function of society is to channel the aggressive drive into constructive and socially acceptable avenues, such as sports, debating, and other forms of competition. If Freud's analysis is correct, then expressing aggression should reduce the aggressive drive. Yet this does not always hold true. Sometimes angry people who are encouraged to express their aggression find their anger dissipating, but nonangry people prodded to express aggression are no calmer than before or actually become more aggressive (Doob & Wood, 1972).

Faced with the twofold evidence that aggression in humans is not an innate response to pain or frustration and that there is no aggressive drive that periodically builds up until it is released, most psychologists today believe that human aggression is largely a learned response. One way we learn aggression is by observing aggressive models, especially models who get what they want (and avoid punishment) when they behave aggressively. For example, in contact sports, acts of aggression are seldom condemned; in fact, they are often hailed (Bredemeier & Shields, 1985). In professional hockey, fistfights between players may elicit as much fan fervor as goal scoring.

4. Do most psychologists feel that aggression is basically learned behavior or an innate drive?

But what if the aggressive model does not come out ahead or even punished for its aggressive actions? The ancient custom of public executions and painful punishments like flogging and the stock arose from the notion that punishing a person for aggressive acts would deter others from committing those acts. However, as we saw in the learning chapter, children who viewed aggressive behavior learned aggressive behavior, regardless of whether the aggressive model was rewarded or punished. The same results were obtained in a study in which children were shown films of aggressive behavior. Those children who saw the aggressive model being punished were less aggressive than those who saw the aggressive model rewarded, but both groups of children were *more* aggressive than those who saw *no* aggressive model at all. So simply seeing an aggressive model seems to increase aggression among children, whether the model is punished or rewarded and whether the model is live or shown on film. These data are consistent with more recent research showing that exposure to cinematic violence of *any* sort causes a small to moderate increase in naturally occurring aggressive behavior among children and adolescents (W. Wood, Wong, & Chachere, 1991).

This research has implications for children growing up in homes where aggression and violence are prevalent. As we mentioned earlier, domestic violence is rampant in the United States: One survey found that in a 12-month period, more than 3 percent of women (1.8 million) had been severely assaulted, with many of these assaults occurring at home (Browne, 1993). Children who witness domestic violence learn aggressive behavior and are more likely to behave aggressively in the future whenever they believe that violence will serve their purposes.

## Sexual Coercion and its Effects

The term *sexual coercion* is used to describe a variety of behaviors. Rape, or sexual assault, is the most serious form of sexual coercion and the most widely studied. Every 5 minutes, somewhere in the United States, a woman reports being raped. In approximately 80 percent of rapes the victim knows the rapist; about half the rape takes place on a date; and about one-third of the time it occurs in the victim's home. It is important to note that these figures refer only to *reported* cases of violent rape. Since many rapes go unreported, the actual numbers are probably considerably higher. But sexual coercion also encompasses the less extreme forms of pressure to have sex known as *sexual harassment*. Harassment includes job-related extortion of sexual favors as well as unwanted and unceasing sexual advances, both verbal and physical (Fitzgerald, 1993). It also includes sexual activity in response to pressure from partners or peers. What are the motives behind sexual coercion? Are perpetrators driven primarily sexual desires, or are power and aggression their underlying motives?

While early research focusing on rapists in prison cited power, anger, and sadism as the principal motives in rape, more recent research, based on a more representative cross section of the population, disputes those early conclusion.

One study found that anger and the desire to inflict pain played a prominent role in only about 20 percent of (the most violent) rapes (Prentky, Knight & Rosenberg 1988). In another 30 percent of rapes, the motivation sprang from a general hatred of women—the rapists sought to degrade and humiliate their victims as a way of exacting revenge for perceived wrongs committed against them by other women. But in nearly half of the cases, sexuality seemed to be the predominant motive. Roughly one-quarter of the rapists studied were men had difficulty controlling their impulses in many areas of their lives. These rapists rarely acted out of anger; rather, they impulsively raped a date or an acquaintance when the opportunity arose, and their primary motivation was sexual. Another 25 percent of the rapists were obsessed with a sexual fantasy that they sought to act out in the rape; many of these men seemed to believe that their victims would eventually enjoy the experience and perhaps even fall in love with them. Because these last two categories of rapes lacked the violence and brutality of the other rapes, the researchers suspected that they were less likely to be reported, so it is possible that many more than half of all rapes are motivated by sexual impulsiveness and sexual fantasies.

Laboratory research tends to confirm that there is a close connection among rape, aggression, and sexuality. Recent studies indicate that for most men sexual violence is not at all arousing; in fact, viewing films simulating forced sex in which the victim was clearly in distress and experiencing pain *decreased* sexual arousal in most men so much that they would not be able to engage in intercourse at all (Barbaree & Marshall, 1991). However, many of these same men became aroused by scenes of sexual violence if they had been drinking, if they had had an argument with a woman before viewing the film, or if the victim seemed to them to be "asking for it."

Like rape, harassment is often an expression of anger and aggression toward women (Fitzgerald, 1993). In some cases of sexual harassment, crude and sexually explicit graffiti are deliberately placed where women will see them. In others, women are subjected to unwanted caresses or comments about their dress or anatomy. In extreme cases, women are pressured or forced into having sex by male colleagues or supervisors. Over one 2-year period, for example, approximately 12,000 female federal employees reported that they were victims of rape or attempted rape by their supervisors or co-workers (U.S. Merit Systems Protection Board, 1993).

Sexual coercion exacts a severe emotional toll. Though the victims of sexual harassment do not necessarily experience the same trauma as rape victims, many of the aftershocks experienced by those who have been raped applies to victims of sexual harassment as well. Sexual coercion places a woman in a state of great conflict. She must first decide whether to report the incident. Women who report a rape are often treated insensitively, even though the treatment of rape victims by police and hospital personnel has improved in recent years. Women who file charges of sexual harassment risk being demoted, fired, or shunned if they come forward. Their accounts are often regarded with indifference or skepticism or are ignored altogether (Fitzgerald, 1993).

From an emotional standpoint, women who have been sexually coerced frequently experience symptoms of posttraumatic stress disorder (PTSD), a serious psychological disorder first identified in soldiers returning from the horrors of the battlefield. (We will examine PTSD in greater depth in chapter on stress.) People suffering from PTSD have difficulty readjusting to normal life and continue to live the traumatic event. They become alienated and unable to trust or form close bonds with others. In addition, they feel guilty and often blame themselves for what has happened. Women who have been raped may become unable to feel parts of their bodies or experience sexual pleasure. They also suffer from depression and lowered self-esteem (Gruber & Bjorn, 1986).

As we have seen, aggression is a learned motive. A number of important social motives are also learned, and we turn to them now.

**Achievement motive** The need to excel, to overcome obstacles; a social motive.

## Achievement

Climbing Mount Everest "because it is there," sending rockets into space, making the dean's list, rising to the top of a giant corporation—all these actions may have mixed underlying motives. But in all of them there is a desire to excel, "to overcome obstacles, to exercise power, to strive to do something difficult as well and as quickly as possible" (H.A. Murray, 1938, pp. 80-81). The desire for achievement for its own sake is dubbed psychologists an **achievement motive**.

As with all learned motives, the need for achievement varies widely from person to person. McClelland (1958) devised several ways to measure this need for achievement. One method analyzes responses to the Thematic Apperception Test, a personality test in which a person looks at drawings of ambiguous situations and is asked to make up stories about them (see the chapter on personality). For example, one picture used in the test shows an adolescent boy sitting at a classroom desk. A book lies open in front of him,

**Power motive** The need to win recognition or to influence or control other people or groups; a social motive.

but the boy's gaze is directed toward the viewer. Subjects' stories about this character are presumed to reflect their own motivations. Therefore, those whose stories involved the boy accomplishing something difficult or unique, setting high standards of excellence for himself, or taking significant pride in his success would score high on the need for achievement. For example, one subject who scored high on the need for achievement responded: "The boy in the picture is trying to reconcile the philosophies of Descartes and Thomas Aquinas—at the tender age of 18. He has read several books on philosophy and feels the weight of the world on his shoulders." In sharp contrast was another response: "Ed is thinking of leaving home for a while in the hope that this might shock his parents into getting along." This second response was from someone who scored low on the need for achievement (Atkinson & Birch, 1970; Atkinson & Raynor, 1975).

Helmreich and Spence (1978) used a self-report questionnaire called the Work and Family Orientation (WOFO) scale to study achievement motivation. They discovered there are three separate but interrelated aspects of achievement-oriented behavior: *work orientation*, the desire to work hard and do a good job; *mastery*, the preference for difficult or challenging feats, with an emphasis on improving one's past performance; and *competitiveness*, the enjoyment of pitting one's skills against those of other people.

There are three separate but interrelated aspects of achievement-oriented behavior: *work orientation*, the desire to work hard and do a good job; *mastery*, the preference for challenging feats with an emphasis on improving one's performance; and *competitiveness*, the enjoyment of seeing how one's skills compare to those of others.

How do individual differences in the three aspects of achievement motivation relate to people's attainment of goals? Surprisingly, Helmreich and Spence discovered that having a high degree of competitiveness may actually interfere with achievement. In one study, students' grade-point averages (GPAs) were compared to their WOFO scores. As you might expect, students who scored low in work, mastery, and competitiveness had lower GPAs. But students who scored high in work, mastery, and competitiveness did *not* have the highest GPAs. It turned out that the students with the highest grades were those who had high work and mastery scores but low competitiveness scores. The counterproductive effect of competitiveness curbs achievement in other groups of subjects, as well, including businesspeople, elementary school students, and scientists. What accounts for this phenomenon? No one knows for sure, but researchers speculate that highly competitive people alienate the very people who would otherwise help them achieve their goals, or that preoccupation with winning distracts them from taking the actions necessary to attain their goals. Or perhaps, as we will see later in this chapter, the overwhelming need to succeed produces a level of arousal that is too high for optimum performance on complex tasks.

From psychological tests and personal histories, psychologists have developed a profile of people with a high level of achievement motivation. These people do best in competitive situations and are fast learners. Driven less by the desire for fame or fortune than by the need to live up to a high, self-imposed standard of performance, they are self-confident, willingly take on responsibility, and do not readily bow to outside social pressures, while they are energetic and allow few things to stand in the way of their goals, but they are also apt to be tense and to suffer from psychophysiological disorders—that is, real physical ailments, such as ulcers and headaches, with psychological origin. They may also feel like impostors even—or especially—when they achieve their goals.

## Power

Another principal learned motive is the **power motive**, which may be defined as the need to win recognition or to influence or control other people or groups. Like the achievement motive, it can be determined from stories written in response to pictures in the Thematic Apperception Test: Stories filled with images that contain images of vigorous action, behavior that greatly affects the lives of others, and a keen interest in reputation or position earn high scores when it comes to the power motive (Winter, 1973).

College students who score high on the need for power tend to occupy "power positions," such as offices in student organizations, residence counseling positions, and membership on key committees. They are inclined to participate in contact sports and pursue careers in teaching, psychology, and business (R. Beck, 1983).

**Affiliation motive** The need to be with others; a social motive.

## Affiliation

Sometimes people want to get away from it all—to spend an evening or a weekend alone, reading, thinking, or just being by themselves. Generally, however, people have a need for affiliation—to be with other people. If they are isolated from social contact for a long time, they may become anxious. Why do human beings seek one another out? How are groups formed, and how does a handful of isolated people become a group?

For one thing, the **affiliation motive** is aroused when people feel threatened. Esprit de corps—the feeling of being part of a sympathetic group—is critical among troops going into a battle, just as a football coach's pregame pep talk fuels the team spirit. Both are designed to make people feel they are working for a common cause or against a common foe.

But affiliative behavior often results from another motive entirely. For example, you may give a party to celebrate land a job because you want to be praised for your achievement. Fear and anxiety may also be closely tied to the affiliation motive. When rats, monkeys, or humans are placed in anxiety-producing situations, the presence of a member of the same species who remain calm will reduce the fear of the anxious ones. If you are nervous on a plane during a bumpy flight, you may strike up a conversation with the calm-looking woman sitting next to you because the agitation of the plane does not seem to be worrying her.

One study of the affiliation motive involved two groups of college students who agreed to participate in psychology experiments. On arriving at the lab, one group was brought into a room filled with ominous-looking equipment. An unsmiling, white-coated scientist warned these students that the experiments would entail "quite painful" electric shocks. The other group was welcomed by a friendly, casually dressed researcher who also told them to expect shocks but who emphasized that each shock would be "more like a tickle than anything unpleasant" (Schachter, 1959). Both groups were informed that the experiment would begin in 10 minutes and that they could either wait alone or with other subjects, as they preferred. More of the subjects who expected painful shocks indicated they wanted to be with other people compared to the subjects who expected a mild shock. And both groups preferred to wait with subjects like themselves: The high-fear group wanted to wait with other people who were also expecting painful shocks, and the low-fear group preferred to wait with other low-fear subjects. On the basis of these and other similar findings, Schachter concluded that one of the reasons people affiliate is their need to interpret unfamiliar situations. Just how scared should they be? Should they refuse to participate? To answer such questions as these, it is not sufficient to say that "misery loves company"; rather, "misery loves *miserable* company"!

A recent theory of affiliation holds that people seek company or solitude depending on how much benefit they expect to derive from being with other people (Rofe, 1984). In ambiguous situations, like the one created by Schachter, people generally gravitate toward others like themselves to help them assess the situation. But in less ambiguous settings, people may actually prefer to be alone or with people who are not facing the same problems. For example, Rofe, Hoffman, and Lewin (1985) found that patients with critical illnesses preferred being with healthy people rather than with other seriously ill patients or by themselves. They also preferred not to talk about their illnesses.

Affiliation behavior (like most behavior) stems from a subtle interplay of internal and external factors. Whether you strike up a conversation with the person sitting next to you on a bumpy airplane flight depends on how friendly you normally are, as well as on how scared you feel at the moment, how calm or nervous your neighbor appears to be, and how turbulent the flight is.

## A HIERARCHY OF MOTIVES

You have probably noticed that our narrative has gradually moved from primitive motives, shared by all animals, to motives that are more sophisticated, complex, and specifically human. Abraham Maslow, a humanistic psychologist, arranged all motives in such a hierarchy, from lower to higher (1954). The lower motives are relatively simple: They spring from bodily needs that *must* be satisfied. As we move higher on Maslow's hierarchy of needs, the motives have more subtle origins: the desire to live as comfortably as possible in our environment, to deal as well as we can with other human beings, and to make the best possible impression on others. Maslow believed that the most highly "evolved" motive in the hierarchy is *self-actualization*—the drive to realize one's full potential. Maslow's hierarchy of motives is illustrated in Figure 9-4.

According to Maslow's theory, higher motives emerge only after the more basic ones have been largely satisfied. This holds true on both an evolutionary and an individual scale. Someone who is starving doesn't care what people think of her table manners.

Maslow's model offers an appealing way to organizing a wide range of motives into a coherent structure. But recent research challenges the universality of his views. Maslow based his hierarchical model on observations of historical figures, famous living individuals, and even friends whom he admired greatly; however, the majority of these people were white males living in Western society. Neher (1991) points out that in many simpler societies people often live on the very edge of survival, yet they form strong and meaningful social ties and possess a firm sense of self-esteem. In fact, Neher points out, difficulty in meeting basic needs can actually *foster* the satisfaction of higher needs: A couple struggling to financially raise a family may grow closer as a result of the experience. Recall also that in our discussion of development during adolescence and early adulthood, we examined some research indicating it is necessary for males to have a firm sense of their own identity (and thus a degree of self-esteem) *before* they can successfully establish the kinds of close relationships with others that satisfy the need for belonging. As a

**Figure 9-4**
**A pyramid representing Maslow's hierarchy of needs.** From bottom to top, the stages correspond to how fundamental the motive is for survival and how early it appears in both the evolution of the species and the development of the individual. According to Maslow, the more basic needs must largely be satisfied before higher motives can emerge.

*Source:* After Maslow, 1954.

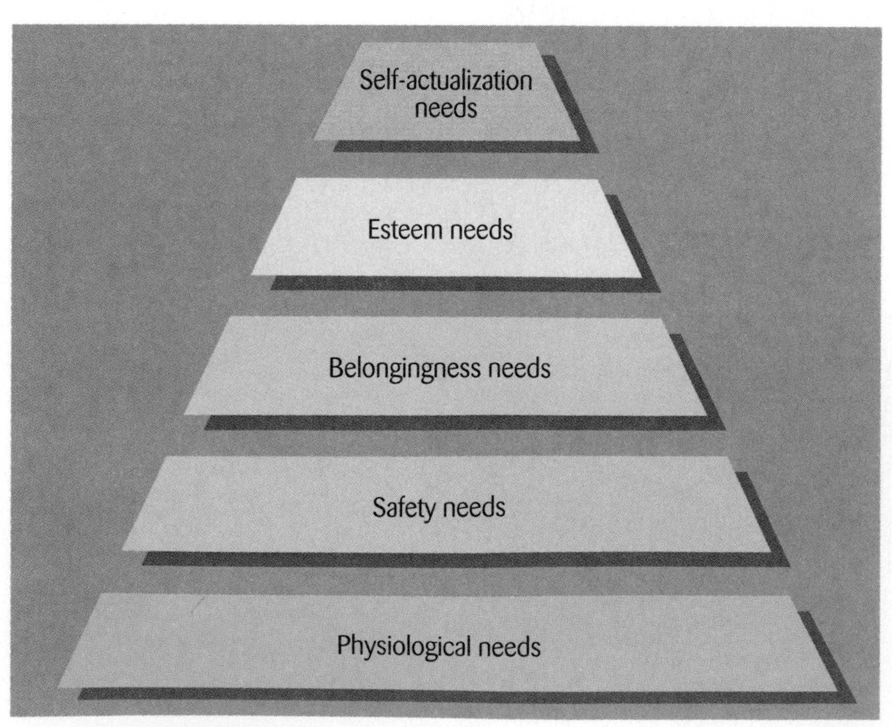

result of such research findings, many psychologists now view of Maslow's model with a measure of skepticism.

## EMOTIONS

In the first part of this chapter, we saw that motives may both arouse and direct our behavior. Emotions do, too. "She shouted for joy," we say, or "I was so angry I could have strangled him."

At the simplest level, we may classify emotions according to whether they make us turn *to* or *away* from objects (Arnold, 1960). Imagine that you overhear this conversation among three people whose television set has just gone out during a midsummer thunderstorm:

> A: Just when the movie was getting good! I've wanted to see it for years, and now *this* happens. (Fiddles with set, to no avail, and turns it off in disgust.) Things like this always happen at the worst time. It makes me furious!
>
> B: I *hate* thunderstorms—I always have. Don't you think we ought to shut off all the lights so we won't attract the lightning? My grandmother used to hide in a closet till a thunderstorm was over, and I don't blame her. She used to say it was God's vengeance for our sins.
>
> C (*Going to window*): Look at it! It's fantastic—the way the blue flashes light up everything! It makes the whole world different. I've always loved thunderstorms—they're so wild and happy. They make me feel liberated and crazy!

A is frustrated and angry: This category of emotions moves us to *approach* something, but in an aggressive or hostile way. *B* is fearful and anxious: These emotions make us want to *avoid* something. C is happy and exhilarate, experiencing a sense of release and joy: These emotions prompt us want to *approach* something in a positive way.

But emotions, like motives, may trigger a chain of complex behavior that goes far beyond simple approach or avoidance reactions. For example, if we are anxious about something, we may collect information about it, ask questions, and then decide whether to approach it, flee from it, or stay and fight it. Imagine a family faced with an anxiety-provoking situation: The husband and wife have both been temporarily laid off from their jobs; several months of severe economic hardship lie ahead. Where should supplementary income be found? How should family goals be adjusted? Will it be possible for the family to survive the crisis without suffering too seriously? Faced with these uncertainties and the anxiety they create, the family decides to tackle the problem through a series of positive strategies. The husband, who is knowledgeable about cars and likes to work with his hands, goes to work for his neighbor, who owns an automobile repair shop. The wife, who managed an office for several years at one time in her life, takes advantage of her former employer's offer to return to a part-time position with her old company. Their daughter accepts a scholarship at a local campus of the state university instead of attending a more expensive private school. In short, the emotional anxiety brought on by this situation has focused the family members on the crisis at hand and triggered a complex sequence of goal-directed behavior in much the same way that motives do.

Of course, our emotions sometimes overwhelm our good sense. Most of us have found ourselves in situations in which we desperately wanted to think rationally but could not because our emotions were get-

**Yerkes-Dodson law** States that there is an optimal level of arousal for the best performance of any task; the more complex the task, the lower the level of arousal that can be tolerated before performance deteriorates.

ting in the way of our concentration. Under what circumstances does emotion hinder what we do, and when does it help? Psychologists agree that there is no single, simple answer; rather, it is largely a question of degree—of both the strength of the emotion and the difficulty of the task. The **Yerkes-Dodson law** puts it this way: The more complex the task, the lower the level of arousal that can be tolerated without interfering with performance. You may feel very angry while boiling an egg, and your anger may not make much difference in how well you perform that task, but the same degree of emotional arousal may interfere with your ability to drive safely. Moreover, although a certain minimal level of arousal is necessary for good performance, a very high level may hamper your performance (see Figure 9-5).

## Basic Emotional Experiences

As we saw, emotions may be broadly grouped according to how they affect our behavior—whether they motivate us to approach or to avoid something. But within these broad groups, how many different emotions are there?

One of the most influential attempts to identify and classify emotions was made by Robert Plutchik (1980). He proposed that animals and human beings experience eight basic categories of emotions that motivate various kinds of adaptive behavior. Fear, surprise, sadness, disgust, anger, anticipation, joy, and acceptance—each of these emotions helps us adjust to the demands of our environment, although in different ways. Fear, for example, underlies flight, which helps protect animals from their enemies; while anger propels animals to attack or destroy.

Emotions adjacent to each other on Plutchik's emotion "circle" (see Figure 9-6) are more alike than those situated opposite each other or that are farther away from each other. Amazement is more closely related to terror than to rage; ecstasy and adoration are more similar to each other than either is to loathing. Moreover, according to Plutchik's model, different emotions may combine to produce an even wider and richer spectrum of experience. Occurring together, anticipation and joy, for example, yield optimism; joy and acceptance fuse into love; surprise and sadness make for disappointment.

Within any of Plutchik's eight categories, emotions vary in *intensity*, represented by the vertical dimensions of the model in Figure 9-7. At the top of the figure—the most intense end of the model—lie rage, vigilance, ecstasy, adoration, terror, amazement, grief, and loathing. As we move

**Figure 9-5**
**Graphs illustrating the Yerkes-Dodson law.** A certain amount of arousal is needed to perform most tasks, but a very high level of arousal interferes with the performance of complicated activities, that is, the level of arousal that can be tolerated is higher for a simple task than for a complex one.

*Source:* After Hebb, 1955.

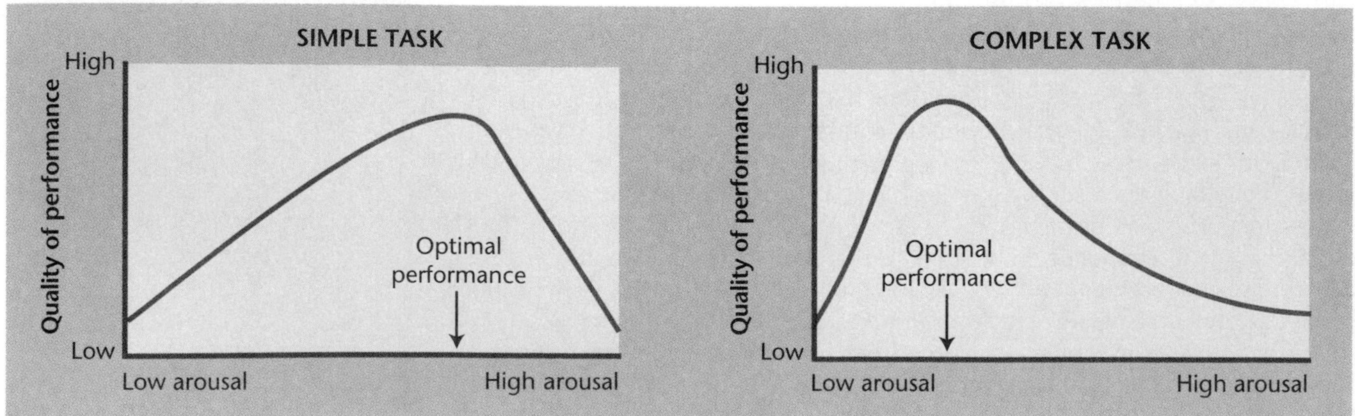

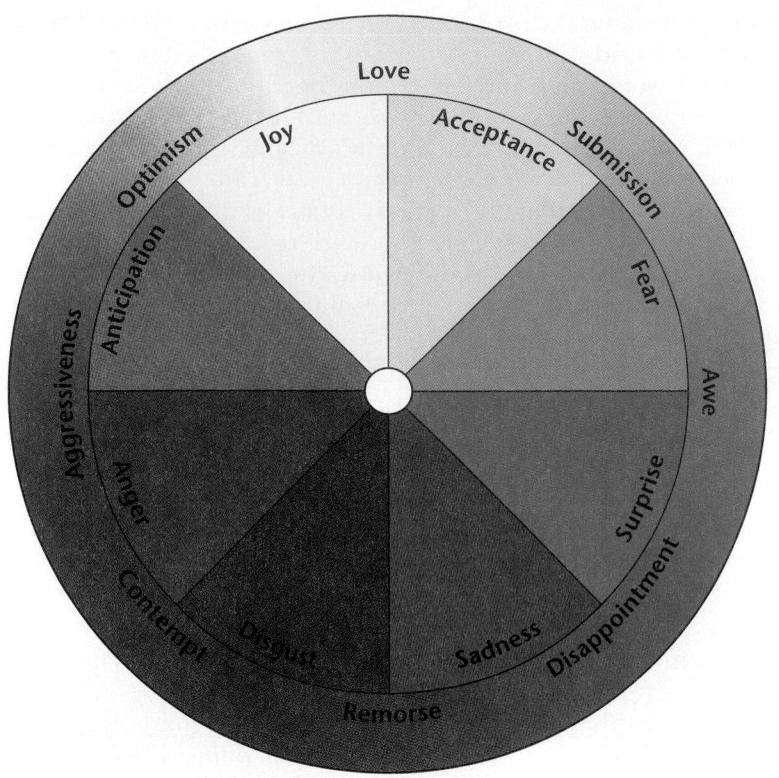


**Figure 9-6**
**Plutchik's eight basic categories of emotion.** Emotions adjacent to each other on Plutchik's emotion "circle" are more alike than those that lie opposite each other or are farther apart. When adjacent emotions are combined, they yield new but related emotions. For example, sadness mixed with surprise leads to disappointment.

*Source:* Plutchik, 1980.

**Figure 9-7**
**Plutchik's three-dimensional model of the eight basic emotions.** Within any of the categories, emotions vary in intensity. Intensity is represented on the vertical dimension of the model, ranging from maximum intensity at the top to a state of deep sleep at the bottom. The model tapers inward at the bottom to indicate that emotions are less clearly distinguishable from one another at low intensities.

*Source:* Plutchik, 1980.

toward the bottom, each emotion becomes less intense, and the distinctions among the emotions become less sharp. Anger, for example, is less intense than rage, and annoyance is even less intense than anger. But all three emotions—annoyance, anger, and rage—are closely related.

Emotional intensity also varies among individuals. At one extreme are people who experience intense joy or deep sadness over what may appear to others to be fairly insignificant events. At the other extreme are those who seem to have almost no emotional reactions, even in the most difficult circumstances. Most of us fall between these two extremes. One study determined that an individual's capacity for emotional intensity appears early in life and remains stable at least through young adulthood (Larsen & Diener, 1985). However, another study concluded that emotional peaks and valleys level out with age; in this research, the average level of emotional intensity for 242 people aged 15 to 70 dropped with each passing decade (Diener, Sandvik, & Larsen, 1985).

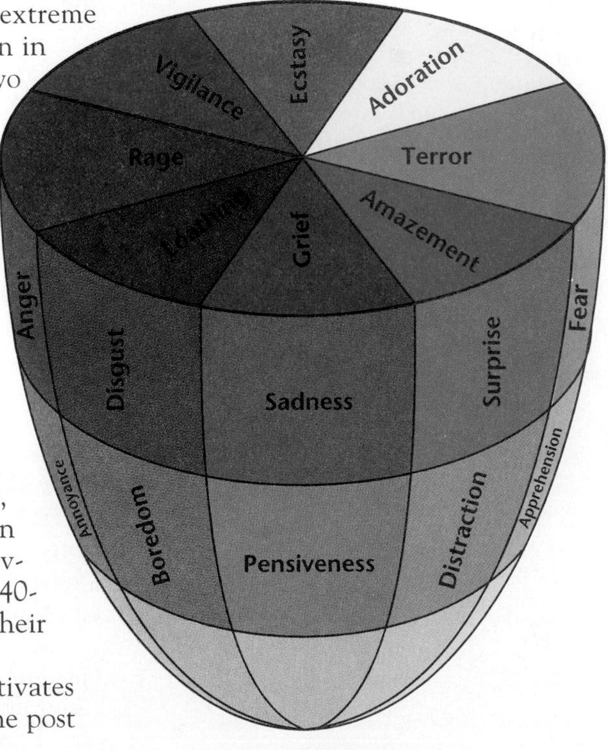


Some emotionally intense people are especially prone to anger and hostility. Physiologically, they frequently have more responsive sympathetic nervous systems, which produce higher levels of adrenaline and noradrenaline, hormones associated with such stress responses as higher blood pressure, increased heart rate, and dilated pupils. Over time, these stress responses may weaken the heart and harden the arteries. One study found much higher levels of low-density lipoprotein, the harmful form of cholesterol, in 40-year-olds who had been identified as chronically angry during their college years (Siegler et al., 1990).

In general, the more intense the emotion, the more it motivates behavior. If you wanted to mail an important letter and got to the post

**James-Lange theory** States that stimuli cause physiological changes in our bodies, and emotions result from those physiological changes.

**Cannon-Bard theory** States that the experience of emotion occurs simultaneously with biological changes.

*True or false*: Different peoples throughout the world categorize emotions in essentially the same way.

office 1 minute after it closed, your prevailing emotion might be anger, and you might respond with a muttered curse. If you only needed to buy some stamps, you would probably feel annoyed and just walk away. But if you wanted to mail an income tax return that had to be postmarked by midnight that night, you might become enraged and start banging on the post office door or perhaps even kicking it.

Thus, although Plutchik identifies only eight categories or families of emotions, within each category the emotions vary in intensity, greatly expanding the range of emotions that we experience. So this very simple model makes it possible to account for all sorts of different emotions and a wide array of associated behaviors.

However, some scientists challenge the universality of Plutchik's model, noting that it may apply only to the emotional experience of English-speaking people. Anthropologists report enormous differences in the ways that disparate cultures view and categorize emotions. Some languages, in fact, do not even have a word for *emotion* (J. A. Russell, 1991a). Other languages differ in the number of words they have to name emotions. While English includes over 2,000 words to describe emotional experiences, there are only 750 such descriptive words in Taiwanese Chinese. One tribal language has only 7 words that could be translated into categories of emotion. Interestingly, words used to name or describe an emotion may influence how that emotion is experienced. For example, in the Tahitian language, there is no direct translation for the concept of sadness. Instead, Tahitians experience sadness in terms of physical illness. As a result, the sadness we feel over the departure of a close friend would be experienced by a Tahitian as exhaustion. Some cultures lack words for *anxiety* or *depression* or *guilt*. Samoans have one word encompassing love, sympathy, pity, and liking—all distinct emotions in our own culture (J. A. Russell, 1991a).

## Theories of Emotion

Why do we feel on top of the world one minute and down in the dumps the next? What causes emotional experiences?

Nineteenth century psychologists William James and Carl Lange proposed in the **James-Lange theory,** that stimuli in the environment (say, seeing a ferocious grizzly bear) cause physiological changes in our bodies (accelerated heart rate, enlarged pupils, deeper or shallower breathing, increased perspiration, a gooseflesh sensation as body hairs stand on end), and emotions arise from those physiological changes. The emotion of fear, then, is simply the awareness of these physiological changes. But even though the physiological changes associated with fear and anxiety differ somewhat from those that accompany anger and aggressiveness (Funkenstein, King, & Drolette, 1953; McGeer and McGeer, 1980), psychologists have not pinpointed distinct bodily states that account for all our various emotions.

Moreover, as we saw in the chapter on physiology and behavior, sensory information about bodily changes flows to the brain through the spinal cord. If bodily changes are the source of emotions, then people with severe spinal cord injuries should experience fewer and less intense emotions. Research, however, has demonstrated that this is no so (Chwalisz, Diener, & Gallagher, 1988). Thus, bodily changes do not cause specific emotions, and may not even be necessary for emotional experience.

An alternative theory of emotions, the **Cannon-Bard theory**, dating back nearly 70 years, holds that emotions and bodily responses occur simultaneously, not one after another. When you see the bear, you feel afraid and you start running—neither of these precedes the other. What you see or otherwise perceive, that is, plays a key role in determining the emotional experience you have.

Recently, cognitive psychologists have developed and extended this idea by contending that our perception or judgment of situations (cognition) is absolutely essential to our emotional experience of those situations (Lazarus, 1982, 1991a, 1991b, 1991c). All emotional states involve arousal of the nervous system, but, according to the **cognitive theory** of emotion, the situation that we are in when we are aroused—the environment—gives us clues as to how we should respond to this general state of arousal. Thus, our cognitions tell us how to label our diffuse feelings in a way that suits our current thoughts and ideas about our surroundings. (See Figure 9-8 for a comparison of these three theories of emotion.)

**Cognitive theory** States that emotional experience depends on one's perception or judgment of the situation one is in.

A fascinating test of the cognitive theory of emotion was undertaken by Spiesman (1965). People were shown a violent, stress-inducing film that aroused strong emotional responses. But Spiesman was able to manipulate people's emotional responses to the film by varying the sound track (the verbal setting of the film). Those who heard a sound track that narrated what was happening in the film responded with more emotion than those who saw the film with no accompanying narration. But those who heard a sound track that described the events in a detached and clinical way and those who heard a sound track that glossed over, denied, or spoke in glowing terms about what was depicted experienced much less emotion than either of the first two groups. These results show that our emotional responses are directly and sharply affected by how we interpret a situation, or how it is interpreted for us.

Some recent attempts to repeat these experiments, however, have failed to yield the same results (Hogan & Schroeder, 1981). In an effort to explain the differences in findings, Pennebaker and Skelton (1981) con-

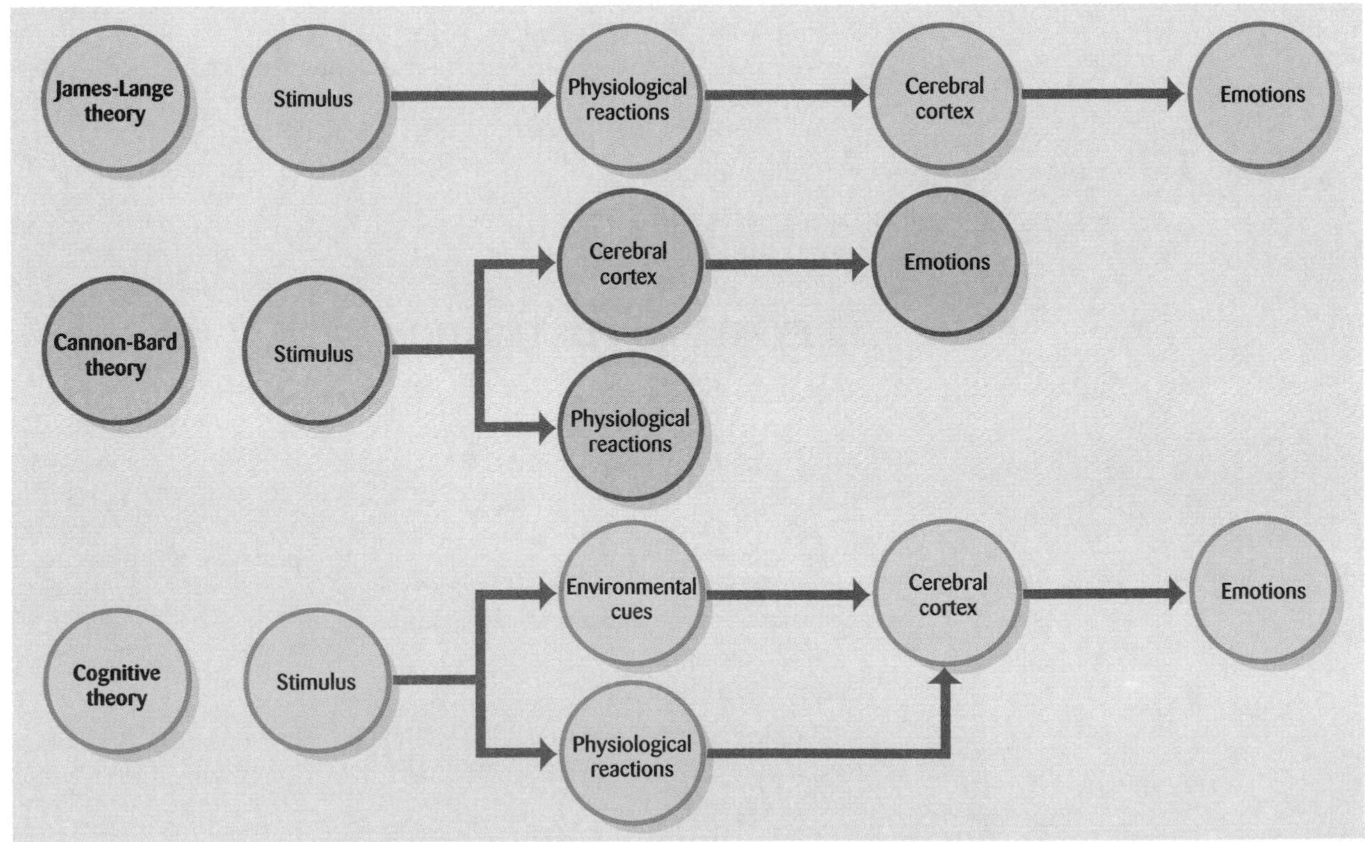


**Figure 9-8**
**The three major theories of emotion.** According to the *James-Lange theory*, the body first responds physiologically to a stimulus, and then the cerebral cortex determines which emotion is being experienced. The *Cannon-Bard theory* holds that impulses are sent simultaneously to the cerebral cortex and the peripheral nervous system; thus, the response to the stimulus and the emotion are experienced at the same time, but independently. *Cognitive theorists* assert that the cerebral cortex interprets physiological changes in the light of information about the situation to determine which emotions we feel.

tended that interpreting emotional states is a two-part process: People respond to emotional arousal with a quick appraisal of their feelings, and then they search for environmental cues to back up their assessment. In the process, they pay greater attention to internal cues that agree with external cues; thus, they tend to experience the kind of emotion they expect to experience.

The cognitive theory of emotion makes a great deal of sense, though some critics reject the idea that feelings must always stem from cognitions. Quoting the poet e. e. cummings, Zajonc argues that "feelings come first." Human infants, he points out, can imitate emotional expressions at 12 days of age, well before they acquire language. Animals rely on their sense of danger to survive: A rabbit doesn't evaluate the possibilities that might account for a rustle in the bushes before it runs away (Zajonc, 1980). Zajonc notes the affective (emotional) system has the ability to respond instantaneously to the situations in which we find ourselves, without taking time to interpret and evaluate those situations. But some affective reaction is fairly diffuse and difficult to explain. When we feel sort of jittery, a cross between nervous and excited, we ask ourselves, "What's going on?" Zajonc (1984) believes that we invent explanations to label feelings: Cognition thus comes *after* emotion.

A direct challenge to the cognitive theory of emotions comes from researcher C. E. Izard (1971, who claims that emotions can be experienced without the intervention of cognition. In his view, a situation such as separation or pain provokes a unique pattern of unlearned facial movements and body postures that may be completely independent of conscious thought (Trotter, 1983). When information about our facial expressions and posture reaches the brain, we automatically experience the corresponding emotion. According to Izard, then, the James-Lange theory was essentially right in suggesting that emotional experience arises from bodily reactions. But Izard's theory stresses facial expression and body posture as crucial to the *experience* of emotion, while the James-Lange theory emphasizes muscles, skin, and internal organs.

Considerable evidence supports the contention that facial expressions do influence emotions (Adelmann & Zajonc, 1989; Ekman & Davidson, 1993; Zajonc, Murphy, & Inglehart, 1989). If further research bolsters Izard's theory, we will be able to say with certainty that a key element in determining our emotional experience is our own expressive behavior, the next topic in this chapter.

## THE EXPRESSION OF EMOTION

Sometimes you are vaguely aware that a person makes you feel uncomfortable. When pressed to be more precise, you might say: "You never know what she is thinking." But you do not mean that you never know her opinion of a film or what she thought about the last election. It would probably be more accurate to say that you do not know what she is *feeling*. Almost all of us conceal our emotions to some extent to protect our self-image or to conform to social conventions. But usually we give off some clues to help others determine what we are feeling.

### Verbal Communication

The simplest way to find out what someone is feeling is to ask. Sometimes we do ask people what they are feeling, with varying results. If your roommate finishes washing the dishes and says acidly, "I hope you are enjoying your novel," the literal meaning of his words is quite clear, but you know very well that he is note expressing pleasure at your choice of reading material. If he were to say, "I am furious that you did not offer to help clean up after dinner," he would be giving you an accurate report of his emotions at that moment.

For many reasons, we may be unable or unwilling to report our emotions accurately. In some situations, people simply cannot pinpoint what they are feeling. A father who abuses his child may sincerely profess affection for the child, yet act in ways that reflect quite different emotions far removed from tender affection—feelings that are hidden from his own awareness. Even when we are aware of our emotions, we sometimes minimize the degree of emotion that we are feeling: We may say we are "a little worried" about an upcoming exam when in fact we are terrified. Or we may deny the emotion entirely, especially if it is negative (hatred toward a parent or sibling, for example). So often what people *say* does not mirror what they are *feeling*. Thus, we must frequently turn to other cues to emotion if we are to understand them fully.

## Nonverbal Communication

"Actions speak louder than words," the saying goes, and people are often more eloquent with their bodies than they realize or intend. We transmit a good deal of information to others through our facial expressions, body postures, and physical distance—in fact, our bodies often send emotional messages that contradict our words.

Here's an example of this process at work. At a county fair, a political rally, or a football game, a pickpocket goes to work. Standing behind someone, the nimble-fingered thief prepares to relieve the person of his wallet. Slowly, the thief's hand moves toward the victim's back pocket and is almost touching the wallet, when suddenly the thief pulls his hand back empty. The pickpocket moves casually through the crowd, whistling. What went wrong? What gave the thief a clue that his intended victim might have been about to reach for his wallet? A pickpocket skillful enough to stay out of jail learns to heed all kinds of signs: The hairs on the back of the victim's neck might have bristled slightly; there might have been an almost imperceptible stiffening of the back, a twitch in a neck muscle, a subtle change in skin color, a trickle of sweat. The victim might not yet have been consciously aware that his pocket was about to be picked, but these signals showed that he was physiologically aware something was afoot.

As we noted earlier, these kinds of physiological changes are not normally outside our control. They tend to function independently of our will—indeed, often against it. (See the Controversies and Online boxes on lie detectors.)

*Facial expressions* are the most obvious emotional indicators. We saw earlier that facial expressions can actually cause some emotional experiences. Facial expressions are also good indicators of the emotions a person is experiencing, from whatever source. We can tell a good deal about a person's emotional state by observing whether that person looks as if he or she is laughing, crying, smiling, or frowning. Many facial expressions are innate, not learned. Children who are born deaf and blind use the same facial expressions as other children do to express the same emotions. Charles Darwin first advanced the idea that most animals share a common pattern of muscular facial movements. For example, dogs, tigers, and humans all bare their teeth in rage. Darwin also observed that expressive behaviors serve a basic biological as well as social function, Darwin's notion that emotions have an evolutionary history and can be traced across cultures as part of our biological heritage laid the groundwork for many modern investigations of emotional expression (Izard, 1982) (see

# CONTROVERSIES

## Truth Is More than Skin Deep: The Lie Detector

Once limited to law enforcement applications, lie detectors—also called *polygraphs*—were for a time being used routinely by corporations, banks, and even fast-food chains to question job applicants about their honesty in past jobs. In 1983, President Ronald Reagan ordered polygraph tests of certain federal employees in an effort to plug leaks of classified or embarrassing information to the press. Then, in December 1988, Congress passed the Employee Protection Act prohibiting the use of polygraphs for random examinations or as part of a preemployment screening process.

The growing use of the polygraph prompted a number of questions: What exactly does a lie detector measure? Do the telltale patterns of inked lines on graph paper necessarily mean that a person is lying? Or do other factors, such as emotional reactions to the content of the questions or the testing situation itself, cause truthful people react as if they were lying?

Lie detectors do not register lies; their readings are based on the fact that lying gives rise to inner emotional conflict that is typically accompanied by specific physiological changes. It is those physiological changes the polygraphs measure. When people lie, they usually experience uncontrollable changes in blood pressure, in breathing, and in the resistance of the skin to electrical current, known as *galvanic skin response*. However, there is no set of responses that definitively indicates that a person has been lying; the pattern of responses varies from person to person (Saxe, 1994).

In the typical lie detector situation, failing the test has serious consequences. Thus, subjects are generally quite nervous and fearful as the blood pressure cuff is strapped to their arm, sensors designed to measure breathing are attached to their chest and stomach, and electrodes are placed on their fingertips to measure galvanic skin response. Because the blood pressure cuff soon starts cutting off circulation, the examination must be completed within 3 to 4 minutes.

Not surprisingly, then, lie detectors are far from error-free perfect when it comes to determining whether someone is lying or telling the truth. Figures vary widely, but according to one estimate, such polygraphs correctly

Figure 9-9). Today psychologists who take an evolutionary approach believe facial expressions served an adaptive function, enabling our ancestors to compete successfully for status, to win mates, and to defend themselves (Ekman, 1992; Tooby & Cosmides, 1990). Facial expressions are probed in greater detail in the chapter on human diversity.

Interestingly, some emotions come through more clearly in facial expressions than others. When Thompson and Meltzer (1964) asked their subjects to fake certain emotions, they found that most people had no trouble showing love, fear, determination, and happiness. Suffering, disgust, and contempt, however, were more difficult to convey convincingly, and these feelings were also tougher for other people to "read." Moreover, very different emotions are easier to tell apart than are related emotions such as fear and surprise (Tomkins & McCarter, 1964).

6. What do psychologists mean by "body language"?

*Body language* is another way by we communicate messages nonverbally. When we are relaxed, we tend to stretch back into a chair; when we are tense, we sit more stiffly with our feet together. Slumping and straightness of the back supply clues about which emotion someone is feeling. In a study similar to the one by Thompson and Meltzer, Beier (1974) videotaped identify only about 75 percent of those who are lying. Unfortunately, about 49 percent of people telling the truth are falsely branded as liars (Horvath, 1977). One major source of error: Galvanic skin response changes in reaction to *all* kinds of emotions, not just those associated with deception (Lykken, 1975). When someone is asked if he committed a murder, the lie detector is likely to surge. But while this reaction may reflect guilt, but it may also signal anxiety, fear, or loathing—all possible reactions to being suspected of murder. If the subject were questioned about marital problems, relationships with parents, or even attitudes toward work, the polygraph might register a similar sharp peak, indicating emotional response, regardless of whether she was telling the truth (Stern et al., 1981). Subjects' feelings about the accuracy of the test also have an impact on the strength of their physiological reactions. The more accurate subjects believes the polygraph to be, the more arousal they are likely to experience when responding deceptively (Saxe, 1994).

It is also fairly easy to fool the polygraph machine, if you know how to do it. Some tactics do not work, however. Conscious efforts not to sweat or not to alter one's respiratory patterns will not succeed. Nor will efforts to increase one's response to control items, such as by clenching one's teeth (Waid & Orne, 1982). But taking tranquilizers does seem to reduce the physiological response to lying. So does not paying attention to the questions. In one experiment, subjects counted backward by sevens during their polygraph examination to distract themselves from the questions, and their lies were undetectable more often than the norm (Waid, Orne, & Orne, 1981).

Personal and social factors may also affect the physiological signs monitored by the machine as well. The galvanic skin response of some people changes quickly and spontaneously, making it more likely that their truthful answers will appear to be lies. Finally, the degree to which examiner and subject are matched in terms of sex, age, race, and ethnicity may also seems to have an impact on polygraph results. In one study, the lie detector failed most often when examiner and subjects shared the same ethnicity, possibly because the subjects felt most at ease in this situation (Waid & Orne, 1981).

Moreover, preconceptions based on individual or social biases may color how officials respond to the results of a lie detector test. Because we know that results are often inaccurate, we must decide whether to trust them in each case. Professor Anita Hill took a polygraph test after testifying that then Supreme Court nominee Clarence Thomas had sexually harassed her. She "passed" the polygraph, but the Senate Judiciary Committee chose to discount the results of her test because of possible inaccuracy. In another case, a death-row inmate who "failed" a lie detector test was executed because the test results were deemed to be true (Saxe, 1994). It may be that in both cases the decisions were justified, but lack of certainty about lie detector results encourages a great deal of subjectivity in deciding whether to accept them—and such decisions can have very serious consequences. Who makes those decisions? On what basis? To what degree are such decisions affected by people's preconceptions? Those who feel the polygraph's unreliability is a serious drawback are convinced that polygraph examinations pose more risks than benefits for society.

It is possible to increase the accuracy of polygraphs by testing only for "guilty knowledge"—that is, knowledge about details of a crime that only the guilty person could know. For example, if the examiner reads off a list of bank names, a guilty suspect should have a stronger physiological reaction to the name of the bank that he or she actually robbed. However, in many of the 500,000 to 1 million lie detector tests conducted each year in the United States, the most sophisticated methods are not used in formulating questions or interpreting results, partly because the vast majority of the 4,000 to 8,000 examiners have had little or no training in physiology or psychology (Lykken, 1975; Saxe, 1994).

subjects acting out six emotions: anger, fear, seductiveness, indifference, happiness, and sadness. While most subjects could portray successfully two out of the six emotions but that the rest of their portrayals were not conscious. One young woman appeared angry no matter which emotion she tried to project; another was invariably seductive.

Body communication also comes through in *personal distance*. The normal conversing distance between people differs from culture to culture. Two Swedes conversing would ordinarily stand much farther apart than would two Arabs or Greeks. Within every culture, there is a personal distance for normal conversation that is generally accepted as appropriate. If someone is standing closer than usual to you, it may indicate aggressiveness or seductiveness; if farther away than usual, it may indicate withdrawal or repugnance.

When having a conversation, Arabs tend to stand closer to one another than most American do when conversing.

Explicit *acts*, of course, serve as nonverbal clues as well. When we receive a 2:00 A.M. telephone call, we expect that the caller has something urgent to say. A slammed door tells us that the person who just left the room is angry. If friends drop in for a visit and you invite them into your living room, you are probably less at ease with them than you are with other friends whom you generally ask to sit down at the kitchen table. *Ges-*

**Figure 9-9**
**Infant facial archetypes.** Working from Charles Darwin's theory that certain emotional and facial expressions have an evolutionary history and are universal, psychologist Carroll Izard believes that he has isolated ten distinct emotions that can be interpreted in the facial expressions of infants. Four characteristic expressions are illustrated here.

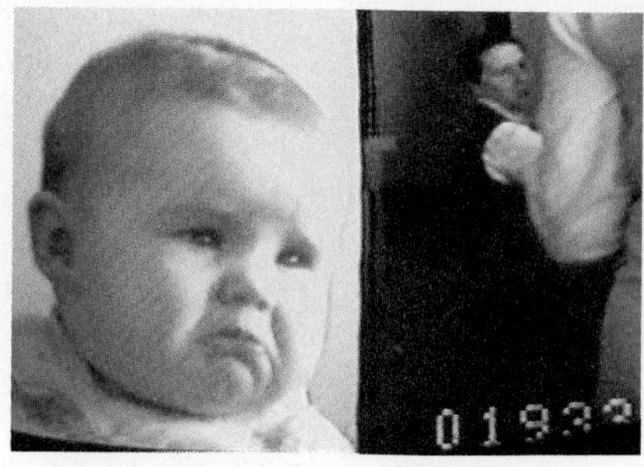

**Sadness**: Brows' inner corners raised, mouth drawn out and down.

**Interest**: Brows raised or knit, mouth softly rounded, lips pursed.

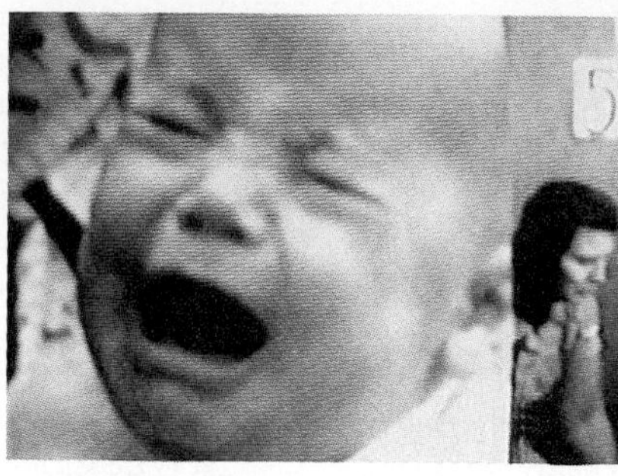

**Distress**: Eyes tightly closed; mouth, as in anger, squared, and angular.

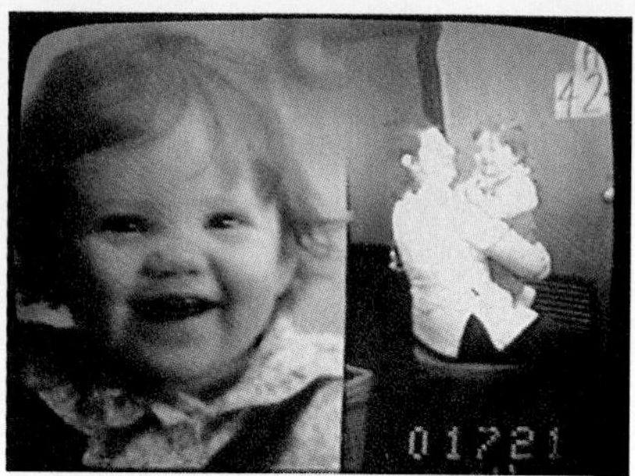


**Joy**: Mouth forms smile, cheeks lifted, twinkle in eyes.

*tures*, such as a slap on the back or an embrace, can also indicate feelings. Whether people shake your hand briefly or for a long time, firmly or limply, tells you something about how they feel about you.

A word of caution is needed here. Although overt behavior may offer a clue to a person's feelings, it is not an *infallible* clue. Laughing and crying sound alike, for example, and we bare our teeth in smiles as well as in snarls. Crying may "mean" sorrow, joy, anger, nostalgia—or that you are slicing an onion. Moreover, as with verbal reports, it is always possible that someone is projecting false clues. We all have done something thoughtlessly—turned our backs, frowned because we were thinking about something else, laughed at the wrong time—that has given offense because these acts were misinterpreted as an expression of an emotion that we were not, in fact, feeling at the time. In all these cases, nonverbal cues do not correspond well to the actual emotions being felt.

Just as people sometimes send out complex and contradictory emotional messages by nonverbal cues, they also differ significantly in their ability to read and decipher such messages. In fact, most people overestimate their ability to interpret nonverbal cues. For example, Ekman and O'Sullivan (1991) studied several hundred "professional lie catchers," including members of the Secret Service, government lie detector experts, judges, police officers, and psychiatrists. With the exception of the psychiatrists, all these groups rated themselves above average in ability to tell if another person was lying. The subjects viewed a set of ten videotapes: Some showed a person lying; others showed a person telling the truth. In

**"How and why should lie detectors be used?"**

Many U.S. institutions have come to depend on lie detectors in a variety of situations. But as our reliance on polygraphs has increased, so have the legal, moral, and scientific questions about their use. In the Controversies box, we looked at such questions as what lie detectors actually register, whether polygraph examinations are error-free, and if people can "beat" them.

What are your feelings on these issues? Do you think lie detectors have a place in business? The government? The courtroom? If so, under what circumstances should polygraphs be administered? Should there be restrictions on their use? If so, what limitations seem necessary to you? Why might these restrictions be needed? After you have thought about these questions, take a few minutes to examine the opinions of some other students, which appear below.

• • • • • • •

**LISA: A person could be termed a liar just because her heart rate went up when her boss walked in or because she was nervous about the test. I think the results and the testing method are too ambiguous for them to be given any real validity.**

**BILL: All evidence used is subject to bias. Lie detectors don't seem a whole lot worse. As long as jurors are informed of percentages of which they are correct, they can decide whether a defendant is guilty beyond a reasonable doubt or not.**

**JOE: I am of the opinion that with well-formed questions, lie detectors can give valuable clues as to what kinds of things the person being tested reacts to the most, and this could in turn lead to other evidence. But I agree that they aren't valid for conviction purposes.**

**ERIN: The worst problem is that despite their lack of reliability, jurors would be likely to place a great deal of stock in lie detectors. Even if they were reminded that they were highly fallible, at least subconsciously I think they would base their opinions on the results too much.**

**ANDRE: I do not think it is our business to decide the role lie detectors play in business—no pun intended. Businesses can generally hire whom they wish—so what they do is their business. I do think they have a place in law and government but should not determine guilt and innocence—they should shed information—not confirm it.**

**STEVE: The sad fact is that in order to appease the general public, a person should take a lie detector test regardless of that person's actual innocence. More often than not, people will assume guilt rather than dignity when a person declines to take the test.**

**SUNI: Personnel recruitment should rely more on the judgment of the personnel manager or how the candidate handles the situation, not on whether he/she is lying or not, since nobody in the business world is speaking the truth all the time. But I think though it is not always reliable, it is sometimes useful in the legal sector.**

**AMY: Maybe a lie detector could be used in court cases where less is at stake, like a civil suit. They shouldn't be the deciding factor of whether or not someone will spend his life in jail.**

**ETHAN: What people have not mentioned . . . is that when hiring in business this [the lie detector's unreliability] is not much of a disadvantage. As long as you screen out the lying people, who cares if you discard some who are not lying? The point is to get as many trustworthy people as possible, and it seems that the lie detector is reasonably accurate at this.**

**BOB: How would businesses use lie detectors? Finding embezzlers has more to do with using the lie detector for law, not business. Would businesses use the detector to test their employees' general character? . . . It seems like an invasion of privacy thing. I think that using the lie detector to find spies and embezzlers is a good thing because 75 percent correctness are fairly good odds.**

**ERIN: But wouldn't the lie detector also be likely to say some people were not lying when they really were? So you would still end up hiring people who weren't trustworthy if you were unlucky? What if someone confessed to a crime but they failed a lie-detector test about the confession? What would people think then?**

**BILL: If rejecting somebody from a job because of not knowing that he was actually telling the truth is helping to give equal opportunity for jobs, then something is whacked. These businesses need all the help they can to be fair when hiring.**

**CARVER: The point is that the polygraph eliminates undesirables. They don't use it to see who would be good at the job, just who would be a risk.**

• • • • • • •

Has reading other students' opinions changed your views? If so, how? What role should the psychology profession play in this area? How would you feel about taking a lie detector test?

every instance when the person was lying, there were telltale changes in that person's behavior that showed up on the videotape. Nonetheless, only the Secret Service agents managed to identify the liars at a better-than-chance rate. Similar results have been obtained with other groups of people (e.g., DePaulo & Pfeifer, 1986).

R. Rosenthal and his colleagues (1974, 1979) developed a test of sensitivity to nonverbal cues—the Profile of Nonverbal Sensitivity (PONS)—that assesses people's ability to judge the meaning of vocal intonations and facial and body movements. Subjects watch a film with an actress or actor portraying various emotional states. Sometimes the portrayal is accompanied by spoken phrases, but certain tones and rhythms identifying them as distinct words have been removed. The viewer then picks one of two possible interpretations of the scene.

The study revealed that women were consistently better than men at accurately deciphering nonverbal cues, although men in the "nurturing" professions—psychiatrists, psychologists, mental hospital aides, and teachers—along with artists, actors, and designers, scored as high as women. The study also showed that sensitivity to nonverbal cues increases with age, most likely because we accumulate more experience in judging vocal tones and observing body movements as we grow older.

Closely related to the ability to read other people's emotions is *empathy*—the arousal of emotion in an observer that is a vicarious response to the other person's situation (Parke & Asher, 1983). Empathy depends not only on one's ability to identify someone else's emotions but also on one's capacity to put oneself in the other person's place and to experience an appropriate emotional response. Just as sensitivity to nonverbal cues increases with age, so does empathy: The cognitive and perceptual abilities required for empathy develop only as a child matures.

## GENDER DIFFERENCES IN EMOTION

**7.** *True or false*: Men generally feel less emotion than women.

Experience tells us that males and females differ considerably in how they express emotion and the emotions they choose to express. As noted in the Chapter 1, for example, men are often perceived as being less emotional than women. But is it that men *feel* less emotion, or are they simply less likely to express the emotions they feel? And are there some emotions that men are *more* likely to express than women?

Recent research sheds some light on these issues. In one study, when men and women saw depictions of people in distress, the men showed little emotion but the women expressed feelings of concern for those in distress (Eisenberg & Lennon, 1983). However, physiological measures of emotional arousal (such as heart rate and blood pressure) showed that the men in the study were actually just as affected as the women were: The men simply inhibited the expression of their emotions, while the women were more open about their feelings. V.E. O'Leary and Smith (1988) point that emotions such as sympathy, sadness, empathy, and distress are often considered to be "unmanly," and boys are trained from an early age to suppress those emotions in public.

In other circumstances, men and women react with very different emotions to the same situation. For example, L. Brody (1985) described one study in which subjects responded to hypothetical situations in which they were betrayed or criticized by another person. Males usually said that they would feel angry: females were likely to report that they would feel hurt, sad, or disappointed.

When men get angry, they tend to interpret the source of their anger as something or someone in the environment around them, and they generally turn their anger outward, against other people and against the situation in which they find themselves. Women, as a rule, are more likely to see themselves as the source of the problem and turn their anger inward, against themselves. Given these gender-specific reactions, it is not surprising that men are four times more likely than women to become violent in the face of life crises, while women are much more likely than men to become depressed.

Some women, however, do allow themselves to feel anger and hostility. As we mentioned earlier, chronic anger—in both women and men—pose a serious health risk. But one study determined that it is far more serious in women who feel angry but do not express their anger (Julius et al., 1986). Tracking a group of women over 18 years, the study found that those who scored high on hostility were three times more likely to die during the course of the study. However, this higher level of risk applied only to subjects who said they got angry in many situations but did not vent their anger. Other subjects who reported frequent bouts of anger, which they expressed, were in the same low risk-group as those who said they rarely or never felt angry.

## LOOKING FORWARD

In the last chapter, we traced the course of human development. In this chapter, we looked at some of the drives, desires, and feelings that characterize human beings. Clearly, without some knowledge of motivation and emotion, we cannot hope to develop a sound understanding of the origins of human behavior. Although we all share certain motives and emotions, the expression of these forces varies from one person to the next. As we explore personality in the next chapter, we will be delving into some of the theories that attempt to explain how and why individuals differ. If we all have motives for achievement, curiosity, affiliation, and power, why do some people strive to achieve while others are content to coast through life? What makes some people chronically angry? Why are some people more sociable than others? Why do some folks have more difficulty with relationships? Why do certain people seek power while others shun it? What makes each of us unique lies at the heart of psychology.

Many of the core questions raised in this chapter pique the interest of contemporary psychologists. To what extent are motives inborn characteristics and to what degree are they culturally determined? What exactly is the relationship between emotion and cognition? Are certain facial expressions universal? How do men and women differ in the ways they experience, interpret, and express emotions? We will address some of these issues in greater detail in the chapter on human diversity.

## SUMMARY

Motivation and emotion help guide our behavior. **Motives** are specific inner needs or wants that arouse an organism and direct its behavior toward a goal. **Emotions** are experiences of feelings such as fear, joy, or surprise, which also underlie behavior.

### PERSPECTIVES ON MOTIVATION

At the turn of the twentieth century, psychologists believed that motivated behavior was caused by **instincts**, specific, inborn behavior patterns characteristic of a species. However, this perspective fell out of favor when scientists realized that human behavior was too changeable and complex to be explained so simply. **Drive-reduction theory** viewed motivated behavior a strategy to ease an unpleasant state of tension or arousal (a **drive**) and return the body to a state of **homeostasis**, or balance. Today scientists assert that an organism seeks to maintain an optimum state of arousal: If arousal is too high, efforts will be made to bring it down; if the level of arousal is too low, we will take action to raise it. In addition to internal motives, goal-oriented behavior is prompted by external stimuli called **incentives**.

## PRIMARY DRIVES

In some instances, a biological need triggers a corresponding state of psychological arousal or tension. This unlearned drive is called a **primary drive**. Hunger, thirst, and sex are the principal primary drives.

### Hunger

Hunger is regulated by two centers in the brain: the hunger center, which stimulates eating, and the satiety center, which reduces the feeling of hunger. Whether level of the simple sugar **glucose** in the blood falls to a certain point, neurons in the hunger center are stimulated. Receptors in the stomach also send signals to the brain. Finally, when food enters the small intestine, a hormone is released that stimulates the satiety center. In addition to these day-to-day regulators, there is another hunger regulator that affects long-term body weight. Both the motivation to eat and overeating are influenced by biological, psychological, cultural, and environmental factors.

Thirst parallels hunger in that both internal and external cues can trigger the thirst drive. Dehydration both inside and outside the cells prompts activation of the thirst drive; so do weather conditions as well as social, psychological, and cultural influences, and other external stimuli.

Weight loss is difficult to achieve and maintain for many obese people because the body appears to have a homeostatic mechanism, known as the **set point**, that regulates metabolism, fat storage, and food intake so as to maintain a preprogrammed weight. Genetic factors also play a major role in determining who is thin and who is overweight.

### Sex

Though not essential to individual survival, sex is nonetheless constitutes a primary drive because it gives rise to reproductive behavior essential for the survival of the species. For both women and men, the hormone **testosterone** exerts the most influence on the sex drive. It is also possible that scents, called **pheromones**, secreted by one sex promote sexual readiness in the other sex. Once arousal begins, the nervous system plays a role in the stimulation of the genitals and other parts of the body.

Psychological influences are at least as important as biological influences in stimulating sexual arousal. People have individual preferences for certain fantasies, pictures, words, music, and so on. Men tend to be aroused by visual cues; women respond more to touch. What we find attractive is also influenced by our culture.

## STIMULUS MOTIVES

Like primary drives, **stimulus motives** are largely unlearned. Stimulus motives place a premium on obtaining information about the environment, but they depend more on external stimuli than on internal states.

### Exploration and Curiosity

Exploration and curiosity are motives activated by the unfamiliar and are directed toward the goal of discovering how the world works. Some psychologists have seen curiosity as an emotion, others as evidence of the need to find meaning in life. It has been linked to creativity.

### Manipulation

Humans and primates need to manipulate objects, to gain both tactile information and a sense of comfort.

### Contact

Contact, the need for affection and closeness, is another important stimulus motive. While manipulation requires active "hands-on" exploration, contact may be passive.

## LEARNED MOTIVES

Some motives are learned rather than innate, but they have just as much of an impact on our behavior as unlearned drives and motives do. Aggression is one important learned motive. Another major class of learned motives, the social motives, center on our relationships with others.

### Aggression

Any behavior that is intended to inflict physical or psychological harm on others is an act of **aggression**. In addition to being a form of behavior, however, aggression is a motive in and of itself. Some psychologists consider aggression part of an unlearned instinct that is triggered by pain and frustration; others see it as an innate drive that must be channeled into constructive avenues. Most contemporary psychologists, however, believe aggression is a learned response, modeled after the aggressive behavior of others, in sports, in movies, on television, or at home. Even when children and adolescents see models of aggressive behavior being punished, the young people tend to behave in a more aggressive manner.

### Sexual Coercion and Its Effects

*Sexual coercion* refers to a variety of behaviors from rape to the less extreme forms of coercion known as *sexual harassment*. Early research on rape, done mostly on imprisoned rapists, found that power, anger, and sadism were the predominant motives behind rapes. More recent research, conducted among the broader population, has concluded that only half of all rapes are motivated by anger, sadism, and hatred. The other half stems from sexual motives.

### Achievement

Psychologists have determined that the **achievement motive** is another learned social motive, underlies the desire to excel, to overcome obstacles, and to strive to do something difficult well. The need for achievement, which varies among individuals, has been measured using the Thematic Apperception Test, a personality test that asks people to make up stories about drawings they are shown, and the Work and Family Orientation scale, a questionnaire that measures work orientation, mastery, and competitiveness. It has been found that a high degree of competitiveness may actually interfere with achievement. People with a strong need to achieve are usually motivated by the desire to live up to a self-imposed high standard of performance.

### Power

The **power motive** is defined as the need to win recognition or to influence or control other people or groups. For instance, college students who score high in the need for power tend to hold important positions in student organizations and committees and pursue careers in fields such as teaching, psychology, and business.

### Affiliation

The **affiliation motive**, the need to be with other people, is especially pronounced when people feel threatened. But we often join groups or establish relationships with other motives in mind. For example, we may choose to get together with others because we want them to praise our achievements or to give us the physical contact we crave.

## A HIERARCHY OF MOTIVES

Abraham Maslow suggested the various motives—learned and unlearned, social and primary drives—can be arranged in a hierarchy. The lower motives are relatively simple: They spring from bodily needs that must be satisfied for survival. Maslow believed that the higher motives, such as the striving to belong or to achieve self-esteem, emerge until the more basic motives have largely been satisfied. The ultimate motive or goal, according to Maslow, is to be *self-actualized*, or the drive to make the most of one's talents and life's possibilities. This view has been challenged by recent research indicating that difficulty in meeting lower needs can actually foster the satisfaction of higher needs.

## EMOTIONS

Emotions, like motives, both arouse and direct our behavior. They prompt us to move toward or away from an object. However, also like motives, emotions may trigger a complex chain of behavior that may promote or interfere with the accomplishment of our goals. According to the **Yerkes-Dodson law**, the more complex the task, the lower the level of arousal that can be tolerated without interfering with performance. If you are highly emotional while you're performing a simple task, your emotional state is of little consequence. If the task is difficult, however, an agitated emotional state may compromise your performance.

### Basic Emotional Experiences

Under Robert Plutchik's classification system for emotions, eight basic categories of emotions motivate various kinds of adaptive behavior. Emotions that are somewhat alike are closer to each other on his emotion circle; those that are quite different (such as sadness and joy) are positioned opposite each other. Within the eight categories, emotions vary in intensity, with the more intense emotion—rage, for example—near the top of the vertical dimension and a less intense version of the same category of emotion—anger, in this case—closer to the bottom. Not all cultures view or categorize emotions this way, however. Some do not even have a word for *emotion*. Others describe feelings by their physical sensations.

### Theories of Emotion

Theories of emotion seek to explain the relationship among the stimuli for an emotion, the bodily responses associated with that emotion, and our thoughts about what we are experiencing. According to the **James-Lange theory**, stimuli bring on physiological changes in our bodies and emotions arise from those physical changes. The **Cannon-Bard theory** states that emotions and bodily response occur simultaneously rather than one after the other. The **cognitive theory** of emotion holds that the situation that we are in when we are aroused—the overall environment—gives us clues that help us interpret this general state of arousal. According to recent research, facial expression may influence emotions apart from cognition.

## THE EXPRESSION OF EMOTION

### Verbal Communication

What people say about what they are feeling often does not accurately reflect their emotions. In some cases, they may not know or be aware of what they are feeling; in others, they may choose to minimize or conceal their feelings.

### Nonverbal Communication

Facial expressions are the most obvious nonverbal emotional indicators. It seems there are certain inborn or universal facial expressions that serve an adaptive function. Body language—our posture, the way we move, our preferred personal distance from others when talking to them—also expresses emotion. Overt behavior, such as slamming a door, is another clue to someone's emotional state.

## GENDER DIFFERENCES IN EMOTION

When confronted with a person in distress, men and women react differently: Women are more likely than men to express emotion about the situation. However, even though the two sexes express emotion in distinct ways, the levels of physiological arousal for men and women are the same. Yet men and women part company when it comes to labeling what they are feeling: Facing the same difficult situation, men report more often that they would feel angry, while women tend to say that they would feel hurt or sad. In a related finding, men are four times more likely than women to be violent; women are much more likely than men to be depressed.

# REVIEW QUESTIONS

## MULTIPLE CHOICE

1. Both ______ and ______ direct our behavior and can activate behavior even without our awareness.

2. Motivation begins with which of the following?

   a. emotion
   b. drive
   c. stimulus
   d. arousal

3. According to drive-reduction theory, the state of balance toward which motivated behavior is directed is called ______ .

4. True of false: Primary motives are not at all affected by learning or experience.

5. In the brain, signals from the ______ center stimulate eating, while those from the ______ center reduce the desire to eat.

6. The hormone ______ stimulates sexual arousal in both men and women.

7. Category of wants or needs that is activated by external stimuli and pushes us to investigate our environment is called______ motives.

8. A person who is willing to contend with the high risks of a career in sales is probably motivated by a high ______ motive.

9. The ______ motive is sometimes aroused when a person needs to be consoled or supported by a group of peers.

10. True or false: According to Maslow, humans are motivated to realize their highest potential.

11. According to the ______ ______ law, there is a relationship between the complexity of a task and the level of emotional arousal that can be tolerated while performing the task.

12. Robert Plutchik asserts that emotions vary in ______, a fact that accounts in part for the great range of emotions we experience.

13. True or false: Cultural differences, particularly language, influence how we experience emotion.

14. Match the following theories of emotion with their definitions:

    ____Cannon-Bard
    ____Cognitive theory
    ____ James-Lange

    a. States that physical reactions come before experienced emotions
    b. Contends that emotions and bodily responses occur simultaneously
    c. Says that emotional experience depends on the perception of a given situation

15. Izard's theory of emotion stresses the importance of:
a. cognition b. expressive behavior

16. Two important nonverbal clues to emotion are ______ ______ and ______ ______.

## CRITICAL THINKING AND APPLICATIONS

17. Recent research confirms that obesity has a much larger genetic component than scientists previously thought. Do you think this finding will change our society's attitudes toward people who are overweight? If so, how? Do you think it will prompt people to think about their own weight problems? If so, how?

18. People who get low grades in school or do poorly on the job are often viewed as lacking motivation. What are some other possible explanations for their substandard performance?

19. Some research reveals that boredom inspires curiosity; other studies show that curiosity is piqued by the new and unknown. Explain why these findings do not contradict each other. How would you apply these concepts in an elementary-school classroom?

20. Think about how you experience and handle feelings of love, anger, and sadness. Do you express all these emotions with equal ease? Do any of these emotions make you uncomfortable? Are your responses to these feelings typical of your gender and culture? In what ways?

*(Answers to the Review Questions can be found in the back of the text.)*

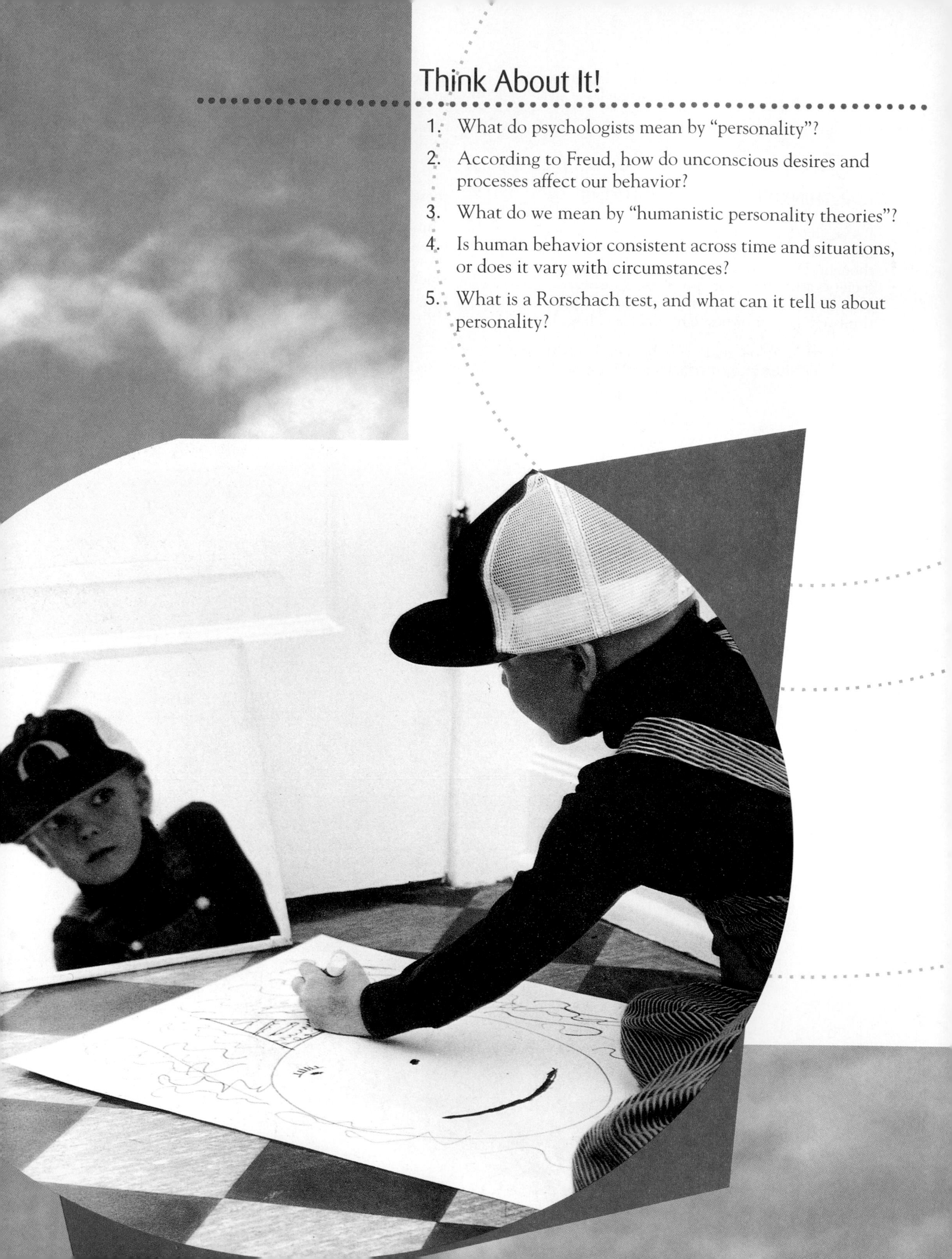

## Think About It!

1. What do psychologists mean by "personality"?
2. According to Freud, how do unconscious desires and processes affect our behavior?
3. What do we mean by "humanistic personality theories"?
4. Is human behavior consistent across time and situations, or does it vary with circumstances?
5. What is a Rorschach test, and what can it tell us about personality?

Psychodynamic Projective Tests Superego Collective Unconscious Expectancies

# PERSONALITY

# 10

## Overview

**Personality** An individual's unique pattern of thoughts, feelings, and behaviors that persists over time and across situations.

**We talk about personality all the time. We describe our best friend as "a fun-loving, but quiet personality," or "kind of a jock, but really gentle." Acquaintances we know less well may elicit a one-dimensional assessment: "He's really arrogant" or "She's a brain." However, these brief characterizations of people do not define their personalities because personality is made up of not one or two outstanding characteristics or abilities but a whole range of them.**

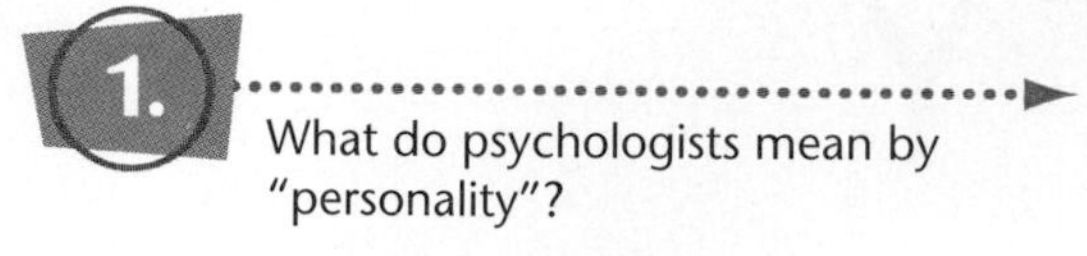

What do psychologists mean by "personality"?

Nonetheless, to study personality and examine it scientifically as psychologists do, it is necessary to define it. Many psychologists define **personality** as an individual's unique pattern of thoughts, feelings, and behaviors that persists over time and across situations. Notice that there are two important parts to this definition. On the one hand, personality refers to *unique differences*, those aspects of a person that distinguish him or her from everybody else. On the other hand, the definition asserts that personality is relatively *stable* and *enduring*—that is, that these unique differences persist through time and across situations. Perhaps you have had the chance to view yourself at various ages in home movies or videos. At each age some of the same characteristics are evident—maybe you are a natural performer, always showing off for the camera, or it could be you are a director type who was telling the camera operator what to do at 4 years of age as well as at 14. We expect people's personalities to be relatively consistent from day to day and from one situation to another; in fact, when that is not so, we generally suspect that something is wrong with the person.

Psychologists approach the study of personality in a number of ways. Some set out to identify the most important characteristics of personality. Others seek to understand why there are differences in personality. Among the latter group, some psychologists identify the family as the most important factor in the development of the individual's personality, while others emphasize environmental influences outside the family and still others see personality as the result of how we learn to think about ourselves and our experiences. Out of these various approaches have come four major categories of personality theories:

- *Psychodynamic theories* place the origins of personality in unconscious, often sexual, motivations and conflicts.
- *Humanistic theories* spotlight positive growth motives and the realization of potential in shaping personality.
- *Trait theories* categorize and describe the ways in which people's personalities differ.
- *Cognitive–social learning theories* find the roots of personality in the ways people think about, act on, and respond to their environment.

To varying degrees, each of these theoretical approaches contributes to our overall understanding of personality.

In this chapter, we will explore the four approaches by examining some representative theories each one has produced. We will see how each theoretical paradigm sheds light on the personality of Jaylene Smith, a young doctor who is having trouble forming close and lasting relationships and who is described in the case that follows. Finally, we will evaluate the strengths and weaknesses of each approach when it comes to understanding personality.

## The Case of Jaylene Smith

Thirty-year-old Jaylene Smith is single and shows plenty of promise as a physician. Yet she has entered therapy because she is troubled by certain aspects of her social life. Acquaintances describe Jay in glowing terms—highly motivated, intelligent, attractive, and charming. But Jay feels terribly insecure and anxious. When asked by a psychologist to pick out some self-descriptive adjectives, Jay selected "introverted," "shy," "inadequate," and "unhappy"—far from an enviable self-image!

Jay was the firstborn in a family of two boys and one girl. Her father is a quiet and gentle medical researcher who married when he was 35 years old. Since his work often allowed him to study at home, he had extensive contact with his children when they were young. He loved all his children but clearly favored Jay. His ambitions and goals for her were extremely high, and as she matured, he responded to her every need and demand almost immediately and with full conviction. He wanted to instill in her a strong desire for achievement. Their relationship remains as close today as it was during Jay's childhood.

Jay's mother, who was 30 years old when she married, worked long hours away from home as a store manager and consequently saw her children primarily at night and on an occasional free weekend. When she came home, Mrs. Smith was tired and had little energy for "nonessential" interactions with her children; instead she devoted her efforts to feeding them (especially the younger ones) and to making certain the house was in order. She had always been career oriented, but she experienced considerable conflict and frustration trying to reconcile her roles as mother, housekeeper, and financial provider. Mrs. Smith was usually amiable toward all her children but tended to argue and fight more with Jay than with the others—at least until Jay was about 6 or 7 years of age (when the bickering subsided). Today their relationship is cordial but lacks the closeness apparent between Jay and Dr. Smith. Interactions between Dr. and Mrs. Smith were sometimes marred by stormy outbursts over seemingly trivial matters. These episodes were always followed by periods of mutual silence lasting for days.

Jay was very jealous of her first brother, who was born when she was 2 years old. Although she does not clearly remember the details of their early relationship, her parents recall that Jay sometimes staged temper tantrums when the new infant demanded and received a lot of attention (especially from Mrs. Smith). The temper tantrums intensified when Jay's second brother was born, just one year after the first. As time went on, the brothers formed an alliance to try to undermine Jay's supreme position with their father. Jay only became closer to her father, while her relationships with her brothers were marked by greater-than-average jealousy and rivalry from early childhood to the present.

Throughout elementary, junior high, and high school, Jay was popular and did well academically. When asked once by a favorite teacher about future goals, she replied confidently, "I plan on going into medicine because I enjoy helping people, particularly when they are sick and must be taken care of." Yet despite Jay's stated lofty goals and ambitions, off and on between the ages of 8 and 17, she had strong feelings of loneliness, depression, insecurity, and confusion—feelings common enough during this age period, but stronger than in most youngsters and very distressing to Jay.

Jay's college days, when she was away from home for the first time, proved exciting and challenging. This was a period of great personal growth for her, but it also caused her much pain. While having new friends and responsibilities gave Jay increased self-confidence and zeal for pursuing

**Psychodynamic theories** Personality theories contending that behavior results from psychological dynamics that interact within the individual, often outside conscious awareness.

a medical career, several unsuccessful romantic involvements proved disheartening and led her to concentrate even more on her studies. The failure to achieve a stable and long-lasting relationship persisted after college and troubled Jay greatly. "After all," she would muse, "aren't people supposed to fall in love and marry? What is wrong with me? Why do I find it impossible to maintain a serious relationship for any length of time?"

Although even-tempered in most circumstances, Jay often has an explosive fit of anger that ends each important heterosexual relationship she has cultivated. Her relationships with other women, while more stable than those with men, are usually casual, uncommitted, and of short duration.

When Jay was 13, she became good friends with a male classmate named Mark. They had many interesting hours of conversation, even though Jay was never able "to be herself" or really express her feelings to Mark. The relationship thrived nonetheless, until one fatal day when a minor disagreement suddenly erupted into a major altercation. Jay ran away and tearfully said that she did not want to see Mark again. Despite Mark's persistent efforts to talk with her and despite the many classes they were in together, Jay refused to have anything further to do with him.

Much later, while finishing her undergraduate education, Jay met Ted, a graduate student some 15 years older than she. At 21, Jay felt that she was falling in love. Their relationship was only about 2 months old when disaster struck. Although Jay and Ted were close and trusted each other, an innocent conversation between Ted and a female classmate triggered Jay's rage. When Jay caught sight of the two together, she turned and hurried away. Ted finally caught up with her, but she screamed angrily in his face that she never wanted to see him again. And she never did.

Thanks to her excellent work in college, Jay was admitted to medical school. After the initial excitement, however, the hard realities of training took hold: She realized she was in for several years of difficult work, intense competition, and the always-present possibility of failure. The severe pressures and workload of medical school forced Jay to pass up potential romantic involvements, although she had many casual friends whom she could always call for brief diversions. While she tried not to dwell on her personal feelings and conflicts during this period of her life, they crept into her consciousness periodically: "I don't deserve to be a doctor"; "I won't pass my exams"; "Who am I, and what do I want from life?"; "Why can't I meet that special person?" At graduation, Dr. and Mrs. Smith were as proud as they could be. Their daughter was now Dr. Jaylene Elizabeth Smith, and she had graduated at the top of her class!

How can we describe and understand Jaylene Smith's personality? How did she become who she is? Why does she feel insecure and uncertain despite her obvious success? Why do her friends see her as charming and attractive, while she describes herself as introverted and inadequate? Each of the several theoretical perspectives on personality provides somewhat different answers to these questions.

## PSYCHODYNAMIC THEORIES

**Psychodynamic theories** see behavior as the end product of psychological dynamics that interact within the individual, often outside conscious awareness. Freud drew on the physics of his day to coin the term *psychodynamics*: As thermodynamics is the study of heat and mechanical energy and how one may be transformed into the other, psychodynamics is the study of psychic energy and how it is transformed and expressed in behavior. Psychodynamic theorists disagreed among themselves about the exact nature of this psychic energy. Some, like Freud, traced it to sexual and aggressive urges; others, like Karen Horney, saw it as rooted in the individual's struggle to deal with dependency. But all psychodynamic theorists share the sense that personality is primarily determined by unconscious processes and can best be understood within the context of life-span development.

**Unconscious** In Freud's theory, all the ideas, thoughts, and feelings of which we are not and normally cannot become aware.

**Psychoanalysis** The theory of personality Freud developed as well as the form of therapy he invented.

**Id** In Freud's theory of personality, the collection of unconscious urges and desires that continually seek expression.

**Pleasure principle** According to Freud, the way in which the id seeks immediate gratification of an instinct.

**Ego** Freud's term for the part of the personality that mediates between environmental demands (reality), conscience (superego), and instinctual needs (id); now often used as a synonym for "self."

## Sigmund Freud

To this day, Sigmund Freud (1856–1939) is the best-known and most influential of the personality theorists. Freud created an entirely new perspective on the study of human behavior. Up to his time, psychology had focused on consciousness—that is, on those thoughts and feelings of which we are aware. Freud, however, stressed the **unconscious**—all the ideas, thoughts, and feelings of which we are not normally aware. Freud's ideas form the basis of **psychoanalysis**, a term that encompasses both the theory of personality that Freud developed and the form of therapy that he invented.

According to Freud, human behavior is based on unconscious instincts, or drives. Some instincts are aggressive and destructive; others, such as hunger, thirst, self-preservation, and sex, are necessary to the survival of the individual and the species. Freud used the term *sexual instincts* to refer not just to erotic sexuality but also to the desire for virtually any form of pleasure. In this broad sense, Freud regarded the sexual instinct as the most critical factor in the development of personality.

**2.** According to Freud, how do unconscious desires and processes affect our behavior?

**HOW PERSONALITY IS STRUCTURED** According to Freud, personality is formed around three structures: the id, the ego, and the superego. The **id** is the only structure present at birth and is completely unconscious (see Figure 10-1). In Freud's view, the id consists of unconscious urges and desires that continually seek expression. It operates according to the **pleasure principle**—that is, it tries to obtain immediate pleasure and avoid pain (see Figure 10-2). As soon as an instinct arises, the id seeks to gratify it. But since the id is not in contact with the real world, it has only two ways of obtaining gratification. One is by reflex actions, such as coughing, which relieve unpleasant sensations at once. Another is through fantasy, or what Freud called *wish fulfillment*: A person forms a mental image of an object or situation that partially satisfies the instinct and relieves the uncomfortable feeling. This kind of thought occurs most often in dreams and daydreams, but it may take other forms. For instance, if someone enrages you and you spend the next half hour imagining all the brilliant things you might say or do to get even with that person, you are engaging in a form of wish fulfillment.

Mental images of this kind provide fleeting relief, but they cannot fully satisfy most needs. Just thinking about being with someone you love may be gratifying, but it is a poor substitute for actually being with that person. Therefore, the id by itself is not very effective at gratifying instincts. It must link up with reality if it is to relieve its discomfort. The id's link to reality is the ego.

Freud conceived of the **ego** as the psychic mechanism that controls all thinking and reasoning activities. The ego operates partly consciously, partly preconsciously, and partly unconsciously. ("Preconscious" refers to material that is not currently in awareness but can easily be recalled.) The ego learns about the external world through the senses and sees to the satisfaction of the id's drives in the external world. In seeking to replace discomfort with comfort, the id acts according to the pleasure principle, while

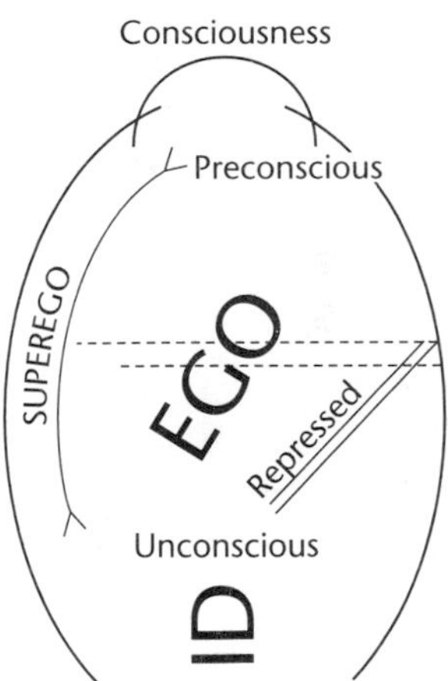


**Figure 10-1**
**The structural relationship formed by the id, ego, and superego.** The *ego* is partly conscious, partly unconscious, and partly preconscious; it derives knowledge of the external world through the senses. The *superego* is also partly conscious, partly unconscious, and partly preconscious. But the *id* is an entirely unconscious structure. The open space beneath the id indicates the limitlessness of the unconscious id.

*Source:* Adapted from *New Introductory Lectures on Psychoanalysis* by Sigmund Freud, 1933, New York: Carlton House.

**Reality principle** According to Freud, the way in which the ego seeks to satisfy instinctual demands safely and effectively in the real world.

**Superego** According to Freud, the social and parental standards the individual has internalized; the conscience and the ego ideal.

**Ego ideal** The part of the superego that consists of standards of what one would like to be.

the ego operates by the **reality principle**: By means of intelligent reasoning, the ego tries to delay satisfying the id's desires until it can do so safely and successfully (see Figure 10-2). For example, if you are thirsty, your ego will attempt to determine how best to obtain something to quench your thirst effectively and safely.

A personality that consisted only of ego and id would be completely selfish. It would behave effectively but unsociably. Fully adult behavior is governed not only by reality but also by morality—that is, by the individual's conscience, or the moral standards the individual develops through interaction with parents and society. Freud called this moral watchdog the **superego**.

The superego is not present at birth. In fact, as young children, we are amoral and do whatever is pleasurable. As we mature, however, we assimilate, or adopt as our own, the judgments of our parents about what is "good" and "bad." In time, the external restraint applied by our parents is completely replaced by our own internal self-restraint. The superego, eventually acting as conscience, takes over the task of observing and guiding the ego, just as the parents once observed and guided the child. Like the ego, it works at both the conscious and the unconscious level.

According to Freud, the superego also compares the ego's actions with an **ego ideal** of perfection and then rewards or punishes the ego accordingly. Unfortunately, the superego is often too harsh in its judgments. An artist dominated by such a punishing superego, for example, may realize the impossibility of ever equaling Rembrandt or Michelangelo and give up painting in despair.

Ideally, our id, ego, and superego work in harmony, the ego satisfying the demands of the id in a reasonable, moral manner approved by the superego. We are then free to love and hate and to express our emotions sensibly and without guilt. When our id is dominant, our instincts are unbridled, and we are apt to endanger both ourselves and society. When our superego dominates, our behavior is checked too tightly, and we are inclined to judge ourselves too harshly or too quickly, impairing our ability to act on our own behalf and enjoy ourselves.

**Figure 10-2**
**How Freud conceived the workings of the pleasure and reality principles.** Note that according to the reality principle, the *ego* uses rational thought to postpone the gratification of the *id* until its desires can be satisfied safely.

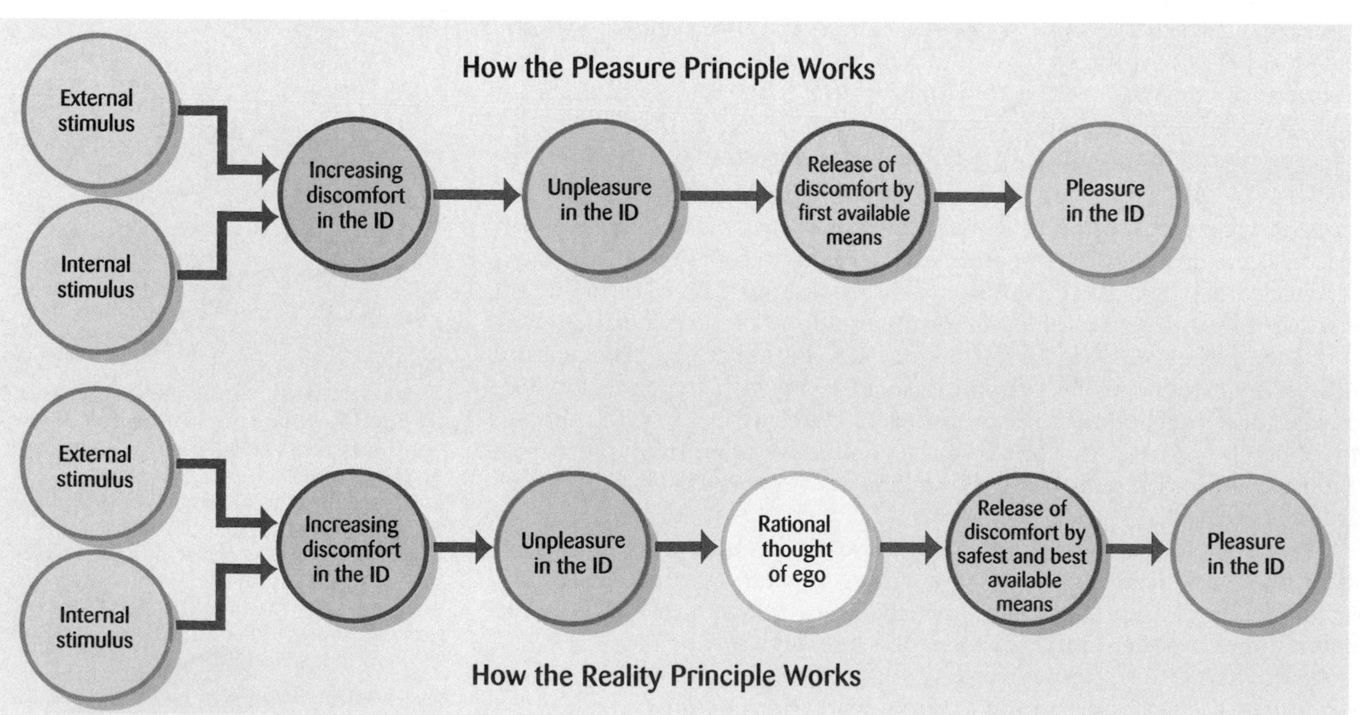

**How Personality Develops** Freud's theory of personality development gives center stage to the way in which the sexual instinct is satisfied during the course of life. Recall that Freud thought of the sexual instinct not just as a desire for sexual activity but, in broader terms, as a craving for sensual pleasure of all kinds. Freud called the energy generated by the sexual instinct **libido**. As infants mature, their libido becomes focused on different sensitive parts of the body. During the first 18 months of life, the dominant source of sensual pleasure is the mouth. At about 18 months, sensuality shifts to the anus; and at about age 3, it shifts again, this time to the genitals. According to Freud, children's experiences at each stage stamp their personality with tendencies that endure into adulthood. If a child is deprived of pleasure (or allowed too much gratification) from the part of the body that dominates a certain stage, some sexual energy may remain permanently tied to that part of the body, instead of moving on in normal sequence to give the individual a fully integrated personality. This is called **fixation**, and as we shall see, Freud believed that it leads to immature forms of sexuality and to certain characteristic personality traits. Let's look more closely at the psychosexual stages that Freud identified and their presumed relationship to personality development.

In the **oral stage** (birth to 18 months), infants, who depend completely on other people to satisfy their needs, relieve sexual tension by sucking and swallowing; when their baby teeth come in, they obtain oral pleasure from chewing and biting. According to Freud, infants who receive too much oral gratification at this stage grow into overly optimistic and dependent adults; those who receive too little may turn into pessimistic and hostile people later in life. Fixation at this stage is linked to such personality characteristics as lack of confidence, gullibility, sarcasm, and argumentativeness.

During the **anal stage** (roughly 18 months to 3 1/2 years) toilet training takes place. If parents are too strict in toilet training, some children throw temper tantrums; they may end up with self-destructive lives as adults. Others become obstinate, stingy, and excessively orderly.

When children reach the **phallic stage** (after age 3), they discover their genitals and develop a marked attachment to the parent of the opposite sex and become jealous of the same-sex parent. Freud called this the **Oedipus complex**, after the character in Greek mythology who killed his father and married his mother. Girls go through a corresponding **Electra complex**, involving possessive love for their fathers and jealousy toward their mothers. Most children eventually resolve these conflicts by identifying with the parent of the same sex. However, Freud contended that fixation at this stage leads to vanity and egotism in adult life, with men boasting of their sexual prowess and treating women with contempt, and women becoming flirtatious and promiscuous. Phallic fixation may also prompt feelings of low self-esteem, shyness, and worthlessness.

At the end of the phallic period, Freud believed, children lose interest in sexual behavior and enter a **latency period**. During this period, which begins at around the age of 5 or 6 and lasts until age 12 or 13, boys play with boys, girls play with girls, and neither sex takes much interest in the other.

At puberty, the individual enters the last psychosexual stage, which Freud called the **genital stage**. At this time, sexual impulses reawaken. In lovemaking, the adolescent and the adult are able to satisfy unfulfilled desires from infancy and childhood. Ideally, immediate gratification of these desires is replaced by mature sexuality, in which postponed gratification, a sense of responsibility, and caring for others all play a part.

**Libido** According to Freud, the energy generated by the sexual instinct.

**Fixation** According to Freud, a partial or complete halt at some point in the individual's psychosexual development.

**Oral stage** First stage in Freud's theory of personality development, in which the infant's erotic feelings center on the mouth, lips, and tongue.

**Anal stage** Second stage in Freud's theory of personality development, in which a child's erotic feelings center on the anus and on elimination.

**Phallic stage** Third stage in Freud's theory of personality development, in which erotic feelings center on the genitals.

**Oedipus complex** and **Electra complex** According to Freud, a child's sexual attachment to the parent of the opposite sex and jealousy toward the parent of the same sex; generally occurs in the phallic stage.

**Latency period** In Freud's theory of personality, a period in which the child appears to have no interest in the other sex; occurs after the phallic stage.

**Genital stage** In Freud's theory of personality development, the final stage of normal adult sexual development, which is usually marked by mature sexuality.

Freud believed that during the *oral stage*, when infants are dependent on others to fulfill their needs, they derive pleasure from the mouth, lips, and tongue.

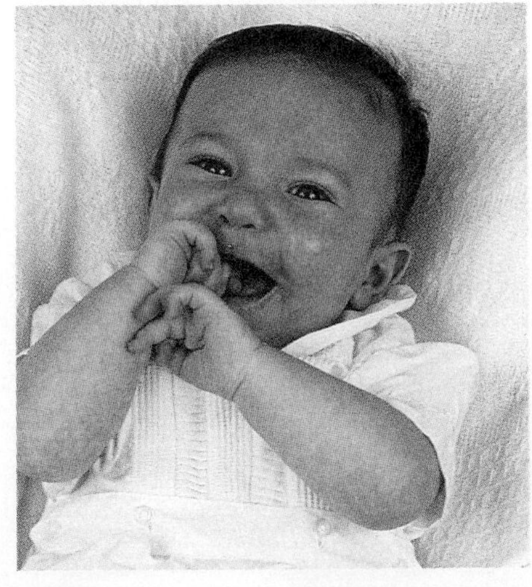

**Personal unconscious** In Jung's theory of personality, one of the two levels of the unconscious; it contains the individual's repressed thoughts, forgotten experiences, and undeveloped ideas.

**Collective unconscious** In Jung's theory of personality, the level of the unconscious that is inherited and common to all members of a species.

**Archetypes** In Jung's theory of personality, thought forms common to all human beings, stored in the collective unconscious.

**Persona** According to Jung, our public self, the mask we put on to represent ourselves to others.

**Anima** According to Jung, the female archetype as it is expressed in the male personality.

**Animus** According to Jung, the male archetype as it is expressed in the female personality.

Freud's male-centered, phallic view of personality development has been assailed by feminists, especially since he also hypothesized that all little girls feel inferior because they do not have a penis. The tendency today is to see penis envy as much less central to female personality development than Freud thought it was (D. Gelman, 1990). In fact, the whole view that male and female personality development proceed along similar lines is being challenged. It may be, for example, that the developmental tasks facing boys are quite different from those facing girls; if this is the case, then the unique developmental tasks encountered by girls may leave them with important skills and abilities that were overlooked or minimized in Freud's theory.

Freud's beliefs, particularly his emphasis on sexuality, were not completely endorsed even by members of his own psychoanalytic school. Carl Jung and Alfred Adler, two early associates of Freud, eventually broke with him and formulated their own psychodynamic theories of personality. Jung accepted Freud's stress on unconscious motivation but expanded the scope of the unconscious well beyond the selfish satisfactions of the id. Adler believed that human beings have positive—and conscious—goals that guide their behavior. Other psychodynamic theorists put greater emphasis on the ego and its attempts to gain mastery over the world. These neo-Freudians, principally Karen Horney and Erik Erikson, also focused more on the influence of social interaction on personality.

## Carl Jung

Carl Jung's (1875–1961) embraced many of Freud's tenets; however, he amplified on them in novel ways. For example, whereas Freud viewed the id as a "cauldron of seething excitations" that the ego has to control, Jung saw the unconscious as the ego's source of strength and vitality. He also believed that the unconscious breaks down into the personal unconscious and the collective unconscious. Within the realm of the **personal unconscious** fall our repressed thoughts, forgotten experiences, and undeveloped ideas, which may rise to consciousness if an incident or sensation triggers their recall.

The **collective unconscious**, Jung's most original concept, comprises the memories and behavior patterns inherited from the past generations. Just as the human body is the product of millions of years of evolution, so too, according to Jung, over the millenia the human mind has developed "thought forms," or collective memories, of experiences that people have had in common since prehistoric times. He called these thought forms **archetypes**. Archetypes appear in our thoughts as typical mental images or mythical representations (see Figure 10-3). Because all people have mothers, for example, the archetype of "mother" is universally associated with the image of one's own mother, with Mother Earth, and with a protective presence. The archetype of "hero" may enter one's thoughts as a primitive tribal chieftain, Joshua at the battle of Jericho, or Nelson Mandela, depending on one's particular moment in history.

Carl Jung

Jung felt that specific archetypes play special roles in shaping personality. The **persona** (an archetype whose meaning stems from the Latin word for mask) is the element of our personality by which we are known to other people—a shell that grows around our inner self. For some people, the public self so predominates that they lose touch with their inner feelings, leading to personality maladjustments.

In Jung's scheme, the archetypes of anima and animus also figure prominently. The **anima** is the female archetype as it is expressed in a man; the **animus** is the male archetype as expressed in the female personality. Thus, Jung considered aggressive behavior in females and nurturing behavior in males as manifestations of, respectively, the animus and the anima.

Jung also divided people into two general attitude types—introverts and extroverts. **Extroverts** turn their attention to the external world. They are "joiners" who take an active interest in other people and in the events going on around them. **Introverts** are more caught up in their own private worlds. They tend to be unsociable and lack confidence in dealing with other people. Everyone, Jung felt, possesses some aspects of both attitude types, but one is usually dominant, while the other remains largely submerged.

**Extrovert** According to Jung, a person who usually focuses on social life and the external world instead of on his or her internal experience.

**Introvert** According to Jung, a person who usually focuses on his or her own thoughts and feelings.

**Compensation** According to Adler, the person's effort to overcome imagined or real personal weaknesses.

While Freud emphasized the primacy of the sexual instincts, Jung stressed people's rational and spiritual qualities. While Freud considered development to be shaped in childhood, Jung thought that psychic development only come to fruition during middle age. Jung brought a sense of historical continuity, to his theories, tracing the roots of human personality back through our ancestral past; yet he also contended that a person moves constantly toward self-realization—toward blending all parts of the personality into a harmonious whole. Both because Jung broke with Freud and because of the symbolism and mysticism that characterize his theories, Jung's ideas have been somewhat neglected by psychologists. Recently, however, he has been "rediscovered" by those convinced of the power of myth.

## Alfred Adler

Alfred Adler (1870–1931) disagreed sharply with Freud's concept of the personality emerging out of the conflict between the id's desire to gratify instinctual impulses and the superego's morality-based restrictions. To Adler, people possess innate *positive* motives and strive for personal and social perfection. One of his earliest theories grew out of personal experience: As a child, Adler was frail and almost died of pneumonia at the age of 5. This early brush with death led him to the concept that personality develops through the individual's attempt to overcome physical weaknesses, an effort he called **compensation.** The blind person who, like Stevie Wonder, cultivates particularly acute auditory abilities and the disabled child who, like the late Wilma Rudolph, surmounts the crippling effects of a disease and goes on to become an athlete exemplify Adler's theory of compensation.

Later on, Adler modified and broadened his views, contending that people seek to overcome *feelings* of inferiority that may or may not have a basis in reality. Such feelings may spring from a child's sense of being inferior to parents, siblings, teachers, or peers. To Adler, birth order made a crucial difference in this sense of inferiority. That is, it does not matter whether second or third children are, in fact, inferior to their older siblings at athletics; what matters is that they *believe* they are. In Adler's view, the attempt to overcome such feelings of inferiority is a principal governor of human behavior and a major determinant of adult personality.

Interestingly, Adler did not consider the feeling of inferiority, as a negative characteristic per se. Rather, he

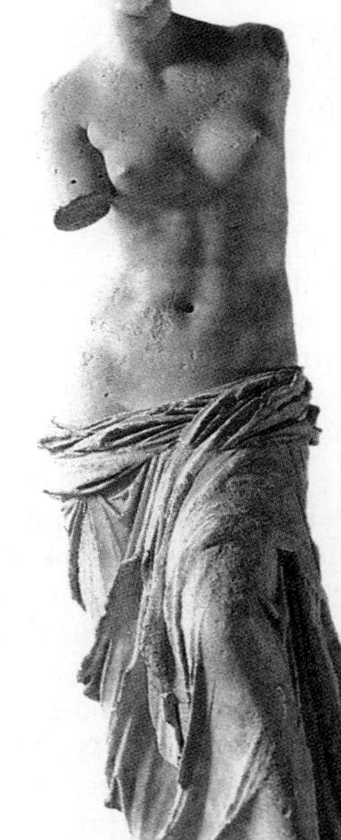

**Figure 10-3**
**The artistic expression of archetypes from the collective unconscious.** Each of these artworks depicts the same mythological female figure—a goddess of love and fertility. At right is a Hellenistic figure of Venus from about 130–120 B.C., and at left is a female idol from Eastern Europe that dates from about 4000 B.C. Despite the obvious differences between the two figures, there are some striking similarities. According to Jung, mythological figures represent *archetypes*, or thought forms stored in a *collective unconscious*. He believed that because archetypes are stored as images that are passed on from generation to generation, they have inspired the artistic imagination throughout the ages.

**Inferiority complex** In Adler's theory, the fixation on feelings of personal inferiority that results in emotional and social paralysis.

thought such feelings often spark positive development and personal growth. Nevertheless some people become so fixated on their feelings of inferiority that they become paralyzed and develop what Adler called an **inferiority complex.**

Unlike Freud, Adler believed that individuals are not controlled by their environment; instead, he contended that we have the capacity to master our own fate. Because of this emphasis on voluntary striving toward positive goals, Adler has been hailed by many psychologists as the father of humanistic psychology, a topic we will explore in greater depth later in this chapter.

**What is the value of examining personality from a variety of perspectives?**

In Chapter 1 we discussed the major schools in the evolution of psychology as a science. In this chapter we focus on the issue of personality, and we see how each of the perspectives examines personality from a different viewpoint. In the specific case of Jaylene Smith we see how each perspective raises different questions and provides us with different insights into the personality of one individual.

Rather than adhere strictly to one perspective, many psychologists today take an eclectic approach, utilizing many perspectives to form a broader view of personality. These scientists do not believe that human behavior can be reduced to simple cause-and-effect explanations; rather, they feel that each discipline contributes pieces to solving the puzzle of human personality and behavior. What are your thoughts on this issue? Which perspective do you find most convincing? Do you rely primarily on one or two perspectives, or do you prefer an *eclectic* approach? As you are considering these questions, take a few minutes to familiarize yourself with these views of some fellow students.

• • • • • • •

**AMY: The humanistic interpretation made sense to me. It stressed the difference between Jay's self-concept and her capacities. Also, the idea that Jay learned to be shy by being rewarded for studying alone made sense.**

**CARVER: Each approach does a good job of explaining Jay's personality, given its particular paradigm. Each of these paradigms is vaguely true in some way. None of them tells us "the way Jay is." They just tell us how Jay seems from one perspective.**

**GREG: By attacking the issue from different angles there is a higher pool of causes to be offered, but I can see how they could cause more confusion. Perhaps Jay would be the best at deciding which interpretation of her problem would be the best and make the most sense since she is most in tune with her experience.**

**MICHAEL: Most of the perspectives made some sense as to some aspect of her life. I think the theories generally are too narrow to account for everything. For instance, Freud's ideas worked well in this case, but in many other cases [they] would not really explain anything. I think it is very valuable to look at a case study from many perspectives, as I believe they are all pieces of one big theory that can explain so much more.**

**GREG: One concern that I have is if some psychologist might be deeply rooted into a certain school of thought. Let's say that you see a psychologist who believes solely in Freudian theories and little else. This type of narrow mindedness seems like it could cause dissent in the academic community of psychology. Definitely there needs to be open mindedness, but then who is actually correct...?**

**ETHAN: One of the things that always strikes me about Freud is that though he shows good predictive ability with his theories (such as being able to predict when Jay was going to stop fighting with her mother), the motivations for these predictions seem absurd. Perhaps what Feud really was is an extremely good observational psychologist.**

• • • • • • •

Now that you have been exposed to the views of other students, have your opinions changed at all? If you want to understand your own behavior and personality, what kind of approach would you use? To what extent should psychologists utilize different perspectives in their work?

## Karen Horney

Karen Horney (1885–1952), another psychodynamic personality theorist who was greatly indebted to Freud, took issue with some of his most prominent ideas, especially his analysis of women and his emphasis on sexual instincts. Based on her experience as a practicing therapist in Germany and the United States, Horney concluded that environmental and social factors are the most important influences in shaping personality, and among these, the most pivotal are the human relationships we experience as children.

In Horney's view, Freud overemphasized the sex drive, leading him to present a distorted picture of human relationships. While sexuality does figure in the development of personality, Horney thought that nonsexual factors, such as the need for a sense of basic security and the response to real or imagined threats, play an even larger role. For example, all people share the need to feel loved and nurtured by their parents, regardless of any sexual feelings they might have about them. Conversely, parents' protective feelings toward their children emerge not only from biological forces but also from the value society places on the nurturance of children.

**Anxiety** In Horney's theory, the individual's reaction to real or imagined threats.

**Neurotic trends** Horney's term for irrational strategies for coping with emotional problems and minimizing anxiety.

Karen Horney

For Horney, **anxiety**—an individual's reaction to real or imagined dangers—is a powerful motivating force. Whereas Freud believed that anxiety usually emerges from sexual conflicts, Horney stressed that feelings of anxiety also originate in a variety of nonsexual contexts. In childhood, anxiety arises because children depend on adults for their very survival. Anxious because they are insecure about receiving continued nurturance and protection, children develop inner protections, or defenses, that provide both satisfaction and security. They experience more anxiety when those defenses are threatened.

As adults, according to Horney (1937), we adopt one of three coping strategies, or **neurotic trends,** that help us deal with emotional problems and ensure safety, albeit at the expense of personal independence: moving toward people (submission), moving against people (aggression), and moving away from people (detachment). Well-adjusted people also experience anxiety and threats to their basic security, but because their childhood environment enabled them to satisfy their basic emotional needs, they were able to develop without becoming trapped in neurotic lifestyles.

Parting company with Freud in another area, Horney was convinced that cultural forces—including social status and social roles—were far more important than biological imperatives when it comes to human development. Advocating a constructive and optimistic understanding of male and female personality, which emphasized that culture and not anatomy determines many of the characteristics that differentiate women from men, she was a forerunner of contemporary thinkers who believe that culture and society can be changed and, in the process, transform human relationships.

## Erik Erikson

Erik Erikson (1902–1994), who studied with Freud in Vienna and who was psychoanalyzed by Freud's daughter, Anna, was another psychodynamic theorist who took a socially oriented view of personality development. Erikson agreed with much of Freud's thinking on sexual development and the influence of libidinal needs on personality. But also important for Erikson was the *quality* of parent-child relationships. Since the family constitutes the child's first brush with society, Erickson believed that children can be disciplined in a way that makes them feel loved or hated. The key is that children should feel their own needs and desires are compatible with

Erik Erikson

those of society as embodied in their family. Only if children feel competent and valuable, in their own eyes and in society's, will they develop a secure sense of identity. This exemplifies how Erikson shifted the focus of Freud's personality theory to ego development.

Erikson (1963) outlined eight stages of personality development (see Figure 10-4) and suggested that success at each stage depends on the person's adjustments in previous stages:

1. *Trust versus mistrust.* During the first year of life, babies are torn between trusting and not trusting their parents. If their needs are generally met, infants come to trust the environment and themselves. This leads to faith in the predictability of the environment and optimism about the future. Frustrated infants become suspicious, fearful, and overly concerned with security.
2. *Autonomy versus shame and doubt.* During their first 3 years, as physical development proceeds, children gain increasing autonomy and begin to explore their surroundings. They learn to walk, hold onto things, and control their excretory functions. If the child repeatedly fails to master these skills, self-doubt may take root. One response to self-doubt is the practice of abiding compulsively by fixed routines. At the other extreme is the hostile rejection of all controls, both internal and external. If parents and other adults belittle a child's ef-

**Figure 10-4**
**Erikson's eight stages of personality development.** Each stage involves its own developmental crisis, whose resolution is crucial to adjustment in successive stages. The first five of the eight stages correspond to Freud's stages of personality development.

*Source:* Adapted from *Childhood and Society* by Erik H. Erikson. Copyright 1950, © 1963 by W. W. Norton & Company, Inc. Renewed 1978 by Erik H. Erikson. Used by permission of W. W. Norton & Company, Inc., and The Hogarth Press.

**Erikson's stages of personality development**

Freud's stages of personality development (Oral through Genital)

| Stage | 1 | 2 | 3 | 4 | 5 | 6 | 7 | 8 |
|---|---|---|---|---|---|---|---|---|
| Oral | Basic trust vs. mistrust | | | | | | | |
| Anal | | Autonomy vs. shame doubt | | | | | | |
| Phallic | | | Initiative vs. guilt | | | | | |
| Latency | | | | Industry vs. inferiority | | | | |
| Genital | | | | | Identity vs. role confusion | | | |
| Young adulthood | | | | | | Intimacy vs. isolation | | |
| Adulthood | | | | | | | Generativity vs. stagnation | |
| Maturity | | | | | | | | Ego integrity vs. despair |

forts, the child may also begin to feel shame and acquire a lasting sense of inferiority.

**Object-relations theories** Psychodynamic theories of personality that emphasize early relations with caregivers as the chief determinant of personality and the basis for subsequent interpersonal relations.

3. *Initiative versus guilt*. Between the ages of 3 and 6, children become increasingly active, undertaking new projects, manipulating things in the environment, making plans, and conquering new challenges. Parental support and encouragement for these initiatives lead to a sense of joy in exercising initiative and taking on new challenges. However, if the child is scolded for these initiatives, strong feelings of guilt, unworthiness, and resentment may take hold and persist.
4. *Industry versus inferiority*. During the next 6 or 7 years, children encounter a new set of expectations at home and at school. They must learn the skills needed to become well-rounded adults, including personal care, productive work, and independent social living. If children are stifled in their efforts to become part of the adult world, they may conclude that they are inadequate, mediocre, or inferior and lose faith in their power to become self-sufficient.
5. *Identity versus role confusion*. At puberty, childhood ends and the responsibilities of adulthood loom just ahead. The critical problem at this stage is to find one's identity. In Erikson's view, identity is achieved by integrating a number of roles—student, sister or brother, friend, and so on—into a coherent pattern that gives the young person a sense of inner continuity or identity. Failure to forge an identity leads to role confusion and despair.
6. *Intimacy versus isolation*. During young adulthood, men and women must resolve a critical new issue: the question of intimacy. To love someone else, Erikson argued, we must have resolved our earlier crises successfully and feel secure in our own identities. To form an intimate relationship, lovers must be trusting, autonomous, and capable of initiative, and must exhibit other hallmarks of maturity. Failure at intimacy brings a painful sense of loneliness and the feeling of being incomplete.
7. *Generativity versus stagnation*. During middle adulthood, roughly between the ages of 25 and 60, the challenge is to remain productive and creative in all aspects of one's life. People who have successfully negotiated the six earlier stages are likely to find meaning and joy in all the major activities of life—career, family, community participation. For others, life becomes a drab routine, and they feel dull and resentful.
8. *Integrity versus despair*. With the onset of old age, people must try to come to terms with their approaching death. For some, this is a period of despair at the loss of former roles, such as employee and parent. Yet, according to Erikson, this stage also represents an opportunity to attain full selfhood. By this, he meant an acceptance of one's life, a sense that it is complete and satisfactory. People who have gained full maturity by resolving the conflicts in all the earlier stages possess the integrity to face death with a minimum of fear.

## Object-relations Theories of Personality

In contrast to Erikson's emphasis on development throughout the lifespan, **object-relations theories** of personality stress the importance of the child's earliest interactions. The object relations school originated in Great Britain with the work of Melanie Klein, W.R.D. Fairbairn, and D. W. Winnicott. Object-relations theorists see children's relations with their caregiver (primary object) during the first 2 years of life as crucial to their personality development (e.g., Fairbairn, 1952; M. Klein, 1948; Winnicott, 1971). They hypothesize that during this time children develop an image of themselves based on the quality of their relationship with their primary caregiver. To the extent that this attachment to the primary caregiver is in some way disturbed, the person may very well experience difficulties in interpersonal relationships as an adult (Bowlby, 1969/1982a). According to object-relations theories, infants do not relate to their caregivers as real people, but rather as objects, and the quality of that relationship (whether gentle, angry, kind, rejecting, distant, constant, or erratic) shapes children's ideas about themselves and the world.

## A PSYCHODYNAMIC VIEW OF JAYLENE SMITH

According to Freud, personality characteristics such as insecurity, introversion, and feelings of inadequacy and worthlessness often arise from fixation at the phallic stage of development. Thus, had Freud been Jay's therapist, he would probably have concluded that Jay has not yet effectively resolved her Electra complex. Working from this premise, he would have hypothesized that Jay's relationship with her father was either very distant and unsatisfying or unusually close and gratifying. We know, of course, that it was the latter.

In all likelihood, Freud would also have asserted that at around age 5 or 6, Jay had become aware that she could not actually marry her father and do away with her mother, as he would say she wished to do. On this point, it is interesting that the arguments and fights between Jay and her mother subsided when Jay was "about 6 or 7 years of age." Moreover, we know that shortly thereafter, Jay began to experience "strong feelings of loneliness, depression, insecurity, and confusion." Clearly, something important happened in Jay's life when she was 6 or 7.

Finally, the continued coolness in Jay's relationship with her mother and the unusual closeness with her father would probably have confirmed Freud's suspicion that Jay has still not satisfactorily resolved her Electra complex. Thus, Freud would have predicted that Jay would have problems making the progression to mature sexual relationships with other men. Jay, of course, is very much aware that she has problems relating to men, at least when these relationships get "serious."

And what does Erikson's theory tell us about Jaylene Smith's personality? Recall that for Erikson, one's success in dealing with later developmental crises depends on how effectively one has resolved earlier crises. Because Jay is having great difficulty in dealing with intimacy (Stage 6), he would have suggested that she is still struggling with problems from earlier developmental stages. Erikson would have looked for the source of these problems in the quality of Jay's relationships with others. We know that her mother "subtly" communicated her own frustration and dissatisfaction to her children and spent little time on "nonessential" interactions with them. These feelings and behavior patterns would not have instilled in a child the kind of basic trust and sense of security that Erikson believed were essential to the first stage of development. In turn, Jay's failure to establish basic trust would complicate her future development. In addition, her relationship with her mother and brothers continued to be less than fully satisfactory. It is not surprising, then, that Jay had some difficulty working through subsequent developmental crises. Although she developed a close and caring relationship with her father, Jay was surely aware that his affection partly depended on her fulfilling the dreams, ambitions, and goals he had for her.

## Evaluating Psychodynamic Theories

Freud's contention that we are not always, or even often, conscious of the underlying causes of our behavior has fundamentally changed the way people view themselves and others. It has also had a lasting impact on history, literature, and the arts. Yet Freud was a product of his time and place. Critics of his theories have pointed out that he was apparently unable to imagine a connection between his female patients' sense of inferiority and their subordinate position in their society. In addition, when patients allegedly told him of sexual abuse they had endured at the hands of family members, Freud initially took these stories at face value but later reversed himself and saw them as fantasies, supporting his theory of the Oedipus and Electra complexes.

This conclusion has been challenged on two fronts. First, given our heightened awareness of the high rates of sexual abuse of children, some critics claim that the stories were probably true, and that Freud's about-face amounted to caving in to the social disapproval of his hypotheses regarding childhood sexuality (Masson, 1984). More disturbingly, there is growing evidence that Freud's patients may never have actually reported instances of sexual abuse to him; rather, it appears that Freud may have *inferred* sexual abuse in their childhoods from their adult symptoms (Cioffi, 1974; Esterson, 1993; Schatzman, 1992).

Psychodynamic views have also been criticized because they are based largely on retrospective (backward-looking) accounts of individuals who have sought treatment rather than on experimental research with "healthy" individuals. Yet it is often difficult to translate psychodynamic personality theories into hypotheses that can be tested experimentally (Cloninger, 1993).

Still, Freud's theory has received some limited confirmation from experimental research. For example, people who eat and drink too much tend to mention oral images when interpreting inkblot tests (Bertrand & Masling, 1969; Masling, Rabie, & Blondheim, 1967). Orally fixated people also seem to depend heavily on others, as Freud predicted (S. Fisher & Greenberg, 1985). In addition, some research indicates that a few characteristics of anally fixated people do tend to appear together; for instance, individuals who are stingy are indeed also likely to be neat (S. Fisher & Greenberg, 1985). However, research has not confirmed that these various personality characteristics stem from the kinds of early-childhood experiences described by Freud. Yet support for Freud's theory comes from more recent research that uses stimuli designed to activate or "trigger" particular unconscious processes (Cloninger, 1993).

The effectiveness of psychoanalysis as a therapy has also been cited as evidence in support of Freud's theories. As we shall see in the chapter on therapies, however, although psychoanalysis has been found to be beneficial in many cases, it does not seem to be any more or less effective than therapies based on other theories (Stiles, Shapiro, & Elliott, 1986).

Erikson's theory of stages of identity has also prompted a good deal of research. The concept of identity resolution has probably attracted the most attention. Waterman, Beubel, and Waterman (1970) looked into whether people who were successful in handling the crises of the first four stages were more likely to achieve a stable source of identity in the fifth stage. Their data suggest that this is indeed the case. Other research has focused on the link between the formation of identity in Stage 5 and the achievement of intimacy in Stage 6. Is it necessary to forge a strong identity in order to achieve intimacy? The answer, again, seems to be yes. Orlofsky, Marcia, and Lesser (1973) found that college men who were the least isolated socially were also those with the clearest sense of self. In a follow-up study of the same group of college men, Marcia (1976) observed that identity continued to be related to intimacy. So, achieving a solid sense of personal identity apparently does pave the way for an individual to cultivate successful personal relationships. Yet another study found the same connection between identity and intimacy for both sexes. Men and women both believe that a positive sense of identity is crucial to achieving satisfactory relationships (Orlofsky, 1978).

**Humanistic personality theory** Any personality theory that asserts the fundamental goodness of people and their striving toward higher levels of functioning.

**Actualizing tendency** According to Rogers, the drive of every organism to fulfill its biological potential and become what it is inherently capable of becoming.

**Self-actualizing tendency** According to Rogers, the drive of human beings to fulfill their self-concepts, or the images they have of themselves.

**Fully functioning person** According to Rogers, an individual whose self-concept closely resembles his or her inborn capacities or potentials.

## HUMANISTIC PERSONALITY THEORIES

What do we mean by "humanistic personality theories"?

Freud believed that personality grows out of the resolution of unconscious conflicts and developmental crises. Many of his followers—including some who modified his theory and others who broke away from his circle—also embraced this basic point of view. But in the theory of Alfred Adler, we glimpsed a very different view of human nature. You will recall that Adler wrote about forces that contribute to positive growth and a move toward personal perfection. For these reasons, Adler is sometimes called the first humanistic personality theorist.

**Humanistic personality theory** emphasizes that we are positively motivated and progress toward higher levels of functioning—in other words, that there is more to human existence than dealing with hidden conflicts. Humanists stress people's potential for growth and change as well as the ways they subjectively experience their lives right now, rather than dwelling on how they felt or acted in the past. As a result, this approach holds all of us personally responsible for our lives and their outcome. Finally, humanists also believe that given reasonable life conditions, people will develop in desirable directions (Cloninger, 1993). Adler's concept of striving for perfection laid the groundwork for later humanistic personality theorists such as Abraham Maslow and Carl Rogers. We discussed Maslow's theory of the hierarchy of needs leading to self-actualization in the previous chapter. We now turn to Rogers's theory of self-actualization.

### Carl Rogers

Humanistic psychologists believe that life is a process of striving to achieve our potential, of opening ourselves to the world around us and experiencing joy in living. Carl Rogers, who died in 1987, was one of the most prominent humanistic theorists who contended that men and women develop their personalities in the service of positive goals. According to Rogers, every organism is born with certain innate capacities, capabilities, or potentialities—"a sort of genetic blueprint, to which substance is added as life progresses" (Maddi, 1989, p. 102). The goal of life, Rogers believed, is to fulfill this genetic blueprint, to become the best of whatever each of us is inherently capable of becoming. Rogers called this biological push toward fulfillment the **actualizing tendency**. While Rogers maintained that the actualizing tendency characterizes all organisms—plants, animals, and humans—he noted that human beings also form images of themselves, or *self-concepts*. Just as we try to fulfill our inborn biological potential, so, too, we attempt to fulfill our self-concept, our conscious sense of who we are and what we want to do with our lives. Rogers called this striving the **self-actualizing tendency**. If you think of yourself as "intelligent" and "athletic," for example, you will strive to live up to those images of yourself.

When our self-concept is closely matched with our inborn capacities, we are likely to become what Rogers called a **fully functioning person**. Such people are self-directed: They decide for themselves what it is they wish to do and to become, even though their choices may not always be sound ones. They are not unduly swayed by other people's expectations for them. Fully functioning people are also open to experience—to their own feelings as well as to the world and other people around them—and thus find themselves "increasingly willing to be, with greater accuracy and depth, that self which [they] most truly [are]" (C. R. Rogers, 1961, pp. 175–176).

According to Rogers, people tend to become more fully functioning if they are brought up with **unconditional positive regard**, or the experience of being treated with warmth, respect, acceptance, and love regardless of their own feelings, attitudes, and behaviors.

**Unconditional positive regard** In Rogers's theory, the full acceptance and love of another person regardless of that person's behavior.

**Conditional positive regard** In Rogers's theory, acceptance and love that are dependent on behaving in certain ways and fulfilling certain conditions.

But often parents and other adults offer children what Rogers called **conditional positive regard**, meaning they value and accept only certain aspects of the child. The acceptance, warmth, and love the child receives from others, then, depends on the child's behaving in certain ways and fulfilling certain conditions. The condition may be expressed explicitly, such as "Daddy won't love you if . . . " or "Mommy doesn't love girls who . . ." But it may also come through subtly, as in statements like "That's a nice idea, but wouldn't you rather do . . . ?" The message here is twofold: The other person finds the child's feelings or behavior questionable and proposes alternatives that are allegedly better for the child. Not surprisingly, one response to conditional positive regard is a tendency to change one's self-concept to include those things that one "ought to be," to become more like the person one is expected to be to win the caregiver's love. In the process, one's self-concept comes to resemble one's inborn capacity less and less, and one's life deviates from the genetic blueprint.

When people lose sight of their inborn potential, they become constricted, rigid, and defensive. They feel threatened and anxious and experience considerable discomfort and uneasiness. Because their lives are directed toward what other people want and value, they are unlikely to experience much real satisfaction in life. At some point, they may realize that they don't really know who they are or what they want.

## A HUMANISTIC VIEW OF JAYLENE SMITH

Humanistic personality theory would focus on the discrepancy between Jay's self-concept and her inborn capacities. For example, Rogers would point out that Jay is intelligent and achievement oriented but nevertheless feels that she doesn't "deserve to be a doctor," worries about whether she will ever be "truly happy," and remembers that when she was 13, she "never was able 'to be herself' and really express her feelings," even with a good friend. Her unhappiness, fearfulness, loneliness, insecurity, and other dissatisfactions similarly stem from Jay's inability to become what she "most truly is." Rogers would suspect that in Jay's life acceptance and love were conditioned on her living up to other people's ideas of what she should become. We know that for most of her life, Jay's father was her primary source of positive regard. We don't know with certainty that Dr. Smith conditioned his love for Jay conditional on her living up to his goals for her, but it seems very possible that he did.

### Evaluating Humanistic Theories

The central tenet of most humanistic personality theories—that the overriding purpose of the human condition is to realize one's potential—is difficult if not impossible to verify scientifically. The resulting lack of scientific rigor is one of the major criticisms of these theories. In addition, some critics claim that humanistic theories present an overly optimistic view of human beings and fail to take into account the evil in human na-

**Personality traits** Dimensions or characteristics on which people differ in distinctive ways.

**Factor analysis** A statistical technique that identifies groups of related objects; used by Cattell to identify trait clusters.

ture. Others contend that the humanistic view fosters self-centeredness and narcissism, and reflects Western values of individual achievement rather than universal human potential.

Nonetheless, Maslow and, especially, Rogers did attempt to test some aspects of their theories scientifically. For example, Rogers studied the discrepancy between the way people perceived themselves and the way they ideally wanted to be. He presented subjects with statements such as "I often feel resentful" and "I feel relaxed and nothing really bothers me." First, his subjects were asked to sort the statements into several piles indicating how well the statements described their real selves. Then they were asked to sort them again, this time according to how well they described their ideal selves. In this way, Rogers discovered that people whose real selves were considerably different from their ideal selves were more likely to be unhappy and dissatisfied. A subsequent study showed that Rogers's client-centered approach to therapy does help to close the gap between a person's real and ideal selves, leading to greater self-acceptance and an ideal self that includes qualities the person already possesses (Butler & Haigh, 1954).

## TRAIT THEORIES

The personality theories we have examined all emphasize the importance of early-childhood experiences and advance a set of principles that accounts for the varieties of human personality. Other personality theorists take a different approach. Instead of concentrating on how personality develops from early childhood on, they focus on the present, describing the ways in which already-developed adult personalities differ from one another. These *trait theorists*, as they are known, assert that people differ according to the degree to which they possess certain **personality traits**, such as dependency, anxiety, aggressiveness, and sociability.

Of course, traits cannot be observed directly, but we can *infer* a trait from how a person behaves. If someone consistently throws parties, goes to great lengths to make friends, and is regularly seen in groups, we might conclude that that person possesses a high degree of sociability.

Our language has many words that describe personality traits. Gordon Allport, along with his colleague H. S. Odbert (1936), went through the dictionary and found nearly 18,000 words that might refer to personality traits. For Allport, traits—or "dispositions," as he called them—are literally encoded in the nervous system as structures that guide consistent behavior across a wide variety of situations. Allport also believed that while traits describe behaviors that are common to many people, each individual personality comprises a unique constellation of traits.

Only about 2,800 of the words on Allport and Odbert's list concern the kinds of stable or enduring characteristics that most psychologists would call personality traits, and when synonyms and near-synonyms are removed, the number of possible personality traits drops to around 200—which is still a formidable list. Psychologist Raymond Cattell (1965), using a statistical technique called **factor analysis**, has demonstrated that when people are rated on those 200 characteristics, various traits tend to cluster in groups. Thus, a person who is described as persevering or determined is also likely to be thought of as responsible, ordered, attentive, and stable and probably would not be described as frivolous, neglectful, and changeable. On the basis of extensive research, Cattell originally concluded that just 16 traits account for the complexity of human personality; later he suggested that it might be necessary to add another 7 traits to the list (R. B.

Cattell & Kline, 1977). According to Cattell, each individual personality consists of a relatively unique constellation of those basic traits.

Other trait theorists think that Cattell used too many traits to classify personality. For example, Tupes and Christal (1961) demonstrated that personality traits can be boiled down to five basic dimensions: extraversion, agreeableness, conscientiousness, emotional stability, and culture. This finding has been confirmed repeatedly in subsequent research (see Table 10-1) (Borgatta, 1964; Botwin & Buss, 1989; Goldberg, 1981, 1982, 1993; W. T. Norman, 1963), although there is some disagreement about whether the fifth dimension should be called "culture" or "openness to experience" (McCrae & Costa, 1985, 1987, 1989) or "intellect" (Digman & Takemoto-Chock, 1981; Peabody & Goldberg, 1989). There is a growing consensus that the "big five" personality dimensions, also known as the *five-factor model*, indeed capture the most salient dimensions of human personality (Funder, 1991; John, 1988).

## A TRAIT VIEW OF JAYLENE SMITH

A psychologist working from the trait perspective would infer certain traits from Jay's behavior. When we observe that Jay chose at an early age to become a doctor, did well academically year after year, and graduated first in her medical-school class, it seems reasonable to infer a trait of "determination" or "persistence" to account for her behavior. Similarly, we

**TABLE 10-1 The "Big Five" Dimensions of Personality**

| | |
|---|---|
| **EXTRAVERSION** | Talkative, bold, boisterous, forceful, assertive, spontaneous, active, demonstrative, energetic, enthusiastic, adventurous, outgoing, outspoken, loud, noisy, ambitious, dominant, sociable. |
| **AGREEABLENESS** | Warm, kind, cooperative, unselfish, flexible, fair, polite, forgiving, helpful, pleasant, affectionate, gentle, good-hearted, sympathetic, trusting, generous, considerate, agreeable. |
| **CONSCIENTIOUSNESS** | Organized, dependable, conscientious, responsible, hardworking, efficient, capable, deliberate, painstaking, precise, practical, thorough, thrifty, cautious, serious, economical, reliable. |
| **EMOTIONAL STABILITY** | Unemotional, unenvious, relaxed, objective, calm, at ease, even-tempered, good-natured, stable, contented, secure, imperturbable, undemanding, steady, placid, peaceful. |
| **CULTURE OR OPENNESS TO EXPERIENCE OR INTELLECT** | Intelligent, perceptive, curious, imaginative, analytical, reflective, artistic, insightful, inventive, wise, witty, refined, creative, sophisticated, knowledgeable, intellectual, resourceful, versatile, original, deep, cultured. |

might reasonably conclude from the previous description of Jay that she also has traits of sincerity, motivation, and intelligence, as well as insecurity, introversion, shyness, and anxiety. These relatively few traits account for a great deal of Jay's behavior, and they also provide a thumbnail sketch of "what Jay is like."

### Evaluating Trait Theories

Traits are the language that we commonly use to describe other people (e.g., as "shy" or "insecure" or "arrogant"). Thus, the trait view of personality has considerable commonsense appeal. Moreover, although psychologists disagree as to the exact number of traits, it is easier to scientifically study personality traits than to study such things as "self-actualization" and "unconscious motives." But trait theories have several shortcomings (Eysenck, 1993; Kroger & Wood, 1993).

First of all, they are primarily descriptive: They seek to delineate the basic dimensions of personality but generally do not try to explain causes (Funder,1991). As you can see from the trait view of Jaylene Smith, trait theory describes and classifies personality, but it tells us little about *why* people are the way they are. Thus, the five-factor theory of personality helps us much the way north-south and east-west axes do in map making (Goldberg, 1993a, cited in Ozer & Reise, 1994)—that is, it helps us to locate personality more precisely. But like a point on a map, it gives us no information about what kind of terrain is there and how it got to be that way.

In addition, some critics argue that the dangers in reducing the diversity and complexity of human nature to just a few traits are greater than the usefulness traits offer in terms of description and classification (Mischel, 1984). Moreover, psychologists disagree about whether 5 traits or 20 traits or even 100 traits are sufficient to capture the complexity of human personality (Funder, 1991). Finally, many psychologists question whether traits are really useful as descriptors and predictors of behavior. If you label a friend "agreeable," does this mean that he or she is agreeable in different situations and all the time? Of course not. But if not, then how useful is the trait designation to begin with? This last question raises the issue of consistency in human behavior, an issue to which we now turn.

## THE CONSISTENCY CONTROVERSY

We have been assuming that behavior is generally consistent across both situations and time. According to this view, an aggressive person is likely to act aggressively in a wide variety of situations and to express belligerence in more or less the same way from day to day and year to year. Such consistently aggressive behavior is evidence for the underlying personality trait, or disposition, of aggression.

Is human behavior consistent across time and situations, or does it vary with circumstances?

But some theorists question whether humans are consistent in their behavior. For example, the marine sergeant who is aggressive toward his recruits may be quite submissive when the captain comes to conduct an inspection, and he may act much more aggressively one day than the next. A given situation, moreover, may elicit similar behavior from a wide variety of people whatever their personality traits. For example, most people wait their turn at a checkout counter no matter how aggressive they may otherwise be. The thesis that human behavior is more often inconsistent than consistent was confirmed by Walter Mischel (1968), who reviewed many studies of personality and found that the consistency of behavior across situations was actually quite low—people act in strikingly different ways across a range of situations. In the past 30 years, Mischel has moderated his position somewhat, conceding that at least *some* behaviors are relatively consistent over time and across situations. For example, intelligence, as measured by intelligence tests, appears to be quite stable over time, as we saw in Chapter 7. Similarly, academic achievement is consistent from course to course and grade level to grade level (Rushton & Endler, 1977). In addition, J. Block (1971) showed that students rated as dependable by high school peers tended to be rated as dependable by independent observers 10 years later. Nonetheless, much human behavior is quite inconsistent across situations and over time. This gives rise to two perplexing questions: Why does behavior usually *appear* to be far more consistent than it actually is? And how can personality theories account for inconsistency in behavior?

Some theorists have answered the first question by asserting that the appearance of consistent personality traits is an illusion. Mischel, for example, noted that behavior sometimes seems to be consistent merely because we see a person only in a limited variety of situations that tend to elicit the same behavior. Moreover, Mischel believes humans have a strong need to find consistency and stability even in the face of inconsistency and unpredictability, to read consistency into the behavior of others even when there is none. According to his research, observers tend to greatly overestimate the consistency of someone's actions and to ignore behaviors that do not square with their preexisting image of that person (Hayden & Mischel, 1976).

As for the second question, it seems clear that only a theory of personality that accounts for both consistencies and inconsistencies in behavior can offer a fully satisfactory explanation of human behavior. One approach to integrating all these elements considers the *interaction* between personal and situational factors (Bowers, 1973; Funder, 1991). In the next section of the chapter, we will look at personality theories that take into account both personal and situational determinants of behavior.

**Cognitive–social learning theories** Personality theories that view behavior as the product of the interaction of cognitions, learning and past experiences, and the immediate environment.

**Expectancies** In Bandura's view, what a person anticipates in a situation or as a result of behaving in certain ways.

**Locus of control** According to Rotter, an expectancy about whether reinforcement is under internal or external control.

Walter Mischel

## COGNITIVE–SOCIAL LEARNING THEORIES

**Cognitive–social learning theorists** believe that people internally organize their expectancies and values to guide their own behavior. This set of personal standards is unique to each one of us, growing out of our own life history. Our behavior is the product of the interaction of cognitions (how people think about a situation and how they view their behavior in that situation), learning and past experiences (including reinforcement, punishment, and modeling), and the immediate environment. For example, Albert Bandura (1977, 1986) asserts that people evaluate a situation according to certain internal **expectancies**, such as personal preferences, and this evaluation affects their behavior. Environmental feedback that follows the actual behavior, in turn, influences future expectancies. In this way, expectancies guide behavior in a given situation, and the results of the behavior in that situation shape expectancies in future situations. For example, two young women trying a video game for the first time may experience the situation quite differently, even if their scores are similarly low. One may find the experience fun and be eager to gain the skills necessary to go on to the next level of games, while the other may be disheartened by getting a low score, assume she will never be any good at video games, and never play again.

To Rotter (1954), **locus of control** is a prevalent expectancy, or cognitive strategy, by which people evaluate situations. People with an *internal* locus of control are convinced they can control their own fate. They

**Self-efficacy** According to Bandura, the expectancy that one's efforts will be successful.

**Performance standards** In Bandura's theory, standards that people develop to rate the adequacy of their own behavior in a variety of situations.

**Reciprocal determinism** In Bandura's personality model, the concept that the person influences the environment and is in turn influenced by the environment.

believe that through hard work, skill, and training, it is possible to find reinforcements and avoid punishments. People with an *external* locus of control do not believe they control their fate. Instead, they are convinced that chance, luck, and the behavior of others determine their destiny and that they are helpless to change the course of their lives (Strickland, 1989). There is some evidence that drug use, inactivity among people suffering from depression, and school truancy are linked to an external locus of control (Lefcourt, 1992). In all these cases, people do not believe that making an effort to be active or productive will bring about any positive consequences.

Both Bandura and Rotter have tried to combine personal variables (such as expectancies) with situational variables in an effort to understand the complexities of human behavior. Both theorists believe that expectancies become part of a person's *explanatory style*, which, in turn, greatly influences behavior. Explanatory style separates optimists from pessimists. It is what causes two beginners who get the same score on a video game to respond so differently.

Some research shows that children as young as 8 years old have already developed a habitual explanatory style (Nolen-Hoeksema, Girgus, & Seligman, 1986). Third-graders were asked to read descriptions of 12 good and 12 bad events and then come up with reasons the events happened. Their scores reflected their degree of pessimism or optimism. Pessimists tended to believe that negative events were due to personal characteristics they could not change; optimists viewed negative events as unfortunate incidents they could remedy. Children with a more pessimistic style were found to be more prone to depression and to do worse on achievement tests.

Albert Bandura

Explanatory style dovetails with **self-efficacy**, a term Albert Bandura has used to describe the degree to which one feels one can meet one's goals. Suppose a math professor has a son and a daughter. Say the son's mathematical aptitude is low, while the daughter is especially gifted in this area. Imagine further that both children develop a **performance standard** that calls for high achievement in mathematics. The son will most likely feel incapable of meeting his standard, while the daughter will almost certainly feel capable of meeting hers. In Bandura's terms, the son will probably develop a low sense of self-efficacy and thus feel generally incapable of meeting his life goals, while the daughter will likely develop a strong sense of self-efficacy. In turn, these explanatory styles will have a profound effect on their behavior.

If all this sounds too pessimistic and deterministic, we must point out that Bandura (1986) also emphasizes people do have the power of self-determination. For example, the frustrated son in the example above might modify his behavior and seek to excel in other areas. He might pursue other academic interests related to mathematics—his original performance standard—but in a field where his talents shine. In this way, performance standards may be modified by experience, affecting future behavior.

People with an *external locus of control* tend to have faith in chance or fate.

Bandura calls such interactions between personalities and their environment **reciprocal determinism**. Personality variables, situational variables, and actual behaviors constantly interact. Certain people may be prone to display aggressive behavior. But whether they will actually behave aggressively is determined by their perception of a given situation, which likely involves other people. Thus, people who are considering acting aggressively will likely ask themselves if they are prepared to cope with aggressive behavior in return. Furthermore, the consequences that follow their aggressive behavior will affect their subsequent behavior in similar situations in the future. They learn where and when it is rewarding to be aggressive. According to Bandura, human personality develops out of this ongoing interaction among personal standards (learned by observation and reinforcement), situations, and behavioral consequences.

## A COGNITIVE–SOCIAL LEARNING VIEW OF JAYLENE SMITH

Jaylene may have *learned* to be shy and introverted because she was rewarded for spending much time by herself studying. Her father probably encouraged her devotion to her studies; certainly, she earned the respect of her teachers. Moreover, long hours of studying helped her avoid the somewhat uncomfortable feelings that she experienced when she was around other people for long periods.

Reinforcement may have shaped other facets of Jay's personality as well. No doubt her father and her teachers reinforced her self-discipline and her need to achieve academically. Even her aggression toward men may have been learned in childhood as a successful coping mechanism. If her hostility put an end to her brothers' taunts and was also rewarded by her father's affection, she may have learned to react with aggression to perceived threats from males in general.

In addition, at least some aspects of Jaylene's personality were formed by watching her parents and brothers and learning subtle lessons from these family interactions. Her aggressive behavior with boyfriends, for example, may have grown out of seeing her parents fight. As a young child, she may have observed that some people deal with conflict by means of outbursts. Moreover, as Bandura's concept of self-efficacy would predict, Jay surely noticed that her father, a "successful medical researcher," enjoyed and prospered in both his career and his family life, while her mother's two jobs as housewife and store manager left her somewhat frustrated and overtired. This contrast may have contributed to Jay's own interest in medicine and to her mixed feelings about establishing a close relationship that might lead to marriage.

### Evaluating Cognitive–social Learning Theories

Cognitive–social learning theories of personality seem to have great potential. They put mental processes back at the center of personality. The key concepts of these theories, such as self-efficacy and locus of control, can be defined and studied scientifically, which is not true of the key concepts of psychodynamic and humanistic theories. Moreover, as we saw in the discussion of the consistency controversy, cognitive–social learning theories help explain why people behave inconsistently, an area where trait approaches fall short. Cognitive–social learning theories of personality have also spawned useful therapies that help people recognize and change a negative sense of self-efficacy or explanatory style. As we will see in Chapter 13, these therapies have been particularly useful in helping people overcome depression.

However, it is still too early to say how well cognitive–social learning theories account for the complexity of human personality. Some critics point out that with the benefit of hindsight, any behavior can be explained as the product of certain cognitions, but that doesn't mean those cognitions were the *causes*—or at least the sole causes—of the behavior.

Just as there is great diversity in the way psychologists view personality, psychologists also disagree on the best way to measure or assess personality, the topic we turn to next.

## SUMMARY TABLE

### Theories of Personality

| Theory | Roots of Personality | Methods of Assessing |
|---|---|---|
| **Psychodynamic** | Unconscious thoughts, feelings, motives, and conflicts; repressed problems from early childhood. | Projective tests, personal interivews. |
| **Humanistic** | A drive toward personal growth and higher levels of functioning. | Objective tests and personal interviews. |
| **Trait** | Relatively permanent dispositions within the individual that cause the person to think, feel, and act in characteristic ways. | Objective tests. |
| **Social Learning Theories** | Determined by past reinforcement and punishment as well as by observing what happens to other people. | Interviews, objective tests, observations. |

## PERSONALITY ASSESSMENT

In some ways, testing personality is much like testing intelligence (see the chapter on intelligence). In both cases, we are trying to measure something intangible and invisible. And in both cases, a "good test" is one that is both reliable and valid: It gives dependable and consistent results, and it measures what it claims to measure. But there are special difficulties in measuring personality.

Personality, as you know, reflects *characteristic* behavior—how people usually react to their environment. In assessing personality, then, we are not interested in someone's *best* behavior. We are interested in *typical* behavior—how a person usually behaves in ordinary situations. Further complicating the measurement process, such factors as fatigue, the desire to impress the examiner, and the fear of being tested can profoundly affect a person's behavior in a personality-assessment situation.

In the intricate task of measuring personality, psychologists use four basic tools: the personal interview; direct observation of behavior; objective tests; and projective tests. We will look at each in turn.

### The Personal Interview

An *interview* is a conversation with a purpose: to obtain information from the person being interviewed. Interviews are often used in clinical settings to find out, for example, why someone is seeking treatment and to help diagnose the person's problem. Such interviews are generally *unstructured*—that is, the interviewer asks the client questions about any material that comes up and asks follow-up questions whenever appropriate. The most effective interviewers are warm, interested in what the respondent has to say, calm, relaxed, and confident (Feshbach & Weiner, 1982; Saccuzzo, 1975). Ideally, the interviewer directs the conversation over a wide range of subjects and encourages the person to discuss his or her experiences, feelings, and attitudes freely. The interviewer also pays attention to the person's behavior—manner of speaking, poise, or tenseness when it comes to certain topics.

**Objective tests** Personality tests that are administered and scored in a standard way.

Because the behavior of the interviewer may color the outcome of unstructured interviews, they are often used in combination with more objective tests of personality.

When conducting systematic research on personality, investigators more often rely on the *structured interview*. Here the order and content of the questions are fixed ahead of time, and the interviewer adheres to the set format. While less personal, this kind of interview allows the interviewer to obtain comparable information from everyone interviewed. Generally speaking, structured interviews draw out information about sensitive topics that might not come up in an unstructured interview.

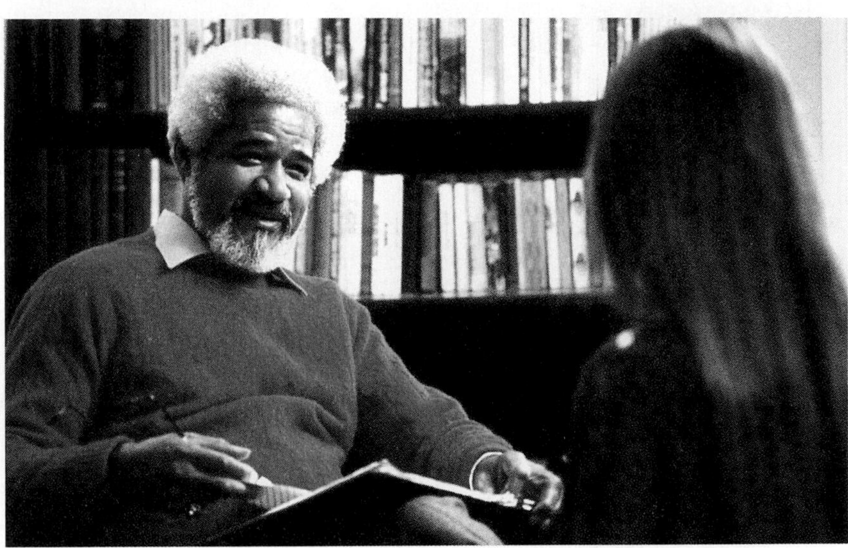

The *personal interview* is a basic tool of personality assessment. The structured interview follows a fixed order and content of questioning.

## Observation

Another way to find out how a person usually behaves is to *observe* that person's actions in everyday situations over a long period of time. Behaviorists and social learning theorists prefer this method of assessing personality because it allows them to see how situation and environment influence behavior as they note the range of behaviors the person is capable of exhibiting. Since most people are self-conscious when they suspect they are being watched, observation works best with young children and with people who have problems with language. But this technique can be used successfully with people of almost any age and in many settings—a company cafeteria, an assembly line, wherever people work or socialize together.

In *direct observation*, observers watch people's behavior firsthand; ideally, their unbiased accounts of the subjects' behavior paint an accurate picture of that behavior. However, an observer runs the risk of misinterpreting the true meaning of an act. For example, the observer may think that children are acting hostile when they are merely protecting themselves from the class bully. An expensive and time-consuming method of research, direct observation may also yield faulty results if, as noted earlier, the presence of the observer affects the subjects' behavior.

In recent years, observation techniques have been refined to address these sources of potential research error. Most observations are now quantified, so if, for example, aggression is being studied, the investigator typically determines in advance what behaviors will be considered aggressive and then counts the frequency with which the subject displays those behaviors. Moreover, experimenters usually *videotape* behavior now. This allows an entire research team to view a person's behavior repeatedly and at various speeds.

## Objective Tests

In an attempt to devise measuring instruments that do not depend on the skills of an interviewer or the interpretive abilities of an observer, psychologists developed **objective tests**, or personality inventories. Generally, these are written tests that are administered and scored according to

**Sixteen Personality Factor Questionnaire** Objective personality test created by Cattell that provides scores on the 16 traits he identified.

**Minnesota Multiphasic Personality Inventory (MMPI)** The most widely used objective personality test, originally intended for psychiatric diagnosis.

a standard procedure. The tests are usually constructed so that the person merely chooses between a "yes" or "no" response or selects one answer among many choices. Objective tests are the most widely used tools for assessing personality, but before we proceed to describe several of them, we must note that they have two serious drawbacks. First, they rely entirely on self-report. Therefore, with people who do not know themselves well, or cannot be entirely objective about themselves, or want to paint a particular picture of themselves, self-report questionnaire results have limited usefulness (Funder, 1991). (In fact, some research indicates that peers who know you well often do a better job characterizing you than you do yourself [Funder, 1987, 1989]!) Second, if subjects have taken other personality questionnaires, their familiarity with the test format may affect a person's responses to the present questionnaire. This is a particular problem on college campuses, where students are likely to participate in multiple research studies, many of which rely on some kind of personality inventory (Council, 1993).

Because of their interest in accurately measuring personality traits, trait theorists favor objective tests. Cattell, for example, developed a 374-question personality test called the **Sixteen Personality Factor Questionnaire**. Not surprisingly, the 16PF (as it is usually called) provides scores on each of the 16 traits identified by Cattell. More recently, objective tests have been developed to assess the "big five" major personality traits described earlier in this chapter (Goldberg, 1993).

The most widely used objective personality test, however, is the **Minnesota Multiphasic Personality Inventory (MMPI)** (Lubin et al., 1985). Published in 1942 by Starke Hathaway and his colleagues at the University of Minnesota, the MMPI was originally developed as an aid in diagnosing psychiatric disorders (Hathaway & McKinley, 1942). The person taking the test is asked to answer "true," "false," or "cannot say" to such questions as "Once in a while I put off until tomorrow what I ought to do today," "At times I feel like swearing," and "There are persons who are trying to steal my thoughts and ideas." Some of the items repeat very similar thoughts in different words: for example, "I tire easily" and "I feel weak all over much of the time." This redundancy contributes to ease of scoring and provides a check on the possibility of false or inconsistent answers.

The MMPI also includes several scales that check the validity of the responses. For example, if a person has answered too many items "cannot say," the test is considered invalid. The L, or lie, scale is scored on 15 items scattered throughout the test. Sample items rated on this scale are "I do not always tell the truth" and "I gossip a little at times." Most of us would have to admit that our answers to these two questions would be "true." People who mark these and many other similar items "false" are probably consciously or unconsciously distorting the truth to present themselves in a more favorable light.

By analyzing people's answers, researchers have extracted a number of personality scales from this test, rating people in terms of masculinity-femininity, depression, and hypochondriasis. These elements of the MMPI are highly regarded as useful tools for differentiating among psychiatric populations (Anastasi, 1982; J. R. Graham & Lilly, 1984). The MMPI is also used to differentiate among more normal personality dimensions, such as extroversion-introversion and assertiveness, but with less success.

To accommodate social changes over the last 50 years, the MMPI was recently revised. Outdated or sexist items ("Sometimes at elections I vote for men about whom I know very little") have been reworded in the MMPI-2, and new items have been added to assess such disorders as Type A behavior, suicidal tendencies, and anorexia nervosa, all of which have received considerable attention in recent years (Butcher et al., 1989). And there are now two versions of the test: The full-length, adult form of the MMPI-2 has 704 items, while the adolescent form has 654 items. Both include 550 items from the original MMPI to ensure that clinical information from the new test does not differ too much from that on the original.

**Projective tests** Personality tests, such as the Rorschach inkblot test, consisting of ambiguous or unstructured material.

**Rorschach test** A projective test composed of ambiguous inkblots; the way people interpret the blots is thought to reveal aspects of their personality.

**Thematic Apperception Test (TAT)** A projective test composed of ambiguous pictures about which a person writes stories.

## Projective Tests

Psychodynamic theorists, who believe that people are often unaware of the determinants of their behavior, put very little faith in objective personality tests that rely on self-reports. Instead, they prefer to use **projective tests** of personality, which generally ask subjects what some essentially meaningless material or a vague picture means to them. Or subjects may be given the lead-in to a sentence, such as "My brother is . . . " and be asked to complete the statement. Many psychologists believe that in devising their own answers, subjects "project" their personality into the test materials, revealing unconscious thoughts and fantasies, such as latent sexual or family problems.

The **Rorschach test** .is the best-known projective personality test. It is named for Hermann Rorschach, a Swiss psychiatrist who in 1921 published the results of his research on interpreting inkblots as a key to personality. (see Figure 10-5). Each inkblot design is printed on a separate card and is unique in form, color, shading, and white space. Subjects are asked to specify what they see in each blot. Test instructions are kept to a minimum so subjects' responses will be completely their own. After interpreting all the blots, subjects go over the cards again with the examiner and explain which part of each blot prompted each response.

**5.** What is a Rorschach test, and what can it tell us about personality?

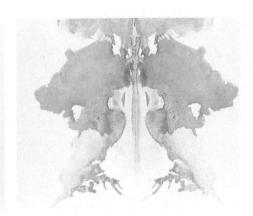

Many psychologists interpret the Rorschach responses intuitively; but it is also possible to score Rorschach responses according to the *form* rather than the content of each subject's responses (Exner, 1986; Lleiger, 1992).

Somewhat more demanding is the **Thematic Apperception Test (TAT),** developed at Harvard by H. A. Murray and his associates. It consists of 20 cards picturing one or more human figures in various poses (see Figure 10-6). The situations depicted in the pictures are deliberately ambiguous. A person is shown the cards one by one and asked to write a complete story about each picture, including what led up to the scene depicted, what the characters are doing at that moment, what their thoughts and feelings are, and what the outcome will be.

Although various scoring systems have been devised for the TAT, examiners usually interpret the stories in the light of their personal knowledge of the subjects. One key in evaluating the TAT is whether the subject identifies with the hero or heroine of the story or with one of the minor

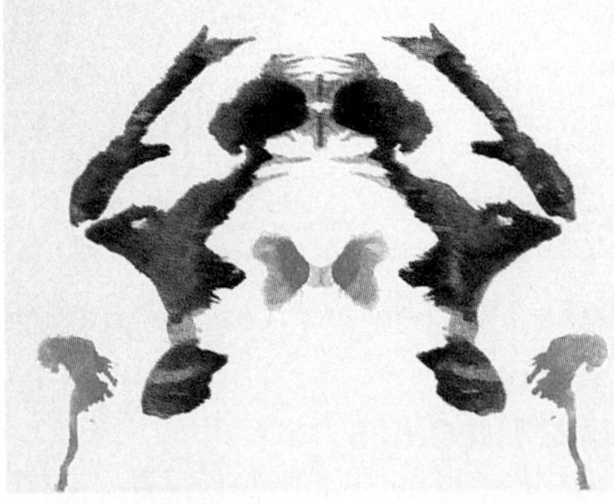

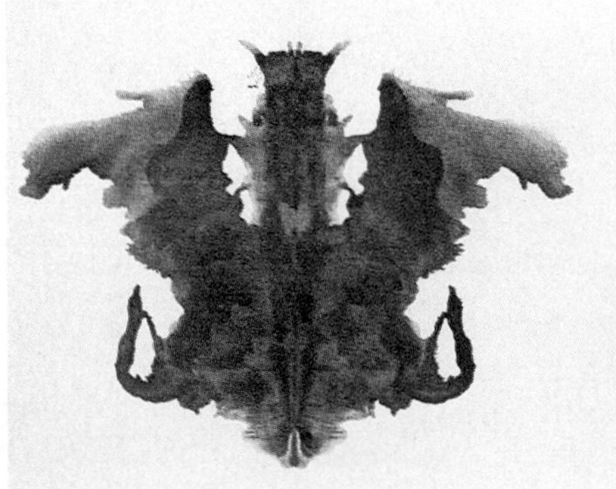

**Figure 10-5**
**Inkblots used in the *Rorschach projective test.***

characters. Then the examiner determines what the attitudes and feelings of the character reveal about the storyteller. The examiner also assesses each story for content, language, originality, organization, and consistency.

**Figure 10-6**
**Revealing stories** A sample item from the *Thematic Apperception Test (TAT),* and a subject making up a story to explain the scene depicted on that card. The examiner must then interpret and evaluate the subject's story.

Certain themes, such as the need for affection, repeated failure, or parental domination, may recur in several plots.

Both the Rorschach and the TAT may open up a conversation between a clinician and a person who is reluctant or unable to talk about personal problems (Oltmanns & Emery, 1995). Both may also provide useful information about motives, events, or feelings of which the person is unaware (Stricker & Healy, 1990). However, because projective tests are often not administered in a standard fashion, their validity and reliability have been called into question (Dawes, 1994; Wierzbicki, 1993). As a result, their use has declined since the 1970s. Still, when interpreted by a skilled examiner, these tests can offer insight into a person's attitudes and feelings.

## LOOKING FORWARD

From Sigmund Freud, with his emphasis on unconscious processes, to contemporary cognitive and social learning theorists, who spotlight the interaction among cognitive processes, learning, and the environment, psychologists have strived to understand the nature of human personality and how personality develops. As we saw in this chapter and will see to a greater extent in the next, how we interpret what happens to us not only affects our personality but also largely determines what actually happens to us. If you tend to believe that finding romance, getting a job, or rebuilding after a flood is within your control, you will probably experience loneliness, joblessness, or a natural disaster very differently from people who believe these things are beyond their control.

In this chapter, we saw that people differ in the ways they interpret and evaluate situations. In the next two chapters, we will learn more about how this process affects physical and mental health, and some of the ways in which the more damaging and debilitating impacts of these cognitions may be treated and changed.

## SUMMARY

Ever since the discipline of psychology began, psychologists have been attempting to define those characteristic thoughts, feelings, and behaviors that persist over time and that distinguish one person from another. **Personality** is a person's unique psychological signature; it signs itself to all the person's actions and marks the person's passage through time.

### PSYCHODYNAMIC THEORIES

**Psychodynamic theories** of personality consider behavior to be the result of psychological dynamics within the individual. Often these dynamics are unconscious processes.

### Sigmund Freud

For Freud, the founder of **psychoanalysis**, our personality is rooted in the dynamics of our **unconscious**—all the ideas, thoughts, and feelings of which we are normally unaware. Freud identified sexual and aggressive instincts as the primary unconscious drives that determine human behavior. These instincts motivate the id, the first of the three personality structures Freud identified. The **id**, the only personality structure present at birth, operates according to the **pleasure principle**, meaning it tries to obtain immediate pleasure and avoid pain.

Since the id is not in direct contact with the real world, it has only two ways of obtaining satisfying its desires: by reflex actions, which immediately relieve unpleasant sensations; and through wish fulfillment, whereby a person forms a mental image of an object that partially gratifies the instinctual drives and relieves the uncomfortable sensations.

The **ego** is the id's link to the real world. It controls all conscious thinking and reasoning activities. The ego operates according to the **reality principle**. By means of intelligent reasoning, the ego delays satisfying the id's desires until it can do so safely and effectively in the real world.

A personality consisting solely of an id and an ego would be completely selfish and could not function effectively within a social structure. Freud's third personality component, the **superego**, acts as the person's moral guardian or conscience and helps the person function in society. It also compares the ego's actions with an **ego ideal** of perfection.

Freud called energy generated by the sexual instinct **libido**. As infants mature, their libido becomes focused on different sensitive parts of the body. A **fixation** occurs if a child is deprived of or receives too much pleasure from the part of the body that dominates one of the five developmental stages—**oral, anal, phallic, latency,** and **genital**—and some sexual energy may lodge in that part of the body. Strong attachment to the parent of the opposite sex and jealousy of the parent of the same sex—which develops during the phallic stage—is termed the **Oedipus complex** in boys and the **Electra complex** in girls. At the end of the phallic stage, the child enters the **latency period**, characterized by a loss of interest in sexual behavior. Finally, at puberty, the individual enters the **genital stage** of mature sexuality.

### Carl Jung

Where Freud saw the id as a seething cauldron of excitations, Carl Jung viewed the unconscious as the ego's source of strength. He believed that the unconscious consisted of two distinct components: the **personal unconscious**, encompassing an individual's repressed thoughts, forgotten experiences, and undeveloped ideas; and the **collective unconscious**, a subterranean river of memories and behavior patterns flowing to us from previous generations. Over the millennia, the human mind has developed certain thought forms, called **archetypes**, which give rise to mental images or mythological representations.

One of the many archetypes Jung described, the **persona**, plays a special role in shaping personality. It is that part of our personality by which we are known to other people, like a mask we put on to go out in public. Two other important archetypes are the **anima**, which is the expression of female traits in a man, and the **animus**, the expression of male traits in a woman. Jung also believed that people generally exhibit one of two attitudes toward the world: **Extroverts** are interested in other people and the world at large, while **introverts** are more concerned with their own private worlds.

### Alfred Adler

Adler believed that people possess innate positive motives and strive toward personal and social perfection. He originally proposed that the principal determinant of personality was the individual's attempt to **compensate** for actual physical weakness, but he later modified his theory to stress the importance of *feelings* of inferiority, whether or not those feelings are justified. When people become so fixated on their feelings of inferiority that they become paralyzed by them, they are said to have an **inferiority complex**. Later still, Adler concluded that strivings for superiority and perfection, both in one's own life and in the society in which one lives, are crucial to personality development. In the course of striving for individual and social perfection, the individual forms a particular set of meanings and beliefs that become her or his style of life.

### Karen Horney

For Horney, anxiety, a person's reaction to real or imagined dangers or threats, is a stronger motivating force than the sexual drive, or libido. She believed that there are several **neurotic trends** or strategies that people use to cope with emotional problems, and that these strategies are reflected in personality types—submissive, aggressive, or detached. By emphasizing that culture and not anatomy determines many of the personality traits that differentiate women from men, Horney also challenged the prevailing notion of her time that biological imperatives underlie the personality characteristics of men and women.

### Erik Erikson

Erikson argued that the quality of the parent-child relationship affects the development of personality because out of this interaction the child either feels competent and valuable and is able to form a secure sense of identity, or feels incompetent and worthless and fails to build a secure identity. Erikson believed that the personality develops over a lifetime. He outlined eight life stages—*trust versus mistrust, autonomy versus shame and doubt, initiative versus guilt, industry versus inferiority, identity versus role confusion, intimacy versus isolation, generativity versus stagnation,* and *integrity versus despair*—and asserted that success in each stage depends on whether adjustments in previous stages went smoothly. Though little of Erikson's theory has been verified through research, some researchers have confirmed that a positive sense of identity is important for achieving intimacy.

### Object-relations Theories of Personality

**Object-relations theories** of personality, which originated in the work of D. W. Winnicott, Melanie Klein, and W.R.D. Fairbairn, point up the importance of the feedback children receive in their relationship with their primary "object" or caregiver. This feedback figures prominently in the view children form of themselves.

### Evaluating Psychodynamic Theories

Psychodynamic theories have had a profound impact on the way we view ourselves and others as well as on the arts. However, some of Freud's theories have been criticized as unscientific and culture-bound, especially penis envy in women and the Oedipus and Electra complexes, which are based on the anecdotal accounts of individuals who felt troubled enough to seek treatment. There is some experimental evidence to support the existence of the unconscious, but this research does not show a clear link between unconscious processes and personality. As a therapy, psychoanalysis has been shown to be beneficial in some cases, but no more so than other therapies.

## HUMANISTIC PERSONALITY THEORIES

Adler's notion of the individual's perpetual striving for perfection laid the groundwork for **humanistic personality theory**.

### Carl Rogers

Rogers contended that people develop their personalities in the service of positive goals. Every organism is born with certain innate potentialities, and all living things strive to become whatever it is they are capable of becoming. This biological push toward fulfillment is called the **actualizing tendency**. In addition to trying to realize our biological potential, we attempt to fulfill our conscious sense of who we are, which Rogers called the **self-actualizing tendency**. A **fully functioning person** is someone whose self-concept closely matches his or her inborn capabilities. Fully functioning people were usually raised with **unconditional positive regard**, or the experience of being valued by other people regardless of their emotions, attitudes, and behaviors. People who are not fully functioning were brought up with **conditional positive regard**—that is, parents and others, accepted and valued only certain aspects of their individuality. Such people tend to deviate from their inborn capacities to construct a personality more in line with how other people see them. People who are not fully functioning are likely to feel threatened and anxious and generally dissatisfied with what they do.

### Evaluating Humanistic Theories

There is a lack of scientifically derived evidence for humanistic theories of personality. In addition, they are criticized fortaking too rosy a view of human nature and forpromoting a view of the self that fosters self-centerness. However, research on humanist therapies, particularly Rogers' client-centered therapy, has shown they do promote self-acceptance.

## TRAIT THEORIES

Trait theorists reject the notion that there are just a few distinct personality types. Instead, they insist that each person possesses a unique constellation of fundamental **personality traits**, which can be inferred from how the person behaves.

Psychologists disagree about how many different personality traits there are. Gordon Allport came up with several thousand words that could be used to describe human personality traits, and he arranged traits in a hierarchy. Raymond Cattell identified 16 basic personality traits by means of a statistical model called **factor analysis**. Recent research suggests that there may be just five global personality traits: extraversion, agreeableness, conscientiousness, emotional stability, and culture.

### Evaluating Trait Theories

Trait theories are primarily descriptive. They provide a way of classifying personalities, but they do not explain why someone's personality developed as it did. Unlike psychodynamic and humanistic theories, however, trait theories have the advantage of being relatively easy to test experimentally, and research does confirm the value of the five-factor model in pinpointing personality.

### The Consistency Controversy

Though most personality theories assume that behavior is consistent across situations and over a lifetime, a number of psychologists have challenged this assumption. They believe that situational variables have a greater effect on behavior than do personality traits. Walter Mischel, for instance, argues that people tend to overestimate the consistency of another person's actions, both because they see that person in only a limited number of situations that elicit similar behavioral responses and because they disregard any behavior that does not correspond to their preexisting image of that person.

### Cognitive–social Learning Theories

**Cognitive–social learning theories** of personality view behavior as the product of the interaction of cognitions, learning and past experiences, and the immediate environment. Albert Bandura maintains that certain internal **expectancies** determine how a person evaluates a situation and that this evaluation has an effect on the person's behavior. **Locus of control** is one prominent expectancy. People with an internal locus of control believe they can control their own fate through their actions, while people with an external locus of control believe their fate rests with chance and the behavior of others. Expectancies prompt people to conduct themselves according to unique **performance standards**, individually determined measures of excellence by which they judge their behavior. Those who succeed in meeting their own internal performance standards develop an attitude Bandura calls **self-efficacy**.

In Bandura's view, behavior arises from a process he calls **reciprocal determinism**, in which personality variables, situational variables, and actual behaviors constantly interact. Personality develops out of the interaction of personal standards, situations, and behavioral consequences. Both Bandura and Mischel believe that people internally organize their expectancies and values in order to control their behavior. Additionally, Mischel has proposed a set of **person variables** that grow out of experience and help to shape future behavior.

### Evaluating Cognitive–social Learning Theories

Cognitive–social learning theories avoid the narrowness of trait and behavioral theories, as well as the reliance on case studies and anecdotal evidence that weakens psychodynamic and humanistic theories. Expectancies and locus of control can be tested scientifically, and they have proved to be useful concepts for predicting health and depression. For example, those who tend to see events as beyond their control are more likely to be depressed and less likely to take care of their health than those who view events as largely under their control. However, correlations such as these do not provide evidence for causes of behavior.

## PERSONALITY ASSESSMENT

Psychologists use four different methods to assess personality: the personal interview, direct observation of behavior, objective tests, and projective tests.

### The Personal Interview

There are two types of personal interviews. During an unstructured interview, the interviewer asks questions about any material that comes up during the course of the conversation as well as follow-up questions where appropriate. In a structured interview, the order and the content of the questions are fixed and the interviewer does not deviate from the format. Structured interviews are more likely to be used when conducting systematic research on personality because they solicit comparable information from all interviewees.

### Observation

Social learning theorists prefer the technique of direct observation of a person over a period of time to determine the environmental influence on that person's behavior. This method of personality assessment has the advantage of not relying on people's self-reports of their behavior. It also gives researchers a good idea of the range of behaviors the subject is capable of. Among the drawbacks of direct observation: It is expensive and time-consuming, the subject's actions may be misinterpreted by the observer, and behavior may be affected by the subject's awareness of being watched.

### Objective Tests

**Objective tests** of personality like the **Sixteen Personality Factor Questionnaire** and the **Minnesota Multiphasic Personality Inventory (MMPI)** are given and scored according to standardized procedures. Since scores are obtained through self-report, there are "truth" questions built into the MMPI that help determine the accuracy of a subject's answers throughout. These tests are inexpensive to use and easy to score.

### Projective Tests

Psychodynamic theorists, who believe that much behavior is determined by unconscious processes, tend to discount tests that rely on self-reports. They are more likely to use **projective tests**, which consist of ambiguous stimuli that can draw out an unlimited number of responses. The **Rorschach test** has ten inkblots that the subject is asked to interpret. The **Thematic Apperception Test (TAT)** uses 20 pictures about which the subject is asked to make up stories.

# REVIEW QUESTIONS

## MULTIPLE CHOICE

1. Personality is the pattern of thoughts, feelings, and behaviors that persists over ______ and ______ and that distinguishes one person from another.

2. Match the following of Freud's terms with their appropriate definitions:

| | |
|---|---|
| ____ Unconscious | a. Energy that comes from the sexual instinct |
| ____ Superego | b. Mediator between reality, the superego, and the id |
| ____ Id | c. Unconscious urges seeking expression |
| ____ Ego | d. That part of the superego concerned with standards |
| ____ Ego ideal | e. Ideas and feelings of which we are normally not aware |
| ____ Libido | f. Moral guardian of the ego |

3. According to Freud, the ______ operates according to the reality principle, while the ______ acts according to the pleasure principle.

4. According to Freud, ______ _______ is the means by which the id partially relieves the discomfort of instinctual drives through formal mental images.

5. Match the following of Jung's terms with their appropriate definitions:

| | |
|---|---|
| ____ Persona | a. Typical mental image or mythical representation |
| ____ Animus | b. Memories and behavior patterns inherited from past generations |
| ____ Collective unconscious | c. Aspect of the personality by which one is known to other people |
| ____ Archetype | d. Expression of male traits in females |

6. Match the following of Adler's terms with their appropriate definitions:

| | |
|---|---|
| ____ Inferiority complex | a. Fixation on or belief in a negative characteristic |
| ____ Compensation | b. Individual's effort to overcome weaknesses |

7. Horney believed that ______ is a stronger source of emotional disturbance than sexual urges.

8. Match Erikson's eight stages of personality development with their appropriate descriptions:

| | |
|---|---|
| ____ Industry versus inferiority | a. The infant appreciates the predictability of the environment and learns optimism about the future. |
| ____ Trust versus mistrust | b. The child gains increasing independence and contact with the environment. |
| ____ Generativity versus stagnation | c. Children become increasingly active, undertake new projects, and manipulate things in the environment. |
| ____ Intimacy versus isolation | d. Children encounter new expectations and begin learning adult skills. |
| ____ Identity versus role confusion | e. Childhood ends and the responsibilities of adulthood loom ahead. |
| ____ Autonomy versus shame and doubt | f. The question of becoming intimate with the opposite sex comes to the fore. |
| ____ Initiative versus guilt | g. The adult faces the challenge of remaining productive and creative. |
| ____ Integrity versus despair | h. Individuals integrate life roles and face impending death. |

9. Rogers believed that people strive to live up to and fulfill their self-image; he called this the ______ tendency.

10. Cognitive–social learning theorists believe that locus of control is a cognitive strategy by which people ________situations.

11. ______ tests require people to fill out questionnaires, which are then scored according to a standardized procedure.

12. In ______ tests of personality, people are shown ambiguous stimuli and asked to describe them or make up a story about them.

## CRITICAL THINKING AND APPLICATIONS

13. One of the key issues addressed by personality theorists is consistency: Does a person behave the same way from one situation to another, or does behavior

vary with circumstances? What are your feelings on this issue?

14. Explain how Jung, Adler, Horney, and Erikson modified Freud's psychodynamic theory of personality.

15. What are the major forms of personality assesssment? Which do you consider the most reliable? The least reliable? Why?

16. Look back at the case study of Jaylene Smith. Which theory, or theories, do you think best explains her behavior? Why do you feel this way?

*(Answers to the Review Questions can be found in the back of the text.)*

## Think About It!

1. *True or false*: Stress is always a response to negative events in our lives.
2. *True or false*: Stressful events almost inevitably involve changes in our lives.
3. What kinds of factors influence whether we find a particular situation stressful?
4. What is meant by "defense mechanisms"? What are some common types of defense mechanisms?
5. Do men generally handle stress better than women do?
6. How can stress lead to physical illness?
7. What is posttraumatic stress disorder? What kinds of events are most likely to trigger this disorder?

# STRESS AND HEALTH PSYCHOLOGY

# 11

## Overview

**Stress** Any environmental demand that creates a state of tension or threat and requires change or adaptation.

**Adjustment** Any effort to cope with stress.

**Let's begin our study of stress and adjustment with a few real-life stories.**

- In 1979, Iranian militants stormed the U.S. embassy in Teheran and took more than 50 Americans hostage. For 444 days, the hostages lived in fear for their lives and endured the humiliations of captivity. To feel less like a prisoner and more like a person in charge of his life, one hostage saved food from meals brought to him by his captors and then played gracious host by offering the saved food to other hostages who visited him in his cell. A diary kept by one prisoner records some other prisoners' strategies: "Al's working on his painting. . . . Dick's walking his daily three miles back and forth across the room, and Jerry's lying on his mattress reading."
- When Eric de Wilde, an orphan, found a bag of jewels worth $350,000 on a Florida railroad track, he thought it was a fairy tale come true. But reporters hounded him, and schoolmates and others kept calling him up with demands and threats. "Life is very difficult for the young man—a lot of things have happened to him in a hurry," said the lawyer whom de Wilde was forced to retain. But when the boy arrived in New York to sell his jewels at a public auction, he conducted himself with such dignified restraint that he managed to maintain his privacy and self-possession.
- When Janet Garcia had her first baby at age 34, she was filled with special joy because she had feared she would never become pregnant. But she found taking care of the baby, on top of all her other responsibilities, exhausting. Her husband, Michael, resented her constant fatigue and the fact that he didn't come first in her life anymore. To alleviate the situation, Janet and Michael drew on their savings to pay for household help and Michael took a more active role in looking after the baby. These measures relieved some of Janet's burden, leaving her with more time and energy for her other responsibilities and for her life with Michael.

These three stories sound quite different, but they have several things in common. First, all involved some degree of **stress**—that is, the people in the stories were faced with significant new demands from their environments that created in them a state of tension or threat that gave rise to a state of tension or threat. Second, the people under stress had to find ways to *cope* with these new events. Finally, in all three situations, the people *adjusted* about as well as could be expected under the circumstances.

Most people must adjust to a life that is less than perfect, a life in which bad events happen and even pleasures come with built-in complications. We need to adapt to stress, not just in the form of crises or unexpected strokes of good fortune, but also in the form of everyday minor demands.

Every **adjustment** is an attempt—successful or not—to balance our desires against the demands of the environment, to weigh our needs against realistic possibilities, and to cope as well as we can within the limits of our situation. The student who fails to get the lead in the school play may quit the production in a huff, accept a smaller role, serve as theater critic for the school paper, or join the debating team. Each response is an adjustment to failure, although some of these responses will probably be less constructive in the long run than others.

How we adjust to the stresses—both major and minor—that we encounter is crucial to our health and the quality of our lives. As we shall see in this chapter and the following one on abnormal psychology, stress can contribute to both psychological and physical illness. In fact, some medical experts believe that all physical ailments, from colds to ulcers to cancer, have a psychological as well as a physical component. For this reason, stress and its effects on people's lives is a key focus of **health psychology**, a subfield of psychology (see Table 1-1, p. 3) concerned with the relationship between psychological factors and physical health and illness. Health psychologists look into why some people manage stress well enough to remain healthy while others become ill, which character traits help people recover from serious illness, and how to promote healthy behaviors. In the process, they study the interaction of biological, psychological, and social factors, an approach we explore in detail in the next chapter.

**Health psychology** A subfield of psychology concerned with the relationship between psychological factors and physical health and illness.

In this chapter, we first delve into the characteristics of different kinds of stressful events. Then we analyze some of the ways people cope with stress, paying particular attention to coping techniques that lessen the harmful effects of stress. Finally, we explore how the body deals with stress and how methods of coping with stressful events can affect health.

## SOURCES OF STRESS

As we have seen, *stress* refers to any environmental demand that creates a state of tension or threat and requires change or adaptation. Many situations prompt us to change our behavior in some way: We stop our car when a traffic light turns red; we switch channels on the television set to avoid a boring program and find and interesting one to watch; we go inside when it starts to rain. Under normal circumstances, these situations are not stressful because they are not accompanied by tension or threat. Now imagine that when the light turned red you were rushing to make an important appointment, or that the person watching TV with you definitely does not want to switch the channel, or that you are about to host a large outdoor party when it starts to rain. Under these conditions, the same events can be quite stressful.

Before we look at some of the major sources of stress, it is worth making several points about stress in general. Some events, such as wars and natural disasters, are inherently stressful. Here the danger is very real: Lives are threatened, and often there is little or nothing people can do to save themselves. But even in inherently stressful situations, the time of greatest stress is not necessarily the time when danger is most imminent; rather, the period when we're *anticipating* the danger is actually the time of greatest stress. S. Epstein (1962) demonstrated this when he studied the effects of anticipated stress on a group of 28 parachutists. Each man was asked to describe his feelings before, during, and after his jump. All reported an increase in fear and the desire to escape as the time for the jump approached. Once the men were in line and realized they could not turn back, however, they calmed down. By the time they reached the most dangerous part of the jump—when they were in free fall and waiting for their chutes to open—their fears had subsided.

Stress is not limited to life-and-death situations, however, nor even to unpleasant or tension-filled situations. The good things that happen to us can also cause stress because they "require change or adaptation if an individual is to meet his or her needs" (C. Morris, 1990, p. 72). A wedding is a stressful as well as an exciting event: Most weddings are very complicated affairs to arrange, and marriage marks a profound change in one's relationships with parents, friends, old boyfriends or girlfriends, and, of course, one's new spouse. A promotion at work is gratifying—but it

*True or false*: Stress is always a response to negative events in our lives.

demands that we relate to new people in new ways, learning to do new things, and perhaps dressing differently and working longer hours.

## Change

2. *True or false*: Stressful events almost inevitably involve changes in our lives.

Notice that all the stressful events we have considered so far involve change. Most people have a strong preference for order, continuity, and predictability in their lives. Therefore, any event, good or bad, that brings about change will be experienced as stressful; by the same token, the stressfulness of various situations can be determined by the amount of change they require. In fact, some questionnaires measure the amount of stress in a person's life by calculating "life changes" that a person has experienced over a specified period of time. For example, the Social Readjustment Rating Scale (SRRS) devised by T.H. Holmes and R.H. Rahe (1967) consists of several dozen events that are assigned a point value depending on the amount of change they require (see Table 11-1). Notice that the stress ratings of events on the SRRS have little to do with whether the events are desirable or undesirable.

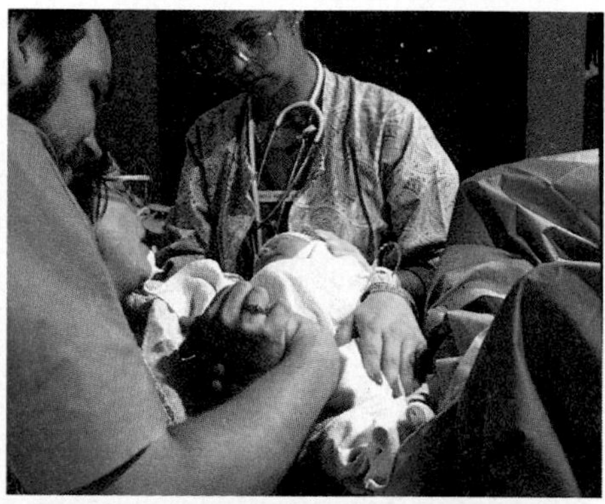

All major life events—whether positive or negative—involve a certain amount of stress.

**TABLE 11-1 Social Readjustment Rating Scale***

| LIFE EVENT | LIFE-CHANGE UNITS |
|---|---|
| Death of one's spouse | 100 |
| Divorce | 73 |
| Personal injury or illness | 53 |
| Marriage | 50 |
| Being fired at work | 47 |
| Retirement | 45 |
| Pregnancy | 40 |
| Gain of a new family member | 39 |
| Change in one's financial state | 38 |
| Death of a close friend | 37 |
| Change to a different line of work | 36 |
| Foreclosure of a mortgage or loan | 30 |
| Change in responsibilities at work | 29 |
| Son or daughter leaving home | 29 |
| Outstanding personal achievement | 28 |
| Beginning or ending school | 26 |
| Change in living conditions | 25 |
| Trouble with one's boss | 23 |
| Change in residence | 20 |
| Change in schools | 20 |
| Change in social activities | 18 |
| Change in sleeping habits | 16 |
| Change in eating habits | 15 |
| Vacation | 13 |

*The SRRS assigns "life-change units" to several dozen stressful events. Holmes and Rahe linked the number of units to risk for medical problems, based on the premise that stress undermines health.

*Source*: From "The social readjustment rating scale," by T.H. Holmes and Rahe, *Journal of Psychosomatic Research, 11*, 1967. Copyright © 1967, Pergamon Press. Reprinted with permission.

## Hassles

Holmes and Rahe's SRRS emphasizes the kind of stress that arises from fairly dramatic, one-time life events. But as other psychologists like Lazarus (Lazarus & De Longis, 1983; Lazarus et al., 1985) have pointed out, much stress

**Pressure** A feeling that one must speed up, intensify, or change the direction of one's behavior or live up to a higher standard of performance.

**Frustration** The feeling that occurs when a person is prevented from reaching a goal.

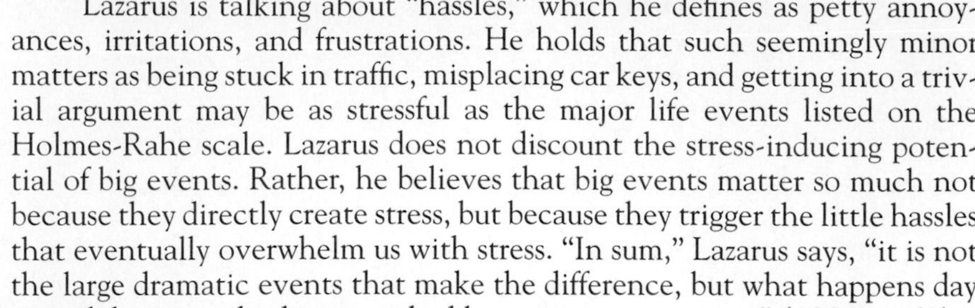

is generated by "chronic or repeated conditions of living—boredom, continuing tension in a family relationship, lack of occupational progress, isolation and loneliness, absence of meaning and commitment" (Lazarus, 1981, p. 60).

Lazarus is talking about "hassles," which he defines as petty annoyances, irritations, and frustrations. He holds that such seemingly minor matters as being stuck in traffic, misplacing car keys, and getting into a trivial argument may be as stressful as the major life events listed on the Holmes-Rahe scale. Lazarus does not discount the stress-inducing potential of big events. Rather, he believes that big events matter so much not because they directly create stress, but because they trigger the little hassles that eventually overwhelm us with stress. "In sum," Lazarus says, "it is not the large dramatic events that make the difference, but what happens day in and day out, whether provoked by major events or not" (1981, p. 62).

We have been looking at external events and situations, both major and minor, as sources of stress. These events are stressful because they give rise to feelings of pressure, frustration, conflict, and anxiety. Let's take a look at how each of these emotional experiences contributes to our overall feeling of stress before we consider the different ways in which people perceive and adjust to stress.

Some psychologists argue that much of the stress we experience arises not from traumatic events, but rather from everyday hassles such as traffic jams.

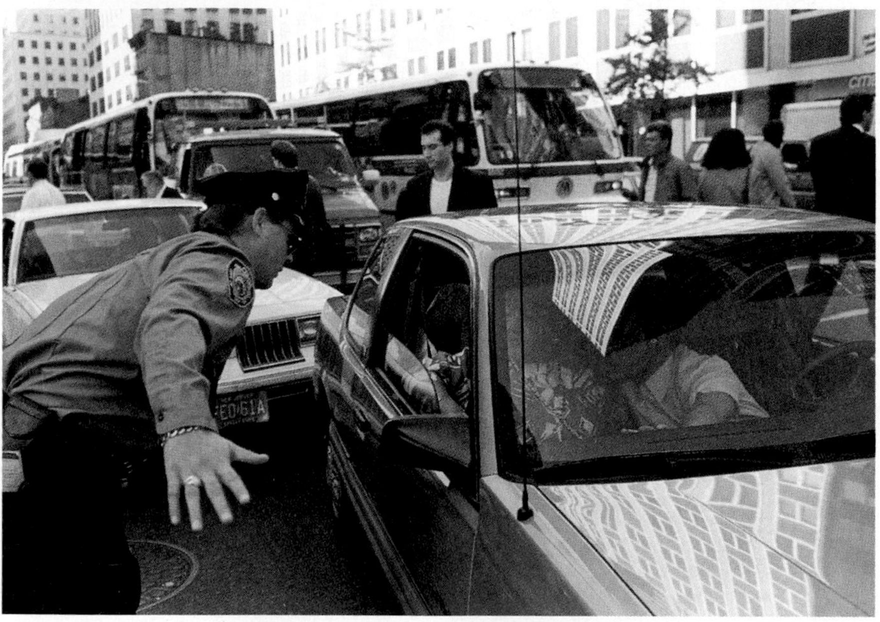

## Pressure

**Pressure**, another common source of stress, occurs when we feel forced to speed up, intensify, or shift direction in our behavior, or when we feel compelled to meet a higher standard of performance (C. Morris, 1990). Pressure may come from within—as when we push ourselves to reach personal standards of excellence—and this internal pressure may be either constructive or destructive. For instance, it may drive us to learn how to play a musical instrument, which may ultimately bring us great pleasure, or it may erode our self-esteem if we set standards for ourselves that are impossible to achieve. Outside demands also give us pressure: We compete for grades, for popularity, for sexual and marital partners, and for jobs. In addition, we're pressured to live up to the expectations of our family and close friends.

## Frustration

**Frustration** also contributes to stress. Frustration occurs when a person is prevented from reaching a goal because something or someone stands in the way. A teenager madly in love with a popular singer may learn that the singer is happily married; a high school student who does poorly on his college boards may not get into his father's alma mater; a woman looking forward to a well-deserved promotion may be denied it for sexist reasons. These people must either give up their goals as unattainable, modify their goals, or find some way to overcome the obstacles blocking their way.

The teenager with the crush on the married singer will probably recover quickly, but the high school student faces a more complex problem. Most likely his first reaction will be to get angry—at himself for not having studied harder, at his father for pushing him to apply to a college that is difficult to get into, at the admissions board for not taking into account the bad cold he had the day he took the college boards. He may not be able to express his anger directly; he may not even realize or admit to himself how disappointed he is. Nevertheless, he must either find a new way to reach his goal or change it by applying to another school with lower acceptance standards. The woman denied the promotion has an even more difficult task. She could protest her company's decision by going through a lengthy and potentially even more frustrating appeals process, or she could seek employment at another company that may or may not prove less sexist, or she could start her own firm.

Morris (1990) identifies five common sources of frustration in American life. *Delays* are annoying because our culture puts great stock in the value of time. *Lack of resources* is especially frustrating to low-income Americans, who cannot afford the new cars or lavish vacations that the mass media tout as every American's due. *Losses*, such as the end of a love affair or a cherished friendship, cause frustration because they often make us feel helpless, unimportant, or worthless. *Failure* generates intense frustration—and accompanying guilt—in our competitive society. As we imagine that if we had done things differently, we might have succeeded, so we feel responsible for our own or someone else's pain and disappointment. *Discrimination* also makes for frustration: Being denied opportunities or recognition simply because of one's sex, age, religion, or skin color is immensely frustrating.

**Conflict** Simultaneous existence of incompatible demands, opportunities, needs, or goals.

**Approach/approach conflict** According to Lewin, the result of simultaneous attraction to two appealing possibilities, neither of which has any negative qualities.

**Avoidance/avoidance conflict** According to Lewin, the result of facing a choice between two undesirable possibilities, neither of which has any positive qualities.

## Conflict

Of all life's troubles, conflict is probably the most common. A student finds that both the required courses she wanted to take this semester are given at the same hours on the same days. We find ourselves in agreement with one political candidate's views on foreign policy, but prefer the domestic programs proposed by the opponent. A boy does not want to go to his aunt's for dinner, but neither does he want to listen to his parents complain about his decision if he stays home.

**Conflict** arises when we face two or more incompatible demands, opportunities, needs, or goals. We can never resolve conflict completely. We must either give up some of our goals, modify some of them, delay our pursuit of some of them, or resign ourselves to not attaining all of our goals. Whatever we do, we are bound to experience some frustration; which adds to the stressfulness of conflicts.

In the 1930s, Kurt Lewin described conflict in terms of two opposite tendencies: *approach* and *avoidance*. When something attracts us, we want to approach it; when something frightens us, we try to avoid it. Lewin (1935) showed how different combinations of these tendencies create three basic types of conflict: approach/approach conflict, avoidance/avoidance conflict, and approach/avoidance conflict.

**Approach/approach conflict** occurs when a person is simultaneously attracted to two appealing goals. For example, a student who has been accepted at two equally desirable colleges or universities, neither of which has any significant drawbacks, will experience an approach-approach conflict in choosing between these two desirable options.

The reverse of this dilemma is **avoidance/avoidance conflict**, in which a person is confronted with two undesirable or threatening possibilities, neither of which has any positive attributes. When faced with an avoidance/avoidance conflict, people usually try to escape the situation altogether. If escape is impossible, their coping method depends on how threatening each alternative is. Most often they vacillate between choosing one threat or the other, like a baseball runner caught in a rundown between first and second base. The player starts to run toward second, then realizes that he will be tagged and turns around, only to realize that he will be tagged on first if he tries to go back there. In no-exit situations like this, people sometimes simply wait for events to resolve their conflict for them.

**Approach/avoidance conflict** According to Lewin, the result of being simultaneously attracted to and repelled by the same goal.

An **approach/avoidance conflict**, in which a person is both attracted to and repelled by the same goal, is the most common form of conflict, and it, too, is often difficult to resolve. According to Lewin, the closer we come to a goal with good and bad features, the stronger grow our desires both to approach and to avoid, but the tendency to avoid increases more rapidly than the tendency to approach. In an approach/avoidance conflict, therefore, we approach the goal until we reach the point at which the tendency to approach equals the tendency to avoid the goal. Afraid to go any closer, we stop and vacillate, making no choice at all, until the situation changes. Most often in real life, we are faced simultaneously with two or more goals, each of which is less than ideal but each of which also has enough positive features to attract us. The existence of multiple goals of this sort simply increases our conflict for on top of the conflict we experience about each goal is piled the conflict we undergo in being forced to choose from among the various goals.

Lewin's three types of conflict are outlined in the Summary Table.

A classic example of avoidance/avoidance conflict is a baseball player trying to avoid being tagged out at either first or second base.

## Self-imposed Stress

So far, we have considered sources of stress outside the individual. However, people sometimes create problems for themselves quite apart from stressful events in their environment. Albert Ellis (Ellis & Harper, 1975) has proposed that many people carry around a set of irrational, self-defeating beliefs that add unnecessarily to the normal stresses of living. For example, according to Ellis, some people believe "It is essential to be loved or approved by almost everyone for everything I do"; for people who share this belief, any sign of disapproval will be a source of considerable stress. Other people believe "I must be competent, adequate, and successful at everything I do"; such people take the slightest sign of failure or inadequacy as evidence that they are worthless human beings. Still other people believe "It is disastrous if everything doesn't go the way I would like"; these people feel upset, miserable, and unhappy when things don't go perfectly. As we will see in the next chapter, Aaron Beck (1967, 1976) believes that many cases of depression arise from self-defeating thoughts such as these.

## Stress and Individual Differences

Some people find it easy to cope with major life stresses, while others find it hard to deal with even minor problems. What accounts for these different responses? The answer seems to lie in individual differences in perceiving and reacting to potentially stressful events.

An obstacle that looks like a molehill to one person looms like a mountain to another. An experienced construction worker thinks nothing

## SUMMARY TABLE

### Types of Conflict

| Type of Conflict | Nature of Conflict |
|---|---|
| **Approach/Approach** | You are attracted to two incompatible goals at the same time. |
| **Avoidance/Avoidance** | Repelled by two undesirable alternatives at the same time, you are inclined to escape, but other factors often prevent such an escape. |
| **Approach/Avoidance** | You are both repelled by, and attracted to, the same goal. |

of eating his lunch perched on a girder hundreds of feet above the ground, but just watching him may make a passerby anxious. One patient facing a serious operation may feel less anxious than someone else visiting a doctor for a routine physical exam. The person who gets fired from a job and the soldier who gets caught behind enemy lines may feel equally threatened. In short, how much stress we experience depends partly on the way we interpret the situation.

Several factors determine whether we find a particular situation stressful (Kessler, Price, & Wortman, 1985). A person who is self-confident, who feels capable of coping with life events, is less likely to find a given situation stressful than someone who lacks self-assurance. For example, students who know they can study when they have to and have done well on exams in the past tend to be calmer the night before an important test than students who have done poorly on previous exams. People who have handled job changes well in the past are likely to find a new change less stressful than those who have had great difficulty adjusting to previous job changes.

**3.** What kinds of factors influence whether we find a particular situation stressful?

Suzanne Kobasa (1979) studied a group of people who either tolerated stress exceptionally well or actually thrived on it. What these stress-resistant people had in common was a trait that Kobasa called *hardiness*: They felt very much in control of their lives, were deeply committed to their work and their own values, and experienced difficult demands from the environment as challenging rather than intimidating. Kobasa's study suggests that people's response to stress depends partly on whether they believe they have some control over events or feel helpless. On the flip side, research cited by M.E.P. Seligman (1975) shows that some people in seemingly hopeless situations not only become apathetic, but when the situation changes, fail to recognize that it is now possible to cope more effectively. They remain passive even when there are opportunities for improving the situation.

Behavior under stress also reflects individual differences. In natural disasters, for example, some people immediately mobilize to save themselves. Others fall apart. Still others are shaken but regain their composure—and ability to respond—almost instantly. And then there are those who refuse to admit that there is any danger. In the next section, we probe how people respond when they are under stress.

## HOW PEOPLE COPE WITH STRESS

Whatever its source, stress calls for adjustment. Psychologists distinguish between two general types of adjustment: direct coping and defensive coping. *Direct coping* refers to any action we take to change an uncomfortable situation. When our needs or desires are frustrated, for example, we attempt to remove the obstacles between ourselves and our goal or we give up. Similarly, when we are threatened, we try to eliminate the source of the threat, either by attacking it or by escaping from it. (See the Highlights box titled "Coping with Exam Stress" for a discussion of how some universities are helping students directly cope with the pressures of final-exam week.)

*Defensive coping* refers to the different ways people convince themselves that they are not really threatened or that they do not really want something they cannot get. A form of self-deception, defensive coping is characteristic of internal, often unconscious conflicts when we are emotionally unable to bring a problem to the surface of consciousness and deal with it directly because it is too threatening. We decide to avoid it out of self-defense.

### Direct Coping

When we are threatened, frustrated, or in conflict, we have three basic choices for coping directly: confrontation, compromise, or withdrawal. We can meet a situation head-on and intensify our efforts to get what we want (confrontation). We can give up some of what we want and perhaps persuade others to give up part of what they want (compromise). Or we can admit defeat and stop fighting (withdrawal).

Take the case of a woman who has worked hard at her job for years but is not promoted. She learns that the reason is her stated unwillingness to move temporarily from the company's main office to a branch office in another part of the country to acquire more experience. Her unwillingness

IGHLIGHTS

#### Coping with Exam Stress

Traditionally, students coping with the stress of final-exam week have been on their own. Some complain they have difficulty forcing themselves to study. Others are afraid that at the critical moment they will fail to remember even the titles, let alone the plots, of Shakespeare's tragedies. Still others stay up late at night, feverishly memorizing the series of events that led to the breakup of the Communist bloc in East Europe while resorting to such caffeine-laden staples as coffee and Coca-Cola or Pepsi to keep going.

Recently, colleges and universities have been rushing to the rescue of exam-beleaguered undergraduates and graduate students by providing aerobics programs, counseling, stress-reduction workshops, and other services designed to ease the pressure of finals. At the University of California at Los Angeles, for instance, stress-reduction workshops teach students to picture themselves calmly answering tough test items. At New York University, students can choose from over 50 programs that are geared to reducing prefinal tension. One group, "Peers Ears," boasts walk-in office hours and a staff of students specially trained to counsel their peers. At Pennsylvania's Swarthmore College, students participate in a campus-wide "Howl" the night before exam week. And at the University of Washington in Seattle, the Hall Health Center's mental-health clinic opens its doors to desperate students during exam week. At this time, the clinic, according to its director, sees more graduate and professional students than undergraduates, more seniors than juniors, and more first-year students than sophomores.

These new approaches have not entirely replaced the old standbys when it comes to coping with exam stress. During exam week at the University of California at Berkeley, for example, the manager of a popular off-campus café still increases his order of coffee from the usual 400 pounds to 550.

**How can we explain the degree of anxiety we associate with different phenomena?**

Why do people tend to overestimate the risks of such hazards as nuclear power, police work, firefighting, hunting, mountain climbing, and skiing, and to underestimate the risks of such hazards as X-rays, swimming, electric power, home appliances, and surgery? In other words, why do we feel little or no anxiety about exposing ourselves to phenomena that, statistically, are significantly dangerous, while flinching from other phenomena that, objectively speaking, pose little risk?

After you have thought about these questions, take a few minutes to examine the opinions of some other students, which appear below.

• • • • • • •

BILL: I think the [dangers] that people underestimate are things that most people see themselves encountering in their lifetime. We all see a possibility of surgery and we certainly all use home appliances and have had X-rays. By falsely acknowledging to ourselves that we will not be harmed by them, we justify why we expose ourselves to them and make handling the stress that they could cause a minuscule problem.

BOB: If one day the news said that telephones lowered life expectancy, people will become afraid of them.

STEVE: We overestimate the risks of nuclear power and police work and firefighting because not many of us know exactly what those jobs entail. We haven't experienced them up close. Like a great person once said, we fear the unknown.

ANDRE: We fear things we encounter less often even though the things we should really fear are those we work with every day.

BILL: I think that if I've been swimming all my life, and have never had a problem (positive reinforcement over and over again), I've been conditioned that there is no risk involved and it's purely pleasurable. There's little or no conditioning involved with nuclear power or firefighting, other than the horror stories we hear on the news, and thus we tend to "play it safe."

KATE: From our experiences and our friends' tales, we learn to fear what seems to be the most outlandish. I've heard of X-rays causing problems only if you have a heck of a lot of them, so I'm not afraid of them. People get them every day, and nothing immediate happens. But skiing is different. My aunt broke her leg doing it.

GREG: Perhaps we fear natural disasters (hunting, mountain climbing, skiing), more than those things that are physically close to us like household appliances.

KEISHA: Exposure is the key here. We are exposed to swimming, electric power, etc., almost on a daily basis. When something seems safe again and again and again, the risk just seems to disappear in our eyes. But when we are separated from something and only see maybe one side of it (on television, for example), that separation causes fear (a fear of the unknown) that elevates our perception of how risky something is.

STEVE: I think that it's all a matter of the things we associate with things. When I think of swimming, I think fun in water. The first thing I think of is not death trap. When we think of nuclear power, we think, exploding and Chernobyl.

AMY: Maybe we underestimate the risks of things like electric power and surgery because we need these things in our lives, and it would be stressful to be afraid every time we walked by the toaster.

BOB: I think that our ignorance of danger has a lot to do with the slot machine thing. The punishment of losing each time we pull the slot is outweighed by the occasional payoff it gives. I guess if the benefits of something are really good, we'll tend to lessen the impact of its bad qualities.

ETHAN: I think a factor of this phenomenon is that many of the hazards people consider dangerous rely on skills that the concerned people don't possess. For instance, the average person knows how to swim or operate home appliances, while he or she would find the idea of firefighting or mountain climbing daunting. The fact that they don't understand the necessary skills causes them to overestimate the risks. Also, perhaps it is partially a defense mechanism to avoid feeling inadequate. People who envy fearless skiers might say, "They're crazy to do that: It's so dangerous!" so that they think they have valid reasons to be afraid.

• • • • • • •

Have the views of other students caused you to revise your own views on this issue? If so, in what way? If not, why not? Which points make the most sense? Why?

to move stands between her and her goal of advancing in her career. She has several choices. Let's look at each in turn.

**Confrontation** Acknowledging a stressful situation directly and attempting to find a solution to the problem or attain the difficult goal.

**Compromise** Deciding on a more realistic solution or goal when an ideal solution or goal is not practical.

**Withdrawal** Avoiding a situation when other forms of coping are not practical.

**CONFRONTATION** **Confrontation** means facing a stressful situation forthrightly, acknowledging to oneself that there is a problem for which a solution must be found, attacking the problem head-on, and pushing resolutely toward one's goal. The hallmark of the "confrontational style" (C. Morris, 1990) is making intense efforts to cope with stress and to accomplish one's aims. This may involve learning skills, enlisting other people's help, or just trying harder. Or it may require steps to change either oneself or the situation. The woman whom we have been describing might decide that if she wants very much to move up in the company, she will have to agree to relocate. Or she might try to change the situation itself in one of several ways. She could challenge the assumption that working at the branch office would give her the kind of experience her supervisor thinks she needs. She could try to persuade her boss that even though she has never worked in a branch office, she nevertheless has acquired enough experience to handle a better job in the main office. Or she could remind her supervisor of the company's stated goal of promoting more women to top-level positions.

Confrontation may also include expressions of anger. Anger may be effective, especially if we really have been treated unfairly and if we express our anger with restraint instead of exploding in rage. A national magazine once reported an amusing, and effective, example of controlled anger in response to an annoying little hassle. As a motorist came to an intersection, he had to stop for a frail old lady crossing the street. The driver of the car behind his honked his horn impatiently, whereupon the first driver shut off his ignition, removed the key, walked back to the other car, and handed the key to the second driver. "Here," he said, "*you* run over her. I can't do it. She reminds me of my grandmother."

**COMPROMISE** **Compromise** is one of the most common, and effective, ways of coping directly with conflict or frustration. We often recognize that we cannot have everything we want and that we cannot expect others to do just what we would like them to do. In such cases, we may decide to settle for less than we originally sought. A young person who has loved animals all his life and long cherished the desire to become a veterinarian may discover in college that he has less aptitude for biology than he thought and that he finds dissecting lab specimens so distasteful that he could never bring himself to operate on animals. He may decide to compromise by becoming an animal technician, a person who assists veterinarians.

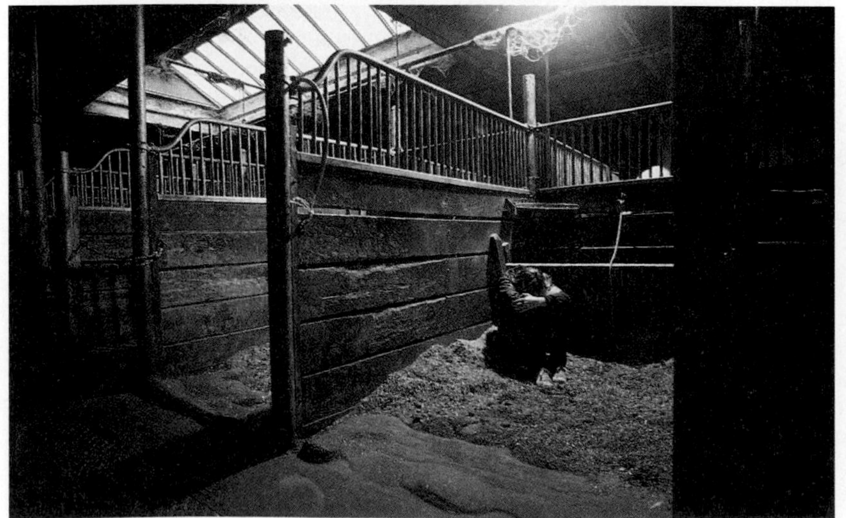

Although at times withdrawal is the most effective way of coping with a difficult situation, if avoidance of difficult situations becomes habitual, the person may be unable to take advantage of more effective solutions.

**WITHDRAWAL** In some circumstances, the most effective way of coping with stress is to withdraw from the situation. A person at an amusement park who is overcome by anxiety just looking at a roller coaster may simply move on to a less threatening ride or may even leave the park entirely. The woman whose promotion depends on temporarily relocating might just quit her job and join another company.

We often disparage **withdrawal** as a craven refusal to face problems. But when we realize that our adversary is more powerful than we are, or that there is no way we can effectively change ourselves, alter the situation, or reach a compromise, and that any form of aggression would be self-destructive, withdrawal is a positive and realistic response. In seemingly hopeless situations, such as submarine and mining disasters, few people panic (Mintz, 1951). Believing there is nothing they can do to save themselves, they give up. If a situation, in fact, is hopeless, resignation may be the most effective way of coping with it.

Perhaps the greatest danger of coping by withdrawal is that the person will come to avoid all similar situations. The person who grew extremely anxious looking at the roller coaster may refuse to go to an amusement park or carnival again. The woman who did not want to take a job at her company's branch office may quit her present job without even looking for a new one. In such cases, coping by withdrawal becomes maladaptive avoidance. Moreover, people who have given up on a situation are in a poor position to take advantage of an effective solution if one should come along. For example, one group of fifth-grade students was given unsolvable problems by one teacher and solvable problems by another. When the teacher who had handed out the "unsolvable" problems later presented the students with problems that *could* be solved, the students were unable to solve them, even though they had solved nearly identical problems given out by the other teacher (Dweck & Reppucci, 1973).

Withdrawal, in whatever form, is a mixed blessing. Although it can be an effective method of coping, it has built-in dangers. The same tends to be true of defensive coping, to which we now turn.

**Defense mechanisms** Self-deceptive techniques for reducing stress, including denial, repression, projection, identification, regression, intellectualization, reaction formation, displacement, and sublimation.

**Denial** Refusal to acknowledge a painful or threatening reality.

## Defensive Coping

Thus far, we have been speaking of coping with stress that arises from recognizable sources. But there are times when we either cannot identify or cannot deal directly with the source of our stress. For example, you return to a parking lot to discover that someone has damaged your new car and then left the scene. Or your vacation trip must be delayed because the airport is buried under 3 feet of new snow. In other cases, a problem is so emotionally threatening that it cannot be faced directly. Perhaps you find out that someone close to you is terminally ill. Or you learn that after 4 years of intensive study you have failed to gain admission to medical school and may have to abandon your lifelong ambition of becoming a doctor.

In all these cases, you are under stress and there is little or nothing you can do to cope with the stress directly. In such situations, people generally turn to **defense mechanisms** as a way of coping. Defense mechanisms are techniques for deceiving oneself about the causes of a stressful situation to reduce pressure, frustration, conflict, and anxiety are reduced. The self-deceptive nature of such adjustments led Freud to conclude that they are entirely unconscious. He was particularly interested in distortions of memory and in irrational feelings and behavior, all of which he considered symptoms of a struggle against unconscious impulses. Not all psychologists accept Freud's interpretation of defensive coping as always springing from unconscious conflicts over which we have little or no control. Often we *realize* that we are pushing something out of our memory or otherwise deceiving ourselves. For example, all of us have blown up at one person when we knew we were really angry at someone else.

What is meant by "defense mechanisms"? What are some common types of defense mechanisms?

Whether or not defense mechanisms operate consciously or unconsciously, they do provide a means of coping with stress that might otherwise be unbearable. Let's take a closer look more closely at some of the major defense mechanisms, which are listed in the Summary Table.

**Denial** One common defense mechanism is **denial**, or the refusal to acknowledge a painful or threatening reality. Lazarus (1969) cites the example of a woman who was near death from severe burns. At first, she was

**Repression** Excluding uncomfortable thoughts, feelings, and desires from consciousness.

depressed and frightened, but after a few days she felt sure she would soon be able to return home and care for her children, even though all medical indications were to the contrary. By denying the extent of her injuries, this woman was able to stay calm and cheerful. She was not merely putting on an act for her relatives and friends: She *believed* that she would recover.

While denial is a positive response in some situations, in other situations, it clearly is not. Students who deny their need to study and instead spend several nights a week at the movies may well fail their exams.

**REPRESSION** The most common mechanism for blocking out painful feelings and memories is **repression**, a form of forgetting that excludes painful thoughts from consciousness. Soldiers who break down in the field often block out the memory of the experiences that led to their collapse (Grinker & Spiegel, 1945). Many psychologists believe that re-

## SUMMARY TABLE

### Defense Mechanisms

| | |
|---|---|
| *Denial* | Refusing to acknowledge a painful or threatening reality: Ray, whose best friend has just been killed in a car accident, insists that it is a case of mistaken identity and that his friend is still alive. |
| *Repression* | Excluding uncomfortable thoughts from consciousness: Lisa, whose grandmother died of breast cancer, is at higher-than-average risk for developing breast cancer herself; still she routinely forgets to do a self-exam. |
| *Projection* | Attributing one's own repressed motives, feelings, or wishes to others: Marilyn is unfairly passed over for a promotion; she denies that she is angry about this, but is certain that her supervisor is angry with her. |
| *Identification* | Taking on the characteristics of someone else to avoid feeling inadequate: Anthony, uncertain of his own attractiveness, takes on the dress and mannerisms of a popular teacher. |
| *Regression* | Reverting to childlike behavior and defenses: Furious because his plan to reorganize his division has been rejected, Bob throws a tantrum. |
| *Intellectualization* | Thinking abstractly about stressful problems as a way of detaching oneself from them: After learning that she has not been asked to a classmate's costume party, Tina coolly discusses the ways in which social cliques form and how they serve to regulate and control school life. |
| *Reaction formation* | Expression of exaggerated ideas and emotions that are the opposite of one's repressed beliefs or feelings: At work, Michael loudly professes that he would never take advantage of a rival employee, though his harassing behavior indicates quite the opposite. |
| *Displacement* | Shifting repressed motives from an original object to a substitute object: Infuriated at his instructor's unreasonable request that he rewrite his term paper, but afraid to say anything for fear he will make the instructor angry, Nelson comes home and yells at his housemates for telling him what to do. |
| *Sublimation* | Redirecting repressed motives and feelings into more socially acceptable channels: The child of parents who never paid attention to him, Bill is running for public office. |

pression is a symptom that the person is struggling against impulses (such as aggression) that conflict with conscious values. For example, most of us were taught in childhood that violence and aggression are wrong. This conflict between our feelings and our values can create stress, and one way of coping defensively with that stress is to repress our feelings—to block out completely any awareness of our underlying anger and hostility.

Denial and repression are the most basic defense mechanisms. In denial, we block out situations we can't cope with; in repression, we block out unacceptable impulses or thoughts. These psychic strategies form the bases for other defensive ways of coping, which we examine now.

**Projection** Attributing one's own repressed motives, feelings, or wishes to others.

**Identification** Taking on the characteristics of someone else to avoid feeling incompetent.

**Regression** Reverting to childlike behavior and defenses.

**Intellectualization** Thinking abstractly about stressful problems as a way of detaching oneself from them.

**PROJECTION** If a problem cannot be denied or completely repressed, we may be able to distort its nature so that we can handle it more easily. One example of this is **projection**, the attribution of one's own repressed motives, ideas, or feelings to others. We ascribe feelings to someone else that we do not want to acknowledge as our own, thus locating the source of our conflict outside ourselves. A corporate executive who feels guilty about the way she rose to power may project her own ruthless ambition onto her colleagues. She is simply doing her job, she believes, while her associates are all crassly ambitious and consumed with power.

**IDENTIFICATION** The reverse of projection is **identification**. Through projection, we *rid* ourselves of undesirable characteristics that we have repressed by attributing them to someone else. Through identification, we *take on* the characteristics of someone else so that we can vicariously share in that person's triumphs and overcome feeling inadequate. The admired person's actions, that is, become a substitute for our own. A father with unfulfilled career ambitions may share emotionally in a son's professional success. When the son is promoted, the father may feel as if *he* has triumphed. Identification is often used as a form of self-defense in situations where a person feels utterly helpless, including being taken as a hostage or being a prisoner in a Nazi concentration camp. Some prisoners gradually come to identify with their guards as a way of defensively coping with unbearable and inescapable stress.

**REGRESSION** People under severe stress may revert to other kinds of childlike behavior through a process called **regression**. Why do people regress? Some psychologists say that it is because an adult cannot stand feeling helpless. Children, on the other hand, feel helpless and dependent every day, so becoming more childlike can make total dependency or helplessness more bearable.

Regression is sometimes used as a manipulative strategy, too, albeit an immature and inappropriate on. Adults who cry or throw temper tantrums when their arguments fail may expect those around them to react sympathetically, as their parents did when they were children.

**INTELLECTUALIZATION** The defense mechanism known as **intellectualization** is a subtle form of denial in which we detach ourselves from our feelings about our problems by analyzing them intellectually and thinking of them almost as if they concerned other people. Parents who start out intending to discuss their child's difficulties in a new school and then find themselves engaged in a sophisticated discussion of educational philosophy may be intellectualizing a very upsetting situation. They appear to be dealing with their problems, but in fact they are not because they have cut themselves off from their emotions.

**Reaction formation** Expression of exaggerated ideas and emotions that are the opposite of one's repressed beliefs or feelings.

**Displacement** Shifting repressed motives and emotions from an original object to a substitute object.

**Sublimation** Redirecting repressed motives and feelings into more socially acceptable channels.

**Reaction Formation** The term **reaction formation** refers to a behavioral form of denial in which people express with exaggerated intensity ideas and emotions that are the opposite of their own. *Exaggeration* is the clue to this behavior. The woman who extravagantly praises a rival may be covering up jealousy over her opponent's success. Reaction formation may also be a way of convincing oneself that one's motives are pure. The man who feels ambivalent about being a father may devote a disproportionate amount of time to his children in an attempt to prove to *himself* that he is a good father.

**Displacement** **Displacement** is the redirection of repressed motives and emotions from their original objects to substitute objects. The man who has always wanted to be a father may feel inadequate when he learns that he cannot have children. As a result, he may become extremely attached to a pet or to a niece or nephew. In an other example of displacement, the woman who must smile and agree with her boss all day may come home and yell at her husband or children.

**Sublimation** **Sublimation** refers to transforming repressed motives or feelings into more socially acceptable forms. Aggressiveness might be channeled into competitiveness in business or sports. A strong and persistent desire for attention might be transformed into an interest in acting or politics.

From the Freudian perspective, sublimation is not only necessary but desirable. People who can transform their sexual and aggressive drives into more socially acceptable forms are clearly better off, for they are able to at least partially gratify instinctual drives with relatively little anxiety and guilt. Moreover, society benefits from the energy and effort such people channel into the arts, literature, science, and other socially useful activities.

We have seen that there are many different ways of coping defensively with stress. Is defensive coping a sure sign that a person is immature, unstable, on the edge of a "breakdown"? Not at all. The effects of prolonged stress may be so severe, as we will see in the next section, that in some cases defensive coping not only contributes to our overall ability to adapt and adjust but even becomes essential to survival. And in less extreme situations, people may rely on defense mechanisms to cope with everyday problems and stress. As Coleman et al. (1987) point out, defenses are "essential for softening failure, alleviating tension and anxiety, repairing emotional hurt, and maintaining our feelings of adequacy and worth" (p. 190). It is only when a defense mechanism interferes with a person's ability to function or creates more problems than it solves that it is considered maladaptive.

People in the lower socioeconomic classes often face greater difficulties than other people but have fewer resources to deal with them.

## Socioeconomic and Gender Differences in Coping with Stress

People use the various coping strategies we have been discussing in different combinations and in different ways to deal with stressful events. In particular, economic and social factors figure not only in the amount of stress that people encounter but also in their ability to cope with that stress. Poor people frequently have to deal with more stress than other people who are better off (N. Adler et al., 1994; S. Cohen & Williamson, 1988; Kessler, 1979). They often live in substandard housing in neighborhoods with high rates of crime and violence. They are more likely than others to experience long-term joblessness, and they face greater obstacles in addressing such basic needs as feeding their children adequately, maintaining good health and securing high-quality medical care, and providing a home.

Moreover, some data indicate that people in low-income groups cope less effectively with stress and that, as a result, stressful events have a harsher impact on their emotional lives (Kessler, 1979; Wills and Langer, 1980). Psychologists have offered several possible explanations for these data. Pearlin and Schooler (1978) suggested that people in lower socioeconomic classes often have fewer means for coping with hardship and stress. In a similar vein, Liem and Liem (1978) concluded that low-income people have fewer people to turn to and fewer community resources to draw on for support during stressful times. In addition, people living in poverty may believe to a greater extent than other people that external factors are responsible for what happens to them and that they have little personal control over their lives (see the discussion of locus of control in the chapter on personality). Finally, there is some evidence that members of low-income groups are more likely to have low self-esteem and to doubt their ability to master difficult situations. All these factors help explain why stress often takes a greater toll on people in lower socioeconomic classes.

**General adaptation syndrome (GAS)** According to Selye, the three stages the body passes through as it adapts to stress: alarm reaction, resistance, and exhaustion.

Gender has also been studied in relation to stress and coping. One study of victims of Hurricane Andrew found that although women reported experiencing more stress than men, when stress was measured physiologically, men and women turned out to be affected equally (T. Adler, 1993b). In another study of 300 couples in which both spouses worked, women and men felt equally stressed by the state of their marriage and jobs and how well their children were doing. However, the women in this study experienced greater stress than men when problems developed in long-term relationships, largely because they were more committed to their personal and professional relationships than the men were (Barnett, 1993; Gore & Colten, 1991).

5. Do men generally handle stress better than women do?

## HOW STRESS AFFECTS HEALTH

The Canadian physiologist Hans Selye (1907–1982) contended that we react to physical and psychological stress in three stages he collectively called the **general adaptation syndrome** (**GAS**, for short) (Selye, 1956, 1976). These three stages are alarm reaction, resistance, and exhaustion.

Stage 1, *alarm reaction*, is the first response to stress. It begins when the body recognizes that it must fend off some physical or psychological danger. Emotions run high. We become more sensitive and alert, our respiration and heartbeat quicken, our muscles tense, and we experience other physiological changes as well. All these changes help us to mobilize our coping resources in order to regain self-control. At the alarm stage, we might use either direct or defensive coping strategies. If neither of these approaches reduces the stress, we eventually enter the second stage of adaptation.

During Stage 2, that of *resistance*, physical symptoms and other signs of strain appear as we struggle against increasing psychological disorganization. We intensify our use of both direct and defensive coping techniques. If our efforts succeed in reducing the stress, we return to a more normal state. But if the stress is extreme or prolonged, we may turn in desperation to inappropriate coping techniques and cling to them rigidly, despite the evidence that they are not working. When that happens, physical and emotional resources are further depleted and signs of psychic and physical wear and tear become even more apparent.

In the third stage, *exhaustion*, we draw on increasingly ineffective defense mechanisms in a desperate attempt to bring the stress under control. Some people lose touch with reality and show signs of emotional disorder or mental illness at this stage. Others show signs of "burnout," including inability to concentrate, irritability, procrastination, and a cynical belief that nothing is worthwhile (Freudenberger, 1983; Freudenberger & Richelson, 1980; Maslach, 1982). Physical symptoms such as skin or stomach problems may erupt, and some victims of burnout turn to alcohol or drugs to cope with the stress-induced exhaustion. If the stress continues, the person may suffer irreparable physical or psychological damage or even death.

One of the most startling implications of Selye's theory is the possibility that prolonged psychological stress can cause disease, or at least make certain diseases worse. This idea is controversial, but recent studies strongly support the belief that psychological factors lie at the root of some of our worst afflictions, including heart disease and diseases of the immune system such as cancer.

6. How can stress lead to physical illness?

How exactly does psychological stress lead to physical illness? There are at least two routes. First, when people experience stress, their hearts, lungs, nervous systems, and other physiological systems are forced to work harder, so it is hardly surprising that when stress is prolonged, people are more likely to experience some kind of physical disorder. The human body is not designed to be exposed for long periods to the powerful biological changes that accompany alarm and mobilization. Second, stress has a powerful negative effect on the body's immune system, and prolonged stress can destroy the body's ability to defend itself from disease. In the following pages, we will examine both of these processes.

## Stress and Heart Disease

Stress is known to be a major contributing factor in the development of coronary heart disease (CHD), the leading cause of death and disability in the United States. Heredity also factors in the likelihood of developing CHD, but even among identical twins, the incidence of CHD is closely linked to attitudes toward work, problems in the home, and the amount of leisure time available (Kringlen, 1981). Having stress on the job predisposes a person to CHD. For instance, London bus drivers, who have to contend with the strain of driving in heavy traffic, are far more likely to have CHD than are London conductors, who merely sell the bus tickets (A. J. Fox & Adelstein, 1978). Generally speaking, life stress and social isolation are significant predictors of mortality among those who have suffered heart attacks for whatever reason (Ruberman et al., 1984).

Individual personality also appears to play an important role in determining who develops heart disease. A great deal of research has been done, for example, on people who exhibit the Type A *behavior pattern*—that is, who respond to life events with impatience, hostility, competitiveness, urgency, and constant striving (M. Friedman & Rosenman, 1959). This pattern of behavior was first identified in the 1950s by cardiologists Meyer Friedman and Ray Rosenman, who devised a structured interview to distinguish Type A people from more easygoing Type B people. The interview not only assesses people's own accounts of their achievement and striving but also attempts to provoke interviewees somewhat because Friedman and Rosenman were convinced that Type A behavior was most likely to surface in stressful situations.

A number of studies have shown that the Friedman and Rosenman structured interview not only does an excellent job of identifying people with Type A behavior (Glass, 1977; T.Q. Miller et al., 1991) but also predicts CHD (Booth-Kewley & Friedman, 1987). For example, one study found that when Type A personalities were being evaluated, subjected to harassment or criticism, or playing video games, their heart rate and blood pressure were much higher than those of Type B personalities under the same circumstances (Lyness, 1993). And high heart rate and high blood pressure are known to contribute to CHD. Other studies maintain that the link between Type A behavior and CHD is less direct—that the tendency toward Type A behavior may influence people to engage in behaviors, such as smoking or overeating, that directly contribute to heart disease (K.A. Matthews, 1988). Based on the preponderance of evidence, it seems clear that Type A behavior (hostility, chronic negative emotions, heavy workload, and fierce competitiveness) does indeed predict heart disease (C.D. Jenkins, 1988).

Since long-term stress increases the likelihood of developing CHD, reducing stress has become part of the treatment used to slow the progress of the disease known as *atherosclerosis*, or blockage of the arteries, which can lead to a heart attack. In one recent study, a group of patients with severe heart disease were placed on a very low fat diet and taught stress-management techniques such as yoga and deep relaxation (Ornish, 1990). In the majority of these patients, blockage of the arteries was significantly reduced. By contrast, less than one-third of a control group that adopted a less rigorous diet and did not systematically practice stress reduction showed improvement.

**Psychoneuroimmunology** A field of medicine that studies the interaction between stress on the one hand and immune, endocrine, and nervous system activity on the other.

## Stress and the Immune System

Because so many people come down with colds or flu after a stressful period in their lives (e.g., after an exam), scientists have long suspected that the functioning of the immune system is also affected by stress. Recall that the immune system does not work independently: It depends on hormones and signals from the brain to tell it what to do. Therefore, the nervous and endocrine systems are also involved in the interactions between stress and the immune system. The relatively new field of **psychoneuroimmunology** studies the interaction between stress on the one hand and immune, endocrine, and nervous system activity on the other (Ader & Cohen, 1993).

Just what sort of changes does stress cause in the endocrine and immune systems and how do these changes affect health? Before we can answer this two-part question, we need to say something about how the immune system works. The immune system defends our body against invading substances, or *antigens*, such as bacteria, viruses, and other microbes. It does so primarily with the help of white blood cells called *lymphocytes*. Dysfunctions of the immune system can have noticeable effects on health. At one extreme are cases of hypersensitivity, or allergy, in which the immune system becomes so hyperactive that it responds to substances that don't represent a threat to health. At the other extreme is acquired immune deficiency syndrome (AIDS), a disease caused by the human immunodeficiency virus (HIV), which disables the immune system, leaving the body unable to defend itself against antigens.

To the extent that stress disrupts the functioning of the immune system, it can impair health. In fact, stress associated with college exams and with depression has been linked to suppressed functioning of the immune system (A. O'Leary, 1990; Oltmanns & Emery, 1994;). Chronic stress, such as caring for an elderly parent or living in poverty, also compromises the body's defenses.

Prolonged stress has been shown to increase vulnerability to cancer. Stress does not *cause* cancer, but it apparently impairs the immune system so that cancerous cells are better able to establish themselves and spread throughout the body. Animal research has demonstrated this connection between stress and cancer. In one study, a group of mice known to be vulnerable to cancer was kept for 400 days in crowded conditions in which they heard noise made by people and other animals. By the end of this period, 92 percent of the mice had developed cancer. By contrast, only 7 percent of a comparable group of mice kept in quiet, low-stress conditions developed cancer. In other animal experiments, cancer was diagnosed earlier and death occurred sooner in mice that received frequent shocks under conditions that made escape impossible (presumably a stressful situation) than in mice that were allowed to cope with the stress of shocks by escaping (B.L. Anderson, 1983).

Studies of humans also show a link between life stress and incidence of cancer. For example, A. O'Leary (1990) reported that people who developed cancer generally had experienced a number of stressful life events in the year before diagnosis. They were also likely to be fatigued and to feel helpless (see the Controversy box titled "Can Illusions Keep You Healthy?"). Interestingly, these people reported less distress and were less likely to express negative emotions, such as anger, than others who had the same number of stressful life events, which suggests that suppressing negative emotions may be more stressful (and less healthful) than expressing them. Of course, cancer treatments themselves are very stressful, which is why many cancer patients plunge into depression. Moreover, some chemotherapy and radiation treatments suppress immune function, so patients who are depressed at their diagnosis must deal with a double blow to the immune system. Some studies indicate that relaxation techniques improve immune functioning, and thus increase survival rates among cancer patients (Andersen et al., 1994), so cancer therapy now often includes stress-reduction components.

Unemployment is a major source of stress, although there are some indications that it does not so much create new psychological difficulties as bring previously hidden ones to the surface.

## SOURCES OF EXTREME STRESS

Stress has a variety of sources, ranging from unemployment to wartime combat, from violent natural disaster to rape. In this section, we look briefly at some major stressors, the effects they have on people, and the coping mechanisms people use to deal with them.

1. *Unemployment.* Joblessness is a major source of stress. One researcher observed that when the jobless rate rises, so do first admissions to psychiatric hospitals, infant mortality, deaths from heart disease, alcohol-related diseases, and suicide (Brenner, 1973, 1979). In a study of aircraft workers who lost their jobs, Rayman and Bluestone (1982) found that many of the workers reported suffering from high blood pressure, alcoholism, heavy smoking, and anxiety. Other studies have found signs of family strain. "Things just fell apart," one worker said after both he and his wife lost their jobs.

People usually react the stress of unemployment in several stages (Powell & Driscoll, 1973). First comes a period of relaxation and relief, in which they take a vacation of sorts, confident they will find another job. Stage 2, marked by continued optimism, is a time of concentrated job hunting. In Stage 3, a period of vacillation and doubt, jobless people become moody, their relationships with family and friends deteriorate, and they scarcely bother to look for work. By Stage 4, a period of malaise and cynicism, they have simply given up.

Although these effects are not universal, they are quite common. Moreover, there are indications that joblessness may not so much create new psychological difficulties as bring previously hidden ones to the surface. Finally, two studies have shown that death rates go up and psychiatric symptoms worsen not just during periods of unemployment but also during short, rapid upturns in the economy (Eyer, 1977; Brenner, 1979). This finding lends support to the idea we brought out earlier—that change, whether good or bad, causes stress.

2. *Divorce and separation.* As Coleman and colleagues (1988) observe, "the deterioration or ending of an intimate relationship is one of the more potent of stressors and one of the more frequent reasons why people seek

psychotherapy" (p. 155). After a breakup, both partners often feel they have failed at one of life's most important endeavors. Strong emotional ties frequently continue to bind the pair. If only one spouse wants to end the marriage, the one initiating the divorce may feel sadness and guilt at hurting a once-loved partner; while the rejected spouse may vacillate between anger, humiliation, and self-recrimination over his or her role in the failure. Even if the decision to separate was mutually agreed upon, ambivalent feelings of love and hate can make life upsetting and turbulent. Thus, people commonly use defensive coping techniques, particularly denial and projection, to cushion the impact of divorce or separation.

## CONTROVERSIES

### Can Illusions Keep You Healthy?

To many people, including most psychotherapists, *illusion* is a bad word. In their view, staying in touch with reality is the hallmark of mental health, and people who cherish too many illusions are not well adjusted.

Shelley E. Taylor (1983) has taken a strikingly different view: "Far from impeding adjustment," she says, "illusion may be essential for adequate coping" (p. 1171). Taylor reached this conclusion after a 2-year study of women with breast cancer. The women who coped best with the stress of disfiguring surgery, painful follow-up treatment, and fear of death proved to be those who constructed comforting illusions about themselves and their illness. Taylor defined illusions as beliefs that were based on an overly optimistic view of the facts or that had no factual basis at all.

In subsequent research, Taylor and Jonathon Brown (1988) expanded on the idea that positive illusions can promote mental and physical health. They found that mentally healthy people distort reality in a way that enhances self-esteem and maintains optimism. In other words, such people tend to overestimate their ability to control or influence chance events and believe—evidence to the contrary notwithstanding—that the future will be better than the present. Taylor and Brown contend that these people are happier, have more friends, and are usually more persistent, creative, and productive than those laboring under no such positive illusions. Their optimistic outlook draws other people to them and also gives them the confidence to pursue their interests.

Still, relying on illusions seems to be a rather risky way of handling stress, for if the illusion is shattered, the person's sense of well-being may collapse as well. Moreover, because illusions are often symptoms of a psychiatric disorder, many psychologists dispute the notion that in certain circumstances they are cornerstones of mental health. When Randall Colvin and Jack Block (1994) reviewed the evidence cited in Taylor and Brown's study as well as in other studies, they found evidence for the beneficial effect of illusions inconclusive. They noted that in one study done on cardiac patients, only those patients whose risk of recurrence of heart disease was not severe seemed to benefit from the illusion that they had the power to prevent another heart attack. Other cardiac patients did not appear to reap any health benefits from illusions of control (Helgeson, 1992).

Another study showed that mothers who overestimated their abilities as caregivers to their children were more prone to depression than those who had no illusion they could be "perfect mothers" (Ainsworth & Wittig, 1969). The beliefs of the mothers in the first group believed they could control their babies' emotional states to an unrealistic degree. As a result, they exhibited more physiological distress when their children cried than did mothers in the second group.

In their response to Colvin and Block's criticism, Taylor and Brown (1994) emphasize that they are not contending that mildly positive illusions cure physical illness, but rather that such illusions foster behaviors (e.g., eating better and taking better care of oneself) that can improve a person's health. They also note that not all illusions are good, and that more illusion is not necessarily better than less.

Although more research needs to be done in this area, one explanation for the different points of view on illusion may be semantic. It seems, at least in some cases, that what Taylor and Brown and others of like mind call illusions are just realistic and positive strategies for dealing with certain health problems. Research has shown, for example, that maintaining an optimistic attitude can have both psychological and physical health benefits (Scheier & Carver, 1993). At what point, though, does an "optimistic attitude" become an illusion?

**Posttraumatic stress disorder (PTSD)** Psychological disorder characterized by episodes of anxiety, sleeplessness, and nightmares resulting from some disturbing event in the past.

3. *Bereavement.* Following the death of a loved one, people generally experience the strong feelings of grief and loss known as *bereavement.* Most people emerge from this experience without suffering permanent psychological harm, but usually not before they pass through a long process that Freud called the "work of mourning." Janis and his colleagues (1969) have described normal grief as beginning with numbness and progressing through months of distress in which anger, despair, intense grief and yearning, depression, and apathy may all come to the fore. During this phase, people in mourning tend to cope defensively with an inescapable and extremely painful reality. In most cases, denial, displacement, and other defense mechanisms allow the survivor to gather strength for the more direct coping efforts that will be necessary later on—such as, in the case of a spouse's death, selling belongings and moving out of the marital home.

4. *Natural and man-made catastrophes.* Natural and man-made catastrophes include floods, earthquakes, violent storms, fires, and plane crashes. Psychological reactions to all stressful events have much in common. At first, in the *shock* stage, "the victim is stunned, dazed, and apathetic," and sometimes even "stuporous, disoriented, and amnesic for the traumatic event." Then, in the *suggestible* stage, victims are passive and quite ready to do whatever rescuers tell them to do. In the third phase, the *recovery* stage, emotional balance is regained, but anxiety often persists and victims may need to recount their experiences over and over again (C. Morris, 1990). Some investigators report that in later stages survivors may feel irrationally guilty because they lived while others died. Said a flight attendant who survived a plane crash, "It's not fair. Everyone else is hurt. Why aren't I?" (*Time*, January 15, 1973, p. 53).

Psychological reactions to natural and man-made disasters have much in common. Victims progress from an initial stage of shock to a suggestible final stage of recovery.

5. *Threatening personal attacks.* While wartime experiences often cause soldiers intense and disabling combat stress, similar reactions—including bursting into rage over harmless remarks, sleep disturbances, cringing at sudden loud noises, psychological confusion, uncontrollable crying, and silently staring into space for long periods—are also frequently seen in survivors of serious accidents and violent crimes such as rapes and muggings. In extreme cases, severely stressful events can cause a psychological disorder known as **posttraumatic stress disorder (PTSD)**. Dramatic nightmares in which the victim reexperiences the terrifying event exactly as it happened are common. So are daytime flashbacks, in which the victim relives the trauma. Oftentimes, victims of PTSD cannot function well in their day-to-day existence, and hence may withdraw from social life and from job and family responsibilities.

7. What is posttraumatic stress disorder? What kinds of people are most likely to experience this disorder?

In some cases, posttraumatic stress disorders set in either right after a traumatic event or within a short time. But in other cases, months or years may go by in which the victim seems to have recovered from the experience, and then, without warning, psychological symptoms appear. In some instances, the symptoms disappear quickly, although they may recur repeatedly; in others, they continue unabated for weeks or months, or even years.

Recovery from posttraumatic stress disorder depends a great deal on the amount of emotional support survivors receive from family, friends, and community. Treatment consists of helping those who have experienced severe trauma come to terms with their terrifying memories. Immediate treatment near the site of the trauma coupled with the expectation that the individual will return to everyday life is often effective. Reliving the traumatic event in a safe setting is also crucial to successful treatment. This helps desensitize people to the traumatic memories haunting them (Oltmanns & Emery, 1995).

## THE WELL-ADJUSTED PERSON

We said at the beginning of the chapter that adjustment refers to any effort to cope with stress. But psychologists disagree about what constitutes *good* adjustment. Some think that means the ability to live according to social norms. Everyone has hostile and selfish wishes; everyone dreams impossible dreams. People who learn to control their forbidden impulses and to limit their goals to those society allows are, by this definition, well adjusted. A woman who grows up in a small town, attends her state university, teaches for a year or two, then settles down to a peaceful family life might be considered well adjusted to the extent that she is living by the predominant values of her community.

Other psychologists disagree strongly with this conformist viewpoint. Barron (1963) argued that "refusal to adjust . . . is very often the mark of a healthy character." Society is not always right. If we accept its standards blindly, we renounce the right to make independent judgments. Barron contends that well-adjusted people *enjoy* the difficulties and ambiguities of life; they do not sidestep them through unthinking conformity. They accept challenges and are willing to endure the pain and confusion these challenges may bring. Because they are confident of their ability to deal with problems in a realistic and mature way, they can admit primitive or childish impulses into their consciousness. Temporary regression does not frighten them. Barron has asserted that flexibility, spontaneity, and creativity, rather than simply fitting in, are signs of healthy adjustment.

Still other psychologists maintain that well-adjusted people have learned to balance conformity and nonconformity, self-control and spontaneity—to adapt flexibility as situations change. They can let themselves go at times, but can control themselves in situations where acting on impulse would run counter to their interests or better judgments. They can change themselves at society's urging, but they work to change society when this strikes them as the better course. Such people know both their strengths and admit their weaknesses, and this realistic assessment underlies an approach to life that is in harmony with their inner selves. They do not feel they must act against their values to be successful. Their self-trust enables them to face conflicts and threats without excessive anxiety and, perhaps more important, lets them risk their feelings and self-esteem in intimate relationships.

We may also evaluate adjustment by using specific criteria, such as the following (C. Morris, 1990), to judge an action:

1. *Does the action realistically meet the demands of the situation, or does it simply postpone resolving the problem?* Various forms of escapism—drugs, alcohol, and even endless fantasizing through books, movies, and television—may divert us from our pain, but they do not address the causes of our difficulties. Thus, too great a reliance on escapism never makes for effective adjustment to a stressful situation.
2. *Does the action meet the individual's needs?* Often we act to reduce external pressures by shortchanging our personal needs. An aspiring ac-

tress may abandon her own career goals to further the goals of her spouse. In the short run, she reduces external pressure, but she may be frustrated and disappointed for the rest of her life. A solution that creates such inner conflict is not an effective adjustment.

3. *Is the action compatible with the well-being of others?* Some people satisfy their needs in ways that hurt others. A young executive who ruthlessly uses people and manipulates co-workers may "get ahead" through such actions. But even if he does succeed in becoming vice president of his company, he may find himself without friends and may fear that his superiors will treat him as his subordinates. Ultimately, this situation can become extremely stressful and frustrating. Good adjustment takes into consideration both individual needs and the well-being of others.

Abraham Maslow, whose humanistic views of personality and hierarchy of needs were discussed in the two previous chapters. takes yet another approach to describing the well-adjusted person. According to Maslow, people who are well adjusted seek to "actualize" themselves—that is, they live in a way that enhances their own growth and fulfillment, regardless of what others may think. After studying a number of famous people and a group of college students, Maslow (1954) compiled a list of traits he believed were characteristic of self-actualizing people. In Maslow's view, well-adjusted individuals perceive people and events realistically and are better able than others to accept uncertainty and ambiguity. Though often quite conventional in behavior, they do not think conventionally; rather, they are creative and spontaneous thinkers. At the same time, self-actualized people set goals for themselves and work, often independently of others, to achieve them.

Self-actualizing people also tend to form deep, close relationships with a few chosen individuals and are generally indifferent to such characteristics as sex, birth, race, color, and religion in responding to other people. Maslow saw this indifference as extending to their own culture as well, enabling self-actualizing individuals to function effectively in various cultural settings. Finally, Maslow noted that people with a sense of humor that is broad and philosophical rather than pointed and hostile stand the best chance of adjusting to stress and achieving the most they can.

As we have seen, there are many standards for judging if a person is well adjusted. A person deemed well adjusted by one standard may not be adjudged so by other criteria. The same holds true when we try to specify what behaviors are "abnormal"—the topic of the next chapter.

## LOOKING FORWARD

Life stresses take many forms: a new baby, a new home, an exam, a flood or fire, a belligerent boss, a noisy neighbor, a traffic jam, a rape, a presentation, the loss of someone we love. Stress can arise from a positive change, a hassle, a frustration, a conflict, or a catastrophe. Whatever the specific event or object, every time we experience stress, we need to adjust to it in some way. We may cope by calling on a friend, resorting to alcohol or drugs, or denying that the problem exists. How we deal with stress influences the degree to which stress disrupts our normal functioning and, ultimately, our health.

Sometimes, however, the stressful event is so threatening that adjusting to it is very difficult or nearly impossible. As we have seen, experiencing, or even witnessing, violence or brutality such as imprisonment in a concentration camp or rape can be so threatening that we need professional help and counseling to adequately cope with the experience. In other cases, personal vulnerabilities may make us susceptible to stress. For example, a cold and remote man with few friends may not notice or be adversely affected by his lack of social life until his wife dies and the loneliness he experiences during this terrible time—and his lack of emotional resources for coping with the situation—send him into a deep depression.

As we noted in the discussion of posttraumatic stress in this chapter and will examine again in the next two chapters, stressful events can precipitate a mental disorder. Oftentimes an individual is predisposed toward a particular disorder—either psychologically, as in the case of the widower we just mentioned, or genetically, as in schizophrenia—but the disorder will be expressed only after the individual is subjected to severe stress. This is not to suggest that stress directly causes psychological disorders any more than it directly causes physical disorders like heart disease or cancer. Yet the interaction between stress and psychological and physiological vulnerability is a theme that runs through many, if not most, psychological disorders.

# SUMMARY

We experience **stress** when we are faced with a tense or threatening situation that requires us to change or adapt our behavior. **Adjustment** refers to any attempt we make to cope with a stressful situation, balancing our needs and desires against the demands of the environment and the realistic possibilities available to us. How we adjust to the stresses in our lives affects our health; prolonged or severe stress can contribute to physical and psychological disorders. **Health psychology** is a subfield of psychology concerned with the relationship between psychological factors and physical health.

## SOURCES OF STRESS

Some life-and-death situations, like war and natural disasters, are inherently stressful. Even events that are usually viewed as positive, like a wedding or a job promotion, may be stressful because they require change or adaptation.

### Change

Because most people have a strong desire to maintain order in their lives, any event that involves change will be experienced as stressful. The Social Readjustment Rating Scale (SRRS) developed by Holmes and Rahe measures how much stress a person has undergone in any given period by assigning a series of life-changing events a point value corresponding to the amount of change each event requires.

### Hassles

Lazarus points out that much stress comes from nonevents or hassles, which he defines as petty annoyances, irritations, and frustrations. Lazarus does not discount the impact of major events, but views them as triggers for the little hassles that lie at the root of stress.

### Pressure

**Pressure** also contributes to stress. Pressure can derive from both internal and external forces; in either case, we feel forced to intensify our efforts or to perform at higher levels.

### Frustration

We feel frustrated when someone or something stands between us and our goal. Five basic sources of **frustration** are delays, lack of resources, losses, failure, and discrimination.

### Conflict

**Conflict** arises when we are faced with two or more incompatible demands, opportunities, needs, or goals. Kurt Lewin sees conflict in terms of *approach* and *avoidance*, and shows how these tendencies combine to characterize three basic types of conflict. Someone who is simultaneously attracted to two incompatible goals, experiences an **approach/approach conflict** in which the person must either make a choice between the two goals or opportunities or modify them so as to take some advantage of both goals. The reverse of this problem is **avoidance/avoidance conflict**, in which a person confronts two undesirable or threatening possibilities. People usually try to escape this kind of conflict, but if escape is impossible, they cope in one of several ways, often by vacillating between the two possibilities. Also difficult to resolve is an **approach/avoidance conflict**, in which a person is both attracted and repelled by the same goal or opportunity. Since both the desire to approach and the desire to avoid the goal grow stronger the nearer people in this dilemma get to the goal, they eventually reach a point where the tendency to approach equals the tendency to avoid and they vacillate until they finally make a decision or until the situation changes.

### Self-Imposed Stress

Sometimes people subject themselves to stress by internalizing a set of irrational, self-defeating beliefs that add unnecessarily to the normal stresses of living. According to Albert Ellis, this kind of self-imposed stress is independent of outside forces.

### Stress and Individual Differences

Why do some people perceive a particular situation as stressful while others are able to take the same situation in stride? Suzanne Kobasa suggests that stress-resistant people share a trait called *hardiness*—a tendency to experience difficult demands as challenging rather than threatening. She also found that people who feel they have some control over an event are far less susceptible to stress than those who feel powerless in the same situation.

## HOW PEOPLE COPE WITH STRESS

People generally adjust to stress in one of two ways: *Direct coping* describes any action people take to change an uncomfortable situation, while *defensive coping* denotes the various ways people convince themselves—through a form of self-deception—that they are not really threatened or do not really want something they cannot get.

### Direct Coping

When we cope directly with a particular threat or conflict, we do it in one of three ways: **confrontation, compromise**, or **withdrawal**. When we confront a stressful situation and admit to ourselves there is a problem that needs to be solved, we may learn new skills, enlist other people's aid, or try harder to reach our goal. Confrontation may also involve expressions of anger. Compromise usually requires adjusting expectations or desires; the conflict is resolved by settling for less than what was originally sought. Sometimes the most effective way of coping with a stressful situation is to distance oneself from it. However, the danger of withdrawal is that it may become a maladaptive habit.

### Defensive Coping

When a stressful situation arises and there is little that can be done to deal with it directly, people often turn to **defense mechanisms** as a way of coping. Defense mechanisms are ways of deceiving ourselves about the causes of stressful events, thus reducing conflict, frustration, pressure, and anxiety. Freud believed that such self-deceptions were entirely unconscious, but many psychologists challenge his assertion, maintaining that oftentimes we realize that we are deceiving ourselves.

**Denial** is the refusal to acknowledge a painful or threatening reality. **Repression** is the blocking out of unacceptable thoughts or impulses from consciousness. When we cannot deny or repress a particular problem, we might resort to **projection**—that is, attributing our repressed motives or feelings to others, thereby locating the source of our conflict outside of ourselves. **Identification** is another form of defensive coping, and may occur in situations that make them feel completely powerless; adopting this technique, people take on the characteristics of a powerful person in order to gain a sense of control.

People under severe stress sometimes revert to childlike behavior. This kind of defensive coping is called **regression**. Because adults can't stand feeling helpless, becoming more childlike can make total dependency or helplessness more tolerable. Sometimes people **intellectualize** their problems in order to emotionally distance themselves from a particularly disturbing situation. **Reaction formation** refers to a behavioral form of denial in which people express with exaggerated intensity ideas and emotions that are the opposite of their own. Through **displacement**, repressed motives and feelings are redirected from their original objects to substitute objects. **Sublimation** involves transforming repressed emotions into more socially accepted forms.

### Socioeconomic and Gender Differences in Coping with Stress

People living in poverty tend to experience greater stress than other people, primarily because the environments in which they live are generally more threatening. In addition, they have fewer resources to draw on in coping with that stress. As a result, they experience more health problems than do people in better financial circumstances. Contrary to popular belief, women and men seem to be equally affected by stress, although women are more likely than men to experience stress when their marriage or other long-term relationships are deeply troubled. This appears to be a sign of greater commitment to the relationship rather than an indication of greater vulnerability to stress.

## HOW STRESS AFFECTS HEALTH

Physiologist Hans Selye contends that people react to physical and psychological stress in three stages that he called the **general adaptation syndrome**

(GAS). In Stage 1, *alarm reaction*, the body recognizes that it must fight off some physical or psychological danger. This recognition results in quickened respiration and heart rate, increased sensitivity and alertness, and a highly charged emotional state, a physical adaptation that augments our coping resources and helps us to regain self-control. If neither direct nor defensive coping mechanisms succeed in reducing the stress, we move on to Selye's second stage of adaptation. During this *resistance stage*, physical symptoms of strain appear as we intensify our efforts to cope both directly and defensively. If these attempts to regain psychological equilibrium fail, psychological disorganization rages out of control until *exhaustion*, Selye's third stage, is reached. In this phase, we use increasingly ineffective defense mechanisms to bring the stress under control. At this point, some people lose touch with reality, while others show signs of "burnout," such as shorter attention spans, irritability, procrastination, and general apathy.

### Stress and Heart Disease

Stress is known to be an important factor in the development of coronary heart disease. Type A behavior pattern, a set of characteristics that includes hostility, urgency, competitiveness, and striving, has been linked to a greater likelihood of CHD. Stress-reduction programs can slow, and sometimes arrest, the progress of CHD.

### Stress and the Immune System

Studies in **psychoneuroimmunology** have shown that stress can suppress the functioning of the immune system, particularly by lowering the levels of lymphocytes, white blood cells that defend the body from antigens such as bacteria and viruses. Prolonged exposure to stress increases the risk of cancer. Stress-reduction techniques can help cancer patients cope with the ravages of radiation therapy and chemotherapy.

## SOURCES OF EXTREME STRESS

Stress derives from a number of sources, including unemployment, divorce and separation, bereavement, crime, and natural disasters. People try to cope with these intense, life-altering events in various ways; most resort to defense mechanisms at one or more stages to allow themselves time to gather their energies for more direct coping efforts later on. Extreme traumas may result in **posttraumatic stress disorder (PTSD)**, a disabling emotional disorder whose symptoms include anxiety, sleeplessness, and nightmares.

## THE WELL-ADJUSTED PERSON

Psychologists are of several minds on what constitutes good adjustment. Some believe that well-adjusted people live according to social norms, having learned to control socially forbidden impulses and limit their goals to those that society sanctions. Other psychologists vehemently disagree with this conformist outlook, contending that blind acceptance of society's standards of behavior is equivalent to renouncing the right to independent judgment. Barron (1963) argues that the refusal to adjust to social norms is the mark of a healthy character. He maintains that well-adjusted people thrive on the difficulties and ambiguities of life; they accept challenges and are willing to endure pain and confusion because they are confident of their ability to deal with problems in a realistic and mature way. Still other psychologists believe that well-adjusted people are those who have learned to balance conformity and nonconformity, self-control and spontaneity. They can change their behavior at society's behest, but they try to change when this strikes them as the better course. Flexibility of this sort signals a realistic assessment of both the world and one's own needs and the conviction that one has chosen to live in harmony with one's inner self. Finally, some psychologists use specific criteria to evaluate a person's ability to adjust, such as how well the adjustment solves the problem and satisfies both personal needs and responds to the needs of others.

# REVIEW QUESTIONS

## MULTIPLE CHOICE

1. The process by which we respond to events that create a sense of physiological or psychological tension or threat is known as ______ .

2. True or false: Both pleasant and unpleasant situations can be stressful.

3. ______ occurs when we feel forced to speed up, intensify, or redirect our behavior, or to meet a higher standard of performance.

4. ______ occurs when people are prevented from achieving a goal.

5. Probably the most common problem to which people must adjust is ______ .

6. Match each type of conflict with its definition:

___ approach/approach
___ avoidance/avoidance
___ approach/avoidance

a. We must choose between two undesired, yet unavoidable, alternatives.
b. We are both attracted and repelled by the same goal.
c. We are attracted to two goals at the same time.

7. True or false: Though living in poverty can lead to an increase in stress, this has no effect on health.

8. There are two general types of coping: ______ and ______.

9. Confronting problems, compromising, or withdrawing from the situation entirely are all forms of ______ coping.

10. ______ coping is a means of dealing with situations that people feel unable to resolve.

11. Match each of the following defense mechanisms with its definition:

_____ Denial
_____ Repression
_____ Projection
_____ Identification
_____ Regression
_____ Intellectualization
_____ Reaction formation
_____ Displacement
_____ Sublimation

a. A form of forgetting
b. Detachment from problems through rational analysis
c. Reversion to less mature, even childlike behavior
d. Exaggerated expression of emotions or ideas that are the opposite of what we really feel or believe
e. Redirection of motives or emotions to other objects
f. Refusal to acknowledge that a painful or threatening situation exists
g. Attributing one's own motives and feelings to others
h. Redirection of motives or emotions into more socially acceptable forms
i. Taking on the characteristics of someone else to share that person's successes and avoid feelings of personal inadequacy.

12. The general adaptation syndrome consists of three stages of reaction to stress: ______, ______, and exhaustion.

13. ______ is the term given to the set of characteristics, such as hostility and a sense of urgency, that many people believe make a person more susceptible to coronary heart disease.

14. True or false: Research so far has been unable to find a connection between stress and the strength of the body's immune system.

## CRITICAL THINKING AND APPLICATIONS

15. Sherry is an air-traffic controller who has recently been coming home from work with terrible headaches. She is a perfectionist and is easily frustrated, but she loves her job and does it well. Recently, she broke up with her boyfriend rather than leave her job and relocate to another city with him. Try to come up with at least two or three hypotheses to explain Sherry's headaches.

16. Are defense mechanisms bad for you, or do they foster good health? Give an example of defensive coping as it applies to a person you know (without using the person's name). Has this defense mechanism helped or hurt the person? Come up with two other strategies for coping—one that seems better and another that seems worse than the one chosen—that this person might have used to cope with the stress that prompted these defense mechanisms.

17. Charlie's father was transferred from New Hampshire to North Dakota in the middle of Charlie's senior year in high school, forcing the family to relocate. By the time he comes home from his

new school, Charlie can barely keep his eyes open. His parents tell him his exhaustion and depression are "all in his head." Charlie doesn't think so. Cite some evidence from this chapter to support his claim.

*(Answers to the Review Questions can be found in the back of the text.)*

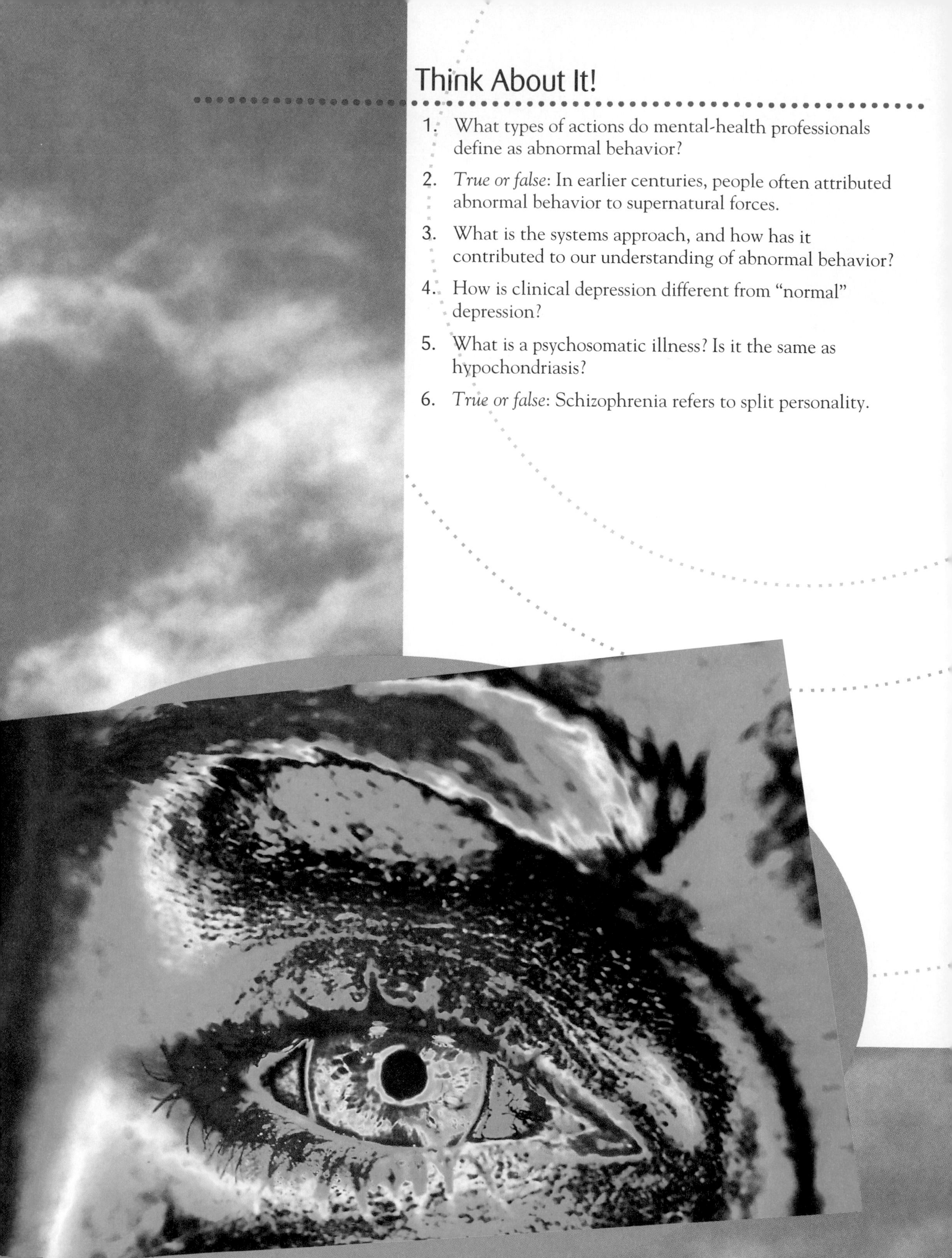

## Think About It!

1. What types of actions do mental-health professionals define as abnormal behavior?
2. *True or false*: In earlier centuries, people often attributed abnormal behavior to supernatural forces.
3. What is the systems approach, and how has it contributed to our understanding of abnormal behavior?
4. How is clinical depression different from "normal" depression?
5. What is a psychosomatic illness? Is it the same as hypochondriasis?
6. *True or false*: Schizophrenia refers to split personality.

Schi... ia Phobia Anxiety ...ination Obsessio... anity Fu

# ABNORMAL BEHAVIOR

# 12

## Overview

**When does behavior become abnormal? The answer to this question is more complicated than it may seem. No one would argue that the man on the street corner claiming to be Jesus Christ or the woman who believes that aliens from outer space are trying to kill her is behaving normally. But what about the members of a religious cult who follow through on a suicide pact? A business executive who happily drinks three martinis every day for lunch? A young woman who feels depressed much of the time but still functions effectively and "keeps up a good front"?**

Many physical diseases can be detected by impartial laboratory tests, but the presence or absence of mental illness cannot be determined so objectively. Whether an individual suffers from an emotional disorder is something of a judgment call, and judgments may differ, depending on a person's perspective.

## SOCIETAL, INDIVIDUAL, AND MENTAL-HEALTH PERSPECTIVES ON ABNORMAL BEHAVIOR

Table 12-1 presents three distinct views of mental health. Each uses different standards to judge normal and abnormal behavior: Society's prevailing standard is whether behavior conforms to the existing social order; the individual's primary criterion is his or her own sense of well-being, mental-health professionals, meanwhile, look chiefly at personality characteristics as well as *personal discomfort* (the person's experience of inner distress) and *life functioning* (the person's success in meeting societal expectations for performance in work or school and in social relationships). Serious personal discomfort and impaired life functioning often go together, but some emotional disorders are characterized by only one or the other problem. Such circumstances complicate the definition of abnormal behavior. Consider the imbalance between personal discomfort and life functioning in each of the following examples:

Not all unusual behaviors are classified as abnormal. Psychologists have developed certain criteria, such as personal discomfort and inadequate life functioning, to help define abnormal behavior.

- A young executive is in a state of profound euphoria. He feels exhilarated, invulnerable, and all-powerful. Suddenly deciding that he's been caught up in a "rat race," he quits his successful job, withdraws his life savings from the bank, and hands out fistfuls of his money on the street corner, telling startled passersby that "it's only paper."
- A 40-year-old successful computer programmer who lives alone is awkward at relating to others. She makes little eye contact, rarely initiates a conversation, and almost always acts "jittery." Inwardly, she feels so tense and restless that she avoids being around people. Often she finds it difficult to sleep at night.
- A 14-year-old boy has been uncontrollable at home and disruptive in school since early childhood. He abuses alcohol and other drugs and frequently steals from stores. As part of his initiation into a gang, he fires a semiautomatic pistol into the air while driving through the territory of a rival gang.

Does each of these brief vignettes describe abnormal behavior? The answer depends, in part, upon whose perspective you adopt. The euphoric

**TABLE 12-1 Viewpoints on Mental Health**

| | STANDARDS/VALUES | MEASURES |
|---|---|---|
| Society | Orderly world in which people assume responsibility for their assigned social roles (e.g., breadwinner, parent), conform to prevailing mores, and meet situational requirements. | Observations of behavior, extent to which a person fulfills society's expectations and measures up to prevailing standards. |
| Individual | Happiness, gratification of needs. | Subjective perceptions of self-esteem, acceptance, and well-being. |
| Mental-health professional | Sound personality structure characterized by growth, development, autonomy, environmental mastery, ability to cope with stress, adaptation. | Clinical judgment, aided by behavioral observations and psychological tests of such variables as self-concept, sense of identity, balance of psychic forces, unified outlook on life, resistance to stress, self-regulation, ability to cope with reality, absence of mental and behavioral symptoms, adequacy in love, work, and play, adequacy in interpersonal relationships. |

*Source*: Reprinted from Strupp & Hadley. Copyright ©1977 by the American Psychological Association. Reprinted by permission of the authors.

young executive certainly feels happy, and the adolescent gang member surely does not think of himself as psychologically impaired. Although society would clearly define their actions as abnormal, from their own perspectives, neither suffers from the sort of personal discomfort that accompanies most abnormal behavior. The opposite is true of the middle-aged computer programmer. Society might judge her behavior as eccentric, but most people would not view her as "abnormal." Her behavior does not violate any essential social rules, and she is functioning adequately. Yet she is clearly experiencing much personal discomfort. From her own perspective, then, something is seriously wrong.

## CATEGORIES AND DIMENSIONS OF ABNORMAL BEHAVIOR

Individual and societal perspectives are in conflict in these cases, but a mental-health professional would have little difficulty concluding that all three people are displaying abnormal behavior. Mental-health professionals define abnormal behavior as involving either maladaptive life functioning *or* serious personal discomfort or both. But now imagine that the facts in each of these cases were slightly different. What if the young executive took a trip around the world or gave his savings to a worthy charity instead of handing out money on the street? What if the middle-aged programmer

What types of actions do mental-health professionals define as abnormal behavior?

**Categorical approach to classification** Dividing mental health and mental illness into categories that are qualitatively different from each other.

**Dimensional approach to classification** Viewing abnormal behavior as different in degree from normal behavior.

were not quite so anxious and honestly preferred being a "loner"? What if the teenager had behaved like a "good kid" until he got involved with the gang members who pressured him to do things he knew were wrong?

These questions raise a second key point about the definition of abnormal behavior. Normal and abnormal behavior often differ only in degree. It is tempting to take a **categorical approach to classification** of emotional disorder and emotional health, dividing mental health and mental illness into categories that are *qualitatively different* from each other—like apples and oranges. However, it is more accurate to think of mental health and mental illness in terms of a **dimensional approach to classification**—where abnormal behavior is viewed as being *quantitatively different* (that is, different in degree) from normal behavior.

You can more readily grasp the important distinction between the categorical and dimensional approaches to classification by thinking about how we classify people's weight. There are no clear dividing lines between normal and abnormal weight, between someone who is underweight or overweight and someone of normal weight. Since the distinction between normal and abnormal weight is a matter of degree, the dividing line between "normal" and "abnormal" is somewhat arbitrary. Still, it is often useful to divide the dimension of weight into categories such as "obese," "overweight," "normal," "thin," and "skinny." In the same way, abnormal behavior differs only quantitatively from normal behavior, but it is often useful to divide the dimension "normal-abnormal" into discrete categories. Nonetheless, it is important to remember that the line separating normal from abnormal behavior is somewhat arbitrary, and that cases are always much easier to judge when they fall at the extreme end of a dimension than when they fall near the dividing line. Remember, too, that individuals, society, and mental-health professionals do not always view abnormality in the same way.

## HISTORICAL VIEWS OF ABNORMAL BEHAVIOR

*True or false*: In earlier centuries, people often attributed abnormal behavior to supernatural forces.

Our distant ancestors in ancient civilizations attributed abnormal behavior to supernatural powers. People who were "possessed" were seen as scared in some societies, their visions construed as messages from the gods. Other cultures felt threatened by signs of madness, ostracizing anyone whose behavior marked them as odd.

In contrast, the Greek physician Hippocrates (c. 450–377 B.C.) proposed that mental illness is like any other sickness—a natural event arising from natural causes. Following this logic, the mentally ill deserved to be treated with the same kind of care and sympathy bestowed on people suffering from physical ailments.

The Middle Ages in Europe witnessed a return to a darkly supernatural view of abnormal behavior, with mentally ill people presumed to be doing the Devil's work. This belief prompted all manner of exorcisms—from the mild to the hair-raising. Some unfortunates were even burned at the stake. As these barbaric practices faded from the scene in the late Middle Ages, public and private asylums were built for the confinement of emotionally disturbed people. Little better than prisons, with some inmates chained down and deprived of food, light, or air to "cure" them, these asylums nonetheless signaled a turn away from viewing the mentally ill as possessed by demons.

In 1793, the Bicêtre Hospital in Paris became the first to abandon questionable and violent medical treatments for the mentally ill. Under the leadership of Philippe Pinel, drastic reforms were made: Patients were released from their chains and allowed to move around the hospital grounds freely, and rooms were made more comfortable and sanitary.

Shortly thereafter, a Boston schoolteacher named Dorothea Dix (1802–1887) led a campaign for humane treatment of mentally ill people throughout America. Her successful efforts turned the few existing asylums in the United States into hospitals and led to the construction of many new institutions with the goal of providing humane care for the mentally ill. Sadly, these hospitals often failed to offer the humane treatment Dix had pressed for, and *deinstitutionalization*—the movement of mental patients out of large hospitals—became a major goal of mental-health care in the latter half of the twentieth century.

**Biological model of abnormal behavior** View that abnormal behavior has a biochemical or physiological basis.

**Psychoanalytic model of abnormal behavior** View that abnormal behavior is the result of unconscious internal conflicts.

## CONFLICTING THEORIES OF THE NATURE, CAUSES, AND TREATMENT OF ABNORMAL BEHAVIOR

Underlying the failed, and sometimes abusive, treatment of mentally disturbed people throughout history has been the lack of understanding of the nature, causes, and treatment of abnormal behavior. Although our knowledge in this area is still inadequate, important advances in understanding abnormal behavior can be traced to the late nineteenth and early twentieth centuries. Three influential but conflicting models of abnormal behavior emerged during this period: the biological model, the psychoanalytic model, and the cognitive-behavioral model.

Dorothea Dix was a nineteenth-century reformer who led a nationwide campaign for humane treatment of mentally ill people.

### The Biological Model

The **biological model of abnormal behavior** holds that such behavior is caused by physiological malfunction (e.g., malfunctioning of the nervous system or the endocrine glands) that is often attributable to hereditary factors. The biological model gained momentum toward the end of the nineteenth century with the discovery of the nature, cause, and treatment of *general paresis*, a disorder characterized by mental and physical symptoms that include severe cognitive impairment and progressive paralysis. Researchers discovered that the massive mental deterioration of paresis was caused by syphilis, a sexually transmitted disease. The discovery of antibiotic medications in the twentieth century gave physicians a way to cure syphilis, and this breakthrough virtually eliminated the disorder. Thus began the search for biological causes—and cures—for all forms of mental disorder.

As we shall see, there is growing evidence that genetic factors predispose people to mental disorders as diverse as schizophrenia, depression, and anxiety. We will also see that some cases of depression and schizophrenia are linked to disturbances in the biochemistry of the nervous system as well. Yet, few contemporary theorists believe that biology alone accounts for all forms of mental illness.

### The Psychoanalytic Model

The **psychoanalytic model of abnormal behavior** was developed by Freud and his followers at the end of the nineteenth and throughout the first half of the twentieth century (see the chapter titled "Personality"). According to this model, behavior disorders are symbolic expressions of unconscious internal conflicts, which generally can be traced to the early years of life. For example, a man who behaves toward women in a violent way may be unconsciously expressing rage at his mother for failing to show affection toward him during his childhood. The psychoanalytic model argues that people must become aware that the source of their problems lies in their childhood and infancy before they can resolve those problems effectively.

**Cognitive-behavioral model of abnormal behavior** View that abnormal behavior is the result of learning and therefore can be unlearned.

**Diathesis-stress model of abnormal behavior** View that people biologically predisposed to a mental disorder (those with a certain diathesis) will tend to exhibit that disorder when subjected to stress.

**Diathesis** Biological predisposition.

**Systems approach to abnormal behavior** View that biological, psychological, and social risk factors combine to produce mental disorders. Also known as the *biopsychosocial model of abnormal behavior.*

The psychoanalytic model is rich in theory. Freud was a brilliant thinker who called attention to the complexity of personality development, including competing human needs (represented by the id, ego, and superego), unconscious cognitive and emotional processes (the unconscious mind), distortions in interpretation and memory (defense mechanisms), and the importance of child development (psychosexual stages of development). Freud and his followers not only profoundly influenced the mental-health disciplines; but also changed patterns of thought in Western culture. Despite its many intricate and appealing ideas, however, the psychoanalytic model has generated only weak scientific evidence to support its theoretical tenets dealing with the causes and effective treatment of mental disorders.

## The Cognitive-behavioral Model

A third model of abnormal behavior grew out of psychological research on learning and cognition during the twentieth century. The **cognitive-behavioral model of abnormal behavior** maintains that, like all behavior, abnormal behavior is the result of learning. From this perspective, fear, anxiety, sexual deviance, and similar behaviors are learned, and they can be unlearned.

As we saw in Chapter 5, learning theory emphasized classical and operant conditioning at first, but cognitive psychologists now highlight the critical role of internal processes (such as expectations and awareness of contingencies) in learned behavior. The cognitive-behavioral model stresses both internal and external learning processes in the development and treatment of abnormal behavior. For example, a bright student who considers himself academically inferior to his classmates and who believes that he doesn't have the ability to perform well on a test does not study with much care or confidence. Naturally, he performs poorly, and his poor test score both punishes his minimal efforts and confirms his belief that he is academically inferior. This student is caught up in a vicious circle (Turk & Salovey, 1985). A cognitive-behavior therapist might therefore set out to modify both the young man's dysfunctional studying behavior and his inaccurate and maladaptive cognitive processes.

The cognitive-behavioral model has resulted in innovations in the treatment of psychological disorders. Still, the model can be readily criticized for its limited perspective, especially its extreme emphasis on purely environmental causes and treatments of abnormal behavior.

## The Diathesis-stress Model and Systems Theory

The three major competing theories have each shed some light on certain types of abnormality, and no doubt each will continue to do so. However, the most exciting recent developments in abnormal psychology emphasize *integration* of the disparate theoretical models to discover specific causes and treatments for all sorts of mental disorders.

The **diathesis-stress model of abnormal behavior** is one promising approach to integrating these theoretical perspectives. This model maintains that a biological *predisposition* called a **diathesis** must combine with some kind of stressful circumstance before the predisposition to a mental disorder shows up as behavior (Rosenthal, 1970). According to this model, some people are biologically prone to developing a particular disorder under stress, while others are not.

The **systems approach to abnormal behavior** is even more promising (Oltmanns & Emery, 1995). This approach examines how biological, psychological, and social *risk factors* combine to produce psychological disorders; for this reason, it is also known as the *biopsychosocial model.* According to this model, emotional problems are "lifestyle diseases" that, much like heart disease and many other physical illnesses, are caused by the interaction of biological risks, psychological stresses, and societal pressures and expectations. We know that heart disease is brought on by a combination of genetic predisposition, stress, characteristic personality styles, poor health behavior, and competitive pressures in our industrialized society. Similarly, according to the systems approach, psychological problems are caused by multiple risk factors that operate in tandem and influence one another. In this chapter, we will follow the systems approach in addressing the causes and treatments of abnormal behavior.

3. What is the systems approach, and how has it contributed to our understanding of abnormal behavior?

## CLASSIFYING ABNORMAL BEHAVIOR

For nearly 40 years, the American Psychiatric Association (APA) has issued an official manual describing and classifying the various kinds of abnormal behavior. This publication, the *Diagnostic and Statistical Manual of Mental Disorders (DSM)*, has gone through four editions: The first appeared in 1952, the second (DSM-II) in 1968, the third (DSM-III) in 1980 (further revised in 1987), and the fourth (DSM-IV) in 1994 (see Table 12-2).

The DSM-IV is intended to provide a complete list of mental disorders, with each category painstakingly defined in terms of significant behavior patterns so that diagnoses based on it will be reliable. *Reliability* means repeatability, and the DSM's most crucial test of reliability is whether different mental-health professionals arrive at the same diagnosis for the same individual—that is, do two or more mental-health professionals agree that one person should be diagnosed with schizophrenia, another with depression, and so on?

Still, the DSM has its critics. Some experts object to the very notion of classifying psychological and behavioral disorders as if they were diseases. Many of these critics argue that a dimensional approach to classification is more accurate—and more humane—than the categorical approach that characterizes the DSM. Others charge that the manual is too medically oriented and that it includes too many kinds of behavior that have nothing to do with mental illness. As the authors of *The Selling of DSM* wrote:

> The expanding scope of mental health, advanced through the ever-growing list of official diagnoses of mental disorders, produces two important political gains for psychiatry: First, if increasing numbers of people have definable mental disorders, the mental health professions can argue that increasing funds should be allocated to conduct research and provide treatment for them. Second, an expanding list of mental disorders that contains everything, including low intelligence, tobacco dependence, antisocial personality, schizophrenia, caffeine intoxication, and childhood misconduct, offers an ideology for understanding a potpourri of dysfunctional or devalued behaviors as medical disorders rather than as diverse forms of social deviance. (Kirk & Kutchins, 1992, p. 238)

Still other critics object to specific DSM categories. The manual already contains hundreds of diagnostic categories, and its appendix offers an additional list of categories that are said to require "further study." Some of these categories are highly controversial. For instance, *premenstrual dysphoric disorder*, described as an increase in sadness, tension, and irritability that occurs in the week before a woman begins to menstruate each month, has been denounced as a sexist attempt to label as "illness" what may actually be a normal psychological reaction to significant biological changes in

**TABLE 12-2 Diagnostic Categories in DSM-IV**

**Disorders Usually First Diagnosed in Infancy, Childhood, or Adolescence**
Examples: mental retardation, learning disorders, autistic disorder, attention-deficit/hyperactivity disorder.

**Delirium, Dementia, and Amnestic and Other Cognitive Disorders**
Examples: delirium, dementia of the Alzheimer's type, amnestic disorder.

**Mental Disorders Due to a General Medical Condition**
Example: psychotic disorder due to epilepsy.

**Substance-Related Disorders**
Examples: alcohol dependence, cocaine dependence, nicotine dependence.

**Schizophrenia and Other Psychotic Disorders**
Examples: schizophrenia, schizoaffective disorder, delusional disorder.

**Mood Disorders**
Examples: major depressive disorder, dysthymic disorder, bipolar disorder.

**Anxiety Disorders**
Examples: panic disorder with agoraphobia, social phobia, obsessive-compulsive disorder, posttraumatic stress disorder, generalized anxiety disorder.

**Somatoform Disorders**
Examples: somatization disorder, conversion disorder, hypchondriasis.

**Factitious Disorders**
Example: factitious disorder with predominantly physical signs and symptoms.

**Dissociative Disorders**
Examples: dissociative amnesia, dissociative fugue, dissociative identity disorder, depersonalization disorder.

**Sexual and Gender-Identity Disorders**
Examples: male erectile disorder, female orgasmic disorder, vaginismus.

**Eating Disorders**
Examples: anorexia nervosa, bulimia nervosa.

**Sleep Disorders**
Examples: primary insomnia, narcolepsy, sleep terror disorder.

**Impulse-Control Disorders**
Examples: kleptomania, pyromania, pathological gambling.

**Adjustment Disorders**
Examples: adjustment disorder with depressed mood, adjustment disorder with conduct disturbance.

**Personality Disorders**
Examples: antisocial personality disorder, borderline personality disorder, narcissistic personality disorder, dependent personality disorder.

the body (Adler, 1990). Similarly, some critics have questioned whether diagnoses currently listed in DSM-IV—for example, *oppositional defiant disorder*, which essentially describes disobedient and angry children—are "mental disorders" at all.

Some of the controversies surrounding the DSM-IV reflect political concerns, while others reflect legitimate scientific disagreements about the nature of abnormal behavior (such as the argument over dimensions and categories). However, controversies over the predominant classification scheme in the mental-health field should not detract from the recognition that much progress has been made in recent years toward understanding the nature, causes, and treatment of many forms of abnormal behavior.

In the remainder of this chapter, we will look at a variety of psychological disorders from the integrative systems perspective. In reading through this material, you may occasionally feel an uncomfortable twinge of personal recognition. This is only natural and nothing to worry about. Much abnormal behavior is simply normal behavior greatly exaggerated or displayed in inappropriate situations.

**Mood disorders** Disturbances in mood or prolonged emotional state.

**Depression** A mood disorder characterized by overwhelming feelings of sadness, lack of interest in activities, and oftentimes, excessive guilt or feelings of worthlessness.

**Psychotic** Marked by defective or lost contact with reality.

## MOOD DISORDERS

As their name suggests, **mood disorders** are characterized by disturbances in *mood* or prolonged emotional state, sometimes referred to as *affect*. Most people have a wide emotional range—that is, they are capable of being happy or sad, animated or quiet, cheerful or discouraged, overjoyed or miserable, depending on the circumstances. In some people with mood disorders, this range is greatly restricted. They seem stuck at one or the other end of the emotional spectrum—either consistently excited and euphoric or consistently sad—whatever the circumstances of their lives. Other people with a mood disorder alternate between the extremes of euphoria and sadness.

The most common mood disorder is **depression**, a state in which a person feels overwhelmed with sadness, loses interest in activities, and displays other symptoms such as excessive guilt or feelings of worthlessness. People suffering from depression are tired and apathetic unable to experience pleasure from activities they once enjoyed. Frequently unable to make the simplest everyday decisions, they may feel as if they have failed utterly in life, and they tend to blame themselves for their problems. Seriously depressed people often have insomnia and lose interest in food and sex. They may have trouble thinking or concentrating—even to the point of finding it difficult to read a newspaper. In very serious cases, depressed people may be plagued by suicidal thoughts or even attempt suicide (see the Highlights box titled "Suicide").

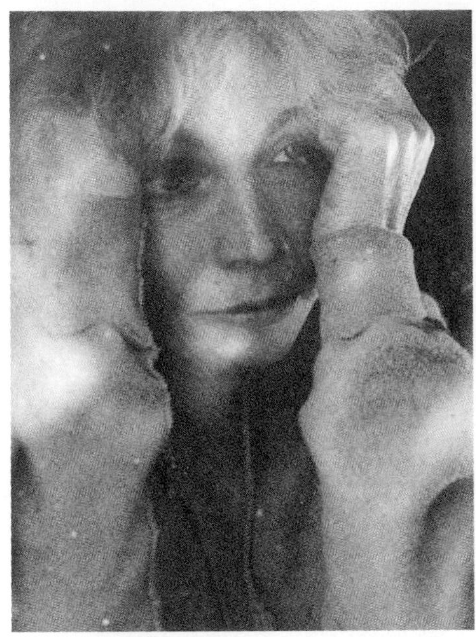

Everyone feels depressed now and then. Psychologists distinguish between the depression we all feel and *clinical depression*, which is serious and long-lasting.

It is important to recognize the difference between *clinical depression* and the "normal" kind of depression that all people experience from time to time. It is entirely normal to become sad when a loved one has died, when you've come to the end of a romantic relationship, when you have problems on the job or at school—even when the weather's bad or you don't have a date for Saturday night. Most psychologically healthy people also get "the blues" occasionally for no apparent reason. But in all these instances, the mood disturbance is either a normal reaction to a "real-world" problem (for example, grief) or passes quickly. Only when depression is serious, lasting, and well beyond the typical reaction to a stressful life event is it classified as a mood disorder (APA, 1994).

How is clinical depression different from "normal" depression?

The DSM-IV distinguishes between two forms of depression. *Major depressive disorder* is an episode of intense sadness that may last for several months; by contrast, *dysthymia* involves less intense sadness (and related symptoms) but persists with little relief for a period of 2 years or more. Some theorists suggest that major depressive disorder is generally caused by a difficult life event, whereas dysthymia has its roots in a physiological disorder, but this is just speculation at this time. It is true, however, that some depressions can become so severe that people become **psychotic**—that is, they lose touch with reality. Consider the following case:

> A 50-year-old widow was transferred to a medical center from her community mental health center, to which she had been admitted three weeks previously with severe agitation, pacing, and handwringing, depressed mood accompanied by severe self-reproach, insomnia and a 6.8 kg [15-pound] weight loss. She believed that her neighbors were against her, had poisoned her coffee, and had bewitched her to punish her because of her wickedness. Seven years previously, after

the death of her husband, she had required hospitalization for a similar depression, with extreme guilt, agitation, insomnia, accusatory hallucinations of voices calling her a worthless person, and preoccupation with thoughts of suicide. (Spitzer et al., 1981, pp. 28–29)

**Mania** A mood disorder characterized by euphoric states, extreme physical activity, excessive talkativeness, distractedness, and sometimes grandiosity.

**Bipolar disorder** A mood disorder in which periods of mania alternate with periods of depression, sometimes with periods of normal mood intervening.

Depression occurs two to three times more frequently in women than in men (Smith & Weissman, 1992).

There are other mood disorders besides depression. One that is less common is **mania**, in which the person becomes euphoric or "high," extremely active, and excessively talkative, and easily distracted. People suffering from mania may also become *grandiose*—that is, their self-esteem is greatly inflated. They typically have unlimited hopes and schemes, but little interest in realistically carrying them out. People in a manic state sometimes become aggressive and hostile toward others as their self-confidence grows more and more exaggerated. At the extreme, people going through a manic episode may become wild, incomprehensible, or violent until they collapse from exhaustion.

Manic episodes rarely appear by themselves; rather, they usually alternate with depression. Such a mood disorder, in which both mania and depression are present, is known as **bipolar disorder**. In bipolar disorder, periods of mania alternate with periods of depression (each lasting from a

## HIGHLIGHTS

### Suicide

In the United States, more than 200,000 people try to commit suicide each year (Rosenhan & Seligman, 1984). More women than men attempt suicide, but more men actually succeed at it, partly because men more often choose violent and lethal means, such as firearms.

Though there has been only a slight increase in the overall suicide rate over the last several decades, the rate of suicide among adolescents and young adults has tripled since 1950. Suicide is now the third leading cause of death in this age group, after accidents and homicides (Blumenthal, 1990). No one has yet offered a convincing explanation for this sudden increase. In part at least, the increase may be due to an erosion of family or social ties and increased feelings of isolation and hopelessness as well as increased depression, drug use and alcoholism among young people and their families (Harris & Liebert, 1991)

There are several dangerous myths concerning suicide. One is the notion that someone who talks about committing suicide will never go through with it. In fact, most people who kill themselves mention their intent beforehand. Comments referring to suicide as"the only way out," for example, should *always* be taken seriously by the person's friends and family. A related misconception is that someone who has attempted suicide and failed is not serious about it or is just trying to attract attention. Often a suicidal person will try again, picking a more deadly method the second or third time around. (And any suicide attempt is a sign that the person is deeply troubled and in desperate need of help.) A third erroneous idea is that those who commit suicide are life's losers—people who have failed vocationally and socially. In fact, many people who kill themselves have prestigious jobs, conventional families, and a good income. Physicians, for example, have a suicide rate several times higher than that for the general population; in this case, the tendency to suicide is probably related to their work stresses.

People considering suicide are overwhelmed with hopelessness. They feel that things *cannot* get better and see no way out of their difficulties. This is depression in the extreme, and it is not a state of mind that someone can easily be talked out of. It does little good to tell suicidal people that things aren't really so bad; they will only take this as further evidence that no one understands their suffering. But most suicidal people *do* want help, however much they may despair of obtaining it. If a friend or family member is leaning toward suicide, make sure that person is not left alone and seek professional help for him or her as soon as possible. Your local community mental-health center is a good starting point, or you can call one of the national suicide hot lines (see telephone numbers listed in the next chapter).

few days to a few months), sometimes with periods of normal mood intervening. Occasionally, bipolar disorder is seen in a mild form: The person has alternating moods of unrealistically high spirits followed by moderate depression. Research indicates that bipolar disorder differs in several ways from unipolar depression. Bipolar disorder is much less common and, unlike depression, which occurs two to three times more frequently in women than in men (Smith & Weissman, 1992), bipolar disorder is equally prevalent in men and women. Bipolar disorder also seems to have a stronger biological component than depression: It is more strongly linked to heredity and is more often treated by drugs (Gershon1990).

**Cognitive distortion** An illogical and maladaptive response to early negative life events that leads to feelings of incompetence and unworthiness that are reactivated whenever a new situation arises that resembles the original events.

## Causes of Mood Disorders

Most psychologists believe that mood disorders stem from a combination of risk factors. Biological factors seem to figure prominently in some cases—for example, bipolar disorders—while psychological factors appear to underlie other cases—such as depression following the experience of a loss. Social factors loom large in still other cases—for example, some instances of depression among women. Although we can identify many of the causative factors, we still do not yet know exactly how they interact to bring on a mood disorder.

BIOLOGICAL FACTORS Genetic factors play a pivotal role in the development of depression, particularly in bipolar disorder (Andreasen et al., 1987; Goodwin & Guze, 1984; Katz & McGuffin, 1993; Kety, 1979). As we saw in Chapter 2, the strongest evidence implicating genetic risk factors comes from studies of twins. If one identical twin is clinically depressed, the other (genetically identical) twin is at substantial risk of becoming clinically depressed as well. Among fraternal twins (who share only about half the same genes), if one twin is clinically depressed, the likelihood is much less that the second twin will also be clinically depressed. But what is it that predisposes some people to a mood disorder?

Promising research has linked mood disorders to certain chemical imbalances in the brain—principally an oversupply or undersupply of certain neurotransmitters, chemicals involved in the transmission of nerve impulses from one cell to another (see the chapter on physiology and behavior) (Delgado, Price, Heninger, & Charney, 1992). For example, medications that are effective in treating mood disorders are known to alter neurotransmitter levels. Moreover, some animal researchers have found that apparently "depressed" behavior in rats (such as decreased effort) can be brought about by lowering their levels of the neurotransmitter norepinephrine (J.M. Weiss, Glazer, & Pohorecky, 1975). Still other evidence ties depression to high levels of hormones released by the endocrine system (E.S. Friedman, Clark, & Gershon, 1992). Yet no conclusive evidence has established a correlation between high or low levels of neurotransmitters and an increased genetic risk for mood disorders. In fact, the chemical imbalance in the brain associated with depression could be caused by stressful life events. Biology affects psychological experience, but psychological experience also alters biological functioning.

PSYCHOLOGICAL FACTORS While a number of psychological factors may bring on severe depression, in recent years research on the causes of this disorder focused on maladaptive **cognitive distortions**. According to Aaron Beck (1967, 1976), during childhood and adolescence some people undergo such wrenching experiences as the loss of a parent, severe difficulties in gaining parental or social approval, or humiliating criticism from teachers and other adults. One response to such emotionally battering experiences is to develop a negative self-concept—a feeling of incompetence or unworthiness that has little to do with reality but is maintained by a distorted and illogical interpretation of real events. When a new situation arises that resembles the situation under which the self-concept was learned, these same feelings of worthlessness and incompetence may surface, triggering depression.

Beck describes several kinds of illogical thinking that may contribute to feelings of depression:

1. *Arbitrary inference.* Individuals arrive at a sweeping conclusion about themselves despite a scarcity or absence of supporting evidence. For example, a man thinks of himself as professionally incompetent because his car won't start on the morning he is scheduled to make an important presentation at work.

2. *Selective abstraction.* The individual jumps to a conclusion based on only one of numerous factors at work in a situation. For example, an athlete blames herself alone for her team's bad performance, though several other members of the team also played poorly.

3. *Overgeneralization.* The individual arrives at a sweeping conclusion based on a single, sometimes trivial, event. For example, a high school student concludes that she is not worthy of admission to the college of her choice because of her poor performance on a pop quiz for which she was not prepared.

4. *Magnification and minimization.* The individual tends to magnify difficulties and failures while minimizing accomplishments and successes. For example, a man who has been driving for 20 years without an accident minimizes his established record of skillful motoring and focuses instead on the nearly imperceptible dent he put in his car while trying to back out of a tight parking space.

Considerable research supports Beck's view of depression. In tests designed to allow respondents to express their immediate thoughts, researchers have found that the thoughts of depressed persons are generally more illogical than the thoughts of people who are not depressed (White, Davison, & White, 1985). Depressed people also seem to perceive and recall information in more negative terms (Roth & Rehm, 1980). However, critics of Beck's theories have pointed out that such negative responses may be the *result* of depression instead of the cause (Hammen, 1985). Still, as we shall see in the next chapter, therapy based on Beck's theories has proved quite successful in the treatment of depression.

**SOCIAL FACTORS** Many social factors figure in mood disorders, particularly difficulties in interpersonal relationships to Freud depression stemmed from excessive and irrational grief over a real or "symbolic" loss. Freud's complex view of how "unresolved grief" is transformed into depression is not supported by current evidence (Crook & Eliot, 1980). However, other theorists have built on the analogy Freud drew between grief and depression, considerable research has established a link between depression and troubled close relationships (Monroe & Simons, 1991). Some theorists have suggested that the greater incidence of depression among women stems from women's tendency to be more relationship-oriented than men are in our society (Gilligan, 1982). Yet not every person who experiences a troubled relationship becomes depressed. As the systems approach would predict, it appears that a genetic predisposition or cognitive distortion is necessary before a distressing close relationship or other significant life stressor will result in a mood disorder.

One further point deserves our attention. People with certain depression-prone genetic or cognitive tendencies may be more likely than others to encounter stressful life events by virtue of their personality and behavior. For example, studies show that depressed people tend to evoke anxiety and even hostility in others (Coyne, 1976), partly because they require more emotional support than people feel comfortable giving (Coyne, 1982). Other people, in turn, tend to avoid those who are depressed, and this shunning may intensify the depression (Lewinsohn & Arconad, 1981). In short, depression-prone and depressed people may become trapped in a vicious circle that is at least partly of their own creation.

## ANXIETY DISORDERS

Although all of us are afraid from time to time, we usually know why we are fearful: Our fear is caused by something appropriate and identifiable, and it passes in time. But in the case of **anxiety disorders**, either people do not know why they are afraid or their anxiety is inappropriate to the circumstances. In either case, their fear and anxiety don't seem to make sense.

Until the publication of DSM-III in 1980, anxiety disorders were grouped as part of the broader diagnostic category of *neurosis*, which also included mood disorders and several other very different problems that we will address shortly. Although the term *neurotic* has passed into everyday language ("I cleaned my room three times this week—I guess that's pretty neurotic!"), psychologists and psychiatrists do not agree on precisely what neurosis means. Therefore, the DSM has dropped the term in favor of more specific diagnostic categories.

Anxiety disorders are subdivided into specific diagnostic categories. One familiar subtype of anxiety disorder is **specific phobia**. A specific phobia is an intense, paralyzing fear of something that perhaps should be feared, but the fear is excessive and unreasonable. In a specific phobia the fear is so great that it leads the person to avoid routine or adaptive activities, and thus interferes with life functioning. For example, it is not inappropriate to be a bit fearful as an airplane takes off or lands, but it is inappropriate to be so afraid of flying that you refuse to get on or even go near an airplane—particularly if your career demands frequent travel. Other common phobias center on animals, heights, closed places, blood, needles, or injury. Some fear of all these things is normal and common, but excessive, intense, paralyzing fear is a sign of specific phobia. Data indicate that about 1 in 10 people in the United States suffers from at least one specific phobia.

Another important subtype of phobia is **social phobia**, which refers to excessive, inappropriate fears connected with social situations or performances in front of other people. Intense fear of public speaking is a common form of social phobia. In other cases, simply talking with people or eating in public causes such severe anxiety that the phobic person will go to great lengths to avoid these situations. As with specific phobias, it is normal to experience some mild fear or uncertainty in many social situations. These fears are only considered to be social phobias when they are excessive enough to interfere significantly with life functioning.

**Agoraphobia** is a much more debilitating type of anxiety disorder than social phobia. *Agoraphobia* is a term formed from Greek and Latin words that literally mean "fear of the marketplace," but the disorder typically involves multiple, intense fears, such as the fear of being alone, of being in public places from which escape might be difficult, of being in crowds, of traveling in an automobile, or of going through tunnels or over bridges. The common element in all these situations seems to be a great

**Anxiety disorders** Disorders in which anxiety is a characteristic feature or the avoidance of anxiety motivates abnormal behavior.

**Specific phobia** Anxiety disorder characterized by intense, paralyzing fear of something.

**Social phobia** An anxiety disorder characterized by excessive, inappropriate fears connected with social situations or performances in front of other people.

**Agoraphobia** An anxiety disorder that involves multiple, intense fears of crowds, public places, and other situations which separate them from sources of security, such as the home.

Excessive fear of heights is an example of a *specific phobia.*

**Panic disorder** An anxiety disorder characterized by recurrent panic attacks in which the person suddenly experiences intense fear or terror without any reasonable cause.

**Generalized anxiety disorder** An anxiety disorder characterized by prolonged vague but intense fears that are not brought on by any particular object or situation.

**Obsessive-compulsive disorder** An anxiety disorder in which a person feels driven to think disturbing thoughts and/or perform senseless rituals.

dread of being separated from sources of security, such as the home or a loved one with whom the person feels safe.

Agoraphobia can greatly interfere with life functioning: Some people are so fearful that they will venture only a few miles from home, while others will not leave their homes at all. Although agoraphobia is less common than specific or social phobia (it affects about 3 percent of the population), because of the severity of its effects, it is more likely to cause the person to seek treatment (L. Robins & Regier, 1991). Interestingly, women are far more likely than men to suffer from agoraphobia. One possible explanation: Traditionally it has been more acceptable for a woman to be housebound. It is also possible that women more readily admit to the problem.

Yet another type of anxiety disorder is **panic disorder**, a problem characterized by recurrent panic attacks. A *panic attack* is a sudden, unpredictable, and overwhelming experience of intense fear or terror without any reasonable cause. During a panic attack, a person may have feelings of impending doom, chest pain, dizziness or fainting, sweating, difficulty breathing, and a fear of losing control or dying. A panic attack usually lasts only a few minutes, but such attacks may recur for no apparent reason. For example:

> A 31-year-old stewardess . . . had suddenly begun to feel panicky, dizzy, had trouble breathing, started to sweat, and trembled uncontrollably. She excused herself and sat in the back of the plane and within ten minutes the symptoms had subsided. Two similar episodes had occurred in the past: the first, four years previously, when the plane had encountered mild turbulence; the second, two years earlier, during an otherwise uneventful flight, as in this episode. (Spitzer et al., 1981, p. 219)

Despite the fact that she has enjoyed a very successful career, singer Carly Simon has suffered from performance anxiety, the fear of performing in front of an audience. This is an example of a *social phobia*.

Panic attacks like this not only cause tremendous fear while they are happening but also leave behind a dread of having another panic attack; this dread can persist for days or even weeks after the original episode. In some cases, in fact, this dread is so overwhelming that it may evolve into agoraphobia: In their efforts to prevent a recurrence of the panic anxiety, some people avoid any situation that might cause anxiety, and cling to people or settings that help keep them calm. In other words, their agoraphobia develops out of their attempt to avoid further panic attacks.

In the various phobias and in panic attacks, the anxiety has a specific source: fear of heights, fear of social situations, or fear of being in crowds. In contrast, **generalized anxiety disorder** is characterized by prolonged vague but intense fears that are not triggered by any particular object or situation. Generalized anxiety disorder perhaps comes closest to the everyday meaning attached to the term "neurotic." Its symptoms include an inability to relax, constantly feeling restless or keyed up, muscle tension, rapid heart beat or pounding heart, apprehensiveness about the future, hypervigilance (constant alertness to potential threats), and sleeping difficulties.

A very different form of anxiety disorder is **obsessive-compulsive disorder**. *Obsessions* are involuntary thoughts or ideas that keep recurring despite all attempts to stop them, while *compulsions* are repetitive, ritualistic behaviors that a person feels driven to perform. Obsessive thoughts are often horrible and exceptionally frightening. One patient, for example, reported that "when she thought of her boyfriend she wished he were dead; when her mother went down the stairs, she 'wished she'd fall and break her neck'; when her sister spoke of going to the beach with her infant daughter [she] 'hoped that they would both drown'" (Carson & Butcher, 1992, p. 190). Truly compulsive behaviors may be equally dismaying to the person who feels driven to perform them. They often take the form of washing or cleaning, as if the compulsive behavior were the person's attempt to "wash away" contaminating thoughts. One patient reported that her efforts to keep her clothes and body clean eventually took up 6 hours of her day, and even then, "washing my hands wasn't enough, and I started to use rubbing alcohol" (Spitzer et al., 1981, p. 137). Another common type of compulsion is checking: repeatedly performing a particular behavior to make sure that something was or was not done in a certain way. For example, a person might feel compelled to check dozens of times whether the doors are locked before going to bed. In a more unusual case, a man became obsessed with the idea that he had run over someone while driving and spent an entire day driving up and down the same piece of highway trying to find the "body" of the person he was convinced he'd run over (D. Holzman, 1986).

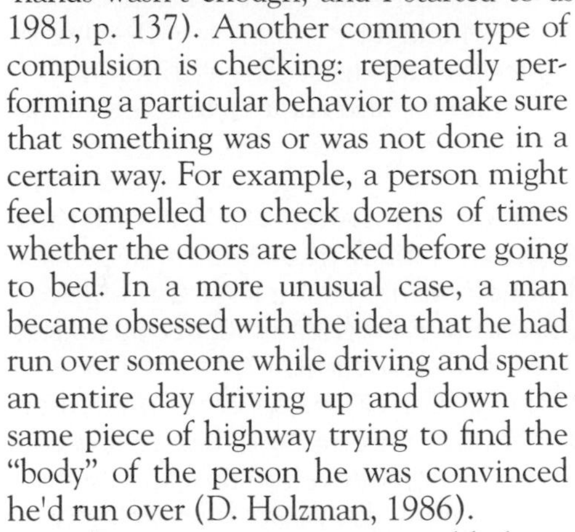

During a panic attack, a person experiences intense fear, including fear of the panic attack itself.

Anyone can experience mild obsessions or compulsions at times. Most of us have occasionally been unable to get a certain song lyric out of our head or have felt that we *had* to walk so as to avoid stepping on cracks in the sidewalk. But in an obsessive-compulsive disorder, the obsessive thoughts and compulsive behavior are of a more serious nature. For example, a man who checks his watch every five minutes when his wife is late coming home is merely being normally anxious. But a man who feels that he must go through his house every hour checking every clock for accuracy, even though he knows there is no reason to do so, is showing signs of an obsessive-compulsive disorder.

Since people beset by obsessions and compulsions often do not seem particularly anxious, you may wonder why this disorder is considered an anxiety disorder. Simply put, if such people try to *stop* their irrational behavior, or if someone else tries to stop them, they experience severe anxiety. In other words, the obsessive-compulsive behavior has developed to keep anxiety down to a tolerable level.

Finally, two types of anxiety disorder can be traced directly to some specific highly stressful event. Some people who have lived through fires, floods, tornadoes, or man-made disasters like an airplane crash experience repeated episodes of fear and terror after the crises is over. If the anxious reaction occurs soon after the event, the diagnosis is *acute stress disorder*. If it takes place long after the event is past, the diagnosis is likely to be *posttraumatic stress disorder* (examined in Chapter 11). Posttraumatic stress disorder is characterized by hyperarousal, avoidance of situations that recall the trauma, and "reexperiencing"—that is, reliving the traumatic event in vivid and frightening detail. Two kinds of traumatic experience are especially likely to bring on acute or posttraumatic stress disorder: exposure to military combat or violent crime among men and rape among women.

## Causes of Anxiety Disorders

A good starting point in considering the origin of anxiety disorders is to recall our discussion of phobias in the chapter on learning. We noted that phobias are often learned after only one fearful event and are extremely difficult to change. We also saw that there is a relatively limited and predictable range of phobic objects: People are more likely to be injured in an automobile accident than by a snake or spider bite, yet snake and spider

**Psychosomatic disorders** Disorders in which real physical illness is largely caused by psychological factors such as stress and anxiety.

phobias are far more common than car phobias. Some theorists, therefore, believe phobias are *prepared responses*—that is, responses that evolution has made us biologically predisposed to acquire through learning so that we seem to be "hard-wired" to associate certain stimuli with intense fears. Consider a young boy who is savagely attacked by a large dog. Because of this experience, he is now terribly afraid of all dogs. Other children who witnessed the attack or just heard about it may also come to fear dogs. Thus realistic fears or cautions are transformed into a phobia.

More generally, and from a more cognitive perspective, research indicates that people who feel they are not in control of stressful events in their lives are more likely to experience anxiety than those who believe they have control over such events. As one real-life example of this, African Americans who live in high-crime areas have a higher incidence of anxiety disorders than other Americans (Neal & Turner, 1991).

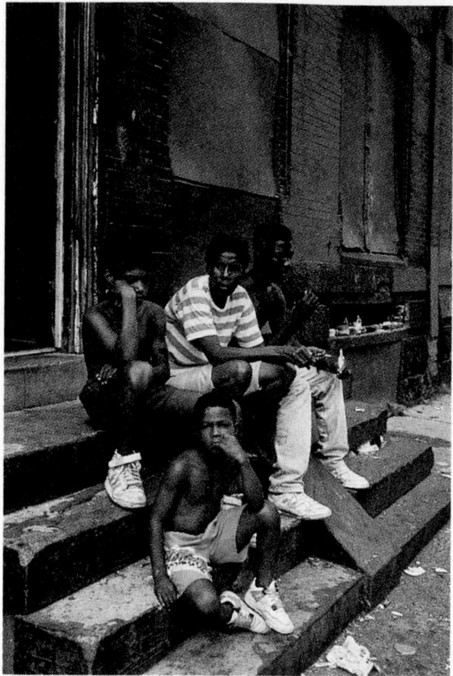

Rates of anxiety disorders among African Americans who live in high-crime areas are higher than among white Americans. According to some experts, a major reason for this difference is that people who live in high-crime areas feel they lack control over stressful life events.

Psychologists working from the biological perspective point out, however, that even when there is the same opportunity to learn phobic or obsessive-compulsive behavior, some people develop unrealistic fears while others do not. To explain this difference, they note that the activity of the autonomic nervous system is involved in all kinds of fear. Moreover, there is considerable evidence that autonomic responsiveness is genetically determined, at least in part. Thus, there is a distinct possibility that a predisposition to anxiety disorders may be inherited (R.B. Cattell, 1965; Eysenck, 1970; Sarason & Sarason, 1987), with some research bolstering this argument by noting that anxiety disorders tend to run in families (Carey & Gottesman, 1981; Kendler et al., 1992; Torgersen, 1983). Yet when it comes to specifying which kinds of anxiety disorders are inherited, the evidence is less conclusive (Oltmanns & Emery, 1995).

Apart from the effects of heredity, some current research draws a link between specific biological factors and panic disorder (DeAngelis, 1990b). In particular, infusions of *lactate*, a by product of intense and rapid breathing, provoke panic attacks in a high percentage of patients. And some people with obsessions and compulsions have brain abnormalities and respond well to treatment with drugs (Schmeck, 1988).

Finally, in tracing the causes of anxiety, we must account for the key role of internal psychological conflicts. Most psychoanalytic theorists focus at length on such conflicts. From the Freudian perspective, unacceptable impulses or thoughts (usually sexual or aggressive in nature) may threaten to overwhelm the ego and break through into full consciousness. The Freudian defense mechanisms protect the conscious mind against such threats, but generate anxiety as a by product. For example, according to the psychoanalytic view, phobias emerge as a result of *displacement*, meaning people redirect their strong feelings from whatever originally aroused them toward something else. Thus, a woman who feels unconsciously threatened by unacceptable feelings of fear toward a spouse might redirect her fear toward elevators or spiders. While we may doubt the validity of specific psychoanalytic interpretations of phobias, inner conflicts—as well as defenses and other internal distortions of these conflicts—certainly seem to play a role in many cases of anxiety and related disorders.

## PSYCHOSOMATIC DISORDERS

To many people, the term *psychosomatic* implies that a condition is not "real," something that exists "only in your head." In fact, **psychosomatic disorders** are *real* physical disorders. The illnesses have a valid physiological basis—there is real physiological damage to the body that can be ascertained through tests. For example, a gastric ulcer (a condition that is widely considered to be psychosomatic in origin) consists of a perforation in the lining of the stomach. The ulcer is real, but the illness is called "psychosomatic" because psychological factors (such as stress and anxiety) are known to play an important role in causing the physical abnormality. In fact, the term *psychosomatic* perfectly captures the interplay of psyche (mind) and soma (body) that characterizes these disorders.

**Somatoform disorders** Disorders in which there is an apparent physical illness for which there is no organic basis.

**Somatization disorder** A somatoform disorder characterized by recurrent, vague somatic complaints without a physical cause.

Scientists used to believe that psychological factors contributed to the development of some physical illnesses, principally ulcers, headaches, allergies, asthma, and high blood pressure, but not others, such as infectious diseases. Today modern medicine leans toward the idea that *all* physical ailments are to some extent "psychosomatic"—in the sense that stress, anxiety, and various states of emotional arousal alter body chemistry, the functioning of bodily organs, and the body's immune system (which is vital to fighting infections). Contemporary physicians recognize that stress and psychological strains can also alter *health behavior*, which includes positive actions such as eating a balanced diet and exercising as well as negative activities like cigarette smoking and excessive alcohol consumption. As we noted earlier in this chapter, both physical and mental illnesses are now viewed as "lifestyle diseases" that are caused by a combination of biological, psychological, and social factors.

What is a psychosomatic illness? Is it the same as hypochondriasis?

Because virtually every physical illness can be linked to psychological stress, DSM-IV does not list psychosomatic disorders separately. Rather, the manual includes physical illnesses only if they are related to a diagnosed mental disorder. For example, a child's asthma may be included in a DSM-IV diagnosis if it is part of broader cluster of symptoms of *separation anxiety disorder*, which comprises various fears of being away from a parent.

## SOMATOFORM DISORDERS

It is important to distinguish between psychosomatic disorders, which involve genuine physical illnesses, and **somatoform disorders**, which are characterized by physical symptoms without any identifiable physiological cause. Despite reassurances to the contrary from physicians, people suffering from somatoform disorders *believe* they are physically ill and report symptoms that sound like those seen in physical illnesses, yet there is no evidence of physical illness. Their problem is somatic (physical) in appearance only, as indicated by the term *somatoform* (somatic in form or appearance). It is important to emphasize that people who suffer from these disorders do not consciously seek to mislead others about their physical condition. The symptoms are real to them; they are not faked or under voluntary control (APA, 1994).

In one kind of somatoform disorder, **somatization disorder**, the person experiences vague, recurring physical symptoms for which medical attention has been sought repeatedly but no organic cause found. Common complaints include back pains, dizziness, partial paralysis, abdominal pains, and sometimes anxiety and depression. The following case is typical:

> An elderly woman complained of headaches and periods of weakness that lasted for over six months. Her condition had been evaluated by doctors numerous times; she was taking several prescription medications, and she had actually undergone 30 operations for a variety of complaints. She was thin, but examination showed her to be within normal limits in terms of physical health (except for numerous surgical scars). Her medical history spanned half a century, and there can be little doubt that she suffered from somatization disorder. (Quill, 1985)

**Conversion disorders** Somatoform disorders in which a dramatic, specific disability has no physical cause but instead can be traced to psychological problems.

**Hypochondriasis** A somatoform disorder in which a person interprets insignificant symptoms as signs of serious illness in the absence of any organic evidence of such illness.

**Body dysmorphic disorder** A somatoform disorder in which a person becomes so preoccupied with his or her imagined ugliness that normal life is impossible.

Another form of somatoform disorder involves complaints of far more bizarre symptoms, such as paralysis, blindness, deafness, seizures, loss of feeling, or false pregnancy. People with such **conversion disorders** have intact, healthy muscles and nerves, yet their symptoms are very real. For example, a person with such a "paralyzed" limb has no feeling in it, even if stuck with a pin. (The term *conversion disorder* comes from the notion that psychological problems are "converted" into physical illness.)

Psychologists also look for evidence that the "illness" resolves a thorny conflict or allows the patient to avoid confronting a difficult situation. For example, a housewife reported serious attacks of dizziness, nausea, and visual disturbances that came on in the late afternoon and cleared up at about 8:00 P.M. After ruling out any physical cause for her problems, a therapist discovered that she was married to an extremely tyrannical man who, shortly after coming home from work in the evening, habitually abused her verbally, criticizing her housekeeping, the meal she had prepared, and so on. Her psychological distress was unconsciously converted to physical symptoms that enabled her to withdraw from this painful situation (Spitzer et al., 1981).

Yet another somatoform disorder is **hypochondriasis**. Here, the person interprets some small symptom—perhaps a cough, bruise, or perspiration—as a sign of a serious disease. Although the symptom may actually exist, there is no reason to believe that the serious illness does. Nevertheless, repeated assurances of this sort have little effect, and the people suffering from hypochondriasis will visit one doctor after another in search of a medical authority who will share their conviction that the symptom means they have a critical illness.

**Body dysmorphic disorder**, or imagined ugliness, is a recently diagnosed and poorly understood type of somatoform disorder that may seriously impair life functioning. One man, for example, felt that people stared at his "pointed ears" and "large nostrils" so much that he eventually could not face going to work—so he quit his job. Clearly people who become that preoccupied with their appearance cannot lead a normal life. Ironically, most people who suffer from this disorder are not ugly or disfigured. They may be average looking or even attractive, but they are unable to evaluate their looks realistically. When they look in the mirror, all they seem to see is their "defect"—greatly magnified. Many people with this disorder seek physical treatment (such as plastic surgery) rather than psychotherapy. For this reason, it may be some time before we know how widespread the disorder is, why people develop it, and what can be done to treat it effectively.

Somatoform disorders (especially conversion disorders) present a challenge for psychological theorists because unconscious processes appear to be at work. Freud concluded that the physical symptoms in these cases were often related to traumatic experiences buried in a patient's past: A woman who years earlier saw her mother physically abused by her father suddenly loses her sight; a man who was punished for masturbating later loses the use of his hand. By developing a handicap, Freud theorized, people accomplish two things. First, they prevent themselves from acting out forbidden desires or repeating forbidden behavior; Freud called this the *primary gain* of the symptom. Second, the symptoms often allow the person to avoid an unpleasant activity, person, or situation; Freud dubbed this the *secondary gain*.

Cognitive behavioral theories of somatoform disorders focus on Freud's notion of secondary gain—that is, they look for ways in which the symptomatic behavior is being rewarded. For example, a person may have learned in the past that aches, pains, and so on can be used to circumvent unpleasant situations. (Timely headaches and stomachaches have "solved" a lot of problems over the years.) Later in life, this person may complain of somatic symptoms to avoid facing unpleasant or stressful situations. Moreover, people who are ill often enjoy a good deal of attention, support, and care, which is indirectly rewarding.

Now we turn to the biological perspective. Research has shown that at least some diagnosed somatoform disorders actually were real physical illnesses that were overlooked or misdiagnosed! For example, one set of follow-up studies indicated that some cases of "conversion disorder" eventually proved to be undiagnosed neurological problems such as epilepsy or multiple sclerosis (Shalev & Munitz, 1986). Still, most cases of conversion disorder cannot be explained by current medical science. These cases pose as much of a theoretical challenge today as they did when conversion disorders captured Freud's attention more than a century ago.

**Dissociative disorders** Disorders in which some aspect of the personality seems separated from the rest.

**Dissociative amnesia** A dissociative disorder characterized by loss of memory for past events without an organic cause.

**Dissociative fugue** A dissociative disorder that involves flight and the assumption of a new identity, with amnesia for past identity and events.

**Dissociative identity disorder** A dissociative disorder in which a person has several distinct personalities that emerge at different times.

## DISSOCIATIVE DISORDERS

**Dissociative disorders** are among the most puzzling forms of mental illness, both to the observer and to the sufferer. *Dissociation* means that part of an individual's personality is separated or dissociated from the rest, and for some reason the person cannot reassemble the pieces. It usually involves memory loss and a complete—though generally temporary—change in identity. More rarely, several distinct personalities are present in one person.

Loss of memory without an organic cause occur in reaction to intolerable experiences. People often block out an event or a period of their lives that has been extremely stressful. During World War II, some hospitalized soldiers could not recall their names, where they lived, where they were born, or how they came to be in battle. But war and its horrors are not the only causes of **dissociative amnesia**. The man who betrays a friend to complete a business deal or the woman who has been raped may also forget—selectively—what has happened. Sometimes an amnesia victim leaves home and assumes an entirely new identity, although this phenomenon, known as **dissociative fugue**, is highly unusual.

Total amnesia, in which people forget everything, is quite rare, despite its popularity in novels and films. In one unusual case of fugue, the police picked up a 42-year-old man after he became involved in a fight with a customer at the diner where he worked. The man reported that he had no memory of his life before drifting into that town a few weeks earlier. Eventually, the authorities discovered that he matched the description of a missing person who had wandered from his home 200 miles away. Just before he disappeared, he had been passed over for promotion at work and had had a violent argument with his teenage son (Spitzer et al., 1981).

Even more bizarre than amnesia is **dissociative identity disorder**—commonly known as *multiple personality*—in which a person has several distinct personalities that emerge at different times. This dramatic disorder, which has been the subject of popular fiction and films, is thought to be extremely rare. In the true multiple personality, the various personalities are distinct people, with their own names, identities, memories, mannerisms, speaking voices, and even IQs. Sometimes the personalities are so separate that they don't know they inhabit a body with other "people"; at other times, the personalities are aware of the existence of other "people" and will even make disparaging remarks about them. Consider the case of Maud and Sara K., two personalities that coexisted in one woman:

> In general demeanor, Maud was quite different from Sara. She walked with a swinging, bouncing gait contrasted to Sara's sedate one. While Sara was depressed, Maud was ebullient and happy. . . . Insofar as she could Maud dressed differently from Sara. . . . Sara used no make-up. Maud used a lot of rouge and lipstick, [and] painted her fingernails

Jane Doe was near death when she was discovered by a Florida park ranger in 1980. She was also suffering from *amnesia* and could not remember her name, her past, or how to read and write. Despite later renewed ties to her past, Jane Doe never regained her memory.

**Depersonalization disorder** A dissociative disorder in which the person suddenly feels changed or different in a strange way.

> and toenails deep red. . . . Sara was a mature, intelligent individual. Her mental age was 19.2 years, IQ, 128. A psychometric done on Maud showed a mental age of 6.6, IQ, 43. (Carson, Butcher, & Coleman, 1988, p. 206)

Actually, this case is typical of dissociative identity disorder in that the personalities contrasted sharply with each another. It is as if the two (and sometimes more) personalities represent different aspects of a single person—one the more socially acceptable, "nice" side of the person, the other the darker, more uninhibited or "evil" side.

The origins of dissociative identity disorder have long puzzled researchers and clinicians. One theory that has gained wide acceptance holds that it develops in response to childhood abuse. The child learns to cope with the abuse through a process of dissociation—by assigning the abuse, in effect, to "someone else," that is, to a personality who is not conscious most of the time (Putnam et al., 1986). One or more of the multiple personalities in almost every case is a child (even when the patient is an adult), a fact that lends support to the notion that child abuse lies at the root of this disorder, and clinicians report a history of child abuse in over three-quarters of documented cases of dissociative identity disorder (C.A. Ross, Norton, & Wozney, 1989).

Other clinical psychologists contend that dissociative identity disorder is not a real disorder at all but an elaborate kind of role playing—feigned in the beginning, and then perhaps genuinely believed in by the patient (Mersky, 1992). However, some intriguing biological data show that in at least some patients with dissociative identity disorder, the various personalities have different blood pressure readings, different responses to medication, different allergies, different vision problems (necessitating several pairs of glasses, one for each personality), and different handedness—all of which would be difficult, if not impossible, to feign. Each personality may also exhibit distinctly different patterns of brain waves (Putnam, 1984).

A far less dramatic (and much more common) dissociative disorder is **depersonalization disorder**. Its essential feature is that the person suddenly feels changed or different in a strange way. Some people feel they have left their bodies, others that their actions have suddenly become mechanical or dreamlike. A sense of losing control over one's own behavior is common, and it is not unusual to imagine changes in one's environment. This kind of feeling may occur as a matter of course during adolescence and young adulthood, when our sense of ourselves and our interactions with others changes rapidly. Only when the sense of depersonalization becomes a long-term or chronic problem or when the alienation from real life impairs normal social functioning should this be classified as a dissociative disorder (APA, 1994). For example, a 20-year-old college student sought professional help after experiencing periods of feeling "outside" himself for 2 years. At these times, he felt groggy, dizzy, and preoccupied. Because he had experienced several of these episodes while driving, he had stopped driving alone. Although he managed to keep up with his studies, his friends began to notice that he seemed "spacey" and overly preoccupied (Spitzer et al., 1981).

Like conversion disorders, dissociative disorders seem to have their origins in unconscious processes. The loss of memory is real in amnesia, fugue, and in many cases of multiple personality disorder as well. The patient often lacks awareness of the memory loss, and memory impairments usually cannot be overcome despite the patient's desire and will to do so. Biological factors may also figure in some of these cases. We know that dissociation and amnesia may stem from physical processes: Memory impairments are often associated with aging and illnesses such as Alzheimer's disease, and dissociative experiences are a common consequence of the ingestion of hallucinogenic drugs such as LSD. Trauma is a psychological factor that looms large in the onset of amnesia and fugue; it also may bring on dissociative identity disorder (Oltmanns & Emery, 1995). Nonetheless, we must admit that all these observations are only early unconfirmed leads in the fascinating mystery of what causes dissociative disorders.

## SEXUAL DISORDERS

Because ideas about what is normal and abnormal in sex vary with the times—and with the individual—psychologists have increasingly narrowed their definition of abnormal sexual behavior. Let us take a closer look at one of the most common sexual disorders—sexual dysfunction.

### Sexual Dysfunction

**Sexual dysfunction** is the loss or impairment of the ordinary physical responses of sexual function. In men, this usually takes the form of **erectile disorder**, the inability to achieve or maintain an erection. In women, it often appears as **female sexual arousal disorder**, the inability to become sexually excited or to reach orgasm. (These conditions were once called "impotence" and "frigidity," respectively, but professionals in the field have rejected these terms as too negative and judgmental.)

While sexual dysfunction may occur during any of a number of points in the sexual response cycle, some people find it difficult or impossible to experience any desire for sexual activity to begin with. **Sexual desire disorders** involve a lack of interest in sex or perhaps an active distaste for it. Low sexual desire is more common in women than in men and may figure in upwards of 40 percent of all sexual dysfunctions (Southern & Gayle, 1982). However, some people simply have a low motivation for sexual activity. Others report no anxiety about or aversion to sex but do exhibit physiological indicators of inhibited desire (Wincze, Hoon, & Hoon, 1978).

**Sexual arousal disorder** refers to the inability to achieve physical arousal or the inability to sustain arousal until the end of intercourse. Among the causes of this disorder are anxiety-provoking attitudes derived from parental or social teaching, fear of pregnancy or inadequate performance, and inexperience on the part of one or both partners.

Still other people experience sexual desire and maintain arousal but are unable to reach **orgasm**, the peaking of sexual pleasure and the release of sexual tension. These people are said to experience **orgasmic disorders**.

Among the other problems that can occur during the sexual response cycle are **premature ejaculation**, which the DSM-IV defines as the male's inability to inhibit orgasm as long as desired, and **vaginismus**, involuntary muscle spasms in the outer part of a woman's vagina during sexual excitement that make intercourse impossible. The occasional experience of such problems is not uncommon; the DSM-IV considers them dysfunctions only if they are "persistent and recurrent."

## PERSONALITY DISORDERS

In the chapter on personality, we learned that personality is the individual's unique and enduring pattern of thoughts, feelings, and behavior. We also noted that, despite having certain characteristic views of the world and ways of doing things, people normally are capable of adjusting their behavior to fit the needs of different situations. But certain people, starting

**Sexual dysfunction** Loss or impairment of the ordinary physical responses of sexual function.

**Erectile disorder** The inability of a man to achieve or maintain an erection.

**Female sexual arousal disorder** The inability of a woman to become sexually aroused or to reach orgasm.

**Sexual desire disorders** Disorders in which the person lacks sexual interest or has an active distaste for sex.

**Sexual arousal disorder** Inability to achieve or sustain arousal until the end of intercourse in a person who is capable of experiencing sexual desire.

**Orgasm** Peaking of sexual pleasure and release of sexual tension.

**Orgasmic disorders** Inability to reach orgasm in a person able to experience sexual desire and maintain arousal.

**Premature ejaculation** Inability of a man to inhibit orgasm as long as desired.

**Vaginismus** Involuntary muscle spasms in the outer part of the vagina that make intercourse impossible.

**Personality disorders** Disorders in which inflexible and maladaptive ways of thinking and behaving, learned early in life, cause distress to the person and/or conflicts with others.

**Schizoid personality disorder** Personality disorder in which a person is withdrawn and lacks feelings for others.

**Paranoid personality disorder** Personality disorder in which the person is inappropriately suspicious and mistrustful of others.

**Dependent personality disorder** Personality disorder in which the person is unable to make choices and decisions independently and cannot tolerate being alone.

**Avoidant personality disorder** Personality disorder in which the person's fears of rejection by others leads to social isolation.

**Narcissistic personality disorder** Personality disorder in which the person has an exaggerated sense of self-importance and an insatiable desire for praise.

at some point early in life, develop inflexible and maladaptive ways of thinking and behaving that are so exaggerated and rigid that they cause serious distress to themselves or problems for others. People with such **personality disorders** range from harmless eccentrics to cold-blooded killers. A personality disorder may also coexist with one of the other problems already examined in this chapter; that is, someone with a personality disorder may also become depressed, develop sexual problems, and so on.

One group of personality disorders is characterized by odd or eccentric behavior. For example, people who exhibit **schizoid personality disorder** lack the ability or desire to form social relationships and have no warm or tender feelings for others. Such loners cannot express their feelings and are perceived by others as cold, distant, and unfeeling. Moreover, they often appear vague, absentminded, indecisive, or "in a fog." Because their withdrawal is so complete, people with schizoid personality disorder seldom marry and may have trouble holding jobs that require them to work with or relate to others (APA, 1994). For example:

> A 36-year-old electrical engineer was "dragged" to a marital therapist by his wife because of his unwillingness to join in family activities, failure to take an interest in his children, lack of affection, and disinterest in sex.. . . The patient's history revealed long-standing social indifference, with only an occasional and brief friendship here and there. (Spitzer et al., 1981, p. 66)

In **paranoid personality disorder**, sufferers are overly suspicious, mistrustful, and hypersensitive to any possible threat or trick. Guarded, secretive, devious, scheming, and argumentative, these people nonetheless see themselves as rational and objective.

Another category of personality disorders is distinguished by anxious and fearful behavior. **Dependent personality disorder** is characterized by an inability to make decisions or to do things independently. Extremely unhappy being alone, these individuals rely on parents, a spouse, friends, or others to make the major choices in their lives. People with **avoidant personality disorder** meanwhile, exhibit timidity, anxiety and fear of rejection. This social anxiety leads to isolation, even though the person with avoidant personality disorder *wants* to have close relationships with other people.

In contrast to the schizoid, paranoid, dependent, and avoidant personality disorders, in which behavior is generally strange or withdrawn, a third cluster of personality disorders is revealed through dramatic flourishes, emotional outbursts, or wildly erratic behavior. People with **narcissistic personality disorder**, for instance, display a grandiose sense of self-importance and a preoccupation with fantasies of limitless success. Such people believe they are extraordinary, need constant attention and admiration, display a sense of entitlement, and tend to exploit others.. They are given to envy and arrogance and lack the ability to really care for anyone else (APA, 1994). For example, a male graduate student sought help because he was having difficulty completing his Ph.D. dissertation. He bragged that his dissertation would revolutionize his field and make him famous—but he had not been able to write much of it yet. He blamed his academic adviser for his lack of progress, called his fellow students "drones," and loudly declared that everyone was jealous of his brilliance. He had frequent brief relationships with women but few lasting friendships (Spitzer et al., 1981).

The word *narcissism* comes from a character in Greek mythology named Narcissus who fell in love with his own reflection in a pool and pined away because he could not reach the beautiful face he saw before him. Although excessive self-esteem would seem to be the prominent problem in narcissistic personality disorder, psychiatrist Otto Kernberg observes that the self-esteem of the narcissistic person is actually very fragile: "The pathological narcissist cannot sustain his or her self-regard without having it fed constantly by the attentions of others" (in Wolfe, 1978, p. 55).

**Borderline personality disorder** is characterized by marked instability—in self-image, mood, and interpersonal relationships. People with this personality disorder are uncomfortable being alone, tend to act impulsively, and often display self-destructive behaviors, including promiscuity, drug and alcohol abuse, and threats of suicide (J.G. Gunderson, 1984). Arkema (1981) reports the following case:

> Ms. C., a 22-year-old unemployed woman, had been assaulted by her boyfriend and had cut both her forearms. . . . [The couple] had been at a nightclub the previous evening. He felt she was dancing too seductively, they argued, and he slapped her in the face. She ran from the club, later cut both arms, became fearful something terrible would happen to her boyfriend, and spent the rest of the night looking for him, damaging her car in the process. . . . In the hospital, with much support, she appeared to understand the advisability of terminating the destructive relationship. As soon as she was free on a pass, however, she would become "desperate" and seek him out again. She observed, "If I have someone else right away I can do it; I can leave him. But it's the only way." (pp. 174–175)

Borderline personality disorder is both common and serious. The available evidence indicates that more women than men suffer from this disorder and that it runs in families (Loranger, Oldham, & Tulis, 1983; McGlashan, 1983).

One of the most widely studied personality disorders is **antisocial personality disorder**. People who exhibit this disorder lie, steal, cheat, and show little or no sense of responsibility, although they often seem intelligent and charming on first acquaintance. The "con man" exemplifies many of the features of the antisocial personality, as do people who compulsively cheat their business partners because they know their partners' weak points. Antisocial personalities rarely show the slightest trace of anxiety or guilt about their behavior. Indeed, they generally blame society or their victims for the antisocial actions that they themselves commit.

Antisocial personalities are responsible for a good deal of crime and violence, as seen in this case history of a person with antisocial personality disorder:

> Although intelligent, the subject was a poor student and was frequently accused of stealing from his schoolmates. At the age of 14, he stole a car, and at the age of 20, he was imprisoned for burglary. After he was released, he spent another two years in prison for drunk driving and then eleven years for a series of armed robberies.
>
> Released from prison yet one more time in 1976, he tried to hold down several jobs but succeeded at none of them. He moved in with a woman whom he had met one day earlier, but he drank heavily (a habit that he had picked up at age 10) and struck her children until she ordered him out of the house at gunpoint. On at least two occasions, he violated his parole but was not turned in by his parole officer. In July of 1976, he robbed a service station and shot the attendant twice in the head. He was apprehended in part because he accidentally shot himself during his escape. "It seems like things have always gone bad for me," he later said. (Spitzer et al., 1983, p. 68)

**Borderline personality disorder** Personality disorder characterized by marked instability in self-image, mood, and interpersonal relationships.

**Antisocial personality disorder** Personality disorder that involves a pattern of violent, criminal, or unethical and exploitative behavior and an inability to feel affection for others.

Like Gary Gilmore, Ted Bundy was a highly intelligent serial killer who, though he may have killed as many as 50 women, apparently felt no guilt or anxiety. Bundy was executed in January 1989.

The subject was Gary Gilmore, and on January 17, 1977, he became the first person to be executed in the United States in 11 years. While awaiting an execution that was postponed several times, he became the subject of numerous news stories detailing his fight for the "right to be executed." He twice attempted suicide.

Approximately 3 percent of American men and less than 1 percent of American women suffer from antisocial personality disorder. Not surprisingly, the prevalence of the disorder is high among prison inmates. One study concluded that 50 percent of the people incarcerated in two prisons had antisocial personalities (Hare, 1983). Not all people with antisocial personality disorder are convicted criminals, however. Many skillfully and successfully manipulate others for their own gain while steering clear of the criminal justice system, as was demonstrated by a researcher who placed the following advertisement in an underground Boston newspaper:

> WANTED: Charming, aggressive, carefree people who are impulsively irresponsible but are good at handling people and at looking after Number One. Send name, address, phone, and short biography proving how interesting you are. . . .(Widom, 1978, p. 72)

Of 73 respondents, about one-third seemed to satisfy the criteria for antisocial personality disorder. Widom found only one difference between prison samples and the people in her study: Her subjects had somehow avoided being apprehended by the police.

Research indicates that antisocial personality disorder stems from a combination of biological predisposition, adverse psychological experiences, and an unhealthy social environment (Moffitt, 1993). Some findings point to heredity as a risk factor for the later development of antisocial behavior (DiLalla & Gottesman, 1991). Impulsive violence and aggression have been traced to abnormal levels of certain neurotransmitters (Virkkunen, 1983). While none of this research is definitive, the weight of evidence does suggest that in some people with antisocial personalities the autonomic nervous system is less responsive to stress. Thus, they are more likely to engage in thrill-seeking behaviors, which can be harmful to themselves or others. In addition, because they respond less emotionally to stressful situations, punishment as a technique of social control is less effective for them than for other people.

Some psychologists feel that emotional deprivation in early childhood predisposes people to antisocial personality disorder. The child for whom no one cares, say psychologists, cares for no one. The child whose problems no one identifies with can identify with no one else's problems. Respect for others is the basis of our social code, but if you cannot see things from the other person's perspective, rules about what you can and cannot do will seem entirely arbitrary.

Family influences may also interfere with the normal learning of rules of conduct in the preschool and school years. Theorists reason that a child who has been rejected by one or both parents is not likely to develop adequate social skills and appropriate social behavior. They also point out the high incidence of antisocial behavior among people with an antisocial parent and suggest that antisocial behavior may be partly learned and partly inherited from parents (L.N. Robins, 1966). Once serious misbehavior begins in childhood, these actions follow a predictable progression: The child's conduct results in rejection by peers and failure in school, leading to affiliation with other children who have behavior problems. By late childhood or adolescence, the deviant patterns that will later show up as a full-blown antisocial personality disorder are well established (G.R. Patterson, DeBaryshe, & Ramsey, 1989).

Cognitive theorists emphasize that in addition to the failure to learn rules and develop self-control, moral development may be arrested among children who are emotionally rejected and inadequately disciplined. For example, between the ages of about 7 and 11, all children are apt to respond to unjust treatment by behaving unjustly toward someone else who is vulnerable. At about age 13, when they are better able to reason in abstract terms, most children begin to think more in terms of fairness than vindictiveness. This works best if new cognitive skills and moral concepts are reinforced by parents and peers (M.W. Berkowitz & Gibbs, 1983).

**Schizophrenic disorders** Severe disorder in which there are disturbances of thoughts, communications, and emotions, including delusions and hallucinations.

**Psychotic** Out of touch with reality.

**Insane** Legal term for mentally disturbed people who are deemed not responsible for their criminal actions.

**Hallucinations** Sensory experiences in the absence of external stimulation.

**Delusions** False beliefs about reality that have no basis in fact.

## SCHIZOPHRENIC DISORDERS

It is a common misconception that schizophrenia means split personality. This is not the case at all. As we have already seen, split personality (or multiple personality) is actually a dissociative identity disorder. The misunderstanding comes from the fact that the root *schizo* comes from the Greek verb meaning "to split." But what is split in schizophrenia is not so much personality as the connections among thoughts.

6. *True or false*: Schizophrenia refers to split personality.

**Schizophrenic disorders** are severe conditions marked by disordered thoughts and communications, inappropriate emotions, and bizarre behavior that lasts for months, even years. People with schizophrenia are out of touch with reality, which is to say they are **psychotic**. Psychotic is sometimes confused with *insane*, but the terms are not the synonymous. **Insane** is the legal term for people who are found not to be responsible for their criminal actions (see the Controversies box titled "The Insanity Defense").

People with schizophrenia often experience **hallucinations**, false sensory perceptions that usually take the form of hearing voices that are not really there.* They also frequently have **delusions**—false beliefs about reality with no basis in fact—that distort their relationships with their surroundings and with other people. Typically, these delusions are *paranoid*: People with schizophrenia believe that someone is out to harm them. They may think that a doctor wishes to kill them or that they are receiving radio messages from aliens invading from outer space. Oftentimes, they regard their own bodies—as well as the outside world—as hostile and alien.

People suffering from schizophrenic disorders frequently exhibit disorganized thought and bizarre communication.

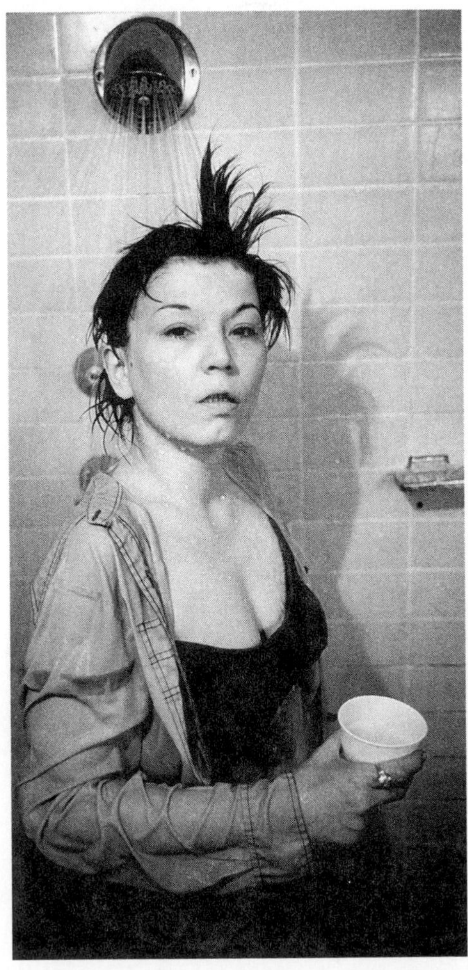

Because their world is utterly different from the one most people live in, people with schizophrenia usually cannot lead anything like a normal life unless they are successfully treated with medication (see Chapter 13). Many people with schizophrenia are unable to communicate with others, because when they speak, their words are incoherent. (See Table 12-3 for the DSM-IV criteria for schizophrenia.) The following case illustrates some of the characteristic features of schizophrenia:

> [The patient is a 35-year-old widow.] For many years she has heard voices, which insult her and cast suspicion on her chastity. . . . The voices are very distinct, and in her opinion, they must be carried by a telescope or a machine from her home. Her thoughts are dictated to her; she is obliged to think them, and hears them repeated after her. She . . . has all kinds of uncomfortable sensations in her body, to which something is "done." In particular, her "mother parts" are turned inside out, and people send a pain through her back, lay ice-water on her heart, squeeze her neck, injure her spine, and violate her. There are also hallucinations of sight—black figures and the altered appearance of people—but these are far less frequent. . . . (Spitzer et al., 1981, pp. 308–309)

*Visual, tactile, or olfactory hallucinations are more likely to indicate substance abuse or organic brain damage than schizophrenia.

**Disorganized schizophrenia** Schizophrenic disorder in which bizarre and childlike behaviors are common.

**Catatonic schizophrenia** Schizophrenic disorder in which disturbed motor behavior is prominent.

**Paranoid schizophrenia** Schizophrenic disorder marked by extreme suspiciousness and complex, bizarre delusions.

**Undifferentiated schizophrenia** Schizophrenic disorder in which there are clear schizophrenic symptoms that don't meet the criteria for any other subtype of the disorder.

**TABLE 12-3 DSM-IV Criteria for Schizophrenia**

A. *Characteristic symptoms.* Two (or more) of the following, each present for a significant portion of time during a 1-month period (or less if successfully treated):

(1) delusions
(2) hallucinations
(3) disorganized speech (e.g., incoherent)
(4) disorganized or catatonic behavior
(5) negative symptoms (e.g., flat affect)

B. *Social/occupational dysfunction*: For a significant portion of the time since the onset of the disturbance, one or more major areas of functioning such as work, interpersonal relations, or self-care are markedly below the level achieved prior to the onset.

C. *Duration*: Continuous signs of the disturbance persist for at least 6 months.

D. *Schizoaffective and Mood Disorder exclusion*: Schizoaffective Disorder and Mood Disorder With Psychotic Features have been ruled out.

E. *Substance/general medical condition exclusion*: The disturbance is not due to the direct physiological effects of a substance (e.g., abuse of a drug or medication) or a general medical condition.

F. *Relationship to a Pervasive Developmental Disorder*: If there is a history of Autistic Disorder or another Pervasive Developmental Disorder, the additional diagnosis of Schizophrenia is made only if prominent delusions or hallucinations are also present for at least a month (or less if successfully treated).

There are actually several kinds of schizophrenic disorders, each of which has different characteristic symptoms.

In **disorganized schizophrenia**, people exhibit some of the more bizarre symptoms of schizophrenia, including inappropriate giggling, grimacing, and frantic gesturing. People suffering from disorganized schizophrenia show a childish disregard for social conventions and may urinate or defecate at inappropriate times or in inappropriate places. They are active but aimless, and they are often given to incoherent conversations.

The primary feature of **catatonic schizophrenia** is a severe disturbance of motor activity. People in this state may remain immobile, mute, and impassive. At the opposite extreme, they become excessively excited, talking and shouting continuously. They may behave in a robotlike fashion when ordered to move, and some have even let doctors mold their arms and legs into strange and uncomfortable positions that they then manage to maintain for hours.

**Paranoid schizophrenia** is marked by extreme suspiciousness and complex delusions. People with paranoid schizophrenia may believe themselves to be Napoleon or the Virgin Mary, or they may insist that Russian spies with laser guns are constantly on their trail because they have learned some great secret. Since they are less likely to be incoherent or to look or act "crazy," these people can appear more "normal" than people with other schizophrenic disorders if their delusions are compatible with everyday life. However, they may become hostile or aggressive toward anyone who questions their thinking or tries to contradict their delusions. Note that this disorder is far more severe than paranoid personality disorder, which does not involve bizarre delusions or loss of touch with reality.

Finally, **undifferentiated schizophrenia** is the classification developed for people who have several of the characteristic symptoms of schizophrenia, such as delusions, hallucinations, or incoherence, yet do not exhibit the typical symptoms of any other subtype of the disorder.

Since schizophrenia is a very serious disorder, considerable research has been directed at trying to discover its causes. As we saw in the chapter

# CONTROVERSIES

## The Insanity Defense

Particularly horrifying crimes—assassinations of public figures, mass murders, and serial murders, for instance—have often been attributed to mental disturbance because it seems to many people that anyone who could commit such crimes must be mentally ill. But to the legal system, this logic poses a dilemma: If people are truly mentally ill, are we justified in holding them responsible for criminal acts? The legal answer to this question is a qualified *yes.* Mentally ill people *are* responsible for their crimes unless they are *insane.* But, what's the difference between the two? Insanity is a legal term, not a psychological one. It is typically applied to defendants who, when they committed the offense with which they are charged, either could not distinguish right from wrong or could not control their behavior.

Actually, when defendants are suspected of being mentally disturbed, another important question must be answered before they are brought to trial: Are they able to understand the charges against them and to participate in their own defense in court? This issue is known as *competency to stand trial.* An accused person is examined by a court-appointed expert and, if found to be incompetent, is sent to a mental institution, often for an indefinite period. If judged to be competent, the person is required to stand trial. At this point the defendant may decide to plead not guilty by reason of insanity—which is an assertion that *at the time of the crime* the defendant lacked substantial capacity to appreciate the criminality of the action (know right from wrong) or to conform to the requirements of the law (control the lawless behavior).

Despite popular belief to the contrary, the insanity plea is used relatively infrequently, serving as a defense in less than 1 percent of serious criminal cases. But it became controversial when it was successfully used by John Hinckley, the man who attempted to assassinate President Ronald Reagan in 1981. Many people were very upset that Hinckley, whose action had been clearly captured on videotape, seemed to escape punishment for his crime by pleading insanity in a jurisdiction (Washington, D.C.) that required the prosecution to prove beyond a reasonable doubt that *he was sane.* (By contrast, most states, as well as the federal courts, place the burden on the defense to prove that the *defendant is insane.*) Since his trial, Hinckley has been confined in a mental hospital.

John Hinckley's successful use of the insanity defense upset many people. The insanity defense raises fundamental questions about the causes of, and responsibility for, harmful behaviors.

When a defendant enters an insanity plea, the court system relies heavily on the testimony of forensic psychologists and psychiatrists to determine the mental state of the defendant at the time of the crime. Because most such trials feature well-credentialed experts testifying both for the defense and for the prosecution, the jury is often perplexed about which side to believe. Furthermore, there is much cynicism about "hired-gun" professionals who receive large fees to appear in court and argue that a defendant is or is not sane. Among psychologists and psychiatrists, opinions differ sharply about the appropriateness of this kind of court testimony. And the public, skeptical about professional jargon, may charge that psychological testimony allows dangerous criminals to "get off" (even though, as we have seen, the insanity plea is only rarely invoked). Actually, those who successfully plead insanity—like John Hinckley—often are confined longer in mental hospitals than they would have been in prison if convicted of their crimes. Therefore, the insanity plea is usually not an easy way out of responsibility for a crime.

**Figure 12-1**
**Average risk of schizophrenia among biological relatives of an individual with schizophrenia.**

*Source:* From *Schizophrenia Genesis: The Origins of Madness* by I.I. Gottesman, 1991, New York: W.H. Freeman and Company. Reprinted with permission.

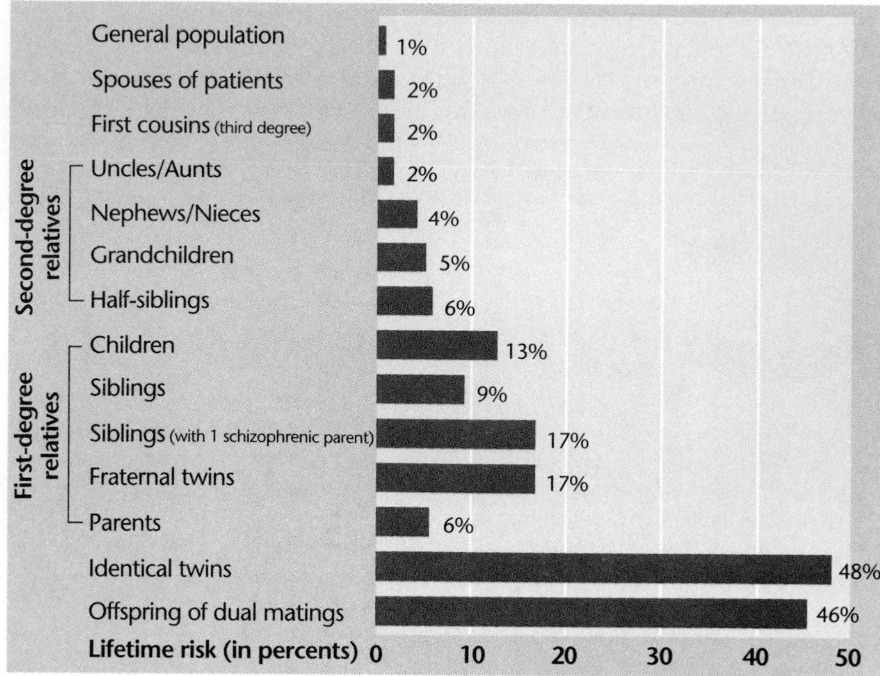


on Physiology and Behavior, it is now clear from a wide range of studies that schizophrenia has a genetic component (Gottesman, 1991). People with schizophrenia are more likely than other people to have children with schizophrenia, even when those children have lived with adoptive parents since early in life (Heston, 1966). And if one identical twin suffers from schizophrenia, the chances are about 1 in 2 that the other twin will also develop schizophrenia; but in cases where a fraternal twin has schizophrenia, only about 15 percent of the time will the other twin also develop schizophrenia (Gottesman, 1991; see Figure 12-1).

These studies reveal that a biological predisposition to schizophrenia may be inherited. Recent research indicates that part of the problem may lie in excessive amounts of the neurotransmitter *dopamine* in the central nervous system (recall our discussion of neurotransmitters in Chapter 2). Drugs that alleviate schizophrenic symptoms also decrease the amount of dopamine in the brain and block dopamine receptors. On the other hand, amphetamines raise the amount of dopamine in the brain, aggravate schizophrenic symptoms, and, if taken in excess, lead to what is called *amphetamine psychosis*, which bears striking similarities to schizophrenia.

Despite the preponderance of evidence for the role of genetics in schizophrenia, studies of identical twins can also be used to identify the importance of *environment* in causing schizophrenia. How? Remember, half the identical twins of people with schizophrenia do *not* develop schizophrenia themselves. Since identical twins are genetically identical, this means that this severe and puzzling disorder *cannot* be caused by genetic factors alone. Environmental factors—ranging from disturbed family relations to drug-taking behavior to biological damage that may occur at any age, even before birth—must also figure in determining whether a person will develop schizophrenia. McGuffin, Reveley, and Holland (1982) reported on a set of identical triplets, all of whom suffered

The Genain quadruplets, pictured here, all developed schizophrenia as adults. Most experts now believe that schizophrenia has a strong genetic component.

from chronic psychotic disorders. But while two of the brothers had severe schizophrenic symptoms and were unable to function even between psychotic periods, the third brother was able to function at a higher level and hold down a job between psychotic periods. His IQ was higher than his two brothers, and his relationship with his family was less troubled. As the systems model indicates, environment and experience can increase or decrease the effects of any inherited tendency. As a result there is often a significant difference in levels of functioning between identical twins (or triplets) afflicted with psychological disorders.

Some psychologists regard family relationships as a key factor in the development of schizophrenia, but evidence bolstering this position is mixed. One study found that if there were communication problems between parents, a good percentage of their children developed schizophrenia (M. Goldstein & Rodnick, 1975). More recent research has discovered that schizophrenic patients whose families display high levels of negative *expressed emotion* are rehospitalized at twice the average rate for people with this disorder (Kavanagh, 1992). Moreover, treatments designed to reduce negative expressed emotion in the families of schizophrenic patients have cut the rates of rehospitalization. Though it is still not clear how—or if—family variables such as communication problems between parents or expressed emotion in family settings interact with biological predispositions to cause some people to develop schizophrenia, the early research in this area looks promising.

A number of studies have demonstrated a relationship between social class and schizophrenia (Neale & Oltmanns, 1980). Schizophrenia is much more common in lower social classes. One theory holds that lower-class socioeconomic environments—which offer little education, opportunity, or reward and put considerable stress on individuals—promote the development of schizophrenia. Another theory speculates that the symptoms of schizophrenia make people to drift downward into the lower socioeconomic classes. There appears to be some truth to both theories.

While clearly quite different in emphasis, the various explanations for schizophrenic disorders are not mutually exclusive. Although genetic factors are universally acknowledged, many theorists believe that it takes a combination of biological, psychological, and social factors to produce schizophrenia (Gottesman, 1991). According to the systems model, genetic factors predispose some people to schizophrenia, and family interaction and life stress activate the predisposition.

## GENDER DIFFERENCES IN ABNORMAL BEHAVIOR

Throughout this chapter, we have proceeded on the assumption that men and women were equally susceptible to mental disorders. There are, however, a number of interesting differences between men and women in this area. Although many studies have concluded that women have a higher rate of psychological disorders than men do, this is an oversimplification. Prevalence rates of mental disorders vary by age, race, ethnicity, marital status, income, and type of disorder. Furthermore, how do we determine the "rate of psychological disorders"? Do we count only people admitted to mental hospitals? Those who receive a formal diagnosis in an outpatient treatment setting? Or all those persons in the general population judged to suffer from mental disorders even if they have not sought treatment or received a formal diagnosis? These questions illustrate how hard it is to make a firm generalization about differences between the sexes.

We do know that more women than men are *treated* for mental disorders. Indeed, as one expert observed, "Women have always been the main

**"Is the insanity defense ever valid?"**

In this chapter, we discuss the controversial insanity defense, which asserts that at the time of the crime the defendant was unable to understand the criminality of his or her act and to conform to the standards of the law. Among the issues the insanity defense raises are whether the mentally ill should be held responsible for their behaviors and whether people who successfully plead insanity and are later "cured" should then be punished by being sent to prison. In addition, because mental illness is a scientific term and insanity a legal one, an individual can be judged mentally ill yet be legally sane, as was the convicted serial killer Jeffrey Dahmer.

Insanity defenses are rare. When a defendant does enter such a plea, the court, as described in the chapter, tends to rely on expert testimony from psychologists and psychiatrists working for both sides. This practice has put psychology at the center of the insanity plea debate.

Do you think insanity should ever be considered a legal defense for criminal acts? Why or why not? After you have thought about these questions, take a few minutes to examine the opinions of some other students, which appear below.

• • • • • • •

**KEISHA: I really don't think it should be called a defense for that implies an excuse. Just because you are considered insane does not mean you are not guilty.**

**PAT: The person is insane. Punishing him or her for being insane will not help. They must receive help, and if this is impossible, then they should be under supervision and cared for, but not punished.**

**TOM: I think if you know you are insane and potentially dangerous it's your societal responsibility to seek help beforehand, not after you've killed five people. If you were cognizant of your insanity, even if not of your act, you should be held to the same standards as everybody else.**

**MICHAEL: I think, by definition, an insane person does not know that he is insane, at least in most cases. It isn't really a loophole: it's not easy to prove that you were insane. . . . In most cases where it is not a genuine case of insanity, this comes out during a trial. . . . It is useless to set them free, as it is useless to throw them in jail, where they do not even understand why they are there, and will not comprehend the idea of punishment.**

**BOB: What is "temporary insanity"? How can you just say that when you killed someone, you were not yourself, but now you're okay? Does anyone who knows something about law know what temporary insanity is exactly? This is what I call a loophole because it seems like an excuse that anyone could use if they wanted to.**

**ANNMARIE: If it can be proven that the person was not thinking rationally and therefore could not control her actions, then punishing the person would be like punishing someone who had a heart attack while driving and hit someone when they lost control of the car.**

**MELISSA: There comes a point where the crimes are so hideous that they should be punished no matter what.**

**KARI: When a person is abused, even if their lives are not immediately in danger, the self-defense case becomes an issue, legally speaking. This is a very tough subject, but really has nothing to do with metal illness. Abuse of all sorts, mental and physical, may change a person's state of mind, but this is not necessarily a case of temporary insanity so much as a reasonable fear of the threat of violence.**

**BOB: I don't think temporary insanity is a good defense because these people also have shown that they have the capacity to do wrong, and when provoked again, they could repeat what they did.**

**AMAL: How can a person be responsible for his actions if he doesn't even know what it means to be responsible? The little boy who kills another child isn't old enough to understand; on TV people spring back to life, should the child assume that the neighbor child would not get up?**

**KEISHA: If you are taking a drug (maybe your doctor prescribed some outdated junk) and you kill someone, whose fault is it?**

• • • • • • •

Did your views change after reading other students' views? If so, how? If not, why? How does your response to this discussion compare with your response to the discussion of alcoholism in Chapter 4? Are the two issues related? What can psychology teach us concerning the causes of human behavior?

consumers of psychotherapy from Freud's era onward" (J.A. Williams, 1987, p. 465). But this does not mean that more women than men have mental disorders, for in our society, it is much more acceptable for women to discuss their emotional difficulties and to seek professional help openly. It may be that mental disorders are equally common among men—or even more common—but that men do not so readily show up in therapists' offices and therefore are not counted in the studies.

All the disorders listed in the DSM-IV (with the exception of a few sexual disorders) affect both men and women. Indeed, those mental disorders for which there seems to be a strong biological component, such as bipolar disorder and schizophrenia, are distributed fairly equally between the sexes. Gender differences tend to be more pronounced in disorders without a strong biological component—that is, disorder in which learning and experience figure more prominently. For example, men are more likely than women to suffer from substance abuse and antisocial personality disorder. Women, on the other hand, are more likely to suffer from depression, agoraphobia, simple phobia, and somatization disorder (Basow, 1986; Russo, 1990). Analyzing these tendencies from the perspective of gender-based socialization, we see how influential gender is in determining who develops which kinds of disorder: When men display abnormal behavior, it is more likely to take the forms of drinking too much and acting aggressively; when women behave in abnormal ways, they are more likely to become fearful, passive, hopeless, and "sick" (Basow, 1986).

One commonly reported difference between the sexes concerns marital status. Men who are separated or divorced or who have never married have a higher incidence of mental disorders than do either women of the same marital status or married men. But married women have higher rates of mental illness than married men. Why is marriage psychologically less beneficial for women than for men?

Here, too, socialization apparently is at work. For women, marriage, family relationships, and child rearing are usually more stressful than they are for men (Basow, 1986). For men, marriage and family provide a haven from the pressures of daily life; for women, they constitute a demanding job. In addition, women are more likely than men to be the victims of incest, rape, and marital battering. As one researcher has commented, "for women, the U.S. family is a violent institution" (Koss, 1990). For some married women, employment outside the home seems to confer the kind of psychological benefits that marriage apparently provides for many men. Work can supply "stimulation, self-esteem, adult contacts, escape from the repetitive routines of housework and child care, and a buffer against stress from family roles" (L. Hoffman, 1989, p. 284). It should be noted that these benefits are likely to be realized only if the woman freely chooses to work, has a satisfying job, receives support from family and friends, and is able to set up stable child-care arrangements (Basow, 1986; Hoffman, 1989). Women who enter the work force because they have to rather than because they want to, whose work is routine or demeaning, or who are responsible for all domestic duties as well as their outside jobs, often find that the economic pressures and the stress of performing two demanding roles put them at risk for psychological disorder.

We saw in the last chapter that the effects of stress are greater to the extent that a person feels alienated, powerless, and helpless. Alienation, powerlessness, and helplessness are more often seen in women than in men. They are especially common experiences among minority women, so it is not surprising that the prevalence of psychological disorders is greater among these women than among other women (Russo & Sobel, 1981). And alienation, powerlessness, and helplessness play an especially critical role in anxiety disorders and depression—precisely the disorders experienced most often by women (Carmen et al., 1981). A 1990 report by a task force of the American Psychological Association noted that the rate of depression among women is twice that of men and ascribed that difference to the more negative and stressful aspects of women's lives, including lower incomes and the experiences of bias and physical and sexual abuse (APA, 1990).

Once past puberty, therefore, women do seem to have higher rates of anxiety disorders and depression than men do, and they are more likely than men to seek professional help for their problems. However, greater stress, due in part to socialization and lower status rather than psychological weakness, apparently accounts for this statistic. Marriage and family life, associated with lower rates of mental disorders among men, introduce additional stress into the lives of women, particularly young women (25 to 45). In some cases, this added stress translates into a psychological disorder.

## LOOKING FORWARD

The study of abnormal behavior is simultaneously one of the most fascinating and most frustrating areas of psychology. From a broad social perspective, abnormal behavior commands our attention, because the pain and lifestyle disruptions experienced by so many individuals result in enormous costs to society. Yet psychologists have come up with few answers to the pressing questions raised by abnormal behavior: What causes psychological disorders? What can be done to reduce their prevalence? Which problems actually constitute mental illness and how should we diagnose these conditions?

Attempts to diagnose abnormal behavior are much more than a "name game." The development of a reliable and valid classification system is as critical to the study of abnormal psychology as it is to any other scientific discipline. Thus, elements of classification constitute one essential and recurring theme in abnormal psychology. A second essential theme concerns theories about the causes of abnormal behavior. Competing biological, psychoanalytic, and cognitive-behavioral models dominated the study of psychological disorders for decades. Today a new theoretical integration called the systems approach is emerging to explain how the interplay among biological, psychological, and social risk factors brings on different types of psychological problems.

## SUMMARY

This chapter briefly describes the history of abnormal behavior and presents an overview of the major categories of mental disorders.

### SOCIETAL, INDIVIDUAL, AND MENTAL-HEALTH PERSPECTIVES ON ABNORMAL BEHAVIOR

Whether an individual suffers from an emotional disorder is, at least in part, a subjective judgment. Mental-health professionals define abnormal behavior as either maladaptive life functioning or serious personal discomfort or both, but normal and abnormal behavior often differ only in degree.

### CATEGORIES AND DIMENSIONS OF ABNORMAL BEHAVIOR

A **categorical approach** to **classification** divides mental health and mental illness into categories that are qualitatively different from each other. However, it may be more accurate to think of mental health and mental illness in terms of a **dimensional approach** that views abnormal behavior as being merely quantitatively different from normal behavior.

### HISTORICAL VIEWS OF ABNORMAL BEHAVIOR

In early societies, mysterious actions were often attributed to supernatural powers. The roots of a more contemporary view of abnormal behavior can be traced to Hippocrates, who maintained that madness was like any other sickness—a natural event arising from natural causes. This approach to mental illness fell into disfavor in the Middle Ages, and it was not until the nineteenth century that abnormal behavior again received systematic scientific attention.

### CONFLICTING VIEWS OF THE NATURE, CAUSES, AND TREATMENT OF ABNORMAL BEHAVIOR

Three influential, conflicting models of abnormal behavior emerged during the late 1800s and early 1900s: the biological, psychoanalytic, cognitive-behavioral models. Each approach has influenced the study and treatment of abnormal behavior, but none can claim to be the decisively correct theory of abnormal psychology.

### The Biological Model

The **biological model of abnormal behavior** states that abnormal behavior has a biochemical or physiological origin. Although research has determined that genetic/biochemical factors underlie mental disorders as diverse as schizophrenia, depression, and anxiety, biology alone cannot account for most mental illnesses.

### The Psychoanalytic Model

The **psychoanalytic model of abnormal behavior**, originally proposed by Freud, holds that abnormal behavior is a symbolic expression of unconscious mental conflicts traceable to early childhood or infancy. For all its richly appealing ideas, this approach has produced little scientific evidence to support its theoretical insights about the causes and effective treatment of mental disorders.

### The Cognitive-Behavioral Model

The **cognitive-behavioral model of abnormal behavior** maintains that mental disorders stem from learning maladaptive ways of behaving and posits that what has been learned can be unlearned. Cognitive-behavioral therapists therefore strive to modify their patients' dysfunctional behavior and inaccurate cognitive processes. The model has been criticized for its extreme emphasis on environmental causes and treatments.

### The Diathesis-stress Model and Systems Theory

The most promising recent development in abnormal psychology is the integration of the major approaches. The **diathesis-stress model of abnormal behavior**, for example, asserts that mental disorders develop when a **diathesis** (biological predisposition to the disorder) is triggered by a stressful circumstance. The **systems approach to abnormal behavior** focuses on how biological, psychological, and social risk factors combine to produce mental disorders. According to this model, emotional problems are "lifestyle diseases" that emerge from a combination of biological risks, psychological stresses, and societal pressures and expectations.

## CLASSIFYING ABNORMAL BEHAVIOR

For nearly 40 years, the American Psychiatric Association has published an official manual describing and classifying the various kinds of abnormal behavior. This publication, the *Diagnostic and Statistical Manual of Mental Disorders (DSM)*, has gone through four editions. The current version, known as the DSM-IV, provides careful descriptions of symptoms of different disorders, but includes little information on causes and treatments.

## MOOD DISORDERS

**Mood disorders** are characterized by disturbances in mood or prolonged emotional state. The most common mood disorder is **depression**, a state in which a person feels overwhelmed with sadness, loses interest in activities, and displays other symptoms such as excessive guilt or feelings of worthlessness. The DSM-IV distinguishes between two forms of depression. *Major depressive disorder* is an episode of intense sadness that may last for several months; by contrast, *dysthymia* involves less intense sadness but persists with little relief for a period of 2 years or more. Some depressions become so intense that people become **psychotic**—that is,they lose contact with reality.

Another, less common mood disorder is **mania**. People suffering from mania become euphoric ("high"), extremely active, excessively talkative, and easily distractible. Manic episodes rarely appear by themselves; rather, they usually alternate with depression. This mood disorder, in which both mania and depression are alternately present, sometimes interrupted by periods of normal mood, is known as **bipolar disorder**.

### Causes of Mood Disorders

Most psychologists believe that mood disorders stem from a combination of biological, psychological, and social factors. *Biological factors*—including genetics and chemical imbalances within the brain—are important in the development of depression and, especially, bipolar disorder. But just as biology affects psychological experience, so does psychological experience alter biological functioning. **Cognitive distortions**, illogical and maladaptive responses to early negative life events, may lead to feelings of incompetence that are reactivated whenever a new situation arises that resembles the original events. This *psychological factor* has been found to operate in many depressed people, though it is uncertain whether the cognitive distortions cause the depression or are caused by it. Finally, *social factors* such as troubled relationships have been linked to mood disorders.

## ANXIETY DISORDERS

In **anxiety disorders**, a person's anxiety is inappropriate to the circumstances. Anxiety disorders have been subdivided into many specific diagnostic categories. One familiar subtype is **specific phobia**, an intense, paralyzing fear of something that it is unreasonable to fear so excessively. Another subtype is **social phobia**, excessive, inappropriate fears connected with social situations or performances in front of other people. **Agoraphobia** is a less common and much more debilitating type of anxiety disorder that involves multiple, intense fears such as the fear of being alone or of being in public places or other situations that require separation from a source of security. **Panic disorder** is characterized by recurrent panic attacks, which are sudden, unpredictable, and overwhelming experiences of intense fear or terror without any reasonable cause. **Generalized anxiety disorder** is defined by prolonged vague but intense fears that are not caused by any particular object or situation. In **obsessive-compulsive disorder,** either involuntary thoughts keep recurring despite the person's attempt to stop them or compulsive rituals become a paralyzing routine that a person feels compelled to perform. Two other types of anxiety disorder are caused by highly stressful events. If the anxious reaction occurs soon after the event, the diagnosis is *acute stress disorder*; if it occurs long after the event is past, the diagnosis is *posttraumatic stress disorder*.

### Causes of Anxiety Disorders

Psychologists working from an evolutionary perspective believe that we are predisposed by evolution to associate certain stimuli with intense fears; this, they contend, is the origin of phobias. Psychologists focusing on biological causes assert that a predisposition to anxiety disorders may be inherited, since these types of disorders tend to run in families. Cognitive psychologists observe that people who believe they have no control over stressful events in their lives are more likely to suffer from anxiety, while psychoanalytic theorists trace anxiety disorders to internal psychological conflicts.

## PSYCHOSOMATIC DISORDERS

**Psychosomatic disorders** are illnesses that have a verifiable physiological basis but are largely caused by psychological factors such as stress and anxiety. In fact, many physicians now recognize that nearly every physical disease can be linked to psychological compromises in the sense that such stress compromises body chemistry, organ functioning, and the immune system.

## SOMATOFORM DISORDERS

**Somatoform disorders** are characterized by physiological symptoms without any identifiable physiological cause. **Somatization disorder** is defined by vague, recurring, physical symptoms (such as back pain, dizziness, and abdominal pains) for which medical attention has been sought repeatedly but no organic cause found. Sufferers from **conversion disorders** have a dramatic, specific disability for which there is no physiological causes. In **hypochondriasis**, the person interprets some small symptom as a sign of a serious disease. **Body dysmorphic disorder**, or imagined ugliness, characterized by extreme dissatisfaction with some part of one's appearance.

## DISSOCIATIVE DISORDERS

In **dissociative disorders**, some part of an individual's personality or memory is separated from the rest. **Dissociative amnesia** refers to loss of at least some significant aspects of memory. When an amnesia victim leaves home and assumes an entirely new identity, the disorder is known as **dissociative fugue**. In **dissociative identity disorder**—commonly called *multiple personality disorder*—a person has several distinct personalities that emerge at different times. **Depersonalization disorder** is diagnosed when the person suddenly feels changed or different in a strange way.

## SEXUAL DISORDERS

The most common form of sexual disorders is sexual dysfunction.

### Sexual Dysfunction

**Sexual dysfunction** is the loss or impairment of the ability to function effectively during sex. In men, this may take the form of **erectile disorder**, the inability to achieve or keep an erection; in women, it often appears as **female sexual arousal disorder**, the inability to become sexually excited or to reach orgasm. **Sexual desire disorders** are those in which the person either lacks sexual interest or has an active aversion to sex. People with **sexual arousal disorder** experience sexual desire but cannot achieve or maintain physical arousal, while those with **orgasmic disorders** experience both desire and arousal but are unable to reach **orgasm**.

## PERSONALITY DISORDERS

**Personality disorders** are enduring, inflexible, and maladaptive ways of thinking and behaving that are so exaggerated and rigid that they cause serious inner distress and/or conflicts with others. One group of personality disorders is characterized by odd or eccentric behavior. For example, people who exhibit **schizoid personality disorder** lack the ability or desire to form social relationships and have no warm feelings for other people; those with **paranoid personality disorder** are inappropriately suspicious of others. Another cluster of personality disorders is distinguished by anxious or fearful behavior. Examples are **dependent personality disorder** (inability to make decisions or do things independently) and **avoidant personality disorder** (social anxiety leading to isolation). A third category of personality disorders is identified by dramatic, emotional, or erratic behavior. For example, people with **narcissistic personality disorder** display a grandiose sense of self-importance. **Borderline personality disorder** is characterized by a marked instability in self-image, mood, and interpersonal relationships. Finally, people with **antisocial personality disorder** lie, steal, cheat, and show little or no sense of responsibility.

## SCHIZOPHRENIC DISORDERS

**Schizophrenic disorders** are severe conditions marked by disordered thoughts and communications, inappropriate emotions, and bizarre behavior that lasts for years. People with schizophrenia are out of touch with reality and usually cannot live anything like a normal life unless they are successfully treated with medication. They often suffer from **hallucinations** (false sensory perceptions) and **delusions** (false beliefs about reality). There are several kinds of schizophrenia disorders, including **disorganized schizophrenia, catatonic schizophrenia, paranoid schizophrenia,** and **undifferentiated schizophrenia**.

## GENDER DIFFERENCES IN ABNORMAL BEHAVIOR

Studies have concluded that women have a higher rate of psychological disorders than men do, especially for the mood and anxiety disorders. There is controversy about what accounts for these differences, but psychologists believe that both socialization and biology underlie these gender-based differences.

# REVIEW QUESTIONS

## MULTIPLE CHOICE

1. True or false: Psychologists can readily distinguish abnormal from normal behavior.

2. Match the model of abnormal behavior with the appropriate explanation or approach:

   ___ biological model
   ____psychoanalytic model
   ____cognitive-behavioral model

   a. Behavior disorders are symbolic expressions of unconscious internal conflicts.
   b. Abnormal behavior is a product of biological, psychological, and social risk factors.
   c. Abnormal behavior is the result of learning and can be unlearned.
   d. Abnormal behavior is caused by heredity, damage to the nervous system, and/or endocrine dysfunction.

3. The DSM-IV is a classification system for mental disorders that was developed by the

   a. American Psychiatric Association.
   b. American Psychological Association.
   c. National Institutes for Mental Health.

4. Which of the following is *not* an anxiety disorder?

   a. specific phobia
   b. dissociative fugue
   c. obsessive-compulsive disorder
   d. posttraumatic stress disorder

5. Mood disorders include the extremes in the two moods of

   a. anger and sadness.
   b. mania and depression.
   c. psychosis and neurosis.

6. True or false: Dissociative disorders involve real damage to the body.

7. ______ is a form of mood disorder that involves less intense sadness than ______ , but the sadness is prolonged for a period of upwards of 2 years.

8. Schizophrenic disorders are characterized by ______ symptoms or loss of contact with reality.

9. Lifelong patterns of relatively "normal" but rigid and maladaptive behavior are called

   a. schizophrenic disorders.
   b. personality disorders.
   c. anxiety disorders.

10. Why doesn't the DSM-IV contain a list of psychosomatic disorders?

11. Although the DSM-IV uses a system of classification, many theorists believe that differences between normal and abnormal behavior are, in fact, ______ .

## CRITICAL THINKING AND APPLICATIONS

12. A client comes to you with what he considers to be a weird and inexplicable complaint. One day, while discussing his marriage plans with his parents and siblings, he began to feel as if someone else, not he, were speaking. He could hear himself, at a distance, acquiescing to demands his mother was making and responding to his father's criticisms of his fiancée. However, he felt as if he were hovering above his own body, observing the goings-on rather than participating in them. He is afraid that he is losing his mind, and wants to know your diagnosis. What name would you give to his experience, and would you consider it a serious disorder at this point?

13. Mood disorders are among the most common psychological problems, and the symptoms of these disorders are at least somewhat familiar to all of us. Use the critical thinking problem above to consider whether abnormal and normal behavior should be viewed in terms of dimensions or categories.

*(Answers to the Review Questions can be found in the back of the text.)*

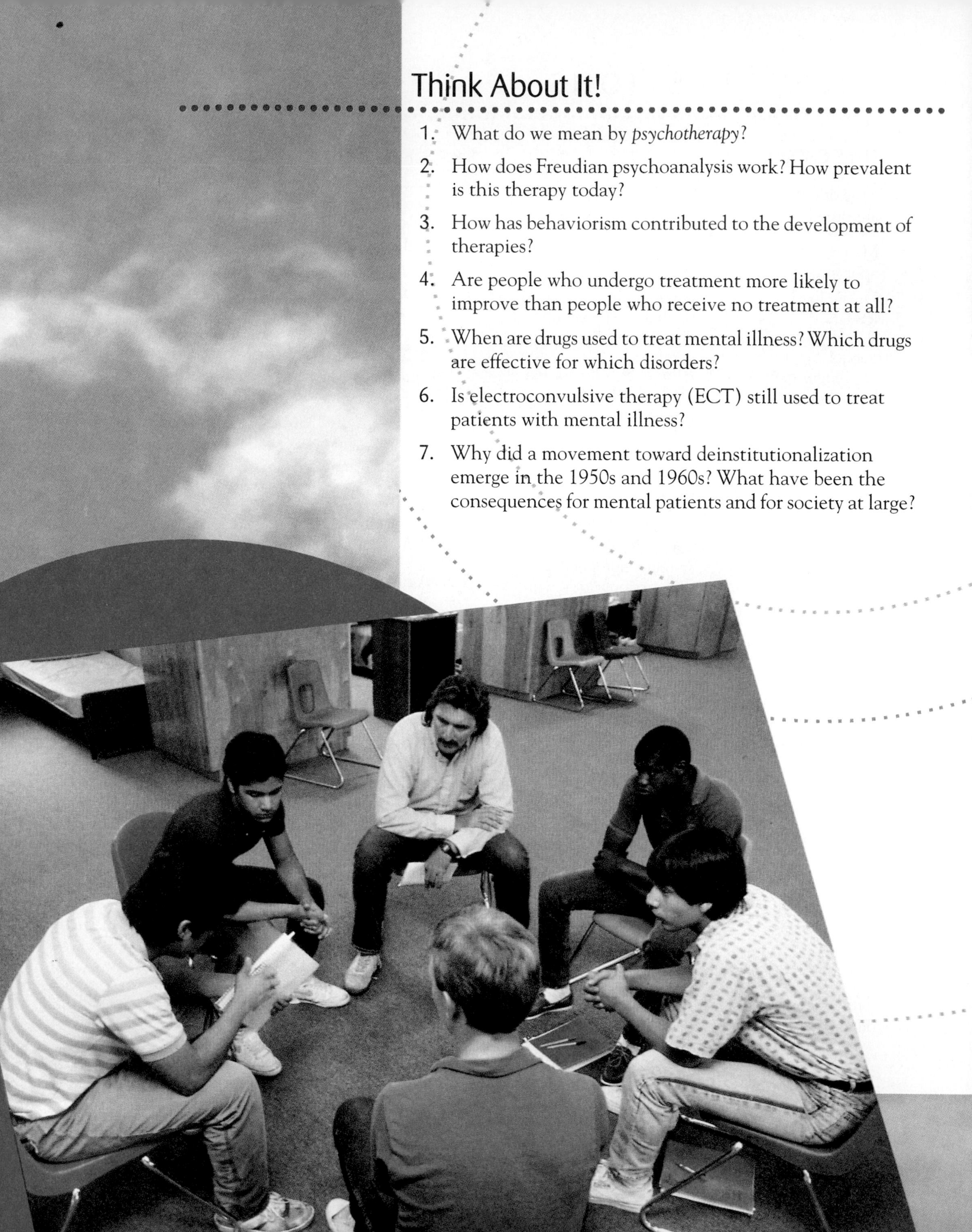

## Think About It!

1. What do we mean by *psychotherapy*?
2. How does Freudian psychoanalysis work? How prevalent is this therapy today?
3. How has behaviorism contributed to the development of therapies?
4. Are people who undergo treatment more likely to improve than people who receive no treatment at all?
5. When are drugs used to treat mental illness? Which drugs are effective for which disorders?
6. Is electroconvulsive therapy (ECT) still used to treat patients with mental illness?
7. Why did a movement toward deinstitutionalization emerge in the 1950s and 1960s? What have been the consequences for mental patients and for society at large?

# THERAPIES

# 13

## Overview

**In Chapter 1, we introduced the concept of psychotherapy, the use of psychological techniques to treat personality and behavior disorders. To many people, psychotherapy still evokes an image of an analyst sitting silently in a chair while a client, reclining on a nearby couch, recounts traumatic events in his or her life. As the anxious client reveals dreams, fantasies, fears, and obsessions, the therapist nods, scribbles in a notebook, and perhaps asks a question or two. The therapist rarely offers the client advice and never reveals details of his or her own personal life.**

**Psychotherapy** The use of psychological techniques to treat personality and behavior disorders.

1. What do we mean by *psychotherapy*?

This cliché of psychotherapy has some truth to it; scenes like this do occur. But there are many other forms of psychotherapy—literally hundreds of variations practiced by several different types of mental-health professionals. And although many therapies have much in common, others bear little resemblance to one another. In some forms of psychotherapy, therapists are very directive, even confrontational, in exploring their clients' thoughts and feelings. Some types of psychotherapy occur outside the therapist's office, as clients confront their fears in real life. Other psychotherapies treat couples or entire families, and still others treat groups of people with similar problems or goals. Later in this chapter we will take a close look at the major types of therapy. Still, we should note now that, in contrast to the popular image of the clinical, detached analyst, most psychotherapists are warm, understanding, and willing to offer at least some direct information and advice.

In addition to holding inaccurate views of therapists, many people are confused about the effectiveness of psychotherapy. Some people who have gone through therapy claim that it changed their lives; others complain that it made little difference. The public's perception of the effectiveness of **psychotherapy** is particularly important now that health-care costs have escalated and treatments of psychological disorders are being monitored more closely in terms of their costs and outcomes.

Although there have been hundreds of scientific studies of the effectiveness of psychotherapy, the issue remains controversial among psychologists as well as the public at large. Some psychologists reject therapy as a vague and poorly defined art. Ironically, there are practicing clinicians who *embrace* the idea of therapy as art, arguing that psychological science is irrelevant to the reality of clinical practice. Scientific clinical psychologists vehemently disagree with the characterization of therapy as either ineffective or an art. These *scientist-practitioners* maintain that certain therapies are highly effective for certain kinds of problems, but acknowledge that effective treatments have not been developed for some psychological problems. They believe the key to effective practice is to apply the right treatment to a particular problem and that a major goal of scientific psychology is to develop new and more effective therapies for all problems.

The future of psychotherapy rests in demonstrating the effectiveness of different treatments for different problems. In this chapter, we survey the major types of therapies used to treat psychological disorders. Included among these treatments are individual psychotherapies employed by clinical psychologists and psychiatrists in private practice and in institutions, as well as group therapies. We also examine research comparing the effectiveness of different forms of psychotherapies and consider the role of medication and other biological therapies. Finally, we discuss the important issues of institutionalization, deinstitutionalization, and prevention.

Our review of individual psychotherapies follows the sequence of their historical development. Insight therapies were developed early in the twentieth century, followed by behavior therapies in the 1960s and 1970s, and more recently by cognitive therapies.

**Insight therapy** A variety of individual psychotherapies designed to give people a better awareness and understanding of their feelings, motivations, and actions in the hope that this will help them adjust.

**Psychoanalysis** An insight therapy, developed by Freud, that is based on the belief that psychological problems are symptoms of inner conflicts repressed during childhood and that the psychoanalyst's task is to help the patient bring these hidden conflicts to conscious awareness so they can be effectively dealt with.

**Free association** A psychoanalytic technique that encourages the patient to talk about whatever thoughts or fantasies come to mind without inhibition.

## INSIGHT THERAPIES

Several of the individual psychotherapies used in both private practice and institutions fall under the heading of **insight therapy**. Although the various insight therapies differ in their details, their common goal is to give people a better awareness and understanding of their feelings, motivations, and actions, in the hope that this will lead to better adjustment. In this section, we consider two major insight therapies as well as some recent developments in the area.

### Psychoanalysis

**Psychoanalysis**, the approach to psychotherapy developed by Sigmund Freud, is based on the belief that anxiety and other problems are symptoms of inner conflicts dating back to childhood. Usually, these problems concern aggressive or sexual drives whose expression was dangerous or forbidden to the child. According to Freud, the impulses repressed by the child lurk in the adult's unconscious mind, where they can give rise to various psychological disorders. Psychoanalysis is designed to bring these hidden feelings to conscious awareness so the person can deal with them more effectively.

In Freudian psychoanalysis, the patient is instructed to talk about whatever comes to mind, with as little editing as possible and without inhibiting or controlling thoughts and fantasies. This process is called **free association**. Freud believed that the resulting "stream of consciousness" would provide insight into the patient's unconscious mind. During the early stages of psychoanalysis, the analyst remains impassive, mostly silent, and out of the patient's sight. In classical psychoanalysis, the patient lies on a couch, while the neutral analyst sits behind him or her. The analyst's silence is a kind of "blank screen" onto which the patient eventually projects unconscious thoughts and feelings.

**2.** How does Freudian psychoanalysis work? How prevalent is this therapy today?

The interview that follows is characteristic of the early stages of psychoanalysis and demonstrates free association. The analyst remains fairly quiet while the patient, a 32-year-old male teacher with recurring headaches, talks about whatever occurs to him:

> *Patient*: This is like my last resort. I've been to so many doctors for this headache. But I tell you . . . I don't want . . . I know that there's something wrong with me though. I've known it since I was a kid. Like I started to tell you, when I was 17, I knew there was something wrong with me, that . . . and I told my father that I needed to see a doctor, and he laughed at me and said it was just foolishness, but he agreed to take me to his doctor, Dr. ——— on 125th Street, and I never went in; I chickened out.
>
> *Therapist*: You chickened out, then. How'd you feel about that chickening out?
>
> *Patient*: I don't know. I don't feel *proud* that I wasn't able to talk over these . . . this feeling I had. . . . I wouldn't have wanted my father to know about my . . . some of my problems. 'Cause my father, he just . . . you know, I told him, my father, that there was something wrong, that I needed help, and he'd laugh at me and, you

**Transference** The patient's carrying over to the analyst feelings held toward childhood authority figures.

know, just to pacify me, you know, he took me to Dr. ———, but I didn't know Dr. ———. He was a friend of my father's, yeah, I don't know if. . . . I don't remember thinking about it, but if I had talked to Dr. ——— about my problems like the problems I talk about in here, and my father found out, he might get pretty mad. Yeah.

*Therapist*: Well, this would be insulting to him? He'd feel it would be a bad reflection on his upbringing of you, if you went to a doctor like this? Would this humiliate him?

*Patient*: Yeah. I've got. . . . My father and I didn't get along too well, and to tell the truth, I was ashamed of my father. He was born in Poland, and he was a self-made man. He went to the University of Warsaw and then Fordham. He was a pharmacist, but he was . . . he didn't care how he dressed. He was all sloppy and dirty, and he was short. He's about five foot one and stoop-shouldered. . . . We used to go to restaurants, my mother and him and me, and he would never leave a tip, never leave a tip, never leave a tip. I used to sneak back and I'd throw a few cents that I might have on the table, but he was so stingy, so tight. When we went on a train, when we went somewhere, I would try to pretend I wasn't with them. I'd want. . . . I'd go in another. . . . I do need some help, and I know I've got to do the talking. That's the hardest part for me, that you won't give me any guidelines, that I have to do everything myself, and you'll analyze me. . . . I didn't ever think I'd. . . . I didn't want to think I was gonna end up here. I hate to think that this is the problem, but. . . . (Hersher, 1970, pp. 135–139)

The consulting room where Freud met his clients. Note the position of Freud's chair at the head of the couch. In order to encourage *free association*, the psychoanalyst has to function as a blank screen onto which the client can project his or her feelings, and this, Freud thought, required staying out of sight of the patient.

Analysis typically proceeds very slowly. After the initial awkwardness wears off, many people enjoy having the chance to talk without interruption and appreciate having someone evidence an interest in their problems. Eventually, they may test their analyst by talking about desires and fantasies they have never revealed to anyone else. But the analyst maintains neutrality throughout the process, showing little of his or her own feelings and personality. When patients discover that their analyst is not shocked or disgusted by their revelations, they are reassured and carry over to their analyst feelings they have toward authority figures from their childhood in a process is known as **transference**. When the patient feels good about the analyst, the process is called *positive transference*.

As patients continue to expose their innermost feelings, they begin to feel increasingly vulnerable. They want reassurance and affection, but their analyst remains silent. Their anxiety builds. Threatened by their analyst's silence and by their own thoughts, patients may feel cheated and perhaps accuse their analyst of being money-grubbing. Or they may suspect that their analyst is really disgusted by their disclosures or is laughing about them behind their backs. This *negative transference* is thought to be a crucial step in psychoanalysis, for it presumably reveals patients' negative feelings toward authority figures and their resistance to uncovering their repressed emotions.

As therapy progresses, the analyst takes a more active role and begins to *interpret* or suggest alternative meanings for patients' feelings, memories, and actions. The goal of interpretation is to help patients gain **insight**—to become aware of what was formerly outside of their awareness. As what was unconscious becomes conscious, patients may come to see how their childhood experiences have determined how they feel and act now. Analysts encourage patients to confront childhood events and recall them fully. As patients relive their childhood traumas, they become able to resolve conflicts they could not resolve in the past. *Working through* old conflicts is thought to provide people with the chance to review and revise the feelings and beliefs that underlie their problems.

**Insight** Awareness of previously unconscious feelings and memories and how they influence present feelings and behavior.

The somewhat more active role of the analyst in the later stages of therapy is demonstrated in the following excerpt (from a session with a different patient from the one we heard from earlier):

> *Therapist*: *(summarizing and restating)* It sounds as if you would like to let loose with me, but you are afraid of what my response would be.
>
> *Patient*: I get so excited by what is happening here. I feel I'm being held back by needing to be nice. I'd like to blast loose sometimes, but I don't dare.
>
> *Therapist*: Because you fear my reaction?
>
> *Patient*: The worst thing would be that you wouldn't like me. You wouldn't speak to me friendly; you wouldn't smile; you'd feel you can't treat me and discharge me from treatment. But I know this isn't so; I know it.
>
> *Therapist*: Where do you think these attitudes come from?
>
> *Patient*: When I was 9 years old, I read a lot about great men in history. I'd quote them and be dramatic, I'd want a sword at my side; I'd dress like an Indian. Mother would scold me: Don't frown; don't talk so much. Sit on your hands, over and over again. I did all kinds of things. I was a naughty child. She told me I'd be hurt. Then, at 14, I fell off a horse and broke my back. I had to be in bed. Mother then told me on the day I went riding not to, I'd get hurt because the ground was frozen. I was a stubborn, self-willed child. Then I went against her will and suffered an accident that changed my life, a fractured back. Her attitude was, "I told you so." I was put in a cast and kept in bed for months.
>
> *Therapist*: You were punished, so to speak, by this accident.
>
> *Patient*: But I gained attention and love from Mother for the first time. I felt so good. I'm ashamed to tell you this: Before I healed, I opened the cast and tried to walk, to make myself sick again so I could stay in bed longer.
>
> *Therapist*: How does that connect up with your impulse to be sick now and stay in bed so much? *(The patient has these tendencies, of which she is ashamed.)*
>
> *Patient*: Oh. . . . *(pause)*
>
> *Therapist*: What do you think?
>
> *Patient*: Oh, my God, how infantile, how ungrownup *(pause)*. It must be so. I want people to love me and be sorry for me. Oh, my God.

**Client-centered** or **person-centered therapy** Nondirectional form of therapy developed by Carl Rogers that calls for unconditional positive regard of the client by the therapist with the goal of helping the client become fully functioning.

How completely childish. It is, *is* that. My mother must have ignored me when I was little, and I wanted so to be loved.

*Therapist*: So that it may have been threatening to go back to being self-willed and unloved after you got out of the cast *(interpretation)*.

*Patient*: It did. My life changed. I became meek and controlled. I couldn't get angry or stubborn afterward.

*Therapist*: Perhaps if you go back to being stubborn with me, you would be returning to how you were before, that is, active, stubborn, but unloved.

*Patient*: *(excitedly)* And, therefore, losing your love. I need you, but after all, you aren't going to reject me. But the pattern is so established now that the threat of the loss of love is too overwhelming with everybody, and I've got to keep myself from acting selfish or angry. (Wolberg, 1977, pp. 560–561)

Our description up to this point applies to traditional, or orthodox, psychoanalysis. But only a handful of people who seek therapy go into traditional analysis. As Freud himself recognized, analysis requires great motivation to change and an ability to deal rationally with whatever the analysis uncovers. Moreover, orthodox analysis may take 5 years or longer, and most traditional analysts feel that at least three, and sometimes five, sessions a week are essential. Few people can afford the orthodox course of psychoanalysis. Another disadvantage of this therapy is that it does not give the immediate help for immediate problems that some people require. Finally, psychoanalysis is not effective with severely disturbed patients.

Though some therapists still use orthodox psychoanalysis, many others believe that it is outdated. Freud invented this technique around the turn of the century. Since then, psychodynamic personality theory has changed significantly, as we saw in the chapter on personality. Many of these changes have led to modifications in psychoanalytic techniques as well as to different approaches to therapy. For example, although Freud felt that to understand the present, one must understand the past, most neo-Freudians encourage their patients to cope directly with current problems in addition to, or as a way of, addressing unresolved conflicts from the past. Neo-Freudians also favor face-to-face discussions with their patients, and most take an active role in the analysis by interpreting patients' statements freely and suggesting topics for discussion.

## Client-centered Therapy

Carl Rogers, the founder of **client-centered** (or **person-centered**) **therapy**, took bits and pieces of the neo-Freudians' views and revised and rearranged them into a radically different approach to therapy. According to Rogers, the goal of therapy is to help people become fully functioning, to open them up to all of their experiences and to all of themselves. Such inner awareness is a form of insight, but for Rogers, the person's insight into current feelings was more important than insight into unconscious wishes with roots in the distant past. Rogers called his approach to therapy *client-centered* because he placed the responsibility for change on the person with the problem. The image of a patient seeking advice from an expert, the doctor, contradicted Rogers's view of therapeutic change. He intentionally used the term *client* rather than *patient* to highlight the more active and equal role he assigned to the person who sought therapy.

Rogers's ideas about therapy are quite specific. As we saw in the chapter on personality, Rogers believed that people's defensiveness, rigidity, anxiety, and other signs of discomfort stem from their experiences of conditional positive regard. They have learned that love and acceptance are contingent on conforming to what other people want them to be. Therefore, the cardinal rule in person-centered therapy is for the therapist to express *unconditional positive regard*—that is, to show true acceptance of clients no matter what clients may say or do. Rogers felt that this was a crucial first step toward getting clients to accept themselves.

Carl Rogers, far right, leading a group therapy session. Rogers was the founder of *client-centered therapy.*

Rather than taking an objective approach, Rogerian therapists try to understand things from the clients' point of view. They are also emphatically *nondirective*. They do not suggest reasons why clients feel as they do or how they might better handle a difficult situation. Instead, they try to reflect clients' statements, sometimes asking questions and sometimes hinting at feelings that clients have not put into words. Rogers felt that when therapists provide an atmosphere of openness and genuine respect, clients can find themselves.

The following excerpt conveys the nondirective approach of client-centered therapy. The client-centered therapist is far more active and understanding than the traditional analyst, but always follows the client's lead in therapy.

> *Client*: I guess I do have problems at school. . . . You see, I'm chairman of the Science Department, so you can imagine what kind of a department it is.
>
> *Therapist*: You sort of feel that if you're in something that it can't be too good. Is that. . . .
>
> *Client*: Well, it's not that I. . . . It's just that I'm. . . . I don't think that I could run it.
>
> *Therapist*: You don't have any confidence in yourself?
>
> *Client*: No confidence, no confidence in myself. I never had any confidence in myself. I—like I told you—like when even when I was a kid I didn't feel I was capable and I always wanted to get back with the intellectual group.
>
> *Therapist*: This has been a long-term thing, then, it's gone on a long time.
>
> *Client*: Yeah, the *feeling* is—even though I know it isn't, it's the feeling that I have that—that I haven't got it, that—that—that—people will find out that I'm dumb or—or. . . .
>
> *Therapist*: Masquerade. . . .

**Short-term psychodynamic psychotherapy** Insight therapy that is time-limited and focused on trying to help clients correct the immediate problems in their lives.

*Client*: Superficial, I'm just superficial. There's nothing below the surface. Just superficial generalities, that. . . .

*Therapist*: There's nothing really deep and meaningful to you.

*Client*: No—they don't know it, and. . . .

*Therapist*: And you're terrified they're going to find out.

*Client*: My wife has a friend, and—and she and the friend got together so we could go out together with her and my wife and her husband. . . . And the guy, he's an engineer and he's you know—he's got it, you know; and I don't want to go, I don't want to go because—because if—if we get together he's liable to start to—to talk about something I don't know, and I'll—I won't know about that.

*Therapist*: You'll show up very poorly in this kind of situation.

*Client*: That I—I'll show up poorly, that I'll—that I'll just clam up, that I. . . .

*Therapist*: You're terribly frightened in this sort of thing.

*Client*: I—I'm afraid to be around people who—who I feel are my peers. Even in pool—now I—I play pool very well and—if I'm playing with some guy that I—I know I can beat, *psychologically*, I can run 50, but—but if I start playing with somebody that's my level, I'm done. I'm done. I—I—I'll miss a ball every time.

*Therapist*: So the . . . the fear of what's going on just immobilizes you, keeps you from doing a good job. (Hersher, 1970, pp. 29–32)

Rogers was not interested in comparing his therapy to others, nor was he concerned simply with statistics on outcomes (such as the percent of clients who recovered). Rather, he wanted to discover those processes or events in client-centered therapy that were associated with positive outcomes. Rogers' interest in the *process* of therapy resulted in important and lasting contributions to the field. For example, it has been found that a therapist's warmth and understanding increase success, no matter what therapeutic approach is used (Frank & Frank, 1991).

## Recent Developments

Although Freud and Rogers originated the two major forms of insight therapy, other therapists have developed hundreds of variations on those themes. As we noted earlier in this chapter, even among mainstream psychoanalysts, there has been considerable divergence from the traditional form of "couch" psychotherapy. Most present-day insight-oriented therapists are far more active and emotionally engaged with their clients than traditional orthodox psychoanalysts thought fit.

Another general trend in recent years is toward shorter-term "dynamic therapy" for most people—usually occurring once a week for a fixed period of time. In fact, **short-term psychodynamic psychotherapy** is increasingly popular among both patients and mental-health professionals. Insight remains the goal of short-term psychodynamic therapy, but the treatment is usually time-limited—for example, to 25 sessions. This movement toward briefer therapy was highlighted by an article published a decade ago in which the authors reviewed more than 30 years of research on various kinds of therapy with more than 2,400 patients (Howard et al., 1986). They found that about half the patients showed improvement after only 8 sessions and that about three-quarters improved within 26 sessions. Thus, regardless of the form of therapy, improvement seemed to occur fairly quickly in most people.

With the trend to a time-limited framework, insight therapies have become more problem- or symptom-oriented. Instead of slowly and patiently trying to construct a "narrative of the psyche"—the aim of traditional Freudian analysis—most contemporary therapists try to help their clients correct the immediate problems in their lives. They see the individual as less at the mercy of early childhood events than the Freudians did, although they do not discount childhood experiences. Still, the focus is on the client's current life situation and relationships. In addition, most contemporary therapists give clients more direct guidance and feedback, commenting on what they are told rather than just listening to their clients in a neutral manner.

Even more notable than the trend toward shorter-term therapy has been the proliferation of behavior therapies in the past few decades. Behavior therapies sharply contrast with insight-oriented approaches: Behavior therapists are more active than psychodynamic therapists; they concentrate on changing people's behavior rather than on increasing their insight into their thoughts and feelings; and they operate within a briefer framework (K.D. O'Leary & Wilson, 1987). In the next section of the chapter, we examine several types of behavior therapy.

**Behavior therapies** Therapeutic approaches that are based on the belief that all behavior, normal and abnormal, is learned, and that the objective of therapy is to teach people new, more satisfying ways of behaving.

**Systematic desensitization** A behavioral technique for reducing a person's fear and anxiety by gradually associating a new response (relaxation) with stimuli that have been causing the fear and anxiety.

## BEHAVIOR THERAPIES

How has behaviorism contributed to the development of therapies?

As we have noted repeatedly throughout this book, behaviorists believe psychology should focus on observable, measurable behavior rather than on thoughts, feelings, and unconscious processes. Unlike insight-oriented therapists, who regard personality disorders as the symptoms of unconscious forces or the products of insufficient awareness or insight, behavior therapists argue that the disorder *is* the problem. They believe that if they can teach people to respond with more appropriate behavior, they have cured the problem.

**Behavior therapies** are based on the belief that all behavior, both normal and abnormal, is learned. Hypochondriacs *learn* that they get attention when they are sick; paranoid personalities *learn* to be suspicious of others. At the same time, behavior therapists assert, in opposition to insight therapists, that the therapist does not need to know exactly how or why people learned to behave abnormally in the first place. The job of the therapist is simply to teach people new, more satisfying ways of behaving.

Behavior therapies also differ from insight therapies in that they attempt to apply basic findings from psychological science, particularly research on learning processes (see Chapter 5), to the treatment of clinical problems. So many behavior therapy techniques are simply applications of behavioral concepts discussed in earlier chapters of this text.

## CLASSICAL CONDITIONING

As we saw in the chapter on learning, *classical conditioning* requires pairing a conditioned stimulus repeatedly with an unconditioned stimulus. If the conditions are right, the conditioned stimulus will eventually produce a conditioned response. Several variations on the classical conditioning approach have been used to treat psychological problems.

DESENSITIZATION, EXTINCTION, AND FLOODING **Systematic desensitization**, a method for gradually reducing fear and anxiety, is one of the oldest behavior therapy techniques (Wolpe, 1990). The method works by gradually associating a new response (relaxation) with stimuli that have been causing anxiety. For example, an aspiring politician might seek therapy because he is very anxious about speaking to crowds. The therapist looks for more details, asking if the man feels more threatened by an audience of 500 than by an audience of 50, more tense when addressing men than when speaking to both men and women, more anxious when talking to friends or to strangers, and so on. Through such explorations, the therapist develops a *hierarchy of fears* for this individual—a list of situations from the least to the most anxiety-provoking.

After establishing a client's hierarchy of fears, the therapist teaches the client how to relax: to clear his or her mind, to release tense muscles, and to be able to produce this relaxation response readily. In some cases, drugs or mild hypnosis is used to aid relaxation. Once a client has mastered the technique of deep relaxation, he or she begins work at the bottom of the hierarchy of fears. The client is told to imagine the least threatening situation on the list and to signal when feeling the least bit tense. At the signal, the therapist tells the client to forget the scene and to concentrate on relaxing. After a short time, the therapist instructs the client to imagine the scene again. This process is repeated until the client feels completely relaxed when imagining that scene. Then the therapist moves on to the next situation in the client's hierarchy of fears and trains the client to be completely relaxed when imagining that situation as well. Therapist and client advance up the hierarchy this way until finally the client can imagine the most fearful situation at the top of the hierarchy without experiencing any anxiety whatsoever. Figure 13-1 illustrates the process of desensitization.

Numerous studies indicate that systematic desensitization helps many people overcome their fears and phobias (Wolpe, 1990). Research suggests, however, that the key to desensitization's success may not be the learning of a new conditioned relaxation response but rather the *extinction* of the old fear response through mere exposure. Recall from Chapter 5 that in classical conditioning extinction occurs when the learned, conditioned stimulus is repeatedly presented without the unconditioned stimulus being present. Thus, if a person repeatedly imagines a frightening situation with-

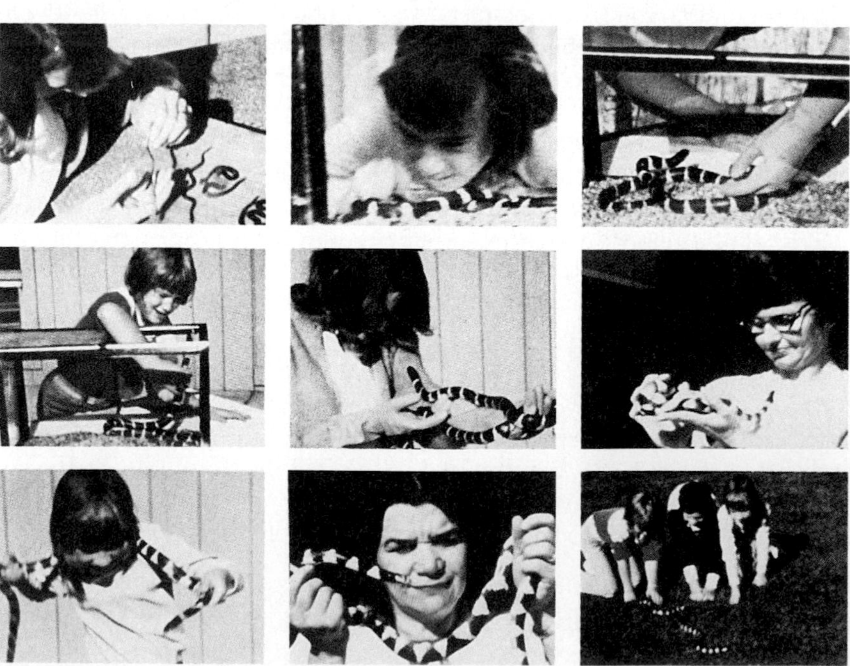

**Figure 13-1**
**Desensitization therapy at work.** The clients in these photographs are overcoming a simple phobia: fear of snakes. After practicing a technique of deep relaxation, clients in desensitization therapy work from the bottom of their *hierarchy of fears* up to the situation that provokes the greatest fear or anxiety. Here, clients progress from handling rubber snakes (top left) to viewing live snakes through a window (top center) and finally to handling live snakes. This procedure can also be conducted vicariously in the therapist's office, where clients combine relaxation techniques with imagining anxiety-provoking scenes.

out actually encountering danger, the fear or anxiety associated with that situation should gradually decline.

Because exposure to the fearful situation seems to be critical for overcoming anxiety, many behavior therapists believe desensitization is more effective when clients gradually confront their fears in the real world rather than merely in their imaginations. People who are deathly afraid of flying, for example, might first simply drive to an airport. When they are able to do this without experiencing fear or anxiety, they may move on to walking around a plane on the ground. When they can do that without anxiety, they may go inside a stationary plane. Eventually, they may take a short flight. This commonsense approach of working step by step through a hierarchy of fears in real life is surely familiar to you. For example, folk wisdom says that if you fall off a horse, the best way to get over your fear of riding is to get right back on the horse and to continue to ride as often as possible until the fear is gone. That's an example of desensitization in the real world.

The technique of *flooding* is a less familiar, and more frightening, method of desensitization through exposure. For some problems, however, extinction works best if exposure occurs soon, at full intensity, and for a prolonged period of time (K.D. O'Leary & Wilson, 1987; Wolpe, 1990). Thus, someone with an obsessive-compulsive disorder may be repeatedly forced to encounter and deal directly with the source of his or her irrational fear. For example, someone with a powerful fear of snakes might be forced to handle dozens of snakes, or someone with an overwhelming fear of spiders might be forced to stroke a tarantula and allow it to crawl up his or her arm. If you think that flooding is an unnecessarily harsh method, it is worth recalling the severity and life impairment that can be caused by untreated anxiety disorders (see Chapter 12).

**Aversive conditioning** Behavioral therapy techniques aimed at eliminating undesirable behavior patterns by teaching the person to associate them with pain and discomfort.

**Behavior contracting** Form of operant conditioning therapy in which the client and therapist set behavioral goals and agree on reinforcements the client will receive upon reaching those goals.

AVERSIVE CONDITIONING Another classical conditioning technique aimed at eliminating undesirable behavior patterns is **aversive conditioning**. This form of behavior therapy, in which therapists teach clients to associate pain and discomfort with the behavior that they want to unlearn, has been used with limited success to treat alcoholism, obesity, and smoking.

At times the therapist uses real physical pain. Some clinics, for example, treat alcoholism by pairing the taste and smell of alcohol with drug-induced nausea and vomiting. Before long, patients feel sick just seeing a bottle of liquor. A follow-up study of nearly 800 patients who completed alcohol-aversion treatment at one clinic in 1978 and 1979 found that 63 percent had maintained continuous abstinence for at least 12 months after treatment (Wiens & Menustik, 1983). Still, the use of aversive conditioning has declined in recent years because its long-term effectiveness has been questioned: Although it can create avoidance in the presence of the certainty of punishment, unwanted behaviors often continue in real-life situations when no such threat exists. Moreover, aversive conditioning is a controversial technique because of its painful nature.

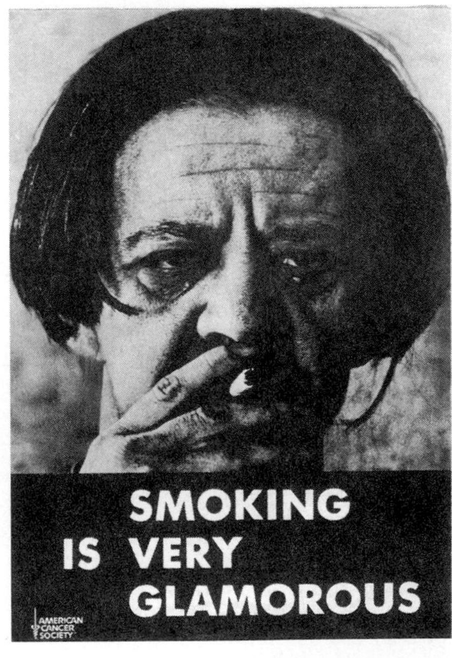

Ads such as this use classical conditioning to link unpleasant stimuli with undesirable behavior. Such ads can help make people aware of positive associations they may have for behavior that is fundamentally undesirable.

OPERANT CONDITIONING As we saw in the chapter on learning, *operant conditioning* techniques are based on the idea that a person learns to behave in different ways when new behaviors are reinforced and old ones ignored or punished. In one form of operant conditioning called **behavior contracting**, the therapist and the client agree on behavioral goals and on the reinforcement that the client will receive when the goals are reached. These goals and reinforcements are often written down in a contract that binds both the client and the therapist as if by legal agreement. The contract specifies the behaviors to be followed, the penalties for not following them, and any privileges to be earned. One such contract

**Token economy** An operant conditioning therapy in which patients earn tokens (reinforcers) for desired behaviors and exchange them for desired items or privileges.

**Modeling** A behavior therapy in which the person learns desired behaviors by watching others perform those behaviors.

**Cognitive therapies** Psychotherapies that emphasize changing clients' perceptions of their life situation as a way of modifying their behavior.

might be: "For each day that I smoke fewer than 20 cigarettes, I will earn 30 minutes of time to go bowling. For each day that I exceed the goal, I will lose 30 minutes from the time that I have accumulated."

Another form of operant conditioning is called the **token economy.** As we mentioned in the chapter on learning, token economies are usually employed in institutions like schools and hospitals, where controlled conditions are most feasible (K.D. O'Leary & Wilson, 1987). Subjects are rewarded with tokens or points for behaviors that are considered appropriate and adaptive; in turn, the tokens or points can be exchanged for desired items and privileges. On the ward of a mental hospital, for example, improved grooming habits might earn points that can be used to purchase special foodstuffs or weekend passes. Token economies have proved effective in modifying the behavior of patients who are resistant to other forms of treatment, such as people with chronic schizophrenia (Paul, 1982; Paul & Lentz, 1977). Interestingly, in some instances, the use of token economies has also led to improved morale among hospital staff (Ullman & Krasner, 1975). Although token economies can be effective in institutions, the positive changes do not always generalize to everyday life outside the hospital or clinic, where adaptive behavior is not always reinforced with tokens and maladaptive behavior is not always ignored or punished.

### Modeling

The behavior therapies we have discussed so far rely on classical and operant conditioning principles to change behavior. But as we saw in the chapter on learning, much human behavior is learned by **modeling**—the process of learning a behavior by watching someone else perform it. Modeling can also be used to treat problem behaviors. In one experiment, Bandura, Blanchard, and Ritter (1969) tried to help people overcome snake phobia by showing them films in which models confronted snakes and gradually moved closer and closer to them. The researchers reported a notable reduction in the observers' fear of snakes. Similar techniques have succeeded in reducing such common phobias as fear of dental work (Melamed et al., 1975). Moreover, a combination of modeling and positive reinforcement was successful in helping schizophrenic patients learn and use appropriate behavior both inside and outside the hospital (Bellack, Hersen, & Turner, 1976). Modeling has also been used to teach retarded people job skills and appropriate responses to problems encountered at work (LaGreca, Stone, & Bell, 1983).

## COGNITIVE THERAPIES

In modeling, people learn a behavior simply by watching others perform it. Thus, as we saw in the last section, people with snake phobia learned how to confront snakes by watching a film of others moving closer and closer to snakes. Cognitive psychologists would point out that in addition to learning a *behavior*, these people also learned from watching the film that snakes are not necessarily dangerous and that one can endure contact with them without suffering ill effects. It might be said that in addition to changing their behavior, these people *changed their way of thinking* about snakes, and that their new way of thinking should lead to more adaptive behavior in the future. It is this simple idea—that people's ideas about the world can be changed and that that will have a beneficial effect on their subsequent behavior—that is at the heart of the **cognitive therapies**.

Cognitive therapists believe that their clients suffer from misconceptions about themselves and the world, and that these misconceptions cause them psychological problems. The task facing cognitive therapists is to identify such erroneous ways of thinking and to correct them. This focus on learning new ways of thinking has many similarities with behavior therapy; in fact, many professionals consider themselves to be *cognitive behavior therapists*, or therapists who combine both cognitive and behavior therapies. Let's examine some of the more popular forms of cognitive therapy.

**Stress-inoculation therapy** A type of cognitive therapy that trains clients to cope with stressful situations by learning a more useful pattern of self-talk.

**Rational-emotive therapy (RET)** A directive cognitive therapy based on the idea that clients' psychological distress is caused by irrational and self-defeating beliefs and that the therapist's job is to challenge such dysfunctional beliefs.

## Stress-inoculation Therapy

As we go about our lives, we talk to ourselves constantly—we propose courses of action to ourselves, comment on our performance, express wishes, and so on. **Stress-inoculation therapy** is a type of cognitive therapy that makes use of this self-talk process to help clients cope with stressful situations (Meichenbaum & Cameron, 1982). Once the stressful situation is identified, the client is taught to suppress any negative, anxiety-evoking thoughts and to replace them with positive, "coping" thoughts. Take a student with exam anxiety who faces every test telling herself: "Oh, another test. I'm so nervous and I'm sure I won't be able to think calmly enough to remember the answers. If only I'd studied more! If I don't get through this course, I'll never graduate!" This pattern of thought is highly dysfunctional because it will only make her anxiety worse. With the help of a cognitive therapist, the student learns a new pattern of self-talk: "I studied hard for this exam and I know the material well. I looked at the textbook last night and reviewed my notes. I should be able to do well. If some questions are hard, they won't all be, and even if it's tough, my whole grade doesn't depend on just one test." Then the client tries out the new strategy in a real situation, ideally one of only moderate stress (like a short quiz). Finally, the client is ready to use the strategy in a more stressful situation (like a final exam). Stress-inoculation therapy works by turning the client's own thought patterns into a kind of vaccine against stress-induced anxiety. This technique, as you might guess, is particularly effective with anxiety disorders.

## Rational-emotive Therapy

Another type of cognitive therapy, one that includes a more elaborate set of assumptions, is known as **rational-emotive therapy (RET)**. According to Albert Ellis (1973), the founder of RET, most people in need of therapy hold a set of irrational and self-defeating beliefs. These include such notions as: they should be competent at everything and liked by everyone; life should always be fair; quick solutions to problems should be available; and their lives should turn out a certain way. The core problem with such beliefs is that they involve absolutes—"musts" and "shoulds" that allow for no exceptions, no room for making mistakes. When people with such irrational beliefs come up against real-life struggles, they often experience excessive psychological distress. For example, when a college student who believes he must be liked by everyone isn't invited to join a fraternity, rather than feeling simply sad and disappointed, he may view the rejection as a catastrophe and become deeply depressed.

In rational-emotive therapy, therapists confront such dysfunctional beliefs vigorously, using a variety of techniques, including persuasion, challenge, commands, and theoretical arguments. Consider the following excerpt from a rational-emotive therapy session:

> *Client*: . . . I always doubt that I have what it takes intellectually. . . .
>
> *Therapist*: Well, let's suppose you haven't. Let's just suppose for the sake of discussion that you really are inferior to some degree, and

you're not up to your fellows—your old peers from childhood or your present peers. Now what's so catastrophic about that, if it were true?

*Client*: Well, this is a fear, I'm not . . . if they found out, then . . . if I can't keep my job teaching, then I . . . I couldn't support my family.

*Therapist*: How long have you been teaching?

*Client*: Seven years.

*Therapist*: So, being inferior, you've done pretty well in keeping your job. You're not that concerned about your job.

*Client*: I know my wife says this. She says that somebody would find me out, but I . . . still feel that I . . . I'm kidding everybody, that I have to be very careful what I say and what I do, because if they should find out that I haven't got it, then I don't know what I would do. If I don't feel that I'm capable of being a teacher, then I shouldn't be a teacher.

*Therapist*: Who said so?

*Client*: I don't know.

*Therapist*: I know. You said so. Don't you think there are lots of teachers in the school system who are not very good teachers?

*Client*: Yes, I know there are a lot of them, and I don't respect them. I don't feel they should be teachers if they aren't qualified.

*Therapist*: So you're saying you don't respect yourself, if you act ineffectively as a teacher. Right?

*Client*: Yes, I wouldn't respect myself.

*Therapist*: Why not?

*Client*: Because if . . . well, it wouldn't be right to say that I'm teaching when . . . if I haven't got the qualifications, if I'm not capable to do the job.

*Therapist*: Let's assume you're a lousy teacher. Now why are you tying up your performance? Lousy teacher, we're assuming now. You are a lousy teacher and may always be a lousy teacher. Why are you tying that aspect of you up with your total self? I am a slob because my teaching is slobbish. Now do you see any inconsistency with that conclusion?

*Client*: No, but I agree that I would be . . . it would be a terrible thing if I were to teach and it wouldn't . . . and I wouldn't be capable. That it wouldn't be right. That would be like I was a fraud.

*Therapist*: But the terrible thing is that you would be a slob, a no-goodnik, a louse who couldn't respect you.

*Client*: It would be dishonest of me.

*Therapist*: Well, yeah. What's terrible about that?

*Client*: Well, it's terrible.

*Therapist*: But according to you, about half or more of the teachers in the school system are not-so-hot teachers. Right?

*Client*: Yes, and if I were the administrator, I would have to do something about that.

*Therapist*: Meaning fire them?

*Client*: Fire them.

*Therapist*: And then who would teach the kids?

*Client*: You mean, if I was the administrator I'd have to. . . .

*Therapist*: Tolerate.

*Client*: To tolerate it. . . . (Hersher, 1970, pp. 64–66)

**Cognitive therapy** Therapy that depends on identifying and changing inappropriately negative and self-centered patterns of thought.

**Group therapy** Type of psychotherapy in which clients meet regularly to interact and help one another achieve insight into their feelings and behavior.

### Beck's Cognitive Therapy

One of the most important and promising forms of cognitive therapy was developed by Aaron Beck (1967) for the treatment of depression. It is usually known simply as **cognitive therapy**, but is sometimes referred to as "Beck's cognitive therapy" to avoid confusion with the broader category of cognitive therapies.

Beck believes that depression results from negative patterns of thought that people develop about themselves. Principally, depressed people interpret events in a distorted way, one that is strongly and inappropriately self-critical. Such people have unrealistic expectations, magnify their failures, make sweeping negative generalizations about themselves from little evidence, notice only negative feedback from the outside world, and interpret anything less than total success as failure. For example, when a salesman loses an important account, he might not react normally, with disappointment, but abnormally, with severe, disabling depression. Why? Because the account loss set off a pattern of negative thoughts in his mind: He is not really a good salesman, he will never find any customers as good as the one he just lost, and he will probably now go bankrupt from lack of income. From there his negative thoughts will continue to spiral into more general areas of his life, and he may conclude that his life is worthless. According to Beck, this downward spiral of negative thoughts and cognitive distortions is at the heart of depression.

Beck's assumptions about the cause of depression are very similar to the assumptions underlying RET, but the style of treatment differs considerably. Cognitive therapists are much less challenging and confrontational than rational-emotive therapists. Instead, they try to help clients examine each dysfunctional thought in a supportive but objectively scientific manner ("Are you *sure* you'll never find any more good customers? What is your evidence for that?"). Like RET, Beck's cognitive therapy has as its goal leading the client to more realistic and flexible ways of thinking.

## GROUP THERAPIES

The therapies we have been discussing thus far involve only two people, a client and a therapist. Some psychologists think that this sort of therapy is less than ideal, for many of the problems that cause people to go into therapy are interpersonal problems. These therapists believe, therefore, that the treatment of several clients simultaneously, or **group therapy**, is preferable to individual therapy. Group therapy allows both client and thera-

**Family therapy** A form of group therapy that sees the family as at least partly responsible for the individual's problems and that seeks to change all family members' behaviors to the benefit of the family unit as well as the troubled individual.

**Marital therapy** Form of group therapy intended to help troubled couples improve their problems of communication and interaction.

pist to see how the client acts around other ordinary people. If a client is painfully anxious and tongue-tied, or chronically self-critical and self-denigrating, or hostile and aggressive toward the opposite sex, these tendencies will show up quickly in a group setting.

Groups have other advantages besides revealing a client's problems more quickly and clearly than individual therapy might. A good group offers a client social support, a feeling that he or she is not the only person in the world with emotional problems. The group can also help the client learn useful new behaviors (how to express feelings, how to disagree without antagonizing others). Interactions with other group members may push the client toward insights into his or her own behavior (seeing how annoying another person's constant complaints are, or how helpful his or her words of encouragement are, can lead the client toward useful behavior change). Finally, because group therapy consists of several clients "sharing" the therapist at once, it is less expensive for each participant than is individual therapy.

There are many kinds of group therapy. Some groups follow the general outlines of the therapies we've already mentioned. Others are oriented toward a specific goal, such as stopping smoking, drinking, or overeating. And some have more open-ended goals—for example, a happier marriage. The *self-help group* is a particularly popular form of group therapy today. You will find information about self-help groups in the Highlights box with that title that appears toward the end of the chapter. A list of some self-help organizations is contained in the Highlights box titled "How to Find Help."

If a member of a family is having problems, it is often a sign that the entire family needs assistance.

## Family Therapy

**Family therapy** is one form of group therapy (Molineux, 1985). Family therapists believe that it is a mistake to treat a client in a vacuum, making no attempt to meet the client's parents, spouse, and children, for if one person in the family is having problems, it is often a signal that the entire family needs assistance. The primary goals of family therapy are improving family communication, encouraging family members to become more empathic, getting members to share responsibilities, and reducing intrafamily conflict. To achieve these goals, all family members must see that they will benefit from changes in their behavior. Family therapists concentrate on changing the ways in which family members satisfy their needs rather than on trying to change those needs or the individual members' personalities (Gurman & Kniskern, 1990).

Family therapy is especially appropriate when there are problems between husband and wife, parents and children, or other family members. It is also called for when clients' progress in individual therapy is slowed by their family for some reason (often because other family members have trouble adjusting to a client's improvement). As Goldenberg (1973) notes, however, not all families benefit from family therapy. Sometimes the problems are too entrenched; in the other cases, important family members may be absent or unwilling to cooperate; in still others, one family member monopolizes sessions to the extent that the therapy becomes unworkable (for example, a bossy and overbearing parent might prevent other family members from getting a word in edgewise). In all these cases, a different therapeutic approach is warranted.

## Marital Therapy

Another form of group therapy is **marital therapy**, which is designed to assist couples who are having difficulties with their relationship. Most marital therapists concentrate on improving the couple's patterns of communica-

# HIGHLIGHTS

## How to Find Help

As we have seen, there is no such thing as therapy in the definitive sense; there are only *therapies*. We discuss the major types of therapies in this chapter, but there are others—many of them syntheses of various techniques and practices. There are probably as many therapies as there are practicing psychotherapists. (For a description of the differences in training among the various types of psychotherapists—from psychiatrists to clinical and counseling psychologists—see "Careers in Psychology" in the chapter on the science of psychology.)

It should be clear by now that therapy and psychological counseling are not just intended to help "crazy" people. Unfortunately, the notion that seeking help for your problems is a sign of weakness or mental illness is hard to dispel. But the fact is that tens of thousands of people are helped by psychological counseling and therapy every year. These people include business executives, artists, sports heroes, celebrities—and students. Therapy is a common, useful aid in coping with daily living.

College is a time of stress and anxiety for many people. The pressure of work, the competition for grades, the exposure to many different kinds of people with unfamiliar views, the tension of relating to peers—all these factors can add up to considerable emotional and physical stress, especially for students who are away from home for the first time. Most colleges and universities have their own counseling services, and many of these are as sophisticated as the best clinics in the country. Most communities also have mental-health programs. As an aid to a potential search for the right counseling service, we include here a list of some of the other available resources for people who would like the advice of a mental-health professional. Many of these services have national offices that, if contacted, will provide you with local branches and the appropriate people to contact in your area.

**For Aid in Locating an Appropriate Self-help Group Near You**

National Self-Help Clearinghouse
25 W. 43rd St., Room 620
New York, NY 10036
(212) 642-2944

**For Alcohol and Drug Abuse**

Alcohol and Drug Problems Association
of North America
444 N. Capitol St. NW, Suite 706
Washington, DC 20001

National Clearinghouse for Alcohol
and Drug Information
P.O. Box 2345
Rockville, MD 20847-2345
(301) 468-2600

Veterans Administration
Alcohol and Drug Dependency Services
810 Vermont Ave. NW
Washington, DC 20420
(202) 535-7316

Association of Halfway Houses of North America
Alcoholism Programs
680 Stewart Ave.
St. Paul, MN 55102
(612) 227-7818

General Service Board
Alcoholics Anonymous, Inc.
P.O. Box 459, Grand Central Station
New York, NY 10163
(212) 870-3400

**For Those with a Friend or Relative Who Has an Alcohol Problem**

Alanon Family Group Headquarters, Inc.
P.O. Box 862
Midtown Station
New York, NY 10018-0862
(212) 302-7240

National Association for Children of Alcoholics
11426 Rockville Pike
Rockville, MD 20852
(301) 468-0985

**For Smoking and Eating Abuses**

Smokenders
4455 E. Camelback Road
Suite D-150
Phoenix, AZ 85018
(602) 840-7414

Stop Teen-Age Addiction to Tobacco
511 East Columbus
Springfield, MA 01105
(413) 732-STAT

Weight and Smoking Counseling Service
(212) 755-4363

Overeaters Anonymous
(213) 936-4206

**For Depression and Suicide**

Mental Health Counseling Hotline
33 East End Ave.
New York, NY 10028
(212) 734-5876

International Association for Suicide Prevention
Suicide Prevention Center
626 South Kingsley Drive
Los Angeles, CA 90005
(213) 381-5111

Payne-Whitney Suicide Prevention Program
425 E. 61st Street
New York, NY 10021
(212) 821-0700

Heartbeat (for survivors of suicides)
2015 Devon St.
Colorado Springs, CO 80909
(719) 596-2575

**For Sexual and Sex-Related Problems**

Sex Information and Education Council
of the United States (SIECUS)
130 W. 42nd St., Suite 350
New York, NY 10036-7802
(212) 819-9770

National Organization for Women Legislative Office
1000 16th St. NW
Washington, DC 20036
(202) 331-0066

National Clearinghouse on Marital and Date Rape
2325 Oak St.
Berkeley, CA 94708
(510) 524-1582 (fee required)

People Against Rape
P.O. Box 5876
Naperville, IL 60567-5876

**For Physical Abuse**

Child Abuse Listening and Mediation (CALM)
P.O. Box 90754
Santa Barbara, CA 93190-0754
(805) 965-2376
(805) 687-7912 (24-hour listening service)

**For Stress**

Anxiety Disorders Association of America
6000 Executive Blvd., Suite 513
Rockville, MD 20852
(301) 231-8368

**For Help in Selecting a Therapist**

Depressives Anonymous: Recovery from Depression
329 E. 62nd St.
New York, NY 10021
(212) 689-2600

**National Mental Health Consumer Self-help Clearinghouse**

311 S. Juniper St., Room 902
Philadelphia, PA 19107
(215) 735-6367

Psychiatric Service Section
American Hospital Association
1 North Franklin St.
Chicago, IL 60606
(312) 422-3000

Mental Health Help Line
(212) 222-7666

**For General Information on Mental Health and Counseling**

The National Alliance for the Mentally Ill
200 N. Glebe Road, Suite 1015
Arlington, VA 22204
(703) 524-7600

The National Mental Health Association
1201 Prince St.
Alexandria, VA 22314-2971
(703) 684-7722

The American Psychiatric Association
1400 K St. NW
Washington, DC 20005
(202) 682-6000

The American Psychological Association
750 1st St., NE
Washington, DC 20002
(202) 336-5500

The National Institute of Mental Health
5600 Fishers Lane
Rockville, MD 20857
(301) 443-4513

tion and mutual expectations. In *empathy training*, for example, each member of the couple is taught to share inner feelings and to listen to and understand the partner's feelings before responding to them. The empathy technique focuses the couple's attention on feelings and requires that they spend more time listening and less time in rebuttal.

Other marital therapists employ behavioral techniques. For example, a couple might be helped to develop a schedule for exchanging specific caring actions. This approach is based on the theory that scheduled exchanges of benefits can result in the learning of behavior that benefits both partners. It isn't terribly romantic, but its supporters point out that any strategy that breaks the cycle of dissatisfaction and hostility in a marriage is an important step in the right direction (Margolin, 1987).

Recently Aaron Beck (1989) described a cognitive marital therapy that helps partners recognize the ways they have been misinterpreting each other's communications. For example, when one spouse says "How's your work going?" the other spouse may take this to mean "I wish you would get a better job" or "I hate the way you're always working late at the office." Or an innocent question about helping around the house can be taken as criticism by the other partner. Misinterpretations like these, which can turn harmless or friendly remarks into criticism or nagging, evoke unnecessary conflict. Cognitive therapy in the marital setting aims at uncovering and undoing such destructive cognitive distortions.

Whatever form of therapy a couple chooses, research indicates that marital therapy for both partners is more effective than therapy for only one of them (Gurman et al., 1986). One study found that when both partners underwent therapy together, 56 percent were still married 5 years later; among those couples who underwent therapy separately, only 29 percent remained married (Cookerly, 1980).

Marital and family therapy are being increasingly used when only one family member has a clear psychological disorder such as schizophrenia, agoraphobia, or, in some cases, depression. The goal of treatment in these circumstances is to help the mentally healthy members of the family cope more effectively with the effects of the disorder or the family unit. The improved coping of the well-adjusted family members may, in turn, help the troubled person compensate for or overcome his or her problems.

## EFFECTIVENESS OF PSYCHOTHERAPY

Although the various therapies we have discussed so far represent different approaches to the goal of improved mental health, they all share one characteristic: All are *psycho*therapies—that is, they use psychological methods to treat disorders. But is psychotherapy *effective*? Is it any better than no treatment at all? And if it is, how *much* better is it?

One of the first investigators to raise questions about the effectiveness of psychotherapy was the British psychologist Hans Eysenck (1952). After surveying 19 published reports covering more than 7,000 cases, Eysenck concluded that therapy significantly helped about two out of every three people. However, he also concluded that "Roughly two-thirds of a group of neurotic patients will recover or improve to a marked extent within about two years of the onset of their illness whether they are treated by means of psychotherapy or not" (p. 322).

Are people who undergo treatment more likely to improve than people who receive no treatment at all?

Eysenck's conclusion that individual psychotherapy was no more effective in treating neurotic disorders than no therapy at all caused a storm of controversy in the psychological community and stimulated considerable research. Ironically, an important but often overlooked aspect of the subsequent debate has little to do with the effectiveness of therapy. Many researchers then, and many investigators today, agree with Eysenck that therapy helps about two-thirds of the people who undergo it. That fact is not much debated. More controversial is the question of what happens to people with psychological problems who do *not* receive formal therapy. For example, Bergin and Lambert (1978) questioned the "spontaneous recovery" rate of the control subjects in the studies Eysenck surveyed. They concluded that only about *one* out of every three people improves without treatment (not

**Eclecticism** Psychotherapeutic approach that recognizes the value of a broad treatment package over a rigid commitment to one particular form of therapy.

the two out of three cited by Eysenck); since twice as many people improve with formal therapy, therapy *is* indeed more effective than no treatment at all. Furthermore, these researchers noted that many people who do not receive formal therapy get real therapeutic help from friends, clergy, physicians, and teachers; thus, it is possible that the recovery rate for people who receive no therapeutic help at all is even less than one-third.

In 1977, a dramatically new approach was taken to the effectiveness question. M.L. Smith and Glass (1977) averaged the results of a large number of studies and concluded that the typical therapy client is better off than 75 percent of untreated controls. But is this result due simply to the fact that the therapy patients believed they would be helped, or is it due to the actual treatment? Landman and Dawes (1982) concluded that while initiating *any* treatment causes a small improvement in most people, actually receiving therapy leads to a much greater improvement. So the effects of therapy are due to more than the mere belief by clients that they are going to get better.

## Effectiveness of Various Forms of Psychotherapy

We have seen that researchers generally agree that psychotherapy is usually effective. This raises a second question: Is any particular form of psychotherapy more effective than the others? Is behavior therapy, for example, more effective than insight therapy? In general, the answer seems to be "not much." Several reviewers have concluded that there are few major differences in the effectiveness of various forms of therapy (Garfield, 1983; Michelson, 1985; M.L. Smith, Glass, & Miller, 1980). Most of the benefit of treatment seems to come from being in *some* kind of therapy, regardless of the particular type. However, this conclusion needs to be interpreted in the light of two cautions.

First, several reviewers have noted that when differences are found among therapies, they almost always favor cognitive or behavior therapies over insight therapies (Eysenck, 1985; Piroleau, Murdock, & Brody, 1983; B.A. Shapiro, 1985). Second, different therapies are not so different in actual practice as in theory (e.g., Sloane et al., 1975). Most insight-oriented therapists are warm and understanding during treatment, and they will offer direct suggestions. Most behavior therapists also are empathic, and although they focus more on the present than the past, they, too, offer interpretations. So, in practice, the differences in therapies are sharply reduced.

Second, as we saw at the beginning of the chapter, some kinds of psychotherapy seem to be particularly appropriate for certain people and problems. Insight therapy, for example, seems to be best suited to people seeking profound self-understanding, relief of inner conflict and anxiety, or better relationships with others. Behavior therapy is probably most appropriate for treating specific anxieties or other well-defined behavioral problem such as sexual dysfunctions. Cognitive therapies have been shown to be effective treatments for depression (Elkin et al., 1989; L.A. Robinson, Berman, & Neimeyer, 1990) and seem to be promising treatments for anxiety disorders as well. The race, culture, ethnic background, and gender of both client and therapist can also influence the effectiveness of therapy.

Clearly, the trend in psychotherapy is toward **eclecticism**—that is, toward a recognition of the value of a broad treatment package rather than commitment to a single form of therapy. Although the eclectic model doesn't guarantee greater effectiveness—unless carefully thought out, it can result in an inconsistent hodgepodge of concepts and techniques that merely confuses clients—the majority of therapists now claim to use an eclectic approach. Eclectic psychologists rely heavily on scientific research to help determine the best treatment for a particular problem.

# BIOLOGICAL TREATMENTS

**Biological treatments** Group of approaches, including medication, electroconvulsive therapy, and psychosurgery, that are sometimes used to treat psychological disorders in conjunction with, or instead of, psychotherapy.

**Antipsychotic drugs** Drugs used to treat very severe psychological disorders, particularly schizophrenia.

**Biological treatments**—a group of approaches including medication, electroconvulsive therapy, and psychosurgery—may be used to treat psychological disorders in addition to, or instead of, psychotherapy. Patients and/or therapists select biological treatments for several reasons. First, therapists sometimes find that they cannot help clients with any of the therapies we have described because the clients are extremely agitated, disoriented, or totally unresponsive to psychotherapy. In these cases, therapists may decide to use some kind of biological treatment to change clients' behavior so they can benefit from psychotherapy. Second, biological treatment is virtually always used for disorders that have a strong biological component. Schizophrenia and bipolar disorder, for example, cannot be effectively treated with psychotherapy, but often do respond to medication. For other disorders like depression, psychotherapy can be effective, but the patient may prefer to take medication because it costs less, is more convenient, and allows them to avoid the stigma of seeing a psychotherapist. Third, biological treatment is often used for clients who are dangerous to themselves and to others, especially if they are residing in institutions where there are only a few therapists for many patients.

Three points deserve mention before we go on. First, psychiatrists (who are physicians) currently are the only mental-health professionals licensed to offer biological treatments. Second, in many cases where biological treatments are used, psychotherapy is also recommended. For example, family therapy alone does little to alter the symptoms of schizophrenia, but when it is used in addition to medicating the patient, the combined treatment greatly reduces the need for hospitalization (Kavanagh, 1992). Third, in recent years, scientists have developed many new medications to treat psychological disorders, and there are many ways of combining biological treatments with psychotherapy. We can only highlight a few of the most widely used biological treatments in this chapter.

## Drug Therapies

Medication is frequently and effectively used to treat a number of different psychological problems (see Table 13-1). In fact, Prozac, a drug used to treat depression, is today the best-selling of all medications—including all drugs used to treat *physical* disorders (like antibiotics).

**5.** When are drugs used to treat mental illness? Which drugs are effective for which disorders?

Two major reasons for the widespread use of drug therapy are the recent development of several effective drugs and the fact that drug therapies cost less than psychotherapy. But critics have suggested there is another reason for the widespread use of drug therapy: our society's "pill mentality" (take a medicine to fix any problem). The medications used to treat psychological disorders are often prescribed by psychiatrists, but more commonly they are prescribed by primary-care physicians such as family practitioners, pediatricians, and gynecologists.

ANTIPSYCHOTIC DRUGS Before the mid-1950s, drugs were not used widely in therapy for psychological disorders because the only available sedatives induced sleep as well as calm. Then the major tranquilizers *reserpine* and the *phenothiazines* were introduced. In addition to alleviating anxiety and aggressive behavior, both drugs reduce psychotic symptoms, such as hallucinations and delusions. Thus they are called **antipsychotic drugs**. Antipsychotic drugs are used primarily in very severe psychological disorders, particularly schizophrenia. They are very effective for treating the "positive symptoms" (like hallucinations) of this incapacitating disorder, but they are less effective with the "negative symptoms" (like social withdrawal).

**TABLE 13-1 Major Types of Psychoactive Medications**

| THERAPEUTIC USE | CHEMICAL STRUCTURE* | TRADE NAME* |
|---|---|---|
| Antipsychotics | Phenothiazines | Thorazine |
| Antidepressants | Tricyclics<br>MAO inhibitors<br>SSRIs | Elavil<br>Nardil<br>Prozac |
| Psychostimulants | Amphetamines<br>Other | Dexedrine<br>Ritalin |
| Antimanic | (not applicable) | Tegretol |
| Antianxiety | Benzodiazepines | Valium |
| Sedatives | Barbiturates | |
| Antipanic | Tricyclics | Tofranil |
| Antiobsessional | Tricyclics | Anafranil |

*The chemical structures and especially the trade names listed in this table are often just one example of the many kinds of medications available for the specific therapeutic use.

*Source*: Klerman et al., 1994.

Lionel Aldridge is a former professional football player who developed schizophrenia. His disorder is now in remission, thanks largely to the use of antipsychotic medications.

How do antipsychotic drugs work? Research with animals indicates that they block dopamine receptors in the brain. Dopamine, you will recall, is a neurotransmitter, and the research on antipsychotic drugs is one of the most important pieces of evidence supporting the hypothesis that schizophrenia is linked in some way to an excess of this neurotransmitter (see Chapter 12). In fact, it has been shown that the effectiveness of antipsychotic medications is directly proportional to their ability to block dopamine receptors (Oltmanns & Emery, 1995).

As the following case study shows, the antipsychotics can sometimes have dramatic effects (Grinspoon, Ewalt, & Shader, 1972):

> Ms. W. was a 19-year-old, white, married woman who was admitted to the treatment unit as a result of gradually increasing agitation and hallucinations over a three-month period. Her symptoms had markedly intensified during the four days prior to admission. . . . She had had a deprived childhood, but had managed to function reasonably well up to the point of her breakdown.
>
> At the outset of her hospitalization, Ms. W. continued to have auditory and visual hallucinations and appeared frightened, angry, and confused. . . . Her condition continued to deteriorate for more than two weeks, at which point medication was begun. . . .
>
> She responded [to thioridazine (Mellaril)] quite dramatically during the first week of treatment. Her behavior became, for the most part, quiet and appropriate, and she made some attempts at socialization. She continued to improve, but by the fourth week of treatment began to show signs of mild depression. Her medication was increased, and she resumed her favorable course. By the sixth week she was dealing with various reality issues in her life in a reasonably effective manner, and by the ninth week she was spending considerable time at home, returning to the hospital in a pleasant and cheerful mood. She was

discharged exactly 100 days after her admission, being then completely free of symptoms.

Although their benefits can be dramatic, antipsychotic drugs also produce a number of undesirable side effects (Van Putten et al., 1981). Blurred vision and constipation are among the common complaints, as are temporary neurological impairments such as muscular rigidity or tremors. A very serious potential side effect is *tardive dyskinesia*, a permanent disturbance of motor control, particularly in the muscles of the face (e.g., uncontrollable smacking of the lips), which can only be partially alleviated with other drugs. The risk of tardive dyskinesia increases with the length of time antipsychotics are taken, which leads to another important point. Antipsychotic drugs do not cure schizophrenia; they only alleviate the symptoms while the patient is taking the drug. This means that most patients with schizophrenia must take antipsychotics for years and years—perhaps for the rest of their lives (Oltmanns & Emery, 1995).

Another problem is that while antipsychotic drugs allow many schizophrenic patients to leave the hospital, the drugs by themselves are of little value in treating the social incapacity and other difficulties these people encounter when trying to adjust to life outside the institution. And since many discharged patients fail to take their medications, relapse is common. (The relapse rate can be reduced if drug therapy is effectively combined with psychotherapy.)

**ANTIDEPRESSANT DRUGS** A second group of drugs is used to combat depression. Until the end of the 1980s, there were only two main types of antidepressant drugs: *monoamine oxidase inhibitors (MAO inhibitors)* and *tricyclics* (named from their chemical properties). Both drugs are thought to work by increasing the concentration of the neurotransmitters serotonin and norepinephrine in the brain (P.A. Berger, 1978). Both are effective for most patients with serious depression, but both produce a number of serious and troublesome side effects. The MAO inhibitors require careful dietary restriction, since they can be lethal in combination with some foods. The tricyclics often cause blurred vision, dry mouth, dizziness, low blood pressure, constipation, and other problems. Because of the seriousness of these side effects, the search has continued for better antidepressant drugs.

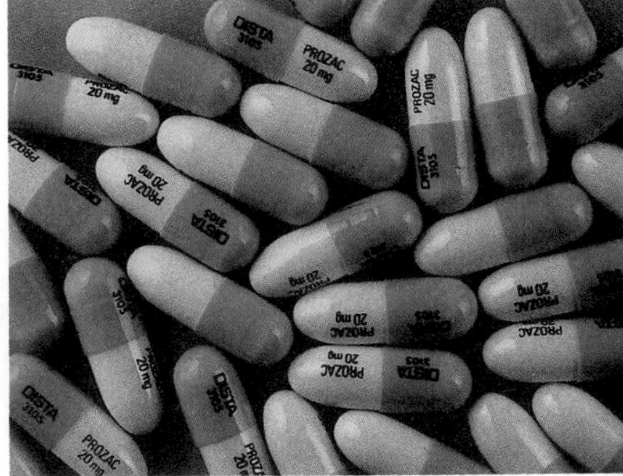

The antidepressant drug Prozac is now the best-selling medication in the United States.

In 1988, Prozac came onto the market. This drug works by reducing the uptake of serotonin in the nervous system, thus increasing the amount of serotonin active in the brain at any given moment. Prozac has fewer side effects than MAO inhibitors or tricyclics, and has been heralded in the popular media as a "wonder drug" for the treatment for depression. There was an early backlash against the medication: Some reports attributed dramatic suicidal or violent actions in people on Prozac, but those stories have since been discredited (Thompson, 1993).

A more pressing question is "How effective is Prozac?" As we have noted, Prozac is now the best selling of all medications, and its widespread use is considered testimony to its effectiveness in alleviating depression. We must view this development with some caution, however. Prozac undoubtedly has helped many depressed people, but often because of its placebo effect—that is, Prozac frequently works because people believe it will work. This fact underscores the very important point that the success of an antidepressant medication does not mean that depression is caused by a "chemical imbalance in the brain." Aspirin relieves headaches, but this does not mean that headaches are caused by a lack of the ingredients in aspirin. Although antidepressants clearly have an important role in the treatment of depression, some therapists are concerned that too many people are trying to solve their emotional or life problems with a pill rather than through their own efforts.

**Electroconvulsive therapy (ECT)** Biological therapy in which a mild electrical current is passed through the brain for a short period, often producing convulsions and temporary coma; used to treat severe, prolonged depression.

LITHIUM Bipolar disorder or manic depression is frequently treated with lithium carbonate. Lithium is not a drug but a naturally occurring salt that helps level out the wild and unpredictable mood swings of manic depression. Although it is effective in approximately 75 percent of cases, lithium is often prescribed along with antidepressants because it is slow to take effect. We do not know exactly how lithium works, but it appears to affect the levels of serotonin and epinephrine in the brain (Oltmanns & Emery, 1995).

OTHER MEDICATIONS There are several medications that can be used to alleviate the symptoms of various psychological problems (see Table 13-1). *Psychostimulants* heighten alertness and arousal. They are also commonly used to treat children with attention-deficit hyperactivity disorder; strangely, in these cases, they have a calming rather than a stimulating effect. As with the antidepressants, some professionals worry that the psychostimulants are being overused. *Antianxiety medications* (for example, Valium) quickly produce a sense of calm and mild euphoria; they are often used to reduce general tension and anxiety, though their addictive potential limits their current use. *Sedatives* produce both calm and drowsiness; they are used to treat agitation or to induce sleep. These drugs, too, also can become addictive. Finally, recent evidence indicates that certain types of antidepressant medications are effective in reducing episodes of panic and alleviating obsessive-compulsive symptoms (Klerman et al., 1994).

## Electroconvulsive Therapy

6. Is electroconvulsive therapy (ECT) still used to treat patients with mental illness?

**Electroconvulsive therapy (ECT)** is most often used for cases of prolonged and severe depression that do not respond to other forms of therapy. The technique of ECT remained largely unchanged for many years: One electrode was placed on each side of the patient's head, and a mild current was turned on for a very short time (about 1.5 seconds). The electrical current passed from one side of the patient's brain to the other, producing a brief convulsion, followed by a temporary loss of consciousness. Muscle relaxants administered in advance prevented dangerously violent contractions. When patients awoke several minutes later, they normally had amnesia for the period immediately before the procedure and remained confused for the next hour or so. With repeated treatments, people often became disoriented, but this condition usually cleared after treatment concluded. Treatment normally consisted of ten or fewer sessions of ECT.

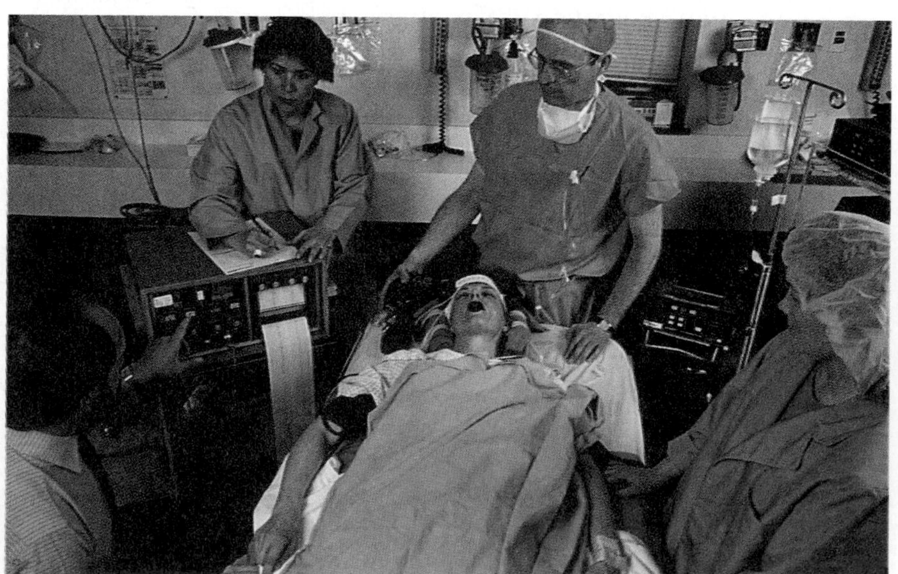

Although no one knows precisely why *electroconvulsive therapy* works, it has been successful in treating cases of severe, prolonged depression.

**"Are biological treatments like psychosurgery and ECT ever justified?"**

In Chapter 12, we discussed the physiological and biological components of abnormal behavior. For example, it is now believed that genetic factors play an important role in depression, anxiety, and schizophrenia, and that some cases of depression and schizophrenia can be traced to biochemical disturbances in the nervous system.

Given the biological basis of certain mental disorders, therapists sometimes resort to biological interventions like psychosurgery and electroconvulsive therapy (ECT) to treat them. Do you think such interventions are ever valid—for example, as an alternative to the death penalty for people who have committed serious crimes? What are the goals of biological treatment? What are the alternatives to using these interventions? To not using these interventions? After you have thought about these questions, take a few minutes to examine the opinions of some other students, which appear below.

• • • • • • •

**BOB: I'm sure that psychosurgery wouldn't end with criminals. It could become like plastic surgery. If people thought that they were a bit too mean to people, they could go to the doctor, and POOF! become the ultimate humanitarian.**

**JOEL: Wouldn't it be better if we POOFED criminals and put them back in society than just locked them up in overcrowded jails with revolving doors?**

**LISA: How do we know that if we remove a portion of the brain with "bad" emotional traits we are not removing any positive emotions traits with it?**

**BILL: What about giving these people [those facing the death penalty] a choice? Say techniques were perfected—if we leave the choice to them, and it's their own risk, it no longer becomes an ethical question for the rest of us. Personally, having my brain operated upon scares me more than the thought of a quick death.**

**ANDRE: I see no real difference between the death penalty and surgery. In both cases, a person dies. One dies physically, but in surgery, you come out a different person, which in a sense is like dying and being reborn.**

**AMY: I suppose electrical stimulation would be warranted if it were some sort of medical treatment, like a new method for treating epilepsy. I don't think criminals should be forced to undergo psychosurgery.**

**JOEL: If serious repeat offenders can be removed from the system by brain transformations, by all means implement it.**

**PAT: Which is more cruel—to be trapped in a body that has lost some small element of free will or to be trapped in a metal cage where a man is treated like a beast?**

**KEISHA: Each person's body is his own, and no government has the right to tamper with it.**

**ETHAN: Perhaps in the pain and suffering of jail these people will actually realize they were WRONG. A distinction they would be unable to make after the surgery.**

**ANDRE: I guess from my research I learned that some people are unchangeable with normal therapy or counseling, so I guess I would go for surgery if it didn't make them a different person.**

**JOEL: The problem with long sentences is that the prisons are overcrowded and that more often than not, because of the overcrowding, criminals "serve" vastly reduced sentences for their crimes. Since we have neglected to eliminate socioeconomic reasons for crime, at least we can utilize psychosurgery to remove the problem repeat offenders from the loop.**

**BILL: Until we understand the root causes of crime, I do not think we should surgically alter someone until we know that it is a genetic rather than a behavioral problem. Behavior-environment problems—even though they may be deep-seated—can be changed.**

**MELISSA: Who would decide what kind of criminals would warrant this kind of "treatment"? Would it be reserved for murders? Child molesters? Rapists? I see great potential for society to use this surgery to turn out people who are close to the social norm.**

**CARVER: All psychosurgery might do is change motivation. As such, it would be similar to psychotherapy.**

**KEISHA: There is no such thing as a perfect society, and psychosurgery provides a "falsely" perfect solution to societal problems.**

• • • • • • •

Now that you've been exposed to other students' views, you might want to reconsider your own views. Do you think psychosurgery is ever warranted? If so, under what circumstances? Would you give permission for psychosurgery to be performed on yourself or anyone else in your family? Why or why not? Do you think psychologists should condemn psychosurgery or remain neutral on this issue?

Recently, an important modification was made to traditional ECT. In this new procedure, called *unilateral ECT*, the electrical current is passed through only one side of the brain. Evidence strongly suggests that unilateral ECT produces fewer side effects, such as memory impairment and confusion, than the traditional method, but is just as effective (Daniel & Crovitz, 1983). In another modification of the traditional method, some therapists use less powerful electric currents, which also seems to lessen the severity of side effects, and limit each stimulation to only one-twenty-fifth of a second.

No one knows exactly why ECT works, but evidence clearly demonstrates its effectiveness. The treatment is especially likely to be used in severe

## SUMMARY TABLE

### Major Perspectives on Therapy

| Type of Therapy | Cause of Disorder | Goal | Techniques |
|---|---|---|---|
| ***Insight therapies*** | | | |
| *Psychoanalysis* | Unconscious conflicts and motives; repressed problems from childhood. | To bring unconscious thoughts and feelings to consciousness; to gain insight. | Free association, dream analysis, interpretation, transference. |
| *Client - Centered Therapy* | Experiences of conditional positive regard. | To help people become fully functioning by opening them up to all of their experiences. | Regarding clients with unconditional positive regard. |
| *Gestalt Therapy* | Lack of wholeness in the personality. | To get people to "own their feelings" and to awaken to sensory experience in order to become whole. | Active rather than passive talk; empty chair techniques; encounter groups. |
| ***Behavior Therapies*** | Reinforcement for maladaptive behavior. | To learn new and more adaptive behavior patterns. | Classical conditioning (systematic desensitization; extinction, flooding); aversive conditioning; operant conditioning (behavior contracting; token economies); modeling. |
| ***Cognitive Therapies*** | Misconceptions; negative, self-defeating thinking. | To identify erroneous ways of thinking and to correct them. | Rational-emotive therapy (rationally examining negative thought patterns); stress-inoculation therapy (consciously replacing negative thoughts with positive, coping thoughts); Beck's cognitive therapy. |
| ***Group Therapies*** | Personal problems are often interpersonal problems. | To develop insight into one's personality and behavior by interacting with others in the group. | Group interaction and mutual support; family therapy; marital therapy; self-help groups. |
| ***Biological Treatments*** | Physiological imbalance or malfunction. | Eliminate symptoms; prevent recurrence. | Electroconvulsive therapy, drugs, psychosurgery. |

cases of depression in which other methods have failed or where medication cannot work quickly enough. Still, ECT has many critics and its use remains controversial. The procedure often produces memory loss, and it is certainly capable of damaging the brain. For these reasons, ECT is best considered a "last resort" treatment when all other methods have failed.

**Psychosurgery** Brain surgery performed to change a person's behavior and emotional state; a biological therapy rarely used today.

## Psychosurgery

**Psychosurgery** refers to brain surgery performed to change a person's behavior and emotional state. This is a drastic step, especially since its effects are difficult to predict. In a *prefrontal lobotomy*, the frontal lobes of the brain are severed from the deeper centers beneath them, on the assumption that in extremely disturbed patients the frontal lobes intensify emotional impulses from the lower brain centers (chiefly the thalamus and hypothalamus). Unfortunately, lobotomies can work with one person and fail completely with another—possibly producing permanent undesirable side effects, such as inability to inhibit impulses or a near-total absence of feeling.

Prefrontal lobotomies are rarely performed today. In fact, no psychosurgical procedures are done nowadays except as desperate measures to control such conditions as intractable psychoses, severe and debilitating disorders that do not respond to any other treatment, and occasionally for pain control in a terminal illness.

# INSTITUTIONALIZATION

For the severely mentally ill, hospitalization has been the treatment of choice in the United States for the past 150 years. The costs of treating mental patients in hospitals are great—about $14 billion a year (Kiesler, 1991).

Several different kinds of hospitals offer care to the mentally ill. General hospitals admit many people suffering from mental disorders, usually for short-term stays until they can be released to their families or to other institutional care. Private hospitals—some nonprofit and some for-profit—offer services to patients with adequate insurance. And for veterans with psychological disorders, there are Veterans Administration hospitals.

When most people think of "mental hospitals," however, it is the large state institutions that come to mind. These public hospitals, many with beds for thousands of patients, were often built in rural areas in the nineteenth century, the idea being that a country setting would calm patients and help restore their mental health. Whatever the good intentions behind the establishment of these hospitals, for most of their history they have not provided adequate care or therapy for their residents. Perpetually underfunded and understaffed, state hospitals have often been little more than warehouses for victims of serious mental illness who were unwanted by their families. Except for new arrivals, who were often intensively treated so they could be quickly discharged, patients received little therapy besides drugs, and most spent their days watching television or staring into space. Under these conditions, many patients became completely apathetic and accepted a permanent "sick role."

The development of effective drug therapies starting in the 1950s led to a number of changes in state hospitals. For one thing, patients who were agitated (engaging in violent behavior, for example) could now be sedated with drugs. Although the drugs often produced lethargy, this was considered an improvement over the use of physical restraints. The second major, and more lasting, result of the new drug therapies was wholesale discharge of patients. As we shall see, however, this movement toward deinstitutionalization created new problems, both for individual patients and for society.

## ALTERNATIVES TO INSTITUTIONALIZATION

**Deinstitutionalization** Policy of treating people with severe psychological disorders in the larger community, or in small residential centers such as halfway houses, rather than in large public hospitals.

### Deinstitutionalization

The advent of antipsychotic drugs in the 1950s created a favorable climate for the policy of **deinstitutionalization**—releasing patients with severe psychological disorders back into the community. The idea of deinstitutionalization was strengthened in 1963, when Congress passed legislation establishing a network of community mental-health centers around the nation. The practice of placing patients in smaller, more humane facilities or returning them under medication to care within the community intensified during the 1960s and 1970s. The many community-based mental-health centers that were starting up at that time seemed to make deinstitutionalization quite feasible. In fact, by 1975, there were 600 regional mental-health centers accounting for 1.6 million cases of outpatient care.

7. Why did a movement toward deinstitutionalization emerge in the 1950s and 1960s? What have been the consequences for mental patients and for society at large?

However, deinstitutionalization has created serious problems in recent years. Discharged patients are often confronted with poorly funded community mental-health centers—or none at all. Many of these ex-patients are poorly prepared to live in the community, and they receive little guidance in coping with the mechanics of daily life. Those who return home can become a burden to their families, especially when they don't get adequate follow-up care. Residential centers, such as halfway houses, vary in quality, but many provide poor medical and psychological care and minimal contact with the outside world. In any case, the dearth of sufficient sheltered housing forces many former patients into nonpsychiatric facilities—often rooming houses located in dirty, unsafe, isolated neighborhoods. They are further burdened by the social stigma that attaches to mental illness; in fact, this may be the largest single obstacle to their rehabilitation (Bassuk & Gerson, 1978). Moreover, although outpatient care is presumed to be a well-established national policy objective in mental health, Medicare, Medicaid, Blue Cross–Blue Shield, and other large insurers typically cover inpatient care completely (or nearly so) but discourage outpatient care by requiring substantial copayments and limiting the number of treatment visits.

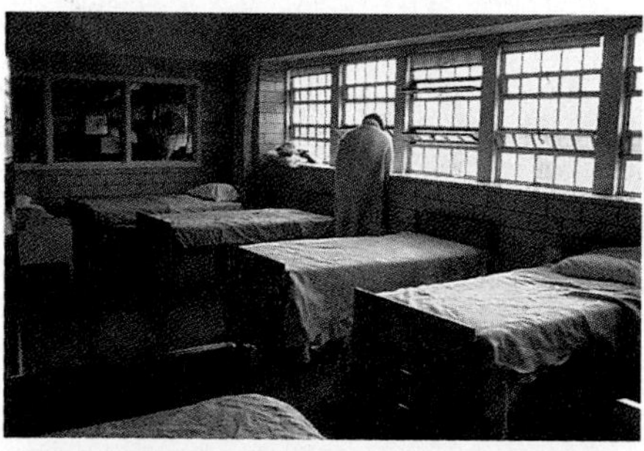

Lacking adequate funding and staff, mental hospitals frequently failed to provide adequate treatment to their residents. Beginning in the 1950s and 1960s, the policy of *deinstitutionalization* led to the release of many individuals. Unfortunately, many of these patients received no follow-up care and ended up living on the streets. Although not all homeless people are mentally ill, estimates suggest that between 10 and 47 percent of homeless persons suffer from some type of mental disorder.

The full effects of the deinstitutionalization of recent decades are not known; few follow-up studies have been done on discharged patients, who are difficult to keep track of for long periods. Still, it is obvious that, though a worthy ideal, deinstitutionalization in practice has had dire effects on patients and society. Many released patients, unable to obtain follow-up care or to find housing, incapable of looking after their own needs, have ended up on the streets. Absent supervision, they have stopped taking the drugs that made their release possible in the first place and have again become psychotic. Every major U.S. city now has a population of homeless mentally ill men and women living in makeshift shelters or sleeping in doorways, bus stations, parks, and other public spaces. Estimates of the percentage of homeless people who are mentally ill run from 10 percent to 47 percent of the total homeless population, which is gauged to be about 600,000 on any given night (I.S. Levine & Rog, 1990). This situation is not only tragic for the mentally ill homeless, who, often incoherent, are easy prey for criminals. It is also contributing to the coarsening of our society, as the general public, finding the constant presence of "crazies" among them unpleasant, has begun to lose compassion for both the homeless and the mentally ill and to pressure public officials to "get them off the street." Most mental-health professionals now agree that many chronically ill patients should not be released to live "in the community" without better planning, more funding, more community support, and ready availability of short-term rehospitalization for those who require it.

## Alternative Forms of Treatment

Deinstitutionalization assumes that institutionalization occurs in the first place. Recently, however, the focus has shifted to forms of treatment that avoid hospitalization altogether. Kiesler (1982a) examined ten controlled studies in which seriously disturbed patients were randomly assigned either to hospitals or to an alternative program. The alternative programs took many forms: patients living at home who were trained to cope with daily activities; a small homelike facility in which staff and residents shared responsibility for residential life; hostels offering therapy and crisis intervention; family crisis therapy; day-care treatment; visits from public-health nurses combined with medication; and intensive outpatient counseling combined with medication. All these alternatives involved daily professional contact and skillful preparation of the community to receive the patients. Even though the hospitals to which some people in these studies were assigned provided very good patient care—probably substantially above average for institutions in the United States—nine out of ten studies found that the outcome was more positive for alternative treatments than for hospitalization. (It is worth noting that hospitalization cost 40 percent more than the alternative programs.) Moreover, the patients who received alternative care were less likely to undergo hospitalization later—which suggests that hospitalizing mental patients is a self-perpetuating process. Many such people "could be treated in alternative settings more effectively and less expensively," Kiesler concludes (1982a, p. 358).

**Prevention** Reducing the incidence of emotional disturbance by eliminating conditions that cause or contribute to mental disorders and substituting conditions that foster mental well-being.

**Primary prevention** Techniques and programs to improve the social environment so that new cases of mental disorders do not develop.

The individuals in this photo are released patients who are producing a newsletter at a community mental-health center. Such centers are an example of an alternative form of treatment.

## Prevention

Yet another approach to mental illness involves efforts to prevent its onset in the first place. **Prevention** refers to reducing the incidence of emotional disturbance in society. This requires finding and eliminating the conditions that cause or contribute to mental disorders and substituting conditions that foster well-being. Prevention takes three forms: primary, secondary, and tertiary.

**Primary prevention** refers to efforts to improve the overall environment so that new cases of mental disorders do not develop. Family planning and genetic counseling are two examples of primary prevention programs. They assist prospective parents to think through such questions as how many children to have and when. They also provide testing to diagnose genetic defects in embryo, and direct parents to treatments, including fetal surgery, that may be able to alleviate defects before the baby is born. Other primary prevention programs aim at increasing personal and social competencies in a wide variety of groups. For example, there are programs designed to help mothers encourage the development of problem-solving skills in their children; other programs have the goal of enhancing competence and adjustment among the elderly. Current campaigns to educate young people about the consequences of drugs are another example of primary prevention.

**Secondary prevention** Programs to identify groups that are at high risk for mental disorders and to detect maladaptive behavior in these groups and treat it promptly.

**Tertiary prevention** Programs to help people adjust to community life after release from a mental hospital.

**Secondary prevention** requires the identification of groups that are at high risk for mental disorders—for example, abused children, people who have recently divorced, and those who have been laid off from their jobs. The main thrust of secondary prevention is *intervention* with such high-risk groups—that is, detecting maladaptive behavior early and treating it promptly. One form of intervention is *crisis intervention*, which includes such programs as suicide hot lines. Another is the establishment of short-term crisis facilities at which a therapist can provide face-to-face counseling and support for high-risk individuals and families.

The main objective of **tertiary prevention** is to help people adjust to community life after they are released from a mental hospital. For example, hospitals often grant passes to encourage patients to leave the institution for short periods of time prior to their release. Other tertiary prevention measures are halfway houses, where patients find support and skills training during the period of transition between hospitalization and full integration into the larger community, and nighttime and outpatient programs that provide supportive therapy while patients live at home and hold down a full-time job. Tertiary prevention also includes efforts to educate the community the patient will reenter.

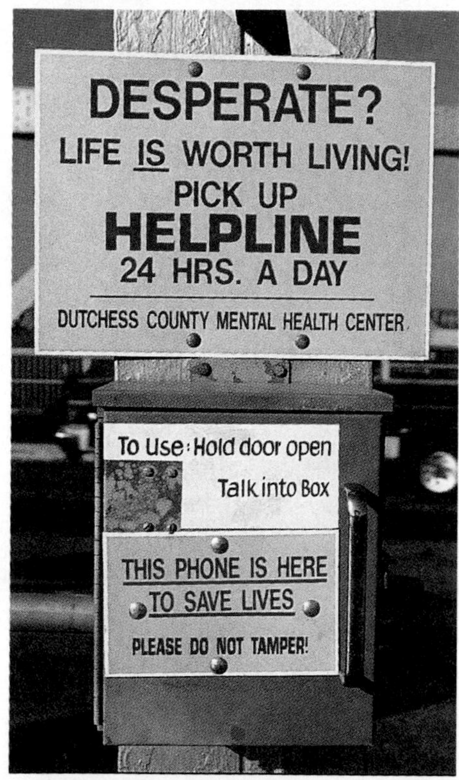


Suicide hot lines and other crisis intervention programs are *secondary prevention* measures designed to serve individuals and groups at high risk for mental disorders.

To illustrate how preventive measures work, let's look at the aftermath of the Hyatt Regency Hotel disaster in Kansas City in 1981. Two aerial walkways in the midst of a crowded "tea dance" suddenly collapsed one Friday evening, killing 111 people and injuring more than 200. The disaster had a major emotional impact on both rescuers and survivors, as well as on hotel and media employees, medical personnel, hotel guests, and families and friends of the dead and injured (Gist & Stolz, 1982). Thus, an estimated 5,000 people were deeply affected by this disaster. Indeed, because virtually all the victims were local, an entire community felt its psychological impact.

By Monday, all the community mental-health centers in the area had organized support group activities. Training was arranged for the professionals and natural caregivers, such as clergy, who would respond to Hyatt-related emotional problems. In addition, a major campaign was undertaken to publicize the availability of psychological services and to "legitimize the expression and acceptance of psychological reactions to the disaster" (Gist & Stolz, 1982, p. 1137). Press releases delivered a consistent message to the community, describing the reactions that were to be expected after such a disaster, emphasizing that they were normal responses that needed to be shared and accepted, and reminding people that help was available.

While this example illustrates the potential of prevention, it also highlights the difficulty and limitations of prevention efforts. How do we know whether such an intervention program had beneficial effects over the long term that would not otherwise have occurred? How realistic are preventive efforts of this sort in other than very unusual, dramatic circumstances? And how can government agencies justify spending taxpayers' dollars on programs that claim to head off problems when we don't know whether those problems would have actually materialized without the programs? These are all questions that will have to be addressed in the years to come.

Other, more specific efforts at prevention, such as genetic counseling, make sense for clear-cut problems like Down syndrome (a well-established cause of mental retardation), but even they are controversial. For example, in cases where definite genetic abnormalities are detected early in pregnancy, selective abortion is an option, but that avenue is fraught with ethical and moral dilemmas. Moreover, as we have seen, disorders such as schizophrenia appear to be caused by a combination of several genes working in combination with certain environmental stresses. Exactly what should a genetic counselor tell a schizophrenic patient about becoming a parent when we know that the patient's risk of having a child with schizophrenia is 10 to 15 percent (compared to 1 percent for the general population)?

# HIGHLIGHTS

## Self-help Groups

This chapter emphasizes the kinds of therapy provided by trained professionals. But there are not enough mental-health professionals to treat everyone who needs or wants therapy (Lieberman, 1986). For example, we saw in Chapter 12 that at any given time, nearly 30 million adult Americans suffer from some form of psychological disorder (Regier et al., 1988); when children and adolescents are counted in, the figure rises to 40–45 million. Only a fraction of those people can be served by mental-health professionals.

Because of this gap in the mental-health system (as well as the high cost of many forms of professional treatment), more and more people faced with life crises are turning to low-cost self-help groups for support and help (Tyler, 1980). By the most conservative estimates, over 6 million adult Americans belong to self-help groups; that number is expected to grow to at least 10 million by the end of the century (M.K. Jacobs & Goodman, 1989).

What are self-help groups and how do they work? Most such groups are small, local gatherings of people who share a common problem or predicament and who provide mutual assistance at a very low cost (M.K. Jacobs & Goodman, 1988; A.H. Katz, 1981). Alcoholics Anonymous is perhaps the best-known self-help group, but there are similar types of groups for people suffering from anorexia, arthritis, cancer, divorce, and drug abuse; for parents whose children have died or are chronically ill or handicapped; for adolescents, retirees, overeaters, compulsive gamblers, AIDS victims, former mental patients, and people suffering from depression or anxiety. In short, there are self-help groups for virtually every conceivable life problem.

Do these self-help groups work? In many cases, apparently they do. Alcoholics Anonymous has developed an enviable reputation for helping people cope with alcoholism. And both the number of self-help groups and their rapid growth in the last two decades testify to their widespread appeal. Research confirms that most group members express strong support for their groups (Riordan & Beggs, 1987), and the few studies that have directly measured the effectiveness of self-help groups have demonstrated that they can indeed be effective (Galanter, 1984; Pisani et al., 1993; Videka-Sherman, 1982).

Though more research is needed before we can say for certain how self-help groups should be used, we already know that such groups play a valuable role in preventing psychological disorders by reaching out to people near the limits of their ability to cope with life stresses. By providing social support—which is particularly important in an age when divorce, geographic mobility, and other factors have reduced the ability of the family to comfort people—and by increasing their members' coping skills through information and advice, self-help groups may significantly reduce the likelihood that people will develop more serious psychological problems and require professional treatment.

To sum up, prevention is clearly cost-effective compared to therapy, but preventive efforts are constrained by several factors: It is very difficult to bring about social change; our scientific knowledge about the causes of abnormal behavior is far from complete; it is very hard to prove conclusively that prevention works; and there are legitimate concerns about forcing people to accept treatments before their problems are manifest.

No more than 2 percent of the money spent on mental health goes for prevention (Albee, 1982). Practically all current efforts are targeted at treatment *after* mental illness develops. As advocates of prevention observe, there are many more disturbed people in this country than could possibly be seen individually by mental-health professionals. Albee (1982), for example, estimates that "the mental health community actually sees fewer than one in five of the seriously disturbed people" (1982, p. 1043). Since treatment programs cannot begin to reach all those in need, it seems only commonsensical to put more effort and funding into preventive programs.

Preventing behavior disorders to begin with rather than treating them after they develop has been the ideal of the mental-health community since 1970 at least, when the final report of the Joint Commission on Mental Health of Children called for a new focus on prevention in mental-health work. Ironically, because preventive programs are usually long-range and indirect, they are often the first mental-health programs to be eliminated in times of economic hardship. Though such cuts are predicated on cost effectiveness, they exemplify the old adage about being penny-wise and pound-foolish.

## GENDER DIFFERENCES IN TREATMENTS

In the previous chapter, we saw that there are some significant gender differences in the prevalence of many psychological disorders. There are also important similarities and differences in the treatment that men and women receive. First, women are more likely than men to be in psychotherapy. In part, this is because women are more willing than men to admit they have psychological problems and need help to solve them. Moreover, psychotherapy is more socially accepted for women than for men (Williams, 1987). Whatever the reasons for the difference, it is estimated that in 1977, 5.6 percent of all females visited ambulatory health-care facilities for treatment of psychological problems, compared to 3.5 percent of males (Russo, 1985). A 1980 national survey arrived at a similar finding: 60 percent of those seeing psychologists and psychiatrists were women (J.H. Williams, 1987).

The treatment given women, in most respects, is the same as that given men. This fact has become somewhat controversial in recent years. Since most therapists are male, and most vocational and rehabilitation programs are male-oriented, some critics of "equal treatment" have claimed that women in therapy are often encouraged to adopt traditional, male-oriented views of what is "normal" or "appropriate"; that male therapists tend to urge women to adapt, adjust, or conform to their surroundings passively; and that male therapists are insufficiently sensitive to the fact that much of the stress women experience comes from trying to cope with a world in which they are *not* treated equally (APA, 1975; J. Asher, 1975). For all these reasons, there has been an increase recently in the number of "feminist therapists," who attempt to help their female clients become aware of the extent to which their problems derive from external controls and inappropriate sex roles, become more conscious of and attentive to their own needs and goals, and develop a sense of pride in their womanhood rather than passively accepting or identifying with the status quo.

We said earlier that in *most* respects women receive the same kinds of treatment men receive. There is, however, one very important difference: Women receive a disproportionate share of drugs prescribed for psychological disorders. Overall, more than 70 percent of all prescriptions written by psychiatrists are for women, although women account for only 58 percent of psychiatrists' office visits (Basow, 1986; Russo, 1985). Similarly, al-though women make up only two-thirds of all cases of depressive disorders, they receive 70 to 80 percent of all antidepression medications. Researchers have not yet identified the reasons for this sex bias in drug prescriptions, but it has become a source of considerable concern. Professionals' willingness to prescribe drugs to women may encourage women to see their problems as having physical causes. Moreover, the readiness to prescribe drugs for women at least partly accounts for women's tendency to abuse prescription drugs more often than men do (Russo, 1985).

Many female clients believe that female therapists are more sensitive to their needs and goals than male therapists are.

As researchers continue to explore these various issues, the American Psychological Association (1978) issued the following guidelines regarding treatment of women in psychotherapy:

1. The conduct of therapy should be free of constrictions based on gender-defined roles, and the options explored between client and practitioner should be free of sex-role stereotypes.

2. Psychologists should recognize the reality, variety, and implications of sex-discriminatory practices in society and should facilitate client examination of options in dealing with such practices.

3. The therapist should be knowledgeable about current empirical findings on sex roles, sexism, and individual differences resulting from the client's gender-defined identity.

4. The theoretical concepts employed by the therapist should be free of sex bias and sex-role stereotypes.

5. The psychologist should demonstrate acceptance of women as equal to men by using language free of derogatory labels.

6. The psychologist should avoid establishing the source of personal problems within the client when they are more properly attributable to situational or cultural factors.

7. The psychologist and a fully informed client mutually should agree on aspects of the therapy relationship such as treatment modality, time factors, and fee arrangements.

8. While the importance of the availability of accurate information to a client's family is recognized, the privilege of communication about diagnosis, prognosis, and progress ultimately resides with the client, not with the therapist.

9. If authoritarian processes are employed as a technique, the therapy should not have the effect of maintaining or reinforcing stereotypic dependency of women.

10. The client's assertive behaviors should be respected.

11. The psychologist whose female client is subjected to violence in the form of physical abuse or rape should recognize and acknowledge that the client is the victim of a crime.

12. The psychologist should recognize and encourage exploration of a woman client's sexuality and should recognize her right to define her own sexual preferences.

13. The psychologist should not have sexual relations with a woman client nor treat her as a sex object.

## CULTURAL DIFFERENCES IN TREATMENTS

Imagine the following scenario: As a Native-American client is interviewed by a psychologist, he stares at the floor. He answers questions politely, but during the entire consultation looks away continually, never meeting the doctor's eye. This body language might lead the psychologist to suppose that the man is depressed or has low self-esteem. Unless, that is, the psychologist knows that in the client's culture not making eye contact is a sign of respect.

This example shows how culture-bound are our ideas of what constitutes normal behavior. When psychotherapist and client come from very different cultures, misunderstandings of speech, body language, and customs are almost inevitable. Even when client and doctor are of the same nationality and speak the same language, there can be striking differences if they belong to different racial and ethnic groups. Some black clients, for example, are wary of confiding in a white therapist—so much so that their wariness is sometimes mistaken for paranoia. For this reason, many black clients seek out a black therapist, a tendency that is becoming more common as larger members of black middle-class people enter therapy (L. Williams, 1989).

One of the challenges for U.S. therapists in recent years has been to treat refugees from foreign countries, many of whom have fled such horrifying circumstances at home that they arrive in the United States exhibiting posttraumatic stress disorder. Not only must these refugees overcome the effects of trauma and flight from it, but they are also faced with the new stresses of settling in a strange country, which often include separation from their families, ignorance of the English language, and inability to practice their traditional occupations. Therapists in such circumstances must learn something of their clients' culture, and often have to conduct interviews through an interpreter—hardly an ideal circumstance for therapy.

In August 1990, the American Psychological Association approved a document titled "Guidelines for Psychological Practice with Ethnic and Culturally Diverse Populations." In it, the APA reminds practitioners that different groups may perform differently on psychological tests, express symptoms in different ways, and relate differently to family members and outsiders than members of the dominant population (Moses, 1990). In 1991, following practitioners' observations that in other countries the "standard" dosages of medication are quite different than in the United States, the National Institutes of Health began a study that attempts to measure the responses of different ethnic groups to several psychiatric medications (DeAngelis, 1991b).

Both these measures should alleviate some of the problems we noted earlier in this section. Ultimately, however, the best solution to the difficulties of serving a multicultural population is to train therapists of many different backgrounds so that members of ethnic, cultural, and racial minorities can choose therapists of their own group if they wish to do so.

## LOOKING FORWARD

Few people doubt the importance of treating—or, preferably, preventing—emotional disorders. Psychological problems create profound personal distress, and disorders like depression, alcohol abuse, and schizophrenia are so disruptive that they are societal as well as personal problems.

Numerous treatments have been developed to treat psychological problems. Unlike many earlier efforts that often offered the same treatment for a variety of disorders, current efforts focus on developing specific treatments for specific problems. A number of these new treatments show promise. Short-term psychodynamic psychotherapies may accomplish more at far less expense than psychoanalysis. Several behavior therapies have proved effective, especially in treating anxiety disorders. Newer cognitive therapies are being developed to treat a variety of problems, and some cognitive approaches are known to be helpful in treating specific disorders like depression. New drugs have also been developed in recent years, and many of these medications can alleviate the symptoms of emotional problems such as obsessive-compulsive disorder, depression, and schizophrenia.

Despite the great promise of a wide array of psychotherapies and medications to treat emotional problems, no one is yet prepared to declare victory in the battle against mental illness. Many existing treatments are only partially effective; others help only a limited number of people. Some disorders have not responded well to any of the treatments developed to date. Future success depends not only on creating new treatments but also on developing a better understanding of the causes of psychological problems. If scientists can uncover the causes of mental disorders, we will be in a much better position to treat and, ultimately, to prevent them.

# SUMMARY

This chapter presents some of the main types of **psychotherapy**, the treatment of personality and behavior disorders by psychological means. It also discusses biological treatments, as well as institutionalization and its alternatives. A theme running through the chapter is the need to develop and use specific treatments for specific types of emotional disorders.

## Insight Therapies

The main goal of **insight therapies** is to give clients a better awareness and understanding of their feelings, motivations, and actions in the hope that this will lead to better adjustment.

### PSYCHOANALYSIS

**Psychoanalysis** is a therapy based on the belief that psychological problems stem from feelings and conflicts repressed during childhood. It is directed toward uncovering what has been repressed through, for example, the process of **free association**, in which the client discloses whatever thoughts or fantasies come to mind without editing or otherwise inhibiting them. In classical psychoanalysis, the patient comes to transfer feelings held toward authority figures from childhood to the analyst in a process known as **transference**. The goal of psychoanalysis is **insight**, or awareness of feelings, memories, and actions from the past that were unconscious but were exerting a strong influence on the patient's present feelings and behavior.

### CLIENT-CENTERED THERAPY

**Client-centered,** or **person-centered, therapy**, founded by Carl Rogers, is built on the idea that therapy should be based on the client's view of the world rather than the therapist's. The therapist's most important task is to provide unconditional positive regard for clients so that they will learn to accept themselves.

### RECENT DEVELOPMENTS

Contemporary insight therapists are more active than traditional psychoanalysts, giving clients direct guidance and feedback. They are also more focused on clients' immediate problems than on their childhood traumas. An especially significant development is the trend to **short-term psychodynamic psychotherapy**, which recognizes that most people can be successfully treated within a time-limited framework.

## Behavior Therapies

**Behavior therapies** are based on the belief that all behavior, normal and abnormal, is learned, and that the objective of therapy is to teach people more satisfying ways of behaving.

### CLASSICAL CONDITIONING

Classical conditioning therapies attempt to evoke a new conditioned response to old stimuli. For example, **systematic desensitization** is a method for gradually reducing irrational fears by imagining—or confronting in real life—increasingly fearful situations while maintaining a relaxed state. Eventually, relaxation replaces fear as a response, perhaps as a result of extinction. Flooding, which subjects the person to feared situations at full intensity and for a prolonged period of time, is a somewhat harsh but highly effective method of desensitization. **Aversive conditioning** has the opposite goal: it conditions a negative rather than a positive response to a stimulus such as the sight or taste of alcohol. Its purpose is to eliminate undesirable behaviors by associating them with pain and discomfort.

### OPERANT CONDITIONING

Operant conditioning techniques work by reinforcing new behaviors and ignoring or punishing old ones. In one such technique called **behavior contracting**, client and therapist agree on certain behavioral goals and on the reinforcement the client will receive upon reaching those goals. In another technique called the **token economy**, tokens are used for positive reinforcement of many different kinds of desired behavior.

### MODELING

In **modeling**, a person learns new behaviors by watching others perform those behaviors. Modeling is a useful technique for teaching any number of behaviors.

## Cognitive Therapies

**Cognitive therapies** aim at changing clients' maladaptive ways of thinking about themselves and the world.

### STRESS-INOCULATION THERAPY

**Stress-inoculation therapy** teaches clients new and positive patterns of self-talk they can use to support themselves through stressful situations.

### RATIONAL-EMOTIVE THERAPY

**Rational-emotive therapy (RET)** is based on the idea that people's emotional problems derive from a set of irrational and self-defeating beliefs they hold about themselves and the world. The therapist vigorously challenges these beliefs until the client comes to see just how irrational and dysfunctional they are.

### BECK'S COGNITIVE THERAPY

Aaron Beck believes that depression results from negative patterns of thought, patterns that are strongly and inappropriately self-critical. His **cognitive therapy** tries to help clients think more positively about themselves and the world.

## Group Therapies

**Group therapies** are based on the idea that psychological problems are at least partly interpersonal problems and are therefore best approached in an interpersonal setting. There are many different kinds of group therapies.

#### FAMILY THERAPY

**Family therapy** is based on the idea that an individual's psychological problems are to some extent family problems. Therefore, the therapist treats the family unit rather than the isolated individual, with the goal of improving communication and empathy among family members and reducing intrafamily conflict.

#### MARITAL THERAPY

**Marital therapy** includes both marriage partners in treatment. It concentrates on improving patterns of communication and interaction between husband and wife. Like family therapy, it attempts to change relationships, not just individuals.

### Effectiveness of Psychotherapy

Most researchers agree that psychotherapy helps about two-thirds of the people treated.

#### EFFECTIVENESS OF VARIOUS FORMS OF PSYCHOTHERAPY

Most kinds of therapy are more effective than no treatment at all, but each kind of therapy works better for some problems and not so well for others. The general trend in psychotherapy is toward **eclecticism**, the use of whatever treatment works best for a particular problem. Increasingly the choice of alternative treatments is guided by evidence on effectiveness.

### Biological Treatments

**Biological treatments**, including medication, electroconvulsive therapy, and psychosurgery, are sometimes used when psychotherapy does not work or when a client has a disorder for which biological treatment is known to be safe and effective. Medication, especially, is very often used in conjunction with psychotherapy.

#### DRUG THERAPIES

Drugs are the most common biological therapies. **Antipsychotic drugs** are valuable in the treatment of schizophrenia; they do not cure the disorder, but they do reduce its symptoms. Side effects can be severe.

Antidepressant drugs alleviate depression, though some have serious side effects. Much of the effectiveness of antidepressants seems to be due to the patient's belief that the drug will work (the placebo effect).

Many other types of medication are used to treat psychological disorders, including antimanic and antianxiety drugs, sedatives, and psychostimultants for children with attention-deficit hyperactivity disorder.

#### ELECTROCONVULSIVE THERAPY

**Electroconvulsive therapy (ECT)** is used for cases of severe depression that do not respond to other treatments. An electric current briefly passed through the brain of the patient produces convulsions and temporary coma.

#### PSYCHOSURGERY

**Psychosurgery** is brain surgery performed to change a person's behavior and emotional state. It is rarely done today, and then only as a last desperate measure on patients with intractable psychoses.

### Institutionalization

Large mental hospitals offer people with severe mental disorders shelter and a degree of care, but there are a number of problems linked with institutionalization, including the tendency of patients to become lethargic and accept a permanent "sick role."

#### ALTERNATIVES TO INSTITUTIONALIZAITON

### Deinstitutionalization

With the advent of antipsychotic drugs in the 1950s, many patients were released from large public hospitals with the idea that they would be cared for in a community setting. But community mental-health centers and other support services proved inadequate to the task. As a result, many former patients stopped taking their medication, became homeless, and ended up suffering from psychosis and living on the street. Thus, although **deinstitutionalization** may have been a good idea in principle, in practice it has not worked out well for many patients or for society.

#### ALTERNATIVE FORMS OF TREATMENT

Alternatives to hospitalization range from living in the family home, with training to cope with daily activities for the mentally ill individual and crisis therapy for the family, to small homelike facilities in which residents and staff share responsibilities. Most alternative treatments involve some medication of the troubled individual and skillful preparation of the family/community. The majority of studies have found more positive outcomes for alternative treatments than for hospitalization.

#### PREVENTION

Prevention refers to efforts to reduce the incidence of mental illness. **Primary prevention** refers to improving the social environment through assistance to parents, education, and family planning. **Secondary prevention** refers to identifying high-risk groups and directing service to them. **Tertiary prevention** refers to helping hospitalized patients return to the community.

### Gender Differences in Treatments

Women are more likely than men to be in psychotherapy; they are also more likely to be given psychoactive medication. Since in traditional therapy, women are often expected to conform to gender stereotypes in order to be pronounced "well," many women have turned to "feminist therapists." The American Psychological Association has issued guidelines to ensure that women receive treatment that is not tied to traditional ideas about appropriate behavior for the sexes.

### Cultural Differences in Treatments

When client and therapist come from different cultural backgrounds or belong to different racial or ethnic groups, misunderstandings can arise in therapy. The APA has issued guidelines to help psychologists deal more effectively with our ethnically and culturally diverse population.

# REVIEW QUESTIONS

## MULTIPLE CHOICE

1. Which of the following is the goal of working through problems in psychoanalysis?
   a. free association
   b. positive transference
   c. countertransference
   d. insight

2. Match the terms at left with the appropriate descriptions at right:

| | |
|---|---|
| ____ Psychoanalysis | a. Aimed at teaching clients to stop misinterpreting events and to see themselves more rationally. |
| ____ Client-centered therapy | b. Based on the idea that anxiety stems from repressed problems from childhood. |
| ____ Cognitive behavior therapy | c. Goal is to help clients become more fully functioning. |
| ____ Rational-emotive therapy | d. Seeks to relieve clients of their misconceptions about themselves and their relationship to their environment. |

3. Rogerian therapists show that they value and accept their clients by providing ______ ______ regard.

4. In contrast with ______ therapies, which seek to increase clients' self-awareness, ______ therapies try to teach people more appropriate ways of acting.

5. A client begins therapy to get rid of an irrational fear of elevators. A technique that the therapist is likely to employ is:
   a. desensitization
   b. behavior contracting

6. The behavior therapy known as ______ ______ discourages undesired behaviors by associating them with pain and discomfort.

7. Family therapists concentrate on changing the needs and personalities of individual family members. T / F

8. Behavior therapy has generally been found to be more effective than insight therapy for most types of problems. T / F

9. Drugs that help to control schizophrenia are called:
   a. barbiturates
   b. tricyclics
   c. lithium
   d. antipsychotics

10. The practice of treating severely mentally ill people in large, state-run facilities is known as ______.

11. Mentally ill people who receive alternative care are less likely to undergo hospitalization later on. T / F

12. The establishment of halfway houses and similar facilities within the community is an example of the movement toward ______ .

13. Crisis intervention and hot lines are two examples of ______ , that is, coping with mental illness before it occurs.

## CRITICAL THINKING AND APPLICATIONS

14. What is the role of insight in traditional psychoanalysis?

15. What are some of the major differences between insight and behavior therapies in the treatment of psychological disorders?

16. What are some of the major differences between behavior and cognitive therapies?

17. Why is it wrong to conclude that depression is caused by a "chemical imbalance in the brain" when antidepressant drugs are known to be effective?

*(Answers to the Review Questions can be found in the back of the text.)*

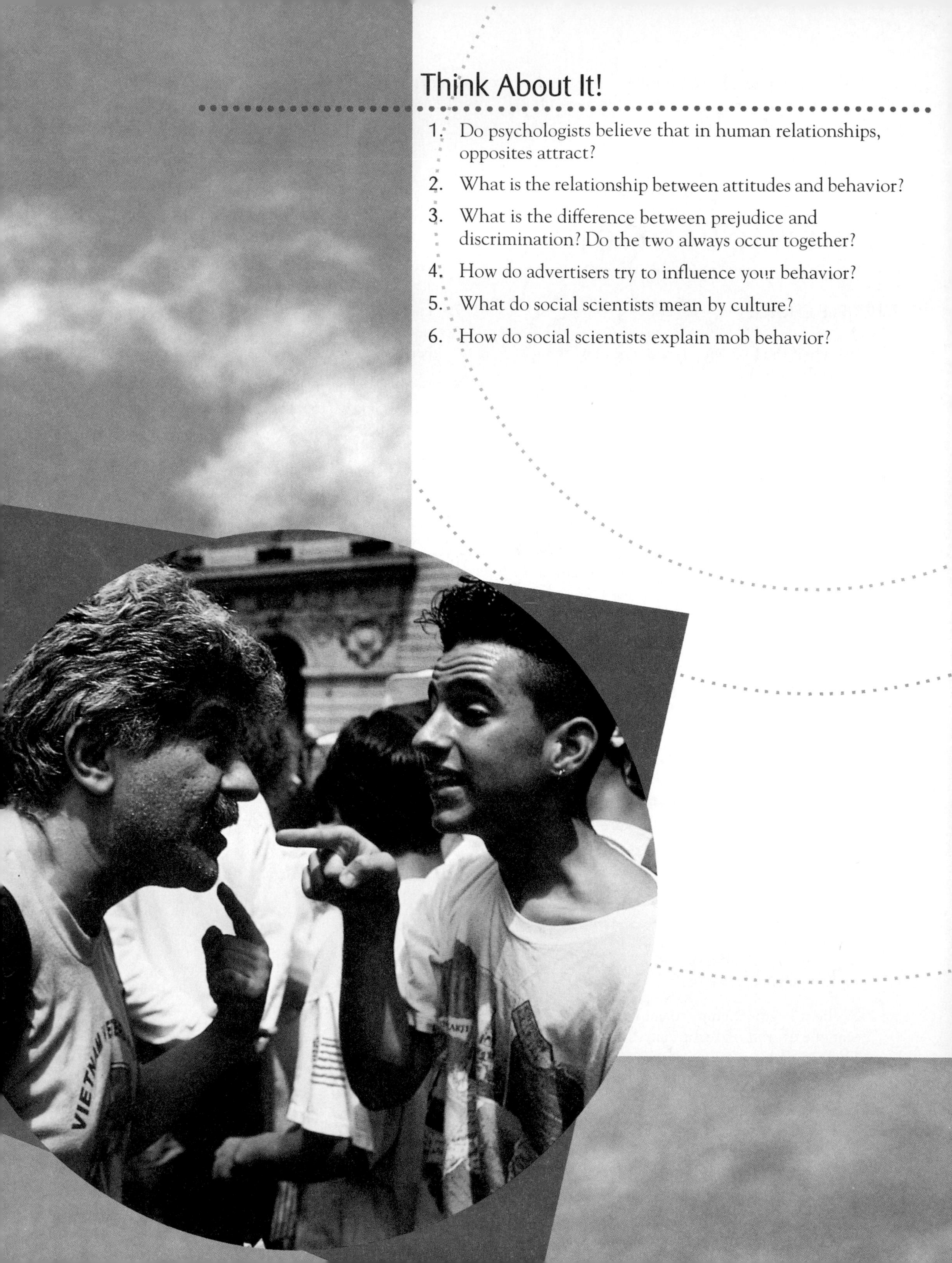

## Think About It!

1. Do psychologists believe that in human relationships, opposites attract?
2. What is the relationship between attitudes and behavior?
3. What is the difference between prejudice and discrimination? Do the two always occur together?
4. How do advertisers try to influence your behavior?
5. What do social scientists mean by culture?
6. How do social scientists explain mob behavior?

# SOCIAL PSYCHOLOGY

# 14

## Overview

**Social psychology** Scientific study of the ways in which the thoughts, feelings, and behaviors of one individual are influenced by the real, imagined, or inferred behavior or characteristics of other people.

**We all spend much of our time alone thinking about our relationships with other people. Why do we like one person and dislike another? What underlie's other people's behaviors as well as our own? Why do we hold particular attitudes and how do our views compare to those of the people around us? We work in groups to solve problems, and we join groups to meet other people and make friends. We hear about the actions of organizations and political parties, and we wonder how—or whether—they will affect our society or the world.**

Social psychologists address the same questions, but they do so with more systematic methods than we use at home in our armchairs. **Social psychology** is the scientific study of the ways in which the thoughts, feelings, and behaviors of one individual are influenced by the real, imagined, or inferred behavior or characteristics of other people.

We begin this chapter by exploring how people form impressions of and make judgments about one another, as well as the factors that influence attraction. Next we consider the ways in which people's attitudes and behaviors are shaped and changed by others. Then our discussion shifts to relationships among people in small groups and large organizations.

## SOCIAL COGNITION

When we are slated to meet someone for the first time, we often try to find out something about that person so we can adjust our expectations and behavior accordingly. Unfortunately, such information is often difficult to come by, so we are forced to form our first impressions of people based on only scanty evidence.

### Impression Formation

How do we form our first impressions of people? What external cues do we use? And how accurate are these first impressions?

**SCHEMATA** When we meet someone for the first time, we notice a number of things about that person—clothes, gestures, manner of speaking, tone of voice, firmness of handshake, and so on. We then draw on these cues to fit the person into ready-made *categories*. No matter how little information we have or how contradictory it is, no matter how many times in the past our initial impressions of people have been wrong, we still classify and categorize people on first encountering them. Associated with each category is a *schema*, which, as we saw in the chapter on memory, is a set of beliefs or expectations about something (in this case, people) that is based on past experience and that is presumed to apply to all the individuals in that category. For example, if a woman is wearing a white coat and has a stethoscope around her neck, we might reasonably categorize her as a doctor and as a result conclude that she is a highly trained professional, knowledgeable about diseases and their cures, qualified to prescribe drugs, and so on. These various conclusions follow from most people's schemata of *doctor*.

Schemata serve a number of important functions. For one thing, they allow us to make inferences about other people. We assume, for example, that a friendly person is likely to be good-natured, to accept a social invitation from us, or to do us a small favor. We may not know these things for sure, but our schema for *friendly person* leads us to make this inference.

As we also saw in the chapter on memory, schemata play a crucial role in how we interpret and remember information. For example, in one study, some subjects were told that they would be receiving information about friendly, sociable men, while other subjects were informed that they would be learning about intellectual men. Both groups were then given the same information about a set of 50 men and asked to say how many of the men were friendly and how many were intellectual. The subjects who had expected to hear about friendly men dramatically overestimated the number of friendly men in the set, and those who had expected to hear about intellectual men vastly overestimated the number of intellectual men in the set. Moreover, each group of subjects forgot many of the details they received about the men that were inconsistent with their expectations (Rothbart, Evans, & Fulero, 1979). In short, the subjects tended to hear and remember what they expected to.

**Primacy effect** The phenomenon that early information about someone weighs more heavily than later information in influencing one's impression of that person.

Schemata can also lure us into "remembering" things about people that we never actually observed. For most of us, shyness, quietness, and preoccupation with one's own thoughts are traits associated with the schema *introvert*. If we notice that Melissa is shy, we are likely to categorize her as an introvert. Later, we may "remember" that she also seemed preoccupied with her own thoughts. In other words, thinking of Melissa as an introvert saves us the trouble of taking into account all the subtle shadings of her personality. But this kind of thinking can easily lead to errors if we attribute to Melissa qualities that belong to the schema but not to her.

When we meet someone for the first time, we may notice a number of things about that person and then use these cues to fit the person into a ready-made category that is associated with a *schema*, a set of beliefs or expectations. How would you categorize the individual in this photo? Would you have guessed that he is Richard Feynman, one of the premier physicists of the twentieth century?

Because other people are so important to us as actual or potential friends, colleagues, and intimate partners, we measure them against our schemata from the moment we meet them. Drawing on our general schemata, we quickly form a first impression. Over time, as we continue to interact with them, we add new information about them to our mental files. However, our later experiences with people generally do not influence us nearly so much as our earliest impressions. The first research on this **primacy effect** was conducted by Solomon Asch (1946). Asch gave subjects one of two lists describing a target person's traits. One list began with positive traits (e.g., "industrious") and ended with negative descriptors (e.g., "stubborn"). The other list presented the same traits in reverse sequence. Subjects who read the positive-to-negative sequence formed more favorable impressions of the people described than did those who read the same list in negative-to-positive sequence. Asch concluded that early impressions of a person create the context for evaluating later information about that person. Thus, if you already like a new acquaintance, you may excuse a flaw or vice you discover later on. Conversely, if someone has made an early bad impression on you, you may refuse to believe subsequent evidence of that person's good qualities.

A more recent explanation of the primacy effect was offered by Susan Fiske and Shelley Taylor (1984), who argued that human thinkers are "cognitive misers." Instead of exerting ourselves to interpret every detail we learn about a person, we are stingy with our mental efforts. Once we have formed an impression about someone, we cease our investigations,

**Self-fulfilling prophecy** Process by which a person's expectation about another elicits behavior from the second person that confirms the expectation.

**Stereotype** Set of characteristics presumed to be shared by all members of a social category.

choosing to believe what we already know—our first impressions—even if we derived them by jumping to conclusions or through prejudice.

If people are specifically warned to beware of first impressions, or if they are encouraged to interpret information about others slowly and carefully, the primacy effect can be weakened or even nullified (Luchins, 1957; Stewart, 1965). Generally speaking, however, the first impression is the lasting impression, and it can affect our behavior even when it is inaccurate. In one study, Mark Snyder and William Swann (1978) asked pairs of subjects to play a competitive game. They told one member of each pair that his or her partner was either hostile or friendly. Players who were led to believe their partner was hostile behaved differently toward the partner than players led to believe their partner was friendly. In turn, those treated as hostile actually began to display hostility. In fact, these people continued to show hostility later on, when they were paired with new players who had no expectations about them. The expectation of hostility it seems, produced actual aggressiveness, and this behavior persisted. When we bring about expected behavior in another person in this way, our impression has become a **self-fulfilling prophecy**.

**STEREOTYPES** A **stereotype** is a set of characteristics believed to be shared by all members of a social category. A stereotype is a special kind of schema that is based on almost any distinguishing feature, including sex, race, occupation, physical appearance, place of residence, and membership in a group or organization (R. D. Hansen, 1984). When our first impressions of people are governed by a stereotype, we tend to infer things about them solely on the basis of their social category and to ignore facts about individual traits that are inconsistent with the stereotype. As a result, we may remember things about them selectively or inaccurately, thereby perpetuating our initial stereotype. For example, with a quick glance at almost anyone, you can classify that person as male or female. Once you have so categorized the person, you may rely more on your stereotype of that gender than on your own perceptions during further interactions with the person. One dominant stereotype of women paints them as emotional, excitable, home oriented, and gentle (Spence, Helmreich, & Stapp, 1975). Thus, you may *expect* a woman to have these qualities—and feel disappointed when you find she does not—merely because your impression is based on a simplistic stereotype rather than on reliable information about a particular individual.

Stereotypes can easily become the basis for self-fulfilling prophecies. Snyder, Tanke, and Berscheid (1976) paired college-aged men and women who were strangers to each other and arranged for each pair to talk by phone. Before the call, each male was given a snapshot, presumably of the woman whom he was about to call. In fact, however, the snapshot was a randomly selected photo of either an attractive or an unattractive woman. Attractiveness carries with it a stereotype that includes sociability and social adeptness. The males in the experiment therefore expected attractive partners to display these qualities and the unattractive partners to be unsociable, awkward, and serious. These expectations produced radically different behavior in the men. Those who believed they were talking to an attractive woman were warm, friendly, and animated; in response, the women acted in a friendly, animated way. The other men spoke to their partners in a cold, reserved manner. In response, the women reacted in a cool, distant manner. Thus, the stereotype took on a life of its own as the perceptions of the men determined their behavior, which in turn subtly forced the women to conform to the stereotype.

So far, we have seen how people form impressions of other people and how those impressions affect their subsequent behavior. But social perception goes beyond simple impression formation. We also try to make sense out of people's behavior, to uncover the reasons they act as they do. This is the subject of the next section.

**Attribution theory** Theory that addresses the question of how people make judgments about the causes of behavior.

## Attribution

Suppose you run into a friend at the supermarket. You greet him warmly, but he barely acknowledges you, mumbles "Hi," and walks away. You feel snubbed and try to figure out why he acted like that. Did he behave that way because of something in the situation? Perhaps you said something that offended him; perhaps he was having no luck finding the groceries he wanted; or perhaps someone had just blocked his way by leaving a cart in the middle of an aisle. Or did something within him, some personal trait such as moodiness or arrogance, prompt him to behave that way? Clearly, in social interaction it makes a difference which of these explanations is correct.

**EXPLAINING BEHAVIOR** Social interaction is filled with occasions like this one that invite us to make judgments about the causes of behavior. Especially when something unexpected or unpleasant occurs, we wonder about it and try to understand it. Social psychologists have discovered that we go about this process of assessment in predictable ways. Their findings and the principles derived from them form the basis of **attribution theory**.

An early attribution theorist, Fritz Heider (1958) argued that a simple or "naíve" explanation for a given behavior attributes that behavior to either internal or external causes, but not both. Thus, you might say a classmate's tardiness was caused by his laziness (a personal factor—an internal attribution) *or* by traffic congestion (a situational factor—an external attribution).

How do we decide whether to attribute a given behavior to causes inside or outside a person? According to another influential attributional theorist, Harold Kelley (1967), we rely on three kinds of information about behavior in determining its cause: distinctiveness, consistency, and consensus. For example, if your instructor asks you to stay briefly after class so she can talk with you, you will probably try to figure out what lies behind her request, by asking yourself three questions.

First, how *distinctive* is the instructor's request? Does she often ask other students to stay and talk (low distinctiveness), or is such a request unusual (high distinctiveness)? If she often asks students to speak with her, you will conclude that she has internal reasons for talking with you. But if her request is highly distinctive, you will conclude that something about you, not her, underlies her request.

Second, how *consistent* is the instructor's behavior? Does she regularly (consistently) ask you to stay and talk (high consistency), or is this a first for you (low consistency)? If she has consistently made this request of you before, you will guess that this occasion is like those others. But if her request is inconsistent with past behavior, you will wonder whether some passing event—perhaps something you said in class—motivated her to request a private conference.

Finally, what is the *consensus* of others' similar behavior: Do your other instructors ask you to stay and talk with them (high consensus), or is this instructor unique in making such a request (low consensus)? If it is common for your instructors to ask to speak with you, this instructor's request is probably due to some external factor. But if she is the only instructor ever to ask to speak privately with you, it must be something about this particular person—an internal motive or concern—that accounts for her behavior.

Your answers to these questions about distinctiveness, consistency, and consensus will help you decide what has caused the behavior in question and how best to respond. If you conclude that the instructor has her

**Fundamental attribution error** Tendency of people to overemphasize personal causes for other people's behavior and to overemphasize situational causes for their own behavior.

**Defensive attribution** Tendency to attribute our successes to our own efforts or qualities and our failures to external factors.

**Just-world hypothesis** Attribution error based on the assumption that bad things happen to bad people and good things happen to good people.

own reasons for wanting to speak with you, you may feel mildly curious for the remainder of class, until you can find out what she wants. But if you think external forces—like your own actions—have prompted her request, you may worry about whether you are in trouble and spend the time until class ends nervously preparing your defense!

**Biases** When making an attribution, you are guessing about the true causes of a particular action. Research shows that these guesses are vulnerable to a number of biases. One significant bias is our general tendency to attribute our own actions to situational factors and the behavior of others to internal or personal factors (E. E. Jones & Nisbett, 1972). So while you might think that an unforeseen bump and icy conditions caused your fall as you skied down the ski hill, your companion might be more inclined to attribute your mishap to your inexperience as a skier or to your carelessness or awkwardness on the slopes. The prosecutor in a trial may try to convince the jury that the defendant "did it on purpose and deserves to be blamed," while the defense attorney may respond by pointing out that her client was "a victim of circumstances and shouldn't be blamed." The tendency to place too much emphasis on personal factors when accounting for other people's actions is so common that one psychologist has termed it the **fundamental attribution error** (L. Ross, 1977).

A related bias is called **defensive attribution**. A number of studies have shown that we tend to credit our successes to our personal abilities while chalking up our failures to forces beyond our control (Zuckerman, 1979). For example, students tend to regard exams on which they do well as good indicators of their abilities and exams on which they do poorly as defective indicators (M. H. Davis & Stephan, 1980). By the same token, studies show that when students do well, teachers are more likely to assume responsibility for their performance than when students perform poorly (Arkin, Cooper, & Kolditz, 1980).

Another kind of attribution error arises from the assumption that the world is just: Bad things happen to bad people, and good things happen to good people. This is called the **just-world hypothesis** (M.J. Lerner, 1980). Thus, when misfortune strikes someone, we often jump to the conclusion that the person deserved it rather than giving full weight to situational factors that may have been responsible. Why do we do this? For one thing, it gives us the comforting illusion that such a thing could never happen to us. For example, by reassigning the blame for a terrible crime from a chance event (something that could happen to us) to the victim's own negligence (a trait that *we*, of course, do not share), we delude ourselves into believing that we could never suffer such a misfortune (Chaikin & Darley, 1973). This may explain why, when we hear of a rape or burglary, we may wonder whether the victim somehow "asked for it." Unfortunately, such self-reassurance neither protects us from a similar fate nor makes us sympathetic or fair-minded toward the victim.

## Interpersonal Attraction

So far, we have seen how people form impressions of one another and judge the causes of their own and others' behavior. The next question we address is: When people meet, what determines if they will like each other? This is the subject of much speculation and even mystification, with popular explanations running the gamut from fate to compatible astrological signs. Romantics believe that irresistible forces propel them toward an inevitable meeting with their beloved, but social psychologists take a more hardheaded view of the matter. They have found that attraction and the tendency to like someone else are closely linked to such factors as *proximity*, *physical attractiveness*, *similarity*, *exchange*, and *intimacy*.

**PROXIMITY** **Proximity** is usually the most important factor in determining attraction. The closer two people live to each other, the more likely they are to interact, and the more frequent their interaction, the more they will tend to like each other. Conversely, two people separated by considerable geographic distance are not likely to ever run into each other, and thus have no chance to develop a mutual attraction.

**Proximity** How close two people live to each other.

Festinger, Schachter, and Back (1950) investigated the effects of proximity on friendship in a housing project for married students at MIT. The project consisted of two-story apartment complexes with five apartments to a floor. The researchers found that 44 percent of the residents were most friendly with their next-door neighbors, while only 10 percent said their best friends lived down the hall. An even smaller number were best friends with an upstairs or downstairs neighbor. Similarly, Nahemow and Lawton (1975) discovered that 93 percent of the residents of an inner-city housing project chose their best friends from the same building. The proximity effect has less to do with simple convenience than with the security and comfort we feel with people and things that have become familiar. Familiar people are predictable and safe—thus more likable (R. F. Bornstein, 1989).

Attraction and the tendency to like someone are closely linked to such factors as *proximity, similar interests and attitudes,* and *rewarding behavior.*

**PHYSICAL ATTRACTIVENESS** Physical attractiveness exerts a powerful influence on the conclusions that we reach about a person's character. Attractive people are presumed to be more intelligent, interesting, happy, kind, sensitive, moral, and successful than people who are not perceived as attractive. They are also thought to make better spouses and to be more sexually responsive (J.S. Brigham, 1980; Dion, 1972; Dion, Berscheid, & Walstef, 1972; J. S. Moore, Graziano, & Millar, 1987).

Not only do we tend to credit physically attractive people with a wealth of positive qualities, but we also tend to like them more than we do less attractive people, in part because physical attractiveness itself is generally considered a positive attribute (Baron & Byrne, 1991). Beauty is perceived to be a valuable asset that can be exchanged for other things in social interactions. We may also believe that beauty has a "radiating effect"—that the glow of others' good looks enhances our own public image (Kernis & Wheeler, 1981).

Whatever its origins, our preoccupation with physical attractiveness has material consequences. Attractive people are often more persuasive when they communicate with others. In addition, other people try harder to please good-looking individuals (Sigall, Page, & Brown, 1971). Moreover, teachers tend to be more lenient when it comes to the undesirable behavior of exceptionally attractive children and to have higher expectations about their intelligence and grades. In general, we give good-looking people the benefit of the doubt: If they don't live up to our expectations during the first encounter, we give them a second chance, ask for a second date, or seek further opportunities for interaction. These reactions can eventually give attractive people substantial advantages in life.

This almost universally favorable attitude toward physical attractiveness can become a self-fulfilling prophecy. Physically attractive people may come to think of themselves as good or lovable because they are continually treated as if they are. Conversely, unattractive people may begin to see themselves as bad or unlovable because they have always been regarded that way—even as children (Aronson, 1992).

**SIMILARITY** Similarity of attitudes, interests, values, backgrounds, and beliefs underlie much interpersonal attractiveness (D. M. Buss, 1985; Gonzales et al., 1983). When we know that someone shares

**Exchange** Concept that relationships are based on trading rewards among partners.

our attitudes and interests, we tend to have more positive feelings toward that person (Byrne, 1961); the higher the proportion of attitudes that two people share, the stronger the attraction between them (Byrne & Nelson, 1965). We value similarity because it is important to us to have others agree with our choices and beliefs. By comparing our opinions with those of other people, we clarify our understanding of and reduce our uncertainty about social situations. Finding that others agree with us strengthens our convictions and boosts our self-esteem (Suls & Fletcher, 1983).

Yet, some bases of similarity are clearly more crucial than others. A shared taste for bran muffins is not as consequential for friendship as a common interest in sports or religion. And the true degree of similarity may not be as important as *perceived* similarity (Marsden, 1966). We often assume that we share attitudes with people who attract us in other ways. Some research indicates that marriage may rest in part on the *illusion* of similarity—that is, spouses tend to perceive more similarity in attitudes between themselves and their partners than in fact exists (Byrne & Blaylock, 1963).

**1.** Do psychologists agree that in human relationships, opposites attract?

If similarity is such a critical determinant of attraction, what about the notion that opposites attract? Aren't people sometimes attracted to others who are completely different from them? Extensive research has failed to confirm this notion. In long-term relationships, where attraction plays an especially important role, people overwhelmingly prefer to associate with other people who are similar to them (D. M. Buss, 1985).

In some cases, when people's attraction seems to be founded on their "differentness," research suggests that their critical qualities are not opposites but complements. *Complementary traits* are needs or skills that complete or balance each other (Hendrick & Hendrick, 1992). For example, a person who likes to care for and fuss over others will be most compatible with a mate who enjoys receiving such attention. These people are not really opposites, but their abilities and desires complement each other to their mutual satisfaction. Complementarity almost always occurs between people who already share similar goals and values and are willing to adapt to each other. True opposites are unlikely even to meet each other, much less interact long enough to achieve such compatibility.

**EXCHANGE** According to the *reward theory of attraction*, we tend to like people who make us feel rewarded and appreciated. But the relationship between attraction and rewardingness is subtle and complex. For example, Aronson's (1992) gain-loss theory of attraction suggests that *increases* in rewarding behavior influence attractiveness more than constant rewarding behavior does. Say if you were to meet and talk with a young man at three successive parties, and if during these conversations that person's behavior toward you changed from polite indifference to overt flattery. You would be inclined to like this person more than if he or she had immediately started to praise you during the first conversation and kept up the stream of praise each time you met. The reverse also holds true: We tend to dislike people whose opinion of us changes from good to bad even more than we dislike those who consistently display a low opinion of us from our first encounter with them.

The reward theory of attraction is based on the concept of **exchange**. In social interactions, two people exchange various goods and resources with each other. For example, you may agree to help a friend paint his apartment in exchange for his preparing dinner for you. Every exchange involves both rewards (you get a free dinner, he gets his apartment painted) and costs (you have to paint first, he has to cook you dinner). As long as both parties find their interactions more rewarding than costly, their exchanges will continue (Clore & Byrne, 1974; A. J. Lott & Lott,

1974). People do seem to "keep score" in their interactions, especially in the early stages of relationships (M. S. Clark & Mills, 1979).

Such exchanges work only insofar as they are fair or equitable. A relationship is based on **equity** when what one person "gets out of it" is equal to what the other gets (Walster, Walster, & Berscheid, 1978). When exchanges are consistently unfair, the one who reaps fewer rewards feels cheated and the one who gains is apt to feel guilty. As a result, the pain and discomfort may undermine the attraction that once drew the two people together. People may come to like one another because of uncontrollable circumstances like proximity and physical attractiveness, but a relationship will only develop and be maintained through the deliberate efforts of both partners to be fair to each other.

**Equity** Fairness of exchange achieved when each partner in the relationship receives the same proportion of benefits to investments.

**Intimacy** The quality of genuine closeness and trust achieved in communication with another person.

**Attitude** Relatively stable organization of beliefs, feelings, and behavior tendencies directed toward something or someone—the attitude object.

**INTIMACY** When does liking someone become something more? Social psychologists have found that love depends on several critical processes in addition to interpersonal attraction. The process of intimacy has sparked particular interest among relationship theorists. **Intimacy** is the quality of genuine closeness and trust achieved in communication with another person. When people communicate, they do more than just interact—they share their deep-rooted feelings and ideas. When you are first getting to know someone, you communicate about "safe," superficial topics like the weather, sports, or shared activities. As you get to know each other better over time, your conversation progresses to more personal subjects: your personal experiences, memories, hopes and fears, goals and failures (Altman & Taylor, 1973).

Self-disclosure—revealing personal experiences and opinions that you might conceal from strangers—is essential to all close relationships.

Intimate communication is based on the process of *self-disclosure* (Jourard, 1964). As you talk with friends, you disclose or reveal personal experiences and opinions that you might conceal from strangers. Because self-disclosure is only possible when you trust the listener, you will seek—and usually receive—a reciprocal disclosure to keep the conversation balanced. For example, after telling your roommate about something that embarrassed you, you may expect him or her to reveal a similar episode; you might even ask directly, "Has anything like that ever happened to you?" Such reciprocal intimacy keeps you "even" and makes your relationship more emotionally satisfying (R. J. Burke, Weir, & Harrison, 1976; Hendrick & Hendrick, 1992). The pacing of disclosure is important. If you "jump levels" by revealing too much too soon—or to someone who is not ready to make a reciprocal personal response—the other person will retreat and communication will go no further.

# ATTITUDES

The phrase "I don't like his attitude" is a telling one. People are often told to "change your attitude" or make an "attitude adjustment." What does this mean? Just what are attitudes? How are they formed? How can they be changed?

## The Nature of Attitudes

An **attitude** is a relatively stable organization of beliefs, feelings, and tendencies toward something or someone—the attitude object. An attitude has three major components: *evaluative beliefs* about the object, *feelings* about the object, and *behavior tendencies* toward the object. Beliefs include facts, opinions, and our general knowledge about the object. Feelings encompass love, hate, like, dislike, and similar sentiments. Behavior tendencies refer to our inclinations to act in certain ways toward the ob-

**Self-monitoring** The tendency to observe a situation for cues about how to react.

ject—to approach it, avoid it, and so on. For example, our attitude toward a political candidate includes our beliefs about the candidate's qualifications and positions on crucial issues and our expectations about how the candidate will vote on those issues. We also have feelings about the candidate—like or dislike, trust or mistrust. And because of these beliefs and feelings, we are inclined to behave in certain ways toward the candidate—to vote for or against the candidate, to contribute time or money to the candidate's campaign, to make a point of attending or staying away from rallies for the candidate, and so forth.

As we will see shortly, these three aspects of an attitude are very often consistent with one another. For example, if we have positive feelings toward something, we tend to have positive beliefs about it and to behave positively toward it. This does not mean, however, that our every action will accurately reflect our attitudes. For example, you may buy a particular product not because you already know you will like it but simply because you want to try something new or because someone recommended it. Let's look more closely at the relationship between attitudes and behavior.

2. What is the relationship between attitudes and behavior?

**ATTITUDES AND BEHAVIOR** The attitudes we voice are not always reflected in our behavior and are not always straightforward. In a classic study, LaPiere (1934) traveled through the United States with a Chinese couple in the early 1930s—a time when prejudice against the Chinese was still running high in this country. He discovered that they were refused service at only one of the 250 hotels and restaurants they visited. Six months later, LaPiere sent a questionnaire to each of these establishments and asked if they would serve Chinese people. Most said they would not. LaPiere therefore concluded that attitudes are not reliable predictors of actual behavior. Subsequent research on the relationship between attitudes and behavior has supported LaPiere's conclusion, particularly with respect to behavior in nonlaboratory settings (Hanson, 1980; Wicker, 1969).

But Fishbein and Ajzen (1975) point out that the apparently weak relationship between attitudes and behavior may be due to improper measurement of either attitudes or behavior or both. For example, LaPiere measured attitudes toward Chinese people in general and then used that to predict specific behavior. If LaPiere had asked about attitudes toward the particular Chinese people who traveled with him rather than about Chinese people in general, the correlation between attitudes and behavior might have been higher.

Other researchers have pointed out that behavior is influenced by many factors besides attitudes (Chaiken & Stangor, 1987). For instance, Ajzen and Fishbein (1980) have argued that behavior is closely linked to a person's intentions. Intentions, in turn, are only partly a product of the person's attitudes; they also reflect his or her acceptance of norms, including social pressures to perform or not to perform the behavior.

Personality traits also underlie behavior. Some people consistently match their actions to their attitudes (R. Norman, 1975). Others have a tendency to override their own attitudes in order to behave properly in a given situation. As a result, attitudes do not predict behavior as well among some people as among others (M. Snyder & Tanke, 1976). In particular, people who are high on **self-monitoring** are especially likely to override their attitudes to behave in accordance with others' expectations. Before speaking or acting, high self-monitors observe the situation for cues about how they should react. Then they try to meet those "demands" rather than behave according to their own beliefs or sentiments. By contrast, low self-monitors express and act on their attitudes with great consistency, showing little regard for situational clues or constraints. For example, a high self-monitor who disagrees with the politics of a respected dinner guest may keep her thoughts to herself in an effort to be polite and agreeable, while a low self-monitor who disagrees might challenge the speaker openly, even though doing so might disrupt the social occasion (M. Snyder, 1974).

**Prejudice** An unfair, intolerant, or unfavorable attitude toward a group of people.

**Discrimination** An unfair act or series of acts taken directed toward an entire group of people or individual members of that group.

**ATTITUDE DEVELOPMENT** How do we acquire our attitudes? Where do they come from? Many of our most basic attitudes derive from early, direct personal experience. Children are rewarded with smiles and encouragement when they please their parents, and are punished through disapproval when they displease them. These early experiences give children enduring positive and negative attitudes toward particular objects (Oskamp, 1977). Attitudes are also formed by imitation. Children mimic the behavior of their parents and peers, and thus acquire attitudes even when no one is deliberately trying to influence their beliefs.

But parents are not the only source of attitudes. Teachers, friends, and even famous people are also important in shaping our attitudes. If a young man joins a fraternity, for example, he may model his behavior and attitudes on those of his fraternity brothers. If a young woman idolizes one of her teachers, she may adopt many of the teacher's attitudes toward controversial subjects, even if they run counter to attitudes expressed by her parents or friends.

The mass media, particularly television, also have a great impact on the formation of attitudes in our society. Television bombards us with messages—not merely through its news and entertainment programs but also through commercials: Violence is commonplace in life. . . women are dependent on men . . . without possessions your life is empty, and so on. Hartmann and Husband (1971) have shown that, without experience of their own against which to measure the merit of these messages, children are particularly susceptible to television as an influence on their social attitudes. They found that white children in England who had little contact with nonwhites tended to associate race relations with conflicts and hostility more often than white children who lived in integrated neighborhoods. The first group of children was informed exclusively by TV news reports that focused on the problems caused by integration.

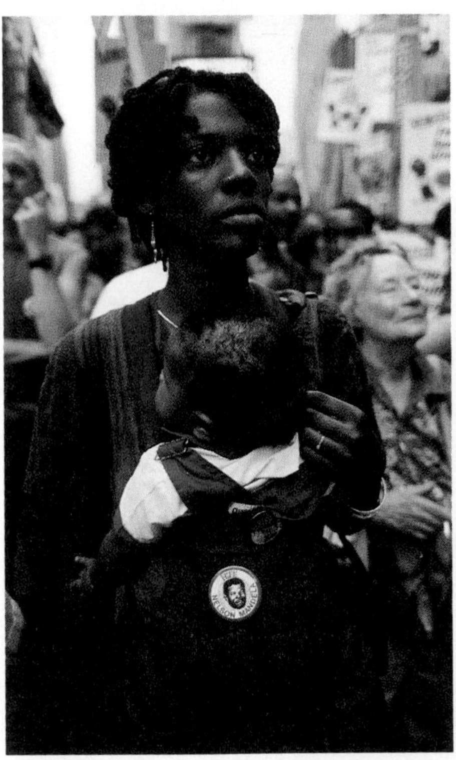

Attitudes are often formed through imitation. Children regularly adopt their parents' attitudes on issues, even when parents don't consciously attempt to influence their children's beliefs.

## Prejudice and Discrimination

Often use interchangeably, the terms *prejudice* and *discrimination* actually refer to different concepts. **Prejudice**—an attitude—is an unfair, intolerant, or unfavorable view of a group of people. **Discrimination**—a behavior—is an unfair act or a series of acts directed against an entire group of people or individual members of that group. To discriminate is to treat an entire class of people in an unfair way.

Prejudice and discrimination do not always occur together. It is possible to be prejudiced against a particular group without openly behaving in a hostile or discriminatory manner toward its members. A racist store owner may smile at a black customer, for example, to disguise opinions that could hurt his business. Likewise, many institutional practices can be discriminatory even though they are not based on prejudice. For example, regulations establishing a minimum height requirement for police officers may discriminate against women and certain ethnic groups whose average height falls below the arbitrary standard even though the regulations do not stem from sexist or racist attitudes.

**3.** What is the difference between prejudice and discrimination? Do the two always occur together?

**PREJUDICE** Like other attitudes, prejudice has three components: beliefs, feelings, and behavior tendencies. Prejudicial beliefs are virtually always stereotypes, and as mentioned earlier in this chapter, reliance on ste-

**Frustration-aggression theory** Theory that under certain circumstances people who are frustrated in their goals turn their anger away from the proper, powerful target toward another, less powerful target it is safer to attack.

**Authoritarian personality** A personality pattern characterized by rigid conventionality, exaggerated respect for authority, and hostility toward those who defy society's norms.

reotypes leads to erroneous thinking about other people. When a prejudiced employer interviews an African American job applicant, for example, the employer may automatically attribute to the job candidate all the traits associated with the negative African-American stereotype. To make matters worse, an individual's positive personal attributes that go against the stereotype are likely to be ignored or quickly forgotten (Allport, 1954).

Along with stereotyped beliefs, prejudicial attitudes are usually marked by strong emotions, such as dislike, fear, hatred, or loathing. Understandably, such negative feelings are likely to prompt the prejudiced person to discriminate against members of the group in question.

**SOURCES OF PREJUDICE** What causes prejudice? According to the **frustration-aggression theory**, prejudices stem from the frustrations experienced by a group low on the social scale (Allport, 1954; Hovland & Sears, 1940). As we noted in the chapter on motivation and emotion, under some circumstances frustration may erupt into anger and hostility. But people who feel exploited and oppressed often are not at liberty to vent their anger against their oppressors, so they may displace their hostility onto those even "lower" on the status scale than themselves in the form of prejudicial attitudes and discriminatory behavior (see the discussion of displacement in the chapter on stress). Historically, for example, violence against Jews has often followed periods of economic unrest or natural catastrophe. Similarly, African Americans in the United States have been scapegoats for the economic frustrations of some lower-income white Americans who feel powerless to improve their own socioeconomic condition. Latinos, Asian Americans, and women are also scapegoated—at times by African Americans. Like kindness, greed, and all other human qualities, prejudice is not restricted to a particular racial or ethnic group.

People with highly prejudiced attitudes tend to be rigidly conventional, preoccupied with power and toughness, and hostile to those who defy social norms.

Another theory locates the source of prejudice in a bigoted or **authoritarian personality**. Adorno and his colleagues (1950) linked prejudice to a complex cluster of personality traits called *authoritarianism*. Authoritarian individuals tend to be rigidly conventional, favoring following the rules and abiding by tradition, and hostile to those who defy those norms. They respect and submit to authority and are preoccupied with power and toughness. Looking at the world through a lens of rigid categories, they are cynical about human nature, fearing, suspecting, and rejecting all groups other than those to which they belong. Prejudice is only one expression of their suspicious, mistrusting approach to life.

There are also cognitive sources of prejudice. As we saw earlier, "cognitive misers" are people who try to simplify and organize their social thinking as much as possible. Too much simplification—*oversimplification*—leads to erroneous thinking, stereotypes, prejudice, and discrimination. For example, a stereotyped view of women as indecisive or weak will prejudice an employer against hiring a qualified woman as a manager. Belief in a just world—where people get what they deserve and deserve what they get—also simplifies one's view of the victims of prejudice as somehow people "deserve" their plight (M. J. Lerner, 1980).

In addition, social psychologists point out that prejudice and discrimination may have their roots in people's attempts to conform in society. If we associate with people who express clear prejudices, we are more likely to go along with their ideas than to resist them. During the 1960s in the South, for example, many restaurant owners maintained that they themselves would not mind serving African-American patrons but claimed that their white customers would not tolerate it (Deaux & Wrightsman, 1984). The pressures of social conformity help explain why children quickly absorb the prejudices of their parents and playmates long before they have formed their own beliefs and opinions on the basis of experience. Peer pressure often makes it "cool" or acceptable to express certain biases rather than to behave tolerantly toward members of other social groups.

**REDUCING PREJUDICE** If people tend to like those who are similar to themselves, can prejudice be reduced by reminding people how similar they are to members of rejected groups? Research seems to offer a qualified yes. Silverman (1974) described various "roommates" to incoming college students. Some subjects were told that they were to choose actual roommates from among the people described. Other subjects were told that they were making hypothetical roommates choices from among the people described. Racial discrimination was far more common in the choice of *actual* roommates than in the choice of *imagined* roommates, even though similarity in attitude and belief still made a difference in both groups.

So how can we encourage people to abandon longstanding or deeply held prejudices? At first glance, the solution might seem obvious: One way to reduce tensions between groups is to bring those groups together. However, as the turbulent history of school desegregation shows us, this solution is not as simple or straightforward as it sounds. Contact between members of two groups *can* undermine prejudicial attitudes, but only if certain conditions are met:

*The members of the groups in contact with one another must have equal status*. When blacks and whites were first integrated in the army and in public housing projects, they had relatively equal status and, as a result, prejudice between them was greatly reduced (Pettigrew, 1969). School desegregation has been less successful because the structure of our school system rewards the economic and academic advantages of white children, giving them an edge over black schoolchildren (Cohen, 1984).

*People must have one-on-one contact with members of the other group*. Simply putting students together in a structured classroom does not change attitudes. Interactions like lunchtime or after-school gatherings with friends must be part of the overall program.

*Groups must come together to cooperate rather than compete*. Because it provides the kind of personal contact just mentioned, as well as common ground and equal status, working together to achieve a common goal helps break down prejudice. Integrated sports teams exemplify this sort of contact. Cooperative learning techniques have also proved to be effective in overcoming prejudice in schools (Johnson, Johnson & Maruyama, 1984; Slavin, 1983). In one study by psychologist Eliot Aronson, the information a class of fifth-graders needed to learn was broken into pieces like a jigsaw puzzle. Each student had to learn a piece of the puzzle and present it to the others (Aronson, Bridgeman & Geffner, 1978). Not only did this method foster cooperation rather than competition, but it also improved self-esteem.

*The social norms should encourage contact*. In many cases, school desegregation took place in a highly charged atmosphere. Busloads of children arrived at their new schools only to face the protests of angry parents and the closed minds of fearful children. These conditions clearly did not promote interpersonal contact. In situations where contact is encouraged by the social norms or by those in positions of authority, prejudicial attitudes are more likely to break down.

While some kinds of intergroup contact can reduce prejudice, simply observing behavior that runs counter to one's stereotypical views goes far toward changing biased views. For example, whites in newly inte-

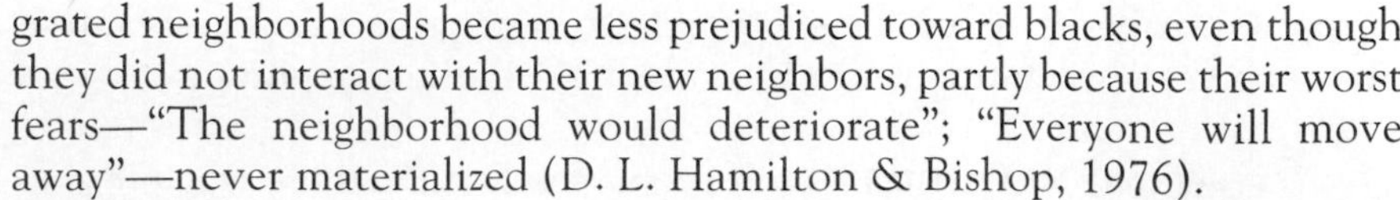

grated neighborhoods became less prejudiced toward blacks, even though they did not interact with their new neighbors, partly because their worst fears—"The neighborhood would deteriorate"; "Everyone will move away"—never materialized (D. L. Hamilton & Bishop, 1976).

Finally, we can train ourselves to be more "mindful" of other people who are different from us. For example, Ellen Langer and her colleagues (1985) taught a group of sixth-graders to be more "mindful" of people with various disabilities by showing them view slides and having them answer such questions as, "How might a handicapped person drive a car?" The students were also encouraged to see people with disabilities as having both strengths and weaknesses. The group showed far less prejudice toward handicapped people after the procedure than before it.

One strategy for overcoming prejudice is for people from different racial and ethnic groups to work together in cooperative, noncompetitive situations.

There are grounds for optimism about efforts to reduce sexism as well (Baron & Byrne, 1991). For example, prejudice against women is disappearing in many job interviews (Graves & Powell, 1988). Moreover, female-dominated jobs are no longer universally seen as deserving of lower compensation than those traditionally occupied by men (Grams & Schwab, 1985). While sexism still narrows the range of women's opportunities, it is less socially acceptable and fashionable today than it once was, and overall it appears to be on the decline.

## Attitude Change

A man watching TV on Sunday afternoon ignores scores of beer commercials but makes a note when a friend recommends a particular imported beer. A political speech convinces one woman to change her vote in favor of the candidate who made it but leaves her next-door neighbor determined to vote against the candidate. Why would a personal recommendation have greater persuasive power than an expensively produced television commercial? How can two people with similar views derive completely different messages from the same speech? What makes one attempt to change attitudes fail and another succeed? More generally, how and why do attitudes change, and how can we successfully resist attitude changes we do not want?

The answers to these questions depend to some extent on the technique used to influence our attitudes. We will look first at attempts to change attitudes through various kinds of persuasive messages.

**The Process of Persuasion** To be persuaded, you must first pay attention to the message; then you must comprehend it; finally, you must accept it as convincing. Consider how each of these steps is accomplished by advertising.

4. How do advertisers try to influence your behavior?

The first step in persuasion is to seize and retain the audience's attention. According to the *reasoned action model* of behavior (Ajzen, 1985), an ad must catch your attention, or you will "filter it out" along with all the other stimuli you ignore every hour of the day. As the competition has stiffened, advertisers have become increasingly creative in seizing your attention. For example, ads that arouse emotions, especially feelings you want to act on, can be memorable and thus persuasive (Engel, Black, & Miniard, 1986). Humor, too, is an effective way to keep you watching or reading an entire ad you would otherwise ignore.

Once an ad grabs your attention, other techniques are used to make you comprehend and accept its message. For example, more and more ads "hook" the audience by involving them in a narrative. A commercial might open with a dramatic scene or situation—for example, two people seemingly "meant" for each other but not yet making eye contact—and the viewer stays tuned to find out what happens. Some commercials even feature recurring characters and story lines so that each new commercial in the series is really the latest installment in a soap opera.

For an ad to affect our behavior, it must first attract our attention.

What if an ad is annoying? Surprisingly, even an ad that rubs you the wrong way can be effective because your irritation with it makes you remember the name of the product (Aaker & Bruzzone, 1985).

With so many clever strategies focused on seizing and holding your attention, how can you shield yourself from unwanted influences and resist persuasive appeals? According to the reasoned action model, even if you do pay attention to a commercial message, you must further comprehend it, accept it, and form an intention to act on it before you will be completely persuaded. One strategy for resisting persuasion, therefore, is to analyze ads to identify which attention-getting strategies are at work. Make a game of deciphering the advertisers' "code" instead of falling for the ad's appeal. And raise your standards for the kinds of messages that are worthy of your attention and commitment.

**The Communication Model** The second and third steps in persuasion—comprehending and then accepting the message—are influenced by both the message itself and the way it is presented. The communication model of persuasion spotlights four key elements to achieve these goals: the source, the message itself, the medium of communication, and characteristics of the audience. Once they have seized your attention, persuaders manipulate each of these factors in hopes of changing your attitudes. Let us take each factor in turn as we can consider what is known about effective persuasion.

The effectiveness of a persuasive message first depends upon its *source*, the author or communicator who appeals to the audience to accept the message. Here credibility makes a big difference (W. J. McGuire, 1985). For example, we are less likely to change our attitude toward the oil industry's antipollution efforts if the president of a major refining company tells us about them than if we hear the same information from an impartial commission appointed to study the situation.

The effectiveness of a persuasive message primarily depends on its source. A prominent celebrity like basketball star Shaquille O'Neal lends credibility to a message, especially among young people.

Recent research indicates that the credibility of the source is most important when we are not inclined to pay attention to the message itself (Cooper & Croyle, 1984; Petty & Cacioppo, 1981, 1986a). In cases where we have some interest in the message, it is the message that plays the greater role in determining whether we change our attitudes (Petty & Cacioppo, 1986b).

Looking next at the message itself, researchers have discovered that we frequently tune out messages that contradict our own point of view. In addition, the more arguments a message makes in support of a position, the more effective that message is (Calder, Insko, & Yandell, 1974), and novel arguments are more persuasive than rehashes of old standbys, heard many times before.

Research has found that *fear* sometimes works well, especially in convincing people to get tetanus shots (Dabbs & Leventhal, 1966), to

**Cognitive dissonance** Perceived inconsistency between two cognitions.

drive safely (Leventhal & Niles, 1965), and to take care of their teeth (Evans et al., 1970). But if the message generates too much fear, it will turn off the audience and have little persuasive effect (Worchel, Cooper, & Goethals, 1991).

Messages designed to persuade are more successful when both sides of an argument are presented because a two-sided presentation generally makes the speaker seem less biased and thus enchances his or her credibility. We have greater respect and trust for a communicator who acknowledges that there is another side to a controversial issue.

When it comes to a choice of *medium*, writing is best suited to making people understand complex arguments, while videotaped or live media presentations are more effective with an audience that already grasps the gist of an argument (Chaiken & Eagly, 1976). Most effective, however, are face-to-face appeals or the lessons of our own experience. Salespeople who sell products door-to-door rely on the power of personal contact.

The most critical factors in changing attitudes—and the most difficult to control—have to do with *audience*. Attitudes are most resistant to change if (1) the audience has a strong *commitment* to its present attitudes, (2) those attitudes are shared by others, and (3) the attitudes were instilled during early childhood by such pivotal groups as the family.

The *discrepancy* between the contents of the message and the present attitudes of the audience also affects how well the message will be received. Up to a point, the greater the difference between the two, the greater the likelihood of attitude change. However, if the discrepancy is *too* great, the audience may reject the new information altogether. The expertise of the communicator is very important in this context: Influence increases with the size of the discrepancy only when the speaker is considered an expert.

Certain personal characteristics make some people more susceptible to attitude change than others. People with low self-esteem are more easily influenced, especially when the message is complex and hard to understand. Highly intelligent people tend to resist persuasion because they can think of counterarguments more easily. When the message is complex, however, only highly intelligent people may be able to follow the logic and hence be influenced by it.

So while attitudes are open to change, they are very difficult to change. Fortunately for advertisers, politicians, and others, attitude change is often less crucial than a shift in behavior—buying Brand X, voting for Jane Smith. In fact, in many cases it is possible to first change behavior and *then* obtain attitude change as a concomitants. We will now explore how behavior can affect attitudes.

**COGNITIVE CONSISTENCY THEORY** One of the more fascinating approaches to understanding the process of attitude change is the theory of **cognitive dissonance** developed by Leon Festinger (1957). Cognitive dissonance exists whenever a person has two contradictory cognitions, or beliefs, at the same time. "I am a considerate and loyal friend" is one cognition; so is "Yesterday I repeated some juicy gossip I heard about my friend Chris." These two cognitions are dissonant—each one implies the opposite of the other. According to Festinger, cognitive dissonance creates unpleasant psychological tension, and this tension motivates the individual to try to resolve the dissonance in some way.

Sometimes changing one's attitude is the easiest way to reduce the discomfort of dissonance. I cannot easily change the fact that I have repeated gossip about a friend. Therefore, it is easier to change my attitude toward my friend. If I conclude that Chris is not really a friend but simply an acquaintance, then my new attitude now fits my behavior—spreading gossip about someone who is *not* a friend does not contradict the fact that I am loyal and considerate to those who *are* my friends.

**Social influence** Process by which others individually or collectively affect one's perceptions, attitudes, and actions.

Discrepant behavior that contradicts an attitude does not necessarily bring about attitude change, however, because there are other ways a person can reduce cognitive dissonance. One alternative is to *increase the number of consonant elements*—that is, the thoughts that support one or the other dissonant cognitions. For example, I might note that the gossip I repeated was pretty interesting, that anyone who had heard it would be concerned and surprised about Chris, and that it would be only natural to discuss it with others in an effort to determine whether it was true. Now my action is less at odds with my attitude toward Chris as a friend. Another option is to reduce the importance of one or both cognitive elements. "The person I repeated the gossip to was Terry, who doesn't really know Chris very well. Terry doesn't care and won't repeat it. It was no big deal and Chris shouldn't be upset about it." By reducing the significance of my behavior, I reduce the dissonance that I experience and so make it less necessary to change my attitude toward Chris.

Our discussion so far has ignored an important question: Why would someone engage in behavior that goes against an attitude in the first place? One answer is that cognitive dissonance is a natural part of everyday life. For example, simply choosing between two or more desirable alternatives leads inevitably to dissonance. Suppose you are in the market for a computer but can't decide between an IBM and a Macintosh. If you choose the IBM, all of its bad features and all the good aspects of the Macintosh contribute to dissonance. After you have bought the IBM, you can reduce the dissonance by changing your attitude: You might decide that the Macintosh keyboard wasn't "quite right" and that some of the "bad" features of the IBM are actually desirable.

You may also engage in behavior at odds with an attitude because you are enticed to do so. Perhaps someone offers you a small bribe or reward: "I will pay you 25 cents just to try my product." Curiously, the larger the reward, the smaller the change in attitude that is likely to result. When rewards are large, dissonance is at a minimum, and attitude change is small, if it happens at all. Apparently, when people are convinced that there is a good reason to do something that goes against their beliefs ("I'll try almost anything in exchange for a large cash incentive"), they experience little dissonance and their attitudes are not likely to shift, even though their behavior may change for a time. However, if the reward is small, just barely enough to induce behavior that conflicts with one's attitude, dissonance will be great, maximizing the chances for attitude change: "I only got 25 cents to try this product, so it couldn't have been the money that attracted me. I must really *like* this product after all." The trick is to induce the behavior that goes against an attitude while leaving people feeling personally responsible for the dissonant act. That way they are more likely to change their attitudes than if they feel they were forced to act in a way that contradicts their beliefs (J. Cooper, 1971; Kelman, 1974).

## SOCIAL INFLUENCE

In social psychology, **social influence** refers to the process by which others—individually or collectively—affect our perceptions, attitudes, and actions (Baron & Byrne, 1991). In the previous section, we examined one form of social influence: attitude change. Next, we'll focus on how behavior is controlled by the presence or actions of others without regard to underlying attitudes.

## Cultural Influence

**Culture** All the goods, both tangible and intangible, produced in a society.

**Cultural truism** Belief that most members of a society accept as self-evidently true.

**Norm** A shared idea or expectation about how to behave.

When we hear the word "culture," we are prone to think of certain forms of art and entertainment, such as classical music or paintings by Old Masters. In fact, as used by social scientists, **culture** refers to *all* the goods produced by a society—both tangible, such as machines, buildings, and literature, and intangible, such as shared beliefs and values. Thus defined, culture exerts an enormous influence on our attitudes and behaviors. Consider for a moment the many aspects of day-to-day living that are derived from culture:

- Your culture dictates how you dress. A Saudi woman covers her entire body and face before venturing outside her home; a North American woman freely displays her face, arms, and legs; and women in some other societies mingle in completely naked (D. G. Myers, 1992).

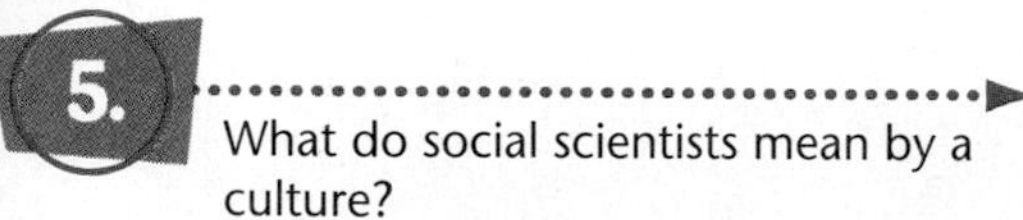

What do social scientists mean by a culture?

- Culture specifies what you eat—and what you do *not* eat. Americans do not eat dog or reptile meat, the Chinese eat no cheese, and the Hindus refuse to eat beef. Culture further guides *how* you eat: with a fork, chopsticks, or your bare hands.
- People from different cultures seek different amounts of personal space. This is the bubble of space or mobile territory one maintains in one's interactions with others. Latin Americans, French people, and Arabs get closer to each other in most types of face-to-face interactions than do Americans, English people, or Swedes (E. T. Hall, 1966).

To some extent, culture influences us through formal instruction. For example, your parents may have reminded you from time to time that certain actions are considered "normal" or the "right way" to behave. But more often cultural lessons are learned through modeling and imitation. One result of such learning is the unquestioning acceptance of **cultural truisms**—beliefs that most members of a society accept as self-evidently true (Aronson, 1992).

We also learn cultural lessons through conditioning. We are rewarded (reinforced) for doing as our companions and fellow citizens do in most situations—for going along with the crowd. This social learning process is one of the chief mechanisms by which a culture transmits its central lessons and values. In the course of comparing and adapting our own behavior to that of others, we learn the norms of our culture. A **norm** is a shared idea or expectation about how to behave. Norms are often steeped in tradition and strengthened by habit. For example, it is "normal" in the United States for women to go into professions like nursing and teaching but not to become construction workers or combat pilots. When visiting a friend in the hospital, you may be surprised and uncomfortable if the nurse in attendance turns out to be a man. Lawmakers and politicians are likewise uncomfortable with images of women flying combat missions into enemy territory—although there is no demonstrable physical reason for assuming that men are better at such work than women.

## Cultural Assimilators

Cultures seem strange to us if their norms are very different from our own. It is tempting to conclude that *different* means "wrong," simply because unfamiliar patterns of behavior can make us feel uncomfortable. To transcend our differences and get along better with people from other cultures, we must find ways to overcome such discomfort. Since cultural norms are learned—not inherited—it is possible to *relearn* or otherwise modify our responses to unfamiliar cultures. For example, if you know that the hand gesture that signifies "okay" in our culture (putting the thumb and forefinger together to form a circle) means something offensive or obscene in another person's culture, you can avoid insulting that person simply by refraining from making that gesture.

One technique for understanding other cultures is the *cultural assimilator*, a strategy for perceiving the norms and values of another group (Baron & Graziano, 1991; Brislin et al., 1986). This technique teaches by example, asking students to explain why a member of another cultural or social group has behaved in a particular manner. For example, why do the members of a Japanese grade school class silently follow their teacher single file through a park on a lovely spring day? Are they afraid of being punished for disorderly conduct if they do otherwise? Are they naturally placid and compliant? Once you understand that Japanese children are raised to value the needs and feelings of others over their own selfish concerns, their orderly, obedient behavior seems not mindless but disciplined and considerate.

Cultural assimilators encourage us to remain open-minded about others' norms and values by challenging such cultural truisms as "My country is always the best" or "Our way is the *only* right way."

**Cultural norm** A behavioral rule shared by an entire society.

**Conformity** Voluntarily yielding to social norms, even at the expense of one's own preferences.

Why do Japanese schoolchildren behave in such an orderly fashion? Check your answer against the text discussion on cultural assimilators.

## Conformity

We have been discussing **cultural norms**, the behavioral rules shared by entire societies. Our behavior is also shaped by the norms of smaller organizations, such as families, teams, and communities. Some norms are written into law or official rules; many more are unwritten expectations enforced by teasing, frowns, ostracism, and other informal means of punishment. Without norms, social life would be chaotic. With them, the behavior of other people becomes fairly predictable despite great differences in underlying attitudes and preferences.

Most instances of uniformity are not cases of conformity. For instance, millions of Americans drink coffee in the morning, but they do not do so as a matter of conforming. They drink coffee because they have learned to like and desire it. **Conformity** implies a conflict between the individual and the group—a conflict that the people resolve by yielding their own preferences or beliefs to the norms or expectations of a larger group.

Since the early 1950s, when Solomon Asch conducted the first systematic study of the subject, conformity has been a major topic of research in social psychology. Asch demonstrated in a series of experiments that under some circumstances people will conform to group pressures even if this forces them to deny obvious physical evidence. His studies ostensibly tested visual judgment by asking people to choose from a card with several lines of differing lengths the line most similar to the line on a comparison card (see Figure 14-1). The lines were deliberately drawn so that the comparison was obvious and the correct choice was clear. All but one of the subjects were confederates of the experimenter. On certain trials these confederates deliberately gave the same wrong answer. This put the lone real subject on the spot: Should he conform to what he knew to be a wrong decision and agree with the group, thereby denying the evidence of his own senses, or should he disagree with the group, thereby risking the social consequences of nonconformity?

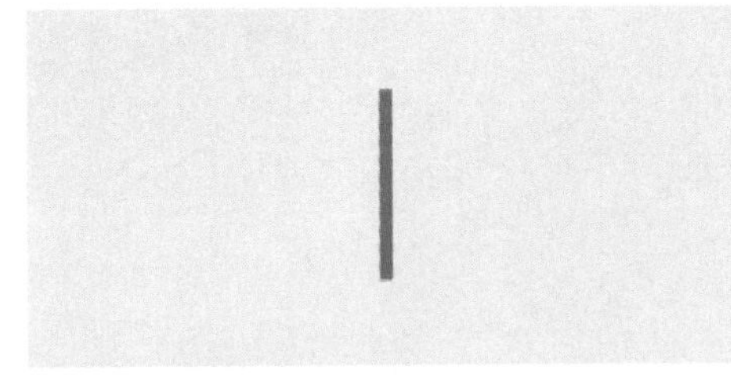

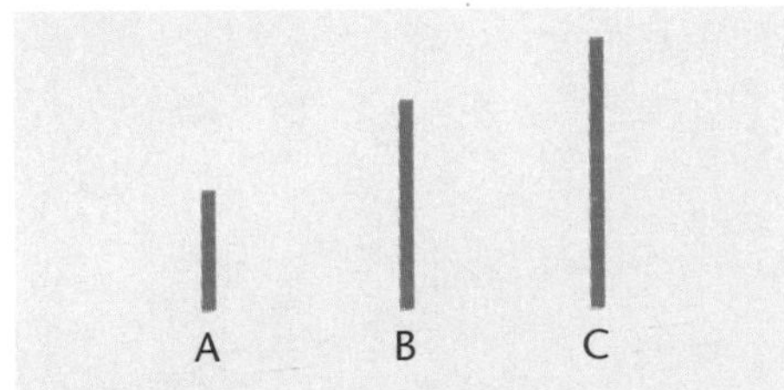


**Figure 14-1**
**Distorting the truth.** In Asch's experiment on *conformity*, subjects were shown a comparison card like the one on the top and were asked which of the three lines on the card at bottom was the most similar.

Overall, subjects conformed on about 35 percent of the trials. There were large individual differences, however, and in subsequent research, experimenters discovered that two sets of factors influence the likelihood that a person will conform: characteristics of the situation and characteristics of the individual.

The *size* of the group is one situational variable that has been studied extensively. Asch (1951) found that the likelihood of conformity increased with expansion of group size until four confederates were present. After that point, the number of others made no difference in the subjects' tendency to ignore the evidence of their own eyes.

**Compliance** Change of behavior in response to an explicit request from another person or group.

Another important situational factor is the degree of *unanimity* in the group. If just one confederate broke the perfect agreement of the majority by giving the correct answer, conformity among subjects in the Asch experiments fell from an average of 35 percent to about 25 percent (Asch, 1956). Apparently, having just one "ally" eases the pressure to conform. The ally does not even have to share the subject's viewpoint—just breaking the unanimity of the majority is enough to reduce conformity (Allen & Levine, 1971).

The *nature of the task* is still another situational variable that affects conformity. For instance, conformity has been shown to vary with the difficulty and the ambiguity of a task. When the task is difficult or poorly defined, conformity tends to be higher (R. R. Blake, Helson, & Mouton, 1956). In an ambiguous situation, individuals are less sure of their own opinion and more willing to conform to the majority view.

Personal characteristics also influence conforming behavior. The more an individual is attracted to the group, expects to interact with it its members in the future, holds a position of relatively low status in the group, and does not feel completely accepted by the group, the more that person tends to conform. The fear of rejection apparently motivates conformity when a person scores high on one or more of these variables.

## Compliance

Conformity is a response to pressure exerted by norms that are generally left unstated. In contrast, **compliance** is a change of behavior in response to an explicit request. The demand may reflect a social norm, as when the doorman at a nightclub informs a jeans-clad prospective customer that proper attire is required. Or the request may be intended to satisfy the needs of the person making it: "Please help me fold the sheets."

Social psychologists have studied several techniques by which people can induce others to comply with their requests. One procedure is based on the so-called *foot-in-the-door effect*. Every salesperson knows that the moment a prospect allows the sales pitch to begin, the chances of making a sale improve greatly. The same effect operates in other areas of life: Once people have granted a small request, they are more likely to comply with a larger one.

In the most famous study of this phenomenon, Freedman and Fraser (1966) approached certain residents of Palo Alto, California, posing as members of a Committee for Safe Driving. Residents were asked to place a large ugly sign reading "Drive Carefully" in their front yards. Only 17 percent agreed to do so. Then other residents were asked to sign a petition calling for more safe-driving laws. When these same people were later asked to place the ugly "Drive Carefully" sign in their yards, an amazing 55 percent agreed to do so. Compliance with the initial small request more than tripled the rate of compliance with the larger request.

Why does the foot-in-the-door technique work so well? One possible explanation is that agreeing to the token act (signing the petition) realigns the subject's self-perception slightly to that of someone who favors the cause. When presented with the larger request, the subject then feels obligated to comply (Snyder & Cunningham, 1975).

Another strategy commonly used by salespeople is the *lowball procedure* (Cialdini et al., 1978). The first step in this procedure is to induce a person to agree to do something. After the commitment to the behavior has been made, the second step is to raise the cost of compliance. Among new-car dealers, lowballing works like this: The dealer persuades the customer to buy a new car by reducing the price well below that offered by competitors. Once the customer has agreed to buy the car, however, the terms of the sale shift abruptly (e.g., the trade-in value promised by the used-car manager is cut), so that in the end the car is *more* costly than it would be at other dealerships. Despite the added costs, many customers follow through on their commitment to buy. Although the original inducement was the low price (the "lowball" the salesperson originally pitched), once committed, the buyer remains loyal to the now-pricier vehicle.

**Obedience** Change of behavior in response to a command from another person, typically an authority figure.

Under certain circumstances, a person who has refused to comply with one request may be more likely to comply with a second. For example, if saying no to the first request made you feel guilty, you may readily seize an opportunity to diminish your guilt by saying yes to something else. This phenomenon has been dubbed the *door-in-the-face effect* (Cialdini et al., 1975). In one study, researchers approached students and asked them to make an unreasonably large commitment: Would they counsel delinquent youths at a detention center for two years? Nearly everyone declined, thus effectively "slamming the door" in the face of the researcher making the request. On then being asked to make a much smaller commitment—supervising children during a trip to the zoo—many of the same subjects quickly agreed. The door-in-the-face effect may work because subjects interpret the smaller request as a concession by the experimenter, and feel pressured to comply in return.

## Obedience

Compliance is agreement to change behavior in response to a request. **Obedience** is compliance with a command. Like compliance, it is a response to an explicit message; but in this case, the message is a direct order, generally from a person in authority, such as a police officer, principal, or parent, who can back up the command with some sort of force if necessary. Obedience embodies social influence in its most direct and powerful form.

Several studies by Stanley Milgram, mentioned in Chapter 1, "The Science of Psychology," showed how far many people will go to obey someone in authority (Milgram, 1963). Recall from that chapter that subjects who agreed to participate in what they believed was a learning experiment administered what they thought were severe electrical shocks to the "learners." What factors influence the degree to which people will do what they are told? Studies in which people were asked to put a dime in a parking meter by people wearing uniforms shows that one important factor is the amount of *power* vested in the person giving the orders. A guard whose uniform looked like that of a police officer was obeyed more often than was a man dressed either as a milkman or as a civilian. Another factor is *surveillance*. If we are ordered to do something and then left alone, we are less likely to obey than if we are being watched. This seems to be true especially when the order involves an unethical act. Most of the subjects still put a dime in the meter when the policeman impersonator was out of sight, but Milgram found that his "teachers" were less willing to give severe shocks when the experimenter was out of the room.

Milgram's experiments revealed other factors that influence a person's willingness to follow orders. When the victim was in the same room as the teacher, obedience dropped sharply. When another "teacher" was present who refused to give shocks, obedience also dropped. But when responsibility for an act was shared, so that the person was only one of many doing it, the degree of obedience was much greater. Executions by firing squads illustrate this principle.

Why do people willingly obey an authority figure, even if means violating their own principles? Milgram (1974) thought that people feel obligated to those in power, first, because they respect their credentials and assume that they know what they are doing, and second, because often-

**"Does the norm of obedience to an authority figure absolve an individual's responsibility for his or her behavior?"**

Recall that earlier chapters focused on the pressures exerted on individuals by groups and peers. In this chapter, we investigate the related issues of conformity, compliance, and obedience—each of which involves a change in an individual's beliefs, preferences, or behaviors in response to some form of external pressure.

Our awareness of the effects of social influence on human behavior raises a number of questions. For example, are individuals fully responsible for their actions, even when those actions have been influenced by group pressure? If so, why? If not, why not? To what extent can we escape from or overcome social or group pressure? To what extent must we compromise and agree to maintain our status as social regulations as accepted members of a society? After you have thought about these questions, take a few minutes to examine the opinions of some other students, which appear below.

• • • • • • •

**ANNMARIE: People should be held accountable for their actions to a certain extent, but I think that some kinds of pressure to "do what I was told to do" create an unfair strain on the person.**

**LEE: Unless you are brainwashed or being completely controlled somehow, the decision to do something is totally up to you, and you're fooling yourself or lying to yourself if you think you can't disobey or don't have a right to.**

**ANN: Just following orders? Nazi Germany anyone?**

**AMY: The choice may be kill someone or be killed, but you still have the opportunity to decide if you will commit murder.**

**MARIA: In sociology, we learned about how people see such nonconformity in gangs and such, but if you look within the gang, the people *are* conforming. It's their lifestyle, their own notion of right and wrong, not just "group pressure." It's "normal" to them (not that they shouldn't be punished for crimes, just that it's understandable).**

**JOSÉ: There are certain cases in which one should not be punished for crimes, such as Nazi soldiers. The higher-ups should be put in hell, but if you're just a foot soldier following the orders of the government, you're no longer acting as yourself.**

**KATE: In the army, the punishment for defying an order is probably worse than the punishment for the heinous act committed because of the order. In real life, one should know what is right, and there are ways to avoid following orders.**

**SUNI: In legal matters, we do not have enough knowledge to make judgments, so we refer to our lawyers and do as they say. Our society is too complex to allow clear-cut responsibility.**

**PAT: Moral decisions in a societal context depend upon many conflicting variables.Do you save yourself or the other guy, et cetera? We always want someone to hold accountable, but such definite, directed responsibility is just not possible in this morally ambiguous world. That's what our judicial system is for, to consider each violation independently, paying attention to all reasons and possibilities so as to take into account the individual human experience.**

**MICHAEL: It all depends on the situation. If two guys go out to kill someone, and the friend chooses to come along, it's one thing. But in Nazi Germany, if you don't follow orders, you die. I know what I would do. Morality sometimes has to come second, behind personal safety. Morality doesn't mean much when you are dead.**

**ANN: It is easy for us to sit here and preach about what we feel is right and moral, but I think that if our conforming meant that we would live or die as a result, then I think that probably most of us would conform, or follow orders, even if it [was] against what we may believe to be right.**

**ETHAN: I would never hold someone responsible for not being a martyr. The people who choose otherwise, however, must understand that they will face the consequences for the alternative they have chosen. If a soldier in Nazi Germany chooses to shoot an innocent so he will not be killed by his commanding officer, that's fine. I cannot expect him to choose otherwise. However, he cannot expect us not to convict him for murder when his crime is discovered.**

• • • • • • •

Now that you have read through other students' ideas, you might want to reconsider your answers to the questions we posed earlier. Do you think that the concept of individual responsibility is stronger in some cultures than in others? How does studying the question of personal responsibility prepare us to deal with issues relating to civil disobedience?

times they have established trust with the people in authority by agreeing to do whatever they ask. Once this happens, subjects may experience conflict over what they are doing, but manage through rationalization to "forget" about it to push the conflict aside and thus minimize it.. The essence of obedience, says Milgram, is that subjects come to see themselves as the agents of *another* person's wishes and therefore not responsible for the obedient actions or their consequences. Once this shift in self-perception has occurred, obedience follows, because in their minds, the subjects have relinquished control of their actions.

Milgram's analysis emphasizes the *power of the situation*: Once subjects volunteered to take part in the study, they became caught up in the bizarre circumstances of the experiment and felt compelled to respond to external forces (the experimenter's commands) rather than internal ones (their own moral opposition to harming others). An alternative explanation was offered by Nissani (1990), who argued that obedient subjects do not succumb to situational forces but rather fail to *perceive* the situation correctly. Thus, in Milgram's study, the subjects began with the belief that the experiment would be safe and the experimenter would be trustworthy. When these assumptions proved false—when the experiment turned out to be dangerous and the experimenter disregarded the victim's obvious suffering—the subject's assumptions were invalidated. But it is hard—sometimes impossible—to change one's beliefs and assumptions quickly, in spite of irrefutable evidence. The real emotional struggle for the obedient subjects, Nissani argues, may not have been in deciding whether to obey malevolent orders, but rather in recognizing that a trusted authority figure proved to be treacherous. (See Online box for a discussion of whether the norm of obedience to an authority figure exonerates individuals of responsibility for their actions.)

## SOCIAL ACTION

The various kinds of social influence we have just discussed may take place between two people, in groups of three or more, or even when no one else is physically present. We refrain from playing our stereo at full volume when our neighbors are sleeping, comply with jury notices that we receive in the mail, and obey traffic signals even when no one is on the road to enforce the social norms that dictate these actions. We now turn our attention to processes that *do* depend on the presence of other people. Specifically, we will examine processes that occur when people interact one-on-one and in groups. The social actions we consider next are *deindividuation*, *helping behavior*, *group decision making*, and *organizational behavior*.

Mob behavior can be explained in part by the phenomenon of *deindividuation*: The more anonymous people feel in a group, the less responsible they feel as individuals for their behavior.

### Deindividuation

We have seen several cases of social influence in which people act differently in the presence of others than they would if they were alone. The most striking and frightening instance of this phenomenon is *mob behavior*. Some well-known violent examples of mob behav-

**Deindividuation** Loss of personal sense of responsibility in a group.

**Altruistic behavior** Helping behavior that is not linked to personal gain.

**Bystander effect** Tendency for an individual's helpfulness in an emergency to decrease as the number of bystanders increases.

ior are the beatings and lynchings of African Americans, the looting that sometimes accompanies urban rioting, and the wanton destruction of property that mars otherwise peaceful protests and demonstrations. After a power outage in New York City in 1977, during which considerable looting took place, some of the looters were interviewed. Strangely, many said they would never have thought of looting had they been alone and others were later shocked by their own behavior.

One reason for such behavior is that people lose their personal sense of responsibility in a group, especially in a group subjected to intense pressures and anxiety. This process is called **deindividuation**, because people respond not as individuals, but as anonymous parts of a larger group. In general, the more anonymous people feel in a group, the less responsible they feel as individuals.

6.

How do social scientists explain mob behavior?

But deindividuation only partly explains mob behavior. Another contributing factor is that, in a group, one dominant and persuasive person can convince people to act through a *snowball effect*: If the persuader convinces just a few people, those few will convince others, who will convince still others, and the group becomes an unthinking mob. Moreover, large groups provide *protection*. Anonymity makes it difficult to press charges. If 2, or even 10, people start smashing windows, they will probably be arrested. If a thousand people do it, very few of them will be caught or punished.

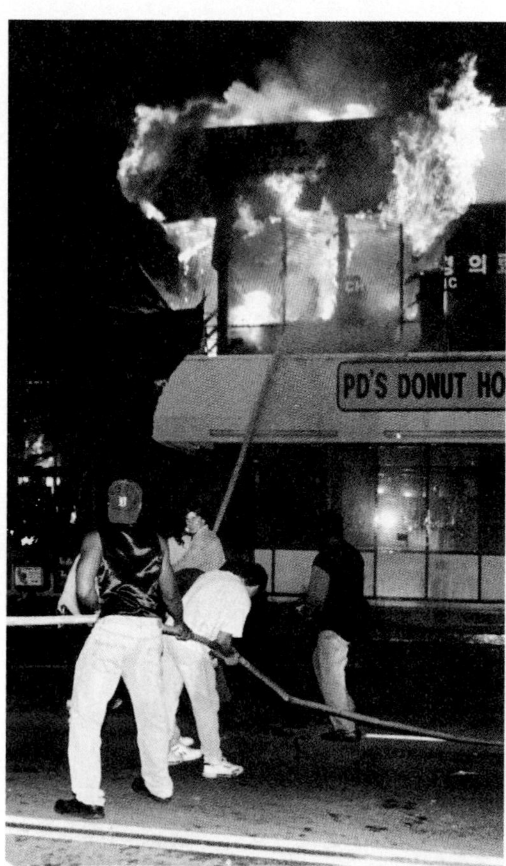


An example of *altruistic behavior*: Civilians help put out a fire in a California shop without expecting reward or recognition for their action.

## Helping Behavior

Research on deindividuation seems to support the unfortunate—and inaccurate—the notion that when people get together they become more destructive and irresponsible than they would be individually. However, human society depends on people's willingness to work together and help one another. In fact, we could cite many instances of cooperation and mutual assistance as examples of human conflict and hostility. If, as we saw in the chapter on motivation and emotion, our willingness to harm others is influenced by social forces, so is our willingness to help others. Why do people help one another—especially strangers?

Our benevolent treatment of others is sometimes motivated by self-interest. We offer our boss a ride home from the office because we know that our next promotion depends on how much he or she likes us. We volunteer to water our neighbors' lawn while they are away because we want to use their pool. But when helpful actions are not linked to such personal gain, it is considered to be **altruistic behavior**. A person who acts in an altruistic way does not expect any recognition or reward in return, except perhaps the good feeling that comes from helping someone in need. Many altruistic acts, including many charitable contributions, are directed at strangers and are made anonymously (M. L. Hoffman, 1977). (See the Highlights box for a look at factors that influenced Gentiles to help Jewish victims of the Holocaust.)

Under what conditions is helping behavior most likely to occur? Like other sociopsychological phenomena, helping is influenced by two sets of variables: those inherent in the situation and those grounded in the individual.

The most important situational variable is the *presence of other people*. In a phenomenon called the **bystander effect,** as the number of passive bystanders increases, the likelihood that any one of them will help someone in trouble decreases. In one experiment, subjects completing a questionnaire heard a taped "emergency" in the next room, complete with a crash and screams. Of those who were alone, 70 percent offered help to the unseen female victim, but of those who waited with a companion—a stranger who did nothing to help—only 7 percent offered help (Latane & Rodin, 1969).

# HIGHLIGHTS

## Altruism and the Holocaust

In 1939, when the German army occupied Warsaw, Poland, the army segregated the city's Jews in a ghetto surrounded by barbed wire. Deeply concerned about the fate of her Jewish friends, a 16-year-old Catholic girl named Stefania Podgórska made secret expeditions into the ghetto with gifts of food, clothing, and medicine. When the Jewish son of her former landlord made a desperate flight from the ghetto to avoid being deported to a concentration camp, Stefania agreed to hide him in her apartment. Throughout Nazi-occupied Europe, only a few thousand non-Jews like Stefania risked their lives to rescue Jews from persecution, deportation, and death. Why did they do what so many millions of others failed to do? What qualities of Stefania's personality enabled her to behave so altruistically, bravely, and competently?

In 1981, several researchers set out to find answers to questions like these and combined their efforts two years later in the Altruistic Personality Project. By 1985, the project had published findings based on interviews with 25 rescuers and 50 survivors, as well as historical documents about the activities of others (Fogelman & Wiener, 1985). The people with whom the researchers spoke came from several countries and differed widely in education and vocation. The rescuers did, however, share one characteristic: They preferred not to see themselves as heroes but instead considered their behavior to be natural.

Although no single personality characteristic emerged, researchers could identify some common threads. For example, rescuers tended to fall into one of two groups: those who were motivated by deeply rooted moral values and felt ethically bound to rescue victims, and those who were attached personally to the victims and sometimes identified with them *emotionally*. These findings support the contention of social psychologist Carol Gilligan (1982) that there are fundamentally two forms of moral reasoning: one based on a sense of justice, the other based on a sense of responsibility and care.

Morally motivated rescuers often harbored intense anti-Nazi attitudes; for some, religious belief played a paramount role in their lives. Those rescuers also tended to help victims regardless of whether they liked or disliked them. On the other hand, emotionally motivated rescuers frequently had strong personal attachments to the people whom they helped—neighbors, for instance. Some helped people whom they scarcely knew but with whom they identified. In certain cases, the empathy sprang from the rescuer's belief that he or she was also vulnerable to persecution. "It is easy to understand what the Jews felt," explained one Ukrainian rescuer, "because Jews and the Ukrainians were in similar positions everywhere" (Fogelman & Wiener, 1985, p. 63).

Despite their varied motivations, the rescuers shared a number of characteristics. Many of them belonged to families with traditions of concern for others outside the family, and many stated that their behavior was strongly guided by their parents' values. Stefania Podgórska cited her parents' belief in religious tolerance. Most rescuers had uncommon capacities for perseverance and unusually strong beliefs in their own competence to risk and survive danger. Stefania and her sister managed to shelter 13 Jews for 2 1/2 years in the attic of their small apartment—and for 7 months of that time, two German nurses and two German soldiers were bivouacked in the apartment!

Another key aspect of the situation is its *ambiguity*. Any factors that make it harder for others to recognize a genuine emergency reduce the probability of altruistic actions. Clark and Word (1974) had a "workman" carry a ladder and a venetian blind past a waiting room in which subjects were sitting. A loud crash soon followed. In this ambiguous situation, the fewer the bystanders, the more likely the workman was to receive help. When he clarified matters by calling out that he was hurt, however, all subjects without exception rushed to his aid.

The *personal characteristics* of bystanders also affect helping behavior. Not all bystanders are equally likely to help a stranger. According to Moriarty (1975), increasing the amount of personal responsibility that one person feels for another boosts the likelihood that help will be extended. In his experiment, subjects were more likely to try to stop the theft of a stranger's property if they had promised to watch the property while the stranger was away than if they had had no contact with the stranger. The amount of *empa-*

**Risky shift** The greater willingness of people in groups to take risks in decision making as opposed to independent individuals deliberating alone.

**Polarization** Shift in attitudes by members of a group toward more extreme positions than the ones held before group discussion.

*thy* that we feel toward another person also affects our willingness to act in a helpful way. Krebs (1975) found that when subjects felt that their values and personalities were similar to a victim's, they were more likely to help, even if that meant jeopardizing their own safety.

*Mood* also makes a difference. A person in a good mood is more likely to help another in need than is someone who is in a neutral or bad mood. Isen and Levin (1972) demonstrated this by leaving a dime in the scoop of a pay phone to put the finder in a good mood. Subjects finding the dime were much more likely than other subjects to help a confederate who dropped a folder full of papers on the sidewalk near the phone booth. Other research indicates that individuals who *fear embarrassment* are less likely to help (McGovern, 1976). Mistakenly offering help to someone who does not really need it can be highly embarrassing. Finally, when others are watching, people who score high on the need for approval are more likely to help than are low scorers (Satow, 1975).

To sum up, we offer help if we are helpful people *or* if the circumstances bring our helpful tendencies to rise to the fore.

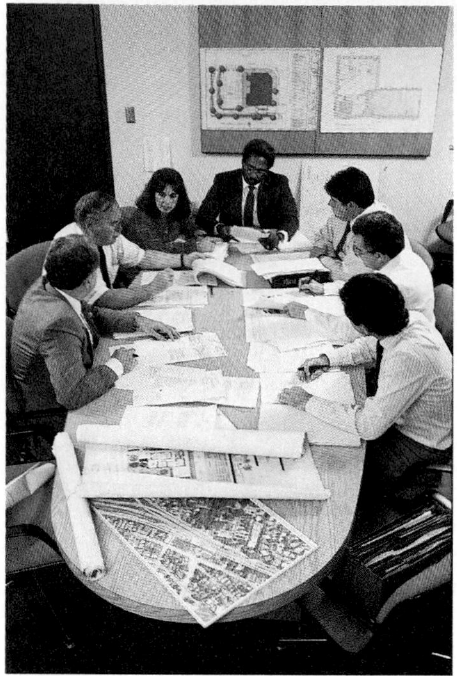

Key business decisions are often made by groups rather than by individuals. Contrary to popular belief, groups sometimes propose a riskier course of action than would be favored by group members working alone. This phenomenon is known as the *risky shift*.

## Group Decision Making

There is a tendency in our society to turn important decisions over to groups. In the business world, key decisions are often made around a conference table rather than behind one person's desk. In politics, major policy decisions are seldom vested in just one person; groups of advisers, cabinet officers, committee members, or aides meet to deliberate and forge a course of action. In the courts, a defendant may request a trial by jury, and for some serious crimes, a jury trial is required by law. And, of course, the nine-member U.S. Supreme Court renders group decisions on issues affecting the entire nation.

**Group Polarization** Why are so many decisions entrusted to groups rather than to individuals? For one thing, we assume that an individual acting alone is more likely to take risks than a group considering the same issue. The assumption that groups make more conservative decisions than individuals remained unchallenged until the early 1960s. At that time, James Stoner (1961) designed an experiment to test this idea. He asked subjects individually to counsel imaginary people who had to choose between a risky but potentially rewarding course of action and a conservative and less rewarding alternative. Next, the advisers met in small groups to discuss each decision until they reached unanimous agreement. Stoner and many other social psychologists were surprised to find that the groups consistently proposed a riskier course of action than that counseled by the group members working alone. This phenomenon is known as the **risky shift**.

Subsequent research has shown that the risky shift is simply one aspect of a more general group phenomenon called **polarization**—the tendency for individuals to become more extreme in their attitudes as a result of group discussion. Groups that begin deliberations on a fairly risky note will move further during discussion than groups inclining to be cautious as they consider an issue (Fraser, 1971).

What causes polarization in decision-making groups? First of all, people discover during discussion that the other group members share their views to a greater degree than they realized. Then, in an effort to be seen in a positive light by the others, at least some group members become strong advocates for what is shaping up to be the dominant sentiment in the group. Arguments leaning toward one extreme or the other not only reassure people that their initial attitudes are correct but also intensify those attitudes so that the group as a whole becomes more extreme in its position. Thus, if you refer a problem to a group to ensure that it will be resolved in a cautious, conservative direction, you should make sure that the members of the group hold cautious and conservative views in the first place.

**Great person theory** Theory that leadership is a result of personal qualities and traits that qualify one to lead others.

**THE EFFECTIVENESS OF THE GROUP** Another reason for assigning so many important problems to groups is the assumption that the members of the group will pool their skills and expertise, and therefore solve the problem more effectively than would any individual member working alone. The adage that "Two heads are better than one" reflects this way of thinking.

In fact, groups are more effective than individuals only under specific circumstances. According to Steiner (1972), the effectiveness of a group depends on three factors: (1) the nature of the task, (2) the resources of the group members, and (3) the interaction among group members. There are many different kinds of *tasks*, each of which demands specific kinds of skills. If the requirements of the task match the skills of the group members, the group is likely to be more effective than any single individual.

Even if task and personnel are perfectly matched, however, the ways in which the people *interact* in the group may reduce the group's efficiency. For example, high-status individuals tend to exert more influence in groups, regardless of their problem-solving abilities. If high-status people are not the most qualified group members to solve the problem, the group may well settle on the wrong solution, even though one or more of the lower-status participants could have come up with the right solution working alone. In one experiment with bomber crews, Torrance (1954) found that the low-status gunners who correctly solved a problem were about six times less likely than the high-status pilots to convince the group that their answer was correct.

One theory of leadership holds that an especially effective leader is the right person in the right place at the right time—as in the case of Martin Luther King's leadership of the civil rights movement in the 1950s and 1960s.

Another factor is group *size*. The larger the group, the more likely it is to include someone who has the skills needed to solve a difficult problem. On the other hand, it is much harder to coordinate the activities of a large group than those of a small group.

Still another variable is the *cohesiveness* of a group. When the people in the group like one another and feel committed to the goals of the group, cohesiveness is high. Under these conditions, members may work hard for the group, spurred on by high morale. But cohesiveness can undermine the quality of group decision making. If the group succumbs to *groupthink* (Janis 1982), according to Irvine Janis, strong pressure to conform prevents people in a cohesive group from expressing critical ideas of the emerging consensus. In such a group, amiability and morale supercede judgment. Members with doubts may hesitate to express them. The result may be disastrous decisions—such as the Bay of Pigs invasion, the Watergate cover-up, or the *Challenger* explosion (Kruglanski, 1986).

**LEADERSHIP** Every group has a leader, but how do group leaders come to the fore? For many years the predominant answer to this question was the **great person theory**, which states that leaders are extraordinary people who assume positions of influence and then shape events around them. In this view, individuals like George Washington, Winston Churchill, and Nelson Mandela were "born leaders" who would have led any nation at any time in history.

Most historians and psychologists now regard this theory as naive because it ignores social and economic factors. An alternative theory holds that leadership emerges when the right person is in the right place at the right time. For instance, in the later 1950s and early 1960s, Dr. Martin

**Industrial/organizational (I/O) psychology** Division of psychology concerned with the application of psychological principles to the problems of human organizations, especially work organizations.

**Hawthorne effect** Principle that subjects will alter their behavior because of researchers' attention and not necessarily because of any specific experimentation.

Luther King, Jr., rose to lead the black civil rights movement. Dr. King was clearly a "great person"—intelligent, dynamic, eloquent, and highly motivated. Yet had the times not been right, according to this theory, it is doubtful that he would have been as successful as he was.

Recently, social scientists have taken a more complex approach to understanding the nature of leadership. Called *transactional view*, this perspective integrates and expands on the great person and the right-place-at-the-right-time theories of leadership. According to transactional theorist Fred Fiedler (1967, 1981), the personal characteristics of aspiring leaders can be grouped into two contrasting *leadership styles: task-oriented leaders* concentrate on doing the task well, even at the expense of worsening relationships among group members, while *relationship-oriented leaders* focus on maintaining group cohesiveness and harmony. Which style works best depends on three factors: the task (whether it is clearly structured or ambiguous; the *relationship* between the leader and the group (a warm, caring relationship or a cool, distant relationship); and *power* (the leader's ability and propensity to exercise power over a group). Fieldler has demonstrated that task-oriented leaders succeed best in situations that are either favorable for leader or very unfavorable—either structured tasks, good leader-member relations, and high leader power, or unstructured tasks, poor leader-member relations, and low leader power. When conditions within the group are only moderately favorable for the leader, the most effective leader is one concerned about maintaining good interpersonal relations.

Summing up, Fieldler notes, "Except perhaps for the unusual case, it is simply not meaningful to speak of an effective or of an ineffective leader; we can only speak of a leader who tends to be effective in one situation and ineffective in another." (Fieldler, 1967, p. 261).

## Organizational Behavior

Much of our behavior is shaped by the places where we work and the various organizations to which we belong. **Industrial organizational (I/O) psychology** spotlights the influence on human interaction of large, complex organizational settings, with special emphasis on behavior in the workplace.

**PRODUCTIVITY** I/O psychologists focus on practical problems such as how to reduce employee turnover, improve worker morale, and increase productivity. One of the first studies of the relationship between productivity and working conditions was conducted in the late 1920s by Elton Mayo and his colleagues, who gradually increased the lighting in the Western Electric Hawthorne plant in Cicero, Illinois. The researchers were testing the hypothesis that better lighting would boost worker output. But their results showed something else entirely: Productivity increased with better lighting, too much lighting, and too little lighting. In what has become known as the **Hawthorne effect,** the workers' behavior changed merely because of the researchers' attention, not as a function of any specific manipulations of workplace conditions.

The methods of Mayo's team have since come under criticism (Parsons, 1974), but their study was one of the first to highlight the importance of psychological and social factors on behavior in the workplace. Since the 1930s, I/O psychologists have attempted to analyze that relationship in more specific terms. For example, recent studies have demonstrated that the psychological requirements of a job are just as critical to understanding productivity as the physical demands of the job (Katzell & Guzzo, 1983). For example, workers whose jobs call for a greater variety of skills are more likely to think of their jobs as meaningful and to exhibit increased motivation and satisfaction; and workers whose jobs entails more autonomous activity generally perceive their jobs as responsible and produce work of a higher quality (Hackman & Oldham, 1976). Thus, motivation, satisfaction, and productivity in the workplace can all be improved by making the right changes in job components.

Research by I/O psychologists has also found that small, cohesive work groups are more productive than large, impersonal ones. Putting this idea into practice, managers of assembly-line workers have developed the *autonomous work group*, replacing the massive assembly line with small groups of workers who produce an entire unit (a whole car, for instance) and periodically alternate their tasks. Additional benefits derived from this approach include greater worker satisfaction, higher-quality output, and decreased absenteeism and turnover (G. D. Jenkins & Gupta, 1983).

**COMMUNICATION AND RESPONSIBILITY** The way communications are handled within an organization also has an impact on organizational efficiency and the attitudes of its members. In organizations where members communicate with just one person in authority, for instance, the communications system becomes centralized. This type of communications scheme typically works well in solving simple problems; complex problems, on the other hand, are better handled in a decentralized way, with group members freely communicating with one another (L. W. Porter & Roberts, 1976).

I/O psychologists have also examined the issue of assigning responsibility for key decisions to work groups. While some groups make better decisions than others, it turns out that group decision-making enhances membership satisfaction in 60 percent of the cases analyzed (Locke & Schweiger, 1979). In a related finding, workplace satisfaction also goes up the more a position allows its occupant to communicate with others. In additional to formal communication, following an organizational chart, workers in most companies develop less formal patterns of communication that bypass established channels.

## LOOKING FORWARD

In the first chapter we defined psychology as the science of behavior and mental processes. In subsequent chapters we isolated many forces and processes that help shape our behavior: memory, cognition, intelligence, physiological processes, and so on. Clearly, however, these phenomenon do not operate in a vacuum. Although on one level we are all individuals, on another level we are all members of a society and are subject to cultural influences. Even our "personal" decisions—what to eat, whom to marry, which occupation to pursue—are shaped to some degree by social and cultural forces. For this reason we have devoted an entire chapter to the study of the ways in which the thoughts and behavior of one individual are influenced by the behaviors of other people.

Social psychology thus provides us with the broader stage on which the drama of human behavior unfolds. In so doing it raises a number of fundamental questions: To what extent are our behaviors shaped by forces that we might not be consciously aware of? Should we attribute other people's behaviors to their personal choices and characteristics or to larger social and economic forces? How and when should we try to change people's attitudes? Can prejudice and discrimination be overcome? How far will people go in conforming to group norms? To what extent must we compromise our individuality to function effectively as members of society? These questions go directly to the heart of who we are and why we behave as we do.

Social psychology also teaches us that groups differ in their norms and behaviors. This raises another basic question: Are any human behaviors truly universal, or do all behaviors vary from one group or culture to another? We will examine this question in the next and final chapter, which deals with human diversity.

## SUMMARY

**Social psychology** is the scientific study of how the thoughts, feelings, and behaviors of one individual are influenced by the real, imagined, or inferred behavior or characteristics of other people. Research in social psychology has concentrated on four topics: social cognition, attitudes, social influence, and social action.

### SOCIAL COGNITION

In thinking about others, we organize our thoughts and feelings to enhance our control and effectiveness in social interactions.

#### Impression Formation

When forming impressions of others, we rely on schemata, sets of expectations and beliefs about different categories of people. Impressions are also affected by the order in which information is acquired. According to the **primacy effect**, first impressions are the strongest. As "cognitive misers," we avoid wasting thought and judge people according to simplistic concepts. One such concept is the **stereotype**, a set of characteristics we presume is shared by all members of a social category or group. Biased treatment of others can bring about the very behavior one expects through the effects of the **self-fulfilling prophecy**.

#### Attribution

People also seek to understand one another by explaining behavior, a process called **attribution**. Attributions can be either internal or external. One theory maintains that attributions are made by analyzing the distinctiveness, consistency, and consensus of a particular behavior pattern. Biases in perception can lead to the **fundamental attribution error**, in which personal (internal) forces are overemphasized as influences on other people's behavior and situational (external factors) are given far more weight in accounting for our own behavior. Just the opposite goes on when we seek to explain our own behavior. **Defensive attribution** motivates us to explain our own actions in ways that protect our self-esteem, that is, we tend to attribute our successes to internal factors and our failures to external factors. The **just-world hypothesis** may lead us to blame the victim when bad things happen to other people.

#### Interpersonal Attraction

People are more attracted to each other when **proximity** brings them into frequent contact. We also like people because of *physical attractiveness*, *similarity* of attitudes, interests, and values, and rewarding **exchanges** that are based on **equity**. Love is an experience based on such factors as **intimacy**, and *trust*.

### ATTITUDES

An **attitude** is a relatively stable organization of one's thoughts, feelings, and behavior tendencies toward something or someone—the attitude object.

#### The Nature of Attitudes

Attitudes can predict behavior, especially if one's actions and expressions are not influenced by other factors like **self-monitoring**. Attitudes are acquired through learning and developed through experience.

#### Prejudice and Discrimination

**Prejudice** is an unfair negative attitude directed against a group and its members; **discrimination** is behavior based on prejudice. One explanation of the roots of prejudice is the **frustration-aggression theory**, which states that people who feel exploited and oppressed displace their hostility toward the powerful onto people who are lower on the social scale than they are. Another theory links prejudice to the **authoritarian personality**, a rigidly conformist and bigoted personality type marked by exaggerated respect for authority and hostility toward those who defy society's norms. A third theory proposes a cognitive source of prejudice—oversimplified thinking about both classes of people and the world. Finally, conformity to the prejudices of one's social group or society explains much individual prejudice.

Prejudice can be reduced by encouraging contact between groups of equal status, one-on-one contacts, and participation in cooperative enterprises, and by changing social norms.

#### Attitude Change

Attitudes are sometimes changed in response to new experiences and persuasive efforts. The first step in the persuasive process is to get the audience's attention. Then, according to the communication model, persuasion is a function of the *source*, the *message* itself, the *medium* of communication, and the characteristics of the *audience*. Attitudes may also be changed when new actions contradict preexisting attitudes (**cognitive dissonance**), according to the cognitive consistency model.

## SOCIAL INFLUENCE

**Social influence** refers to the idea that behavior can be controlled by the presence and actions of others without regard to underlying attitudes.

### Cultural Influence

The **culture** in which we are immersed—all the tangible products of our society as well as its shared beliefs and values—teaches us what to value and how to behave. Culture dictates differences in beliefs, diet, dress, and personal space. In the course of adapting our behavior to that of others, we learn the **norms** of our culture. We accept **cultural truisms** without questioning their validity. Through techniques like the **cultural assimilator**, however, we can learn to understand and accept the perspective of people from different cultures.

### Conformity

Besides **cultural norms**, the behavioral rules shared by an entire society, there are norms that pertain to smaller organizations within the society, and these, too, shape our behavior. Voluntary yielding of one's own preferences or beliefs to norms is called **conformity**. Research by Solomon Asch and others has shown that characteristics of the situation and characteristics of the individual influence the likelihood of conformity.

### Compliance

Compliance is a change in behavior in response to an explicit request from another person or group. Some techniques used to get others to comply are the *foot-in-the-door effect*, the *lowball procedure*, and the *door-in-the-face effect.*

### Obedience

Classic work by Stanley Milgram showed that many subjects were willing to obey orders to administer harmful shocks to other people. This **obedience**, or compliance to a command, was more in evidence when the authority figure was physically close and apparently legitimate, and when the victim was distant and thus easier to punish. According to Milgram, obedience is brought on by the constraints of the situation, but another interpretation holds that subjects are unable to mentally shift gears to abandon their belief that the authority figure is credible and trustworthy.

## SOCIAL ACTION

Social actions depend on the presence of other people—as victims, recipients, and sources of influence.

### Deindividuation

Immersion in a group may lead to **deindividuation**, the loss of a sense of personal responsibility that makes possible violent, irresponsible behavior. Immersion in a large group shields individuals with a cloak of anonymity to group members and promotes the arousal to action.

### Helping Behavior

Help without expectation of reward is considered **altruistic behavior**. Helping is constrained by situational factors like the presence of other passive bystanders, a phenomenon known as the **bystander effect**. Personal characteristics that induce helping are empathy with the victim and good mood. Studies of those who helped Holocaust victims revealed a variety of motivations, including strongly held moral values, attachment to the victims, family support and encouragement, and a bedrock belief in religious tolerance.

### Group Decision Making

Groups are often entrusted with problem solving in the expectation that they will be more careful and responsible than lone individuals. Research on the **risky shift** and the broader phenomenon of **polarization** shows that group deliberation actually enhances members' tendencies toward extreme solutions, leaning toward risk or caution. Group effectiveness depends on such factors as the nature of the task, the group's resources, and how members interact. Group cohesiveness can lead to *groupthink*, a pattern of thought characterized by self-deception and the manufacture of consent through conformity to group values.

According to the **great person theory**, leadership is a function of personal traits that qualify one to lead others. An alternative theory attributes leadership to being in the right place at the right time. According to the *transactional view*, traits of the leader and traits of the group interact with certain aspects of the situation to determine what kind of leader will come to the fore. Fred Fiedler focused on two contrasting leadership styles (task-oriented and relationships-oriented). The effectiveness of each one depends on the nature of the task, the relationship of the leader with group members, and the leader's power over the group.

### Organizational Behavior

**Industrial/organizational (I/O) psychology** studies behavior in organizational environments like the workplace. Studies of productivity have revealed that worker output increases as a result of researchers' attention, a phenomenon called the **Hawthorne effect**. I/O findings have also led organizations to establish *autonomous work groups* to replace less efficient assembly-line arrangements. Productivity and morale may also be improved by increasing worker responsibility and facilitating communication in the workplace.

# REVIEW QUESTIONS

## MULTIPLE CHOICE

1. The scientific study of how thoughts, feelings, and behavior of one individual are influenced by the real, imagined, or inferred behavior or characteristics of other people is called ______ psychology.
2. When we first meet someone, we use cues to fit that person into preexisting categories called ______. Sometimes we think and behave in accordance with a ______, a set of characteristics thought to be shared by all the people who belong to a particular social group.
3. The ______ effect exists to the extent that the first information we receive about someone weighs more heavily than later information in the impressions we form.
4. The inferences we make about the behavior of other people is addressed by:

   a. psychology
   b. social psychology
   c. attribution theory
   d. cognitive dissonance
5. Which of the following has *not* been established as a factor that encourages people to like each other?

   a. proximity
   b. attractiveness
   c. complementary attitudes and interests
   d. intimacy
6. A(n) ______ is a fairly stable organization of beliefs, feelings, and behavioral tendencies directed toward some object such as a person or group.
7. True or fales: The best way to predict behavior is to measure attitudes.
8. Prejudice and discrimination can be formed and sustained by people's attempts to ______ to society.
9. ______ ______ theory maintains that a state of unpleasant tension arises from the clashing of two incompatible cognitions.
10. According to cognitive dissonance theory, when there is a discrepancy between a person's behavior and attitudes, it is often easiest for the person to change ______ to reduce the dissonance.

    a. attitudes
    b. behavior
    c. neither attitudes nor behavior
    d. intentions
11. Match each of the following terms with its definition:

    _____ Social influence
    _____ Compliance
    _____ Obedience
    _____ Conformity

    a. Voluntarily yielding to social norms, even at the expense of one's own preferences
    b. A change of behavior in response to a command from another person
    c. A change of behavior in response to an explicit request from another person or from a group
    d. Any actions performed by one or more persons to change the attitudes, behavior, or feelings of others
12. If group members are inclined to take risks, then the group decision is likely to be riskier than arrived at by individuals acting alone. This phenomenon is known as the ______ ______.

13. A shift in attitudes by members of a group toward more extreme positions than those they held before group discussion is called ______ .

14. The effectiveness of a group depends on three factors: (1) the nature of the ______ , (2) the resources of the group members, and (3) the ______ among group members.

15. True or false: All groups have a leader, whether a formal one or an informal one.

16. True or false: Worker satisfaction is not related to the position a person occupies within an organization.

## CRITICAL THINKING AND APPLICATIONS

17. What is a self-fulfilling prophecy? How does this concept apply to human relationships?

18. What do we mean by internal versus external attribution? Which approach would you be more likely to adopt in trying to explain other people's behavior?

19. What are some of the key factors that determine interpersonal attraction according to social psychologists?

20. Think of an advertisement that influenced your decision to purchase something. What kind of message did the ad convey? How was this message communicated? Why did you respond to it? Were you aware at the time that the ad was designed to elicit this response? Is advertising inherently dishonest and manipulative, or does it sometimes serve a useful purpose?

*(Answers to the Review Questions can be found in the back of the text.)*

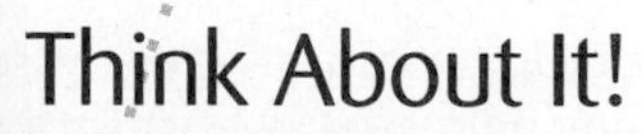

## Think About It!

1. Do psychologists agree that men have greater mathematical skills than women have?
2. What is "emotional labor," and why is it more common among females than among males?
3. What is the difference between an individualist and a collectivist culture? In which category is the United States generally placed?
4. Can people from one culture understand the facial expressions of people from very different cultures?
5. Do people in collectivist cultures exhibit higher levels of conformity than people in individualist cultures?
6. How do management styles in Japanese businesses reflect a collectivist approach to leadership? How do they differ from traditional management styles in the United States?

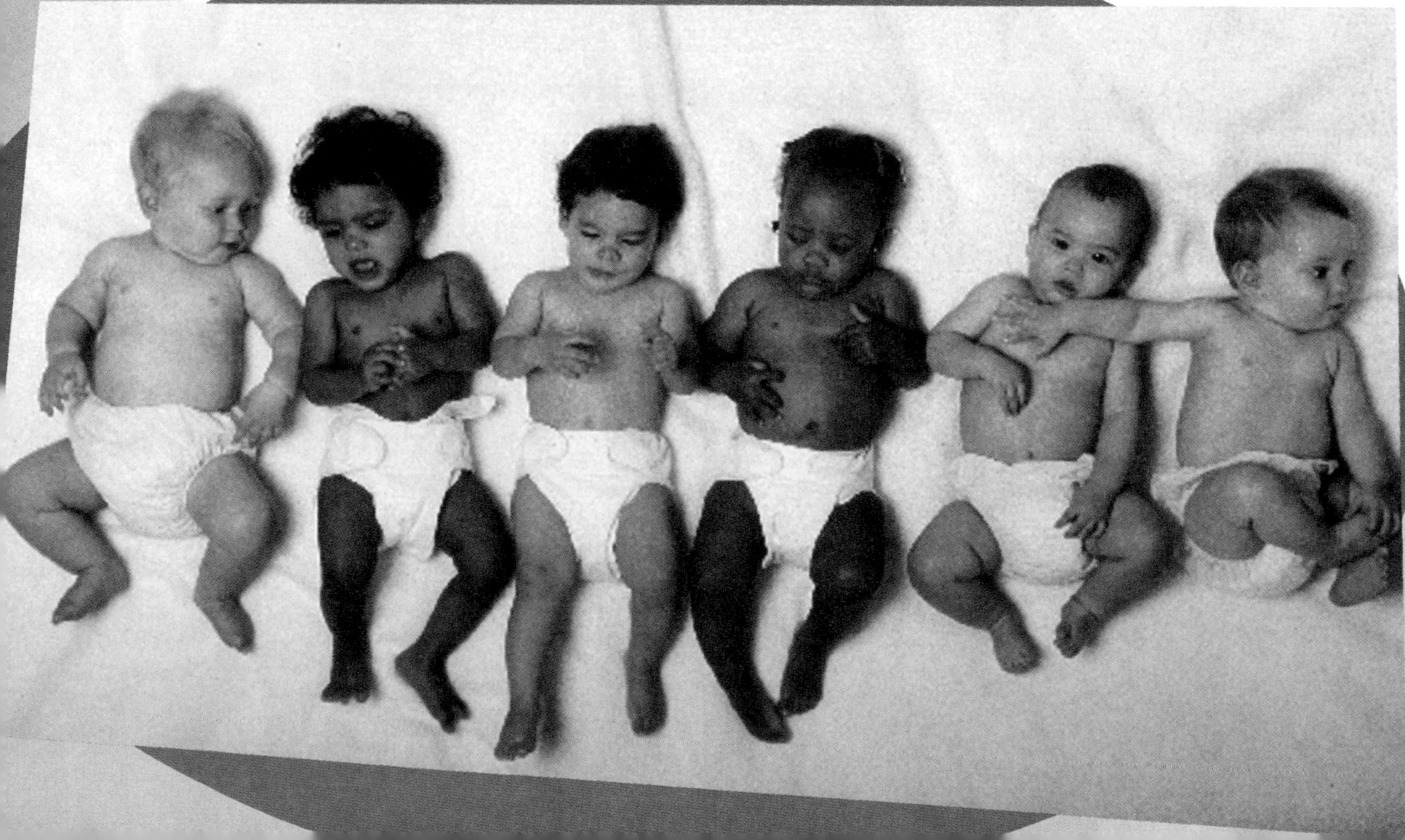

# Human Diversity

# 15

## Overview

**Many years ago it was very exciting for a child to have a pen pal from a different country. You would write a letter to your friend, go to the post office to buy strange-looking airmail envelopes with extra postage, and then mail off your letter and wait for a reply. Several weeks later an envelope would arrive, covered with odd stamps from another land. Upon receiving the first letter, you might not be sure from the writer's name whether your pen pal was a boy or a girl; you'd have to gauge this person's gender from the things said in the letter, the activities and hobbies your new friend liked, or the tone of the writing. The two of you would trade tales of lives that probably seemed very different, and over time you would develop a sense of what daily life in your pen pal's culture was like. The mystery remained, of course, since most people never met their pen pals in person, let alone got a chance to live life as the pen pal lived it.**

Today the idea of having a pen pal seems quaint rather than exciting to American children. Technological advances have eliminated much of the mystery about daily life in faraway places. Television allows us to participate vicariously in the lives and customs of people who live virtually anywhere in the world, and jet travel makes it possible for us to visit almost any country in less than 24 hours. A Canadian can now correspond with someone in Denmark simply by sending electronic mail over the Internet. In the near future, an American child will simultaneously be able to speak with and see her grandmother in Guatemala using a videophone. In short, the world has shrunk.

This realization holds a lesson for psychology. Psychologists once believed that basic psychological processes such as thinking, feeling, and behaving were pretty much the same everywhere in the world and that any departures from what "most people" did either weren't significant or weren't worth studying. As we have seen, however, psychologists' knowledge about "most people" was for a long time based primarily on research using white male subjects in the United States and Western Europe. There were, of course, scattered exceptions to this way of thinking. Wilhelm Wundt, one of the originators of experimental psychology (see Chapter 1), published several volumes on "folk psychology," or the study of various peoples and their habits. In the early days of psychology, there was also some communication among anthropologists, sociologists, and psychologists studying cultural practices. And, as we have seen, a number of female psychologists challenged the predominantly male orientation of the discipline. But only in recent years have many psychologists taken up the systematic study of how people differ by gender, ethnic or racial background, and culture.

Why should psychologists study human diversity? Psychology claims to be "the scientific study of behavior and mental processes," so psychologists would be doing a disservice to the scientific community, and the general public, if they continued to base their conclusions on studies of only a narrow segment of the population. It would be as if biologists who studied only the life cycles of frogs were proposing conclusions concerning how all living things are born, grow, and die: These conclusions would be scientifically invalid and of very limited value. Certainly we can learn a lot about basic life processes by studying a single species, just as we can learn a lot about human beings by examining subgroups of people that are readily

To understand human behavior fully, we must appreciate the rich diversity of human beings throughout the world.

available. But to gain a fuller understanding of human behavior and mental processes, we must appreciate the rich diversity in behavior and mental processes that exists within the human species.

Let us suppose you accept the foregoing argument. Still, you may ask: Why should *I* be interested in learning about human diversity? The answer is all around you. Our major cities are populated by people from diverse backgrounds, with diverse values and goals, living side by side. As we saw in the previous chapter, proximity does not always produce harmony; sometimes it leads to aggression, prejudice, and conflict. Understanding the behavior of people from diverse backgrounds gives us the tools to reduce some of these interpersonal tensions. The differences between males and females are also important to understand. Advertisers' images of the sexes are widely accepted, yet they may have little basis in fact. For example, stereotypes about how the "typical male" looks and acts or the "accepted social roles" for females often lead to confusion and misunderstandings between the sexes. Knowing the scientific bases of human diversity will allow you to separate fact from fiction in your daily interactions with people. Moreover, once you understand how and why groups differ in their values, behaviors, approaches to the world, thought processes, and responses to situations, you will savor the diversity around you. Finally, the more you comprehend the extent of human diversity, the more you will appreciate the many universal features of humanity.

In previous chapters, we explored what is different and what is similar among *individuals*. For example, we examined differences in personality characteristics, intelligence, and levels of motivation, and we explored similarities in biological functioning and developmental stages. In this chapter, we are concerned with exploring psychological differences and similarities among *groups* of people—males and females and members of

**Gender stereotypes** General beliefs about characteristics that men and women are presumed to have.

**Gender roles** Behaviors that we expect each gender to engage in.

different cultural and ethnic groups. We will begin our discussion with a consideration of how men and women are alike and how they differ, after which we'll turn to research comparing various cultures.

## GENDER DIVERSITY

Let's first consider some of the common terms we use to refer to sexual differences: "women and men," "males and females," "feminine and masculine," "gender and sex." *Women* and *men*, the most basic terms on this list, are generally used to distinguish which person is being referred to, as in "Who is that man over there?" or "What does that woman do for a living?" *Male* and *female* refer to one's biological makeup, the physical and genetic facts of being one sex or the other. Some people (e.g., Unger & Crawford, 1992) use the term *sex* to refer exclusively to biological differences in anatomy, genetics, or physical functioning and *gender* to refer to the psychological and social meanings attached to being biologically male or female. This distinction can be difficult to maintain, however, since we are all biological beings interacting in a social world. Because distinguishing what is biologically produced from what is socially influenced is almost impossible, in our discussion of these issues we will use the terms *sex* and *gender* interchangeably.

In contrast, the terms *masculine* and *feminine* have distinct psychological and social meanings. "Masculine" preferences, attributes, and interests are those that are typically associated with being a male in our society, whereas "feminine" preferences, attributes, and interests are those associated with being a female. These terms are based on people's perceptions about the sexes (and indeed, about themselves) rather than on biological facts, which raises the question of stereotypes, to which we now turn.

### Gender Stereotypes

Many popular beliefs concerning differences between the sexes are based on **gender stereotypes**: characteristics that are assumed to be typical of each sex. John Williams and Deborah Best (1990) studied gender stereotypes cross-culturally by surveying college students as well as 5-, 8-, and 11-year-old children from 30 countries. The children read or were told a story about a person and were then asked to indicate the person's gender. The college students were asked which of 300 characteristics were more associated with being male and which with being female. The choices included such common traits as "adventurous," "dependent," "kind," "patient," and "tough." Williams and Best found strong consistency across cultures regarding which characteristics described males and females. For example, in most cultures, men were seen as dominant, strong, and aggressive, whereas women were viewed as affectionate, emotional, and soft-hearted.

Beyond our stereotypes about what males and females "typically" are like, we have general beliefs about **gender roles,** behaviors that we expect males and females to engage in. For example, common gender roles for women in most cultures are to take care of children and family, cook meals, and do laundry. Men, on the other hand, are expected to hold a paying job, provide resources, and drive the car whenever the family goes somewhere.

Gender stereotypes and gender roles usually operate together in our evaluation of the sexes. For example, your stereotype of males as courageous or resourceful might lead you to expect a man to fill the role of "protector" or "person in charge." Stereotypes and role expectations such as these are not always accurate; in fact, some lack even a kernel of truth. However, they are encountered daily by most of us, whether we be children interacting on the playground ("You hit like a girl!"), women experiencing discrimination in the workplace, or men pressured to "succeed." They are also reinforced through the media and through the use of sexist language (see the Controversies and Online boxes in Chapter 7), sometimes in insidious ways. Here are a few examples: Images of men and women appear very differently in newspaper and magazine photographs; those of men tend to stress the face, whereas those of women emphasize the body (D. Archer, Iritani, Kimes, & Barrios, 1983). Television commercials that rely on "expert" voice-over narrations almost invariably use a man (R.S. Craig, 1992). And numerous studies have demonstrated that when we use the word "man" generically ("mankind" instead of "humankind"; "fireman" instead of "fire fighter"), it is rarely interpreted to mean "both sexes." Study after study has shown that when "man" is used in this sense, people think only of male human beings (C. Miller & Swift, 1991).

**Meta-analysis** A way of statistically combining the results of several independent research studies to form an overall conclusion.

Our expectations concerning gender roles often reflect traditional gender stereotypes. What were your initial reactions to these photos?

Generalizations are undeniably an important "cognitive shorthand"; the point about stereotypes is that they are *over*generalizations. Habitually relying on stereotypes rather than paying attention to an individual's personal characteristics can lead to mistaken impressions, false beliefs, and misbegotten conclusions about a person. Since our stereotypes about men and women are so firmly fixed and so potentially damaging, they need to be examined scientifically.

One direct approach to analyzing gender stereotypes and roles is simply to ask: "How are the sexes alike, and how do they differ?" Many laypeople believe that there are vast, well-documented sex differences in most behaviors and abilities, but this is far from true, as we shall see in the following sections where we examine some of the areas in which researchers have investigated diversity between the genders. Before we start, however, you should know that psychologists have increasingly relied on a research strategy called **meta-analysis** to evaluate the size and direction of differences between groups. This technique is described in the Highlights box and is illustrated in Figure 15-1 on page 561. You should also know that the issue of whether psychologists should report on gender diversity *at all* has sparked some debate. As discussed in the accompanying Controversies box, some psychologists argue that disseminating information on gender differences only fuels stereotypes about the sexes, while others maintain that the more valid information we have about the similarities and differences between the sexes, the better able we will be to counter fake stereotypes.

## Gender and Cognitive Skills

As we discussed in Chapter 7, *cognition* refers to a variety of mental processes that involve thinking, reasoning, memory, learning, and intelligence. The relationship between gender and cognitive abilities is controversial. Many laypeople assume that males and females differ significantly in intelligence, verbal skills, mathematical performance, and other cognitive abil-

## HIGHLIGHTS

### Combining Research Findings Across Studies: Using Meta-Analysis in Psychological Research

In several places in this chapter, we present findings from reviews of psychological research in which a research team has summarized a wide selection of literature on a topic in order to reach some conclusions on that topic. There are several crucial decisions to be made in such a process: Which research reports should be included? How should the information be summarized? What questions might be answered after all the available information is gathered?

Traditionally, psychologists reviewing the literature in a particular area relied on the *box-score method* to reach conclusions. That is, after collecting all the relevant research reports, the researcher simply counted the number supporting one conclusion or the other, much like keeping track of the scoring in nine innings of a baseball game (hence the term "box score"). For example, if there were 200 studies of gender differences in aggressive behavior, researchers might find that 120 of them showed that males were more aggressive than females, 40 showed the opposite pattern, and 40 showed no evidence of gender differences. On the basis of these box scores, the reviewer might conclude that males are more likely than females to act aggressively.

Today researchers tend to rely on a more sophisticated strategy known as *meta-analysis*. Meta-analysis provides a way of statistically combining the results of individual research studies to reach an overall conclusion. In a single experiment, each participant contributes data to help the researcher reach a conclusion. In a meta-analysis, each published study contributes data to help the reviewer reach a conclusion, as Figure 15-1 illustrates. Rather than relying on the raw data of individual participants, meta-analysis treats the results of entire studies as its raw data. Meta-analysts begin by collecting all available research reports that are relevant to the question at hand. Next they statistically transform these results into a common scale for comparison. That way differences in sample size (one study might have used 50 participants, another 500), in the magnitude of an effect (one study might have found a small difference, another a more substantial one), and in experimental procedures (which might vary from study to study) can be examined using the same methods. The key element in this process is its statistical basis. Rather than keeping a tally of "yeas" and "nays," meta-analysis allows the reviewer to determine both the strength and the consistency of a research conclusion. For example, instead of simply concluding that there were more studies that found a particular gender difference, the reviewer might determine that the genders differ by six-tenths of a percentage point, or that across all the studies the findings are highly variable.

Meta-analysis has proved to be a valuable tool for psychologists interested in reaching conclusions about a particular research topic. By systematically examining patterns of evidence across individual studies that vary in their conclusions, psychologists are able to gain a clearer understanding of the findings and their implications.

ities. Others believe that the sexes are basically alike in cognitive abilities, that thinking is thinking, regardless of who is doing it. This issue has become increasingly important as women work in ever-larger numbers. Employment statistics show that many occupations are dominated by one gender or the other. Engineering, for example, has traditionally been almost exclusively a male field (e.g., U.S. Bureau of the Census, 1984). Is it possible that this occupational difference and others like it reflect underlying gender differences in cognitive skills?

In 1974, psychologists Eleanor Maccoby and Carol Jacklin published a review of psychological research on gender differences in a number of areas. Using the box-score method, they found no differences at all between males and females in most of the studies they examined. But a few differences did appear in the area of cognitive abilities: Girls tended to have greater verbal ability, and boys tended to exhibit greater spatial and mathematical abilities.

The existence of such cognitive disparities became so widely accepted that these differences are cited as one of the best-established facts of psychology to this day (Hyde, Fennema, & Lamon, 1990; Hyde & Linn, 1988). Yet a close examination of the research literature, including much recent work,

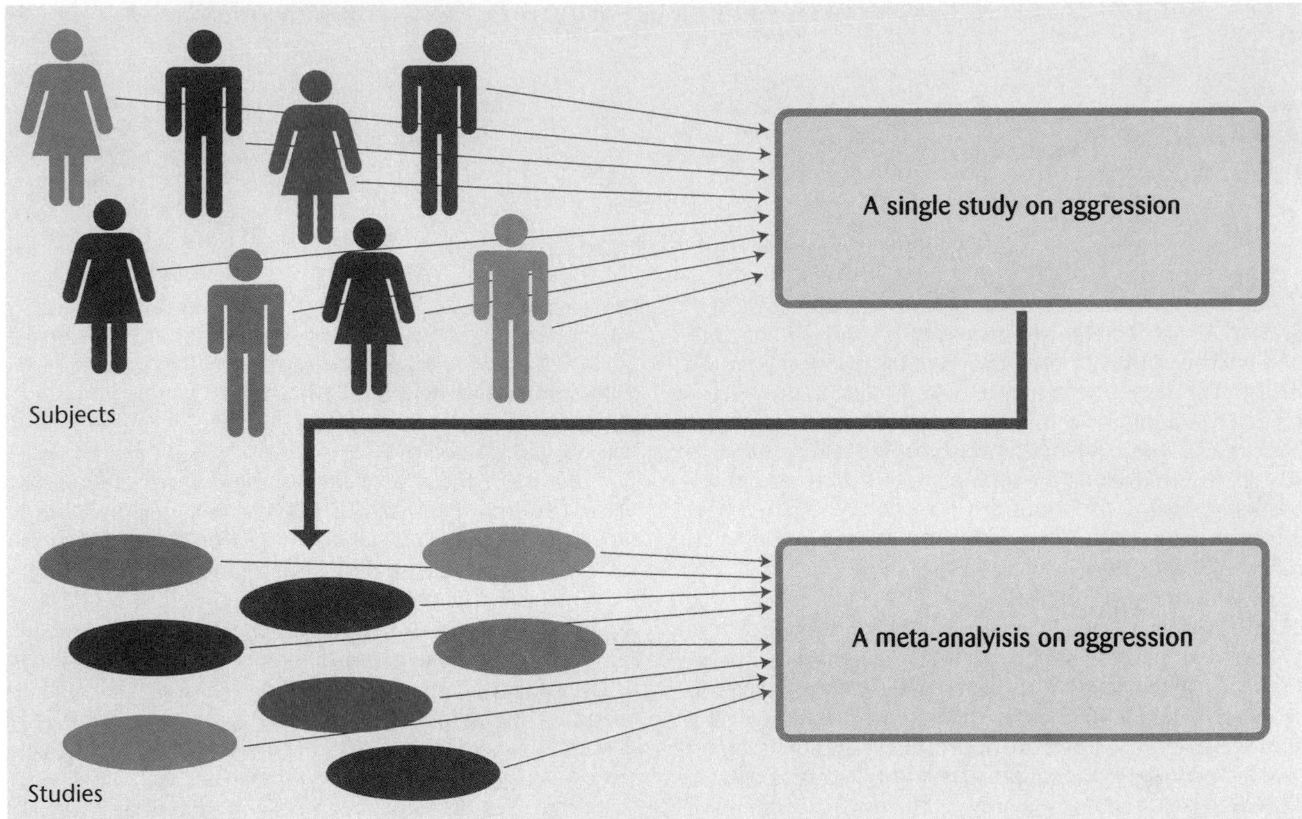


**Figure 15-1**

**Meta-analysis.** Meta-analysis enables researchers to combine the results of individual studies to reach an overall conclusion.

indicates that gender differences in verbal and mathematical ability are virtually nonexistent. For example, Janet Shibley Hyde and her colleagues performed a meta-analysis of 165 research studies involving more than a million people in which gender differences in verbal ability were examined. They concluded that "there are no gender differences in verbal ability, at least at this time, in American culture, in the standard ways that verbal ability has been measured" (Hyde & Linn, 1988, p. 62). A similar review of 100 research studies on mathematical ability involving more than 3 million people showed that in the general population "females outperformed males by only a negligible amount. . . . Females are superior in computation, there are no gender differences in understanding of mathematical concepts, and gender differences favoring males in problem solving do not emerge until the high school years" (Hyde et al.,1990, pp. 139, 151).

1. Do psychologists agree that men have greater mathematical skills than women have?

Males apparently do have an advantage over females in spatial abilities (Halpern, 1992). Spatial tasks include mentally rotating an object and mentally estimating horizontal and vertical dimensions (see Figure 7-2 on p. 239). These skills are particularly useful in solving certain engineering, architecture, and geometry problems. (They are also handy in deciding how to arrange furniture in your new apartment or how to fit all those suitcases into the trunk of your car!)

What should we conclude from these findings? First, differences between males and females seem to be restricted to specific cognitive skills. Scores on tests such as the Stanford-Binet or the WAIS reveal *no* gender differences in general intelligence (Halpern, 1992). Second, gender differences in specific cognitive abilities typically are small—and, in fact, may be disappearing. Finally, the origins of the differences that do exist are still unclear.

## CONTROVERSIES

### Should We Report Sex Differences at All?

Whenever psychologists conduct research, they have several options concerning the sharing of their results with one another and with the general public. How should the research findings be framed? Should all conclusions be given equal weight? How much detail should be included for each result? These are questions to be addressed in any research report, such as the journal articles and book chapters referred to throughout this textbook. Recently a new issue has been raised: How and when should psychologists report evidence of sex differences?

Maureen McHugh, Randi Koeske, and Irene Frieze (1986), writing about the potential problem of sexism in the research process, suggested that unexamined assumptions about the sexes can contaminate psychological research by influencing the way theories are developed, how some research questions are approached, and the manner in which findings regarding the behavior of males and females are reported. For example, some early theories of intelligence (e.g., Thorndike, 1903) held that women differed substantially from men in their intellectual skills. For a long time, such theories were used to argue against admitting women to colleges and universities or treating them equally once they were admitted (see the Highlights Box titled "Missing: Women in Psychology?" in Chapter 1). McHugh, et al., suggested several guidelines that psychologists might follow when interpreting and reporting their findings. One of their recommendations was that "sex-related differences that have not been replicated or have not been predicted by . . . a theoretical model may not be appropriate . . . for published research" (p. 883)—which implies that only expected, well-confirmed sex differences should be published. Presumably, this guideline would prevent the reporting of haphazard or chance findings of sex differences and thus establish a firm foundation upon which to base conclusions.

Social psychologist Alice Eagly (1987a), of Purdue University, proposed a different approach. Rather than reporting only well-confirmed sex differences, Eagly suggested that psychologists should report on comparisons between the sexes routinely and with the same precision they exercise in other types of research. She offered several reasons for this recommendation. First, if psychologists begin to censor themselves by reporting only those sex differences that flow from a theory, many potentially important findings that don't fit with current theories will go unrecognized. Theories and explanations of behavior change, so today's theoretical outlook may be outdated 10 years from now. Therefore, a sex difference that may not be appreciated in the current theoretical climate might prove to be a quite informative finding at some future date. If that sex difference goes unreported, however, we will never know it exists and is significant.

Furthermore, if only well-established sex differences were reported, there would be less chance of replicating newer findings because researchers would be unable to compare their results to results that have not been reported. Finally, if published reports were limited to sex differences the researchers had predicted ahead of time, many null results—findings of no differences between the sexes—would go unreported. Usually a theory predicts that a difference *will* be found, not that there will be *no difference*. Therefore, if a predicted difference was *not* found, the researchers may be reluctant to report that fact. However, the absence of differences can be quite informative. If 20 research reports predicted a sex difference and none of them found it, then perhaps no difference exists. This null result could prove important to our understanding of males and females, so it certainly should be announced.

Social psychologist Roy Baumeister (1988) of Case Western Reserve University has suggested an alternative strategy: By *not* reporting or focusing on sex differences, we can disarm political and social factions inclined to use that kind of information to perpetuate gender stereotypes and myths. If psychologists don't accentuate differences between the sexes, he believes, the general public may shed its notion that the sexes differ markedly. Baumeister also points out that media reports of scientific findings often exaggerate the size or importance of a difference, so that a small sex difference often balloons into a major news item. He advocates that psychologists strive for a "sex-neutral psychology of people" (p.1094). In response, Eagly (1990) has argued that until the women's movement, psychologists spent little time investigating or reporting sex differences, yet gender stereotypes flourished among the general public. Eagly also points out that *any* scientific finding runs the risk of being misinterpreted in the popular media.

This issue is far from resolved. How do you think we should treat findings that the sexes differ in some respects? Do you believe that acknowledging these differences in a research report does more harm than good?

Are biological factors primarily at work? Or do cultural factors, such as the socialization of boys and girls, hold the answer? Recent research has identified several factors that discourage females from pursuing careers in mathematics and science. For example, Chipman , Krantz, and Silver, (1992) found that women avoid careers in mathematics and science partly because of *mathematics anxiety*. Girls and college women are more likely than males to agree with such statements as "I dread mathematics class," perhaps because they do not receive the same amount of encouragement from teachers, peers, and family members to believe they have mathematical ability. Chipman et al., suggest that "a program that reduced mathematics anxiety, or enhanced confidence, could have a striking influence on the study of science among able college women" (p. 295). This type of research suggests that occupational and career differences may be an outgrowth of different socialization of boys and girls.

For years, people assumed that males exhibited greater mathematical abilities than females. Research evidence, however, indicates that gender differences in both mathematical and verbal ability are virtually nonexistent.

## Gender and Emotion

Intuitive. Emotional. Insightful. In touch with feelings. We use these phrases more often to describe women than men. In the chapter on motivation and emotion, we saw that the sexes differ in how they express emotion and respond emotionally to an event. For example, when confronted with betrayal or criticism, men more often report feeling angry, while women report feeling sad, hurt, or disappointed. Men are also less likely than women to express emotion about an event. In this section, we examine some other gender differences in the area of emotional experience.

At the most basic level there are two aspects to communicating emotion: (1) sending an emotional message (through facial expressions, tone of voice, posture, and so on); and (2) perceiving the emotional content of a message sent by someone else. According to the stereotype, women are more expressive than men, which suggests they should be better "senders" of emotional information. Furthermore, the popular notion of "women's intuition" suggests that women should be better than men at perceiving or "decoding" the emotional expressions of others—for instance, figuring out what is being communicated by a brief facial expression. Research indicates that these stereotypes have a kernel of truth. After conducting a meta-analysis of studies in this area, Judith Hall (1984) concluded that women are more skilled than men at decoding the facial expressions, body cues, and tones of voice of others. Several explanations could account for these gender differences (Taylor, Peplau, & Sears, 1994). One is that many women are the primary caregivers for preverbal infants and as such they need to become more attuned than men to the subtleties of emotional expressions. Some have even suggested that this skill is genetically programmed into females. Another explanation is based on the social power held by women and men. Because women historically have occupied less powerful positions in society, they may have felt the need to become acutely attuned to the emotional displays of others, particularly those in more powerful positions (namely, men). Indeed, Sara Snodgrass (1992) found that regardless of gender, followers are more sensitive to the emotions of leaders than vice versa.

The fact that men are more likely than women to hold positions of power may affect emotional experience in other ways as well. In the types of jobs traditionally held by women, workers are often called upon to regulate, manage, or otherwise alter their emotional expression. Sociologist Arlie Hochschild (1983) described this process as *emotional labor*. In a study of flight attendants, the majority of whom were women, Hochschild found clear guidelines regarding which emotions were to be displayed, to whom, by whom, and how often. Most of the flight attendants feel they

**2.** What is "emotional labor," and why is it more common among females than among males?

were being robbed of genuine emotional experiences on the job: ". . . [I]n the flight attendant's work, smiling is separated from its usual function, which is to express a personal feeling, and attached to another one—expressing a company feeling" (p. 127). Hochschild also noted that jobs that are high in emotional labor—such as secretaries, registered nurses, cashiers, social workers, and bank tellers—tend to be filled by women.

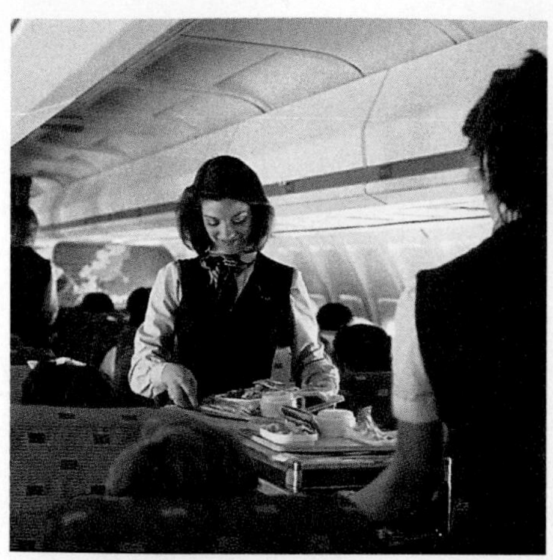

Jobs that require a great deal of emotional labor—such as flight attendant—traditionally have been filled by women.

## Gender and Social Behavior

Having examined gender diversity in thinking and feeling, we turn now to a consideration of gender and social behavior. Are men and women similar or different in the ways they interact with other people? And if there are gender differences in social behavior, what conclusions can we reach about their origins?

**AGGRESSION** A popular belief holds that men are more aggressive than women. There is ample evidence from everyday observations supporting this stereotype. Across cultures and at every age, males are more likely than females to behave aggressively. Moreover, men are more likely than women to murder, to favor capital punishment, to use force to achieve their goals, and to prefer aggressive sports such as hockey, football, and boxing.

The research literature confirms this belief. Two meta-analyses reviewed more than 100 studies of aggression and concluded that males are more aggressive than females both verbally (e.g., taunts, insults, threats) and (especially) physically (e.g., hitting, kicking, fighting) (Eagly & Steffen, 1986; Hyde, 1986). These gender differences tended to be greater in real-life, naturalistic settings than in controlled laboratory settings (Hyde, 1986).

Is the gender difference in aggression biological or social in origin? The answer is not simple. On the one hand, certain biological factors contribute to aggressive behavior. As we saw in Chapter 2, testosterone (a sex hormone found predominantly in males) plays a role in aggression and violence, whereas estrogen (a hormone found predominantly in females) apparently does not. At the same time, it also seems clear that our society encourages greater aggressiveness in boys than in girls. Boys are more likely than girls to be given toy guns or to be rewarded for behaving aggressively; girls are more likely than boys to feel guilty for behaving aggressively or to expect parental disapproval for their aggressive behavior (Perry, Perry, & Weiss, 1989). These findings suggest that early socialization plays a key role in the type and amount of aggression that is seen. Perhaps the most accurate conclusion is that both biological and social factors contribute to aggressive behavior.

Research seems to confirm the belief that males are more aggressive than females verbally and, especially, physically. Higher rates of aggression among males probably reflect both biological differences and gender differences in socialization.

**HELPING BEHAVIOR** As we saw in the chapter on social psychology, the likelihood that people will exhibit helping behavior is affected by characteristics of both the individual and the situation. Does the willingness to provide help also vary by gender? A meta-analysis of the research literature on gender diversity in helping behavior concluded that men were generally more likely than women to offer help (Eagly & Crowley, 1986). The researchers noted, however, that men are more likely to offer assistance when the situation calls for heroism or chivalry toward a stranger, especially if the person in need of help is female or if an audience is present. In fact, most of the studies they reviewed looked at only this type of behavior (i.e., dramatically helping a stranger in need). Notice that this behavior is consistent with the traditional male gender role. The researchers suggested that women may be more helpful than men in situations that call for nurturance, comforting, or caregiving (which also reflect a gender role), such as offering assistance to a loved one. Because very few of the research studies reviewed investigated this other types of helping behavior, it is not surprising that males were found to exhibit more helping behavior. Subsequent studies have shown that women are more likely to be the primary caregivers in a family (Unger & Crawford, 1992) and are more prone than men to offer social support (e.g., advice, encouragement, nurturance) to others (Shumaker & Hill, 1991). This is true partly because women tend to have broader social networks of friends and confidants than men do (thereby enlarging the circle within which support can be offered and received), and partly because both women and men tend to turn to women when seeking social support. Which sex is more helpful? The answer depends on the type of help being considered.

**CONFORMITY** As we discussed in the chapter on social psychology, conformity refers to voluntarily yielding to social norms, even at the expense of one's own preferences. A popular notion is that women are more conforming than men, perhaps because they are more sensitive to the dynamics of interaction and therefore more willing to promote harmony. A meta-analysis of the relevant research literature found a slight overall tendency for females to be more easily influenced than males (Eagly, 1987b). This is especially evident in conformity studies involving group pressure, such as the Asch study described in the previous chapter. However, study results are markedly inconsistent: Where one study reports substantial sex differences in conformity proneness, another finds no evidence of this at all. Therefore, any conclusions concerning sex differences in conformity must be treated with great caution.

**LEADERSHIP** Although more and more women have been elected to serve as mayors, governors, and members of Congress in recent years, the United States still does not seem close to electing a female president. And in the business world, it is still rare to see a woman in a top-level management position. Why do men outnumber women by a large margin in leadership positions throughout the society?

One possible explanation is that women and men practice different leadership styles. Basing their ideas on traditional gender stereotypes, some people have proposed that women have a more group-oriented, participatory approach to leadership, whereas men practice a more instrumental, autocratic style. If the male approach is more successful than the female approach, this could account, at least in part, for the far greater numbers of men in positions of authority. When Alice Eagly and her colleagues investigated this issue by examining the results of hundreds of research studies on leadership (Eagly & Johnson, 1990; Eagly & Karau, 1991; Eagly, Makhijani, & Klonsky, 1992; Eagly, Karau, & Makhijani, 1995), they found mixed support for leadership stereotypes. For example, females did tend to provide more democratic leadership than males did, perhaps because of their better interpersonal skills and greater willingness to seek input from group members (Eagly & Johnson, 1990). However, contrary to the stereotype, men were not more likely to be in leadership positions that required getting the job done and women in leadership positions that required promoting harmony among group members. Moreover, Eagly et al.(1992) found very little support for the notion that women who exercise leadership are evaluated more negatively than men who do so, and Eagly et al. (1995) discovered no evidence that men are more effective leaders overall than women are. Thus, the research data do not support the argument that different styles of leadership account for the scarcity of women in leadership positions. Rather, the data indicate that both men and women can be capable, effective leaders, winning the praise of their followers and meeting the demands of the tasks at hand.

Why, then, are so few women in leadership positions? Although the answer is complex, the key may be found in our stereotypes and role expectations. Many people expect women to be nurturant and compassionate. A woman manager who adopts the stereotypically male role of dominance and autocracy may violate expectations and thus be held to an unfairly high standard of performance or be evaluated harshly. In the studies by Eagly and her colleagues cited earlier, women were indeed more likely to receive negative evaluations when they adopted traditionally "masculine" leadership styles—that is, when they were autocratic or task-oriented. They were also considered less effective in relatively "masculine" leadership roles that required directing and controlling people rather than cooperating with and getting along with people. Against these odds women may be unable to retain leadership positions in traditionally male-dominated settings. Furthermore, because society still expects women to be the primary caregivers to children, many women involved in their careers find themselves caught in a bind of conflicting expectations and competing demands on their time. This role conflict, coupled with unfair evaluations, may limit women's opportunities to secure and hold leadership positions.

Janet Reno, who has served as attorney general in the Clinton administration, is an example of a woman who rose to an important leadership position. The argument that men are more effective leaders than women is not supported by the research evidence and therefore cannot account for the relative scarcity of women in leadership roles.

### Gender Diversity: Summing Up

Several conclusions arise from our investigation of gender diversity. First, although there are some psychological differences between the sexes, they are not as significant as many people suppose. In fact, it is reasonable to say that men and women are much more alike than they are different. Second, the finding that there are some differences between the sexes does not mean that all males or all females are committed to particular ways of behaving. Remember, these are *group* differences. There is much more variability within a gender than across genders; thus, some males are highly sensitive to nonverbal cues, just as some females are highly aggressive. In short, the existence of some differences *between* the sexes should not obscure the fact that there are far greater differences *within* each sex. Finally, psychologists still have much work to do in this area in terms of documenting the diversity between the sexes (i.e., discovering other areas in which males and females behave differently or similarly) and explaining such diversity (i.e., examining the roles of biology and social factors in producing the behaviors). Although gender differences undoubtedly arise from the interaction of both nature and nurture, we are far from certain about the exact contributions of each.

## CULTURAL DIVERSITY

Let's briefly consider the case of Traci, an African-American undergraduate spending her junior year as an exchange student in Japan. Although Traci thought of herself as a sophisticated, cultured person, every day of that year brought her surprises and new insights. Attitudes toward work, family relations, interpersonal communication, values, and goals seemed very different from the ones she was used to. For example, she couldn't understand why her host family interacted with one another the way they did, or why their daughter, Keiko, who was about Traci's age, seemed to have such different aspirations and values. Even daily activities, such as going to the market, asking directions, and taking a weekend trip to the country, seemed to be done in novel ways. Traci could understand why her physical surroundings were very different; it was the *cultural* differences that puzzled her the most. She was experiencing what is sometimes called **culture shock**—"a personal disorientation that accompanies exposure to an unfamiliar way of life" (Macionis, 1993, p. 62). From culture to culture, people differ in their ethnic, racial, and family backgrounds as well as in their values and traditions. If we are unfamiliar with the customs of a particular culture, we may become confused about which behaviors are appropriate within that culture. In the following pages, we will explore what social scientists mean by culture and examine the psychological diversity that exists among cultures.

**Culture shock** Feeling disoriented or uncertain when exposed to an unfamiliar way of life.

**Race** A subpopulation of a species, defined according to an identifiable dimension (i.e., geographic location, skin color, hair texture, genes, facial features).

## Race and Ethnicity

Traci and her hosts obviously belong to a single species: the human species. However, laypeople (and some psychologists) often speak of Asians, Latinos, Native Americans, African Americans, Caucasians, and Pacific Islanders as distinct races, implying fundamental differences among these peoples. A **race** is usually defined as a subpopulation of a species (in this case, humans) who share some biological and genetic similarities and who have reproduced among themselves (Betancourt & López, 1993; J. Diamond, 1994; Macionis, 1993). Furthermore, members of different races generally have distinct physical characteristics, such as hair color or type, skin pigmentation, and facial features. At one time it might have been reasonable to talk about races as distinct groups, given the isolated geographic regions some peoples occupied and the identifiable physical characteristics they developed in adapting to those regions. Today, however, many scientists do not consider race a valid scientific concept because humans have so frequently migrated, intermarried, and commingled. Consequently, genetic characteristics that were once specific to a group of individuals in a particular region were spread widely across a much larger area. All contemporary societies are populated by people with rich genetic mixtures, so it is difficult to argue that human beings now differ substantially on a genetic basis. Furthermore, the physical characteristics that were once thought to "define" membership in a racial group are somewhat arbitrary. Race classification has often been based on melanin (the substance that produces differences in the color of skin, hair, and eyes), but humans could just as easily be classified several other dimensions. For example, some people have a genetic resistance to malaria and others do not; some people can digest milk products and others cannot; and some people have fingerprint patterns that form spirals, while others have patterns that form loops and still others exhibit patterns that form arches (J. Diamond, 1994). We could posit any number of different "races" based these other classification schemes.

Because it is so difficult to define "race" exactly, most psychologists have abandoned the term as a fundamental scientific concept (e.g., Dole, 1995), although racial categories are still used by social scientists and public officials for demographic purposes or for purposes of formulating public policy. (Think of the many forms you've completed that asked you to check off a box identifying yourself as a member of one racial group or another.) Race still has a role in psychology, however, because it can form an important part of a person's self-identity. Identifying with a socially or politically recognized racial group—for example, feeling strongly about oneself as an Asian American—can affect an individual's behavior, attitudes, and cognitive processes. This type of self-identification is even more apparent in the related concept of ethnicity. Whereas race refers to an

**Ethnicity** A common cultural heritage, including religion, language, and/or ancestry, that is shared by a group of individuals.

**Ethnic identity** That aspect of an individual's self-concept that is based on his or her awareness of being a member of a particular ethnic group.

individual's biological heritage, **ethnicity** refers to a common cultural heritage that is shared by a group of people (Macionis, 1993). Members of an ethnic group may have common ancestors, language, or religion or feel a kinship based on traditional social practices. For example, a person of Danish ancestry living in Florida may share the traditions and viewpoints of her compatriots in Denmark (the ethnic group to which she belongs). At the same time, she may identify herself on a questionnaire as Caucasian (the racial group with which she identifies), all the while residing in Florida (the cultural setting where these behaviors are taking place). As you can see, the concepts of race, ethnicity, and culture are closely interrelated.

What effect does ethnicity have on behavior? Ethnic identity can form a part of the individual's self-concept. **Ethnic identity** refers to that aspect of one's self-concept that is based on identifying oneself as a member of a particular ethnic group. Our Danish friend may feel strongly about her ethnic background and build on that identification as a foundation for her overall self-concept. In turn, this view of herself can influence her choice of interaction partners (she may seek out other Danish people), the activities she engages in (she may participate in activities associated with her ethnic group), and her cognitions about herself (seeing herself as a person who is Danish first and a resident of the United States second). Research shows that a strong sense of ethnic identity is linked to high self-esteem (Phinney, 1991), but only when the individual also feels a positive association with the mainstream culture he or she is living in. In other words, holding a strong ethnic identity and being assimilated to the larger culture (e.g., seeing oneself as a Dane in the United States) is a positive combination.

## What Is a Culture?

As we saw in the previous chapter, culture refers to the tangible goods produced in a society, such as art, inventions, literature, and consumer goods. But it also refers to intangible processes such as shared beliefs, values, attitudes, traditions, and behaviors that are communicated from one generation to the next within a society (Barnouw, 1985). These cultural values, traditions, and beliefs in turn give rise to characteristic rules or norms that govern the behavior of people in that society, including what foods they eat, whom they may marry, and what they do on Saturday nights. These few examples should give you an idea of the extent to which cultural norms contribute to cultural diversity; we will see more examples in the pages that follow.

Diversity can exist within a culture as well as among cultures. This scene is from Nairobi, the capital of Kenya.

Moreover, there is room for diversity within a dominant culture in the form of *subcultures*, "cultural patterns that distinguish some segment of a society's population" (Macionis, 1993, p. 75). Texans, psychology professors, persons with AIDS, African-American women, homeless people, and teenagers all form subcultures within U.S. society. These subcultures have their own norms, values, and rituals, which may or may not be similar to those of the dominant culture. Moreover, many nations (such as the United States) are composed of various peoples with different backgrounds and traditions. Although we identify certain ideas, products, and behaviors as distinctly "American,"

we are actually a nation of great diversity—within our borders there are many well-formed subcultures of immigrants and their offspring.

Cultures and subcultures can vary in very many ways, but researchers usually prefer to compare them on certain specific dimensions or characteristics that summarize or capture many of the large number of differences. For example, cultures can be categorized according to "power distance"—the perceived distance between those at the upper reaches of the social structure and those at the bottom—and "uncertainty avoidance"—the tendency to avoid situations whose outcome is unknown (Hofstede, 1980). One very important and widely used dimension is *individualism/collectivism* (see the Highlights box titled "Measuring Individualism/Collectivism at a Personal Level"). Cultures high in individualism, such as the United States, see the

**3.** What is the difference between an individualist and a collectivist culture? In which category is the United States generally placed?

# HIGHLIGHTS

## Measuring Individualism/Collectivism at a Personal Level

*Individualism/collectivism* is an important dimension along which cultures vary. People living in individualist cultures emphasize self-reliance, independence, and achieving personal goals, even at the expense of the goals of a larger group (such as family or work group). In comparison, people in collectivist cultures put a premium on the goals of their group and often strive for harmonious social relations with other group members. Many of these people's activities and motives are determined by group memberships.

This cultural distinction can also be seen at the individual level. Some people tend to perceive themselves as independent individualists—this is called *idiocentrism*—whereas others emphasize interpersonal relationships—this is called *allocentrism*. You can score your own idiocentric/allocentric tendencies by rating your agreement or disagreement with the following statements, which were taken from measures developed by Harry Triandis and his colleagues. Answer each item using the following 5-point rating scale.

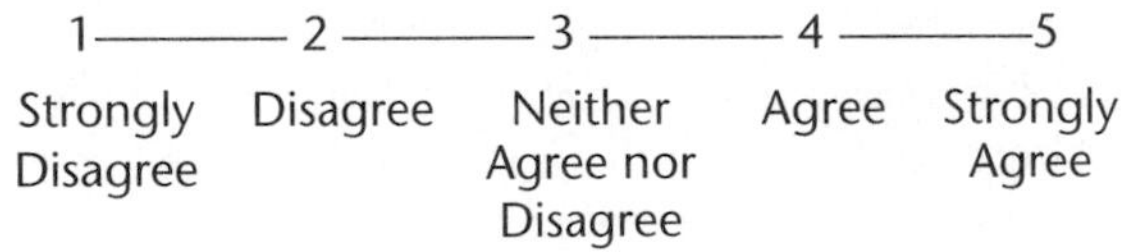


1. If the group is slowing me down, it is better to leave it and work alone.
2. I like to live close to my friends.
3. Only those who depend on themselves get ahead in life.
4. I would help within my means if a relative told me that he or she was in financial difficulty.
5. Success is the most important thing in life.
6. When I choose an intimate friend, I pay a lot of attention to the views of my acquaintances.
7. I am not to blame when one of my close friends fails.
8. My parents' opinions are important in my choice of a relationship partner.
9. It is foolish to try to preserve resources for future generations.
10. When my co-workers tell me personal things about themselves, we are drawn closer together.

Add up your ratings on the odd-numbered items and then do the same for the even-numbered items. Agreeing more strongly with the odd-numbered items reflects an idiocentric orientation; while agreeing more strongly with the even-numbered items reflects an allocentric orientation.

Although people living in individualistic cultures tend to be idiocentric and those living in collectivist cultures tend to be allocentric, there are numerous exceptions. The match (or mismatch) between an individual's level of idiocentrism/allocentrism and the individualism/collectivism of that person's culture is an important predictor of behavior. As Triandis put it, "Allocentric persons in collectivist cultures feel positive about accepting in-group norms and do not even raise the question of whether or not to accept them. However, idiocentric persons in collectivist cultures feel ambivalent and even bitter about acceptance of in-group norms" (Triandis, Bontempo, Villareal, Asai, & Lucca, 1988, p. 325).

*Sources*: H. C. Triandis, R. Bontempo et al. (1988), Individualism and collectivism: Cross-cultural perspectives on self-ingroup relationships. *Journal of Personality and Social Psychology, 54*, 323–338. See also H. C. Triandis et al. (1985), Allocentric versus idiocentric tendencies: Convergent and discriminant validation. *Journal of Research in Personality, 19*, 395–415.

individual person as the basic unit of society and thus foster individual decision making and action. Members of individualist societies have social relationships with many different individuals and groups. In contrast, cultures high in collectivism see the group as the basic unit of society and foster group cohesion and input. Members of collectivist societies have close relationships only with others in similar circumstances who share their goals and fate. Although there are some exceptions, the United States and most European societies emphasize individualism, whereas societies in Latin America, Asia, and Africa tend to be collectivist.

Before we consider the ways in which cultural differences such as these affect psychological processes, a comment on methodology is in order. Studying cultural diversity presents some unique problems. Cultures often differ in language, making translation a potential problem. Cultural norms concerning willingness to help strangers also differ, thus complicating the researcher's job of data collection. And some cultures are simply less accessible than others: Psychologists know relatively little about the nomads of the Gobi desert, for example. Researchers studying other cultures are also confronted by unique ethical issues: They must be sensitive to cultural traditions and avoid passing judgment on cultural practices or using research methods that disrupt lifestyles. Suppose, for example, you want to determine whether the members of two cultures differ in overall intelligence. You decide to use an intelligence test to measure those differences, and indeed it turns out that there are significant differences in average test scores between the two cultures. Assuming for the moment that your test is a valid measure (recall our discussion in the intelligence chapter of the criticisms of intelligence tests), you might conclude that there is a cultural difference in overall intelligence. However, there are other circumstances and plausible explanations you would have to consider before you could validly reach that conclusion. Social psychologist Harry Triandis (1994) described some of the difficulties researchers studying intelligence across cultures often encounter (see Table 15-1 for details). These range from practical matters (such as the way instructions are presented) to theoretical issues (such as the motivation of the participants or the meaning they assign to such evaluations) to ethical concerns (such as the perceived intrusiveness of some questions).

So far we have discussed how scientists define culture and analyze cultural practices. In the following section, we examine how the psychological processes of members of various cultures are similar and how they are different. Here we are relying on the work of psychologists who have made cross-cultural comparisons as well as on the studies of anthropologists and sociologists interested in these issues. Much of the research we discuss uses Americans as a comparison group, largely because behavior in the United States has been so well studied. This trend is changing as psychologists begin to expand their questions of interest and as more and more psychologists from other cultures report their findings. As we did when examining gender diversity, we will organize our discussion around the general topics of human thought, feeling, and behavior.

## Culture and Cognition

Cultural context can have a profound effect on cognitive processes. Consider Traci's experiences. She had spent many years in a U.S. school system, where she had been taught certain techniques of memorization, various ways of putting information together, and general attitudes about how to study and do well in a learning environment. As we saw earlier, Traci's experiences as a foreign exchange student opened her eyes to the diversity in the world around her. This was especially evident in the class-

**TABLE 15-1 Methodological Considerations in Cross-Cultural Research**

Suppose you studied intelligence (using an IQ test) in two distinct cultures and found differences in the two sets of scores you obtained. Before you concluded that there is a meaningful difference in intelligence levels across the two cultures, you would need to eliminate rival hypotheses or other likely explanations for the findings. Harry Triandis, a distinguished social psychologist interested in cultural diversity, outlines some likely rival hypotheses in the study of intelligence (Triandis, 1994, pp. 57–61).

| | |
|---|---|
| 1. The two cultures may have a different definition of "intelligence." | One culture may define intelligence as "being skilled at solving verbal, quantitative, and analytic problems," whereas another culture may define intelligence as "knowing how to treat different people politely in different situations" or "respecting the traditions of our elders." Applying the same definition and measuring instrument to both groups may not be appropriate. |
| 2. The instructions may not be understood the same way. | One culture may be less familiar with the format, techniques, or type of responses called for by the testing situation. If so, the culture that understands the testing situation better will likely perform better. |
| 3. The levels of motivation in the two samples may be different. | Tasks that one culture finds engaging and important may not be interpreted the same way by another culture. For example, members of other cultures may not understand why Americans are so motivated to solve analogies and fill in tiny circles with a No. 2 pencil on a scholastic performance test. |
| 4. The reactions to the experimenter may be different. | Various cultural norms regarding cooperation with "distinguished visitors," "invited guests," or "suspicious outsiders" may contribute in part to the differences in test scores between the two cultures. |
| 5. The meaning of the test situation is not always the same. | The test taker's interpretation of the test and its uses can affect performance. For example, in hierarchical societies such as Japan or India, responses may differ according to whether test takers think the results will be used for pure research or as a method of job placement, or will be shared with teachers or family members. |
| 6. Some people panic in test situations and thus do very badly. | This is true within any culture, but levels of test anxiety, nervousness, or uncertainty may also vary across cultures. |
| 7. Response sets differ across cultures. | Members of some cultures may respond to test items in a polite way, in an extreme way, in a defensive way, in an honest way, and so on. |
| 8. The two samples, in the two cultures, may not have been strictly equivalent. | In order to isolate cultural differences, you need to establish that the two samples are roughly equivalent in terms of gender, age, educational background, family background, rural or urban environment, religion, social class, and so on. |
| 9. The ethical acceptability of the method may not have been the same. | Questions that seem harmless to members of one culture may be offensive to members of a different culture. Also, the way in which the experimenter interacts with the test participants may not be as acceptable to members of both cultures. |

*Source*: Adapted from *Culture and social behavior* (pp. 57–61) by Triandis, 1994. Copyright © by McGraw Hill, Inc. Reprinted by permisison of the publisher.

room. She found it difficult to understand why her fellow students studied so hard, how they could remember information she'd barely noticed, or why they blamed themselves for doing poorly on an impossibly difficult exam. Our discussion of culture and cognition may provide some answers to clear up some of her perplexity, for in this section we examine findings regarding cultural diversity in categorization, memory processes, academic performance, and attributional style.

**CATEGORIZATION** We learned in Chapter 7 that categorization is a basic cognitive act that helps us form concepts. Categorizing birds, trees, furniture, or occupations helps us to develop a prototype of those concepts and thus speeds our processing of new, incoming information. All known cultures use categories (Kluckholn, 1954), but what information gets included in a given category, and how the categories are shaped by experience, can differ substantially from one culture to another. Cross-cultural psychologist David Matsumoto provides an example of how these differences can affect perception, cognition, and behavior:

> We have probably all seen imported, handmade, brass pitchers of various designs and sizes. Once, after dinner with a Persian friend at an American's home, we all gathered in the living room. After a moment, our Persian friend turned red, giggled, and looked embarrassed, but didn't say anything. When the host left the room a few minutes later, the Persian pointed out a large ornate brass pitcher with a long spout that was sitting on a coffee table as a decoration. It had been made in the Middle East where toilet paper is scarce and people clean themselves after going to the bathroom by using such pitchers to pour water on themselves. So what was a prized decoration to our host was an embarrassment to my friend. (Matsumoto, 1995, p. 52)

As this example illustrates, two people perceiving the same object may assign it to very different categories!

Cultures differ even in the extent to which they categorize very basic information, such as colors or shapes. We all know that a circle, an oval, and an ellipse belong together, whereas a triangle is not part of that group. However, what we "all know" may not be universally held. For example, the Dani, a people who live in the highlands of New Guinea, do not have names for geometric shapes. Nonetheless, cognitive psychologist Eleanor Rosch (1973) found that the Dani learned geometric categories more easily when presented with a prototypical example (such as a square) than when presented with a less prototypical example (a crudely drawn irregular square). Similarly, the Dani use only two color terms, which correspond roughly to "light" and "dark." When Rosch presented them with prototypical colors (a pure red), the Dani were able to learn the color categories more readily than when presented with nonprototypical colors (a reddish brown).

These findings indicate that category concepts based on prototypes are learned quickly, even when the categories are not part of one's culture or language. In addition, Berlin and Kay (1969) found another regularity in color terms. If a culture's language has only two color names, these names will refer to black and white. If the language has three terms, the third invariably refers to red, and if it has a fourth term, it will refer to either yellow or green. More complex languages add blue and then brown, and if a language has more than seven color terms, it will include names for pink, purple, orange, and gray.

Taken together, these findings support two basic principles. First, there are some universal aspects to categorization. Members of all cultures, for example, either have or can easily learn categories for basic colors, shapes, and other icons (such as facial expressions, discussed below). These are areas in which members of different cultures are likely to have had similar experiences (Matsumoto, 1995). Second, where cultural experiences differ, there are likely to be differences in categorization. This diversity is partly responsible for the different world-views of various cultures. If members of different cultures use very different concepts and categories as a result of their different experiences, then they will probably think about the world and organize experiences in very different ways, which can, in turn, lead to significant differences in behavior.

**MEMORY** Many researchers believe that culture has a profound effect on memory. For example, Jayanthi Mistry and Barbara Rogoff (1994) note that remembering has practical consequences for one's daily life, that it takes place within a particular context, and that it is influenced by the values and customs of a given culture. Each of these factors has an influence on what people remember and how easily they recall it. For example, in many Western cultures, being able to recite a long list of words or numbers, to repeat the details of a scene, and to provide long lists of facts and figures about historical events are all signs of a "good memory." In fact, tasks such as these are often used to test people's memory abilities. What we should realize is that these kinds of memory tasks reflect the type of learning, memorization, and categorization skills taught in Western schools. Members of other cultures often perform poorly on such memory tests because the exercises seem odd or foreign to them. In contrast, consider the memory skills of a person living in a society where cultural information is passed on from one generation to the next through a rich oral tradition. The individual may be able to recite the deeds of the culture's heroes in verse or rattle off the lines of descent of families, larger lineage groups, and elders. Or perhaps the individual has a storehouse of information about the migration of animals or the life cycles of plants that helps people obtain food and know when to harvest crops. An oral tradition of epic poetry (D'Azevedo, 1982), detailed recollection of the workings of nature, and the ability to recite long genealogies (Bateson, 1982) all demonstrate impressive memory skills. Note that all these memory feats involve material that is highly significant to the culture.

Frederic Bartlett, whose experiments with memory were discussed in Chapter 6, anticipated this view of memory long ago. Bartlett (1932) related a tale of a Swazi cowherd who had a prodigious memory for facts and figures about cattle. The cowherd could recite, with virtually no error, the selling price, type of cattle bought, and circumstances of the sale for purchases dating back several years. Bartlett explained that in Swazi culture the care and keeping of cattle are very important in daily life, and many cultural practices focus on the economic and social importance of cattle. In contrast, he reported, Swazi children did no better than his young European subjects in recalling a 25-word message. Stripped of its cultural significance, their memory performance was not exceptional.

**ACADEMIC PERFORMANCE** There is a growing concern in the United States that the academic preparation of American students is inadequate compared to that of students in other countries. To what extent is this concern valid?

Harold Stevenson (Stevenson, 1992, 1993; Stevenson, Chen, & Lee, 1993) has investigated the differences in academic performance among members of various cultures. In 1980, he and his colleagues (Stevenson, Lee, & Stigler, 1986) studied first- and fifth-graders in American, Chinese, and Japanese elementary schools. At that time, the Japanese and Chinese students at both grade levels far surpassed the American students in mathematics, and the Chinese also were more proficient readers . A decade later, when the study was repeated with a new group of fifth-graders, the researchers discovered even greater differences in mathematical proficiency between American students on the one hand and Japanese and Chinese students on the other (Stevenson et al., 1993). The reading vocabulary scores of the three groups also showed changes. In 1980, Chinese fifth-graders scored the highest on vocabulary, whereas Japanese students scored the lowest. Among the 1990 fifth-graders, however, the Japanese students performed the best, and American students had dropped to the lowest position. In 1990, the research team also studied the original first-graders in the three cultures, who

**"How does cultural experience affect our ability to learn and remember things?"**

Learning and remembering are such basic human functions that we are tempted to consider them innate. Indeed, as we have seen, some scholars argue that certain aspects of memory operate independently of the individual's cultural setting. Still, much evidence suggests that culture exerts a major influence on memory. Recall from the earlier chapters on memory and learning that we tend to place new information into established categories and prototypes in order to make sense of and recall this information. Many scholars maintain that what types of information we consider important and the kinds of categories we use vary according to our cultural background. As we have noted in the text, material that is important to Americans might be unimportant to members of a preliterate society, and vice versa. Indeed, as Bartlett demonstrated in his studies involving Native-American folk tales (see the chapter on memory), people sometimes reconstruct memories in ways that make these memories more familiar or relevant to their lifestyle.

Can you think of some types of information that are easily remembered in our culture but that might be difficult for members of other cultures to encode? In what ways does cultural experience prepare us to remember some things easily but not other things? After you have thought about these questions, take a few minutes to examine the opinions of some other students, which appear below.

• • • • • • •

**GREG: Most people in American society can recognize different models of cars, since the automobile is supposedly an American obsession and a very useful means of transportation. An aborigine living in Australia might have a bit more difficulty, though, when asked to distinguish between a Yugo and a Porsche.**

**BOB: In our TV culture, I think we memorize things that are laid out in front of us. On Sundays, sports events on TV always have stats ready to show their audience.**

**LEE: I think Americans tend to remember public figures like movie stars, since they are connected to entertainment and we are almost an "entertainment culture."**

**MARIA: I think remembering has a lot to do with language, which is directly related to culture and its needs. For example, Eskimos have tons more words for snow than there are in English for it, and Chinese people have at least 10 different words for rice.**

**MICHAEL: Whatever is important and used frequently in a culture gets remembered. If you see snow all the time, you will be able to remember different kinds. In a computerized society like ours, you have to remember ID numbers, phone numbers, bank card numbers, addresses, and so on. Beads aren't especially important in our society, so we aren't going to remember series of them.**

**CARVER: What we value, we remember.**

**SUNI: I think we tend to remember not just the things we value . . . but most importantly, things that interest us. Why do we tend to remember the lines of the movie, gossip about the celebrities and stats of the sportsmen much more easily? Because these things interest us. Also, I think the media play an important role in deciding what kind of things different cultures tend to remember.**

**KARI: In class, we have discussed extensively how memory is linked to certain "clues" or pathways of remembering particular things—as if memory is divided into particular areas. Since different cultures remember or know different things, doesn't it follow that they have different paths of memory?**

**AMY: I've heard that it's much easier for a child to learn another language than for an adult. Why should this be? Do they just have more space available in LTM [long-term memory]?**

**GREG: It would seem only logical that during those earlier years that your mind be more of a sponge than it is when you are 80 years old. Language would be one of the things that is easily absorbed. My younger cousins were raised in families where two languages were spoken and seemed to have no problem with multiple definitions and words to go along with, let's say, the word "apple." Thus, I assume that having grown up with two languages, it was easy for them to learn.**

**SUNI: I think mastering more languages definitely helps recalling. I think this has a lot to do with the differences in structures of different languages. For example, I always remember long digits or numbers in Chinese because the pronunciation is much shorter, so it's easier to memorize and recall.**

• • • • • • •

Now that you have been exposed to other students' ideas, you might want to reconsider your answers to the questions raised earlier. To what extent is memory an innate, universal feature of the human mind, and to what extent does it vary from culture to culture? How does studying the effects of culture on memory prepare us to deal with human diversity issues?

were now in the eleventh grade. This allowed a comparison of the academic performance of this group across the decade. The results showed that American students retained their low status on mathematics performance, while the Asian students still scored higher.

Recalling Triandis's cautions about cross-cultural research discussed earlier in this chapter, we must consider whether these findings could be flawed by systematic differences in the way the students were selected or measured—differences that somehow put the American students at a disadvantage. However, that explanation does not seem to account for the findings in this case: The researchers were careful to take their measurements at the same time during the school year, under the same testing conditions, and with equivalent test items. Moreover, the American students were from school districts in Minnesota, a state that not only ranks high nationally in mathematics achievement but that also has the highest percentage in the nation of students who graduate from high school (Stevenson et al., 1993). So, if anything, the Americans were in a strong position to show up well in these cross-cultural comparisons. Another possible explanation for the results is differences in curriculum: Perhaps the Chinese and Japanese schools demand less from their students or cover more rudimentary material at the various grade levels. Unfortunately, this explanation also falls apart when examined, for the demands on the Asian students related to reading and vocabulary were far greater than those on the American students. To read successfully, the average Chinese fifth-grader must have learned several thousand characters in the Chinese alphabet, and Japanese fifth-graders must know Chinese characters, two sets of symbols for the syllables in Japanese, and the Roman alphabet as well (Stevenson, 1992).

It is safe to assume, then, that the assessment procedures were not biased against U.S. students. So how might we account for the disparities in test scores? One advanced explanation singles out cultural attitudes toward ability and effort. Stevenson and his colleagues (1993) asked students, their parents, and their teachers whether they thought effort or ability had a greater impact on their academic performance. From first through eleventh grade, American students disagreed that "everyone in my class has about the same natural ability in math" and clearly thought that "studying hard" had little impact on performance. These responses seem to reflect a belief that performance on mathematics tests is primarily a matter of innate ability: Students who lack this ability cannot improve their scores very much no matter how hard they study. The American mothers expressed a similar view. Similarly, 41 percent of the American eleventh-grade teachers thought "innate intelligence" was the most important factor in mathematics performance. To a much greater extent, Asian students, parents, and teachers believed that effort and "studying hard" were important factors in scoring high on tests.

Asians and Americans clearly held different opinions concerning the origins of academic performance, and these culturally influenced views of the respective importance of effort and innate ability can have profound consequences on the way children (and their parents) approach the task of learning. Children who believe that learning is ability-based may conclude that working hard and exerting effort will have little effect on their academic success and therefore may not make much of an effort to learn. By comparison, students who believe that academic success can be achieved through hard work and diligence are more likely to work hard and make an extra effort to do well. In fact, both effort and ability are important to academic achievement: Even the brightest students will not get far without making an effort to develop, refine, and direct their intellectual abilities, but there is a limit to what students can achieve academically through sheer effort and hard work. On the whole, Americans subscribe to the

**Social cognition** Knowledge and understanding concerning the social world and the people in it (including oneself).

value of effort and hard work, just as Asians agree that ability is an important factor in success. But in the academic domain, the widespread perception among Americans that ability is the key ingredient to success may be doing more harm than good.

Several lines of evidence suggest that the nature of the educational system is also critical for explaining the origin and nature of the cultural differences in academic performance. First, when the eleventh-grade American, Japanese, and Chinese schoolchildren were tested on general information that they could have learned outside of school, all three groups earned nearly identical test scores. This suggests that American students are just as competent as their Asian counterparts at learning information that does *not* originate solely in the school curriculum. Second, when the students' mothers were polled, 79 percent of the American mothers thought the schools were doing a "good" or "excellent" job of educating their children, and over 80 percent pronounced the level of curriculum difficulty "just right." Mothers of Chinese and Japanese students were more critical of their schools' performance. Third, American mothers and students were satisfied with the students' academic performance, even though, as we have seen, it was low compared to the other groups. Finally, Stevenson (1992, 1993) has proposed that the structure of the school day and the role of the teacher might contribute to cultural differences in student performance. Asian students spend more time in school each day than American students do. However, much of this additional time is taken up by longer lunch periods, more frequent recesses, and after-school clubs and activities. Contrast this with a typical American school day, in which the student arrives, begins classes, has a single recess and short lunch, then leaves soon after the last class ends. Stevenson suggests that the diversity of activities in Asian schools contributes to students' liking and wanting to attend school each day and therefore indirectly contributes to academic achievement. Moreover, teachers in Asian schools typically are better trained in educational methods and teaching strategies, have more time to spend with students, and are required to do fewer course preparations than American teachers. This suggests that Chinese and Japanese teachers have more time, energy, and skills to work closely and actively with their pupils.

**ATTRIBUTION** Psychologists have also examined cultural diversity in the attribution process. As we saw in the previous chapter, attribution theory deals with people's explanations for their own (or another's) behaviors, emotions, or outcomes of events. Attributions are a type of **social cognition**, ways of thinking about and interpreting information from the social world. We also saw that people tend to attribute behavior either to external or internal causes and that these attributions are sometimes flawed or biased. For example, people are prone to overestimate the internal causes of another's behavior (the *fundamental attribution error*). In their own case, however, people tend to overestimate internal factors when they are successful and external factors over which they have no control when they fail (the *self-serving bias*, also known as *defensive attribution*).

Historically, most of the research on attribution theory has been conducted in Western cultures. Do the basic principles of attribution apply to people in other cultures as well? The answer is *no*. We have already noted some cultural differences in attributions made for academic performance: Asian students, their parents, and their teachers tend to attribute good academic performance to effort (studying hard), whereas Americans tend to attribute it to ability (innate intelligence). These differences in attributional style extend beyond classroom performance and help explain how people from different cultural backgrounds make sense of the data in their social worlds. Kashima and Triandis (1986), for example, reported that

Japanese students studying in the United States usually explained failure as a lack of effort (an internal attribution) and attributed their successes to the assistance they received from others (an external attribution). Research data also suggest that the fundamental attribution error may not be as pervasive as once believed. Researchers are finding that in some cultures people are much less likely to attribute behavior to internal personal characteristics; they place more emphasis on the role of external, situational factors in explaining both their own behavior and that of others (Cousins, 1989; Markus & Kitayama, 1991. For example, J. Miller (1984), in comparing the descriptions of others given by Indian and American college students, found that the Americans used three times as many trait descriptions (i.e., internal attributions) and the Indians used twice as many context-related explanations. This suggests that the Indian respondents were not overestimating the role of internal causal factors but were instead giving appropriate weight to the external factors that influence behavior.

So far we have seen that cognitive processes can be heavily influenced by the cultural context in which they occur. In the next section, we examine cultural influences on emotional processes.

## Culture and Emotion

Emotional experiences across cultures are similar in certain ways and very different in others. The death of a loved one, for example, is sure to produce feelings of grief and sadness in all cultures. Similarly, being unexpectedly attacked will produce fear and surprise in anyone. In contrast, the feelings experienced after a job promotion are likely to differ depending upon one's cultural values and the meaning one attaches to personal success. If you perceive your work as an individual effort, you will no doubt feel proud, happy, and perhaps boastful when you are promoted. If, however, you see your success as reflecting the efforts of your group, you will still be happy, but you will probably be more humble about taking individual credit for the success, perhaps even ashamed.

To psychologists, the key issue is how the larger defining elements of cultures help shape the emotional experiences of members of those cultures. Some of the diversity across cultures in experiencing emotions is consistent with the distinctions between individualism and collectivism we mentioned earlier. For example, Hazel Markus and Shinobu Kitayama (1991) report that the English language has many terms for self-focused emotions (e.g., anger, sadness), whereas the Japanese language has many terms for other-focused emotions (e.g., sympathy, empathy). This difference parallels the predominantly individualist orientation of most English-speaking cultures and the collectivist orientation of Japanese culture. The emotions of people in collectivist cultures also tend to be shorter in duration than those of individualists (Markus & Kitayama, 1991). For example, David Matsumoto and his colleagues found that American college students reported experiencing emotions that lasted longer, were more intense, and were accompanied by more bodily symptoms than emotions reported by Japanese students (Matsumoto, Kudoh, Scherer, & Wallbott, 1988). Finally, Matsumoto et al. (1988) suggest that, in general, "collective cultures will foster emotional displays of their members that maintain and facilitate group cohesion, harmony, or cooperation to a greater degree than individualistic cultures" (p. 132). How a cultural dimension like individualism/collectivism might explain these differences is just now being investigated, largely because research on how various cultures define, acknowledge, and experience emotions is relatively recent. Most of the well-established findings in the psychology of emotions come from studies of emotional expression within a single culture.

**Communicating Emotion** There are many ways of communicating emotions. As we discussed in the chapter on motivation and emotion, we can use verbal channels of communication (e.g., speech), nonverbal channels (e.g., facial expressions, body posture, tone of voice, hand gestures, eye contact), or both to let someone know what we're feeling. Among the nonverbal channels, facial expressions seem to communicate the most specific information. While hand gestures or posture can communicate general emotional states (e.g., "feeling bad"), the complexity of the muscles in the face allows facial expressions to communicate very specific feelings (e.g., feeling sad, angry, or fearful). That is why researchers studying cultural differences in emotional communication have focused on facial expressions.

Some researchers have argued that across cultures, peoples, and societies, the face looks the same whenever certain emotions are expressed; this is known as the *universalist* position. Charles Darwin subscribed to this view, arguing that part of our common evolutionary heritage was to use the same expressions to convey the same emotions. In contrast, other researchers support the *culture-learning* position, which holds that facial expressions of emotion are learned within a given culture and therefore may differ greatly from one culture to the next. In sum, the universalist position predicts that the same emotion will elicit the same facial response from people in many different cultures, whereas the culture-learning position predicts that the facial responses will be quite different. Which view is more accurate?

Paul Ekman and Wallace Friesen, who have been studying this question for several decades, have produced a wealth of information regarding how emotions are expressed and understood in a cultural context (Ekman & Friesen, 1986; Ekman et al., 1987). They have concluded that at least seven primary emotions are accompanied by universal facial expressions: happiness, sadness, anger, surprise, fear, disgust, and contempt. For example, in one set of studies, Ekman and Friesen (1969) showed photographs of faces expressing the first six of those emotions to people in Argentina, Brazil, Japan, Chile, and the United States. They found very high rates of agreement across cultures about which emotion was being displayed. Carroll Izard (1980) conducted similar studies in England, Germany, Switzerland, France, Sweden, Greece, and Japan with similar results. These studies seem to support the universalist position: Regardless of culture, subjects tended to agree on which emotions people were expressing facially. However, this research does not completely rule out the culture-learning view. Because the subjects were all members of developed countries that likely had been exposed to one another through movies, magazines, and tourism, they might simply have become familiar with the facial expressions seen in other cultures. A stronger test was needed that reduced or eliminated this possibility.

**4.** Can people from one culture understand the facial expressions of people from very different cultures?

This test was made possible by the discovery of several contemporary cultures that had been totally isolated from Western culture for most of their existence. Members of the Fore and the Dani cultures of New Guinea, for example, had their first contact with anthropologists only a few years before Ekman's research took place, so they provided a nearly perfect opportunity to test the universalist/culture-learning debate. If members of these cultures, who had little or no experience with Western peoples, gave the same interpretation of facial expressions and produced the same expressions on their own faces as people in Western cultures, there would be much stronger evidence for the universality of facial expressions of emotion. Ekman and his colleagues (Ekman & Friesen, 1971; Ekman, Sorenson, & Friesen, 1969) presented members of the Fore culture with three photographs of people from outside their culture and asked them to point to the picture that represented how they would feel in a certain situation. For example, if a subject was told "Your child has died and you feel very sad," he or she would have the opportunity to choose which of the three

**Display rules** Culture-specific rules that govern how, when, and why facial expressions of emotion are displayed.

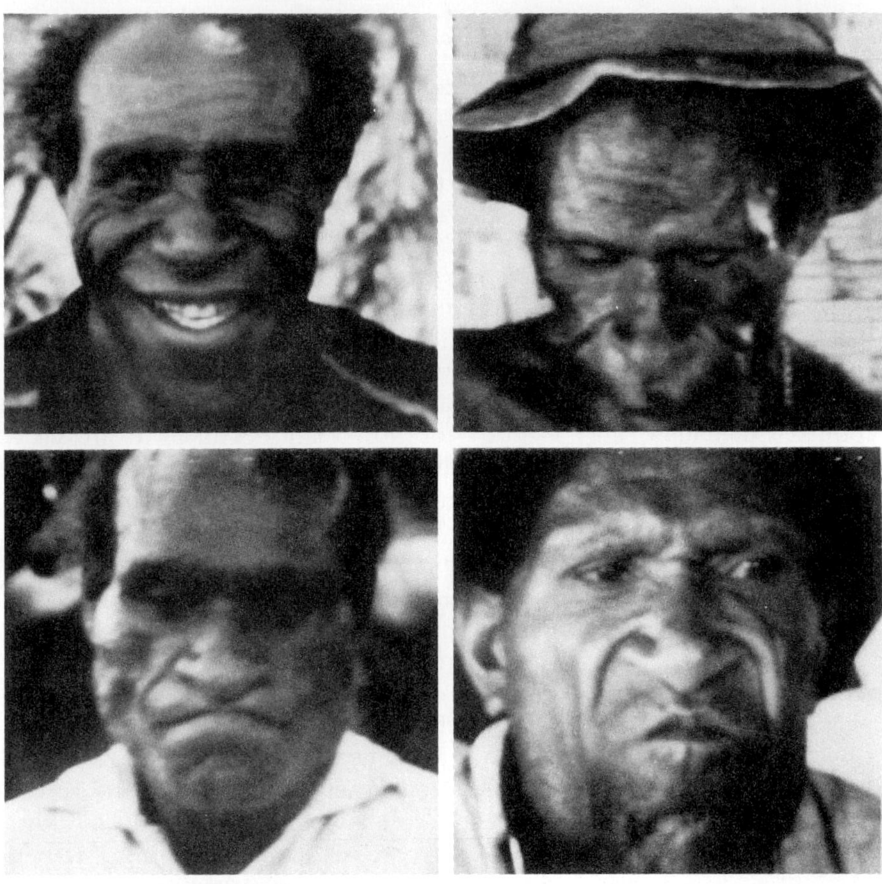

Can you identify the emotions being expressed by this man from New Guinea? The finding that U.S. college students could recognize the emotional expressions of people who had been largely isolated from Western cultures—and vice versa—lent support to the *universalist* position of facial expression.

*Source:* From P. Ekman and W.V., Friesen, "Unmasking the Face", Englewood Cliffs, NJ, Prentice Hall, 1975, pg. 27.

pictures most closely corresponded to sadness. The results indicated very high rates of agreement regarding which facial expressions showed which emotions. So even members of these isolated groups were able to identify correctly the emotional expressions of people with whom they had had virtually no previous contact. Moreover, when photographs of the Fore and Dani posing the primary emotions were shown to college students in the United States, the same high agreement was found: Americans, who had had no prior experience with these groups, were able to identify the emotional expressions on their faces (Ekman & Friesen, 1975). In summary, it appears that facial expressions of primary emotions are indeed universal.

If this is true, why are people so often confused about the emotions being expressed by people in other cultures? For example, Traci sometimes had difficulty figuring out what her hosts were feeling. She might sense they were disappointed about some decision she had made, yet they continued to smile. If facial expressions reliably convey emotional states, why did her Japanese hosts appear to be pleased at her mistakes?

The answer lies in a principle Ekman and Friesen (1975) have called **display rules**. Display rules refer to the circumstances under which it is appropriate for people to show emotion on their faces. In essence, display rules help govern which emotions get displayed, by whom, to whom, and under what conditions. Some common display rules are to intensify, deintensify, mask, or neutralize one's expression. You practice *intensification* when you exaggerate your facial expression and *deintensification* when you mute your facial expression. For example, when showing greater joy than you are actually experiencing at a surprise party your friends have thrown for you, you are following the intensification display rule that dictates "Look happy and thrilled when people unexpectedly do nice things for you." *Masking* is a quite different display rule: Here you are feeling one emotion but showing a completely different one. Smiling when you are feeling sad is an example. Finally, *neutralizing* means keeping a "poker face," or showing a blank expression regardless of what you are feeling. Following this rule might be appropriate in situations that require you to be "strong and silent."

Although facial expressions of primary emotions have a universal quality, display rules differ substantially from culture to culture. Ekman demonstrated this in a study of Japanese and American college students (Ekman, Friesen, & Ellsworth, 1972). These students watched graphic films of surgical procedures, either by themselves or in the presence of an experimenter. Unbeknownst to them, the students' facial expressions were secretly videotaped as they viewed the films. The results showed that when the students were by themselves, both the Japanese and the Americans showed facial expressions of disgust (precisely the emotion the films were intended to elicit). This supports the universality of facial expressions: Members of two very different cultures showed virtually the same facial expression in response to the same emotional event. But when the subjects watched the film in the presence of an experimenter, the two groups displayed different responses. American students continued to show disgust on their faces, but the Japanese students showed facial expressions that were more neutral, even somewhat pleasant.

Why the sudden switch? The answer lies in the different use of display rules by members of the two cultures. The Japanese norm says "Don't display strong negative emotion in the presence of a respected elder" (in this case, the experimenter). Americans typically don't honor this display rule; hence, they expressed their true emotions whether they were alone or with someone else. Similarly, Traci's hosts undoubtedly were displeased with some of her decisions, but they displayed positive emotions out of respect for their guest. The general rule that Traci learned was this: Knowledge of both the universal expression of emotions *and* the particular rules operating in a culture is important for understanding what others are feeling.

**OTHER FORMS OF NONVERBAL COMMUNICATION** We have seen that facial expressions of primary emotions have a universal quality. Is this true of all forms of nonverbal communication? No. Hand gestures, for example, vary from one culture to another. This is especially true of *emblems*, or hand gestures that have a specific meaning (H.G. Johnson, Ekman, & Friesen, 1975). Giving someone the "thumbs up," for example, or circling your thumb and index finger in an "OK" sign, or flashing a friend two fingers in a "V" shape all have well-defined meanings within U.S. culture. Outside this cultural context, however, these emblems may either be meaningless or take on very different meanings. In some cases, this can be troublesome. In the early 1970s, for instance, Leonid Brezhnev, then general secretary of the Communist Party of the USSR, visited the United States as part of a process entered into by the two superpowers to improve their relations. In the following excerpt, Ekman comments on Brezhnev's use of emblems in his public appearances with President Richard Nixon.

> When Brezhnev visited the United States he and Nixon would use emblems to communicate the "spirit of détente." Nixon typically would use the American hand-wave, a greeting emblem. Brezhnev in these appearances would clasp his hands together with arms extended, raising his clasped hands up to the region in front of his face. This is a Soviet emblem for friendship. Unfortunately, he did not know . . . that this performance is an American emblem for "I am the winner," employed almost exclusively in the context of boxing matches. Research on the emblem repertoire and cross-national contrasts could help eliminate such miscommunications. (Ekman, 1976, p. 24)

Cultures also differ in the amount of touch that takes place among people, the distance between people who are interacting, and the amount of eye contact that is appropriate between friends, business partners, loved ones, and strangers. However, Irenäus Eibl-Eibesfeldt (1972) has identified one form of eye contact that is almost universal: the "brow-raise" greeting used when a friend approaches (Figure 15-2). The next time a friend approaches you, watch to see if he or she uses this greeting.

## Culture and Social Behavior

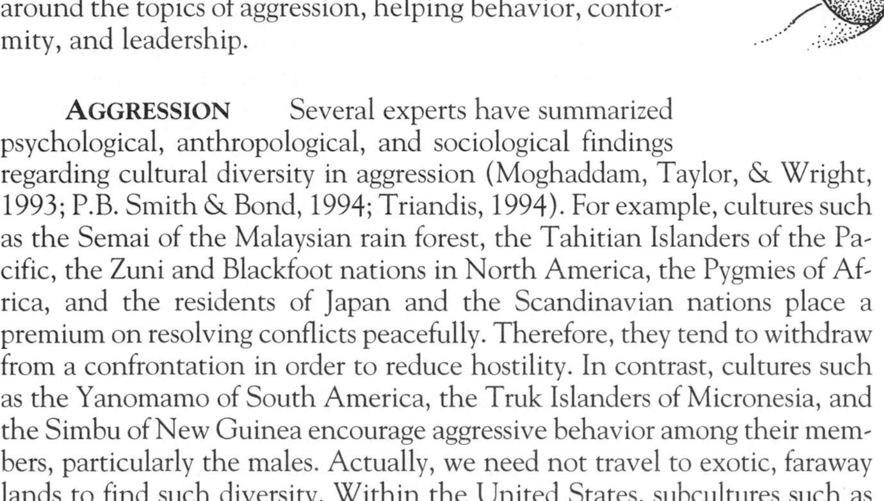

One reason psychologists study cultural diversity is that culture is closely interrelated with social behavior. In fact, social behavior—people's interactions with one another on a regular basis—largely defines a culture, for this is the mechanism by which values, traditions, and cultural learning are transmitted. Thus, to understand people's behaviors, we need to understand the cultural context in which these behaviors occur. Our discussion will focus on some of the better-researched aspects of social behavior, particularly those areas that highlight what is similar and what is different across cultures. As we did when discussing gender diversity, we will organize our observations around the topics of aggression, helping behavior, conformity, and leadership.

**Figure 15-2**
People throughout the world use the "brow-raise" greeting when a friend approaches.

**AGGRESSION** Several experts have summarized psychological, anthropological, and sociological findings regarding cultural diversity in aggression (Moghaddam, Taylor, & Wright, 1993; P.B. Smith & Bond, 1994; Triandis, 1994). For example, cultures such as the Semai of the Malaysian rain forest, the Tahitian Islanders of the Pacific, the Zuni and Blackfoot nations in North America, the Pygmies of Africa, and the residents of Japan and the Scandinavian nations place a premium on resolving conflicts peacefully. Therefore, they tend to withdraw from a confrontation in order to reduce hostility. In contrast, cultures such as the Yanomamo of South America, the Truk Islanders of Micronesia, and the Simbu of New Guinea encourage aggressive behavior among their members, particularly the males. Actually, we need not travel to exotic, faraway lands to find such diversity. Within the United States, subcultures such as Quakers, the Amish, the Mennonites, and the Hutterites have traditionally valued nonviolence and peaceful coexistence. This contrasts markedly with attitudes and practices in the larger American culture.

Cultural differences in aggressiveness are reflected in statistics on violent crimes. Despite the presence of a few nonviolent subcultures, the United States struggles with violent crime rates that are shockingly high compared to those of other nations. The murder rate in Norway, for example, is estimated at 0.9 per 100,000 people; in Finland and China, it is 1.1 per 100,000. In contrast, in the United States, the murder rate is 8.6 per 100,000 people (Triandis, 1994). The United States also reports higher rates of rape and vandalism.

These striking cultural differences in aggressive behavior suggest that aggression is very much influenced by learning that takes place within a particular cultural context and by cultural norms and values. Consider the relatively nonaggressive cultures we just described. Most of them are collectivist societies that emphasize the good of the group over the desires of the individual. Members of collectivist societies are more likely to seek compromise or to withdraw from a threatening interaction because of their concern for maintaining group harmony. In contrast, members of individualist societies are more likely to follow the adage "Stand up for yourself." Michael Bond and his colleagues have provided some research evidence that links the individualist/collectivist orientation of a culture with aggressive behavior (Bond, Wan, Leung, & Giacolone, 1985). In a study of verbal aggression, Chinese students in Hong Kong and American students in the United States heard a manager insult either a superior or a subordinate, who was either in that person's work group or outside of it. Consistent with the more collectivist orientation of their culture, the Chinese students were more likely to perceive the high-status manager who insulted the subordinate as behaving legitimately in that situation. Also, the Chinese students were likely to view an insult within the manager's group as more appropriate than one directed at someone in an out-group. These findings suggest that the interpretation of what is aggressive and what is not depends to a large extent on the cultural background of the persons involved.

Finally, we should note that one of the best-established cross-cultural findings regarding aggression has already been discussed: Study after study has found that across cultures males are more aggressive than females. Maccoby and Jacklin (1974) reached this conclusion in their review of gender differences, as did Whiting and Whiting (1975) in a famous study of six very different cultures. Bacon, Child, and Barry (1963) reported that in 48 nonindustrialized societies males were found to commit the majority of criminal acts. And Goldstein and Segall(1983) noted that increases in crime rates in the United States closely paralleled increases in the population of 14- to 24-year-old males. Are higher rates of aggression among males due to socialization and learning, or do they indicate some biological underpinning? Testosterone levels in males are at their highest in the age group 14 to 24, and, as we noted earlier in this chapter, testosterone is related to aggression and violence in males. Recall, however, that the different socialization of males and females also plays a role in aggressive behavior. Like most of the complex behaviors we have reviewed in this book, aggression undoubtedly depends on the interaction of nature and nurture.

**HELPING BEHAVIOR** People often assume that there is a "helping personality," or a single personality trait that determines who is helpful and who is not. In the chapter on social psychology, we saw that this is unlikely; several conditions, both individual and situational, combine to determine when help will be offered. Similarly, it's doubtful that there is such a thing as a "helpful culture"—that is, a society, nation, or group whose members are invariably "more helpful" than those of other groups. Psychologists have instead focused on the cultural factors that make helping more or less likely to take place. As you might imagine by now, individualism/collectivism is an important dimension in this area: It seems plausible that members of individualist cultures feel less obligated to help other people than members of collectivist cultures do. Miller, Bersoff, and Harwood (1990) investigated this intuitive conclusion in a study using Indian and American subjects. Participants were presented with helping scenarios involving either a stranger, a friend, or a close relative whose need was either minor, moderate, or extreme. There were no cultural differences in cases of extreme need; members of both groups reported being equally willing to help. But the two groups did differ in cases of minor need; almost three times as many Indians as Americans felt obligated to help in a scenario involving a close friend or a stranger asking for minor assistance.

Triandis (1994) points out, however, that even within collectivist cultures the prediction of when help will be offered can be problematic.

Some members of collectivist societies are reluctant to offer help to anyone outside of their in-group; they are therefore less likely to help strangers. Other cultures treat a stranger as a member of their group until that person's exact status can be determined.

**CONFORMITY** A Chinese proverb states that "if one finger is sore, the whole hand will hurt." In a collectivist culture such as China, community and harmony are very important. Although members of all societies show a tendency to conform, it would seem that members of collectivist cultures should more frequently conform to the will of a group than members of noncollectivist cultures would. Psychologists who have studied this question have utilized tests similar to those conducted by Solomon Asch, which you read about in the previous chapter. Recall that in Asch's study about 35 percent of American male college students agreed with a group's opinion that was obviously wrong. Asch's research was conducted in a relatively individualist culture. What if the same experiment were repeated in a more collectivist culture?

Several researchers have performed just such studies. Researchers in individualist cultures other than the United States typically found fairly high conformity rates; for example, 24 percent of Belgian and Dutch students conformed in the Asch situation, compared to 35 percent of male American students. However, the levels of conformity in collectivist cultures often proved higher than those found by Asch. In collectivist societies as diverse as Fiji, Zaire, Hong Kong, Lebanon, Zimbabwe, Kuwait, Japan, and Brazil, conformity rates ranged from 25 percent among Japanese students to 51 percent among students in Zimbabwe (P.B. Smith & Bond, 1994, p. 152). In a novel extension of this approach, Berry (1967) demonstrated that conformity was greater in farming societies (where members are more dependent upon one another for long-term group survival) than in hunting and gathering societies (where people must exercise a good deal of independence to survive).

Not all the research data support the existence of a simple link between collectivism/individualism and conformity, however. Perrin and Spencer (1989) did not find evidence among British students of the type of conformity Asch found, and although Williams and Sogon (1984) reported that Japanese subjects showed a high tendency to conform when they were among friends, Frager (1970) found evidence of nonconformity among Japanese subjects when the confederates in the Asch situation were strangers. (In fact, in this situation, Japanese participants often deliberately gave the wrong response even when the majority opinion was correct.)

Given these somewhat conflicting data, what conclusion can we reach about the universality of social influence? The fact that rates of conformity in the Asch situation were relatively high across a variety of cultures suggests that there may be some kind of universal conformity norm. But the fact that conformity was especially high within collectivist societies suggests that the tendency toward conformity is heightened or lessened by a specific cultural context. As psychologists gain a better understanding of the differences among cultures, the answers to the questions "What is universal about social influence?" and "What is culturally determined?" should become clearer.

5. Do people in collectivist cultures exhibit higher levels of conformity than people in individualist cultures?

**LEADERSHIP** The individualist/collectivist distinction also seems to pertain to cross-cultural differences in leadership and group behavior. Leaders are leaders only if they have followers. Therefore, an examination of both leadership style *and* the composition of the group being led will inform us about cross-cultural diversity in this area.

In the previous chapter, we saw that some leaders are primarily *task-oriented* (focused on the goals or work demands of the group), while others are more *relationship-oriented* (focused on promoting harmony and good feeling among the group members). This distinction seems to be a main operating principle in most work groups in the United States: Someone explicitly appointed manager, foreperson, or crew chief is charged with making sure the job gets done, while someone else usually emerges informally to act as the relationship-oriented specialist who tells jokes, remembers everyone's birthday, smoothes disputes, and generally maintains morale (Bales, 1951). In the Western world, this division of leadership is often the primary operating mode of both formal work groups and less formal social groups. Indeed, it seems sensible, but it is not the only approach to leadership. Consider a collectivist culture that values cooperation and interdependence among group members. In such an environment, it is unlikely that individuals would emerge to serve specific functions within a group. Although one member may be named "the manager," there is less need for individuals to have clearly defined roles as "this type of leader" or "that type of leader" because the emphasis is always on the group's goals and the group's output.

6. How do management styles in Japanese businesses reflect a collectivist approach to leadership? How do they differ from traditional management styles in the United States?

Leadership in American businesses is presently being transformed through the introduction of a management style that has proved successful in Japan and other Eastern collectivist cultures (J.W. Dean & Evans, 1994; McFarland, Senn, & Childress, 1993). This approach emphasizes input from all group members regarding decision making, small work teams that promote close cooperation among members, and a style of leadership in which managers receive much the same treatment as any other employee. In the West, it is not uncommon for executives to have their own parking spaces, dining facilities, fitness and social clubs, as well as separate offices and independent schedules. This privileged style of management is considered very strange by most Japanese executives. In many Eastern cultures, managers and executives share the same facilities as their workers, hunt for parking spaces like everyone else, and eat and work side by side with their employees. Interestingly, the Japanese model has effectively combined the two leadership approaches—task-oriented and relationship-oriented—into a single overall style. By being a part of the group, the leader can simultaneously work toward and direct the group's goals, while also contributing to the group's morale and social climate. Misumi (1985) has found that combining these roles is an effective strategy for Japanese leaders in such diverse workplaces as banks, bus companies, shipyards, coal mines, and government offices.

## LOOKING FORWARD

We began this book by noting how microscopic cellular processes and tiny chemical reactions could produce substantial changes in behavior. We progressed through discussions of how biology influences behavior, how the internal world of the mind operates, how humans grow and develop physically and psychologically, how the personality of individuals is studied, and how groups can affect our behavior. At each step we have added layers of understanding to our knowledge of how the thoughts, feelings, and behaviors of humans take place. In this chapter, we have extended that progression, to examine the diversity found in different groups and the ways in which they interact with one another. In some cases, our understanding of the basic processes at work is quite complete. In many other cases, we simply don't have enough evidence to conclude why different groups of people behave as they do. These cases include why females and males have different reactions to the same event and why tribal New Guineans and urban Americans share some thoughts and feelings. Psychologists are actively researching these issues, and as the second 100 years of psychology unfold, we hope to have better answers and better insights. The world is becoming a smaller place. Understanding the psychology of the people who populate it—all the people—will make it a more livable place for everyone.

# SUMMARY

The study of human diversity focuses on both the psychological differences and the psychological similarities among groups of people. Understanding human diversity broadens our understanding of human behavior in general.

## GENDER DIVERSITY

Females and males obviously differ in their biological makeup. There are also some psychological, social, and behavioral differences between the sexes, though these are often exaggerated by gender stereotypes and gender role expectations.

### Gender Stereotypes

**Gender stereotypes** are general beliefs about characteristics that men and women are presumed to have—for example, men are assertive and dominant, whereas women are gentle and considerate of others. **Gender roles** refer to beliefs about behaviors we expect men and women to engage in, such as men being economic providers and women caregivers. These stereotypes are often inaccurate overgeneralizations.

Studies of the actual gender diversity between men and women rely on **meta-analysis**, a technique for statistically combining the results of individual studies to form an overall conclusion. Meta-analyses have been performed in the areas of cognitive skills, emotion and communication, and social behavior.

### Gender and Cognitive Skills

Women and men show no gender differences in verbal ability. Women show a slight advantage in mathematical skills, and men show a slight advantage in spatial abilities. Overall, men and women do not differ significantly in general intelligence, as measured by scores on standardized tests.

### Gender and Emotion

Women have an advantage over men in decoding or understanding the emotional content of the nonverbal messages of others. They also have traditionally held occupations that are high in emotional labor. Flight attendants, secretaries, nurses, and cashiers are often called upon to regulate their true emotions in performing their jobs.

### Gender and Social Behavior

Men and women show diversity in their social interactions. Men, for example, are more aggressive than women and also tend to offer assistance more often, although women excel in providing social support and nurturance. Women tend to be slightly more conforming than men, although there is great variability across research studies in this area. Men and women are equally able to meet the demands of being effective leaders, though there may be some variation in their leadership styles. In each of these cases—aggression, helping, conformity, and leadership—it is unclear to what extent gender stereotypes and expectations play a role in producing the diversity. For example, men may appear more helpful because of social expectations about male heroism, while women may seem more conforming because of the way research questions in this area have been framed.

### Gender Diversity: Summing Up

Although the sexes differ in some ways, these differences are typically small. Moreover, there is much greater behavioral diversity within each sex than there is between the sexes. Psychologists still need to do much work on documenting and understanding the origins of gender diversity.

## CULTURAL DIVERSITY

There is much human diversity to be found in cultures around the world. When we encounter an unfamiliar way of life, we may experience **culture shock**, or a sense of disorientation about what constitutes appropriate behavior and practices.

### Race and Ethnicity

A **race** is a subpopulation that is defined on the basis of some identifiable characteristics. Racial classifications have long been based on such biological characteristics as skin color, facial features, genetics, and hair texture, or on habitation in a geographic region. Today many scientists believe race is an invalid scientific concept because contemporary societies are populated by people with rich genetic mixtures.

**Ethnicity** refers to a common cultural heritage that is shared by a group of people. **Ethnic identity** refers to that aspect of one's self-concept that is based on identifying oneself as a member of a particular group.

## WHAT IS A CULTURE?

Culture refers to the tangible goods produced in a society, such as art, literature, inventions, and consumer goods, as well as to such intangible processes as shared beliefs, values, attitudes, traditions, and behaviors communicated from one generation to the next. Subcultures are groups with their own norms, values, and rituals that exist within the larger culture. Cultures can differ in an astounding number of ways. To simplify cross-cultural comparisons, researchers often look at a few basic dimensions along which cultures vary, particularly individualism/collectivism. Individualist cultures value personal independence and place a premium on individual decision making and action. Collectivist cultures emphasize interdependence, group cohesion, and close relationships among group members.

### Culture and Cognition

Members of different cultures vary in the ways they perform basic cognitive tasks, such as categorizing or remembering information. Some cultures have only a few categories for shapes or colors, whereas others have a wider range. Members of some cultures have very good memories for information and events that directly affect their daily lives, whereas people in other cultures perform better on rote memorization tasks (such as those in a grammar school classroom). A few general principles apply. First, cultural customs and practices tend to influence what gets remembered and how events get categorized. These cultural influences affect the way people act on the information stored in memory and what they will include within a given category. Second, there is some universality to these cognitive activities. Despite cultural influences, in areas where experiences are similar, categorization and memory show more similarity across cultures.

Cultural diversity operates also in people's attributions for a variety of behaviors. For example, collectivist cultures tend to see a good academic performance as the result of effort, whereas individualist cultures tend to attribute academic success to innate ability. Moreover, biases in making internal or external attributions for behavior (such as the fundamental attribution error) seem to differ across cultures.

### Culture and Emotion

The individualism/collectivism dimension helps to predict diversity across cultures in the experience of emotion. Members of collectivist cultures, for example, tend to have many terms for other-focused emotions, have emotions of shorter duration, and promote emotional displays that are designed to maintain group cohesion.

The expression of emotions in a cultural context has received a great deal of attention from researchers. Facial expressions of the primary emotions have a universal quality: The face shows a similar expression for a given emotion regardless of the cultural background of the expressor. These findings, which held in studies of several cultures, both literate and preliterate, run counter to the culture-learning view, which suggests that facial expressions of emotion are learned within a particular culture.

Overlaying the universal expression of emotion are **display rules**, which govern when it is appropriate to show emotion: to whom, by whom, and under what circumstances. These do tend to differ from culture to culture. Common display rules include intensification, deintensification, masking, and neutralizing.

Finally, other forms of nonverbal communication show greater variability from culture to culture than facial expressions do. Hand gestures, such as emblems, can be quite culture-specific. Understanding the way emotion is communicated in a cultural context, then, requires knowing both the universal aspects of such communication and the cultural rules that govern in the specific communication setting.

### Culture and Social Behavior

Studies of cultural diversity in aggression, helping, conformity, and leadership have revealed the individualism/collectivism dimension of these behaviors. Collectivist cultures, for example, encourage harmony in interpersonal relationship and so tend to be less tolerant of aggressive acts that disrupt that harmony. We would also expect collectivist cultures to show greater rates of conformity and helping behavior, but the research findings in these areas are mixed. Finally, the traditional division of task-oriented leadership and relationship-oriented leadership is not as strongly maintained among members of collectivist cultures. Small work teams, in which all members provide input for key decisions and in which managers are seen as having nearly equal status with other group members, may foster an interdependent approach to leadership and group behavior.

# REVIEW QUESTIONS

## MULTIPLE CHOICE

1. Match each of the following terms with its correct definition:

____ masculine
____ feminine
____ gender stereotypes
____ gender roles

a. general beliefs about characteristics that men and women are presumed to have
b. general beliefs about behaviors we expect men and women to engage in
c. preferences, attributes, and interests typically associated with being a male
d. a description of one's biological and genetic make-up

2. Arrange the following steps so that they form the correct sequence of activities for performing a meta-analysis:
   a. taking detailed notes on the findings of each study
   b. publishing the overall results in a journal article or book chapter
   c. gathering all the available relevant research studies
   d. reaching an overall conclusion about the research area
   e. defining an area in which to conduct the meta-analysis
   f. statistically combining the results of the available studies

3. In which of the following areas do women *not* show more of the behavior than men?

   a. understanding nonverbal cues
   b. mathematical computation
   c. physical aggressiveness
   d. conformity

4. Being called upon to manage, alter, or regulate one's emotional expressions as a component of one's occupation is called ______ .

5. Which of the following statements most accurately summarizes research on gender differences in helping behavior?
   a. Males and females are equally likely to offer heroic help to a person in a life-threatening situation.
   b. The type of help being offered plays an important role in determining which gender is more helpful.
   c. The number of studies that have found more helping among males is roughly equal to the number of studies finding more helping among females.
   d. Males are more likely than females to offer social support.

6. In summarizing gender differences, it is important to remember that there is much greater variability ______ genders than there is ______ genders.

   a. within/across
   b. across/between
   c. across/within
   d. between/across

7. ______ refers to the disorientation we sometimes feel when encountering a way of life different from our own.

8. Match each of the following terms with an example that illustrates it:

   ____ Power distance
   ____ Masculinity
   ____ Uncertainty avoidance
   ____ Collectivism

   a. Valuing productivity and competition in business
   b. Living with members of one's extended family
   c. Having a distinct "upper class" and "lower class"
   d. Preferring the routine of a daily schedule

9. A person who values independence would score high on ______ , whereas a culture that values independence among its members would be high on ______ .

10. "I did poorly on the exam because I didn't exert enough effort in studying." This is an example of an ______ attribution, which is likely to be offered by a member of a ______ culture.

11. Showing an emotional expression on one's face that is different from the emotion one is actually feeling is an example of

    a. intensification
    b. deintensification
    c. masking
    d. neutralizing

12. Following the ______ view of emotion means believing that facial expressions of emotion differ from one culture to another.

13. The distinction between a task leader and a relationship leader is more likely to be maintained among members of ______ cultures.

## CRITICAL THINKING AND APPLICATIONS

14. Initial contacts with the Fore and Dani presented a once-in-a-lifetime opportunity to test the universalist and culture-learning views of emotional expression. Because these cultures had developed in isolation from the rest of the world, there was little opportunity for their members to learn the facial expressions of members of other cultures. Isolated cultures are extremely difficult to find in the 1990s. Can you suggest other ways to study facial expressions of emotion that would address the universalist/culture-learning debate?

15. If you've traveled to other cultures, you may have experienced culture shock. Many cultures seem to differ radically from our own, but none do so in all regards. Some aspects of daily life might be very different, while others might be quite similar to what you're used to. Compile a list of areas in which you think other cultures might be very different and a list of areas in which they might be similar to your own dominant culture. It might help you to choose just one other culture for comparison. It also might be useful to write down areas in your own dominant culture that you're especially curious about.

16. Choose a topic from a previous chapter in this textbook (e.g., depth perception, altered states of consciousness, classical conditioning, eyewitness testimony, social development, achievement motivation, coping, schizophrenia). After reading the suggestions given in Table 15-1, describe the special considerations you would feel compelled to address in designing a research study of your topic that compares members of different cultures.

*(Answers to the Review Questions can be found in the back of the text.)*

# APPENDIX A: MEASUREMENT AND STATISTICAL METHODS

## Overview

**Statistics** A branch of mathematics that psychologists use to organize and analyze data.

**Nominal scale** A set of categories for classifying objects.

**Ordinal scale** Scale indicating order or relative position of items according to some criterion.

**Interval scale** Scale with equal distances between the points or values, but without a true zero.

Most of the experiments described in this book involve measuring one or more variables and then analyzing the data statistically. The design and scoring of all the tests we have discussed are also based on statistical methods. **Statistics** is a branch of mathematics. It provides techniques for sorting out quantitative facts and ways of drawing conclusions from them. Statistics let us organize and describe data quickly, guide the conclusions we draw, and help us make inferences.

Statistical analysis is essential to conducting an experiment or designing a test, but statistics can only handle numbers—groups of them. To use statistics, the psychologist first must measure things—count and express them in quantities.

## SCALES OF MEASUREMENT

No matter what we are measuring—height, noise, intelligence, attitudes—we have to use a scale. The data we want to collect determine the scale we will use and, in turn, the scale we use helps determine the conclusions we can draw from our data.

**NOMINAL SCALES** If we decide to classify a group of people by the color of their eyes, we are using a **nominal scale**. We can count how many people have blue eyes, how many have green eyes, how many have brown eyes, and so on, but we cannot say that one group has more or less eye color than the other. The colors are simply different.

A nominal scale is a set of arbitrarily named or numbered categories. If we look up how many Republican, Democratic, and Independent voters registered in a certain congressional district in the last election year, we are using a nominal scale. Since a nominal scale is more of a way of classifying than of measuring, it is the least informative kind of scale. If we want to compare our data more precisely, we will have to use a scale that tells us more.

**ORDINAL SCALES** If we list horses in the order in which they finish a race, we are using an **ordinal scale**. On an ordinal scale, data are ranked from first to last according to some criterion. An ordinal scale tells the order, but nothing about the distances between what is ranked first and second or ninth and tenth. It does not tell us how much faster the winning horse ran than the horses that placed or showed. If a person ranks her preferences for various kinds of soup—pea soup first, then tomato, then onion, and so on—we know what soup she likes most and what soup she likes least, but we have no idea how much better she likes tomato than onion, or if pea soup is far more favored than either one of them.

Since we do not know the distances between the items ranked on an ordinal scale, we cannot add or subtract ordinal data. If mathematical operations are necessary, we need a still more informative scale.

**INTERVAL SCALES** An **interval scale** is often compared to a ruler that has been broken off at the bottom—it only goes from, say, 51/2 to 12. The intervals between 6 and 7, 7 and 8, 8 and 9, and so forth are equal, but there is no zero. A thermometer is an interval scale—even though a certain degree registered on a Fahrenheit or Centigrade thermometer specifies a certain state of cold or heat, there is no such thing as no temperature at all. One day is never twice as hot as another; it is only so many equal degrees hotter.

An interval scale tells us how many equal-size units one thing lies above or below another thing of the same kind, but it does not tell us how many times bigger, smaller, taller, or fatter one thing is than another. An intelligence test cannot tell us that one person is three times as intelligent as another, only that he or she scored so many points above or below someone else.

**Ratio scale** Scale with equal distances between the points or values and with a true zero.

**Central tendency** Tendency of scores to congregate around some middle value.

**Mean** Arithmetical average calculated by dividing a sum of values by the total number of cases.

**Median** Point that divides a set of scores in half.

**Mode** Point at which the largest number of scores occurs.

**RATIO SCALES** We can only say that a measurement is two times as long as another or three times as high when we use a **ratio scale**, one that has a true zero. For instance, if we measure the snowfall in a certain area over several winters, we can say that six times as much snow fell during the winter in which we measured a total of 12 feet as during a winter in which only 2 feet fell. This scale has a zero—there may be no snow.

## MEASUREMENTS OF CENTRAL TENDENCY

Usually, when we measure a number of instances of anything—from the popularity of TV shows to the weights of 8-year-old boys to the number of times a person's optic nerve fires in response to electrical stimulation—we get a distribution of measurements that range from smallest to largest or lowest to highest. The measurements will usually cluster around some value near the middle. This value is the **central tendency** of the distribution of the measurements.

Suppose, for example, you want to keep 10 children busy tossing rings around a bottle. You give them three rings to toss each turn, the game has six rounds, and each player scores one point every time he or she gets the ring around the neck of the bottle. The highest possible score is 18. The distribution of scores might end up like this: 11, 8, 13, 6, 12, 10, 16, 9, 12, 3.

What could you quickly say about the ring-tossing talent of the group? First, you could arrange the scores from lowest to highest: 3, 6, 8, 9, 10, 11, 12, 12, 13, 16. In this order, the central tendency of the distribution of scores becomes clear. Many of the scores cluster around the values between 8 and 12. There are three ways to describe the central tendency of a distribution. We usually refer to all three as the *average*.

The arithmetical average is called the **mean**—the sum of all the scores in the group divided by the number of scores. If you add up all the scores and divide by 10, the total number of scores in this group of ring tossers, you find that the mean for the group is 10.

The **median** is the point that divides a distribution in half—50 percent of the scores fall above the median, and 50 percent fall below. In the ring-tossing scores, five scores fall at 10 or below, five at 11 or above. The median is thus halfway between 10 and 11—10.5.

The point at which the largest number of scores occurs is called the **mode**. In our example, the mode is 12. More people scored 12 than any other.

### Differences Between the Mean, Median, and Mode

If we take many measurements of anything, we are likely to get a distribution of scores in which the mean, median, and mode are all about the same—the score that occurs most often (the mode) will also be the point that half the scores are below and half above (the median). And the same point will be the arithmetical average (the mean). This is not always true, of course, and small samples rarely come out so symmetrically. In these cases, we often have to decide which of the three measures of central tendency—the mean, the median, or mode—will tell us what we want to know.

For example, a shopkeeper wants to know the general incomes of passersby so he can stock the right merchandise. He might conduct a rough survey by standing outside his store for a few days from 12:00 to 2:00 and asking every tenth person who walks by to check a card showing the gen-

**Frequency distribution** A count of the number of scores that fall within each of a series of intervals.

eral range of his or her income. Suppose most of the people checked the ranges between $15,000 and $25,000 a year. However, a couple of the people made a lot of money—one checked $100,000–$150,000 and the other checked the $200,000-or-above box. The mean for the set of income figures would be pushed higher by those two large figures and would not really tell the shopkeeper what he wants to know about his potential customers. In this case, he would be wiser to use the median or the mode.

Suppose instead of meeting two people whose incomes were so great, he noticed that people from two distinct income groups walked by his store—several people checked the box for $15,000–$17,000, and several others checked $23,000–$25,000. The shopkeeper would find that his distribution was bimodal. It has two modes—$16,000 and $24,000. This might be more useful to him than the mean, which could lead him to think his customers were a unit with an average income of about $20,000.

Another way of approaching a set of scores is to arrange them into a **frequency distribution**—that is, to select a set of intervals and count how many scores fall into each interval. A frequency distribution is useful for large groups of numbers; it puts the number of individual scores into more manageable groups.

Suppose a psychologist tests memory. She asks 50 college students to learn 18 nonsense syllables, then records how many syllables each student can recall 2 hours later. She arranges her raw scores from lowest to highest in a rank distribution:

| | | | | | |
|---|---|---|---|---|---|
| 2 | 6 | 8 | 10 | 11 | 14 |
| 3 | 7 | 9 | 10 | 12 | 14 |
| 4 | 7 | 9 | 10 | 12 | 15 |
| 4 | 7 | 9 | 10 | 12 | 16 |
| 5 | 7 | 9 | 10 | 13 | 17 |
| 5 | 7 | 9 | 11 | 13 | |
| 6 | 8 | 9 | 11 | 13 | |
| 6 | 8 | 9 | 11 | 13 | |
| 6 | 8 | 10 | 11 | 13 | |

The scores range from 2 to 17, but 50 individual scores are too cumbersome to work with. So she chooses a set of two-point intervals and tallies the number of scores in each interval:

| INTERVAL | TALLY | FREQUENCY |
|---|---|---|
| 1–2 | \| | 1 |
| 3–4 | \|\|\| | 3 |
| 5–6 | ~~\|\|\|\|~~ \| | 6 |
| 7–8 | ~~\|\|\|\|~~ \|\|\|\| | 9 |
| 9–10 | ~~\|\|\|\|~~ ~~\|\|\|\|~~ \|\|\| | 13 |
| 11–12 | ~~\|\|\|\|~~ \|\|\| | 8 |
| 13–14 | ~~\|\|\|\|~~ \|\| | 7 |
| 15–16 | \|\| | 2 |
| 17–18 | \| | 1 |

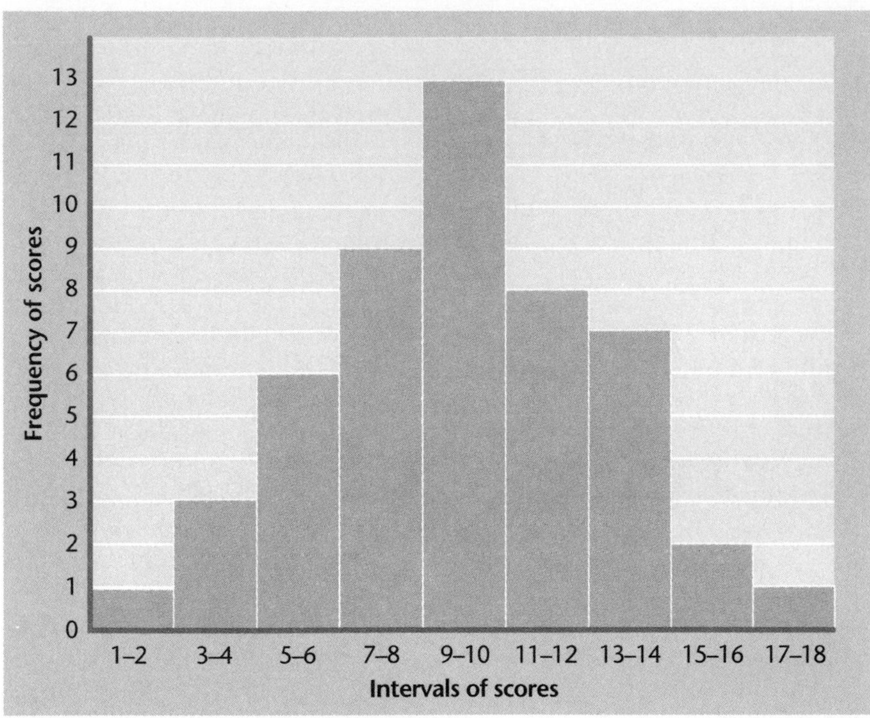


**Frequency histogram** Type of bar graph that shows frequency distributions.

**Frequency polygon** Type of line graph that shows frequency distributions.

**Figure A-1**
**A frequency histogram for a memory experiment.** The bars indicate the frequency of scores within each interval.

Now she can tell at a glance what the results of her experiment were. Most of the students had scores near the middle of the range, and very few had scores in the high or low intervals. She can see these results even better if she uses the frequency distribution to construct a bar graph—a **frequency histogram**. Marking the intervals along the horizontal axis and the frequencies along the vertical axis would give her the graph shown in Figure A-1. Another way is to construct a **frequency polygon**, a line graph. A frequency polygon drawn from the same set of data is shown in Figure A-2. Note that the figure is not a smooth curve, since the points are connected by straight lines. With many scores, however, and with small intervals, the angles would smooth out, and the figure would resemble a rounded curve.

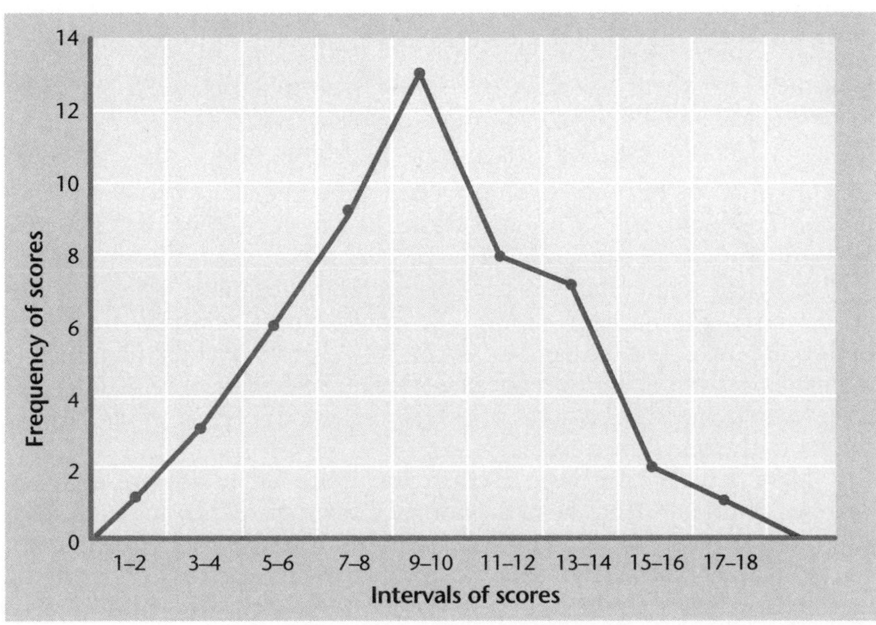


**Figure A-2**
**A frequency polygon drawn from data used in Figure A-1.** The dots, representing the frequency of scores in each interval, are connected by straight lines.

**Normal curve** Hypothetical bell-shaped distribution curve that occurs when a normal distribution is plotted as a frequency polygon.

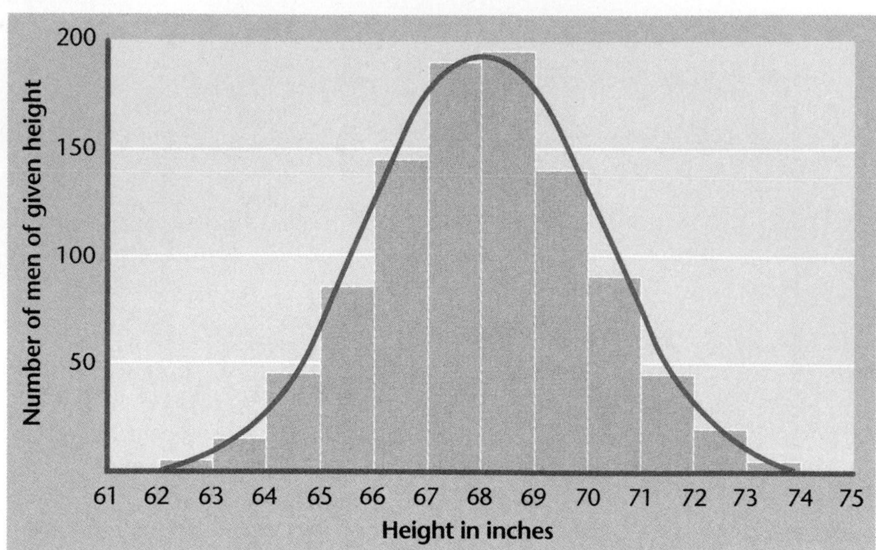


**Figure A-3**
**A normal curve,** based on measurements of the heights of 1,000 adult males.

*Source:* From Hill, 1966.

## The Normal Curve

Ordinarily, if we take enough measurements of almost anything, we get a *normal distribution*. Tossing coins is a favorite example of statisticians. If you tossed 10 coins into the air 1,000 times and recorded the heads and tails on each toss, your tabulations would reveal a normal distribution. Five heads and five tails would occur most often, six heads/four tails and four heads/six tails would be the next most frequent, and so on down to the rare all heads or all tails.

Plotting a normal distribution on a graph yields a particular kind of frequency polygon, called a **normal curve**. Figure A-3 shows data on the heights of 1,000 men. Superimposed over the gray bars that reflect the actual data is an "ideal" normal curve for the same data. Note that the curve is absolutely symmetrical—the left slope parallels the right slope exactly. Moreover, the mean, median, and mode all fall on the highest point on the curve.

The normal curve is a hypothetical entity. No set of real measurements shows such a smooth gradation from one interval to the next, or so purely symmetrical a shape. But because so many things do approximate the normal curve so closely, the curve is a useful model for much that we measure.

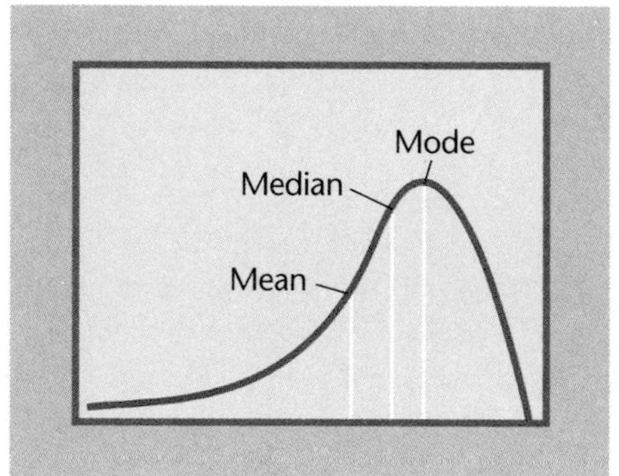


**Figure A-4**
**A skewed distribution.** Most of the scores are gathered at the high end of the distribution, causing the hump to shift to the right. Since the tail on the left is longer, we say that the curve is skewed to the left. Note that the *mean, median,* and *mode* are different.

## Skewed Distributions

If a frequency distribution is asymmetrical—if most of the scores are gathered at either the high end or the low end—the frequency polygon will be *skewed*. The hump will sit to one side or the other, and one of the curve's tails will be disproportionately long.

If a high-school mathematics instructor, for example, gives her students a sixth-grade arithmetic test, we would expect nearly all the scores to be quite high. The frequency polygon would probably look like the one in Figure A-4. But if a sixth-grade class is asked to do advanced algebra, the scores would probably be quite low. The frequency polygon would be very similar to the one shown in Figure A-5.

Note, too, that the mean, median, and mode fall at different points in a skewed distribution, unlike in the normal curve, where they coincide. Usually, if you know that the mean is greater than the median of a distribution, you can predict that the frequency polygon will be skewed to the right. If the median is greater than the mean, the curve will be skewed to the left.

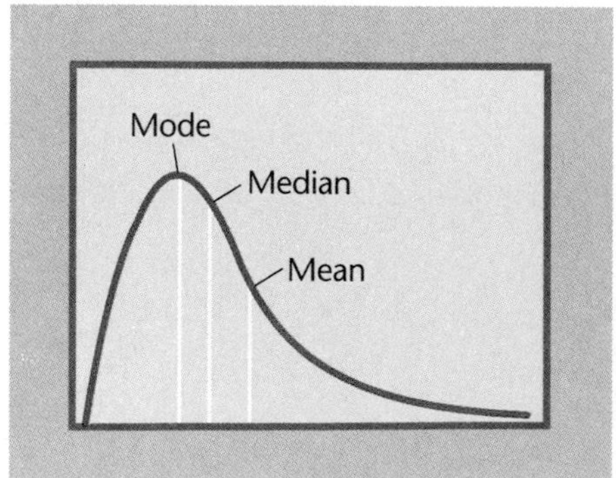


**Figure A-5**
In this distribution, most of the scores are gathered at the low end, so the curve is skewed to the right. The *mean, median,* and *mode* do not coincide.

## Bimodal Distributions

We have already mentioned a bimodal distribution in our description of the shopkeeper's survey of his customers' incomes. The frequency polygon for a bimodal distribution has two humps—one for each mode. The mean and the median may be the same (Figure A-6) or different (Figure A-7).

**Range** Difference between the largest and smallest measurements in a distribution.

# MEASURES OF VARIATION

Sometimes it is not enough to know the distribution of a set of data and what their mean, median, and mode are. Suppose an automotive safety expert feels that too much damage occurs in tail-end accidents because automobile bumpers are not all the same height. It is not enough to know what the average height of an automobile bumper is. The safety expert also wants to know about the variation in bumper heights: How much higher is the highest bumper than the mean? How do bumpers of all cars vary from the mean? Are the latest bumpers closer to the same height?

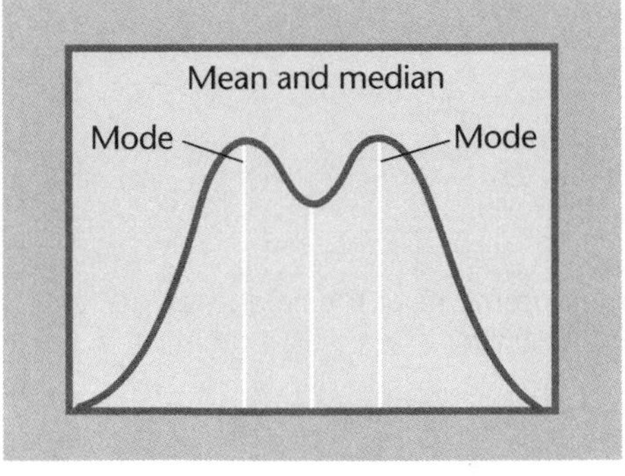


**Figure A-6**
A bimodal distribution in which the *mean* and the *median* are the same.

## Range

The simplest measure of variation is the **range**—the difference between the largest and smallest measurements. Perhaps the safety expert measured the bumpers of 1,000 cars two years ago and found that the highest bumper was 18 inches from the ground, the lowest only 12 inches from the ground. The range was thus 6 inches—18 minus 12. This year the highest bumper is still 18 inches high, the lowest still 12 inches from the ground. The range is still 6 inches. Moreover, our safety expert finds that the means of the two distributions are the same—15 inches off the ground. But look at the two frequency polygons in Figure A-8—there is still something the expert needs to know, since the measurements cluster around the mean in drastically different ways. To find out how the measurements are distributed around the mean, our safety expert has to turn to a slightly more complicated measure of variation—the standard deviation.

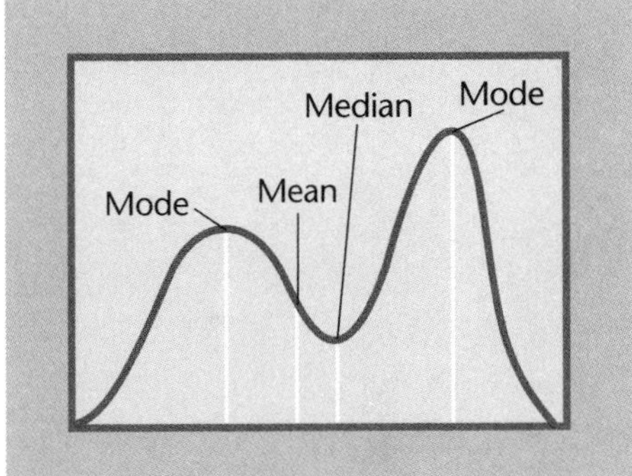


**Figure A-7**
In this bimodal distribution, the *mean* and *median* are different.

**Figure A-8**
**Frequency polygons for two sets of measurements of automobile bumper heights.** Both are normal curves, and in each distribution the *mean*, *median*, and *mode* are 15. But the variation from the mean is different, causing one curve to be flattened and the other to be much more sharply peaked.

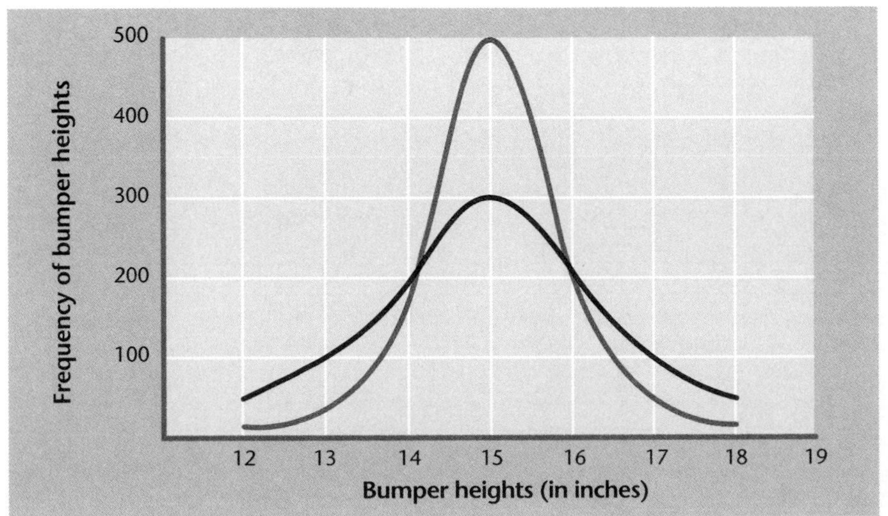

**Standard deviation** Statistical measure of variability in a group of scores or other values.

| Number of scores = 10 | | Mean = 7 |
|---|---|---|
| Scores | Difference from mean | Difference squared |
| 4 | 7 − 4 = 3 | $3^2 = 9$ |
| 5 | 7 − 5 = 2 | $2^2 = 4$ |
| 6 | 7 − 6 = 1 | $1^2 = 1$ |
| 6 | 7 − 6 = 1 | $1^2 = 1$ |
| 7 | 7 − 7 = 0 | $0^2 = 0$ |
| 7 | 7 − 7 = 0 | $0^2 = 0$ |
| 8 | 7 − 8 = − 1 | $-1^2 = 1$ |
| 8 | 7 − 8 = − 1 | $-1^2 = 1$ |
| 9 | 7 − 9 = − 2 | $-2^2 = 4$ |
| 10 | 7 − 10 = − 3 | $-3^2 = 9$ |

Sum of squares = 30

÷

Number of scores = 10

Variance = 3

Standard deviation = $\sqrt{3} = 1.73$

**Figure A-9**
Step-by-step calculation of the *standard deviation* for a group of 10 scores with a mean of 7.

## The Standard Deviation

The **standard deviation**, in a single number, tells us much about how the scores in any frequency distribution are dispersed around the mean. Calculating the standard deviation is one of the most useful and widely used statistical tools.

To find the standard deviation of a set of scores, we first find the mean. Then we take the first score in the distribution, subtract it from the mean, square the difference, and jot it down in a column to be added up later. We do the same for all the scores in the distribution. Then we add up the column of squared differences, divide the total by the number of scores in the distribution, and find the square root of that number. Figure A-9 shows the calculation of the standard deviation for a small distribution of scores.

In a normal distribution, however peaked or flattened the curve, about 68 percent of the scores fall between one standard deviation above the mean and one standard deviation below the mean (see Figure A-10).

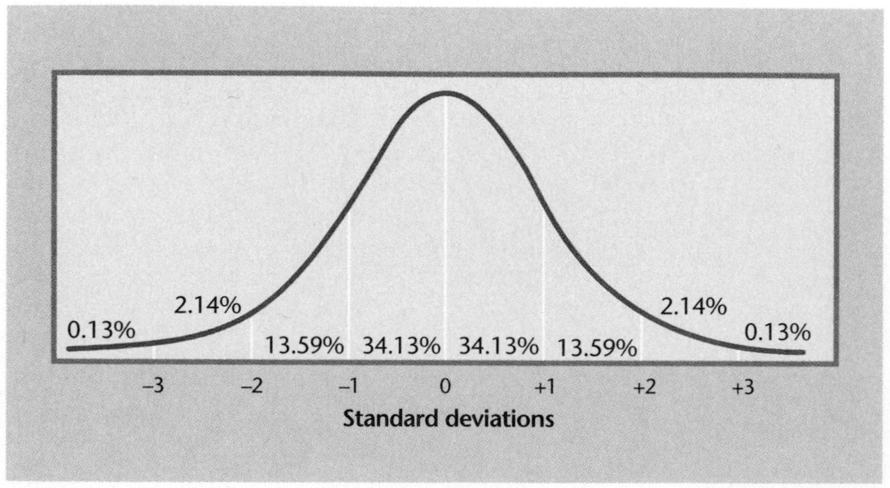


**Figure A-10**
**A normal curve,** divided to show the percentage of scores that fall within each *standard deviation* from the *mean.*

Another 27 percent fall between one standard deviation and two standard deviations on either side of the mean, and 4 percent more between the second and third standard deviations on either side. Overall, then, more than 99 percent of the scores fall between three standard deviations above and three standard deviations below the mean. This makes the standard deviation useful for comparing two different normal distributions.

Now let us see what the standard deviation can tell our automotive safety expert about the variations from the mean in the two sets of data. The standard deviation for the cars measured 2 years ago is about 1.4. A car with a bumper height of 16.4 is one standard deviation above the mean of 15; one with a bumper height of 13.6 is one standard deviation below the mean. Since the engineer knows that the data fall into a normal distribution, he or she can figure that about 68 percent of the 1,000 cars he measured will fall somewhere between these two heights: 680 cars will have bumpers between 13.6 and 16.4 inches high. For the more recent set of data, the standard deviation is just slightly less than 1. A car with a bumper height of about 14 inches is one standard deviation below the mean; a car with a bumper height of about 16 is one standard deviation above the mean. Thus, in this distribution, 680 cars have bumpers between 14 and 16 inches high. This tells the safety expert that car bumpers are becoming more similar, although the range of heights is still the same (6 inches), and the mean height of bumpers is still 15.

**Scatter plot** Diagram showing the association between scores on two variables.

## MEASURES OF CORRELATION

Measures of central tendency and measures of variation can be used to describe a single set of measurements—like the children's ring-tossing scores—or to compare two or more sets of measurements—like the two sets of bumper heights. Sometimes, however, we need to know if two sets of measurements are in any way associated with each other—if they are *correlated.* Is parental IQ related to children's IQ? Does the need for achievement relate to the need for power? Is watching violence on TV related to aggressive behavior?

One fast way to determine if two variables are correlated is to draw a **scatter plot**. We assign one variable (X) to the horizontal axis of a graph, the other variable (Y) to the vertical axis. Then we plot a person's score on one characteristic along the horizontal axis and his or her score on the second characteristic along the vertical axis. Where the two scores intersect, we draw a dot. When several scores have been plotted in this way, the pattern of dots tells if the two characteristics are in any way correlated with each other.

If the dots on a scatter plot form a straight line running between the lower left-hand corner and the upper right-hand corner, as they do in Figure A-11a, we have a perfect *positive correlation*—a high score on one of the characteristics is always associated with a high score on the other one. A straight line running between the upper-left-hand corner and the lower-right-hand corner, as in Figure A-11b, is the sign of a perfect *negative correlation*—a high score on one of the characteristics is always associated with a low score on the other one. If the pattern formed by the dots is cigar shaped in either of these directions, as in Figure A-11c, we have a modest correlation—the two characteristics are related but not highly correlated. If the dots spread out over the whole graph, forming a circle or a random pattern, as they go in Figure A-11d, there is no correlation between the two characteristics.

A scatter plot can give us a general idea if a correlation exists and how strong it is. To describe the relation between two variables more pre-

**Correlation coefficient** Statistical measure of the strength of association between two variables.

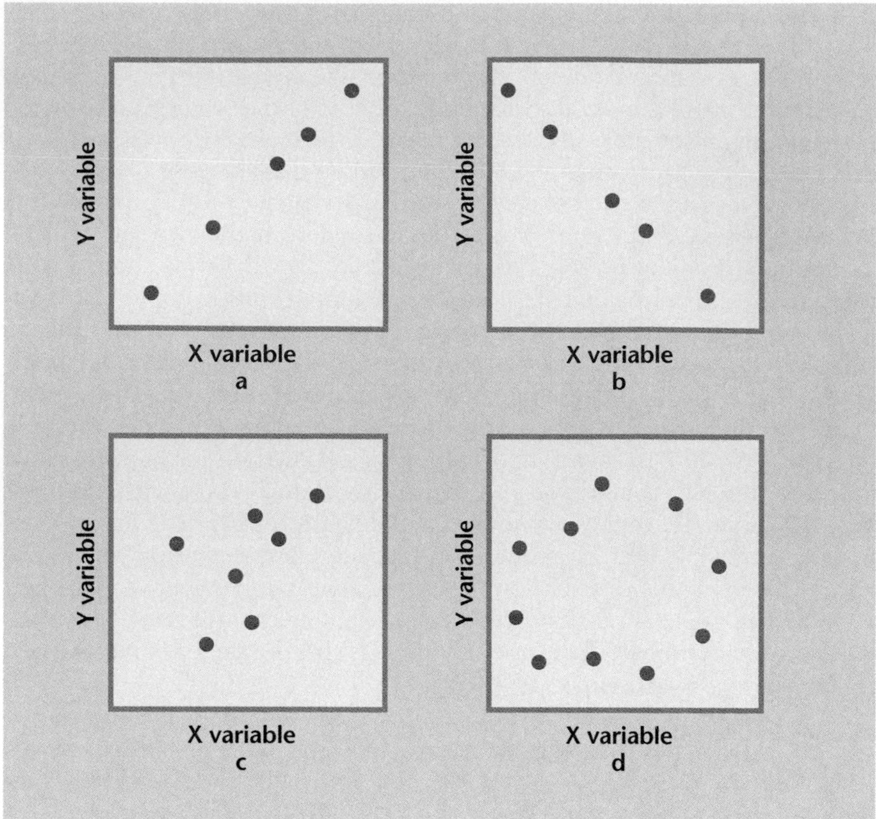


**Figure A-11**
*Scatter plots* can be used to give a rough idea of the strength and direction of correlation. Plot *a* shows a perfect *positive correlation*; plot *b* shows a perfect *negative correlation*. Plot *c* shows a moderate positive correlation, but in plot *d* there is no correlation at all.

cisely, we need a **correlation coefficient**—a statistical measure of the degree to which two variables are associated. The correlation coefficient tells us the degree of association between two sets of matched scores—that is, to what extent high or low scores on one variable tend to be associated with high or low scores on another variable. It also provides an estimate of how well we can predict from a person's score on one characteristic how high he or she will score on another characteristic. If we know, for example, that a test of mechanical ability is highly correlated with success in engineering courses, we could predict that success on the test would also mean success as an engineering major.

Correlation coefficients can run from +1.0 to –1.0. The highest possible value (+1.0) indicates a perfect positive correlation—high scores on one variable are always and systematically related to high scores on a second variable. The lowest possible value (–1.0) means a perfect negative correlation—high scores on one variable are always and regularly related to low scores on the second variable. In life, most things are far from perfect, so most correlation coefficients fall somewhere between +1.0 and –1.0. A correlation smaller than ±.20 is considered insignificant, from ±.20 to ±.40 is low, from ±.40 to ±.60 is moderate, from ±.60 to ±.80 is high, and from ±.80 to ±1.0 is very high. A correlation of zero indicates that there is no correlation between two sets of scores—no regular relation between them at all.

Correlation tells us nothing about causality. If we found a high positive correlation between participation in elections and income levels, for example, we still could not say that being wealthy made people vote or that voting made people wealthy. We would still not know which came first, or if some third variable explained both income levels and voting behavior. Correlation only tells us that we have found some association between scores on two specified characteristics.

**Significance** Probability that results obtained were due to chance.

## USING STATISTICS TO MAKE PREDICTIONS

Behind the use of statistics is the hope that we can generalize from our results and use them to predict behavior. We hope, for example, that we can use the record of how well a group of rats run through a maze today to predict how another group of rats will do tomorrow, that we can use a person's scores on a sales aptitude test to predict how well he or she will sell life insurance, that we can measure the attitudes of a relatively small group of people about pollution control to indicate what the attitudes of the whole country are.

First we have to determine if our measurements are representative and if we can have confidence in them. In Chapter 1, we discussed this problem when we considered the problem of proper sampling.

### Probability

Errors based on inadequate sampling procedures are somebody's fault. Other kinds of errors occur randomly. In the simplest kind of experiment, a psychologist will gather a representative sample, split it randomly into two groups, and then apply some experimental manipulation to one of the groups. Afterward, the psychologist will measure both groups and determine if the experimental group's score is now different from the score of the control group. But even if there is a large difference between the scores of the two groups, it may still be wrong to attribute the difference to the manipulation. Random effects might influence the results and introduce error.

Statistics give the psychologist many ways to determine precisely if the difference between the two groups is really significant, if something other than chance produced the results, and if the same results would be obtained with different subjects. These probabilities are expressed as measures of **significance**. If the psychologist computes the significance level for the results as .05, he or she knows that there are 19 chances out of 20 that the results are not due to chance. But there is still 1 chance in 20—or a .05 likelihood—that the results are due to chance. A .01 significance level would mean that there is only 1 chance in 100 that the results are due to chance.

# ANSWERS TO REVIEW QUESTIONS

## CHAPTER 1

**1.** scientific; **2.** describe, explain, predict, and control; **3.** naturalistic observation; **4.** independent-dependent; **5.** c—experimenter bias; **6.** correlational; **7.** observer bias; **8.** predicting and explaining; **9.** random and representative; **10.** d—failure to follow federal regulations can result in penalties; **11.** 1800s; **12.** E structuralism, A functionalism, D behaviorism, H psychoanalysis, C existential psychology, F humanistic psychology, B Gestalt psychology, G cognitive psychology; **13.** reinforcement; **14.** psychotherapy; **15.** behavior and mental processes; **16.** "Critical thinking in psychology" involves both analytical and integrative thinking. Making effective use of information about human behavior can benefit you in your personal relationships as well as your professional life; **17.** Correlational research could be done to compare number of pages of notes per class period to test scores. You could also set up an experiment with 3 sets of subjects who are assigned to take small, medium, or a large amount of notes during a one hour lecture. The subjects would then be given a test over the material. The mean test scores of the three groups could be compared; **18.** Keeping an open mind about the study would be important until the study is replicated with women and various ethnic groups. The results may be accurate for other groups but we can not be sure at this point; **19.** Personal answer but research should not be done if animals suffer unnecessarily.

## CHAPTER 2

**1.** D neuron, A nerve, C axon, B dendrite; **2.** positive-negative; **3.** B relative refractory; **4.** F; **5.** neurotransmitters; **6.** B Amphetamines, A Curare, LSD, and Atropine, C Antidepressant; **7.** peripheral; **8.** D hypothalamus; 9 A thalamus; **10.** parietal, frontal; **11.** D parathyroid; **12.** C corpus callosum; **13.** left; **14.** left, right; **15.** hormones; **16.** True; **17.** After reading this chapter the biological perspective of psychology processes probably seems more feasible; **18.** We can now study a living brain through the use of PET, SPECT, MEG, CT scans, MRI, and examine both the structure and function. These methods can be useful after brain damage, psychological problems, difficulty thinking or when behavioral problems exist; **19.** It may turn out that most psychological disorders have a biological component. Denying someone access to drugs when there is a biological basis could possibly be compared to denying insulin to someone with diabetes; **20.** Similar behaviors have been observed in identical twins even if they have never met.

## CHAPTER 3

**1.** B difference; **2.** D cornea, H pupil, A iris, F lens, B fovea, E retina, G rod, C cone; **3.** A dark adaptation; **4.** B blind spot; **5.** hue, saturation, and brightness; 6 B subtractive; **7.** red, green, blue; 8 C Opponent-process theory; **9.** 2 oval window, 1 anvil, 4 cochlea, 5 auditory nerve, 3 round window; **10.** B frequency theory, A volley principle, C place theory; **11.** taste buds—sweet, sour, salty, and bitter; **12.** culture, experience, expectancy, motivation; **13.** B releasing endorphins; **14.** perception; **15.** figure–ground; **16.** D similarity, C continuity, B common fate, E proximity, A closure; **17.** B retinal disparity, M texture gradient M shadowing, B convergence, M motion parallax, M accommodation, B stereoscopic vision, M linear perspective, M superposition; **18.** A monaural; **19.** apparent; **20.** The fovea is the site of the sharpest vision; 21. Our eyes are very sensitive to movement, especially in our side vision; 22. The kinesthetic senses provide specific information about muscles movement, changes in posture, and strain on muscles and joints. The vestibular senses control equilibrium and create an awareness of body position. Playing any sport requires both systems; **23.** Taste preferences are culturally taught and there is a loss of taste buds throughout our lifespan; **24.** The flavor and taste of an onion are very different. Some foods smell strange but have great flavor (some people would say this about garlic); **25.** Beecher (1972) noted that only 25 percent of soldiers wounded during battle requested pain medication, whereas more than 80 percent of surgical patients requested medication for comparable wounds. These factors also influence other senses; **26.** Personal response.

## CHAPTER 4

**1.** altered states of; **2.** attention; **3.** sexual and aggressive; **4.** F; **5.** paradoxical; **6.** REM rebound; **7.** C insomnia, B apnea, A narcolepsy; **8.** sympathetic nervous; **9.** suggestibility; **10.** depressant-stimulant; **11.** barbiturates; **12.** C crack; **13.** D Alcohol, A Amphetamines, F Barbituates, H Opiates, C Cocaine, E Hallucinogens; **14.** Some areas of consciousness can be studied with scientific methods while other areas are very abstract; **15.** Some psychologists believe dreams offer insights into our innermost thoughts, while other psychologists believe dreams are just the result of neural processes; **16.***(Your personal response.)*

## CHAPTER 5

**1.** conditioning; **2.** before; **3.** A CS and US; **4.** information; **5.** spontaneous recovery; **6.** stimulus generalization; **7.** operant (or instrumental) conditioning; **8.** shaping; 9 B negative reinforcement; **10.** 1 food, 2 money, 2 diploma, 1 sex; **11.** A positive reinforcement; 12 B negative reinforcement; **13.** FI , FR , VR , VI ; **14.** cognitive map; **15.** A insight; **16.** A CS provides new information; **17.** C both a and b; **18.** vicarious punishment; **19.** vicarious or observational learning; **20.** insight learning in animals, cognitive map learning in animals, observational learning in animals; **21.** The dill pickle is the unconditioned stimulus and salivation and mouth puckering are the unconditioned responses. The picture in your mind of the dill pickle is the conditioned stimulus which then leads to the conditioned response of salivation; **22.** Fearful sounds and painful experiences are the unconditioned stimuli. Aversion and fear would be the responses. Eventually just the thought of going to the dentist becomes the conditioned stimulus which triggers the response of fear; **23.** Classical conditioning involves association. Either fear or relief could become associated with the sound of a siren depending on what we experienced after hearing a siren; **24.** Answers could include such things as; going to Introductory Psychology to receive a grade, working to receive a paycheck; **25.** Giving the dog treats when he doesn't bark and withholding treats when he does bark. Extinction could involve stopping any behavior (like giving attention) which might be reinforcing the barking; **26.** Cognitive maps are mental images of whole areas. We use these when getting around campus to different classes or around town running errands. **27.** The program "Scared Straight" involves teenagers hearing from inmates what it is like in prison. The teenagers do not have to go to prison to learn that it is not where they want to be.

## CHAPTER 6

**1.** sensory registers; **2.** attention; **3.** "cocktail party"; **4.** short-term; **5.** decay–interference; **6.** rote; **7.** elaborative; **8.** semantic–episodic; **9.** interference; **10.** proactive; **11.** eidetic; **12.** survey, question, read, recite, review; **13.** T; **14.** infantile amnesia; **15.** Accuracy of any eyewitness testimony is difficult to determine because an individual's perceptions can alter memory significantly. Getting an account of the event from several people may help to clarify what really occurred. Her memory of the accident could be altered if carefully chosen words were used to lead here to recall the experience a certain way; **16.** Flashbulb memories are the experience of remembering vividly a certain event and the incidents surrounding them even after a long time as passed. Flashbulb memories may not be accurate because they undergo reconstruction and become less accurate over the years until they do not even resemble what actually occurred; **17.** Semantic memory contains facts and information, whereas, episodic memory is made up of specific events that have personal meaning for us. Implicit memories are stored unintentionally. These memories can be of both facts and experiences.

## CHAPTER 7

**1.** cognition; **2.** words, images, and concepts; **3.** _A_ concepts; **4.** True; **5.** True; **6.** _C_ algorithm, _A_ heuristics, _B_ hill climbing, _E_ means-end analysis, _D_ working backward; **7.** _D_ hill climbing; **8.** compensatory; **9.** set; **10.** functional fixedness; **11.** noncompensatory; **12.** _B_ the stakes are high; **13.** phonemes–morphemes–sentences; **14.** language; **15.** linguistic relativity hypothesis; **16.** transformations; **17.** confirmation bias, **18.** _D_ Cattell, _C_ Spearman, _A_ Sternberg, _B_ Thurston, _E_ Gardner; **19.** componential–experiential–contextual; **20.** IQ–100–Binet-Simon Scale; **21.** T; **22.** Wechsler Adult Intelligence Scale–Revised (WAIS-R); **23.** group tests, _C_ Wechsler Adult Intelligence Scale; **24.** performance–culture-fair; **25.** reliable; **26.** validity; **27.** school; **28.** _A_ creativity; **29.** _A_ take risks and like their own problems, **30.** The compensatory model of decision making analyzes if the attractive features of something you are deciding on can compensate for the unattractive features; **31.** *(Your personal response.)*

## CHAPTER 8

**1.** longitudinal; **2.** F; **3.** T; **4.** T; **5.** sensory-motor (mainly flex activity), preoperational (can use symbols but are very egocentric), concrete operations (logical but not yet abstract), formal operations (abstract thinking); **6.** Shortly after they are born or hatched, some young animals form a strong bond to the first moving object they see. This is called imprinting, and is important for their survival; **7.** attachment; **8.** socialization; **9.** 10 1/2, 12 1/2; **10.** menarche; **11.** F; **12.** F; **13.** leaving home; **14.** The unborn baby is affected by his or her environment. Everything that Serena ingests is passed on to the fetus. The fetus is very much "awake" already. He or she is physically active and most of his or her senses are already functioning. **15.** signs of anorexia nervosa: intense fear of becoming obese, distorted body image, very low weight, and in females the absence of three consecutive menstrual cycles–signs of bulimia: binge eating, self-induced vomiting, excessive worry about body shape–The prevalence of eating disorders seems to be associated with media emphasis on thin body images. **16.** Millions of American children under the age of 5 are now being cared for in day-care centers, in preschools, or in a relative's house. Research indicates that any secure, fun, and stimulating environment is more likely to produce healthy children; **17.** According to a recent survey, 37 percent of married people over 60 have sex at least once a week.

## CHAPTER 9

**1.** motives and emotions; **2.** _C_ stimulus; **3.** homeostasis; **4.** F; **5.** hunger–satiety; **6.** testosterone; **7.** stimulus; **8.** achievement; **9.** affiliation; **10.** T; **11.** Yerkes-Dodson; **12.** intensity; **13.** T: **14.** _B_ Cannon-Bard, _C_ cognitive theory, _A_ James-Lange; **15.** _B_ expressive behavior; **16.** facial and expressions and body language; **17.** Obesity having a genetic component should lead to less judgmental and discriminatory treatment; however, it is questionable if society will change; **18.** Other possible explanations for low performance levels could be learning disabilities, brain damage, numerous negative past experiences related to performance; **19.** Boredom leads some people to explore their environment; and most people have an innate reaction to novel stimuli. These two ideas represent different components of curiosity. Children need both time and an interesting environment to stimulate their curiosity; **20.** *(Your personal response.)*

## CHAPTER 10

1. time and situations; **2.** _E_ unconscious, _C_ id, _F_ superego, _B_ ego, _D_ ego ideal, _A_ libido; **3.** ego–id; **4.** wish fulfillment; **5.** _C_ persona, _D_ animus, _B_ collective unconscious, _A_ archetype; **6.** _A_ inferiority complex, _B_ compensation; **7.** anxiety; **8.** _D_ industry versus inferiority, _A_ trust versus mistrust, _G_ generativity versus stagnation, _F_ intimacy versus isolation, _E_ identify versus role confusion, _B_ autonomy versus shame and doubt, _C_ initiative versus guilt, _H_ integrity versus despair; **9.** self-actualizing; **10.** evaluate; **11.** objective; **12.** projective; **13.** your personal feelings; **14.** Jung contended that libido represents all the life forces, not just the sexual ones. He saw the unconscious as the ego's source of strength and vitality. Adler believed that individuals possess innate positive motives and strive toward personal and social perfection. Horney concluded that environmental and social factors are the most important influences in shaping personality. Erikson took a socially oriented view of personality development. He also extended his interest to development throughout the life cycle; **15.** The major forms of personality assessment are observation, objective tests, and projective tests. Behaviorists and social learning theorists prefer observation. Objective tests were devised so as not to be dependent on the skill or interpretation of the psychologist. Psychodynamic theorists put little faith in objective personality tests because they

believe the unconscious determinant of behavior; **16.** *(Your personal feelings.)*

## CHAPTER 11

**1.** the stress response (or sympathetic nervous system response); **2.** T; **3.** pressure; **4.** frustration; **5.** conflict; **6.** _C_ approach/approach, _A_ avoidance/avoidance, _B_ approach/avoidance; **7.** F; **8.** direct, defensive; **9.** direct; **10.** defensive; **11.** _F_ denial, _A_ repression, _G_ projection, _I_ identification, _C_ regression, _B_ intellectualization, _D_ reaction formation, _E_ displacement, _H_ sublimation; **12.** alarm-resistance, exhaustion; **13.** Type A personality; **14.** F; **15.** Sherry's headaches could be related to the stress experienced by air-traffic controllers, or her perfectionism, or the recent loss of her boyfriend. The problem could also be stress overload by the combination of stresses; **16.** Defense mechanisms are not always bad. Denial can sometimes keep us trying at something when, if we faced the actual odds against us, we might have given up; **17.** The General Adaptation Syndrome theory of a person's response to stress describes the end result of stress as physical exhaustion.

## CHAPTER 12

**1.** F; **2.** _D_ biological model, _A_ psychoanalytic model, _C_ cognitive-behavioral model, _B_ diathesis-stress model; **3.** a. American Psychiatric Association; **4.** b. dissociative fugue; **5.** b. mania and depression; **6.** F; **7.** dysthymia, major depressive disorder; **8.** psychotic; **9.** b. personality disorders; **10.** Psychosomatic disorders are real physical disorders, with a valid physical basis; **11.** just a matter of normal behavior greatly exaggerated or displayed in inappropriate situations; **12.** He may be experiencing a dissociative disorder. It becomes serious when he can not-control it and it interferes with his life; **13.** Dimension (magnitude) is more important because psychology symptoms are experienced by most people, but these symptoms do not interfere with their lives in any significant way.

## CHAPTER 13

**1.** d–insight; **2.** _B_ psychoanalysis, _C_ client-centered therapy, _D_ cognitive behavior therapy, _A_ rational-emotive therapy; **3.** unconditional positive; **4.** insight–behavior; **5.** A–desensitization; **6.** aversion conditioning; **7.** F; **8.** F; **9.** d–antipsychotics; **10.** institutionalization; **11.** T; **12.** deinstitutionalization; **13.** prevention; **14.** Psychoanalysis focuses on reversing the process of repression so hidden feelings can be dealt with more effectively; **15.** Insight therapy focuses on using free association to uncover inner conflicts dating back to childhood. Behavior therapies are based on the belief that all behavior is learned, and they focus on teaching people, new ways of behaving; **16.** Cognitive therapists believe that in addition to changing behavior, clients also change their way of thinking about themselves and the world; **17.** The chemical imbalance may be a result of another process rather than the cause.

## CHAPTER 14

**1.** social; **2.** schemata—stereotype; **3.** primacy; **4.** c—attribution theory; **5.** c—complementary attitudes and interests; **6.** attitude; l **7.** F; **8.** conform; **9.** cognitive dissonance; **10.** a—attitudes; **11.** _D_ social influence, _C_ compliance, _B_ obedience, _A_ conformity; **12.** risky shift; **13.** polarization; **14.** task—interaction; **15.** T; **16.** F; **17.** Self-fulling prophecy is a process in which a person's expectation about another elicits behavior from the second person that confirms the expectation. Our expectations and treatment of others influence our relationships significantly; **18.** Internal versus external attribution refer to how people make judgments about the causes of behavior. Internal is a quality within the person, whereas external refers to an outside circumstance; **19.** Some key factors that determine interpersonal attraction are: proximity, physical attractiveness, similarity, exchange, and intimacy; **20.** Advertising can be useful or it can be dishonest and manipulative, depending on the ethics of the developers.

## CHAPTER 15

**1.** _C_ masculine, _D_ female, _A_ gender stereotypes, _B_ gender roles; **2.** rank order—e, c, f, a, d, b: **3.** _C_ physical aggression; **4.** emotional labor; **5.** _D_ males are more likely than females to offer social support; **6.** _A_ within/across; **7.** Cultural shock; 8 _C_ power distance, _A_ masculinity, _D_ uncertainty avoidance, _B_ collectivism; **9.** idiocentrism/individualism; **10.** internal/collective; **11.** _C_ masking; **12.** culture-learning position; **13.** individualist; Critical Thinking and Applications; **14.** Culture and emotional expression can also be studied by analyzing emotions which appear to be expressed differently in different cultures and determine what, if any, cultural connections correlate with the differences. (There could be many correct answers to this question.); **15.** answers vary depending on cultures being analyzed; **16.** answers vary depending on topic chosen for research study.

# GLOSSARY

**Absolute refractory period** A period after firing when a neuron will not fire again no matter how strong the incoming messages may be. [p. 37]

**Absolute threshold** The least amount of energy that can be detected as a stimulation 50 percent of the time. [p. 79]

**Achievement motive** The need to excel, to overcome obstacles; a social motive. [p. 361]

**ACTH** Hormone released by the anterior pituitary; it stimulates hormone production of the adrenal cortex. [p. 63]

**Actualizing tendency** According to Rogers, the drive of every organism to fulfill its biological potential and become what it is inherently capable of becoming. [p. 398]

**Adaptation** Adjustment of the senses to the level of stimulation they are receiving. [p. 80]

**Additive color mixing** The process of mixing lights of different wavelengths to create new hues. [p. 90]

**Adjustment** Any effort to cope with stress. [p. 418]

**Adoption studies** Research carried out on children adopted at birth by parents not related to them to determine the relative influence of heredity and environment on human behavior. [p. 70]

**Adrenal cortex** Outer covering of the two adrenal glands that releases hormones important for dealing with stress. [p. 63]

**Adrenal glands** Two endocrine glands located just above the kidneys. [p. 63]

**Adrenal medulla** Inner core of the adrenal glands that also releases hormones to deal with stress. [p. 63]

**Aerial perspective** Monocular cue to distance and depth based on the fact that more distant objects are likely to appear hazy and blurred. [p. 110]

**Affiliation motive** The need to be with others; a social motive. [p. 363]

**Afterimage** Sense experience that occurs after a visual stimulus has been removed. [p. 86]

**Aggression** Behavior aimed at doing harm to others; also the motive to behave aggressively. [p. 358]

**Agoraphobia** An anxiety disorder that involves multiple, intense fears of crowds, public places, and other situations which separate people from sources of security, such as the home. [p. 459]

**Alcohol** Depressant that is the intoxicating ingredient in whiskey, beer, wine, and other fermented or distilled liquors. [p. 143]

**Algorithm** A step-by-step method of problem solving that guarantees a correct solution. [p. 243]

**All-or-none law** Principle that the action potential in a neuron does not vary in strength; the neuron either fires at full strength or it does not fire at all. [p. 37]

**Altered state of consciousness (ASC)** Mental state that differs noticeably from normal waking consciousness. [p. 124]

**Altruistic behavior** Helping behavior that is not linked to personal gain. [p. 544]

**Alzheimer's disease** A disorder common in late adulthood that is characterized by progressive losses in memory and cognition and changes in personality and that is believed to be caused by a deterioration of the brain's structure and function. [p. 337]

**Amniocentesis** Technique that involves collecting cells cast off by the fetus into the fluid of the womb and testing them for genetic abnormalities. [p. 70]

**Amphetamines** Stimulant drugs that initially produce "rushes" of euphoria often followed by sudden "crashes" and, sometimes, severe depression. [p. 152]

**Amplitude** The magnitude of a wave; in sound, the primary determinant of loudness. [p. 92]

**Anal stage** Second stage in Freud's theory of personality development, in which a child's erotic feelings center on the anus and on elimination. [p. 389]

**Anima** According to Jung, the female archetype as it is expressed in the male personality. [p. 390]

**Animus** According to Jung, the male archetype as it is expressed in the female personality. [p. 390]

**Anorexia nervosa** A serious eating disorder that is associated with an intense fear of weight gain and a distorted body image. [p. 325]

**Anterior pituitary** Part of the pituitary known as the "master gland" because it produces numerous hormones that trigger the action of other glands; it regulates body growth and also affects motives and emotions. [p. 62]

**Antipsychotic drugs** Drugs used to treat very severe psychological disorders, particularly schizophrenia. [p. 503]

**Antisocial personality disorder** Personality disorder that involves a pattern of violent, criminal, or unethical and exploitative behavior and an inability to feel affection for others. [p. 469]

**Anxiety disorders** Disorders in which anxiety is a characteristic feature or the avoidance of anxiety motivates abnormal behavior. [p. 459]

**Anxiety** In Horney's theory, the individual's reaction to real or imagined threats. [p. 393]

**Apnea** Sleep disorder characterized by breathing difficulty during the night and feelings of exhaustion during the day. [p. 137]

**Approach/approach conflict** According to Lewin, the result of simultaneous attraction to two appealing possibilities, neither of which has any negative qualities. [p. 423]

**Approach/avoidance conflict** According to Lewin, the result of being simultaneously attracted to and repelled by the same goal. [p. 424]

**Archetypes** In Jung's theory of personality, thought forms common to all human beings, stored in the collective unconscious. [p. 390]

**Association areas** Areas of the cerebral cortex where incoming messages from the separate senses are combined into meaningful impressions and outgoing messages from the motor areas are integrated. [p. 45]

**Attachment** Emotional bond that develops in the first year of life that makes human babies cling to their caregivers for safety and comfort. [p. 308]

**Attention** Selection of some incoming information for further processing. [p. 205]

**Attitude** Relatively stable organization of beliefs, feelings, and behavior tendencies directed toward something or someone—the attitude object. [p. 529]

**Attribution theory** Theory that addresses the question of how people make judgments about the causes of behavior. [p. 525]

**Auditory nerve** The bundle of neurons that carries signals from each ear to the brain. [p. 93]

**Authoritarian personality** A personality pattern characterized by rigid conventionality, exaggerated respect for authority, and hostility toward those who defy society's norms. [p. 532]

**Autonomic nervous system** The part of the peripheral nervous system that carries messages between the central nervous system and the internal organs. [p. 58]

**Autonomy** Sense of independence; a desire not to be controlled by others. [p. 308]

**Availability** A heuristic by which a judgment or decision is based on information that is most easily retrieved from memory. [p. 250]

**Aversive conditioning** Behavioral therapy techniques aimed at eliminating undesirable behavior patterns by teaching the person to associate them with pain and discomfort. [p. 493]

**Avoidance training** Learning a desirable behavior to prevent the occurrence of something unpleasant such as punishment. [p. 172]

**Avoidance/avoidance conflict** According to Lewin, the result of facing a choice between two undesirable possibilities, neither of which has any positive qualities. [p. 423]

**Avoidant personality disorder** Personality disorder in which the person's fears of rejection by others leads to social isolation. [p. 468]

**Axon** Single long fiber extending from the cell body; it carries outgoing messages. [p. 34]

**Axon terminal or synaptic knob** Knob at the end of an axon terminal branch. [p. 38]

**Babbling** A baby's language that consists of repetition of consonant-vowel combinations. [p. 304]

**Barbiturates** Potentially deadly depressants, first used for their sedative and anticonvulsant effects, now used only to treat such conditions as epilepsy and arthritis. [p. 149]

**Basilar membrane** Vibrating membrane in the cochlea of the inner ear; it contains sense receptors for sound. [p. 92]

**Behavior contracting** Form of operant conditioning therapy in which the client and therapist set behavioral goals and agree on which reinforcements the client will receive upon reaching those goals. [p. 493]

**Behavior genetics** Study of the relationship between heredity and behavior. [p. 64]

**Behavior therapies** Therapeutic approaches that are based on the belief that all behavior, normal and abnormal, is learned, and that the objective of therapy is to teach people new, more satisfying ways of behaving. [p. 491]

**Behaviorism** School of psychology that studies only observable and measurable behavior. [p. 19]

**Beta endorphin** One of the endorphins, a natural painkiller released by the body. [p. 63]

**Biased sample** Sample that does not truly represent a whole population. [p. 13]

**Binaural cue** Cue to sound location that involves both ears working together. [p. 111]

**Binet-Simon Scale** The first test of intelligence, developed for testing children. [p. 258]

**Binocular cues** Visual cues requiring the use of both eyes. [p. 109]

**Biographical or retrospective study** Method of studying developmental changes by reconstructing subjects' past through interviews and investigating the effects of past events on current behaviors. [p. 291]

**Biological model of abnormal behavior** View that abnormal behavior has a biochemical or physiological basis. [p. 451]

**Biological treatments** Group of approaches, including medication, electroconvulsive therapy, and psychosurgery, that are sometimes used to treat psychological disorders in conjunction with, or instead of, psychotherapy. [p. 503]

**Bipolar cells** Neurons that have only one axon and one dendrite; in the eye, these neurons connect the receptors on the retina to the ganglion cells. [p. 84]

**Bipolar disorder** A mood disorder in which periods of mania alternate with periods of depression, sometimes with periods of normal mood intervening. [p. 456]

**Blind spot** Place on the retina where the axons of all the ganglion cells leave the eye and where there are no receptors. [p. 87]

**Blocking** A process whereby prior conditioning prevents conditioning to a second stimulus even when the two stimuli are presented simultaneously. [p. 183]

**Body dysmorphic disorder** A somatoform disorder in which a person becomes so preoccupied with his or her imagined ugliness that normal life is impossible. [p. 464]

**Borderline personality disorder** Personality disorder characterized by marked instability in self-image, mood, and interpersonal relationships. [p. 469]

**Brain stem** The top of the spinal column; it widens out to form the hindbrain and midbrain. [p. 44]

**Brainstorming** A problem-solving strategy in which an individual or a group produces numerous ideas and evaluates them only after all ideas have been collected. [p. 248]

**Brightness constancy** Perception of brightness as the same, even though the amount of light reaching the retina changes. [p. 106]

**Brightness** The nearness of a color to white as opposed to black. [p. 89]

**Bulimia** An eating disorder characterized by binges of eating followed by self-induced vomiting. [p. 325]

**Bystander effect** Tendency for an individual's helpfulness in an emergency to decrease as the number of bystanders increases. [p. 544]

**Cannon-Bard theory** States that the experience of emotion occurs simultaneously with biological changes. [p. 368]

**Case study** Intensive description and analysis of a single individual or just a few individuals. [p. 7]

**Catatonic schizophrenia** Schizophrenic disorder in which disturbed motor behavior is prominent. [p. 472]

**Categorical approach to classification** Dividing mental health and mental illness into categories that are qualitatively different from each other. [p. 450]

**Central nervous system** Division of the nervous system that consists of the brain and spinal cord. [p. 42]

**Cerebellum** Two hemispheres in the hindbrain that control certain reflexes and coordinate the body's movements. [p. 44]

**Cerebral cortex** The outer surface of the two cerebral hemispheres that regulate most complex behavior. [p. 44]

**Chromosomes** Pairs of threadlike bodies within the cell nucleus that contain the genes. [p. 65]

**Chunking** Grouping of information into meaningful units for easier handling by short-term memory. [p. 207]

**Classical or Pavlovian conditioning** Type of learning in which a response naturally elicited by one stimulus comes to be elicited by a different, neutral stimulus. [p. 162]

**Client-centered or person-centered therapy** Nondirectional form of therapy developed by Carl Rogers that calls for unconditional positive regard of the client by the therapist with the goal of helping the client become fully functioning. [p. 488]

**Clique** Group of adolescents with similar interests and strong mutual attachment. [p. 321]

**Cocaine** Drug derived from the coca plant that, while producing a sense of euphoria by stimulating the sympathetic nervous system, also leads to anxiety, depression, and addictive cravings. [p. 152]

**Cochlea** Part of the inner ear containing fluid that vibrates, which in turn causes the basilar membrane to vibrate. [p. 92]

**Cognition** The processes whereby we acquire and use knowledge. [p. 236]

**Cognitive dissonance** Perceived inconsistency between two cognitions. [p. 536]

**Cognitive distortion** An illogical and maladaptive response to early negative life events that leads to feelings of incompetence and unworthiness that are reactivated whenever a new situation arises that resembles the original events. [p. 457]

**Cognitive learning** Learning that depends on mental processes that are not directly observable. [p. 186]

**Cognitive map** A learned mental image of a spatial environment that may be called on to solve problems when stimuli in the environment change. [p. 186]

**Cognitive psychology** School of psychology devoted to the study of mental processes in the broadest sense. [p. 22]

**Cognitive theory** States that emotional experience depends on one's perception or judgment of the situation one is in. [p. 369]

**Cognitive therapies** Psychotherapies that emphasize changing clients' perceptions of their life situation as a way of modifying their behavior. [p. 494]

**Cognitive therapy** Therapy that depends on identifying and changing inappropriately negative and self-centered patterns of thought. [p. 497]

**Cognitive-behavioral model of abnormal behavior** View that abnormal behavior is the result of learning and therefore can be unlearned. [p. 452]

**Cognitive–social learning theories** Personality theories that view behavior as the product of the interaction of cognitions, learning and past experiences, and the immediate environment. [p. 403]

**Cohort** Group of people born during the same period in historical time. [p. 290]

**Collective unconscious** In Jung's theory of personality, the level of the unconscious that is inherited and common to all members of a species. [p. 390]

**Color constancy** Inclination to perceive familiar objects as retaining their color despite changes in sensory information. [p. 106]

**Colorblindness** Partial or total inability to perceive hues. [p. 90]

**Compensation** According to Adler, the person's effort to overcome imagined or real personal weaknesses. [p. 391]

**Compensatory model** A rational decision-making model in which choices are systematically evaluated based on various criteria. [p. 248]

**Compliance** Change of behavior in response to an explicit request from another person or group. [p. 540]

**Componential intelligence** According to Sternberg, the ability to acquire new knowledge, to solve problems effectively. [p. 256]

**Compromise** Deciding on a more realistic solution or goal when an ideal solution or goal is not practical. [p. 428]

**Concept** A mental category for classifying objects, people, or experiences. [p. 239]

**Concrete-operational stage** In Piaget's theory, the stage of cognitive development between 7 and 11 years of age, in which the individual can attend to more than one thing at a time and can understand someone else's point of view, though thinking is limited to concrete matters. [p. 301]

**Conditional positive regard** In Rogers's theory, acceptance and love that are dependent on behaving in certain ways and fulfilling certain conditions. [p. 399]

**Conditioned food or taste aversion** Conditioned avoidance of poisonous food even if there is a lengthy interval between eating the food and becoming ill and even if there is only one pairing of conditioned and unconditioned stimuli. [p. 167]

**Conditioned response (CR)** After conditioning, the response an organism produces when only a conditioned stimulus is presented. [p. 164]

**Conditioned stimulus (CS)** Originally neutral stimulus that is paired with an unconditioned stimulus and eventually produces the desired response in an organism when presented alone. [p. 164]

**Conditioning** The acquisition of specific patterns of behavior in the presence of well-defined stimuli. [p. 162]

**Cones** Receptor cells in the retina responsible for color vision. [p. 83]

**Confirmation bias** The tendency to look for evidence in support of a belief and to ignore evidence that would disprove a belief. [p. 251]

**Conflict** Simultaneous existence of incompatible demands, opportunities, needs, or goals. [p. 423]

**Conformity** Voluntarily yielding to social norms, even at the expense of one's own preferences. [p. 539]

**Confrontation** Acknowledging a stressful situation directly and attempting to find a solution to the problem or attain the difficult goal. [p. 428]

**Consciousness** Our awareness of various cognitive processes, such as sleeping, dreaming, concentrating, and making decisions. [p. 124]

**Content validity** Refers to a test's having an adequate sample of the skills or knowledge it is supposed to measure. [p. 264]

**Contextual intelligence** Sternberg's term for the ability to select contexts in which you can excel, to shape the environment to fit your strengths. [p. 256]

**Contingency** A reliable "if-then" relationship between two events such as a CS and US. [p. 183]

**Control group** In a controlled experiment, the group not subjected to a change in the independent variable; used for comparison with the experimental group. [p. 10]

**Convergence** A visual depth cue that comes from muscles controlling eye movement as the eyes turn inward to view a nearby stimulus. [p. 111]

**Convergent thinking** Thinking that is directed toward one correct solution to a problem. [p. 248]

**Conversion disorders** Somatoform disorders in which a dramatic, specific disability has no physical cause but instead can be traced to psychological problems. [p. 464]

**Cooperative play** Two or more children engaged in play that requires interaction. [p. 310]

**Cornea** The transparent protective coating over the front part of the eye. [p. 83]

**Corpus callosum** Band of nerve fibers that connects the two cerebral hemispheres and coordinates their activities. [p. 48]

**Correlation** Relationship between two or more variables. [p. 9]

**Correlational method** Research technique based on the naturally occurring relationship between two or more variables. [p. 8]

**Creativity** The ability to produce novel and unique socially valued ideas or objects. [p. 277]

**Criterion-related validity** Validity of a test as measured by comparing the test score with independent measures of what the test is designed to assess. [p. 265]

**Critical period** Time when certain internal and external influences have a major effect on development; at other periods, the same influences will have little or no effect. [p. 292]

**Cross-sectional study** Method of studying developmental changes by examining groups of subjects who are of different ages. [p. 290]

**Cultural norm** A behavioral rule shared by an entire society. [p. 539]

**Cultural truism** Belief that most members of a society accept as self-evidently true. [p. 538]

**Culture** All the goods, both tangible and intangible, produced in a society. [p. 538]

**Culture shock** Feeling disoriented or uncertain when exposed to an unfamiliar way of life. [p. 567]

**Culture-fair tests** Intelligence tests designed to eliminate cultural bias by minimizing assessment of skills and values that vary from one culture to another. [p. 262]

**Dark adaptation** Increased sensitivity of rods and cones in darkness. [p. 86]

**Daydreaming** Alteration in consciousness that occurs seemingly without effort, typically when we want to momentarily escape the demands of the real world. [p. 126]

**Decay theory** A theory that argues that the passage of time causes forgetting. [p. 209]

**Decibel** Unit of measurement for the loudness of sounds. [p. 92]

**Deep structure** The underlying meaning of a sentence. [p. 237]

**Defense mechanisms** Self-deceptive techniques for reducing stress, including denial, repression, projection, identification, regression, intellectualization, reaction formation, displacement, and sublimation. [p. 429]

**Defensive attribution** Tendency to attribute our successes to our own efforts or qualities and our failures to external factors. [p. 526]

**Deindividuation** Loss of personal sense of responsibility in a group. [p. 544]

**Deinstitutionalization** Policy of treating people with severe psychological disorders in the larger community, or in small residential centers such as halfway houses, rather than in large public hospitals. [p. 510]

**Delusions** False beliefs about reality that have no basis in fact. [p. 471]

**Dendrites** Short fibers that branch out from the cell body and pick up incoming messages. [p. 34]

**Denial** Refusal to acknowledge a painful or threatening reality. [p. 429]

**Deoxyribonucleic acid (DNA)** Complex molecule that is the main ingredient of chromosomes and genes and forms the code for all genetic information. [p. 65]

**Dependent personality disorder** Personality disorder in which the person is unable to make choices and decisions independently and cannot tolerate being alone. [p. 468]

**Dependent variable** In an experiment, the variable that is measured to see how it is changed by manipulations in the independent variable. [p. 10]

**Depersonalization disorder** A dissociative disorder in which the person suddenly feels changed or different in a strange way. [p. 466]

**Depressants** Chemicals that slow down behavior or cognitive processes. [p. 143]

**Depression** A mood disorder characterized by overwhelming feelings of sadness, lack of interest in activities, and oftentimes, excessive guilt or feelings of worthlessness. [p. 455]

**Desensitization therapy** Conditioning technique designed to gradually reduce anxiety about a particular object or situation. [p. 166]

**Developmental norms** Ages by which an average child achieves various developmental milestones. [p. 297]

**Developmental psychology** Study of the changes that occur in people from birth through old age. [p. 290]

**Diathesis** Biological predisposition. [p. 452]

**Diathesis-stress model of abnormal behavior** View that people biologically predisposed to a mental disorder (those with a certain diathesis) will tend to exhibit that disorder when subjected to stress. [p. 452]

**Difference threshold or just noticeable difference (jnd)** The smallest change in stimulation that can be detected 50 percent of the time. [p. 80]

**Dimensional approach to classification** Viewing abnormal behavior as different in degree from normal behavior. [p. 450]

**Discrimination** An unfair act or series of acts taken directed toward an entire group of people or individual members of that group. [p. 531]

**Disorganized schizophrenia** Schizophrenic disorder in which bizarre and childlike behaviors are common. [p. 472]

**Displacement** Shifting repressed motives and emotions from an original object to a substitute object. [p. 432]

**Dissociative amnesia** A dissociative disorder characterized by loss of memory for past events without an organic cause. [p. 465]

**Display rules** Culture-specific rules that govern how, when, and why facial expressions of emotion are displayed. [p. 579]

**Dissociative disorders** Disorders in which some aspect of the personality seems separated from the rest. [p. 465]

**Dissociative fugue** A dissociative disorder that involves flight and the assumption of a new identity, with amnesia for past identity and events. [p. 465]

**Dissociative identity disorder** A dissociative disorder in which a person has several distinct personalities that emerge at different times. [p. 465]

**Divergent thinking** Thinking that meets the criteria of originality, inventiveness, and flexibility. [p. 248]

**Dominant gene** Member of a gene pair that controls the appearance of a certain trait. [p. 65]

**Double-blind procedure** Experimental design, useful in studies of the effects of drugs, in which neither the subject nor the researcher knows at the time of administration which subjects are receiving an active drug and which are receiving an inactive substitute. [p. 143]

**Dreams** Vivid visual and auditory experiences that occur primarily during REM periods of sleep. [p. 131]

**Drive** State of tension or arousal brought on by biological needs. [p. 349]

**Drive-reduction theory** Theory that motivated behavior is aimed at reducing a state of bodily tension or arousal and returning the organism to homeostasis. [p. 349]

**Eclecticism** Psychotherapeutic approach that recognizes the value of a broad treatment package over a rigid commitment to one particular form of therapy. [p. 502]

**Ego** Freud's term for the part of the personality that mediates between environmental demands (reality), conscience (superego), and instinctual needs (id); now often used as a synonym for "self." [p. 387]

**Ego ideal** The part of the superego that consists of standards of what one would like to be. [p. 388]

**Egocentric** Unable to see things from another's point of view. [p. 300]

**Eidetic imagery** The ability to reproduce unusually sharp and detailed images of something one has seen. [p. 226]

**Elaborative rehearsal** The linking of new information in short-term memory to familiar material stored in long-term memory. [p. 211]

**Electroconvulsive therapy (ECT)** Biological therapy in which a mild electrical current is passed through the brain for a short period, often producing convulsions and temporary coma; used to treat severe, prolonged depression. [p. 506]

**Elevation** Monocular cue to distance and depth based on the fact that the higher on the horizontal plane an object is, the farther away it appears. [p. 110]

**Embryo** Developing human between 2 weeks and 3 months after conception. [p. 292]

**Emotion** Feeling, such as fear, joy, or surprise, that underlies behavior. [p. 348]

**Endocrine glands** Glands of the endocrine system that release hormones into the bloodstream. [p. 60]

**Endocrine system** Internal network of glands that release hormones directly into the bloodstream to regulate body functions. [p. 33]

**Epinephrine** Adrenal hormone that is released mainly in response to fear and that causes the heart to beat faster. [p. 63]

**Episodic memory** Portion of long-term memory that stores more specific information that has personal meaning. [p. 212]

**Equity** Fairness of exchange achieved when each partner in the relationship receives the same proportion of benefits to investments. [p. 529]

**Erectile disorder** The inability of a man to achieve or maintain an erection. [p. 467]

**Ethnic identity** That aspect of an individual's self-concept that is based on his or her awareness of being a member of a particular ethnic group. [p. 568]

**Ethnicity** A common cultural heritage, including religion, language, and/or ancestry, that is shared by a group of individuals. [p. 568]

**Evolutionary psychology** An approach to, and subfield of, psychology that is concerned with the origins of behaviors and mental process, their adaptive value, and the purposes they continue to serve. [p. 22]

**Exchange** Concept that relationships are based on trading rewards among partners. [p. 528]

**Existential psychology** School of psychology that focuses on the meaninglessness and alienation of modern life, and how these factors lead to apathy and psychological problems. [p. 20]

**Expectancies** In Bandura's view, what a person anticipates in a situation or as a result of behaving in certain ways. [p. 403]

**Experiential intelligence** Sternberg's designation of the ability to adapt creatively in new situations, to use insight. [p. 256]

**Experimental group** In a controlled experiment, the group subjected to a change in the independent variable. [p. 10]

**Experimenter bias** Expectations by the experimenter that might influence the results of an experiment or their interpretation. [p. 10]

**Explicit memory** Memory for information that was intentionally committed to memory or intentionally retrieved from memory. [p. 213]

**Extinction** Decrease in the strength or frequency of a learned response due to failure to continue pairing the US and CS (classical conditioning) or to withholding of reinforcement (operant conditioning). [p. 176]

**Extrovert** According to Jung, a person who usually focuses on social life and the external world instead of on his or her internal experience. [p. 391]

**Factor analysis** A statistical technique that identifies groups of related objects; used by Cattell to identify trait clusters. [p. 400]

**Family studies** Studies of heritability in humans based on the assumption that if genes influence a certain trait, close relatives should be more similar on that trait than distant relatives. [p. 67]

**Family therapy** A form of group therapy that sees the family as at least partly responsible for the individual's problems and that seeks to change all family members' behaviors to the benefit of the family unit as well as the troubled individual. [p. 498]

**Female sexual arousal disorder** The inability of a woman to become sexually aroused or to reach orgasm. [p. 467]

**Fetus** Developing human between 3 months after conception and birth [p. 292]

**Figure** Entity perceived to stand apart from the background. [p. 102]

**Fixation** According to Freud, a partial or complete halt at some point in the individual's psychosexual development. [p. 389]

**Fixed-interval schedule** Reinforcement schedule in which the correct response is reinforced after a fixed length of time since the last reinforcement. [p. 183]

**Fixed-ratio schedule** Reinforcement schedule in which the correct response is reinforced after a fixed number of correct responses. [p. 184]

**Flashbulb memory** A vivid memory of a certain event and the incidents surrounding it even after a long time has passed. [p. 223]

**Forebrain** Top part of the brain, including the thalamus, hypothalamus, and cerebral cortex. [p. 44]

**Formal-operational stage** In Piaget's theory, the stage of cognitive development between 11 and 15 years of age, in which the individual becomes capable of abstract thought. [p. 301]

**Fovea** Area of the retina that is the center of the visual field. [p. 83]

**Fraternal twins** Twins developed from two separate fertilized ova and therefore different in genetic makeup. [p. 68]

**Free association** A psychoanalytic technique that encourages the patient to talk about whatever thoughts or fantasies come to mind without inhibition. [p. 485]

**Frequency** The number of cycles per second in a wave; in sound, the primary determinant of pitch. [p. 92]

**Frontal lobe** Part of the cerebral cortex that is responsible for voluntary movement; it is also important for attention, goal-directed behavior, and appropriate emotional experiences. [p. 46]

**Frustration** The feeling that occurs when a person is prevented from reaching a goal. [p. 422]

**Frustration-aggression theory** Theory that under certain circumstances people who are frustrated in their goals turn their anger away from the proper, powerful target toward another, less powerful target it is safer to attack. [p. 532]

**Fully functioning person** According to Rogers, an individual whose self-concept closely resembles his or her inborn capacities or potentials. [p. 398]

**Functional fixedness** The tendency to perceive only a limited number of uses for an object; it interferes with the process of problem solving. [p. 246]

**Functionalist theory** Theory of mental life and behavior that is concerned with how an organism uses its perceptual abilities to function in its environment. [p. 18]

**Fundamental attribution error** Tendency of people to overemphasize personal causes for other people's behavior and to overemphasize situational causes for their own behavior. [p. 526]

**Ganglion cells** Neurons that connect the bipolar cells in the eyes to the brain. [p. 87]

**Gate control theory** Theory that a "neurological gate" in the spinal cord controls the transmission of pain messages to the brain. [p. 101]

**Gender constancy** The realization by a child that gender cannot be changed. [p. 311]

**Gender identity** A little girl's knowledge that she is a girl, and a little boy's knowledge that he is a boy. [p. 310]

**Gender roles** Behaviors that we expect each gender to engage in. [p. 558]

**Gender stereotypes** General beliefs about characteristics that men and women are presumed to have. [p. 558]

**General adaptation syndrome (GAS)** According to Selye, the three stages the body passes through as it adapts to stress: alarm reaction, resistance, and exhaustion. [p. 433]

**Generalized anxiety disorder** An anxiety disorder characterized by prolonged vague but intense fears that are not brought on by any particular object or situation. [p. 460]

**Genes** Elements that control the transmission of traits; they are found on the chromosomes. [p. 65]

**Genetics** Study of how traits are passed from one generation to the next. [p. 64]

**Genital stage** In Freud's theory of personality development, the final stage of normal adult sexual development, which is usually marked by mature sexuality. [p. 389]

**Gestalt psychology** School of psychology that studies how people perceive and experience objects as whole patterns. [p. 20]

**Giftedness** Refers to superior IQ combined with demonstrated or potential ability in such areas as academic aptitude, creativity, or leadership. [p. 276]

**Glial cells or glia** Cells that form the myelin sheath; they insulate and support neurons by holding them together, removing waste products, and preventing harmful substances from passing from the bloodstream into the brain. [p. 35]

**Glucose** Simple sugar that is the main source of body energy. [p. 351]

**Gonads** The reproductive glands—testes in males and ovaries in females. [p. 62]

**Graded potential** A shift in the electrical charge in a tiny area of a neuron. [p. 37]

**Grammar** The language rules that determine how sounds and words can be combined and used to communicate meaning within a language. [p. 237]

**Grasping reflex** Reflex that causes newborn babies to close their fists around anything that is put in their hands. [p. 293]

**Great person theory** Theory that leadership is a result of personal qualities and traits that qualify one to lead others. [p. 547]

**Ground** Background against which a figure appears. [p. 102]

**Group tests** Written intelligence tests administered by one examiner to many people at one time. [p. 261]

**Group therapy** Type of psychotherapy in which clients meet regularly to interact and help one another achieve insight into their feelings and behavior. [p. 497]

**Growth spurt** A rapid increase in height and weight that occurs during adolescence. [p. 315]

**Hallucinations** Sensory experiences in the absence of external stimulation. [p. 471]

**Hallucinogens** Any of a number of drugs, such as LSD and mescaline, that distort visual and auditory perception. [p. 154]

**Hammer, anvil, stirrup** The three small bones in the middle ear that relay vibrations of the eardrum to the inner ear. [p. 92]

**Hawthorne effect** Principle that subjects will alter their behavior because of researchers' attention and not necessarily because of any specific experimentation. [p. 548]

**Health psychology** A subfield of psychology concerned with the relationship between psychological factors and physical health and illness. [p. 419]

**Heredity** The transmission of traits from one generation to the next. [p. 64]

**Hertz (Hz)** Cycles per second; unit of measurement for the frequency of waves. [p. 92]

**Heuristics** Rules of thumb that help in simplifying and solving problems, although they do not guarantee a correct solution. [p. 243]

**Higher-order conditioning** Conditioning based on previous learning; the conditioned stimulus serves as an unconditioned stimulus for further training. [p. 182]

**Hill climbing** A heuristic problem-solving strategy in which each step moves you progressively closer to the final goal. [p. 244]

**Hindbrain** Brain area containing the medulla, pons, and cerebellum. [p. 43]

**Holophrases** One-word sentences, commonly used by children under 2 years of age. [p. 304]

**Homeostasis** State of balance and stability in which the organism functions effectively. [p. 349]

**Hormones** Chemical substances released by the endocrine glands; they help regulate bodily activities. [p. 60]

**Hue** The aspect of color that corresponds to names such as red, green, and blue. [p. 89]

**Humanistic personality theory** Any personality theory that asserts the fundamental goodness of people and their striving toward higher levels of functioning. [p. 398]

**Humanistic psychology** School of psychology that emphasizes nonverbal experience and altered states of consciousness as a means of realizing one's full human potential. [p. 22]

**Hypnosis** Trancelike state in which the subject responds readily to suggestions. [p. 138]

**Hypochondriasis** A somatoform disorder in which a person interprets insignificant symptoms as signs of serious illness in the absence of any organic evidence of such illness. [p. 464]

**Hypothalamus** Forebrain region that governs motivation and emotional responses. [p. 44]

**Hypotheses** Specific, testable predictions derived from a theory. [p. 4]

**Id** In Freud's theory of personality, the collection of unconscious urges and desires that continually seek expression. [p. 387]

**Identical twins** Twins developed from a single fertilized ovum and therefore identical in genetic makeup at the time of conception. [p. 67]

**Identification** Taking on the characteristics of someone else to avoid feeling incompetent. [p. 431]

**Identity crisis** Period of intense self-examination and decision making; part of the process of identity formation. [p. 320]

**Identity formation** Erikson's term for the development of a stable sense of self necessary to make the transition from dependence on others to dependence on oneself. [p. 320]

**Image** A mental representation of a sensory experience. [p. 239]

**Imaginary audience** Elkind's term for adolescents' delusion that they are constantly being observed by others. [p. 319]

**Implicit memory** Memory for information that either was unintentionally committed to memory or was unintentionally retrieved from memory. [p. 213]

**Imprinting** Form of primitive bonding seen in some species of animals; the newborn animal has a tendency to follow the first moving thing (usually its mother) it sees after it is born or hatched. [p. 307]

**Incentive** External stimulus that prompts goal-directed behavior. [p. 350]

**Independent variable** In an experiment, the variable that is manipulated to test its effects on the other, dependent variables. [p. 10]

**Industrial/organizational (I/O) psychology** Division of psychology concerned with the application of psychological principles to the problems of human organizations, especially work organizations. [p. 548]

**Inferiority complex** In Adler's theory, the fixation on feelings of personal inferiority that results in emotional and social paralysis. [p. 392]

**Information retrieval** A problem-solving strategy that requires only the recovery of information from long-term memory. [p. 243]

**Insane** Legal term for mentally disturbed people who are deemed not responsible for their criminal actions. [p. 471]

**Insight** Awareness of previously unconscious feelings and memories and how they influence present feelings and behavior. [p. 487]

**Insight** Learning that occurs rapidly as a result of understanding all the elements of a problem. [p. 188]

**Insight therapy** A variety of individual psychotherapies designed to give people a better awareness and understanding of their feelings, motivations, and actions in the hope that this will help them adjust. [p. 485]

**Insomnia** Sleep disorder characterized by difficulty in falling asleep or remaining asleep throughout the night. [p. 136]

**Instinct** Inborn, inflexible, goal-directed behavior that is characteristic of an entire species. [p. 349]

**Insulin and glucagon** Hormones that work in opposite ways to regulate the level of sugar in the blood. [p. 61]

**Intellectualization** Thinking abstractly about stressful problems as a way of detaching oneself from them. [p. 431]

**Intelligence** A general term referring to the ability or abilities that figure in learning and adaptive behavior. [p. 254]

**Intelligence quotient (IQ)** A numerical value given to intelligence that is determined from the scores on an intelligence test; based on a score of 100 for average intelligence. [p. 259]

**Intelligence tests** Tests designed to measure a person's general mental abilities. [p. 254]

**Interference theory** A theory that argues that interference from other information causes forgetting. [p. 209]

**Intermittent pairing** Pairing the conditioned stimulus and the unconditioned stimulus on only a portion of the learning trials. [p. 175]

**Interneurons or association neurons** Neurons that carry messages from one neuron to another and do most of the work of the nervous system. [p. 34]

**Intimacy** The quality of genuine closeness and trust achieved in communication with another person. [p. 529]

**Introvert** According to Jung, a person who usually focuses on his or her own thoughts and feelings. [p. 391]

**Ions** Electrically charged particles found both inside and outside of the neuron. [p. 36]

**Iris** Colored part of the eye. [p. 83]

**James-Lange theory** States that stimuli cause physiological changes in our bodies, and emotions result from those physiological changes. [p. 368]

**Just-world hypothesis** Attribution error based on the assumption that bad things happen to bad people and good things happen to good people. [p. 526]

**Kinesthetic senses** Senses of muscle movement, posture, and strain on muscles and joints. [p. 97]

**Language acquisition device** An internal mechanism for processing speech that is "wired into" all humans. [p. 305]

**Latency period** In Freud's theory of personality, a period in which the child appears to have no interest in the other sex; occurs after the phallic stage. [p. 389]

**Latent learning** Learning that is not immediately reflected in a behavior change. [p. 186]

**Law of effect** Thorndike's theory that behavior consistently rewarded will be "stamped in" as learned behavior, and behavior that brings about discomfort witll be stamped out. [p. 170]

**Learning** The process by which experience or practice results in a relatively permanent change in behavior or potential behavior. [p. 162]

**Learning set** Ability to become increasingly more effective in solving problems as more problems are solved. [p. 189]

**Lens** Transparent part of the eye inside the pupil that focuses light onto the retina. [p. 83]

**Libido** According to Freud, the energy generated by the sexual instinct. [p. 389]

**Light adaptation** Decreased sensitivity of rods and cones in bright light. [p. 86]

**Limbic system** Ring of structures around the brain stem; it plays a role in learning and emotional behavior. [p. 56]

**Linear perspective** Monocular cue to distance and depth based on the fact that two parallel lines seem to come together at the horizon. [p. 110]

**Linguistic relativity hypothesis** Whorf's contention that patterns of thinking are determined by the specific language one speaks. [p. 252]

**Locus of control** According to Rotter, an expectancy about whether reinforcement is under internal or external control. [p. 403]

**Longitudinal study** Method of studying developmental changes by examining the same group of subjects two or more times, as they grow older. [p. 290]

**Long-term memory (LTM)** Portion of memory that is more or less permanent, corresponding to everything we "know." [p. 211]

**Lysergic acid diethylamide (LSD)** Hallucinogenic or "psychedelic" drug that produces hallucinations and delusions similar to those occurring in a psychotic state. [p. 154]

**Mania** A mood disorder characterized by euphoric states, extreme physical activity, excessive talkativeness, distractedness, and sometimes grandiosity. [p. 456]

**Marijuana** A mild hallucinogen that produces a "high" often characterized by feelings of euphoria, a sense of well-being, and swings in mood from gaiety to relaxation; may also cause feelings of anxiety and paranoia. [p. 155]

**Marital therapy** Form of group therapy intended to help troubled couples improve their problems of communication and interaction. [p. 498]

**Maturation** Automatic biological unfolding of development in an organism as a function of the passage of time. [p. 297]

**Meditation** Any of various methods of concentration, reflection, or focusing of thoughts undertaken to suppress the activity of the sympathetic nervous system [p. 137]

**Medulla** Part of the hindbrain that controls such functions as breathing, heart rate, and blood pressure. [p. 43]

**Menarche** First menstrual period. [p. 316]

**Menopause** Time in a woman's life when menstruation ceases. [p. 334]

**Mental representation** Mental image or symbol (such as a word) used to think about or remember an object, a person, or an event. [p. 300]

**Mental retardation** Condition of significantly subaverage intelligence combined with deficiencies in adaptive behavior. [p. 274]

**Meta-analysis** A way of statistically combining the results of several independent research studies to form an overall conclusion. [p. 559]

**Midbrain** Region between the hindbrain and the forebrain; it is important for hearing and sight, and it is one of several places in the brain where pain is registered. [p. 44]

**Midlife crisis** A time when adults discover they no longer feel fulfilled in their jobs or personal lives and attempt to make a decisive shift in career or lifestyle. [p. 334]

**Midlife transition** According to Levinson, a process whereby adults assess the past and formulate new goals for the future. [p. 334]

**Minnesota Multiphasic Personality Inventory (MMPI)** The most widely used objective personality test, originally intended for psychiatric diagnosis. [p. 408]

**Mnemonics** Techniques that make material easier to remember. [p. 225]

**Mnemonist** Someone with highly developed memory skills. [p. 225]

**Modeling** A behavior therapy in which the person learns desired behaviors by watching others perform those behaviors. [p. 494]

**Monaural cue** Cue to sound location that requires just one ear. [p. 111]

**Monocular cues** Visual cues requiring the use of one eye. [p. 109]

**Mood disorders** Disturbances in mood or prolonged emotional state. [p. 455]

**Morphemes** The smallest meaningful units of speech, such as simple words, prefixes, and suffixes. [p. 236]

**Motive** Specific need, desire, or want, such as hunger, thirst, or achievement, that prompts goal-oriented behavior. [p. 348]

**Motor or efferent neurons** Neurons that carry messages from the spinal cord or brain to the muscles and glands. [p. 34]

**Motor projection areas** Areas of the cerebral cortex where response messages from the brain to the muscles and glands begin. [p. 46]

**Myelin sheath** White fatty covering found on some axons. [p. 34]

**Narcissistic personality disorder** Personality disorder in which the person has an exaggerated sense of self-importance and an insatiable desire for praise. [p. 468]

**Narcolepsy** Hereditary sleep disorder characterized by sudden nodding off during the day and sudden loss of muscle tone following moments of emotional excitement. [p. 137]

**Naturalistic observation** Research method involving the systematic study of animal or human behavior in natural settings rather than in the laboratory. [p. 6]

**Negative reinforcer** Any event whose reduction or termination increases the likelihood that ongoing behavior will recur. [p. 170]

**Neonate** Newborn baby. [p. 292]

**Nerve** Group of axons bundled together [p. 34]

**Nervous system** The brain, the spinal cord, and the network of nerve cells that transmit messages throughout the body. [p. 33]

**Neural impulse or action potential** The firing of a nerve cell. [p. 37]

**Neurons** Individual cells that are the smallest unit of the nervous system. [p. 34]

**Neurotic trends** Horney's term for irrational strategies for coping with emotional problems and minimizing anxiety. [p. 393]

**Neurotransmitters** Chemicals released by the synaptic vesicles that travel across the synaptic space and affect adjacent neurons. [p. 38]

**Noncompensatory model** A decision-making model in which weaknesses in one or more criteria are not offset by strengths in other criteria. [p. 249]

**Non-REM (NREM) sleep** Non–rapid-eye-movement stages of sleep that alternate with REM stages during the sleep cycle. [p. 130]

**Norm** A shared idea or expectation about how to behave. [p. 538]

**Obedience** Change of behavior in response to a command from another person, typically an authority figure. [p. 541]

**Objective tests** Personality tests that are administered and scored in a standard way. [p. 407]

**Object permanence** The concept that things continue to exist even when they are out of sight. [p. 299]

**Object-relations theories** Psychodynamic theories of personality that emphasize early relations with caregivers as the chief determinant of personality and the basis for subsequent interpersonal relations. [p. 395]

**Observational or vicarious learning** Learning by observing other people's behavior. [p. 189]

**Obsessive-compulsive disorder** An anxiety disorder in which a person feels driven to think disturbing thoughts and/or perform senseless rituals. [p. 460]

**Occipital lobe** Part of the cerebral hemisphere that receives and interprets visual information. [p. 45]

**Oedipus complex and Electra complex** According to Freud, a child's sexual attachment to the parent of the opposite sex and jealousy toward the parent of the same sex; generally occurs in the phallic stage. [p. 389]

**Olfactory bulb** The smell center in the brain. [p. 95]

**Olfactory epithelium** Nasal membranes containing receptor cells sensitive to odors. [p. 95]

**Operant behavior** Behavior designed to operate on the environment in a way that will gain something desired or avoid something unpleasant. [p. 169]

**Operant or instrumental conditioning** Type of learning in which behaviors are emitted (in the presence of specific stimuli) to earn rewards or avoid punishments. [p. 162]

**Opiates** Drugs, such as opium and heroin, derived from the opium poppy, that dull the senses and induce feelings of euphoria, well-being, and relaxation. Synthetic drugs resembling opium derivatives are also classified as opiates. [p. 150]

**Opponent-process theory** Theory of color vision that holds that three sets of color receptors (yellow-blue, red-green, black-white) respond to determine the color you experience. [p. 90]

**Optic chiasm** Point near the base of the brain where some fibers in the optic nerve from each eye cross to the other side of the brain. [p. 87]

**Optic nerve** The bundle of axons of ganglion cells that carries neural messages from each eye to the brain. [p. 87]

**Oral stage** First stage in Freud's theory of personality development, in which the infant's erotic feelings center on the mouth, lips, and tongue. [p. 389]

**Organ of Corti** Structure on the surface of the basilar membrane that contains the receptor cells for hearing. [p. 93]

**Orgasm** Peaking of sexual pleasure and release of sexual tension. [p. 467]

**Orgasmic disorders** Inability to reach orgasm in a person able to experience sexual desire and maintain arousal. [p. 467]

**Oval window** Membrane across the opening between the middle ear and inner ear that conducts vibrations to the cochlea. [p. 92]

**Overtones** Tones that result from sound waves that are multiples of the basic tone; primary determinant of timbre. [p. 92]

**Pancreas** Organ lying between the stomach and small intestine; it secretes insulin and glucagon. [p. 61]

**Panic disorder** An anxiety disorder characterized by recurrent panic attacks in which the person suddenly experiences intense fear or terror without any reasonable cause. [p. 460]

**Papillae** Small bumps on the tongue that contain taste buds. [p. 97]

**Parallel play** Two children playing side by side at the same activities, paying little or no attention to each other; the earliest kind of social interaction between toddlers. [p. 310]

**Paranoid personality disorder** Personality disorder in which the person is inappropriately suspicious and mistrustful of others. [p. 468]

**Paranoid schizophrenia** Schizophrenic disorder marked by extreme suspiciousness and complex, bizarre delusions. [p. 472]

**Parasympathetic division** Branch of the autonomic nervous system; it calms and relaxes the body. [p. 59]

**Parathormone** Hormone that controls the levels of calcium and phosphate in the blood and tissue fluids. [p. 60]

**Parathyroids** Four tiny glands embedded in the thyroid; they secrete parathormone. [p. 60]

**Parietal lobe** Part of the cerebral cortex that responds primarily to sensations of touch and bodily position. [p. 46]

**Peer group** A network of same-aged friends and acquaintances who give one another emotional and social support. [p. 320]

**Perception** Process of creating meaningful patterns from raw sensory information. [p. 78]

**Perceptual constancy** Tendency to perceive objects as stable and unchanging despite changes in sensory stimulation. [p. 104]

**Perceptual illusion** Illusion due to misleading cues in stimuli that cause us to create perceptions that are inaccurate or impossible. [p. 112]

**Performance standards** In Bandura's theory, standards that people develop to rate the adequacy of their own behavior in a variety of situations. [p. 404]

**Performance tests** Intelligence tests that minimize the use of language. [p. 262]

**Peripheral nervous system** Division of the nervous system that connects the central nervous system to the rest of the body. [p. 42]

**Persona** According to Jung, our public self, the mask we put on to represent ourselves to others. [p. 390]

**Personal fable** Elkind's term for adolescents' delusion that they are unique, very important, and invulnerable. [p. 319]

**Personal unconscious** In Jung's theory of personality, one of the two levels of the unconscious; it contains the individual's repressed thoughts, forgotten experiences, and undeveloped ideas. [p. 390]

**Personality** An individual's unique pattern of thoughts, feelings, and behaviors that persists over time and across situations. [p. 384]

**Personality disorders** Disorders in which inflexible and maladaptive ways of thinking and behaving, learned early in life, cause distress to the person and/or conflicts with others. [p. 468]

**Personality traits** Dimensions or characteristics on which people differ in distinctive ways. [p. 400]

**Phallic stage** Third stage in Freud's theory of personality development, in which erotic feelings center on the genitals. [p. 389]

**Pheromone** Chemical that communicates information to other organisms through smell. [p. 96]

**Pheromones** Substances secreted by some animals; when scented they enhance the sexual readiness of the other sex. [p. 354]

**Phonemes** The basic sounds that make up any language. [p. 236]

**Physical illusion** Illusion due to distortion of information reaching receptor cells. [p. 112]

**Pineal gland** A gland located roughly in the center of the brain that appears to regulate activity levels over the course of a day. [p. 61]

**Pitch** Auditory experience corresponding primarily to frequency of sound vibrations, resulting in a higher or lower tone. [p. 92]

**Pituitary gland** Gland located on the underside of the brain; it produces the largest number of the body's hormones. [p. 61]

**Placebo** Chemically inactive substance used for comparison with active drugs in experiments on the effects of drugs. [p. 143]

**Placenta** Organ by which an embryo or fetus is attached to its mother's uterus and that nourishes it during prenatal development. [p. 292]

**Pleasure principle** According to Freud, the way in which the id seeks immediate gratification of an instinct. [p. 387]

**Polarization** Shift in attitudes by members of a group toward more extreme positions than the ones held before group discussion. [p. 546]

**Polarization** The condition of a neuron when the inside is negatively charged relative to the outside; for example, when the neuron is at rest. [p. 36]

**Polygenic inheritance** Process in which several genes interact to produce a certain trait; responsible for our most important traits. [p. 65]

**Pons** Part of the hindbrain that connects the cerebral cortex at the top of the brain to the cerebellum. [p. 44]

**Positive reinforcer** Any event whose presence increases the likelihood that ongoing behavior will recur. [p. 170]

**Posterior pituitary** Part of the pituitary that affects thirst, sexual behavior, and perhaps paternal and maternal behavior. [p. 61]

**Posttraumatic stress disorder (PTSD)** Psychological disorder characterized by episodes of anxiety, sleeplessness, and nightmares resulting from some disturbing event in the past. [p. 438]

**Power motive** The need to win recognition or to influence or control other people or groups; a social motive. [p. 362]

**Prejudice** An unfair, intolerant, or unfavorable attitude toward a group of people. [p. 531]

**Premature ejaculation** Inability of a man to inhibit orgasm as long as desired. [p. 467]

**Prenatal development** Development from conception to birth. [p. 292]

**Preoperational stage** In Piaget's theory, the stage of cognitive development between 2 and 7 years of age, in which the individual becomes able to use mental representations and language to describe, remember, and reason about the world, though only in an egocentric fashion. [p. 300]

**Pressure** A feeling that one must speed up, intensify, or change the direction of one's behavior or live up to a higher standard of performance. [p. 422]

**Prevention** Reducing the incidence of emotional disturbance by eliminating conditions that cause or contribute to mental disorders and substituting conditions that foster mental well-being. [p. 511]

**Primacy effect** The phenomenon that early information about someone weighs more heavily than later information in influencing one's impression of that person. [p. 523]

**Primary drive** Physiologically based unlearned motive, such as hunger. [p. 350]

**Primary prevention** Techniques and programs to improve the social environment so that new cases of mental disorders do not develop. [p. 511]

**Primary reinforcer** Reinforcer that is rewarding in itself, such as food, water, and sex. [p. 182]

**Proactive interference** Process by which old material already in memory interferes with new information. [p. 215]

**Problem representation** The first step in solving a problem; it involves interpreting or defining the problem. [p. 241]

**Projection** Attributing one's own repressed motives, feelings, or wishes to others. [p. 431]

**Projective tests** Personality tests, such as the Rorschach inkblot test, consisting of ambiguous or unstructured material. [p. 409]

**Prototype** According to Rosch, a mental model containing the most typical features of a concept. [p. 240]

**Proximity** How close two people live to each other. [p. 527]

**Psychoactive drugs** Chemical substances that change moods and perceptions. [p. 141]

**Psychoanalysis** An insight therapy, developed by Freud, that is based on the belief that psychological problems are symptoms of inner conflicts repressed during childhood and that the psychoanalyst's task is to help the patient bring these hidden conflicts to conscious awareness so they can be effectively dealt with. [p. 485]

**Psychoanalytic model of abnormal behavior** View that abnormal behavior is the result of unconscious internal conflicts. [p. 451]

**Psychodynamic theories** Personality theories contending that behavior results from psychological dynamics that interact within the individual, often outside conscious awareness. [p. 386]

**Psychology** The scientific study of behavior and mental processes. [p. 4]

**Psychoneuroimmunology** A field of medicine that studies the interaction between stress on the one hand and immune, endocrine, and nervous system activity on the other. [p. 435]

**Psychosomatic disorders** Disorders in which real physical illness is largely caused by psychological factors such as stress and anxiety. [p. 462]

**Psychosurgery** Brain surgery performed to change a person's behavior and emotional state; a biological therapy rarely used today. [p. 509]

**Psychotherapy** The use of psychological techniques to treat personality and behavior disorders. [p. 484]

**Psychotic** Marked by defective or lost contact with reality. [p. 455]

**Puberty** Onset of sexual maturation, with accompanying physical development. [p. 315]

**Punisher** A stimulus that follows a behavior and decreases the likelihood that the behavior will be repeated. [p. 170]

**Punishment** Any event whose presence decreases the likelihood that ongoing behavior will recur. [p. 171]

**Pupil** Small opening in the iris through which light enters the eye. [p. 83]

**Race** A subpopulation of a species, defined according to an identifiable dimension (i.e., geographic location, skin color, hair texture, genes, facial features). [p. 567]

**Random sample** Sample in which each potential subject has an equal chance of being selected. [p. 13]

**Rational-emotive therapy (RET)** A directive cognitive therapy based on the idea that clients' psychological distress is caused by irrational and self-defeating beliefs and that the therapist's job is to challenge such dysfunctional beliefs. [p. 495]

**Reaction formation** Expression of exaggerated ideas and emotions that are the opposite of one's repressed beliefs or feelings. [p. 432]

**Reality principle** According to Freud, the way in which the ego seeks to satisfy instinctual demands safely and effectively in the real world. [p. 388]

**Receptor cell** Specialized cell that responds to a particular type of energy. [p. 83]

**Receptor site** A location on a receptor neuron into which a specific neurotransmitter fits like a key into a lock. [p. 38]

**Recessive gene** Member of a gene pair that can control the appearance of a certain trait only if it is paired with another recessive gene. [p. 65]

**Reciprocal determinism** In Bandura's personality model, the concept that the person influences the environment and is in turn influenced by the environment. [p. 404]

**Regression** Reverting to childlike behavior and defenses. [p. 431]

**Reinforcement** Anything that follows a response and makes that response more likely to recur. [p. 20]

**Reinforcer** A stimulus that follows a behavior and increases the likelihood that the behavior will be repeated. [p. 170]

**Relative refractory period** A period after firing when a neuron is returning to its normal polarized state and will fire again only if the incoming message is much stronger than usual. [p. 37]

**Reliability** Ability of a test to produce consistent and stable scores. [p. 263]

**REM (paradoxical) sleep** Sleep stage characterized by rapid eye movement; it is during this stage that most vivid dreaming occurs. [p. 130]

**Representative sample** Sample carefully chosen so that the characteristics of the subjects correspond closely to the characteristics of the larger population. [p. 13]

**Representativeness** A heuristic by which a new situation is judged on the basis of its resemblance to a stereotypical model. [p. 250]

**Repression** Excluding uncomfortable thoughts, feelings, and desires from consciousness. [p. 430]

**Response acquisition** "Building phase" of conditioning during which the likelihood or strength of the desired response increases. [p. 174]

**Response generalization** Giving a response that is somewhat different from the response originally learned to that stimulus. [p. 181]

**Resting potential** Electrical charge across a neuron membrane when sodium ions concentrate on the outside and potassium ions concentrate on the inside. [p. 36]

**Reticular formation (RF)** Network of neurons in the hindbrain, midbrain, and part of the forebrain whose primary function is to alert and arouse the higher parts of the brain. [p. 55]

**Retina** Lining of the eye containing receptor cells that are sensitive to light. [p. 83]

**Retinal disparity** Binocular distance cue based on the difference between the images cast on the two retinas when both eyes are focused on the same object. [p. 110]

**Retroactive interference** Process by which new information interferes with old information already in memory. [p. 215]

**Retrograde amnesia** The inability to recall events immediately preceding an accident or injury, but without loss of earlier memory. [p. 211]

**Risky shift** The greater willingness of people in groups to take risks in decision making as opposed to independent individuals deliberating alone. [p. 546]

**Rods** Receptor cells in the retina responsible for night vision and perception of brightness. [p. 83]

**Rooting reflex** Reflex that causes a newborn baby to turn its head toward something touching its cheek and to grope around with its mouth. [p. 293]

**Rorschach test** A projective test composed of ambiguous inkblots; the way people interpret6146 the blots is thought to reveal aspects of ther personality. [p. 409]

**Rote rehearsal** Retaining information in STM simply by repeating it over and over. [p. 210]

**Round window** Membrane between the middle ear and inner ear that equalizes pressure in the inner ear. [p. 92]

**Sample** Selection of cases from a larger population. [p. 12]

**Saturation** The vividness or richness of a hue. [p. 89]

**Schedule of reinforcement** In operant conditioning, the rule for determining when and how often reinforcers will be delivered. [p. 183]

**Schema (plural: schemata)** Set of beliefs or expectations about something that is based on past experience. [p. 217]

**Schizoid personality disorder** Personality disorder in which a person is withdrawn and lacks feelings for others. [p. 468]

**Schizophrenic disorders** Severe disorder in which there are disturbances of thoughts, communications, and emotions, including delusions and hallucinations. [p. 471]

**Scientific method** An approach to knowledge that relies on collecting data, generating a theory to explain the data, producing testable hypotheses based on the theory, and testing those hypotheses empirically. [p. 4]

**Secondary prevention** Programs to identify groups that are at high risk for mental disorders and to detect maladaptive behavior in these groups and treat it promptly. [p. 512]

**Secondary reinforcer** Reinforcer whose value is learned through association with other primary or secondary reinforcers. [p. 182]

**Selection studies** Studies that estimate the heritability of a trait by breeding animals with other animals that have the same trait. [p. 67]

**Self-actualizing tendency** According to Rogers, the drive of human beings to fulfill their self-concepts, or the images they have of themselves. [p. 398]

**Self-efficacy** According to Bandura, the expectancy that one's efforts will be successful. [p. 404]

**Self-fulfilling prophecy** Process by which a person's expectation about another elicits behavior from the second person that confirms the expectation. [p. 524]

**Self-monitoring** The tendency to observe a situation for cues about how to react. [p. 530]

**Semantic memory** Portion of long-term memory that stores general facts and information. [p. 211]

**Semantics** The criteria for assigning meaning to the morphemes in a language. [p. 237]

**Sensation** Experience of sensory stimulation. [p. 78]

**Sensory or afferent neurons** Neurons that carry messages from sense organs to the spinal cord or brain. [p. 34]

**Sensory projection areas** Areas of the parietal lobe where messages from the sense receptors are registered. [p. 46]

**Sensory registers** Entry points for raw information from the senses. [p. 203]

**Sensory-motor stage** In Piaget's theory, the stage of cognitive development between birth and 2 years of age, in which the individual develops object permanence and acquires the ability to form mental representations. [p. 299]

**Set** The tendency to perceive and to approach problems in certain ways. [p. 245]

**Set point** A homeostatic mechanism in the body that regulates metabolism, fat storage, and food intake so as to maintain a preprogrammed weight. [p. 352]

**Sex-role awareness** Knowledge of what behavior is appropriate for each gender. [p. 311]

**Sex-typed behavior** Socially prescribed ways of behaving that differ for boys and girls. [p. 311]

**Sexual arousal disorder** Inability to achieve or sustain arousal until the end of intercourse in a person who is capable of experiencing sexual desire. [p. 467]

**Sexual desire disorders** Disorders in which the person lacks sexual interest or has an active distaste for sex. [p. 467]

**Sexual dysfunction** Loss or impairment of the ordinary physical responses of sexual function. [p. 467]

**Shape constancy** Tendency to see an object as the same shape no matter what angle it is viewed from. [p. 106]

**Shaping** Reinforcing successive approximations to a desired behavior. [p. 176]

**Short-term memory (STM)** Working memory; briefly stores and processes selected information from the sensory registers. [p. 206]

**Short-term psychodynamic psychotherapy** Insight therapy that is time-limited and focused on trying to help clients correct the immediate problems in their lives. [p. 490]

**Sixteen Personality Factor Questionnaire** Objective personality test created by Cattell that provides scores on the 16 traits he identified. [p. 408]

**Size constancy** Perception of an object as the same size regardless of the distance from which it is viewed. [p. 105]

**Skinner box** Box often used in operant conditioning of animals that limits the available responses and thus increases the likelihood that the desired response will occur. [p. 175]

**Social cognition** Knowledge and understanding concerning the social world and the people in it (including oneself). [p. 576}

**Social influence** Process by which others individually or collectively affect one's perceptions, attitudes, and actions. [p. 537]

**Social learning theory** View of learning that emphasizes the ability to learn by observing a model or receiving instructions, without firsthand experience by the learner. [p. 189]

**Social motive** Learned motive associated with relationships among people, such as the needs for affiliation, achievement, and power. [p. 358]

**Social phobia** An anxiety disorder characterized by excessive, inappropriate fears connected with social situations or performances in front of other people. [p. 459]

**Social psychology** Scientific study of the ways in which the thoughts, feelings, and behaviors of one individual are influenced by the real, imagined, or inferred behavior or characteristics of other people. [p. 522]

**Socialization** Process by which children learn the behaviors and attitudes appropriate to their family and their culture. [p. 309]

**Solitary play** A child engaged in some activity alone; the earliest form of play. [p. 310]

**Somatic nervous system** The part of the peripheral nervous system that carries messages from the senses to the central nervous system and between the central nervous system and the skeletal muscles. [p. 58]

**Somatization disorder** A somatoform disorder characterized by recurrent, vague somatic complaints without a physical cause. [p. 463]

**Somatoform disorders** Disorders in which there is an apparent physical illness for which there is no organic basis. [p. 463]

**Sound waves** Changes in pressure caused when molecules of air or fluid collide with one another and then move apart again. [p. 91]

**Specific phobia** Anxiety disorder characterized by intense, paralyzing fear of something. [p. 459]

**Spinal cord** Complex cable of neurons that runs down the spine, connecting the brain to most of the rest of the body. [p. 56]

**Split-half reliability** A method of determining test reliability by dividing the test into two parts and checking how well the scores match on both parts. [p. 263]

**Spontaneous recovery** The reappearance of an extinguished response after the passage of time, without further training. [p. 178]

**Stanford-Binet Intelligence Scale** Terman's adaptation of the Binet-Simon Scale. [p. 259]

**Stepping reflex** Reflex that causes newborn babies to make little stepping motions if they are held upright with their feet just touching a surface. [p. 293]

**Stereoscopic vision** Combination of two retinal images to give a three-dimensional perceptual experience. [p. 110]

**Stereotype** Set of characteristics presumed to be shared by all members of a social category. [p. 524]

**Stimulants** Drugs, including amphetamines and cocaine, that stimulate the sympathetic nervous system and produce feelings of optimism and boundless energy. [p. 150]

**Stimulus discrimination** Learning to respond to only one stimulus and to inhibit the response to all other stimuli. [p. 180]

**Stimulus generalization** Transfer of a learned response to different but similar stimuli. [p. 180]

**Stimulus motive** Unlearned motive, such as curiosity or activity, that prompts us to explore or change the world around us. [p. 356]

**Strain studies** Studies of the heritability of behavioral traits using animals that have been inbred to produce strains that are genetically very similar to one another. [p. 66]

**Stress** Any environmental demand that creates a state of tension or threat and requires change or adaptation. [p. 418]

**Stress-inoculation therapy** A type of cognitive therapy that trains clients to cope with stressful situations by learning a more useful pattern of self-talk. [p. 495]

**Structuralism** School of psychology that stresses the basic units of experience and the combinations in which they occur. [p. 18]

**Subgoals** Intermediate, more manageable goals used as one heuristic strategy to make it easier to reach the final goal. [p. 244]

**Subjects** Individuals whose reactions or responses are observed in an experiment. [p. 10]

**Sublimation** Redirecting repressed motives and feelings into more socially acceptable channels. [p. 432]

**Substance abuse** A pattern of drug use that diminishes the ability to fulfill responsibilities at home or at work or school, that results in repeated use of a drug in dangerous situations, or that leads to legal difficulties related to drug use. [p. 142]

**Substance dependence** A pattern of compulsive drug taking that results in tolerance, withdrawal symptoms or other specific symptoms for at least a year. [p. 142]

**Subtractive color mixing** The process of mixing pigments, each of which absorbs some wavelengths of light and reflects others. [p. 90]

**Sucking reflex** Reflex that causes the newborn baby to suck on objects placed in its mouth. [p. 293]

**Superego** According to Freud, the social and parental standards the individual has internalized; the conscience and the ego ideal. [p. 388]

**Superposition** Monocular distance cue in which one object, by partly blocking a second object, is perceived as being closer. [p. 109]

**Surface structure** The particular words and phrases used to make up a sentence. [p. 237]

**Surveys** Questionnaires or interviews administered to a selected group of people. [p. 8]

**Swallowing reflex** Reflex that enables the newborn baby to swallow liquids without choking. [p. 293]

**Sympathetic division** Branch of the autonomic nervous system; it prepares the body for quick action in an emergency. [p. 59]

**Synapse** Area composed of the axon terminal of one neuron, the synaptic space, and the dendrite or cell body of the next neuron. [p. 38]

**Synaptic space or synaptic cleft** Tiny gap between the axon terminal of one neuron and the dendrites or cell body of the next neuron. [p. 38]

**Synaptic vesicles** Tiny sacs in a synaptic knob that release chemicals into the synapse. [p. 38]

**Syntax** The rules for arranging words into grammatically correct sentences. [p. 238]

**Systematic desensitization** A behavioral technique for reducing a person's fear and anxiety by gradually associating a new response (relaxation) with stimuli that have been causing the fear and anxiety. [p. 491]

**Systems approach to abnormal behavior** View that biological, psychological, and social risk factors combine to produce mental disorders. Also known as the biopsychosocial model of abnormal behavior. [p. 452]

**Tactic of elimination** A problem-solving strategy in which possible solutions are evaluated according to appropriate criteria and discarded as they fail to contribute to a solution. [p. 247]

**Taste buds** Structures on the tongue that contain the receptor cells for taste. [p. 97]

**Temperament** Term used by psychologists to describe the physical/emotional characteristics of the newborn child and young infant; also referred to as personality. [p. 293]

**Temporal lobe** Part of the cerebral hemisphere that helps regulate hearing, smell, balance and equilibrium, and certain emotions and motivations. [p. 45]

**Tertiary prevention** Programs to help people adjust to community life after release from a mental hospital. [p. 512]

**Testosterone** Hormone that is the primary determinant of the sex drive in both men and women. [p. 354]

**Texture gradient** Monocular cue to distance and depth based on the fact that objects seen at greater distances appear to be smoother and less textured. [p. 110]

**Thalamus** Forebrain region that relays and translates incoming messages from the sense receptors, except those for smell. [p. 44]

**Thematic Apperception Test (TAT)** A projective test composed of ambiguous pictures about which a person writes stories. [p. 409]

**Theory of multiple intelligences** Howard Gardner's theory that there is not one intelligence, but rather many intelligences, each of which is relatively independent of the others. [p. 257]

**Theory** Systematic explanation of a phenomenon; it organizes known facts, allows us to predict new facts, and permits us to exercise a degree of control over the phenomenon. [p. 4]

**Threshold of excitation** The level an impulse must exceed to cause a neuron to fire. [p. 37]

**Thrill seekers** apparently need a different level of stimulation than other people. Thrill-seeking behaviors defy the theory of drive reduction. [p. 350]

**Thyroid gland** Endocrine gland located below the voice box; it produces the hormone thyroxin. [p. 60]

**Thyroxin** Hormone that regulates the body's rate of metabolism. [p. 60]

**Timbre** Quality or texture of sound; caused by overtones. [p. 92]

**Token economy** An operant conditioning therapy in which patients earn tokens (reinforcers) for desired behaviors and exchange them for desired items or privileges. [p. 494]

**Tolerance** Phenomenon whereby higher doses of a drug are required to produce its original effects or to prevent withdrawal symptoms. [p. 142]

**Traits** Characteristics on which organisms differ. [p. 64]

**Transference** The patient's carrying over to the analyst feelings held toward childhood authority figures. [p. 486]

**Trial and error** A problem-solving strategy based on the successive elimination of incorrect solutions until the correct one is found. [p. 243]

**Triarchic theory of intelligence** Sternberg's theory that intelligence involves mental skills (componential aspect), insight and creative adaptability (experiential aspect), and environmental responsiveness (contextual aspect). [p. 256]

**Trichromatic theory** Theory of color vision that holds that all color perception derives from three different color receptors in the retina (usually red, green, and blue receptors). [p. 90]

**Twin studies** Studies of identical and fraternal twins to determine the relative influence of heredity and environment on human behavior. [p. 67]

**Unconditional positive regard** In Rogers's theory, the full acceptance and love of another person regardless of that person's behavior. [p. 399]

**Unconditioned response (UR)** Response that takes place in an organism whenever an unconditioned stimulus occurs. [p. 164]

**Unconditioned stimulus (US)** Stimulus that invariably causes an organism to respond in a specific way. [p. 164]

**Unconscious** In Freud's theory, all the ideas, thoughts, and feelings of which we are not and normally cannot become aware. [p. 387]

**Undifferentiated schizophrenia** Schizophrenic disorder in which there are clear schizophrenic symptoms that don't meet the criteria for any other subtype of the disorder. [p. 472]

**Vaginismus** Involuntary muscle spasms in the outer part of the vagina that make intercourse impossible. [p. 467]

**Validity** Ability of a test to measure what it has been designed to measure. [p. 264]

**Variable-interval schedule** Reinforcement schedule in which the correct response is reinforced after varying lengths of time following the last reinforcement. [p. 184]

**Variable-ratio schedule** Reinforcement schedule in which a varying number of correct responses must occur before reinforcement is presented. [p. 184]

**Vestibular senses** Senses of equilibrium and body position in space. [p. 97]

**Vicarious reinforcement and vicarious punishment** Reinforcement or punishment experienced by models that affects the willingness of others to perform the behaviors they learned by observing the models. [p. 190]

**Visual acuity** The ability to distinguish fine details visually. [p. 85]

**Visualizing** A problem-solving strategy in which principles or concepts are drawn, diagrammed, or charted so that they can be better understood. [p. 247]

**Vomeronasal organ (VNO)** Location of receptors for pheromones in the roof of the nasal cavity. [p. 96]

**Waking consciousness** Mental state that includes the thoughts, feelings, and perceptions that occur when we are awake and reasonably alert. [p. 124]

**Weber's law** The principle that the jnd for any given sense is a constant fraction or proportion of the stimulation being judged. [p. 81]

**Wechsler Adult Intelligence Scale–Revised (WAIS–R)** Individual intelligence test developed especially for adults; measures both verbal and performance abilities. [p. 260]

**Wechsler Intelligence Scale for Children–Third Edition (WISC–III)** Individual intelligence test developed especially for school-aged children; measures verbal and performance abilities and also yields an overall IQ score. [p. 261]

**Withdrawal** Avoiding a situation when other forms of coping are not practical. [p. 428]

**Withdrawal symptoms** Unpleasant physical or psychological effects that follow the discontinuance of a dependence-producing substance. [p. 142]

**Working backward** A heuristic strategy in which the problem solver works backward from the desired goal to the given conditions. [p. 245]

**Yerkes-Dodson law** States that there is an optimal level of arousal for the best performance of any task; the more complex the task, the lower the level of arousal that can be tolerated before performance deteriorates. [p. 366]

# REFERENCES


Aaker, D.A., & Bruzzone, D.E. (1985). Causes of irritation in advertising. *Journal of Marketing, 49*, 47–57.

Aaronson, D., & Scarborough, H.S. (1976). Performance theories for sentence coding: Some quantitative evidence. *Journal of Experimental Psychology: Human Perception and Performance, 2*, 56–70.

Aaronson, D., & Scarborough, H.S. (1977). Performance theories for sentence coding: Some quantitative models. *Journal of Verbal Learning and Verbal Behavior, 16*, 277–304.

Abramov, I., & Gordon, J. (1994). Color appearance: On seeing red or yellow, or green, or blue. *Annual Review of Psychology, 45*, 451–485.

Abramson, L.Y., & Alloy, L.B. (1981). Depression, non-depression, and cognitive illusions: A reply to Schwartz. *Journal of Experimental Psychology, 110*, 436–447.

Acredolo, L.P., & Hake, J.L. (1982). Infant perception. In B.B. Wolman (Ed.), *Handbook of developmental psychology* (pp. 244–283). Englewood Cliffs, NJ: Prentice-Hall.

Adams, D.B., Gold, A.R., & Burt, A.D. (1978). Rise in female-initiated sexual activity at ovulation and its suppression by oral contraceptives. *New England Journal of Medicine, 299*, 1145–1150.

Adams, G.R., & Gullota, T. (1983). *Adolescent life experiences.* Monterey, CA: Brooks/Cole.

Adams, J.L. (1980). *Conceptual blockbusting: A guide to better ideas* (2nd ed.). New York: Norton.

Adams, J.S. (1965). Inequity in social exchanges. In L. Berkowitz (Ed.), *Advances in experimental social psychology.* New York: Academic Press.

Adelmann, P.K., & Zajonc, R.B. (1989). Facial efference and the experience of emotion. *Annual Review of Psychology, 40*, 249–280.

Ader, R., & Cohen, N. (1993). Psychoneuroimmunology: Conditioning and stress. *Annual Review of Psychology, 44*, 53–85.

Adler, N., Boyce, T., Chesney, M.A., Cohen, S., Folkman, S., Kahn, R.I., & Syme, S.L. (1994). Socioeconomic status and health. The challenge of the gradient. *American Psychologist, 49*, 15–24.

Adler, N., & Matthews, K. (1994). Health psychology: Why do some people get sick and some stay healthy? *Annual Review of Psychology, 45*, 229–259.

Adler, T. (1990, January). PMS diagnosis draws fire from researchers. *APA Monitor*, p. 12.

Adler, T. (1993a, May). Raising the cigarette tax can lower smoking rates. *APA Monitor*, p. 15.

Adler, T. (1993b, July). Men and women affected by stress, but differently. *APA Monitor*, pp. 8–9.

Adorno, T.W., Frenkel-Brunswick, E., Levinson, D.J., & Sanford, R.N. (1950). *The authoritarian personality.* New York: Harper & Row.

Agras, W.S. (1987). *Eating disorders: Management of obesity, bulimia and anorexia nervosa.* Elmsford, NY: Pergamon.

Agras, W.S., & Kraemer, H. (1983). The treatment of anorexia nervosa. Do different treatments have different outcomes? *Psychiatric Annuals, 13*, 928–935.

Aiken, L.R. (1988). *Psychological testing and assessment* (6th ed.). Boston: Allyn & Bacon.

Ainslie, G. (1975). Specious reward: A behavioral theory of impulsiveness and impulse control. *Psychological Bulletin, 82*, 463–496.

Ainsworth, M.D., Blehar, M.C., Waters, E., & Wall, S. (1978). *Patterns of attachment.* New York: Halstead Press.

Ainsworth, M.D.S. (1977). Attachment theory and its utility in cross-cultural research. In P.H. Leiderman, S.R. Tulkin, & A. Rosenfields (Eds.), *Culture and infancy: Variation in the human experience.* New York: Academic Press.

Ainsworth, M.D.S., & Wittig, B.A. (1969). Attachment and exploratory behavior of one-year olds in a strange situation. In B.M. Foss (Ed.), *Determinants of infant behavior* (Vol. 4., pp. 111–136). London: Methuen.

Ajzen, I. (1985). From intentions to actions: A theory of planned behavior. In J. Kuhl & J. Beckman (Eds.), *Action-control: From cognition to behavior* (pp. 11–39). Heidelberg: Springer-Verlag.

Ajzen, I., & Fishbein, M. (1980). *Understanding attitudes and predicting behavior.* Englewood Cliffs, NJ: Prentice-Hall.

Akil, H., & Watson, S.J. (1980). The role of endogenous opiates in pain control. In H.W. Kosterlitz & L.Y. Terenius (Eds.), *Pain and society.* Weinheim: Verlag Chemie.

Alan Guttmacher Institute. (1990). *Adolescent sexuality.* New York: Alan Guttmacher Institute.

Albee, G.W. (1982). Preventing psychopathology and promoting human potential. *American Psychologist, 37*, 1043–1050.

Albus, M. (1989). Cholecystokinin. *Progress in Neuro-Psychopharmacology and Biological Psychiatry, 12*(Suppl.), 5–21.

Allen, V.L., & Levine, J.M. (1971). Social support and conformity: The role of independent assessment of reality. *Journal of Experimental Social Psychology, 7*, 48–58.

Allport, G.W. (1954). *The nature of prejudice.* New York: Anchor.

Allport, G.W. (1965). *Letters from Jenny.* New York: Harcourt, Brace & World.

Allport, G.W., & Odbert, H.S. (1936). Trait-names: A psycholexical study. *Psychological Monographs, 47*(1, Whole No. 211).

Altman, I., & Taylor, D.A. (1973). *Social penetration: The development of interpersonal relationships.* New York: Holt, Rinehart & Winston.

Amabile, T.M. (1983). The social psychology of creativity: A comparative conceptualization. *Journal of Personality and Social Psychology, 45*, 357–376.

Amabile, T.M., Hennessey, B.A., & Grossman, B.S. (1986). Social influences on creativity: The effects of contracted-for reward. *Journal of Personality and Social Psychology, 50*, 14–23.

American Psychological Association (APA). (1994). *Diagnostic and statistical manual of mental disorders* (4th ed.). Washington, DC: American Psychiatric Press.

American Psychological Association (APA). (1953). *Ethical standards of psychologists.* Washington, DC: American Psychological Association.

American Psychological Association (APA). (1975). Report of the task force on sex bias and sex-role stereotyping in psychotherapeutic practice. *American Psychologist, 30,* 1169–1175.

American Psychological Association (APA). (1978). Guidelines for therapy with women. *American Psychologist, 33,* 1122–1123.

American Psychological Association (APA). (1982). *Ethical principles in the conduct of research with human participants.* Washington, DC: American Psychological Association.

American Psychological Association (APA). (1985). *Ethical principles in the conduct of research with human participants.* Washington, DC: American Psychological Association.

American Psychological Association (APA). (1990). *Task force on women's depression* (Final Report). Washington, DC: American Psychological Association.

American Psychological Association (APA). (1992). *Big world, small screen.* Washington, DC: American Psychological Association.

American Psychological Association (APA). (1993). *Violence and youth.* Washington, DC: American Psychological Association.

Anastasi, A. (1982). *Psychological testing* (5th ed.). New York: Macmillan.

Anastasi, A. (1989). *Psychological testing* (6th ed.). New York: Macmillan.

Anch, A.M., Browman, C.P., Mitler, M.M., & Walsh, J.K. (1988). *Sleep: A scientific perspective.* Englewood Cliffs, NJ: Prentice-Hall.

Anderson, A.E., (Ed.). (1990). *Males with eating disorders.* New York: Brunner/Mazel.

Anderson, B.L. (1983). Primary orgasmic dysfunction: Diagnostic considerations and review of treatment. *Psychological Bulletin, 93,* 105–136.

Anderson, R.C., & Pichert, J.W. (1978). Recall of previously unrecallable information following a shift in perspective. *Journal of Verbal Learning and Verbal Behavior, 17,* 1–12.

Andreasen, N.C., Rice, J., Endicott, J., Coyell, W., Grove, W.M., & Reich, T. (1987). Familial rates of affective disorder. *Archives of General Psychiatry, 44,* 451–469.

Andrews, J.A., & Lewinsohn, P.M. (1992). Suicidal attempts among older adolescents: Prevalence and co-occurrence with psychiatric disorders. *Journal of the American Academy of Child and Adolescent Psychiatry, 31,* 655–662.

Angier, N. (1990, May 15). Cheating on sleep: Modern life turns America into the land of the drowsy. *New York Times,* Sec. B.

Angier, N. (1992, May 20). Is there a male menopause? Jury is still out. *New York Times,* p. A1.

Anthony, J.C., & Aboraya, A. (1992). The epidemiology of selected mental disorders in later life. In J.E. Birren, R.B. Sloane, & G.D. Choen (Eds.), *Handbook of mental health and aging* (2nd ed., pp. 3–143). San Diego, CA: Academic Press.

Antonarakis, S.E. (1991). Parental origin of the extra chromosome in trisomy 21 as indicated by analysis of DNA polymorphisms. *New England Journal of Medicine, 324,* 872–876.

Aranya, N., Kushnir, T., & Valency, A. (1986). Organizational commitment in a male dominated profession. *Human Relations, 39,* 433–438.

Archer, D., Iritani, B., Kimes, D.D., & Barrios, M. (1983). Face-ism: Five studies of sex differences in facial prominence. *Journal of Personality and Social Psychology, 45,* 725–735.

Archer, R.F. (1992). Review of the Minnesota Multiphasic Personality Inventory–2. In J.J. Kramer & J. C. Conoley (Eds.) *The eleventh mental measurements yearbook.* Lincoln: University of Nebraska Press.

Arkema, P.H. (1981). The borderline personality and transitional relatedness. *American Journal of Psychiatry, 138,* 172–177.

Arkin, R.M., Cooper, H., & Kolditz, T. (1980). A statistical review of literature concerning the self-serving attribution bias in interpersonal influence situations. *Journal of Personality, 48,* 435–448.

Arnett, J. (1991, April). *Sensation seeking and egocentrism as factors in reckless behaviors among a college-age sample.* Paper presented at the meeting of the Society for Research in Child Development, Seattle, WA.

Arnold, M.B. (1960). *Emotion and personality* (2 vols.). New York: Columbia University Press.

Aronson, E. (1992). *The social animal* (6th ed.). New York: Freeman.

Aronson, E., Bridgeman, D.L., & Geffner, R. (1978). Interdependent interactions and prosocial behavior. *Journal of Research and Development in Education, 12,* 16–27.

Aronson, E., Cookie, S., Sikes, J., Blaney, N., & Snapp, M. (1978). *The jigsaw classroom.* Beverly Hills, CA: Sage.

Asch, S.E. (1946). Forming impressions of personality. *Journal of Abnormal and Social Psychology, 41,* 258–290.

Asch, S.E. (1951). Effects of group pressure upon the modification and distortion of judgments. In H. Guetzkow (Ed.), *Groups, leadership, and men.* Pittsburgh: Carnegie Press.

Asch, S.E. (1956). Studies of independence and conformity: I. A minority of one against a unanimous majority. *Psychological Monographs, 70*(9, Whole No. 416).

Ash, R.A., Levine, E.L., & Sistrunk, F. (1983). The role of jobs and job-based methods in personnel and human resources management. *Research in Personnel and Human Resources Management, 1,* 45–84.

Asher, J. (1975, April). Sex bias found in therapy. *APA Monitor,* pp. 1, 5.

Aslin, R.N., & Smith, L.B. (1988). Perceptual development. *Annual Review of Psychology, 39,* 435–473.

Aston, R. (1972). Barbiturates, alcohol and tranquilizers. In S.J. Mule & H. Brill (Eds.), *The chemical and biological aspects of drug dependence.* Cleveland, OH: CRC Press.

Atchley, R.C. (1976). *The sociology of retirement.* Cambridge, MA: Schenkman.

Atkinson, J.W., & Birch, D. (1970). *The dynamics of action.* New York: Wiley.

Atkinson, J.W., & Raynor, J.O. (1975). *Motivation and achievement.* Washington, DC: Winston.

Attili, G., Vermigli, P., & Travaglia, G. (1991). Cultural variability and temperament: The difficult child. *Eta Evolutiva, 40,* 128–131.

Aveizer, O., IJ'zendoom, V., Sagi, A., & Schuengel, C. (1994). "Children of the dream" revisited: 70 years of collective early child care in Israeli kibbutzim. *Psychological Bulletin, 116,* 99–116.

Azzi, R., Fix, D.S.R., Keller, R.S., & Rocha e Silva, M.I. (1964). Exteroceptive control of response under delayed reinforcement. *Journal of the Experimental Analysis of Behavior, 7*, 159–162.

Babkoff, H., Caspy, T., Mikulincer, M., & Sing, H.C. (1991). Monotonic and rhythmic influences: A challenge for sleep deprivation research. *Psychological Bulletin, 109*, 411–428.

Bachtold, L.M., & Werner, E.E. (1973). Personality characteristics of creative women. *Perception and Motor Skills, 36*, 311–319.

Bacon, M.K., Child, I.L., & Barry, H., III. (1963). A cross-cultural study of correlates of crime. *Journal of Abnormal and Social Psychology*, 66, 291–300.

Baddeley, A.D. (1986). *Working memory*. Oxford: Clarendon Press.

Baddeley, A.D. (1987). Amnesia. In R.L. Gregory (Ed.), *The Oxford companion to the mind* (pp. 20–22). Oxford: Oxford University Press.

Baddeley, A.D., & Hitch, G. (1974). Working memory. In G.H. Bower (Ed.), *The psychology of learning and motivation* (Vol. 8). New York: Academic Press.

Bahrick, H.P. (1984). Semantic memory in permastore: Fifty years of memory for Spanish learned in school. *Journal of Experimental Psychology: General, 113*, 1–31.

Bahrick, H.P., & Hall, L.K. (1991). Lifetime maintenance of high school mathematics content. *Journal of Experimental Psychology: General, 120*, 20–33.

Bahrick, H.P., Bahrick, P.O., & Wittlinger, R.P. (1974, December). Those unforgettable high school days. *Psychology Today*, pp. 50–56.

Bailey, A., LeCouteur, A., Gottesman, I., Bolton, P., Simonoff, E., Yuzda, E., & Rutter, M. (in press). Autism as a strongly genetic disorder: Evidence from a British twin study. *Psychological Medicine*.

Bailey, J.M., & Pillard, R.C. (1991). A genetic study of male sexual orientation. *Archives of General Psychiatry, 48*(12), 1089–1096.

Bailey, J.M., Pillard, R.C., Neale, M.C., & Agyei, Y. (1993). Heritable factors influence sexual orientation in women. *Archives of General Psychiatry, 50*(3), 217–223.

Baldwin, A.Y. (1985). Programs for the gifted and talented: Issues concerning minority populations. In F.D. Horowitz & M. O'Brien (Eds.), *The gifted and talented: Developmental perspectives*. Washington, DC: American Psychological Association.

Bales, R.F. (1951). Interaction Process Analysis: *A method for the study of small groups*. Reading, MA: Addison-Wesley.

Bandura, A. (1962). Social learning through imitation. In M.R. Jones (Ed.), *Nebraska Symposium on Motivation*. Lincoln: University of Nebraska Press.

Bandura, A. (1965). Influence of models' reinforcement contingencies on the acquisition of imitative responses. *Journal of Personality and Social Psychology, 1*, 589–595.

Bandura, A. (1973). *Aggression: A social learning analysis*. Englewood Cliffs, NJ: Prentice-Hall.

Bandura, A. (1977). *Social learning theory*. Englewood Cliffs, NJ: Prentice-Hall.

Bandura, A. (1986). *Social foundations of thought and action: A social cognitive theory*. Englewood Cliffs, NJ: Prentice-Hall.

Bandura, A., Blanchard, E.B., & Ritter, B. (1969). Relative efficacy of desensitization and modeling approaches for inducing behavioral, affective, and attitudinal changes. *Journal of Personality and Social Psychology, 13*, 173–199.

Banyai, E.I., & Hilgard, E.R. (1976). A comparison of active-alert hypnotic induction with traditional relaxation induction. *Journal of Abnormal Psychology, 85*, 218–224.

Barbaree, H.E., & Marshall, W.L. (1991). The role of male sexual arousal in rape: Six models. *Journal of Consulting and Clinical Psychology*, 59, 621–630.

Barber, B.L., & Eccles, J.E. (1992). Long-term influence of divorce and single parenting on adolescent family- and work-related values, behaviors and aspirations. *Psychological Bulletin, 111*, 108–126.

Barglow, P., Vaughn, B.E., & Molitor, N. (1987). Effects of maternal absence due to employment on the quality of infant-mother attachment in a low-risk sample. *Child Development, 58*, 945–954.

Barkley, R.A. (1990). *Hyperactive children: A handbook for diagnosis and treatment* (2nd ed). New York: Guilford.

Barlow, D.H. (1988). *Anxiety and its disorders: The nature and treatment of anxiety and panic*. New York: Guilford.

Barnett, (1993).

Barnouw, D. (1985). *Culture and personality*. Chicago: Dorsey Press.

Baron, R.A., & Byrne, D. (1991). *Social psychology: Understanding human interaction* (6th ed.). Boston: Allyn & Bacon.

Barret, G.V., & Depinet, R.L. (1991). A reconsideration of testing for competence rather than for intelligence. *American Psychologist, 46*, 1012–1024.

Barrett-Connor, E., & Bush, T.L. (1991). Estrogen and coronary heart disease in women. AMA, *Journal of the American Medical Association, 265*(14), 1861–1867.

Barron, F. (1963). *Creativity and psychological health*. Princeton, NJ: Van Nostrand.

Barron, F., & Harrington, D.M. (1981). Creativity, intelligence, and personality. *Annual Review of Psychology, 32*, 439–476.

Barsalou, L.W. (1983). Ad hoc categories. *Memory & Cognition, 11*, 211–227.

Barsalou, L.W. (1987). The instability of graded structure: Implications for the nature of concepts. In U. Neisser (Ed.), *Concepts and conceptual development* (pp. 101–140). Cambridge, UK: Cambridge University Press.

Bartlett, F.C. (1932). *Remembering: A study in experimental and social psychology*. New York: Macmillan.

Bartoshuk, L.M. (1974). Taste illusions: Some demonstrations. *Annuals of the New York Academy of Sciences, 237*, 279–285.

Bartoshuk, L.M., & Beauchamp, G.K. (1994). Chemical senses. *Annual Review of Psychology, 45*, 419–449.

Baruch, F., & Barnett, R. (1986). Role quality, multiple role involvement, and psychological well-being in mid-life women. *Journal of Personality and Social Psychology, 51*, 578–585.

Basow, S.A. (1986). *Gender stereotypes: Traditions and alternatives* (2nd ed.). Pacific Grove, CA: Brooks/Cole.

Bateson, G. (1982). Totemic knowledge in New Guinea. In U. Neisser (Ed.), *Memory observed: Remembering in natural contexts*. San Francisco: Freeman.

Baum, A., Schaeffer, M.A., Lake, C.R., Fleming, R., & Collins, D.L. (1985). Psychological and endocrinological correlates of chronic stress at Three Mile Island. In R. Williams (Ed.),

*Perspectives on behavioral medicine* (Vol. 2). Orlando, FL: Academic Press.

Baumeister, R.F. (1988). Should we stop studying sex differences altogether? *American Psychologist, 43*, 1092–1095.

Baumrind, D. (1972). Socialization and instrumental competence in young children. In W.W. Hartup (Ed.), *The young child: Reviews of research* (Vol. 2). Washington, DC: National Association for the Education of Young Children.

Baumrind, D. (1985). Research using intentional deception. *American Psychologist, 40*, 165–174.

Baxter, D.W., & Olszewski, J. (1960). Congenital insensitivity to pain. *Brain, 83*, 381.

Bayley, N. (1956). Individual patterns of development. *Child Development, 27*, 45–74.

Beaton, A. (1985). *Left side—right side: A review of the laterality research*. New Haven, CT: Yale University Press.

Beatty, S.E., & Hawkins, D.I. (1989). Subliminal stimulation: Some new data and interpretation. *Journal of Advertising, 18*, 4–8.

Bédard, J., & Chi, M.T.H. (1992). Expertise. *Current Directions in Psychological Science, 1*, 135–139.

Beck, A.T. (1967). *Depression: Clinical, experimental and theoretical aspects*. New York: Harper (Hoeber).

Beck, A.T. (1976). *Cognitive therapy and emotional disorders*. New York: International Universities Press.

Beck, A.T. (1989). *Love is never enough*. New York: Harper & Row.

Beck, R. (1983). *Motivation: Theories and principles* (2nd ed.). Englewood Cliffs, NJ: Prentice-Hall.

Beecher, H.K. (1972). The placebo effect as a nonspecific force surrounding disease and the treatment of disease. In R. Jansen, W.D. Kerdel, A. Herz, C. Steichele, J.P. Payne, & R.A.P. Burt (Eds.), *Pain, basic principles, pharmacology, and therapy*. Stuttgart: Thieme.

Beier, E.G. (1974, October). Nonverbal communication: How we send emotional messages. *Psychology Today*, pp. 53–56.

Bellack, A.S., Hersen, M., & Turner, S.M. (1976). Generalization effects of social skills training in chronic schizophrenics: An experimental analysis. *Behavior Research and Therapy, 14*, 391–398.

Belsky, J., Lang, M.E., & Rovine, M. (1985). Stability and change in marriage across the transition to parenthood: A second study. *Journal of Marriage and the Family, 97*, 855–865.

Belsky, J., & Rovine, M. (1988). Nonmaternal care in the first year of life and infant parent attachment security. *Child Development, 59*, 157–167.

Bem, S.L. (1989). Genital knowledge and gender constancy in preschool children. *Child Development, 60*, 649–662.

Benin, M.H., & Agostinelli, J. (1988). Husbands' and wives' satisfaction with the division of labor. *Journal of Marriage and the Family, 50*, 349–361.

Bennett, W., & Gurin, J. (1982). *The dieter's dilemma: Eating less and weighing more*. New York: Basic Books.

Benson, H. (1975). *The relaxation response*. New York: William Morrow.

Benson, H., Alexander, S., & Feldman, E.L. (1975). Decreased premature ventricular contractions through use of the relaxation response in patients with stable ischemic heart disease. *Lancet, 2*, 380–382.

Benson, H., Kotch, J.B., Crassweller, K.D., & Greenwood, M.M. (1979). The relaxation response. In D. Goleman & R. Davidson (Eds.), *Consciousness: Brain, states of awareness and mysticism*. New York: Harper & Row.

Benson, H., Wallace, R.K. (1972). Decreased drug abuse with transcendental meditation—a study of 1,862 subjects. In C.J.D. Zarafonetis (Ed.), *Drug abuse*. Philadelphia: Lea & Febiger.

Benton, D., & Roberts, G. (1988). Effect of vitamin and mineral supplementation on intelligence of a sample of schoolchildren. *Lancet, 1*, 14–144.

Berger, P.A. (1978). Medical treatment of mental illness. *Science, 200*, 874–981.

Berger, R.J. (1969). The sleep and dream cycle. In A. Kales (Ed.), *Sleep: Physiology and pathology*. Philadelphia: Lippincott.

Bergin, A.E., & Lambert, M.J. (1978). The evaluation of therapeutic outcomes. In S.L. Garfield & A.E. Bergin (Eds.), *Handbook of psychotherapy and behavior change: An empirical analysis*. New York: Wiley.

Berke, R.L. (1990, February 14). Survey shows use of drugs by students fell last year. *New York Times*, Sec. A.

Berkowitz, L. (1983). Aversively stimulated aggression. *American Psychologist, 38*, 1135–1144.

Berkowitz, M.W., & Gibbs, J.C. (1983). Measuring the developmental features of moral discussion. *Merrill-Palmer Quarterly, 29*, 399–410.

Berlin, B., & Kay, P. (1969). *Basic color terms: Their universality and evolution*. Berkeley: University of California Press.

Berndt, T.J., & Perry, T.B. (1990). Distinctive features and effects of friendship in early adolescent friendships. In R. Montemayor (Ed.), *Advances in adulthood research* (pp. 269–287). Greenwich, CT: JAI Press.

Berntson, G.G., Cacippo, J.T., & Quigley, K.S. (1993). Cardiac psychophysiology and autonomic space in humans: Empirical perspectives and conceptual implications. *Psychological Bulletin, 114*(2) 296–322.

Berry, J.W. (1967). Independence and conformity in subsistence level societies. *Journal of Personality and Social Psychology, 7*, 415–518.

Bersoff, D.N. (1981). Testing and the law. *American Psychologist, 36*, 1047–1056.

Bertenthal, B.I. (1992). Infants' perception of biomechanical motions: Intrinsic image and knowledge based on constraints. In C. Ganrud (Ed.), *Visual perception and cognition in infancy*, Hillsdale, NJ: Erlbaum.

Bertrand, S., & Masling, J. (1969). Oral imagery and alcoholism. *Journal of Abnormal Psychology, 74*, 50–53.

Betancourt, H., & López, S.R. (1993). The study of culture, ethnicity, and race in American psychology. *American Psychologist, 48*, 629–637.

Bettelheim, B. (1943). Individual and mass behavior in extreme situations. *Journal of Abnormal Psychology, 38*, 417–452.

Bettelheim, B. (1960). *The informed heart*. New York: Free Press.

Bettelheim, B. (1967). *The children of the dream*. London: Collier-Macmillan.

Bhatt, R.S., Wasserman, E.A., Reynolds, W.F., & Knauss, K.S. (1988). Conceptual behavior in pigeons: Categorization of both familiar and novel examples from four classes of natural and artificial stimuli. *Journal of Experimental Psychology: Animal Behavior Processes, 14*, 219–324.

Bialystock, E. (1988). Levels of bilingualism and levels of linguistic awareness. *Developmental Psychology, 24*, 650–567.

Biederman, I. (1987). Recognition by components: A theory of human image understanding. *Psychological Review, 95*, 115–147.

Birch, H.G., & Rabinowitz, H.S. (1951). The negative effect of previous experience on productive thinking. *Journal of Experimental Psychology, 41*, 121–125.

Birren, J.E. (1983). Aging in America: Role for psychology. *American Psychologist, 38*, 298–299.

Bjorklund, D.F. (1989). *Children's thinking, developmental function and individual differences*. Pacific Grove, CA: Brooks/Cole.

Blake, R. (1993). Cats perceive biological motion. *Psychological Science, 4*, 54–57.

Blake, R.R., Helson, H., & Mouton, J. (1956). The generality of conformity behavior as a function of factual anchorage, difficulty of task and amount of social pressure. *Journal of Personality, 25*, 294–305.

Blakeslee, S. (1994, October 5). Yes, people are right. Caffeine is addictive. *New York Times*.

Blanck, D.C., Bellack, A.S., Rosnow, R.L., Rotheram-Borus, M.J., & Schooler, N.R. (1992). Scientific rewards and conflicts of ethical choices in human subjects research. *American Psychologist, 47*, 959–965.

Bliss, T.V., & Dolphin, A.C. (1982). What is the mechanism of long-term potentiation in the hippocampus? *Trends in Neurosciences, 5*, 289–290.

Block, J. (1971). *Lives through time*. Berkeley, CA: Bancroft.

Block, J., & Robbins, R.W. (1993). A longitudinal study of consistency and change in self-esteem from early adolescence to early adulthood. *Child Development, 64*, 902–923.

Bloom, L. (1970). *Language development: Form and function in emerging grammar*. Cambridge, MA: MIT Press.

Blum, J.M. (1979). *Pseudoscience and mental ability: The origins and fallacies of the IQ controversy*. New York: Monthly Review Press.

Blum, K., Noble, E.P., Sheridan, B.J., Montgomery, A., Ritchie, T., Jagadeeswaran, P., Nogami, H., Briggs, A.H., & Cohn, J.B. (1990). Allelic association of human dopamine D2 receptor gene in alcoholism. *JAMA, Journal of the American Medical Association, 263*, 2055–2060.

Blumenthal, S.J. (1990). Youth suicide: The physician's role in suicide prevention. JAMA, *Journal of the American Medical Association, 264*(24), 3194–3196.

Bokert, E. (1970). *The effects of thirst and related auditory stimulation on dream reports*. Paper presented to the Association for the Physiological Study of Sleep, Washington, DC.

Bolles, R., & Fanselow, M. (1982). Endorphins and behavior. *Annual Review of Psychology, 33*, 87–101.

Bolles, R.C. (1972). Reinforcement, expectancy, and learning. *Psychological Review, 79*, 394–409.

Bolos, A.M., Dean, M., Lucas-Derse, S., Ramsburg, M., Brown, G.L., & Goldman, D. (1990). Population and pedigree studies reveal a lack of association between the dopamine D2 receptor gene and alcoholism. *JAMA, Journal of the American Medical Association, 264*, 3156–3160.

Bond, M.H., Wan, K.C., Leung, K., & Giacolone, R.A. (1985). How are responses to verbal insult related to cultural collectivism and power distance? *Journal of Cross-Cultural Psychology, 16*, 111–127.

Booth-Kewley, S., & Friedman, H.S. (1987). Psychological predictors of heart disease: A quantitative review. *Psychological Bulletin, 101*, 343–362.

Borbély, A. (1984). *Secrets of sleep*. New York: Basic Books.

Borgatta, E.F. (1964). The structure of personality characteristics. *Behavioral Science, 9*, 8–17.

Boring, E.G., Langfeld, H.S., & Weld, H.P. (1976). *Foundations of psychology*. New York: Wiley.

Bornstein, M.H., & Lamb, M.E. (1988). *Developmental psychology: An advanced textbook* (2nd ed.). Hillsdale, NJ: Erlbaum.

Bornstein, R.F. (1989). Exposure and affect: Overview and meta-analysis of research, 1968–1987. *Psychological Reports, 106*, 265–289.

Botwin, M.D., & Buss, D.M. (1989). The structure of act report data: Is the five factor model of personality recaptured? *Journal of Personality and Social Psychology*.

Bouchard, C., Tremblay, A., Despres, J.P., Nadeau, A., Lupien, P.J., Theriault, G., Dussault, J., Moorjani, S., Pinault, S., & Fournier, G. (1990). The response to long-term overfeeding in identical twins. *New England Journal of Medicine, 322*, 1477–1482.

Bouchard, T.J., Jr. (1984). Twins reared together and apart: What they tell us about human diversity. In S.W. Fox (Ed.), *Individuality and determinism* (pp. 147–178). New York: Plenum.

Bouchard, T.J., Jr., Lykken, D.T., McGue, M., Segal, N.L., & Tellegen, A. (1990). Sources of human psychological differences: The Minnesota study of twins reared apart. *Science, 250*, 223–228.

Bourne, L.E., Dominowski, R.L., Loftus, E.F., & Healy, A.F. (1986). *Cognitive process* (2nd ed.). Englewood Cliffs, NJ: Prentice-Hall.

Bouton, M.E. (1993). Context, time and memory retrieval in the interference paradigms of Pavlovian conditioning. *Psychological Bulletin, 114*, 80–99.

Bouton, M.E. (1994). Context, ambiguity and classical conditioning. *Current Directions in Psychological Science, 3*, 49–52.

Bowden, S.C. (1990). Separating cognitive impairment in neurologically asymptomatic alcoholism from Wernicke-Korsakoff's syndrome: Is the neuropsychological distinction justified? *Psychological Bulletin, 107*, 355–366.

Bower, G.H. (1973, October). How to . . . uh . . . remember. *Psychology Today*, pp. 63–70.

Bower, G.H., & Mann, T. (1992). Improving recall by recoding interfering material at the time of recall. *Journal of Experimental Psychology: Learning, Memory, and Cognition, 18*, 1310–1320.

Boyatzis, R. (1982). *The competent manager*. New York: Wiley.

Brainerd, C.J. (1978). The stage question in cognitive-developmental theory. *Behavioral and Brain Sciences, 2*, 172–213.

Brandon, T.H. (1994). Negative affect as motivation to smoke. *Current Directions in Psychological Science, 3*, 33–37.

Braveman, N.S., & Bornstein, P. (Eds.). (1985). *Annuals of the New York Academy of Sciences*: Vol. 443. Experimental assessments and clinical applications of conditioned food aversions. New York: New York Academy of Sciences.

Bray, G.A. (1986). Effects of obesity on health and happiness. In K.D. Brownell & J.P. Foreyt (Eds.), *Handbook of eating disorders: Physiology, psychology, and treatment of obesity, anorexia, and bulimia* (pp. 3–44). New York: Basic Books.

Bredemeier, B., & Shields, D. (1985, October). Values and violence in sports today. *Psychology Today*, pp. 23–32.

Breedlove, S.M. (1994). Sexual differentiation of the human nervous system. *American Review of Psychology*, *45*, 389–418.

Breer, H., & Boekhoff, I. (1991). Odorants of the same class activate different second messenger pathways. *Chemical Senses*, *16*, 19–29.

Brehm, S.S. (1992). *Intimate relationships* (2nd ed.). Boston: McGraw-Hill.

Breland, K., & Breland, M. (1972). The misbehavior of organisms. In M.E.P. Seligman & J.L. Hager (Eds.), *Biological boundaries of learning*. Englewood Cliffs, NJ: Prentice-Hall.

Brenneis, B. (1970). Male and female modalities in manifest dream content. *Journal of Abnormal Psychology*, *76*, 434–442.

Brenner, M.H. (1973). *Mental illness and the economy*. Cambridge, MA: Harvard University Press.

Brenner, M.H. (1979). Influence of the social environment on psychopathology: The historic perspective. In J.E. Barrett (Ed.), *Stress and mental disorder*. New York: Raven Press.

Brewer, W.F., & Nakamura, G.V. (1984). The nature and function of schemas. In R.S. Wyer & T.K. Srull (Eds.), *Handbook of social cognition*. Hillsdale, NJ: Erlbaum.

Brigham, C.C. (1923). *A study of American intelligence*. Princeton, NJ: Princeton University Press.

Brigham, J.C. (1980). Limiting conditions of the "physical attractiveness stereotype": Attributions about divorce. *Journal of Research in Personality*, *4*, 365–375.

Brislin, R.W., Cushner, K., Cherries, C., & Yong, M. (1986). *Intercultural interactions: A practical guide*. Beverly Hills, CA: Sage.

Broadbent, D.E. (1958). *Perception and communication*. New York: Pergamon.

Brock, T.C., & Balloun, J.L. (1967). Behavioral receptivity to dissonant information. *Journal of Personality and Social Psychology*, *6*, 413–428.

Brody, J. (1992, December 9). For mothers who also work, rewards may outweigh success. *New York Times*, p. B2.

Brody, J.E. (1986, August 19). Widely used mental test undergoing treatment. *New York Times*, p. C1.

Brody, J.E. (1987, August 26). For children of alcoholics, many broken promises. *New York Times*, p. 16.

Brody, J.E. (1990, May 10). Personal health: On menopause and the toll that loss of estrogens can take on a woman's sexuality. *New York Times*, Sec. B.

Brody, L. (1985). Gender differences in emotional development: A review of theories and research. In A.J. Stewart & M.B. Lykes (Eds.), *Gender and personality: Current perspectives on theory and research* (pp. 14–61). Durham, NC: Duke University Press.

Bronfenbrenner, U. (1977). Toward an experimental ecology of human development. *American Psychologist*, *32*, 513–531.

Bronfenbrenner, U. (1986). Ecology of the family as a context for human development: Research perspectives. *Developmental Psychology*, *22*, 723–742.

Brooks-Gunn, J., & Lewis, M. (1984). The development of early visual self-recognition. *Developmental Review*, *4*, 215–239.

Brooks-Gunn, J. (1993). *Adolescence*. Paper presented at the meeting of the Society for Research in Child Development, Kansas City, MO.

Brooks-Gunn, J. (1977). The development of early visual self-recognition. *Developmental Review*, *4*, 215-239.

Brown, A.S. (1991). A review of the tip-of-the-tongue experience. *Psychological Bulletin*, *109*, 204–223.

Brown, B., & Grotberg, J.J. (1981). Head Start: A successful experiment. *Courrier*. Paris: International Children's Centre.

Brown, E.R., & Zuckerman, B. (1991). The infant of the drug abusing mother. *Pediatric Annals*, *20*, 555–558.

Brown, P.L., & Jenkins, H.M. (1968). Autoshaping of the pigeon's key peck. *Journal of Experimental and Analytical Behavior*, *11*, 1–8.

Brown, R. (1958). *Words and things*. New York: Free Press/Macmillan.

Brown, R. (1973). *A first language: The early stages*. Cambridge, MA: Harvard University Press.

Brown, R., & Kulik, J. (1977). Flashbulb memories. *Cognition*, *5*, 73–99.

Brown, R., & McNeill, D. (1966). The "tip of the tongue phenomenon." *Journal of Verbal Learning and Verbal Behavior*, *8*, 325–337.

Brown, R.W., & Lenneberg, E.H. (1954). A study in language and cognition. *Journal of Abnormal and Social Psychology*, *49*, 454–462.

Browne, A. (1993). Violence against women by male partners. Prevalence, outcomes and policy implications. *American Psychologist*, *48*, 1077–1087.

Brownell, K.D., & Rodin, J. (1994). The dieting maelstrom. Is it possible and advisable to lose weight? *American Psychologist*, *49*, 781–791.

Bruch, C.B. (1971). Modification of procedures for identification of the disadvantaged gifted. *Gifted Child Quarterly*, *15*, 267–272.

Bruch, H. (1980). *The golden cage: The enigma of anorexia nervosa*. New York: Random House.

Brumberg, J.J. (1988). *Fasting girls: The emergence of anorexia nervosa as a modern disease*. Cambridge, MA: Harvard University Press.

Brunner, H.G., Nelen, M., Breakfield, X.O., & Ropers, H.H. (1993). Abnormal structures associated with a point mutation in the structural gene for monoamine oxidase A. *Science*, *263*, 578–580.

Buchanan, C.M., Eccles, J.S., & Becker, J.B. (1992). Are adolescents the victims of raging hormones: Evidence for activational effects of hormones on moods and behavior at adolescence. *Psychological Bulletin*, *111*, 67–107.

Buck, L., & Axel, R. (1991). A novel multigene family may encode odorant receptors: A molecular basis for odor recognition. *Cell (Cambridge, Mass.)*, *65*, 175–187.

Budzynski, T., Stoyva, J., & Adler, C. (1970). Feedback-induced muscle relaxation: Application to tension headache. *Journal of Behavior Therapy and Experimental Psychiatry*, *1*, 205–211.

Buhrich, N., Theile, N., Yaw, A., & Crawford, A. (1979). Plasma testosterone, serum FSH, and serum LH levels in transvestism. *Archives of Sexual Behavior*, *8*, 49–54.

Bukowski, W.M., Gauze, C., Hoza, B., & Newcomb, A.F. (1993). Differences in consistency between same-sex and other-sex peer relationships during early adolescence. *Developmental Psychology*, *2*, 255–263.

Burke, D.M., McKay, D.G., Worthley, J.S., & Wade, E. (1991). On the tip of the tongue: What causes word finding failures in young and older adults? *Journal of Memory and Language, 30*, 542–579.

Burke, R.J., Weir, T., & Harrison, D. (1976). Disclosure of problems and tensions experienced by marital partners. *Psychological Reports, 38*, 531–542.

Bushman, B.J. (1993). Human aggression while under the influence of alcohol and other drugs: An integrative research review. *Current Directions in Psychological Science, 2*, 148–152.

Bushman, B.J., & Cooper, H.M. (1990). Effects of alcohol on human aggression: An integrative research review. *Psychological Bulletin, 107*, 341–354.

Buss, D.M. (1985). Human mate selection. *American Scientist, 73*, 47–51.

Butcher, J.N., Dahlstrom, W.G., Graham, J.R., Telegen, A., & Kaemmer, B. (1989). *Minnesota Multiphasic Personality Inventory: II. Manual for administration and scoring*. Minneapolis: University of Minnesota Press.

Butler, R.N. (1963). The life review: An interpretation of reminiscence in the aged. *Psychiatry, 26*, 63–76.

Butler, R.N., & Lewis, M.I. (1982). *Aging and mental health: Positive psychological and biomedical approaches*. St. Louis, MO: Mosby.

Byrd, K.R. (1994). The narrative reconstructions of incest survivors. *American Psychologist, 49*, 439–440.

Byrne, D. (1961). Interpersonal attraction and attitude similarity. *Journal of Abnormal and Social Psychology, 62*, 713–715.

Byrne, D. (1977). The imagery of sex. In J. Money & H. Masaph (Eds.), *Handbook of sexology*. New York: Elsevier/North Holland.

Byrne, D., & Blaylock, B. (1963). Similarity and assumed similarity of attitudes between husbands and wives. *Journal of Abnormal and Social Psychology, 67*, 636–640.

Byrne, D., & Nelson, D. (1965). Attraction as a linear function of properties of positive reinforcements. *Journal of Personality and Social Psychology, 1*, 659–663.

Byrne, D., & Wong, T.J. (1962). Racial prejudice, interpersonal attraction, and assumed dissimilarity of attitudes. *Journal of Abnormal and Social Psychology, 65*, 246–253.

Cahill, L., & McGaugh, J.L. (1990). Amygdaloid complex lesions differentially affect retention of tasks using appetitive and aversive reinforcement. *Behavior Neuroscience, 104*, 532–543.

Cain, W.S. (1981, July). Educating your nose. *Psychology Today*, pp. 48–56.

Cain, W.S. (1982). Odor identification by males and females: Predictions versus performance. *Chemical Senses, 7*, 129–142.

Caine, S.B., & Koob, G.F. (1994). Effects of mesolimbic dopamine depletion on responding maintained by cocaine and food. Special issue: Contributions of Joseph V. Brady. *Journal of the Experimental Analysis of Behavior, 61*, 213–221.

Calder, B.J., Insko, C.A., & Yandell, B. (1974). The relation of cognitive and memorial processes to persuasion in simulated jury trial. *Journal of Applied Social Psychology, 4*, 62–92.

Caldwell, J.D., Jirikowski, G.F., Greer, E.R., & Pedersen, C.A. (1989). Medial preoptic area oxytocin and female sexual receptivity. *Behavioral Neuroscience, 103*, 655–662.

Calvert, S., & Cocking, R. (1992). Health promotion through mass media. *Journal of Applied Developmental Psychology, 13*, 143–149.

Campeau, S., Miserendino, M.J.D., & Davis, M. (1992). Intra-amygdala infusion of the N-methyl-D-aspartate receptor antagonist AP5 blocks retention but not expression of fear-potentiated startle to an auditory conditioned stimulus. *Behavioral Neuroscience, 106*, 569–574.

Campos, J.L., Langer, A.,& Krowitz, A. (1970). Cardiac responses on the visual cliff in prelocomotor human infants. *Science, 170*, 196–197.

Capron, C., & Duyme, M. (1989). Assessment of effects of socio-economic status on IQ in a full cross-fostering study. *Nature (London), 340*, 552–554.

Carey, G., & Gottesman, I.I. (1981). Twin and family studies of anxiety, phobic, and obsessive disorders. In D.F. Klein & J. Rabkin (Eds.), *Anxiety: New research and changing concepts*. New York: Raven Press.

Carlson, N. (1994). *Physiology of behavior*, (5th ed.). Boston: Allyn & Bacon.

Carmen, E.H., Russo, N.F., & Miller, J.B. (1981). Inequality and women's mental health: An overview. *American Journal of Psychiatry, 138*, 1319–1330.

Carmody, D. (1990, March 7). College drinking: Changes in attitude and habit. *New York Times*, Sec. B.

Carroll, J.B., & Horn, J.L. (1981). On the scientific basis of ability testing. *American Psychologist, 36*, 1012–1020.

Carroll, J.M., Thomas, J.C., & Malhotra, A. (1980). Presentation and representation in design problem solving. *British Journal of Psychology, 71*, 143–153.

Carskadon, M., & Dement, W. (1982). Current perspectives on daytime sleepiness. *Sleep*, 5(Suppl. 2), 73–81.

Carson, R.C., Butcher, J.N., & Coleman, J.C. (1988). *Abnormal psychology and modern life* (8th ed.). Glenview, IL: Scott, Foresman.

Caspi, A., & Elder, G.H., Jr. (1986). Life satisfaction in old age: Linking social psychology and history. *Journal of Psychology and Aging, 1*, 18–26.

Cattell, J.M. (Ed.). (1906). *American men of science: A biographical directory*. New York: Science.

Cattell, R.B. (1965). *The scientific analysis of personality*. Baltimore: Penguin.

Cattell, R.B. (1971). *Abilities: Their structure, growth, and action*. Boston: Houghton Mifflin.

Cattell, R.B., & Kline, P. (1977). *The specific analysis of personality and motivation*. New York: Academic Press.

Cavanaugh, J.C. (1990). *Adult development and aging*. Belmont, CA: Wadsworth.

Celis, W. (1994, June 8). More college women drinking to get drunk. *New York Times*, p. B8.

Centers for Disease Control. (1991). Attempted suicide among high school students—United States, 1990. *JAMA, Journal of the American Medical Association*, 266(14), 1911.

Chaiken, S., & Eagly, A.H. (1976). Communication modality as a determinant of message persuasiveness and message comprehensibility. *Journal of Personality and Social Psychology, 34*, 605–614.

Chaiken, S., & Stangor, C. (1987). Attitudes and attitude change. *Annual Review of Psychology, 38*, 575–630.

Chaikin, A.L., & Darley, J.M. (1973). Victim or perpetrator? Defensive attribution of responsibility and the need for order and justice. *Journal of Personality and Social Psychology, 25*, 268–275.

Chase, W.G., & Ericsson, K.A. (1981). Skilled memory. In J. Anderson (Ed.), *Cognitive skills and their acquisition*. Hillsdale, NJ: Erlbaum.

Chase, W.G., & Simon, H.A. (1973). Perception in chess. *Cognitive Psychology, 4*, 55–81.

Chasnoff, I., Griffith, D.R., Frier, C., & Murray, J. (1992). Cocaine/poly drug use in pregnancy: Two year follow-up. *Pediatrics, 89*, 284–289.

Cherry, C. (1966). *On human communication: A review, a survey, and a criticism* (2nd ed.). Cambridge, MA: MIT Press.

Chipman, S.F., Krantz, D.H., & Silver, R. (1992). Mathematics anxiety and science careers among able bodied college women. *Psychological Science, 5*, 292–295.

Chodorow, N.J. (1978a). Mothering, object-relations, and the female oedipal configuration. *Feminist Studies, 4*, 137–158.

Chodorow, N.J. (1978b). *The reproduction of motherhood: The psychoanalysis and sociology of gender*. Berkeley: University of California Press.

Chodorow, N.J. (1989). *Feminism and psychoanalytic theory*. New Haven, CT: Yale University Press.

Chomsky, N. (1957). *Syntactic structures*. The Hague: Mouton.

Chomsky, N. (1965). *Aspects of the theory of syntax*. Cambridge, MA: MIT Press.

Christensen, F. (1986). *Pornography: The other side*. Unpublished paper, University of Alberta.

Church, D.K., Siegel, M.A., & Foster, C.D. (1988). *Growing old in America*. Wylie, TX: Information Aids.

Chwalisz, K., Diener, E., & Gallagher, D. (1988). Autonomic arousal feedback and emotional experience: Evidence from the spinal cord injured. *Journal of Personality and Social Psychology, 54*, 820–828.

Cialdini, R.B., Cacioppo, J.T., Bassett, R., & Miller, J.A. (1978). Lowball procedure for producing compliance: Commitment then cost. *Journal of Personality and Social Psychology, 36*, 463–476.

Cialdini, R.B., Vincent, J.E., Lewis, S.K., Catalan, J.,Wheeler, D., & Darby, B.L. (1975). A reciprocal concessions procedure for inducing compliance: The door-in-the-face technique. *Journal of Personality and Social Psychology, 21*, 206–215.

Clanan, A.D.(1966). Sexual difficulties after 50, a panel discussion. *Canadian Medical Association Journal*, 207–219.

Claparéde, E. (1951). Recognition and "me-ness." In D. Rapaport (Ed.), *Organization and pathology of thought* (pp. 58–75). (original work published 1911)

Clark, M.S., & Mills, J. (1979). Interpersonal attraction in exchange and communal relationships. *Journal of Personality and Social Psychology, 37*, 12–24.

Clark, R.D., & Word, L.E. (1974). Where is the apathetic bystander? Situational characteristics of the emergency. *Journal of Personality and Social Psychology, 29*, 279–287.

Clarke-Stewart, K.A. (1989). Infant day care, maligned or malignant? *American Psychologist, 44*, 266–273.

Clausen, J.A. (1975). The social meaning of differential physical and sexual maturation. In S.E. Dragastin & G.H. Elder, Jr. (Eds.), *Adolescence in the life cycle: Psychological change and social context* (pp. 25–47). New York: Wiley.

Cloninger, S.C. (1993). *Theories of personality. Understanding persons*. Englewood Cliffs, NJ: Prentice-Hall.

Clore, G.L., Bray, R.B., Atkin, S.M., & Murphy, P. (1978). Interracial attitudes and behavior at a summer camp. *Journal of Personality and Social Psychology, 36*, 107–116.

Clore, G.L., & Byrne, D. (1974). A reinforcement-affect model of attraction. In T.L. Huston (Ed.), *Foundations of interpersonal attraction* (pp. 143–170). New York: Academic Press.

Cohen, A., & Raffal, R.D. (1991). Attention and feature integration: Illusory conjunctions in a patient with a parietal lobe lesion. *Psychological Science, 2*, 106–110.

Cohen, A.G., & Gutek, B.A. (1991). Differences in the career experiences of members of two APA divisions. *American Psychologist, 46*, 1292–1298.

Cohen, D.B. (1973). Sex, role orientation and dream recall. *Journal of Abnormal Psychology, 82*, 246–252.

Cohen, D.B. (1974, May). Repression is not the demon who conceals and hoards our forgotten dreams. *Psychology Today*, 50–54.

Cohen, D.B. (1976). Dreaming: Experimental investigation of representation and adaptive properties. In G. Schwartz & D. Shapiro (Eds.), *Consciousness and self-regulation*. New York: Plenum.

Cohen, E.G. (1984). The desegregated school: Problems in status, power and interethnic climate. In N. Miller & M.B. Brewer (Eds.), *Groups in contact: The psychology of desegregation* (pp. 77–96). New York: Academic Press.

Cohen, M.L., Seghorn, T., & Calmas, W. (1969). Sociometric study of the sex offender. *Journal of Abnormal Psychology, 74*, 249–255.

Cohen, S., & Williamson, G.M. (1988). Stress and infectious disease in humans. *Psychological Bulletin, 109*, 5–24.

Cohen, L.D. (1991). Sex differences in the course of personality development: A meta-analysis. *Psychological Bulletin, 109*(2), 252–266.

Cole, N.S. (1981). Bias in testing. *American Psychologist, 36*, 1067–1077.

Colegrove, F.W. (1982). Individual memories. *American Journal of Psychology, 10*, 228–255. (Original work published in 1899). (Reprinted in *Memory observed: Remembering in natural contexts*, by V. Neisser, Ed. San Francisco: Freeman.)

Coles, C. (1992).

Colvin, C.R., & Block, J. (1994). Do positive illusions foster metal health? An examination of the Taylor and Brown formulation. *Psychological Bulletin, 116*, 3–20.

Condry, J., & Condry, S. (1976). Sex differences: A study in the eye of the beholder. *Child Development, 47*, 812–819.

Conger, J.J., & Petersen, A.C. (1991). *Adolescence and youth* (4th ed.). New York: Harper Collins.

Conrad, R. (1972). Short-term memory in the deaf: A test for speech coding. *British Journal of Psychology, 63*, 173–180.

Cook, M., Mineka, S., Wolkenstein, B., & Laitsch, K. (1985). Observational conditioning of snake fear in unrelated rhesus monkeys. *Journal of Abnormal Psychology, 94*, 591–610

Cook, R. (1991). *The experimental analysis of cognition in animals*. Paper presented at the meeting of the Psychonomic Society, San Francisco.

Cookerly, J.R. (1980). Does marital therapy do any lasting good? *Journal of Marital and Family Therapy*, *6*, 393–397.

Cooper, A.J. (1969). A clinical study of coital anxiety in male potency disorders. *Journal of Psychosomatic Research*, *13*, 143–147.

Cooper, J. (1971). Personal responsibility and dissonance. *Journal of Personality and Social Psychology*, *18*, 354–363.

Cooper, J., & Croyle, R.T. (1984). Attitudes and attitude change. *Annual Review of Psychology*, *35*, 395–426.

Cooper, J.R., Bloom, F.E., & Roth, R.H. (1991). *The biochemical basis of neuropharmacology* (6th ed.). Oxford: Oxford University Press.

Cooper, R., & Zubek, J. (1958). Effects of enriched and restricted early environments on the learning ability of bright and dull rats. *Canadian Journal of Psychology*, *12*, 159–164.

Coren, S., Porac, C., & Ward, L.M. (1984). *Sensation and perception* (2nd ed.). Orlando, FL: Academic Press.

Coren, S., Ward, L.M., & Enns, J.T. (1994). *Sensation and perception* (4th ed.). Orlando, FL: Harcourt Brace.

Costa, P.T., & McCrae, R.R. (1980). Still stable after all these years: Personality as a key to some issues in adulthood and old age. In P.B. Baltes & O.G. Brim (Eds.), *Lifespan development and behavior* (Vol. 3). New York: Academic Press.

Cotton, J.L., & Tuttle, J.M. (1986, January). Employee turnover: A meta-analysis and review with implications for research. *Academy of Management Review*, pp. 55–70.

Cotton, N.S. (1979). The familial incidence of alcoholism. *Journal of Studies on Alcohol*, *40*, 89–116.

Council, J.R. (1993). Context effects in personality research. *Current Directions*, *2*, 31–34.

Cousins, S. (1989). Culture and self-perception in Japan and in the United States. *Journal of Personality and Social Psychology*, *56*, 124–131.

Cowan, N. (1988). Evolving conceptions of memory storage, selective attention, and their mutual constraints within the human information-processing system. *Psychological Bulletin*, *104*, 163–191.

Coyne, J.C. (1976). Depression and the responses of others. *Journal of Abnormal Psychology*, *85*, 186–193.

Coyne, J.C. (1982). A critique of cognitions as casual entities with particular reference to depression. *Cognitive Therapy and Research*, *6*, 3–13.

Cox, D.J., Sutphen, J., Borowitz, S., & Dickens, M.N. (1994). Simple electromyographic biofeedback treatment for chronic pediatric constipation/encopresis: Preliminary report. *Biofeedback & Self Regulation*, *19*(1), 41–50.

Craig, R.S. (1992). The effect of television day part and gender portrayals in television commercials. *Sex Roles*, *26*, 197–211.

Craighead, L. (1990). Supervised exercise in behavioral treatment for moderate obesity. *Behavior Therapy*, *20*, 49–59.

Craik, F.I.M., & Lockhart, R.S. (1972). Levels of processing: A framework for memory research. *Journal of Verbal Learning and Verbal Behavior*, *11*, 671–684.

Craik, F.I.M., & Watkins, M.J. (1973). The role of rehearsal in short-term memory. *Journal of Verbal Learning and Verbal Behavior*, *12*, 599–607.

Crick, F., & Mitchison, G. (1983). The function of dreamsleep. *Nature (London)*, *304*(5922), 111–114.

Critchlow, B. (1986). The powers of John Barleycorn: Beliefs about the effects of alcohol on social behavior. *American Psychologist*, *41*, 751–764.

Crockenberg, S.B. (1980). Creativity tests: A boon or boondoggle for education? *Review of Educational Research*, *42*, 27–44.

Cronbach, L.J. (1990). *Essentials of psychological testing* (5th ed.). New York: Harper Collins.

Crook, T., & Eliot, J. (1980). Parental death during childhood and adult depression: A critical review of the literature. *Psychological Bulletin*, *87*, 252–259.

Crovitz, H.F., & Schiffman, H. (1974). Frequency of episodic memories as a function of their age. *Bulletin of the Psychonomic Society*, *4*, 517–518.

Crowther, J.H., Tennenbaum, D.L., Hobfoll, S.E., & Stephens, M.A.P. (Eds.). (1992). *The etiology of bulimia nervosa: The individual and family context*. Washington, DC: Hemisphere.

Crutchfield, R.A. (1955). Conformity and character. *American Psychologist*, *10*, 191–198.

Crystal, D.S., Chen, C., Fuligini, A.J., Stevenson, H., Hus, C., Ko, H., Kitamura, S., & Kimura, S. (1994). Psychological maladjustments and academic achievement: A cross-cultural study of Japanese, Chinese, and American high school students. *Child Development*, *65*, 738–753.

Cumming, E., & Henry, W.E. (1961). *Growing old: The process of disengagement*. New York: Basic Books.

Cutler, B.L., & Penrod, S.D. (1988). Improving the reliability of eyewitness identification: Lineup construction and presentation. *Journal of Applied Psychology*, *73*, 281–290.

Cynader, M., Timney, B.N., & Mitchell, D.E. (1980). Period of susceptibility of kitten visual cortex to the effects of monocular deprivation extends beyond six months of age. *Brain Research*, *191*, 545–550.

Dabbs, J.M., & Leventhal, H. (1966). Effects of varying the recommendations in a fear-arousing communication. *Journal of Personality and Social Psychology*, *4*, 525–531.

Dabbs, J.M., Jr., & Morris, R. (1990). Testosterone, social class, and antisocial behavior in a sample of 4,462 men. *Psychological Science*, *1*, 209–211.

Dabbs, J.M., Jr., Ruback, R.B., Frady, R.L., & Hopper, C.H. (1988). Saliva testosterone and criminal violence among women. *Personality and Individual Differences*, *9*, 269–275.

Dadona, L., Hendrickson, A., & Quigley, H.A. (1991). Selective effects of experimental glaucoma on axonal transport by retinal ganglion cells to the dorsal lateral geniculate nucleus. *Investigations in Ophthalmology & Visual Science*, *32*, 1593–1599.

Dahlström, W.G. (1993). Tests: Small samples, large consequences. *American Psychologist*, *48*, 393–399.

Daley, S. (1991, January 9). Girls' self-esteem is lost on way to adolescence, new study finds. *New York Times*, Sec. B.

Damasio, A.R., Tranel, D., & Damasio, H. (1990a). Face agnosia and the neural substrates of memory. *Annual Review of Neuroscience*, *13*, 89–109.

Damasio, A.R., Tranel, D., & Damasio, H. (1990b). Individuals with sociopathic behavior caused by frontal damage fail to respond autonomically to social stimuli. *Behavioral Brain Research*, *41*, 81–94.

D'Amato, M.R., & Van Sant, P. (1988). The person concept in monkeys (*Cebus apella*). *Journal of Experimental Psychology: Animal Behavior Processes*, *14*, 32–55.

Darnton, N. (1992, January 13). A split verdict on America's marital future. *Newsweek*, p. 52.

Daniel, W.F., & Crovitz, H.F. (1983). Acute memory impairment following electroconvulsive therapy: 2. Effects of electrode placement. *Acta Psychiatrica Scandinavica, 67*, 57–68.

Daniell, H.W. (1971). Smokers' wrinkles: A study in the epidemiology of "Crow's feet." *Annals of Internal Medicine, 75*, 873–880.

Dannemiller, J.L., & Stephens, B.R. (1988). A critical test of infant pattern preference models. *Child Development, 59*, 210–216.

Darley, J.M., & Latané, B. (1968). Bystander intervention in emergencies. *Journal of Personality and Social Psychology, 8*, 377–383.

Darwin, C. (1872). *The expression of the emotions in man and animals*. London: John Murray.

Davidson, T.L., Aparicio, J., & Rescorla, R.A. (1988). Transfer between Pavlovian facilitators and instrumental discriminative stimuli. *Animal Learning and Behavior, 16*, 285–291.

Davis, M.H., & Stephan, W.G. (1980). Attributions for exam performance. *Journal of Applied Social Psychology, 10*, 235–248.

Dawes, R.M. (1988). *Rational choice in an uncertain world*. San Diego, CA: Harcourt Brace Jovanovich.

Dawes, R.M. (1993). Prediction of the future versus understanding of the past. *American Journal of Psychology, 106*, 1–24.

Dawes, R.M. (1994). *House of cards: The collapse of modern psychotherapy*. New York: Free Press.

D'Azevedo, W.A. (1982). Tribal history in Liberia. In U. Neisser (Ed.), *Memory observed: Remembering in natural contexts*. San Francisco: Freeman.

Dean, J.W., Jr., & Evans, J.R. (1994). *Total quality: Management, organization, and strategy*. St. Paul, MN: West Publishing Company.

Dean, S.R. (1970). Is there an ultraconscious? *Canadian Psychiatric Association Journal, 15*, 57–61.

DeAngelis, T. (1990a, June). Quality of child care counts, panel affirms. *APA Monitor*, p. 20.

DeAngelis, T. (1990b, August). NIMH educational effort aimed at panic disorder. *APA Monitor*, p. 13.

DeAngelis, T. (1991a, June). Hearing pinpoints gaps in research on women. *APA Monitor*, p. 8.

DeAngelis, T. (1991b, August). Ethnic groups respond differently to medication. *APA Monitor*, p. 28.

Deaux, K., & Wrightsman, L. (1984). *Social psychology in the 80s* (4th ed.). Monterey, CA: Brooks/Cole.

DeCasper, A.J., & Fifer, W.P. (1980). Of human bonding: Newborns prefer their mother's voice. *Science, 208*, 1174–1176.

DeCasper, A.J., & Spence, M.J. (1986). Prenatal maternal speech influences newborns' perception of speech sounds. *Infant Behavior and Development, 9*, 133–150.

DeFreitas, B., & Schwartz, G. (1979). Effects of caffeine in chronic psychiatric patients. *American Journal of Psychiatry, 136*, 1337–1338.

de Groot, A.D. (1965a). Perception and memory versus thought: Some old ideas and recent findings. In B. Kleinmuntz (Ed.), *Problem solving: Research, method, and theory*. New York: Wiley.

de Groot, A.D. (1965b). *Thought and choice in chess*. The Hague: Mouton.

Deikman, A.J. (1973). Deautomatization and the mystic experience. In R.W. Ornstein (Ed.), *The nature of human consciousness*. San Francisco: Freeman.

DeKay, W.T., & Buss, D.M. (1992). Human nature, individual differences and the importance of context: Perspectives from evolutionary psychology. *Current Directions in Psychological Science, 1*, 184–189.

DeLeon, P.H., Fox, R.E., & Graham, S.R. (1991). Prescription privileges: Psychology's next frontier? *American Psychologist, 46*, 384–393.

DeLong, F., & Levy, B.I. (1974). A model of attention describing the cognitive effects of marihuana. In L.L. Miller (Ed.), *Marijuana: Effects on human behavior*. New York: Academic Press.

DeMaris, A., & Rao, K.V. (1992). Premarital cohabitation and subsequent marital stability in the United States: A reassessment. *Journal of Marriage and the Family, 54*, 178–190.

Dember, W.N. (1965). The new look in motivation. *American Scientist, 53*, 409–427.

Dember, W.N., Earl, R.W., & Paradise, N. (1957). Response by rats to differential stimulus complexity. *Journal of Comparative and Physiological Psychology, 50*, 514–518.

Dement, W.C. (1965). An essay on dreams: The role of physiology in understanding their nature. In F. Barron (Ed.), *New directions in psychology* (Vol. 2). New York: Holt, Rinehart & Winston.

Dement, W.C. (1974). *Some must watch while some must sleep*. San Francisco: Freeman.

Dement, W.C., Cohen, H., Ferguson, J., & Zarcone, V. (1970). A sleep researcher's odyssey: The function and clinical significance of REM sleep. In L. Madow & L.H. Snow (Eds.), *The psychodynamic implications of the physiological studies of dreams*. Springfield, IL: Charles C. Thomas.

Dement, W.C., & Wolpert, E. (1958). Relation of eye movements, body motility, and external stimuli to dream content. *Journal of Experimental Psychology, 55*, 543–553.

Dennerstein, L., & Burrows, G.D. (1982). Hormone replacement therapy and sexuality in women. *Clinics in Endocrinology and Metabolism, 11*, 661–679.

Denney, N.W. (1984). A model of cognitive development across the life span. *Developmental Review 4*, 171–191.

Dennis, W., & Dennis, M.G. (1940). The effect of cradling practices upon the onset of walking in Hopi children. *Journal of Genetic Psychology, 56*, 77–86.

DePaulo, B.M., & Pfeifer, R.L. (1986). On-the-job experience and skill detecting deception. *Journal of Applied Social Psychology, 16*, 249–267.

Desiher, R.W. (1993). Gay and lesbian youth. In P.H. Tolan & B.J. Cohler (Eds.), *Handbook of clinical research and practice with adolescents* (pp. 249–280). New York: Wiley.

DeValois, R.L., & DeValois, K.K. (1975). Neural coding of color. In E.C. Carterette & M.P. Friedman (Eds.), *Handbook of perception: Seeing* (Vol. 5). New York: Academic Press.

Devane, W.A., Dysarz, F.A., III, Johnson, M.R., Melvin, L.S., & Howlett, A.C. (1988). Determination and characterization of a cannabinoid receptor in rat brain. *Molecular Pharmacology, 34*, 605-613.

Devane, W.A., Hanus, L., Breuer, A., Pertwee, R.G., Stevenson, L.A., Griffin, G., Gibson, D., Mandelbaum, A., Etinger, A., & Mechoulam, R. (1992). Isolation and structure of a brain constituent that binds to the cannabinoid receptor. *Science, 258*, 1946–1949.

DeWitt, K. (1991, August 28). Low test scores renew debate on TV. *New York Times*, Sec. B.

Diamond, J. (1994). Race without color. *Discover, 15*, 82–92.

Dickinson, A., & Mackintosh, N.J. (1978). Classical conditioning in animals. *Annual Review of Psychology, 29*, 587–612.

Diener, E., Sandvik, E., & Larsen, R.J. (1985). Age and sex effects for emotional intensity. *Developmental Psychology, 21*, 542–546.

Dietz, W.H., Jr. (1987). Childhood obesity. *Annals of the New York Academy of Sciences, 499*, 47–54.

Digman, J.M., & Takemoto-Chock, N.K. (1981). Factors in the natural language of personality: Re-analysis, comparison, and interpretation of six major studies. *Multivariate Behavioral Research, 16*, 149–170.

DiLalla, L.F., & Gottesman, I.I. (1991). Heterogeneity of causes for delinquency and criminality: Lifespan perspectives. *Development and Psychopathology, 1*, 339–349.

Dill, S. (1994, January 16). Babies' grunts may have meaning. *Associated Press*.

Dilon, S. (1994, October 21). Bilingual education effort is flawed, study indicates. *New York Times*, p. A20.

DiMatteo, M.R., & Friedman, H.S. (1982). *Social psychology and medicine*. Cambridge, MA: Oelgeschlager, Gunn, & Hain.

Dion, K.K. (1972). Physical attractiveness and evaluations of children's transgressions. *Journal of Personality and Social Psychology, 24*, 285–290.

Dion, K.K., Berscheid, E., & Walster, E. (1972). What is beautiful is good. *Journal of Personality and Social Psychology, 24*, 285–290.

Doherty, W.J., & Jacobson, N.S. (1982). Marriage and the family. In B.B. Wolman (Ed.), *Handbook of developmental psychology* (pp. 667–680). Englewood Cliffs, NJ: Prentice-Hall.

Dohrenwend, B.P., & Shrout, P.E. (1985). "Hassles" in the conceptualization and measurement of life stress variables. *American Psychologist, 40*, 780–785.

Dole, A.A. (1995). Why not drop race as a term? *American Psychologist, 50*, 40.

Domjan, M. (1987). Animal learning comes of age. *American Psychologist, 42*, 556–564.

Domjan, M., & Purdy, J.E. (in press). Animal research in psychology: More than meets the eye of the general psychology student. *American Psychologist.*

Donatelle, R.J., & Davis, L.G. (1993). *Access to health* (2nd ed.). Englewood Cliffs, NJ: Prentice-Hall.

Donchin, E. (1987). Can the mind be read in the brain waves? In F. Farley & C. Null (Eds.), *Using psychological science: Making the public case* (pp. 25–42). Washington, DC: Federation of Behavioral, Psychological, and Cognitive Sciences.

Doob, A.N., & Wood, L. (1972). Catharsis and aggression: The effects of annoyance and retaliation on aggressive behavior. *Journal of Personality and Social Psychology, 22*, 156–162.

Dotto, L. (1990). *Losing sleep*. New York: William Morrow.

Doty, R.L. (1989). Influence of age and age-related diseases on olfactory function. *Annals of the New York Academy of Sciences, 561*, 76–86.

Doty, R.L., Applebaum, S., Zusho, H., & Settle, R.G. (1985). Sex differences in odor identification ability: A cross-cultural analysis. *Neuropsychologia, 23*, 667–672.

Doty, R.L., Shaman, P., Applebaum, S.L., Giberson, R., Siksorski, L., & Rosenberg, L. (1984). Smell identification ability: Changes with age. *Science, 226*, 1441–1443.

Dovidio, J.F., Evans, N., & Tyler, R.B. (1986). Racial stereotypes: The contents of their cognitive representations. *Journal of Experimental Social Psychology, 22*, 22–37.

Downs, H. (1994, August 21). Must we age? *Parade Magazine*, pp. 3, 5, 7.

Drago, F., Pedersen, C.A., Caldwell, J.D., & Prange, A.J. (1986). Oxytocin potently enhances novelty-induced grooming behavior in the rat. *Brain Research, 368*, 287–295.

Druckman, D., & Bjork, R.A. (Eds.). (1991). *In the mind's eye: Enhancing human performance*. Washington, DC: National Academy Press.

Dumaine, B. (1990, May 7). Who needs a boss? *Fortune*, p. 52.

Dunkle, T. (1982, April). The sound of silence. *Science*, pp. 30–33.

Dweck, C.S., & Reppucci, N.D. (1973). Learned helplessness and reinforcement responsibility in children. *Journal of Personality and Social Psychology, 25*, 109–116.

Dyk, P.K. (1993). Anatomy, physiology and gender issues in adolescence. In T.P. Gullota, G.R. Adams, & R. Montemayor (Eds.), *Adolescent sexuality: Advances in adolescent development (pp. 35–36)*. Newbury Park, CA: Sage.

Eagly A.H. (1978). Sex differences in influenceability. *Psychological Bulletin, 85*, 86–116.

Eagly, A.H. (1983). Gender and social influence: A social psychological analysis. *American Psychologist, 38*, 971–981.

Eagly, A.H. (1987a). Reporting sex differences. *American Psychologist, 42*, 756–757.

Eagly, A.H. (1987b). *Sex differences in social behavior: A social-role interpretation*. Hillsdale, NJ: Erlbaum.

Eagly, A.H. (1990). On the advantages of reporting sex comparisons. *American Psychologist, 45*, 560–562.

Eagly, A.H., & Carli, L.L. (1981). Sex of researchers and sex-typed communications as determinants of sex differences in influenceability: A meta-analysis of social influence studies. *Psychological Bulletin, 90*, 1–20.

Eagly, A.H., & Crowley, M. (1986). Gender and helping behavior: A meta–analytic review of the social psychological literature. *Psychological Bulletin, 100*, 283-308.

Eagly, A.H., & Johnson, B.T. (1990). Gender and leadership style: A meta-analysis. *Psychological Bulletin, 108*, 233–256.

Eagly, A.H., & Karau, S.J. (1991). Gender and the emergence of leaders: A meta-analysis. *Journal of Personality and Social Psychology, 60*, 685–710.

Eagly, A.H., Karau, S.J., & Makhijani, M.G. (1995). Gender and the effectiveness of leaders: A meta-analysis. *Psychological Bulletin, 117*, 125–145.

Eagly, A.H., Makhijani, M.G., & Klonsky, B.G. (1992). Gender and the evaluation of leaders: A meta-analysis. *Psychological Bulletin, 111*, 3–22.

Eagly, A.H., & Steffen, V.J. (1986). Gender and aggressive behavior: A meta-analytic review of the social psychological literature. *Psychological Bulletin, 100*, 309–330.

East, P., & Felice, M.E. (1992). Pregnancy risk among the younger sisters of pregnant and childbearing adolescents. *Developmental and Behavioral Pediatrics, 13*, 128–136.

Eccles, J. Midgley, C., Wigfield, A., Buchanan, C.M., Reuman, D., Flanagan, C., & MacIver, D. (1993). Development during adolescence: The impact of stage-environment fit on young adolescents' experiences in school and families, *American Psychologist, 2*, 90–101.

Eccles, J.C. (1983). Attributional processes as mediators of sex differences in achievement. *Journal of Educational Equality and Leadership, 3*, 19–27.

Eckerman, C.O., Davis, C.C., & Didow, S.M. (1989). Toddlers' emerging ways of achieving social coordinations with a peer. *Child Development, 60*, 440–453.

Eibl-Eibesfeldt, I. (1972). *Love and hate*. New York: Holt, Rinehart & Winston.

Eimas, P.D., & Tartter, V.C. (1979). The development of speech perception. In H.W. Reese & L.P. Lipsitt (Eds.), *Advances in child development and behavior* (Vol. 13). New York: Academic Press.

Einhorn, H.J. (1980). Learning from experience and suboptimal rules in decision making. In T.S. Wallsten (Ed.), *Cognitive processes in choice and decision behavior*. Hillsdale, NJ: Erlbaum.

Eisenberg, N. (1989, April). *The development of prosocial moral reasoning in childhood and mid-adolescence*. Paper presented at the meeting of the Society for Research in Child Development, Kansas City, MO.

Eisenberg, N., & Lennon, R. (1983). Sex differences in empathy and related capacities. *Psychological Bulletin, 94*, 100–131.

Ekman, P. (1976). Movements with precise meanings. *Journal of Communication, Sum*, pp. 14–26.

Ekman, P. (1992). An argument for basic emotions. *Cognition and Emotion, 6*, 169–200.

Ekman, P., & Davidson, R.J. (1993). Voluntary smiling changes regional brain activity. *Psychological Science, 4*, 342–345.

Ekman, P., & Friesen, W.V. (1969). The repertoire of nonverbal behavior—Categories, origins, usage, and coding. *Semiotica, 1*, 49–98.

Ekman, P., & Friesen, W.V. (1971). Constants across cultures in the face and emotion. *Journal of Personality and Social Psychology, 17*, 124–129.

Ekman, P., & Friesen, W.V. (1975). *Unmasking the face*. Englewood Cliffs, NJ: Prentice-Hall.

Ekman, P., & Friesen, W.V. (1986). A new pan-cultural facial expression of emotion. *Motivation and Emotion, 10*, 159–168.

Ekman, P., Friesen, W.V., & Ellsworth, P. (1972). *Emotion in the human face*. Elmsford, NY: Pergamon.

Ekman, P., Friesen, W.V., O'Sullivan, M., Chan, A., Diacoyanni-Tarlatzis, I., Heider, K., Krause, R., LeCompte, W.A., Pitcairn, T., Ricci-Bitti, P.E., Scherer, K., Tomita, M., & Tzavaras, A. (1987). Universals and cultural differences in the judgments of facial expressions of emotion. *Journal of Personality and Social Psychology, 53*, 712–717.

Ekman, P., & O'Sullivan, M. (1991). Who can catch a liar? *American Psychologist, 46*, 913–920.

Ekman, P, Sorenson, E.R., & Friesen, W.V. (1969). Pancultural elements in facial displays of emotion. *Science, 164*, 86–88.

Elkin, I., Shea, T., Watkins, J.T., Imber, S.D., Sotsky, S.M., Collins, J.F., Glass, D.R., Pikonis, P.A, Leber, W.R., Docherty, J.P., Fiester, S.J., & Parloff, M.B. (1989). National Institute of Mental Health treatment of depression collaborative research program: General effectiveness of treatments. *Archives of General Psychiatry, 46*, 971–982.

Elkind, D. (1968). Cognitive development in adolescence. In J.F. Adams (Ed.), *Understanding adolescence*. Boston: Allyn & Bacon.

Elkind, D. (1969). Egocentrism in adolescence. In R.W. Grinder (Ed.), *Studies in adolescence* (2nd ed.). New York: Macmillan.

Ellis, A. (1973). *Humanistic psychotherapy: The rational emotive approach*. New York: Julian Press.

Ellis, A., & Harper, R.A. (1975). *A new guide to rational living*. North Hollywood, CA: Wilshire Book Co.

Emmorey, K. (1994). Sign language. In *Encyclopedia of human behavior* (Vol. 4, pp. 193–204). San Diego, CA: Academic Press.

Engel, J.F., Black, R.D., & Miniard, P.C. (1986). *Consumer behavior*. Chicago: Dryden Press.

Engen, T. (1982). *The perception of odors*. New York: Academic Press.

Eppley, K.R., Abrams, A.I., & Shear, J. (1989). Differential effects of relaxation techniques on trait anxiety: A meta-analysis. *Journal of Clinical Psychology, 45*, 957–974.

Epstein, A.N., Fitzsimmons, J.T., & Simons, B. (1969). Drinking caused by the intracranial injection of angiotensin into the rat. *Journal of Physiology, 200*, 98–100.

Epstein, R., Kirshnit, C.E., Lanza, R.P., & Rubin, L.C. (1984). "Insight" in the pigeon: Antecedents and determinants of an intelligent performance. *Nature (London), 308*, 61–62.

Epstein, S. (1962). The measurement of drive and conflict in humans: Theory and experiment. In M.R. Jones (Ed.), *Nebraska Symposium on Motivation*. Lincoln: University of Nebraska Press.

Epstein, S. (1994). Integration of the cognitive and the psychodynamic unconscious. *American Psychologist, 49*, 709–724.

Erdley, C.A., & D'Agostino, P.R. (1988). Cognitive and affective components of automatic priming effects. *Journal of Personality and Social Psychology, 54*, 741–747.

Erickson, D. (1990, November). Electronic earful: Cochlear implants sound better all the time. *Scientific American*, pp. 132, 134.

Ericsson, K.A., & Chase, W.G. (1982). Exceptional memory. *American Scientist, 70*, 607–615.

Erikson, E.H. (1963). *Childhood and society* (2nd ed.). New York: Norton.

Erikson, E.H. (1968). *Identity: Youth in crisis*. New York: Norton.

Eron, L.D. (1982). Parent-child interaction, television violence, and aggression of children. *American Psychologist, 37*, 197–211.

Evans, C. (1983). *Landscapes of the night: How and why we dream*. New York: Viking Press.

Evans, L.I., Rozelle, R.M., Lasater, T.M., Dembroski, R.M., & Allen, B.P. (1970). Fear arousal, persuasion and actual vs. implied behavioral change: New perspective utilizing a real-life dental hygiene program. *Journal of Personality and Social Psychology*, 16, 220–227.

Exner, J.E. (1986). *The Rorschach: A comprehensive system* (2nd ed., Vol. 1). New York: Wiley.

Exner, J.E., & Weiner, I.B. (1982). *The Rorschach: A comprehensive system*. New York: Wiley.

Eyer, J. (1977). Prosperity as a cause of death. *International Journal of Health Services, 7*, 125–150.

Eysenck, H.J. (1952). The effects of psychotherapy: An evaluation. *Journal of Consulting and Clinical Psychology, 16*, 319–324.

Eysenck, H.J. (1970). *The structure of human personality* (3rd ed.). London: Methuen.

Eysenck, H.J. (1985). *The decline and fall of the Freudian empire*. London: Pelican.

Eysenck, H.J. (1993). Commentary on Goldberg. *American Psychologist, 48*, 1299–1300.

Fairbairn, W.R.D. (1952). *Psychoanalytic studies of the personality*. London: Routledge & Kegan Paul. (from Westen, 1991)

Fallon, A., & Rozin, P. (1985). Sex differences in perceptions of desirable body states. *Journal of Abnormal Psychology, 84*, 102–105.

Falls, W.A., Miserendino, M.J.D., & Davis, M. (1992). Extinction of fear-potentiated startle: Blockade by infusion of an NMDA antagonist into the amygdala. *Journal of Neuroscience, 12*, 854–863.

Fantz, R.L., Fagan, J.F., & Miranda, S.B. (1975). Early visual selectivity. In L.B. Cohen & P. Salapatek (Eds.), *Infant perception: From sensation to cognition* (Vol. 1). New York: Academic Press.

Farah, M.J. (1992). Is an object an object an object? Cognitive and neuropsychological investigations of domain specificity in visual object recognition. *Current Directions in Psychological Science*, 164–169.

Farber, S. (1981, January). Telltale behavior of twins. *Psychology Today*, pp. 58–62, 79–80.

Farthing, C.W. (1992). *The psychology of consciousness*. Englewood Cliffs, NJ: Prentice-Hall.

Feinson, M.C. (1986). Aging widows and widowers: Are there mental health differences? *International Journal of Aging and Human Development, 23*, 244–255.

Feldman, R.E. (1968). Response to compatriot and foreigner who seek assistance. *Journal of Personality and Social Psychology, 10*, 202–214.

Ferguson, C.A., & Macken, M.A. (1983). The role of play in phonological development. In K.E. Nelson (Ed.), *Children's language* (Vol. 4). Hillsdale, NJ: Erlbaum.

Feshbach, S., & Weiner, B. (1982). *Personality*. Lexington, MA: D.C. Heath.

Festinger, L. (1957). *A theory of cognitive dissonance*. Evanston, IL: Row, Peterson.

Festinger, L., Schachter, S., & Back, K. (1950). *Social pressures in informal groups: A study of human factors in housing*. New York: Harper & Row.

Fiedler, F.E. (1967). *A theory of leadership effectiveness*. New York: McGraw-Hill.

Fiedler, F.E. (1981). Leadership effectiveness. *Behavioral Scientist, 24*, 619–623.

Field, T.M. (1986). Interventions for premature infants. *Journal of Pediatrics, 109*, 183–191.

Fischman, J. (1985, September). Mapping the mind. *Psychology Today*, pp. 18–19.

Fishbein, M., & Ajzen, I. (1975). *Belief, attitude, intention and behavior: An introduction to theory and research*. Reading, MA: Addison-Wesley.

Fisher, S., & Greenberg, R.P. (1985). *The scientific credibility of Freud's theories and therapy*. New York: Columbia University Press.

Fiske, S.T., & Taylor, S.E. (1984). *Social cognition*. Reading, MA: Addison-Wesley.

Fitch, J.H. (1962). Men convicted of sexual offenses against children. *British Journal of Criminology, 3*, 18–37.

Fitts, P.M., & Jones, R.E. (1947). *Psychological aspects of instrument display: I. Analysis of 270 "pilot-error" experiences in reading and interpreting aircraft instruments*. (Report No. TSEAA-694-12A). Dayton, OH: Aero Medical Laboratory, Air Material Command.

Fitzgerald, L.F. (1993). Sexual harassment. Violence against women in the workplace. *American Psychologist, 48*, 1070–1076.

Flavell, J.F. (1986). The development of children's knowledge about the appearance-reality distinction. *American Psychologist, 41*, 418–425.

Fleishman, E.A., & Harris, E.F. (1962). Patterns of leadership behavior related to employee grievances and turnover. *Personnel Psychology, 15*, 43–56.

Flexser, A.J., & Tulving, E. (1978). Retrieval independence in recognition and recall. *Psychological Review, 85*, 153–171.

Fliegler, L.A., & Bish, C.E. (1959). The gifted and talented. *Review of Educational Research, 29*, 408–450.

Flynn, J.R. (1984). The mean IQ of Americans: Massive gains 1932 to 1978. *Psychological Bulletin, 95*, 29–51.

Flynn, J.R. (1987). Massive IQ gains in 14 nations: What IQ tests really measure. *Psychological Bulletin, 101*, 171–191.

Flynn, J.R. (1988). The decline and rise of scholastic aptitude scores. *American Psychologist, 43*, 479–480.

Fogelman, E., & Wiener, V.L. (1985, August). The few, the brave, the noble. *Psychology Today*, pp. 60–65.

Ford, B.D. (1993, December). Emergenesis: An alternative and a confound. *American Psychologist*, p. 1294.

Foulkes, D. (1982). *Children's dreams*. New York: Wiley.

Fouts, R.S. (1973). Acquisition and testing of gestural signs in four young chimpanzees. *Science, 180*, 978–980.

Fox, A.J., & Adelstein, A.M. (1978). Occupational mortality: Work or way of life. *Journal of Epidemiology and Community Health, 32*, 73–78.

Fox, L.H. (1981). Identification of the academically gifted. *American Psychologist, 36*, 1103–1111.

Frank, J.D., & Frank, J.B. (1991). *Persuasion and healing* (3rd ed.). Baltimore: Johns Hopkins University Press.

Frager, R. (1970). Conformity and anticonformity in Japan. *Journal of Personality and Social Psychology, 15*, 203–210.

Fraser, C. (1971). Group risk-taking and group polarization. *European Journal of Social Psychology, 1*, 7–30.

Frederickson, N. (1986). Toward a broader conception of human intelligence. *American Psychologist, 41*, 445–452.

Freedman, J.L., & Fraser, S.C. (1966). Compliance without pressure: The foot-in-the-door technique. *Journal of Personality and Social Psychology, 4*, 195–202.

Freud, S. (1900). *The interpretation of dreams*. In J. Strachey (Ed.), *The standard edition of the complete psychological works of Sigmund Freud* (Vol. 5). London: Hogarth Press.

Freud, S. (1909). Analysis of a phobia in a five-year-old boy. In J. Strachey (Ed), *The standard edition of the complete psychological works of Sigmund Freud* (Vol. 10). London: Hogarth Press.

Freud, S. (1933). *New introductory lectures on psychoanalysis*. New York: Carlton House.

Freudenberger, H.J. (1983). The public lectures. *APA Monitor*, p. 24.

Freudenberger, H.J., & Richelson, G. (1980). *Burnout: The high cost of high achievement*. New York: Bantam.

Freudenheim, M. (1988, December 12). Workers' substance abuse is increasing, survey says. *New York Times*, Business Sec.

Frezza, M., di Padova, C., Pozzato, G., Terpin, M., Baraona, E., & Lieber, C.S. (1990). High blood alcohol levels in women: The role of decreased gastric alcohol dehydrogenase activity and first-pass metabolism. *New England Journal of Medicine, 322*, 95–99.

Friedman, E.S., Clark, D.B., & Gershon, S. (1992). Stress, anxiety, and depression: Review of biological, diagnostic, and nosologic issues. *Journal of Anxiety Disorders, 6*, 337–363.

Friedman, H.S., & Booth-Kewley, S. (1988). Validity of the Type A construct: A reprise. *Psychological Bulletin, 104*, 381–384.

Friedman, M., & Rosenman, R.H. (1959). Association of specific overt behavior patterns with blood and cardiovascular findings: Blood cholesterol level, blood clotting time, incidence of arcus senilis and clinical coronary artery disease. *JAMA, Journal of the American Medical Association, 169*, 1286–1296.

Frieze, I., Fisher, J, Hanusa, B., McHugh, M., & Valle, V. (1978). Attributions of success and failure in internal and external barriers to achievement in women. In J. Sherman & F. Denmark (Eds.), *Psychology of women: Future of research*. New York: Psychological Dimensions.

Friman, P.C., Allen, K.D., Kerwin, M.L.E., & Larzelere, R. (1993). Changes in modern psychology. *American Psychology, 48*, 658–664.

Froman, L. (1986). Work motivation. In H. Petri (Ed.), *Motivation*. Belmont, CA: Wadsworth.

Frumkin, B., & Ainsfield, M. (1977). Semantic and surface codes in the memory of deaf children. *Cognitive Psychology*, 9, 475–493.

Funder, D.C. (1987). Errors and mistakes: Evaluating the accuracy of social judgment. *Psychological Bulletin, 101*, 75–90. (from Funder, 1991)

Funder, D.C. (1989). Accuracy in personality judgment and the dancing bear. In D.M. Buss & N. Cantor (Eds.), *Personality psychology: Recent trends and emerging directions*. New York: Springer-Verlag. (from Funder, 1991)

Funder, D.C. (1991). Global traits: A neo-Allportian approach to personality. *Psychological Science, 2*, 31–39.

Funkenstein, D.H., King, S.H., & Drolette, M. (1953). The experimental evocation of stress. In *Symposium on Stress*. Division of Medical Sciences of the National Research Council and Army Medical Services Graduate School of Walter Reed Army Medical Center. Washington, DC: U.S. Government Printing Office.

Furstenberg, F.F., Jr., Brooks-Gunn, J., & Chase-Lansdale, L. (1989). Teenaged pregnancy and childbearing. *American Psychologist, 44*, 313–320.

Gable, M., Wilkens, H.T., Harris, L., & Feinberg, R. (1987). An evaluation of subliminally embedded sexual stimuli in graphics. *Journal of Advertising, 16*, 25–31.

Gaertner, S.L., & McLaughlin, J.P. (1983). Racial stereotypes: Associations and ascriptions of positive and negative characteristics. *Social Psychology Quarterly, 46*, 23–30.

Gagnon, J.H., Laumanm, E.O., Michael, R.T., & Kolata, G. (1994). *Sex in America: A definitive study*. Boston: Little, Brown.

Galef, B.G. (1993). Functions of social learning about food: A causal analysis of effects of diet novelty on preference transmission. *Animal Behaviour, 46*(2), 257–265.

Gallistel, C.R. (1981). Bell, Magendie, and the proposals to restrict the use of animals in neurobehavioral research. *American Psychologist, 36*, 357–360.

Gallup, G.G., Jr. (1985). Do minds exist in species other than our own? *Neuroscience and Biobehavioral Reviews, 9*, 631–641.

Gannon, L., Luchetta, T., Rhodes, K., Pardie, L., & Segrist, D. (1992). Sex bias in psychological research. *American Psychologist, 47*, 389–396.

Garber, H., & Heber, R. (1982). Modification of predicted cognitive development in high risk children through early intervention. In D.K. Detterman & R.J. Sternberg (Eds.), *How and how much can intelligence be increased?* (pp. 121–137). Norwood, NJ: Ablex.

Garcia, J., Hankins, W.G., & Rusiniak, K.W. (1974). Behavioral regulation of the milieu in man and rat. *Science, 185*, 824–831.

Garcia, J., Kimeldorf, D.J., Hunt, E.L., & Davies, B.P. (1956). Food and water consumption of rats during exposure to gamma radiation. *Radiation Research, 4*, 33–41.

Garcia, J., & Koelling, R.A. (1966). Relation of cue to consequence in avoidance learning. *Psychonomic Science, 4*, 123–124.

Gardner, H. (1982). *Developmental psychology* (2nd ed.). Boston: Little, Brown.

Gardner, H. (1983a). *Frames of mind: The theory of multiple intelligences*. New York: Basic Books.

Gardner, H. (1983b, May). Prodigies' progress. *Psychology Today*, pp. 75–79.

Gardner, H. (1993). *Multiple intelligences: The theory in practice*. New York: Basic Books.

Gardner, R.A., & Gardner, B.T. (1969). Teaching sign language to a chimpanzee. *Science, 165*, 664–672.

Gardner, R.A., & Gardner, B.T. (1975). Evidence for sentence constituents in the early utterances of child and chimpanzee. *Journal of Experimental Psychology: General, 3*, 244–267.

Gardner, R.A., & Gardner, B.T. (1977). Comparative psychology and language acquisition. In K. Salzinger & R. Denmark (Eds.), *Psychology: The state of the art*. New York: New York Academy of Sciences.

Garfield, S.L. (Ed.). (1983). Special section: Meta-analysis and psychotherapy. *Journal of Consulting and Clinical Psychology, 51*, 3–75.

Garfinkel, P.E., & Garner, D.M. (1982). *Anorexia nervosa: A multidimensional perspective*. New York: Brunner/Mazel.

Gazzaniga, M.S., Fendrich, R., & Wessinger, C.M. (1994). Blindsight reconsidered. *Current Directions in Psychological Science*, 93–96.

Geldard, F.A. (1972). *The human senses* (2nd ed.). New York: Wiley.

Gelman, D. (1990, October 29). A fresh take on Freud. *Newsweek*, pp. 84–86.

Gelman, D. (1994, June 13). Reliving the painful past. *Newsweek*, pp. 20–22.

Genesee, F. (1994). Bilingualism. In V.S. Ramachandran (Ed.), *Encyclopedia of human behavior* (Vol. 1, pp. 383–393). San Diego, CA: Academic Press.

Gentner, D., & Stevens, A.L. (1983). *Mental models*. Hillsdale, NJ: Erlbaum.

Gentry, J., & Eron, L.D. (1993). American Psychological Association Commission on Violence and Youth. *American Psychologist, 48*, 89.

Gergen, K.J. (1973). The codification of research ethics—views of a Doubting Thomas. *American Psychologist, 28*, 907–912.

Gershon, E.S. (1990). Genetics. In F.K. Goodwin & K.R. Jamison (Eds.), *Manic depressive illness* (pp. 373–401). New York: Oxford University Press.

Gesell, A., & Thompson, H. (1929). Learning and growth in identical infant twins: An experimental study by the method of co-twin control. *Genetic Psychology Monographs*, 6, 1–125.

Getzels, J.W. (1975). Problem finding and the inventiveness of solutions. *Journal of Creative Behavior*, 9, 12–18.

Getzels, J.W., & Jackson, P. (1962). *Creativity and intelligence*. New York: Wiley.

Giambra, L. (1974, December). Daydreams: The backburner of the mind. *Psychology Today*, pp. 66–68.

Gibbs, R. (1986). On the psycholinguistics of sarcasm. *Journal of Experimental Psychology: General, 115*, 3–15.

Gilbert, E.H., & DeBlassie, R.R. (1984). Anorexia nervosa: Adolescent starvation by choice. *Adolescence, 19*, 839–853.

Gilbert, L.A. (1994). Current perspectives on dual-career families. *Current Directions in Psychological Science, 3*, 101–105.

Gilligan, C. (1982). *In a different voice: Psychological theory and women's development*. Cambridge, MA: Harvard University Press.

Gilligan, C. (1992). *Joining the resistance: Girls' development in adolescence*. Paper presented at the meeting of the American Psychological Association, Montreal.

Gilligan, C., & Attanucci, J. (1988). Two moral orientations: Gender differences and similarities. *Merrill-Palmer Quarterly, 34*, 223–237.

Gilovich, T. (1991). *How we know what isn't so: The fallibility of human reason in everyday life*. New York: Free Press.

Ginsberg, H. (1972). *The myth of the deprived child*. Englewood Cliffs, NJ: Prentice-Hall.

Gist, R., & Stolz, S. (1982). Mental health promotion and the media. *American Psychologist, 37*, 1136–1139.

Glass, D.C. (1977). *Behavior patterns, stress, and coronary disease*. Hillsdale, NJ: Erlbaum.

Glenberg, A., Smith, S.M., & Green, C. (1977). Type I rehearsal: Maintenance and more. *Journal of Verbal Learning and Verbal Behavior, 16*, 339–352.

Glucksberg, S., & King, L.J. (1967). Motivated forgetting mediated by implicit verbal chaining: A laboratory analog of repression. *Science, 158*, 517–519.

Goldberg, L.R. (1981). Language and individual differences: The search for universals in personality lexicons. In L. Wheeler (Ed.), *Review of personality and social psychology* (Vol. 2, pp. 141–165). Beverly Hills, CA: Sage.

Goldberg, L.R. (1982). From ace to zombie: Some explorations in the language of personality: In C.D. Spielberger & J.N. Butcher (Eds.), *Advances in personality assessment* (Vol. 1, pp. 203–234). Hillsdale, NJ: Erlbaum.

Goldberg, L.R. (1993). The structure of phenotypic personality traits. *American Psychologist, 48*, 26–34.

Goldenbert, H. (1973) *Contemporary clinical psychology*. Monterey, CA: Brooks/Cole.

Goldman, M.S., Brown, S.A., Christiansen, B.A., & Smithy, G.T. (1991). Alcoholism and memory: Boradening the scope of alcohol-expectancy research. *Psychological Bulletin, 110*, 137–146.

Goldsmith, H.H., & Harman, C. (1994). Temperament and attachment: Individuals and relationships. *Current Directions in Psychological Sciences*, pp. 53–56.

Goldstein, A.P., & Segall, M.H. (1983). *Aggression in global perspective*. New York: Pergamon.

Goldstein, M., & Rodnick, E. (1975). The family's contribution to the etiology of schizophrenia: Current status. *Schizophrenia Bulletin, 14*, 48–63.

Gonzales, M.H., Davis, J.M., Loney, G.L., Lukens, C.K., & Junghans, C.M. (1983). Interactional approach to interpersonal attraction. *Journal of Personality and Social Psychology, 44*, 1192–1197.

Goodall, J. (1971). *In the shadow of man*. New York: Dell.

Goodman, P.S., Rukmini, D., & Hughson, T.L. (1988). Groups and productivity: Analyzing the effectiveness of self-managing teams. In J.P. Campbell, R.J. Campbell, & Associates (Eds.), *Productivity in organizations* (pp. 295–327). San Francisco: Jossey-Bass.

Goodwin, D.W., & Guze, S.B. (1984). *Psychiatric diagnosis* (3rd ed.). New York: Oxford University Press.

Gore, S., & Colten, M. (1991). Gender, stress, and distress: Social-relational influences. In J. Eckenrode (Ed.), *The social context of coping*. New York: Plenum.

Gottesman, I.I. (1991). *Schizophrenia genesis*. San Francisco: Freeman.

Gottesman, I.I., & Shields, J. (1982). *The schizophrenic puzzle*. New York: Cambridge University Press.

Graf, P. (1990). Life-span changes in implicit and explicit memory. (30th Annual Meeting of the Psychonomic Society Symposium: Implicit memory: Multiple perspectives [1989, Atlanta, GA].) *Bulletin of the Psychonomic Society, 28*, 353–358.

Graf, P., Squire, L.R., & Mandler, G. (1984). The information that amnesic patients do not forget. *Journal of Experimental Psychology: Learning, Memory and Cognition, 10*, 164–178.

Graham, J.R., & Lilly, R.S. (1984). *Psychological testing*. Englewood Cliffs, NJ: Prentice-Hall.

Graham, S. (1992). Most of the subjects were white and middle class. *American Psychologist, 47*, 629–639.

Grams, R., & Schwab, D.P. (1985). An investigation of systematic gender-related error in job evaluation. *Academy of Management Journal, 28*, 279–290.

Graves, L.M., & Powell, L.M. (1988). An investigation of sex discrimination in recruiters' evaluations of actual applicants. *Journal of Applied Psychology, 73*, 20–29.

Graziadei, P.P.C., Levine, R.R., & Graziadei, G.A.M. (1970). Plasticity of connections of the olfactory sensory neuron: Regeneration into the forebrain following bulbectomy in the neonatal mouse. *Neuroscience, 4*, 713–728.

Greaves, G.B. (1980). Psychosocial aspects of amphetamine and related substance abuse. In J. Caldwell (Ed.), *Amphetamines and related stimulants: Chemical, biological, clinical and sociological aspects*. Boca Raton, FL: CRC Press.

Green, L., Fry, A.F., & Myerson, J. (1994). Discounting of delayed rewards: A life-span comparison. 5, 33–36.

Green, P., Paelke, G., & Clack, K. (1989). *Instrument panel controls in sedans: What drivers prefer and why*. Ann Arbor, MI: UMTRI.

Greenberg, R., & Pearlman, C. (1967). Delirium tremens and dreaming. *American Journal of Psychiatry, 124*, 133–142.

Greene, R.L. (1987). Effects of maintenance rehearsal on human memory. *Psychological Bulletin, 102*, 403–413.

Greenfield, P.M., & Savage-Rumbaugh, E.S. (1984). Perceived variability and symbol usage: A common language-cognition interface in children and chimpanzees (Pan Troglodytes). *Journal of Comparative Psychology, 98*, 201–218.

Greenfield, P.M., & Smith, J.H. (1976). *The structure of communication in early language development*. New York: Academic Press.

Greenough, W.T. (1992). Animal rights replies distort(ed) and misinform(ed). *Psychological Science, 3*, 142.

Greenstein, T.H. (1993). Maternal employment and child behavioral outcomes. *Journal of Family Issues, 14*, 323–354.

Greenwald, A.G., Spangenberg, E.R., Pratkanis, A.R., & Eskenazi, J. (1991). Double-blind tests of subliminal self-help audiotapes. *Psychological Science, 2*, 119-122.

Gregory, R.L. (1978). Eye and brain: The psychology of seeing (3rd ed.). New York: McGraw-Hill.

Greif, E.B., & Ulman, K.J. (1982). The psychological impact of menarche on early adolescent females: A review of the literature. *Child Development, 53*, 1413–1430.

Grilo, C.M., & Pogue-Geile, M.F. (1991). The nature of environmental influences on weight and obesity: A behavior genetic analysis. *Psychological Bulletin, 110*, 520–537.

Grinker, R.R., & Spiegel, J.P. (1945). *War neurosis*. Philadelphia: Blakiston.

Grinspoon, L., Ewalt, J.R., & Shader, R.I. (1972). *Schizophrenia: Pharmacotherapy and psychotherapy*. Baltimore: Williams & Wilkins.

Groth, A.N., & Birnbaum, J.J. (1979). *Men who rape: The psychology of the offender*. New York: Plenum.

Groth, A.N., Burgess, A.W., & Maelstrom, L.L. (1977). Rape: Power, anger and sexuality. *American Journal of Psychiatry, 134*, 1239–1243.

Gruber, J.E., & Bjorn, L. (1986). Women's responses to sexual harassment: An analysis of sociocultural, organizational, and personal resource models. *Social Science Quarterly, 67*, 814–826.

Gruetzner, H. (1988). *Alzheimer's: A caregiver's guide and sourcebook*. New York: Wiley.

Guérin, D. (1994). *Fussy infants at risk*. Paper presented at the meeting of the American Psychological Association, Los Angeles.

Guilford, J.P. (1961). Factorial angles to psychology. *Psychological Review, 68*, 1–20.

Guilford, J.P. (1967). *The nature of human intelligence*. New York: McGraw-Hill.

Gunderson, J.G. (1984). *Borderline personality disorder*. Washington, DC: American Psychiatric Press.

Gunderson, V.M., Yonas, A., Sargent, P.L., & Grant-Webster, K.S. (1993). Infant macaque monkeys respond to pictorial depth. *Psychological Science, 4(2)* 93–98.

Gunne, L.M., & Anggard, E. (1972). Pharmical kinetic studies with amphetamines—relationship to neuropsychiatric disorders. *International Symposium on Pharmical Kinetics*, Washington, DC.

Gurman, A.S., & Kniskern, D.P. (Eds.). (1991). *Handbook of family therapy* (Vol. 2). New York: Brunner/Mazel.

Gurman, A.S., Kniskern, D.P., & Pinsof, W.M. (1986). Research on the process and outcome of marital and family therapy. In S.L. Garfield & A.E. Bergin (Eds.), *Handbook of psychotherapy and behavior change* (3rd ed., pp. 565–624). New York: Wiley.

Guthrie, E.R. (1952). *The psychology of learning* (rev. ed.). New York: Harper & Row.

Gwirtsman, H.E. (1984). Bulimia in men: Report of three cases with neuro-endocrine findings. *Journal of Clinical Psychiatry, 45*, 78–81.

Haber, R.N. (1969, April). Eidetic images. *Scientific American*, pp. 36–44.

Haberman, C. (1994, October 12). Bringing up baby: Job for Kibbutz? *New York Times*, p. A6.

Hack, M., Breslau, N., Weissman, B., Aram, D., Klein, N., & Borawski, E. (1991). Effect of very low birth weight and subnormal head size on cognitive abilities at school age. *New England Journal of Medicine, 325*, 231–237.

Hackett, R.D. (1989). Work attitudes and employee absenteeisms: A synthesis of the literature. *Journal of Occupational Psychology, 62*, 235–248.

Hackman, J.R., & Oldham, G.R. (1976). Motivation through the design of work: Test of a theory. *Organizational Behavior and Human Performance, 16*, 250–279.

Haefele, J.W. (1962). *Creativity and innovation*. New York: Reinhold.

Hakuta, K. (1987). Degree of bilingualism and cognitive ability in mainland and Puerto Rican children [Special issue: Schools and development]. *Child Development, 58*, 1372–1388.

Hall, E.T. (1966). *The hidden dimension*. New York: Doubleday.

Hall, G.S. (1904). *Adolescence: Its psychology and its relations to physiology, anthropology, sex, crime, religion and education* (Vol. 1). New York: Appleton-Century-Crofts.

Hall, J.A. (1978). Gender effects in decoding nonverbal cues. *Psychological Bulletin, 85*, 845–875.

Hall, J.A. (1984). *Nonverbal sex differences: Communication accuracy and expressive style*. Baltimore: Johns Hopkins University Press.

Hall, J.A., & Halberstadt, A.G. (1986). Smiling and gazing. In J.S. Hyde & M.D. Linn (Eds.), *The psychology of gender: Advances through meta-analysis* (pp. 136–158). Baltimore: Johns Hopkins University Press.

Hallahan, D., Kauffman, J., & Lloyd, J. (1985). *Introduction to learning disabilities* (2nd ed.). Englewood Cliffs, NJ: Prentice-Hall.

Halpern, D.F. (1992). *Sex differences in cognitive abilities* (2nd ed.). Hillsdale, NJ: Erlbaum.

Hamer, D.H., Hu, S., Magnuson, V.L., & Hu, N. (1993). A linkage between DNA markers on the X chromosome and male sexual orientation. *Science, 261*, 321–327.

Hamilton, D.L., & Bishop, G.D. (1976). Attitudinal and behavioral effects of initial integration of white suburban neighborhoods. *Journal of Social Issues, 32*, 47–67.

Hamilton, J.A., Haier, R.J., & Buchsbaum, M.S. (1984). Intrinsic enjoyment and boredom coping scales: Validation with personality evoked potential and attentional measures. *Personality and Individual Differences, 5*(2), 183–393.

Hammen, C.L. (1985). Predicting depression: A cognitive-behavioral perspective. In P. Kendall (Ed.), *Advances in cognitive-behavioral research and therapy* (Vol. 4). New York: Academic Press.

Hampson, E., & Kimura, D. (1992). Sexual differentiation and hormonal influences on cognitive function in humans. In J.B. Becker, S.M. Breedlove, & D. Crews (Eds.), *Behavioral endocrinology*. Cambridge, MA: MIT Press.

Hampson, J., & Nelson, K. (1993). The relation of maternal language to variation in rate and style of language acquisition. *Journal of Child Language, 20*, 313–342.

Hansen, R.D. (1984). Person perception. In A.S. Kahn (Ed.), *Social psychology*. Dubuque, IA: Wm. C. Brown.

Hanson, D.J. (1980). Relationship between methods and findings in attitude-behavior research, *Psychology, 17*, 11–13.

Harburg, E., DiFranceisco, W., Webster, D.W., Gleiberman, L., & Schork, A. (1990). Familial transmission of alcohol use: II. Imitation of and aversion to parent drinking (1960) by adult offspring (1977)—Tecumseh, Michigan. *Journal of Studies on Alcohol, 51*, 245–256.

Harburg, E., Gleiberman, L., DiFranceisco, W., Schork, A. & Weissfeld, L.A. (1990). Familial transmission of alcohol use: III. Impact of imitation/non-imitation of parent alcohol use (1960) on the sensible/problem drinking of their offspring (1977). *British Journal of Addiction, 85*, 1141–1155.

Hardaway, R.A. (1991). Subliminally activated symbiotic fantasies: Facts and artifacts. *Psychological Bulletin, 107*, 177–195.

Hare, R.D. (1983). Diagnosis of antisocial personality disorder in two prison populations. *American Journal of Psychiatry, 140*, 887–890.

Harlow, H.F. (1949). The formation of learning sets. *Psychological Review, 56*, 51–65.

Harlow, H.F. (1958). The nature of love. *American Psychologist, 13*, 673–685.

Harlow, H.F., & Zimmerman, R.R. (1959). Affectional responses in the infant monkey. *Science, 130*, 421–432.

Harrell, R.F., Woodyard, E., & Gates, A.I. (1955). *The effect of mother's diet on the intelligence of the offspring*. New York: Teacher's College, Columbia Bureau of Publications.

Harrington, D.M., Block, J.H., & Block, J. (1987). Testing aspects of Carl Rogers's theory of creative environments: Child-rearing antecedents of creative potential in young adolescents. *Journal of Personality and Social Psychology, 52*, 851–856.

Harris, J.R., & Liebert, R.M. (1991). *The child: A contemporary view of development* (3rd ed.). Englewood Cliffs, NJ: Prentice-Hall.

Hartmann, E. (1984). *The nightmare*. New York: Basic Books.

Hartmann, P., & Husband, C. (1971). The mass media and racial conflict. *Race, 12*, 267–282.

Hass, R.G. (1981). Effects of source characteristics on cognitive responses in persuasion. In R.E. Petty & J.T. Cacioppo (Eds.), *Attitudes and persuasion: Classic and contemporary approaches*. Dubuque, IA: Wm. C. Brown.

Hathaway, S.R., & McKinley, J.C. (1942). A multiphasic personality schedule (Minnesota): III. The measurement of symptomatic depression. *Journal of Psychology, 14*, 73–84.

Hauri, P. (1970). Evening activity, sleep mentation, and subjective sleep quality. *Journal of Abnormal Psychology, 76*, 270–275.

Hauri, P. (1982). *Sleep disorders*. Kalamazoo, MI: Upjohn.

Hayden, T., & Mischel, W. (1976). Maintaining trait consistency in the resolution of behavioral inconsistency: The wolf in sheep's clothing? *Journal of Personality, 44*, 109–132.

Hayes, C., & Hayes, K. (1951). The intellectual development of a home-raised chimpanzee. *Proceedings of the American Philosophical Society, 95*, 105–109.

Hayes, J.R., & Simon, H.A. (1976).The understanding process: Problem isomorphs. *Cognitive Psychology, 8*, 165–190.

He, L. (1987). Involvement of endogenous opioid peptides in acupuncture analgesia. *Pain, 31*, 99–122.

Hearst, E. (1975). The classical-instrumental distinction: Reflexes, voluntary behavior, and categories of associative learning. In W.K. Estes (Ed.), *Handbook of learning and cognitive processes: Vol. 2. Conditioning and behavior theory*. Hillsdale, NJ: Erlbaum.

Heath, R.C. (1972). Pleasure and brain activity in man. *Journal of Nervous and Mental Disease, 154*, 3-18.

Heath, S.B. (1989). Oral and literate traditions among black Americans living in poverty. *American Psychologist, 44*, 367–373.

Heatherton, T.F., & Baumeister, R.F. (1991). Binge eating as escape from self-awareness. *Psychological Bulletin, 110*, 86–108.

Hebb, D.O. (1955). Drives and the CNS (conceptual nervous system). *Psychological Review, 62*, 243–254.

Hebb, D.O. (1958). The motivating effects of exteroceptive stimulation. *American Psychologist, 13*, 109–113.

Heber, R., Garber, H., Harrington, S., & Hoffman, C. (1972). *Rehabilitation of families at risk for mental retardation*. Madison: University of Wisconsin, Rehabilitation Research and Training Center in Mental Retardation.

Hechtman, L. (1989). Teenage mothers and their children: Risks and problems: A review. *Canadian Journal of Psychology, 34*, 569–575.

Heider, E.R. (1972). Universals in color naming and memory. *Journal of Experimental Psychology, 93*, 10–20.

Heider, E.R., & Oliver, D.C. (1972). The structure of the color space in naming and memory in two languages. *Cognitive Psychology, 3*, 337–354.

Heider, F. (1958). *The psychology of interpersonal relations*. New York: Wiley.

Heiman, J.R. (1977). A psychophysiological exploration of sexual arousal patterns in females and males. *Psychophysiology, 14*, 266–274.

Hellige, J.B. (1990). Hemispheric asymmetry. *Annual Review of Psychology, 41*, 55–80.

Helmreich, R., & Spence, J. (1978). The Work and Family Orientation Questionnaire: An objective instrument to assess components of achievement motivation and scientific attainment. *Personality and Social Psychology Bulletin, 4*, 222-226.

Helms, J.E. (1992). Why is there no study of cultural equivalence in standardized cognitive ability testing? *American Psychologist, 47*, 1083–1101.

Helson, R. (1971). Women mathematicians and the creative personality. *Journal of Consulting and Clinical Psychology, 36*, 210–220.

Henderson, N.D. (1982). Human behavior genetics. *Annual Review of Psychology, 33*, 403–440.

Hendrick, S., & Hendrick, C. (1992). *Liking, loving and relating* (2nd ed.). Pacific Grove, CA: Brooks/Cole.

Henriques, J.B., & Davidson, R.J. (1990). Regional brain electrical asymmetries discriminate between previously depressed and healthy control subjects. *Journal of Abnormal Psychology, 99*, 22–31.

Herberg, L.J., & Rose, I.C. (1990). Excitatory amino acid pathways in brain stimulation reward. *Behavioural Brain Research, 39*, 230–239.

Herdt, G., & Boxer, A. (1993). *Children of horizons*. Boston: Beacon Press.

Hergenhahn, B.R., & Olson, M.H. (1993). *An introduction to theories of learning* (4th ed.). Englewood Cliffs, NJ: Prentice-Hall.

Herkenham, M., Lynn, A.B., Little, M.D., Johnson, M.R., Melvin, L.S., deCosta, B.R., & Rice, K.C. (1990). Cannabinoid receptor localization in brain. *Proceedings of the National Academy of Sciences of the U.S.A., 87*, 1932–1936.

Herman, C.P., Policy, J., & Silver, R. (1979). Effects of an observer on eating behavior: The induction of sensible eating. *Journal of Personality, 47*, 85-99.

Herman, J., & Hirschman, L. (1981). Families at risk for father–daughter incest. *American Journal of Psychiatry, 38*, 967–970.

Herman, L.M., Richards, D.G., & Wolz, J.P. (1984). Comprehension of sentences by bottlenosed dolphins. *Cognition, 16*, 1–90.

Heron, W. (1957). The pathology of boredom. *Scientific American, 199*, 52–56.

Herrnstein, R.J., & Mazur, J.E. (1987). Making up our minds: A new model of economic behavior. *The Sciences, 27*, 40–47.

Herrnstein, R.J., & Murray, C. (1994). *The bell curve*. New York: Free Press.

Hersey, P., & Blanchard, K.H. (1988). *Management of organizational behavior*. Englewood Cliffs, NJ: Prentice-Hall.

Hersher, L. (Ed.). (1970). *Four psychotherapies*. New York: Appleton-Century-Crofts.

Heston, L.L. (1966). Psychiatric disorders in foster-home-reared children of schizophrenic mothers. *British Journal of Psychiatry, 112*, 819–825.

Heyes, C.M., Jaldow, E., & Dawson, G.R. (1993). Observational extinction: Observation of nonreinforced responding reduces resistance to extinction in rats. *Animal Learning & Behavior, 21*, 221–225.

Hilgard, E.R. (1965). *Hypnotic susceptibility*. New York: Harcourt Brace Jovanovich.

Hilgard, E.R. (1974, November). Hypnosis is no mirage. *Psychology Today*, pp. 121–128.

Hilgard, E.R. (1980). Consciousness in contemporary psychology. *Annual Review of Psychology, 31*, 1–26.

Hilgard, E.R. (1986). *Divided consciousness: Multiple controls in human thought and action*. New York: Wiley.

Hilgard, E.R., Hilgard, J.R., & Kaufmann, W. (1983). *Hypnosis in the relief of pain* (2nd ed.). Los Altos, CA: Kaufmann.

Hillier, L., Hewitt, K.L., & Morrongiello, B.A. (1992). Infants' perception of illusions in sound locations: Researching to sounds in the dark. *Journal of Experimental Child Psychology, 53*, 159–179.

Hobbs, N., & Robinson, S. (1982). Adolescent development and public policy. *American Psychologist, 37*, 212–223.

Hobson, J.A., & McCarley, R. (1977). The brain as a dream state generator: An activation–synthesis hypothesis of the dream process. *American Journal of Psychiatry, 134*, 1335–1348.

Hochberg, J. (1978). *Perception* (2nd ed.). Englewood Cliffs, NJ: Prentice-Hall.

Hochschild, A.R. (1983). *The managed heart*. Berkeley: University of California Press.

Hodges, J.R., Salmon, D.P., & Butters, N. (1992). Semantic memory impairment in Alzheimer's disease: Failure of access or degraded knowledge? *Neuropsychologia, 30*, 301–314.

Hofferth, S.L., Brayfield, A., Beich, S., & Holcomb, P. (1990). *National Child Care Survey*. Washington, DC: Urban Institute.

Hoffman, H.S., & Depaulo, P. (1977). Behavioral control by an imprinting stimulus. *American Scientist, 65*, 58–66.

Hoffman, L. (1989). Effects of maternal employment in the two-parent family. *American Psychologist, 44*, 283–292.

Hoffman, L.W. (1977). Changes in family roles, socialization, and sex differences. *American Psychologist, 32*, 644-657.

Hoffman, M. (1991). Unraveling the genetics of fragile X syndrome. *Science, 252*, 1070.

Hoffman, M.L. (1977). Personality and social development. *Annual Review of Psychology, 28*, 295–321.

Hofstede, G. (1980). *Culture's consequences*. Beverly Hills, CA: Sage.

Hogan, R., & Schroeder, D. (1981, July). Seven biases in psychology. *Psychology Today*, pp. 8–14.

Holland, C.A., & Rabbitt, P.M.A. (1990). Ageing memory: Use versus impairment. *British Journal of Psychology, 82*, 29–38.

Hollister, L.E. (1986). Health aspects of cannibis. *Pharmacological Reviews, 38*, 1–20.

Holmes, D.S. (1984). Meditation and somatic arousal reduction: A review of the experimental evidence. *American Psychologist, 39*, 1–12.

Holmes, T.H., & Rahe, R.H. (1967). The social readjustment rating scale. *Journal of Psychosomatic Research, 11*, 213.

Holzman, D. (1986, September 15). An obsessive trouble in mind. *Insight*, p. 62.

Holyoak, K.J., & Spellman, B.A. (1993). Thinking. *Annual Review of Psychology, 44*, 265–315.

Honeybourne, C., Matchett, G., & Davey, G.C. (1993). Expectancy models of laboratory preparedness effects: A UCS-expectancy bias in phylogenetic and ontogenetic fear-relevant stimuli. *Behavior Therapy, 24*, 253–264.

Honts, C.R. (1994). Psychophysiological detection of deception. *Current Directions in Psychological Science, 3*, 77–82.

Horn, J. (1983). The Texas Adoption Project: Adopted children and their intellectual resemblance to biological and adoptive parents. *Child Development, 54*, 268–275.

Horney, K. (1937). *The neurotic personality of our time*. New York: Norton.

Horowitz, F.D., & O'Brien, M. (Eds.). (1985). *The gifted and talented: Developmental perspectives*. Washington, DC: American Psychological Association.

Horowitz, F.D., & O'Brien, M. (1986). Gifted and talented children: State of knowledge and directions for research. *American Psychologist, 41*, 1147–1152.

Horvath, F.S. (1977). The effect of selected variables on interpretation of polygraph records. *Journal of Applied Psychology, 62*, 127–136.

Hovland, C.I., & Sears, R.R. (1940). Minor studies in aggression: VI. Correlation of lynchings with economic indices. *Journal of Abnormal and Social Psychology*, 9, 301–310.

Howard, K.I., Kopta, S.M., Krause, M.S., & Orlinsky, D.E. (1986). The does-effect relationship in psychotherapy. *American Psychologist, 41*, 159–164.

Hubel, D.H. (1963). The visual cortex of the brain. *Scientific American, 209*, 54–62.

Hubel, D.H., & Livingstone, M.S. (1987). Segregation of form, color, and stereopsis in primate area 18. *Journal of Neuroscience*, pp. 3378–3415.

Hubel, D.H., & Livingstone, M.S. (1990). Color and contrast sensitivity in the lateral geniculate body and primary visual cortex of the macaque monkey. *Journal of Neuroscience, 10*, 2223–2237.

Hubel, D.H., & Wiesel, T.N. (1959). Receptive fields of single neurons in the cat's striate cortex. *Journal of Physiology (London), 148*, 574–591.

Hubel, D.H., & Wiesel, T.N. (1979). Brain mechanisms of vision. *Scientific American, 241*, 150–162.

Hudspeth, A.J. (1983). The hair cells of the inner ear. *Scientific American, 248*, 54–64.

Huebner, A.M., Garrod, A., & Snarey, J. (1990). *Moral development in Tibetan Buddhist monks: A cross-cultural study of adolescents and young adults in Nepal*. Paper presented at the meeting of the Society for Research in Adolescence, Atlanta, GA.

Hummel, J.E., & Biederman, I. (1992). Dynamic binding in a neural network for shape recognition. *Psychological Review*, 99, 480–517.

Humphrey, G.K., Goodale, M.A., & Gurnsey, R. (1991). Orientation discrimination in a visual form agnosic: Evidence from the McCollou gh effect. *Psychological Science, 2*(5), 331–335.

Humphreys, L.G. (1992). Commentary: What both critics and users of ability tests need to know. *Psychological Science, 3*, 271–274.

Hunt, M. (1974). *Sexual behavior in the 1970s*. Chicago: Playboy Press.

Huston, A.C., Watkins, B.A., & Kunkel, D. (1989). Public policy and children's television. *American Psychologist, 44*, 424–433.

Huttenlocher, J., Smiley, P., & Charney, R. (1983). Emergence of action categories in the child: Evidence from verb meanings. *Psychological Review*, 90, 72–93.

Hyde, J.S. (1982). *Understanding human sexuality* (2nd ed.). New York: McGraw-Hill.

Hyde, J.S., Fennema, E., & Lamon, S.J. (1990). Gender differences in mathematics performance: A meta-analysis. *Psychological Bulletin, 107*, 139–155.

Hyde, J.S., & Linn, M.C. (1988). Gender differences in verbal ability: A meta-analysis. *Psychological Bulletin, 104*, 53–69.

Iaffaldano, M.T., & Muchinsky, P.M. (1985). Job satisfaction and job performance: A meta-analysis. *Psychological Bulletin, 97*, 251–273.

Inhelder, B., &Piaget, J. (1958). *The growth of logical thinking from childhood to adolescence* (A. Parson & S. Milgram, Trans.). New York: Basic Books.

Insel, T.R., & Harbaugh, C.R. (1989). Lesions of the hypothalamic paraventricular nucleus disrupt the initiation of maternal behavior. *Physiology & Behavior, 45*, 1033–1041.

Irwin, R.J., & Whitehead, P.R. (1991). Towards an objective psychophysics of pain. *Psychological Science, 2*, 230–235.

Isen, A.M., & Levin, P.F. (1972). The effect of feeling good on helping: Cookies and kindness. *Journal of Personality and Social Psychology, 21*, 384–388.

Ivancevich, J.M., & Matteson, M.T. (1980). *Stress and work: A managerial perspective*. Glenview, IL: Scott, Foresman.

Izard, C.E. (1971). *The face of emotion*. New York: Appleton-Century-Crofts.

Izard, C.E. (1980). Cross-cultural perspectives on emotion and emotion communication. In H.C. Triandis & W.J. Lonner (Eds.), *Handbook of cross-cultural psychology* (Vol. 3). Boston: Allyn & Bacon.

Izard, C.E. (1982). The psychology of emotion comes of age on the coattails of Darwin. *Contemporary Psychology, 27*, 426–429.

Jacklin, C.N. (1989). Female and male: Issues of gender. *American Psychologist, 44*, 127–133.

Jacobs, G.H. (1993). The distribution and nature of color vision among the mammals. *Biological Review of the Cambridge Philosophical Society*, 68, 413–471.

Jacobs, M.K., & Goodman, G. (1989). Psychology and self-help groups: Predictions on a partnership. *American Psychologist, 44*, 536–545.

Jacobsen, P.B., Bovbjerg, D.H., Schwartz, M.D., & Andrykowski, M.A. (1994). Formation of food aversions in patients receiving repeated infusions of chemotherapy. *Behaviour Research & Therapy*, 38, 739–748.

Jamal, M. (1981). Shift work related to job attitudes social participation and withdraw behavior: A study of nurses and industrial workers. *Personnel Psychology, 34*, 535–547.

James, W. (1890). *The principles of psychology*. New York: Holt.

Jamison, K.R. (1989). Mood disorders and patterns of creativity in British writers and artists. *Psychiatry, 52*, 125–134.

Janis, I. (1982). *Groupthink: Psychological studies of policy decisions and fiascoes* (2nd ed.). Boston: Houghton Mifflin.

Janis, I.L., Mahl, G.G., & Holt, R.R. (1969). *Personality: Dynamics, development and assessment*. New York: Harcourt Brace Jovanovich.

Janofsky, M. (1994, December 13). Survey reports more drug use by teenagers. *New York Times*, p. A1.

Jenkins, C.D. (1988). Epidemiology of cardiovascular diseases. *Journal of Consulting and Clinical Psychology*, 56, 324–332.

Jenkins, G.D., Jr., & Gupta, N. (1983, August). *Success and tensions in a "new design" organization*. Paper presented at the meeting of the American Psychological Association, Anaheim, CA.

Jensen, A.R. (1969). How much can we boost IQ and scholastic achievement? *Harvard Educational Review, 39*, 1–123

Jensen, A.R. (1992). Commentary: Vehicles of *g*. *Psychological Science, 3*, 275–278.

Jensen, A.R. (1995). Psychological research on race differences. *American Psychologist, 50*, 41–42.

Jirikowski, G.F., Caldwell, J.D., Pilgrim, C., Stumpf, W.E., & Pedersen, C.A. (1989). Changes in immunostaining for oxytocin in the forebrain of the female rate during late pregnancy, parturition and early lactation. *Cell Tissue Research, 256*, 411–417.

Johansson, G. (1975). Visual motion perception. *Scientific American, 232*, 76–88.

Johansson, G., von Hofsten, C., & Jansson, G. (1980). Event perception. *Annual Review of Psychology, 31*, 27–64.

John, O.P. (1988, April). *Personality assessment in the 1990s: Issues and challenges*. Paper presented at the meeting on Emerging Issues in Personality Psychology, University of Michigan.

Johnson, C., Lewis, C., Love, S., & Stuckey, M. (1984). Incidence and correlates of bulimic behavior in a female high school population. *Journal of Youth and Adolescence, 13*, 15–26.

Johnson, D. (1990). Can psychology ever be the same again after the human genome is mapped? *Psychological Science, 1*, 331–332.

Johnson, D.W., Johnson, R.T., & Maruyama, G. (1984). Effects of cooperative learning: A meta-analysis. In N. Miller & M.B. Brewer (Eds.), *Groups in contact: The psychology of desegregation* (pp. 187–212). New York: Academic Press.

Johnson, H.G., Ekman, P., & Friesen, W.V. (1975). Communicative body movements: American emblems. *Semiotica, 15*, 335–353.

Johnson, M.K., & Raye, C.L. (1981). Reality monitoring. *Psychological Review, 88*, 67–85.

Johnson-George, C., & Swap, W. (1982). Measurement of specific interpersonal trust: Construction and validation of a scale to assess trust in a specific order. *Journal of Personality and Social Psychology, 43*, 1306–1317.

Johnson-Laird, P.N., & Wason, P.C. (1970). A theoretical analysis of insight into a reasoning task. *Cognitive Psychology, 1*, 134–148.

Jones, C.P., & Adamson, L.B. (1987). Language use and mother-child-sibling interactions. *Child Development, 58*, 356–366.

Jones, E.E., & Nisbett, R.E. (1972). The actor and the observer: Divergent perceptions of the causes of behavior. In E.E. Jones, D.E. Kanouse, H.H. Kelley, R.E. Nisbett, S. Valins, & B. Weiner (Eds.), *Attribution: Perceiving the causes of behavior*. Morristown, NJ: General Learning Press.

Jones, M.C. (1924). Elimination of children's fears. *Journal of Experimental Psychology, 7*, 381–390.

Jones, R. (1978). Marihuana: Human effects. In L.L. Iverson, S. Iverson, & S.H. Snyder (Eds.), *Handbook of psychopharmacology* (Vol. 12). New York: Plenum.

Jones, R.T., & Benowitz, N. (1976). The 30-day trip: Clinical studies of cannabis tolerance and dependence. In M.C. Braude & S. Szara (Eds.), *Pharmacology of marijuana* (Vol. 2). New York: Academic Press.

Jourard, S.M. (1964). *The transparent self*. Princeton, NJ: Van Nostrand Reinhold.

Julius, M., Harburg, E., Cottington, E.M., & Johnson, E.H. (1986). Anger-coping types, blood pressure, and all-cause mortality: A follow-up in Tecumseh, Michigan (1971–1983). *American Journal of Epidemiology, 124*, 220–233.

Kagan, J., Reznick, J.S., Snidman, N., Gibbons, J., & Johnson, M.O. (1988). Childhood derivatives of inhibition and lack of inhibition to the unfamiliar. *Child Development, 59*, 1580–1589.

Kagan, J., & Snidman, N. (1991). Infant predictors of inhibited and uninhibited profiles. *Psychological Science, 2*(1), 40–44.

Kagan, J., Snidman, N., & Arcus, D.M. (1992). Initial reactions to unfamiliarity. *Current Directions, 1*(6), 171–174.

Kalat, J.W. (1988). Biological psychology (3rd ed.). Belmont, CA: Wadsworth.

Kales, A., Wilson, T., Kales, J.D., Jacobson, A., Paulson, M.J., Kollar, E., & Walter, R.D. (1976). Measurements of all night sleep in normal elderly persons: Effects of aging. *Journal of the American Geriatrics Society, 15*, 405–414.

Kales, J.D., Kales, A., Soldatos, C.R., Caldwell, A.B., Charney, D.S., & Martin, E.D. (1980). Night terrors: Clinical characteristics and personality patterns. *Archives of General Psychiatry, 137*, 1413–1417.

Kamin, L.J. (1969). Selective association and conditioning. In N.J. Mackintosh & W.K. Honig (Eds.), *Fundamental issues in associative learning*. Halifax: Dalhousie University Press.

Kantrowitz, B., Rosenberg, D., Rogers, P., Beachy, L., & Holmes, S. (1993, November 1). Heroin makes an ominous comeback. *Newsweek*.

Kaplan, W.S., & Novorr, M.J. (1994). Age and season of birth in sudden infant death syndrome in North Carolina, 1982–1987: No interaction. *American Journal of Epidemiology, 140*, 56–58.

Kashima, Y., & Triandis, H.C. (1986). The self-serving bias in attributions as a coping strategy: A cross-cultural study. *Journal of Cross-Cultural Psychology*, 17, 83–98.

Kassebaum, N.L. (1994). Head Start: Only the best for America's children. *American Psychologist, 49*, 123–126.

Katz, A.H. (1981). Self-help and mutual aid: An emerging social movement? *American Review of Sociology, 7*, 129–155.

Katz, R., & McGuffin, P. (1993). The genetics of affective disorders. In D. Fowles (Ed.), *Progress in experimental personality and psychopathology research*.

Katzell, R.A., & Guzzo, R.A. (1983). Psychological approaches to productivity improvements. *American Psychologist, 38*, 468–472.

Katzman, R., & Terry, R.D. (1983). *The neurology of aging*. Philadelphia: F.A. Davis.

Kaufman, L. (1979). *Perception: The world transformed*. New York: Oxford University Press.

Kavanaugh, D.J. (1992). Recent developments in expressed emotion and schizophrenia. *British Journal of Psychiatry, 160*, 601–620.

Kelley, H.H. (1967). Attribution theory in social psychology. In D. Levine (Ed.), *Nebraska Symposium on Motivation*. Lincoln: University of Nebraska Press.

Kellogg, W.N. (1968). Communication and language in the home-raised chimpanzee. *Science, 162*, 423–427.

Kelley, J.B. (1982). Divorce: The adult perspective. In B.B. Wolman (Ed.), *Handbook of developmental psychology* (pp. 734–750). Englewood Cliffs, NJ: Prentice-Hall.

Kelman, H.C. (1974). Attitudes are alive and well and gainfully employed in the sphere of action. *American Psychologist, 230*, 310–324.

Kendler, K.S., Neale, M.C., Kessler, R.C., Heath, A.C., & Eaves, L.J. (1992). Generalized anxiety disorder in women: A population-based twin study. *Archives of General Psychiatry, 49*, 267–272.

Kernis, M.H., & Wheeler, L. (1981). Beautiful friends and ugly strangers: Radiation and contrast effects in perception of same-sex pairs. *Personality and Social Psychology Bulletin, 7*, 617–620.

Kessler, R.C. (1979). Stress, social status, and psychological distress. *Journal of Health and Social Behavior, 20*, 259–272.

Kessler, R.C., Price, R.H., & Wortman, C.B. (1985). Social factors in psychopathology: Stress, social support, and coping processes. *Annual Review of Psychology, 36*, 531–572.

Kety, S.S. (1979). Disorders of the human brain. *Scientific American, 241*, 202–214.

Khantzian, E.J. (1990). Self-regulation and self-medication factors in alcoholism and the addictions: Similarities and differences. *Recent Developments in Alcoholism, 8*, 255–271.

Kiesler, C.A. (1982). Mental hospitals and alternative care: Noninstitutionalization as a potential public policy for mental patients. *American Psychologist, 37*, 349–360.

Kiesler, C.A. (1991). Changes in general hospital psychiatric care, 1980–1985. *American Psychologist, 46*, 416–421.

Kihlström, J.F. (1985). Hypnosis. *Annual Review of Psychology, 36*, 385–418.

Kihlström, J.F. (1987). The cognitive unconscious. *Science, 237*, 1445–1452.

Kihlström, J.F., & Harackiewicz, J.M. (1982). The earliest recollection: A new survey. *Journal of Personality, 50*, 134–148.

Kihlström, J.F., & McConkey, K.M. (1990). William James and hypnosis: A centennial reflection. *Psychological Science, 1*, 174–178.

Kim, D.O. (1985). Functional roles of the inner and outer-hair-cell subsystems in the cochlea and brain stem. In C.J. Berlin (Ed.), *Hearing science: Recent advances*. San Diego, CA: College Hill.

Kimble, G.A. (1993). A modest proposal for a minor revolution in the language of psychology. *Psychological Science, 4*, 253–255.

Kimmel, D.C. (1974). *Adulthood and aging*. New York: Wiley.

Kimura, D. (1985, November). Male brain, female brain: The hidden difference. *Psychology Today*, pp. 50–58.

Kimura, D., & Hampson, E. (1994). Cognitive pattern in men and women is influenced by fluctuations in sex hormones. *Current Directions in Psychological Science*, 57–61.

Kinsey, A.C., Pomeroy, W.B., & Martin, C.E. (1948). *Sexual behavior in the human male*. Philadelphia: Saunders.

Kinsey, A.C., Pomeroy, W.B., Martin, C.E., & Gebhard, P.H. (1953). *Sexual behavior in the human female*. Philadelphia: Saunders.

Kirchner, W.H., & Towne, W.F. (1994). The sensory basis of the honeybee's dance language. *Scientific American, 270*, 74–80.

Kirk, S.A., & Kutchins, H. (1992). The selling of DSM: *The rhetoric of science in psychiatry*. New York: de Gruyter.

Klatzky, R.L. (1980). *Human memory: Structures and processes* (2nd ed.). San Francisco: Freeman.

Kleiger, J.H. (1992). A conceptual critique of the EA: es comparison in the Comprehensive Rorschach System. *Psychological Assessment, 4*, 288–296.

Klein, G.S. (1951). The personal world through perception. In R.R. Blake & G.V. Ramsey (Eds.), *Perception: An approach to personality*. New York: Ronald Press.

Klein, M. (1948). *Contributions to psychoanalysis, 1921–1945*. London: Hogarth Press. (from Westen, 1991)

Kleinhesselink, R.R., & Edwards, R.E. (1975). Seeking and avoiding belief-discrepant information as a function of its perceived refutability. *Journal of Personality and Social Psychology, 31*, 787–790.

Kleinmuntz, D.N. (1991). Decision making for professional decision makers. *Psychological Science, 2*, 135, 138–141.

Klerman, G.L., Weissman, M.M., Markowitz, J.C., Glick, I., Wilner, P.J., Mason, B., & Shear, M.K. (1994). Medication and psychotherapy. In A.E. Bergin & S.L. Garfield (Eds.), *Handbook of psychotherapy and behavior change* (4th ed., pp. 734–782). New York: Wiley.

Klinger, E. (1990). Daydreaming: *Using waking fantasy and imagery for self-knowledge and creativity*. New York: J.P. Tarcher.

Kluckholn, C. (1954). Culture and behavior. In G. Lindzey (Ed.), *Handbook of social psychology* (Vol. 2, pp. 921–976). Cambridge, MA: Addison-Wesley.

Kobasa, S.C. (1979). Stressful life events, personality, and health: An inquiry into hardiness. *Journal of Personality and Social Psychology, 37*, 1–11.

Kohlberg, L. (1969). Stage and sequence: The cognitive–developmental approach to socialization. In D.A. Goslin (Ed.), *Handbook of socialization theory and research*. Chicago: Rand McNally.

Kohlberg, L. (1979). *The meaning and measurement of moral development* (Clark Lectures). Worcester, MA: Clark University.

Kohlberg, L. (1981). *The philosophy of moral development* (Vol. 1). San Francisco: Harper & Row.

Kohler, W. (1927). *The mentality of apes*. New York: Liveright.

Kolata, G. (1992, November 16). New views on life spans alter forecast on elderly. *New York Times*, p. A1.

Kolbert, E. (1991, October 11). Sexual harassment at work is pervasive, survey suggests. *New York Times*, Sec. A.

Kolodny, R.C., Masters, W.H., & Johnson, V.E. (1979). *Textbook of sexual medicine*. Boston: Little, Brown.

Komatsu, L.K. (1992). Recent views of conceptual structure. *Psychological Bulletin, 112*, 500–526.

Kondrasuk, J.N. (1981). Studies in MBO effectiveness. *Academy of Management Review, 6*, 419–430.

Kosambi, D.D. (1967). Living prehistory in India. *Scientific American, 216*, 105.

Koss, M.P. (1990). Violence against women. *American Psychologist, 45*, 374–380.

Kosslyn, S.M. (1980). *Image and mind*. Cambridge, MA: Harvard University Press.

Kosslyn, S.M. (1987). Seeing and imaging in the cerebral hemispheres: A computational approach. *Psychological Review, 94*, 148–175.

Kosslyn, S.M. (1994). *Image and brain*. Cambridge, MA: MIT Press.

Kosslyn, S.M., & Koenig, O. (1992). *The wet mind*. New York: Free Press.

Koulack, D., & Goodenough, D.R. (1976). Dream recall and dream recall failure: An arousal-retrieval model. *Psychological Bulletin, 83*, 975–984.

Krebs, D. (1975). Empathy and altruism. *Journal of Personality and Social Psychology, 32*, 1134–1140.

Kringlen, E. (1981). Stress and coronary heart disease. *Twin research 3: Epidemiological and clinical studies*. New York: Alan R. Liss.

Kroger, R.O., & Wood, L.A. (1993). Reification, "faking" and the Big Five. *American Psychologist, 48*, 1297–1298.

Kruglanski, A.W. (1986, August). Freeze-think and the Challenger. *Psychology Today*, pp. 48–49.

Kübler-Ross, E. (1969). *On death and dying*. New York: Macmillan.

Kübler-Ross, E. (1975). *Death: The final stage of growth*. Englewood Cliffs, NJ: Prentice-Hall.

Kuhl, P.K., Williams, K.A., & Lacerda, F. (1992). Linguistic experience alters phonetic perception in infants by 6 months of age. *Science, 255*, 606–608.

Kuhn, D. (1991). Thinking as argument. *Harvard Educational Review, 62*, 155–178.

Kulik, J., & Brown, R. (1979). Frustration, attribution of blame, and aggression. *Journal of Experimental Social Psychology,15*, 183–194.

Kunkel, D. (1988). Children and host-selling television commercials. *Communication Research, 15*, 71–92.

Labouvie-Vief, G. (1986). Modes of knowledge and the organization of development. In M.L. Commons, L. Kohlberg, F.A. Richards, & J. Sinott (Eds.), *Beyond formal operations: 3. Models and methods in the study of adult and adolescent thoughts*. New York: Praeger.

Lachman, S.J. (1984). *Processes in visual misperception: Illusions for highly structured stimulus material*. Paper presented at the 92nd annual convention of the American Psychological Association, Toronto, Canada.

LaGreca, A.M., Stone, W.L., & Bell, C.R., III. (1983). Facilitating the vocational-interpersonal skills of mentally retarded individuals. *American Journal of Mental Deficiency, 88*, 270–278.

Lakoff, G. (1987). *Women, fire and dangerous things*. Chicago: University of Chicago Press.

Lambert, W.W., Solomon, R.L., & Watson, P.D. (1949). Reinforcement and extinction as factors in size estimation. *Journal of Experimental Psychology, 39*, 637–641.

Lampl, M., Veidhuis, J.D., & Johnson, M.L. (1992). Saltation and stasis: A model of human growth. *Science, 258*, 801–803.

Lande, R. (1993). The video violence debate. *Hospital and Community Psychiatry, 44*, 347–351.

Landesman, S., & Butterfield, E.C. (1987). Normalization and deinstitution of mentally retarded individuals: Controversy and facts. *American Psychologist, 42*, 809–816.

Landman, J.C., & Dawes, R.M. (1982). Psychotherapy outcome: Smith and Glass' conclusions stand up under scrutiny. *American Psychologist, 37*, 504–516.

Landy, F.J. (1985). *Psychology of work behavior*. Homewood, IL: Dorsey.

Landy, F.J., & Farr, J.L. (1980). Performance ratings. *Psychological Bulletin, 87*, 72–107.

Langer, E.J., Bashner, R.S., & Chanowitz, B. (1985). Decreasing prejudice by increasing discrimination. *Journal of Personality and Social Psychology, 49*, 113–120.

LaPiere, R.T. (1934). Attitudes versus actions. *Social Forces, 13*, 230–237.

Larsen, R.J., & Diener, E. (1985). A multi-trait multimethod examination of affect structure: Hedonic level and emotional intensity. *Personality and Individual Differences, 6*, 631–636.

LaRue, A., & Jarvik, L. (1982). Old age and biobehavioral changes. In B.B. Wolman (Ed.), *Handbook of developmental psychology* (pp. 791–806). Englewood Cliffs, NJ: Prentice-Hall.

LAS. (no date). Piaget challenged: Babies see world as we do.

Lasch, C. (1979). *The culture of narcissism*. New York: Norton.

Lashley, K.S. (1950). In search of the engram. *Symposia of the Society for Experimental Biology, 4*, 454–482.

Latané, B., & Rodin, J. (1969). A lady in distress: Inhibiting effects of friends and strangers on bystander intervention. *Journal of Experimental Social Psychology, 5*, 189–202.

Lavond, D.G., Jeansok, J.K., & Thompson, R.F. (1993). Mammalian brain substrates of aversive classical conditioning. *Annual Review of Psychology, 44*, 317–342.

Lazarus, R.S. (1969). *Patterns of adjustment and human effectiveness*. New York: McGraw-Hill.

Lazarus, R.S. (1981, July). Little hassles can be hazardous to health. *Psychology Today*, pp. 58–62.

Lazarus, R.S. (1982). Thoughts on the relations between emotion and cognition. *American Psychologist, 37*, 1019--1024.

Lazarus, R.S. (1991a). Cognition and motivation in emotion. *American Psychologist, 46*, 352–367.

Lazarus, R.S. (1991b). Progress on a cognitive-motivational-relational theory of emotion. *American Psychologist, 46*, 819–834.

Lazarus, R.S. (1991c). *Emotion and adaptation*. New York: Oxford University Press.

Lazarus, R.S., & De Longis, A. (1983). Psychological stress and coping in aging. *American Psychologist, 38*, 245–254.

Lazarus, R.S., & De Longis, A., Folkman, S. & Gruen, R. (1985). Stress and adaptional outcomes. *American Psychologist, 40*, 770–779.

Leary, W.E. (1990, January 25). Risk of hearing loss is growing, panel says. *New York Times*, Sec. B.

Leccese, A.P. (1991). *Drugs and society*. Englewood Cliffs, NJ: Prentice-Hall.

LeDoux, J.E., Iwata, J., Pearl, D., & Reis, D.J. (1986). Disruption of auditory but not visual learning by destruction of intrinsic neurons in the rat medical geniculate body. *Brain Research, 371*, 395–399.

LeDoux, J.E., Farb, C., & Ruggiero, D.A. (1990). Topographic organization of neurons in the acoustic thalamus that project to the amygdala. *Journal of Neuroscience, 10*, 1043–1054.

Lee, G.P., Loring, D.W., Dahl, J.I., & Meador, K.J. (1993). Hemispheric specialization for emotional expression. *Neuropsychiatry, Neuropsychology, & Behavioral Neurology*, 6(3), 143–148.

Lefcourt, H.M. (1992). Durability and impact of the locus of control construct. *Psychological Bulletin, 112*, 411–414.

Lehman, D.R., Lempert, R.O., Nisbett, R.E. (1988). The effects of graduate training on reasoning: Formal discipline and thinking about everyday-life events. *American Psychologist, 43*, 431–442.

Leibowitz, H.W., & Owens, D.A. (1977). Nighttime driving accidents and selective visual degradation. *Science, 197*, 422–423.

Leigh, B.C. (1989). In search of the seven dwarves: Issues of measurement and meaning in alcohol expectancy research. *Psychological Bulletin, 105*, 361–373.

Leigh, B.C., & Stacy, A.W. (1991). On the scope of alcohol expectancy research: Remaining issues of measurement and meaning. *Psychological Bulletin, 110*, 147–154.

LeMagnen, J. (1952). Les phéromones olfactosexuals chez le rat blanc. *Archives des Sciences Physiologiques*, 6, 295–332.

Lemish, D., & Rice, M.L. (1986, June). Television as a talking picture book: A prop for language acquisition. *Journal of Child Language, 13*, 251–274.

Lenhardt, M.L., Skellett, R., Wang, P., & Clarke, A.M. (1991, July 5). Human ultrasonic speech perception. *Science*, 82–85.

Leonard, J.M., & Whitten, W.B. (1983). Information stored when expecting recall or recognition. *Journal of Experimental Psychology: Learning, Memory, and Cognition*, 9, 440–455.

Lerner, M.J. (1980). *The belief in a just world: A fundamental delusion*. New York: Plenum.

Lev, M. (1991, May). No hidden meaning here: Survey sees subliminal ads. *New York Times*, Sec. C.

LeVay, S. (1991). A difference in hypothalamic structure between heterosexual and homosexual men. *Science, 253*, 1034–1038.

Leventhal, H., & Niles, P. (1965). Persistence of influence for varying duration of exposure to threat stimuli. *Psychological Reports, 16*, 223–233.

Levine, I.S., & Rog, D.J. (1990). Mental health services for homeless mentally ill person: Federal initiatives and current service trends. *American Psychologist, 45*, 963–968.

Levine, S., Johnson, D.F., & Gonzales, C.A. (1985). Behavioral and hormonal responses to separation in infant rhesus monkeys and mothers. *Behavioral Neuroscience*, 99, 399–410.

Levinson, B.M. (1959). Traditional Jewish cultural values and performance on the Wechsler tests. *Journal of Educational Psychology*, 50, 177–181.

Levinson, D.J. (1978). *The seasons of a man's life*. New York: Knopf.

Levinson, D.J. (1986). A conception of adult development. *American Psychologist, 41*, 3–13.

Levinson, D.J. (1987). *The seasons of a woman's life*. New York: Knopf.

Lewin, K.A. (1935). *A dynamic theory of personality* (K.E. Zener & D.K. Adams, Trans.). New York: McGraw-Hill.

Lewin, T. (1994a, May 18). Boys are more comfortable with sex than girls are, survey finds. *New York Times*, p. A10.

Lewin, T. (1994b, October 7). Sex in America: Faithfulness thrives after all. *New York Times*, p. A1.

Lewin, T. (1994c, October 12). Men whose wives work earn less, studies show. *New York Times*, p. A1.

Lewinsohn, P.M., & Arconad, M. (1981). Behavioral treatment in depression: A social learning approach. In J. Clarkin & H. Glazer (Eds.), *Behavioral and directive treatment strategies*. New York: Garland.

Lewy, A.J. (1992). (Paper in issue of Chronobiology International in fall of 1992; mentioned by Jane Brody in New York times on 111/3/92; page B1.)

Lewy, A.J. (pre-1992 ref regarding effect of sunlight on pineal gland—probably about 1980—kin Brody article above).

Lieberman, M. (1986). Self-help groups and psychiatry. *American Psychiatric Association Annual Review, 5*, 744–760.

Liem, R., & Liem, J.V. (1978). Social class and mental illness reconsidered: The role of economic stress and social support. *Journal of Health and Social Behavior, 19*, 139–156.

Limber, J. (1977). Language in child and chimp. *American Psychologist, 32*, 280–295.

Lindsay, D.S. (1993). Eyewitness suggestibility. *Current Directions in Psychological Science, 2*, 86–89.

Lindsay, D.S., & Johnson, M.K. (1989). The eyewitness suggestibility effect and memory for source. *Memory & Cognition, 17*, 349–358.

Lindsay, P.H., & Norman, D.A. (1977). *Human information processing* (2nd ed.). New York: Academic Press.

Linn, R.L. (1982). Admissions testing on trial. *American Psychologist*, 37, 279–291.

Lisspers, J., Ost, L., & Skagerberg, B. (1992). Clinical effects of biofeedback treatment in migraine: The relation to achieved self-control and pretreatment predictors. *Scandinavian Journal of Behaviour Therapy*, 21(4), 171–190.

Livingstone, M.S., & Hubel, D.H. (1988a). Do the relative mapping densities of the magno- and parvocellular systems vary with eccentricity? *Journal of Neuroscience*, 8, 4334–4339.

Livingstone, M.S., & Hubel, D.H. (1988b). Segregation of form, color, movement, and depth: Anatomy, physiology, and perception. *Science*, 340, 740–749.

Livingstone, M.S., Rosen, G., & Drislane, F. (1991). *Proceedings of the National Academy of Sciences of the U.S.A.*

Locke, E.A., & Schweiger, D.M. (1979). Participation in decision-making: One more look. In B. Staw (Ed.), *Research in organizational behavior* (Vol. 1). Greenwich, CT: JAI Press.

Locke, E.A., Shaw, K.N., Saari, L.M., & Latham, G.P. (1981). Goal setting and task performance: 1969–1980. *Psychological Bulletin*, 90, 125–152.

Loehlin, J.C. (1989). Partitioning environmental and genetic contributions to behavioral development. *American Psychologist, 44*, 1285–1292.

Loehlin, J.C., & Nichols, R.C. (1976). *Heredity, environment, and personality*. Austin: University of Texas Press.

Loehlin, J.C., Willerman, L., & Horn, J.M. (1988). Human behavior genetics. *Annual Review of Psychology, 39*, 101–133.

Loewenstein, G. (1994). The psychology of curiosity: A review and reinterpretation. *Psychological Bulletin, 116*, 75–98.

Loftus, E.F. (1983). Silence is not golden. *American Psychologist*, 38, 564–572.

Loftus, E.F. (1993a). The reality of repressed memories. *American Psychologist, 48,* 518–537.

Loftus, E.F. (1993b). Psychologists in the eyewitness world. *American Psychologist, 48,* 550–552.

Loftus, E.F., & Hoffman, H.G. (1989). Misinformation and memory: The creation of new memories. *Journal of Experimental Psychology: General, 118,* 100–114.

Loftus, E.F., & Palmer, J.C. (1974). Reconstruction of automobile destruction: An example of the interaction between language and memory. *Journal of Verbal Learning and Verbal Behavior, 13,* 585–589.

Logue, A.W., Ophir, I., & Strauss, K.E. (1981). The acquisition of taste aversions in humans. *Behavior Research and Therapy, 19,* 319–333.

Loranger, A.W., Oldham, J.W., & Tulis, E.H. (1983). Familial transmission of DSM-III borderline personality disorder. *Archives of General Psychiatry, 40,* 795–799.

Lorenz, K. (1935). Der Kumpan inder Umwelt des Vogels. *Journal of Ornithology, 83,* 137–213, 289–413.

Lorenz, K. (1968). *On aggression.* New York: Harcourt.

Lott, A.J., & Lott, B.E. (1974). The role of reward in the formation of positive interpersonal attitudes. In T.L. Huston (Ed.), *Foundations of interpersonal attraction* (pp. 171–192). New York: Academic Press.

Lovibond, P.F., Siddle, D.A., & Bond, N.W. (1993). Resistance to extinction of fear-relevant stimuli: Preparedness or selective sensitization? *Journal of Experimental Psychology: General, 122,* 449–461.

Lubin, B., Larsen, R.M., & Matarazzo, J.D. (1984). Patterns of psychological test usage in the United States: 1935–1982. *American Psychologist, 39,* 451–454.

Lubin, B., Larsen, R.M., Matarazzo, J.D., & Seever, M. (1985). Psychological test usage patterns in five professional settings. *American Psychologist, 40,* 857–861.

Lubinski, D., & Benbow, P.C. (1992). Gender differences in abilities and preferences among the gifted: Implications for the math-science pipeline. *Current Directions in Psychological Science, 1,* 61–66.

Lucas, O.N. (1975). The use of hypnosis in hemophilia dental care. *Annals of the New York Academy of Sciences, 240,* 263–266.

Luchins, A. (1957). Primacy-recency in impression formation. In C. Hovland, W. Mandell, E. Campbell, T. Brock, A. Luchins, A. Cohen, W. McGuire, I. Janis, R. Feierbend, & N. Anderson (Eds.), *The order of presentation in persuasion.* New Haven, CT: Yale University Press.

Luria, A.R. (1968). *The mind of a mnemonist* (L. Solotaroff, Trans.). New York: Basic Books.

Lykken, D.T. (1975, March). Guilty knowledge test: The right way to use a lie detector. *Psychology Today,* pp. 56–60.

Lykken, D.T., McGue, M., Tellegen, A., & Bouchard, T.J., Jr. (1992). Emergenesis: Genetic traits that may not run in families. *American Psychologist, 47,* 1565–1577.

Lynch, G., Muller, D., Seubert, P., & Larson, J. (1988). Long-term potentiation: Persisting problems and recent results [United States Air Force School of Aerospace Medicine Symposium: Basic questions in neuroscience (1987, San Antonio, Texas)]. *Brain Research Bulletin, 21,* 364–372.

Lyness, S.A. (1993). Predictors of differences between Type A and B individuals in heart rate and blood pressure reactivity. *Psychological Bulletin, 114,* 266–295.

Lynn, S.J., & Rhue, J.W. (1988). Fantasy proneness, hypnosis, developmental antecedents, and psychopathology. *American Psychologist, 43,* 35–44.

Lytton, H., & Romeny, D.M. (1991). Parents' differential socialization of boys and girls: A meta-analysis. *Psychological Bulletin, 109*(2), 267–296.

Maccoby, E.E. (1990). Gender and relationships: A developmental account. *American Psychologist, 45,* 513–520.

Maccoby, E.E., & Jacklin, C.N. (1974). *The psychology of sex differences.* Stanford, CA: Stanford University Press.

Macionis, J.J. (1993). *Sociology* (4th ed.). Englewood Cliffs, NJ: Prentice-Hall.

Mackavey, W.R., Malley, J.E., & Stewart, A.J. (1991). Remembering autobiographically consequential experiences: Content analysis of psychologists' accounts of their lives. *Psychology and Aging, 6,* 50–59.

MacKinnon, D.W. (1962). The nature and nurture of creative talent. *American Psychologist, 17,* 484–495.

Mackworth, N. (1965). Originality. *American Psychologist, 20,* 51–66.

MacLean, P.D. (1970). The limbic brain in relation to the psychoses. In P. Black (Ed.), *Physiological correlates of emotion* (pp. 129–146). New York: Academic Press.

MacLeod, D.I.A. (1978). Visual sensitivity. *Annual Review of Psychology, 29,* 613–645.

Maddi, S.R. (1989). *Personality theories: A comparative approach* (5th ed.). Homewood, IL: Dorsey.

Maier, N.R.F. (1931). Reasoning in humans: II. The solution of a problem and its appearance in consciousness. *Journal of Comparative Psychology, 12,* 181–194.

Makstein, N.K., McLaughlin, A.M., & Rogers, C.M. (1979, September). *Sexual abuse and the pediatric setting: Treatment and research implications.* Paper presented at the meeting of the American Psychological Association, New York.

Maloney, M.P., & Ward, M.P. (1976). *Psychological assessment: A conceptual approach.* New York: Academic Press.

Manfredi, M., Bini, G., Cruccu, G., Accornero, N., Beradelli, A., & Medolago, L. (1981). Congenital absence of pain. *Archives of Neurology (Chicago), 38,* 507–511.

Mansnerus, L. (1992, October 4). Smoking: Is it a habit or is it genetic? *New York Times,* Good Health Magazine, p. 14.

Marcia, J.E. (1976). Identity six years after: A follow-up study. *Journal of Youth and Adolescence, 5,* 145–160.

Marcia, J.E. (1980). Identity in adolescence. In J. Adelson (Ed.), *Handbook of adolescent psychology.* New York: Wiley.

Margolin, G. (1987). Marital therapy: A cognitive-behavioral-affective approach. In N.S. Jacobson (Ed.), *Psychotherapists in clinical practice* (pp. 232–285). New York: Guilford.

Markovic, B.M., Dimitrijevic, M., & Jankovic, B.D. (1993). Immunomodulation by conditioning: Recent developments. *International Journal of Neuroscience, 71*(1–4, 231–249.

Markus, H.R., & Kitayama, S. (1991). Culture and self: Implications for cognition, emotion, and motivation. *Psychological Review, 98,* 224–253.

Marland, S.P. (1972). *Education of the gifted and talented: Report to the Congress of the United States by the U.S. Commissioner* of *Education*. Washington, DC: U.S. Government Printing Office.

Marlatt, G.A., & Rohsenow, D.J. (1980, December). The think–drink effect. *Psychology Today*, pp. 60–69, 93.

Marlin, N.A. (1983). Second-order conditioning using a contextual stimulus as S1. *Animal Learning and Behavior, 11*, 290–294.

Marr, D. (1982). *Vision*. San Francisco: Freeman.

Marsden, E.N. (1966). Values as determinants of friendship choice. *Connecticut College Psychological Journal, 3*, 3–13.

Martin, R.L., Roberts, W.V., & Clayton, P.J. (1980). Psychiatric status after a one-year prospective follow-up, *JAMA, Journal of the American Medical Association, 244*, 350–353.

Marvin, R.S. (1975). *Aspects of the pre-school child's changing conception of his mother*. Unpublished.

Maslach, C. (1982). *Burnout*. Englewood Cliffs, NJ: Prentice-Hall.

Masling, J., Rabie, L., & Blondheim, S.H. (1967). Obesity, level of aspiration, and Rorshach and TAT measures of oral dependence. *Journal of Consulting Psychology, 31*, 233–239.

Maslow, A.H. (1954). *Motivation and personality*. New York: Harper & Row.

Mason, W.A., & Lott, D.F. (1976). Ethnology and comparative psychology. *Annual Review of Psychology, 27*, 129–154.

Massaro, D.W., & Cowan, N. (1993). Information processing models: Microscopes of the mind. *Annual Review of Psychology, 44*, 383–425.

Massimini, F., Czikszentmihalyi, M., & Della Fave, A. (1988). Flow and biocultural evolution. In M. Czikszentmihalyi & I.S. Czikszentmihalyi (Eds.), *Optimal experience: Studies of flow in consciousness* (pp. 60–81). New York: Cambridge University Press.

Masson, J.M. (1984). *The assault on truth: Freud's suppression of the seduction theory*. New York: Farrar, Strauss, & Giroux.

Masters, W.H., & Johnson, V.E. (1970). *Human sexual inadequacy*. Boston: Little, Brown.

Masters, W.H., Johnson, V.E., & Kolodny, R.C. (1982). *Human sexuality*. Boston: Little, Brown.

Mateer, C.A., Polen, S.B., & Ojemann, G.A. (1982). Sexual variation in cortical localization of naming as determined by stimulation mapping. *Behavioral and Brain Sciences, 5*, 310–311.

Matsuda, L.H., Lolait, S.J., Brownstein, M.J., Young, A.C., & Bonner, T.I. (1990). Structure of a cannabinoid receptor and functional expression of the cloned CDNA. *Nature, 346*, 561–564.

Matsumoto, D. (1995). *People: Psychology from a cultural perspective*. Pacific Grove, CA: Brooks/Cole.

Matsumoto, D., Kudoh, T., Scherer, K., & Wallbott, H.G. (1988). Emotion antecedents and reactions in the U.S. and Japan. *Journal of Cross-Cultural Psychology, 19*, 267–286.

Matthews, K.A. (1988). Coronary heart disease and Type A behaviors: Update on and alternative to the Booth-Kewley and Friedman (1987) quantitative review. *Psychological Bulletin, 104*, 373–380.

Maurer, D., & Maurer, C. (1988). *The world of the newborn*. New York: Basic Books.

Mayberry, R.I., & Eichen, E.B. (1991). The long-lasting advantage of learning sign language in childhood: Another look at the critical period for language acquisition. *Journal of Memory and Language, 30*, 486–512.

Mayer, D.J., & Watkins, L.R. (1984). Multiple endogenous opiate and nonopiate analgesia systems. In L. Kruger & J.C. Liebeskind (Eds.), *Neural mechanisms of pain*. New York: Raven Press.

Mayer, R.E. (1983). *Thinking, problem solving, cognition*. San Francisco: Freeman.

Mayo, E. (1933). *The human problems of an industrial civilization*. New York: Macmillan.

Mazur, J.E. (1989). *Learning and behavior*. Englewood Cliffs, NJ: Prentice-Hall.

Mazur, J.E. (1991). Choice with probabilistic reinforcement: Effects delay and conditioned reinforcers. *Journal of the Experimental Analysis of Behavior, 55*, 63–77.

Mazur, J.E. (1993). Predicting the strength of a conditioned reinforcer: Effects of delay and uncertainty. *Current Directions in Psychological Science, 2*, 70–74.

Mazur, J.E. (1994). *Learning and behavior* (3rd ed). Englewood Cliffs, NJ: Prentice-Hall.

McBurney, D.H., & Collings, V.B. (1984). *Introduction to sensation/perception* (2nd ed.). Englewood Cliffs, NJ: Prentice-Hall.

McCall, R.B. (1979). *Infants*. Cambridge, MA: Harvard University Press.

McClearn, G.E., Plomin, R., Gora-Maslak, G., & Crabbe, J.C. (1991). The gene chase in behavioral science. *Psychological Science, 2*, 222–229.

McClelland, D.C. (1958). Methods of measuring human motivation. In J.W. Atkinson (Ed.), *Motives in fantasy, action and society: A method of assessment and study*. New York: Van Nostrand.

McClelland, D.C. (1973). Testing for competence rather than for "intelligence." *American Psychologist, 28*, 1–14.

McClelland, D.C. (1993). Intelligence is not the best predictor of job performance. *Current Directions in Psychological Science, 2*, 5–7.

McClelland, D.C., & Atkinson, J.W. (1948). The projective expression of needs: I. The effect of different intensities of the hunger drive on perception. *Journal of Psychology, 25*, 205–222.

McClintock, M.K. (1971). Menstrual synchrony and suppression. *Nature (London), 229*, 244–245.

McClintock, M.K. (1978). Estrous synchrony and its mediation by airborne chemical communication (*Rattus norvegicus*). *Hormones & Behavior, 10*, 264–276.

McClintock, M.K. (1984). Estrous synchrony: Modulation of ovarian cycle length by female pheromones. *Physiology & Behavior, 32*, 701–705.

McCloskey, M., & Egeth, H.E. (1983). Eyewitness identification: What can a psychologist tell a jury? *American Psychologist, 38*, 550–563.

McCollough, C. (1965). Color adaptation of edge detectors in the human visual system. *Science, 149*, 1115–1116.

McCormick, D.A., CLark, G.A., Lavond, D.G., & Thompson, R.F. (1982). Initial localization of the memory trace for a basic form of learning. *Proceedings of the National Academy of Sciences of the U.S.A., 79*, 2731–2735.

McCrae, R.R., & Costa, P.T., Jr. (1985). Updating Norman's "adequate taxonomy": Intelligence and personality dimensions in natural language and in questionnaires. *Journal of Personality and Social Psychology*, *49*, 710–721.

McCrae, R.R., & Costa, P.T., Jr. (1987). Validation of the five-factor model of personality across instruments and observers. *Journal of Personality and Social Psychology*, *52*, 81–90.

McCrae, R.R., & Costa, P.T., Jr. (1989). More reasons to adopt the five-factor model. *American Psychologist*, *44*, 451–452.

McDonald, K.A. (1990, September 26). Ape is found capable of learning and creating grammatical rules. *Chronicle of Higher Education*, p. A5.

McFarland, L.J., Senn, L.E., & Childress, J.R. (1993). *21st century leadership: Dialogues with 100 top leaders*. Los Angeles: The Leadership Press.

McGeer, P.L., & McGeer, E.G. (1980). Chemistry of mood and emotion. *Annual Review of Psychology*, *31*, 273–307.

McGlashan, T.M. (1983). The borderline syndrome: I. Testing three diagnostic system. *Archives of General Psychiatry*, *40*, 1311–1318.

McGothlin, W.H., & West, L.J. (1968). The marijuana problem: An overview. *American Journal of Psychiatry*, *125*, 370–378.

McGovern, L.P. (1976). Dispositional social anxiety and helping behavior under three conditions of threat. *Journal of Personality*, *44*, 84–97.

McGuffin, P., Reveley, A., & Holland, A. (1982). Identical triplets: Non-identical psychosis? *British Journal of Psychiatry*, *140*, 1–6.

McGuire, W.J. (1985). Attitudes and attitude change. In G. Lindzey & E. Aronson (Eds.), *Handbook of social psychology*. Reading, MA: Addison-Wesley.

McHugh, M.D., Koeske, R.D., & Frieze, I.H. (1986). Issues to consider in conducting nonsexist psychological research: A guide for researchers. *American Psychologist*, *41*, 879–890.

McKean, K. (1985, April). Of two minds: Selling the right brain. *Discover*, pp. 30–41, 60.

McKim, W.A. (1986). *Drugs and behavior: An introduction to behavioral pharmacology*. Englewood Cliffs, NJ: Prentice-Hall.

McLaughlin, C.L., Peikin, S., & Boile, C. (1984). Decreased pancreatic CCK receptor binding and CCK-stimulated amylase release in Jucker obese rats. *Physiology & Behavior*, *32*, 961–965.

McLellan, J.A., Haynie, D., & Strauss, D. (1993). *Membership in high school crowd clusters and relationships with family and friends*. Paper presented at the meeting of the Society for Research in Child Development, New Orleans, LA.

McMurray, G.A. (1950). Experimental study of a case of insensitivity to pain. *Archives of Neurology and Psychiatry*, *64*, 650.

McNamara, H.J., Long, J.B., & Wike, E.L. (1956). Learning without response under two conditions of external cues. *Journal of Comparative and Physiological Psychology*, *49*, 477–480.

McNeill, D. (1972). *The acquisition of language: The study of developmental psycholinguistics*. New York: Harper & Row.

Mead, M. (1928). *Coming of age in Samoa: A psychological study of primitive youth for Western civilization*. New York: Morrow Quill Paperbacks.

Mednick, A. (1993, May). Worlds' women familiar with a day's double shift. *APA Monitor*, p. 32.

Mednick, S.A. (1962). The associative basis of creativity. *Psychological Review*, *69*, 220–232.

Meglino, B.M., DeNisi, A.S., Youngblood, S.A., & Williams, K.J. (1988). Effects of realistic job previews: A comparison using an enhancement and a reduction preview. *Journal of Applied Psychology*, *73*, 259–266.

Meichenbaum, D., & Cameron, R. (1982). Cognitive-behavior therapy. In G.T. Wilson & C.M. Franks (Eds.), *Contemporary behavior therapy: Conceptual and empirical foundations*. New York: Guilford.

Melamed, B.G., Hawes, R.R., Heiby, E., & Glick, J. (1975). Use of filmed modeling to reduce uncooperative behavior of children during dental treatment. *Journal of Dental Research*, *54*, 797–801.

Meltzoff, A.N. (1988). Imitation of televised models by infants. *Child Development*, *59*(5), 1221–1229.

Meltzoff, A.N., & Moore, M.K. (1985). Cognitive foundations and social functions of imitation and intermodal representation in infancy. In J. Mehler & R. Fox (Eds.), *Neonate cognition: Beyond the blooming, fuzzing confusion*. Hillsdale, NJ: Erlbaum.

Melzack, R. (1973). *The puzzle of pain*. New York: Basic Books.

Melzack, R. (1980). Psychological aspects of pain. In J.J. Bonica (Ed.), *Pain*. New York: Raven Press.

Melzack, R. (1992, April). Phantom limbs. *Scientific American*, pp. 120–126.

Menzel, E.W. (1974). A group of young chimpanzees in a one-acre field. In A.M. Schrier & F. Stollnitz (Eds.), *Behavior of nonhuman primates* (Vol. 5, pp. 83–153). New York: Academic Press.

Mercer, T.B., & Lewis, J.G. (1978). Using the system of multicultural assessment (SOMPA) to identify the gifted minority child. In A.Y. Baldwin, G.H. Gear, & L.J. Lucito (Eds.), *Educational planning for the gifted: Overcoming cultural, geographic, and socioeconomic barriers*. Reston, VA: Council for Exceptional Children.

Mersky, H. (1992). The manufacture of personalities: The production of multiple personality disorder. *British Journal of Psychiatry*, *160*, 327–340.

Meyer, G.E., & Hilterbrand, K. (1984). Does it pay to be "Bashful"? The seven dwarfs and long term memory. *American Journal of Psychology*, *97*, 47–55.

Meyer, J.K., & Reter, D.J. (1979). Sex reassignment. *Archives of General Psychiatry*, *36*, 1010–1015.

Meyer, R.E., & Mirin, S.M. (1979). *The brain stimulus*. New York: Plenum.

Michael, R.P., Bonsall, R.W., & Warner, P. (1974). Human vaginal secretions: Volatile fatty acid content. *Science*, *186*, 1217–1219.

Michelson, L. (Ed.). (1985). Meta-analysis and clinical psychology [Special issue]. *Clinical Psychology Review*, *5*(1).

Middlebrooks (1994, May). Cortical sound localization. *Science*.

Milgram, S. (1963). Behavioral study of obedience. *Journal of Abnormal and Social Psychology*, *67*, 371–378.

Milgram, S. (1974). *Obedience to authority: An experimental view*. New York: Harper & Row.

Miller, C., & Swift, K. (1991). *Words & women: New language in new times*. New York: Harper Collins.

Miller, G.A. (1956). The magical number seven plus or minus two: Some limits on our capacity for processing information. *Psychological Review*, *63*, 81–96.

Miller, G.A., Galanter, E., & Pribram, K. (1962). *Plans and the structure of behavior*. New York: Holt, Rinehart & Winston.

Miller, J. (1984). Culture and the development of everyday social explanation. *Journal of Personality and Social Psychology, 46*, 961–978.

Miller, J.G., Bersoff, D.M., & Harwood, R.L. (1990). Perceptions of social responsibilities in India and the United States: Moral imperatives or personal decisions? *Journal of Personality and Social Psychology, 58*, 33–47.

Miller, N., & Campbell, D. (1959). Recency and primacy in persuasion as a function of the timing of speeches and measurements. *Journal of Abnormal and Social Psychology, 59*, 1–9.

Miller, P.A., Kliewer, W., & Burkeman, D. (1993, March). *Effects of maternal socialization on children's learning to cope with divorce*. Paper presented at the biennial meeting of the Society for Research in Child Development, New Orleans, LA.

Miller, T.Q., Turner, C.W., Tindale, R.S., Posavac, E.J., & Dugoni, B.L. (1991). Reasons for the trend toward null findings in research on Type A behavior. *Psychological Bulletin, 110*, 469–485.

Milner, B. (1959). The memory defect in bilateral hippocampal lesions. *Psychiatric Research Reports, 11*, 43–52.

Minton, H.L., & Schneider, F.W. (1980). *Differential psychology*. Monterey, CA: Brooks/Cole.

Mintz, A. (1951). Nonadaptive group behavior. *Journal of Abnormal and Social Psychology, 46*, 150–159.

Mischel, W. (1968). *Personality and assessment*. New York: Wiley.

Mischel, W. (1981). *Introduction to personality*. New York: Holt, Rinehart & Winston.

Mischel, W. (1984). On the predictability of behavior and the structure of personality. In R. Zucker et al. (Eds.), *Personality and the prediction of behavior*. New York: Academic Press.

Miserendino, M.J.D., Sananes, C.B., Melia, K.R., & Davis, M. (1990). Blocking of acquisition but not expression of conditioned fear-potentiated startle by NMDA antagonists in the amygdala. *Nature (London), 345*, 716–718.

Mistry, J., & Rogoff, B. (1994). Remembering in cultural context. In W.W. Lonner & R. Malpass (Eds.), *Psychology and culture* (pp. 139–144). Boston: Allyn & Bacon.

Misumi, J. (1985). *The behavioral science of leadership: An interdisciplinary Japanese leadership program*. Ann Arbor: University of Michigan Press.

Mittleman, G., Whishaw, I.Q., Jones, G.H., Koch, M., & Robbins, T.W. (1990). Cortical, hippocampal, and striatal mediation of schedule-induced behaviors. *Behavioral Neuroscience, 104*, 399–409.

Moffitt, T.W. (1993). Adolescence-limited and life-course-persistent antisocial behavior: A developmental taxonomy. *Psychological Review, 100*, 674–701.

Moghaddam, F.M., Taylor, D.M., & Wright, S.C. (1993). *Social psychology in cross-cultural perspective*. New York: Freeman.

Molineux, J.B. (1985). *Family therapy: A practical manual*. Springfield, IL: Charles C. Thomas.

Moncrieff, R.W. (1951). *The chemical senses*. London: Leonard Hill.

Monroe, S.M., & Simons, A.D. (1991). Diathesis-stress theories in the context of life stress research: Implications for the depressive disorders. *Psychological Bulletin, 110*, 406–425.

Moore, J.S., Graziano, W.G., & Millar, M.G. (1987). Physical attractiveness, sex-role orientation, and the evaluation of adults and children. *Personality and Social Psychology Bulletin, 13*, 95–102.

Moore, T.E. (1982). Subliminal advertising: What you see is what you get. *Journal of Marketing, 46*, 38–47.

Moore-Ede, M.C., Czeisler, C.A., & Richardson, G.S. (1983). Circadian timekeeping in health and disease: I. Basic properties of circadian pacemakers. *New England Journal of Medicine, 309*, 469–476.

Moriarty, T. (1975). Crime, commitment and the responsive bystander: Two field experiments. *Journal of Personality and Social Psychology, 31*, 370–376.

Morris, C. (1990). *Contemporary psychology and effective behavior* (7th ed.). Glenview, IL: Scott, Foresman.

Morris, N.M., & Udry, J.R. (1978). Pheromonal influences on human sexual behavior. *Journal of Biosocial Science, 10*, 147–159.

Morrison, A. (1983). A window on the sleeping brain. *Scientific American, 249*, 94–102.

Moses, S. (1990, December). Sensitivity to culture may be hard to teach. *APA Monitor*, p. 39.

Moses, S. (1991, April). New paradigms of science inquiry may help women. *APA Monitor*, p. 36.

Moskowitz, B.A. (1978). The acquisition of language. *Scientific American, 239*, 92–108.

Mozel, M.M., Smith, B., Smith, P., Sullivan, R., & Swender, P. (1969). Nasal chemoreception in flavor identification. *Archives of Otolaryngology, 90*, 367–373.

Muchinsky, P.M. (1986). Personnel selection methods. *International Review of Industrial and Organizational Psychology, 1*, 37–70.

Muir, D.W. (1985). The development of infants' auditory spatial sensitivity. In S. Trehub & B. Schneider (Eds.), *Auditory development in infancy*. New York: Plenum.

Mumford, M.D., & Gustafson, S.B. (1988). Creativity syndrome: Integration, application, and innovation. *Psychological Bulletin, 103*, 27–43.

Murphy, J.M. (1976). Psychiatric labeling in cross-cultural perspective. *Science, 191*, 1019–1028.

Murray, H.A. (1938). *Explorations in personality*. New York: Oxford University Press.

Murray, H.G., & Denny, J.P. (1969). Interaction of ability level and interpolated activity in human problem solving. *Psychological Reports, 24*, 271–276.

Murstein, B.J. (1986). *Paths to marriage*. Beverly Hills, CA: Sage.

Myers, D.G. (1992). *Social psychology* (4th ed.). Boston: McGraw-Hill.

Nahemow, L., & Lawton, M.P. (1975). Similarity and propinquity in friendship formation. *Journal of Personality and Social Psychology, 32*, 205–213.

Nakahara, D., Ozaki, N., Miura, Y., Miura, H., & Nagatsu, T. (1989). Increased dopamine and serotonin metabolism in rat nucleus accumbens produced by intracranial self-stimulation of medial forebrain bundle as measured by in vivo microdialysis. *Brain Research, 495*, 178–181.

National Commission on Marijuana and Drug Abuse (NCMDA). (1973a). *Drug use in America: Problem in perspective*. Washington, DC: U.S. Government Printing Office.

National Commission on Marijuana and Drug Abuse (NCMDA). (1973b). *Drug use in America: Problem in perspective. Technical papers—appendix*. Washington, DC: U.S. Government Printing Office.

National Science Foundation. (1994). *Characteristics of doctoral scientists and engineers in the United States: 1991* (pp. 94–307). Arlington, VA: NSF.

Neal, A., & Turner, S.M. (1991). Anxiety disorders research with African Americans: Current status. *Psychological Bulletin, 109*(3), 400–410.

Neale, J.M., & Oltmanns, T.F. (1980). *Schizophrenia*. New York: Wiley.

Neher, A. (1991). Maslow's theory of motivation: A critique. *Journal of Humanistic Psychology, 31*, 89–112.

Neisser, U. (1967). *Cognitive psychology*. New York: Appleton-Century-Crofts.

Neisser, U. (1982). *Memory observed: Remembering in natural contexts*. San Francisco: Freeman.

Neitz, J., Neitz, M., & Jacobs, G.H. (1993). More than three cone pigments among people with normal color vision. *Vision Research, 33*, 117–122.

Neuberg, S.L. (1988). Behavioral implications of information presented outside of conscious awareness: The effect of subliminal presentation of trait information on behavior in the Prisoner's Dilemma Game. *Social Condition*, 6, 207–230.

Neugarten, B.L. (1977). Personality and aging. In I. Birren & K.W. Schaie (Eds.), *Handbook of the psychology of aging*. New York: Van Nostrand.

Newell, A., & Simon, H.A. (1972). *Human problem solving*. Englewood Cliffs, NY: Prentice-Hall.

Newlin, D.B., & Thomson, J.B. (1990). Alcohol challenge with sons of alcoholics: A critical review and analysis. *Psychological Bulletin, 108*, 383–402.

Newman, B.M. (1982). Mid-life development. In B.B. Wolman (Ed.), *Handbook of developmental psychology* (pp. 617–635). Englewood Cliffs, NJ: Prentice-Hall.

Newman, P.R. (1982). The peer group. In B.B. Wolman (Ed.), *Handbook of developmental psychology* (pp. 526–536). Englewood Cliffs, NJ: Prentice-Hall.

Nickerson, R.S., & Adams, M.J. (1979). Long-term memory for a common object. *Cognitive Psychology, 11*, 287–307.

Nielsen, G.D., & Smith, E.E. (1973). Imaginal and verbal representative in short-term recognition of visual forms. *Journal of Experimental Psychology, 101*, 375–378.

Nisbett, R.E., Fong, G.T., Lehman, D.R., & Cheng, P.W. (1987). Teaching reasoning. *Science, 238*, 625–631.

Nissani, M. (1990). A cognitive reinterpretation of Stanley Milgram's observations on obedience to authority. *American Psychologist, 45*, 1384–1385.

Noden, M. (1994, August 8). Dying to win. *Sports Illustrated*, p. 52.

Nolen-Hoeksema, S., Girgus, J.S., & Seligman, M.E.P. (1986). Learned helplessness in children: A longitudinal study of depression, achievement, and explanatory style. *Journal of Personality and Social Psychology, 51*, 435–442a.

Norman, D.A., & Bobrow, D.C. (1976). Active memory processes in perception and cognition. In C. Cofer (Ed.), *The structure of human memory* (pp. 114–132). San Francisco: Freeman.

Norman, R. (1975). Affective-cognitive consistency, attitudes, conformity, and behavior. *Journal of Personality and Social Psychology, 32*, 83–91.

Norman, W.T. (1963). Toward an adequate taxonomy of personality attributes: Replicated factor structure in peer nomination personality ratings. *Journal of Abnormal and Social Psychology, 66*, 574–583.

Norris, F.H., & Murrell, S.A. (1990). Social support, life events, and stress as modifiers of adjustment to bereavement by older adults. *Psychology and Aging, 45*, 267–275.

Norris, P.A. (1986). On the status of biofeedback and clinical practice. *American Psychologist, 41*, 1009–1010.

Novak, M.A. (1991, July). "Psychologists care deeply" about animals. *APA Monitor*, p. 4.

O'Connell, A., & Russo, N. (Eds.). (1990). *Women in psychology: A bibliographic sourcebook*. Westport, CT: Greenwood Press.

O'Connor, N., & Hermelin, B. (1987). Visual memory and motor programmes: Their use by idiot savant artists and controls. *British Journal of Psychology, 78*, 307–323.

Offer, D., & Offer, J. (1975). *From teenager to young manhood*. New York: Basic Books.

Offermann, L., & Gowing, M. (1990). Organizations of the future. *American Psychologist, 45*(2), 95–108.

Office of Educational Research and Improvement. (1988). *Youth indicators, 1988*. Washington, DC: U.S. Government Printing Office.

Ojemann, G., Ojemann, J., Lettich, E., & Berger, M. (1989). Cortical language localization in left, dominant hemisphere: An electrical stimulation mapping investigation in 117 patients. *Journal of Neurosurgery, 71*, 316–326.

Oldenburg, D. (1992, April 29). *Research is clear: TV violence does affect children. Ann Arbor News*, p. B4.

Olds, J., & Milner, P. (1954). Positive reinforcement produced by electrical stimulation of septal area and other regions of rat brain. *Journal of Comparative Physiological Psychology, 47*, 419–427.

O'Leary, A. (1990). Stress, emotion, and human immune function. *Psychological Bulletin, 108*, 363–382.

O'Leary, K.D., & Wilson, G.T. (1987). *Behavior therapy: Application and outcome*. Englewood Cliffs, NJ: Prentice-Hall.

O'Leary, V.E., & Smith, D. (1988, August). *Sex makes a difference: Attributions for emotional cause*. Paper presented at the meeting of the American Psychological Association, Atlanta, GA.

Olio, K. (1994). Truth in memory. *American Psychologist, 49*, 442–443.

Oliver, M.B., & Hyde, J.S. (1993). Gender differences in sexuality: A meta-analysis. *Psychological Bulletin, 114*, 29–51.

Olton, D.S., & Noonberg, A.R. (1980). *Biofeedback: Clinical applications in behavioral science*. Englewood Cliffs, NJ: Prentice-Hall.

Olton, D.S., & Samuelson, R.J. (1976). Remembrance of places passed: Spatial memory in rats. *Journal of Experimental Psychology, 2*, 97–115.

Orlofsky, J.L. (1978). Identity formation, *N* achievement, and fear of success in college men and women. *Journal of Youth and Adolescence, 7*, 49–62.

Orlofsky, J.L., Marcia, J.E., & Lesser, I.M. (1973). Ego identity status and the intimacy versus isolation crisis of young adulthood. *Journal of Personality and Social Psychology, 27,* 211–219.

Ortar, G. (1963). Is a verbal test cross-cultural? *Scripta Hierosolymitana, 13,* 219–235.

Oskamp, S. (1977). *Attitudes and opinions.* Englewood Cliffs, NJ: Prentice-Hall.

Oswald, I. (1973). Is sleep related to synthetic purpose? In W.P. Koella & P. Levin (Eds.), *Sleep: Physiology, biology, psychology, psychopharmacology, clinical implications.* Basel, Switzerland: Karger.

Oswald, I. (1974). Pharmacology of sleep. In O. Petre-Quadens & J.S. Schlag (Eds.), *Basic sleep mechanism.* New York: Academic Press.

Ozer, D.J., & Reise, S.P. (1994). Personality assessment. *Annual Review of Psychology, 45,* 357–388.

Pace, R. (1994, July 28). Christy Henrich, 22, gymnast plagued by eating disorders. *New York Times,* p. A12.

Packard, R.G. (1970). The control of "classroom attention": A group contingency for complex behavior. *Journal of Applied Behavior Analysis, 3,* 13–28.

Paikoff, R.L., & Brooks-Gunn, J. (1991). Do parent-child relationships change during puberty? *Psychological Bulletin, 110*(1), 47–66.

Pakkenberg, B. (1993, November 13). Study published in 11/13/93 issue of *Lancet.*

Paludi, M.A., & Gullo, D.F. (1987). The effect of sex labels on adults' knowledge of infant development. *Sex Roles, 17,* 19–30.

Panksepp, J. (1986). The neurochemistry of behavior. *Annual Review of Psychology, 37,* 77–107.

Paris, S.G., & Weissberg, J.A. (1986). Young children's remembering in different contexts: A reinterpretation of Istomina's study. *Child Development, 57,* 1123–1129.

Parke, R.D., & Asher, S.R. (1983). Social and personality development. *Annual Review of Psychology, 34,* 465–509.

Parker, E.S., Birnbaum, I.M., & Noble, E.P. (1976). Alcohol and memory: Storage and state dependency. *Journal of Verbal Learning and Verbal Behavior, 15,* 691–702.

Parker, J.G., & Asher, S.R. (1987). Peer relations and later personal adjustment: Are low-accepted children at risk? *Psychological Bulletin, 102,* 357–389.

Parker, K.C.H., Hanson, R.K., & Hunsley, J. (1988). MMPI, Rorschach, and WAIS: A meta-analytic comparison of reliability, stability, and validity. *Psychological Bulletin, 103,* 367–373.

Parkes, C.M. (1976). Components of the reaction to loss of limb, spouse, a home. *Journal of Psychosomatic Research, 16,* 343–349.

Parsons, H.M. (1974). What happened to Hawthorne? *Science, 183,* 922–932.

Patterson, F. (1978). The gestures of a gorilla: Language acquisition in another pongid. *Brain and Language, 5,* 72–97.

Patterson, F.G.P. (1980). Innovative uses of language by a gorilla: A case study. In K.E. Nelson (Ed.), *Children's language* (Vol. 2). New York: Gardner Press.

Patterson, F.G.P. (1981). *The education of Koko.* New York: Holt, Rinehart & Winston.

Patterson, F.G.P., & Cohn, R.H. (1990). Language acquisition by a lowland gorilla: Koko's first ten years of vocabulary development. *Word, 41,* 97–143.

Patterson, G.R, & Bank, L. (1989). Some amplifying mechanisms for pathologic processes in families. In M.R. Gunnar & E. Thelen (Eds.), *Systems and development: The Minnesota Symposia on Child Psychology* (Vol. 22). Hillsdale, NJ: Erlbaum.

Patterson, G.R., DeBaryshe, B.D., & Ramsey, E. (1989). A developmental perspective on antisocial behavior. *American Psychologist, 44,* 329–335.

Paul, G.L. (1982). *The development of a "transportable" system of behavioral assessment for chronic patients.* Invited address, University of Minnesota, Minneapolis.

Paul, G.L., & Lentz, R.J. (1977). *Psychosocial treatment of chronic mental patients: Milieu versus social learning programs.* Cambridge, MA: Harvard University Press.

Paulson, P.C. (1990, November). The fine art of sleeping well. *University Health Service Bulletin,* pp. 1–2.

Pavlov, I.P. (1927). *Conditional reflexes* (G.V. Anrep, Trans.). London: Oxford University Press.

Peabody, D., & Goldberg, L.R. (1989). Some determinants of factor structures from personality-trait descriptors. *Journal of Personality and Social Psychology, 57,* 552–567.

Pearlin, L.I., & Schooler, C. (1978). The structure of coping. *Journal of Health and Social Behavior, 19,* 2–21.

Pedlow, R., Sanson, A., Prior, M., & Oberklaid, F. (1993). Stability of maternally reported temperament from infancy to 8 years. *Developmental Psychology, 29,* 998–1007.

Pekala, R.J., & Kumar, V.K. (1984). Predicting hypnotic susceptibility by a self-report phenomenological state instrument. *American Journal of Clinical Hypnosis, 27,* 114–121.

Pekala, R.J., & Kumar, V.K. (1986). The differential organization of the structures of consciousness during hypnosis and a baseline condition. *Journal of Mind and Behavior, 7,* 515–539.

Pennebaker, J.W., & Skelton, J.A. (1981). Selective monitoring of physical sensations. *Journal of Personality and Social Psychology, 41,* 213–223.

Pereira, J. (1994, September 23). Oh boy! In toyland, you get more if you're male. *Wall Street Journal,* p. A1.

Perls, F.S. (1969). *Gestalt theory verbatim.* Lafayette, CA: People Press.

Perrin, S., & Spencer, C.P. (1989). Independence or conformity in the Asch experiment as a reflection of cultural and situational factors. *British Journal of Social Psychology, 20,* 205–210.

Perry, D.G., Perry, L.C., & Weiss, R.J. (1989). Sex differences in the consequences that children anticipate for aggression. *Developmental Psychology, 25,* 312–319.

Persson-Blennow, I., & McNeil, T.F. (1988). Frequencies and stability of temperament types in childhood. *Journal of the American Academy of Child and Adolescent Psychiatry, 27,* 619–622.

Pert, C.B., & Snyder, S.H. (1973). The opiate receptor: Demonstration in nervous tissue. *Science, 179*(6), 1011–1014.

Peskin, H. (1967). Pubertal onset and ego functioning. *Journal of Abnormal Psychology, 72,* 1–15.

Peterson, C., Vaillant, G.E., & Seligman, M.E.P. (1988). Explanatory style as a risk factor for illness. *Cognitive Therapy and Research, 12,* 119–132.

Peterson, L.R., & Peterson, M.J. (1959). Short-term retention of individual verbal items. *Journal of Experimental Psychology, 58,* 193–198.

Pettigrew, T.F. (1969). Racially separate or together? *Journal of Social Issues, 25*, 43–69.

Petty, R.E., & Cacioppo, J.T. (1981). *Attitudes and persuasion: Classic and contemporary approaches*. Dubuque, IA: Wm. C. Brown.

Petty, R.E., & Cacioppo, J.T. (1986a). The elaboration likelihood model of persuasion. In L. Berkowitz (Ed.), *Advances in experimental social psychology* (Vol. 19). Orlando, FL: Academic Press.

Petty, R.E., & Cacioppo, J.T. (1986b). *Communication and persuasion: Central and peripheral routes to attitude change*. New York: Springer-Verlag.

Pfeiffer, E. (1977). Sexual behavior in old age. In E.W. Busse & E. Pfeiffer (Eds.), *Behavior and adaptation in late life*. Boston: Little, Brown.

Phares, E.J. (1984). *Introduction to personality*. Columbus, OH: Charles E. Merrill.

Phelps, L., & Bajorek, E. (1991). Eating disorders of the adolescent: Current issues in etiology, assessment, and treatment. *School Psychology Review, 20*, 9–22.

Phillips, A.G., Coury, A., Fiorino, D., LePiane, F.G., Brown, E., & Fibiger, H.C. (1992). *Annals of the New York Academy of Sciences, 654*, 199–206.

Phillips, D.A., McCartney, K., Scarr, S., & Howes, C. (1987). Selective review of infant day care research: A cause for concern. *Zero to Three, 7*(3), 18–21.

Piaget, J. (1967). *Six psychological studies*. New York: Random House.

Piaget, J. (1969). The intellectual development of the adolescent. In G. Caplan & S. Lebovici (Eds.), Adolescence: *Psychosocial perspectives*. New York: Basic Books.

Piaget, J., & Inhelder, B. (1956). *The child's conception of space* (F.J. Langdon & E.L. Lunzer, Trans.). London: Routledge & Kegan Paul.

Pick, A.D. (1980). Cognition: Psychological perspectives. In H.C. Triandis & W.J. Lonner (Eds.), *Handbook of cross-cultural psychology* (Vol. 3). Boston: Allyn & Bacon.

Pierce, J.P. et al. (1994). *Tobacco use in California: An evaluation of the Tobacco Control Program, 1989–1993*. La Jolla: University of California, San Diego.

Pinel, J. (1993). *Biopsychology* (2nd ed.). Boston: Allyn & Bacon.

Piontelli, A. (1989). A study on twins before and after birth. *International Review of Psycho-Analysis, 16*(4), 413–426.

Piroleau, L., Murdock, M., & Brody, N. (1983). An analysis of psychotherapy versus placebo studies. *Behavioral and Brain Sciences, 6*, 275–310.

Pi-Sunyer, F.X. (1987). Exercise effects on calorie intake. *Annals of the New York Academy of Sciences, 499*, 94–103.

Plomin, R. (1989). Environment and genes: Determinants of behavior. *American Psychologist, 44*, 105–111.

Plomin R. (1990). The role of inheritance in behavior. *Science, 248*, 183–188.

Plomin, R., Corley, R., DeFries, J.C., & Fulker, D.W. (1990). Individual differences in television watching in early childhood: Nature as well as nurture. *Psychological Science 1*(6), 371–377.

Plomin, R., DeFries, J.C., & McClearn, G.E. (1990). *Behavioral genetics: A primer* (2nd ed.). New York: Freeman.

Plomin, R., & Rende, R. (1991). Human behavioral genetics. *Annual Review of Psychology, 42*, 161–190.

Plutchik, R. (1980). *Emotion: A psychoevolutionary synthesis*. New York: Harper & Row.

Poincaré, H. (1924). *The foundations of science* (G.B. Halstead, Trans.). London: Science Press.

Policy, J., Herman, C.P., Hackett, R., & Kuleshnyk, I. (1983). *The effects of personal and public monitoring of consumption on eating in restrained and unrestrained subjects*. Unpublished manuscript, University of Toronto.

Pope, H.G., Jonas, J.M., Hudson, J.I., Cohen, B.M., & Gunderson, J.G. (1983). The validity of DSM-III borderline personality disorder. *Archives of General Psychiatry, 40*, 23–30.

Poppel, E., Held, R., & Frost, D. (1973). Residual visual function after brain wounds involving the central visual pathways in man. *Nature (London), 243*, 295–296.

Porter, L.W., & Lawler, E.E. (1968). *Managerial attitudes and performance*. Homewood, IL: Richard D. Irwin.

Porter, L.W., & Roberts, K.H. (1976). Communication in organizations. In M.D. Dunnette (Ed.), *Handbook of industrial and organizational psychology*. Chicago: Rand McNally.

Porter, R.H., Balogh, R.D., Cernoch, J.M., & Franchi, C. (1986). Recognition of kin through characteristic body odors. *Chemical Senses, 11*, 389–395.

Porter, R.H., Cernich, J.M., & McLaughlin, F.J. (1983). Maternal recognition of neonates through olfactory cues. *Physiology & Behavior, 30*, 151–154.

Postman, L. (1975). Verbal learning and memory. *Annual Review of Psychology, 26*, 291–335.

Povinelli, D.J. (1993). Reconstructing the evolution of mind. *American Psychologist, 48*, 493–509.

Powell, D.H., & Driscoll, P.F. (1973). Middle class professionals face unemployment. *Society, 10*(2), 18–26.

Powers, S.I, Hauser, S.T., & Kilner, L.A. (1989). Adolescent mental health. *American Psychologist, 44*, 200–208.

Premack, D. (1971). Language in chimpanzees. *Science, 172*, 808–822.

Premack, D. (1976). *Intelligence in ape and man*. Hillsdale, NJ: Erlbaum.

Premack, D. (1983). Animal cognition. *Annual Review of Psychology, 34*, 351–362.

Premack, D. (1986). *Gavagai! Or the future history of the animal language controversy*. Cambridge, MA: MIT Press.

Prentky, R.A., Knight, R.A., & Rosenberg, R. (1988). Validation analyses on a taxonomic system for rapists: Disconfirmation and reconceptualization. *Annals of the New York Academy of Sciences, 528*, 21–40.

Preti, G., Cutler, W.B., Garcia, C.R., Huggins, G.R., & Lawley, J.J. (1986). Human auxiliary secretions influence women's menstrual cycles: The role of donor extract from females. *Hormones & Behavior, 20*, 474–482.

Prince, V., & Bentler, P.M. (1972). Survey of 504 cases of transvestism. *Psychological Reports, 31*, 903–917.

Prior, M., Smart, D., Sanson, A., & Obeklaid, F. (1993). Sex differences in psychological adjustment from infancy to 8 years. *Journal of the American Academy of Child and Adolescent Psychiatry, 32*, 291–304.

Pryor, K. (1981, April). The rhino likes violets. *Psychology Today*, pp. 92–98.

Pulaski, M.A.S. (1974, January). The rich rewards of make believe. *Psychology Today*, pp. 68–74.

Putnam, F.W. (1984). The psychophysiological investigation of multiple personality: A review. *Psychiatric Clinics of North America, 7*, 31–39.

Putnam, F.W., Guroff, J.J., Silberman, E.D., Barban, L., & Post, R.M. (1986). The clinical phenomenology of multiple personality disorder: Review of 100 recent cases. *Journal of Clinical Psychology, 47*, 285–293.

Quadagno, D.M. (1987). Pheromones and human sexuality. *Medical Aspects of Human Sexuality, 21*, 149–154.

Quadrel, M.J., Prouadrel, Fischoff, B., & Davis, W. (1993). Adolescent (In)vulnerability. *American Psychologist, 2*, 102–116.

Quill, T.E. (1985). Somatization disorder: One of medicine's blind spots. *JAMA, Journal of the American Medical Association, 254*, 3075–3079.

Raine, A., Lencz, T., Reynolds, G.P., Harrison, G., Sheard, C., Medley, I., Reynolds, L.M., & Cooper, J.E. (1992). An evaluation of structural and functional prefrontal deficits in schizophrenia: MRI and neuropsychological measures. *Psychiatry Research Neuroimaging, 45*, 123–137.

Rachlin, H., Logue, A.W., Gibbon, J., & Frankel, M. (1986). Cognition and behavior in studies of choice. *Psychological Review, 93*, 33–45.

Rayman, P., & Bluestone, B. (1982). *The private and social response to job loss: A metropolitan study*. Final report of research sponsored by the Center for Work and Mental Health, National Institute of Mental Health.

Ree, M.J., & Earles, J.A. (1992). Intelligence is the best predictor of job performance. *Current Directions in Psychological Science, 1*, 86–89.

Reed, S.F., Ernst, G.W., & Banerji, R. (1974). The role of analogy in transfer between similar problem states. *Cognitive Psychology, 6*, 435–450.

Reed, S.K. (1988). *Cognition: Theory and applications*. Monterey, CA: Brooks/Cole.

Reed, S.K. (1992). *Cognition: Theory and applications* (3rd ed.). Pacific Grove, CA: Brooks/Cole.

Regier, D.A., Boyd, J.H., Burke, J.D., Jr., Rae, D.S., Myers, J.K., Kramer, M., Robbins, L.N., George, L.K., Karno, M., & Locke, B.Z. (1988). One-month prevalence of mental disorders in United States based on 5 epidemiologic catchment area sites. *Archives of General Psychiatry, 45*, 977–986.

Reis, S.M. (1989). Reflections on policy affecting the education of gifted and talented students, past and future perspectives. *American Psychologist, 44*, 399–408.

Reisenzein, R., & Schonpflug, W. (1992). Stumpf's cognitive-evaluative theory of emotion. *American Psychologist, 47*, 34–45.

Rempel, J.K., & Holmes, J.G. (1986, February). How do I trust thee? *Psychology Today*, pp. 23–84.

Rempel, J.K., Holmes, J.G., & Zanna, M.P. (1985). Trust in close relationships. *Journal of Personality and Social Psychology, 49*, 95–112.

Renzulli, J.S. (1978). What makes giftedness? Reexamining a definition. *Phi Delta Kappan*, 60, 180–184, 216.

Reschly, D.J. (1981). Psychology testing in educational classification and placement. *American Psychologist*, 36, 1094–1102.

Rescorla, R.A. (1966). Predictability and number of pairings in Pavlovian fear conditioning. *Psychonomic Science, 4*, 383–384.

Rescorla, R.A. (1967). Pavlovian conditioning and its proper control procedures. *Psychological Review, 74*, 71–80.

Rescorla, R.A. (1988). Pavlovian conditioning: It's not what you think. *American Psychologist, 43*, 151–160.

Rescorla, R.A. (1992). Hierarchical associative relations in Pavlovian conditioning and instrumental training. *Current Directions in Psychological Science, 1*, 66–70.

Rescorla, R.A., & Solomon, R.L. (1967). Two-process learning theory: Relationships between Pavlovian conditioning and instrumental learning. *Psychological Review, 74*, 151–182.

Rice, B. (1979, September). Brave new world of intelligence testing. *Psychology Today*, pp. 27–38.

Richards, R., Kinney, D.K., Benet, M., & Merzel, A.P. (1988). Assessing everyday creativity: Characteristics of the lifetime creativity scales and validation with three large samples. *Journal of Personality and Social Psychology, 54*, 476–485.

Richards, R., Kinney, D.K., Lunde, I., & Benet, M. (1988). Creativity in manic-depressives, cyclothymes, their normal relatives, and control subjects. *Journal of Abnormal Psychology, 97*, 281–288.

Richardson, G.S., Miner, J.D., & Czeisler, C.A. (1989–1990). Impaired driving performance in shiftworkers: The role of the circadian system in a multifactional model. *Alcohol, Drugs & Driving*, 5(4), 6(1), 265–273.

Riger, S. (1992). Epistemological debates, feminist voices. *American Psychologist, 47*, 730–740.

Riordan, R.J., & Beggs, M.S. (1987). Counselors and self-help groups. *Journal of Counseling and Development, 65*, 427–429.

Roberts, A.H.(1985). Biofeedback: Research, training, and clinical roles. *American Psychologist, 40*, 938–941.

Roberts. R.M., & Kreuz, R.J. (1994). Why do people use figurative language? *Psychological Science, 5*, 159–163.

Robins, L.N. (1966). *Deviant children grown up: A sociological and psychiatric study of sociopathic personality*. Baltimore: Williams & Wilkins.

Robins, L.N., Helzer, J.E., Weissman, M.M., Orvaschel, H., Gruenberg, E., Burke, J.D., Jr., & Regier, D.A. (1984). Lifetime prevalence of specific psychiatric disorders in three sites. *Archives of General Psychiatry, 41*, 949–958.

Robins, L.N., & Regier, D.A. (1991). *Psychiatric disorders in America: The Epidemiologic Catchment Area Study*. New York: Free Press.

Robins, L.N., Schoenberg, S.P., Holmes, S.J., Ratcliff, K.S., Benham, A., & Works, J. (1985). Early home environment and retrospective recall: A test for concordance between siblings with and without psychiatric disorders. *American Journal of Orthopsychiatry, 55*, 27–41.

Robinson, L.A., Berman, J.S., & Neimeyer, R.A. (1990). Psychotherapy for the treatment of depression: A comprehensive review of controlled outcome research. *Psychological Bulletin, 108*, 30–49.

Rodin, J. (1981a). Current status of the internal-external hypothesis for obesity. *American Psychologist, 36*, 361–371.

Rodin, J. (1981b). Understanding obesity: Defining the samples. *Personality and Social Psychology Bulletin, 7*, 147–151.

Rodin, J. (1985). insulin levels, hunger, and food intake: An example of feedback loops in body weight regulation. *Health Psychology, 4,* 1–24.

Rodin, J., Striegel-Moore, R.H., & Silberstein, L.R. (1985, July). *A prospective study of bulimia among college students on three U.S. campuses.* First unpublished progress report, Yale University, New Haven, CT.

Rofe, Y. (1984). Stress and affiliation: A utility theory. *Psychological Review, 91,* 251–268.

Rofe, Y., Hoffman, M., & Lewin, I. (1985). Patient affiliation in major illness. *Psychological Medicine, 15,* 895–896.

Rogers, C.R. (1961). *On becoming a person: A therapist's view of psychotherapy.* Boston: Houghton Mifflin.

Rogers, D. (1980). *The adult years: An introduction to aging.* Englewood Cliffs, NJ: Prentice-Hall.

Roitblatt, H.L., Penner, R.H., & Nachtigall, P.E. (1990). Matching-to-sample by an echolocating dolphin *(Tursiops truncatus). Journal of Experimental Psychology: Animal Behavior Processes, 16,* 85–95.

Rokeach, M., & Mezei, L. (1966). Race and shared belief as factors in social choice. *Science, 151,* 167–172.

Rolls, B.J., Wood, R.J., & Rolls, E.T. (1980). The initiation, maintenance and termination of drinking. In J.M. Sprague & A.N. Epstein (Eds.), *Progress in psychobiology and physiological psychology* (Vol. 9). New York: Academic Press.

Romeo, F. (1984). Adolescence, sexual conflict, and anorexia nervosa. *Adolescence, 19,* 551–557.

Rosch, E.H. (1973). Natural categories. *Cognitive Psychology, 4,* 328–350.

Rosch, E.H. (1978). Principles of categorization. In E.H. Rosch & B.B. Lloyd (Eds.), *Cognition and categorization.* Hillsdale, NJ: Erlbaum.

Rosen, R.C., & Rosen, L. (1981). *Human sexuality.* New York: Knopf.

Rosenthal, D. (1970). *Genetic theory and abnormal behavior.* New York: McGraw-Hill.

Rosenthal, E. (1992, October 15). Headache? You skipped your coffee. *New York Times,* p. A8.

Rosenthal, E. (1993, February 28). Patients in pain find relief, not addiction, in narcotics. *New York Times,* p. A1.

Rosenthal, R., Archer, D., DiMatteo, M.R., Koivumaki, J.H., & Rogers, P.L. (1974, September). Body talk and tone of voice: The language without words. *Psychology Today,* pp. 64–68.

Rosenthal, R., Hall, J.A., Archer, D., DiMatteo, M.R., & Rogers, P.L. (1979). The PONS test: Measuring sensitivity to nonverbal cues. In S. Weitz (Ed.), *Nonverbal communication* (2nd ed.). New York: Oxford University Press.

Rosenzweig, M.R., & Bennett, E.L. (1976). Enriched environments: Facts, factors, and fantasies. In L. Petrinovich & J.L. McGaugh (Eds.), *Knowing, thinking, believing,* 179–214. New York: Plenum.

Rosenzweig, M.R., Bennett, E.L., & Diamond, M.C. (1972). Brain changes in response to experience. *Scientific American, 226*(2), 22–29.

Rosenzweig, M.R., & Leiman, A.L. (1982). *Physiological psychology.* Lexington, MA: D.C. Heath.

Ross, C.A., Norton, G.R., & Wozney, K. (1989). Multiple personality disorder: An analysis of 236 cases. *Canadian Journal of Psychiatry, 34,* 413–418.

Ross, L. (1977). The intuitive psychologist and his shortcomings: Distortions in the attribution process. In L. Berkowitz (Ed.), *Advances in experimental social psychology* (Vol. 10). New York: Academic Press.

Rossi, E.I. (1973). The dream protein hypothesis. *American Journal of Psychiatry, 130,* 1094–1097.

Roth, D., & Rehm, L.P. (1980). Relationships among self-monitoring processes, memory, and depression. *Cognitive Therapy and Research, 4,* 149–157.

Rothbart, M., Evans, M., & Fulero, S. (1979). Recall for confirming events: Memory processes and the maintenance of social stereotypes. *Journal of Experimental Social Psychology, 15,* 343–355.

Rotter, J.B. (1954). *Social learning and clinical psychology.* Englewood Cliffs, NJ: Prentice-Hall.

Rovner, S. (1990, December 25). The empty nest myth. *Ann Arbor News,* p. D3.

Ruberman, J.W., Weinblatt, E., Goldberg, J.D., & Chaudhary, B.S. (1984). Psychological influences on mortality after myocardial infarction. *New England Journal of Medicine, 311,* 552–559.

Ruble, D.N., Fleming, A.S., Hackel, L.S., & Stangor, C. (1988). Changes in the marital relationship during the transition to first time motherhood: Effects of violated expectations concerning division of household labor. *Journal of Personality and Social Psychology, 55,* 78–87.

Ruble, D.N., Parsons, J.E., & Ross, J. (1976). Self-evaluative responses of children in an achievement setting. *Child Development, 47,* 990–997.

Rumbaugh, D.M. (1977). *Language learning by a chimpanzee.* New York: Academic Press.

Rumbaugh, D.M. (1990). Comparative psychology and the great apes: Their competence in learning, language, and numbers. *Psychological Record, 40,* 15–39.

Rumbaugh, D.M., & Savage-Rumbaugh, E.S. (1978). Chimpanzee language research: Status and potential. *Behavior Research Methods and Instrumentation, 10,* 119–131.

Rumbaugh, D.M., von Glaserfeld, E., Warner, H., Pisani, P., & Gill, T.V. (1974). Lana (chimpanzee) learning language: A progress report. *Brain and Language, 1,* 205–212.

Rumelhart, D.E., & McClelland, J.L. (Eds.). (1986). *Parallel distributed processing: Explorations in the neurostructure of cognition.* Cambridge, MA: MIT Press.

Rushton, J.P. (1995). Construct validity, censorship, and the genetics of race. *American Psychologist,50,* 40–41.

Rushton, J.P., & Endler, N.S. (1977). Person by situation interactions in academic achievement. *Journal of Personality, 45,* 297–309.

Russell, D.E.H. (1986). The incidence and prevalence of intrafamilial and extrafamilial sexual abuse of female children. *Child Abuse and Neglect, 7,* 133–146.

Russell, J.A. (1991). Culture and the categorization of emotions. *Psychological Bulletin, 110,* 426–450.

Russell, M.J., Switz, G.M., & Thompson, K. (1980). Olfactory influences on the human menstrual cycle. *Pharmacology, Biochemistry, and Behavior, 13,* 737–738.

Russell, T.G., Rowe, W, & Smouse, A.D. (1991). Subliminal self-help tapes and academic achievement: An evaluation. *Journal of Counseling and Development, 69,* 359–362.

Russo, N.F. (1985). *A woman's mental health agenda.* Washington, DC: American Psychological Association.

Russo, N.F. (1990). Overview: Forging research priorities for women's mental health. *American Psychologist, 45,* 368–373.

Russo, N.F., & Denmark, F.L. (1987). Contributions of women to psychology. *Annual Review of Psychology, 38,* 279–298.

Russo, N.F., & Sobel, S.B. (1981). Sex differences in the utilization of mental health facilities. *Professional Psychology, 12,* 7–19.

Ryan, S. (1974). *A report on longitudinal evaluations of preschool programs: Vol. 1. Longitudinal evaluations.* (DHEW Publication No. OHD 74-24). Washington, DC: Office of Human Development.

Saccuzzo, D.P. (1975). What patients want from counseling and psychotherapy. *Journal of Clinical Psychology, 31,* 471–475.

Salamone, J.D., Kurth, P.A., McCullough, L.D., & Sokolowski, J.D. (1993). The role of brain dopamine in response initiation: Effects of haloperidol and regionally specific dopamine depletions on the local rate of instrumental responding. *Brain Research, 629*(1–2), 218–226.

Salkind, N.J. (1983). The post-divorce father-child relationship: A review of research findings. In J. Cassety (Ed.), *Child support in the United States: Research and public policy.*

Salthouse, T.A. (1991). Mediation of adult age differences in cognition by reductions in working memory and speed of processing. *Psychological Science, 2*(3), 179–183.

Sananes, C.B., & Davis, M. (1992). N-methyl-D-aspartate lesions of the lateral and basolateral nuclei of the amygdala block fear-potentiated startle and shock sensitization of startle. *Behavioral Neuroscience, 106,* 72–80.

Sanford, R.N. (1937). The effects of abstinence from food upon imaginal processes: A further experiment. *Journal of Psychology, 3,* 145–159.

Sarason, I.G., & Sarason, B.R. (1987). *Abnormal psychology: The problem of maladaptive behavior* (5th ed.). Englewood Cliffs, NJ: Prentice-Hall.

Satow, K.K. (1975). Social approval and helping. *Journal of Experimental Social Psychology, 11,* 501–509.

Sattler, J.M. (1975). *Assessment of children's intelligence.* New York: Holt, Rinehart & Winston.

Sattler, J.M. (1982). *Assessment of children's intelligence and special abilities* (2nd ed.). Boston: Allyn & Bacon.

Sattler, J.M. (1988). *Assessment of children* (3rd ed.). San Diego, CA: M. Sattler.

Savage-Rumbaugh, E.S. (1990). Language acquisition in a nonhuman species: Implications for the innateness debate. *Developmental Psychobiology, 23,* 599–620.

Savage-Rumbaugh, E.S. (1993). *Language comprehension in ape and child.* Chicago: University of Chicago Press.

Savage-Rumbaugh, E.S., McDonald, K., Sevcik, R.A., Hopkins, W.D., & Rubert, E. (1986). Spontaneous symbol acquisition and communicative use by pygmy chimpanzees *(Pan paniscus). Journal of Experimental Psychology: General, 115,* 211–235.

Saxe, L. (1994). Detection of deception. Polygraph and integrity tests. *Current Directions in Psychological Science, 3,* 69–73.

Scarr, S. (1993). Ebbs and flows of evolution in psychology. *Contemporary Psychology, 38,* 458–462.

Scarr, S., & Weinberg, R. (1983). The Minnesota Adoption Study: Genetic differences and malleability. *Child Development, 54,* 260–267.

Schaal, B. (1986). Presumed olfactory exchanges between mother and neonate in humans. In J.L. Camus & J. Conler (Eds.), *Ethology and psychology.* Toulouse: Private IEC.

Schachter, S. (1959). *The psychology of affiliation: Experimental studies of the sources of gregariousness.* Stanford, CA: Stanford University Press.

Schachter, S. (1971a). Some extraordinary facts about obese humans and rats. *American Psychologist, 26,* 129–144.

Schachter, S. (1971b, April). Eat, eat. *Psychology Today,* pp. 44–47, 78–79.

Schacter, D.L., Cooper, L.A., Tharan, M., & Rubens, A.B. (1991). Preserved priming of novel objects in patients with memory disorders. *Journal of Cognitive Neuroscience, 3,* 117–130.

Schaefer, H.H., & Martin, P.L. (1966). Behavioral therapy for "apathy" of hospitalized patients. *Psychological Reports, 19,* 1147–1158.

Schaie, K.W. (1984). Midlife influences upon intellectual functioning in old age. *International Journal of Behavioral Development, 7,* 463–478.

Schaie, K.W. (1994). The course of adult intellectual development. *American Psychologist, 4,* 304–313.

Schally, A.V., Kastin, A.J., & Arimura, A. (1977). Hypothalamic hormones: The link between brain and body. *American Scientist, 65,* 712–719.

Schanberg, S.M., & Field, T.M. (1987). Sensory deprivation stress and supplemental stimulation in the rat pup and preterm human neonate. *Child Development, 58,* 1431–1447.

Scheier, M.F., & Carver, C.S. (1993). On the power of positive thinking: The benefits of being optimistic. *Current Directions 2,* 26–30.

Schiffman, H.R. (1982). *Sensation and perception: An integrated approach* (2nd ed.). New York: Wiley.

Schleidt, M., & Genzel, C. (1990). The significance of mother's perfume for infants in the first weeks of their life. *Ethology & Sociobiology, 11,* 145–154.

Schmeck, H.M., Jr. (1988, March 8). Researchers link region in brain to obsessive disorder. *New York Times,* Sec. C.

Schnell, L., & Schwab, M.E. (1990). Axonal regeneration in the rat spinal cord produced by an antibody against myelin-associated neurite growth inhibitors. *Nature (London), 343,* 269–272.

Schoenthaler, S.J., Amos, S.P., Eysenck, H.J., Peritz, E., & Yudkin, J. (1991). Controlled trial of vitamin-mineral supplementation: Effects on intelligence and performance. *Personality and Individual Differences, 12,* 251–362.

Schroeder, S.R., Schroeder, C.S., & Landesman, S. (1987). Psychological services in educational setting to persons with mental retardation. *American Psychologist, 42,* 805–808.

Schulz, D.A. (1984). *Human sexuality* (2nd ed.). Englewood Cliffs, NJ: Prentice-Hall.

Schwab, M.E., & Catoni, P. (1988). Oligodendrocytes and CNS myelin are nonpermissive substrates for neurite growth and fibroblast spreading in vitro. *Journal of Neuroscience, 8,* 2381–2393.

Schwartz, B. (1989). *Psychology of learning and behavior* (3rd ed.). New York: Norton.

Schwartz, G.E. (1974, April). TM relaxes some people and makes them feel better. *Psychology Today*, pp. 39–44.

Schweinhart, L.J., Barnes, H.V., & Weikart, D.P. (1993). *Significant benefits: The High/Scope Perry Study through age 27* (Monographs of the High/Scope Educational Research Foundation, No. 10). Ypsilanti, MI: High/Scope Press.

Schweinhart, L.J., & Weikart, D.P. (1980). Young children grow up: The effects of the Perry Preschool Program on youths through age 15. *Monographs of the High/Scope Educational Research Foundation* (Series No. 7).

Scott, K.G., & Carran, D.T. (1987). The epidemiology and prevention of mental retardation. *American Psychologist, 42*, 801–804.

Scupin, R. (1995). *Cultural anthropology* (2nd ed.). Englewood Cliffs, NJ: Prentice-Hall.

Seamon, J.G., & Kenrick, D.T. (1992). *Psychology*. Englewood Cliffs, NJ: Prentice-Hall.

Sears, D.O. (1994). On separating church and lab. *Psychological Science, 5*, 237–239.

Seligman, J., Rogers, P., & Annin, P. (1994, May 2). The pressure to lose. *Newsweek*, pp. 60, 62.

Seligman, M.E., & Schulman, P. (1986). Explanatory styles as a predictor of productivity and quitting among life insurance sales agents. *Journal of Personality and Social Psychology, 50*, 832–838.

Seligman, M.E.P. (1972). Phobias and preparedness. In M.E.P. Seligman & J.L. Hager (Eds.), *Biological boundaries of learning*. Englewood Cliffs, NJ: Prentice-Hall.

Seligman, M.E.P. (1975). *Helplessness: On depression, development, and death*. San Francisco: Freeman.

Seligmann, J., et al. (1992, February 3). The new age of aquarius. *Newsweek*, p. 65.

Selman, R. (1981). The child as friendship philosopher. In S.R. Asher & J.M. Gottman (Eds.), *The development of children's friendships*. New York: Cambridge University Press.

Selye, H. (1976). *The stress of life* (rev. ed.). New York: McGraw-Hill.

Semrud-Clikeman, M., & Hynd, G.W. (1990). Right hemispheric dysfunction in nonverbal learning disabilities: Social, academic, and adaptive functioning in adults and children. *Psychological Bulletin, 107*, 196–209.

Shalev, A., & Munitz, H. (1986). Conversion without hysteria: A case report and review of the literature. *British Journal of Psychiatry, 148*, 198–203.

Shapiro, B.A. (1985). Recent applications of meta-analysis in clinical research. *Clinical Psychology Review, 5*, 13–34.

Shapiro, K. (1991, July). Use morality as basis for animal treatment. *APA Monitor*, p. 5.

Shepard, R.N. (1978). Externalization of mental images and the act of creation. In B.S. Randhawa & W.E. Coffman (Eds.), *Visual learning, thinking, and communicating*. New York: Academic Press.

Shepard, R.N, & Metzler, J. (1971). Mental rotation of three-dimensional objects. *Science, 171*, 701–703.

Shepherd, G.M. (1994). *Neurobiology* (3rd ed.). Oxford: Oxford University Press.

Shields, J. (1977). Genetics and alcoholism. In G. Edwards & M. Grant (Eds.), *Alcoholism: New knowledge and new responses*. London: Croom Helm.

Shiffrin, R.M., & Cook, J.R. (1978). Short-term forgetting of item and order information. *Journal of Verbal Reasoning and Verbal Behavior, 17*, 189–218.

Shneidman, E. (1989). The Indian summer of life: A preliminary study of septuagenarians. *American Psychologist, 44*(4), 684–694.

Shover, L.R., Friedman, J.M., Weiler, S.J., Heiman, J.R., & LoPiccolo, J. (1982). Multiaxial problem-oriented system for sexual dysfunctions. *Archives of General Psychology, 39*, 614–619.

Shreeve, J. (1994). Terms of estrangement. *Discover, 15*, 82–92.

Shumaker, S.A., & Hill, D.R. (1991). Gender differences in social support and physical health. *Health Psychology, 10*, 102–111.

Shwalb, B.J., Shwalb, D.W., & Shoji, J. (1994). Structure and dimension of maternal perceptions of Japanese infant temperament. *Developmental Psychology, 30*, 131–141.

Siegel, L. (1993). Amazing new discovery: Piaget was wrong. *Canadian Psychology, 34*, 239–245.

Siegel, R. (1989). *Intoxication: Life in pursuit of artificial paradise*. New York: E.P. Dutton.

Siegel, R.K. (1977). Hallucinations. *Scientific American, 237*, 132–140.

Siegel, R.K. (1982). Cocaine smoking. *Journal of Psychoactive Drugs, 14*, 271–359.

Siegler, I.C., Zonderman, A.B., Barefoot, J.C., & Williams, R.B. (1990). Predicting personality in adulthood from college MMPI scores: Implications for follow-up studies in psychosomatic medicine. *Psychosomatic Medicine, 52*, 644–652.

Sigall, H., Page, R., & Brown, A.C. (1971). Effect of expenditure as a function of evaluation and evaluator attractiveness. *Representative Research in Social Psychology, 2*, 19–25.

Silverman, B.I. (1974). Consequences, racial discrimination, and the principle of belief congruence. *Journal of Personality and Social Psychology, 29*, 497–508.

Simmons, J., & Mares, W. (1983). *Working together: Employee participation in action*. New York: Knopf.

Simon, H.A. (1974). How big is a chunk? *Science, 165*, 482–488.

Simon, H.A. (1979). *Models of thought*. New Haven, CT: Yale University Press.

Simon, H.A. (1992). What is an "explanation" of behavior? *Psychological Science 3*, 150–161.

Singer, J.L. (1975). *The inner world of daydreaming*. New York: Harper Colophon.

Singer, J.L., & Singer, D.G. (1983). Psychologists look at television: Cognitive, developmental, personality, and social policy implications. *American Psychologist, 38*, 826–834.

Singular, S. (1982, October). A memory for all seasonings. *Psychology Today*, pp. 54–63.

61% of Americans call drug use "immoral," survey reports. (1990, February 27). *Ann Arbor News*, pp. A1, A9.

Skeels, H.M. (1938). Mental development of children in foster homes. *Journal of Consulting Psychology, 2*, 33–43.

Skeels, H.M. (1942). The study of the effects of differential stimulation on mentally retard children: A follow-up report. *American Journal of Mental Deficiencies, 46*, 340–350.

Skeels, H.M. (1966). Adult status of children with contrasting early life experiences. *Monographs of the Society for Research in Child Development, 31*(3), 1–65.

Skinner, B.F. (1938). *The behavior of organisms*. New York: Appleton-Century-Crofts.

Skinner, B.F. (1948). *Science and human behavior*. New York: Macmillan.

Skinner, B.F. (1957). *Verbal behavior*. Englewood Cliffs, NJ: Prentice-Hall.

Skinner, B.F. (1987). Whatever happened to psychology as the science of behavior? *American Psychologist, 42*, 780–786.

Skinner, B.F. (1989). The origins of cognitive thought. *American Psychologist, 44*, 13–18.

Skinner, B.F. (1990). Can psychology be a science of mind? *American Psychologist, 45*, 1206–1210.

Slavin, R.E. (1983). *Cooperative learning*. New York: Longman.

Sloane, R.B., Staples, F.R., Cristol, A.H., Yorkston, N.J., & Whipple, K. (1975). Short-term analytically oriented psychotherapy versus behavior therapy. *American Journal of Psychiatry, 132*, 373–377.

Smith, A.L., & Weissman, M.M. (1992). Epidemiology. In E.S. Paykel (Ed.), *Handbook of affective disorders* (2nd ed., pp. 111–130). New York: Guilford.

Smith, C.T. (1985). Sleep states and learning: A review of the animal literature. *Neuroscience & Biobehavioral Reviews, 9*, 157–168.

Smith, C.T., & Kelly, G. (1988). Paradoxical sleep deprivation applied two days after end of training retards learning. *Physiology & Behavior, 43*, 213–216.

Smith, C.T., & Lapp, L. (1986). Prolonged increase in both PS and number of REMS following a shuttle avoidance task. *Physiology & Behavior, 36*, 1053–1057.

Smith, G.P., & Gibbs, J. (1976). Cholecystokinin and satiety: Theoretic and therapeutic implications. In D. Novin, W. Wyrwicka, & G. Bray (Eds.), *Hunger: Basic mechanics and clinical implications*. New York: Raven Press.

Smith, J.F., & Kida, T. (1991). Heuristics and biases: Expertise and task realism in auditing. *Psychological Bulletin, 109*, 472–489.

Smith, M.L., & Glass, G.V. (1977). Meta-analysis of psychotherapy outcome studies. *American Psychologist, 32*, 752–760.

Smith, M.L., Glass, G.V., & Miller, T.I. (1980). *The benefits of psychotherapy*. Baltimore: Johns Hopkins University Press.

Smith, P.B., & Bond, M.H. (1994). *Social psychology across cultures: Analysis and perspectives*. Boston: Allyn & Bacon.

Smollar, J., & Youniss, J. (1989). Transformations in adolescents' perceptions of parents. *International Journal of Behavioral Development, 12*, 71–84.

Snodgrass, S.E. (1992). Further effects of role versus gender on interpersonal sensitivity. *Journal of Personality and Social Psychology, 62*, 154–158.

Snyder, M. (1974). Self-monitoring of expressive behavior. *Journal of Personality and Social Psychology, 30*, 526–537.

Snyder, M., & Cunningham, M.R. (1975). To comply or not comply: Testing the self-perception explanation of the "foot-in-the-door" phenomenon. *Journal of Personality and Social Psychology, 31*, 64–67.

Snyder, M., & Swann, W.B., Jr. (1978). Behavioral confirmation in social interaction: From social perception to social reality. *Journal of Experimental Social Psychology, 14*, 148–162.

Snyder, M., & Tanke, E.D. (1976). Behavior and attitude: Some people are more consistent than others. *Journal of Personality, 44*, 501–517.

Snyder, S.H. (1977). Opiate receptors and internal opiates. *Scientific American, 236*, 44–56.

Snyderman, M., & Rothman, S. (1987). Survey of expert opinion on intelligence and aptitude testing. *American Psychologist, 42*, 137–144.

Sokal, M.M. (1992). Origins and early years of the American Psychological Association, 1890–1906. *American Psychologist, 47*, 111–122.

Sommers, C.H. (1994, April 3). The myth of schoolgirls' low self-esteem. *Wall Street Journal*, p. 4.

Sorensen, R.C. (1973). *Adolescent sexuality in contemporary America*. New York: World.

Southern, S., & Gayle, R. (1982). A cognitive behavioral model of hypoactive sexual desire. *Behavioral Counselor, 2*, 31–48.

Spanos, N.P. (1986). Hypnotic behavior: A social-psychological interpretation of amnesia, analgesia, and "trance logic." *Behavioral and Brain Sciences, 9*, 449–502.

Spanos, N.P., & Chaves, J.F. (1989). *Hypnosis. The cognitive-behavioral perspective*. Buffalo, NY: Prometheus Books.

Spence, J.T., Helmreich, R.L., & Stapp, J. (1975). Ratings of self and peers on self-role attributes and their relation to self-esteem and conceptions of masculinity and femininity. *Journal of Personality and Social Psychology, 32*, 29–39.

Sperling, G. (1960). The information available in brief visual presentations. *Psychological Monographs, 74*, 1–29.

Sperry, R.W. (1964). The great cerebral commissure. *Scientific American, 210*, 42–52.

Sperry, R.W. (1968). Hemisphere disconnection and unity in conscious awareness. *American Psychologist, 23*, 723–733.

Sperry, R.W. (1970). Perception in the absence of neocortical commissures. In *Perception and its disorders* (Res. Publ. A.R.N.M.D., Vol. 48). New York: The Association for Research in Nervous and Mental Disease.

Sperry, R.W. (1988). Psychology's mentalists paradigm and the religion/science tension. *American Psychologist, 43*, 607–613.

Spettle, C.M., & Liebert, R.M. (1986). Training for safety in automated person-machine systems. *American Psychologist, 41*, 545–550.

Spiegel, D., Bierre, P., & Rootenberg, J. (1989). Hypnotic alteration of somatosensory perception. *American Journal of Psychiatry, 146*, 749–754.

Spiesman, J.C. (1965). Autonomic monitoring of ego defense process. In N.S. Greenfield & W.C. Lewis (Eds.), *Psychoanalysis and current biological thought*. Madison: University of Wisconsin Press.

Spitzer, R.L., Skodal, A.E., Gibbon, M., & Williams, J.B.W. (1981). *DSM-III case book*. Washington, DC: American Psychiatric Association.

Spitzer, R.L., Skodal, A.E., Gibbon, M., & Williams, J.B.W. (1983). *Psychopathology: A casebook*. New York: McGraw-Hill.

Spoendlin, H.H., & Schrott, A. (1989). Analysis of the human auditory nerve. *Hearing Research, 43*, 25–38.

Springer, S.P., & Deutsch, G. (1989). *Left brain, right brain* (3rd ed.). New York: Freeman.

Spyraki, C., Fibiger, H.C., & Phillips, A.G. (1982). Attenuation by haloperidol of place preference conditioning using food reinforcement. *Psychopharmacology, 77,* 379–382.

Squire, L.R., Knowlton, B., & Musen, G. (1993). The structure and organization of memory. *Annual Review of Psychology, 44,* 453–495.

Squire, S. (1983). *The slender balance: Causes and cures for bulimia, anorexia, and the weight loss/weight gain seesaw.* New York: Putnam.

Steele, C.M., & Josephs, R.A. (1990). Alcohol myopia: Its prized and dangerous effects. *American Psychologist, 45,* 921–933.

Stein, D.D., Hardyck, J.A., & Smith, M.B. (1965). Race and belief: An open and shut case. *Journal of Personality and Social Psychology, 1,* 281–289.

Steinberg, K.K. et al. (1991). A meta-analysis of the effect of estrogen replacement therapy on the risk of breast cancer. *JAMA, Journal of the American Medical Association, 265*(15), 1985–1990.

Steiner, J.A., (1972). A questionnaire study of risk-taking in psychiatric patients. *British Journal of Medical Psychology, 45,* 365–374.

Steiner, J.E. (1979). Facial expressions in response to taste and smell stimulation. In H.W. Reese & L.P. Lipsitt (Eds.), *Advances in child development and behavior* (Vol. 13). New York: Academic Press.

Steinhausen, H.C., Willms, J., & Spohr, H. (1993). Long-term psychopathological and cognitive outcome of children with fetal alcohol syndrome. *Journal of the American Academy of Child and Adolescent Psychiatry, 32,* 990–994.

Stern, R.M., Breen, J.P., Watanabe, T., & Perry, B.S. (1981). Effect of feedback of physiological information on responses to innocent associations and guilty knowledge. *Journal of Applied Psychology,* 66, 677–681.

Sternberg, R.J. (1982, April). Who's intelligent? *Psychology Today,* pp. 30–39.

Sternberg, R.J. (1985a). *Beyond IQ: A triarchic theory of human intelligence.* New York: Cambridge University Press.

Sternberg, R.J. (1985b). A triangular theory of love. *Psychological Review, 93,* 119–135.

Sternberg, R.J. (1986). *Intelligence applied.* Orlando, FL: Harcourt Brace Jovanovich.

Sternberg, R.J. (1992). Ability tests, measurements and markets. *Journal of Educational Psychology, 84,* 134–140.

Sternberg, R.J., Conway, B.E., Ketron, J.L., & Bernstein, M. (1981). People's conceptions of intelligence. *Journal of Personal and Social Psychology, 41,* 37–55.

Sternberg, R.J., & Davidson, J.E. (1985). Cognitive development in the gifted and talented. In F.D. Horowitz & M. O'Brien (Eds.), *The gifted and talented: Developmental perspectives.* Washington, DC: American Psychological Association.

Sternberg, R.J., & Davidson, J.E.(Eds.). (1986). *Conceptions of giftedness.* New York: Cambridge University Press.

Sternberg, R.J., & Lubart, T.I. (1992). Buy low and sell high: An investment approach to creativity. *Current Directions in Psychological Science, 1,* 1–5.

Sternberg, R.J., & Wagner, R.K. (1993). The g-ocentric view of intelligence and job performance is wrong. *Current Directions in Psychological Science, 2,* 1–5.

Stevens, G., Gardner, S. (1982). *Women of psychology: Expansion and refinement* (Vol. 1). Cambridge, MA: Schenkman.

Stevens, S.S. (1961). To honor Fechner and repeal his law. *Science, 133,* 80–86.

Stevens, S.S. (1962). The surprising simplicity of sensory metrics. *American Psychologist, 17,* 29–39.

Stevenson, H.W. (1992). Learning from Asian schools. *Scientific American,* 70–76.

Stevenson, H.W. (1993). Why Asian students still outdistance Americans. *Educational Leadership,* 63–65.

Stevenson, H.W., Chen, C., & Lee, S.-Y. (1993). Mathematics achievement of Chinese, Japanese, and American children: Ten years later. *Science, 259,* 53–58.

Stevenson, H.W., Lee, S.-Y., & Stigler, J.W. (1986). Mathematics achievement of Chinese, Japanese, and American children. *Science, 231,* 693-697.

Stewart, R.H. (1965). Effect of continuous responding on the order effect in personality impression formation. *Journal of Personality and Social Psychology, 1,* 161–165.

Stiles, W.B., Shapiro, D.A., & Elliott, R. (1986). "Are all psychotherapies equivalent?" *American Psychologist, 41,* 165–180. (from Myers, 1992)

Stinnett, M., Carter, L.M., & Montgomery, J.E. (1972). Older persons' perceptions of their marriages. *Journal of Marriage and the Family, 34,* 665–670.

Stock, M.B., & Smythe, P.M. (1963). Does undernutrition during infancy inhibit brain growth and subsequent intellectual development? *Archives of Disorders in Childhood, 38,* 546–552.

Stone, L.J., & Church, J. (1984). *Childhood and adolescence: A psychology of the growing person* (5th ed.). New York: Random House.

Stone, R.A., & Deleo, J. (1976). Psychotherapeutic control of hypertension. *New England Journal of Medicine, 294,* 80–84.

Stoner, J.A.F. (1961). *A comparison of individual and group decisions involving risk.* Unpublished master's thesis, School of Industrial Management, MIT Press.

Straub, R.O., Seidenberg, M.S., Bever, T.G., & Terrace, H.S. (1979). Serial learning in the pigeon. *Journal of the Experimental Analysis of Behavior, 32,* 137–148.

Strickland, B.R. (1989). Internal-external control expectancies. From contingency to creativity. *American Psychologist, 44,* 1–12.

Strupp, H.H., & Hadley, S.W. (1977). A tripartite model of mental health and therapeutic outcomes: With special reference to negative effects on psychotherapy. *American Psychologist, 32,* 187–196.

Study links alcohol use to earlier death. (1990, October 2). *Ann Arbor News,* p. C1.

Stunkard, A.J., Harris, J.R., Pedersen, N.L., & McClearn, G.E. (1990). The body-mass index of twins who have been reared apart. *New England Journal of Medicine, 322,* 1483–1487.

Suddath, R.L., Christison, G.W., Torrey, E.F., & Casanova, M.F. (1990). Anatomical abnormalities in the brains of monozygotic twins discordant for schizophrenia. *New England Journal of Medicine, 322,* 789–794.

Suedfeld, P.E. (1975). The benefits of boredom: Sensory deprivation reconsidered. *American Scientist, 63,* 60–69.

Suedfeld, P.E., & Borrie, R.A. (1978). Altering states of consciousness through sensory deprivation. In A. Sugerman &

R. Tarter (Eds.), *Expanding dimensions of consciousness*. New York: Springer.

Suga, N. (1990, June). Bisonar and neural computation in bats. *Scientific American*, 60–66, 68.

Suls, J., & Fletcher, B. (1983). Social comparison in the social and physical sciences: An archival study. *Journal of Personality and Social Psychology*, *44*, 575–580.

Takaki, A., Nagai, K., Takaki, S., & Yanaihara, N. (1990). Satiety function of neurons containing CCKK-like substance in the dorsal parabrachial nucleus. *Physiology & Behavior*, *48*, 865–871.

Takami, S., Getchell, M.L., Chen, Y., Monti-Bloch, L., & Berliner, D.L. (1993). Vomeronasal epithelial cells of the adult human express neuron-specific molecules. *Neuro Report*, *4*, 374–378.

Talland, G.A. (1968). *Disorders of memory and learning*. Baltimore: Penguin.

Tanner, J.M. (1973). Growing up. *Scientific American*, *235*, 34-43.

Tanner, J.M. (1978). *Foetus into man: Physical growth from conception to maturity*. Cambridge, MA: Harvard University Press.

Taylor, S.E. (1983). Adjustment to threatening events. *American Psychologist*, *38*, 1161–1173.

Taylor, S.E. (1991). *Health psychology* (2nd ed.). New York: McGraw-Hill.

Taylor, S.E., & Brown, J.D. (1988). Illusion and well-being: A social psychological perspective on mental health. *Psychological Bulletin*, *103*, 193–210.

Taylor, S.E., & Brown, J.D. (1988). Positive illusions and well-being revisited: Separating fact from fiction. *Psychological Bulletin*, *116*, 21–27.

Telch, C.F., Agras, W.S., Rossiter, E.M., Wilfley, D, & Kenardy, J. (1990). Group cognitive-behavioral treatment for the nonpurging bulimic: An initial evaluation. *Journal of Consulting and Clinical Psychology*, *58*, 629–635.

Terman, L.M. (1925). *Mental and physical traits of a thousand gifted children: Genetic studies of genius* (Vol. 1). Stanford, CA: Stanford University Press.

Terrace, H.S. (1979). *Nim: A chimpanzee who learned sign language*. New York: Knopf.

Thomas, A., & Chess, S. (1977). *Temperament and development*. New York: Brunner/Mazel.

Thompson, D.F., & Meltzer, L. (1964). Communication of emotional intent by facial expression. *Journal of Abnormal and Social Psychology*, *68*, 129–135.

Thompson, T. (1993, November 21). *The wizard of Prozac: A pilgrimage to the center of a medical debate*. *Washington Post*, pp. F1-F5.

Thorndike, E.L. (1898). Animal intelligence. *Psychological Review Monograph*, *2*(4, Whole No. 8).

Thorndike, E.L. (1903). *Heredity, correlation, and sex differences in ability: Vol. 11. Columbia University contributions to philosophy, psychology, and education*. New York: Columbia University Press.

Thurstone, L.L. (1938). Primary mental abilities. *Psychometric Monographs*, *1*.

Timberlake, W., & Farmer-Dougan, V.A. (1991). Reinforcement in applied settings: Figuring out ahead of time what will work. *Psychological Bulletin*, *110*, 379–391.

Tolman, E.C. (1938). The determiners of behavior at a choice point. *Psychological Review*, *45*, 1-41.

Tolman, E.C., & Honzik, C.H. (1930). Introduction and removal of reward, and maze performance in rates. *University of California Publications in Psychology*, *4*, 257–275.

Tomarken, A.J., Davidson, R.J., & Henriques, J.B. (1990). Resting frontal brain asymmetry predicts affective responses to films. *Journal of Personality and Social Psychology*, *59*, 791–801.

Tomkins, S.S., & McCarter, R. (1964). What and where are the primary affects: Some evidence for a theory. *Perceptual and Motor Skills*, *18*, 119–158.

Tooby, J., & Cosmides, L. (1990). The past explains the present: Emotional adaptations and the structure of ancestral environments. *Ethology and Sociobiology*, *10*, 29–50.

Torgersen, S. (1983). Genetic factors in anxiety disorders. *Archives of General Psychiatry*, *40*, 1085–1089.

Torrance, E.P. (1954). Leadership training to improve air-crew group performance. *USAF ATC Instructor's Journal*, *5*, 25–35.

Torrey, E.F., Bowler, A.E., Taylor, E.H., & Gottesman, I.I. (1994). *Schizophrenia and manic-depressive disorder: The biological roots of mental illness as revealed by the landmark study of identical twins*. New York: Basic Books.

Tower, R.B., Singer, D.G., Singer, L.J., & Biggs, A. (1979). Differential effects of television programming on preschoolers' cognition, imagination, and social play. *American Journal of Othopsychiatry*, *49*, 265–281.

Tranel, D., Damasio, A.R., & Damasio, H. (1988). Intact recognition of facial expression, gender, and age in patients with impaired recognition of face identity. *Neurology*, *38*, 690–696.

Treaster, J.B. (1993, April 14). Drug use by younger teen-agers appears to rise, counter to trend. *New York Times*, p. A1.

Treaster, J.B., (1994, February 1). Survey finds marijuana use is up in high schools. *New York Times*, p. A1.

Treisman, A.M. (1960). Contextual cues in selective listening. *Quarterly Journal of Experimental Psychology*, *12*, 242–248.

Treisman, A.M. (1964). Verbal cues, language and meaning in selective attention. *American Journal of Psychology*, *77*, 206–219.

Treisman, A.M. (1986). Features and objects in visual processing. *Scientific American*, *255*, 114–125.

Treisman, A.M., Cavanagh, P., Fischer, B., Ramachandran, V.S., & von der Heydt, R. (1990). Form perception and attention: Striate cortex and beyond. In L. Spillman & J.S. Werner (Eds.), *Visual perception*. San Diego, CA: Academic Press.

Triandis, H.C. (1994). *Culture and social behavior*. New York: McGraw-Hill.

Triandis, H.C., Bontempo, R., Villareal, M.J., Asai, M., & Lucca, N. (1988). Individualism and collectivism: Cross-cultural perspectives on self-ingroup relationships. *Journal of Personality and Social Psychology*, *54*, 323–338.

Triandis, H.C., Leung, K., Villareal, M.J., & Clack, F.L. (1985). Allocentric versus idiocentric tendencies: Convergent and discriminant validation. *Journal of Research in Personality*, *19*, 395–415.

Trice, A.D. (1986). Ethical variables? *American Psychologist*, *41*, 482–483.

Trotter, R.J. (1983, August). Baby face. *Psychology Today*, pp. 12–20.

Tryk, H.E. (1968). Assessment in the study of creativity. In P. McReynolds (Ed.), *Advances in psychological assessment* (Vol. 1). Palo Alto, CA: Science and Behavior Books.

Tryon, R.C. (1940). Genetic differences in maze-learning abilities in rats. In *39th Yearbook: Part I. National Society for the Study of Education*. Chicago: University of Chicago Press.

Tulving, E. (1972). Episodic and semantic memory. In E. Tulving & W. Donaldson (Eds.), *Organization and memory*. New York: Academic Press.

Tulving, E. (1985). How many memory systems are there? *American Psychologist, 40*, 385–398.

Tulving, E., & Patkau, J.E. (1962). Concurrent effects of contextual constraint and word frequency on immediate recall and learning of verbal material. *Canadian Journal of Psychology, 69*, 344–354.

Tulving, E., & Schacter, D.L. (1990). Priming and human memory systems. *Science, 247*, 301–306.

Tupes, E.C., & Christal, R.W. (1961). Recurrent personality factors based on trait ratings. *USAF ASD Technical Report*, No. 61-97.

Turk, D.C., & Salovey, P. (1985). Cognitive structures, cognitive processes, and cognitive behavior modification: II. Judgments and inferences of the clinician. *Cognitive Therapy and Research, 9*, 19–34.

Turkheimer, E. (1991). Individual and group differences in adoption studies of IQ. *Psychological Bulletin, 110*, 392–405.

Turnage, J. (1990). The challenge of new workplace technology for psychology. *American Psychologist, 45*(2), 171–178.

Turnbull, C.M. (1961). Observations. *American Journal of Psychology, 1*, 304–308.

Tversky, A., & Kahneman, D. (1973). Availability: A heuristic for judging frequency and probability. *Cognitive Psychology, 5*, 207–232.

Tyler, L.E. (1980). The next twenty years. *The Counseling Psychologist, 8*, 19–21.

Ullman, L.P., & Krasner, L. (1975). *A psychological approach to abnormal behavior* (2nd ed.). Englewood Cliffs, NJ: Prentice-Hall.

Ulrich, R., & Azrin, N. (1962). Reflexive fighting in response to aversive stimulation. *Journal of Experimental Analysis of Behavior, 5*, 511–520.

Unger, R., & Crawford, M. (1992). *Women and gender: A feminist psychology*. New York: McGraw-Hill.

U.S. Bureau of the Census. (1980). *Statistical abstract of the United States*. Washington, DC: U.S. Government Printing Office.

U.S. Bureau of the Census. (1981). *Statistical abstract of the United States*. Washington, DC: U.S. Government Printing Office.

U.S. Bureau of the Census. (1983). *Statistical abstract of the United States*. Washington, DC: U.S. Government Printing Office.

U.S. Bureau of the Census. (1984). *Statistical abstract of the United States*. Washington, DC: U.S. Government Printing Office.

U.S. Bureau of the Census. (1990). *Statistical abstract of the United States* (110th ed.). Washington, DC: U.S. Government Printing Office.

U.S. Bureau of the Census. (1991). *Global aging*. Washington, DC: U.S. Government Printing Office.

U.S. Merit Systems Protection Board. (1993). *Sexual harassment of federal workers: Is it a problem?* Washington, DC: U.S. Government Printing Office.

Usher, J.A., & Neisser, U. (1993). Childhood amnesia and the beginnings of memory for four early life events. *Journal of Experimental Psychology: General, 122*, 155–165.

Vaillant, G.E. (1977). *Adaptation to life*. Boston: Little, Brown.

Valkenburg, P.M., & van der Voort, T.H.A. (1994). *Psychological Bulletin, 116*, 316–339.

Van Natta, P., Malin, H., Bertolucci, D., & Kaelber, C. (1985). The influence of alcohol abuse as a hidden contributor to mortality. *Alcohol, 2*, 535–539.

Van Putten, T., May, P.R.A., Marder, S.R., & Wittman, L.A. (1981). Subjective response to antipsychotic drugs. *Archives of General Psychiatry, 38*, 187–190.

Vaughn, M. (1993, July 22). Divorce revisited. *Ann Arbor News*, p. C4.

Videka-Sherman, L. (1982). Effects of participation in a self-help group for bereaved parents: Compassionate friends. *Prevention in Human Services, 1*(3), 69–77.

Vigersky, R. (1977). *Anorexia nervosa*. New York: Raven Press.

Vignolo, L.A., Boccardi, E., & Caverni, L. (1986). Unexpected CT-scan findings in global aphasia. *Cortex, 22*, 55–69.

*Violence & youth: Psychology's response*. (1993). Washington, DC: American Psychological Association.

Virkkunen, M. (1983). Insulin secretion during the glucose tolerance test in antisocial personality. *British Journal of Psychiatry, 142*, 598–604.

Vogel-Sprott, M. (1967). Alcohol effects on human behavior under reward and punishment. *Psychopharmacologia, 11*, 337–344.

Vogel-Sprott, M. (1992). *Alcohol tolerance and social drinking: Learning the consequences*. New York: Guilford.

Vokey, J.R., & Read, J.D. (1985, November). Subliminal messages: Between the devil and the media. *American Psychologist, 40*, 1231–1239.

von Frisch, K. (1974). Decoding the language of the bee. *Science, 185*, 663–668.

von Hofsten, C., & Fazel-Zandy, S. (1984). Development of visually guided hand orientation in reaching. *Journal of Experimental Child Psychology, 38*, 208–219.

Wachs, T.D., & Smitherman, C.H. (1985). Infant temperament and subject loss in a habituation procedure. *Child Development, 56*, 861–867.

Wagner, R.K., & Sternberg, R.J. (1986). Tacit knowledge and intelligence in the everyday world. In R.J. Sternberg & R.K. Wagner (Eds.), *Practical intelligence* (pp. 51–83). New York: Cambridge University Press.

Waid, W.M., Orne, E.C., & Orne, M.T. (1981). Selective memory for social information, alertness, and physiological arousal in the detection of deception. *Journal of Applied Psychology, 66*, 224–232.

Waid, W.M., & Orne, M.T. (1981). Cognitive, social, and personality processes in the physiological detection of deception. In L. Berkowitz (Ed.), *Advances in experimental social psychology* (Vol. 14). New York: Academic Press.

Waid, W.M., & Orne, M.T. (1982). The physiological detection of deception. *American Scientist, 70*, 402–409.

Walk, R.D., & Gibson, E.J. (1961). A comparative and analytical study of visual depth perception. *Psychological Monographs*, No. 75.

Walker, L.J. (1991). Sex differences in moral development. In W.M. Kurtines & J. Gerwitz (Eds.), *Handbook on moral behavior and development* (Vol. 2, pp. 333–364). Hillsdale, NJ: Erlbaum.

Walker, P.C., & Johnson, R.F.Q. (1974). The influence of presleep suggestions on dream content: Evidence and methodological problems. *Psychological Bulletin, 81*, 362–370.

Wallace, A.F.C. (1961). On being just complicated enough. *Proceedings of the National Academy of Sciences of the U.S.A., 47*, 458–464.

Walster, E., & Festinger, L. (1962). The effectiveness of "overheard" persuasive communications. *Journal of Abnormal and Social Psychology, 65*, 395–402.

Walster, E., Walster, G.W., & Berscheid, E. (1978). *Equity: Theory and research*. Boston: Allyn & Bacon.

Walters, J.M., & Gardner, H. (1986). The theory of multiple intelligences: Some issues and answers. In R.J. Sternberg (Ed.), *Practical intelligence* (pp. 163–182). New York: Cambridge University Press.

Walton, G.E., Bower, N.J.A., & Bower, T.G.R. (1992). Recognition of familiar faces by newborns. *Infant Behavior and Development, 15*, 265–269.

Walton, G.E., & Bower, T.G.R. (1993). Newborns form "prototypes" in less than 1 minute. *Psychologia Science, 4*, 203–206.

Wanous, J.P. (1980). Organizational entry: *Recruitment, selection and socialization of newcomers*. Reading, MA: Addison-Wesley.

Warr, P., & Perry, G. (1982). Paid employment and women's psychological well-being. *Psychological Bulletin, 91*, 498–516.

Washburn, M.F. (1916). *Movement and mental imagery: Outlines of a motor theory of the complexer mental processes*. Boston: Houghton Mifflin.

Wason, P.C. (1966). Reasoning. In B.M. Foss (Ed.), *New horizons in psychology* (pp. 135–151). Harmondsworth: Penguin.

Wason, P.C., & Evans, J. St. B.T. (1975). Dual processes in reasoning? *Cognition, 3*, 141–154.

Wasserman, E.A. (1993). Comparative cognition: Beginning the second century of the study of animal intelligence. *Psychological Bulletin, 113*, 211–228.

Wasserman, E.A., Kledinger, R.E., & Bhatt, R.S. (1988). Conceptual behavior in pigeons: Categories, subcategories, and pseudocategories. *Journal of Experimental Psychology: Animal Behavior Processes, 14*, 219–324.

Waterman, C.K., Bleubel, M.E., & Waterman, A.S. (1970). Relationship between resolution of the identity crisis and outcomes of previous psychosocial crises. *Proceedings of the Annual Convention of the American Psychological Association*, 5(Pt. I), 467–468.

Watson, D.L., & Tharp, R.G. (1985). *Self-directed behavior* (4th ed.). New York: Norton.

Watson, J.B. (1919). *Psychology from the standpoint of a behaviorist*. Philadelphia: Lippincott.

Watson, J.B. (1930). *Behaviorism*. New York: Norton.

Watson, J.B., & Rayner, R. (1920). Conditioned emotional reactions. *Journal of Experimental Psychology, 3*, 1–14.

Waugh, N., & Norman, D.A. (1960). Primary memory. *Psychological Review, 72*, 89–104.

Webb, W.B., & Agew, H.W. (1975). Are we chronically sleep deprived: *Bulletin of the Psychonomic Society, 6*, 47–48.

Webb, W.B., & Levy, C.M. (1984). Effects of spaced and repeated total sleep deprivation. *Ergonomics, 27*, 45–58.

Webster, D.W., Harburg, E., Gleiberman, L., Schork, A., & DiFranceisco, W. (1989). Familial transmission of alcohol use: I. Parent and adult offspring alcohol use over 17 years—Tecumseh, Michigan. *Journal of Studies on Alcohol, 50*, 557–566.

Weinstein, S. (1968). Intensive and extensive aspects of tactile sensitivity as a function of body part, sex, and laterality. In D.R. Kenshalo (Ed.), *The skin senses*. Springfield, IL: Charles C. Thomas.

Weintraub, M.I. (1990). High-impact aerobic exercises and vertigo—a possible cause of vestibulopathy. *New England Journal of Medicine, 323*, 1633.

Weiskrantz, L. (1978). Visual function within the hemianopic field following early cerebral hemidecortication in man: II. Pattern discrimination. *Neuropsychologia, 16*, 1–13.

Weiskrantz, L. (1986). *Blindsight*. Oxford: Clarendon Press.

Weiss, B.A., & Reynolds, S. (1992). Generation of neurons and astrocytes from isolated cells of the adult mammalian nervous system. *Science, 255*, 1707–1710.

Weiss, J.M., Glazer, H.I., & Pohorecky, L.A. (1975). Coping behavior and neurochemical changes: Alternative explanation for the original "learned helplessness" experiments. In G. Serban & A. Ling (Eds.), R*elevance of the animal model to the human*. New York: Plenum.

Weiss, S.J. (1979). The language of touch. *Nursing Research, 28*, 76–80.

Wells, G.L. (1993). What do we know about eyewitness identification? *American Psychologist, 48*, 553–571.

Werker, J.F. (1989). Becoming a native listener. *American Scientist, 77*, 54–59.

Westen, D. (1991). Social cognition and object relations. *Psychological Bulletin, 109*, 429–455.

White, J., Davison, G.C., & White, M. (1985). *Cognitive distortions in the articulate thoughts of depressed patients*. Unpublished manuscript, University of Southern California, Los Angeles.

Whiting, B.B., & Whiting, J.W.M. (1975). *Children of six cultures—A psychocultural analysis*. Cambridge, MA: Harvard University Press.

Whorf, B.L. (1956). *Language, thought, and reality*. New York: MIT Press–Wiley.

Whyte, W.H. (1956). *The organizational man*. New York: Simon & Schuster.

Wickelgren, W.A. (1977). *Learning and memory*. Englewood Cliffs, NJ: Prentice-Hall.

Wickelgren, W.A. (1979). *Cognitive psychology*. Englewood Cliffs, NJ: Prentice-Hall.

Wicker, A. (1969). Attitudes vrsus actions: The relationship of verbal and overt behavioral responses to attitude objects. *The Journal of Social Issues, 25*, 1–78.

Widom, C.S. (1978). A methodology for studying noninstitutionalized psychopaths. In R.D. Hare & D.A. Schalling (Eds.), *Psychopathic behavior: Approaches to research*. Chichester: Wiley.

Wielkiewicz, R.M., & Calvert, C.R.X. (1989). *Training and habilitating developmentally disabled people: An introduction*. Newbury Park, CA: Sage.

Wiens, A.N., & Menustik, C.E. (1983). Treatment outcome and patient characteristics in an aversion therapy program for alcoholism. *American Psychologist, 38*, 1089–1096.

Wierzbicki, M. (1993). *Issues in clinical psychology: Subjective versus objective approaches*. Boston: Allyn & Bacon.

Wiesel, T.N., & Hubel, D.H. (1963). Effects of visual deprivation on morphology and physiology of cells in the cat's geniculate body. *Journal of Neurophysiology, 26*, 978–993.

Wilcoxon, H.C., Dragoin, W.B., & Kral, P.A. (1971). Illness-induced aversions in rat and quail: Relative salience of visual and gustatory cues. *Science, 171*, 826–828.

Will, G. (1993, April 6). How do we turn children off to the violence caused by TV? Wise up parents. *Philadelphia Inquirer*, p. A1.

Williams, J.E., & Best, D.L. (1990). *Sex and psyche: Gender and self viewed cross-culturally*. Newbury Park, CA: Sage.

Williams, J.H. (1987). *Psychology of women: Behavior in a biosocial context* (3rd ed.). New York: Norton.

Williams, L. (1989, November 22). Psychotherapy gaining favor among blacks. *New York Times*.

Williams, T.P., & Sogon, S. (1984). Group composition and conforming behavior in Japanese students. *Japanese Psychological Research, 26*, 231–234.

Willis, S.L. (1985). Towards an educational psychology of the elder adult learner: Intellectual and cognitive bases. In J.E. Birren & K.W. Schaie (Eds.), *Handbook of the psychology of aging* (2nd ed.). New York: Van Nostrand.

Willis, S.L., & Schaie, K.W. (1986). Training the elderly on the ability factors of spatial orientation and inductive reasoning. *Psychology and Aging, 1*, 239–247.

Wilson, G.D. (1987). An ethological approach to sexual deviation. In G.D. Wilson (Ed.), *Variant sexuality: Research and theory* (pp. 84–115). London: Croom Helm.

Wilson, R.S. (1983). The Louisville Twin Study: Developmental synchronies in behavior. *Child Development, 54*, 298–316.

Wilson, T.D., & Schooler, J.W. (1991). Thinking too much: Introspection can reduce the quality of preferences and decisions. *Journal of Personality and Social Psychology, 60*, 181–192.

Wilson, W., & Hunter, R. (1983). Movie-inspired violence. *Psychological Reports, 53*, 435–441.

Wimer, R.E., & Wimer, C.C. (1985). Animal behavior genetics: A search for the biological foundations of behavior. *Annual Review of Psychology, 36*, 171–218.

Wincze, P., Hoon, E.F., & Hoon, P.W. (1978). Multiple measure analysis of women experiencing low sexual arousal. *Behavior Research and Therapy, 16*, 43–49.

Winget, C., Kramer, M., & Whitman, R.M. (1972). Drams and demography. *Canadian Psychiatric Association Journal, 17*, 203–208.

Winnicott, D.W. (1971). *Playing and reality*. New York: Basic Books. (from Westen, 1991)

Winter, D.G. (1973). *The power motive*. New York: Free Press.

Winter, D.G. (1976, July). What makes the candidates run? *Psychology Today*, pp. 45–49, 92.

Witkin, A.H., Dyk, R.B., Faterson, H.F., Goodenough, D.R., & Karp, S.A. (1962). *Psychological differentiation*. New York: Wiley.

Witt, D.M., & Insel, T.R. (1991). A selective oxytocin antagonist attenuates progesterone facilitation of female sexual behavior. *Endocrinology (Baltimore), 128*, 3269–3276.

Wolberg, L.R. (1977). *The technique of psychotherapy* (3rd ed.). New York: Grune & Stratton.

Wolf, M., Mees, H., & Risley, T. (1964). Application of operant conditioning procedures to the behavior problems of an autistic child. *Behavior Research Therapy, 1*, 304–312.

Wolfe, L. (1978, June). Why some people can't love. *Psychology Today*, p 55.

Wolff, C.T., Friedman, S.B., Hofer, M.A., & Mason, J.W. (1964). Relationship between psychological defenses and mean urinary 17-hydroxycorticosteroid excretion rates: I. A study of parents of fatally ill children. *Psychosomatic Medicine, 26*, 576–591.

Wolkowitz, O.M., Gertz, B., Weingartner, H., & Beccaria, L. (1990). Hunger in humans induced by MK-329, a specific peripheral-type cholecystokinin receptor antagonist. *Biological Psychiatry, 28*, 169–173.

Wolpe, J. (1973). *The practice of behavior therapy* (2nd ed.). New York: Pergamon.

Wolpe, J. (1982). *The practice of behavior therapy* (3rd ed.). New York: Pergamon.

Wolpe, J., & Rachman, S. (1960). Psychoanalytic evidence: A critique of Freud's case of little Hans. *Journal of Nervous and Mental Diseases, 130*, 198–220.

Wood, J.M., & Bootzin, R.R. (1990). The prevalence of nightmares and their independence from anxiety. *Journal of Abnormal Psychology, 99*, 64–68.

Wood, P.B. (1962). *Dreaming and social isolation*. Unpublished doctoral dissertation, University of South Carolina, Columbia.

Wood, W., Wong., F.Y., & Chachere, J.G. (1991). Effects of media violence on viewers' aggression in unconstrained social interaction. *Psychological Bulletin, 109*, 371–383.

Woodward, K.L., & Springen, K. (1992, August 22). Better than a gold watch. *Newsweek*, p. 71.

Worchel, S, Cooper, J., & Goethals, G.R. (1991). *Understanding social psychology* (5th ed.). Pacific Grove, CA: Brooks/Cole.

Wu, T.-C., Tashkin, D.P., Djahed, B., & Rose, J.E. (1988). Pulmonary hazards of smoking marijuana as compared with tobacco. *New England Journal of Medicine, 318*, 12–28.

Wyatt, W.J. (1993, December). Identical twins, emergenesis, and environments. *American Psychologist*, pp. 1294–1295.

Wyrwicka, W. (1988). Imitative behavior: A theoretical view. *Pavlovian Journal of Biological Science, 23*, 125–131.

Wysocki, C.J., & Meredith, M. (1987). *The vomeronasal system*. New York: Wiley.

Yamamoto, K., & Chimbidis, M.E. (1966). Achievement, intelligence, and creative thinking in fifth grade children: A correlational study. *Merrill-Palmer Quarterly, 12*, 233–241.

Yerkes, R.M. (1948). Psychological examining in the United States Army. In W. Dennis (Ed.), *Readings in the history of psychology* (pp. 528–540). New York: Appleton-Century-Crofts.

Yoder, J.D., & Kahn, A.S. (1993). Working toward an inclusive psychology of women. *American Psychologist, 48*, 846–850.

Zajonc, R.B. (1980). Feeling and thinking: Preferences need no inferences. *American Psychologist, 35*, 151–175.

Zajonc, R.B. (1984). On the primacy of affect. *American Psychologist, 39*, 117–129.

Zajonc, R.B., Murphy, S.T., & Inglehart, M. (1989). Feeling and facial efference: Implications of the vascular theory of emotion. *Psychological Review, 96*.

Zamansky, H.S., & Bartis, S.P. (1985). The dissociation of an experience: The hidden observer observed. *Journal of Abnormal Psychology, 94*, 243–248.

Zametkin, A.J., Nordahl, T.W., Gross, M., & King, A.C., et al. (1990). Cerebral glucose metabolism in adults with hyperactivity of childhood onset. *New England Journal of Medicine, 323*, 1361–1366.

Zeki, S. (1992). The visual image in mind and brain. *Scientific American, 267*(3), 68–76.

Zeki, S. (1993). *A vision of the brain*. London: Blackwell.

Zigler, E., & Styfco, S.J. (1994). Head Start: Criticisms in a constructive context. *American Psychologist, 49*, 127–132.

Zimbardo, P.G. (1969). The human choice: Individuation, reason, and order versus deindividuation, impulse and chaos. In N.J. Arnold & D. Levine (Eds.), *Nebraska Symposium on Motivation*. Lincoln: University of Nebraska Press.

Zucker, R.A., & Gomberg, E.S.L. (1990). Etiology of alcoholism reconsidered: The case for a biopsychosocial process. *American Psychologist, 41*, 783–793.

Zuckerman, M. (1979). Attribution of success and failure revisited, or: The motivational bias is alive and well in attribution theory. *Journal of Personality, 47*, 245–287.

Zwislocki, J.J. (1981). Sound analysis in the ear: A history of discoveries. *American Scientist, 245*, 184–192.

# PHOTO CREDITS

## CHAPTER 1

Rafael Macia/Photo Researchers, Inc., xxii; Zigy Kaluzny/Tony Stone Images, 4; Gerd Ludwig/Woodfin Camp & Associates, 5; Breese/Gamma-Liaison, Inc., 6; Jeff Greenberg/Picture Cube, Inc., 7; T. Kitamona/Agence France - Press, 9 (top); Lee Snyder/The Image Works, 9 (bottom); UPI/Bettmann, 13; Mrs. Alexandra Milgram, 15; Jim Amos/Photo Researchers, Inc., 16; Keystone View Co., Inc. of NY, 17; New York Public Library, 18 (top); Österreichische National-Bibliothek, Wien (Vienna, Austria), 18 (bottom); Archive Photos, 19; G. Paul Bishop, 20.

## CHAPTER 2

Mark Harmel/FPG International, 30; Biophoto Association/Science Source/Photo Researchers, Inc., 34; J&L Weber/Peter Arnold, Inc., 35; E.R. Lewis, Y.Y. Zeevi, T.E. Everhart/University of California at Berkeley - E.R. Lewis, 38; Rick Browne/Stock Boston, 39; Dr. Marcus Raichle/Mallinckropt Institute of Radiology, St. Louis, 16 (text column); The Warren Anatomical Museum/Harvard Medical School, 46(margin); Dan McCoy / Rainbow, 48; Mazziotta ET/Photo Researchers, Inc., 50; Richard T. Nowitz/Photo Researchers, Inc., 53 (top); Catherine Pouedras/Science Photo Library/Photo Researchers, Inc. 53 (bottom); Science Photo Library/Photo Researchers, Inc., 54; Howard Sochurek/Woodfin Camp & Associates, 55 (top); Dan McCoy/Rainbow, 55 (bottom); Giboux/Gamma-Liaison, Inc., 62; CNR/SPL/Science Source/Photo Researchers, Inc., 65 (top); CNRI/Science Photo Library/Photo Researchers, Inc., 65 (bottom); Dr. Gopal Murtl/Photo Researchers, Inc., 67; Hiller/Monkmeyer Press, 68; B. Daemmrich/The Image Works, 68 (top); Mike Mazzachi/Stock Boston, 68 (bottom).

## CHAPTER 3

George Hall/Woodfin Camp & Associates, 76; D. Jennings/The Image Works, 79; Don Wong/Science Source/Photo Researchers, Inc., 84; Photo Courtesy E.R. Lewis, University of California, Berkeley, E.R. Lewis, Y.Y. Zeevi, T.E. Everhart 85; Drs. Michael E. Phelps, John C. Mazziotta, UCLA School of Medicine, 88; PH Archives, 89; Fritz Goro/Life Magazine, Time Warner, Inc., 90; Dann Coffey/The Image Bank, 91; Dorothy Littell Greco/The Image Works, 94; D. Carroll/The Image Bank, 96; Gianni Giansanti/Sygma, 98; H.M.S. Images/The Image Bank, 99; Ronald C. James, 103 (top); John R. MacGregor/Peter Arnold, Inc., 103 (bottom); M.C. Escher Heirs/Cordon Art B.V., 104 (text column); Kaiser Porcelain, Ltd., 104 (margin); Dr. Peter Thompson, University of York, 106; M.C. Escher Heirs/Cordon Art B.V., 114.

## CHAPTER 4

Don Farber/Woodfin Camp & Associates, 122; Will & Deni McIntyre, Photo Researchers, Inc., 128; Philippe Plailly/Science Photo Library/Photo Researchers, Inc., 129; Philippe Plailly/Science Photo Library/Photo Researchers, Inc., 129; Philippe Plailly/Science Photo Library/Photo Researchers, Inc., 129; Philippe Plailly/Science Photo Library/Photo Researchers, Inc., 129; Philippe Plailly/Science Photo Library/Photo Researchers, Inc., 129; Philippe Plailly/Science Photo Library/Photo Researchers, Inc., 129; Marc Chagall/The Museum of Modern Art, 132; Carl Frank/Photo Researchers, Inc., 139; John Ficara/Woodfin Camp & Associates, 140 B. Riha/Gamma-Liaison, Inc., 142 Kenneth Murray/Photo Researchers, Inc. 144 (top) ; Joan Liftin/Actuality Inc., 144 (bottom); Stanley Rowin/Picture Cube, Inc., 153 (top); Leduc/Monkmeyer Press, 153 (bottom); Kal Muller/Woodfin Camp & Associates, 154.

## CHAPTER 5

James Schnepf/Liaison International, 160; Daemmrich/The Image Works, 162; Marian and Robert Bailey/Electric Science Productions, 173 (top); Ken Karp/New York University, 173 (bottom); Sepp Seitz/Woodfin Camp & Associates, 175; Reuters/Bettmann, 176 (top); William R. Sallaz/Duomo Photography, Inc., 176 (bottom); Andre Nadeau/Explorer/Photo Researchers, Inc., 181; Bob Daemmrich/Stock Boston, 185; Hank Morgan/Photo Researchers, Inc., 187; Kohler, 188; Lawrence Migdale/Photo Researchers, Inc., 189.

## CHAPTER 6

Garry Gay/The Image Bank, 200; Paul Simcock/The Image Bank, 204; Charles Harbutt/Actuality Inc., 210; Jeff Isaac Greenberg/Photo Researchers, Inc., 212; Dorothy Littell Greco/Stock Boston, 213; Andy Levin/Photo Researchers, Inc., 216; UPI/Bettmann, 218; Shahn Kermani/Gamma-Liaison, Inc., 219; NASA Headquarters, 223; Bob Daemmrich/Stock Boston, 226.

## CHAPTER 7

Elizabeth Crews/Stock Boston, 234; Charles Gupton/Stock Boston, 236; Bryan Yablonsky/Duomo Photography, Inc., 244; Kagan/Monkmeyer Press, 250; Smithsonian Institution, 252; Gamma-Liaison, Inc., 258; Bettmann, 259; Merrim/Monkmeyer Press, 261 (left); Forsyth/Monkmeyer Press, 261 (right); Goodwin/Monkmeyer Press, 266; Stephanie Maze/Woodfin Camp & Associates, 270; Jeff Greenberg/Photo Researchers, Inc., 271 (left); M&E Bernheim/Woodfin Camp & Associates, 271 (right); Pam Driscol Gallery, 275; Raphael Gaillarde/Gamma-Liaison, Inc., 277.

## CHAPTER 8

Stephen Simpson/FPG International, 288; Tom McHugh/Photo Researchers, Inc., 292; Journal of the American Medical Association, 1976, Vol 235, 1458–1460. Courtesy James W. Hanson, MD, 293; Spencer Grant/Gamma-Liaison, Inc., 298 (top left); Nancy Rader/Cornell University, 298; PH Archives, 298 (center left); Lew Merrim/Monkmeyer Press, 298 (top center); John Eastcott/The Image Works, 298 (top right); Shackman/Monkmeyer Press, 298 (bottom left); John Coletti/Stock Boston, 298 (bottom right); Bettmann, 299; Laura Dwight/Peter Arnold, Inc., 300; Nina Leen/Time Life Books, 308; Tom McCarthy/Picture Cube, Inc., 314; Gabe Palmer/The Stock Market, 321; Barbara Burnes/Photo Researchers, Inc., 322; AP/Wide World Photos, 325; Sylvain Grandadam/Tony Stone Images, 328; Bob Daemmrich/Stock Boston, 329; Wally Mc-Namee/Woodfin Camp & Associates, 335; Bob Daemmrich/ The Image Works, 336; Leinwand/Monkmeyer Press, 337.

## CHAPTER 9

Focus on Sports, 346; Johnny Johnson/Tony Stone Images, 349; Ellis Herwig/Stock Boston, 350; Dr. Neal E. Miller, 351; Camermann/The Image Works, 352 (bottom); W. Hill, Jr./The Image Works, 352 (top); Bernard Boutrit/Woodfin Camp & Associates, 356; University of Wisconsin, Harlow Primate Laboratory, 357; Daemmrich/The Image Works, 358; Reuters/Bettmann, 359; Blair Seitz © 88'/Photo Researchers, Inc., 362; Sandy Clark/FPG International, 372; Robert Azzi/Woodfin Camp & Associates, 373; Joe McNally, 374 (top left); Joe McNally, 374 (top right); Joe McNally, 374 (bottom left); Joe McNally, 374 (bottom right).

## CHAPTER 10

Jeffry Myers/FPG International, 382; Tom McCarthy/Picture Cube, Inc., 389; UPI/Bettmann, 390; Erich Lessing/Art Resource, 391 (left); Erich Lessing/Art Resource, 391 (right); Culver Pictures, Inc., 393; Jon Erickson/PH Archives, 394; Joe Pineiro/PH Archives, 403; PH Archives, 404 (top); Bob Daemmrich/Stock Boston, 404 (bottom); Jeff Kaufman/FPG International, 407; PH Archives, 409; Harvard University Press, 410 (left); Ken Karp, 410 (right).

## CHAPTER 11

Steve Goldberg/Monkmeyer Press, 416; Le Duc/Monkmeyer Press, 420 (top left); Schaefer/Monkmeyer Press, 420 (top right); Eric Roth/Picture Cube, Inc., 420 (bottom); Reuters/Bettmann, 422; David Madison/Duomo, 424; Richard Hutchings/Photo Researchers, Inc., 428; Goodwin/Monkmeyer Press, 433; Crandall/The Image Works, 436; Lester Sloan/Woodfin Camp & Associates, 438.

## CHAPTER 12

Scott Camazine/Photo Researchers, Inc., 446; Daemmrich/Stock Boston, 448; Library of Congress, 451; Mel Digiacomo/The Image Bank, 455; Jan Halaska/Photo Researchers, Inc., 459; Pamela Frank/Everett Collection, 460; John Lei/Stock Boston, 461; Lester Sloan/Woodfin Camp & Associates, 462; Susan Greenwood/Gamma Liaison, Inc., 465; UPI/Bettmann, 469; Mary Ellen Mark Library, 471; UPI/Bettmann, 473; Dr. Monte Buchsbaum, 474.

## CHAPTER 13

Bob Daemmrich/Stock Boston, 482; The Freud Museum/Sygma, 486; Michael Rougier/Life Magazine, Time Warner, Inc., 489; Courtesy Albert Bandura, 492; American Cancer Society, 493; Bob Daemmrich/Stock Boston, 498; Focus on Sports, 504; Gary Retherford/Photo Researchers, Inc., 505; James Wilson/Woodfin Camp & Associates, 506; Eric Roth, Picture Cube, Inc., 510 (top); Laima E. Druskis, 510 (bottom); Rhoda Sidney/Stock Boston, 511; M. Antman/The Image Works, 512; Erich Hartmann/Magnum Photos, Inc., 514.

## CHAPTER 14

R. Lord/The Image Works, 520; California Institute of Technology, 523; Frank Siteman/Stock Boston, 527 (top); Lawrence Migdale/Photo Researchers, Inc., 527 (bottom); Sidney/The Image Works, 529; Jacques Chenet/Woodfin Camp & Associates, 531; L. Kolvoord/The Image Works, 532; Jeff Greenberg/Picture Cube, Inc., 534; Scolney/Monkmeyer Press, 535 (top); DeBobigny/Gamma-Liaison, Inc., 535 (bottom); H. Gans/The Image Works, 539; AP/Wide World Photos, 543; Reuters/Bettmann, 544; Michal Heron/Woodfin Camp & Associates, 546; William Langley/FPG International, 547.

## CHAPTER 15

Comstock, 554; Travelpix © 1989/FPG International, 557 (top left); Robert Caputo/Stock Boston, 557 (top center); Arvind Garg/Gamma-Liaison, Inc., 557 (top right); B. Gerard/Gamma-Liaison, Inc., 557 (bottom left); Frank Siteman/Picture Cube, Inc., 557 (bottom center); John Eastcott/YVA Momatiuk/The Image Works, 557 (bottom right); Cary Wolinsky/Stock Boston, 559 (left); Philippe Brylak/Gamma-Liaison, Inc., 559 (right); Russell Dian/Monkmeyer Press, 563; Mark Reinstein © 1987/FPG International, 564 (top); Anthony Johnson/Picture Cube, Inc., 564 (bottom); AP/Wide World Photos, 566; Robert Caputo/Robert Caputo, 568; P. Ekman and W.V. Friesen, 579.

# NAME INDEX

# SUBJECT INDEX